Germany

Do you wish to roam farther and farther?
See! The Good lies so near.
Only learn to seize good fortune,
For good fortune's always here.

Goethe, *Erinnerung*

Travel Publications

38 Clarendon Road - WATFORD Herts WD1 1SX - U.K.
Tel. (01923) 415 000
www.michelin-travel.com
TheGreenGuide-uk@uk.michelin.com

Manufacture Française des Pneumatiques Michelin

Société en commandite par actions au capital de 2 000 000 000 de francs
Place des Carmes-Déchaux – 63000 Clermont-Ferrand (France)
R.C.S. Clermont-Fd B 855 200 507

© Michelin et Cie, Propriétaires-éditeurs, 2000
Dépôt légal août 2000 – ISBN 2-06-000008-4 – ISSN 0763-1383

Printed in the EU 08-00/3.1

Compogravure : MAURY Imprimeur S.A., Malesherbes
Impression et brochage : AUBIN, Ligugé.

Cover design : Carré Noir, Paris 17ᵉ arr.

THE GREEN GUIDE:
The Spirit of Discovery

*The exhilaration of new horizons,
the fun of seeing the world, the
excitement of discovery: this is what
we seek to share with you. To help you
make the most of your travel experience,
we offer first-hand knowledge and turn
a discerning eye on places to visit.
This wealth of information gives
you the expertise to plan your own
enriching adventure. With THE GREEN
GUIDE showing you the way, you can
explore new destinations with confidence
or rediscover old ones.
Leisure time spent with THE GREEN
GUIDE is also a time for refreshing
your spirit, enjoying yourself,
and taking advantage of our selection
of fine restaurants, hotels
and other places for relaxing.
So turn the page and open a window
on the world. Join THE GREEN GUIDE
in the spirit of discovery.*

Contents

Statue of the knight Roland, Bremen

Beach chair for windy days

Practical information   551

Moritzburg Castle

Werner OTTO Reisefotografie, Oberhausen

Wooden sculpture

Werner OTTO Reisefotografie, Oberhausen

Maps
and plans

COMPANION PUBLICATIONS

Michelin maps 415 to 420 at a scale of 1:300 000
- with alphabetical index

Town plan of Berlin no 33
- a practical and complete map of the city at a scale of 1:10 000, showing the main through streets, one-way streets, car parks, main public buildings, post offices
- an alphabetical street index
- practical information for visiting Berlin...

and if you are driving to Germany

Michelin Road Atlas to Europe
- with an alphabetical index, 74 town plans and local suburban maps

Michelin map 987 on a scale of 1:1 000 000

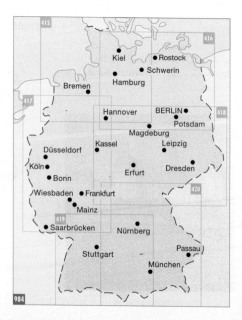

List of maps and plans

Local maps

Town plans

Museums and monuments

Using this guide

- The summary maps on the following pages are designed to assist you in planning your trip: the **Map of principal sights** identifies major sights and attractions, the **Touring programmes** propose regional driving itineraries and the **Places to stay map** points out pleasant holiday spots.

- We recommend that you read the **Introduction** before setting out on your trip. The background information it contains on history, the arts and traditional culture will prove most instructive and make your visit more meaningful.

- The main towns and attractions are presented in alphabetical order in the **Sights** section. In order to ensure quick, easy identification, original place names have been used throughout the guide. The clock symbol ⊘, placed after monuments or other sights, refers to the **Admission times and charges** section at the end of the guide, in which the names appear in the same order as in the Sights section.

- A new feature of this guide is the **blue pages** which list hotels and restaurants for the major towns in Germany, as well as other tips for using public transportation, having an evening on the town and finding entertainment. The addresses on these pages will guide you, for example, to inexpensive lodgings, a welcoming *Gasthof*, or a pleasant place to sit and enjoy a glass of beer.

- The **Practical information** section offers useful addresses for planning your trip, seeking accommodation, indulging in outdoor activities and more; opening hours and admission prices for monuments, museums and other tourist attractions; festival and carnival dates; suggestions for thematic tours on scenic railways and through nature reserves etc.

- The **Index** lists attractions, famous people and events, and other subjects covered in the guide.

Let us hear from you. We are interested in your reaction to our guide, in any ideas you have to offer or good addresses you would like to share. Send your comments to Michelin Tyre PLC, Michelin Travel Publications, 38 Clarendon Road, Watford, Herts WD1 1SX, U.K. or thegreenguide-uk@uk.michelin.com

Werner OTTO Reisefotografie, Oberausen

Key

★★★ **Worth a journey**

★★ **Worth a detour**

Tourism

⊘	Admission Times and Charges listed at the end of the guide	►►	Visit if time permits
	Sightseeing route with departure point indicated	**AZ B**	Map co-ordinates locating sights
	Ecclesiastical building		Tourist information
	Synagogue – Mosque		Historic house, castle – Ruins
	Building (with main entrance)		Dam – Factory or power station
■	Statue, small building		Fort – Cave
‡	Wayside cross		Prehistoric site
◎	Fountain		Viewing table – View
	Fortified walls – Tower – Gate	▲	Miscellaneous sight

Recreation

	Racecourse		Waymarked footpath
	Skating rink		Outdoor leisure park/centre
	Outdoor, indoor swimming pool		Theme/Amusement park
	Marina, moorings		Wildlife/Safari park, zoo
	Mountain refuge hut		Gardens, park, arboretum
	Overhead cable-car		Aviary, bird sanctuary
	Tourist or steam railway		

Additional symbols

	Motorway (unclassified)		Post office – Telephone centre
0 **0**	Junction: complete, limited		Covered market
	Pedestrian street		Barracks
I═══I	Unsuitable for traffic, street subject to restrictions		Swing bridge
	Steps – Footpath		Quarry – Mine
	Railway – Coach station		Ferry (river and lake crossings)
	Funicular – Rack-railway		Ferry services: Passengers and cars
	Tram – Metro, Underground		Foot passengers only
Bert (R.)...	Main shopping street	③	Access route number common to MICHELIN maps and town plans

Abbreviations and special symbols

J	Law courts (Justizgebäude)	**T**	Theatre (Theater)
L	Provincial government (Landesregierung)	**U**	University (Universität)
M	Museum (Museum)	ⓐ	Hotel
POL.	Police (Polizei)		Park and Ride
R	Town hall (Rathaus)	℗	Covered parking
		19	Federal road (Bundesstraße)

NB: The German letter ß (eszett) has been used throughout this guide.

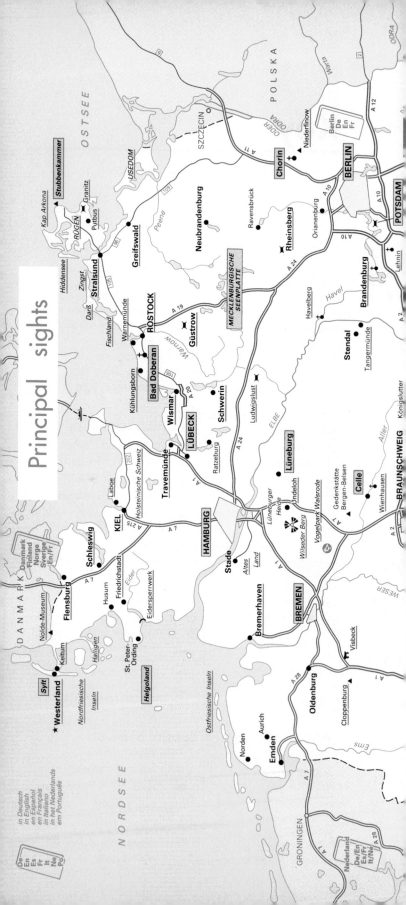

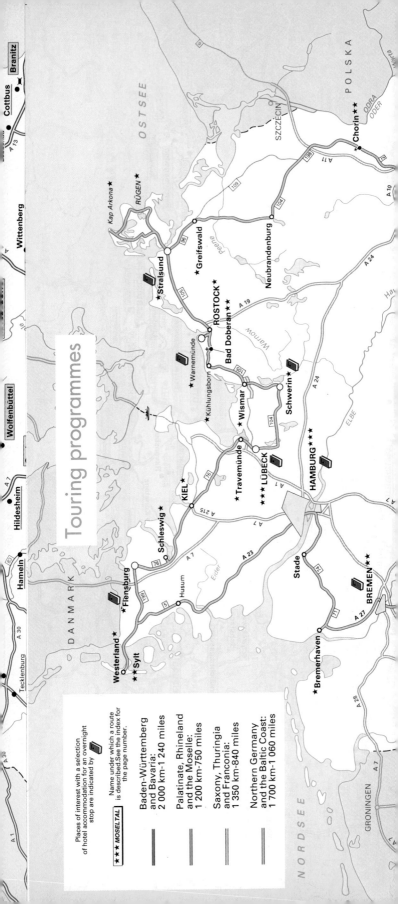

Touring programmes

MOSELTAL ★★★ — Places of interest with a selection of hotel accommodation for an overnight stop are indicated by ■

Name under which a route is described See the index for the page number.

Baden-Württemberg and Bavaria:
2 000 km-1 240 miles

Palatinate, Rhineland and the Moselle:
1 200 km-750 miles

Saxony, Thuringia and Franconia:
1 350 km-840 miles

Northern Germany and the Baltic Coast:
1 700 km-1 060 miles

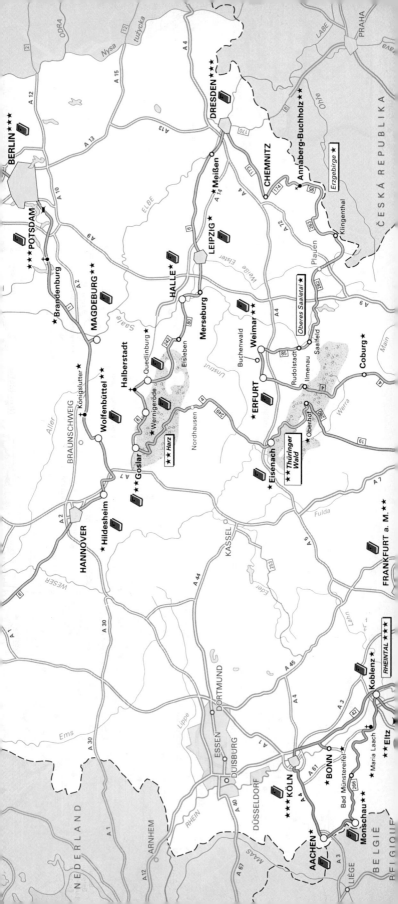

Rostock Town Hall

Introduction

Landscapes

At the heart of Europe, bordered by the Alps to the south and by the Baltic Sea to the north, Germany is virtually without natural frontiers to the east and the west. Such a lack of barriers, and the subsequent accessibility to outside influences has had a profound effect on the country's history and civilization.

Modern Germany covers an area of 356 000km²/139 000sq mi. Geologically and geographically, this vast area is divided into three separate regions. In the **north**, the immense **Germano-Polish Plain**, formed by the glaciation of the Quaternary Era, owes the fact that it was scarcely touched by the Hercynian and Alpine mountain-building movements to the resistance of its crystalline bedrock.

In the **centre**, during the Primary Era, the formidable **Hercynian folding** created a complex of minor massifs – now smoothed by erosion and for the most part wooded – separated by geographic depressions. The most important of these Hercynian massifs are the Black Forest, the Rhenish schist massif, and – encircling Bohemia – the Böhmerwald, the Bavarian Forest, the Erzgebirge (or metal-bearing mountains) and the Sudeten Mountains. On the edges of this Hercynian zone accumulated the coal-bearing deposits of the Ruhr and Silesia which led to the industrial expansion of the 19C. The sedimentary basin of Swabia-Franconia, its vast area drained by the Main and the Neckar, offers a less dramatic landscape; abutting the Black Forest on the west and the Swabian Jura to the south, the limestone plateau is patterned with lines of hills sculpted according to the resistance of the varied strata.

In the **south**, the Alpine portion of Germany is delimited by the **Pre-Alps**, where the debris torn up and crushed during the final exertions of Quaternary glaciation formed the Bavarian plateau – a huge area stretching in a gentle slope as far as the Danube.

THE SCENERY

Northern Germany

Lower Rhine Valley and Westphalia – Lush, green and flat, protected from flooding, the plain of the Lower Rhine, with its cosy houses, brings to mind the landscape of the neighbouring Netherlands. There is similar scenery around Münster, on the Westphalian plain, where the farmlands patterned by hedges and trees offer the additional attraction of many moated castles (Wasserburgen).

Great Northern Plain – Despite its apparent monotony, this enormous area (which extends eastwards into Poland but is confined, so far as Germany is concerned, between the Ems and the Oder) does offer a certain variety of landscapes.
In the south, below the Weser and Harz foothills, the Börde country lies between the Weser and the Elbe – a region covered by an alluvial topsoil whose fertility is legendary. Farms and market gardens flourish in this densely populated zone, which is favoured also with mineral deposits rich in iron and potassium.
Further north, on either side of the Elbe, is the Geest – a region with little to recommend it geographically, since it was covered by the Scandinavian glaciers right up to Paleolithic times. This has resulted in poor drainage and soils that are too sandy; between Berlin and the Baltic, the Mecklenburg plateau is scattered with shallow lakes interspersed with morainic deposits that bear witness to the prolonged glacial presence.
The Spree and the Havel, meandering through the flatlands, supply the lakeland regions of the Spreewald and Potsdam.
West of the Lower Weser, and in the Worpswede neighbourhood north of Bremen, peat bogs (Moore) alternate with very wet pastureland. Most of the peat moors are now under cultivation, after drainage using Dutch methods.
The nature reserve south of Lüneburg, however, has preserved for all time a typical stretch of the original moorland.

The Baltic Coast – The German section of the Baltic Coast, which stretches from Flensburg all the way to the Stettin Haff, is a murrain landscape, which, in addition to very flat parts also has a few elevations that rise above the 100m/320ft mark. Because of the relatively limited tidal differences of the on average 55m/1 760ft deep Baltic Sea, the coastline has only been subject to little change. That's why numerous cities with long traditions have evolved here. Between the bays of Lübeck and Kiel lies the Holsteinische Schweiz (Holstein Switzerland), the hilly and lake-dotted remainders of a ground and end murrain from the Ice Age. The arms of the sea, which are the fjords and bays left over from the glaciers of the last Ice Age cut deep into the land and form excellent natural harbours. Their banks lined with beaches, forests and little fishing villages. Further to the east, the Baltic Coast is marked by shallow, water-filled inlets from the post-Ice Age period. Four islands lie offshore, the largest is the water-washed Rügen.

North Sea Coast – Because of the winds and waves, the North Sea Coast between the Netherlands and Denmark is constantly undergoing change. The tides (every 12hr 25min 53s) raise and lower the water level by 2m/6.4ft to 3m/9.6ft. Several island groups lie out off shore in the "Watt", a 5x30km/3x18mi strip of land that is washed by the sea when the tide is in, but is above sea level at ebb times. The Watt ecosystem is home to nearly 2 000 species, from sea lions to almost invisible creatures 1/10 of a millimetre in size. A strip of marshland created over centuries lies along the coast. Once upon a time, the tides used to bring in animal and plant particles together with find sand, which formed a fertile base for agriculture in the marshlands. The less fertile, hilly "Geest" lying beyond is made up of glacial deposits: sand, gravel and clay. Broad moors have formed in the depressions, some of which have been turned over to farming. Germany's two largest seaports, Hamburg and Bremen, lie at the inner ends of the funnel-shaped Elbe and Weser estuaries.

Dikes

The flat North Sea Coast is protected by dikes made of clay and sand. This made the land fit for habitation. Building of the dikes, an important cultural job, was started in the 11C. At the beginning, only ring-shaped walls were erected, barely 3m/10ft high and 10m/32ft thick. For a modern dike (around 9m/29ft high), a 90m/290ft strip of land is needed, because the outside of the dike must be as flat as possible to let the waves roll themselves out rather than crash with full power against the wall of the dike. Care of the surface is important. The ground must be well trodden and growth must be kept low. That's why sheep are often found grazing along the dikes: they keep the grass short and their steps pack down the ground.

Central Germany

The Rhenish Schist Massif – This ancient geological mass, cut through by the Rhine – the only real channel of communication between the north and south of the country – the Lahn and the Moselle, comprises the highlands known as the Eifel, the Westerwald, the Taunus and the Hunsrück. They share the same inhospitable climate and the same evidence of volcanic activity as witness the crater lakes, known as the Maare, of the Eifel plateau.

The Eifel will be familiar to motoring enthusiasts as the home of the Nürburgring Grand Prix race circuit. The Upper Sauerland, a thickly wooded, mountainous region (alt 841m/2 760ft), with its many dams, acts as a water reserve for the Ruhr industrial area.

Mountains of Upper Hessen and the Weser – Between the Rhenish schist massif and the forest of Thuringia (Thüringer Wald) lies a confused amalgam of heights, some of them volcanic (Vogelsberg, Rhön), and depressions which have been used as a highway, linking north and south, by German invaders throughout the ages. Between Westphalia and the north, the Weser Mountains – extended westwards by the Teutoburger Wald – form a barrier that is breached at the Porta Westfalica, near Minden. Further to the east, the Erzgebirge (metal-bearing mountains) form a natural frontier with the Czech Republic.

Harz Mountains – This relatively high range (alt 1 142m/3 747ft at the Brocken) has a typical mountain climate, characterized by heavy snowfalls in winter.

Southern Germany

Plain of the Upper Rhine – Between Basle and the Bingen Gap, a soil of exceptionally fertile loess, accompanied by a climate which combines light rainfall, an early spring and a very hot summer, has produced a rich agricultural yield (hops, corn and tobacco) and a terrain highly suitable for the cultivation of vines. The whole of this low-lying, productive tract has become a crossroads for the rest of Europe, which is why certain towns – Frankfurt, for instance – have profited internationally from their development.

Black Forest – This crystalline massif (alt 1 493m/4 899ft at the Feldberg), which overlooks the Rhine Gap, is relatively well populated. The region's healthy climate and many thermal springs, with their attendant, highly reputed spa resorts, draw large numbers of tourists here every year.

Swabian-Franconian Basin – Franconia, formed by vast, gently undulating plateaux, is bordered on the southeast by the small limestone massif of the Franconian Jura which produces Germany's finest building stone, and to the north and northeast by the heavily wooded crystalline ranges flanking Bohemia and Thuringia.

Swabia, once ruled by the kings of Württemberg, offers a great variety of landscapes – barred to the south by the blue line of the Swabian Jura, which rises to 874m/2 867ft. Small valleys, enlivened by orchards and vineyards, alternate here with the gentle slopes of wooded hillsides.

Garmisch-Partenkirchen with the Zugspitze range

The Alps and the Bavarian Plateau – The Bavarian Alps and the Alps of Allgäu offer impressive contrasts between the sombre green of their forests and the shades of grey colouring their rocks and escarpments, which make an impressive sight when seen against the backdrop of a brilliant blue sky. The Zugspitze, the highest point in Germany, reaches an altitude of 2 962m/9 720ft.

Torrents such as the Isar, the Lech and the Iller, gushing down from the mountains throughout the ages, have carved out wide corridors with broad, flat floors suitable for the cultivation of the land and the development of towns (Ulm, Augsburg and Munich).

NATURE AND CONSERVATION

The preservation of natural assets, particularly of trees, is of prime concern to Germans.

The Forest – The colossal forests of the old Germania are of course no more than a memory, but the long survival of feudal customs and the difficulties of adapting undergrowth to the establishment of pastureland have resulted, over the centuries, in a remarkable preservation of wooded countryside. Such regions, gravely threatened today by pollution, are now the subject of protective measures greatly supported in their application by the ecological conscience of the great majority of the German people. Forests of deciduous trees flourish above all in the centre of the country, in the zone of the Hercynian massifs. In the Westerwald, the Thüringer Wald, the Weser Mountains and the land around Kassel, there are still magnificent beechwoods. Clumps of beech and spruce predominate in the Swabian Jura, the Harz and the heights of the Black Forest. Superb oaks cover the Spessart and the Reinhardswald, while the homogeneous carpet of conifers is found mainly in the Alps.

The Parks – Whether it be a municipal park or the grounds of a spa, an English garden at Munich or one in the formal French style at Brühl, a Romantic fantasy like Linderhof or a contemporary design such as can be found in the Ruhr, all German parks have one thing in common, the impeccable standard of their upkeep. Every other year, one of these great parks hosts the National Horticultural Exhibition or Bundesgartenschau.

> The **lime tree**, symbol of poetic inspiration and of youth, is widely prevalent throughout Germany, growing with its fellows around a village square or giving welcome shade along urban thoroughfares. Numerous solitary lime trees can be found standing in silent commemoration of the poetic reverie of great writers such as Goethe or Schiller, or the musings of statesmen such as Bismarck.

In Germany there are many **natural parks** (Naturparks), the details and extent of which can be found in Michelin maps 415 to 420. These must not be confused with the great number of **nature reserves** (Naturschutzgebiete), which are less extensive and frequently play a scientific role justifying certain restrictions of access. The natural parks are kept, especially in forest regions, specifically for the pleasure of walkers. The biggest are in the Altmühl Valley, in Swiss Franconia and the Bergstraße-Odenwald. The Pfälzer Wald is limited in the south by France's North Vosges Regional Park; that of the southern Eifel (Südeifel), which also straddles a frontier, includes the Grand Duchy of Luxembourg's "Little Switzerland". Between Berlin and the Oder lies the Märkische Schweiz.

There are also national parks in Germany. Among them are the Watten-Meer on the North Sea Coast, the Bavarian Forest in the southeast, Swiss Saxony (Sächsische Schweiz) in the east and the Hochharz in the north centre.

Apart from these official parks, all mountain ranges of any importance and most woods near holiday resorts are crisscrossed with public footpaths, well signposted and – if they qualify as a *Waldlehrpfad* – posted with information on local flora and fauna.

Four seasons

Continuous interaction between oceanic and continental air masses determines the atmospheric conditions over Germany, producing a climate notable for its instability – even turbulence – especially in the north of the country. The months which are the least cloudy, although not necessarily the warmest, are normally April and May in coastal regions, June and September in the interior.

Throughout the year, the climate is bracing and breezy on the North Sea Coast, a little milder on the Baltic. But beach life tends to be active because of the prevailing west winds.

From April onwards, the Rhine Valley and southern Germany as a whole enjoy calm, mild weather brightened with the blossom of fruit trees and orchards. On the shores of Lake Constance, in the valleys of the Inn and the Salzach, the arrival of the Föhn – a cool, dry south wind blowing violently down from the Alps – hastens the approach of springtime.

Summer in the centre of the country is marked by a rapid rise in temperature, particularly in the sheltered depressions of the Hercynian massifs (the plains of the Upper Rhine for instance), where the heat can become heavy and thundery. At such times holidaymakers are especially glad of the bathing facilities and the various forest walks on offer. In the Alps, the climate at this time of the year is very variable, depending on the orientation of valleys, the direction of local winds, which way the slopes face etc.

Often enough in late October and mid-November the sun reappears in a kind of Indian summer, known locally as the *Altweibersommer* (old women's summer), which enhances autumn tints marvellously, particularly in southern Germany. But night falls fast. From the first chill days of winter, the Bavarian Alps, the Allgäu, the Black Forest, the Sauerland and the Harz begin to be hidden beneath a carpet of snow.

Overview
of modern Germany

A Federal State – Subdivided throughout history into different regions that were largely autonomous, owing allegiance to no single capital (prior to 1945 Berlin was only capital of the Reich for just over 70 years), Germany has naturally gravitated towards a governmental structure that is federal in origin.

The **Basic Law** established in 1949 guarantees the liberty of the individual and defines the principles underlying the institutions of the Republic. The Federal Parliament is composed of two chambers: the **Bundestag**, a national assembly of 500 members elected by universal suffrage, is invested with legislative power, chooses the Chancellor, and controls the government; the **Bundesrat**, a federal council comprising 41 members drawn from the local governments administering the Länder, or provinces, is concerned with certain aspects of legislative power, particularly when they affect the Länder.

At the head of the Federal government, the Chancellor, who is invested with wide-ranging powers, defines the broad lines of policy. The Federal President (Bundespräsident) is elected by a Federal Assembly. It is he who concludes treaties with foreign states, decides upon or revokes the appointment of judges and Federal functionaries as well as Federal ministers suggested by the Chancellor, and verifies that the laws of the Constitution are respected.

The Federal Republic comprises 16 **Länder** (11 of which formed the old West Germany plus the five added in 1990 which were re-constituted from the 15 districts of the former East German Democratic Republic – *see table*). Each Land organises its constitution within the terms of the Basic Law. Apart from questions concerning the Federal authority – foreign affairs, defence matters, financial policy – each enjoys wide powers, notably in the spheres of education, culture and professional training. They are responsible, in addition, for the application of Federal laws and numerous administrative functions.

Industrial Dynamism – Despite the devastation inflicted during the final years of the Second World War and the dismantling of industrial potential demanded by the Allies after the capitulation of Hitler's Reich, the Federal Republic has raised itself to the position of the world's fourth industrial power and the second biggest exporter. This success is the result of a **social market economy**, linking private enterprise to social progress, in which unions and management work together as partners.

The decline of Germany's traditional iron and steel industry has been compensated by dynamic advances in the fields of mechanics (machine-tools, electro-technology) and automobile construction (the world's third largest producer). Numerous smaller businesses maintain the reputation of the country's optical industry and its talent for the manufacture of precision machinery. Craftwork too occupies an important place in the economy, as exemplified in the annual Munich International Fair, the largest in the world.

Progressive Cities – The political disintegration of the old Germany raised many provincial cities to the status of local capital. The absence, for almost a half-century, of a single national capital dealing in both political and economic matters, as well as the federal character of institutions in West Germany in general, permitted a certain number of cities to develop an unexpected industrial and cultural influence.

Major centres such as Cologne, Düsseldorf, Hanover, Frankfurt and Munich, not to mention also Dresden and Leipzig, each with its own university, theatre and symphony orchestra, organize a packed annual programme of festivals, congresses and commercial fairs which confirms their position as trail-blazers in modern cultural affairs, as well as winning them international acclaim.

THE LÄNDER

	AREA	POPULATION	CAPITAL
Baden-Württemberg	35 751km² 13 530sq mi	9 400 000	Stuttgart
Bayern (Bavaria)	70 555km² 27 213sq mi	11 000 000	München (Munich)
Berlin	883km² 341sq mi	3 400 000	Berlin
Brandenburg	26 000km² 10 036sq mi	2 700 000	Potsdam
Bremen	404km² 156sq mi	682 000	Bremen
Hamburg	755km² 292sq mi	1 600 000	Hamburg
Hessen	21 114km² 8 106sq mi	5 600 000	Wiesbaden
Mecklenburg-Vorpommern (Mecklenburg-West Pomerania)	22 500km² 8 685sq mi	2 100 000	Schwerin
Niedersachsen (Lower Saxony)	47 344km² 18 258sq mi	7 200 000	Hannover (Hanover)
Nordrhein-Westfalen (Rhineland-Westfalia)	34 070km² 13 124sq mi	16 900 000	Düsseldorf
Rheinland-Pfalz (Rhineland-Palatinate)	19 849km² 7 662sq mi	3 700 000	Mainz
Saarland (Saar)	2 570km² 965sq mi	1 100 000	Saarbrücken
Sachsen (Saxony)	17 000km² 6 562sq mi	4 900 000	Dresden
Sachsen-Anhalt (Saxony-Anhalt)	25 000km² 9 650sq mi	3 000 000	Magdeburg
Schleswig-Holstein	15 729km² 6 060sq mi	2 600 000	Kiel
Thüringen (Thuringia)	15 209km² 5 867sq mi	2 500 000	Erfurt

Traditional Costumes – These have tended to be less common since the Second World War. Nevertheless, men in Upper Bavaria still wear leather shorts, a Loden cloth jacket with horn buttons, and the famous "Tyrolean hat" adorned with a tuft of chamois beard or badger's tail, an outfit which makes a tremendous impression on tourists. In the Schwalm region (Alsfeld, Ziegenhain and Marburg), women still sometimes wear the traditional short flared skirt and white stockings. At festivals such as the Schwalm Salad Fair, young women wear heavy, tight-fitting ceremonial costumes embroidered in brilliant colours and crowned with a tiny red hood – as in the well-known Grimms' fairy tale.

To see other regional costumes – for example, those of the Black Forest, the Kleinwalsertal or the region of Forchheim – it is usually necessary to attend a carnival, pageant or local fête.

The **Dirndl**, worn by women in Bavaria, is not in fact attached to any specific folklore or tradition. But the charm of the gathered skirt, the puff-sleeved bodice, and the colourful pinafore ensures a demand for the costume as a souvenir.

FROM THE MIDDLE AGES

After the Treaty of Verdun in AD 843, Germany united from the Baltic Sea to the Alps all those peoples sharing a common language and culture. Faced with constant incursions from the barbarians, a number of powerful princes asserted their authority, and it was from among these that eventual kings of Germany were elected. It was Otto I, who was finally created "Emperor" by the Pope.

	ARCHITECTURE	SCULPTURE / PAINTING	MUSIC
-1000	St. Michaeliskirche, HILDESHEIM	• Wall paintings (OBERZELL, Reichenau Island)	
	SPEYER Cathedral TRIER Cathedral (west front)		
-1100	Abbey Church, MARIA LAACH	• Wall paintings, ALPIRSBACH	
		• Lectern, FREUDENSTADT	HARTMANN von AUE
-1200	BAMBERG and NAUMBURG Cathedrals St. Gereon, COLOGNE WORMS Cathedral (west chancel) COLOGNE Cathedral	• Shrine of the Magi, (COLOGNE Cathedral) • Knight of BAMBERG • Statues of the Margrave Ekkehardt and his wife Uta, (NAUMBURG Cathedral)	REINMAR MINNESÄNGER WALTHER von der VOGELWEIDE
-1300	Marienkirche, LÜBECK FREIBOURG Cathedral (west tower: belfry and spire)		
-1400	ULM Cathedral (west front)		MASTERSINGERS
-1500	HEIDELBERG Castle St. Annenkirche, ANNABERG	V. STOSS, T. RIEMENSCHNEIDER, HOLBEIN the YOUNGER, H.B. GRIEN, M. GRÜNEWALD, S. LOCHNER, M. SCHONGAUER, P. VISCHER, A. DÜRER, A. ALTDORFER, CRANACH the ELDER	J. WALTHER, H. SACHS, H. FINCK
-1600	• Rathaus AUGSBOURG	E. HOLL, A. ELSHEIMER, MERIAN	
-1700	• Zwinger, DRESDEN	A. SCHLÜTER, E. Q. ASAM, B. PERMOSER	H. SCHÜTZ, D. BUXTEHUDE
-1800	• Sanssouci, POSTDAM • OTTOBEUREN Abbey • WIES Church	C.D. FRIEDRICH, BIEDERMEIER	C.-P.-E. BACH, W.-A. MOZART, G.-F. HÄNDEL, J. HAYDN, C.-W. GLUCK, J.-S. BACH, G.-P. TELEMANN
-1900	• NEUSCHWANSTEIN Castle		L. van BEETHOVEN, C.-M. von WEBER, R. SCHUMANN, R. WAGNER, F. MENDELSSOHN, J. BRAHMS, G. MAHLER, H. WOLF, R. STRAUSS
-2000	D. BÖHM, W. GROPIUS, P. BEHRENS, C.F. SCHINKEL, M.D. PÖPPELMANN, G. KNOBELSDORFF, C. D. ASAM, B. NEUMANN, D. ZIMMERMANN, BAROQUE, ROCOCO, ROMANTIC Movement, BAUHAUS	E.L. KIRCHNER, A. von HILDEBRAND, E. BARLACH, J. BEUYS, M. BECKMANN, M. LIEBERMANN, O. DIX, MARC, M. ERNST, JUGENDSTIL	P. HINDEMITH, K.-H. STOCKHAUSEN, K. WEILL

Otto I became the founder of the Holy Roman Empire. For a long time after that, the control of the Papacy itself was the Empire's principal objective, but when this policy failed and the organization was reduced just to Germany, the different territorial principalities grew stronger and the "Empire" shrank in fact to what in time developed into an elective monarchy.

LITERATURE	RELIGION AND PHILOSOPHY	HISTORY	ECONOMY, SCIENCES AND TECHNOLOGY	
		SAXON DYNASTY **Ottonian Emperors** **SALIAN DYNASTY**	Growth of trade Founding of the monasteries	—1000—
SONG OF THE NIBELUNGEN	POPE GREGORY VII • CANOSSA 1077	Henry IV		
HEINRICH von VELDEKE				—1100—
GOTTFRIED de STRASSBOURG	Concordat of Worms (1122)	**House of HOHENSTAUFEN** Conrad III Emperor Frederick I Barbarossa	• Demographic growth • Expansion towards the East	
WOLFRAM von ESCHENBACH	ALEXANDER III	TEUTONIC ORDER 1190 Third Crusade	• Working of the mineral deposits in Silesia and Thuringia	—1200—
Master ECKHART	ALBERTUS MAGNUS	Sixth Crusade	• HANSEATIC LEAGUE: growth of Baltic trade	
H. SUSO		Frederick II (King of Sicily)		
J.TAULER		Rudolph I of Habsburg	• Growth of towns	—1300—
		House of LUXEMBOURG		
		Charles IV The Golden Bull	• Famines • BLACK DEATH 1349 • Demographic decline	
				—1400—
	Concil of Constance The Hussite Controversy	Sigismund	• GUTENBERG	
		House of HABSBURG	Powerful Merchant Families (The FUGGERS and the WELSERS)	
M. LUTHER	1517: Luther exhibits his 95 "theses" on the door of the Church at Wittenberg 1521: Luther is excommunicated 1530: Confession of Augsburg 1546: death of Luther	Maximilian I (1493-1519) acquires the duchy of Burgundy and the rich Netherlands by marriage	• Rapid urban expansion	—1500—
PARACELSUS		Maximilian I		
A. GRYPHIUS / F. FISCHART	H. SACHS	Emperor Charles V • Peace of AUGSBURG 1555		
M. OPITZ		Rudolf II		
J. J. GRIMMELSHAUSEN				—1600—
D. C. LOHENSTEIN		Matthias II • THIRTY YEARS WAR	• KEPLER: astronomical telescope	
	W. G. LEIBNIZ	• Peace of WESTPHALIA 1648 Revocation of the Edict of Nantes : French Huguenots arrive	• LEIBNIZ: differential and integral calculus	—1700—
J. C. GOTTSCHED	J. G. von HERDER	**Rise of BRANDEBURG and PRUSSIAN Rulers THE HOHENZOLLERN**	• BÖTTGER: Saxon porcelain • FAHRENHEIT: mercury thermometer	
G. E. LESSING / F. G. KLOPSTOCK / C. WIELAND	E. KANT	• Seven Years War		—1800—
F von SCHILLER / H. von KLEIST / E. T. A. HOFFMANN / J. W. von GOETHE / J. von EICHENDORFF / NOVALIS	J. G. FICHTE / G. W. F. HEGEL	• Confederation of the Rhine • Chancellor Otto von Bismarck • North German Confederation	• DRAIS: draisienne (prototype of the bicycle)	
H. HEINE / J. and W. GRIMM	K. MARX / F ENGELS	• SECOND REICH	• HAHNEMANN: homeopathy • G. DAIMLER and K. BENZ: internal combustion engine • DIESEL engine	—1900—
G. HAUPTMANN / T. MANN / H. HESSE	A. SCHOPENHAUER / F. NIETZSCHE	FIRST WORLD WAR • Weimar Republic	• RÖNTGEN: X-rays • PLANCK: quantum theory • EINSTEIN: theory of relativity • O. HAHN: nuclear fission	
B. BRECHT / H. BÖLL / G. GRASS	M. HEIDEGGER / E. HUSSERL / K. JASPERS	• THIRD REICH SECOND WORLD WAR • TREATY OF GERMAN REUNIFICATION		—2000—

(Vertical side labels: Investiture Controversy; Counter-Reformation; HANSEATIC LEAGUE; AUFKLÄRUNG)

History

The Origins

The earliest evidence of human life on German territory today is the lower jaw bone dating back over 500 000 years of the so-called Homo Heidelbergiensis, which was discovered near Heidelberg in 1907. The Middle Paleolithic Age (200 000-40 000 BC) is considered the age of the Neanderthal Man *(see DÜSSELDORF: Excursions)*. The first "modern people", the Homo Sapiens, who lived from hunting, fishing and gathering, lived during the Late Paleolithic, an epoch of the Stone Age within the last Ice Age. During he Neolithic Era, people began to settle in village-like communities, where they lived for a while, grew plants and began raising animals.

The last prehistoric period, the Iron Age, began around 1 000 BC, following the Bronze Age, thus named because that material was widely used to make implements, weapons and jewellery. The Iron Age is divided up into the La-Tène Culture and the Hallstatt Culture. Economic and political power started becoming more concentrated, evidence from graves suggests a stratified social system.

La-Tène Culture

The name for this cultural epoch supported by Celtic tribes (5C-1C BC) originated at an excavation site on Neuenburg Lake in Switzerland. Over 2 500 objects were found there, grave furnishings and treasures. The focal area of the La-Tène Culture is in south-western Germany, along the northern edge of the Alps and in the Main-Mosel area. Protective forts for the people grew into city like settlements, the first north of the Alps. The advance of Germanic tribes and the expansion of the Roman Empire brought the La-Tène Culture to an end.

Germans and Romans

In the first millennium before Christ, Germanic tribes began resettling towards Central Europe. The occurrence and extent of this movement was under the auspices of numerous population groups of various origins and cultural levels living in the area between the northern German flatlands and the central mountain ranges. The first written reference to "Germania" is in the works of the Roman author **Poseidonius** (1C BC). Caesar, too, ("De Bello Gallico") used this term to describe the non-Gallic regions north of the Alps.

The wars conducted by the Kimbers and the Teutons against the Romans around 100 BC were the first military conflicts between German tribes and the Roman civilization. The expansion of the western German tribes was stopped in connection with the conquering of Gaul by **Caesar** (58-55 BC).The foreign political ideas of Emperor Augustus and his predecessors also covered the inclusion of Germania into the Roman Empire all the way to the Elbe, an objective that was never met.

During the 1C AD, the **Limes** was built, a 550km/330mi fortified line that sealed the Roman sphere of influence from the Rhine to the Danube. Skirmishes did break out every now and then, but there were also alliances, trade and cultural exchanges. New towns arose where the Roman camps stood and at river crossings (eg Köln, Koblenz, Regensburg).

Late Antiquity, the Germans and Christianity blended to form occidental Middle Ages. In the 2C-3C AD, the large tribes like the Franks, the Saxons and the Allemans merged. The military kingdoms of the age of the Völkerwanderung gave way to early medieval government by personal association.

AD 9	Three Roman legions under general Varus are annihilated by Germanic troops under the command of the Cheruscans prince Arminius *(see DETMOLD)*, which results in the Romans relinquishing their bastions on the right bank of the Rhine.
314	One year after announcing the Edict of Tolerance, Emperor Constantine establishes the first bishopric on German territory in Trier.
375	Beginning of the Völkerwanderung, the "movement of the peoples": The Huns drive the Goths (East Germans) to the west. The former "Imperium Romanum" falls apart to form partial empires.
800	End of the West Roman Empire brought about by Odoaker, the East German general. He is in turn murdered by the Ostrogoth Theodorich.

The Frankish Empire

The tribal union of the Franks – a West German tribe in the estuary of the Rhine – expanded slowly towards the south. These erstwhile confederates of Rome (settled allies), developed into the most important factor at the beginning of the Middle Ages thanks to the creation of large powers introduced by the Merovingians around 500. Their king, Clovis I, mopped up the final remains of the West Roman Empire and converted to Christianity. In the 7C, the Merovingians lost their hegemony to the dynasty later referred to as the Carolingians, who had held the court function of palatines.

Charlemagne's Empire

After being crowned Emperor in St Peter's Cathedral in Rome in 800, Charlemagne stepped in the shoes of the Roman emperors. His empire stretched from the Spanish border to the Elbe, from Rome all the way to the English Channel. Besides the "Carolingian Renaissance", as this Golden Age was called, the most important aspect of his reign was the setting up of a working administrative structure. In disposing of the independent duchies and the tribal states, Charlemagne introduced a county constitution. At the top of each administrative district stood an officer of the king chosen from the Frankish Imperial aristocracy, which ensured the coherence of the empire. The vulnerable borders were secured against attack by setting up border marches under margraves invested with special powers. Emissaries with royal powers watched over the Imperial administration. The king constantly travelled through the empire and visited the "Pfalzen", which grew into major economic and cultural centres, or used the "guesting" option in the Imperial monasteries.

Since the 8C, the general term "thiutisk" had developed from a linguistic derivation of the word for tribe to describe the peoples speaking Germanic languages – as opposed to Latin or later French. There was still no supra-regional language spoken to the east of the Rhine, the area that considered itself the Frankish Empire until the 11C. In the 10C, the term "Regnum Teutonicorum" appeared for the first time as the name for the ruling association of a number of tribes in the Eastern Frankish Empire. During the 11C and 12C it slowly established itself as a term.

751	Pope Zacharias agrees to the deposition of the last of the Merovingian kings, Childeric III, in favour of the palatine Pippin. Three years later the Pope places Rome under the protection of the Frankish kings.
768	Charlemagne becomes the ruler. He conquers, amongst others, the Lombards, divides up Bavaria and defeats the Saxons after a long war.
800	Coronation of Charlemagne in Rome. The emperor thus legally assumes sovereignty over the former empire.
843	The Treaty of Verdun divides the Carolingian Empire amongst Charlemagne's grandchildren. The East Frankish Kingdom is given to Ludwig the German. The final division of the Carolingian Empire, that paved the way to Germany and France, is determined by the treaties of Mersen (870) and Verdun/Ribemont (879-80).
911	The East Franks elect the Frankish duke Konrad to become their king, thereby separating themselves from the West Franks.

The Holy Roman Empire

The Roman-German Empire consisted of an elective monarchy. The elected king – who also had to have hereditary rights – became emperor only after being crowned by the Pope. From the 11C onwards, the emperor could rely on being king of not only Germany and Italy, but also of Burgundy. An especially "German" Imperial concept gave way to a Roman-universal idea of an emperor, a fact underscored as of 1157 by the additional title "sacrum Imperium". During the time of the Staufer dynasty, in the mid 13C, the claim to rule in Italy came to an end. In the 15C, the term "Holy Roman Empire of the German Nation" was finally established, implying the politically active community of the German Imperial estates, who acted as a counterweight to the Kaiser.

Kunsthist. Museum, Vienna

Crown of the Holy Roman Empire

27

Ruling this huge empire, which during the High Middle Ages stretched from Sicily all the way to the Baltic, was extremely difficult without the benefit of central administrational organs and the technical, financial and military wherewithal. By granting land and various privileges (eg customs rights), responsibility for the administration, security and expansion of the empire was placed in the hands of the Imperial aristocracy.

Beginning in the second half of the 11C, the **"Investiture Controversy"** pitted the Pope against the Emperor on the issue of the right to invest the bishops. This weakened the empire and shook up the Christian world. The dispute was ended by the Concordat of Worms (1122), which proclaimed that ecclesiastical dignities had to be separated from bestowed worldly goods. The position of the bishops became similar to that of the princes, since they became vassals of the empire.

Over time, these vassals of the Kaiser gradually accumulated more and more power owing to the establishment of heredity of the fiefs and regalia, which in the long term weakened the empire; this paved the way to the rise of numerous small and some larger territorial states, such as Bavaria and Saxony. The regional ruling of the princely territorial states replaced the personal union state resulting in the federal structure that remains typical of Germany to this day.

962	In Rome, Otto the Great revives the Imperial title and the Pope crowns him emperor. The Saxon duke had already been crowned king in 936. The Otto dynasty rules until the death of Henry II in 1024, and is followed by that of the Salians (Franks).
1073	Pope Gregory VII elected. This church reformer disputes the legitimacy of secular power of decision in affairs of the church. The dramatic crux of the conflict was the penitent journey to Canossa (1077) by King Henrich IV to receive absolution from the Pope, who had excommunicated him.
1152-1190	Rule of the Staufer emperor Frederick I Barbarossa, who once again strengthened Imperial power *(Restauratio Imperii)* – and who captured the duchies of Bavaria and Saxony from the Guelph duke Henry the Lion (see BRAUNSCHWEIG) after a long dispute – and did what he could to limit papal power to the religious sector.
1212-1250	Frederick II stays in southern Italy and Sicily for much of his reign, the area north of the Alps held little interest for him. Two Imperial edicts (1220-31)confirm the power over the territories of the secular and religious princes.
1254-1273	The years extending between he death of Konrad IV and the election of Rudolf of Habsburg are known as the Interregnum. It was a time of lawlessness and rule by force under "foreign" kings and anti-kings, which once and for all took away the typically high Middle Ages power and universal meaning of the empire.

The Golden Bull

Beginning in the 10C, the number of electors for the king began to decline, while at the same time the election itself became more regulated legally and formalised. Finally, in 1356, the Golden Bull promulgated an Imperial law to regulate the election of the king, defining an institutional framework and limiting the power of the empire. Thenceforth, the king would be elected by a college of three religious electors (the Archbishops of Mainz, Köln and Trier) and four secular ones (the kings of Bohemia, the Margrave of Brandenburg, the Duke of Saxony and the Palatine of the Rhein), and then later crowned emperor. The election was to take place in Frankfurt/Main, and the coronation in Aachen, confirmation by the Pope was no longer necessary. This law, announced by the Luxembourg emperor Charles IV is considered the empire's first constitution and a basis for a federal system of state. The power of the electors grew, because they were granted even more extensive privileges, such as the indivisibility of the electoral territories, sole jurisdiction and sovereignty over the land and the securing of dynastic heredity.

The Late Middle Ages

After the Interregnum, the power of the **Habsburgs** grew. The dynasty succeeded in building up tremendous family power, and by the 15C they had consolidated that power – though now and then the powerful Luxembourgs, Nassaus and Wittelsbach families also succeeded in slipping a king onto the throne. The Kaisers got into the habit of trying to have a son elected king during their lifetime in order to keep the highest ranking in their own dynasties. But during the Renaissance, the Imperial crown surrendered its holiness.

The Emperor and the seven Prince-Electors (c 1370)

During the Late Middle Ages, the "Hoftage", the Imperial meetings, became the **Reichstag** – a meeting of the good 350 secular and religious Imperial estates – signalling the beginning of the sharp dualism between the emperor and his estates that followed. At the Reichstag in Worms (1495), fundamental reform decisions were passed that created the preconditions for transforming the Reich into a unified legal and pacified territory. The proclamation of the "Ewiger Landfrieden" (Eternal Peace in the land) prohibited all feuds and personal justice, creating a new legal basis. A Permanent Imperial Chamber Court was there to ensure compliance and to carry out enforcement. After a long debate between Emperor Maximilian I and the Imperial Estates, a reform of the Imperial finances was pushed through raising the "Common Penny", a combination of wealth tax, income tax and poll tax. Later Reichtags divided up the empire into supra-regional administrative units – the Reichskreise, or Imperial districts. In 1663, the Permanent Reichstag was set up in Regensburg.

Inspired by the ideas of the Humanists, the concept and consciousness of a "German nation" began to arise on a political as well as a cultural level, which was legitimised thanks to the rediscovery and collection of literary monuments, such as "Germania" by Tacitus. Until around 1500, it was the "deutsche Lande" (German lands) that were always mentioned, but around that time, the term "Deutschland" in the singular cropped up for the first time.

1273	After a warning from the Pope, the electors chose Count Rudolf von Habsburg (dynastic power in the Breisgau, Alsace and Aargau, amongst others) to be king.
1346-1378	Charles IV of Luxembourg in power as the most important ruler of the Late Middle Ages.
1386	Founding of the University of Heidelberg, the oldest in Germany.
1414-1418	Council of Konstanz; the largest church meeting of the Middle Ages until then.
1438	After the death of the last of the Luxembourg emperors, the electors chose the Habsburg duke Albert V to become King Albert II.
c 1450	Invention of book printing with movable type by Johann Gutenberg from Mainz; flourishing and spreading of Humanism.
1452	During a military campaign by Frederick III, the last coronation of an emperor in Rome takes place.
1493	Maximilian I becomes king. As of 1508 he is the "elected Roman Emperor". His successors adopt the Imperial title immediately after the royal crowning in Aachen, thereby avoiding the difficult and dangerous journey to Rome along with their courts.
1519-1556	Kaiser Charles V, Maximilian's grandchild, gathers the greatest amount of power during his term (in terms of size, population and wealth) since the Carolingians.

The Reformation and the Thirty Years War

In 1503, **Martin Luther** (1483-1546) entered the Augustinian monastery of Erfurt. A dedicated cleric, he was tormented by the problem of salvation. Appointed Professor of Theology, he found in the Holy Scriptures (c 1512-13) his answer: "We cannot earn forgiveness for our sins through our deeds, only God's mercy justifies us in our faith in it". Man's salvation, therefore – Luther argued – lies entirely within the gift, or Grace, of God. This concept led him to attack the Church's dealing in indulgences and,

29

The Hanseatic League

The Hanseatic League existed between the mid 12C and the mid 17C. Its basic structure had already been outlined by around 1300, an alliance of 30 larger and 100 smaller cities to safeguard their joint interests in shipping and trade. This union of cities went through its Golden Age in the 14C under the leadership of Lübeck. At that point it included over 100 cities and was the most significant economic factor in northern Germany. After the Thirty Years War, the Hanseatic tradition only continued in Hamburg, Lübeck and Bremen.

on 31 October 1517, he nailed 95 "theses" condemning such practices and reminding the Faithful of the primordial importance of the sacrifice on the Cross and the Grace of God on the doors of Wittenberg Church.

Luther was denounced in the court of Rome, refused to retract, and in 1521 burned the Papal Bull threatening him with excommunication. Subsequently he attacked the institutions and hierarchy of the Church and objected to the primacy of the clergy in spiritual matters, arguing the universal priesthood of Christians conferred by baptism.

Lausat/EXPLORER, Paris

Martin Luther - a 16C coloured picture

Refusing to retract once more before the Diet of Worms (1521), where he had been summoned by Charles V, he was then placed under a ban of the Empire. His works were condemned as well.

The patronage of Frederick the Wise, Duke of Saxony, enabled him to continue work on a translation of the Bible considered to be the first literary work in modern German. The Edict of Worms was confirmed in 1529 – and even hardened by an additional ruling forbidding any religious reform.

The Council of Trent (1545-63) resulted in the renewal of Catholicism and the Counter Reformation, which was resolutely supported by the Kaiser. The internal struggles of the Protestants and the feud between Rudolf II and his brother Matthias put an end to the Peace of Augsburg. The Protestant Union led by the Electorate of the Palatinate now faced the Catholic League with the Duchy of Bavaria at its head. The Bohemian Rebellion of 1618 led to he outbreak of the **Thirty Years War**, which began as a religious conflict among the estates and soon engulfed all of Europe.

The war, which was almost exclusively fought on German territory, devastated huge tracts of land, caused general havoc, left the cities in piles of rubble and ash and finally ruined all economic life in the countryside. By the end of the war, only the individual territorial states showed some form of gain in authority at the cost of the empire, whose significance dwindled.

1530	Invited by Charles V to meet in Augsburg; theologians of the opposing faiths fail to agree, and Melanchthon draws up in the name of the Lutherans the "Confession of Augsburg" which becomes the charter of the new Protestantism.
1555	The Peace of Augsburg established a compromise, and Lutheran Protestantism was officially recognised as an equal to Catholicism. The empire thereby lost its sovereignty over religious matters to the territories. The basic pronouncement, *Cujus regio ejus religio* – to each state the religious faith of its people – is one of the legal principles of the religious peace.
1618	The Bohemian estates refuse to recognise the Archduke Ferdinand, the successor of Emperor Matthias, as the Bohemian king. Instead, they elect the Protestant Elector Frederick V from the Palatinate to be their ruler. After the Defenestration of Prague, the situation became more tense and ultimately led to the outbreak of the Thirty Years War.
1618-1623	The first phase of the war (Bohemian-Palatinate War) is decided by the defeat of Frederick V at the battle of Weißen Berg in 1620 against an army commanded by Tilly.

1625-1629	Phase two (the Danish-Dutch War) ends with Denmark's Protestant soldiers being defeated by Imperial troops under Wallenstein.
1630-1635	Sweden enters the war on the Protestant side (Swedish War). King Gustav Adolph II dies in the battle near Lützen.
1635-1648	France, under the leadership of Richelieu, now begins to participate actively in the alliance with Bernhard von Weimar (French-Swedish War). Previously France had avoided open war against the Habsburg countries – whom she felt encircled by – and had simply paid subsidies.
1648	Peace of Münster and Osnabrück after four years of negotiations (see Münster). An eighth elector is created for the Rhineland Palatinate after it becomes known that Bavaria will be allowed to keep the electoral position it took from the Palatinate during the war.
1688-1697	Palatinate War of Succession. Louis XIV lays claim to the left bank of the Rhine; French troops under Louvois devastate the Palatinate.

The Rise of Prussia

In 1415, Burgrave Frederick of Hohenzollern was granted the Electorate of Brandenburg. The Duchy of Prussia, 203 years later also came under the authority of his dynasty. Frederick William (1640-88), the Great Elector, turned the small country into the strongest, best governed northern German state thanks to successful power policies, deprivation of the estates' power, a centralised administration and the creation of a standing army. He also extended the country by adding eastern Pomerania, which he received in the Peace of Westphalia. After the revocation of the Edict of Nantes in France, thousands of Huguenots fled to Brandenburg and built up the economic basis for the rise of Berlin.

His grandson, King Frederick William I continued the good works by laying the foundations to the Prussian military and official state. Fulfilment of ones duty, industriousness, economy and strict discipline on the part of the soldiers were some of the aspects of this state inspired by the "Soldier King".

His son, **Frederick the Great** (1740-86), took the throne in a country with an exemplary administration, and within a few years, he turned it into the second power of the empire. The Silesian War and the Seven Years War got him Silesia and the division of Poland extended his power eastwards. This connoisseur and lover of music and literature, the friend and correspondent of Voltaire, was considered an "enlightened ruler" and had a high reputation among European scholars especially at the beginning of his incumbency. The rule of "Old Fritz" left Prussia with a well organised administration and a close relationship between the king and the nobles, which all formed the cornerstone of Prussian power.

1701	Elector Frederick III is crowned Frederick I King of Prussia in Königsberg.
1740-48	War of Austrian Succession/Silesian Wars: The legality of the Pragmatic Sanction (1713) pronounced by Charles VI is disputed. The war is triggered by Frederick II's troops marching into Silesia.
1756-63	The Seven Years War, during which Prussia joins forces with England against the Kaiser, France and Russia. By the end of the war, Prussia was the fifth European power; the system of power will guide Europe's fate until the outbreak of the First World War.

Prussian reforms: the revolution from above

The reforms already prepared by the General Land Law of 1794, were initially set in motion by Baron von Stein, and, after his dismissal, by Baron von Hardenberg. The two men went about installing new structures for government and society virtually by decree and with almost revolutionary energy. Abolition of serfdom by the Edict of 1807 was of particular importance, as was the lifting of guild compulsion and the introduction of a free crafts market. Educational reforms followed, resulting in the founding of the University in Berlin by Wilhelm von Humboldt (1810) and a military reform. Other reforms included the emancipation of the Jews and the modernisation of the administration.

The Way to a German National State

Since 1792, war raged between France and the other powers of Europe. The Peace of Lunéville, signed in 1801, resulted in the loss of the territories of the left bank of the Rhine. The **Decision of the Deputation of German Estates** (1803) destroyed the political and legal foundations of the old Empire: Dissolution, secularisation and harmonisation of almost all religious and smaller states and of most of the Imperial towns. The beneficiaries were Bavaria, Prussia, Baden and Württemberg. They gained territory, and the latter two were even given Elector ranking. 16 of the south and western German states left the Imperial Union and founded the Rhine Union in 1806 in Paris under the protection of France.

At the **Congress of Vienna** (1814-15), the geographical reorganisation of Europe was discussed and decided upon by all the princes present. The political principles of the conference involved restoration of the political status quo of 1792, legitimising the demands of the Ancien Regime, and solidarity of the princes in combating revolutionary ideas and movements.

The Deutscher Bund

The Deutscher Bund, or German Confederation, a loose federation with little authority and function, was founded by the German Union Act of 1815 out of 39 (politically autonomous) individual states – including four free cities. The kings of Holland, Denmark and the Netherlands were also members. Prussia and Austria were also involved with only part of their territories. The Bundestag (Parliament) consisted of 11 representatives named by the governments. This group met in Frankfurt and was presided over by Austria. Prince Metternich, who came from the Rhineland, played a decisive role in this union after he became the chancellor of Austria. In collaboration with Prussia, he mercilessly crushed the libertarian and national movements. The restoration policies of the Bundestag gave rise to a period of extreme calm (Biedermeier period).

Ever since the 18C, a process of growing together of literature, philosophy, art and music had been taking place in the various German states giving rise to a single German cultural nation that preceded patriotism. The ideals of the French Revolution, the end of the Holy Roman Empire, the experience of French occupation and the reforms all created a backdrop for the growth of a 19C movement that sought a free, unified German national state. One important stage on the way to unity was – taking an economic detour – the foundation of the German Zollverein (Customs Union) at the behest of Prussia.

On 31 March 1848, a pre-Parliament met in Frankfurt and decided to convoke a National Convention, which opened on 18 May in the Paulskirche in Frankfurt. The aim was to pass a liberal constitution and to solve the tough question of what the future state should look like. On the table were the greater German solution, with the Habsburg empire under Austrian leadership, and the smaller German solution, ie without Austria, but with a Hohenzollern emperor at the top. The latter was finally voted in. However, the Prussian king Frederick William IV refused the Imperial crown brought to him by a delegate from the Paulskirche Parliament.

Otto von Bismarck, appointed Minister-President of Prussia in 1862, needed no more than eight years to bring about unification under Prussian rule. With the loyalty of an elite bourgeoisie born through the advances of industrialisation and science in his back – and also in the neutrality of Napoleon III – he aggressively pursued a policy of war. After joining Austria in defeating Denmark in 1864, Prussia then declared war on her German ally and defeated the Imperial troops at the battle of Sadowa. This ended Austrian-Prussian dualism for good. A year later, Bismarck created the North German Alliance, consisting of all German states north of the Main River: Hanover, Hessen and Schleswig-Holstein already belonged to Prussia. The Franco-Prussian War of 1870-71 completed the task of unification.

1806	Napoleon marches into Berlin. Emperor Francis II of Austria surrenders the Roman-German Imperial Crown ending the Holy Roman Empire of the German nation going back to Charlemagne.
1813	Prussia commands the Coalition in the Wars of Liberation against Napoleon, who is defeated in the Battle of Nations at Leipzig.
1814-1815	Congress of Vienna: foundation of the German Confederation; Holy Alliance between Russia, Prussia and Austria.
1819	The Decisions of Karlsbad include press censorship, prohibitions of the fraternities, monitoring of the universities.
1833/34	Founding of the German Customs Union (Zollverein), an economic unification of most German states – except Austria – under Prussian leadership.
1835	First German railway line is opened between Nürnberg and Fürth.
1848	Unrest in France in February spread to Mannheim first and then, in March, to all German states. But the revolution quickly turns into a bourgeois reform movement.

FORMATION OF GERMAN UNITY
(1866-1871)

Kingdom of Prussia in 1865	
Prussian annexations in 1866	
Limits of German Empire in 1871	—
K= Kingdom	GD = Grand Duchy
D = Duchy	● = Free City

The German Empire

The immediate cause of the Franco-Prussian War of 1870 was the claim by the House of Hohenzollern (Leopold von Hohenzollern-Sigmaringen) to the Spanish throne. Bismarck succeeded in kindling national pride on both sides of the border. France then declared war on Prussia. The southern states united with the states of the North German Union led by Prussia. The German princes all stood against France as they had signed secret alliances with Prussia. After the victory of Sedan (2 September), the southern states opened negotiations with Prussia on the issue of German unification. The first years following the founding of the German Reich were marked by an exceptional economic boom, also known as the **Gründerzeit**. One reason for this was the 5 billion francs in reparations that the French had been forced to pay. Combined with the advantages of the larger boundary free economic area and measures to standardise coins, measures and weights, this gave rise to wild developments in the financial, industrial, construction and traffic sectors.

1871	On 18 January, William I is crowned German Emperor in the Mirror Room of Versailles. Imperial Germany, enlarged by the acquisition of Alsace-Lorraine, remains in theory a federation – but it is in fact under Prussian domination. Germany goes from an agricultural to an industrial economy.
1888	William II succeeds his father Frederick II.
1890	After numerous altercations, the Emperor forces Bismarck's resignation. The demographic explosion, added to overheated industrial development leads the Kaiser to play dangerous power politics. The Kaiser's unabashed expansionary policies and dangerous foreign policy decisions provoke the enmity of England, Russia and France.

The First World War and the Weimar Republic

Erupting into an international atmosphere crackling with tension, the assassination of the Austrian Archduke Ferdinand and his wife at Sarajevo on 28 June 1914 unleashed a chain reaction; the pent up frustrations discharged for the next four years on Europe's battlefields. Austria's declaration of war against Serbia mobilised the Great Powers of Europe. Germany's plans fo a war on two fronts originated with a former chief of the General Staff named Von Schlieffen. Ignoring Belgium's neutrality, German troops moved into France. The advance was halted at the River Marne. Slow trench warfare began. On the eastern front German troops under General Hindenburg occupied large sections of Russian territory.

After the November revolution, which dwindled in early 1919 due to the unrest caused by the Spartacists, the model of a liberal democratic state with a strong president was able to get established. On 11 August 1919, Germany adopted a Republican Constitution in Weimar, where the National Convention was meeting. This "republic without republicans" had to shoulder the heavy burden of assuming the obligations of the Treaty of Versailles, which took effect in 1920: This meant recognising guilt for war, diminishing of state territory (loosing important agrarian and industrial areas), loss of colonies, demilitarisation and high reparations.

The only truly republican parties accepting the constitution, the SPD (Social Democrats), the Centre Party and the DDP (German Democratic Party) had a parliamentary majority after 1920. All in all, the Weimar Republic had 16 governments, every eight and a half months on average, the government changed. A galloping inflation broke out fairly soon, brought about by an economic crisis, by difficulties in getting the industrial sector working again and by high government debt: the bourgeoisie was ruined, all financial assets that had not been invested in land or real estate was worth nothing.

Development of bread prices (1kg/2lb)

December 1919: 0.80DM
December 1921: 3.90DM
December 1922: 163.15DM
April 1923: 474DM
July 1923: 3 465DM
August 1923: 69 000DM
September 1923: 1 512 000DM
October 1923: 1 742 000 000DM
December 1923: 399 000 000 000DM

Germany experienced fairly tranquil years from 1924 to 1929, even though the republic did have to deal with major internal and external burdens. In spite of continuously high unemployment figures, an economic upswing did take place, thanks to the Dawes payment plan, the end of the occupation of the Ruhr area and high influx of capital – thanks to the commitment of American investors. Germany was even accepted into the League of Nations (1926) during the incumbency of Chancellor and Foreign minister Gustav Stresemann. A year earlier in Locarno, Germany and France signed a pact pledging not to use violent means to revises boarders – a corresponding agreement could not be signed for the eastern boarders.

However, the Weimar Republic was then swept into the world economic crisis of 1929. High foreign debt, sharp decline in exports, inflation and dramatic unemployment figures all led to the growth of radical political parties, especially the German National Socialist Worker's Party after 1930. They presented a concept that states that to solve the social problems, a "Volksgemeinschaft", ie a people's community, based on race was needed. The Nazi storm-troops and Communist groups increasingly fought it out in the street. The high social strata and the business community saw in Adolf Hitler a bulwark against Communism: on 30 January 1933, almost 10 years after his first attempt at taking power, Hitler was named Chancellor of the Reich by the president Von Hindenburg; it was the end of the Weimar Republic.

1914	On 3 August, Germany declares war on France and Russia.
1917	Russia, shaken by the Bolshevik revolution, asks for an armistice. In the West the United States, whose merchant marine had been attacked by German U-boats, declares war on the Reich.
1918	On 28-29 October, the sailors of the High Sea Fleet mutiny in Wilhelmshaven, the long-awaited revolution breaks out in Germany, worker and soldier councils are formed throughout the country. But the revolution is suppressed by the temporary government of Friedrich Ebert in collaboration with the highest army officers. On 9 November, William II abdicates, Philip Scheidemann proclaims a republic. Two days later, Matthias Erzberger signs the armistice in Compiègne.

The National Convention meets in Weimar, Friedrich Ebert (SPD) is named its first President (1 February); Versailles Peace Treaty is signed (28 June).

Occupation of the Ruhr region on 11 January by France, because Germany has fallen behind on reparation payments. Followed by passive resistance in the Ruhr. The NSDAP (the national Socialist German Workers' Party) attempts a coup in Munich on 8-9 November led by Adolf Hitler, who had joined the party in 1919. The coup is foiled, Hitler is sentenced to jail, but released in 1924.

After the death of Friedrich Ebert, the former Field Marshall General Paul von Hindenburg is elected President.

After an electoral defeat in the Reichstag (Parliament) come a number of presidial cabinets (Brüning, Von Papen, Von Schleicher), ie governments without parliamentary majorities.

At the Reichstag elections in July, the NSDAP becomes the strongest party with almost 38% of the votes. Together with the Communists, the Nazis have an absolute majority, which lets the radical parties block any parliamentary majorities they please.

The Nazi dictatorship and the Second World War

No sooner had the NSDAP taken power under the leadership of Hitler than it began to organise a totalitarian dictatorship and eliminating all democratic rules. In a climate of propaganda, intimidation and terror on the part of the SA, SS and Gestapo, all parties, associations and social organisations were liquidated or dissolved, with the exception of the churches. The NSDAP was declared the sole legal party. Opponents were thrown into concentration camps and murdered. Via the process of taking power and standardising society, the party penetrated every single level of state government, from local to national. A kind of coexistence did remain which was marked by crossing authorities that remained one of the main characteristics of the Nazi state. Art and literature were subjected to censorship: "Degenerate art" was forbidden forcing numerous artists into exile.

The Nürnberg Laws promulgated at the Reich party rally (September 1935) endowed the persecution of the Jews with final, systematic, racist characteristics: prohibitions, loss of civil rights and mass arrests were the instruments of the anti-Semitic ideology. Already on 1 April 1933, the NSDAP ordered a "boycott of the Jews" and thus initiated the gradual expulsion of Germany's 500 000 Jews from public life. In the night of 9-10 November 1938, the Nazis organised a pogrom ("Reichskristallnacht"): synagogues, Jewish apartments and shops were damaged or destroyed. The improved worldwide economic situation helped reduce the number of unemployed as did a programme of public works (motorways, drainage schemes) that had already been planned earlier, a policy of rearmament, and the recruitment of young people into para-statal organisations. In 1942, the National Socialist Reich stood at the zenith of its power: materially speaking and otherwise, many Germans had profited up until that point.

The assault on Poland on 1 September 1939, began the Second World War. Preparations for an annihilation war had already been going full steam since 1936. The aim was to do away with other peoples and build up a greater European area dominated by "Aryan" Eurasians. But the war reached the Germans as soon as the British and the Americans began dropping explosive and incendiary bombs on war-related and residential targets. By the end of the war, Germany lay in ruins, the bulk of the inhabitants were suffering from undernourishment and millions had been chased out of the eastern regions. With the liberation of the concentration camps, the world at large discovered with horror with what cruelty and minute care the Nazis had indeed carried out their policy of genocide against the Jews.

1933	After the fire of the Reichstag on 27 February 1933, for which the Communists are blamed – one suspects that the arsonists actually came from the ranks of the NSDAP itself – the basic political laws of the Weimar constitution are annulled. The Emergency Laws of 1933 give Hitler and his government the power to ignore the Reichstag and the President. On 4 April, a law standardising all the states is passed.
1934	After the death of Hindenburg, Hitler takes over his duties and calls himself henceforth "Führer and Chancellor of the Reich;" the Wehrmacht swears its oath to him.
1936	Illegal occupation of the demilitarised zone of the Rhineland.
1938	On 4 February, Hitler personally takes over supreme command of the Wehrmacht. On 13 March, "Anschluß" ("Attachment") of Austria to the German Reich, confirmed thereafter by a vote. In the Munich Agreement (September), London and Paris give Hitler permission to incorporate the Sudetenland to the German Reich.
1939/40	Non-aggression pact signed between Germany and the Soviet Union on 23 August 1939. Secret additional protocol stipulates establishment of mutual spheres of interest in Eastern Europe. The Wehrmacht begins a victorious campaign into wide areas of Western and Northern Europe. Britain alone can resist. The Wehrmacht supports Italian troops in North Africa.
1941	Hitler attacks Russia in a massive annihilation war, while the Balkans are overrun.
1942	In January, the mass-murder in extermination camps in the east of the Jews living under German occupation is decided at the Wannsee Conference.
1943	After the defeat at Stalingrad, the Soviet army begins its counter-attack. The Americans, involved in the conflict since the Japanese attack on Pearl Harbour (December 1941), land in Sicily in July.
1944	Allied landings in Normandy (June). On 20 July, Hitler narrowly escapes a bomb attack planned by his Colonel von Stauffenberg. Allies land in southern France.
1945	On 30 April, Hitler commits suicide. Unconditional surrender is signed on 7-9 May in Reims and Berlin-Karlshorst. On 5 June it is announced that executive power is now in the hands of representatives of the four victorious nations and will be conducted by them jointly.

1945	Germany and Berlin are divided into four zones of occupation. According to the agreement, American and British forces pull out of Saxony, Thuringia and Mecklenburg and redeploy in the western sector of Berlin. At the Potsdam Conference *(see Potsdam)* the victorious powers decide to demilitarise Germany, to denazify it, democratise it and administer it jointly.
1946	Amalgamation of the British and American zones (bizone).
1948	End of the Four-Power administration of Germany after the Soviet delegate leaves the Allied Controlling Council (20 March). Soviet blockade of the western sectors of Berlin, the city is supplied by the airlift.
1949	Creation (23 May) of the **Federal Republic** in the three western zones. The Soviet zone becomes (7 October) the **German Democratic Republic**. Under the leadership of Konrad Adenauer, Chancellor until 1963, and Ludwig Erhard, Minister of Economic Affairs, the Federal Republic enjoys a spectacular economic rebirth and re-establishes normal international relations. Soviet leadership (the so-called Stalin note); to create a single, neutral, democratic Germany.
1961	Construction of the "Berlin Wall" (12-13 August).
1972	Signature of a treaty between the two Germanies, a milestone in Chancellor Willy Brandt's (chancellor from 1969-74) policy of openness towards the East (Ostpolitik).
1989	Citizens of East Germany occupy West German embassies in Prague, Budapest and Warsaw with the aim of travelling to West Germany. Ever since the opening of the border between Austria and Hungary, a veritable mass flight begins. On 4 November, the largest demonstration ever takes place in East Berlin, involving over one million people. In the night of 9-10 November, the inner German border is opened, the Wall becomes permeable. On 7 December, the Round Table meets for the first time as an institution of public control, with representatives from the political parties and the citizens' movements.
1990	Treaty of reunification drawn up; on 3 October the German Democratic Republic joins the Federal Republic of Germany according to Article 23 of the Basic law. On 2 December, the fist joint German parliamentary elections take place.
1991	The Bundestag decides by a narrow majority that Berlin will become the capital and seat of government of a reunited Germany.
1994	By September, Soviet troops have withdrawn from all the provinces of the former East Germany, and the last Allied troops leave Berlin.
1999	After the Federal President's move to Berlin, it's the turn of the Bundestag, the government's second organ. On 19 April, the Plenary Room of the Reichstag building is officially opened with a session of the Bundestag.

INTER NATIONES, Bonn

Konrad Adenauer

Art and architecture

Germany's geographical location and eventful history have left it open to the influence of artistic currents from the rest of Europe – mainly French in the Gothic period and Italian in the Renaissance period. The originality of German art manifests itself above all in the sumptuous decoration of the Baroque abbeys in Bavaria.

ROMANESQUE ARCHITECTURE (9C-12C)

Pre-Romanesque architecture – In Germany, as elsewhere in the Christian West, religious architecture developed from the adaptation of Roman lay basilicas, the long halls of worship now oriented towards the east and ending in an apse. The central portion is raised above two or four side aisles and the whole covered with a plain wooden ceiling.

The Carolingian period is marked by the building of churches with two chancels. The western chancel sometimes forms part of another characteristic feature: the **Westwerk**, a tall square tower of military appearance onto which the nave is securely anchored. The Westwerk – at Corvey for instance – frequently constitutes almost a church in itself. Such large, tall chapels, opening on the nave via galleries sometimes several storeys high, were traditionally reserved for the emperor.

Ottonian architecture (10C and early 11C) – The restoration of imperial power by Otto I in 962 was accompanied by a revival of religious architecture in Saxony and in the regions of the Meuse and Lower Rhine. The huge churches erected during this period were characterized by deeply projecting transepts and wide aisles. As yet, they had no stone vaulting. An alternation of piers and columns broke up the uniformity of the aisles, which were not yet divided by bays. The churches of St. Michaelis at Hildesheim and St. Cyriacus at Gernrode are the best examples of buildings of this period.

Rhineland Romanesque style – At Cologne and in the surrounding countryside, several churches feature a distinctive ground plan with a triple apse designed in the form of a cloverleaf. These trefoil extensions are adorned on the outside with blind arcades and a "dwarf gallery" (Zwerggalerie) – a motif of Lombard origin. In the Middle Rhine region, the style achieves its full splendour in the majestic "imperial" cathedrals of Speyer, Mainz and Worms. Typical of these cathedrals are floor plans with a double chancel and neither ambulatory nor apsidal chapels, but sometimes with a double transept; an elevation featuring numerous towers; and a richly decorated façade with Zwerggalerien, blind arcades and Lombard bands (vertical motifs in low relief with small blind arcades linking them at the top). A characteristic of these Rhineland towers is a pointed roof in the form of a bishop's mitre, the base decorated with a lozenge pattern. Towards the end of the 11C, the architects of the cathedral at Speyer took the bold step of constructing ribbed stone vaulting over the nave. The churches of Limburg and Andernach and the cathedral at Naumburg, which were built with pointed rib vaulting early in the 13C, mark the transition from Romanesque to Gothic.

GOTHIC ARCHITECTURE (13C-16C)

The most famous example of Gothic architecture in Germany is the cathedral at Cologne, with its vast interior, two tall slender towers framing the façade in the French style and its soaring pointed vaulting. Also inspired by the French Gothic style are the cathedrals of Regensburg, Freiburg-im-Breisgau, Magdeburg and Halberstadt. Further manifestations of French influence are the Cistercian

JÜRGENS OSTEUROPA, Köln

Münster, Bad Doberan

37

monasteries built in such profusion between 1150 and 1250. Their churches, usually without towers or belfries and often later modified in the Baroque manner, were habitually designed with squared-off chancels flanked by rectangular chapels. The abbey of Maulbronn is one of very few monastic complexes preserved in almost its entirety still extant in Europe.

East of the Elbe, the most imposing edifices were brick built, complete with buttresses and flying buttresses. Typical of this brick Gothic style (known in German as Backsteingotik) are the Nikolaikirche at Stralsund, the Marienkirche in Lübeck, the town halls of those two cities, Schwerin Cathedral and the abbey church at Bad Doberan.

Late Gothic architecture (Spätgotik) – This style, which dominated church architecture for centuries (14C, 15C and 16C), manifested itself in Germany with the widespread construction of **hall-churches**, usually with vaulting divided by purely decorative ribs forming stars or intricate groining, a charming contrast to the bareness of the walls. St. Annenkirche at Annaberg-Buchholz epitomises the style which allowed artists to demonstrate their virtuosity freed from all architectonic considerations.

These hall-churches are completely different from those constructed on the basilical plan at the end of the Romanesque period. The aisles are now the same height as the nave, separated from it only by tall columns. The most famous examples – extra-tall buildings erected at the end of the Gothic period – are the Frauenkirche in Munich and the Georgskirche, Dinkelsbühl.

Secular architecture in the Late Middle Ages – Commercial prosperity among merchants and skilled craftsmen in the 14C and 15C led to the construction in town centres of impressive town halls and beautiful half-timbered private houses, frequently adorned with painting and sculpture. Examples of such projects are still to be seen in Regensburg, Goslar, Rothenburg ob der Tauber and Tübingen.

THE RENAISSANCE (c 1520-1620)

The Renaissance, eclipsed by the troubles of the Reformation, is no more than a minor episode in the history of German architecture. Italian influence in this period is restricted to southern Germany: elegant Florentine arcading, for instance, was used by Jakob Fugger the Rich as decoration for his funerary chapel at Augsburg (1518); the Jesuits, building the Michaelskirche in Munich (1589), were clearly inspired by their own Sanctuary of Jesus (Gesù) in Rome. Northern Germany was influenced by Flemish and Dutch design. In the rich merchants' quarters many storeyed gables, such as those of the Gewandhaus in Brunswick, boast rich ornamentation in the form of obelisks, scrollwork, statues, pilasters etc. The castle at Güstrow and the old town of Görlitz are important examples of Renaissance influence, while Celle, Wolfenbüttel, Bückeburg and Hamelin are saturated with the particular charm of the so-called "Weser Renaissance".

BAROQUE ARCHITECTURE (17C-18C)

Characterized by an irregularity of contour and a multiplicity of form, the German Baroque seeks, above all, the effect of movement and contrast. Taken to its extreme, the style becomes Rococo, where the fantasy element is employed mainly as

decoration. From the mid 17C, Baroque influence was most marked in Roman Catholic southern Germany, encouraged by the Counter-Reformation's exaltation of dogmatic belief in Transubstantiation, the cult of the Virgin Mary and the saints, and in general all manifestations of popular piety.

Enterprising abbots set about rebuilding their abbeys to plans so ambitious that they would stupefy modern minds. Masons, painters, sculptors and stucco-workers were thus offered extraordinary opportunities. Stucco designs – worked with an amalgam of lime, plaster and wet sand that could be modelled to give a three-dimensional effect – covered every available surface.

The Masters of German and Danubian Baroque – The blossoming of the Baroque style owes much to the **Vorarlberg School** (1680-1750), of which the masters remain largely anonymous, so great was the group's cooperative spirit. These architects, working chiefly in Swabia but also in Bavaria, Switzerland and even Alsace, lavished a great deal of care on the lines and perspectives of their single naves.

A hall-church – St. Georgskirche; Dinkelsbühl 1) Central nave 2) Side aisle 3) Network vaulting

However, there were also exceptionally talented individuals, in Bavaria especially, who displayed equal skill across a variety of techniques, and who tended to prefer subtle ground plans, such as a round or oval focal shape. Johann Michael Fischer (Dießen, Zwiefalten and Ottobeuren), the Asam brothers (Weltenburg and the Asamkirche in Munich) and Dominikus Zimmermann (Steinhausen and Wies) were the virtuosi of this Bavarian School.

The Baroque movement in Franconia, patronized by the prince-bishops of the Schönborn family, who owned residences in Mainz, Würzburg, Speyer and Bamberg, was closely linked with the spread of similar ideas in Bohemia. The Dientzenhofer brothers decorated the palaces in Prague as well as the one in Bamberg. Perhaps the greatest of all Baroque architects was Balthazar Neumann, who worked for the same prelates, and whose breadth of cultural knowledge and creativity, enriched by his contact with French, Viennese and Italian masters, far surpassed that of his contemporaries.

The west front at Ottobeuren
Abbey Church

In Saxony, the Zwinger Palace in Dresden (joint masterpiece of the architect Pöppelmann and the sculptor Permoser) is a consummate example of German Baroque with Italian roots; the refinement of the Rococo decor in the Schloß Sanssouci at Potsdam is even more astonishing, given the reputed Prussian tendency towards austerity – but is explained by the periods of study undertaken in France and Italy by the architect Knobelsdorff.

Churches – A sinuous movement, generally convex in line, animates the façades, while the superposition of two pediments, different in design, adds vitality to the whole. The façades are additionally adorned with twin domed towers (a single tower in the case of pilgrimage churches). The later the church, the more detached are the towers.

Huge galleries stand above the lateral chapels, at the height of pilaster capitals with jutting abaci. Chapels and galleries stop at the level of the transept, giving it a much greater depth. Clerestory windows, opening at the level of the gallery, allow plenty of light to enter.

Bohemian and Franconian Baroque is typified by **complex vaulting**, round or oval bays being covered by complicated structures in which the transverse arches bow out in horse-shoe shape, only to meet in their keystones.

The **altarpiece** or reredos, focal point of the church furnishing, is treated monumentally, its design architecturally that of a triumphal arch. The arch, in carved wood or stucco, frames either a large painting or a group of statuary. Columns twisted into spiral form accentuate the sense of movement which characterizes Baroque art, and back lighting from a hidden source, with its contrasts of brightness and shadow, is equally typical of the style.

Vaulting at Vierzehnheiligen

Profuse and asymmetric ornamentation is a typical feature of the **Rococo** style.

Palaces – The one-storey construction of these country residences was often lent additional importance by being built on a raised foundation. The focal point was a half-circular central bloc with the curved façade facing the garden. Monumental stairways with several flights and considerable theatrical effect are often the centrepieces of the larger German castles and palaces built in the 18C. The staircase, embellished with arcaded galleries and a painted ceiling, leads to the first floor state room which rises majestically to a height of two storeys. Such elaborate arrangements characterize many of the great abbeys of this period, often complemented by that other ceremonial room, the library.

THE ARRIVAL OF NEO-CLASSICISM

The example of Versailles inspired in Germany a new style of court life, particularly in the Rhineland and the Berlin of Frederick II. Many French architects were employed by the Electors of the Palatinate, of Mainz, of Trier and of Cologne; mainly, they produced plans for country mansions with names such as Monrepos ("my rest") or Solitude.

State staircase at Schloß
Pommersfelden

Features such as unadorned pediments, balustrades at the base of the roofs, columned porticoes at the main entrance, all indicate a desire for unobtrusive elegance outside, while the interior decoration, carried out with a lighter touch, confined itself to cornucopias of flowers mingled with Rococo motifs that were now a little more discreet. From 1750 on, Winckelmann's work on the art of Antiquity, and the excavations taking place at Pompeii, threw a new light on Greco-Roman architecture. A new fashion arose, in which architects favoured the Doric style, the plainest of all, coupled with a preference for the colossal – pilasters and columns of a single "order" no longer stood one storey high but always two. Symmetrical balance and a purely static line became the ideal to such an extent that, in some churches, a false pulpit was added to balance the genuine preacher's eyrie. As well as churches, abbeys and castles, skilled craftsmen now turned their attention to commemorative monuments and museums – a new sign of their interest in the past – especially in Berlin where Schinkel, the master of the colonnade, was active. Interior decoration showed a preference for sculptured motifs such as garlands, urns, vases and friezes of pearls.

By 1830, the neo-Classical movement had become sterile; it was superseded, except in Munich, by a renewed interest in the Gothic which became, for the Romantics, emblematic of "the old Germany". The **Biedermeier** taste – lightweight, cushioned furniture with flowing lines, glass-fronted cabinets for the display of knick-knacks – corresponded perhaps with the later Edwardian style in England.

The year 1850 marks the beginning of the **Gründerzeit** (Founders' Period), when wealthy industrialists fell for pretentious reproductions of medieval or Renaissance furniture. Similiar pieces were to be found also in public buildings such as the Reichstag in Berlin.

MODERN AND CONTEMPORARY MOVEMENTS

At the beginning of the 20C, **Jugendstil** ("Style 1900") or Art Nouveau became the vogue in Germany, largely due to mass production of well-made furniture. Of far greater importance to Germany was the growth of the idea that there could be an aesthetic for industrial design, promoted by such pioneers as Peter Behrens, Mies van der Rohe and Walter Gropius. After the First World War, Gropius was appointed head of the **Bauhaus** (see p 42).

Urban growth and the reparation of war damage after the Second World War called for the building or rebuilding of many churches, and architects such as Dominikus Böhm and Rudolf Schwartz were among the craftsmen who were brought to light by this renewal of interest in sacred work, many of their designs being markedly austere. New concepts, too, characterized the construction of municipal and cultural enterprises such as Hans Scharoun's Philharmonia in Berlin and the Staatsgalerie in Stuttgart by British architect James Stirling – buildings of an architectural audacity only made possible by the development of entirely new materials and construction techniques.

GERMANY'S GREAT ARTISTS

Architects and Sculptors (blue lettering) – **Painters and Engravers** (1)

15C

Stefan Lochner (d 1451) – This leading master of the Cologne School is famous for his Madonnas with sweet expressions, executed in an exquisitely delicate palette, generally on a gold background (**Adoration of the Magi**, Cologne Cathedral; **Virgin and Rose Bush**, Wallraf-Richartz-Museum/Museum Ludwig, Cologne).

Veit Stoß (c 1445-1533) – Sculptor, painter and engraver with a distinctive, powerful style; one of the greatest woodcarvers of his age (**Angel's Greeting**, Lorenzkirche, Nuremberg; **Reredos of the Nativity**, Bamberg Cathedral).

Tilman Riemenschneider (1460-1531) – Outstanding sculptor and woodcarver of his age whose intricate works are executed with great finesse and richness of expression (**Tomb of Henry II the Saint**, Bamberg Cathedral; **Adam and Eve**, Mainfränkisches Museum, Würzburg; **Altarpiece to the Virgin**, Herrgottskirche, Creglingen).

The Master of St Severinus (late 15C) – The intimacy and iridescent colours of his works reflect Netherlandish influence (**Christ before Pilate**, Wallraf-Richartz-Museum/Museum Ludwig, Cologne).

The Master of the Life of the Virgin (late 15C) – Painter of minutely observed, vivid works, influenced by Van der Weyden (**Vision of St Bernard**, Wallraf-Richartz–Museum/Museum Ludwig, Cologne).

Friedrich Herlin (d 1500) – Picturesque and precise Realist, also influenced by Van der Weyden (**Almswomen at Prayer**, Stadt-museum, Nördlingen).

---

(1) Artists in the 16C were, as a rule, both painters and engravers.

16C

Matthias Grünewald (c 1460-1528) – An inspired painter, producing works of great emotional intensity on religious subjects, in particular the Crucifixion (**Crucifixion**, Staatliche Kunsthalle, Karlsruhe; **Virgin and Child**, Stuppach parish church).

Albrecht Dürer (1471-1528) – A humanist, deeply affected by the reformation, and the greatest artist of the German Renaissance; his religious scenes and portraits are of an extraordinary intensity; he produced a profusion of wonderful drawings and engravings with a masterful richness of detail (**The Four Apostles, Self-Portrait with Cloak**, Alte Pinakothek, Munich; **Charlemagne**, Germanisches Nationalmuseum, Nuremberg).

Lucas Cranach the Elder (1472-1553) – Master of an important studio; portraitist of the most eminent men of the Reformation, but also famous for his paintings of beautiful women, many of whom he depicts nude apart from a large hat and a strategically draped but diaphanous wisp of fabric. His works reflect a strong sense of the wonders of nature allying him with the painters of the Danube School (**Portrait of Martin Luther**, Germanisches Nationalmuseum, Nuremberg).

Venus in a Landscape by Lucas Cranach the Elder

RÉUNION DES MUSÉES NATIONAUX, Paris

Albrecht Altdorfer (1480-1538) – Leading member of the Danube School and one of the earliest landscape painters. His use of chiaroscuro creates dramatic and moving works (**Battle of Alexander at Issus**, Alte Pinakothek, Munich).

Hans Baldung Grien (c 1485-1545) – Master painter and graphic artist achieving his effects by the use of unusual colours and dramatic lighting (**Altarpiece: The Coronation of the Virgin**, Freiburg Cathedral).

Hans Holbein the Younger (1497-1543) – Author of religious compositions and portraits of a striking realism (**The Nativity and the Adoration of the Magi**, Freiburg Cathedral, **Portrait of the Merchant Georg Gisze**, Museum Dahlem, Berlin).

17C

Adam Elsheimer (1578-1610) – Elsheimer's mythological and biblical paintings were often small scale but exquisitely worked and his influence is apparent in the work of numerous French and Italian artists (**The Flight into Egypt**, Alte Pinakothek, Munich).

Elias Holl (1573-1646) – Architect responsible for the most important buildings of the Renaissance in Germany (**Rathaus, Augsburg**).

Andreas Schlüter (c 1660-1714) – Master of Baroque sculpture in northern Germany, who produced some powerful sculptures in stone (**Statue of the Great Elector**, Schloß Charlottenburg, Berlin; **Masks of Dying Warriors**, Zeughaus, Berlin).

The Merians (17C) – A family of engravers specializing in plates illustrating German towns.

18C

Balthasar Permoser (1651-1732) – Sculptor to the Court of Dresden. His masterful works in the exuberant style of the Italian Baroque reflect the lengthy periods he spent in Rome, Florence and Venice (**Wallpavillon** and **Nymphenbad**, Zwinger, Dresden).

Matthäus Daniel Pöppelmann (1662-1736) – Architect-in-Chief to Augustus the Strong, he worked in Prague, Vienna and Italy before designing his masterpiece, the **Zwinger**, in Dresden, an epitome of the Late Baroque style.

Dominikus Zimmermann (1685-1766) – Architect of the most successful churches in the Bavarian Rococo style (**Churches of Wies and of Steinhausen**).

Balthasar Neumann (1687-1753) – Architect and engineer. Technical virtuosity and the innate harmony of his compositions made him a master of the Baroque style (**Vierzehnheiligen Church**).

The Asam Brothers – The sculptor Egid Quirin (1692-1750) and his brother, the painter and architect Cosmas Damian Asam (1686-1739) provide a splendid example of the collaboration between artists during the Baroque period (**Asamkirche**, Munich).

Georg Wenzeslaus von Knobelsdorff (1699-1753) – Official architect and friend of Frederick the Great; master of the Rococo (**Berlin Opera House; Schloß Sanssouci**, Potsdam).

19C

Caspar David Friedrich (1774-1840) – Great German Romantic painter, who had a particular genius for landscape painting (**The Monk by the Sea, The Cross on the Mountain,** Private Apartments, Charlottenburg, Berlin; **Rambler Above a Sea of Clouds**, Kunsthalle, Hamburg).

Karl Friedrich Schinkel (1781-1841) – Architect whose long, elegant neo-Classical colonnades typify the cityscape of central Berlin (**Neue Wache, Altes Museum** and **Schauspielhaus**).

Wilhelm Leibl (1844-1900) – Master of Realism (**Three Women in Church**, Kunsthalle, Hamburg; **Portrait of Frau Gedon**, Neue Pinakothek, Munich).

Adolf von Hildebrand (1847-1921) – As a monumental sculptor, his measured taste is in contrast to the excesses of most 19C artists (**Wittelsbach Fountain**, Munich).

Max Liebermann (1847-1935) – Leading German Impressionist painter (**Jewish Street in Amsterdam**, Wallraf-Richartz-Museum/Museum Ludwig, Cologne).

20C

Ernst Barlach (1870-1938) – His monumental, tormented sculptures in wood and bronze are characteristic of the Expressionist school (**The Angel**, Antoniterkirche, Cologne; **Frieze of the Listeners**, Ernst-Barlach-Haus, Hamburg; **The Singer**, Ratzeburg).

Dominikus Böhm (1880-1955) – Pioneer of a new type of religious architecture (**Church of Maria Königin**, Cologne; **Church of St. Wolfgang**, Regensburg).

The Bauhaus – School of Architecture and Applied Arts founded in Weimar then transferred to Dessau where it was directed from 1925 to 1928 by Walter Gropius (1883-1969). The marriage of all plastic arts with architecture, breaking down the division between monumental and decorative elements, was the fundamental theme uniting the members of this school, which soon attracted a host of exceptionally talented avant-garde painters and sculptors *(see DESSAU and WEIMAR)*.

The Expressionists – German Expressionism introduced an emotionally charged, often violent or tragic vision of the world to modern painting. The movement owed much to Van Gogh and the Norwegian painter Edvard Munch (1863-1944), whose work had a marked influence in Germany. See the works of **Emil Nolde** (1867-1956) at Seebüll; and of Expressionism in general at the Brücke-Museum, Berlin. The **Brücke** (Bridge) Group united from 1905 to 1913 such painters as Erich Heckel, Ernst Ludwig Kirchner, Karl Schmidt-Rottluff – whose work, with its passion for pure colour, recalls that of the Fauves in France.

Der Blaue Reiter (The Blue Rider Movement) – Association of Expressionist artists founded in Munich in 1911 by Kandinsky and Marc, later to be joined by Macke and Klee. Although the work of the artists involved differed widely, they were united by a general aim to free art from the constraints of reality, thus opening the way to abstraction (**Deer in the Forest** by **Franz Marc**, Orangerie Staatliche Kunsthalle, Karlsruhe; **The Dress Shop** by **August Macke**, Folkwang-Museum, Essen).

Neue Sachlichkeit (New Objectivity) – An artistic movement affecting all the arts which grew up after 1923, aiming to produce a realistic illustration of social facts and phenomena (**War** by **Otto Dix**, 1932, Albertinum in Dresden).

STAATLICHE KUNSTHALLE, Karlsruhe

Deer in the Forest by Franz Marc

Second half of the 20C – The mood of disillusionment in the wake of the First World War also found its expression in the anarchic nihilism of the **Dada** movement, of which Kurt Schwitters (1887-1948) was the main exponent in Germany. After the Second World War, Abstract art was advocated by West German artists such as Willi Baumeister, Julius Bissier and Ernst Wilhelm Nay (who formed the Zen group), not least because it was far removed from the style of art favoured by the Nazi regime. In the early 1950s, Otto Greis, Bernhard Schultze, Hans Kreutz and Karl-Otto Götz formed the Quadriga group, representing German **Art Informel** (linked with Tachisme), while the members of **Gruppe Zero** (Heinz Mack, Otto Piene, Günther Uecker), formed in 1957, concentrated on light, movement and material objects in their work. A high point of abstract painting in Germany was the Documenta II exhibition held in Kassel in 1959 (the **Documenta** exhibition dedicated to contemporary art takes place every four years, generally in Kassel, and is just one of the initiatives of the German art scene to "demystify" modern art).

The 1960s saw a turning point in German artistic creativity. **Gruppe Zebra** (Dieter Asmus, Nikolaus Störtenbecker, Dietmar Ullrich), took up the credo of New Objectivity against German Abstract art. Konrad Klapheck used a hyper-realistic style to depict objects and machines from everyday life in his cool, almost clinical paintings.

A giant of the German art scene and one of the most influential avant-garde artists in Europe was **Joseph Beuys**. In the 1960s and 1970s, together with the artists of his entourage (school of Constructivist Sculpture in Düsseldorf), he strove to create a direct relationship between the artist and the viewing public in his Happenings and Performances, and to redefine the role of art and the artist in contemporary society (works by Beuys can be found in the Kunsthalle in Hamburg, the Neue Nationalgalerie in Berlin, the Hessisches Landesmuseum in Darmstadt and the Staatsgalerie in Stuttgart).

At the end of the 1970s, the term **"Neue Wilde"** (New Savages) was coined for a group of neo-Expressionist painters as diverse as their subject matter, who included **Georg Baselitz**, **Jörg Immendorff**, **Anselm Kiefer**, Markus Lüpertz, AR Penck, **Sigmar Polke** and Gerhard Richter. This new generation of German artists managed to break through onto the international scene, exploring the theme of Germany stripped of all illusion and using their art to examine the age in which they lived. Many contemporary artists are experimenting with media arising from developments in technology, such as video.

Social Realism dominated art in **East Germany** until well into the 1960s and 1970s, although there have been signs of growing experimentation since 1970. Artistic creativity on the whole took ideologically sound themes as its subjects (workers, historical themes). The painters of Leipzig in particular won international acclaim. Among the most prominent painters of this new variation of social Realism are Bernhard Heisig, Wolfgang Mattheuer, Willi Sitte and Werner Tübke, whose enormous panoramic paintings of the German Peasant's War (at Bad Franken-hausen) belong to the most monumental creations in painting. In East Germany in the years leading up to reunification, non-conformist artists were also given the opportunity to express themselves.

Literature

Great philosophers' names appear in **bold** type.

Middle Ages

9C	The Lay of Hildebrand.
Late 12C	National folk saga of the Nibelungen.
13C	Wolfram von Eschenbach writes *Parzifal* – an epic poem recounting a knight's quest for the Holy Grail (chalice said to have contained the blood of Christ).
1170-1228	Walther von der Vogelweide, knight and greatest of the Minnesänger or troubadours, raises Middle High German lyric poetry to its loftiest heights.
Early 16C	Chronicle of the comic adventures of practical joker Till Eulenspiegel.

The Reformation and the Thirty Years War

Only at the end of the Reformation and after the devastation wrought by the Thirty Years War was German literature, indeed any cultural activity, in a position to continue its development.

1534	Luther finishes his translation of the Bible, recognised as the first literary work written in modern German.
1669	Grimmelshausen publishes his account of the fortunes and misfortunes of the lovable rogue Simplicissimus, in a picaresque novel *(Schelmenroman)* considered to be the greatest of its age.

"Aufklärung" (Age of Enlightenment)

1646-1716	**Leibniz**, philosopher, mathematician and linguist, writes his *Theodicy* in French and in Latin; he invents differential calculus with no knowledge of Newton's work on the subject.
1729-1781	Lessing sets down the principles of the new German theatre *(Hamburg Theory of Drama)*; in defiance of Aristotle, he writes the first German tragedies in domestic, "non-aristocratic" settings (Bürgerliches Trauerspiel, eg *Emilia Galotti*).
1724-1804	**Kant** defines the balance between liberty and morality: man finds liberty in submission to "the categorical imperative".

"Sturm und Drang" and Classicism

In reaction to the strict rationalism of the Aufklärung, the "Sturm und Drang" movement exalts freedom, emotion and nature. Johann Wolfgang von Goethe (1749-1832), a universal genius (science, poetry, philosophy, theatre), eventually tempers this fashionable enthusiasm with a proposal for the more disciplined, classical ideal of a noble, serene and harmonious humanity.

Johann Wolfgang von Goethe

Lausat/EXPLORER, Paris

1759-1805	Schiller, poet and dramatist, writes historical dramas *(Don Carlos, Wallenstein, Maria Stuart* and *Wilhelm Tell)* which are undisguised hymns to liberty.
1774	*The Sorrows of Young Werther*, the novel in the form of correspondence (Part One), which traces the doomed passion of a young man increasingly unable to identify with the world around him, makes the young Goethe's reputation.
1788	Returning from Italy, Goethe publishes his great classical dramas: *Iphigenie auf Tauris, Egmont* and *Torquato Tasso*.
1796 and 1821	Goethe's *Wilhelm Meister* – a Bildungsroman (novel of educational development) in two parts.
1808 and 1832	*Faust (Parts I and II)*, a drama in verse containing the quintessence of Goethe's philosophy, drawing on a lifetime's wealth of experience, considered by many to be the greatest work of German literature.

The Romantic movement (1790-1850)

This movement, part of a Europe-wide one, but which reflects certain deep-rooted aspects of the German character, charts the individual soul's quest for the infinite in all its forms. It is the movement of Me, incorporating, besides literature, the fine arts, philosophy, politics and religion. Heidelberg, Jena and Berlin are centres from which the movement blossoms. The Romantic can create his own world from reality or from fantasy and he is able to turn whatever he likes into poetry. The subconscious becomes a subject for serious study and Romantic subjectivism leads to popular interest in the supernatural and religious mysticism.

1770-1831	**Hegel** defines the historical conscience and dialectic.
1772-1801	Novalis, poet and mystic, exalts the art and religion of the Middle Ages; his "Blue Flower symbol" (*Heinrich von Ofterdingen*) comes to represent the Absolute, or object of Romantic longing.
1805	Publication of *The Child with the Magic Horn (Des Knaben Wunderhorn)*, a collection of popular folk poems.
1810	Heinrich von Kleist writes *The Prince of Homburg*, a play about a man of action led away by his dreams. Von Kleist also publishes (1804) *The Marquise of O...* one of a collection of eight powerful novellas.
1812	First publication of *Grimms' Fairy Tales*.
1776-1822	ETA Hoffmann explores the world of fantasy and the supernatural in his vivid tales.

Naturalism and political realism

The disillusioned idealism of the Romantic Movement is succeeded by a search for realism and, after 1848, by historical materialism and social-critical literature.

1797-1856	Heinrich Heine, the "defrocked Romantic", poet of the *Loreley*, mingles a bitter irony with the heated emotions of a liberal "Young Germany".
1788-1860	**Arthur Schopenhauer**, pessimistic theorist of the human will as slave-master, propounds pity as the only antidote to life's suffering.
1813-1863	Hebbel composes powerful tragedies (*Maria Magdalena*, *Agnes Bernauer*).
1848	**Karl Marx** and **Friedrich Engels** publish their *Communist Manifesto*.
1862-1946	Gerhart Hauptmann develops Naturalist, social-critical drama (*The Weavers*).

The modern period

1844-1900	**Friedrich Nietzsche** denounces, in lyrical language, the decadence of humanity, praising a future "super-man" freed from slavish, accepted (especially Christian) morality (*Thus Spoke Zarathustra*).
1868-1933	Stefan George publishes poems which, in their formal perfection, ally him with the French Symbolists.
1875-1955	Thomas Mann, novelist (*Buddenbrooks*, *Dr Faustus*, *The Magic Mountain* and *Death in Venice*).
1877-1962	Hermann Hesse's preoccupation with psychoanalytical issues and most particularly the conflicting sides of man's nature produces some masterly novels (*Der Steppenwolf*, *Narziß und Goldmund*, *The Glass Bead Game*).
1883-1924	Franz Kafka, symbolic novelist of the nightmarish and the absurd (*The Trial*, *Metamorphosis*, *The Castle* and *America*).
1898-1956	Bertolt Brecht, social-critical dramatist who experimented with radical new forms of theatre (*The Threepenny Opera*, *Mother Courage*, *Galileo* and *Caucasian Chalk Circle*).
c 1900-1930	Austrian poets Rainer Maria Rilke and Hugo von Hofmannsthal represent the peak of lyrical impressionism.
1900-1983	Anna Seghers, exiled since 1933, returns to East Germany after the war and questions the relationship between art and reality.
1920-1950	The Existentialist movement (**Husserl, Heidegger, Jaspers**).

National Socialism forced numerous poets and writers into exile (Walter Benjamin, Alfred Döblin, Lion Feuchtwanger, Else Lasker-Schüler, Thomas and Heinrich Mann, Carl Zuckmayer, Stefan Zweig). Others, such as Gottfried Benn (1886-1956) and Ernst Jünger (1895-1998), to avoid being penalised opted for the "inward emigration" undertaken by dissenting authors, who rather than expressing their disapproval of the Nazi regime withdrew into silence, or strictly non-political writing, or in one or two bolder cases seemingly non-political work open to a political interpretation on closer examination (eg Jünger's *Auf den Marmorklippen*, 1939).

Post-1945 literature

Twelve years under National Socialist rule had broken the flow of literary creation in Germany, necessitating repair work in this domain too. The association of authors known as **Gruppe 47** (after the year of its founding), which centred around Hans Werner Richter and Alfred Andersch, was instrumental in putting Germany back onto the map as far as world literature was concerned. This loosely associated group of writers served as a forum for reading, discussion and criticism, until its last conference in 1967, exerting a lasting and formative influence on the contemporary German literary scene. Authors associated with Gruppe 47 included Paul Celan, Heinrich Böll (Nobel Prize winner in 1972), Günter Grass, Siegfried Lenz, Peter Weiss and Hans Magnus Enzensberger. By the end of the 1950s, works of international standing were being produced: Günter Grass' masterpiece *The Tin Drum*; Uwe Johnson's *Speculations about Jakob*; Heinrich Böll's *Billiards at Half Past Nine*; and Martin Walser's first novel *Marriages in Philippsburg*.

Increasing politicisation was what finally put an end to Gruppe 47's activities.

Authors not associated with Gruppe 47 were hard at work also; Arno Schmidt developed a highly original and well-received body of work, while Wolfgang Koeppen produced some wickedly satirical novels on contemporary society. The literature of the 1960s was characterised by a wave of social criticism, but by the 1970s German literary concerns were withdrawing to a newly discovered "inner contemplation". A particularly prolific amount of good writing was produced by women during the 1970s and 1980s (Gabriele Wohmann, Karin Struck, Verena Stefan).

In the world of **theatre**, dominated initially by the dramatic theory of Bertolt Brecht, a new band of writers began to make their presence felt, with works by Tankred Dorst (*Toller*, 1968), Peter Weiss (*Hölderlin*, 1971) and Heinar Kipphardt. Rolf Hochhuth was particularly successful with his "documentary dramas" in which he examines contemporary moral issues (*The Representative*, 1963), and Botho Strauß, the most widely performed modern German dramatist, has won international acclaim with plays such as *The Hypochondriac* (1972), *The Park* (1983) and *Final Chorus* (1991).

The division of Germany was naturally reflected in German literature. In the old **East German Republic**, the leadership viewed literature's raison d'être as the contribution it might make to the socialist programme for educating the masses. The Bitterfelder Weg, a combined propaganda exercise and literary experiment launched at the Bitterfeld chemical factory in 1959 as part of the East German Republic's cultural programme under Walter Ulbricht, was intended to unite art and everyday life and break down class barriers. Factory visits were organised for writers, so that they could observe the workers and then portray them glowingly in their novels, poems or plays, while the workers themselves were encouraged to write about their lives. The results of the project were mixed, and although it gave authors a clearer idea of the primitive conditions under which most of the East German labourforce was obliged to work, those who wrote too honestly about what they saw laid themselves open to the censor's pen. Poetry was the literary form least easily subject to the censorship of the Communist Party and the State, and poets such as Peter Huchel, Johannes Bobrowski and Erich Arendt produced some remarkable work. During the 1970s, Günter Kunert, Reiner Kunze, Sarah Kirsch and Wolf Biermann all made a name for themselves. Biermann's expatriation from the DDR in 1976 provoked a storm of protest and hundreds of expulsions and emigrations. From the early 1960s the prose work of Günter de Bruyn, Stefan Heym and Erwin Strittmacher was widely appreciated, and Christa Wolf became the new Anna Seghers, winning equal approbation in both Germanies. Important contributions to the theatre were made by playwrights Ulrich Plenzdorf, Peter Hacks and above all Heiner Müller (*The Hamlet Machine*, 1978).

Any overview of German literature since the Second World War must, of course, acknowledge the enormous contribution made by Max Frisch and Friedrich Dürrenmatt, of Switzerland, and Ilse Aichinger, Ingeborg Bachmann and Thomas Bernhard of Austria.

Music

Middle Ages

12C and 13C	The Minnesänger, minstrels and troubadours who included in their number aristocratic knights such as **Wolfram von Eschenbach** and **Walther von der Vogelweide**, draw inspiration from French lyric poetry for their songs (Minnesang meaning love song).
14C and 15C	The Meistersinger (Master singers) organize themselves into guilds. They introduce polyphony to German music (**Heinrich von Meißen** and **Hans Sachs**).

Luther (1483-1546) and the precursors of Bach

In the wake of the Reformation German music begins to develop an individual identity. The new liturgy requires a new musical form: the chorale. Sung in German, rather than Latin, this eventually gives rise to the German cantata and oratorio.

1529	Chorale *Eine Feste Burg* (words by Luther, music by **Johann Walther**).
1645	*The Seven Words of Christ*, by **Heinrich Schütz**, shows Italian influence (Monteverdi).
1637-1707	**Dietrich Buxtehude** (Danish composer who was organist at the Marien-kirche in Lübeck) organizes the first concerts of sacred music.

Bach (1685-1750)

His consummate skill as a composer, his genius for invention and his mastery of counterpoint enable **Johann Sebastian Bach** to excel in every kind of music he writes.

Eichhorn/EXPLORER, Paris

Johann Sebastian Bach

1717-23	Kapellmeister at court of Cöthen. *The Brandenburg Concertos.*
1723	Following his appointment as "Cantor" at St Thomas School, Leipzig, Bach's duties include the composition of a cantata for every Sunday service, as well as the supervision of services at four other churches. He also taught Latin and voice and still found time left over to write his own instrumental and vocal works.
1722-44	*The Well-Tempered Clavier.*

Music of the Baroque period

1685-1759	**Georg Friedrich Händel**, inspired and prolific Composer to the Courts of Hanover and St James (London), excels in both opera and oratorio (*The Messiah*, 1742).
1681-1767	**Georg Philipp Telemann**, influenced by French and Italian composers, turns from counterpoint to harmony. He initiates public concerts.
Middle of 18C	Musicians of the **School of Mannheim** help establish the form of the modern symphony. **Carl Philipp Emmanuel Bach** (1714-88) popularizes the sonata in its classic form. Appearance in Germany of the **Singspiel**, a type of popular operetta in which dialogue is interspersed with songs in the form of Lieder.
1743	Berlin's first Opera House is built.
1714-87	**Christoph Willibald Gluck** provokes the enthusiasm of the innovators – and the horror of fans of traditional, Italian-inspired opera – by staging, in Paris, his *Iphigenia in Aulis* and *Orpheus*.

The Viennese School – Haydn and Mozart

The work of these two great Austrian composers constitutes the highlight of the Classical period. **Joseph Haydn** (1732-1809), a prolific composer whose talents produce a vast output of music of all types, lays down the classical form of the symphony and the string quartet in four movements. **Wolfgang Amadeus Mozart** (1756-91) perfects both these forms, writing over 600 compositions (later catalogued by Köchel) during his short lifetime, including 41 symphonies, numerous concertos, string quartets and sonatas and some truly immortal operas.

Beethoven (1770-1827)

With his innovative harmonizations, **Ludwig van Beethoven** develops a highly individual style and transforms existing forms of music, heralding the Romantic movement. The depth of his inspiration, ranging from pure introspection to a wider belief in the force and universality of his art, emanates from his work with extraordinary power, perhaps most particularly in his symphonies, moving and majestic works, considered to be the principle expression of his genius – and certainly the most popular.

1824 | First performance of the magnificent *Ninth Symphony*.

The Romantics

1797-1826 | Austrian composer **Franz Schubert** focused much creative energy on the Lied (song), blending folk and classical music in a unique style. His music brought Romantic music to its first high point.

1786-1826 | **Carl Maria von Weber** creates Germany's first Romantic opera, *Freischütz* (1821), paving the way for the characters of Wagnerian drama.

1809-47 | **Felix Mendelssohn-Bartholdy**, although espousing classical musical forms, reveals himself as more Romantic at heart in his shorter lyrical compositions. An early success was his *Midsummer Night's Dream* overture, and his *Hebrides* overture and *Scottish Symphony* were inspired by a tour he made in Scotland.

1810-56 | **Robert Schumann**, passionate and lyrical in turn, but brought up in the Germanic tradition, strives to reconcile a classical heritage with personal expression.

1833-97 | **Johannes Brahms** exemplifies a more introverted style of German Romanticism. His compositions span a variety of musical forms and include the great choral work *German Requiem*.

Richard Wagner (1813-83)

EXPLORER, Paris

Richard Wagner

Richard Wagner revolutionises German opera, claiming that music should be subservient to the dramatic action, being there to create "atmosphere" and a "backdrop of sound" without which the opera's message could not be fully conveyed. Orchestration thus becomes of paramount importance. Libretto and plot unfold continuously, to preserve dramatic reality. Wagner introduces the use of "leit-motifs" – musical phrases used recurrently to denote specific characters, moods or situations – making them essential to the continuity of the action. The strongly German significance of Wagner's works can for some listeners compromise their universality.

1848 | *Lohengrin*.

1876 | Inauguration of the Bayreuth Festival Theatre with *The Ring (Rheingold, Walküre, Siegfried, Götterdämmerung)*.

1882 | *Parsifal*.

Late 19C

At the end of the 19C, **Gustav Mahler** (1860-1911), Czech-Austrian composer and creator of the symphonic Lied, and Austrian **Hugo Wolf** (1850-1903) develop a new musical language which forms a bridge between Romanticism and Dodecaphony. **Richard Strauss** (1864-1949) unites a certain harmonic audacity with a dazzling and multifaceted style.

Contemporary Music

Contemporary musical experimentation is derived principally from the Austrian school of atonal, or serial (especially 12-note systems) music **(Arnold Schönberg, Alban Berg, Anton von Webern)**. **Paul Hindemith** (1893-1963), on the other hand, remains faithful to a traditional national style.

1895-1982 | **Carl Orff's** innovative ideas about music education (Orffsches Schulwerk, 1930-33) win him international acclaim. His theatrical compositions combine drama, speech and song in a fascinating rhythmic framework (*Carmina Burana*).

1921	Berg's *Wozzeck*.
1900-1950	**Kurt Weill**, influenced at the beginning of his career by the atonal composers, returns under the impact of jazz to tonal music, and composes *The Threepenny Opera* (1928) in collaboration with Brecht.
1901-1983	The compositions – mainly opera and ballet music – of **Werner Egk**, a student of Carl Orff, reveal the influence of Igor Stravinsky and Richard Strauss.

If **Wolfgang Fortner** (1907-87) is influenced initially by Hindemith, he nonetheless later turns to modal 12-note serial music. His mature works introduce electronic elements into his musical compositions.

Bernd Alois Zimmermann (1918-70) perceives past, present and future as one, and the multiple layers of reality are reflected in his composition technique. Quotations and collage are particularly important to him. His major work is the opera *The Soldiers*. From 1950, a younger generation of musicians develops the potential of electronic music under the aegis of **Karlheinz Stockhausen** (b 1920). **Hans Werner Henze** (b 1926) creates expressive operas, in which modernity and tradition, and atonality and tonality are combined. **Wolfgang Rihm** (b 1952), like Henze, a student of Fortner, also mixes traditional stylistic elements with new techniques in his extremely complex musical language.

Stage and screen

Few countries can boast a cultural life so intense, so decentralized and involving so great a proportion of the population as modern Germany.

Music and the theatre

Amateur orchestras as well as highly regarded professional organizations proliferate all over the country: the Berlin Philharmonic, the Gewandhaus Orchestra of Leipzig, the Bamberg Symphony Orchestra and resident radio station orchestras (Südwestfunk, Norddeutscher Rundfunk 3, Westdeutscher Rundfunk 3), and thus perpetuate a strong musical tradition.

This decentralization is equally characteristic of drama and the lyric arts. It is due to the founding of theatres by the sovereigns of the 17C and 18C and, subsequently, by the wealthier classes living in the big towns in the 19C.

Among the most important centres concentrating on music and the lyric arts, Bayreuth is celebrated for performances of the works of Wagner; Berlin, Hamburg, Dresden, Leipzig and Stuttgart for opera and ballet; and Nuremberg for organ music. Stuttgart again is renowned for choral singing, and Munich for the music of Bach and Richard Strauss. Donaueschingen, Darmstadt and Kassel are noted for performances of works by contemporary composers.

Cinema

The creation in 1917 of UFA (Universum Film Aktiengesellschaft) a production company of considerable means, plus the emergence of an expressionist movement linked with the troubled post-war political and social scene, produced the golden age of German cinema. Aside from the more lavish productions, the period is marked by the work of directors **Robert Wiene** (*The Cabinet of Dr Caligari*, 1919), **Fritz Lang** (*Dr Mabuse*, 1922; *Metropolis*, 1925) and **Friedrich Wilhelm Murnau** (*Nosferatu the Vampire*, 1922; *Faust*, 1926). Georg Wilhelm Pabst's *Lulu* (1929) and *The Blue Angel* of Josef von Sternberg (1930), with **Marlene Dietrich**, marked a change of direction towards realism.

This adventurous spirit was quenched with the arrival of the Third Reich, in which the cinema became no more than a tool in the service of an ideology. *The Gods of the Stadium* (**Leni Riefensthal**, 1938) – a glorification of the 1936 Berlin Olympics – and *Jud Süß* (Veit Harlan, 1940) remain the most striking examples. The period immediately after the Second World War was a cultural desert for the German cinema.

In the 1960s and 1970s makers of "New German cinema" rose up in the wake of the French "nouvelle vague", seeking to distance themselves from old-style cinema with its run-of-the-mill commercial superficiality. Films made by **Werner Herzog** (*Young Törless*, 1966) and Alexander Kluge (*Artists at the Top of the Big Top: Disorientated*, 1968) quickly met with success. It was not long – the mid 1970s – before this younger generation had reestablished German cinema on an international scale. **Volker Schlöndorff** made *The Lost Honour of Katharina Blum* (in collaboration with Margarethe von Trotta, 1975), and *The Tin Drum* (1979). Werner Herzog went on to explore a fantastic, often quite exotic world in *Aguirre, Wrath of God* (1972), *Nosferatu the Vampyre* (1979), and *Fitzcarraldo* (1982). A prominent figure in the Munich School of film-making was **Rainer Werner Fassbinder** (1945-1982), who also worked in television, and who was responsible for a considerable number of excellent films: *Fear Eats the Soul (Angst essen Seele auf)* (1973), *The Marriage of Maria Braun* (1978), *Berlin Alexanderplatz* (a 14-part television series, 1980), to name but a few. Other Munich film-makers included **Wim Wenders**: *The American Friend* (1977), *Paris, Texas* (1984) and *Wings of Desire* (1987). Important and innovative women film directors include **Margarethe von Trotta** (*Rosa Luxemburg*, 1986; *Das Versprechen*, 1995) among others. Wolfgang Peterson's fantasy world in *The Neverending Story* (1984) was a resounding commercial success. **Edgar Reitz** won international acclaim with his film epic *Heimat* (1984) and its sequel *Heimat II* (1993). However, West German cinema was, and still is, characterised by a strongly individual narrative feel which perhaps makes it less approachable to outsiders.

In order to draw attention, German film did need the refreshing voice of a **Doris Dörrie** who, with *Men... (Männer)* (1985) and *Bin ich schön?* (1987), reduced the Zeitgeist to a humorous point. But even the great success of Caroline Link's 1996 *Jenseits der Stille* and Tom Tykwer's 1999 *Lola rennt* can't hide the fact that German film is hardly being recognised internationally anymore.

The Marriage of Maria Braun made by Rainer Werner Fassbinder

It is difficult to summarize East German cinema, since like all other art forms it was compelled by the state to fulfil a didactic function. Thus a number of films were made taking literary classics as their theme, since directors felt unable to confront issues relevant to contemporary East Germany. Konrad Wolf made his mark on three decades of East German film-making, with films such as *Sterne* (1958), which won him recognition worldwide. In *Solo Sunny* (1979), he put the case for individualism, thus paving the way for a breakthrough in the East German film industry. Egon Günther made the highly successful *Der Dritte* (1971), while the greatest hit of the East German Film Industry Cooperative (DEFA) was Heiner Carow with *Die Legende von Paul und Paula* (1973). 1984 was a particularly fruitful year, with Hermann Zschoche's *Hälfte des Lebens*, Iris Gusner's *Kaskade Rückwärts*, and Helmut Dzuiba's *Erscheinen Pflicht*. One of the leading East German film-makers of the 1970s and 1980s was Rainer Simon (*Das Luftschiff*, 1982, *Die Frau und der Fremde*, 1985). Finally, Lothar Warneke studied the problems of everyday life and of dismantling rigid ideological points of view (*Bear Ye One Another's Burdens (Einer trage des Anderen Last)*, 1988). In contrast to the West German film industry, East German film-makers produced a number of delightful, well directed children's films (*Ottokar der Weltverbesserer*, 1976).

Michelin publications :
   more than 220 maps, atlases and town plans ;
   12 editions of The Red Guide to hotels and restaurants in European countries ;
   more than 200 editions of The Green Guide in 8 languages to destinations around the world.

Fairy tales and legends

Snow White and the Seven Dwarfs – In the original story, written by the **Brothers Grimm**, the traditional costume worn by the dwarfs is in fact that used by miners in the Middle Ages.

Rübezahl – A giant with a red beard, who goes round putting wrongs right. Sometimes he appears in the form of a rich merchant, sometimes as a collier in rags.

The Witches of Brocken – On the first night of May (Walpurgisnacht), they assemble for a Sabbath on the summit of the Brocken, in the Harz – a legend immortalized by a scene in Goethe's *Faust*.

Pöppele of Hohenkrähen – From his castle perched high on a rock this character surveys the highway and plots the downfall of travellers – preferably nobles or important officials.

The Heinzelmännchen – Elves who helped the craftsmen of Cologne by coming secretly at night to do their work – but who disappeared, never to return, when discovered by a woman who lay in wait to see them.

The Seven Swabians – A somewhat harsh caricature of some people from Swabia, which recounts how they set out to conquer the world, but scattered and fled when confronted by a hare.

Baron Münchhausen – The real Baron Münchhausen (1720-97), who fought with the Russian army against the Turks, is said to have wildly overstated his military prowess, regaling his guests with extraordinarily tall stories. The fanciful adventures he relates include a journey to the centre of the earth, a moon safari, and absurdly exaggerated deeds of heroism on the high seas. Rudolph Erich Raspe (a German exile in England at the end of the 18C) compiled a version of Münchhausen's exploits in English, *Baron Münchhausen's Narrative of his Marvellous Travels and Campaigns in Russia*, inflating the original stories still further into the realms of the unreal.

Till Eulenspiegel *(see BRAUNSCHWEIG)*, the **Pied Piper of Hamelin** *(see HAMELN)*, the **Nibelungen** and the **Loreley** *(see RHEINTAL)* are the principal characters of other, no less celebrated, legends.

Food and drink

German food is more varied and better balanced than is generally supposed, and the composition and presentation of meals are in themselves original.

Breakfast **(Frühstück)** – there is plenty of it – includes cold meats and cheese with some of Germany's tremendous variety of breads and rolls, and invariably a soft-boiled egg. Lunch **(Mittagessen)** usually begins with soup, followed by a fish or meat main course always accompanied by a salad (lettuce, cucumber, shredded cabbage). For the evening meal **(Abendessen)**, there will be a choice of cold meats **(Aufschnitt)**, delicatessen and cheeses, with a selection of different types of bread and/or rolls.

Certain dishes are served all over the country: **Wiener Schnitzel** (veal cutlet

Eel soup (a speciality from Hamburg)

fried in breadcrumbs), **Eisbein** (salted knuckle or shin of pork), **Sauerbraten** (beef in a brown sauce) and **Gulasch** (either in the form of soup or as a stew) are the most popular.

Beer and Wine – Germans are justifiably proud of their national beverage, produced by nearly 1 200 breweries throughout the country. Brewing techniques respect a purity law *(Reinheitsgebot)* decreed in 1516, whereby nothing but barley, hops and plain water may be used in the fabrication of **beer** (with the addition, today, of yeast).

German vineyards cover 69 000ha/170 500 acres, extending from Lake Constance to the Siebengebirge, and from Trier to Würzburg. The growers produce a great variety of wines from a wide range of grapes – as the visitor may discover in most bars and restaurants, sampling them by the glass *(offene Weine)*.

Notable among the **white wines** – 80% of production – are the vigorous Rieslings of the Middle Rhine and those of the Moselle, Saar and Ruwer rivers, aromatic and refreshing; the high quality, delicate wines of the Rheingau; full-bodied and elegant Nahe wines; the potent wines of Franconia, verging sometimes on the bitter; and the many and varied wines of Baden and Württemberg. Among the **red wines**, particularly choice examples come from Rheinhessen and Württemberg, not forgetting the vigorous, well-balanced reds of the Palatinate and, above all, the wines of the Ahr, paradise of the Spätburgunder.

SOME REGIONAL SPECIALITIES

Bavaria and Franconia
Leberknödel: Large dumplings of liver, bread and chopped onion, served in a clear soup.
Leberkäs: Minced beef, pork and liver, cooked as a galantine.
Knödel: Dumplings of potato or soaked bread.
Haxen: Veal or pork trotters.
Schlachtschüssel: Breast of pork, liver sausage and black pudding, served with pickled cabbage and dumplings.
Rostbratwürste: Small sausages grilled over beechwood charcoal.

Baden-Württemberg
Schneckensuppe: Soup with snails.
Spätzle: Egg-based pasta in long strips.
Maultaschen: Pasta stuffed with a mixture of meat and spinach.
Geschnetzeltes: Slices of veal in a cream sauce.

Rhineland-Palatinate
Sauerbraten: Beef marinated in wine vinegar, served with potato dumplings.
Reibekuchen: Small potato pancakes with apple or blueberry sauce.
Hämchen: Pork trotters with pickled cabbage and mashed potato.
Saumagen: Stuffed pork belly with pickled cabbage.
Schweinepfeffer: Highly seasoned, spicy pork in the form of a ragout, thickened with blood.
Federweißer: Partially fermented new wine, customarily accompanied by an onion tart.

Hessen and Westphalia
Sulperknochen: Ears, trotters and tail of pork, served with pickled cabbage and pease pudding.
Töttchen: Ragout of brains and calf's head, cooked with herbs.
Pickert: Sweet potato cakes with raisins.

Thuringia
Linsensuppe mit Thüringer Rotwurst: Lentil soup with Thuringian sausages.

Saxony
Rinderzunge in Rosinen-Sauce: Calf's tongue in a grape sauce.
Dresdener Stollen: Raisin cake.

Lower Saxony and Schleswig-Holstein
Aalsuppe: Sweet-and-sour soup, made of eels, prunes, pears, vegetables, bacon and seasoning.
Labskaus: Favourite sailor's dish, basically beef, pork and salted herrings with potatoes and beetroot, the whole topped with cucumber and fried egg.
Buntes Huhn: Salt beef on a bed of diced vegetables.
Schlesisches Himmelreich: Pickled pork with dried fruit.

WORLD HERITAGE LIST

In 1972, the United Nations Educational, Scientific and Cultural Organization (UNESCO) adopted a Convention for the preservation of cultural and natural sites. To date, more than 150 States Parties have signed this international agreement, which has listed over 500 sites "of outstanding universal value" on the World Heritage List. Each year, a committee of representatives from 21 countries, assisted by technical organizations (ICOMOS – International Council on Monuments and Sites; IUCN – International Union for Conservation of Nature and Natural Resources; ICCROM – International Centre for the Study of the Preservation and Restoration of Cultural Property, the Rome Centre), evaluates the proposals for new sites to be included on the list, which grows longer as new nominations are accepted and more countries sign the Convention. To be considered, a site must be nominated by the country in which it is located.

The protected cultural heritage may be monuments (buildings, sculptures, archeological structures etc) with unique historical, artistic or scientific features; groups of buildings (such as religious communities, ancient cities); or sites (human settlements, examples of exceptional landscapes, cultural landscapes) which are the combined works of man and nature of exceptional beauty. Natural sites may be a testimony to the stages of the earth's geological history or to the development of human cultures and creative genius or represent significant ongoing ecological processes, contain superlative natural phenomena or provide a habitat for threatened species.

Signatories of the Convention pledge to cooperate to preserve and protect these sites around the world as a common heritage to be shared by all humanity.

Some of the most well-known places which the World Heritage Committee has inscribed include: Australia's Great Barrier Reef (1981), the Canadian Rocky Mountain Parks (1984), The Great Wall of China (1987), the Statue of Liberty (1984), the Kremlin (1990), Mont-Saint-Michel and its Bay (France, 1979), Durham Castle and Cathedral (1986).

UNESCO World Heritage sites in Germany are:

Aachen	Cathedral
Bamberg	Historic Town
Brühl	Schloß Augustusburg and Falkenlust
Dessau and Weimar	Bauhaus architecture
Eisleben and Wittenberg	Martin Luther memorials
Goslar	Historic Town and Rammelsberg Mines
Grube Messel	Fossil deposits
Hildesheim	St. Michaeliskirche and Cathedral
Köln	Cathedral
Lorsch	Abbey and Altenmünster
Lübeck	Hanseatic City
Maulbronn	Abbey
Potsdam and Berlin	Sanssouci Palaces and Parks, Schloß Glienicke and Pfaueninsel
Quedlinburg	Old Town, Abbey Church and Castle
Speyer	Cathedral
Trier	Roman Monuments, Cathedral and Liebfrauenkirche
Völklingen	Ironworks
Weimar	Classical Weimar
Wies	Pilgrimage Church
Würzburg	Residenz

Neuschwanstein Castle

Sights

AACHEN★

AIX-LA-CHAPELLE – Nordrhein-Westfalen

Population 253 000
Michelin map 417 N 2

Aachen, situated among the northern foothills of the Ardennes, is the most westerly town in Germany. Its hot springs, already famous in the time of the Celts, were transformed into thermal baths by the Romans ("Aquae Grani"). Under Charlemagne, Aachen became the capital of the Frankish Empire.

Today, the city is an important industrial centre with a renowned college of technology.

Charlemagne (747-814) – King of the Franks from the year 768, Charlemagne (known as Karl der Große to the Germans) chose Aachen as a permanent site for the Frankish Court – which had until then been held by him and his ancestors wherever there was the latest war or good hunting. In AD 800, Charlemagne was crowned Holy Roman Emperor. He then conquered the Saxons and the Bavarians, consolidating his frontiers north of the Pyrenees to resist invasions by Moors, Slavs and Danes.

Charlemagne's Court became a fountain-head of wisdom, culture and Christianity, which spread throughout his realm. The emperor brought to the West the treasures of Latin civilization and culture as well as the advantages of a centralized government.

Charlemagne was buried at Aachen, in the Octagon of the Palatine chapel (Pfalzkapelle).

The Imperial City – Between 936 and 1531, thirty princes were crowned King of Germania in the cathedral at Aachen. In 1562 the town lost the status of Coronation City to Frankfurt.

SIGHTS

★★ **Dom (Cathedral)** ⊙ – At the heart of the town is the **Charlemagne's Palatine chapel** (Pfalzkapelle), built around 800, consisting of an octagonal domed central section surrounded by a 16-sided gallery modeled on the Byzantine palace churches. It was the first construction of this type seen north of the Alps. The Gothic chancel, started in 1355, was consecrated in 1414, on the 600th anniversary of the Emperor's death. The Aachen cathedral was the first German construction to be placed on the list of UNESCO's World Heritage Sites.

Exterior – *Starting at the Katschhof (north side), walk around the cathedral.* One after another the chapel of St.-Nicholas (pre-1487), the chapel of Charles-Hubert (1455-74), with its Flamboyant portal, and finally the chancel (standing at a height of 51m/167ft till the tip of the cross) bearing 19C statues between the clerestory windows, come into view.

From the Münsterplatz *(south side)*, there is a good view of the largest remain of the Carolingian church, crowned now with a 16-sided cupola dating from the 17C. Also on this side are three chapels: St.-Matthias (1414) and St.-Anne (pre-1449), both Gothic, and the Hungarian chapel (1756-1817). The Carolingian entrance hall (west building) on the cathedral courtyard is closed by **bronze doors** embellished with lions' heads (c 800).

Interior – The octagon is surrounded by a two-storey ambulatory with bronze grilles dating from the Carolingian period masking the spaces between the columns on the upper level. The dome is richly decorated with 19C mosaics. From the centre hangs a magnificent **chandelier★★** *(currently being restored)* in copper, donated by Emperor Frederick I Barbarossa (1165). To the right of the two piers in front of the chancel is a 14C statue of the Virgin of Aachen.

Modern stained-glass windows illuminate the chancel aisle. On the right, above the door leading to the sacristy, is the **ambo of Henry II★★★** – a small pulpit in gilded copper, decorated with precious stones (early 11C). The Carolingian high altar is adorned with a **Pala d'Oro★★★** – a sumptuous, gold altar front decorated with scenes from the Passion and Christ in Majesty (c 1020). Behind the altar is the **Shrine of Charlemagne★★★** (Karlsschrein: 1200-15), a reliquary containing the bones of the Emperor which is masterfully hand-worked in gilded and embossed silver. On the upper floor of the west yoke is the **Throne of Charlemagne★** *(only visible during the guided tour; gathering point in the cathedral's treasury).* This perfectly intact throne is made of plain, assembled marble slabs. After being elected and consecrated, 30 Roman-German kings climbed upon this throne and were officially enthroned. Over time, thousands of pilgrims have squeezed through the narrow aperture underneath the throne to take part in the Aachen Shrine Pilgrimage (Aachener Heiligtumsfahrt), which has been held every seven years since 1349 (next deadline is 2000).

★★★ **Domschatzkammer** (Treasury) ⊙ – *Access via Klostergasse.*

This is one of the most important church treasures north of the Alps and is also a unique collection of precious items culled from the history of the cathedral. In 1995 the treasury was entirely redesigned. It now consists of 100 outstanding artworks arranged over 600m²/6 457sq ft and grouped into five topical sections.

Charlemagne's Church: The centre of attention here is the silver and gold **Bust Reliquary of Charlemagne** (post-1349) donated by Karl IV. *The Liturgy at the Aachen Cathedral*: this section focuses on the **Cross of Lothair** (990), encrusted with precious stones, and the so-called **Aachen Altar** (ca 1520). *The Coronation Church*: of particular note is the unique ivory situla (ca AD 100). *The Relics and the Aachen Pilgrimage*: the reliquaries and the Hungarian donations are the finest items. The section entitled The

Cross of Lothair, from the Cathedral Treasury, Aachen

HUBER, Garmisch-Partenkirchen

Cathedral as a Marian Church has a host of fine paintings and sculptures in store. The wealth of textiles is shown around the Cappa Leonis (pre-1520) on the lower floor.

Rathaus (Town hall) ⊙ **(R)** – The town hall was built in the 14C, on the site of Charlemagne's palace, of which the squat Granus tower remains on the corner of Krämerstraße. The façade of the tower, decorated with statues of the kings and emperors crowned at Aachen, overlooks the market place, with its **fountain** and statue of Charlemagne.

The Peace Treaty of 1748, which ended the War of Spanish Succession, was signed in the **White Room** (Weißer Saal), embellished with Italian stuccowork (c 1727), on the right of the entrance. On the left, the **Council Chamber** (Ratssaal) is clad with panelling executed in 1730 by a master woodworker of Liège. From the staircase, there is a fine view of the cathedral.

On the upper floor, the **Coronation Chamber** (Krönungssaal), with its ogive vaulting, was used for the royal banquets when kings were crowned. Of the eight 19C **frescoes of Charlemagne** by the local painter Alfred Rethel, only five remain. In a showcase on the eastern side of the chamber, **copies of the crown jewels** are on display, along with valuable Charlemagne's sword, lance, crown, and accoutrements; the originals have been kept at the Hofburg in Vienna since the French Revolution.

This Coronation Chamber is the venue for the annual awarding of the Aachen Charlemagne Prize for best efforts towards the unification of Europe.

★ **Couven-Museum** ⊘ – On the site of the medieval public weigh-house Aachen architect Couven built this bourgeois mansion for the pharmacist Andreas Monheim. The museum displays exhibits of a century's worth of middle-class domestic life in Aachen. There is a remarkable variety and quality of furniture on show, as well as some magnificent chimney-pieces and Italian stuccowork. Besides a collection of tiles, the museum houses a pharmacy – the Adler-Apotheke – in which chocolate was made for the first time ever in Aachen in 1857.

★ **Suermondt-Ludwig-Museum** ⊘ – *Wilhelmstraße 18.*
New and old complement each other perfectly in this late-19C villa to which was added a modern annex. The tour of this museum follows a different chronological order from the norm – from present to antiquity. First, the ground floor exhibits a collection of **contemporary art** ranging back to the 19C and 18C and neo-Classicism. On the first floor, the display focuses on Dutch, German, Spanish and Italian painting from the 17C back to the 15C. The collection of **Late Gothic sculpture** is particularly highly prized. The second floor contains displays of **stained glass** and craftwork.

Ludwig Forum für Internationale Kunst (Ludwig International Art Forum) ⊘ – *Jülicherstraße 97-109. Leave via the Peterstraße.*
A former umbrella factory, in its time the biggest in Europe, is the unexpected site for this remarkable collection of modern art. The handsome brick building (1928) is a splendid example of the Bauhaus style, which has lost nothing of its original character despite its change in role. Founded by a local industrialist named Ludwig and his wife, both connoisseurs and patrons of the arts, the exhibition includes works by Nam June Paik and Horst Antes *(The Seven Monuments of Desire)*. Also on display are works by Duane Hanson *(Supermarket Lady)*, Roy Lichtenstein, Georg Baselitz, Jonathan Borowsky *(Ballerina Clown)* and Jörg Immendorf *(Brandenburger Tor)*. Theatrical performances (events also include dance, music, film and video) and a park displaying sculptures add to the interest of the Forum, opened in 1991 with the intention of creating a cultural meeting place.

EXCURSION

Kornelimünster – *10km/6mi to the southeast.*
This suburb of Aachen, with its slate-roofed, blue and grey stone houses, in the valley of the Inde is typical of small towns in the Eifel region. In the centre is the old abbey church of **Kornelimünster**★, an unusual construction with five naves (14C-16C), which dates back to a Benedictine church of the Carolingian period. The galleries above the chancel *(east side)* were added in the 17C, the octagonal Kornelius chapel in the early 18C. The furnishings in the Gothic interior (ogive vaulting, painted ceilings) are essentially Baroque; note particularly the Baroque **high altar**, subsequently modified (c 1750) by JJ Couven in the Rococo style. On the left there is a stone statue of St Kornelius (c 1460).

The **collection of relics**★ belonging to the church (valuable ancient cloths, a 1360 bust of the saint in embossed silver etc) attract a large number of pilgrims in September of each year. There is a fine **view** of the church, the abbey and the town from the Romanesque-Gothic church of St.-Stephanus (in a burial ground on a height to the north).

The chapter on art and architecture in this guide gives an outline of artistic creation in Germany, providing the context of the buildings and works of art described in the Sights section.
This chapter may also provide ideas for touring.
It is advisable to read it at leisure/before setting out.

Deutsche ALPENSTRASSE★★★

GERMAN ALPINE ROAD – Bayern

Michelin maps 419 X 13-18/420 X 14-22

From Lindau to Berchtesgaden, from Lake Constance (Bodensee) to the Königssee, this splendid scenic route runs through the foothills of the Allgäu and the Bavarian Alps, passing on the way such heights as the Zugspitze (2 962m/9 718ft) and the Watzmann (2 712m/8 898ft). One of the attractions of the trip is the fact that it allows the traveller both to enjoy the splendours of mountain scenery and visit such renowned monuments as the Wieskirche and the castles of Ludwig II of Bavaria, near Füssen. To cover the whole itinerary, allow three days.

★DAS ALLGÄU

1 From Lindau to Füssen *112km/70mi – half a day*

The landscape at this stage of the tour is not so much Bavarian as Alemannic. The farmers of the region have made their mountain countryside into the great cheese manufacturing area of Germany.

★★ **Lindau** – *See LINDAU.*

Paradies – Engineers have given this name to a viewpoint between Oberreute and Oberstaufen, built halfway around a sweeping curve from which, far off to the southwest, the distant Appenzell Alps in Switzerland (Säntis and Altmann) can be seen.

Oberstaufen – This charming resort, at the foot of the Hochgrat massif (1 834 m/6 017ft), has some interesting ski slopes.
The road now continues over Immenstadt and Sonthofen to Hindelang.

★ **Hindelang** – Together with its neighbour, Bad Oberdorf, this flower-decked village is a holiday centre and spa (sulphurous waters) from which mountain walks can be enjoyed in summer, and skiing on the slopes of the Oberjoch in winter.
Above Hindelang, the climb of the **Jochstraße**★ affords a variety of views over the jagged limestone summits of the Allgäu Alps. From the **Kanzel**★ viewpoint, almost at the summit, admire the panorama embracing the Ostrach Valley and the surrounding mountains.
Descending on the far side, the road crosses the valley of the Wertach, skirts the Grüntensee and passes near the large Pfronten ski resort before it arrives at Füssen.

★ **Füssen** – *See FÜSSEN.*

ENJOYING YOUR TOUR OF THE ALPS

OBERSTAUFEN

Bayerischer Hof – Hochgratstraße 2, ☎ 0 83 86/49 50, Fax 0 83 86/49 54 14. Single rooms from 90DM. Generous centre for rest and wellness with an indoor pool carved into the rock. Centrally located.

Traube – In Thalkirchdorf (6km/3.5mi east), ☎ 0 83 25/92 00, Fax 0 83 25/9 20 39. Single rooms from 98DM. The inn dates from 1767 (half-timbered), casual style.

Alpenkönig – Kalzhofer Straße 25, ☎ 0 83 86/9 34 50, Fax 0 83 86/43 44. Single rooms from 120DM. Well managed hotel with wellness area.

Allgäu Sonne – Am Stiessberg 1, ☎ 0 83 86/70 20, Fax 0 83 86/78 26. Single rooms from 140DM. Wonderful location with grandiose panoramic view. Very generous relaxation and wellness area.

Lindner Parkhotel – Argenstraße 1, ☎ 0 83 86/70 30, Fax 0 83 86/70 37 44. Single rooms from 165DM. First-class hotel on the spa's common. Large rooms and suites. Restaurants in Alpine style.

HINDELANG

Obere Mühle – Bad Oberdorf, Ostrachstraße 40, ☎ 0 83 24/28 57, Fax 0 83 24/86 35. Rustic and cozy country inn dating back to the year 1433 (no rooms). The range includes anything from simple collations to solid regional cooking.

Alpengasthof Hirsch – Bad Oberdorf, Kurze Gasse 18, ☎ 0 83 24/3 08, Fax 0 83 24/81 93. Single rooms from 60DM. Cozy rooms, good cuisine.

Romantikhotel Bad-Hotel Sonne – Marktstraße 15, ☎ 0 83 24/89 70, Fax 0 83 24/98 74 99. Single rooms from 105DM. 400-year-old Allgäu inn decorated with traditional murals.

A FEW SUGGESTIONS FOR OBERAMMERGAU

Feldmeier – Ettaler Straße 29, ☎ 0 88 22/30 11, Fax 0 88 22/66 31. Single rooms from 90DM. Hotel is in rustic style, family-run, apartments available.

Alte Post – Dorfstraße 19, ☎ 0 88 22/91 00, Fax 0 88 22/91 01 00. Single rooms 100DM. 17C inn, former post-house with traditional murals, agreeable and stylish restaurant.

Turmwirt – Ettaler Straße 2, ☎ 0 88 22/9 26 00, Fax 0 88 22/14 37. Single rooms 100DM. Comfortable inn close to the centre of town.

★THE AMMERGAU

② From Füssen to Garmisch-Partenkirchen

95km/59mi – half a day

★ **Hohenschwangau and Neuschwanstein★★★ (Royal Castles of Bavaria)** – *About 2hr walking and sightseeing. See HOHENSCHWANGAU and NEUSCHWANSTEIN.* The road bypasses the salient of the Ammergau Alps to the north and then crosses a stretch of country that is seamed and broken up by the moraines deposited when the ancient Lech glacier withdrew. This rolling countryside is punctuated by the "onion" domes crowning the belfries of village churches.

Steingaden – The former abbey of the Steingaden Premonstratensians, founded in the 12C, still boasts its remarkable minster, though the **abbey church★** was modified in the 18C in the Baroque style. Only the outside, with its massive towers and Lombardy arcading, still has its original thick-set Romanesque appearance. The Gothic entrance is enriched with a painted genealogy of the House of Welf, the original founders of the abbey. The sobriety of the stuccowork embellishing the whole of the chancel contrasts sharply with the brightness of that in the wide nave, which is enhanced by finely painted motifs. Furnishings in both the Baroque and Rococo styles – pulpit, organ loft, altarpieces, statues – lend the interior a certain theatrical quality, as if symbolizing the triumph of decoration over architecture.

★★ **Wieskirche** – *See WIESKIRCHE.*

Rottenbuch – First built as an Augustinian monastery, the **Mariä-Geburts-Kirche★** (Church of the Nativity of the Virgin) was entirely remodelled in the Baroque and Rococo styles in the 18C. The stucco here embodies the virtuosity of the School of Wessobrunn, of which Joseph and Franz Schmuzer were among the masters. Frescoes by Matthäus Günther harmonise perfectly with the extravagantly sculpted decor. The pulpit, organ loft and altars by Franz Xaver Schmädl are heavily adorned with statues and giltwork in pure Rococo tradition.

★ **Echelsbacher Brücke (Echelsbacher Bridge)** – Since 1929, this audacious reinforced concrete structure has spanned the Ammer gorge, which at this point is 76m/250ft deep. Walk to the middle of the bridge to get the most impressive view of the gorge.

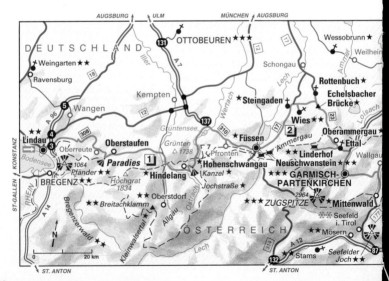

* **Oberammergau** – This small town of peasants and craftsmen, encircled by the wooded foothills of the Ammergau, owes its fame to the internationally-renowned **Passion Play**, which is performed only once every 10 years (next performance: 2000). The play, involving 1 100 amateur actors drawn from the local population, lasts an entire summer's day. The tradition derives from a vow made by the inhabitants in 1633, after a plague epidemic had miraculously been cut short.

Passion Play, Oberammergau

The Klinger/Gemeinde Oberammergau

** **Linderhof** – *See Schloß LINDERHOF.*

Ettal – A blossoming of the Benedictine tradition, added to local veneration of a statue of the Virgin attributed to Giovanni Pisano, explain the vast dimensions of Ettal Abbey, founded by the Emperor Ludwig IV "the Bavarian" in 1330.

The sole example of its kind in Germany, the original abbey church was a Gothic building with a polygonal floor plan. The present construction is due to the Baroque architect Enrico Zucalli, who built the façade and the chancel (1710-26). Joseph Schmuzer of the School of Wessobrunn *(see above)* added the dome after the church was gutted by a fire in 1774. The **frescoes** on the inside of this dome, a masterpiece of Rococo, are the work of Johann Jakob Zeiller.

The road now rejoins the Loisach Valley. To the south, the Wetterstein range appears, with the summits of the Zugspitze, the Dreitorspitze and the pyramid peak of the Alpspitze. Carry onto Garmisch-Partenkirchen.

*** **Garmisch-Partenkirchen** – *See GARMISCH-PARTENKIRCHEN.*

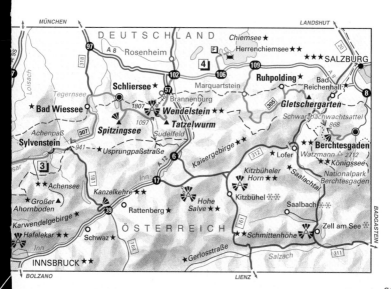

★THE UPPER ISAR VALLEY AND THE LAKE DISTRICT

③ From Garmisch-Partenkirchen to Schliersee

105km/66mi – one day

★ **Mittenwald** – *See GARMISCH-PARTENKIRCHEN: Excursions.*
At Wallgau, the route joins the upper valley of the Isar *(toll road as far as Vorderriß)*, a wild, bleak stretch of open country.

Sylvenstein-Staudamm (Sylvenstein Dam) – Built to regulate the excessive flooding of the Isar, this earthwork dam with its waterproof core has created a huge reservoir, from which water is drawn off to supply an underground power station. The road crosses the wooded Achenpaß *(going 2km/1.2mi into Austria)* and then plunges down towards the Tegernsee.

★ **Bad Wiessee** – An elegant resort, both a fashionable holiday centre and a major spa (iodine, sulphur, fluorine springs), Bad Wiessee is pleasantly situated on the shores of Lake Tegernsee in cultivated, green semi-Alpine surroundings.

★ **Schliersee** – Beside the lake of the same name, this small community – together with the town districts of Fischhausen, Neuhaus and Spitzingsee *(see itinerary below)* – offers interesting possibilities for a short stay. The **St. Sixtus Parish Church**★ (Pfarrkirche) is a former Collegiate of the Chapter of Our Lady in Munich, rebuilt in the Baroque style between 1712 and 1714. Both the frescoes on the vaulting and the delicate stucco were executed by Johann-Baptist Zimmermann (1680-1758), brother of the architect of the Wieskirche *(See WIESKIRCHE).*

★④ THE SUDELFELD AND THE CHIEMGAU MOUNTAINS

From Schliersee to Berchtesgaden

172km/107mi – one day

Spitzingsee – A little less than 1mi from the summit, the steep access road offers a fine **overall view**★ of the Fischhausen-Neuhaus plain and Lake Schliersee. Soon afterwards, the road comes to a stop by the Spitzingsee.
Shortly (3km/2mi) before Bayrischzell, the road passes the lower terminal of a cableway leading to the summit of the Wendelstein *(the trip can also be made by rack-railway, starting from Brannenburg-Inntal – see below).*

Tatzelwurm-Wasserfall – *15min there and back on foot.*
From the "Naturdenkmal Tatzelwurm" car park, a footpath leads to this impressive cascade.

★★ **Wendelstein** – *There are two ways of getting to the summit of the Wendelstein. Either take the cableway from Bayrischzell-Osterhofen terminal (journey time about 7min), or take the rack-rail*way, **Wendelstein-Zahnradbahn** ⊘, *leaving from the lower station at Brannenburg-Inntal (journey time about 25min).*
Ruggedly grinding its way up increasingly steep slopes, the little train finally reaches an altitude of 1 738m/5 702ft. The rest of the climb is on foot up a path carved out of the bedrock. The summit (1 838m/6 030ft) is crowned by a solar observatory and a chapel built in 1718.
Going back 230 million years, the Wendelstein was a coral reef lying many hundreds of miles south of its present location. It has been declared a "Geo-Park" because of its quite singular geological makeup, and there are four geological trails (Geo-Wanderwege) that have been indicated with explanatory panels for visitors to follow. We particularly recommend the Gipfelweg, a circuit of the summit which takes about 2hr 30min.
The **panorama**★★ visible from the top encompasses, from east to west, the mountains of the Chiemgau, the Loferer and the Leoberger Steinberge, the Kaisergebirge range with its jagged peaks, and the glacial crests of the Hohe Tauern.
From the Wendelstein terminal, our route winds down the valley of the Inn and then follows the Munich-Salzburg motorway, which skirts the southern shore of the **Chiemsee**★. After Marquartstein, the road passes through a succession of tortuous, steep-sided valleys, running out finally above the Reit Basin, at the foot of the Zahmer Kaiser.
Turning back towards the east, the Alpenstraße cuts through a long corridor past a series of dark-watered lakes.

★ **Ruhpolding** – This resort, very popular with holiday-makers, is well known for upholding local traditions, crafts and folklore. The most precious artwork in the parish church of St.-George is a Romanesque statue of the Virgin Mary dating from the 12C housed in a golden casing on the right-hand side altar.

WHERE TO STAY IN THE LAKE DISTRICT

BAD WIESSEE

Freihaus Brenner – Freihaus 4, ☎ 0 80 22/8 20 04, Fax 0 80 22/8 38 07. Typical mountain inn (without rooms) beautifully situated above the town. View of the lake and the mountains. Menu from 25DM.

Landhaus Midas – Setzbergstraße 12, ☎ 0 80 22/8 11 50, Fax 0 80 22/9 95 77, single rooms from 93DM.

Lederer am See – Bodenschneidstraße 9, ☎ 0 80 22/82 90, Fax 0 80 22/82 92 00. Single rooms from 118DM. Very beautifully situated on a peninsula along the lake-side promenade. First-class hotel with all amenities, indoor pool, sauna and beach.

SCHLIERSEE

Terofal – Xaver-Terofal-Platz 2, ☎0 80 26/40 45, Fax 0 80 26/26 76. Single rooms from 75DM. Inn in the heart of Schlersee, carefully decorated in peasant style.

Seeblick – Carl-Schwarz-Straße 1, ☎0 80 26/40 31, Fax 0 80 26/40 33. Single rooms from 80DM. Country hotel with a casual atmosphere.

HOTELS IN RUHPOLDING

Alpina Feriendomizil – Niederfeldstraße 17, ☎ 0 86 63/9905, Fax 086 63/8 81 50. Single rooms from 80DM. Quiet location. Nice, cosy rooms.

Sporthotel am Westernberg – Am Wundergraben 4, ☎ 0 86 63/16 74, Fax 0 86 63/638. Single rooms from 99DM. Situated above the town. Rooms from rustic to elegant. Nice views. Complete line of sports offered, from riding to tennis.

Berggasthof Weingarten – Weingarten (3km/2mi westward), ☎ 0 86 63/16 74, Fax 0 86 63/57 83. Single rooms from 76DM, attractively situated with a beautiful vista. Rustic furnishings. Very good value.

Gletschergarten – *15min there and back on foot.*
Opened up by the building of the road, this "garden of glaciers" forms a natural museum of glacial erosion. A prolongation of the Tauern glacier, moving along the Saalach Valley *(see Michelin Green Guide Austria)*, once transported huge blocks of crystalline rock which striated or excavated the rolling, rocky surface of the land.
After the Schwarzbachwacht pass (alt 868m/2 848ft) a sharp contrast is noticeable between the severe, wooded valley of the River Schwarzbach and the open pastureland on the Ramsau side. At a number of places, the descent offers an opportunity to appreciate fine **panoramas★★**, revealing the "teeth" of the Hochkalter biting into the white surface of the Blaueis (along with the Höllentalferner, in the Zugspitze massif, the only glacier in Germany) and the bulk of the Watzmann.
The German Alpine Road ends at Berchtesgaden.

★★ Berchtesgaden – *See BERCHTESGADEN.*

ALSFELD★

Hessen
Population 18 000
Michelin map 417 N 11

Alsfeld, first mentioned in 1069, arose from the territorial policies of the Langraves of Thuringia. In 1247, this town straddling the River Schwalm (between the Knüll Range and the Vogelsberg mountain) was turned over to the County of Hessen. Its convenient location and the policies of its rulers – in addition to its inhabitants economic performance in crafts and trade – paved the way to its rapid rise. This in turn led to active construction activities, especially in the late Middle Ages and Renaissance.
Conscientious care for the many half-timber houses in the narrow and tortuous streets ensured the survival of the historic city center. In 1975, the Year of Monument Protection, Alsfeld was awarded the distinction of model city for the successful renovating of its old town ensemble.

Nach Foto Erich Müller

The Marktplatz, Alsfeld

SIGHTS

★ **Marktplatz** – The northeast corner of this square, where the Rathaus and the Weinhaus (recognizable by its stepped gable) are over-looked by the church tower, is quite delightful. Twin, spired turrets surmount the façade of the 1516 **Rathaus**★ (town hall), half-timbered above stone arcades that once served as a covered market. Diagonally opposite stands a solid stone house with a two-storey oriel window at one corner. Known as "the Wedding House" (Hochzeitshaus), this interesting building dates from 1565. Its two gables, set at right angles, are embellished with festoons and scrollwork typical of the First Renaissance in Germany.

Rittergasse – This street, leaving the square on the side opposite the Rathaus, has two of the most interesting **old houses**★ in Alsfeld. The Neurathhaus at no 3 is a particularly fine example of projecting half-timbering in the Baroque style, while the Minnigerode-Haus at no 5, which is built of stone, conserves its original spiral staircase within. This masterpiece of carpentry rises without any support from the walls around a tall, twisted tree trunk.

Walpurgiskirche – The church is early Gothic, still with its original furnishings. Note the wooden galleries and the beautifully carved central panel of a Late Gothic high altar in the chancel depicting the Crucifixion and four other scenes from the life of Jesus. The Romanesque baptismal font with reliefs showing scenes from the life of Christ is also worthy of note.

In the small square to the north of the church there is a house adorned with modern graffiti and a fountain presided over by a goose-girl in Schwalm costume. Noticed in the neighbourhood of Alsfeld by the Brothers Grimm, a costume of this type was used by them as a model for the clothes worn by Little Red Riding Hood.

ALTENBURG

Thüringen
Population 44 000
Michelin map 418 N 21

Altenburg was recorded for the first time in the year 976. It was expanded to become an imperial palace under the Hohenstaufen emperors – Kaiser Friedrich Barbarossa stayed there on many occasions – and the settlement raised to the status of a free imperial city. In 1329, it fell into the hands of the Margraves of Meißen, and from 1603 to 1672 and again from 1826 to 1918 Altenburg was the residence of the dukes of Saxe-Altenburg. During the intervening period, it was the residence of the dukes of Saxe-Gotha. The town was one of the few to escape relatively unscathed from the damages wrought during the Second World War. However, in the decades after the war a good many streets and houses were demolished or fell into disrepair. Projects are afoot to put a stop to this process. The town's hillside location, with steep streets running up and down hill, lends Altenburg a certain charm and affords visitors some pretty views.

The home of the playing card – Altenburg is well known among the card-playing fraternity, since playing cards have been manufactured here for four centuries. The town is also birthplace of the popular German card game Skat, which evolved from other card games between 1810 and 1818.

SIGHTS

★ **Rathaus and Markt (Town hall and market square)** – The elongated market square with its handsome town houses is dominated by the town hall. This was built between 1562 and 1564 by Weimar architect **Nikolaus Grohmann**, and is one of the most remarkable Renaissance buildings in Germany. An eight-storey staircase tower with an onion-domed roof crowns the edifice, which is further adorned by a wealth of sculpted decoration on the round oriel windows and doorways. Note the so-called "Gaffköpfe" (gaping heads), which are most probably representations of the aldermen at the time the town hall was built. On the west side of the market square stands the **Brüderkirche**, with charming Jugendstil (Art Nouveau) mosaic work on the church façade.

Brühl – *Northeast of the market square.*
The Brühl, the oldest square in the town, is located at the foot of the **St. Bartholomäuskirche**. The square features an ornate Baroque building, the **Seckendorffsche Palais**, dating from 1724, and diagonally opposite, the Baroque **Administrative Court** (Amtsgericht) built in 1725. In between the two stands a fountain, the **Skatbrunnen**, which was erected in 1903.

Schloß (Castle) – High above the town, perched on a rocky outcrop, stands the castle, which is particularly imposing when seen from the southwest. The various castle buildings, arranged around a great courtyard, represent nine centuries of architectural evolution. Remarkable, too, is the **Schloßkirche**★, a Late Gothic church with a beautiful starry vault in the main nave. The chancel is roofed with stellar-vaulting. The richly decorated Baroque interior contains an interesting organ built by **Gottfried Heinrich Trost** in 1738. The castle, which was the scene of the legendary kidnapping of the Prince of Saxony in 1455 (Friedberg), now houses the **Schloß- und Spielkartenmuseum** ⊘. Walk through the extensive castle grounds (Schloßpark) to the north to get to the Lindenau-Museum.

★★ **Lindenau-Museum** ⊘ – The Saxon statesman, astronomer and art collector **Bernhard August von Lindenau** (1779-1854) bequeathed a valuable collection to his native town which is housed in a building dating from 1873. The bequest has earned Altenburg its reputation among connoisseurs of art. In particular the remarkable collection of **antique ceramics** (7C-2C BC) and a series of plaster casts replicating Greek masterpieces testifies to Von Lindenau's excellent artistic judgement.
The jewel of the exhibition is perhaps the collection of **Italian Primitive painting**★★, which is the most comprehensive of its kind outside Italy, including 180 canvases dating from the 13C-16C, principally by the schools of Florence and Siena. The variety, quality and range of paintings in this section are astounding.
One or two examples of European painting from the 16C-18C, most notably German painting from the 19C (charming *Girl with Basket of Flowers* by **Ferdinand von Rayski**) and the present, lend a note of contrast to the exhibition as a whole.

Flight into Egypt by Lorenzo Monaco

Staatl. Lindenau-Museum

AMBERG

Bayern

Population 43 000
Michelin map 420 R 19

In the 14C and 15C, Amberg had an important role to play as a commercial centre on the route from Nuremberg to Prague. The large number of rich burghers' houses, tightly packed between the ramparts, testify today to that prosperity. A modern town has evolved around that ancient, picturesque nucleus, still very well preserved in its green setting.

The two arches of the old fortified bridge, reflected in the water of the river below, form two perfect circles – reminiscent of a pair of spectacles. This image, which can be appreciated best from the Ring Bridge, in the south, and the footpath skirting the Arsenal (Zeughaus) to the north, is known as the **"Stadtbrille"** (town spectacles) and has come to stand as a symbol for Amberg.

Marktplatz – Closing off this square, the **Rathaus** (14C and 16C town hall) displays a Gothic gable above a charming Renaissance balustrade. Opposite is the **St.-Martinskirche**, a powerful 15C Gothic construction to which a tower of almost 100m/328ft was added in the 18C. Three huge naves, supported by elegant columns, make this the largest church in the Upper Palatinate after the cathedral in Regensburg.

★ **Deutsche Schulkirche (Salesian Church)** – This church, built at the end of the 17C by Wolfgang Dientzenhofer, is covered by graceful Rococo decorations, most of them the work of Amberg's own master craftsmen (1738-58). Original features include the curious position of the altar niches flanking the triumphal arch, and an organ loft in the form of a shell.

Wallfahrtskirche Maria-Hilf (Chapel of Mary-the-Helper) – This votive chapel was built as a thanksgiving gesture at the end of a plague epidemic which ravaged the region in 1634 (see also Oberammergau Passion Play). Vault **frescoes★**, painted by CD Asam in his youth, illustrate this tragic event and the subsequent pilgrimages.

ANNABERG-BUCHHOLZ★

Sachsen

Population 24 000
Michelin map 418/420 O 23 – Local map see ERZGEBIRGE

After the discovery of significant lodes of silver and tin ore on the Schreckenberg (Fear Mountain) in 1491 and 1496, Annaberg and Buchholz – which were governed by different families and were only united in 1945 – experienced an economic boom; at the peak period, 600 mines were pumping wealth into the capital of the Erzgebirge (Ore Mountains). During that time, there lived a man in Annaberg, whose name has literally become proverbial: **Adam Ries**, or Riese (1492-1559), wrote about the mountains and headed Annaberg's School of Arithmetic. In the 16C, lace production replaced silver mining, whose yield had been dwindling, as Annaberg's most important economic sector.

After the Second World War, some mining resumed briefly, ending in 1958; deposits of uranium were mined by the SDAG Wismut to be used in nuclear weapons; the so-called Wismut-Halden (slag heaps). Nowadays Annaberg-Buchholz is the centre of the food industry, trimming and electronic switches.

★★ **St.-Annenkirche** – Built in a relatively short time (1499-1525), this church with three naves is one of the most successful and impressive examples of Saxony's Flamboyant Gothic style. Twelve tall, thin pillars soar into the ribs of the vaulting, which consists of seven looping stars in a row and each yoke is covered by a "blossom baldaquin". This superb vault composition was the work of Jakob Heilmann from Schweinfurt. The parapets of the galleries on the side walls are embellished with scenes from the Old and New Testaments.

At the far end of the church, in the left-hand wall, is the **"Schöne Tür"★★** (beautiful door), a brilliantly multicoloured portal originally designed for another church. It was made by Hans Witten in 1512. The **pulpit★★** (1516) is the work of the sculptor F Maidburg. Note the relief figure representing a miner. A similar reference to Annaberg's old activity lies in the painted panels to be found behind the **Miners' Reredos★** (Bergmannsaltar, c 1520). Placed in the left-hand chapel of the chancel, these depict the various stages of work in a mine of that period.

Erzgebirgsmuseum mit Besucherbergwerk ⊙ – This museum retraces local history, in particular that of the mining industry, and contains varied collections of local crafts and folklore. An interesting category of exhibit, peculiar to the region, is the so-called Weihnachtsberge, or mechanical models of the mine combined with Nativity and forest scenes, which illustrate the customs of the Erzgebirge. Scenes such as these were made mainly at the end of the 19C and beginning of the 20C and used to decorate the family home during the Christmas period.

Vaulting in St. Annenkirche, Annaberg-Buchhloz

JÜRGENS OSTEUROPA, Köln

Annexed to the museum is the **Im Gößner mine**, which went into production at the height of Annaberg's economic prosperity c 1498 and from which silver was extracted for a quarter of a century. The entrance shaft is in the courtyard of the museum. The section open to the public is 260m/285yd long and is reached via metal steps.

Technisches Museum Frohnauer Hammer (Frohnau Forge) ⊘ – Once a flour mill, this old building was turned into a workshop for the striking of coins when silver was discovered in the region; it was subsequently transformed into a blacksmith's forge. Hydraulically-operated bellows and power-hammers (100, 200 and 300kg/220, 440, 660lb) can be seen there today.

EXCURSION

★ **Erzgebirge** – *See ERZGEBIRGE.*

ANSBACH

Bayern

Population 40 000
Michelin map 419/420 S 15

The mainly Baroque city of Ansbach in Franconia is a peaceful place which owes its foundation to the Hohenzollerns. The Margraves of the House of Hohenzollern's Frankish line settled in Ansbach and Bayreuth as early as the 13C. Since then the two towns have often been associated in history – the Ansbach-Bayreuth Dragoons, for example, fought under Frederick the Great.
On the female side, the cultivated Margravines of the 18C, one of whom – Friederike Luise – was a sister of Queen Wilhelmina *(Bayreuth)* and Frederick the Great, made the life of the Ansbach Court almost as brilliant as that of Bayreuth.

SIGHTS

★ **Residenz (Castle)** ⊘ – This 14C fortress was enlarged and transformed in the Franconian Baroque style by Gabrieli, architect to the Court of Vienna, and Retti, at the behest of the Margraves of Brandenburg-Ansbach (1705-50). The façade, with its sober lines and simple decoration, is imposing. The interior – symmetrical like the inside of most German Baroque palaces – is especially remarkable for: the princes' apartments (Fürstenzimmer); the **Porcelain Gallery**★★ (Gekachelter Saal), which is lined in some 2 800 Ansbach pottery tiles, lightly and delicately designed with rural motifs; the **Hall of Mirrors**★ (Spiegelkabinett) and its unbelievable profusion of china ornaments and gilded woodwork; the Family Gallery (Familienzimmer), exhibiting portraits of the Hohenzollerns; and the Gobelins Gallery, with three tapestries woven after cartoons by Charles Le Brun.

Kaspar Hauser

In the spring of 1828, an unfortunate young man of about 15 years of age was discovered in Nuremberg marketplace. He had apparently been kept shut up in a dark room and deprived of all contact with the outside world for as long as he could remember, with the result that his behaviour was that of a virtual savage and his ability to communicate with his fellow men severely impaired. This "foundling wild boy", whose sad tale and mysterious origins aroused sympathy and a certain curiosity in all who heard of him, was eventually given the name Kaspar Hauser by those who took him into their care.

Hauser lived in Ansbach from 1831 until his untimely and violent end – he was stabbed by a stranger in 1833. Until relatively recently, legend had it that he must have been the prince and heir of the grand ducal house of Baden. However, this rumour was finally squashed by a DNA test carried out in 1996. The question of Hauser's real identity remains to be solved ... His legend, with its human, psychological and social implications as well as its political aspect, has inspired a wealth of literature and there is even a Kaspar Hauser research foundation. He has also been the subject of several films, such as that directed by Werner Herzog in 1974 (*Jeder für sich und Gott gegen alle*, entitled *The Enigma of Kaspar Hauser* in English).

On the far side of the esplanade, the castle park extends away to the site of the Baroque **Orangery**, which contains a monument to the rather enigmatic Kaspar Hauser – thought to have been the son of Karl Ludwig Friedrich, Grand Duke of Baden – who was fatally wounded here in 1833.

St.-Gumbertus-Kirche – The origins of this church go back to the 8C when the freeborn gentleman Gumbertus founded a Benedictine monastery here; it was turned into a canons regular foundation in the 11C. The Romanesque construction of 1280 was rebuilt as a margravine foundation and court church. Of particular interest is the Chapel of the Knights of the Swan (St. Georgskapelle des Schwanenritterordens, entrance *left behind the altar*). It was built in the 16C with coats of arms and funerary shields, epitaphs and the 1484 Marian altar, which belonged to the Order – which had been founded in 1440 by Friedrich II, Prince Elector of Brandenburg. From 1660 onward the Hohenzollerns were buried in the vault under the chapel, which has architectural remains from the early-Romanesque chancel (1039).

ASCHAFFENBURG

Bayern
Population 65 000
Michelin map 417 Q 11

At the end of the 10C, Aschaffenburg came under the rule of the Archbishopric of Mainz. The town, which lies in a meander of the River Main on the western edge of the legend-filled Spessart, became the second residence of the powerful Archbishops and Prince Electors of Mainz. Renowned landscape and garden architects in the 18C built numerous parks, which still give the town a verdant ambience to this day.

Aschaffenburg became Bavarian in 1814 in the wake of the Congress of Vienna, after the Electorate had been dissolved 11 years prior by the decision of the Deputation of the German Estates (see History). King Ludwig I praised it as the "Bavarian Nice" – also because of its mild climate. Two of its economic pillars today are the clothing industry and automobile accessories. Germany's first driving school was established here in 1904, Mr Kempf's "Autolenkschule".

SIGHTS

* **Schloß Johannisburg (Castle)** – Built on the site of a medieval fortress destroyed in the mid 16C, this huge red-sandstone castle is in the form of a hollow square quartered by lantern towers. The architect commissioned by the bishops to design it was Georg Ridinger of Strasbourg. Constructed from 1605 to 1614, the castle was the pioneer example of the charmingly decorated style that came to be known as German Renaissance. Inside the walls, the steeply sloping roofs of the three-storey wings are dominated by the massive square towers and the 14C keep, retained from the old fort. The central portion of the three façades is topped by dormers adorned with shell niches, pilasters and obelisks – a typical Renaissance concept.

The **State gallery** (Staatsgalerie) ⊘ is on the first floor of the castle, in the wing nearest the river. Apart from 17C Dutch masters (Aert de Gelder), paintings are exhibited by – among others – Hans Baldung Grien (Golgotha) and members of the school of Lucas Cranach the Elder. In the **Paramentenkammer**, vestments and liturgical objects used during the 17C and 18C in the Archdiocese of Mainz may be viewed. Between the West Tower and the old keep is the **chapel** (Schloßkirche). The Franconian sculptor Hans Juncker was responsible for the splendid **altar★**, richly decorated with motifs in relief and alabaster figurines (1609-14). The Second World War did leave some damage.

On the second floor is a **collection of architectural models** of ancient buildings, made in cork. These formed part of the "Collection of Corkery" amassed by Archbishop KT von Dalberg between 1802 and 1806. The **Royal Apartments** in the riverside wing contain late-18C and early-19C furniture, landscape paintings and portraits of the princes who lived there. Finally the **Municipal Museum** (Städtisches Schloßmuseum) ⊘ displays examples of religious art and craftwork from the 15C to the present day, and several collections illustrating the history of Aschaffenburg.

Walk through the castle grounds (Schloßgarten) to reach the **Pompeianum**. This is a reconstruction of the house of Castor and Pollux at Pompeii, built by Ludwig I of Bavaria on the bank overlooking the river.

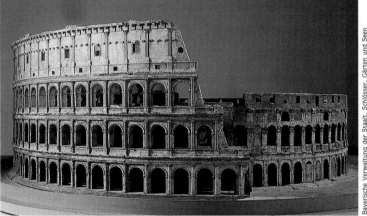

Bayerische Verwaltung der Staatl. Schlösser, Gärten und Seen

Cork model of the Roman Coliseum in Schloß Johannisburg

Stiftskirche – Well situated at the top of a monumental Baroque stairway, this Romano-Gothic church has an oddly asymmetric appearance from the outside, owing to the overshadowing peristyle which flanks the west front and the northern aisle. The oldest part is the long 12C nave (the tower was not completed until c 1490). The Romanesque west door (early 13C) is decorated in pretty plant motifs; on the tympanum in the arch stands a Christ as Judge over the Worlds framed by the two patron saints of the church, the apostle Peter and the Pope and martyr Alexander.

The focus of interest in the interior is on the works of art. **Grünewald's The Lamentation** (1525), the predella of an altarpiece now lost, is on display in a glass case: from 1516 until the outbreak of the Peasant War, this artist acted as the court painter to the Prince-Electors of Aschaffenburg. In the left-hand side wall of the Romanesque nave is a **Romanesque crucifix**, which dates to around AD 980 and is considered one of the most important sculptures of its era. The right-hand transept contains a Resurrection (1520) by Lucas Cranach the Elder, that on the left a Gothic Crucifixion (c 1520). In the **Maria-Schnee-Kapelle** (Chapel of Our Lady of the Snow) is a copy of Grünewald's famous painting of the Virgin Mary, which was taken from the church in the 16C and is now at Stuppach. The late Romanesque **cloister** is supported on 64 columns whose capitals are as varied as they are original.

ENVIRONS

Park Schönbusch – *3km/2mi to the west.*
In the middle of this shady 18C park, which is laid out with ornamental ponds, canals, islets and follies (Temple of Friendship), there is a small and delightful **country manor** (Lustschlößchen) built for the archbishops of Mainz around 1780 and decorated in the Empire style.

From the Hall of Mirrors on the first floor, there is a fine **view** of the castle, with the wooded heights of the Spessart massif in the background.

AUGSBURG★★

Bayern
Population 265 000
Michelin map 419/420 U 16

Tacitus wrote of Augsburg that it was "the most splendid colony in all the province of Rhaetia". Situated on the Romantic Road (Romantische Straße), the town today is both a busy industrial centre and a cultural place boasting numerous constructions from the Renaissance period.

HISTORICAL NOTES

Roman origins – Founded in 15 BC by Drusus and Tiberius, the stepsons of Emperor Augustus, Augsburg is, along with Trier and Cologne, one of the oldest cities in Germany. It became a trading centre on the road to Italy and, at the fall of the Roman Empire, an Episcopal See. By the end of the 13C it was a Free Imperial City and the seat of the Diet.

The Fuggers – At the end of the 15C, Augsburg – which already had a population of 50 000 – became a centre of high finance and banking. This was due to the Fuggers and the Welsers, two local dynastic families who – so it was said – shared the known world between them so far as money and trade were concerned. History has preserved the name of Jakob Fugger the Rich (1459-1529), renowned as the Empire's banker and even better known as the financier of the Habsburgs. Charles V himself once received from this powerful man the rebuke: "It is well known that, without my help, Your Majesty would no longer wear the crown of the Holy Roman Empire." The debt of the Habsburgs to their Augsburg bankers, never settled, has been estimated at four million ducats.

The Augsburg Confession – In 1530 Charles V, disturbed by the growing strength of the Reformation in many states of the Empire, called an Imperial Diet at Augsburg with the hope of dissipating the religious troubles. The Protestants, inspired by Luther, thereupon proclaimed in a celebrated "Confession" the basic tenets of their belief. The statement was rejected, and it was not until the **Peace of Augsburg** in 1555 that Protestants in Germany won the freedom of worship.

The name of the town was once more inscribed in the history books in 1686 with the creation of the **Augsburg League** – an alliance between the Habsburgs and Prussia aimed against Louis XIV, who had revoked the Edict of Nantes.

The Pine Cone – This emblem, an ancient fertility symbol, appears on the city's arms, and indeed through the years Augsburg has flowered with the ideas and talents of artists and humanists. They include Holbein the Elder (d 1525), Hans Burgkmair (1473-1541), and Martin Schongauer, son of Augsburg goldsmith Konrad Peutinger. Augsburg's emergence as "the city of the German Renaissance" is due to the architect Elias Holl (1573-1646). Mozart's father was born in Augsburg, and some of the great composer's glory, too, has been reflected on the town. The famous playwright and poet Bertolt Brecht was born in Augsburg in 1898.

By the 18C, the textile manufacturing industry was flourishing. The 19C was marked by the production (1893-7) of the first diesel engine.

SIGHTS

★ **Fuggerei** (Y) – This name was bestowed in 1519 on the quarter founded by Jakob Fugger the Rich to house the town's poor. The eight streets in the Fuggerei are lined by 53 gabled houses. The district has its own church and its own administration. Each evening the four gateways to the quarter are closed, as they always have been. This housing settlement, the first of its kind in the world, still welcomes citizens in need as it did in the 16C, charging them only a token rent but placing on them the moral obligation of praying for the souls of the founders.

★ **Maximilianstraße** (Z) – Lined by mansions and private houses built by the wealthier burghers of Augsburg during the Renaissance, this street offers today one of the most majestic vistas of Old Germany. Many façades have been extensively restored. Three bronze Renaissance fountains adorn the street.

★ **Münster St.-Ulrich und St.-Afra** (Z) – This former Benedictine abbey church, founded c 1500, lies adjacent to a Protestant church of the same name. The core of the building, high and impressive, is separated from the three aisles by a fine Baroque screen. The ribbed vaulting is well lit by the clerestory windows and at the far end are three Baroque altars: in the choir, the Altar of the Nativity, to the right, the Altar of the Resurrection and to the left the Pentecostal Altar. At the transept crossing is a bronze group of the Crucifixion dating from 1607.

Among the chapels on the north side, St.-Simpert's is furnished with a Gothic baldachin and a balcony surmounted by terracotta **Statues of the Saints**★.

The juxtaposition of the two churches, one Catholic, one Protestant, each with the same name, is characteristic of Augsburg. The two **Heilig-Kreuz-Kirchen** (Y D) are another example.

Banqueting Hall in the Schaezler-Palais, Augsburg

Städt. Kunstsammlungen Augsburg

Städtische Kunstsammlungen (Municipal Art Gallery) ⊘ (**Z M¹**) – *Entrance: Maximilianstraße 46.*
The **Schaezler-Palais** galleries (1767) are the first to be passed through (Deutsche Barockgalerie). Paintings by masters of German Baroque are on display here. The enormous **banqueting hall**★★ (Festsaal) is noteworthy for a ceiling lavishly decorated with Rococo frescoes and stuccowork, and wall panelling adorned in the same style.
Beyond this, a second gallery, the Staatsgalerie Alter Kunst (**Z M²**) exhibits paintings by 15C and 16C Augsburgan and Swabian masters, including a votive portrait of *The Schwarz Family* by Hans Holbein the Elder and the famous *Portrait of Jakob Fugger the Rich* by Albrecht Dürer.
Works by Van Dyck, Tiepolo and Veronese can be seen on the **second floor**.
Right beside the Schaetzler-Palais is the **New Gallery in the Höhmannhaus**, which presents modern art in changing exhibitions.

Rathaus (Town hall) (**Y R**) – This vast Renaissance building is by Elias Holl. Two onion-domed towers frame a pediment adorned with the traditional pine cone. The **Perlachturm** (**Y**), on the left, was originally a Romanesque watchtower. It was expanded three times over the course of the centuries. When the Alps can be seen from the top of it, a yellow flag is flown.
Inside, the town hall's Golden Room (Goldener Saal), with its restored coffered ceiling, can be visited.

St.-Anna-Kirche (**Y B**) – This church was formerly part of a Carmelite convent where Martin Luther found sanctuary when he arrived in Augsburg in 1518. The Late Gothic architecture contrasts with the Rococo stuccowork and frescoes.
The **Fugger Funeral Chapel**★ (Fuggerkapelle) is considered to be the first example of the Italian Renaissance style in Germany. It dates from 1518. Blind arcades at the back of the chapel frame four sculptured scenes: centre, above the recumbent figures, The Resurrection, and Samson Wrestling with the Philistines after Dürer; at each side, the arms of the House of Fugger, from which the fleur-de-lis is reproduced on the pavement.

71

AUGSBURG

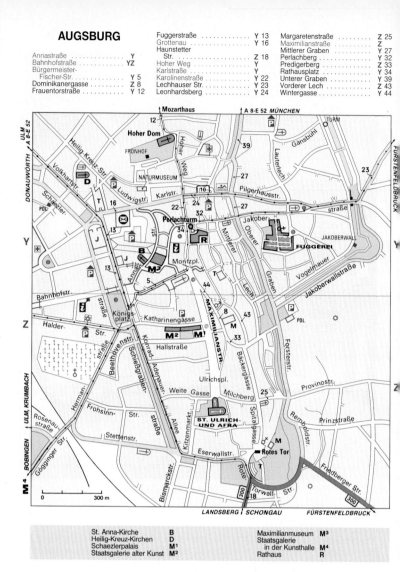

St. Anna-Kirche	B	Maximilianmuseum	M³
Heilig-Kreuz-Kirchen	D	Staatsgalerie	
Schaezlerpalais	M¹	in der Kunsthalle	M⁴
Staatsgalerie alter Kunst	M²	Rathaus	R

In the church there are paintings by Lucas Cranach the Elder: *Jesus, the Friend of Little Children (at the high altar in the main chancel);* a portrait of Martin Luther and the Prince-Elector Johann-Friedrich of Saxony.

The **Goldsmiths' Chapel** (Goldschmiedekapelle), on the north side of the chancel, dating from the 15C, has retained its original Gothic structure and murals.

Maximilianmuseum ⊘ (Y M³) – This museum, which is housed in a Renaissance town palace, contains significant collections on Augsburgs art and cultural history (sculptures, crafts) and outstanding works of goldsmithery.

Dom (Cathedral) (Y) – The church was rebuilt in Gothic style in the 14C. Outside, note the Gothic south door to the chancel (Südportal des Chores) or **Virgin's Door**★★ (Jungfrauen-Portal), and also the Romanesque **bronze panels**★ (Türflügel) dating to the first half of the 11C. They are embellished with 32 bas-relief sculptures illustrating scenes and characters from the Old Testament and mythology (provisionally displayed within the cathedral at the present time). Inside the church, the tall nave is flanked by double side aisles. The chancel, at its eastern extremity, has a double ambulatory with Gothic chapels added. Four of the altars in the nave are adorned with **panel paintings**★ (Tafelgemälden) by Holbein the Elder (on the left: *Birth of the Virgin Mary* and *Entry Into the Temple;* on the right, *The Offering Refused* and *The Presentation*). The clerestory windows on the south side of the nave contain stained-glass **Windows of the Prophets**★ (Prophetenfenster – 12C) which are very rigid in style. The alabaster panes surrounding them are modern.

Mozarthaus (Mozart Family House) ⊘ (Y) – *Leave by Frauentorstraße.*
Documents and other exhibits emphasize the Swabian origins of the Mozart family and the life and work of father and son.

From this house, by way of the Stephingerberg and the Müllerstraße, the tree-lined promenade bordering the moats which follow the line of the ancient ramparts can be reached.

Rotes Tor (Red Gate) (Z) – This is a group of 16C fortified buildings with two vaults and a central courtyard, remodelled by Elias Holl in 1622. The tower overlooking the town is circled by bands of decoration between the engaged pillars. At the foot of the tower is an open-air theatre *(operatic performances late June to late July)*.

★ **Staatsgalerie in der Kunsthalle (State Gallery)** ⊙ **(M⁴)** – *Leave by Imhofstraße (Z)*. The Gallery at Wittelsbach Park exhibits great works of German art from the 19C and 20C. Among the painters displayed are outstanding representatives of Impressionism in Germany such as Lovis and Corinth (*The Three Graces*, 1903) or Max Slevogt, as well as Franz von Stuck and Franz von Lenbach.

The German Expressionists and the art of the Classical Moderns form another focus of the gallery. Self-portraits and typical compositions are used to exemplify the artists of the Bridge Group *(die Brücke)* (Ernst Ludwig Kirchner, Otto Müller, Max Pechstein, Karl Schmitt-Rottluff) and of the Blauer Reiter group (Wassily Kandinsky, Franz Marc, Gabriele Münter). In addition there are sculptures and paintings by other important protagonists of the Classical Moderns such as Hans Arp, Max Beckmann, Paul Klee, Wilhelm Lehmbruck or August Macke. The paintings of the Informal School can be explored by way of two of its most significant representatives: Emil Schumacher and Bernard Schultze.

A separate annex has been reserved for contemporary art, where young artists mainly from southern Germany are exhibited. Photography is also displayed.

Alphabetical order...?
In the German alphabet, ä = ae, ö = oe and ü = ue.

BAD

See under proper name

BADEN-BADEN★★

Baden-Württemberg
Population 50 000
Michelin map 419 T 8 – Local map see SCHWARZWALD
Plan of the conurbation in the current Michelin Red Guide Deutschland

Sheltered between the Black Forest and the Baden vineyards, Baden-Baden is one of the most elegant German health resorts. One of the town's premier attractions is the "Caracalla-Therme", a beautiful balneal establishment **(CY)** (for public enjoyment).

Spa and Casino – In Roman times the Emperor Caracalla came frequently to Baden-Baden to cure his rheumatism.

In the 12C, the town became the seat of the Zähringer branch of the Margraves of Baden. In the 16C, the great Paracelsus, one of the founders of modern pharmacy, came to take care of the Margrave.

By the 19C, a casino launched by the Frenchman Jacques Bénazet, a theatre and opera house (opened in 1862), and a racecourse organised by the Paris Jockey Club had transformed the town into the summer capital of Europe.

In the gardens of the spa park, behind the white Corinthian columns of the **Kurhaus (BZ)**, glittering balls and concerts are held, and the gaming rooms are always crowded. Nearby in the same park (Kurgarten) is the Drinking Hall **(Trinkhalle) (BY)**, embellished with murals illustrating the legends of the Baden countryside.

SIGHTS

★★ **Lichtentaler Allee (BZ)** – This, the most beautiful promenade in Baden-Baden, runs beside the River Oos, flowing here over an artificial bed, and recalls irresistibly the 19C parades of carriages, complete with crinolines, parasols and gentlemen in tall hats. The shade of the esplanade has seen many an historical figure: Napoleon III, his wife the Empress Eugénie, Queen Victoria, Bismarck and Dostoevski, to name a few, strolled along here. In 1861, an unsuccessful attempt was even made on the life of the then King of Prussia, later Kaiser Wilhelm I. Originally these were oaks, planted more than 300 years ago, but the exotic species – azaleas, magnolias, silver poplars, tulip trees – have been added since. On the left, beyond the swimming pool, is the **Gönneranlage★ (BZ)**, a pretty park with fountains and pergolas flanking a rose garden.

ACCOMMODATION

BUDGET

Am Markt – Marktplatz 18; ☎ 0 72 21/2 70 40, Fax 0 72 21/27 04 44. 26 rooms, single rooms from 55DM. Very well-kept family operation near the Stiftskirche.

Auerhahn – Geroldsauer Straße 160; ☎ 0 72 21/74 35, Fax 0 72 21/74 32. 28 rooms, single rooms from 96DM. Comfortable typically Baden inn in Baden-Baden-Geroldsau.

Waldhorn – Beuerner Straße 54; ☎ 0 72 21/722 88, Fax 0 72 21/7 34 88. 12 rooms, single rooms from 100DM. Rustically comfortable country inn in Baden-Baden-Oberbeuern.

OUR SELECTION

Schweizer Hof – Lange Str. 73; ☎ 0 72 21/3 04 60, Fax 0 72 21/30 46 46. 29 rooms, single rooms from 100DM. Hotel with individually furnished rooms.

Atlantic – Sophienstraße 2a; ☎ 0 72 21/36 10, Fax 0 72 21/2 62 60. 51 rooms, single rooms from 120DM. Centrally located on Lichtentaler Allee vis-a-vis from the theatre.

Bad-Hotel Zum Hirsch – Hirschstraße 1; ☎ 0 72 21/93 90, Fax 0 72 21/3 81 48. 58 rooms, single rooms from 152DM. Hotel with a long tradition, classical decoration with stylish furniture.

TREAT YOURSELF!

Steigenberger Europäischer Hof – Kaiserallee 2; ☎ 0 72 21/93 90, Fax 0 72 21/2 88 31. 130 rooms, single rooms from 202DM. Classic grand hotel with four suites.

Quisisana – Bismarckstraße 21; ☎ 0 72 21/36 90, Fax 0 72 21/36 92 69. 60 rooms, single rooms from 240DM. This hotel is located in a former villa furnishings are modern and individual.

Brenner's Park-Hotel – Schillerstraße 6; ☎ 0 72 21/90 00, Fax 0 72 21/3 87 72. 100 rooms, single rooms from 358DM. Baden-Baden's top address.

RESTAURANTS

BUDGET

Molkenkur – Quettigstraße 19; ☎ 0 72 21/3 32 57. Main dishes from 10.50DM. In a former dairy with a beautiful terrace.

Münchner Löwenbräu – Gernsbacher Straße 9; ☎ 0 72 21/2 23 11. Main dishes from 13DM. Brewery restaurant with solid home cooking.

La Provence – Schloßstraße 20; ☎ 0 72 21/2 55 50. Main dishes from 18.50DM. Mediterranean atmosphere under a beautiful vaulting.

OUR SELECTION

Klosterschänke – On the road to Steinbach, via Fremersbergstraße; ☎ 0 72 21/2 58 54. Main dishes from 14.80DM. Rustic wood house, the cuisine is regional and Italian. The terrace has a delightful view of th Rhine valley.

La Casserole – Gernsbacher Straße 18; ☎ 0 72 21/2 22 21. Main dishes from 19.50DM. Small, Alsatian restaurant with rustic decor.

Medici – Augustaplatz 8; ☎ 0 72 21/20 06. Main dishes from 28DM. High-class establishment with antique-like decor. In addition to the restaurant section, it has an American bar and the Cigar Cabinet. The terrace offers a very nice view of the Lichtentaler Allee.

TREAT YOURSELF!

Papalangi – Lichtentaler Straße 13; ☎ 0 72 21/3 16 16. Main dishes from 19.50DM (lunch) and 30DM (supper). Restaurant with modern ambience, with a changing exhibition of paintings.

Le Jardin de France – Rotenbachtalstraße 10, ☎ 0 72 21/3 00 78 60. Main dishes from 35DM. Modern elegant restaurant with French cuisine.

Zum Alde Gott – Weinstraße 10, ☎ 0 72 23/55 13. Main dishes from 37DM. Rustic restaurant in Baden-Baden-Neuweier in a country manor. Regional and international range of dishes.

Friedrichsbad (CY) – The Roman-Irish steam bath in Friedrichsbad is an interesting experience. The elegance and style of the Belle Epoque is still apparent in this neo-Renaissance bathing palace, which is nonetheless discreetly equipped with the very latest in technology. Those with a couple of hours to spare should try out the various installations which make up these baths; the reward is an unbeatable feeling of relaxation and well-being. Things can get quite heated here, however, as the hot air baths can reach temperatures of almost 70°C/158°F; as a result the thermal steam baths can seem somewhat "cooler". A highlight of the visit is the round thermal massage bath in a magnificent domed room. Not surprisingly, the Friedrichsbad has provided a magical setting for a number of films.

Friedrichsbad, Baden-Baden

H.O. Volz/Baden-Baden Marketing GmbH

Neues Schloß (New Castle) (CY) – Built by the Margraves of Baden at the time of the Renaissance, the castle has been partly transformed into the **Zähringer Museum**, where local history can be traced through exhibits in the state rooms and salons. From the terrace, there is a fine **view** of the town, with the Stiftskirche in the foreground.

Stiftskirche (CY) – The Margraves of Baden were all buried in this church from the 14C to the 18C. The chancel contains a wealth of artfully decorated tombs ranging from the Late Gothic to the Rococo period. The massive body of Margrave Leopold Wilhelm, represented for posterity as resting on a divan (left, late 17C), and the sheer opulence of the funerary monument of Ludwig the Turk (right, 1753) stand in stark contrast to the simplicity of the **sandstone Crucifix★**, which draws all the attention from its position on the façade of the chancel. This 1467 masterpiece by Niclaus Gerhaert von Leyden is considered one of the outstanding examples of sculpture from the late Middle Ages thanks to the highly detailed representation of the body that still fascinates the beholder to this very day.
A must is the filigreed Late Gothic tabernacle (late 15C).

Römische Badruinen (Roman Baths) ⊘ – Beneath the **Römerplatz (CY)**, excavations have unearthed the ruins of a Roman bathhouse (note particularly the hypocaust underfloor heating system).

EXCURSIONS

★ **Yburg Ruins** – *6km/3.5mi to the southwest. Leave by Friedrichstraße (BZ).*
From the tower *(110 steps)* there is a **vast panorama★★** over the Rhine plain, with the Baden vineyards in the foreground.

★ **Autobahnkirche (Motorway Church)** – *8km/5mi to the west. Leave by Langestraße.*
Placed under the patronage of St Christopher, patron saint of travellers, this modernistic church is the work (1976-78) of the architect F Zwingmann and the painter-sculptor E Wachter. The design presents a harmonious blend of the plastic arts and architecture. Sculptures and stained glass panels are devoted to biblical and symbolic themes.

Merkur – *2km/1.2mi to the east. Leave by Markgrafenstraße (CZ).*
From the upper terminal of the cable-car take the lift to the top of the lookout tower (Aussichtsturm); the broad **view★** takes in Baden-Baden, the Rhine Valley to the west, the Murg Valley to the east and (on a clear day) the Vosges.

BADEN-BADEN

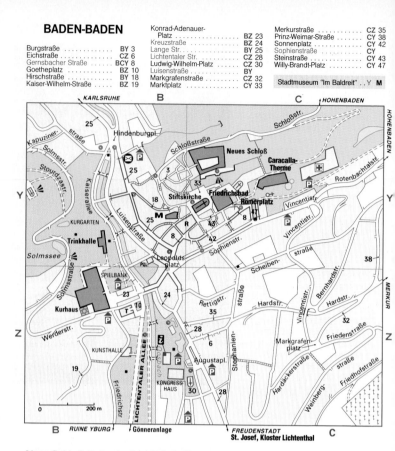

Altes Schloß Hohenbaden (Ruins); Ebersteinburg – *Round tour of 13km/8mi: about 1.5hr. Leave Baden-Baden by the Schloßstraße (CY).*
The old castle of Hohenbaden was built by the Margraves of Baden, who, however, moved to the Neues Schloß (New Castle) at the end of the 15C. One year later it burned down. The parapet commands a view over the town and valley.
Afterwards, climb to the top of the Ebersteinburg keep for a view of the foothills of the Black Forest.

★ **Baden Vineyards** – *30km/19mi: 1.5hr. Leave by the Kaiser-Wilhelm-Straße and then the Fremersbergstraße. Once outside the town, follow the signposts "Badische Weinstraße".*
The **Badische Weinstraße**★★★ twists sinuously from village to village as it winds through the vineyards on the lower slopes of the Black Forest.

Leave the Weinstraße at Altschweir and return to Altwindeck.

★ **Burg Altwindeck** – This ancient fort, built on a circular plan, has been transformed into a restaurant with panoramic views. From its precincts there is a wide **view**★ of the plain.

Sasbach – *15min on foot there and back. Leave the car opposite the Hotel Linde and walk into the park surrounding the Turenne monument.*
An obelisk and plinth with inscriptions in German, French and Latin mark the spot where, in 1675, a fatal cannon-ball ended the glorious career of Turenne – the French hero charged by Louis XIV with the defence of Alsace against the Imperial forces, during the conquest of Franche-Comté.

★★★ **Schwarzwald-Hochstraße (Black Forest Crest Road)** – See SCHWARZWALD.

BADENWEILER★

Badenweiler lies on a slope at the mouth of a valley in the southern foothills of the Black Forest with a view both of the Rhine Valley and the Vosges. It has been known for its thermal waters and gentle climate since time immemorial. This spa and holiday town attracts people seeking rest and recuperation, healing or at least relief from rheumatic and articulatory complaints or cardio-vascular problems.

★★ **Kurpark (Spa Park)** – The rolling parkland abounds in subtropical plants and splendid trees: Cedars and cypresses mingle with enormous sequoias. The park also contains the impressive ruins of some Roman baths, the largest and best-preserved north of the Alps. A climb up to the ruins of the old fort brings with it a fine **view**★ of the resort, the Rhine Valley and the Vosges.

EXCURSIONS

★ **Blauen** – *8km/5mi to the southeast, then 15min on foot there and back.*
From the viewing tower, rising above the woods at the top of a hill, there is a remarkable **panorama**★★ over the plain – the parallel ribbons of the Rhine and the Grand Canal of Alsace can easily be distinguished – and the tree-covered humps of the Vosges. The bare summit to the northeast is the Belchen. On a clear day the Alps appear in the south.

★ **Schloß Bürgeln** ⊘ – *10km/6.2mi to the south.*
This gentleman's residence, set in beautifully kept, terraced gardens, was built in 1762 for the abbots of St.-Blasien. The property overlooks the last undulations of the Black Forest, several reaches of the Rhine, and part of the city of Basle. Inside, there are beautiful examples of stuccowork in the Rococo style.

★ **Burg Rötteln** – *27km/17mi to the south.*
The Oberburg, defensive nucleus of this fortress, is reached by a series of ramps and a drawbridge. The Green Tower (Grüner Turm), which overlooks the whole complex, has been restored and modified into a look-out tower.
From the tower, the view includes the Wiese Valley (which eventually fades into the outskirts of Basel), the wooded massif of the Blauen in the Basel Jura, the gentler slopes of the Black Forest and, far off on the horizon, the Swiss Alps.

BAMBERG★★

It was Emperor Henry II the Saint (1002-24) who transformed this Imperial residence into a flourishing episcopal city.
From the 12C onwards, as was the case with all episcopal towns, the clergy, installed in the higher part, traded on their authority and came into conflict with the burghers who had settled in the valley, on the island, around the Grüner Markt and in the Sand quarter. The quarrel ended in the 16C with the ecclesiastics prevailing. Then gradually the schism healed and the 18C found all parts of town being equally endowed with prestigious buildings in the new Baroque style under the Schönborn bishops.
The sculptor **Tilman Riemenschneider** (1460-1531) and the **Dientzenhofer** family, draughtsmen of distinction, were the most famous products of the city.
Bamberg is the town the Germans feel by far the most affinity for, as a poll suggests. It is a work of art in itself, with 2 300 protected constructions that range from the Romanesque to the Baroque period. The UNESCO paid its respects by putting Bamberg on the World Heritage list in 1993.
Among Bamberg's many gastronomic specialities visitors should sample carp (Karpfen) prepared to a traditional local recipe, and "smoked beer" (Rauchbier).

CATHEDRAL PRECINCTS *allow 2hr*

The Domplatz is lined by the cathedral itself, the Neue Residenz (18C) and the Alte Hofhaltung, which houses the Historical Museum.

★★ **Dom (Cathedral)** (BZ) – Transitional Gothic in style, the cathedral is characterised by its two apses. That to the east, the Georgenchor, the older, stands raised upon a terrace with a fine balustrade, its cornices worked in a chequered pattern; that to the west, the Peterschor, is entirely Gothic. Four towers quarter the two choirs.

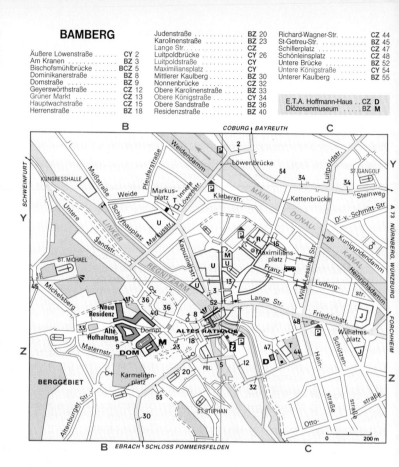

The design, inherited from the original Ottonian edifice, exemplifies the reticence of the Empire's powerful ecclesiastical institutions when faced with the innovations of French Gothic.

The finest of the cathedral entrances is the **Fürstenportal** (Princes' Doorway), on the Domplatz. It comprises 10 recessed arches supported on fluted, ribbed or chevroned columns which alternate with statue-columns representing prophets with apostles on their shoulders.

Enter the church through the Adamspforte, which is decorated with diamond and dogtooth carving (the statues which used to adorn it are in the Diocesan Museum). From east to west, the progression from Romanesque to Gothic is at once apparent. Two choirs, noticeably raised because of the crypts built beneath them, enclose a single nave whose walls – with neither triforium nor galleries – attest to the conservatism of the prevailing style. Underneath the eastern choir, the crypt is huge: three Romanesque naves with heavily ribbed vaulting supported on powerful columns. Beneath the western choir is the tomb of the Bamberg archbishops, whose basic features are those of the re-excavated western crypt of the original cathedral of Heinrich.

Masterpieces of early German Gothic sculpture are on view in the cathedral.

1) Equestrian statue of **The Knight of Bamberg**★★★ (Bamberger Reiter), a 13C representation of an unidentified king (possibly St Stephen, first King of Hungary and brother-in-law of Henry II), symbolizing an idealized view of the Middle Ages – much as Bayard, the "blameless and fearless knight" of France stands for the same chivalrous ideals.

2) Celebrated statuary group, The Visitation (note the features of St Elizabeth). The group, and the Knight on his horse, are the work of an artist strongly influenced by the French School, particularly that of Reims.

The Knight of Bamberg

3) The **tomb**★★★ of Henry II the Saint and Cunegunda (St. Heinrichs-Grab) stands in the centre of the nave, at the entrance to the eastern choir. It took Tilman Riemenschneider 14 years to complete the tomb. The following scenes can be identified, circling the tomb: Cunegunda's ordeal by fire under suspicion of adultery; Cunegunda's dismissal of dishonest workmen; death of Henry II the Saint; the weighing of the Emperor's soul before St Lawrence; St Benedict miraculously operating on the Emperor for gallstones.

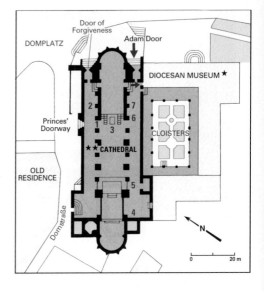

4) Reredos of The Nativity (1523) by Veit Stoß.

5) Funerary statue of a bishop (Friedrich von Hohenlohe).

6) Statue representing The Church.

7) Remarkable statue symbolizing The Synagogue, in the form of a blindfolded woman.

★ **Diözesanmuseum (Diocesan Museum)** ⊘ **(BZ M)** – *Access through the cathedral.*
The collections displayed include lapidary remains, among them statues of Adam and Eve, the former giving his name to one of the cathedral doorways *(see above)*, and the cathedral treasury, rich in imperial and pontifical vestments.

Alte Hofhaltung (Old Residence) (BZ) – *The courtyard is open until dusk.*
This was formerly the episcopal and imperial palace (10C-11C). Its façade, with carved gables, oriel window and corner turret date, along with the doorway, from the Renaissance. The delightful **inner courtyard**★★ (Innenhof) is bordered by half-timbered Gothic buildings with steeply sloping roofs and picturesque, flower-decked wooden galleries.
Opposite the entrance, take a covered alleyway which leads to a small square surrounded by houses once inhabited by the canons.

Follow Domstraße back to the Domplatz.

Neue Residenz (New Residence) ⊘ **(BZ)** – This palace, the largest building in Bamberg, comprises four main blocks: two, bordering the Obere Karolinenstraße, were constructed in the early 17C and are Renaissance in style; the two wings on the Domplatz are Baroque. They were started in 1695 by the architect Leonard Dientzenhofer, on the orders of Lothar Franz von Schönborn, Prince-Elector of Mainz and Bishop of Bamberg.
The palace boasts its own mystery. One morning in 1815, a corpse was found beneath the windows. It was the body of Marshal Berthier, retired to Bavaria after the return of Napoleon from the Isle of Elba. Accident, murder or suicide? The question has never been answered.
On the first floor, works of the German masters are on view (Master of the Life of the Virgin, Hans Baldung Grien etc). The Imperial Apartments on the second floor are among the finest in the Residenz, with beautiful parquet floors, Baroque furniture and authentic Gobelins tapestries. The Emperors' Hall is outstanding for its portraits and its allegorical frescoes. From the palace rose garden, there is a **fine view**★ of the town and the former Benedictine abbey of St. Michael.
Follow the Karolinenstraße to the lay quarter of the old town, built on the banks of the River Regnitz (note the statues of the Virgin Mary on the house corners).

★ **Altes Rathaus (Old town hall) (BZ)** – Standing alone on an islet in the river, this unusual building was remodelled in the 18C. In addition to the town hall proper, with its façades decorated with a perspective fresco, there is a bridge tower and

Altes Rathaus, Bamberg

a small half-timbered house, known as the Rottmeisterhaus, balanced on one of the bridge's pontoons leading to the islet. From the Untere Brücke – the bridge at the lower end of the islet – there is a good view of the old fishermen's cottages along the river bank.

E.T.A. Hoffmann-Haus (Hoffmann's House) ⊘ **(CZ D)** – This tiny house in the Schillerplatz occupies a special place in the memory of the poet ETA Hoffmann (1776-1822), whose tales, set to music by the Franco-German composer Jacques Offenbach *(The Tales of Hoffmann)*, made him a celebrity worldwide. Hoffmann lived here from 1809 to 1813, in three small rooms. The poet dreamed up the first few of his fantastic tales and some of his poems in the "Poetenstübchen". A museum contains information on Hoffmann's activities as writer, musician and caricaturist.

EXCURSIONS

★ **Ebrach** – *35km/22mi to the west.*
The **Old Abbey** (currently used as a prison), founded in 1127 as the first Cistercian monastery to the right of the Rhine and not completed until the end of the 13C, was extensively remodelled in the Baroque fashion, first by JL Dientzenhofer and then by Balthasar Neumann.
The ground plan of the **abbey church**★ – which was built between 1200 and 1285 in Early Gothic style with a right-angled ambulatory – with its flat-ended chancel was directly inspired by that of Cîteaux (the first abbot of Ebrach was closely tied to St Bernard, who was active in that Burgundian monastery). A rose window

The Bamberg Christmas Crèche Circuit

It is not only during summer that Bamberg has something to offer tourists. An increasing number of people choose to visit the town in winter, during the Advent period (and up to 6 January) to take advantage of a particularly seasonal attraction on offer here – the **Bamberg Christmas Crèch Circuit** (Bamberger Krippenweg), which takes in 30 or so churches, museums and squares featuring highly original, decorative crib scenes.

The circuit begins in the cathedral with the altar to the Virgin Mary by Nürnberg master Veit Stoß, and continues to the Maternkapelle and the Obere Pfarre, in which the scenes portrayed include events from the Annunciation to the Wedding at Cana. The Bamberg cribs come in all shapes and sizes – from the enormous crib in Schönleinsplatz with life-size figures in traditional local costume, to the tiny peepshow crib in the church of St. Gandolf. There is an astonishing variety of cribs on display – encompassing the modern crib scene in St Stephan's, the lovingly arranged figures (over 200 of them) in the crib scene at St Martin's and the marvellous 18C crib in the Siechenkapelle – each with its own unique charm to commend it.

Bamberg crib scenes are largely set against backgrounds featuring some aspect of the local environment, such as half-timbered Franconian houses, the outline of the town of Bamberg itself, or a grotto in Franconian Switzerland, which lends them a distinctive "local flavour". The 400 year old tradition of crib-making is carefully nurtured and handed on to future generations in a special training college, the Bamberger Krippenbauschule.

NB Leaflets on the Bamberg Christmas Crèche Circuit are available from the tourist office (Fremdenverkehrsamt).

7.6m/25ft in diameter illuminates the façade. Inside, there are fine Rococo railings, a Baroque organ in the choir, and a Renaissance altarpiece *(north transept)* illustrating the Vision of St Bernard.

★ **Schloß Pommersfelden** ⊘ – *21km/12mi to the south.*
Designed by Dientzenhofer and Hildebrandt and built for Bishop Lothar Franz von Schönborn between 1711 and 1718, this castle is one of the most outstanding examples in Germany of a Baroque palace.
A rapid tour permits the visitor to admire the galleried **state staircase**★ *(see illustration p).* The paintings on the ceiling represent the Olympian gods and the four quarters of the globe. On the ground floor, an artificial grotto opening onto the garden perpetuates a Renaissance tradition. The marble hall on the first floor, lined with stucco pilasters, is decorated with frescoes by Rottmayr.
A longer visit would include the Elector's apartments with their small painting gallery and a hall of mirrors.

Forchheim – *25km/15.5mi to the south.*
St. Martins-Pfarrkirche here stands amid an imposing group of half-timbered houses. Inside are eight **paintings**★ (15C), once part of an altarpiece. Seven of them illustrate on one side the legend of St Martin – commemorated with a procession each year on the 11 November – and on the other side scenes from the Passion. The **palace** (Pfalz), a crude Gothic edifice dating from the 14C, was built on the site of a former Carolingian castle.

BAUTZEN★

Sachsen
Population 47 000
Michelin map 418 M 27

Bautzen owes much to a situation from which one can see as far as the horizon in three different directions – it is built on a rock outcrop skirted by the winding course of the Spree. There is an especially picturesque view of the town from the bridge (Friedensbrücke), combining the cathedral (Dom St. Peter), the castle (Ortenburg), a network of narrow streets and an ancient fountain which serves as an emblem for the municipality. There are many **Sorbian** families in Bautzen – descendants of a western Slav people settling between the Elbe and the Neisse (mainly in south Brandenburg and east Saxony) after the migrations of the 6C. The Sorbian language is still taught in local schools and numerous folk traditions – the decoration of eggs at Easter, the wearing of tall embroidered headdresses, the use of Sorbian national costume for festivals and holidays – perpetuate the identity of this ethnic minority.

SIGHTS

Hauptmarkt – The old market square is surrounded by fine burghers' houses and a three-storey town hall – built around 1730 by Johann Christoph Naumann. Its asymmetrically positioned tower is crowned by a wonderful helm roof. Reichenstraße leads from the market square to the **Reichenturm** ⊙ (Tower of the Rich), a 56m/179ft leaning tower that offers an excellent view of the city.

★ **Dom St.-Peter** – This hall-church with three naves (1213-1497) is the sole place of worship in the region to be used both by Roman Catholics and by Protestants (Catholic Masses in the chancel; Protestant services in the main nave). Construction began at the beginning of the 13C. In the middle of the 15C the southern part of the structure was enlarged, and the Late Gothic windows date from this period – construction of the hall choir gave rise to the elbow in the axis, which is clearly visible from within and without. In 1664, the 85m/279ft tower was crowned with a Baroque cupola.

Inside the cathedral, note the large wood Crucifix (1714) by Balthazar Permoser, and the Princes' Loggia (1674) in the Protestant section. The Baroque (1724) high altar in the chancel (St Peter Receiving the Keys) is the work of GA Pellegrini.

Follow the road that runs past the cathedral as far as the monastery.

Those parts of the **monastery** that remain standing date from 1683. The southern façade with its imposing portal (1753-55) is particularly fine. The armorial bearings of the monastery are displayed between the rounded pediments.

Now follow the Schloßstraße.

Alte Wasserkunst and Michaelkirche, Bautzen

Ortenburg – Where Ortenburg stands today, there once stood a fortified complex that was completed around AD 600 and was expanded as a frontier fort in 958 by Heinrich I. Two devastating fires in the early 15C destroyed the construction. The Hungarian king Matthias Corvinus had the fortress rebuilt from scratch in Late Gothic style between 1483 and 1486 (the Lausitz region was an Hungarian province from 1469 to 1490). A portrait in relief of the Hungarian king can still be distinguished on the tower of the north wing. The Thirty Years War also left profound scars, which were removed by renovations that were performed after 1648. In the midst of the Baroque Age, in the year 1698, three Renaissance gables were added to the castle, a veritable anachronism.

Serbski Muzej (Sorbian Museum) ⊙ – *In the former Salt House, an annex of Ortenburg castle added in 1782.*
Numerous exhibits, including the distinctive traditional costume with its large elaborate headdress, illustrate the history, culture and way of life of the Sorbians. *The museum will be closed for construction purposes from November 2000 to about March 2002.*

★ **Town ramparts** – The medieval ramparts are very well maintained and shape the silhouette of the town. A walk along the town walls provides visitors with an idea of what it must have been like in the Middle Ages. The ruins of the **Nikolaikirche** and the cemetery of the same name are especially worth a visit.

★ **Alte Wasserkunst** ⊙ – This formidable defensive and water tower has been standing since 1558. Although it is difficult to believe, it actually supplied the town with water up to 1965. The workings of this technical monument, with its seven storeys and an impressive pumping system (graphically explained) are extremely interesting.

EXCURSION

From Bautzen to Zittau – *44km/27mi*
(on B 178)

★ **König-Friedrich-August-Turm** ⊙ – *In Löbau (in the southwest of the town across Herwigsdorfer Straße).* The 28m/92ft high cast iron viewing tower is the only one of its kind in Europe. Some 6 000 individual grey cast iron parts and a total weight of 70t combine to produce a filigree masterpiece. Three platforms, heights 12, 18 and 24m/39, 59 and 78ft, afford the visitor a wonderful view, quite in keeping with the tower's motto: "The further the view, the freer the heart".

★ **Obercunnersdorf** – *Turn right 3km/1.8mi to the south of Löbau.* The entire village is a protected monument, as it is a self-contained development of **post-and-beam frame houses**. Some of the 250 or so houses are open to visitors. *(See ZITTAUER GEBIRGE: The post-and-beam frame house).*

Herrnhut – The town has acquired world renown through the Evangelical brotherhood of the same name. The members of this community, which was founded in Mähren in 1457, were persecuted for their beliefs, took refuge here in 1772 and founded the town. This resulted in the

R. Chérey/MICHELIN

König-Friedrich-August-Turm
in Löbau

self-contained method of building described as "Herrnhuter Baroque", which is expressed in the municipal building, the castle and entire streets of houses. A folklore museum documents the educational work of the brethren, which is still practised in 22 countries within five continents.

Zittau – *See ZITTAUER GEBIRGE.*

BAYERISCHER WALD ★

BAVARIAN FOREST – Bayern
Michelin map 420 S 20-T 23

The south-western edge of the Bayerischer Wald begins in the plain of the Danube between Regensburg and Passau. In the northwest, it turns into the Böhmerwald, where one finds the highest mountains; the Großer Arber and the Großer Rachel, 1 456m/4 777ft and 1 453m/4 767ft respectively. The landscape is of low mountains, with rounded off summits, wild and romantic rock bastions and isolated, comb-like river valleys and broad depressions. The Pfahl is a geological peculiarity, a stretch of quartz between 50m and 100m wide and 150km/90mi long. Europe's largest protected forest area stretches over 13 300ha/32 865 acres on both sides of the German-Czech border over an ancient base of gneiss and granite (the Bayerischer Wald is one of the world's oldest mountain ranges. Dark pine forests cover the summits, mixed forest of pine, beech and fir grow along the slopes. The centre of the region is the National Park founded in 1970. Forestry was gradually stopped to let the forest grow as nature wanted it to. The natural quality of the woods have drawn a wide species of animals. Besides tourism, agriculture (with emphasis on the wood industry) is the most important economic sector for the communities in the Bayerischer Wald.

ROUND TOUR STARTING FROM BODENMAIS 66km/41mi – 3hr

★ **Bodenmais** – This unique town with a healing climate lies in a pastureland at the southern foot of the Großer Arber. A subsoil rich in sulphur and magnetic rock has been exploited since the 15C. From Kötzting onwards, the road mounts the pastoral Weißer Regen Valley within sight of the peaks of the Osser.
Motorists continue climbing as far as the Lamer Winkel, a hollow of woods and upland meadows at the head of the valley. A panoramic drive across the mountainside, enlivened by a closer view of the Großer Arber, terminates this part of the journey (highest point: Brennes-Sattel, alt 1 030m/3 380ft).

★ **Hindenburg-Kanzel** – A **look-out point**★ offers a fine view of the Lamer Winkel and the Arber.

★★ **Großer Arber** – *From the lower* **chair-lift** ⊘ *terminal, 1hr there and back, of which 20min chair-lift and 30min there and back on foot.*
From the upper terminal, continue to climb on foot. At the top there are two rocky crags. That on the left (above a small chapel) overlooks the Schwarzer Regen depression, with an extended **view**★★ of the frontier region of the southeast. The right-hand rock (surmounted by a cross) affords a splendid view of the Lamer Winkel and the wooded undulations of the forest to the north.
The **Großer Arbersee**★, a dark, romantic lake surrounded by pines, is passed on the right as the road goes down, winding through the tree-covered foothills on the southern slopes of the Arber. On the way, there are several magnificent **viewpoints**★ commanding the Zwiesel basin, the Falkenstein and the Großer Rachel.

BAYREUTH★

Bayern
Population 72 000
Michelin map 420 Q 18

Bayreuth is the town of Wagner. Built between the wooded heights of the Fichtelgebirge and the curious, desolate landscape of Swiss Franconia, it existed peacefully for hundreds of years before a series of events starting in the 18C placed it once and for all on the world map. First of all, it was chosen as a residence for the Margraves of Brandenburg-Bayreuth, with all the prominence attached to the life of the court; later it became one of Europe's architectural capitals of Baroque and Rococo; and today the town is the Holy Grail to Wagner fans who come here from the four corners of the world.

HISTORICAL NOTES

Princess Wilhelmina – The Margravine Wilhelmina, daughter of the King-Sergeant, sister of Frederick the Great and lifelong friend of Voltaire, was one of the most cultivated women of the 18C. She could have married royalty, but it was decided instead that she should marry Margrave Friedrich of Brandenburg-Bayreuth. Finding him rather a dull man, she gathered cultivated figures around her, creating a more stimulating environment in which her talents might flower.
Her life (1709-58) marked the most brilliant period in Bayreuth's history. A gifted artist, writer, composer, architect and decorator, dilettante and patroness of the fine arts, the Princess was responsible for the blossoming of "Bayreuth Rococo" – a highly personal style whose garlands and flowers differed markedly from the more rustic French Rococo then in vogue.

Wagner and Liszt – It is often said that many of Wagner's masterworks would never have seen the light of day if it had not been for the influence of Liszt. The two innovators of musical expression, stimulated by mutual admiration and drawn closer by family ties (Wagner married Liszt's daughter Cosima in 1870), were united again even in death: the tomb of Liszt, who died during one of the first festivals in 1886, is in the Bayreuth cemetery (Stadtfriedhof via Erlanger Straße – Y), while the remains of Wagner, who died three years earlier in Venice, repose in the gardens of the Villa Wahnfried.

The Festival – Creator of a new musical form, Richard Wagner searched on his many wanderings for the ideal place to present his works. He chose Bayreuth in 1872. With the support of Ludwig II of Bavaria, he had the Festival Theatre (Festspielhaus) built to his own design. It was inaugurated in 1876 with a performance of *The Ring*.

The festival tradition established by the maestro was continued after his death, thanks to the tenacity of Cosima and, subsequently, his son Siegfried, his grandson Wieland (d 1966) and Wolfgang Wagner today. Each year the world's greatest exponents of the Wagnerian ethos retransmit the immortal message to an audience of spellbound enthusiasts.

SIGHTS

★ **Markgräfliches Opernhaus (Margraves' Opera House)** ⊘ (Y) – The Margravine Wilhelmina was responsible for the building of this theatre between 1745 and 1748. The austere façade, hemmed in between 18C burghers' houses, is designed with a projecting centre-section, divided into three parts on its upper floors by four columns that stand on a balcony.

The interior, constructed entirely of wood, attains with the stage and apron an astonishing depth of 72m/236ft. There used to be no seats in the stalls, as that part of the auditorium was reserved for dancing. The three galleries are subdivided into boxes, the most luxurious – beneath a canopy bearing the crown of Prussia and the arms of the local Margraves – being the Royal Box. The decoration, by Giuseppe and Carlo Galli-Bibiena, brilliant artists from Bologna, is of an exuberant richness. Their reds, greens and browns harmonize perfectly with the abundance of gilded stuccowork which winds around the columns, frames medallions and festoons the candelabra hanging over each box. This Baroque Court theatre is one of the best preserved in Germany.

Bayer. Verwalt. der Staatl. Schlösser, Gärten u. Seen

Markgräfliches Opernhaus, Bayreuth

Schloßkirche (Castle Church) (Y **A**) – The single aisle, painted rose-pink and decorated with stuccowork by Pedrozzi (1756), is a visual delight. A closed oratory beneath the organ contains the tombs of the Margrave Friedrich, the Margravine Wilhelmina and their daughter.

Neues Schloß (New Castle) ⊘ (Z) – Wishing to make Bayreuth into a second Potsdam, Wilhelmina created this palace between 1753 and 1754, unifying and remodelling a number of existing buildings.

The **interior decoration★**, of a fascinating elegance, was executed by the stucco-master Pedrozzi, greatly influenced by the Princess, whose delight in the airy, flowered Rococo style is everywhere in evidence. Wilhelmina, whose private apartments were on the first floor of the north wing, concerned herself particularly with the decor of the Mirror Room, the Japanese Room and the old Music Room.

BAYREUTH

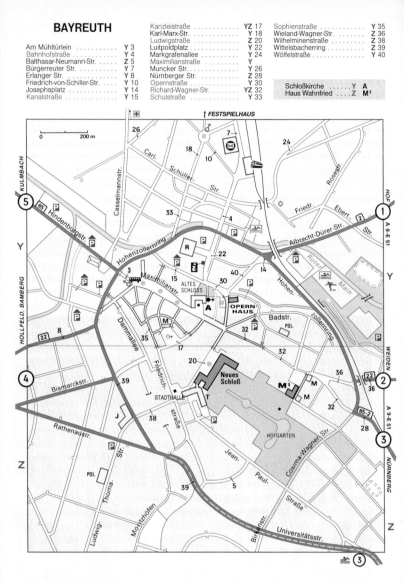

The solemnity of her husband's apartments in the south wing is alleviated by the decorative fantasy of the Palm Chamber, whose panels are carved to resemble exotic trees, and of another room designed to look like an arbour. On the ground floor of the north wing is a **museum of Bayreuth porcelain**.

★ **Haus Wahnfried/Richard-Wagner-Museum** ⊙ (Z M¹) – The Villa Wahnfried (Supreme Peace), which the composer lived in from 1874 onwards, and which was owned by his family until 1966 is still one of the main centres of Wagnerian pilgrimage. The only remaining original feature of the house is the façade. Collections on display in the museum evoke the maestro's life and work (furniture, manuscripts, pianos and death mask) as well as the history of the Bayreuth Festival (construction of the Festival Theatre, costumes and scenery). At the end of the garden, in front of a rotunda, Richard and Cosima lie beneath a simple plaque on the edge of the Hofgarten.

Festspielhaus (Festival Theatre) ⊙ – *Leave by Karl-Marx-Straße* (Y 18).
The theatre is intended to concentrate all the attention on the dramatic action. Even the music, rising from a camouflaged orchestra pit, is no more than a fluid complement to the story. The acoustics have been worked out to the point where even the fabric of the seats (padding is forbidden) and the density of the human audience is taken into account.

★ **Schloß Eremitage** (Hermitage Castle) ⊙ – *4km/2.5mi to the east by* ② *on the town plan.*
The **Schloßpark**★, in which the unexpected and the fantastic manifest themselves in the manner of an English garden, is suffused with memories of Princess Wilhelmina. The **old castle** (Altes Schloß), surrounded by geometric flower beds,

was built in 1715 and remodelled by the Margravine, who was given it as a gift by her husband, in 1736. There is a particularly interesting, if only for its somewhat original decoration, **Chinese Mirror Cabinet** (Chinesisches Spiegelkabinett) in which Wilhelmina wrote her memoirs. Note the curious lower grotto opening onto the inner courtyard, and the hermitage of the Margrave Friedrich. Nearby is the artificial ruin of a theatre constructed in 1743.

The **new castle** (Neues Schloß), designed on a semicircular plan, was rebuilt after 1945. In the centre, the Temple of the Sun contains an image of Apollo in his golden chariot.

EXCURSIONS

★★ ① **Swiss Franconia (Fränkische Schweiz) and Sanspareil** – *Round tour of 105km/65mi – allow one day*
Southwest of Bayreuth, far from the main road and rail arteries, an undulating plateau gashed by deep valleys forms the northern extremity of the Franconian Jura. Heavy erosion of this porous limestone shelf has resulted in a landscape of dolomitic relief, pitted with many caves.

Tüchersfeld – The houses of this village are dispersed among an astonishing series of rocky pinnacles.

Pottenstein – The castle, a former residence of the Elector-Bishops of Bamberg, overlooks the town. There are many natural curiosities (gorges, caves etc) in the neighbourhood.

Teufelshöhle ⊘ – The most famous karst cave of Swiss Franconia is adorned with impressive stalactites and stalagmites. The exit through a maze of towering Jura cliffs is most picturesque.

★ **Gößweinstein** – The Circuit of **Marienfelsen** (*about 45min there and back on foot, leaving the castle to follow the signposts: Marienfels-Schmitt-Anlagen*) leads, through undergrowth strewn with picturesque rocks, to several fine **viewpoints**★★ over the deep valley of the Wiesent.

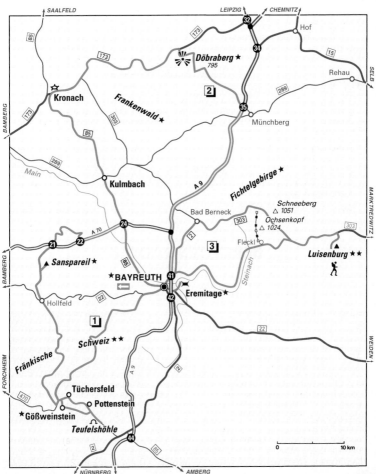

In the town, the **Pilgrimage Church** (Wallfahrtskirche), built between 1730 and 1739 by Balthasar Neumann, contains on the upper part of the high altar an early-16C Gothic group of the Trinity.

★ **Sanspareil and Burg Zwernitz** ⊙ – After the completion of the hermitage in Bayreuth, Margravine Wihelmina and Margrave Friedrich turned their attention to an old hunting estate, converting it into an impressive **rock garden**★ which they named Sanspareil (Without equal). At the edge of the grove stands an **Oriental building**, fitted out in the Bayreuth Rococo style making it an example of Frankish court art. Further architectonic features of this 17ha/42 acre park include caves, grottoes and ruined theatres.

The earliest documentary evidence of **Burg Zwernitz** (of which there is a good view from the keep) dates from 1156. From 1338, the fortress was the property of the Hohenzollern, then in 1810 it fell to Bavaria. It contains furnishings, and a selection of cutting and stabbing weapons from the 16C-18C.

★ ② **The Franconian Mountains (Frankenwald)** – *Round tour of 125km/78mi – allow 5hr*

★ **Döbraberg** – *45min there and back on foot.* Climb to the look-out tower (795m/2 608ft). The majestic **panorama**★ extends as far as the mysterious depths of the Thuringian Mountains in the north, and the Fichtelgebirge in the south, which enclose the Hof Basin.

Kronach – **Festung Rosenberg**, one of the largest medieval fortresses in Germany, towers over the small town of Kronach and the wooded heights of the Frankenwald. Star-shaped bastions surround the nobly designed 16C-18C fortress buildings.

Kulmbach – This industrial town, once the seat of the Hohenzollern Margraves of Franconia, is famous today for its strong beers (Echt Kulmbacher, Bayrisch Gfrorns).
The **Plassenburg**★ ⊙, an impressive medieval fortress in an excellent state of preservation, surprises the visitor with the contrast between the defensive look of its exterior buildings and the delightful elegance of its **Renaissance courtyard**★★ surrounded on three sides by tiered galleries. Various collections are on display in the refurnished apartments, the most interesting being that of **tin soldiers**★ from the **Deutsches Zinnfigurenmuseum** ⊙, the largest collection of its kind in the world with more than 300 000 pieces grouped in 150 dioramas. The Landschaftsmuseum Obermain (Upper Main Landscape Museum) and the Staatliche Sammlungen Collections are also located in the Plassenburg.

★ ③ **The Fichtelgebirge** – *Round tour of 92km/57mi – allow about 5hr*
The route follows the Steinach Valley, penetrating deeply into the pine-covered granite massif of the Fichtelgebirge. Above Fleckl, a cable-car climbs the **Ochsenkopf** (1 024m/3 360ft), one of the highest peaks in the massif, which is crowned by a television tower.

★★ **Luisenburg** – This labyrinth of enormous granite boulders, in situ or fallen, eroded into round shapes or piled on top of each other, can be walked through along a pine-shaded, hilly path *(blue arrows indicate the way up, red the way down)*. Several look-out points along the way afford varying views of the Fichtelgebirge.

Return to Bayreuth on B 303, which passes through the small spa of Bad Berneck.

BERCHTESGADEN★★

Bayern
Population 8 200
Michelin map 420 X 22 – Local map see Deutsche ALPENSTRASSE

The basin of Berchtesgaden is enclosed on three sides by the mountain chains of the Watzmann, the Steinernes Meer and the Hagengebirge, the whole complex forming a salient that penetrates deeply into Austria. Apart from these natural barriers, a number of historical events explain the unusual frontier situation. The development of the area, and of the small town of Berchtesgaden itself, is linked with the importance of a priory of Augustinian monks, which became a pivot of the Bavarian political machine at a time when the grasping archbishops of Salzburg were becoming too demanding. Secularized in 1803, the priory and its lands were definitively incorporated into the kingdom of Bavaria six years later. Berchtesgaden was chosen as a holiday retreat by Adolf Hitler, who built his notorious "Eagle's Nest" sanctuary on the Kehlstein.
Journey's end on the German Alpine Road (Deutsche Alpenstraße) and departure point for many other tourist excursions, Berchtesgaden is intensely busy throughout the summer. The town is dominated by the bulk of the Watzmann (2 712m/8 900ft).

OUR RECOMMENDATIONS FOR BERCHTESGADEN

Fischer – Königsseer Straße 51, ☎ 0 86 52/95 50, Fax 0 86 52/6 48 73. Single rooms from 39DM. Rustic holiday hotel on the road to the Königsee.

Grenzgasthaus Neuhäusl – (7km/4mi east on the Roßfeld-Höhenringstraße) Wildmoos 45, ☎ 0 86 52/94 00, Fax 0 86 52/6 46 37. Single rooms from 65DM. Perched at 850m/2 789ft with a wonderful view of the Untersberg and Kehlstein.

Alpenhotel Denninglehen – (7 km/4mi east on the Roßfeld-Höhenringstraße) Am Priesterstein 7, ☎ 0 86 52/94 00, Fax 0 86 52/6 46 37. Single rooms from 105DM. At 900m/2 953ft altitude, rooms partly with peasant furniture, view of the mountains.

SIGHTS

* **Schloßplatz** – This square is the heart of Berchtesgaden. On the western side are the so-callled Getreidekasten, the former granary, remodelled and furnished with an arcaded gallery in the 16C. The church front and the façade of the old priory, now known as the castle, complete the delightful picture.

Stiftskirche St. Peter und Johannes – The church, whose foundations are Romanesque, is interesting because of the comparison with St Zeno's at Bad Reichenhall, for it too was originally built for Augustinian monks. A Lombard influence manifests itself in the façade, where an alternation of stone in different colours makes a decorative pattern. The towers were rebuilt in the last century after a fire. The interior of the building is distinguished by early-16C network vaulting in the nave, and by a chancel some 200 years older, much higher and of a purer Gothic style.

Schloß (Castle) ⊙ – At the time of the commendatory prelates, the monks' priory did indeed become a sumptuous palace. From 1923 onwards, it was the home of the Crown Prince Rupert, former commander-in-chief of the Bavarian forces during the First World War and head of the House of Wittelsbach until his death in 1955. The Prince embellished the palace with furniture and art treasures, opening to the public his collections of weapons, French tapestries and Nymphenburg porcelain. German wood sculptures of the 15C and 16C, including two altar images by Tilman Riemenschneider, and examples of oriental art are also on view.

Cloister – Conserving its Romanesque galleries on three sides, the 13C cloister has a variety of columns – circular, polygonal or twisted, garnished with latticework, plant designs and capitals with foliated scrolls.

* **Dormitory** (Dormitorium) – A fine Gothic hall with two aisles. Note among other examples of religious art, 12 magnificent busts from the stalls of Weingarten Basilica (1487).

Museum – Worth special attention here are the two Renaissance rooms on the first floor (Italian furniture of the 15C and 16C), and the row of eight interconnected Seigneurs' rooms (Herrenzimmer) which offer an attractive glimpse into the 19C and its Biedermeier style.

* **Salzbergwerk (Salt Mines)** ⊙ – Exploitation of the Berchtesgaden salt mines, started in 1517, brought prosperity to a region which was once very poor. The salt rock is washed by fresh water and the resulting brine (Sole), containing 27% salt, is piped to Bad Reichenhall to be refined.
The tour, in miner's overalls, includes a trip through the galleries in a small train, a vertiginous 34m/112ft scramble down (luckily there are steps for those who prefer) to the salt caves, the crossing by raft of an illuminated underground lake, and a documentary film show on salt extraction.
A room arranged as a salt museum exhibits the machinery, based on the hydraulic pump, invented by the engineer Georg von Reichenbach for raising the brine to the pipeline.

EXCURSIONS

** **Obersalzberg and the Kehlstein** ⊙ – 4km/2.5mi, there is a shuttle service by bus between Obersalzberg and the Kehlstein.
After the abortive putsch of 1923 and the end of his prison sentence, Hitler, linked by friendships and family ties to the region, settled in Obersalzberg. When the Nazis seized power in 1934, the new Chancellor started an increasingly ambitious plan to enlarge and enhance the chalet (Berghof) which he had acquired. Subsequently, the sanctuary of "the lonely man of Berchtesgaden" became the stage for a number of expertly manipulated diplomatic receptions, notably that for the Austrian Chancellor, Dr Schuschnigg, on 12 February, 1938, and that for British Prime Minister Neville Chamberlain on 15 September the same year.

The greater part of the Berghof buildings were destroyed in an American air raid on 25 April, 1945, prior to their capture on 4 May by a detachment of the French 2nd Armoured Division operating with the 101st US Airborne Division.

Obersalzberg – With the exception of the Platterhof – a "People's Hotel" where the faithful could be lodged, at Hitler's behest, for the nominal sum of a single mark – the ruins of all the other buildings comprising the Nazi sanctuary have been razed. A documentation centre on the history of the mountain has been opened, though its emphasis will be the years 1933 to 1945.

★★ **The Kehlstein** – The bus climbs an impressively narrow road★★★ blasted from the bedrock on the craggy spur of the Kehlstein. At the end of the road *(reserve seats for the return journey)*, a lift ascends the final 100m/328ft. On the summit there

U. Watzmann/ZEFA, Paris

Chapel of St. Bartholomä, Königssee

is now a tearoom (Tee-haus) on the premises of the old Eagle's Eyrie (Adlerhorst) – which Hitler was given by the Nazi party as a 50th birthday present, but where he went to stay only rarely. The **panorama**★★ *(climb a little higher up the crest)* extends over the neighbouring peaks and, on the far side of Salzburg, the rolling, rounded Pre-Alps of Salzkammergut, hard against the massif of Dachstein, glittering with small glaciers.

★★ **Königssee** ⊘ – *5km/ 3mi to the south, then about 2hr in a boat.*
This long, narrow lake, with its dark waters and steep banks, is one of the most romantic sites in Bavaria. Dominated on the west by the giant escarpments of the Watz-mann, and the rocky base of the Steinernes Meer to the south, the lake narrows at St. Bartho-lomä, making a **picturesque scene**★, where visitors can go ashore to admire the pretty **chapel of St. Bartho-lomä** with its triple apse and explore the interesting old houses nestling in a dense thicket of chestnuts.

From the landing-stage at Salet, a 15min walk brings the visitor to the Obersee, below the Teufelshörner at the circular end of the valley. From here the Röthbach falls, hurtling down from a height of 400m/1 312ft, can be seen.

★★ **Roßfeld-Höhenringstraße** ⊘ – *Round tour of 29km/18mi to the east of Berchtesgaden – about 1hr 30min.*
The Roßfeld road, which is open year round, reaches the lip of the crest and runs above the Austrian valley of the Salzach. It overlooks the Tennengebirge. The Dachstein, still recognisable by its glaciers, fills in the background. On the other side of the ridge there is a wonderful view of the countryside around Berchtesgaden and Salzburg and of the great massive of the Hoher Göll, the Kehlstein and the Untersberg.
From the Hennenkopf car park, it is only a few minutes' climb to the beacon and the Hennenkopf Cross at 1 551m/5 089ft. The road plunges down from the crest after the Roßfeldhütte (Inn) and winds through the charming, wooded valleys of the Oberau region.

★ **Hintersee** – *12km/8mi to the west.*
The road climbs the narrow Ramsau Valley to reach this lake framed by the steep-sided domes of the Reiteralpe and the Teeth of Hochkalter. The eastern shore, and the "enchanted forest" (Zauberwald) bordering it, together with the shady banks of the rapids feeding the lake, are greatly appreciated by ramblers.

BERGSTRASSE

Baden-Württemberg and Hessen
Michelin map 417 R 10

This road running at the foot of the low, scrub-covered mountains of the Odenwald has given its name to a strip of sunny hillsides sloping towards the Rhine Valley. Orchards flourish on this fertile tract, and its ideal position assures the marketing of fruit earlier than anywhere else in the region. The old villages and small towns of the Bergstraße are surrounded by typical Rhineland scenery.

FROM HEIDELBERG TO DARMSTADT *58km/36mi – about 3hr*

Weinheim – This town, embraced in the north and the east by ridges up to 400m/1300ft, is the first to draw in the Spring on the Bergstraße. Weinheim was given civic rights in 1264 and developed from an agricultural community to the large seat of local government it is today. The old town has a remarkable number of old houses to show, including the attractive Altes Rathaus (old town hall) on Marktplatz (about 1577) and the Büdinger Hof (Judengasse 15-17). The former Schloß (castle), which serves as the town hall today, abuts the castle park, which is in English style and boasts Germany's largest cedar tree. Adjacent to the park is the 50ha/124 acres **Exotenwald★** (Exotic Forest), which was laid out between 1872 and 1884. It has a wonderful stand of trees. The **ruins of Burg Windeck** and the **Wachenburg** (castle completely restored at the beginning of the 20C) are enthroned above the town.

Heppenheim an der Bergstraße – The **Marktplatz★**, or Großer Markt, owes its charm to two wooden buildings with corner oriel windows: the Liebig pharmacy and the 16C town hall. The square is dominated by a vast Neo-Gothic church, nicknamed "the Bergstraße Cathedral".

Lorsch – Of the great abbey founded in 774, there now exist at the east end of the town only the church narthex and the **Torhalle★** ⊘, a triumphal arch in Carolingian style, which has now been added to the list of Unesco World Heritage sites. Above the columns with their composite capitals is an impressive wall adorned with blind, cowled bays and sandstone marquetry in red and white. The old abbey buildings house a **museum complex** with sections on the history of the abbey and on local folklore, as well as a tobacco museum. Behind the church, there is a wide view of the Rhine plain in the direction of the Odenwald.

Bensheim-Auerbach – This "town of flowers and wine" is justly proud of its pretty **old town** (Altstadt). Beautiful half-timbered houses are to be found principally in the Marktplatz, and along the Haupstraße and the Wambolterhof-straße. In a sheltered valley is the **Fürstenlager★★**, once the summer residence of the Landgraves of Hessen. The park surrounding the building (Herrenhaus) is planted with tropical trees and studded with pavilions and symbolical monuments in the late 18C style. A little further north, **Auerbacher Schloß** ⊘ commands a view over the whole region.

BERLIN★★★

Berlin
Population 3 500 000
Michelin map 416/418 I 23-24

Berlin, for so long a symbol of the world's division into two opposing camps, owes its economic and cultural dynamism today to the fact that both the Federal Republic and what used to be called East Germany were determined to use the city as a shop window for their respective ways of life for 30 years. This made Berlin what it is today, a modern metropolis with lively economic and cultural life (details in The Green Guide Berlin).

HISTORICAL NOTES

In the 13C Cölln and Berlin were small towns built respectively on a sandy island and on the east bank of the River Spree, each inhabited by fishermen and travelling merchants. The first castle to be constructed on Cölln was completed in 1451. Nineteen years later it became the permanent residence of the Hohenzollern family – and it was the Hohenzollern Electors of Brandenburg who were politically responsible for the evolution of Berlin as a capital city.

Ph. Gajic/MICHELIN

Equestrian statue of the Great Elector by Andreas Schlüter

The Great Elector (1640-88) – Frederick-William of Brandenburg found Berlin largely deserted at the end of the Thirty Years War. The great commander, who had in 1675 succeeded in beating the Swedish army at Fehrbellin, was also a very capable administrator. Emulating the Dutch (he had spent his youth in Holland), he constructed quays along the banks of the Spree and established many laws making Berlin a healthy and well-governed town.

The construction of a canal between the Spree and the Oder stimulated commerce, but Frederick Wilhelm's most important contribution was to open Berlin to the French Huguenots after the Revocation of the Edict of Nantes in 1685. The arrival of a massive contingent – approximately one Huguenot for every five Berliners – transformed the city, strengthening its influence on its neighbours through the increased number of craftsmen, theologians, doctors, scholars and others now living there.

Berlin in the Age of Enlightenment (18C) – The first King of Prussia, Frederick I, built the palace of Charlottenburg for his wife, Sophie-Charlotte. He entrusted the work to Andreas Schlüter, a sculptor of genius (c 1660-1714) who had worked mainly at the Royal Palace and the Arsenal.

Frederick was succeeded by **Frederick-William I** (1713-40), known to history as the **King-Sergeant** because of his punctilious administration and a policy of systematic recruitment which laid the foundations of Prussian military power. He was less interested in the embellishment of Berlin than in making it more powerful. He ordered a new town, Friedrichstadt, to be laid out beyond the old city bastions. Commanding access to this were three monumental squares: the Quarré (Pariser Platz), the Oktogon (Leipziger Platz near Potsdamer Platz – **GY**) and the Rondell (Belle Alliance, later Mehringplatz – **GY**). Draconian measures accelerated the development and peopling of the district, which is cut by such wide arteries as the Leipziger Straße, the most lively street of pre-war Berlin, the Friedrichstraße and the Wilhelmstraße (now the Toleranzstraße), the Whitehall of the Reich.

ENJOYING YOUR STAY IN BERLIN

Telephone prefix – 0 30

Auskünfte – *Berlin Tourismus Marketing GmbH*, ☎ 25 00 25 Monday-Friday 8am-8pm, Saturday-Sunday 9am-6pm. **Information office**: Europa-Center, Monday-Saturday 8.30am-8.30pm, Sunday 10am-6pm; Brandenburger Tor, south wing, Monday-Sunday 9.30am-6pm; Tegel airport, opposite flight deck 0, Monday-Sunday 5am-10.30pm; KaDeWe, Reisecenter (travel centre) ground floor, Monday-Friday 8am-8pm, Saturday 9am-4pm. The fotnightly city magazines *Zitty* and *Tip* and the monthly *Berlin-Programm* provide information on events of all kinds. Berlin's major dailies have a weekly insert featuring a calendar of events. Tickets are available up to three weeks before the performance at *Berlin Tourismus Marketing*. The numerous theatre box offices are the best place to buy tickets when in town.

Post offices with special opening times – Post office 120 in Budapester Straße (opposite the Europa-Center) is open Monday-Saturday 8am-midnight and Sunday 10am-midnight, post office 519 at Tegel airport, 1st floor, Monday-Friday 7am-9pm, Saturday-Sunday 8am-8pm.

Daily papers – Berliner Morgenpost, Tagesspiegel, Berliner Zeitung, taz, BZ.

Internet – http://www.berlin.de; http://www.berlinonline.de; http://www.berlin-info.de; http://www.d-berlin.de

Public transport

The **BVG** (Berliner Verkehrs-Betriebe) is the umbrella organization for streetcars, buses and underground trains, ☎ 1 94 49 daily 6am-11pm. Transportation for the region around Berlin and the S-Bahn are operated by the **VBB** (Verkehrsverbund Berlin-Brandenburg) in conjunction with the BVG, ☎ 25 41 41 41 Monday-Friday 8am-4pm. Information is available at the BVG-Pavillon on Hardenbergplatz (Bahnhof Zoo) 6.30am-8.30pm and at many U-Bahn and S-Bahn stations. Berlin and its environs (eg Potsdam) are divided into three fare zones. For rides within the city, you need a ticket for Zone AB. Tickets are available in all U-Bahn and S-Bahn stations, in streetcars, at ticket vending machines and from bus drivers.

Normal fare (valid 2hr) 3.90DM, day ticket 7.80DM, group day ticket for two adults and up to three children 20DM (day cards are valid from the time of punching until 3am next morning).

The **Welcome Card** costs 29DM (valid 72hr) lets an adult with up to three children use the entire VBB network; it also gives discounts for selected theatres, museums, attractions and city tours. The card is available at BVG outlets and at the information offices of the *Berlin Tourismus Marketing*.

The heavy construction activity in Berlin can lead to delays and to some detours in local transportation.

Tip: Bus number 100 that shuttles between Bahnhof Zoo and Alexanderplatz, connecting the two city centres, passes by many of Berlin's sights.

City tours

City tours – *Severin & Kühn* (☎ 8 80 41 90), *Bus-Verkehr-Berlin* (☎ 8 85 98 80), *Berliner-Bären-Service* (☎ 35 19 52 70) and *Berolina* (☎ 88 56 80 03) all drive the City-Circle: 2hr tours with explanations via headphones. Every 30min beginning at 10am. You can join or leave the tour at various places. Departure from Kurfürstendamm (between Joachimsthaler Straße and Fasanenstraße) and Alexanderplatz in front of the Forum-Hotel. 3-4hr tours at 10am and 2pm. **City foot tours** with various historical, topical and contemporary themes are offered by: *Kulturbüro* (☎ 4 44 09 36), *art:berlin* (☎ 85 72 81 82) and *Stattreisen* (☎ 4 55 30 28).

Boat tours – *Stern- und Kreisschiffahrt* (☎ 5 36 36 00) offers rides through the historic centre of the city beginning in the Nikolaiviertel (1hr); tours through the inner city by way of the Spree and Landwehr canals (3hr 30min) beginning at the Jannowitzbrücke and Schloßbrücke; and rides on the Havel from Wannsee to Potsdam/Lange Brücke (1hr 15min).

Shopping

Tauentzienstraße/Kurfürstendamm and the *Potsdamer Platz Arkaden* offer good shopping. Berlin's most famous department stores are the *KaDeWe* (Tauentzienstraße 221), a gigantic selection in a luxurious setting, and *Galeries Lafayette* (Friedrichstraße 207), a reasonable priced shop in an amazing architectural setting. **Exclusive shops** are located on Fasanenstraße and Friedrichstraße.

Art galleries in the west half of the city have collected around Savignyplatz, on Fasanenstraße Pariser Straße; in the east half of the city between Oranienburger Straße and Rosa-Luxemburg-Platz.

Antiques are best bought around Eisenacher Straße/Kalckreuthstraße, on Fasanenstraße, around Bleibtreu-, Pestalozzi-, and Knesebeckstraße and in the arches of the S-Bahn at Friedrichstraße.

Flea markets - Flea and art market, Straße des 17. June, Saturday-Sunday 10am-5pm, flea markets in Wilmersdorf, Fehrbelliner Platz, Saturday-Sunday 8am-4pm, Berlin art and nostalgia market on Museums Island, Saturday-Sunday 11am-5pm.

Markets - Market on Winterfeldplatz, Wednesday and Saturday 8am-2pm; Maybachufer (Turkish weekend market), Tuesday and Friday noon-6.30pm.

Hotels

BUDGET

Econtel - Sömmeringstraße 24 (Charlottenburg); ☎ 34 68 10, Fax 34 68 11 63. 205 rooms, single rooms from 147DM. Modern hotel right at the X9 airport bus stop (Tegel).

Am Wilden Eber - Warnemünder Straße 19 (Wilmersdorf); ☎ 8 23 30 71, Fax 82 44 03. 15 rooms, single rooms from 120DM. Small establishment right near Grunewald.

Kastanienhof - Kastanienallee 65 (Mitte); ☎ 44 30 50, Fax 44 30 51 11. 36 rooms, single rooms from 130DM. This hotel located in a typical residential home is especially well situated for exploring Prenzlauer Berg.

OUR SELECTION

Luisenhof - Köpenicker Straße 92 (Mitte); ☎ 2 41 59 06, Fax 2 79 29 83. 27 rooms, single rooms from 210DM. Elegant furnishings in an historical builiding.

Hecker's Hotel - Grolmanstraße 35 (Charlottenburg); ☎ 8 89 00, Fax 8 89 02 60, 72 rooms. Single rooms from 280DM. Contemporarily furnished hotel right in the midst of Charlottenburg's nicest spot.

art'Hotel Ermelerhaus - Wallstraße 70 (Mitte); ☎ 24 06 20, Fax 25 06 22 22. 95 rooms, single rooms from 235DM. restored patrician's house with a modern annex. Artworks are regularly exhibited.

Berlin-Plaza - Knesebeckstraße (Charlottenburg); ☎ 88 41 30, Fax 88 41 37 54. 131 rooms, single rooms from 199DM. Centrally situated on Kurfürstendamm, inexpensive weekend prices.

TREAT YOURSELF!

Kempinski Hotel Bristol - Kurfürstendamm 27 (Charlottenburg); ☎ 88 43 40, Fax 8 83 60 75. 301 rooms, single rooms from 399DM. The Berlin address for the tops in luxury in the western half of the city.

Adlon - Unter den Linden 77 (Mitte); ☎ 2 26 10, Fax 22 41 22 22. 337 rooms, single rooms from 479DM. recently built luxury hotel in a dream location at Pariser Platz, right at the Brandenburger Tor.

Four Seasons - Charlottenstraße 49 (Mitte); 2 03 38, Fax 20 33 61 66. 204 rooms, single rooms from 446DM. This exteriorly simple construction by Kleihues at Gendarmenmarkt has a splendid interior.

Restaurants

BUDGET

Alte Pumpe - Lützowstraße 42 (Tiergarten); ☎ 26 48 42 65. Main course from 14.50DM. Modern café-restaurant with regional cuisine.

Lutter & Wegner - Charlottenstraße 56 (Mitte); ☎ 2 02 95 40. Main course from 18DM (lunch) and 28DM (supper). Bistro with Austrian inspiration, at Gendarmenmarkt.

Marjellchen - Mommsenstraße 9 (Charlottenburg); ☎ 8 83 26 76. Main course from 19.50DM. Robust Silesian and East Prussian cuisine.

Nußbaum - Bundesplatz 6 (Wilmersdorf); ☎ 8 54 50 20. Main course from 7.50DM (lunch) and 12.50DM (supper). Traditional Berlin cuisine "like home".

OUR SELECTION

Kaiserstuben - Kupfergraben 6a (Mitte); ☎ 20 45 29 80. Main course from 41DM. Top restaurant near the Museumsinsel(Museum Island).

Funkturm-Restaurant - Messedamm 22 (Charlottenburg); ☎ 30 38 29 96. Main course from 25DM. Dining with a wonderful view of the western city districts and the Grunewald.

Borchhardt - Französische Straße 47 (Mitte); ☎ 20 38 71 10. Main course from 30DM. Noble dining room with tall columns.

TREAT YOURSELF!

Bamberger Reiter – Regensburger Straße 7 (Schöneberg); ☎ 2 18 42 82. Main course from 56DM. Comfortable luxury restaurant in several rooms.

Harlekin – Lützowufer 15 (Tiergarten); ☎ 25 47 88 58. Main course from 49DM. Modern hotel-restaurant in the *Hotel Esplanade*.

Cafés, pubs and bars

The "scene" in Berlin is very decentralised; there are numerous quarters and streets where life is hopping *(details in The Green Guide Berlin)*: in Charlottenburg around Savignyplatz and on the Ku'Damm; in Schöneberg around Winterfeldplatz; in Kreuzberg around Chamissoplatz, on Oranienstraße and Wiener Straße and along the Landwehrkanal; in Berlin-Mitte at Friedrichstraße, in the Nikolaiviertel and around the Hackescher Markt and in Prenzlauer Berg around Kollwitzplatz and along Kastanienallee.

CAFÉS

Leysieffer – Kurfürstendamm 118 (Charlottenburg). Ku'Damm flair in this traditional café with a comprehensive line of cakes.

Café Einstein – Kurfürstenstraße 58 (Tiergarten).
Viennese coffee-house in a turn-of-the-century villa.

Operncafé – Unter den Linden 5 (Mitte). In the former Prinzessinnenpalais (Princess Palace), with a beautiful terrace open in the warm season.

Pasticceria und Rosticceria Italiana – Leibnizstraße 45 (Charlottenburg). Every cake here is a little work of art.

Tele-Café – Panoramastraße 1 (Mitte). The café in the Television Tower (200m/640ft of the ground) turns on its axis once every 30min.

COCKTAIL BARS

Harry's New York Bar – Lützowufer 15 (Tiergarten). This elegant bar is located in the *Grand Hotel Esplanade*. It's the kind of place where contracts and stock market deals are discussed at the next table.

Bar am Lützowplatz – Lützowplatz 7 (Tiergarten). Barkeepers mix excellent drinks at a very long bar in this fine cocktail haunt.

Galerie Bremer – Fasanenstraße 37 (Wilmersdorf). A cosy, twilit cocktail bar is tucked away in the back room of the gallery.

BEER GARDENS

Café am Neuen See – Lichtensteinallee 1 (Tiergarten). A beer garden with about 1 000 seats right in the zoo (Tiergarten). It is quite a good imitation of the Munich original considering the locality.

Kastanie – Schloßstraße 22 (Charlottenburg). A small beer garden on the road leading up to Charlottenburg Palace. Boules is played on the strip of lawn opposite in summer, giving it all a bit of a French flavour.

Golgatha – In Viktoriapark at the Katzbachstraße/Kreuzbergstraße intersection (Kreuzberg). Beer garden next to the Kreuzberg right beneath the National Monument (Nationaldenkmal). The atmosphere can become turbulent here.

Prater Biergarten – Kastanienallee 7-9 (Prenzlauer Berg). Beer garden right in the middle of Prenzlauer Berg.

Henkelmann/Archiv

PUBS

Irish Harp Pub – Giesebrechtstraße 15 (Charlottenburg). Guiness is the favourite drink here, but the list of whiskies is not to be ignored.

Kilkenny-Irish-Pub – Hackescher Markt (Mitte). A pub situated right in one of the S-Bahn arches.

The Shannon – Apostel-Paulus-Straße 34 (Schöneberg). Everything here revolves around the Emerald Isle.

CAFÉ-KNEIPEN IN CHARLOTTENBURG

Schwarzes Café – Kantstraße 148. Only closed from 3am Monday to Tuesday noon. The atmosphere in this cult café recalls the good old days of West Berlin.

Zillemarkt – Bleibtreustraße 48a. This establishment is located in one of the nicest parts of Charlottenburg, at a former cobble-stoned junk market.

Café Hardenberg – Hardenbergstraße 10. The ultimate meeting place for students of the Technische Hochschule and the College of Arts (Hochschule der Künste). It is always filled to the brim and busy.

Voltaire – Stuttgarter Platz 14. Everyone enjoys the relaxing atmosphere here, from the Hausfrau weighed down by shopping to the local men's group. The menu has just the right thing to eat for any time of day or night.

CAFÉ-KNEIPEN IN MITTE

StäV – Schiffbauerdamm 8. The gathering spot for the Bonn crowd is already in place. The *StäV* stands for "Ständige Vertretung", ie permanent representative, a reference to the title of the diplomatic representatives of the formerly two German states in Bonn and Berlin.

Deponie – Georgenstraße 3. Popular and populous "Kneipe" in rustic garb in one of the S-Bahn arcades of the city train (Stadtbahn).

Aedes – Rosenthaler Straße 40-41. Café in the midst of the Hackesche Höfe. An ideal place to keep an eye on the parade of visitors.

Hackbarths – Auguststraße 49a.
Corner "Kneipe" for the young crowd: artistic and international flair.

Entertainment

THEATRE

Berliner Ensemble – Bertold-Brecht-Platz 1 (Mitte); ☎ 2 82 31 60. This over 100-year-old building is where Bertold Brecht staged the *Threepenny Opera* in 1928 (it was called Theater am Schiffbauerdamm then). He also founded the Berliner Ensemble, which has had its home base here since 1954.

Deutsches Theater – Schumannstaße 13a (Mitte); ☎ 28 44 12 21. Thomas Langhoff top-notch theatre in the house's three stages; the repertory ranges from classical to contemporary.

Schaubühne am Lehniner Platz – Kurfürstendamm 153 (Wilmersdorf); ☎ 89 00 23. The Schaubühne has used this stage since 1981. Its greatest hits were directed by Peter Stein during the West Berlin days.

Volksbühne – Rosa-Luxemburg-Platz (Mitte); ☎ 2 47 76 94. Provocative material under the leadership of Frank Castorf. Besides theatre, the Volksbühne in the Red & Green Salon (Roter & Grüner Salon) also hosts events.

Komödie/Theater am Kurfürstendamm – Kurfürstendamm 206-209 (Charlottenburg); ☎ 47 99 74 30/40. Serious boulevard theatre, frequently using actors from television productions.

OPERA, BALLET, OPERETTA AND MUSICALS

Deutsche Oper Berlin – Bismarckstraße 35 (Charlottenburg); ☎ 3 43 84 01. The Charlottenburg opera house originally stood here. After the war the building was rebuilt.

Staatsoper Unter den Linden – Unter den Linden 5 (Mitte); ☎ 20 35 45 55. The oldest and most magnificent opera house in Berlin harks back to Frederick II.

Komische Oper – Behrenstraße 55-57 (Mitte); ☎ 47 99 74 00. Walther Felsenstein founded the theatre in 1947 in this building; many of the interesting stagings by Harry Kupfer can be seen here.

Theater des Westens – Kantstraße 12 (Charlottenburg); ☎ 31 90 30. Berlin's major musical productions are staged in this grand building from the Wilhelminian days.

VARIETY, REVIEW AND CABARET

Friedrichstadtpalast – Friedrichstraße 107 (Mitte); ☎ 23 26 2 26. This is the place to get a flavour of the sinful spirit of the 1920s: terrific review theatre.

Chamäleon Variété – Rosenthaler Straße 40-41 (Mitte); ☎ 2 82 71 18. A colourfully mixed programme in the Hackesche Höfe.

Wintergarten-Variété – Potsdamer Str. 96 (Tiergarten); ☎ 2 30 88 20. Classic variety show with scintillating artists.

CONCERTS

Konzerthaus Berlin (Schauspielhaus am Gendarmenmarkt) – Gendarmenmarkt (Mitte); ☎ 203 09 21 01/02. Berlin's most beautiful concert hall.

Philharmonie und Kammermusiksaal – Herbert-von-Karajan-Straße 1 (Tiergarten); ☎ 25 48 81 32. Home of the Berlin Philharmonic.

JAZZ

A-Trane – Bleibtreustraße 1 (Charlottenburg); ☎ 3 12 94 93. Jazz in all its styles.

B-Flat – Rosenthaler Straße 13 (Mitte); ☎ 2 80 62 49. Best jazz establishment among the "in" clubs in Mitte.

Mies – Greifswalder Straße 212-213 (Prenzlauer Berg); ☎ 44 00 81 40. Fairly new establishment.

CLUBS, DISCOTHEQUES & LIVE MUSIC

Knaack Club – Greifswalder Straße 224 (Prenzlauer Berg); ☎ 4 42 70 60. Backyard club on several floors, young crowd.

SO 36 – Oranienburger Straße 190 (Kreuzberg); ☎ 6 15 26 01. The place to still find punkers and other activists from revolutionary days past.

Tresor/Globus – Leipziger Straße 126a/Ecke Wilhelmstraße (Mitte); ☎ 2 29 06 11. Techno in the former treasury room of the Wertheim department store near Potsdamer Platz.

WMF – Johannisstraße 19-21.(Mitte); ☎ 28 38 88. Techno institution from the days of the Wall's fall.

CINEMA

Numerous cinema houses have settled around the Gedächtniskirche. The largest multiplex with 19 theatres is the *Cinemaxx* on Potsdamer Platz. The IMAX cinema house is also located here. The interesting program movie houses are otherwise mainly located in Kreuzberg, Schöneberg, Mitte and Prenzlauer Berg.

Special dates

International Film Festival in February, *Theatertreffen* in May, *Love Parade* in July, *Berliner Festival Weeks* in September, *Jazz-Fest* in November.

Frederick II the Great (1740-86) continued this civic effort, adding monuments along the famous Unter den Linden and the Forum Fredericianum (Bebelplatz). To fulfil his ambitions, he enlisted the aid of Knobelsdorff (1699-1753), an architect as much inspired by the Rococo tradition (Sanssouci) as by the Antique (Opera).

The evolution towards neo-Classicism continued until 1835. The monuments of Berlin were finally completed by the Brandenburg Gate (1789) and the Neue Wache (1818), among others.

Towards Bismarck's Berlin – Berlin found its soul for the first time when the high patriotism inaugurated by the professors of the University, founded in 1810 by Wilhelm von Humboldt, was allied to the king of Prussia's call to arms in 1813 when he joined the Allies against Napoleon.

The city benefited from the growing prestige of the Prussian Reich and, as a favoured subject, developed its industrial life under the forceful direction of such great advisers as August Borsig, "the locomotive king", Werner von Siemens (1816-92), the pioneer electrical engineer and Emil Rathenau, the founder of the giant AEG. Although official projects like the Reichstag were pretentious, the number of open spaces increased as the residential suburbs moved westwards towards Grunewald forest. By 1871, Berlin had become the capital of the Empire and numbered almost one million inhabitants.

Greater Berlin – In 1920 the city united, under a single administration, six urban suburbs, seven towns, 59 villages and 27 demesnes to form a unit of four million inhabitants. Despite the upheavals from which Germany was still suffering, the 1920s was an exciting period in Berlin, intellectually and artistically in particular.

BERLIN UND UMGEBUNG

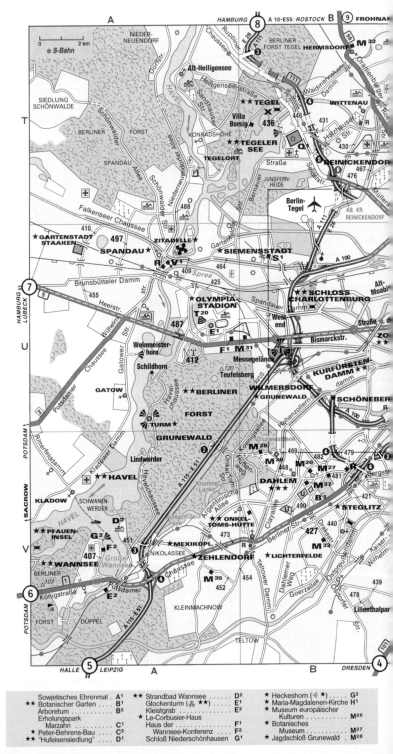

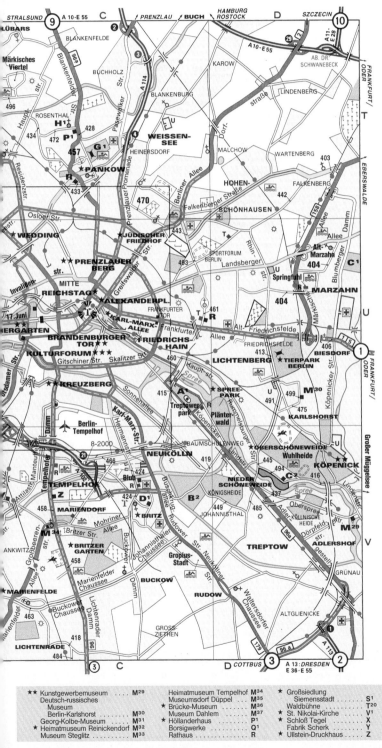

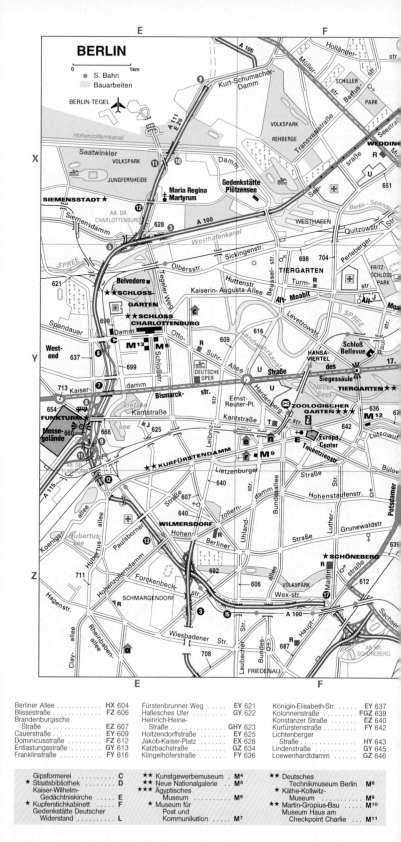

In this guide town plans show the main streets and the way to the sights; local maps show the main roads and the roads on the recommended tour.

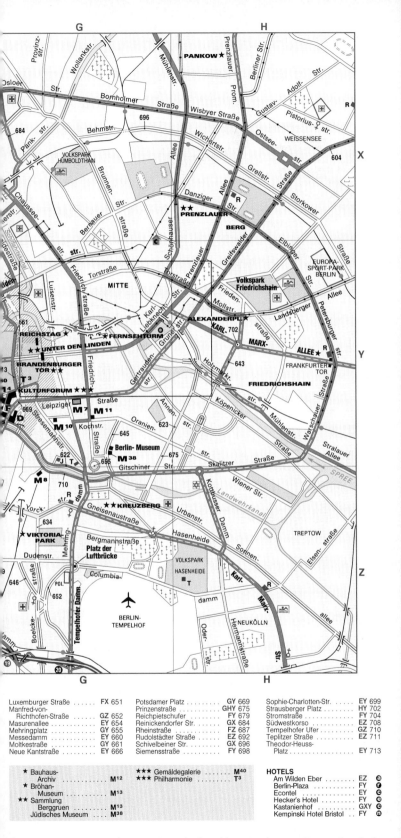

★ Bauhaus-Archiv	**M**¹²	★★★ Gemäldegalerie .... **M**⁴⁰
★ Bröhan-Museum	**M**¹³	★★★ Philharmonie .... **T**³
★★ Sammlung Berggruen	**M**¹³	
Jüdisches Museum	**M**³⁸	

HOTELS

Am Wilden Eber	**EZ**	❸
Berlin-Plaza	**FY**	❼
Econtel	**EY**	❻
Hecker's Hotel	**FY**	❾
Kastanienhof	**GXY**	❿
Kempinski Hotel Bristol	**FY**	⓭

Street names appear on the map or can be found by using the co-ordinates given in the caption below.

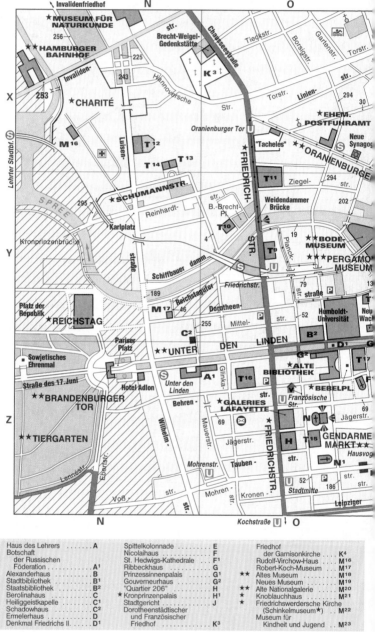

The chapter on Practical Information at the end of the guide lists:
local or national organisations providing additional information,
recreational sports,
thematic tours,
suggested reading,
events of interest to the tourist,
admission times and charges.

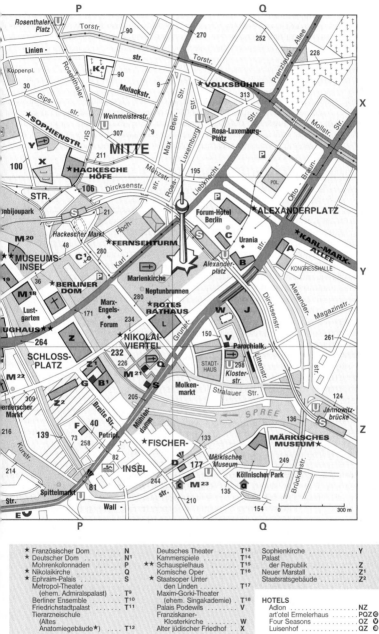

*Michelin maps (scale 1/200 000), which are revised regularly, indicate:
golf courses, sports stadiums, racecourses, swimming-pools, beaches, airfields, scenic routes,
public and long-distance footpaths, viewpoints, forest parks, interesting sights...
The perfect complement to the The Green Guide for planning holidays and leisure time.
Keep current Michelin Maps in the car at all times*

Berlin newspapers set the tone for newspapers all over Germany.
Films made in Berlin won international acclaim thanks to such directors as Ernst Lubitsch, Fritz Lang, Carl Mayer, Georg-Wilhelm Pabst and the actors Emil Jannings and Marlene Dietrich (*The Blue Angel, Maidens in Uniform* etc).

The theatre, rejuvenated by Max Reinhardt (1873-1943), also flourished brilliantly. In 1928 Bertolt Brecht's *Threepenny Opera* was premiered in what was called the Theater am Schiffbauerdamm.. The blossoming of this talent was interrupted by the advent of the Hitler regime, when, along with the persecution of the Jews, a wealth of the country's artistic and literary heritage was forbidden or destroyed in the name of the campaign against "degenerate art" – that is to say all schools of writing, painting and sculpture judged by the Nazis as "decadent".

The Taking of Berlin – The final communiqué of the Yalta Conference in February 1945 announced that Berlin would be occupied after the war by the major powers.
From 21 April to 3 May, Berlin was a battlefield: the Red Army commanded by Generals Zhukov and Koniev against the remnants of the German army. The Soviet troops advanced through the defence lines, destroying everything above ground, including 120 of Berlin's 248 bridges. At last, able to crawl out of their hiding places, the inhabitants learned of the final capture of the Reichstag and the suicide of Hitler (30 April 1945).

Berlin divided – After the German capitulation had been signed in Berlin on 8 May, the four victorious allies (Great Britain, the United States, France and the Soviet Union) took over the administration of Greater Berlin.
The political evolution of the (eastern) Soviet Sector, visualised by the occupants as the potential kernel of a future People's Democratic Republic, nevertheless very rapidly began to hinder the municipal administration as a whole.
Political pressures, vetoes, and various incidents built up an increasing tension. Municipal Councillors unaligned with the concept of State Socialism walked out of the City Hall and formed a rival council at Schöneberg. The foreign representatives on the Allied Control Commission no longer took their seats. From 1948 onwards, the eastern sector found itself isolated.
The Berlin Blockade, provoked by Russian opposition to a currency reform introduced in the western sectors, was beaten by the Berlin Airlift (26 June 1948 to 12 May 1949). The split was aggravated by the proclamation in 1949, in the east, of the German Democratic Republic, the popular uprising of 17 June 1953 and its defeat, the influx of refugees into West Berlin, and numerous other incidents.
On 13 August 1961 the eastern authorities ruled out all communication between the two parts of Berlin. A few days later the construction of the "Wall" began – following with implacable exactitude the theoretical borderline of the Soviet zone marked on the maps.
From then on, on either side of a concrete barrier 160km/99.4mi long and 4m/13ft high, augmented by barbed wire, watchtowers and sentry posts, the two parts of the city evolved separately, each motivated by an ideological pattern opposed to the other. Attempts to pass from East to West through this hermetically sealed cordon ended more often than not in tragedy.

The "fall" of the Wall – A night of wild celebration, especially around the Brandenburg Gate, followed the official "opening" of the Berlin Wall during the evening of 9 November 1989: the eastern authorities, bowing to increased pressure from public protest movements, had finally agreed to re-establish the right of free passage between the two Germanies.
In June 1991, the Bundestag voted that Berlin should become capital of the united Germany.
For a certain time, nevertheless, the two halves of the once-divided city will preserve certain particularities: "socialist" town-planning, for instance, with its broad avenues and grandiose residential units, is a constant reminder of the political climate and community which produced it. And the traces of the wall, in the mind as much as on the ground, will only fade slowly, as a scar that remains too long unhealed.

LIFE IN BERLIN

An outdoor city – Berlin, the biggest city in Germany, occupies an area eight times greater than Paris. Devastated in the last months of the war, the capital lost much of its historical heritage.
But thanks to the famous architects (Le Corbusier, Scharoun and others) involved in its reconstruction, a modernistic town, served by broad arteries linking different quarters separated by vast green belts, has emerged from the ruins of 1945.
The River Havel has been widened in its course through the woods to form lakes (Tegeler See, Stössensee, Großer Wannsee). More than one third of the city's surface is covered by forests, parks and waterways.

A lively cultural scene – Before the Second World War, the centre of the city's life was concentrated around the Potsdamer Platz and the Friedrichstraße. Today the liveliest part of Berlin is around the Kurfürstendamm, the Gedächtniskirche (memorial church) and the Alexanderplatz complex. Night-life centred on the **Kreuzberg hill** (GZ) has more of a cosmopolitan, anti-establishment flavour.

Deservedly, the city enjoys a worldwide reputation for the quality and diversity of entertainment it offers, particularly during the annual festivals of music, theatre and cinema.

During the past 300 years, Berlin has welcomed a large number of immigrants (French Huguenots after the Revocation of the Edict of Nantes, refugees from Poland, and Bohemia), all of whom have contributed to the emergence of a "typical" Berliner, lively, tolerant, with a sardonic sense of humour directed against the world around him.

After Theodore Hosemann in the Biedermeier period, Heinrich Zille (1858-1923) caught this character exactly in a series of spicy sketches satirizing the everyday life of Berlin's "little people".

Because of this intermixture of populations, Berlin restaurants offer – along with such Brandenburger specialities as pig's knuckles (Eisbein) with sauerkraut and pease-pudding – a great variety of dishes from the international cuisine. Berliners term a tankard of lager beer a "Berliner Molle", and a darker beer with a dash of raspberry syrup or woodruff a "Berliner Weiße mit Schuß".

★★ HISTORIC CENTRE *See plan*

The itinerary starts from the Reichstag and then follows the celebrated Unter den Linden, which until the war was the capital's busiest, most lively avenue.

★ **Reichstag (NY)** – This massive neo-Renaissance style palace by Paul Wallot was inaugurated in 1894 and has housed the sessions of the new Diet of the Empire (an Assembly elected through universal suffrage) ever since.

It was gutted by a fire in 1933 and heavily damaged in 1945 during the Battle of Berlin. In 1954 the famous cupola – which Kaiser Wilhelm II had called the apex of tastelessness – was dynamited. The building was restored during the 1970s, albeit without the cupola. On 4 October 1990, it housed the inaugural session of the Parliament of reunified Germany. In 1995 the artist **Christo** wrapped the Reichstag in silver plastic sheeting which was left in place for a fortnight, giving rise to a veritable popular fest as all Berlin flocked to see the work. Finally, building work began again, this time based on the design of British architect Sir Norman Foster. Initially he had decided to forgo the cupola, but was forced to accede to the demands of the conservative CDU/CSU parliamentary faction and so came up with a glass cupola whose complete lightness stands in sharp contrast to the massive building beneath it. Supported by 12 columns, it draws light into the Plenary Hall by way of a mirrored spindle. An exciting thing is being able to access the cupola via a ramp that leads to a **Panorama Platform★★**. The Bundestag is expecting up to 700 000 visitors per year.

On 19 April 1999, the Members of Parliament were able to convene in plenary session in the new Reichstag for the first time.

★★ **Brandenburger Tor (Brandenburg Gate) (NZ)** – This triumphal arch, the very emblem of Berlin, was nevertheless for almost three decades the symbol of the city's division: the structure was integrated into the Wall, which followed a north-south axis here towards the Potsdamer Platz.

There is a vast perspective westward towards Straße des 17 Juni and the Victory Monument (Siegessäule), and eastward towards the Unter den Linden.

Six Doric columns, incorporated into the stonework of the arch, support an antique-style entablature. Inspired by the Propylaea of the Parthenon, the gate was built by Carl Gotthard Langhans in 1789 and surmounted by the famous Victory Quadriga of Gottfried Schadow (1793).

The original group, a post-war reconstruction, was removed to Paris after one of Napoleon's campaigns and returned to Berlin in 1814.

★★ **Unter den Linden (NOZ)** – The famous avenue "under the lime trees", conceived by the Great Elector Frederick-William in 1647, is bordered from the Friedrichstraße intersection onwards by monuments of the 17C and 19C.

Alte Bibliothek (Old Library) (OZ) – Designed by GF Boumann the Younger in the Viennese Baroque style for the royal book collection, this library was inaugurated in 1780. Because of its rounded shapes, the Alte Bibliothek has been nicknamed the "commode" by the people of Berlin.

On the right, take the Charlottenstraße to rejoin the Gendarmenmarkt.

★★ **Gendarmenmarkt (OZ)** – This is undoubtedly the most beautiful square in Berlin, named after the King-Sergeant Frederick Wilhelm I's "Gens d'Armes" regiment, which had stables here. In this square, the Schauspielhaus, an elegant theatre built by Schinkel in 1821, is bounded on the south side by the German cathedral,

Gendarmenmarkt

Deutscher Dom★, and on the north by the French cathedral, **Französischer Dom★**, both early-18C churches decorated by Karl Gontard during the reign of Frederick the Great.

The German cathedral houses the exhibition "**Fragen an die deutsche Geschichte**" (Questions for German History), which used to be in the Reichstag.

★★ **Schauspielhaus** (Theatre, **T¹⁵**) This is the work of Karl Friedrich Schinkel, whose principal inspiration was Greek antiquity; evidence of this is the portico supported by six pillars. The world premiere of Carl Maria von Weber's Freischütz was performed here. After being destroyed during the war, the theatre was rebuilt in compliance with the rules of classicist architecture. The interior was not redone, since the building was scheduled for use as a concert house, though the concert halls did end up magnificently in the end. The monument of Schiller standing in front of the main staircase is an 1871 work by the Berlin sculptor Reinhold Begas.

St. Hedwigs-Kathedrale (**OZ F¹**) - According to the latest research, Georg Wenzeslaus von Knobelsdorff drafted the plans for this Cathlic church, which was built between 1743 and 1773. It was closely modelled on the Pantheon in Rome. Since Frederick II had been victorious in capturing Silesia, the church was dedicated to St Hedwig, the patron saint of Silesia.

★ **Staatsoper** (State Opera House) (**OZ T¹⁷**) - Built by Knobelsdorff between 1740 and 1743 on the site of the "Forum Fredericianum", the Opera House was the only one of three projected buildings - the other two were a palace and a fine arts academy - to be completed. It burned down in 1843; Langhans' reconstruction follows the original plans. Destroyed again during the Second World War, the State Opera House was rebuilt in historicist style between 1951 and 1955.

Humboldt-Universität (**OY**) - The palace of Frederick II's brother, Prince Heinrich, built by J Boumann the Elder in 1753, was transformed into a university in 1810. On the left side of the entrance, a statue of one of its founders, Wilhelm von Humboldt, faces that of his brother, the geographer Alexander von Humboldt, on the other. A famous **equestrian statue** of Frederick the Great, by Christian Daniel Rauch, stands in the centre of the avenue.

Neue Wache (New Guardhouse) (**OY**) - This small, exquisitely proportioned memorial, designed by Schinkel in 1818, is in the form of a temple with Doric columns, wedged between two massive pillars. It was consecrated in 1966 as a Monument to the Victims of Fascism and Militarism.

Ph. Gajic/MICHELIN

Since 1993, it has been designated the leading memorial for Germany, a "place of remembrance for the victims of war and violence". The interior houses a larger than life sculpture by Käthe Kollwitz: *Mother with Dead Son.*

★★ **Zeughaus (Arsenal) (PY)** – Berlin's most important Baroque edifice, erected between 1695 and 1706. It houses the **German Historical Museum**★★, which will probably remain closed until 2002.

During this period, the building will be subjected to a comprehensive technical renovation programme and will be extended with a light-filled exhibition hall and an entrance area in the form of a glass newel designed, as a commission by former Federal Chancellor Helmut Kohl, by the star American architect and Gropius student IM Pei. During the rebuilding process, the inner courtyard will receive a glass roof, another design by the architect.

During this period, the exhibits will be displayed in the Kronprinzenpalais (Palace of the Crown Prince) opposite or in the Martin-Gropius-Bau (Martin Gropius House).

★ **Friedrichswerdersche Kirche** ⊘ **(PZ M²¹)** This impressive brick church was built from 1824 to 1830 following the two-towered neo-Gothic designs of Karl Friedrich Schinkel. It houses the **Schinkelmuseum**★, with sculptures by this multi-talented artist, who left his mark on the cityscape in a way that none other has. There is also various literature on Schinkel's work as well as works from Berlin's classicist period.

Cross the Spree and carry onto the Museumsinsel (described below). On the left stands Berlin Cathedral.

★ **Berliner Dom** ⊘ **(PY)** – This imposing building in the Italian Renaissance style was constructed between 1894 and 1905. Its magnificent **interior**★★ exudes the impression of might and power; the cathedral can seat congregations of 1 500. In the southern part of the church is the **splendid sarcophagus** of Frederick I and his second wife Sophie Charlotte, a work by Andreas Schlüter. Part of the **cathedral crypt** is open to the public. It contains over 90 sarcophagi with the remains of five centuries of the Prussian-Brandenburg Hohenzollern family.

At this point it is possible to prolong your walk to take a look at the modern districts around the Alexanderplatz.

★ **Alexanderplatz (QY)** – The name of this square derives from Tsar Alexander's visit to Berlin in 1805. An important public transport junction and immense commercial centre, the square – known as "Alex" by locals – acts as a focus of

Ph. Gajic/MICHELIN

St. Marienkirche and the Fernsehturm

city life in the eastern sector of Berlin. The **Marienkirche (PY)** (end of the 14C: 15C Danse Macabre fresco in the tower; Baroque pulpit by Schlüter) looks flimsy indeed at the foot of the 365m/1 198ft **Fernsehturm**★ (Television Tower). The revolving sphere at the top of the tower houses a restaurant and a panoramic viewing platform.

South of the square stands the **Rotes Rathaus**★ (Red Town Hall) **(PY)**, built from 1861 to 1869 entirely of bricks sporting a 97m/310ft tower.

★ **Nikolaiviertel (PZ)** – With its narrow cobbled streets and its old taverns, this quarter of restored period houses – including the **Knoblauch house**★ ⊘ (Knoblauchhaus - *Poststraße 23*) and the **Ephraim palace**★ ⊘ – between the Rathaus and the Spree, and between the Rathausstraße and Mühlendamm, seems like a country town transported to the heart of the city. The quarter is dominated by the neo-Gothic bell-towers of the **Nikolaikirche**★ **(Q)**, the oldest church in Berlin.

The old Romanesque basilica, with its Gothic chancel (1379), was transformed into a brick-built Gothic hall-church after the great fire which ravaged the city in 1380. Inside, there is a **permanent exhibition**★ ⊘ of the Stadtmuseum of Berlin outlining the history of the church and its significance as a creative hub and burial place of major Berlin personalities. Its interior decoration includes remarkable tombs and sacred paintings and sculptures ranging from the Gothic period to the 18C.

The Museums of Berlin

The Altes Museum, the first museum to grace Berlin, was built in 1830 by Karl Friedrich Schinkel. It was followed during the rule of Frederick Wilhelm IV by the Neues Museum and Nationalgalerie on the Museumsinsel. Wilhelm von Bode, director of the Berlin museums from 1906 onward, made a major contribution to the further organisation of the city's collections, using his energy and far-sightedness to bring them to the attention of connoisseurs worldwide.

Reconstruction of the destroyed museums began after the Second World War. The collections had either been protected from destruction or confiscated by the victorious powers. Some had been pillaged. The post-war situation, with Germany divided and the city under Allied control also resulted in the dividing of the museum collections. When the German Reich vanished so did Prussia, and it was then formally dissolved by Law no 46 of the Allied Control Council passed in 1947. Prussia's heritage was kept in both halves of Germany. The Stiftung Preußischer Kulturbesitz (Foundation for Prussian Cultural Property) was founded in the west in 1957, while the heritage in the east gathered at the traditional spot: the "Museumsinsel" (Museum Island).

To clarify the current situation (at the time of going to press), there follows a brief outline of the individual museums regrouped under the **Staatliche Museen zu Berlin** ⊙:

in Charlottenburg

Gallery of Romanticism
(Nationalgalerie)
Schloß Charlottenburg,
Knobelsdorff-Flügel
U-Bahn: Sophie-Charlotte-Platz
and Richard-Wagner-Platz,
Bus: X 21, 26, 109, 110, 145
Museum of Pre-and Proto-History
Schloß Charlottenburg, Langhansbau
U-Bahn: Sophie-Charlotte-Platz
and Richard-Wagner-Platz,
Bus: X 21, 26, 109, 110, 145
Egyptian Museum and Papyrus Collection
Schloßstraße 70
U-Bahn: Sophie-Charlotte-Platz
and Richard-Wagner-Platz,
Bus: X 21, 26, 109, 110, 145
Berggruen Collection – Picasso and his times
Schloßstraße 1
U-Bahn: Sophie-Charlotte-Platz
and Richard-Wagner-Platz,
Bus: X 26, 109, 110, 145
Reproductions workshop
Sophie-Charlotten-Str. 17-18
Bus: X 26, 110, 145, 149

in Berlin city centre

Museumsinsel:
Pergamonmuseum with
■ Middle East Museum
■ Collection of Antiquities
■ Museum of Islamic Art
Entrance Kupfergraben
■ Art Library
Library in Pergamonmuseum
Bodemuseum (closed until 2004)
■ Museum of Late Antique
and Byzantine Art
■ Sculpture Collection
■ Numismatic Collection
Entrance Monbijoubrücke
Alte Nationalgalerie (closed until 2001)
Entrance Bodestraße
Altes Museum

■ Antique Collection
Entrance Lustgarten
U-Bahn: and S-Bahn:Friedrichstraße,
S-Bahn: Hackescher Markt,
Tram: 1, 2, 3, 4, 5, 13, 15, 53
Bus: 100, 157, 257, 348
Friedrichswerdersche Kirche
Schinkelmuseum (Nationalgalerie)
Werderstraße
U-Bahn: Hausvogteiplatz,
Bus: 100, 142, 147, 257, 348.

in Berlin-Dahlem

Entrance Lansstraße 8
■ Museum of Ethnography
■ Museum of Indian Art (closed until 2001)
■ Museum of Far Eastern Art (closed until 2001)
U-Bahn: Dahlem-Dorf
Bus: X 11, 101, 110, 183
Museum europäischer Kulturen (of European Cultures)
im Winkel 6/8
U-Bahn: Dahlem-Dorf,
Bus: X 11, 101, 110, 183

In the Kulturforum in Berlin-Tiergarten

Gemäldegalerie (Fine Arts Gallery)
Neue Nationalgalerie
Kupferstichkabinett (Copperplate engraving cabinet) – drawings and prints
Museum of Decorative Arts
Art Library
U-Bahn: Kurfürstenstraße,
U-Bahn: and S-Bahn: Potsdamer Platz
Bus: 129, 142, 148, 248, 348

In Berlin-Köpenick

Museum of Decorative Arts (closed until 2001)
Schloß Köpenick, Schloßinsel
S-Bahn: Spindlersfeld und Köpenick,
Bus: 167, 168, 169, 360
Tram: 26, 60, 62, 67, 68

Besides these great National Museums there is a wealth of other buildings which contribute to the outstanding variety of museum collections which Berlin has to offer.

★★★ MUSEUMSINSEL

Created at the instigation of Frederick-William III at the beginning of the 19C, this huge museum complex was the home until the Second World War of the fabulously rich collections of the National Museums of Berlin.

★★★ **Pergamonmuseum** ⊙ **(OY)** – *Entrance Kupfergraben.*
The museum building, completed in 1930, is divided into three sections (we indicate, for each one, the main centres of interest; plan at the entrance).

Future outlook for the National Museums of Berlin

The museum complex in Dahlem, with the Museum of Ethnography and the Museums for Indian and Far Eastern Art, will be extended as a centre of non-European culture.
The Alte Nationalgalerie has been closed since 1997 (until presumably 2001). The collection, devoted to 19C art, will at some point be housed in the Galerie der Romantik in Schloß Charlottenburg.
A competition has been launched for the redesign of the Museumsinsel. This project will involve reconstruction of the Neues Museum – destroyed during the Second World War – by David Chipperfield. It will take over the Egyptian Museum collections.

The Babylonian Processional Way (detail) in the Pergamonmuseum

– **Collection of Antiquities**★★★ (Antikensammlung): **altar of Pergamon**★★★, a masterpiece of Hellenistic art, dedicated to Zeus (2C BC); richly ornate **gateway to the Milet market**★★ (AD 2C); Greek and Roman sculptures; objets d'art and mosaics.

– **Middle East Museum**★ (Vorderasiatisches Museum): **Processional Way and Gate of Ishtar**★★ from ancient Babylon, 580 BC (rooms 8 and 9); Plinth of Asachadon, 7C BC (room 3); brick façade of the Temple of the Goddess Irmin at Uruk (Sumerian period); bas-relief sculptures of the Temple of Assurnasirpal II at Kalchu, 9C BC (rooms 10 and 11).

– **Museum of Islamic Art**★★ (Museum für Islamische Kunst): façade of Omayyade Castle, Mchatta (8C), east Jordan; painted and lacquered panelling from a house in Aleppo (early 17C); miniatures (15C-17C).

★★ **Alte Nationalgalerie** (National Gallery) ⊘ (**PY M²⁰**) – *Entrance Bodestraße.*
This building (1867-76), designed by Friedrich August Stüler will probably remain closed for renovations until 2001 at which time it will house paintings and sculptures from the 19C.

★★ **Bode-Museum** ⊘ (**OY**) – *Entrance Monbijoubrücke.*
This splendid edifice completed in 1904 at the tip of Museumsinsel closed in mid-1999 for five years for a thorough renovation and restructuring of the interiors. The idea is now to make the best of the outstanding potential of the building, with its three exhibition floors and four interior courtyards. When it is reopened for its 100th anniversary in 2004, the Bode-Museum will house the entire reunited **Sculpture Collection** including the **Museum of Late Antique and Byzantine Art** (Museum für Spätantike und Byzantinische Kunst), as well as the **Numismatic Collection**, which portrays the history of coins and money.
The exhibition concept is scheduled to document the history of European sculpture from the end of antiquity to early classicism using very strictly selected items from the large inventory. It is certainly something to look forward to.

★★ **Altes Museum** (Old Museum) ⊘ (**PY M¹⁸**) – *Entrance Lustgarten.*
Berlin's first public museum, built by Schinkel between 1824 and 1830. The main entrance, which is 87m/285ft long and boasts 18 ionic columns, is a masterpiece of neo-Classical art. Inside, note particularly the frescoes decorating the cupola (rotunda). The building, severely damaged during the war, was reconstructed between 1951 and 1966; the granite basin (7m/23ft diameter) in front of the museum was originally intended for the inside of the rotunda. Nowadays, the ground floor houses the **Antikensammlung** (Collection of Antiquities), specifically the smaller items (the monumental works are located in the Pergamonmuseum). The tour of Ancient Greek art and cultural history begins with the marble idols from the Cyclades (3 millennium BC). It then covers the Archaic Period (7C-5C BC), Hellenism and finally the Roman Empire. Several themes such as *Heroes, the Greek City, Sports and the Greeks, Holiness* are treated in 30 special compartments.

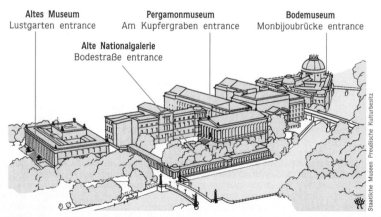

Altes Museum
Lustgarten entrance

Pergamonmuseum
Am Kupfergraben entrance

Bodemuseum
Monbijoubrücke entrance

Alte Nationalgalerie
Bodestraße entrance

The **antique jewellery** (Antiker Schmuck, located in two treasure chambers) is fascinating as well. It includes the gold discoveries from Vettersfelde (c 500 BC), from Tarent (3C BC) and the **Hildesheimer Silberfund**★★★ (Hildesheim Silver Discovery) from the Roman era.

The upper storey has been reserved for more temporary exhibitions.

★TIERGARTEN DISTRICT

The oldest park in the city stretches almost 3km/2mi from Ernst-Reuter-Platz to the Brandenburg Gate. Originally a royal hunting reserve, it was transformed – thanks to the celebrated landscape architect Peter Joseph Lenné (1789-1866) – into a delightful park in the English style. The Hanse residential quarter **(FY)**, a model of town planning which lies to the north, was reconstructed in 1957 by 14 world-famous architects.

Siegessäule (Victory Column) ⓥ **(FY)** – All of 67m/222ft high, this landmark monument, surmounted by a Victory, commemorates the campaigns of 1864, 1866 and 1870. From the top *(285 steps)*, there is an aerial **view**★ of the Spree, the Hanse complex, the Tiergarten, the Brandenburg Gate, Unter den Linden, the Berlin Rathaus and the 12km/8mi perspective that extends to the shores of the Havel.

Schloß Bellevue (FY) – Built in the neo-Classical style by Boumann in 1785, this was the summer palace of Frederick the Great's younger brother, Prince Augustus-Ferdinand. Today it is the official residence of the President of the Republic. The ground floor and first floor can be visited.

Behind the castle there is a 20ha/50-acre park, the western sector being laid out in the English fashion.

Ph. Gajic/MICHELIN

Zoologischer Garten

★★★ **Zoologischer Garten (Zoological Gardens)** ⓥ **(FY)** – *Main entrance: Hardenbergplatz.* Situated in the heart of Berlin, this zoo, gathering together 13 000 creatures from more than 1 400 species, is one of the largest in the world.

The **Aquarium** ⓥ *(entry via the zoo or directly from Budapester Straße)* displays an important collection of approximately 650 species. On the first floor are the widely renowned crocodile hall and the terrarium.

★★★ KULTURFORUM IM TIERGARTEN

★★★ Gemäldegalerie ⓥ **(GY M⁴⁰)**

The collection was born from the collecting passion of the Great Elector and Frederic the Great. However, it was **Wilhelm von Bode**, director of the Gemäldegalerie beginning in 1890, who so indefatigably pushed for new acquisitions, so that by the outbreak of the First World War, an almost complete collection of European painting from the 13C to the 18C had been brought together.

The move into the Gemäldegalerie at the Kulturforum in the summer of 1998 and the converging of the inventory put an end to 50 years of division and provisional states. In spite of losses to the war, the collection today is still considered one of the finest in the world, with representative works from all stylistic periods and schools.

GEMÄLDEGALERIE

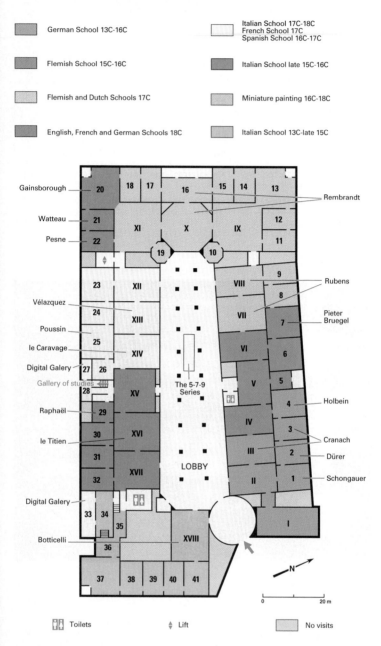

The modest building was conceived by the architects Heinz Hilmer and Christoph Sattler in such a way that all the rooms receive light from above. The 53 rooms are arranged in a horseshoe around a central foyer and provide space for over 1 100 paintings. The Study Gallery on the ground floor displays another 30 valuable works.

Rather than try the patience of the reader with a full inventory, the following list highlights some of the works from the individual schools:

German School, 13C-16C (Rooms I-III, Gallery 1-4):

Darmstädter Passion masters (active c 1440-60): panel of a rood altar; Hans Multscher: *Wurzacher Altar*, 1437 (Room I)

Hans Baldung Grien: *Three Kings Altar*, 1506-07; *Virgin and Child and an Angel*, c 1539 (Room II)

Lucas Cranach the Elder *Winged Altar-piece with the Day of Judgment*, c 1524; *Venus und Amor*, c 1530 (Room III)

The Life of Christ in 35 panels, Cologne c 1410-20; Martin Schongauer: *The Birth of Christ*, c 1480 (Gallery 1)

Several paintings by Albrecht Dürer, including: *Portrait of Hieronymus Holzschuher*; smaller works by Albrecht Altdorfer; Hans Baldung Grien: *Portrait of an Old Man*, c 1518-19; (Gallery 2)

Lucas Cranach the Elder: *Adam and Eve*, 1533; *Rest During the Flight into Egypt*, 1504 (Gallery 3)

Hans Holbein the Younger: *The Merchant Georg Gisze*, 1532; several works by Hans Burgkmair; Christoph Amberger: *Sebastian Münster*, c 1552 (Gallery 4)

Dutch School, 15C-16C (Rooms IV-VI, Gallery 5-7):

Several remarkable altars by Rogier van der Weyden, including the *Mittelburg Altar*, c 1445 (Room IV)

Works by Gerard David; Hans Memling: *Virgin Enthroned with Child*, c 1480-90; Hugo van der Goes: *Adoration of the Kings*, c 1470 (Room V)

Jan Gossaert: *Portrait of a Nobleman*, c 1530 (Room VI)

Petrus Christus: *Portrait of a Young Woman*, c 1470; Jan van Eyck: *The Madonna in Church*, c 1425 (Gallery 5)

Quinten Massys: *Enthroned Madonna*, c 1525; Joachim Patenier: *Rest During the Flight into Egypt*, c 1520 (Gallery 6)

Peter Bruegel the Elder: *Sayings from the Netherlands*, 1559 (Gallery 7)

Flemish and Dutch Schools, 17C, Rubens, Rembrandt (Rooms VII-XI, Gallery 8-19):

Peter Paul Rubens: *Child with a Bird*, c 1629-30; Antonin van Dyck: *Portrait of a Wealthy Genoan Couple*, 1621-23; Jacob Jordaens: *Abduction of Europa*, c 1615-1616 (Room VII)

Peter Paul Rubens: *Virgin and Child*, c 1625-28; Jan Davids de Heem: *Fruit and Flower Cartridge*, 1651 (Room VIII)

Matteus Stom: *Sarah leads Abraham to Hagar*; *Esau Sells his Birth Right* (Room IX)

Rembrandt: *Self-portrait*, 1634; *Simson Threatens his Father-in-law*, 1635; *Moses Shatters the Decalogue*, 1659 (Room X)

Jacob van Ruisdael: *Oaks by the Lake with Water Lilies*, c 1665-69; Meindert Hobbema: *Village Street under Trees*, c 1663. (Room XI)

Jan Brueghel the Elder: *Flower Bouquet*; still-life paintings by Osias Blert und Balthasar van der Ast. (Gallery 8)

Small landscapes by Peter Paul Rubens; Daniel Seghers: *Flower Garland* (Gallery 9)

Works by Peter Paul Rubens and his circle (Gallery 10)

Roelant Savery: *Paradise*, 1626 (Gallery 11)

Landscapes by Jan van Goyen, Pieter de Molijn, Salomon van Ruysdael (Gallery 12)

Frans Hals: *Singing Child with Flute*, c 1623-25; several portrais of men and women (Gallery 13)

Landscapes an cityscapes by Jan van Goyen (Gallery 14)

Landscapes von Jacob van Ruisdael (Gallery 15)

Rembrandt: *Susanna and the two Old Men*, 1647; *Joseph and Potiphar's wife*, 1655; Rembrandt's circle: *The Man with the Golden Helmet*, c 1650-55 (Gallery 16)

Gerard ter Borch: *Fatherly Advice*, c 1654-55 (Gallery 17)

Jan Vermeer van Delft: *The Glass of Wine*, c 1661-62 (Gallery 18)

Philip van Dyk: *The Lute Player* (Gallery 19)

English, French and German Schools, 18C (Gallery 20-22):

Thomas Gainsborough: *The Marsham Children*, 1787; Joshua Reynolds: *Lady Sunderlin*, 1786 (Gallery 20)

Jean Antoine Watteau: *The Dance*, c 1719; Jean Baptiste Siméon Chardin: *The Painter*, 1737 (Gallery 21)

Several works by Antoine Pesne, including *Frederic the Great as Crown Prince*, c 1739 (Gallery 22)

Italian School, 17C-18C., French School, 17C, Spanish School 16C-17C (Rooms XII-XIV, Galleries 23-26, 28):

Francesco Guardi: *Balloon Rising*, 1784; *Canal Grande in Venice*, c 1745; Canaletto: *Canal Grande with View of the Rialto Bridge*; various vignettes of Venice (Room XII)

Diego Velázquez: *Portrait of a Lady*, c 1630-33; Francisco de Zurbarán: *Don Alonso Verdugo de Albornoz*, c 1635; several paintings by Murillo (Room XIII)

Caravaggio: *Amor as Victor*, 1601-02; Simon Vouet: *Ablutions of Venus*, c 1625-27 (Room XIV)

Angelika Kaufmann: several works, including: *Bacchantin*, before 1786; Anton Raphael Mengs: *Self-portrait*, c 1778-79 (Gallery 23)

Luigi Crespi: *Elisabetta Cellesi*, 1732 (Gallery 24)

Claude Lorrain: *Ideal Roman Landscape*, c 1635-36; Nicolas Poussin: *Self-portrait*, 1649 (Gallery 25)

Georges de La Tour: *Peasant Couple Eating Peas*, c 1622-25 (Gallery 26)

Biblical scenes by Jacopo Amigoni (Gallery 28)

Italian School, late 15C-16C (Rooms XV-XVII, Galleries 29-32):

Parmigianino: *Christ's Baptism*, c 1519; Correggio: *Leda with the Swan*, c 1532 (Room XV)

Tizian: *Venus with the Organist*, c 1550-52; *Portrait of a Bearded Young Man*, c 1525; Tintoretto: *Virgin and Child*, 1570-75 (Room XVI)

Giovanni Battista Moroni: *The Duke of Albuquerque*, 1560; (Room XVII)

Raffael: various Madonas, including the *Madonna Terranuova*, c 1505 (Gallery 29)

Florentine artists: Alessandro Alori, Bronzino, Giorgi Vasari (Gallery 30)

Cariani: *Portrait of a Young Woman Resting*, c 1520-24 (Gallery 31)

Lorenzo Lotto: portraits of men (Gallery 32)

Miniature School (Gallery 34):

Lucas Cranach the Elder: *Katharina von Bora*, c 1525

Italian School, 13C-late 15C (Room XVIII, Gallery 35-41):

Botticelli: *Saint Sebastian*, 1474; *Maria with Child and Singing Angels*, c 1477; *Virgin Enthroned*, 1484-85; Antonio de Pollaiuolo: *Portrait of a Young Woman*, c 1465

Gemäldegalerie Antonio del Pollaiuolo – Portrait of a Young Woman

J. P. Anders/Gemäldegalerie – Preußischer Kulturbesitz

Works by Ercole de Roberti (Gallery 35)

Marco Zoppo: *Virgin Enthroned with Child*, 1471 (Gallery 36)

Cima da Conegliano: *Virgin and Child and a Patron*, c 1492-94; several works by Giovanni Bellini (Gallery 37)

Andrea Mantegna: *Representation of Christ in the Temple*, c 1465-66; Carlo Crivelli: *Virgin Enthroned with Child* (Gallery 38)

Fra Angelico: *The Day of Judgement*; Fra Filippo Lippi: *Virgin Adoring the Child*, c 1459 (Gallery 39)

Lorenzo Monaco: several paintings including *The Last Supper*, 1390 (Gallery 40)

Taddeo Gaddi: several works including *Triptych*, 1334; maters of St Magdalena: *Virgin Enthroned with Child and Angels*, c 1270 (Gallery 41)

Study Gallery

Top-notch paintings from all schools are also exhibited here, including some very beautiful still-life paintings: Jan Fyt: *Still-life with Fish and Fruit*; Jan Davidsz de Heem: *Still-life with Fruit and Lobster*; Pieter Claesz: *Still-life with a Drinking Vessel and Fruit*.

★★ **Kunstgewerbemuseum (Museum of Decorative Arts)** ⊙ **(GY M⁴)** – *Matthäikirchplatz*. This new three-storey building by the architect Rolf Gutbrod, completed in 1985, offers a broad survey of decorative art from the Middle Ages to contemporary industrial design.

Gallery I *(ground floor)* is devoted to the Middle Ages. Just inside the entrance, the Enger-Herford (Westphalia) **Treasure of Dionysius** is displayed. This includes a remarkable reliquary purse encrusted with precious stones (second half of the 8C).

5-7-9

The three-naved foyer of the Gemäldegalerie, a wonderfully designed space, boasts a single work of art: a sculpture by the American conceptual sculptor Walter De Maria entitled *The 5-7-9 Series*. It consists of 27 polygonal, highly polished steel staffs ordered in three rows in a granite water basin. The pentagonal, heptagonal and nonagonal staffs have been put together according to all kinds of mathematical combinations. This work of art is a good conclusion to a visit to the Gemäldegalerie, it compels the beholder to come down to earth, to think playfully or merely to pause and rest.

In the centre of the gallery, the **Guelph Treasure**★★★ is displayed. The reliquary here is in the form of a Byzantine church with a dome (Cologne c 1175).
It is thought to have held the head of St Gregory, brought back from Constantinople in 1173. The portable St Elbertus altar dates from the same period. The Guelph Cross (11C) almost certainly came from northern Italy.
Gallery II *(ground floor)*: Italian furniture and majolica from the 14C to the 16C, Venetian glassware from the 16C to the 17C; Gallery III *(ground floor)*: **Lüneburg's municipal silver**★★★ (Late Gothic and Renaissance) and jewellery from Nuremburg; Gallery IV *(first floor)*: the splendid **Pommern Cabinet** and its contents (card games, draughts, measuring instruments, articles of toiletry from the 15C to the 17C); Gallery V *(first floor)*: 17C-18C porcelain from China and Germany (Meissen, Berlin), Chinese lacquer cabinets; Gallery VI *(first floor)*: Biedermeier and Jugendstil objets d'art, panelled glass from Schloß Wiesentheid in Franconia (1724); Gallery VII (first floor): porcelain, earthenware (glazed) and glass from the Jugendstil (Art Nouveau) and Art Deco periods. Galleries IX and X (basement) exhibit the largest existing permanent collection of international design in Germany (furniture, domestic appliances etc).
A second exhibition of decorative arts is to be found in Schloß Köpenick; however, it will only open in 2001 after renovations. In the meantime, especially fine pieces are displayed at the Museum of Decorative Arts at Matthäiplatz, including the **great silverware buffet**★★ from the Knights' Hall of the Berliner Schloß and David Roentgen's **writing pulpit**★.

* **Kupferstichkabinett und Sammlung der Zeichnungen und Druckgraphik (Prints and Drawings Collection)** ⊙ **(GY F)** – *Matthäikirchplatz*.
About 80 000 drawings and 520 000 prints from the Middle Ages to the present make up this collection, which is one of the most significant of its kind in the world.
Representative of the Old Masters of the 14C-18C are **Dürer**, **Brueghel the Elder**, **Rembrandt** and **Botticelli**; of the 19C-20C, Goya, Daumier, Menzel, Kollwitz and Picasso. The collection includes medieval manuscripts and illuminations, incunabula and illustrated books from the 15C-20C, as well as sketch books (Knobelsdorff). The collection is being held in reserve, but it is possible to consult works from this in the reading room after registering.
Since 1994, the Matthäikirchplatz has been home to the **Kunstbibliothek (GY F)**, a particularly richly stocked art library. Part of its function as a public reference library includes hosting special exhibitions.

★★ **Neue Nationalgalerie (New National Gallery)** ⊙ **(GY M⁵)** – *Potsdamer Straße 50*.
This steel and glass structure, designed in 1968 by **Mies van der Rohe**, houses paintings and sculptures from the 20C.
The collections include important work from the classic European Modern art movements and the American art of the 1960s and 1970s. The exhibition begins with the heralds of **Expressionism** (Gauguin, Munch, Holder) and the impressive gallery of work by artists of the **Brücke** (Kirchner, Schmidt-Rottluff, Heckel,

Pillars of Society by George Grosz

Nationalgalerie – Preußischer Kulturbesitz

Otto Müller) provides the first of many highlights. There follow numerous works by Lovis Corinth, Oscar Kokoschka, Wilhelm Lehmbruck and Ernst Barlach. French Cubism is represented by Picasso and Juan Gris. Other artists with work on display include members of the **Bauhaus** (Schlemmer, Kandinsky), George Grosz (*Pillars of Society*), **Paul Klee** (*Boats Leaving*) and the Surrealist **Max Ernst**. Group Zero, the New Realists, and American painters provide the high points of contemporary art, with Barnett Newman's *Who's Afraid of Red, Yellow and Blue IV*, 1969-70.

Among the sculptures gracing the interior of the gallery and the terrace, note *The Washerwoman* by Renoir, Calder's *Heads and Tails*, and the elegant statue of *Maja* by Gerhard Marcks. More recent works have been displayed in the **Hamburger-Bahnhof Museum – für Gegenwart** (Hamburg Train Station – Contemporary Art Museum).

*** Philharmonie ⊘ (GY) – *Herbert-von-Karajan-Straße 1.*

The roof of this boldly asymmetrical building by Hans Scharoun (1963) is in the form of a giant wave. The Berlin Philharmonic Orchestra, directed from 1954 to 1989 by Herbert von Karajan, plays here – the musicians sit in the middle of the auditorium, surrounded by tiered rows of seats that can accommodate up to 2 400 people. Von Karajan's successor is Claudio Abbado who has a contract until the year 2002; Simon Rattle will then take over.

The **Chamber Music Hall** (1988), built beside the Philharmonia by Scharoun and his pupil Edgar Wisniewski, can seat an audience of 1 150. Here, the roof is shaped like a tent.

The **Musical Instruments Museum**★ ⊘ is housed in an annexe (*Tiergartenstraße 1*), also designed by Scharoun and Wisniewski. Keyboard instruments, strings and percussion dating back to the 16C can be seen in this museum.

The massive **National Library**★ (Staatsbibliothek preußischer Kulturbesitz), which faces the Neue Nationalgalerie and houses some 3.7 million volumes, is also the work of Scharoun.

Gedenkstätte Deutscher Widerstand (Monument to German Resistance) ⊘ (GY L) – *Stauffenbergstraße 13-14.*

The monument stands inside the former army headquarters. This is where Claus Schenk, Count of Stauffenberg, had his office, which served as the planning centre for the attempted overthrow of Hitler on 20 July 1944. An exhibition describes German resistance to the Nazis.

Kaiser-Wilhelm-Gedächtniskirche

★ KURFÜRSTENDAMM DISTRICT

★★ **Kurfürstendamm** (EFY) – In the 16C, the Kurfürstendamm was no more than a simple path allowing the Prince Electors to reach the Grunewald hunting lodge. It was Bismarck who transformed it, between 1882 and 1886, into the prestigious thoroughfare known to Berliners today as the "Ku'damm". Along its 3.5km/2mi length, the boulevard unites the cafés, restaurants, theatres, cinemas, art galleries, luxury hotels, nightclubs and fashionable boutiques that make this area the centre of cosmopolitan high life in the capital.

★★ **Kaiser-Wilhelm-Gedächtniskirche** ⊘ (FY E) – This neo-Romanesque church was built between 1891 and 1895 as a memorial to the Emperor Wilhelm I. It was badly damaged during the Second World War, but the ruins were preserved – now a symbol of Berlin – as a reminder of the horrors of conflict. The shattered tower has been incorporated in a modernistic complex (1959-61) of pierced concrete modules in polygonal form, lit by 20 000 blue glass windows designed by Gabriel Loire and made in Chartres.

The former entrance beneath the tower has been arranged as a **Memorial Hall**. An exhibition traces the history of the church, recalls the victims of the war, and pleads for reconciliation.

On the ceiling and walls, mosaics (1906) to the glory of the Hohenzollerns and the Empire are in a good state of preservation.

Tauentzienstraße (FY) – This is the fashionable shopping street where the "KaDeWe", said to be the largest department store in Europe, is situated. The abbreviation stands for Kaufhaus des Westens: Big Store of the West. Behind the Gedächtniskirche at the beginning of the street is the **Europa-Center**, a shopping and business complex which also offers restaurants, cinemas and the famous cabaret "Die Stachelschweine" (The Porcupines).

The water-clock on the Blumenhof is by the Frenchman Bernard Gitton. From the roof of this building, 100m/328ft above the street *(lift to the 20th floor then staircase for the last two storeys)* there is a fine **view★** over the centre of the city.

The fountain in the square between the Gedächtniskirche and the Europa-Center, with its bronze sculptures and exotic figures, symbolises the terrestrial globe. Berliners call it simply **"Wasserklops"**.

★★ SCHLOß CHARLOTTENBURG ⊘ (EY) *allow one day*

Charlottenburg was the favourite retreat of Queen Sophie-Charlotte, wife of Frederick I. With the philosopher-mathematician Leibniz she founded, in 1700, a scientific society which later became the Royal Academy of Science and Fine Arts. Building started in 1695. The original castle was small, but it was soon enlarged, and a dome was added in 1710. The modern, gilded figure of fortune on top of this cupola serves as a weathervane.

Charlottenburg was abandoned by the King-Sergeant, but Frederick II had a new east wing (Neuer Flügel) added by Knobelsdorff, whose peristyled forefront was the sole decorative motif. Later, Queen Louise, the wife of Frederick-William III, lived in the castle.

In the **Cour d'honneur★** stands an equestrian statue of the Great Elector, the masterpiece of Andreas Schlüter (1703).

Central Block – Built between 1695 and 1713 by the architects Arnold Nehring and Eosander Göthe for Queen Sophie-Charlotte.

★★ **Apartments of Frederick I and Sophie-Charlotte** (Historic Rooms) ⊘ **(1)** – *Guided tours only: 1hr.* The itinerary traverses several sombre galleries adorned with portraits of the Royal Family by **Antoine Pesne** (1683-1757), a French painter summoned to the Court by Frederick I, who remained its official portraitist for 46 years. Note particularly, in the apartments of Frederick I, his study, with the portrait of King Stanislas Leszczynski of Poland by Pesne. The room is decorated in red damask. See also the huge courtroom. In the apartments of Sophie-Charlotte, tapestries woven by Charles Vigne in Berlin and richly carved furniture (consoles, mirrors, fire screens with Chinese motifs) evoke the memory of the "Philosopher-Queen".

★★ **Porcelain Room** (Porzellankabinett) **(2)** – The visitor cannot fail to be impressed by the richness and beauty of the vases, figurines and plates on view here, most of which are Chinese.

★ **Chapel (3)** – Restored. Facing the altar, the enormous Royal baldaquin (canopy). Decorated pilasters frame medallions on the side walls.

1st floor – Take the elegant staircase by Eosander Göthe. The salons on this floor contain several tapestries by Philippe Mercier of Berlin, views of the city by the painters Fechhelm and Gaertner, and large decorative vases. In the south-east

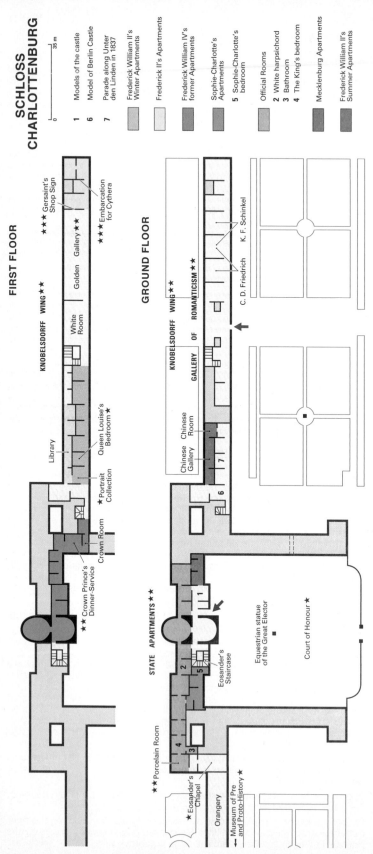

SCHLOSS CHARLOTTENBURG

0   35 m

1   Models of the castle
6   Model of Berlin Castle
7   Parade along Unter den Linden in 1837

Frederick William II's Winter Apartments
Frederick II's Apartments
Frederick William IV's former Apartments
Sophie-Charlotte's Apartments
5   Sophie-Charlotte's bedroom
Official Rooms
2   White harpsichord
3   Bathroom
4   The King's bedroom
Mecklenburg Apartments
Frederick William II's Summer Apartments

FIRST FLOOR

★★★ Gersaint's Shop Sign

★★★ Embarcation for Cythera

KNOBELSDORFF WING ★★

Golden Gallery ★★

White Room

Library

Queen Louise's Bedroom ★

★ Portrait Collection

★★ Crown Prince's Dinner-Service

Crown Room

★★ Porcelain Room

GROUND FLOOR

K. F. Schinkel

C. D. Friedrich

KNOBELSDORFF WING ★★

GALLERY OF ROMANTICISM ★★

Chinese Gallery

Chinese Room

7

6

STATE APARTMENTS ★★

Eosander's Staircase

Equestrian statue of the Great Elector

Court of Honour ★

★★ Eosander's Chapel

Orangery

← Museum of Pre and Proto-History ★

118

arcade of the Oval Salon, a plate-glass window reveals the Insignia of the Prussian Crown (sceptres, globes) together with the swords of the Elector Princes (15C and 16C). To the north, there is a view over the park.

★★ **Knobelsdorff Wing** – The eastern or new wing (Neuer Flügel) was built between 1740 and 1748 as a counterpart to the Orangery.

Summer Apartments (4) – *Ground floor*. The two Chinese rooms and the Etruscan room on the garden front were used by Frederick-William II. On the street side, Frederick-William III's apartments contain works dating from the Napoleonic Wars (Jacques Louis David: *Napoleon Traversing the Great St Bernard Pass*; Ludwig Elsholz: scenes from the wars of liberation) in addition to Royal portraits and the death mask of Queen Louise.

Solitary Tree by Caspar David Friedrich

J. P. Andero/Nationalgalerie preußlscher Kulturbesitz

★★ **Gallery of Romanticism** (Nationalgalerie) ⓥ **(5)** – *Ground floor*. Works by the great Romantic painters of the early 19C can be seen to the right of the entrance hall. The collection of works by **Caspar David Friedrich** is the most significant in the world (23 canvases). Works such as *The Abbey in the Oak Forest*★★★, *Woman at her Window*, *Solitary Tree* or *The Watzmann* mark important stages in the development of this master of German Romanticism. Important landscapes by the painter-architect **Karl Friedrich Schinkel** and by **Carl Blechen** can also be seen. One room is reserved for the Nazarenes (scenes from the Bible).

In the Biedermeier section on the left of the entrance, pictures by **Carl Spitzweg**, Moritz von Schwind and Ferdinand Georg Waldmüller are on display.

Royal Apartments and Banqueting Halls – *First floor*. The result of a collaboration between Knobelsdorff and the sculptor and interior decorator Johann August Nahl, these still present today the impact of "Frederician Rococo" manifested in equally grandiose style at Sanssouci. The galleries exhibit masterpieces, essentially by **French painters of the 18C**★★, collected by Frederick II.

Principal Apartment of Frederick II (6) – Some idea of the private life of a monarch can be gleaned from these rooms. A medallion portrait of Frederick the Great himself hangs in the study. It was executed by Knobelsdorff.

In the **library**, display cupboards contain works from Potsdam; in a glass case there is a selection from the King's priceless collection of snuffboxes. One room is embellished with Italian landscapes, another with Beauvais tapestries (cartoon motifs by François Boucher). On the side towards the city are the **Winterkammer**★ apartments, in which Frederick II's successors (Frederick-William II and Frederick-William III) had their winter quarters. These impressive neo-Classical suites are adorned with Gobelin tapestries in warm tones and beautiful inlaid parquet floors. In **Queen Louise's Bedchamber**★ the pearwood sideboard for flowers and the bed itself were designed by Schinkel.

White Room (Weißer Saal) **(7)** – This huge salon in the central portion of the wing served as a banqueting hall and throne room. The walls are clad with pink marble. The ceiling frescoes, painted by Hans Trier in 1973, express in abstract fashion the ethereal atmosphere of Pesne's original (destroyed) design: *The Marriage of Peleus and Thetis*.

Charlottenburg

★★ **Golden Gallery (8)** – In this superb example of Prussian Rococo, Knobelsdorff renounces the severe, purely architectural approach in favour of decoration. The pink vaulting and spring green walls of the 42m/138ft-long gallery recall the palette of Watteau, one of Frederick II's favourite painters. The Rococo ornamentation impresses above all in the gilded stucco surrounding the mirrors, along the walls and around the embrasures, above the doors and on the ceiling. Here, representations of cherubs, the elements and the four seasons are entwined with the decorative scrolls, garlands, foliage and cornucopia above.

Second Apartment of Frederick II (9) – Frederick the Great appears to have had a preference for this series of rooms at the eastern extremity of the wing. It is here that the most remarkable examples of his collection of paintings are hung. **Watteau's** *Shop Sign*★★★ (painted for his friend, the art dealer Gersaint, in 1720) was acquired by the King in 1745 to decorate the **concert hall**, where it remains today.

Also in the concert hall are two celebrated works by Jean-Baptiste Chardin: *The Letter Sealer* and *The Supplier (Die Köchin)*. The adjoining room contains one of Watteau's versions of the *Embarcation for Cythera*★★★ series.

West Wing (Orangery) – This Orangery wing was built by Eosander Göthe between 1701 and 1707. The theatre at the far end is later; it was built by Langhans (1788-91).

★ **Museum of Pre- and Proto-History** (Museum für Vor- und Frühgeschichte) ⊘ **(A)** – Excellent dioramas and exhibits from archeological digs give an overview of the pre- and proto-history of Europe. An entire floor has been devoted to exhibitions about the Iron Age, the Hallstatt Culture, Lausitz Culture, La-Tène Culture and to the Ibero-Celts. The Roman Empire, Late Antiquity, the Middle Ages and Eurasias Ages of Bronze and Iron are also well represented.

★★ **Schloßgarten (EY)** – Landscaped in English style under Frederick-William II, this green space is an oasis of tranquillity amid the bustle of the city. To the west, at the end of a yew and cypress walk, is a small **mausoleum**★ in the form of a temple, built in 1810 by Heinrich Gentz. It contains the tombs of Frederick-William III, Queen Louise, the Emperor Wilhelm I and Queen Augusta.

The **Schinkel Pavilion**★ *(between the east end of the Knobelsdorff Wing and the castle bridge)* was built by Schinkel in 1824 as a personal residence for Frederick-William III. It is carried out in the Pompeian style very popular in Berlin at that time. Almost all the interior decoration was also designed by Schinkel. The pavilion is a splendid setting for the two biscuit porcelain statuettes of Queen Louise and her sister Frederika (1796) and Queen Louise of Prussia (1802), by **Johann Gottfried Schadow.**

North of the lake, in the direction of the Spree, is a **Belvedere**★ designed by Langhans. It houses an **historic exhibition**★ of the Royal Berlin Porcelain Manufactory founded in 1751 (Rococo tableware). Start the tour on the third floor – view of the castle.

AROUND SCHLOß CHARLOTTENBURG

Stühler Buildings – The two domed buildings on the other side of Schloßstraße from the palace were erected by Friedrich August Stühler between 1851 and 1859 as guard barracks for the royal bodyguards. The Berggruen Collection is housed in the western building, the Egyptian Museum is still located in the eastern one.

★★ **Berggruen Collection** ⊙ – **Picasso and his Times** (Sammlung Berggruen) (**EY**) – Schloßstraße 1, in the western Stühler Building. The collection leant to Berlin by the former Parisian art dealer Heinz Berggruen comprises mostly works by Picasso. All aspects of his œuvre are displayed: tableaux (*The Yellow Pullover*, 1929), sculptures (*Head of Fernande*, 1909), drawings and gouaches. There are also works by Cézanne, Van Gogh, Matisse, Braque, Laurens, Giacometti and African tribal art. Virtually the whole of the second floor is devoted to **Paul Klee**.

★★★ **Egyptian Museum and Papyrus Collection** (Ägyptisches Museum und Papyrussammlung) ⊙ (**EY M⁶**) – The collections of the Egyptian Museum nin the eastern Stühler building retrace, in the main, the historical and cultural evolution of Egypt during the time of the Pharaohs. Quality takes precedence over quantity, with the result that only works of particular beauty and value are on show, in a well-appointed display. The highlights of the exhibition are the impressive **ebony head of the Queen Teje**★★ (18th Dynasty), the unusually expressive Green Head of a priest (c 300 BC), and the world-famous **Bust of Queen Nefertiti**★★★ (painted plaster over limestone – 1350 BC), exerting the magical fascination on the onlooker that has won the bust its reputation as the best-known work of Egyptian art. The entire Egyptian Museum is to be moved to the Museumsinsel in 1999 and to be exhibited in the north wing of the Pergamonmuseum until it can be moved into the Neues Museum. A "Centre for Photography" is scheduled for the eastern Stühler Pavilion.

Bust of Queen Nefertiti

M. Büsing/Ägyptisches Museum – Preußischer Kulturbesitz

★ **Bröhan-Museum** ⊙ (**EY M¹³**) – Schloßstraße 1a. This exhibition, based on a private collection, presents arts, crafts and industrial design from the Paris World Fair of 1889 until the 1930s (Jugendstil, Art Deco). Note, in particular, furniture from the French cabinet-makers in the 1920s (JE Ruhlmann), the art of French glass-makers (Marinot and Gallé), and the porcelain (Berlin, Meissen, Copenhagen and Sèvres). Do not miss, either, the paintings of the Berlin Secession (Hans Baluscheck, Karl Hagemeister and W Jaeckel) or the paintings and sculpture of the Franco-Polish Cubist, Jean Lambert-Rucki.

Those interested in Jugendstil and Art Deco should be sure to visit this excellent exhibition, well laid out on three floors.

Gipsformerei (**EY C**) – 17-18 Sophie-Charlotten-Straße. The plaster replication workshop of the National Museum of Berlin, which contains 6 500 figures, is located near Schloß Charlottenburg. It is one of the largest in the world, alongside those of the British Museum and of the Louvre, France. An impressive selection of busts, masks and figures are on sale in the salesroom.

MUSEUMSZENTRUM DAHLEM ⊙ (**BV**)

The great amount of space left after the 1998 move of the Gemäldegalerie is ideal for the collections of the Ethnographic Museum, the Museum of Far Eastern Art and the Museum of Indian Art.

★★★ **Museum für Völkerkunde (Museum of Ethnography)** – Lansstraße entrance. The collections in this museum, comprising some 400 000 objects, are among the most impressive of their kind in the world.

★★★ **Ancient American Cultures Section** – Stone sculptures and **steles** from the Mayan civilization (Cozumalhuapa, Guatemala); **sacred and secular Aztec statuary** (human sacrifice cup); anthropomorphic ceramics and pre-Inca cloths in multicoloured designs from Peru. The **Gold Room**★★★ displays magnificent jewels and exquisitely engraved cult objects dating from the 7C BC to the 11C AD.

Bröhan-Museum

★★ **Oceania Section** (Südsee) – Among exhibits gathered during sea voyages in the Pacific since the end of the 18C note the **painted masks** and **wooden sculptures** from New Guinea, the spectacular **Oceanian boats**, and the magnificent ochre and red feathered cloak of the king of Hawaii.

★ **Southern Asia and the Far East Section** – Exhibits from South-east Asia, India and Sri Lanka, including masks, puppets and Chinese shadow theatre figures evoke the culture of this region. Indonesia is represented by a sizeable collection of carved and painted figures used in religious ceremonies and textiles.

★★ **North and West Africa Section** – The most interesting objects in this collection include **terracotta heads** from Ife (Nigeria), **bronzes** from the ancient kingdom of Benin, and Berber jewellery. There are also some interesting sculptures in wood from Cameroon.

★★ **Museum für Indische Kunst (Museum of Indian Art)** – *Lansstraße entrance.*
Extensive archeological collections from India, Nepal, Tibet and South-east Asia. The art of Central Asia is represented by the unusual **Turfan collection**, named after an oasis in Chinese Turkestan (on the Silk Road). *The museum is closed for renovations until 2001.*

★ **Museum für Ostasiatische Kunst (Museum of far-Eastern Art)** – *Lansstraße entrance.*
Archeological exhibits, art and decorative arts from China, Japan and Korea. The display includes items made of bronze, stone, wood, ivory, lacquer and ceramic dating from the 3C BC to the present. Highlights of the exhibition are Chinese and Japanese painting and calligraphy, and Oriental woodcuts. There is a magnificent Chinese imperial throne made from jacaranda wood inlaid with mother-of-pearl on a gold and lacquer background (dating from the second half of the 17C). *The museum is closed for renovations until 2001.*

★ **Museum europäischer Kulturen (Museum of European Cultures)** ⊘ **(BV M²⁶)** – *Im Winkel 6-8.*
No lesser figure than Virchow brought his influence to bear on the foundation of the then "Museum for German Folk Costumes and Products of Home Industries" in 1889. After the Second World War, a second ethnographic museum was founded in the eastern part of the city. The two collections have been joined in the Dahlem museum building since 1992.
The museum collects items from folk culture from the 16C to the present. Ever since the 1990s, more and more pieces are being purchased from neighbouring European countries. In the summer of 1999, after refurbishing and take-over of the "Europe" department of the Ethnographic Museum, the museum was once again opened to the public. *The tour begins on the first floor.*
First floor: This permanent exhibition focuses on the *Fascination of the Image* and has "cultural contacts in Europe" as a main topic. It shows the reception of images, beginning with the wonderful artistry of individually created religious artworks, printed images as the basis for paintings on the walls of living rooms, furniture and other household items, all the way to the mass commodities of our times.
Ground floor: Images are placid here in the context of the three world religions, Judaism, Christianity and Islam. The image's social role in the 19C and 20C is then highlighted. And finally, the visitor is shown the image of foreign cultures in comparison to their own images.

ADDITIONAL SIGHTS

* Museum für Post und Kommunikation (Museum of Post and Telecommunications) ⊙
(FY M⁷) – *Leipziger-Str. 16.*
The museum has a wonderful setting in the historic building of the former
Reichspost Museum. This magnificent edifice from the Wilhelminian days, which
was the world's first postal museum when it was built, presents the past, present
and future of communications.

** Deutsches Technikmuseum Berlin (Berlin German Transport and Technical Museum) ⊙
(GZ M⁸) – *Trebbinerstraße 9.*
The very setting of this museum merits a visit, as it was once the main Anhalt
goods depot. The now disused buildings and station land have been converted into
a transport and technical museum. Technical progress is presented as part of the
cultural evolution of mankind in a series of vivid displays and 14 exhibition
departments. Air and space travel, road traffic and maritime transport are all
represented, along with the application of technology to the media, photography
and energy production. The **Railway Section**** – particularly well represented –
includes a selection of locomotives, some of them dating back to the very earliest
rail transport. In the **Spectrum**, 250 experiments demonstrate scientific
phenomena to visitors.

Open-air section of the Transport and Technical Museum

** Hamburger Bahnhof – Museum für Gegenwart ⊙ **(NX)** – *Invalidenstraße
50-51.*
Hamburg Station, the only one of Berlin's first generation of railway stations to
have survived, was built in 1845-47. It was closed in 1884 and later became the
home of the Transport and Construction Museum, for which it had a striking
purpose-built metal hall added to it. This is now the focal point of the new museum
designed by architect Paul Kleihues, which houses works of art from 1960
onwards. The core of it is made up of the private collection of Dr Erich Marx. Ever
since the Hamburger Bahnhof opened in 1996, it has become the most popular
museum of contemporary art in Berlin.
The great hall contains works by Anselm Kiefer (Census, 1991), Richard Long
(Berlin Circle) and Mario Merz ("Water-drop" glass igloo) and a work in nails by
Günther Uecker. The long gallery with its glazed ceiling houses superb works by
Cy Twombly, Robert Rauschenberg and Andy Warhol from the Marx collection.
A whole room is devoted to Joseph Beuys and his installations (Biennale-
Installation Tramstop, 1976)

* Käthe-Kollwitz-Museum ⊙ **(FY M⁹)** – *Fasanenstraße 24.*
A broad survey of the works of the talented graphic artist and sculptress Käthe
Kollwitz (1867-1945), in which – to quote Romain Rolland – "the trials and
tribulations of simple folk are reflected". Her series of engravings *The Weavers'
Revolt* (1893-97) and *The Peasants' War* (1903-08), the wood engravings titled

War (1922-23) and *The Proletariat* (1925), as well as the self-portraits and the late series of lithographs labelled *Death*, all mark milestones in the Kollwitz career.

Well-known posters from the 1920s such as *Nie wieder Krieg (No More War)* underline the artist's political and humanistic commitment. The sculptures are exhibited on the upper floor, among them the *Muttergruppe (Mother Group)* in bronze (1924-37). Also on display is a large bronze seated statue of the artist herself, by Gustav Seitz (1957). One of the museum's concerns is also to show the – much less well known – brighter side of this artist.

★★ **Martin-Gropius-Bau (GY M¹⁰)** – *Stresemannstraße 110*.
This building in the form of a cube (1881) was originally conceived by Martin Gropius and Heino Schmieden as a home for the Royal Museum of Decorative Arts. Its reconstruction, after heavy war damage, was begun in 1978. The neo-Classical style shows the influence of Schinkel. The interior, with its majestic columned hall, is a living proof of the expertise of Prussian designers during the Founders' Period or Gründerzeit. Important special exhibitions take place here. Until 1998, the **Berlinische Galerie** was located here, the Regional Museum for Modern Art, Photography and Architecture. It will be redeployed in the Schultheiss Brewery in Berlin-Kreuzberg (Methfesselstraße 28-48). But the attractive brewery will have to be refurbished for more artistic pursuits. Opening is scheduled for the autumn of 2001.

"Topographie des Terrors" ("Topography of Terror") ⊘ – Adjacent to the Gropius building lies an area known as the **Prinz-Albrecht-Gelände** (after the old Prinz-Albrecht-Straße). From 1939 on, this was the Reich security and secret police centre, grouping the headquarters of the SS, the Gestapo and the SD (Sicherheitsdienst: Security Service). In the 1980s, on what had been considered just a stretch of wasteland, the foundations of the centre's prison building were unearthed.
In 1992 a competition was called for a new building for the planned international documentation and meeting place of the "Topographie des Terrors" Foundation. The winner was the Swiss architect Peter Zumthor, who also designed the avant-garde art house in Bregenz (Vorarlberg, Austria). The building is supposed to be completed by the end of 2000. Until then the documentation in the excavations along Niederkirchnerstraße can be visited as an open-air exhibition.

★ **Viktoria Park** – In the middle of this district is the highest "natural" piece of ground (66m/216ft) in the city. The hillock is surmounted by Karl Friedrich Schinkel's monument to the "Wars of Liberation". There is a panoramic view of Berlin from the terrace.

Luftbrückendenkmal (Airlift Memorial) (GZ) – The three west-facing arcs of this structure symbolise the three air corridors still open to the Allies during the Berlin Blockade to supply the city with its necessities.

Berlin-Museum (GY) – The exterior sections of this one-time Administrative Court, where ETA Hoffmann worked, have been restored in the original Baroque style. On the pediment, allegorical figures representing Justice and Misery surmount the Prussian coat of arms. The permanent exhibition is closed as the Berlin Museum is currently being restructured. Reopening is planned for the autumn of 2000.

Jewish Museum Berlin (GY M³⁸) – The American architect Daniel Libeskind designed this spectacular lightning-shaped new building. The museum, which can be accessed over the foyer of the Berlin Museum, is due to be completed by the autumn of 2000. Until then it will be possible to be guided on weekends through the building, which is shaped like a broken Star of David. This veritable labyrinth, with empty rooms that lead nowhere, is in itself a symbol for the annihilation of the Jewish-German culture.
The permanent exhibition will trace the history of the Jews in Germany from the earliest provable documents to the present. The significance of the Jews for the development of Berlin from the 18C to the 20C will be given a special accent in the presentation, whereby the emphasis will be on the Shoa, the Holocaust during the Nazi era.

Museum Haus am Checkpoint Charlie (Berlin Wall Museum) ⊘ **(GY M¹¹)** – Documentation on the building of the Berlin Wall and attempts to cross it, as well as on the movements for human and civil rights are on display. Works of art on these themes and authentic objects that were used to help in overland and underground escapes are also presented.

★ **Märkisches Museum/Stiftung Stadtmuseum Berlin (March Museum/Foundation City Museum of Berlin)** ⊘**(QZ)** – This picturesque complex of buildings gathered around two interior courtyards was built between 1899 and 1908 borrowing from the typical Gothic and Renaissance architecture of the March of Brandenburg. The museum displays the historical and cultural development of Berlin from the fist

---

The Wall

The border complex known simply as the "Berlin Wall" divided the city's western districts from the eastern half and from the surrounding area. Watchtowers, barbed wire and self-shooting gadgets have all long gone; on the erstwhile deathstrip, construction sites, parks or wild growth have appeared. Only few traces remain of the once divided city, such as the watchtower at the Schlesische Tor, used as a museum for "Forbidden Art", or walled-in house entrances at Heidelberger Straße in the Treptow district. Remains of the actual wall can only be seen in a few places.

The longest stretch of the wall is the "East Side Gallery" in Friedrichshain. The graffiti art completed by various artists in the 1990s is in poor shape these days. More central is the bit of wall in the shadow of the former Prussian House of Parliament between the Detlev-Rohwedder-Haus (built as Göring's Reichs Air Ministry) and the grounds of the "Topography of Terror". As in no other place, the various eras of the last century of Berlin history converge here. The future of the short wall sections on Leipziger Platz along Stresemannstraße is uncertain.

Bernauerstraße remains a symbol of the inhumanity of the wall. In 1998, the **Berlin Wall Memorial** (Gedenkstätte Berliner Mauer) was opened on land from the cemetery of the Sophie Community (corner of Bernauerstraße/Ackerstraße). The romantic, park-like Invaliden Cemetery was also in the border area, a wall section of which still remains along the canal behind it.

---

traces of a prehistoric settlement to the immediate present. Three floors of special exhibitions on various aspects of Berlin history will be shown until completion of extensive renovation activities.

A copy of the larger-than-life 1474 sandstone figure of Brandenburger Roland, symbol of civic liberties and privileges, stands before the entrance to the museum.

Volkspark Friedrichshain (HY) – Rubble from the battle-scarred city has enabled two artificial hills to be constructed in this leisure park. Homely characters from German folklore surround the fountains playing in the "Fairy Basin" (Märchenbrunnen).

Sowjetisches Ehrenmal (Soviet Memorial) (CU) – This monument in Treptower Park was erected in memory of the Red Army soldiers who fell during the Battle of Berlin.

★★ **Kunstgewerbemuseum (Museum of Decorative Arts) (DV M²⁹)** – *In Schloß Köpenick (Schloßinsel).*

A visit to this museum takes the visitor into the old-world provincial charm of the "green" Köpenick suburb, southeast of the city centre and far from the hectic bustle of international tourism.

The museum is situated in a Baroque mansion built by the Dutch architect Rutger von Langerfeld. The **furniture** is specially interesting (chests, cabinets, writing desks and tables, many of them inlaid with marquetry: 16C-19C). Note also the **panelled room**★ from Haldenstein castle (Switzerland, 16C) and the **writing pulpit**★ by David Roentger (Neuwied, 1779), on which the marquetry represents the Seven Liberal Arts of Frederick II.

The **Treasury**★ *(ground floor, on the left)* contains jewellery and 16C gold plate and Baroque silverware. In the Heraldry Room *(Wappensaal, second floor, on the right)* 18C porcelain – including Frederick II's breakfast service – is on display. In the room behind is the great **silver sideboard**★★ from the Knights' Room in the old Castle of Berlin (made by J Ludwig and A Biller, the famous silversmiths of Augsburg, between 1695 and 1698). Beside this is a **cask**★ (Münzfaß, 1719) decorated with 686 talers (old German coins) and 46 medals.

The museum is closed for renovations until autumn 2001. During that period, some of the outstanding pieces such as the silver sideboard and Roentgen's writing pulpit will be exhibited in the Decorative Arts Museum.

★★ **Großer Müggelsee** – *Leave by the Köpenicker Landstraße (DV).*

The largest of the Berlin lakes. From the terrace at the top of the tower: broad view of the surrounding lakes and woods.

★★ **Botanischer Garten (Botanical Gardens)** ⊙ **(BV B¹)** – *Königin-Luise-Straße 6-8.*

It's 43ha/106 acres make it the world's largest botanical garden – vegetation from the temperate zone of the northern hemisphere, planted out geographically from mountains to plains. There are rare species (trees and shrubs) in the Arboretum, while 16 greenhouses display a wealth of tropical and subtropical plants on a total of 6 000m²/64 000sq ft. The **Botanical Museum**★ (Botanisches Museum) ⊙ **(M²⁷)** shows the evolution of flora in all its diversity. Numerous utility plants are shown, as are funeral offerings discovered in Ancient Egyptian tombs. At the entrance, there is a cross-section from an 800-year-old Sequoia tree.

Inside one of the greenhouses of the Botanical Gardens

★ **Brücke-Museum** ⊘ (BV M³⁶) – *Bussardsteig 9.*
This museum contains works by members of the Brücke, the most important school of German Expressionists.
The movement was founded in Dresden in 1905, by a group of students who wished to create an expressive art by the deformation of lines and the use of violent colours.
In 1911, the group moved to Berlin, where it disbanded two years later. The greater part of the oil paintings, watercolours, sculptures and drawings on display is the work of **Karl Schmidt-Rottluff** and Erich Heckel. Max Pechstein, Otto Mueller, Ernst Ludwig Kirchner and Emil Nolde are also represented.

★★ **Grunewald** (AUV) – A hunting reserve of the Prince-Electors in the 16C, this forest of oak, pine and silver birch covers an area of 3 100ha/745 acres. Wild boar, stags and deer still roam freely here.
The Grunewald is bounded on the east by a chain of small lakes, interspersed with residential areas. Beside one of these lakes, the Lake of Grunewald, is the elegant **Jagdschloß Grunewald**★ ⊘ (BV M²⁸), a hunting pavilion built in 1542 by Caspar Theyss for the Elector Prince Joachim II. The building overlooks a courtyard surrounded on three sides by outbuildings (**Jagdzeugmagazin**) and bordered by 100-year-old beech trees. 160 years later, the original Renaissance mansion was redone in Baroque style for the Prussian king Frederick I. Among the paintings on view, note the nine gripping scenes of The Passion from the studio of Lucas Cranach the Elder, as well as Flemish and Dutch work of the 17C (among others: Van Dyck, Jordaens, Jan Steen, *Portrait of Caesar* by Rubens).
The western boundary of the Grunewald is formed by **Havel lake**★★ (AV). Beside this runs the picturesque Havelchaussee road, which leads, a little further south, to the beaches of the **Wannsee**★★ (AV), a favourite place for Berlin bathers in the summer.

★★ **Pfaueninsel (Peacock Island)** (AV) – *Access by boat, leaving from the landing-stage at the end of Nikolskoer Weg (service on demand).*
Landscaped gardens studded with small, picturesque buildings offer a perfect example of late-18C taste on this isle on the Havel.
The **castle**★ ⊘ (1794-97), left incomplete in accordance with the taste for false "ruins" at the beginning of the Romantic period, displays souvenirs of Queen Louise in a number of salons panelled and floored with exotic woods.

★ **Funkturm (Radio Tower)** ⊘ (EY) – This 150m/492ft structure, known to Berliners as the "Beanpole", is indissolubly linked to the city and has become its mascot. At a height of 126m/413ft, reached by a lift which travels at 4mps/13ftps, there is a viewing platform offering a **panorama**★★★ of Berlin.

★ **Olympia-Stadion** ⊘ (AU) – From the top of the campanile (77m/286ft) *(lift)* there is a view of the former 132ha/316-acre Reich Sports Ground. The stadium, built for the 1936 Olympic Games, was used for propaganda purposes by the

Hitler regime. A plan is in place to build a roof over the stadium (for 500 million DM) and to add a retractable stage for 77 000 spectators. Soccer spectators could get up to 4m/13ft from the pitch. For track and field meets, the lower ring could be sunken in. The project is scheduled to be finished in 2003.

* **Bauhaus-Archiv (Museum für Gestaltung)** ⊙ (FY M¹²) – *Klingelhöfersstraße 14.*
The building housing this museum was constructed in 1979 after the original designs of **Walter Gropius**, the founder of the Bauhaus.
The Bauhaus School is known predominantly for its work in the field of architecture (Walter Gropius, Mies van der Rohe), but it exerted a strong influence too on the plastic arts;

Pfaueninsel

through the everyday objects it designed (furniture, the first tubular steel chairs by Marcel Breuer, tapestries, ceramics), it was the precursor of contemporary design. Attempting to make art a component of day to day life through the uses of technology, the Bauhaus called into question the traditional function of art itself. In this museum, apart from industrial products and craftwork, one can see sculptures and paintings (including montages) by Schlemmer, Moholy-Nagy, Feininger, Kandinsky and Klee, as well as models, experimental typography for posters and adverts, and drawings from the Bauhaus School.

Kirche Maria Regina Martyrum ⊙ (EX) – Built in 1963 by Hans Schädel and Friedrich Ebert as a memorial to the victims of National Socialism, this church is entered via a Ceremonial Courtyard whose sombre walls of grey basalt evoke captivity and death. One of them is embellished by the Stations of the Cross, by OH Hajek. Passing below *The Woman of the Apocalypse*, a sculpture by F König, one reaches the crypt, which is shrouded in half-light: only the front wall emerges

Wannsee

from the dark, with a warm golden tint. Beneath König's Pietà is engraved the epitaph: "To all the Martyrs refused a grave – to all the Martyrs whose graves are unknown." Go to the upper part of the church.

A soft light indirectly illuminates one part or another of an immense coloured fresco by Georg Meistermann, representing the passage of night (death, evil) into day (the Redemption). To the right of the altar, there is a Gothic Madonna dating from 1320.

Gedenkstätte Plötzensee (Memorial) ⊘ **(FX)** – The memorial to victims of the Nazi regime occupies the former execution chamber in Plötzensee prison. Between 1933 and 1945 over 3 000 prisoners sentenced to death by Nazi justice were murdered here, dying under the guillotine or by hanging.

★ **Schloß Tegel (Humboldt-Schloß)** ⊘ **(BT)** – *Adelheidallee 19-20*.
A 16C manor house transformed by Schinkel for Wilhelm von Humboldt into a small neo-Classical mansion (1821-24). Low-relief sculptures on the four corner towers represent the gods of the four winds. Inside: antique sculptures and family souvenirs.

★ **Spandauer Zitadelle (AU)** – The Spandau citadel was built in the second half of the 16C on the site of a medieval castle (12C) at the confluence of the Havel and the Spree. Right-angled bastions occupy the four corners of the square, brick-built keep – a break with tradition in comparison with the old, round bastions used until that time. Spandau is the sole example north of the Alps of this so-called "Italian" system of fortification. In the course of its turbulent history, the citadel has been assaulted successively by Swedish, Austrian, French, Russian and Prussian troops, but it is best-known as a state prison.

A drawbridge leads to the gateway. Armorial bearings painted on the pediment represent the different provinces of Prussia.

Pediment on the doorway of the Spandauer Zitadelle

Julius Tower (Juliusturm) – *Skirt the right-hand side of the building*. Sole remnant of the original castle, this 32m/105ft keep has become the emblem of Spandau. It was here, in 1874, that the authorities stored the 120 million DM in gold demanded from France as war reparations after the defeat of 1870. The entrance is guarded by an impressive system of bolts. Inside the tower, 145 steps lead to a look-out point with a panoramic view. The external walls on the southern side of the citadel are studded with Jewish gravestones bearing 13C and 14C Hebraic inscriptions. They were salvaged from the Spandau Jewish cemetery sacked in 1510. A **Museum of Local History** ⊘ has been installed inside the citadel *(entrance via the footbridge)*.

★ **St. Nikolai-Kirche** ⊘ **(AUV)** – This hall-church is one of the last Gothic buildings in brick to remain in Berlin. The piers support ribbed barrel vaulting over the naves and star vaults above the choir. The entrance to the north chapel in the polygonal choir is surmounted by a handsome **Crucifixion Group** (1540) in polychrome carved wood. The magnificent **Renaissance altar**★ (painted limestone and stucco) was a gift from the military architect, Count Rochus de Lynar. The central panel represents The Last Supper. Above it is a striking version of The Last Judgement. On either side there are likenesses of the donor's family. Note the gilded Baroque pulpit, which is finely carved, and the baptismal font cast in bronze (1398).

EXCURSIONS

★★★ **Potsdam** – *19km/12mi to the west. See POTSDAM*.

Oranienburg – *31km/19mi to the north by ⑨ on the plan*.
The Concentration Camp of Sachsenhausen, now a memorial – **Gedenkstätte und Museum Sachsenhausen** ⊘, dates from 1936. More than half the people imprisoned there perished. The various aspects of the history of the concentration camp are

shown in changing and permanent exhibitions at the original sites. The **Museum Baracke 28** opened in 1997 is a special exhibition on the fate of the Jewish prisoners.

A tour of the camp *(follow the plan distributed at the entrance)* gives some idea of the implacable organisation of the Nazi concentration system, whose cynical approach is exemplified by the slogan still above the entrance gates: "Arbeit macht frei" (Work brings Freedom).

The camp inspectorate ("Inspektion der KZ"), a feature common to all the concentration camps within the German Reich, contains a display on the National Socialists' various crimes against humanity, such as medical experimentation on prisoners and their planned "final solution" for the extermination of the Jews.

After the camp had been liberated in August 1945, the Soviets set up "No 7" forced-labour camp here; an exhibition and a commemorative stone to the victims are in the main courtyard.

BERNKASTEL-KUES ★

Rheinland-Pfalz

Population 7 200

Michelin map 417 Q 5 – Local map see MOSELTAL

This double town straddles the River Moselle at the confluence of the Tiefenbach, a stream which has gouged a ravine through the Hunsrück schist. Bernkastel-Kues is in the largest single wine-growing region of Germany – spread over the slopes flanking a wide bend in the Moselle (Moselschleife) and continuing as far as Graach and Zeltingen. The grapes are 95 % of the Riesling variety. The town has numerous cellars where one can try the wine. many visitors come during the first weeks in September This is a famous wine-growing area, gay and animated during the first week in September to celebrate the Middle Moselle Wine Festival. As for the rest of the year, wine remains the focus of attention on the calendar of events.

The town, filled with beautiful half-timbered houses, is dominated by the ruin of Landshut fortress.

SIGHTS

★ **Markt** – Colour-washed houses, most of them half-timbered, surround this small, sloping square in the middle of which is the 17C **St Michael fountain** (Michaelsbrunnen).

St. Nikolaus-Hospital (Cusanusstift) ⊙ – *On the Kues side of the river.*

Founded in 1447 by **Cardinal Nicholas of Kues** (or Nikolaus Cusanus) (1401-64), a humanist and theologian, the hospice was built to house people in need. The number of lodgers was restricted to a symbolic 33 – the age of Christ at his death – a tradition still respected today.

Admire the Late Gothic cloister, the chapel with its fine 15C reredos, and the copy in bronze of the Cardinal's tombstone (the original is in Rome, at San Pietro in Vincoli). On the left, entering the chapel, note the fresco depicting The Last Judgement and, on the right, **the tombstone of Clara Cryftz**, the prelate's sister.

The **library** houses almost 400 manuscripts and early printed works, in addition to astronomical instruments used by the founder.

EXCURSION

Burg Landshut – *3km/2mi to the southeast towards Longkamp and uphill to the right.*

The castle, built on a rocky promontory, was the property of the archbishops of Trier from the 11C. It has been in ruins ever since the War of the Orléans Succession. From the ruin there is a fine **panoramic view ★★** over the bend in the Moselle, above which even the steepest slopes are planted with vines.

OUR SELECTION

Moselblümchen – Schwanenstraße 10, ☎ 0 65 31/23 35, Fax 0 65 31/96 70 50. Single rooms from 87DM. Modern rooms. Inexpensive, with its own butcher.

Behrens – Schanzstraße 9, ☎ 0 65 31/95 04, Fax 0 65 31/9 50 44 46. Single rooms from 75DM. Family feeling.

Zur Post – Gestade 17, ☎ 0 65 31/9 67 00, Fax 0 65 31/76 33. Single rooms from 87DM. Traditional, renovated hotel. Very pleasant rooms.

BODENSEE★★

LAKE CONSTANCE – Baden-Württemberg and Bayern

Michelin map 419 W 10-X 13

With the immensity of its horizons, sometimes lost in the summer haze, and a climate mild enough to permit tropical vegetation in the more favoured sites, Lake Constance, or the Bodensee as it is known to German speakers, attracts a multitude of German holidaymakers, who regard it as their local "Riviera".

With an area of 53 000ha/210sq mi, the lake is only marginally smaller than Lake Geneva, biggest of the Alpine waterways. A wide choice of boat services provides many possibilities for cruises and excursions; the most frequent of these services run from the ports of Constance, Überlingen, Meersburg, Friedrichshafen, Lindau and Bregenz. The lakeside roads offer numerous vistas of the lake with the Alps, in clear weather, as an impressive background.

The islands of **Reichenau**★, on the Untersee, and **Mainau**★★, on the Überlingersee, are described under *KONSTANZ: Excursions.*

FROM ÜBERLINGEN TO LINDAU

56km/35mi - allow 4hr

★ **Überlingen** – *See ÜBERLINGEN.*

★ **Birnau** – The present church was built between 1746 and 1750 on a terrace overlooking the lake, the Cistercians of Salem having entrusted the work to Peter Thumb, Master of the Vorarlberg School.

The building's Rococo charm is most evident in the architectural design, the painted decoration of the interpenetrating oval spaces and curved surfaces over the single aisle, the flattened dome above the chancel, and the cupola surmounting the apse. Halfway up the walls, an elegant gallery is supported on corbels, the bosses of which are embellished with Rococo cartouches. Pilgrims venerate the early-15C Virgin above the tabernacle on the high altar.

Birnau - The church

★ **Meersburg** – This former residence of Prince-Archbishops and now centre of tourism to which visitors flock from Spring to late Autumn is perched above the lake shore. The stylish upper town (Oberstadt) is centred on the **Marktplatz**★, from which the **Steigstraße**★, bordered by half-timbered old houses, offers delightful views of the lake.

STAYING IN MEERSBURG

Löwen – Marktplatz 2, ☎ 0 75 32/4 30 40, Fax 0 75 32/43 41 10. Single rooms from 85DM. 15C inn right on the market square.

Hotel 3 Stuben – Kirchstraße 7, ☎ 0 75 32/8 00 90, Fax 0 75 32/13 67. Single rooms from 145DM. Restored half-timbered house with modern furnishings, in the heart of the old town, starred restaurant with good cuisine.

For further recommendations see Überlingen and Lindau

Annette von Droste-Hülshoff, a poetess born in Westphalia in 1797, died in 1848 in her apartments in the Meersburg, the so-called **Altes Schloß**. This massive construction with over 100 rooms and walls up to 3m/10ft thick dominates the little town. It was purchased in 1838 – and saved from total ruin – by Josef von Laßberg, an antiquity specialist and the brother-in-law of Annette von Droste-Hülshoff, who came to live here in 1841. The two small tower rooms where she wrote some of her finest poetry can be visited. The memory of the author of the *Judenbuche (The Jew's Beech)* is honoured both here and in the **Droste-Museum** *(Fürstenhäusle, Stettener Straße)*. From the terrace of the **New Castle** there is a **panorama**★ of Lake Constance and the Säntis massif.

Friedrichshafen – Friedrichshafen, the second largest town on Lake Constance after Constance itself, is an important and lively port. Friedrichshafen also likes to be called the "Fair and Zeppelin town", in praise of its importance as an industrial centre and the birthplace of the dirigible. The lakeside offers one of the longest and prettiest promenade-quays. Friedrichshafen is the point of departure for boat excursions to the Rhine falls in Schaffhausen or to the "flower island" Mainau and the stilt houses in Unteruhldingen *(see Überlingen)*.

Zeppelin-Museum ⊘ – This museum located in the former harbour train station is devoted to Count Ferdinand Zepelin (1838-1917) who developed the dirigibles named after him in Friedrichshafen. Part of the legendary "Hindenburg", which exploded in Lakehurst in 1937, has been reconstructed, allowing visitors to grasp to some extent the dream of technology and luxury which it represented.
An art department housing works from the Middle Ages to contemporary times is attached to the museum. It portrays the interaction between art and technology.

Wasserburg – This much-visited village is squeezed onto a narrow peninsula jutting out into the lake. Appreciate it on foot, walking to the tip of the promontory.

★★ **Lindau im Bodensee** – *See LINDAU IM BODENSEE.*

The Bodensee seen from a Zeppelin – exclusive enjoyment

Dirigibles have started being built again in Friedrichshafen. In September 1997, the Zeppelin Neuer Technologie (NT) undertook its maiden journey. The airship sails at speeds of up to 130kmh/78mph, 97 years after the very first Zeppelin journey. It is small in comparison to its predecessors: 75m/240ft long with a volume of about 8 200m³/268 000cu ft. The LZ 129 Hindenburg was 245m/784ft long and had a volume of 200 000 m³, which is over 6.5 million cu ft. Inert helium gas is used to keep it in the air. This 12-seater is available to well-heeled tourists for a sightseeing trip over the Bodensee. The seating capacity is scheduled to increase to 40 soon.

BONN★

Nordrhein-Westfalen
Population 312 000
Michelin map 417 N 5

This city is placed at the gateway to the romantic Middle Rhine region. The site has been inhabited since it was a camp for Roman legionaries, but it was not until the 16C that the town became important as the residence of the electors and archbishops of Cologne. In the 18C, the fortifications were transformed into a Baroque residence. In 1949, Bonn was chosen as the "provisional" capital of the new West German Federal Republic, which resulted in its becoming a major city.
The parliamentary buildings are located in a well-off residential area on the banks of the Rhine, to the southeast of town. The **Villa Hammerschmidt** – the official headquarters of the Federal President before it was moved to Berlin – and the **Palais**

Schaumburg (used for diplomatic functions) are set in well-tended parkland. The neighbouring offices of the old Bundeskanzler (until the move to Berlin) were purpose-built in 1976. The two chambers of the ex-West German Federal Parliament sat in the **Bundeshaus**, while the government administrators had their offices in the office block nearby.

Bonn, whose status as German capital could never be more than provisional, nevertheless fulfilled that role for 40 years and became in the process a true seat of government. Even after the official transferring of the Federal Government to Berlin in the autumn of 1999, eight ministries remained in Bonn.

The whole town, including the Rhine and the surrounding countryside, can be seen from the **Alter Zoll** (CZ). The **view**★ of the river and the Siebengebirge range (see below) is particularly attractive in late afternoon and early evening. From the foot of the bastion, riverside promenades beckon those with time for a leisurely stroll (this is the departure point also for boat trips).

The Youth of Beethoven – Precursor of the great stream of Romantic music, **Ludwig van Beethoven** (1770-1827) was born and grew up in the quarter around the **church of St. Remigius** (CYZ). At 13, Beethoven was already an accomplished musician, playing violin, viola and harpsichord in the orchestra attached to the brilliant Court of the Elector. When he was 22, a fervent admirer of Mozart and Haydn, he left Bonn for good, arriving in Vienna with only his virtuosity at the piano as an asset.

The **Beethovenhalle** (CY), a bold example of modern architecture, is the impressive setting for Bonn's annual international Beethoven Festival. The architect was Siegfried Wolske.

SIGHTS

★ **Rheinisches Landesmuseum** (BZ M) – This museum offers an overview of the history, culture and art of the Middle and Lower Rhine region, from prehistory to the present, is traced on three floors. Closed for restoration until spring 2001.

The **Prehistoric Section** (Urgeschichtliche Abteilung) (1st floor) shows, the skull of the celebrated Neanderthal Man, interesting artefacts from the Stone and Bronze Ages and La Tène culture (weapons, metalwork, jewellery found in tumuli etc). The department of **Roman Antiquities**★ (Römische Abteilung) is particularly well endowed. Note the Altars to the Matrons, a cult popular with Roman soldiers stationed in the Rhinelands. The consecrational altar (AD 164) of the Matrons, discovered beneath Bonn Cathedral in 1928, clearly shows the distinguishing characteristic of these benevolent deities: a huge round headdress.

A masterpiece of Roman craft is the **Sun God Mosaic** (c 250 AD), which shows the Sun God in his chariot, surrounded by the signs of the Zodiac. Large memorial stones, such as that for Marcus Caelius found at Xanten (early 1C AD) illustrate funerary cults. Among the treasures of this particularly rich collection, admire also the delightful **bronze statuettes** (Venus, Diana, Hercules etc) and the **glassware**, often decorated with chased or spun motifs. Explanatory panels, illuminated illustrations and dioramas bring to life such facets of the city's early history as military service, building, water supply, traffic control and day-to-day existence in that period.

Pride of place in the **Frankish Section** is reserved for a reconstruction of a chieftain's tomb (c 600 AD). Weapons and above all jewellery are among the sepulchral gifts. The section from the **Middle Ages to the Present** displays arts and crafts from the Romanesque era to the 19C. Well represented are Romanesque sculpture (chancel parclose from Gustorf, 1130-40); sculptures carved from wood; and above all the **Gothic paintings** (Master of the Life of St Ursula, Master of St Severin, Barthel Bruyn the Elder, Derick Baegert etc); **Dutch painting** of the 16C and 17C.

★ **Münster** (Collegiate Church) (BCZ) – The former Stiftskirche St. Cassius und Florentius grew out of a cultic place dating to the second half of the 3C and then room churches from the 5C AD and the Carolingian era. The 11C-13C is what marks the architecture of the church today, stylistic elements from the Romanesque and Gothic eras are harmoniously interwoven.

The Romanesque baptismal font and the Romanesque stone carvings at the stairway to the choir are worthy of especial note, as is the c 1200 graffito drawing depicting the Madonna standing between St. Casius and Florentius. A fresco (c 1300) shows the Virgin Mary's welcome in heaven. The sacristy was built in 1619, whilst the rest of the furnishings are mostly from the Baroque period or the end of the 19C.

Under the high chancel is a three-naved crypt (1040) with a shrine to the martyrs. The atmospheric Romanesque **cloister**★ (c 1150) is considered one of the best-preserved examples of its day in Germany.

Beethovenhaus (Beethoven's Birthplace) ⊙ (CY D) – Beethoven was born in this house in the old town of Bonn in 1770. It has been a museum since 1890, showing authentic documents relating to the life and opus of the great composer. These

BONN

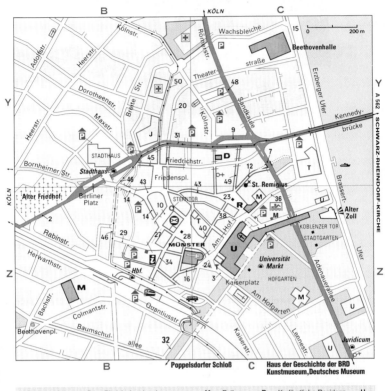

Beethovenhaus ... **D**   Rheinisches Landesmuseum ... **M**   Rathaus ... **R**   Kurfürstliche Residenz ... **U**

include portraits of Beethoven and his friends, original hand-written documents, his instruments (grand piano, string instruments), his listening horns and life and death masks of the master.

Rathaus (Town Hall) (CZ R) – A charming Rococo building (1738) with a pink and grey façade and a fine outside staircase with two flights.

Kurfürstliche Residenz (Electors' Residence) (CZ U) – The lawns of the **Hofgarten** park make a fine setting for this long Baroque building (1697-1725). Since 1818 the palace has housed the university.

★ **Haus der Geschichte der Bundesrepublik Deutschland** ⊘ – *Adenauerallee 250*. This is the first museum of contemporary history to be opened in Germany. Great efforts have been made to present recent history in an interesting way – with displays making full use of modern audio-visual technology such as video screens, interactive control panels and electronic buttons. Older visitors will be able to retrace the historical events of their youth, while the younger generations, for whom this museum already seems to be a popular attraction, watch fascinated as the past unfolds before their eyes. Economic and social history are just as interestingly portrayed as recent cultural and political evolution. From Konrad Adenauer's official Mercedes, to an ice-cream parlour or a cinema from the 1950s, no item of potential historical interest is left out. Even the rough wooden seats used by Mikhail Gorbachev and Helmut Kohl during their summit meeting in the Kaukasus Platz in 1990 are to be seen here. The evolution of the former East German Republic (DDR) is unfolded at the same time as that of the former West German Republic (BDR).
During construction work, a **Roman cellar** was uncovered, which was incorporated into the museum *(basement level)*. Should visitors find that the two labourers standing on the balcony in front of the library do not look exactly enthusiastic about setting to work, then they should not be surprised as the sculpture group is the work of contemporary Realist artist **Duane Hansen**.

Rocket-carrier by Daimler-Benz, Deutsches Museum Bonn

★ Kunstmuseum Bonn (Bonn Museum of Art) ⊘ – *Friedrich-Ebert-Allee 2.*
The charm of Axel Schulter's exciting architecture lies not so much in the façade as in the interior of this spacious building, adorned with a particularly elegant circular staircase. The ground floor houses works by the Expressionists, with particular emphasis on the œuvre of **August Macke**, who lived in Bonn. In the adjoining rooms are exhibitions of German art since 1945 (Nay, Emil Schumacher, Günther Uecker). On the first floor each room is devoted to a particular artist, among others Gerhard Richter, Anselm Kiefer, Georg Baselitz, AR Penck, Marcus Lüpertz. Three rooms are devoted to the constructions of Joseph Beuys alone. From room 15, which contains the work of Gerhard Richter, there is a delightful **view** of the neighbouring **National Art Gallery and Exhibition Hall** ⊘ (Kunst- und Ausstellungshalle der Bundesrepublik Deutschland) by Viennese architect Gustav Peichl with three spires representing science, art and technology. It is used for changing exhibitions on graphic arts, science, technology and architecture.
The 16 pillars in front of the building symbolise the 16 Federal German states.

Deutsches Museum Bonn ⊘ – *Ahrstraße 45.*
This museum, which is an offshoot of the famous museum in Munich, has as its theme "Research and Technology in Germany since 1945", a particularly exciting period in the history of technology. Technological advances in both the former West and East Germanies are covered here. Modern media presentations, video and videophones present a comprehensive picture of German technology and its combination of tradition and innovation.

Poppelsdorfer Schloß (BZ) – The design of this building was entrusted to the French architect **Robert de Cotte**. It was built between 1715 and 1753. A splendid dual carriageway avenue, bordered by chestnut trees and divided by a broad grass strip (the **Poppelsdorfer Allee, BZ 32**), links it to the electoral castle.
The outer façade, with its three wings, reflects a classical French influence, while the inner courtyard, bordered by a semicircular colonnade, is more Italian in style. At the back, on level ground where a moat once flowed, are the university's **Botanical Gardens**.

Alter Friedhof (Old Cemetery) (BZ) – Artists, scholars and celebrities are buried here. One can visit the graves of Robert and Clara Schumann, Beethoven's mother, Ernst Moritz Arndt, August Wilhelm von Schlegel, and others.

OUTSKIRTS

★ Schwarz-Rheindorf – *Leave by the Kennedy bridge (CY).*
This **two-storey chapel★** in Romanesque style was consecrated in 1151. The lower chapel contains expressive murals with scenes depicting the Four Mysteries of Christ from the Book of Ezekiel. The upper chapel has a throne for the emperor like its model, the Pfalzkapelle in Aachen.

Bad Godesberg – With its comfortable villas and many parks (Redoute, Draitschbrunnen), this rich residential suburb south of the city is the seat of ministries and international organizations. The **riverside walk** between the Rhine ferry landing-stages is very popular. The Petersberg Hotel and the Drachenfels ruins overlook the heavy flow of traffic on the river.
The ruins of **Godesburg Castle** ⊘, built in the 13C by the Prince-Electors of Cologne, stand on a basalt outcrop in the town centre. From the keep, there is a fine **panoramic view★** of Godesberg, the Bonn depression northwards as far as Cologne, and the Siebengebirge massif.

EXCURSIONS

★ **Siebengebirge (The Seven Mountains)** – This massif, which reaches an altitude of 460m/1 472ft and is the Rhine's northernmost wine-growing region, rises opposite Bad Godesberg on the eastern bank of the Rhine. Its name (seven mountain range) comes from the seven prominent summits that were once almost all crowned by a castle. These hills and volcanic cones, surrounded by Germany's oldest nature protection area, are favourites with local day-trippers and holidaymakers in search of that old romantic Rhine feeling. It is readily available in the towns and culturally significant buildings such as the chancel ruin of Heisterbach Monastery and in the picturesque inns and wine establishments.

At the foot of the range, bordering the Rhine, are the localities of **Bad Honnef-Rhöndorf** (house of Konrad Adenauer) and **Königswinter**, from where a **funicular** ⊙ rises to the jagged **Drachenfels★** ruins. It was here, so the legend has it, that Siegfried, the hero of the *Nibelungen*, slew the dragon and then bathed in its blood to render himself invulnerable.

From the terrace, near the ruins of the castle tower, the visitor can admire a vast **panorama★★** comprising (from left to right) the Weserwald and Eifel plateaux, Bad Godesberg, Bonn, and finally Cologne.

Halfway up the Drachenfels is the neo-Gothic Schloß Drachenburg, built at the end of the 19C in the middle of a park.

Remagen – *23km/14mi to the south. Leave by the Adenauerallee* (**CZ**).

Passing Mehlem, one sees on the right the ivy covered ruins of **Rolandsbogen**, and, on the left, the island of **Nonnenwerth**, linked to it by legend.

The origin of the small town of Remagen goes back to a Roman fortified camp. Finds from that period are exhibited in the **Roman Museum** (Römisches Museum) at *Kirchstr.9*, the former 16C Knechtstedener Chapel. Remagen became famous when its **bridge** across the Rhine fell into American hands almost intact on 7 March 1945 – the first time the Americans had been able to establish a bridgehead east of the river. Then days later, the bridge collapsed under the weight of armoured vehicles. The remaining towers are today the site of a Peace Museum, **Friedensmuseum** ⊙, tracing the history of the bridge and the battles of March 1945. In the town itself, see the **parish church**: its outer wall is furnished with **double Romanesque doors** – a carriage entrance and one for pedestrians. The reliefs which embellish the arches represent sirens and fantastic beasts.

BRAUNSCHWEIG

BRUNSWICK – Niedersachsen
Population 260 000
Michelin map 416/418 J 15

Brunswick was already considered a striving industrial region at the beginning of the Industrial Revolution, and it remains so to this day, with focus on engineering, tool and car manufacturing and the production of optical equipment. The Technical University, one of the best in the country, arose from the Collegium Carolinum, where astronomer, physicist and mathematician **Carl-Friedrich Gauß** once did his research. In addition, other scientific research institutions and federal offices, such as the Federal Air-Travel Agency, have also settled here and collaborate closely with local companies – especially in the future-oriented areas of biochemistry and high technology. The first soccer match on the European continent was held here. After the devastation of the Second World War, the inner city was rebuilt according to modern urban concepts.

HISTORICAL NOTES

Till Eulenspiegel Country – Memories of the famous jester and buffoon, Till Eulenspiegel, spread far and wide from the beginning of the 16C by storytellers and minstrels, are especially cherished in his native Brunswick. He was born c 1300 in **Schöppenstedt**, 23km/14mi southeast of the city, where there is a small museum in his honour.

A Cultured Court – Brunswick ceased being a princely residence after the death of Henry the Lion, but the Court was reinstated in 1753 by a younger branch of the House of Brunswick. In 1807, after its conquest by Napoleon, the region was added to the ephemeral kingdom of Westphalia. The young Stendhal (Henri Beyle) spent almost two years in Brunswick at this time, first as Commissioner for War, and subsequently as Steward of the Emperor's Domains.

Patrons of the arts were numbered among the later Brunswick princes: it was Karl II who invited Goethe to stage the first performance of *Faust* in the city in 1828.

Stadt Braunschweig

The Lion of Brunswick

The Lion of Brunswick – In 1166, having boosted the House of Guelph to the summit of political power in Germany, Henry the Lion, Duke of Bavaria and Saxony, settled permanently in Brunswick. Frederick Barbarossa, offended at Henry's meteoric rise, summoned him before the Diet. When "the Lion" refused to appear, he stripped him of everything except his personal properties between the Upper Weser and the Lower Elbe. Henry the Lion died in 1195. The lion sculpture on Burgplatz, the first large freestanding sculpture to be installed north of the Alps, dates to that period.

SIGHTS

★ **Dom (Cathedral)** – The Westwerk supports two octagonal towers, linked the whole way up by a Gothic bell gable (1275) which acts as a campanile. This general design was later copied by other churches in the city. The original Romanesque church built by Henry the Lion has groined vaulting with the weight reduced by sizeable cut-outs. The aisles on the north side create a Late Gothic hall with spiral columns turned in alternate directions. The choir and transept are decorated with 13C painted murals. Note especially: the massive seven-branched c 1180 **candelabrum**★ (Bronzeleuchter) in the choir, a donation by Henry the Lion; and the impressive mid-12C cross by Master Imervard in the northern side nave whose **Christ**★ is severely folded clothed, in a long-sleeved shirt. Another Romanesque work of art is the **Marian Altar**, which was consecrated in 1188. A part of the relics were set into the central post. An outstanding example of Saxon sculpting is the **tomb** of Henry the Lion and his second wife, Matilda of England, located in the central nave. In the main crypt beneath the chancel, an independent three-naved church, are the tombs of the Guelph princes.

Altstadtmarkt – One steps back in time when visiting this district, where the old municipal institutions of Brunswick's merchant quarter can be seen. The old **town hall** (Altstadtrathaus) is built with stepped gables, the two wings set at right angles to one another (13C-15C). The buttresses of buildings facing the square support statues of the princes of Saxony and the House of Guelph. In the middle of the Poststraße is the **Drapers' Hall** (Gewandhaus), the building with the town's most decorated gable (Late Renaissance). Four principal floors rise above the street, and these are surmounted by four further pediment levels. The divisions of the gable are softened by inverted consoles, statuettes and globes topped by stone spikes.

Martinikirche – St. Martini, the Hanseatic church at Altstadtmarkt, is the burghers' counterpart to the Brunswick cathedral. For centuries it was the city's richest church. This can still be seen in its architecture and in the artworks inside. The church serves as a "little history of German art", as it were. It begins in the Romanesque period with 12C towers, continues with the Gothic period (transept façade from 1320, St Anne altar of 1434). The wealthy furnishings begin in the Renaissance and end in the Baroque age with the high altar (1722-25). The group of epitaphs from the 16C and 17C suggests the connection to the powers that be (monuments to mayors, jurists, officers). Indeed, St. Martini represents power and pride of the Hanseatic League and its merchants as no other church in northern Germany.

Herzog Anton-Ulrich-Museum ⊘ – The painting gallery is mainly devoted to Flemish and Dutch Masters of the 17C: Rembrandt (*Family Portrait, Stormy Landscape*), Rubens, Vermeer, Ruysdael. Worth attention also are the 16C German painters (Cranach the Elder, Holbein the Younger, Adam Elsheimer), and the 15C Italian artists (Palma Vecchio, Giorgione).
Works ranging from the time of Dürer to the present day are on display in the gallery of drawings and engravings (Kupferstichkabinett). A department of Baroque and Renaissance decorative arts completes the museum collections (furniture, bronze statuettes, ivories and watches in the first case; majolica and Limoges enamels in the second).

Medieval Art Collection in the Burg Dankwarderode ⊙ – This collection of church plate, on display in the ducal castle, includes a reliquary of the arm of St Blaise (patron saint of the cathedral and protector of the Guelphs), the imperial robes of King Otto IV, and the Gospels from the church of St. Ägidius.

EXCURSION

Königslutter am Elm – *20km/12mi to the east.*
On the fringe of the lovely beech forests of the Elm, Königslutter is renowned for its former abbey (Abteikirche) better known as the **Imperial Cathedral★** (Kaiserdom). This is a Romanesque basilica with three naves and five apses revealing northern Italian influence. The principal nave is embellished with a fine, Lombard-inspired, **carved decoration★★** (the hunting frieze). The north doorway is original: it comprises three lobes upheld by twisted columns, each supported by a lion. Kaiser Lothar, the patron and founder of the Kaiserdom, who laid the cornerstone together with his wife Rihenza, is buried in the church.
The north gallery of the **cloister★** consists of two Romanesque naves with groined vaulting resting on elaborate fluted, trellised and chevroned columns.

BREMEN★★

Bremen
Population 552 000
Michelin map 415 G 10

Bremen, at the inner end of the long Weser estuary, and Bremerhaven, its outer harbour 59km/37mi downstream, together form a remarkable port system. Bremen itself is Germany's oldest maritime city. It had market rights from 965; in 1358 it joined the Hanseatic League; in 1646 it was declared a Free Imperial city; and direct trading with America began as early as 1783. By tradition it is a cotton and coffee town, its Cotton Exchange ranks with Liverpool's as a world authority.
Bremen is also a town of culture, where the Weser Renaissance architectural style blossomed. For those interested in food, the city specialities are chicken ragout (Kükenragout), Vegesack herring (Vegesacker Matjeshering), and black pudding with cabbage (Braunkohl mit Pinkelwurst).

Die Bremischen Häfen (The Harbours) ⊙ – The Bremen harbour group (including Bremen City and Bremerhaven) provides employment directly or indirectly for over 25% of the city's population. With a turnover of over 34 million tonnes (1997), these harbours are the largest in Germany after Hamburg.
Bremen specialises in the importation of raw materials:

> **Coffee bean city**
>
> Bremen's close links with coffee date back over three centuries. The first ever coffee house in German-speaking countries was built here in 1673, before those in Vienna and Hamburg. Half of all the cups of coffee drunk in Germany are brewed from beans imported via the port at Bremen.

timber, copper ore, wool, cotton, coffee, tobacco, cereals and cocoa. By far the most important of its activities is however the handling of container transport and cars. In 1997 about 1.7 million containers passed through the Wilhelm-Kaisen-Terminal, Europe's largest container transhipment terminal, and over one million motor vehicles went through the docks. The harbour group of Bremerhaven is Europe's leading port for the turn-around of vehicles.

OLD BREMEN

★★ **Marktplatz (Z)** – The market square, its wide expanse surrounded by the finest buildings in the city, lies in the heart of the old town. The centre is marked by a giant 10m/33ft **statue of Roland** beneath a Gothic canopy (1404). The knight bears the sword of justice and a shield adorned with the imperial eagle.
The **Schütting (A)**, a restrained but elegant 16C building, used to house Bremen's Guild of Merchants. The decoration of its façade shows a Flemish influence.

★ **Rathaus (Town hall)** ⊙ **(Z R)** – The main building is Gothic, its upper floors crowned by decorative gables – part of a 17C transformation made in the Weser Renaissance style. The three-storey principal façade rises from an arcaded gallery emphasized by a richly carved balustrade. Above this, tall windows alternate with statues of Charlemagne and the Seven Electors (copies: the Gothic originals are in the Focke-Museum). Three Renaissance gables embellish the top floor.

At the corner of the west wing is a bronze group by the modern sculptor Gerhard Marcks representing the *Animal Musicians of Bremen* (a pyramid formed by an ass, a dog, a cat, and a cockerel) – characters from a popular fairy tale by the Brothers Grimm.

Interior – A splendid **spiral staircase**★★ (Wendeltreppe) in carved wood (1620) adorns the first floor Council Chamber. The room's Renaissance decoration recalls connections with the law courts *(The Judgement of Solomon)* and with the sea (models of boats). The **Guildhall** (Güldenkammer) – a small council chamber renovated between 1903 and 1905 by Heinrich Vogeler – is noteworthy for its sumptuous leather wall hangings enriched with gold.

The Ratskeller (wine cellar) serves exclusively German wines from 600 different vineyards.

★ **St. Petri-Dom** (Z) – In general, the cathedral presents much the same massive appearance as it did in the 11C, but traces of the 16C and 19C rebuilding are clearly evident in the exterior detail.

Inside, against the first left-hand pillar of the raised chancel, stands a fine 16C **Virgin and Child**★. Among the 16C carvings on the organ balustrade can be seen, in the middle, the figures of Charlemagne and Willehad, the first Bishop of Bremen, who both carry a small replica of the cathedral as it looked in 1500. Beneath the organ loft, the 11C western crypt houses Romanesque capitals and a magnificent bronze **baptismal font**★★ (Taufbecken, c 1220). A small organ by Gottfrid Silbermann also stands here, the only one outside Saxony. The eastern crypt, which dates to the age of the early Salian Franks boasts important capitals adorned with checkerboard ornamentation and mythological animals.

At the end of the right-hand aisle, a gallery from the **cathedral museum** (Dom-Museum) displays items recovered from tombs beneath the nave – in particular, medieval vestments and a priceless 13C bishop's crozier.

In a small room in the southern nave is the tomb of the famous Baron Knigge, who lived in Bremen from 1790 until his death in 1796.

The inner courtyard leads to the **Lead Cellar** (Bleikeller), which displays eight mummified bodies in glass coffins. The mummification is a result of the extremely dry air in the cellar.

Pfarrkirche Unserer Lieben Frauen (Church of Our Lady) (Z B) – The bare interior of this hall church (construction began in 1229), which, except for the 1709 chancel, shows no decoration, is relieved by rounded ogive vaulting dating to the construction period. The four main stained-glass windows, on Biblical themes, were executed between 1966 and 1979 by Alfred Manessier.

A simple crypt with a groined vault and a single central pillar dating from the preceding church (St. Veit), which has been traced to 1020 and therefore represents the oldest built-up space in Bremen.

Stadtwaage (Weigh-House) (Z D) – A lovely 16C building constructed with alternating layers of brick and embossed stone.

★ **Böttcherstraße** (Z) – This narrow street, running from the Marktplatz to the River Weser, was built between 1923 and 1933 by the industrialist Ludwig Roselius, who had become wealthy through the coffee trade. While architects Runge and Scotland took the local building style as their inspiration, Bernhard Hoetger gave free rein to his imagination, drawing on the Expressionist style with Jugendstil (Art Nouveau) and Art Deco overtones. The tall, gabled buildings of this highly original street house art galleries, museums, a theatre, bookshops and taverns. Between two of the gables, a porcelain carillon chimes at noon, 3pm and 6pm.

★ **Paula-Modersohn-Becker-Museum** ⊘ (Z E) – The Paula Modersohn-Becker house was built by Bernhard Hoetger and provides the ideal setting for the display of paintings, drawings and graphic work by Becker-Modersohn (1876-1907), one of the pioneers of modern art. The first and second floors of the house are given over to the varied work of Bernhard Hoetger, who made a name for himself as a sculptor.

The **Museum in the Roselius-Haus**, a merchant's mansion dating from 1588, contains examples of domestic decor, luxurious furnishings and furniture, paintings and craftwork from the 12C to 19C. Works from Cranach the Elder's studio and a Lamentation group by Tilman Riemenschneider are the high points of this collection built up by Roselius.

Atlantishaus (No 2) (Z F) – This 1931 block, decorated with the signs of the zodiac, has an unusual spiral staircase made of concrete and glass.

Not far from there, beyond the Martinistraße, on the banks of the Weser, is the 13C-14C hall-church of St. Martini ⊘.

BREMEN

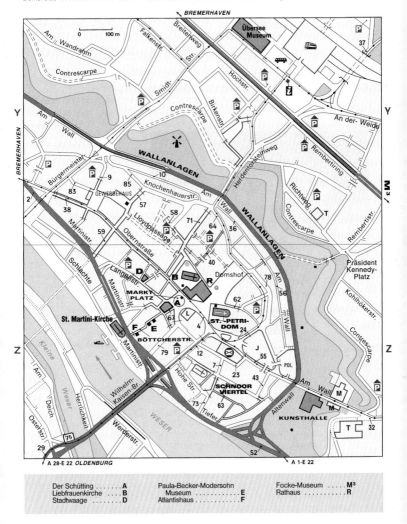

Der Schütting .... A	Paula-Becker-Modersohn Museum .... E	Focke-Museum ..... M³
Liebfrauenkirche ..... B	Atlantishaus .... F	Rathaus .... R
Stadtwaage .... D		

ADDITIONAL SIGHTS

★ **Wallanlagen (Rampart Promenade)** (YZ) – The walk includes a delightful green belt where the ancient bastions used to be. The working windmill here puts a picturesque accent on the area.

★ **The Schnoor** (Z) – The cottages in this quarter, once the homes of fisherfolk, are all that remains of Old Bremen. In styles ranging from the 15C to the 19C, they have all been restored and are now used as art galleries, antique shops, restaurants and craft boutiques. The narrow streets of the quarter, popular with tourists, are very busy after dark.

★ **Kunsthalle (Art Gallery)** ⊘ (Z) – An outstanding collection of 19C and 20C French and German art is the main attraction here. On display are works by: Courbet, Delacroix and the Barbizon School; Menzel, Leibl, Beckmann; the French Impressionists and their German counterparts, in particular Liebermann and Corinth; artists of the Worpswede School *(see below)*, notably Paula Becker-Modersohn and her husband Otto Modersohn. Earlier periods of European art are illustrated

139

by 15C Old Masters, and by Rubens, Terborch, Rembrandt, Tiepolo, Maulbertsch etc up to Picasso. In the print room (Kupferstichkabinett) are over 230 000 prints and drawings of exceptional quality from Dürer's day to the present.

Übersee-Museum (Overseas Museum) ⊙ **(Y)** – Well-displayed exhibits in this museum are devoted to Oceania, Japan, Southeast Asia, India, Africa, China and Australia. The best items, either original or in the form of scale models, relate to living conditions (a Papuan village, a Chinese house completely furnished), to occupations (fishing boats), and to customs and beliefs (legendary masks, effigies of ancestors, objects of worship). There is even a miniature Shinto temple and a Zen garden.

On the first floor there is a collection of masks from Black Africa. The second floor is concerned with the economic life of Bremen and in particular its port activities.

★★ **Focke-Museum** ⊙ **(Y M³)** – *Leave via the Rembertiring (Y).*

This regional museum (Focke-Museum) nestled amid parkland covers the artistic and cultural evolution of Bremen and its surroundings. It houses all these treasures from 1000 years of Bremen history in four historic buildings and one modern main house.

The newly opened Main House (Haupthaus) holds some particularly noteworthy objects in the entrance hall underlining some topics that have remained important to Bremen to this day: the Bremen house, the Weser, Bremen silverware, car and shipbuilding. This is followed by a chronological tour that begins at the finds from the archbishops' tombs in the Dom to medieval sculptures and the splendidly carved furniture from the Reformation. The history of the city is closely knitted with a colourful cultural history depicted in painted vistas and people, images and models of ships, day-to-day equipment and decorative arts; This underlines the unique qualities of the region and the independence of the city. Shipping and trade are just one aspect of the sea-oriented history of this ancient Hanseatic town.

Glass goblet (mid 19C), Focke-Museum

Focke-Museum, Bremen

Return to the ground floor.

The prehistoric collections from the region can be seen in a thatched annex. A farmhouse – a Lower German hall house from Mittelsbüren built around 1586 – on the museum grounds is devoted to the inland areas of Bremen. A permanent exhibition here depicts the history of this village, which had to give way to a steel mill in 1955. The Tarnstedter Scheune (Tarnstedt Barn) shows the products of rural work.

Haus Riensberg also belongs to the museum (*right from the lane leading to the Focke-Museum*). This house built in the second half of the 18C was once an estate and summer residence for upper class Bremen families. It displays the collections covering bourgeois lifestyle, toys, portraits of Bremen burghers and collections with supra-regional significance of Fürstenberg porcelain and European glass art.

EXCURSION

Worpswede – *24km/15mi north – about 1hr 30min. Leave Bremen by the Rembertiring (Y).*

Isolated at one time in a desolate landscape of peat moors, the village of Worpswede attracted at the end of the 19C a colony of artists, notable among whom were Paula Becker-Modersohn, her husband and the poet Rainer Maria Rilke. Since then, galleries, studios and craft workshops have multiplied. Odd, asymmetrical buildings such as the Worpswede Café and the Niedersachsenstein First World War Memorial illustrate the avant-garde ideas and innovations of the architects allied to the group.

BREMERHAVEN*

Bremen

Population 132 000
Michelin map 415 F 9
Town plan in the current Michelin Red Guide Deutschland

Bremerhaven, founded at the mouth of the Weser estuary in 1827, is Bremen's deep-sea port and one of Europe's major gateways to the ocean (see also Bremen – Die Bremischen Häfen).

The **Columbuskaje ship terminal**, once the home of transatlantic luxury liners, now handles ferries and cruise ships, while north of the town there is an immense specialized basin (Kaiser Wilhelm Container Terminal), protected from the tides, designed for the rapid turnaround of ore freighters and container ships.

The **fishing port** (Fischereihafen), in the southern part of Bremerhaven, harbours half of Germany's trawler fleet.

Visit the famous fish auction, held in the Fischauktionshallen sheds from 7am, Mondays to Fridays.

Deutsches Schiffahrtsmuseum, Bremerhaven

★★ **Deutsches Schiffahrtsmuseum (National Maritime Museum)** ⊘ – The idea behind the museum was to examine and portray German maritime history in all fields from its beginning in prehistory right up to the present time. This has been achieved in an open-air museum and by exhibits displayed in a museum that was designed by Hans Scharoun.

Basement – Liners with staterooms from 1897 to 1999; paddle steamer "Meißen" with its boiler and engine rooms; bridge and controls of the nuclear-powered freighter Otto Hahn, built in 1968; steel hulls from the origins until today; harbour activities for freight and containers; "miniport" with remote controlled ship models.

Ground floor – The age of the great sailing ships (16C-19C); especially large models of sailing ships, dioramas and harbour models.

First floor – Navigation by sun and stars, ocean maps and marine markers. German navy from 1848 till today with the pocket "Seehund" class U-boat (1944). Sport boats with sails, oars, or paddles.

Koggehalle – The medieval navy with the Hanseatic cog built in 1380 in Bremen excavated in 1962 during bulldozing work in the Weser. Rhine ship of the Oberländer type, sunk 1 000 years ago near Krefeld. Exhibitions on shipping archeology and the preservation of wet wood. The beginning of shipping until the Vikings, with reconstruction of the world's oldest known boats (over 10 000 years old), ships on rock paintings, the battering ram of a Roman ship, the continued history of the Viking boats into the 20C.

141

Exhibition in the annex – Fleets of sports boats, fishing boats, farmers' boats and salvaging boats. History of marine and polar research with tide calculators, depiction of deep-sea diving and polar expeditions, whaling and deep-sea fishing, whale skeleton and fish auction.

Freilichtmuseum (Open-Air Museum) ⊘ – Eight historic craft are preserved in the Old Port. Moored in the dock basin are: the sailing ship Grönland, which accompanied the first German polar expedition in 1868; the three-master *Seute Deern* (Germany's last wooden sailing ship, 1919); the lightship *Elbe III* (1909); the ocean-going salvage tug *Seefalke*; the small Antarctic whaler *Rau IX*; the inland coastal ship *Emma* from the Oderhaff; the high-speed patrol launch *Kranich*. On shore are the tug *Stier* (with forward propulsion using Voith-Schneider propellers, the concrete ship Paul Kossel (1920), an experimental hydroplane (1953) and a Walter engine (for U-boats) that can run without outside air; and various harbour equipment such as cranes, harbour lights etc.

Technikmuseum U-Boot Wilhelm Bauer (Submarine Museum) ⊘ – Launched in January 1945, this submarine (U 2450) was scuttled on 4 May, shortly before the German capitulation.
It was refloated in 1957 to serve as an experimental unit. A visit to the museum gives some idea of the technical complexity of a submarine as well as the way of life aboard one.

Deichpromenade – From the top of the breakwater (converted into a promenade) on the south side of the Geeste estuary, it is possible to see the mouth of the Weser and watch the great diversity of ships sailing by.

Zoo am Meer (Aquarium) ⊘ – This zoo on the outer dyke of the Weser specialises in animals from northern latitudes and the world's oceans. A special feature is the aquarium with fish from the North Sea. Out in the open-air section of the zoo, polar bears (for which this zoo is one of the most successful breeding centres in the world) can be seen playing around in the company of sea-lions, seals, penguins and a variety of sea birds.

EXCURSION

Cuxhaven – *39km/24mi to the north.*
At the mouth of the Elbe, Cuxhaven is not only Germany's second fishing port but also a control point for navigation in the estuary and a seaside resort. There is an excellent **observation point**★ on the **Alte Liebe** (Old Love) Pier (the name derives from a mispronunciation of *Olivia* – the name of a ship that sank close inshore in 1732, whose wreck was for a time used as a primitive landing-stage). At the far end of the breakwater marking the geographic – if not the hydrographic – limits of the Elbe estuary stands the **Kugelbake**, a huge beacon no longer used but known to sailors the world over. From here there is a splendid **view**★ of the river mouth and the open sea.

Wrackmuseum (Wreck Museum) ⊘ – This museum vividly retraces maritime losses and the hazards of navigation in the dangerous waters of the German bight and the Elbe, Weser and Ems estuaries.

Schloß BRUCHSAL★★

Baden-Württemberg

Michelin map 419 S 9 – 17km/11mi north of Karlsruhe

Bruchsal, residence of the last four prince-bishops of Speyer, is blessed with a pretentious **Baroque palace** comprising something like 50 dwellings or annexes (reconstructed after the total destruction of 1945). Maximilian von Welsch was the architect of this vast complex, begun in 1720 on the orders of the Prince-Bishop Damian Hugo von Schönborn. The main road from Karlsruhe to Heidelberg runs through the extensive palace grounds.

Central Block ⊘ – Pride of place here is held by a magnificent **staircase**★★ with an oval well designed by Balthasar Neumann in 1731. Rococo stucco decorates the dome above it. The state apartments **(Regional Museum)** have items from the original furnishings on display. Apart from silver and porcelain tableware, portraits of the prelates can be seen and, above all, **tapestries** from the 16C to the 18C. These, fabricated in the renowned workshops of Holland and France (Beauvais), include a series representing scenes from ancient Greece.
At the west end of the castle's main block, the Gartensaal – a vaulted room with a marble floor – opens onto the **park** (Hofgarten). When they were at their best, blazing with formal flowerbeds in the French manner, the gardens boasted a broadwalk that extended as far as the river, 16km/10mi away.

** Museum Mechanischer Musikinstrumente

(Mechanical Musical Instruments Museum) ⊘ – *In the main building. Guided tour of about 1hr, with demonstration of instruments.*

This department of the Regional Museum derives from a private collection and includes about 400 instruments ranging from the 18C to the present day, most of them worked by cylinders, pricked-out metal or cardboard, or rolls of paper. Cinema organs, "Barbary organs", and pianolas (mechanical pianos operated by perforated "piano-rolls") are also represented. Note particularly the "household" **organs** and **orchestrions** (in 19C England Aeolian Orchestrelles – machines resembling an oversize upright piano, complete with manual keyboard and stops for different "voices" – wind-operated by means of pedals). Orchestrions were often conceived as two-part instruments, imitating both piano and violin via their organ pipes. Before the arrival of the phonograph, such machines usually provided the music in taverns and at fairs. Many of the instruments were decorated with mechanical figures. The philharmonic organ by Freiburg manufacturer Welte was intended for the *Titanic*, but was not delivered in time for the fateful voyage. Examples from Leipzig and the Black Forest are well represented here.

Music-Box Victory (1942)

T. Goldschmidt/BADISCHES LANDESMUSEUM

Städtisches Museum (Municipal Museum) ⊘ – *Southern part of the main block, on the attic floor.*

The museum is divided up into five areas: The paleontological collection, which also contains minerals from Bruchsal and its surrounding area; the prehistoric department with regional finds from the Late Stone Age (mainly from the Michelsberger Culture) and Iron Ages and from the Roman period to the end of the Middle Ages; the Bruchsal penal system; the numismatic and medal collections of the former state of Baden, the Palatinate and the Prince-Episcopate of Speyer.

BRÜHL

Nordrhein-Westfalen

Population 41 500

Michelin map 417 N 4

This town to the south of Cologne is widely known for its castles, which are open to the public as museums and have been placed on the UNESCO's World heritage list.

** SCHLOSS AUGUSTUSBURG ⊘ *tour: 1hr*

The Rococo castle was built by Westphalian master-builder Johann Conrad Schlaun and Bavarian court architect François Cuvilliés between 1725 and 1768, for the Archbishop and Elector of Cologne Clemens August. This prominent figure, originally from Wittelsbach, was appointed to an impressive number of different offices: in addition to being Archbishop and Elector of Cologne, he was also Bishop of Hildesheim, Münster and Osnabrück and Paderborn, Grand Master of the Teutonic Order. Augustusburg Castle was his favourite residence, at which he was able to indulge his passion for hunting and could hold court in magnificent style. Accordingly, the castle was sumptuously furnished.

★★ **Staircase** – The Würzburg court architect **Balthasar Neumann** produced one of his most beautiful compositions in this splendid staircase. The marble stuccowork, used in abundance, is in shades of greyish-green and yellowish-orange. Four powerful, vivacious supporting figures are grouped around each pillar and hold up the vault. The staircase is edged with an elaborate, wrought-iron railing, the work of Johann Georg Sandtener, as is the lantern light overhead. The stuccowork by Guiseppe Artario and the **ceiling fresco**★ by Carlo Carlone are in celebration of the Prince and of the House of Wittelsbach.

★★ **Interior** – A good two dozen rooms can be visited.

Large new suite: This suite comprises a garden room with ceiling fresco by Carlo Carlone, a dining room with gallery and elaborate ceiling and wall paintings, a magnificent **audience chamber**★, with a wonderful ceiling decorated in 1750 with stuccowork by Giuseppe Artario and paintings by Joseph Billieux, and a bedroom with fine wood panelling. The pulpit desk here, made by Johann Caspar Winkhler, is the most valuable piece of furniture known from the Prince's possessions.

Summer suite: The rooms in this suite are all on the ground floor and were intended for use on hot summer days. In order to reinforce the airy impression, the floors are covered in blue and white tiles from Rotterdam, which are laid in attractive patterns. The rooms feature beautiful stucco ceilings, exquisitely painted over-doors, various costly items of furniture and numerous paintings which are associated with the family of the Prince and also with his love of hunting.

Yellow suite: The yellow suite was principally used by Clemens August as his private residence. Cuvilliés designed the rooms in the Regence style, and they are adorned with stucco ceilings with rosettes, damask wall hangings and panelling with gilded ornamental woodcarvings. The furniture here too is beautiful.

★ **Garden** – The Lenôtre student Dominique Girardet designed the garden in 1727-28. The most important part of the garden is the large decorative garden with reflecting pond embraced by alleys to the south of the castle. The two-part embroided ridge is considered to be one of the most authentic examples of classical French landscape architecture. The French garden gradually gives way to a country park that was designed around 1840 by Peter Joseph Lenné.

★ SCHLOß FALKENLUST ⊙

Some 2.5km/1.5mi from Schloß Augustusburg. Go past the mirror pond and over Falkenluster Allee. A 20min slide show with synchronised sound provides an insight into the history of the building and the appointments of this castle.

This captivating little Rococo castle owes its creation to the Prince's passion for hunting. Clemens August considered hunting with falcons in particular to be his own personal privilege and pursued it with great enthusiasm.

The two-storey plastered building with its belvedere and lantern roof is designed in an absolutely symmetrical shape.

Ground floor: The vestibule houses life-sized statues; the salon, which was intended for hunting parties, is tiled with blue and white tiles from Rotterdam and the

Phantasialand, Brühl

dining room is wood panelled and richly decorated with stuccowork and rocaille. The small **japanned room**★ with its lacquered paintings, a beautiful portrait of the Prince and richly gilded stucco ceiling is most impressive.

The **staircase** is covered with blue and white tiles right up to ceiling height.

Upper floor: The Elector's private rooms were located here. Their lavish and costly furnishings are captivating; in particular the small **mirrored room**★ with its blue-edged panels and gilded carved frames is a masterpiece.

ADDITIONAL SIGHTS

Schloßkirche – The present parish church of Maria zu den Engeln is linked to Augustusburg Castle through the Orangery. Its high altar made of coloured stucco-marble was made by Balthasar Neumann and the sculptor Johann Wolfgang van der Auvera.

★ **Phantasialand** ⊙ – *On the southern edge of the town.* The 28ha/69 acre leisure park, which is famous for its rides, offers many attractions within four themed areas: log flumes with drops of up to 16m/52ft, the **Colorado Adventure**, a wild roller-coaster reaching speeds of up to 50kph/30mph, a mountain and Grand Canyon train and a monorail jet.

The attraction of the **Viva Mexico silver mine** is its miners' village and 120 life-size, moving figures.

Visitors can enjoy a **Wild West Stunt Show** in the Super Globe, an ice show in the Arena di Fiesta and a computer-generated electronics show in the Tanagra Theatre.

Galaxy★ offers a flight simulation through the universe, and an intergalactic experience also awaits visitors in the **Space Center**, one of the largest indoor roller-coasters in the world. Magicians are at work in the brilliant **Wintergarten Show**★ *(seats can be booked at the Wintergarten box office)*, where the large-scale illusions featuring white tigers are a special attraction.

BRUNSWICK

See BRAUNSCHWEIG

BÜCKEBURG

Niedersachsen

Population 20 500

Michelin map 417 J 11

Bückeburg, which lies in the northern foothills of the Weser mountains, received its town rights in 1609 from Count Ernst von Holstein-Schaumburg. He also made Bückeburg a residence town. A large number of Renaissance buildings bear witness to this glorious period during which the town was the capital of the small, well-administered state of Schaumburg-Lippe. Even after 1918, when the last ruling Prince of Schaumburg-Lippe resigned, Bückeburg remained the capital of an independent state; but after 1946 it was dissolved and allotted first to Westphalia and then to newly formed Lower Saxony. Some official agencies remained in Bückeburg, the entire Department of Justice, for example, and the State Archives.

★ **Schloß (Castle)** ⊙ – *Before visiting the castle proper, visitors are advised to walk into the park, on the right of the state entrance.* From here, across velvet lawns beyond the moat, a splendid example of German First Renaissance architecture is visible in the gabled **façade**★ with its semicircular pediments. The overall effect is majestic.

Pass through the early-17C monumental gateway, then to the main courtyard and beyond that to a small inner courtyard surrounded on three sides by a Renaissance balcony. This is the earliest (16C) part of the castle.

During the tour, visitors see some of the rooms, decorated with luxurious furniture, tapestries and Old Master paintings, and the castle chapel, adorned with fine late Renaissance woodwork. An arcaded framework with decorative pediments supports the pulpit – placed, in accordance with Lutheran traditions, in the middle of the nave, facing the sumptuous Princes' Gallery. The highlight of the tour is undoubtedly the Golden Room (Goldener Saal) with the famous "Doorway of the Gods" (Götterpforte) made in 1604. The White Room features a beautiful stucco ceiling adorned with weapon and trophy motifs.

At the edge of the park is the **Mausoleum** built between 1911 and 1915 by Adolf von Schaumburg-Lippe, the last ruling Prince. Its cupola is decorated with a gigantic golden mosaic.

BÜCKEBURG

* **Stadtkirche (Church)** – This was one of the first great religious buildings to be designed expressly for the Lutheran sect (1615). The massive façade is symmetrically divided, in Renaissance style, by an alternation of cornices and vertical elements, but several features – the false bull's-eye windows, for example – hint already at the Baroque. There is a fine bronze font inside that was made by Adrian de Vries in 1615.

* **Hubschraubermuseum (Helicopter Museum)** ⊘ – *Sableplatz.*
From Leonardo da Vinci to the present day, first in theory and then in practice, the evolution of this flight technique is illustrated by numerous models and over 40 actual helicopters. Some, like the BO-46, designed to fly at more than 400kmph/249mph, have yet to go beyond the experimental stage.

EXCURSION

Besucherbergwerk ⊘ – **Kleinenbremen (Mining Museum)** – *3km/2mi to the south. Be sure to wear warm clothing.*
Worked from 1883 to 1982, this mine had produced one million tons of iron ore by 1952. Visitors go through enormous excavations, supported by huge pillars, before being shown the different systems of extraction which were utilized. Annexed to the mine is a **museum** on the history of mining and geology.

BURGHAUSEN★★

Bayern
Population 19 000
Michelin map 420 V 22

The town, whose centre still retains its medieval aspect, lies within a curve of the River Salzach, where it forms the frontier between Bavaria and Austria. Above the old town is the castle, built on a quite exceptional **site**★★ – a long, narrow, rocky spur separating the Salzach from the Wöhrsee.
The dukes of Bavaria, seigneurs since the 12C, made Burghausen into the biggest fortress in Germany: the defence system, reinforced at the beginning of the 16C in the face of a threatened invasion by the Turks, stretches for more than 0.8km/0.5mi.

Burghausen

★★ **Burg (Castle)** ⊘ – *Allow about 2hr 30min walking and sightseeing.*
Leaving the car in the Stadtplatz, follow the road which circles the cliff at the southern extremity of the spur and pass beneath the **Wöhrenseeturm**. Beyond the lake, a steep path leads to the outer line of fortifications. From here, the ramparts stepped up the Eggenberg hill, on the far side, are visible. A wooden footbridge

– fine view of the old town below, and the Salzach – carries the path across a moat to arrive at the **Georgstor**, or St George's Gate. This is set in the innermost ring of battlements, which protect the last small courtyard at the castle's centre.

The full strategic value of Burghausen becomes apparent: the lower town with its main square lined with brilliantly coloured house façades, onion-domed churches and the fortifications linking the castle with the Eggenberg, and, as far as the eye can see, the Salzach Valley winding through the hills.

There are two museums in the main block.

Burgmuseum und Gemäldegalerie (Castle Museum and Painting Gallery) – The former ducal apartments (15C-17C furniture) house an interesting collection of paintings from the Bavarian School. On the first floor are works by, among others, the Master of the Passion of Freising (c 1500). Battle scenes painted by Hans Werl (c 1600) are noteworthy on the second floor – especially a huge canvas depicting the Battle of Ampfing (1322), at which the Emperor Ludwig of Bavaria vanquished his rival Frederick the Handsome of Habsburg. From the **observation platform** *(62 steps higher up)*, there is a splendid panoramic **view**★ of Burghausen, the Salzach and the surrounding hills.

The Gothic **chapel** *(in the same wing)* has elegant star vaulting.

Stadtmuseum (Municipal Museum) – This is installed in the apartments once reserved for the Duchess *(west side of the main block)*. The main exhibit traces the history of Burghausen. It includes a scale model of the town and castle in the 16C. Also on display are examples of local folk art, craftwork and peasant furniture.

Returning directly to the Stadtplatz via the **Burgsteig** *(a ramp between the castle entrance and the Georgstor)*, there is a particularly fine view of the old town: the onion-domed church towers rising above brilliantly coloured house façades are typical of the regions watered by the Inn and the Salzach.

It is also possible to reach the castle by car: there is a parking space on the flat area to the north of the spur.

EXCURSIONS

Marienberg – *4km/2.5mi to the south.*
Here there is a Rococo pilgrims' church (1764) almost square in plan. Inside, the dome over the central part of the building is adorned with a fresco painted by Martin Heigel: a boat (symbol of the Church) lies beneath the Holy Trinity, surrounded by celebrated members of the Founding Fathers. In the centre of the ornate high altar is an Early Baroque Virgin Mary in Glory.

★ **Raitenhaslach** – *6km/4mi to the south.*
Red-marble tombstones enshrining the memory of abbots from the 15C to the 18C can be seen in this 12C Cistercian church, which was modified in the Baroque style in the late 17C. The life of St Bernard of Clairvaux is illustrated in the fine **ceiling paintings**★ (1739) by Johannes Zick of Lachen, near Ottobeuren (1702-62). The same artist executed the paintings on the sumptuous high altar (Assumption of the Virgin Mary). The Baroque artist Johann Michael Rottmayr painted the pictures in the first two side chapels and of the Sebastian and Bartholomew chapels. The stucco work is by M Zick; the abundant bright blue stucco decoration on the chancel arch is particularly striking.

Tittmoning – *16km/10mi to the south.*
On the west bank of the Salzach, across the water from Austria, Tittmoning preserves the remains of its medieval fortifications and a castle which was once the residence of the Prince-Bishops of Salzburg. Two old fortified gateways give access to the wide **Stadtplatz**, which is bordered by houses with ridge roofs masked by perpendicular copings. Brightly painted façades, some decorated with gilded figures, wrought iron signs, oriel windows and emblazoned fountains add considerable style to the ensemble.

Altötting – *21km/13mi to the northwest.*
This pilgrimage centre consecrated to the Virgin is one of the oldest in Bavaria and draws more than 700 000 people to the town each year. The Miraculous Virgin stands in a silver niche on the altar of the octagonal **Holy Chapel** (Heilige Kapelle). In the Late Gothic **Parish Church** (Stiftskirche), there are two fine pieces in the Treasury (Schatzkammer): a splendid Flemish ivory crucifix dating from 1580, and a masterpiece of goldsmith's work (c 1404) – a small gold horse, the **Goldenes Rößl**★, given to Charles VI of France by his wife, Isabella of Bavaria, which he subsequently pledged against a loan from his brother-in-law, Ludwig the Bearded, Duke of Bavaria-Ingolstadt. It was given to the Chapel of Mercy (Gnadenkapelle) of Altötting in 1509.

Johann Tzerklaes, Count of Tilly (1559-1632), a famous general on the side of the Catholic League in the Thirty Years War, is buried in the crypt *(entrance through the cloisters)*.

CELLE★★

Niedersachsen
Population 74 000
Michelin map 415/416/418 I 14
Town plan in the current Michelin Red Guide Deutschland

From 1378 to 1705, Celle was the official residence of the Lüneburg branch of the dukes of Guelph, who had been banished from their original ducal seat by the firm burghers of the salt town to the north. With its carefully preserved centre of 16C-18C half-timbered houses, Celle retains today the air of an aristocratic retreat.

The Three Ladies of Celle – Eléonore d'Olbreuse, a beautiful Huguenot from the old French province of Poitou, seduced Georg-Wilhelm, last of the Guelph dukes to live in Celle, and became the town's chatelaine in 1676. As Duchess, she opened the Court to influences from her own country. The beautiful French-style garden (Französischer Garten) in the southern part of the town stands as her memorial.

Sophia-Dorothy, Eléonore's daughter (1666-1726), was married for reasons of state to her cousin, the future George I of England – a union which produced, first, George II, and subsequently a daughter who became the mother of Frederick the Great. Sophia's love affair with Count Philip of Königsmark was discovered, and she was banished for the rest of her life to Ahlden Castle.

From 1772 to 1775, a third doomed adventuress, **Caroline Matilda of England**, wife of the eccentric Christian VII of Denmark, expiated in Celle Castle her ill-advised affair with Struensee, the all-powerful minister and King's favourite. There is a monument to her in the French Garden.

★★ OLD TOWN *allow 1hr*

The half-timbered houses of Celle are distinguished by a superpositioning of crow-stepped gables. Well-preserved buildings of this type can be seen in the Neue Straße, the Zöllnerstraße and the Poststraße (note the richly carved **Hoppenerhaus**, which dates from 1532). A recess widening the narrow Kalandgasse allows more space for the 1602 **old college** (Lateinschule), remarkable for the luxuriant ornamentation of its posts and wooden beams engraved with biblical slogans. The **Rathaus** (town hall) is in different Renaissance styles. The north gable, built in 1579 by craftsmen who came from the banks of the Weser, is heavily scrolled and bristles with fantastic pinnacles (The Weser Renaissance).

ADDITIONAL SIGHTS

Schloß (Castle) ⊙ – This rectangular fortress, flanked by massive corner towers, boasts roofs in the shape of ribbed helmets. The eastern façade, overlooking the town, is designed with dormer windows topped by rounded pediments – a characteristic of the Weser Renaissance style.

The castle **chapel★** (Hofkapelle) is Renaissance in origin; the ogive vaulting dates from the late 15C. The chapel was modified in the late 16C by the Flemish painter Martin de Vos, whose Crucifixion adorns the altar. With galleries that are both open and glassed-in, the chapel is a peculiar item. Nearby is the **Schloßtheater**, built in 1674 to an Italian design and said to be the oldest court theatre in Germany. A permanent exhibition from the Bomann Museum in the eastern wing documents the history of the kingdom of Hanover.

Bomann-Museum ⊙ – *Schloßplatz.*
The permanent exhibitions in this museum cover the folklore of Lower Saxony and the history of the town of Celle. In the centre of the local history section is also a display on the history of the former kingdom of Hanover.

★ **Stadtkirche (Church)** – This dark and originally Gothic church was considerably renovated in rich Baroque style by Italian stuccoworkers between 1676 and 1698. Especially noteworthy are the 1613 **Altar**, which combines Renaissance features with Baroque elements, the 1565-66 **Fürstenstuhl** (Prince's Seat) beneath the organ and the 1610 **baptismal font**. The remains of dukes from the Celle branch of the House of Guelph lie in the **princes' vault** beneath the chancel. The commemorative stones are above in the chancel itself.

EXCURSION

★ **Kloster Wienhausen** ⊙ – *10km/6mi to the south.*
This Cistercian abbey, founded in 1233 by Henry the Lion's daughter-in-law, has been occupied since the Reformation by a small community of Protestant canonesses. Among the piously preserved relics are a stone statue (1280) of the founder, and 13C wooden figures of the Virgin of Wienhausen and Christ

Resurrected. The **Nuns' Choir** is embellished with fine early-14C **mural paintings**★. During restoration work in 1953, a collection of trinkets was discovered beneath the wooden floor of the choir – penknives, spectacles, small notebooks etc hidden there by the nuns 500 years before to keep them from the hands of the Reformers *(the trinkets are on display in a small museum).*

Once a year, for 11 days only, starting on the Friday after Whitsun, the convent holds an exhibition of its famous **tapestries**, woven by the nuns in medieval times *(the museum is closed during this period).*

CHEMNITZ

Sachsen

Population 300 000
Michelin map 418 N 22

Chemnitz, a major city with a history going back over 800 years, is the economic and intellectual centre of Saxony's most densely populated area. The town lies on an eponymous river in the midst of an attractive sylvan landscape at the foot of the Erzgebirge massif.

The development of Saxony's third largest city began with the foundation of a Benedictine monastery, St Mary's, some time around 1136 on Schloßberg. The establishment of a state bleachery in 1357 and the resulting bleaching monopoly turned Chemnitz into one of the most significant centres of the textile industry in Germany. The first cotton mills were built around 1800, with the onset of the Industrial Age and the development of engineering. Chemnitz became known as "Saxony's Manchester" in the 19C. The industrial monuments and the residential quarters from the "Gründerzeit" period are unique.

From Fritz Heckert to Karl Marx – With such a history, it is hardly surprising that Chemnitz became one of the most militant centres of the German workers' movement.

Fritz Heckert, born in Chemnitz in 1884 and co-founder of the German Communist Party after the failed revolution of November 1918, was one of the driving forces behind this movement. From 1953 to 1990, the town was known as Karl-Marx-Stadt.

SIGHTS

Brückenstraße (EU) – With the Straße der Nationen (Avenue of Nations), which it crosses, this fine street is one of the two main arteries around which the new city centre was conceived. It is in this quarter that the impressive apartment blocks and modern buildings such as the Hotel Kongreß, the Kongreßhalle (Conference Palace) and the central post office can be found.

The imposing **Karl Marx Monument** (12.5m/40ft high) of Ukrainian granite, designed by Lew Kerbel in 1971, stands in front of a huge plaque bearing in several languages the last words of the Communist Manifesto: "Workers of the world, unite!"

Returning in a southerly direction, the visitor passes a series of panels decorated with bas-relief sculptures illustrating the history of the workers' movement.

Altes Rathaus (Old town hall) (EU R) – Painstakingly rebuilt after 1945, this building has a fine Gothic façade, remodelled at the beginning of the 17C. There is a Renaissance doorway at the foot of the tower. To the east stands the Neues Rathaus (new town hall) built at the beginning of the 20C with a Jugendstil interior.

Museum für Naturkunde (Natural History Museum) ⊘ **(EU M¹)** – The main exhibit here is a **"Petrified Forest"**★, in the open air, formed by the trunks of trees geologically turned to stone some 250 million years ago. The museum itself is currently undergoing reorganisation. The insectarium and section on the nature and landscape of the Chemnitz region are open to the public.

Kunstsammlungen Chemnitz (Fine Arts Collection of Chemnitz) ⊘ **(EU M¹)** – German painting and sculpture of the 19C and 20C (Dresden Romantic School, German Impressionism and Expressionism). The artist most prominently represented is Karl Schmidt-Rottluff, born in Chemnitz in 1884 and a member from 1905 to 1913 of the Die Brücke movement. The textile and arts and crafts collections include furniture and handicrafts by Jugendstil (Henry van de Velde, Vienna Workshops), Art Deco and contemporary artists.

Schloßkirche (Castle Church) (ET) – Once part of a Benedictine abbey founded in 1136, this building was transformed into a hall-church at the beginning of the 16C.

There is an elegantly carved Late Gothic doorway (now transferred to the interior, on the south wall). In the northern chancel is a poignant painted wood **Flagellation Group**★ by Hans Witten (1515), that is more than 3m/10ft high.

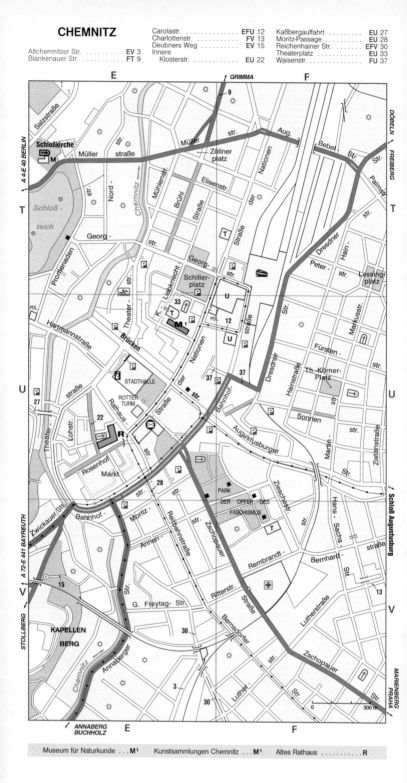

CHEMNITZ

Museum für Naturkunde ... **M¹**   Kunstsammlungen Chemnitz ... **M¹**   Altes Rathaus .... **R**

The chapter on art and architecture in this guide gives an outline of artistic creation in Germany, providing the context of the buildings and works of art described in the Sights section.
This chapter may also provide ideas for touring.
It is advisable to read it at leisure/before setting out.

EXCURSION

★ Schloß Augustusburg – *15km/9mi to the east, via Erdmannsdorf.*
The Elector of Saxony Augustus I built this hunting lodge (c 1570) on top of
Schellenberg hill (515m/1 690ft). In the chapel, the high altar is adorned with a
painting by Lucas Cranach the Younger (1571), showing the Elector surrounded
by his 14 children.
The **Museum of Game and Ornithology★** (Museum für Jagdtier und Vogelkunde) ⊙
presents the fauna of the nearby mountains in reconstructions of their natural
habitat (dioramas). A series of murals (16C) in the "Hasensaal" illustrate *The
Victory of the Hares over the Hunters.*
The castle also houses a **Motorcycle Museum★★** (Motorradmuseum) ⊙ which gives
an overview of more than a century of motorcycles and is one of the most
comprehensive in Europe, placing particular emphasis on illustrating the technical
evolution of this means of transport.

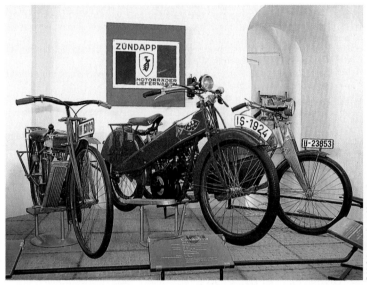

Motorcycle Museum, Schloß Augustusburg

CHIEMSEE★

Bayern

Michelin map 420 W 21 – Local map see Deutsche ALPENSTRASSE

Known as the "Bavarian Sea", the Chiemsee (pronounced Keem-zay) is the largest of
the province's lakes, with a surface area of 82km/32sq mi. Its calm waters lie
between gently sloping, rush-covered banks on one side, and the foothills of the
Bavarian Alps, clearly visible to the south, on the other. Two islands, not far from
the west bank, are worth a visit. They are named the Herreninsel (gentlemen's isle)
and Fraueninsel (ladies' isle). On the former is an extraordinary castle, which took
Versailles for inspiration; on the latter, an abbey.
Summer resorts popular with water sports enthusiasts line the banks of the lake, in
particular **Prien**, the busiest, and **Seebruck**.
The Salzburg-Munich motorway runs close to the Chiemsee's flat, marshy southern
extremity, but it is from the northern bank, between Rimsting and Seebruck, that
the most interesting vistas – with the Alpine peaks as a colourful backdrop – can be
seen.

THE ISLANDS

*From the motorway (Bernau exit), approach the lake from the west, and make
for the* **Prien-Stock landing-stage** ⊙. *Allow 15min for the trip to the Herreninsel,
30min for that to the Fraueninsel.*

Herreninsel – Existence of a monastery on the island goes back to the 8C already.
Around 1130, an Augustine canons order was founded by the archbishop of
Salzburg. The decline during the Reformation was followed by a Golden Age with

intensive construction that resulted in the Domstiftskirche St. Sebastian und Sixtus. Sections of the old monastery walls have remained intact, the so-called **Altes Schloß**. The history of the Herreninsel is presented in these old walls, now a museum. The island, for the most part wooded, is famous for its castle.

The young King Ludwig II of Bavaria bought the whole of this island in 1873 to save it from a systematic deforestation, but also because he wanted to build a sumptuous palace there.

★★ **Schloß Herrenchiemsee** ⊘ – Construction on the **Neues Schloß** (New Castle) in the paradisiac solitude of this generally forest-covered island started in 1878 and continued until 1886. Ludwig II's visit to Versailles in 1867 had greatly strengthened his admiration for Louis XIV, "the Sun King", and his Court; the castle on his island would be a replica of Versailles. The death of the King on June 12, 1886, who had spent only one week in the castle, put an end to the dream – by which time 20 million DM had already been spent and the royal coffers were empty.

The resemblance between the original and the copy is striking: the Latona fountain stands in the middle of formal French-style gardens; the huge façade is adorned with columns and crowned by a flat roof with balustrade in the Italian style; the apartments include a State Bedroom and a **Hall of Mirrors**, both of which are magnificent.

The southern wing of the building houses the **König Ludwig II Museum**, which documents the fairytale king's life.

NB Visitors to Schloß Herrenchiemsee should be prepared to queue for up to one or more hours in high season.

Fraueninsel – Although it is small, this islet boasts a charming fishing village and an ancient Benedictine **monastery** whose 13C church was rebuilt in the Gothic style in the 15C. The interior is decorated in Baroque style with a high altar dating from 1694. A particularly striking feature of the church is its free-standing octagonal bell-tower, whose foundations date from the 11C and were once used as a refuge. The onion-dome was added in 1626.

Kloster CHORIN★★

Brandenburg

Michelin map 416 H 25

The majestic ruins of Chorin Abbey stand framed against a backdrop of trees on the banks of the Amtssee. The original abbey, financed by the Margraves of Brandenburg, was built from 1273 by Cistercian monks from the abbey at Lehnin *(see POTSDAM)*. As early as c 1825, the architect Karl Friedrich Schinkel drew the attention of the king of Prussia to the historical interest of the ruins and persuaded him to start a project to save the site. Now partially restored, Chorin Abbey is one of the finest examples of a brick building in northern Germany. This peaceful site hosts a festival of classical music during the summer.

For further information on the Cistercians, see Introduction: Art and also MAUL-BRONN.

★★ ABBEY ⊘ 30min

Church – The monks from Lehnin adopted the same basilical ground plan with three naves at Chorin, but with one or two modifications on their home church. The sanctuary was extended by the addition of a heptagonal apse, the nave no longer featured twin bays, the transverse and cross ribs were supported on clustered columns rather than piers, and the rectangular pillars are softened by slender engaged colonnettes. As it now stands, the building is missing its south wall.

The west front, with a very strong vertical articulation, combines severity and elegance: flanked by two staircase turrets are three windows, separated by buttresses and surmounted by a rose window, while the upper section of the façade features an attractive array of gables and blind arcading.

Conventual buildings – *Currently under restoration.* The west wing, reserved for the lay-brothers, and the east wing, reserved for the clerics (along with the south wing, which is no longer extant), are original.

The abbot's residence, brewery and the remains of a mill are also open to visitors.

EXCURSION

Schiffshebewerk Niederfinow ⊘ – *18km/11mi south on Bundesstraße no 2. On arrival in Eberswalde, just before the level crossing, turn left towards Liepe. The walk starts from the Tageskasse kiosk by the road, from where you follow the signs "Aufgang".*

This mechanical hoist for ships was built from 1927-34 on the canal linking the Oder and the Havel. It is an enormous construction (60m/200ft tall) designed to carry barges (up to 1 000t loaded weight) and pleasure boats up or down a difference in level of 36m/120ft. The craft are steered into a basin 85m/280ft long by 12m/40ft wide by 2.5m/8ft deep, which is then raised or lowered by means of a set of steel cables and a concrete counterweight. The entire operation takes about 20min. The reinforced concrete platform supporting the hoist is sunk into the ground to a depth of 20m/65ft.

From the east terrace, there is a good **view** of the internal mechanism of the hoist and, from the other side, of the Oder Valley.

Technical data

Material and cost: 72 000m³/2.4 million cu ft concrete, 14 000t steel; 27.5 million Reichsmark.

Overall size (without the canal bridge): 60m/192ft high, 94m/301ft long, 27m/86ft wide.

Basin size: 85m/272ft long, 12m/38ft wide, 2.50m/8ft deep, 4 290t.

Average **speed** lifting and dropping: 12cmps/0.5inps, total time 5min.

Concrete counterweights: 192 weighing 21t each, using 455kW electric motors.

Steel hawsers: 256 each 52mm diameter, running in pairs through 128 double-ridged rings with a diameter of 3.50m/11ft each.

Ships and freight: 10 000 per year, total of 4 million tonnes.

COBURG★

Bayern

Population 44 000
Michelin map 418/420 P 16

Ever since the 1920 referendum, this former royal residence and small duchy wedged between the Upper Main Valley and the Thüringer Wald (Turingian Forest) has been a part of Bavaria (not Turingia). It can be assumed that it was the site of a royal estate already back in the 9C or 10C. Johann Casimir (1586-1633), the first ruler of the diminutive state of Saxony-Coburg had a knack for setting up an exemplary justice and administrative system and laid the foundations for an orderly governmental system. Coburg's Renaissance townscape, surmounted by a mighty fortress, dates to this period. The next significant influence on Coburg's architectural look was provided by the dukes in the 19th century.

Coburg fortress

From that time onward, the noble dynasty of Saxony-Coburg was either directly related to or married into all European royal families. The marriage between Edward, the Duke of Kent, and the Coburg princess Victoire produced the famous Queen Victoria; she, in turn, married a cousin: Prince Albert of Saxony-Coburg.

This little town, which was once just a stone's throw from Germany's border with East Germany, is now aiming to develop the Coburg-Rödental-Neustadt-Sonneberg axis and the Coburg-Rodach-Hildburghausen into a productive economic area along with its Thuringian neighbours.

VESTE COBURG (FORTRESS) *allow 3hr*

This complex, which can be seen from afar, is one of the largest fortresses in Germany with a triple ring of fortified walls. The original castle dated from the 11C, but the present structure is 16C, the epoch of Johann Casimir. The buildings, with high roofs punctuated by dormer windows, are set in a park.

* **Kunstsammlungen (Art Collections)** ⓥ – These collections consist mainly of the possessions of the dukes of Coburg and are fine examples of their kind in Europe. The Steinerne Kemenate wing houses Luther's room, the Great Hall (Große Hofstube) dating from 1501 which was used for jousting tournaments and the Horn Room (1632), which contains some fine medieval and early modern works of art. In the central wing (Carl-Eduard-Bau), there is a display of decorative arts, glassware and engravings. The Duchess' Building (Herzoginbau) houses an interesting display of gilded carriages, weapons and modern ceramic ware.

ADDITIONAL SIGHTS

* **Gymnasium Casimirianum** – Opposite the Moritzkirche, this high school building, with its Baroque turret and lantern (1605), is the finest example of Renaissance civil architecture in Coburg.

Schloß Ehrenburg ⓥ – This castle was the official residence of the dukes of Coburg from 1547 to 1918. Only the south block facing the Steinstraße dates from the original Renaissance palace built in 1547. After a fire in 1690 the castle was rebuilt. Its interior thus features elements of the Baroque, although the façade facing the Schloßplatz was remodelled in the early 19C in the English neo-Gothic manner.

The castle rooms are adorned with sumptuous furniture in the Empire and Biedermeier styles. Visitors should not miss Queen Victoria's apartments, the rich stucco ornamentation by Italian masters in the Gobelins Room (French tapestries), the Red Room and the Great Hall, and also in the castle chapel. There is a paintings gallery with works by German and Dutch masters.

EXCURSIONS

Schloß Callenberg ⓥ – *6km/3.6mi north of Coburg via B 303, then B 4, take the Rodach exit*. The **Callenberg castle** has been the property of the dukes of Coburg since the 16C. It was restored in the 19C, in the neo-Gothic style, and the Coburg family continued to live their until the 20C. The art works collected by the family are now on display there. The historic building is furnished with some fine pieces by David Rœntgen, and the paintings and decorative objects representing four centuries of acquisition are tastefully displayed.

Schloß Rosenau ⓥ – *7km/4mi northeast of Coburg, in Rödental*.
This castle in its picturesque setting is a fine example of neo-Gothic architecture. Duke Ernst I, who had the medieval fortress rebuilt in 1808, is also responsible for the English-style landscaped gardens. Prince Albert, the future Prince Consort of Queen Victoria of Great Britain, was born in this castle in 1819. The ducal apartments and reception rooms are open to the public (neo-Gothic mural paintings and tracery, fine Viennese Biedermeier style furniture). The **orangery** houses a museum of modern glassware, one of the most comprehensive collections of its kind in Europe.

Kloster Banz – *26km/16mi to the south*.
Banz is the holy mountain of Franconia. In the 6C, the Franks, having subdued the tribes of Thuringia, settled in the region and introduced the Cult of St Denis, protector of the Merovingian dynasty. In 1120 Bishop Otto of Bamberg declared the martyr saint patron of this abbey.
The **abbey church**★, completed in 1719 according to plans by Johann Dientzenhofer, has interior roofing of bewildering complexity. The principal dome breaks down into a series of niches that frame a central, tapering space; the wide supporting arches, themselves out of true and springing from keys, emphasize the virtuosity of this layout. The Baroque abbey towers, looking out over the valley of the Main, are balanced by the silhouette of **Vierzehnheiligen Church**★★, built on the opposite slope. There is a fine **view**★ from the terrace.

COLOGNE★★★
See KÖLN

CONSTANCE★
See KONSTANZ

Lake CONSTANCE★★
See BODENSEE

COTTBUS
Brandenburg
Population 125 000
Michelin map 418 K 27

Cottbus, of which mention is first made in 1156, was originally a Slav fortress. Its position at the point where the Salzstraße from Halle to Silesia crosses the Spree, generated the establishment of a merchant settlement there as early as the 12C. In the mid 15C control of Cottbus passed to Brandenburg. The town's wealth came from trade and from textile manufacture, and was consolidated in the 19C and 20C when mining of the nearby brown coal deposits began. As the focal point of Lower Lusitania, the cultural life of the town has blossomed.
Today Cottbus enjoys a "green town" image and boasts a number of parks.

★★SCHLOSS AND PARK BRANITZ (BZ) tour 3hr

The former Branitz estate had belonged to the family since 1696 when Hermann von Pückler-Muskau took up permanent residence here. He had just had to sell Muskau *(see Excursion)*, but was unable to abandon the great passion of his life, garden design. Future generations reaped the benefits, since in Branitz Park he created a jewel in garden design.

Terrace, Schloß Branitz

Schloß Branitz ⊘ – The proceeds from the sale of Muskau enabled Prince Pückler to have the castle, which was built in 1772 by Gottfried Semper, converted and sumptuously fitted out. Large parts of the structure remain.
Interior – The **vestibule**, which is hung with many portraits (16C-18C), functions as a portrait gallery. The **dining room** with its neo-Renaissance style furniture of quality and distinction, was designed by the owner himself. In the charming music room a porcelain stove bearing the royal coat of arms draws particular attention. The **library**, in which Pückler spent time every day, and which houses its original stock of books together with a huge 7t chandelier, is noteworthy. Pückler's great fondness for oriental and exotic styles is evident on the first floor.

155

COTTBUS

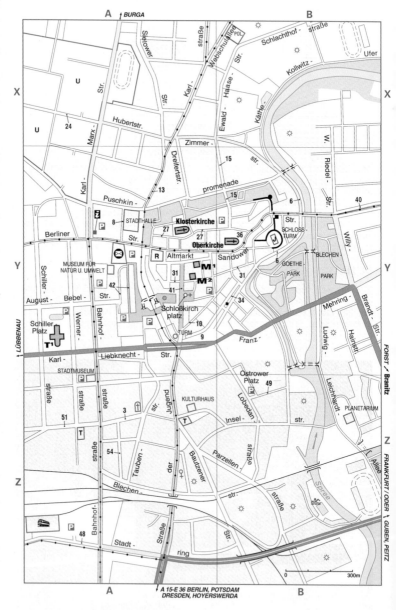

Some rooms house an art gallery featuring paintings by **Karl Blechen**, the Romantic painter born in Cottbus.

In front of the castle are the former Tudor style **royal stables**, in which short-term exhibitions are housed, and the cavalier's house, which is used today as a café. An attractive bower courtyard, with terracotta reliefs based on designs by Bertel Thorvaldsen and cast zinc figures, extends between these two buildings. On the side facing the garden it opens out into a terrace featuring two bronze griffins.

Park – The park covers an area of 90ha/222 acres, into which the elevations, watercourses and lakes had to be incorporated, since the river landscape as a framework did not already exist here as it did in Muskau. The soil from the excavation of the lakes was piled up to form hills and pyramids. Pückler placed particular emphasis on the alternation between open spaces, groups of trees and individual specimens, ditches and pools.

Impoverished Prince seeks Financial Backing

"A garden in the grand style is simply a picture gallery, and pictures need frames".

Hermann, Prince of Pückler-Muskau was born in Muskau in 1785. He studied law for a time and had a brief career as an officer, but did not really have any clearly directed ambition. He was a spendthrift throughout his life, and even while young he accumulated such debts that the family estate came under threat. His father's desperation was such that he even attempted to have his son legally declared incapable of managing his own affairs.

Hermann first discovered his true calling during some lengthy trips, in particular when he came upon the magnificent parklands of England. As a result he started designing the Muskau estate park in 1815. He worked on this project for 30 years, interrupted by further trips to England, North Africa and the Orient, from where he even brought back to Muskau an extremely young Ethiopian slave, Machbuba. Unfortunately the charming young girl died a few months later and he is said to have grieved for her deeply.

His marriage for money (in 1817) to Lucie von Hardenberg, who was nine years his senior, was harmonious, although the Prince divorced her a few years later, in order to marry for money once again (this time the marriage did not actually take place), since he had of course used up all his first wife's money for Muskau Park. Despite all their troubles, the pair remained inseparable until Lucie's death in 1858.

As a Liberal, albeit with anticlerical views, the Prince did not fit any particular mould, and rubbed his peers up the wrong way on more than one occasion. At some point he discovered a further gift, that of writing elegantly and well. As a result he published a few books, mainly travelogues, with which he was extremely successful. The considerable income which he received from these was of course immediately invested in his garden.

When he had to part from Muskau in 1845, at the age of 60, following the threat of its seizure, he took up a new project, Branitz Park, on which he worked for the remaining 25 years of his life.

Only a few of the very many structures and carvings which used to enliven the park remain, namely the gilded bust of Henriette Sontag, the Venus of Capua in the castle lake, the Orangery and the Tudor style park forge.

Tumulus – Prince Pückler had quite individual views on living and dying. He wanted his corpse to be decomposed using caustic soda, potash and lime. In accordance with his wishes, his remains were interred in the 11m/36ft high tumulus in the pyramid lake, which was covered in wild vines.

ADDITIONAL SIGHTS

Altmarkt – This long square provides a picture of relative uniformity, although the houses in it are in different styles, as Baroque curved gables make way for more simple neo-Classical façades.

★ **Niederlausitzer Apotheken-Museum** ⊘ (AY M¹) – In the over 400-year-old Löwenapotheke, or lion apothecary, in the old market, visitors have the good fortune to be able to see apothecary's establishments from several centuries, including a dispensary from the 19C, a drugs cellar, a Galenic laboratory from the early days of the apothecary and a herb and equipment store.

★ **Wendisches Museum** ⊘ (AY M²) – This extremely interesting Sorbian museum is housed in a perfectly restored bourgeois house dating from the 18C. It depicts and explains 1 500 years of Slavian history in Germany. The Wends (Sorbs) settled in the early Middle Ages between the Saale and the Lusitanian Neiße, and have retained their languages and culture right up to the present time. The many elaborate **costumes**★ are a major feature of the museum.

Since the exhibition is presented in a highly vivid manner, visitors leave the museum with a whole wealth of information about this ethnic group.

Oberkirche St. Nikolai ⊘ (BY) – The Late Gothic church with its three naves of equal height was built in the 15C and 16C, although the lower part of the massive west tower dates from an earlier building. The white plastered interior and the high windows produce an impression of great brightness. The beautiful star-ribbed vault is a particular decorative feature. The high and narrow altar created in 1661 by Andreas Schultze stands between the ambulatory pillars. The church houses some noteworthy Renaissance tombs.

The tower *(156 steps)* affords a wonderful **view** over the town.

Klosterkirche (AY) – The church of the former Franciscan monastery was built at the beginning of the 14C. The brick building has a long nave with an extension to the south. In addition to a **double tomb★** (c 1320) which depicts Fredehelm von Cottbus and his wife Adelheid, there is also a larger-than-life-sized Crucifix dating from the same period. The wooden pulpit beneath it is richly decorated and probably dates from the last quarter of the 17C.

Staatstheater (AY T¹) – The only **Late Jugendstil theatre** in Germany which is still in existence and still in use, richly decorated with curves, projections, extensions and three-dimensional decorations, is well worth a visit. It was designed in 1908 by the Berlin architect Bernhard Sehring.

EXCURSION

Bad Muskau – *45km/28mi to the southeast of Cottbus, via B 115.*
This little spa town on the Polish frontier is especially famous for the huge **Muskau Park★★**, the creation of which (1815-45) was the life's work of Prince Pückler, the Prince of Muskau at the time. He spent one million Taler on the country park over this 30 year period. He finally ran out of money and had to sell the estate. Of the original 545ha/1 350 acres, which extended along both sides of the Neiße, only around 200ha/500 acres remain today on the German side.
The history of the park can be experienced in the old castle which has been rebuilt, **Altes Schloß** ⊙ (beautiful Renaissance portal).
The ruins of the Neues Schloß produce an almost theatrical effect. This castle was converted in the neo-Renaissance style for Prince Friedrich of the Netherlands, who owned it from 1846. It was destroyed in 1945 and has only gradually been restored over the past years. The basic construction will be completed in 2000.

DARMSTADT

Hessen
Population 140 000
Michelin map 417/419 Q 9

The former capital of the Grand Duchy of Hesse-Darmstadt, now a thriving industrial centre (machine tools, armoured glass, electronic equipment and chemicals) lies close to the Odenwald massif. It has long been renowned also as a cultural centre, thanks to the endeavours of a succession of enlightened princes who were lovers of art – of Jugendstil notably, at the end of the last century.
Numerous institutions continue the tradition today, in particular the German Academy of Language and Poetry (Deutsche Akademie für Sprache und Dichtung), and the Institute of Industrial Design (Rat für Formgebung).

SIGHTS

★ Hessisches Landesmuseum ⊙ – *Plan of different museum sections available at the entrance.*
Main block – *Ground floor, right:* excellent choice of **medieval altar paintings** (Ortenberg and Reidberg), with works by Stefan Lochner and Lucas Cranach the Elder.
Ground floor, left: craftwork and religious sculptures. Note especially the liturgical accessories, medieval enamels, and **sculptured ivory** from Syria, Byzantium, Holland, Italy and Germany itself (of particular interest: the marquetry room from Chiavenna, Lombardy – c 1580).
Second level: Flemish and Dutch painting (Brueghel, Rembrandt, Rubens), 19C German painting (Schwind, Böcklin, Stuck), and the famous **Werkkomplex of Beuys**.
Basement: religious art (stained glass) and Jugendstil (ceramics, silver, glassware, furniture).
In the main building are the zoological and geological-paleontological sections and the graphics collection.
Annexe – *Ground floor:* representative collection of Expressionist painting.
Basement: German Impressionism, French "New Realism", art of the 1980s and 1990s.

Mathildenhöhe – This is the site on which the Grand Duke Ernst Ludwig founded, in 1899, the colony of Darmstadt artists known as the Künstlerkolonie. It united painters, sculptors and architects anxious to work together in search of a "total art" corresponding to the Jugendstil ideals of Art Nouveau. Outstanding were the architects Joseph Olbrich and Peter Behrens and the sculptor Bernhard Hoetger. The dwellings and workshops grouped near the Russian chapel formed in 1901 the centre of an exhibition titled "A Document on German Art". The ensemble, with its terraces and pergolas, is typical of this movement seeking new forms of expression. The **Wedding Tower** (Hochzeitsturm), built in 1908 to celebrate the marriage of the Grand Duke, overlooks the whole site. Inside are two mosaics (allegories on the subject of Love).

Darmstadt – Mathildenhöhe

Schloß (Castle) ⓥ – The former residence of the Landgraves, in the town centre, comprises two separate buildings: the New Castle (Neuschloß, 1716-26), a Rémy Delafosse design with its symmetrical façade fronting the market place; and the Old Castle (Altschloß 16C and 17C), an edifice with voluted gables and the family coat of arms on the gateway which leads to an inner courtyard.

In the **Castle Museum** (Schloßmuseum), family collections on view include splendid carriages, furniture, silver and, in the picture gallery, Holbein the Younger's *Darmstadt Madonna*.

Prinz-Georg-Palais ⓥ – This onetime summer residence of the Landgraves (built in 1710) houses the Grand Dukes' most valuable **porcelain collection**★. The table services and ornaments belong to the ducal family and constitute one of the largest collections of porcelain from the ducal factory at Kelsterbach, as well as from other German and Russian factories. Almost all the pieces were gifts from the royal and imperial families of Europe.

The **Prinz-Georg-Garten** has been preserved as a work of art of landscape gardening. It is a unique example in Hessen of a historical garden laid out in formal geometric patterns following late-18C principles of landscape gardening. The garden is roughly 2ha/5 acres in area and contains both useful and decorative plants arranged in formal flowerbeds divided by clipped yew borders. It features a number of charming ornamental elements (summer house, tea pavilion, ponds etc) and an orangery.

EXCURSION

Jagdschloß Kranichstein ⓥ – *5km/3mi to the northeast.*
The **hunting museum**★ in this small hunting lodge has assembled an interesting collection of weapons, trophies and pictures.

DESSAU

Sachsen-Anhalt
Population 93 000
Michelin map 418 K 20

Dessau, which is situated between the Elbe and the Mulde, was founded in the 12C and first appears in the record books in the year 1213. Its favourable position along major trading routes contributed to its development, especially since in 1474 it became the seat of a collateral line of the Princes of Anhalt.

After its heyday during the 16C and 18C, the early 20C was also a period of great significance for the town, since it was here that Hugo Junkers developed his gas engines and heating equipment and the first entirely metal passenger aircraft in the world. A new chapter was written in 1925, which made a name for the town worldwide, since it was in this year that the Bauhaus School of Design moved from Weimar to Dessau.

DESSAU

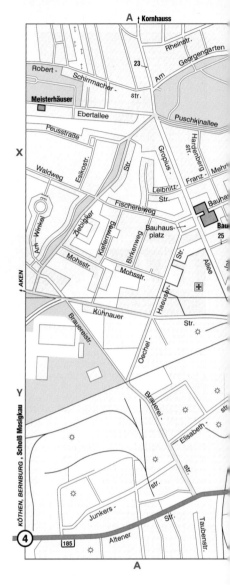

A colourful local figure – Der alte Dessauer, Prince Leopold I von Anhalt-Dessau (1676-1747) was an original character, since he married the daughter of an apothecary in the face of considerable opposition. He was apparently uncouth, and as a Prussian Field Marshal, who excelled himself during the War of the Spanish Succession and the Silesian War, was receptive to all things military. He made a great contribution to the establishment and the discipline of the Prussian army, which inherited from him the iron ramrod and in-step marching. Although he did not compose the Dessau March, he is witness to its popularity. He was ill-disposed towards any form of pomp. His 50 year rule was characterized by a lively building and colonisation policy. He contributed to the prosperity of the small principality by promoting the economy and administration, by reclaiming land using flood protection measures and by drying out swamps.

The "Gartenreich" – His grandson, Leopold III Friedrich Franz (1740-1817), made the Elbe meadows into a garden landscape which was quite unique within Europe, extending as far as **Wörlitz★★** *(see WÖRLITZER PARK)*, and which inspired famous people of his age with great enthusiasm. The enlightened Prince pursued his reforms, to the benefit of the 36 000 inhabitants of the area, with considerable zeal. He had taken progressive England as his model, and made every effort to renew and modernise agriculture, dyking and manufacturing. Although of little political significance, a model state arose in the shadow of Prussia.

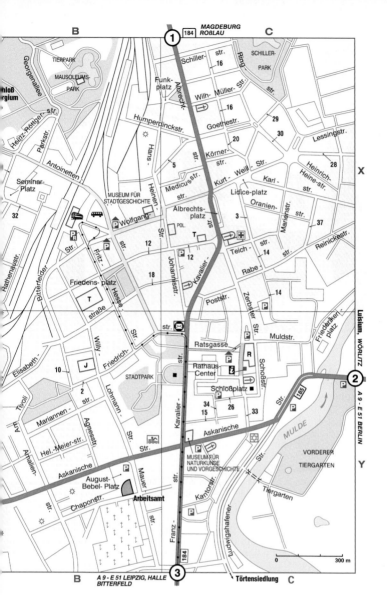

★★ THE BAUHAUS LEGACY (AX)

Since a great number of Bauhaus buildings have survived in Dessau, UNESCO made the town a world cultural heritage site in 1996.

Bauhausgebäude ⊘ – The "Design Academy" built on the basis of plans by Walter Gropius was opened in 1926 and displays all the features of the so-called Bauhaus style: cubic blocks, no visible supports at the corners of the building, glazed façades.

Meisterhäuser – Walter Gropius drew up plans for a small development of three semi-detached houses for the masters (Bauhaus professors) Laszlo Moholy-Nagy and Lyonel Feininger, Georg Muche and Oskar Schlemmer, Paul Klee and Wassily Kandinsky, together with a detached house for himself, and these were built between 1925-26 on a wooded site. Two of the masters' houses and half of a semi-detached house, the so-called **Feiningerhaus** ⊘, remain. The residential and workshop house designed by the artist in 40 colour shades, in which he lived with his family from 1926 to 1932, currently houses the **Kurt Weill Centre**, which is dedicated to the composer who was born in Dessau in 1900.

It is well worth visiting the rooms, which were restored in 1994 with every detail given careful consideration. Only in this way can one appreciate what ground-breaking ideas the Bauhaus realised in its demand for "light and air", at a time when people were still living in the shadow of the departing 19C.

Feiningerhaus, Dessau

Arbeitsamt (BY) – This semicircular flat-roofed building, a fine example of functional architecture, was designed by Walter Gropius in 1928.

Kornhaus (AX) – The restaurant situated on the banks of the Elbe was built in 1929 on the basis of plans by Hermann Baethe and Carl Fieger.

Tortensiedlung (CY) – Although hardly any of the 314 terraced houses in this development described as a "cake" have remained unchanged, it is still possible to recognise the unmistakable Bauhaus style of this model development, which was intended to relieve the housing shortage at the time and to afford workers a cheap opportunity to own their own homes.

Other Bauhaus buildings – Stahlhaus and Haus Fieger (both on Südstraße), Konsumgebäude (1 Am Dreieck) and Laubenganghäuser (Peterholzstraße).

ADDITIONAL SIGHTS

Georgium (BX) – The castle built by Friedrich Wilhelm von Erdmannsdorff for Prince Johann Georg lies in the broad George gardens and, together with the extremely varied park architecture, forms a most attractive focal point. The Georgium houses a picture gallery, the **Anhaltische Gemäldegalerie Dessau** ⊙, an excellent collection of German paintings from the 15C to the 19C, with works by Lucas Cranach the Elder (princes' altar) and Hans Baldung Grien, and of Frankfurt painting from the 18C and Dutch artists from the 15C to the 17C (Peter and Jan Brueghel, Peter Paul Rubens, Jan van Goyen).

EXCURSIONS

★ **Luisium** ⊙ – *In Waldersee, via ②, 4km/2.5mi east of Dessau.* The attractive little neo-Classical castle constructed by Friedrich Wilhelm von Erdmannsdorff was built for Princess Luise von Anhalt-Dessau between 1774 and 1778. The interior was designed as a temple to female virtue, a hint at the Princess herself. The rooms are decorated with ceiling paintings and murals in gentle colours and enchanting compositions. This little architectural gem nestles in a generously proportioned, atmospheric country park, with views of most of the park buildings which are modelled on Greco-Roman times. The castle stands in the centre of the "garden kingdom", the crowning glory of which is **Wörlitz**★★ *(see WÖRLITZER PARK).*

★ **Schloß Mosigkau** ⊙ – *On ④, Bundesstraße 185, around 5km/3mi southwest of Dessau.* The summer residence, built between 1752 and 1757 on the basis of plans by the Dessau architect Christian Friedrich Damm, was used as a residence, up to the time of her death, by Princess Anna Wilhelmine, the unmarried daughter of Leopold I. The two-storey three-winged building, flanked by gentlemen's houses of the same height, is a successful example of the Rococo style, and forms a particularly attractive ensemble with its garden and exotic plants in tubs. The central projections of both frontages are emphasised by pairs of Ionic columns and crowned with a monogrammed scroll between a putto and a female figure; it represents summer on the garden side and autumn on the courtyard side.

H. Fräßdorf/Kulturstiftung Dessau-Wörlitz

Luisium – Ballroom

Although the castle remained unscathed, the pleasance suffered considerable damage during the war. It is planned to gradually restore it to its former glory. It is already possible to "roam" in the **maze** in the front left-hand side of the garden. The rooms in the castle are richly furnished and hung with paintings. Silk and damask hangings, panelling, white inlaying and stucco ceilings afford a bright and gay picture of the Rococo period.

★ **Gartensaal** – The colours in the castle gallery are delicate, the stucco-marble being golden yellow and delicate green, whilst the ceiling with its white stuccowork is also green. The mirrors between the windows are as old as the building itself, as are the pedestal table and the chandeliers. The impressive collection of paintings fills the entire interior and front walls, and the works are hung in their original form. Works include principally Flemish and Dutch paintings (Peter Paul Rubens, Anthony van Dyck, Jan Brueghel).

The yellow room and the library are panelled and decorated with beautiful rocaille patterning. The reception room on the upper floor includes some charming stuccoes by Carlo Bossi.

Das Bauhaus

The most important art school of the 20C was founded in Weimar in 1919 as a "State Bauhaus", in which architecture, painting and sculpture, including all ancillary trades, were to be taught. Its first Director was **Walter Gropius**.

As soon as the elections in 1924 brought extreme right-wing Conservatives to power, the days of the Bauhaus in Weimar were numbered. However, other towns had recognised the significance of this unique institution and applied to become its home.

Dessau was finally selected by the Bauhaus Masters. They were able to realise their plans here in a whole range of buildings and objects. This was the start of a period of fruitful work, during which the ideas associated with the new style of living took shape in the Bauhaus workshops. Marcel Breuer for example, in collaboration with the local Junkers factory, created his legendary tubular steel furniture, and Marianne Brandt and Max Krajewski produced lamps of timeless elegance. In 1932 however the Bauhaus in Dessau was closed following a decision by the municipal council, at the instigation of the Nazis.

The director at the time, **Mies van der Rohe**, resolved to move to Berlin and to continue to run the Bauhaus as a private school, but this too was closed by the Nazis on 12 April 1933.

This act sealed the fate of the institution, although its revolutionary ideas were internationally accepted. It is impossible to imagine 20C international architecture without the Bauhaus.

DETMOLD

Nordrhein-Westfalen
Population 75 000
Michelin map 417 K 10

The chronicles speak of a victory by Charlemagne against the Saxons in the year 783 near a place called "Theotmalli", which, it is assumed, is the origin of the settlement. The actual foundation of the town called "Detmelle" on the north-eastern edge of the Teutoburger Wald on the Paderborn-Lemgo trade route around 1260. During the Soester Feud and as a result of a fire in 1547, large sections of the city were destroyed. Except for a small interruption, Detmold remained a residence first of the counts of Lippe and after 1789 of the princes of Lippe. In addition to the service sector, Detmold's economy nowadays is dominated by the furniture and metal industries.

The centre of the old town, which is filled with beautiful half-timbered houses from the 16C and 17C, is Marktplatz. The pretty carvings, the oriels and gables. that adorn the facades are particularly remarkable.

Residenzschloß (Castle) ⊘ – The little sandstone gables with semicircular pediments that adorn the façade of this 16C building are in early German Renaissance style. In the interior courtyard the corbelled Renaissance gallery with artistic stone carvings links the two corner towers. Souvenirs, the gifts of foreign royalty, enrich the apartments inside. The outstanding porcelain collection includes a service presented by the Empress Josephine to the Princess Pauline zur Lippe, and fine 17C tapestries illustrating, after cartoons by Charles Le Brun, the life of Alexander the Great.

Residenzschloß, Detmold

* **Westfälisches Freilichtmuseum (Westphalian Open-Air Museum)** ⊘ – 100 historic buildings from shed to noble residence have been rebuilt on these 100ha/2 471 acre grounds of verdant cultural landscape and furnished with the appropriate furniture. The result is a wonderful portrayal of Westphalian rural life from the past 500 years, including gardens, fields and pets.

* **Hermannsdenkmal (Arminius Monument)** ⊘ – This commemorates the victory in the year AD 9 of the local hero Arminius over the Roman legions, after he had united the tribes living in what are now Westphalia and Hessen. There is a **view*** of the surrounding forest, the town of Detmold and the Weser hills from the gallery (75 steps).

EXCURSION

★ **Externsteine** ⊙ – *In Horn-Bad Meinberg, about 12km/7mi south of Detmold.* In a forest setting beside a lake, this curious group of eroded sandstone rocks was once a place of worship for Germanic peoples, and subsequently, in the Middle Ages, a Christian pilgrimage. In the 11C a replica of the Holy Places of Jerusalem was constructed for the pilgrims. The most extraordinary sight is a **low relief**★★ of the Descent from the Cross, carved in the 12C from the living rock. Rare in Germany, this work is an example of Romanesque sculpture with a Byzantine influence.

Bad DOBERAN

Mecklenburg-Vorpommern
Population 11 500
Michelin map 416 D 19

The town developed around a Cistercian monastery founded in 1771. The little health resort is characterised by its classicistic architecture, with buildings which were erected between 1800 and 1825 for the visitors of the Baltic spa town of Heiligendamm. At the time, Bad Doberan was the summer residence of the Mecklenburg court.

The principal sight is the cathedral (Münster).

★★ CATHEDRAL ⊙

The former Cistercian monastery church, which was built between 1294 and 1368 and is one of the most beautiful examples of the north German brick Gothic style. In accordance with the architecture of the Order, a mighty window decorates the towerless western façade. Flemish style chapels radiate out from the chancel with its ambulatory. The only decoration in this building, whose clear lines are so characteristic of the Cistercian order, is the clover leaf arched friezes made of black glazed stone under the roof.

Interior – Brick also dominates here, toned down by the colourful painted triforium between the archway and the clerestory. Ogive vaulting covers the three naves of the basilica, which radiates harmonic slenderness. The sumptuous decor reflects the church's significance as the place of burial of the Mecklenburg dukes. The **high altar**★, a filigree Lübeck wood carving dating from the year 1310, shows Old and New Testament scenes. The **rood altar** dating from 1370 and the mighty **triumphal cross**★ which is part of it (depicted as the Tree of Life) have Christ on one side (for the lay-brothers) and Mary on the other (for the monks). The Late Gothic needle-shaped oak **tabernacle**★, which must be the oldest in Germany, originates from the same period. The **candelabra of Our Lady** features a charming Madonna with a crescent moon (symbolising chastity) in a glory; this outstanding work dates from the year 1290. Two side-aisle windows with 14C Gothic **stained glass** are also worth a closer look.

Tombs of the Mecklenburg ducal house stand in the chapels around the chancel.

EXCURSIONS

Heiligendamm – *6.5km/4mi northwest.* A magnificent row of lime trees borders the road from Bad Doberan to the spa resorts of Heiligendamm and Kühlungsborn. An alternate route is via a narrow-gauge railway known as "Molli". Heiligendamm was founded by the Duke of Mecklembourg in 1793. The architecture is typical of spa resorts of the period; the main building was built in 1814-16, and the many elegant houses along Prof.-Vogel-Straße bear witness to the luxurious past of this town where the wealthy came to "take the waters".

★ **Kühlungsborn** – *14km/8mi northwest.* A beach resort and spa, Kühlungsborn has become one of the most popular holiday destinations on the Baltic shore, thanks to the miles of beaches and the vast pine forest.

Consult the Places to Stay map at the beginning of this guide to select the a stopover or holiday destination. The map offers the following categories :
  Short holidays
  Weekend breaks
  Overnight stops
  Resorts
Depending on the region, this map also shows marinas, ski areas, spas, centres for mountain expeditions, etc.

DONAUESCHINGEN[★]

Baden-Württemberg
Population 20 000
Michelin map 419 W 9

This small town in the middle of the Baar, a fertile basin between the Black Forest and the Swabian Jura, stands at the confluence of two rivers, the Breg and the Brigach. From this fact stems the German proverb "Brigach und Breg bringen die Donau zuweg" – roughly, "from small streams great rivers flow". This is because after the confluence the united streams are known as the Danube.

Leading the way in music – The annual Festival of Contemporary Music, founded in 1921, soon became famous worldwide, thanks to the participation of such musicians as Richard Strauss, Arnold Schönberg and Anton von Webern. The concerts, relayed by the Südwestfunk radio station, gained a much wider public for composers like Pierre Boulez, Iannis Xenakis and Karlheinz Stockhausen.

SIGHTS

Source of the Danube – The monumental fountain **(Donauquelle)** was built in the castle park in the 19C. It is considered the official source of the Danube, which has another 2 840km/1 775mi to flow until its estuary.

Fürstenberg-Sammlungen (Princely Collections) ⊘ – These are on display in a building on the Karlsplatz. The exhibitions on geology, mineralogy, paleontology and zoology on the ground floor and first floor are special among collections of natural history in Germany. The presentation and the furnishings date to the founding days of the museum (1868).

★**Gemäldegalerie** (picture gallery) – *On the second floor*. In the large room on the right are works by 15C and 16C Swabian masters such as Bartholomäus Zeitblom and, above all, the very fine **Altarpiece of The Passion**★★ (Passions-altar) by Hans Holbein the Elder. The gallery on the left is devoted to other Swabian painters, including the Master of Sigmaringen. Adjacent rooms exhibit pictures by Cranach

Donaueschingen – Donauquelle

the Elder and Younger, Hans von Kulmbach, the Master of Meßkirch etc. Contemporary art is represented by some outstanding items such as works by Anselm Kiefer.

The Blue Danube

On its course to the Black Sea, from its source in the Black Forest, the Danube flows through or along the border of 10 different countries: Germany, Austria, the Slovak Republic, Hungary, Croatia, Yugoslavia, Bulgaria, Romania, Moldavia and the Ukraine. The beauty of the river and some of the countryside through which it flows has inspired many a poet, musician and artist.

Perhaps the most famous tribute to the Danube, however, is *The Blue Danube* waltz composed in 1867 by Viennese maestro Johann Strauss the Younger (1825-99) – just one of over 400 waltzes he composed during his lifetime.

Schloß (Castle) ⊘ – Remodelled in the 19C, the home of the Fürstenberg princes retains the luxurious amenities of the period, enriched now with gold and silver plate, porcelain and fine Beauvais and Brussels tapestries.

Pfarrkirche (Parish church) – The parish church was built in the Baroque style between 1724 and 1747. The architect was Maximilian Kanka from Bohemia, a student of Dientzenhofer. The unified Baroque furnishing is noteworthy. The so-called Madonna of Donauschingen (1525) by the master Hans Loy, which is located in the first (south) bay is most noteworthy.

DORTMUND

Nordrhein-Westfalen

Population 610 000

Michelin map 417 L 6 – Local map see RUHRGEBIET

Dortmund was first mentioned around 885 and was given market rights even before the year 900. Documents prove its status as an Imperial City since 1220, and as such was a flourishing town during the Middle Ages. As in many places, however, the Thirty Years War left deep scars, so that by 1648 only 2 000 people lived here. The actual boom period began in the mid 19C with the start of the Industrial Revolution. Ever since, Dortmund has been marked by coal, steel and beer. Nevertheless, as an economic hub, the city did put its money on innovation and research. Trade, insurance companies and the service sector have now long been economic buttresses for the city.

Culture, too, is high up on the agenda: evidence of this lies in the large number of museums, galleries and stages as well as in the markets and festivals. Dortmund is a lively city with a great deal to do.

SIGHTS

★ **Westfalenpark** ⊘ – The two main centres of attraction in this 70ha/173-acre park are the **Television Tower** (Fernsehturm "Florian") and the **Rose Garden** (Deutsches Rosarium), which cultivates some 3 200 varieties from all over the world. The tower is 220m/722ft high (31m/102ft higher than the Telecom Tower in London). At a height of 137m/450ft there is a revolving platform with a restaurant and a terrace from which there is a superb **panorama**★ of the Ruhr and the Sauerland.

★ **Reinoldikirche** – *In the Ostenhellweg, near the market.*
This triple-aisle basilica dating from the early Gothic period has interesting furnishings, which include a 15C sculpted reredos, probably a Burgundian work, that represents the life of Christ and the Crucifixion. Of particular interest is the highly skilled bronze **eagle pulpit** (Adlerpult), a work originating in the Maas Valley around 1450. Note the 14C wood statue of St Reynold, patron saint of the town, on the north side of the chancel, and a late-15C statue of Charlemagne on the south.

Marienkirche ⊘ – *Opposite the Reinoldikirche.*
This Romanesque basilica dating to 1170 with a Gothic chancel (1350) houses the **Berswordt Altar** (c 1395) in the northern flanking aisle, representing the Passion of Christ in finest artistry. It is only surpassed in beauty by the **Altar of Our Lady**★ (1420) by Conrad von Soest. This work, a masterpiece of the soft style, radiates in golden, blue and red hues. The golden statue of the Virgin in the chancel, a Romanesque sculpture dating to 1230, still has its radiant medieval colours.

Petrikirche – *In the Westenhellweg.*
This 14C hall-church is famous for its **carved reredos**★, created in 1521 by members of the Guild of St Luke of Antwerp. Including the high altar itself, the work measures 6x7.5m/20x25ft. It incorporates 633 carved and gilded figures and 54 paintings.

Propsteikirche – *Entrance from the Westenhellweg, via Mönchenwordt.*
Another hall-church. This one, restored after the Second World War, contains a **triptych** by Derick and Jan Baegert (c 1490). Open, this reveals, from left to right, the Holy Family, the Adoration of the Magi and the Crucifixion.

Brauereimuseum (Brewery Museum) ⊘ – *On the grounds of the former Dortmunder Kronen brewery, at no 85, Märkische Straße (entrance on the corner of Landgrafenstraße).*
Alongside a permanent exhibition on 5 000 years of beer-related history, this museum presents a survey of the evolution of breweries during the 100 years from the mid 19C to the mid 20C. Two complete **brewing installations** (1928 and 1936) can be viewed at work on the ground floor.

Museum für Kunst und Kulturgeschichte (Museum of Art and Civilization) ⓥ – *At no 3, Hansastraße.*
The exhibits here, displayed chronologically, cover such diverse subjects as the history of Dortmund (many items from archeological digs); religious art at the end of the Middle Ages; houses and furniture in different periods; and 19C painting (Berlin Secession, CD Friedrich, 20C design). The section devoted to the Romanesque epoch contains the **Dortmund Treasure★** (Dortmunder Goldschatz) – a collection of 444 gold coins, dating for the most part from the 4C AD.

Museum am Ostwall ⓥ – *At no 7, Ostwall.*
Works by the greatest exponents of German Expressionism are on view here: paintings by Paula Becker-Modersohn, Jawlensky, Macke, Nolde, Müller and Rohlfs; sculptures by Barlach, Kolbe and Kollwitz. There is also a big display of international art from the years 1960-80, in particular the installations of Wolf Vostell, Robert Filliou, Milan Knizak and Joseph Beuys. Contemporary art is honoured in permanent and special exhibitions.

DRESDEN★★★

Sachsen
Population 480 000
Michelin map 418 M 25 – Local map see SÄCHSISCHE SCHWEIZ

Thanks to an exceptional artistic and architectural heritage and its position in the heart of Saxony, on the banks of the Elbe and at the gates of "Swiss Saxony" *(Sächsische Schweiz)*, Dresden has become one of the most popular and important tourist centres in Germany.

"The Florence of the Elbe" – Originally a Slav town, germanised in the 12C by the Margraves of Meißen, Dresden remained a possession of the Albertine succession from the partition of Saxony in 1485 until 1918.
The major development of the city took place during the first half of the 18C, in the reigns of the Electors Augustus II the Strong (Frederick-Augustus I) and Augustus III (Frederick-Augustus II). To them we owe the magnificent Baroque ensemble of the Zwinger, the Japanese Palace and the Hofkirche (the Court church), as well as outstanding collections of paintings and objets d'art. These, completed by the work of 19C and 20C German painters – Dresden was the cradle of German Expressionism – make the city one of Europe's most prestigious artistic centres. On the cultural side, the Staatskapelle and the Staatsoper orchestras enjoy a worldwide reputation.

The Night of the Apocalypse – A few months before the end of the Second World War, on the night of 13-14 February 1945, Dresden was the target of one of the Allies' most destructive air raids, designed to break the morale of the population. Three successive waves of heavy bombers left the blackened skeletons of the city's principal monuments emerging from a waste of smoking ruins, and a death-toll of between 35 000 and 135 000 (because the city was filled with refugees, the exact toll is unknown). 75% of the city was destroyed.
Restoration of Dresden's historic patrimony – in particular the miraculous reconstitution of the Zwinger – and the rebuilding of residential quarters traversed by wide new thoroughfares have given the town a special quality marrying modern urbanism with this ancient heritage. The **Prager Straße** (Z), linking the old town with the quarter around the railway station, is the most typical example of this contemporary town planning, with imposing modern blocks on each side of a broad pedestrian mall.

Glockenspielpavillon, Zwinger

AROUND TOWN

Prefix – 0 351

Information – *Dresden Werbung & Tourismus GmbH*, ☎ 49 19 21 00 Monday to Friday 8am-7pm, Saturday 10am-4pm, Sunday 10am-2pm. **Information offices**: Schinkelwache at Theaterplatz, Monday-Friday 10am-6pm, Saturday 10am-4pm, Sunday 10am-2pm; Prager Straße 2a, Monday-Friday 10am-6pm, Saturday 10am-4pm. The city magazines *SAX-Das Dresdner Magazin* and *BLITZ! Dresden* (free of charge), published every four weeks, provide information on events taking place in Dresden. The *Kulturkalender*, which appears monthly and is available in hotels, at tourist information offices and cultural venues, is also a good source of information. Ticket sales at *Dresden Werbung und Tourismus*, ☎ 49 19 22 33.

Post offices with special opening hours – Postamt 1, Königsbrücker Straße 21-29, Monday-Friday 8am-7pm, Saturday 9am-1pm.

Daily papers – Sächsische Zeitung, Dresdner Neueste Nachrichten.

Internet – http://www.dresden-tourist.de; http://www.cityguide-dresden.de; http://www.dresden-tourist.de; http://www.dresden-online.de

Public transport

The network of the Dresdner Verkehrsbetriebe **(DVB)** is clear and well-structured, ☎ 8 57 10 11 round the clock. Information is available at the service centres at the main train station and at Postplatz, Monday-Friday 7am-7pm, Saturday-Sunday 8am-6pm; Pirnaischer Platz and Albertplatz, Monday-Friday 7am-7pm, Saturday 8am-4pm. The DVB is integrated into the Verkehrsverbund Oberelbe **(VVO)**, which also covers the region known as "Saxon Switzerland" (Sächsische Schweiz), the eastern Erzgebirge mountains and parts of the Oberlausitz area, ☎ 85 26 50 Monday-Friday 7am-8pm, Saturday-Sunday 7am-7pm. Tickets at the service centres, vending machines at the stations and in the trams and buses; normal fare is 2.70DM (1hr), ticket with four rides 10DM, day ticket 8DM, family day ticket for two grown ups and up to four children 12DM.

The **Dresden-City-Card** for 27DM (valid 48hr) lets an adult use all buses and trams and Elbe ferries in Dresden, plus free entry to 11 museums of the State Art Collections and discounts for other museums; also includes discounts for trips through the city and with steamers. The **Dresden-Regio-Card** for 45DM (valid 72hr) includes free rides on the S-Bahn trains along the Elbe to eg Meißen, Pirna and Königstein and discounts for rides on various narrow-gauge trains. The two cards are available at tourist offices, in numerous hotels and in the service centres of the DVB.

City tours

City tours – *Dresden Tour*, conducted by *Stadtrundfahrt Dresden* ☎ 8 99 56 50: 1hr 30min tours every 30min beginning 9.30am April-October, every 60 hour beginning at 10am November-March. Departure Augustusbrücke/Schloßplatz and 11 other stops such as Königstraße, Frauenkirche and Dr.-Külz-Ring. The *Super Dresden Tour* includes, besides the bus tour, a walk through the city's historic centre (departure from Augustusbrücke daily 10.30am, noon, 1.30pm, November-April Saturday only); The *Sempertour* also includes a tour through the opera house (daily 12.30pm and 1.30pm). The *Dresdner Verkehrsbetriebe* offers its own *Original Dresden Tour* by tram beginning at Postplatz, daily 10am-2pm every hour; book at ☎ 8 57 22 01. **Foot tours** through the historic inner city are arranged by *Stadtrundfahrt Dresden* as well: departure from Augustusbrücke 10.30am, noon and 1pm daily. (November-March Saturday only). Theme tours on foot are organised by *igeltours – Dresdens andere Stadtführung* ☎ 8 04 45 57.
Schiffahrten: The *Sächsische Dampfschiffahrts GmbH und Co. Conti, Elbschiffahrts KG* ☎ 86 60 90 offers rides on the Elbe in authentic old paddle-wheel steamers and in modern ships between Meißen and "Saxon Switzerland".

Shopping

Dresden's main shopping streets are Prager Straße (with department stores), Wilsdruffer Straße and Altmarkt in the old town, Königstraße **(exclusive shops)** and Hauptstraße, both in the inner Neustadt. **Art galleries** and **antiques** are to be found mostly in the Neustadt, on König- und Hauptstraße and in the quarter between Bautzener Straße, Königsbrücker Straße and Alaunplatz.
Flea markets are held at the Elbemarkt, Käthe-Kollwitz-Ufer/Albert-Brücke, May-October 9am-2pm and at the World Trade Centre on Ammon-/Freiberger Straße, every second Sunday of the month, 8am-4pm.

Markets – Altmarkt, mornings at 8am, daily except for Sunday. The Spring Market is held here in May, the Autumn Market in September and the famous Striezelmarkt in December.

Hotels

BUDGET

Wenotel – Schlachthofring 24; ☎ 4 97 60, Fax 4 97 61 00. 82 rooms, single rooms starting at 114DM. Simple, functional construction in the Ostrageheg of Friedrichstadt.

Landhaus Lockwitzgrund – Lockwitzgrund 100; ☎ 2 71 00 10, Fax 27 10 01 30. 12 rooms, single rooms starting at 95DM. Small hotel in rustic style in Lockwitz, good regional cuisine.

Elbterrassen Wachwitz – Altwachwitz 14; ☎ 26 96 10, Fax 2 69 61 13. 8 rooms, single rooms starting at 95DM. Small house under protection order as a monument, directly on the Elbe in Wachwitz.

OUR SELECTION

Schloß Eckberg – Bautzner Straße 134, ☎ 8 09 90, Fax 8 09 91 99. 84 rooms, single rooms starting at 170DM. This hotel complex located in a neo-Gothic castle is in a generous park right on the banks of the Elbe in Loschwitz.

Bayerischer Hof – Antonstraße 35; ☎ 82 93 70, Fax 8 01 48 60. 50 rooms, single rooms starting at 165DM. Elegantly furnished hotel in Neustadt, near the Marienbrücke.

Martha Hospiz – Nieritzstraße 11; ☎ 8 17 60, Fax 8 17 62 22. 50 rooms, single rooms starting at 90DM. Traditional inn in Neustadt, inexpensive rooms in the older section.

TREAT YOURSELF!

Kempinski Hotel Taschenberg – Taschenberg 3; ☎ 4 91 20, Fax 4 91 28 12. 213 rooms, single rooms starting at 370DM. Elegant grand hotel in the Baroque Palace, built by Augustus the Strong for Countess Anna Constanze von Cosel, vis-à-vis the Zwinger and the Opera.

Bülow Residenz – Rähnitzgasse 19; ☎ 8 00 30, Fax 8 00 31 00. 30 rooms, single rooms starting at 290DM. Comfortable, elegantly furnished city hotel in Neustadt with Dresden's best restaurant.

Radisson SAS Gewandhaus Hotel – Ringstraße 1; ☎ 4 94 90, Fax 4 94 94 90. 97 rooms, single rooms starting at 375DM. The hotel is once again in beautiful shape after a thorough restoration, centrally located in the old town.

Restaurants

BUDGET

Landhaus Lockwitzgrund – Lockwitzgrund 100; ☎ 2 71 00 10. Main dishes starting at 22DM. Good regional cuisine.

Feldschlößchen Stammhaus – Budapester Straße 30; ☎ 4 71 88 55. Main dishes starting at 10DM. The 100-year-old utility house of the erstwhile Feldschlößchen main house (Stammhaus) was opened in 1998 as a gastronomic establishment. Information on Dresden's brewing tradition is exhibited in the tower.

Café & Restaurant Pfund – Bautzner Straße 79; ☎ 8 08 08 22. Main dishes starting at 13.50DM. Café-restaurant on the first floor of the *Pfunds Molkerei* (see "Neustadt").

OUR SELECTION

Opernrestaurant – Theaterplatz 2; ☎ 4 91 15 21. Main dishes starting at 25DM. Classically furnished restaurant with wonderful location in the old town.

Fischgalerie – Maxstraße 2; ☎ 4 90 35 06. Main dishes starting at 28DM. The restaurant is near Postplatz; serves excellent salt- and fresh-water fish.

König Albert – Königstraße 26; ☎ 8 04 48 83. Main dishes starting at 26DM. Small restaurant in bistro style with Mediterranean and regional cuisine.

Ars Vivendi – Bürgerstraße 14; ☎ 8 40 09 69. Main dishes starting at 30DM. Creative cuisine in a cellar with vaulted ceiling.

TREAT YOURSELF!

Restaurant Caroussel – Rähnitzgassse 19; ☎ 8 00 30. Main dishes starting at 45DM. Elegant restaurant with fine creative cuisine in the Hotel Bülow Residenz.

Gourmet – Merbitzer Straße 53; ☎ 4 25 50. Main dishes starting at 45DM. Modernised Saxon cuisine in the Romantik Hotel Pattis in Dresden-Kemnitz.

Cafés, Kneipen and bars

The old town and the inner Neustadt have numerous cafés, bistros and restaurants. Many of the good hotels in Dresden have cocktail bars. The alternative-student scene has gathered in the outer Neustadt. The Pieschen district is also quite lively.

CAFÉS IN OLD TOWN

Café Börse – Prager Straße 8a. New, modern coffee house on Prager Straße, right next to the Deutsche Bank.

Café Kreuzkamm – Altmarkt 18. This old and traditional pastry shop returned to the place of its birth (in 1825) right after the fall of the Wall.

Italienisches Dörfchen – Theaterplatz 3. In wonderful rooms, with columns, stucco, and ceiling paintings providing the perfect backdrop for enjoying the home-made delights.

Vestibül im Taschenbergpalais – Taschenberg 3. Cakes, tortes and small dishes are served in this most inviting room with columns.

BREWERIES & BEER GARDENS

Ballhaus Watzke – Kötzschenbrodaer Straße 1. Brewery restaurant is right on the riverbank in historic rooms with a large beer garden. The first floor boasts a wonderfully restored ballroom holding 550 people.

Brauhaus am Waldschlößchen – Am Brauhaus 8b. Dresden beers, "Waldschlößchen Dunkel" and "Waldschlößchen Hefe" are brewed right here.

Fährgarten Johannstadt – Käthe-Kollwitz-Ufer 23b. This oasis in the Elbe Fields (Elbwiese) has been serving beer and barbecued food since 1920.

Biergarten im Schillergarten – Am Schillergarten 9. The wonderful view of the Blaues Wunder is what drags legions of people to this place, especially in good weather.

WINE CELLARS

Besoffenes Huhn – Altenberger Straße 43. Vintage and often little known wines are served here until 3am.

Weinstube Rebstock – Niederwaldstraße 10. 95 different wines, including many from Saxony and almost all German wine-growing areas are served here.

GOING OUT IN NEUSTADT

Blue Note – Görlitzer Straße 26. For the nighthawks, the ne'er tired, musicians and lovers of jazz, blues and rock'n roll.

Café 100 – Alaunstraße 100. One of the last survivors of the Kneipen scene boom from the days of the fall of the wall.

Mondfisch – Louisenstraße 37. Very diverse interior decoration with, among others, ship lights, twirling rotor blades and blue walls. The atmosphere in the front part of this Jugendstil establishment is lively, in the back it's more quiet, with straight music.

Oscar – die Filmkneipe – Böhmische Straße 30. Props, technology and film posters from around the world form the framework to this Kneipe.

Café Europa – Königsbrucker Straße 68. This bistro is open 23hr a day.

Frank's Bar – Alaunstraße 80. It is hard to choose among the 200 cocktails served in this little, chic bar.

Entertainment

THEATRE

Staatsschauspiel Dresden – Theatre at the Zwinger, Ostra-Allee 3; ☎ 4 91 35 55, toll-free 0800 4 91 35 00. Other stages of the Staatsschauspiel Dresden are the Theater Oben, the Schloßtheater and the TiF (Theater in der Fabrik).

Komödie Dresden – Freiberger Straße 39; ☎ 86 64 10. Theatre and more.

Projekttheater Dresden – Louisenstraße 41; ☎ 8 04 30 41. Experimental and performances.

OPERA, BALLET, OPERETTA AND MUSICALS

Semperoper – Theaterplatz 2; ☎ 4 91 17 30 (ticket sales at the Schinkelwache on Theaterplatz). The famous Semperoper is the home of the Saxon State Opera Dresden and the Staatskapelle Dresden.

Staatsoperette – Pirnaer Landstraße 31; ☎ 2 07 99 29. The repertoire ranges from *Fledermaus* by Johann Strauß to *Aspects of Love* by Andrew Lloyd Webber.

VARIETY, REVUE AND CABARET

Dresdens Kabarett-Theater "Die Herkuleskeule" – Sternplatz 1; ☎ 4 92 55 55. Even 10 years after the fall of the wall, this extremely popular ensemble has lost none of its bite.

bebe-Kabarett-Theater – Clara-Zetkin-Straße 44; ☎ 4 12 13 75. Humorous and profound material.

Theaterkahn Dresdner Brettl – Terassenufer, at the Augustbrücke; ☎ 496 94 50. The programme here is very diverse and multifaceted: theatre, cabaret and chansons.

CONCERTS

Kulturpalast – Schloßstraße 2; ☎ 4 86 60. This edifice, built in the 1960s, is not only the venue for concerts by the Dresdner Philharmonic but also for various other musical events.

Kreuzkirche – Altmarkt; ☎ 4 96 58 07. Home of the traditional Kreuz choir.

JAZZ

Tonne – Am Brauhaus; ☎ 8 02 60 17. Concert venue for international jazz-ensembles, but also or blues and folk.

CLUBS, DISCOTHEQUES & LIVE MUSIC

Bärenzwinger – Brühlscher Garten; ☎ 4 95 14 09. This student club located beneath the Brühlschen Terassen has been in existence since the 1960s and has an interesting programme.

Yenidze – Weißeritzstraße 3; ☎ 4 94 00 64. This building on the grounds of the former cigarette factory was constructed at the beginning of the 20C in the shape of a mosque. The Magic is located in its cellars.

CINEMA

The largest multiplex with 15 theatres is located in the UFA-Palast (built by the Viennese architect team Coop Himmelblau) at Prager Straße. Many off movie houses have settled in the outer Neustadt.

Special events

Steamer parade in May, *International Dixieland Festival* mid-May, *Dresdner Musikfestspiele* in July, *Striezelmarkt* in December.

HISTORIC CENTRE

*** **Zwinger** – *The best view of the whole complex is gained if you go in via the Glockenspielpavillon on Sophienstraße.*

Augustus the Strong's original idea was to build, on the site of a former fortress, a simple orangery. But his architect, **Matthäus Daniel Pöppelmann** (1662-1736), brought such breadth of vision to the project that its conception changed in the course of construction and it ended up as an enormous esplanade surrounded by galleries and pavilions. On every side, an impressive succession of windows and arcades with rounded arches lends the composition as a whole its rhythmic unity. The main appeal of this jewel of German Baroque lies in the harmonization of architectural work with sculptures from the studio of **Balthasar Permoser** (1651-1732), a Bavarian artist strongly influenced by his visits to Italy.

The huge rectangular courtyard has two semi-elliptical extensions which include the **Wallpavillon**★★ (Rampart Pavilion) and the **Glockenspielpavillon** (Carillon Pavilion). It is in the former that the intimate relationship between sculpture and architecture most admirably expresses itself. Not a single transverse wall breaks up the soaring lines of these verticals animated by the exuberance and vigour of Atlantes with the face of Hermes, drowned in a sea of vegetation. Crowning the pavilion, **Hercules Carrying the World** is the only work personally signed by Permoser.

Steps from the Wallpavillon lead to the terrace on which Pöppelmann's **Nymphenbad**★★ (Bath of the Nymphs) can be seen. It was undoubtedly in Italy that the artist found inspiration for this marvellous set piece, in which a subtle blend between the inorganic representation of nature – grotto work and fountains – and the grace of feminine forms creates an atmosphere that is irresistibly sensual.

The southwest side of the complex is closed off by the elegant **Zwinger Gallery**, best seen from the outside, passing beneath the **Kronentor** (Crown Gate).

This latter, embellished with statues representing the four seasons, comprises two superposed arcades surmounted by an onion-shaped dome, which terminates in four eagles supporting the Polish crown.

The **Semper Gallery**, built in 1847 by **Gottfried Semper** (1803-79), occupies the northeast side of the Zwinger reserved since 1728 for the exhibition of the royal collections. Of the Baroque ensemble as a whole – two-storey pavilions linked by one-storey galleries – the Anglo-German critic Sir Nikolaus Pevsner wrote: "What exultation in these rocking curves, and yet what grace! It is joyful but never vulgar; vigorous, boisterous perhaps, but never crude... of an inexhaustible creative power, with ever new combinations and variations of Italian Baroque forms placed against each other and piled above one another."

★★★ **Gemäldegalerie Alter Meister** (Old Masters Gallery) ⊘ – *Semper Gallery*.

This collection of paintings built up by Augustus II the Strong and his successor Augustus III is one of the best of its kind in the world. The most important masters from the Italian Renaissance and the Baroque period as well as Dutch and Flemish painters from the 17C are represented:

Ground floor:

Gallery 1: Tapestries after sketches by Raphaël.

Galleries 2-4: Numerous vedute (townscapes which are detailed and realistic enough for the town in question to be identified) by Bernardo Bellotto, otherwise known as Canaletto Bellotto, who painted Dresden and Pirna with extraordinary precision of detail in the mid 18C, to the extent that many of his paintings were used as a guideline during the reconstruction of Dresden after the Second World War. This makes an ideal introduction to a visit to Dresden.

Galleries 5-6: Paintings by Dresden masters Johann Alexander Thiele, a landscape painter and etcher who is credited with the invention of pastel painting in colours across the spectrum, rather than the black, white and red tones that had been used until then, and Christian Wilhelm Ernst Dietrich, a painter and etcher who produced an extraordinary variety of work, mainly in the style of 17C masters.

1st floor:

Galleries 101-102: Works by Silvestre and Canaletto Belotto.

Galleries 104-106 and 108-111: Flemish and Dutch painting from the 16C-17C. Note in particular Rembrandt's *Self-portrait with Saskia* (Gallery 106), Rubens' *Bathsheba*, and Vermeer's *Girl Reading a Letter by the Window* (Gallery 108).

Gallery 107: Paintings by the Early Netherlandish (Jan van Eyck is represented by a marvellous triptych) and Early German (masterpieces by Holbein, Cranach the Elder and Dürer) schools.

Gallery 112: 17C French painting (Claude Lorrain, Nicolas Poussin).

Galleries 113-121: 16C Italian painting. Works by Veronese, Tintoretto, Giorgione *(Sleeping Venus)*, Titian and Correggio, are on display in galleries 117-119 which are lit from above. A highlight of the collection is Raphaël's most famous portrayal of the Virgin and Child, the *Sistine Madonna*, in gallery 117.

Gallery 116: Paintings by Botticelli, Mantegna and Pintoricchio *(Portrait of a Boy)*.

2nd floor:

Gallery 201: pastel painting. Jean-Étienne Liotard's *Chocolate Girl* is particularly captivating. World's largest collection of works by Rosalba Carrieras (75 pastels).

Gallery 202: 18C French painting (Rigaud, Silvestre, Watteau).

Galleries 203-207: 18C Italian painting with works by Tiepolo and Crespi.

Galleries 208-210: Spanish painting (El Greco, Ribera, Murillo, Zurbarán, Velázquez).

GEMALDEGALERIE

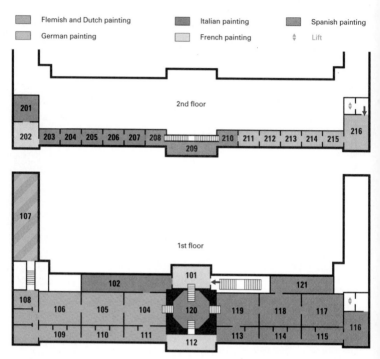

Galleries 211-216: 17C and 18C German painting (Elsheimer's *Jupiter and Mercury with Philemon and Baucis*, small in scale but exquisitely executed, in gallery 211). The exhibition reaches the threshold of the 19C in gallery 216, which contains works by Angelica Kauffmann and Anton Graff.

To help you get your bearings: Italian paintings are hung on a red background, Dutch and Flemish on a green background, and Spanish and French on a grey background.

★★ **Rüstkammer** (Armoury) ⓥ – *Semper Gallery*.
Even those not particularly interested in armour will appreciate this fascinating exhibition of what must be among the finest handcrafted armour, which was collected by the princely dynasty of the Wettiner. This abundant inventory includes 1 300 objects from the 15C to the 19C, including royal gifts and a collection of oriental and Far Eastern weapons and a gallery of rifles. The **suits of armour** are most impressive, and include the work of one of the most famous Augsburg armourers Anton Peffenhauser. The ceremonial suit of armour for King Erik XIV of Sweden, the work of Eliseus Libaert of Antwerp, is particularly ornate, and includes an equally sumptuous set of armour for the King's horse. There is also a unique display of children's armour, worn by the little princes during children's jousting tournaments at the Saxon court. Particularly intelligent is the joint exhibition of weapons and costumes, since the two were inseparable in courtly representation. Other parts of the exhibition not to be missed include the collections of **jousting tournament weapons, guns** and **pistols**.

★★ **Porzellansammlung** (Porcelain Collection) ⓥ – *Entrance on Sophienstraße*.
This gallery displays not only the products of the famous factory at Meißen, but also porcelain acquired by Augustus the Strong from Japan and China (from the best period in the 19C). Do not miss the "giant animal room" on the upper floor, including characters by Kirchner and Kändler of Meißen (first half of the 18C). There is also space devoted to **Johann Friedrich Böttger**, a potter who profited from the discovery of kaolin deposits nearby to create (1708) in Europe a porcelain modelled on that of the Far East. His first attempts to colour glazes are particularly interesting. The largest room displays Meissen tableware of the 18C and a carillon of 52 porcelain bells.

★★ **Mathematisch-Physikalischer Salon** (Salon of Mathematics and Physic) ⓥ – *Northwest corner pavilion* – The inventive genius of scientists in past ages is documented in the clocks and instruments of the 16C and 19C. The first floor displays sun, sand, oil, artistic and automatic clocks, standing clocks, wall clocks, table clocks and pocket watches as well as marine chronometers.

On the lower floor are earth and astronomic globes, a variety of measuring, optical, astronomic and meteorological instruments, calculators and drawing aids, "weights and measures", air pumps and burning machines.

On the way to the **Theaterplatz** *(Y 52) – note the equestrian statue of King John (1854-73) in the centre of the square – the road passes the* **old town watchtower** *(Altstädter Wache), which was designed by Schinkel.*

★★ **Semperoper (Opera)** – Built between 1871 and 1878 by Manfred Semper based on plans designed by his father Gottfried – Professor of Architecture at Dresden responsible for the previous edifice, destroyed by fire in 1869 – the present opera house owes its form to the Italian Renaissance.

The tiered façade comprises two storeys of arcades, surmounted by a third in recess. Each side wall is furnished with twin niches, occupied on the left by statues of Shakespeare and Sophocles, on the right, Molière and Euripides.

★★ **Katholische Hofkirche (Cathedral)** – This enormous basilican edifice was built between 1738 and 1754 following the conversion of the Albertines to Roman Catholicism, the condition of their accession to the Polish throne. Its 5 000m²/53 820sq ft floor area makes it the largest church in Saxony. The building, strongly influenced by Italian Baroque, is dominated by an 86m/282ft belltower and decorated with statues of the saints and apostles, mainly on the attics. The nave is separated from the side aisles by a semicircular ambulatory opening onto four oval chapels. Above the high altar, a fine painting (1765) by Anton Raphael Mengs depicts the Ascension. The pulpit was executed by Permoser in 1722, while the organ was the last work (1750-55) of the master craftsman Gottfried Silbermann. The tombs of several kings and princes of Saxony can be seen in the crypt.

Schloß (Castle) – Most of this Renaissance-style building, once the official residence of the Court, is in the process of being restored.

That part of the exterior façade linking the west wing to the Johanneum is covered by a colossal mosaic, **The Procession of Dukes★** (Fürstenzug, 1906). Composed in tiles of Meissen porcelain, the work represents a parade, in chronological order, of all the ducal members of the house of Saxe-Wettin. It measures 102x957m/335x3 140ft. The inner façade is formed by the **Langer Gang★**, a series of 22 Tuscan arcades enclosing the stable courtyard.

The **Johanneum (M¹)** (left of the Schöne Pforte entrance, a gateway in the Renaissance style) was itself once used as the stables. It now houses a **Transport Museum** (Verkehrsmuseum), where collections of vintage cars and motor cycles join a display outlining the evolution of public transport.

Leaving the Johanneum, cross the Neumarkt towards the ruins of the Frauenkirche.

Frauenkirche – This mighty domed building, the principal work of the architect George Bähr, was built from 1726. The famous 23.5m/77ft diameter dome, which so characterizes the silhouette of the town, was completed in 1738. The place of worship was the most important testimony to Protestant church building, right up until it fell victim to the air attacks of 13 and 14 February 1945. The sea of flames heated up the sandstones to such an extent that they burst and the eight pillars were no longer able to bear the weight of the 5 800t stone dome. On the morning of 15 February it collapsed with such force that the floor of the church was broken open. The ruin of the Frauenkirche symbolised the destruction of the town and stood as a witness and memorial until after the reunification of Germany.

The restoration of the Frauenkirche

The restoration work finally began in 1993, after a good deal of procrastination, not least due to the immense costs involved. The work will cost over 250 million DM and can only be partially paid for by donations and marketing campaigns. In this respect however, a great deal of imagination has been demonstrated: coins, clocks with a minute piece of stone from the church, documents and concerts will all contribute to the restoration work. By 1998, the donated figure stood at 160 million DM. A few figures serve to indicate just what a huge project this is: 8 390 façade, wall and ceiling blocks, one quarter of its total surface, were found in the rubble of the Frauenkirche, but only 10 percent of them were undamaged. In addition there are 90 000 back-up blocks available, which will of course also be used in the construction together with damaged but still usable blocks. It has been possible to allocate, survey and photograph the blocks, with the aid of 10 000 old photographs and the original building plans, before they are assigned to their final location. They are recorded in a database which includes 90 000 electronically stored pictures.

The restoration work, which gains 7.5m/24.5ft in height every year, should be completed on time for the celebrations marking the 800 year anniversary of the founding of Dresden in 2006. The lower church or **crypt**, with its stone altar by the English artist Anish Kapoor in the centre and the tomb of the master builder George Bähr, was completed in August 1996. Services are held on Fridays and Sundays, with so-called restoration concerts being held on Saturdays. The church will seat 2 200 and is set to become an "international meeting place".

Go onto the **Brühlsche Terrasse (Y 6)**, laid out on the site of ancient fortifications, where there is a **view**★ of the Elbe and the Neustadt quarter, on the river's east bank.

Albertinum – This one-time arsenal was transformed, in 1884-85, into a museum.

★★★ **Gemäldegalerie Neuer Meister** (Gallery of 19C and 20C Painters) ⊘ – A visit to these rooms permits the visitor to gauge the richness and diversity of German art from the Romantics (**Casper David Friedrich**, *Two Men Contemplate the Moon*; **AL Richter**, *The Crossing of the Elbe*) to the Biedermeier (**Carl Spitzweg**, *The Hook and Line Fisherman*); from the Bourgeois Realists (**Adolf von Menzel**, *Sermon in the Old Church of the Berlin Monastery*) to the so-called "Deutsch-Römer" (**Arnold Böcklin**, *A Summer's Day*; **Wilhelm Leibl**, *Portrait of the Baron von Stauffenberg*) and the painters of Jugendstil (**Fritz von Uhde**, *The Nativity*). The Impressionists are represented by their leading lights: **Max Slevogt**, *Scenes of Egyptian Life*; **Max Liebermann**, *Portrait of Alfred von Berger*; **Lovis Corinth**, *The Painter's Model*.

The Brücke movement, spearhead of German Expressionism, was born in Dresden at the beginning of this century. The group, a spin-off from Fauvism, is notably represented by **Karl Schmidt Rottluff**, *After the Bath*; and **Max Pechstein**, *A Baltic Landscape*.

Two triptychs illustrate in a gripping way the "revolutionary" German school operating between the wars: *War* (1929-32) by **Otto Dix**, a denunciation without concession of the cruelty and folly of the warlike mentality; and *The Thousand-Year Reich* (1935-38), a vision both ironic and prophetic of the new National Socialist regime by **Hans Grundig**.

The remaining rooms are devoted to painters from the international avant-garde and painters from Dresden and Saxony.

★★★ **Grünes Gewölbe** (Green Vault Collections) ⊘ – From 1723 to 1729, Augustus the Strong redesigned the treasury rooms in the western wing of the Dresden Castle turning them into a treasure chamber museum, called *Die Geheime Verwahrung*,

The Thousand-Year Reich by Hans Grundig

War and the painter

Otto Dix, born in Dresden in 1891 to a working-class family, volunteered for the war and had first-hand experience of the horrors of war for three years. Like George Grosz, with whom he studied in Dresden, Dix was interested in the human being as an individual. His particularly penetrating sense of observation let him depict people with merciless realism in the details, faces and hands ruined by the war. His tableaux, inspired by the old masters such as Grünewald, are filed with criticism of the political and social condition. They are comparable to Karl Grüne's 1923 film *Die Straße*. In 1927, Dix was named professor at the Dresden Academy of Art. Between 1928 and 1932, he painted the triptych *Der Krieg* (War; see **Gallery of 19C and 20C Painters**). In 1933, he was fired, and a year later was prohibited from exhibiting his works. He moved to the Bodensee, where he died in 1969.

---

the Secret Safekeeping, accessible by the public. The name green vault soon became popular owing to the green colour originally used on some of the architectural elements. The great ruler kept masterpieces of the jewellery and goldsmithing art here that were later supplemented with outstanding works of ivory, rare stone carvings and bronze statuettes. In the wake of the chaos left by the Second World War, the treasure was put in care of the Albertinum; about half of the inventory is still kept here in rooms of different colour.

Green room: Displays mostly goldsmithery from the 16C and 17C that had been created for the Elector's table or display cases. The masters were mostly from Nürnberg, Augsburg, Leipzig, or Dresden.

Blue room: Works of amber and ivory. Of particular note is the ivory regatta dating to 1620 and a large cabinet from Königsberg (Kaliningrad). Colourful vessels with precious stones and quartz crystal works are exhibited in wall display cases.

Red room: The room is devoted to precious works that Augustus the Strong purchased from contemporary artists in order to bind them to the court. The works by the court jeweller **Johann Melchior Dinglinger** are outstanding: a golden coffee set, the **Court State of the Grand Mogul,** Diana's Bath and the famous Moor with the Emerald Step.

Yellow room: This room is devoted to jewellery: sets consisting of diamonds, emeralds, sapphires and topazes, representative jewellery from the queen's collection. The case with the microscopic carvings from the Dresden Kunstkammer (Art Chamber) is a must; the most famous piece is the cherry stone bearing the 185 carved heads, a work dating to 1589.

When restoration work is finished on the castle, the treasures of the Green Vault will return to their original place.

★ **Stadtmuseum Dresden** ⊘ (Y M⁴) – Installed in the **Landhaus** – an elegant palazzo built from 1770 to 1775 in the Classical and Late Baroque styles, with elements of Rococo – this exhibition retraces the stages of Dresden's development and the principal facts of its history. There are works by contemporary Dresden artists and exhibits from the history of firefighting.

★ **Kreuzkirche** – The original church, the city's oldest (early 13C), was remodelled in the Baroque style after its destruction (1760) during the Seven Years War. The damage inflicted during the Second World War has been repaired on the outside of the church, but the inside strikes visitors with quite a shock since it has so far only been roughly plastered over. The Kreuzkirche is home to the Kreuzchor, a world famous choir.

NEUSTADT QUARTER (EAST BANK)

The **Hauptstraße (X 19),** which links the Albertplatz and the Neustädter Markt – dominated by the gilded **equestrian statue**★ (X E) of Augustus the Strong – was the object, after the catastrophe of 1945, of a tasteful restoration scheme which managed to preserve several 18C dwellings.

The Neustadt quarter, where the styles of the residences range from Baroque via neo-Classicism to buildings from the Gründerzeit period of rapid industrial expansion (it is in fact the largest quarter in Germany to date from this period), is becoming increasingly popular among both residents and tourists. Shops are being restored and opened, the quarter houses numerous restaurants, antique shops and arts and crafts businesses, and art galleries and bookshops are all setting up here.

★ **Japanisches Palais (Japanese Palace) (X)** – Built between 1715 and 1737 under the direction of Pöppelmann, this huge quadrilateral was designed to display Augustus the Strong's collection of Meissen tableware. The oriental-style roofs of the corner pavilions lend the place its Asiatic character. On the side nearest the Elbe, there is a pleasant garden with a **view** of the river's west bank.

DRESDEN

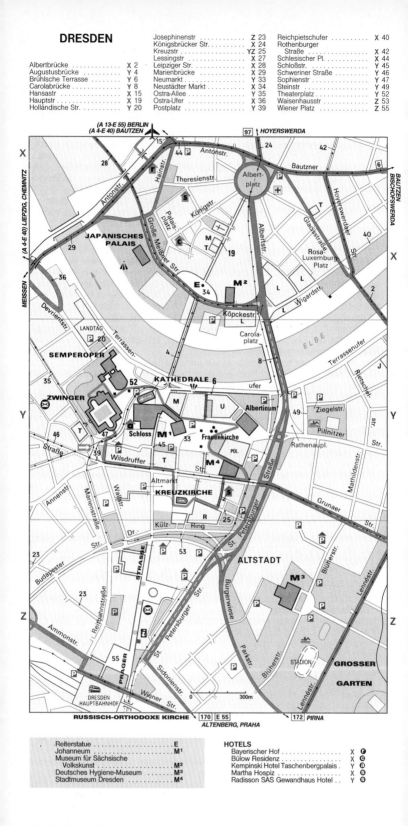

★ **Museum für Sächsische Volkskunst** (Museum of Saxon Arts and Crafts) ⊘ (X M²) –
This collection is located in the oldest Renaissance building in the city, the 1568
Jägerhof (Hunters Court). It displays works mainly of Saxon folk art, painted
furniture, works of pottery and basketry, blue prints and tableware, as well as
Saxon and Sorb folkloric costumes and lacework, toys and carvings from the
Erzgebirge, Christmas decorations and folk art by miners.

Pfunds Molkerei – *79 Bautzner Straße*. The retail shop of the dairy established
by the Pfund brothers in 1880 is described as "the most beautiful dairy in the
world". The shop lies in the heart of the Dresdner Neustadt quarter. The
interior★, which dates from 1892 and has been kept intact, comprises coloured,
hand-painted tiles from the industrial expansion period, which cover all the
walls, the ceiling and the floor. The scenes relating to the dairy business are
based on the motif of the grotesque which was so popular during the
Renaissance. Playing putti and landscapes with pastoral idylls are displayed on
the frieze below the ceiling. Luxuriant floral ornamentations decorate the walls.
The shop counter with its "till" currently sells speciality cheeses from all around
the world.

ADDITIONAL SIGHTS

★ **Großer Garten** (Z) – This huge public park is traversed by a broad walk leading
to a **Palace** (1678-83) in the Baroque style. On either side there are groups of
statuary, a zoo, botanical gardens and an open-air theatre, all in a pleasant sylvan
setting.

★ **Russisch-orthodoxe Kirche** (Z) – *Leave to the south, left of the railway station*.
The designers of this colourful church, built in 1874, were inspired by Russian
architecture of the 17C.

Deutsches Hygiene-Museum ⊘ (Z M³) – *Lingnerplatz 1*.
Karl August Lingner, who invented Odol mouthwash, was instrumental in the
founding of this highly original museum in 1912. The main focus of the exhibition
is the human body. In the current climate of awareness about health and ecology,
the clearly displayed information seems more relevant than ever. One of the main
features of the permanent exhibition is the "glass person" (Gläserner Mensch),
giving an insight into the structure and functioning of the human body. Other
excellent special exhibitions treat cultural and current themes. In short, this
unusual museum stimulates both young and old alike to experiment and find out
more about how their bodies work.

EXCURSIONS

★ **Schloß Moritzburg** ⊘ – *14km/9mi to the northwest, via Hansastraße* (X).
Built by the Duke Moritz on one of the Royal Saxon Hunting Reserves in 1542-46,
this was originally designed to be no more than a simple hunting lodge in the
Renaissance style. However, it was considerably refashioned between 1723 and
1736 by Matthäus Daniel Pöppelmann, at the request of Frederick-Augustus I
(1670-1733), who had wanted to transform it into a Baroque château. Adjoining
the present striking edifice, with four wings and imposing ochre and white corner
towers (the colours of the Baroque in Saxony), are an artificial lake and a large
park. The stone sculptures (urns, cupids and statues of hunters) on the
balustrades of the entrance drive and on the terrace are the work of JC Kirchner
and B Thomae. Inside the castle there is a **Baroque Museum** (Barockmuseum)
displaying furniture of the period, and three main galleries containing an
impressive collection of trophies. The castle chapel was built between 1661 and
1672 by WC von Klengel (1630-91) and integrated by Pöppelmann into the
remodelled building. The small **Pheasantry Pavilion** (Fasanenschlößchen) – *a 30min
walk away, currently under restoration* – houses a museum of ornithology. It was
built between 1769 and 1782.

★ **Schloß Pillnitz** ⊘ – *15km/9.5mi to the southeast, via Bautznerstraße* (X).
Pöppelmann, favourite architect of the Electors, was responsible for this pleasure
palace too. Designed between 1720 and 1724, the **Riverside Palace** (Wasserpalais)
was originally built on the east bank of the Elbe. The Late Baroque predilection
for Chinese motifs is apparent in the roof treatment. A new castle, between the
waterside structure and the **Upper Palace** (Bergpalais) was built between 1818 and
1826 under the architect Schuricht, following a fire which gutted the Renaissance
building.
There is a **Decorative Arts Museum** (Kunstgewerbe-Museum Dresden) in the upper
and riverside palaces. Furniture, gilded bronzes, Baroque faience, silverware,
glassware and Asiatic porcelain are on display, with special emphasis on the

China-Japan-Saxony connection. In addition, applied arts of all genres are shown, from the Gothic period till today. The products of the German Werkbund are especially representative of the 20C, though current fashions in design are also included.

The park was transformed into an English-style garden in 1778. A lagoon was added, a circular pavilion or gazebo a year later, and then a Chinese pavilion (one of the most perfect copies of Chinese architecture in Europe) in 1804. The banks of the Elbe offer attractive riverside walks. The islet opposite the gardens is a bird reserve, inhabited by grey herons.

*** **Swiss Saxony** – *See SÄCHSISCHE SCHWEIZ.*

* **Meißen** – *See MEISSEN.*

DÜSSELDORF*

Nordrhein-Westfalen
Population 570 000
Michelin map 417 M 14

Once a fishing village on the east bank of the Rhine, Düsseldorf today is one of the most important economic centres of Germany. The development of the city, which lies at the confluence of the Rhine and the Düssel, has been given an added administrative importance since it was established, in 1946, as the capital of the Rhineland-Westphalia Land.

HISTORICAL NOTES

Düsseldorf first acquired city status in the 13C when it was chosen as the official residence of the dukes of Berg. Four centuries later, the family of the electors of the Neuburg-Palatinate settled there and the fame of the city spread. This was largely due to the energy and intelligence of the family's most famous member, Johann Wilhelm (Elector from 1690 to 1715). Patron and apostle of the Baroque, **Jan Wellem**, as he was known, surrounded himself with a brilliant court of musicians, painters and architects who transformed Düsseldorf into a true city of the arts.

After the French Revolution, Napoleon created the town capital of the Grand Duchy of Berg, and it became a minor Paris. Murat, and then Jerome Bonaparte were its first rulers. In 1815 it seceded to Prussia.

Heinrich Heine (1797-1856) – Heine, son of a Bolkerstraße merchant, lived in Düsseldorf throughout his youth, deeply impressed by the presence of the French and the personality of Napoleon. In his *Memories of Childhood* he expressed his admiration of France with characteristic verve, at once biting and melancholic. A poet who was also a willing pamphleteer, eternal traveller, defender of liberalism, a Francophile and a genuine European, Heine once described himself as "a German nightingale which would have liked to make its nest in Voltaire's wig".

A Musical City – Among the musicians who have given Düsseldorf its enviable reputation as an artistic centre are Robert Schumann and Felix Mendelssohn-Bartholdy. **Schumann** (1810-56) was appointed conductor of the municipal orchestra in 1850. Living for four years in a house in the Bilker Straße (**DZ**), he was already seriously in prey of a nervous illness, attempting to drown himself in the Rhine in 1854. His friend **Mendelssohn** (1809-47) brilliantly directed the city's Rhine Festival. He made his first journey to England in 1829, conducting his own *Symphony in C Minor* at the London Philharmonic Society.

LIFE IN DÜSSELDORF

The Head Office of the Ruhr – Seat of one of Germany's most important stock exchanges, Düsseldorf is not only the country's second banking and financial centre but also administrative capital for most of the Rhineland industries. All these functions are exemplified in the **Dreischeibenhaus** (Thyssen Building) (**EY E**). Practically all business and commercial transactions concerning the Ruhr and surrounding cities are negotiated in an area between the Kasernenstraße (**DZ**) and the Berliner Allee (**EZ**).

The World of Fashion – Exhibitions, fairs and collections of haute couture several times a year maintain Düsseldorf's reputation as a "minor Paris" and fashion capital of Germany. The CPD (Collections Premiere Düsseldorf) is the largest fashion trade show in the world, with 2 200 exhibitors from over 40 countries. A walk along the chestnut-lined **Königsallee*** (**EZ**) (popularly known as "the Kö") demonstrates that the reputation is deserved. Everything that is elegant in the town centres on this graceful promenade. With its boutiques and arcades, its cafés and restaurants, built on either side of the old moat.

DÜSSELDORF

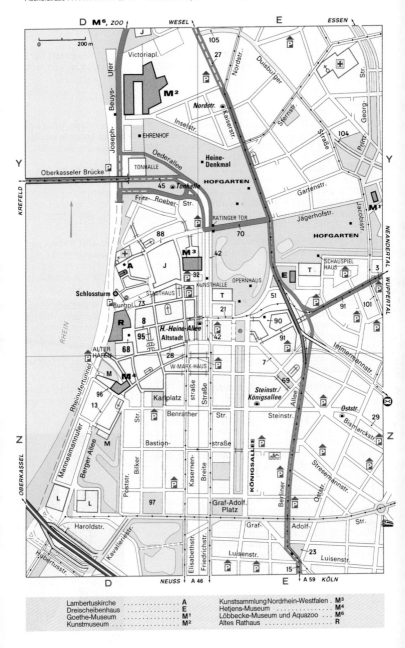

Lambertuskirche	A
Dreischeibenhaus	E
Goethe-Museum	M¹
Kunstmuseum	M²

Kunstsammlung Nordrhein-Westfalen	M³
Hetjens-Museum	M⁴
Löbbecke-Museum und Aquazoo	M⁶
Altes Rathaus	R

A new concept in travel planning.
When you want to calculate a trip distance or visualise a detailed itinerary ; when you need information on hotels,
restaurants or campsites, consult Michelin on the Internet.
Visit our Web site to discover our full range of services for travellers:
www.michelin-travel.com.

DÜSSELDORF

Food – It is in the taverns typical of the old town that regional specialities can best be appreciated: Blutwurst mit Zwiebeln (black pudding with onions); Halve Hahn (caraway cheese eaten with strong local mustard); and Röggelchen (small rye bread rolls). On Friday evenings, there is a tradition of eating Reibekuchen, a kind of savoury potato cake. **Altbier**, the still, dark brown ale of the region, is brewed in Düsseldorf.

The Way Ahead – Düsseldorf plays an increasingly important role in economic relations linking Germany with the Far East. Japanese firms alone have 300 branches in the city.

This strong Oriental presence is reinforced by the existence of the **Japanese Cultural Center** in the Immermannstraße (**EYZ**) and the Taiwan Trade Center, near the central station.

SIGHTS

Old Town (DEY) – This riverside quarter, with its taverns and bars jam-packed from the earliest hours of the evening, is known as "**the biggest boozer in Europe**". It is here that the "**Radschläger**" – local street urchins and buskers who perform outdoor acrobatics for a few pennies – can be found.

The **Bolkerstraße (DY 8)**, birthplace of Heinrich Heine (no 53), is the busiest and liveliest of the city's pedestrian precincts. The neighbourhood is equally linked with the story of the tailor Wibbel, who attended his own funeral after switching identities to escape a prison sentence. This folklore legend is recalled by the figures of the Schneider-Wibbel-Gasse carillon clock (**DY 95**), which operates at 11am, 1pm, 3pm, 6pm and 9pm.

Marktplatz (DY 68) – Separated from the Rhine only by the **Altes Rathaus (DY R)** (late-16C town hall), this square is embellished with the bronze equestrian statue (early 18C) of the famous Jan Willem. There is a good view of the river from the Burgplatz adjoining this square to the north, in the shadow of the **Schloßturm**, a free-standing tower.

Lambertuskirche (DY A) – This huge 14C Gothic hall-church is distinguished by a spire that is both leaning and twisted. The interior decoration is basically Baroque. A finely worked Late Gothic ciborium – a canopy or baldaquin above the altar – can be seen in the northern part of the chancel. The remains of 15C wall paintings are visible on the south wall.

At the far end of the nave there is a Pietà (c 1420) in a modern (1975) setting. The bronze entrance door is by Ewald Mataré.

* **Schloß Jägerhof and the Hofgarten (DEY)** – The Hofgarten park forms a shady continuation of the Königsallee, northwest towards the riverside museum quarter and east as far as **Schloß Jägerhof**. This delightful building, one-time home of the Electors Master of the Hunt, dates from the 18C. The French architect Nicolas de Pigage contributed to the plans. Today the mansion houses the **Goethe-Museum* (EY M¹)**, which displays the author's manuscripts, autographs, drawings and engravings, as well as busts and first editions of his works. On the second floor, a sumptuous apartment provides a perfect setting for the **Dr Schneider Private Collection**: note especially the Augsburg gold and silver plate and the Meissen porcelain. Napoleon Hill, in the park, is crowned with a small Maillol bronze entitled *Harmony* – in fact a modest monument to Heine.

Les Glycines by Emile Gallé, Kunstmuseum, Düsseldorf

* **Kunstmuseum (Fine Arts Museum)** ⊘ **(DY M²)** – Romantics of the Düsseldorf School (Cornelius, Schirmer, Achenbach, Rethel) dominate the important painting gallery in this museum. There is equal exposure for Impressionists and members of the German Expressionist movement (Corinth, Kandinsky, Jawlensky, Macke, Klee, Kirchner and Nolde). Space is also devoted to contemporary art (painting, sculpture and objets d'art), in particular that of the 1960s. The museum is also home to an interesting collection of medieval sculpture, and an outstanding collection of **glassware**** which includes glass from Roman times to the present from both Europe and the Far East, and a large amount of Jugendstil glassware. Other museum departments include an **Oriental section** (with Islamic decorative arts and textiles) and an extensive **graphics collection** (80 000 prints and original engravings from the 15C-20C; works not displayed can be viewed in the reading room).

★ **Kunstsammlung Nordrhein-Westfalen** (Rhineland-Westphalia Art Collection) ⊘ **(DY M³)** – Designed by the Danish architects Dissing and Weitling, this modern building houses a 20C art collection including works by Picasso, Braque, Léger, Chagall, Ernst, Beuys and **Paul Klee** – who was the Fine Arts Professor in Düsseldorf from 1930 to 1933. Ninety-two of the artist's pictures are exhibited in rotation.

★ **Hetjens-Museum** (Deutsches Keramik-Museum) ⊘ **(DZ M⁴)** – This collection of 12 000 ceramic objects from all over the world covers a time span of 8 000 years. This is the only special interest museum of its kind in the German-speaking countries to present one of the oldest work materials used by the human for both utility as well as artistic purposes.

★ **Löbbecke-Museum und Aquazoo** ⊘ – *Kaiserwerther Straße 380, in the North Park, via the Hofgartenufer* **(DY M⁶)**.
This building houses under a single roof the Löbbecke Natural History Museum (insects, molluscs, reptiles) and an aquazoo. No less than 80 aquariums serve as home to all types of aquatic creatures including sharks and seals, and 62 terrariums display reptiles and insects. Instructive explanations familiarise the visitor with all kinds of life in a marine element, and its ecological importance. A **Tropical Hall** in the middle of the building (crocodiles, monkeys and butterflies) can be crossed by means of a footbridge.

EXCURSIONS

Neuss – *10km/6mi to the southwest. Leave Düsseldorf via Elisabethstraße.*
The 13C **Quirinusmünster**★ with its trefoil apse is one of the last Rhenish Romanesque constructions of importance. The exterior is marked by the quadratic tower with its pyramidal roof and the octagonal tower above the transept crossing topped by a cupola flanked by four little quadratic towers with diamond-shaped roofs. The shell form of the church's clerestory windows, as well as unusual mingling of round and pointed arches, marks the transition in Germany to the Gothic style. From the raised chancel there is a good view of the aisles.

★ **Schloß Benrath** ⊘ – *10km/6mi to the southeast.*
This exemplary Late Baroque building was designed by Nicolas de Pigage from 1755 to 1770 as a country palace for Carl Theodor, Prince Elector of the Palatinate.
Two subsidiary wings and two gatehouses flank a central pavilion. The interior is decorated in a style which is transitional between Rococo and Early Classicism, and fitted with elegant late-18C furniture.
The **park**★ was also designed by Pigage and laid out in the formal French style. It extends west as far as the Rhine. The deer garden contains century-old trees and is crisscrossed by avenues which intersect to form star patterns. Other parts of the park feature large lakes and flower ridges.

Neandertal – *14km/9mi to the east, via Am Wehrhahn.*
The deep and steep-sided valley of the Düssel owes its name to the Calvinist poet Joachim Neander (1650-80), who liked to use it as a retreat. It was here, in a grotto since destroyed, that the famous skeleton of **Neanderthal Man**, 60 000 years old, was discovered in 1856. A plaque on a triangular rock *(on the right-hand side of the road, 3km/2mi beyond the motorway underpass)* marks the site of the cave.

Neanderthal Museum ⊘ – *12km/7mi eastwards in Neandertal, Talstraße 300.*
This museum, opened in 1996 not far from the Neandertal excavation site, gives an overview of the history of human evolution. There is a striking reconstruction of our ancestor: from a skull, a computer was able to calculate how the features would have looked. Silicon and modern technological skill were then combined to create a life-size model of prehistoric man.

Michelin on the Net: www.michelin-travel.com.
Our route planning service covers all of Europe – twenty-one countries and one million kilometres of highways and byways – enabling you to plot many different itineraries from wherever you are. The itinerary options allow you to choose a preferred route – for example, quickest, shortest, or Michelin recommended.
The network is updated three times weekly, integrating ongoing road works, detours, new motorways, and snowbound mountain passes.
The description of the itinerary includes the distances and travelling times between towns, selected hotels and restaurants.

Kloster EBERBACH★★

Abbaye d'EBERBACH – Hessen

Michelin map 417 P 8 – 18km/11mi west of Wiesbaden

The former Cistercian abbey, the only sister foundation of Clairvaux in Germany apart from Himmerod in the Eifel, lies in a charming valley in absolute isolation. The abbey still emanates the peace and invitation to contemplation sought by its founders. In 1135, when St Bernard was still alive, the Cistercian monks from Burgundy came here and laid the foundation stone for one of the best kept medieval monasterial establishments in Germany.
The abbey was secularised in 1803 and became a wine-growing property.

TOUR ⊙

Abbey church – Built in two stages, in 1145-60 and then 1170-86, it is a Roman cross vaulted basilica with three naves; its austere appearance is characteristic of Cistercian architecture. Gothic chapels with beautiful tracery windows were built on the south side between 1310 and 1340. A number of remarkable **tombs**★ dating from the 14C to the 18C bear witness to the church's significance as a burial place.

Abbey buildings – These are grouped around the **cloister**★, which was built in the mid 13C and 14C. Only the portal remains of the **monks' refectory** which was built before 1186. Rebuilt in 1720, the room is impressive, with a magnificent stucco ceiling by Daniel Schenk from Mainz (1738).
The lay brothers' refectory contains a collection of mighty **winepresses**★★, documenting the wine producing tradition of the abbey which has endured for over 800 years. The oldest press dates from the year 1668.
The **monks' dormitory**★, which is around 85m/279ft long and which dates back mainly to the period around 1250-70, is remarkable. The double-naved, ribbed vaulted room was built with a slightly rising floor, and the columns were shortened accordingly, so that it appears longer than it is. The **chapter-house** was built prior to 1186. A particularly beautiful star-ribbed vault from the year 1345 should not be missed. The stylised plant decoration dates back to 1500.
The dormitory leads to the **abbey museum** on the upper floor, which contains a display on the history of the abbey and of the Cistercian Order.

EICHSTÄTT★★

Bayern

Population 13 000

Michelin map 419/420 T 17

Eichstätt, a small episcopal city – and seat of a Catholic university – that never suffered wartime damage or industrialisation, lies on a meander in the midst of the Altmühl Valley. The bishopric was already founded in the 8C by Willibald, who had been asked by Bonifatius to perform missionary work in Eichstätt. The town owes its Baroque character to the reconstruction following the burning of the town (except for the cathedral) by the Swedes in 1634 during the Thirty Years War. Many of the roofs are covered with limestone slabs (from Solnhofen) peculiar to the region.
Though the metaphor may seem unsuitable, it nevertheless does express what the city and parish of Eichstätt has become and remains to this day thanks to the "handwriting" of the former Episcopal building director Karljosef Schattner: a "Mecca" of uncompromising, contemporary architecture, such as the new Pedagogical University and the refurbishing of the Summer Residence as a university building.

★**EPISCOPAL QUARTER** (BISCHÖFLICHER RESIDENZBEZIRK) *1hr 30min*

Dom (Cathedral) – The nave and the eastern chancel date from the 14C, though large parts of it are Romanesque, Early Gothic or Baroque. The main entrance is via a Gothic door decorated with polychromatically set statues. The west face is Baroque.
Inside, the most fascinating feature is the late-15C **Pappenheim Reredos**★★, almost 9m/30ft high and of Jura limestone, in the north aisle. The representation of the Crucifixion with its attendant figures is a masterpiece of religious sculpture. In the west chancel is a seated statue of **St Willibald** (Bishop of Eichstätt in the 8C) as an old man, the major work of local sculptor Loy Hering (1514).
Go through the south transept to the Mortuarium.

★**Mortuarium** – This funerary chapel, forming the west wing of the cloister, is a late-15C Gothic hall with two naves. Handsome tombstones pave the floor. A twisted column ends each line of pillars supporting the groined vaulting. The so-called "Beautiful Column" is very finely worked. Four **stained-glass windows** in the east wall are by Hans Holbein the Elder (c 1500). There is a 16C Crucifixion on the south wall by Loy Hering.

EICHSTÄTT

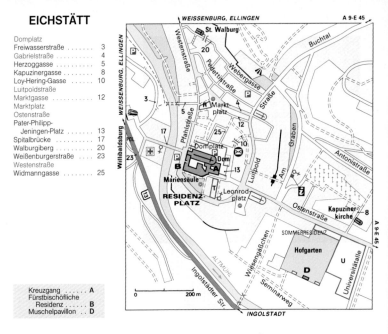

Diocesan Museum (Diözesanmuseum) ⊙ – *Upper floor, above the chancel.*
The long history of the Diocese is illustrated by means of pictures, maps, vestments, liturgical accessories and statues in stone and wood. In the Bishop's Room, note **St Willibald's Chasuble**, the oldest liturgical vestment in the See – a Byzantine work dating probably from the 12C.
Reliquaries, chalices, monstrances and other examples of religious art are on view in the **treasury**.

★ **Cloister (A)** – This element was a 15C addition to the cathedral. The stone tracery of the windows is richly decorated.

★ **Residenzplatz** – The southeast corner is the best place from which to obtain a general view of this irregularly shaped square which nevertheless displays a striking unity. Lawns carpet the centre; Rococo palaces surround it. The south side is bordered by four imposing houses with decorated gables and entrances guarded by atlantes. Facing them is the southern wing of the Residence and, on the west side, the former Vicar-General's mansion. The **Virgin's Column** in the immediate foreground (Mariensäule) rises from a fountain surrounded by cherubs.

Fürstbischöfliche Residenz (Former Episcopal Residence) ⊙ **(B)** – (Local administration office). The main entrance opens onto a magnificent staircase with a Baroque banister and painted ceiling.

ADDITIONAL SIGHTS

Hofgarten – This park was designed in the style of an English garden by Eugene de Beauharnais, the son-in-law of Napoleon created Duke of Leuchtenberg and Prince of Eichstätt by King Maximilian of Bavaria. It extends in front of the summer residence of the Prince-Bishops. Three delightful pavilions adjoin the south wall. In the centre, the **Shell Pavilion**★ (Muschelpavillon) **(D)**, with its fountain and stuccowork, is a true shrine to the Rococo style.

Kapuzinerkirche – One of the chapels in this 17C church contains a 12C copy of the Holy Sepulchre in Jerusalem.

St.-Walburg – The interior of this Benedictine monastery church (built 1629-31) is discreetly decorated with Wessobrunn stuccoes. From the balcony outside the main doorway there is an attractive view over the roofs of the old town to the Altmühl Valley.

Willibaldsburg – *Access via route B 13 and the Burgstraße.*
This 14C castle, unfinished until the beginning of the 17C, occupies a dominant position on a height overlooking the river in the western part of the town. Inside the castle, note the **well** (Tiefer Brunnen), 75m/246ft deep *(access through the courtyard)*. From the top of the crenellated tower *(98 steps)* there is a **view** of the fortifications, the town and the river.

★ **Jura-Museum** ⊙ – The geological history of the Franconian Jura is traced in this museum. Most of the fossils on display (ammonites, crustaceans, fish, reptiles and dragonflies) were discovered in the limestone beds of neighbouring Soln-

Jura-Museum, Eichstätt

Archaeopteryx, Jura-Museum

hofen. An interesting comparison can be made between these fossil animals and those to be found in an aquarium. The museum's prize exhibit is the complete fossilized skeleton of an Archaeopteryx (prehistoric ancestor of birds). A link between the reptile and the bird in the evolution of species, this extremely rare example was found in 1951 near Workerzell, northwest of Eichstätt.

Museum für Ur- und Frühgeschichte (Museum of Early History) ⊙ – The exhibits here chart the history of settlers and settlements in the valley of the Altmühl from the epoch of hunters and crop-gatherers to the Middle Ages. Note especially the objects found in archeological digs which relate to iron-working during the Hallstatt civilization, the collection of Ancient Roman artefacts and a double grave from the Merovingian period.

EXCURSIONS

Weißenburg – *24km/15mi to the northwest.*
At the limit of the ancient Roman province of Rhaetia, Weißenburg was an important garrison town. The **Roman Baths**★ (Römische Thermen) ⊙, discovered in 1977 and a **Roman Museum** (Römermuseum) ⊙ – note particularly the fine **collection of bronze**★, and the porta decumana, a perfectly reconstructed fortified gateway, in the Kastell Biriciana – testify to its significant past. Weißenburg's historical old town centre is worth a visit for the 15C Gothic town hall and the market square, Luitpoldstraße (the Holmarkt or Wood Market) with its elegant merchants' houses.
The **Ellinger Tor**, to the north of the town, is an interesting gateway once part of the surrounding 14C ramparts. The **Andreaskirche** has an elegant Late Gothic chancel built at the beginning of the 15C. Near the church, on Martin-Luther-Platz, is the **The Imperial City Museum of Weißenburg** (Reichsstadtmuseum Weißenburg) located in historic walls. It documents the history of the city with special emphasis on the Imperial period – a title that Weißenburg held until 1802.

Ellingen – *3km/2mi to the north of Weißenburg.*
This locality owes its fame to the Teutonic Knights, whose Commander for Franconia was based in this small town from the 13C until Napoleon's dissolution of the Order in 1809.
The **castle** (Schloß) (1718-1725) comprises an inner courtyard framed by four imposing wings, one of which is entirely occupied by the church.
The huge twin-flight **main staircase**★ links the different apartments with a frigid solemnity.

Neues Fränkisches Seenland – The building of the Danube Canal and the channel linking the waters of the Danube and Altmühl has created an area with three lakes (Altmühl-, Brombach- and Rothsee), north of Weißenburg, which is ideal for relaxation and recreation.

EIFEL★

Nordrhein-Westfalen and Rheinland-Pfalz
Michelin map 417 O-P 4

The Eifel, geographically an eastward extension of the Ardennes, is the largest and most complex of the four Rhineland schist massifs. An undulating plateau at an average altitude of 600m/1 970ft, the region is deeply gashed by the Ahr, the Rur and the Kyll rivers, which meander through picturesque wooded valleys.
The **Upper Eifel** (Hocheifel), in the centre, shows traces of ancient volcanic activity, with basalt crests (Hohe Acht: 747m/2 450ft), tufa deposits, hot springs and lakes (Maare).
The **Schnee-Eifel**, the most rugged and isolated of the four, forms a sombre barrier along the Belgian frontier, northwest of Prum. Much of it rises to 700m/2 300ft.

The **North Eifel**, a landscape of moors and forests cut by deep valleys, is romantic and attractive. The touristic Seven Lakes sector extends in the northwest to the Upper Fagnes (Hohes Venn), a marshy tableland belonging more to the Ardennes than the Eifel.

The **South Eifel**, bordering Luxembourg's "Little Switzerland", is a region of picturesque valleys with small villages among the trees.

Ahr Wines – The vineyards bordering this river, planted with Burgundian stock on schistous slopes, produce dark-red wines late in the season, which are at their best when drunk almost warm.

FROM BAD MÜNSTEREIFEL TO MANDERSCHEID

145km/90mi – one day

This excursion follows the busy valley of the Ahr, climbs to the rolling, forested immensity of the Upper Eifel, and then snakes between the volcanic lakes of the Maare.

★ **Bad Münstereifel** – Surrounded by massive **ramparts**★ (Stadtbefestigung), the town still boasts a quantity of old houses and monuments. The **Stiftskirche St.-Chrysanthus und Daria** is an outstanding abbey church recalling St.-Pantaleon in Cologne because of the two towers flanking its 11C Romanesque west front.

A few miles east of Münstereifel, the road passes, on the left, a giant **radio-telescope**, rejoins the Ahr at Kreuzberg and continues along the winding valley. The telescope is 100m/328ft in diameter and its parabolic depth is 21m/69ft.

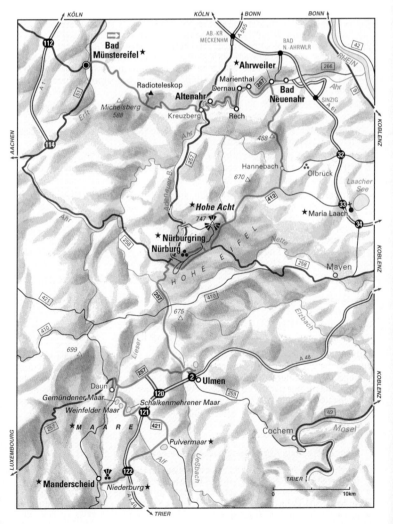

Altenahr – On a site between two bends in the river, Altenahr is an excursion centre dominated by the scattered ruins of the 12C **Burg Are**. There is an attractive view from the upper terminal of the chair-lift.

The valley, in which vineyards now alternate with rock outcrops, plays host to a number of wine producing villages: **Rech**, on either side of its Roman bridge; **Dernau** with its "wine fountain"; **Marienthal** and its ruined convent.

Bad Neuenahr-Ahrweiler – The old town of **Ahrweiler**★ still retains its medieval gates and its fortifications. Half-timbered houses line the narrow, pedestrian-only streets of the town centre. While building a road a **Roman villa** was discovered that was in excellent condition. It is now a museum.

The spa at Bad Neuenahr *(as you leave the town, on the east)*, much favoured by diabetics, produces the celebrated "Apollinaris" sparkling mineral water.

Leaving Ahrweiler, the road climbs swiftly towards the forest before it runs out over a rolling highland area.

★ **Hohe Acht** – *30min on foot there and back.*
From the viewpoint at the top of the tower *(75 steps)* erected at the highest point of the Eifel (747m/2 451ft), there is a superb **panorama**★★ to delight the eye – a vast landscape slashed by deep valleys above which the only prominent points are Nürburg Castle to the southwest and, in the opposite direction, the ruins of Olbrück in front of the distant Siebengebirge (Seven Mountains).

Nürburg – *30min on foot there and back.*
A much-restored ruin in the middle of a rugged **landscape**★ which can be admired to the best advantage from the top of the keep.

★ **Nürburgring** – *See NÜRBURGRING.*

Ulmen – A pretty volcanic crater lake between the village and a ruined castle.

★ **The Maare** – The ancient volcanic region of the Maare starts at Daun. The lakes which distinguish it, of modest dimensions, mark the upheavals which occurred in the volcanic areas of the Upper Eifel in the Tertiary era. Gas pressure produced explosions, creating craters with neither cone nor lava but only a surrounding circle of cinders. The water which has gathered within these craters has formed lakes that are both deep and calm. *Follow the brown signposts with the word "Maare".*

Gemündener Maar – A small, sombre green lake at the bottom of a wooded funnel, very popular in summer with bathers and canoe enthusiasts.

Weinfelder Maar and Schalkenmehrener Maar – These two lakes fill craters well clear of the road, one on either side.

★ **Pulver Maar** – A perfect circle in form, this is the most beautiful lake in the area. After the motorway underpass, the route leaves the plateau to follow the pretty, steep-sided valley that leads to Manderscheid.

★ **Manderscheid** – Arriving from Daun, stop at Niedermanderscheid and climb up to the **Niederburg**★ ruins. From the top of the castle keep, there is a fine **view**★ over the village to the Oberburg ruins and the Lieser Valley. Return to the car and drive as far as the Pension Burgenblick. From here, take the footpath which leads to the **viewpoint**★★, the so-called Kaisertempelchen (little Imperial temple) overlooking the Oberburg and Niederburg ruins.

EINBECK★

Niedersachsen

Population 29 400
Michelin map 417/418 K 13

In the Middle Ages, no less than 700 small breweries in this former Hanseatic town supplied the whole of Germany with "Einpöckisches Bier" (from which the modern name Bockbier is derived). Situated between the Harz mountains and the Weser, Einbeck still retains part of its medieval fortifications, but a more attractive heritage is a collection of almost 400 half-timbered 16C houses, 100 of which are in the old town centre, richly decorated with multicoloured carvings.

★★ **Half-timbered Houses** *1hr*

Most of these half-timbered dwellings are near the old market place.

★★ **Marktplatz** – Note first of all the two houses on the corner of the Münsterstraße: the Brodhaus (1552), and especially the Ratsapotheke (1590), an impressive building which has – like most of the old houses – ventilated attics which served as lofts for hops and barley. Opposite is the town hall (Rathaus), its three projecting fronts crowned with unusual pointed roofs.

* **Ratswaage (Weigh-House)** – The well preserved façade of this ancient weigh-bridge exhibits an embellishment typical of the burghers' houses in Einbeck: fan-shaped, palm-leaf motifs, beaded and twisted mouldings to frame doors and traverses, friezes festooned with garlands.

** **Tiedexerstraße** – *Start behind the church tower (Marktkirche)*.
The gables and façades on either side of this street offer an especially pleasing perspective.

Marktstraße – Note particularly the **Eickesches Haus**** *(no 13 in the street, on the corner of the Knochenhauerstraße)*. Erected between 1612 and 1614, this wooden construction ignores the traditional local style and imitates the stone mansions of the Renaissance. Carved panels represent the virtues and the artistic muses in an allegorical cycle; statues and expressive masks adorn the uprights and the beam-ends.

EXCURSIONS

Bad Gandersheim – *22km/14mi to the northeast.*
The birthplace of Roswitha von Gandersheim, Germany's first (10C) poetess, is today an appreciated hot spring and salt-water spa. The twin octagonal towers of the **cathedral**★, buttressing the 11C central façade, overlook the historic town centre. Inside are two very fine **altars**, one 15C and the other 16C. Around the market place are many well-preserved half-timbered houses (especially those dating from the 16C) and the **Renaissance town hall**, which adjoins the Moritzkirche.

Alfeld – *24km/15mi to the north.*
It is above all the **Alte Lateinschule** which makes a detour to this town on the banks of the Leine worthwhile.
Today this half-timbered old school building, which dates from 1610 and is adorned with carved figures, is the site of a **local museum** (Stadtmuseum) ⊘ with an annexe featuring a collection of exotic stuffed animals. The dioramas display animals that are either extinct or in danger of extinction.

EISENACH★

Thüringen
Population 45 000
Michelin map 418 N 14 – Local map see THÜRINGER WALD

Eisenach was founded at the end of the 12C by Ludwig I, first of the Landgraves of Thuringia. The town, on the north-western edge of the Forest of Thuringia, is indissolubly linked with the Fortress of **Wartburg**, which not only symbolises but also externalises the very spirit of German civilization.

At the Heart of Germany – At the beginning of the 13C, the Minnesänger (troubadours) took part in the legendary jousts in the Wartburg – a custom which inspired the theme of Wagner's opera *Tannhäuser*. It was at Eisenach that Luther studied and in the Wartburg that he later translated the New Testament under the patronage of the Duke of Saxony. **Johann Sebastian Bach** was born there in 1685, when the town was the seat of the dukes of Saxe-Eisenach, who were obliged to relinquish it in 1741 to the house of Saxe-Weimar.
In 1817, the Wartburg fortress was the site of a manifestation by student corporations designed to stimulate patriotism and progressive ideas. Fifty years later (1869) the "Eisenach Declaration" marked the creation by August Bebel and Wilhelm Liebknecht of the German Social Democrat Party.

MARKT (BY)

Schloß – The sober Baroque façade of the castle seals off the northern side of the market place. This former residence of the dukes of Saxe-Weimar now houses the **Thuringian Museum** ⊘ (porcelain, faience and regional glassware of the 18C and 19C; paintings and drawings from the 19C and 20C; Rococo banqueting hall).
During restoration work on the castle, the Thuringian Museum is closed. The interesting exhibition on Medieval Art in Thuringia is on display in the Predi-gerkirche during this period, Predigerplatz 2.

Rathaus (R) – The town hall is a three-storey 16C building in both Baroque and Renaissance styles, restored after a disastrous fire in 1636. Note the (slightly) leaning tower.

Georgenkirche – This triple-aisle 16C hall-church contains the tombs of several Landgraves of Thuringia. Luther preached here on 2 May 1521, despite the fact that he was officially banned from the Holy Roman Empire, and Johann Sebastian Bach was baptized in this church on 26 March 1685.

EISENACH

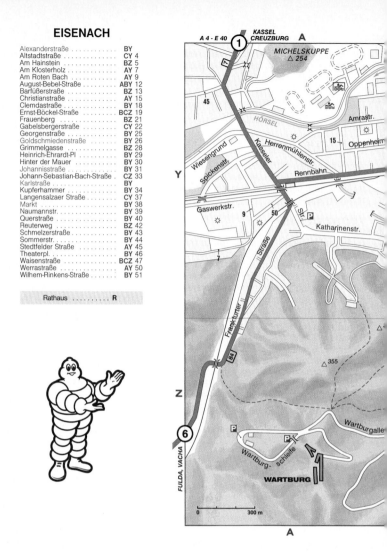

Predigerkirche – The church, an Early Gothic (late-13C building), now houses the wooden **sculpture collection★** formerly in the Thuringian Museum *(see above)*. The carvings date from the 12C to the 16C.

Lutherhaus ⊘ – It was in this fine late-14C house that Luther lived between 1498 and 1501, while he was a student at the School of Latin. The display includes historical rooms, paintings and literature retracing the history of the Reformation.

OTHER SIGHTS

Bachhaus ⊘ (BZ) – *From the Lutherhaus, return along the Lutherstraße as far as the Frauenplan.*
Ambrose Bach, himself a musician and an eminent citizen of Eisenach, owned the house at no 21 Frauenplan, which is believed to have been the birthplace of the great composer. The interior of the house provides fascinating insights into the life-style of a late-17C burgher. Manuscripts, scores and portraits recall not only Johann Sebastian Bach but several other members of the family, all of them composers. Every visitor is given a sampling from the historical keyboard instruments in the instrument room.

Automobilbaumuseum ⊘ (BY) – *Rennbahn 6-8.* This museum on the grounds of the former Eisenacher Automobilwerk (1896-1991) documents a local motorcar construction industry which is over 100 years old, and which has close links with the name Wartburg and Dixi, although BMW manufactured its cars in Eisenach between 1928 and 1941. The Wartburg, so popular in the former East German Republic, was manufactured here from 1955; the last model left the production line in 1991.

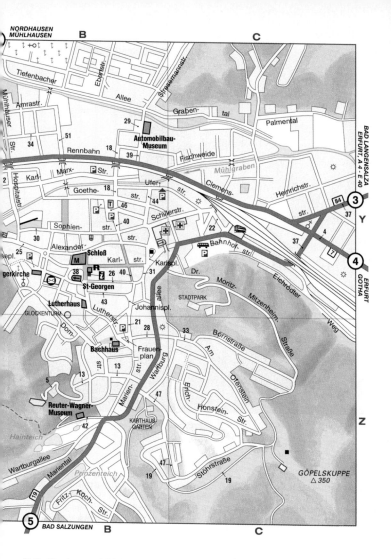

Fritz-Reuter- und Richard-Wagner-Museum ⊘ (BZ) – *Follow the Wartburgallee southwards as far as the Reuterweg.*
The villa in which Fritz Reuter lived from 1863 to 1874 can be viewed. It was while he was living here that this most significant of Lower German poets, most of whose work is written in "Plattdeutsch" (Low German), excited the wrath of the Prussian authorities by participating in the Liberal Students' Movement.
The Richard-Wagner-Museum is also located in the villa. This second most comprehensive collection after Bayreuth illustrates the life and work of the composer.

★★ WARTBURG (AZ) *2hr*

Leave the car in the car park half way up the hill, from where it is a 15min walk up to the fortress.

Perched on a rocky spur, the fortress shows clearly that it combines elements from several different periods. The visitor passes first beneath the porch of an entrance lodge, the oldest parts of which date from the 12C. Beyond this, the **outer courtyard** (Erster Burghof) is framed by half-timbered buildings erected in the 15C and 16C.
A second, inner courtyard leads to the most interesting parts of the fortified complex. On the left, the **Palais★**, where the Landgraves lived, piles three storeys one upon the other, the whole garnished with early-13C arcading.
The fortified wall and south tower give a panoramic **view★** of Eisenach, the Forest of Thuringia and the Rhön foothills.

Wartburg, Eisenach

Interior ⊙ *Guided tours: 1hr.*

Successively, one passes through the **Knights' Hall** (Rittersaal), where the vaulting is supported by an outsize central pillar; the **dining room**, with a grand fireplace and a beamed ceiling; **Elizabeth's boudoir and gallery**, with mosaics (1902-06) and frescoes (Moritz von Schwind, 1854) recalling the life of the King of Hungary's daughter; the Burgkapelle (fortress chapel), the **Hall of the Troubadours**, with Von Schwind's huge fresco illustrating episodes from the epic jousts of the Minnesänger in the Wartburg; the **Landgraves' Courtroom**, with a central pillar illustrating the plunging flight of eagles; the **Great Banqueting Hall**, decorated in a style popular in the mid 19C, today a backdrop for concerts in the Wartburg.

Finally, the tour ends in the **Wartburg Museum**, which displays selected works from the Wartburg foundation's collections. There are several paintings by Lucas Cranach the Elder.

Following the watch-path, the last thing to see is **Luther's Room** (Lutherstube).

EXCURSION

★★ **The Thuringian Forest** – *See THÜRINGER WALD.*

EMDEN

Niedersachsen
Population 53 000
Michelin map 415 F 5

The silting up of the Ems estuary in the 16C struck the port of Emden a fatal blow. The subsequent construction of dykes, however, together with the opening of the Dortmund-Ems and the Ems-Jade canals, have enabled the town to regain its position as the chief maritime port of Lower Saxony, specializing in shipbuilding and the export of new cars. Large freighters sail into the inner harbour to transport iron ore destined for the Ruhr, and there are now installations for the processing of North Sea gas.

Emden is the departure point for a daily service to the isle of Borkum, and for tours of the East Frisian islands *(see FRIESLAND)*.

* **Ostfriesisches Landesmuseum (East Friesian Museum)** ⓥ – *In the former town hall.*

Items excavated in peat bog digs, models of the port and fishing boats and paintings by the Dutch School evoke the colourful history of the town.

Pride of place is given to the collection of the former **Rüstkammer★★**: weapons and armours of the burgher militia from 1500 to the 18C and old reproductions that give the history of the art of designing and building weapons. From the bell-tower, there is a view of the harbour and surrounding countryside.

Harbour – *Ratsdelf.* The oldest section is the harbour gateway built in 1635 and bearing the Latin inscription "God is bridge, harbour and sailing wind for Emden". In the historical harbour basin you can see a **herring lugger**, the *Deutsche Bucht*, a **firefighting museum-ship** (1917), with a museum on the history of shipping, and the **marine emergency cruiser** *Georg Breusing* (1963-68); this is the place to find out more about marine salvage operations.

Blue Horses by Franz Marc,
Kunsthalle Emden

* **Kunsthalle in Emden – Stiftung Henri und Eske Nannen (Art Gallery)** ⓥ – *Hinter dem Rahmen 13; to the northwest of town.*

The post-modern red-brick building houses the sizeable collection of works of art by the German Expressionists and Neue Sachlichkeit, gathered together during his lifetime by founder of *Stern* magazine Henri Nannen, who was born in Emden. The exhibition includes contemporary painting and sculpture.

ALONG THE STÖRTEBEKERSTRASSE *156km/97mi*

Krummhörn – This area of bogs that has been inhabited for millennia is marked by so-called **"Warf"** villages. A "Warf" is a hill artificially put up to protect people from floods. The churches built of tuff and brick were erected at the highest point of the Warf from which the network of streets gathered, connected by radial avenues (the "Lohnen"). One particularity of the churches in the region are the 600-year-old organs they contain. One particularly noteworthy Warfen-village is **Rysum**; its church contains a Late Gothic organ from the 15C which is considered the world's oldest playable organ. The sight to see in **Pewsum** is the romantically located Manningaburg (late 15C), surrounded by a moat and boasting a collection on East Friesian fortresses and chiefs. In the Middle Ages, the heads of powerful family dynasties – who, thanks to land ownership and success in trade, had achieved positions of power in the East Friesian villages – were called chiefs. The cruciform church in **Pilsum**, with its mighty crossing tower, is one of the best-kept and most beautiful Late Romanesque religious constructions (c 1200) in the region.

Other notable "Warf" villages are Loquard, Campen, Groothusen and Eilum.

Greetsiel – This picturesque fishing and artist village has a typical Friesian look, with a fleet of crab catchers, carefully restored gable houses and the two windmills. At the eastern edge of the centre, which boasts numerous watercourses, is the **National Park house** offering a wealth of information about the Wattenmer and its living beings.

Norden – The large Marktplatz, with its stand of trees, is not only the attractive centre of the "city behind the dike", but also the centre of the sights and burgher houses. It's here that the imposing **Ludgerkirche** stands, built in fits and starts between the 13C and 15C. It has a Romanesque nave and a free-standing bell-tower. Inside is the Late Gothic sacristy and the heavily decorated Baroque organ by Arp Schnitger (1868-92) with a wonderful sound. On the other side of the plaza is the palace-like **Mennonite church** and the "Dree Süsters" from 1617. Beyond the Bundestrase 72 is the **old town hall** (Altes Rathaus) from the 16C with the **museum of local culture** (Heimatmuseum) and the **East Friesian Tea Museum** (Ostfriesisches Teemuseum – with a comprehensive documentation on the history of tea). The Thelkammer is also in the town hall. This room was used for meetings of the Theelacht, a guild of hereditary farmers existing for 1 100 years. Haus Schöningh on Osterstraße, a richly decorated patrician house from the Renaissance, which was built in 1576, deserves special attention.

Dornum – Of the three chief's fortresses of Dornum built before 1400, only two were rebuilt after the town's destruction in 1514, one of which is the Beningsburg. The **castle**, a four-winged Baroque construction, stands in the midst of an extensive park.

Esens – The Late Classicist **Magnuskirche** (built 1848-54) in the charming little rural town of Esen, is Ostfriesland's largest church. The attentively worked, grandiose sandstone sarcophagus inside belonging to the knight of Sibet-Attena, who died in 1473, is particularly impressive. The **Holarium** on Kirchplatz teaches its visitors something about holography, and lets them delve into the magic of three-dimensional images and sculptures.

Neuharlingersiel – This fishing village is not only the oldest (first mentioned in documents in 1693) but also one of the most beautiful ports of the North Sea coastline. Watching the busy activities of the yachts and cutters from one of the benches is an enjoyable pastime. The carefully gathered objects of the **Buddelschiff-museum** (a bottled-ship museum) is worth visiting.

Drive back to Eden over Esens and **Aurich**.

ERFURT★

Thüringen
Population 212 000
Michelin map 418 N 17

In the year 742, Wynfrith, a missionary arriving from England who was later canonized as St Boniface, created a bishopric at Erfurt which was soon joined to that of Mainz.

From the Middle Ages onward, the town's position on the important trade route linking the Rhine with Russia lent it such commercial consequence that it was incorporated into the Hanseatic League in the 15C. Erfurt thus became an essential part of the connection uniting Central Europe with the powerful ports of the north. Erfurt has been the capital of the state of Thuringia since 1990.

Spirituality and Humanism – The numerous steeples and bell-towers rising above the roofs of the town bear witness to the religious activity in Erfurt under the influence of the Archbishop-Electors of Mainz.

After the Dominican **Master Eckhart**, established in Erfurt from 1303 as Provincial of Saxony, the town was host two centuries later to the young **Martin Luther**. Eckhart was the instigator of what developed into the Rhineland spiritual mystic. Luther studied philosophy at the university – considered to be the cradle of German Humanism – entered the Augustine monastery in 1505 and left six years later to establish himself in Wittenberg.

The Congress of Erfurt – With the aim of persuading the Czar Alexander I to "neutralise" Austria while he pursued his Spanish campaign, Napoleon received the Russian ruler in Erfurt with great pomp and ceremony from 27 September to 14 October 1808. His plan, backed up with a demonstration of force, was only partly successful: all he could get was a promise of Russian military aid in the case of Austrian aggression. During the 17-day conference, Napoleon met Goethe several times, the two men sharing a mutual admiration, and subsequently made him a Chevalier de la Légion d'Honneur.

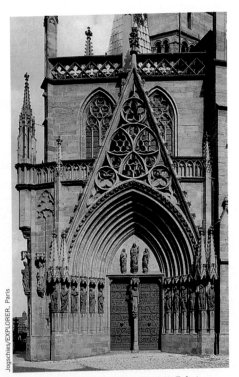

Jogschies/EXPLORER, Paris

Northwest door of the cathedral, Erfurt

ERFURT

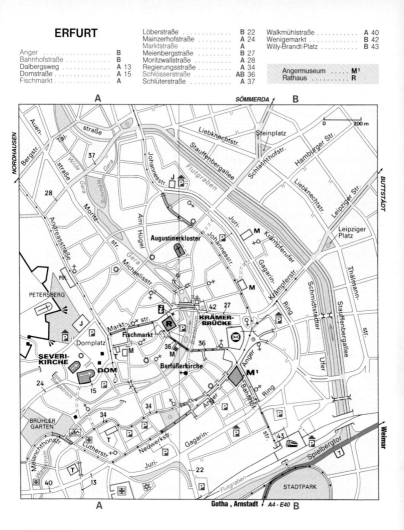

SIGHTS

★★ Dom St. Marien (Cathedral) (A) – The original Romanesque basilica, built in 1154 on a hill occupied by the citadel, was added to in the mid 14C – a portal at the entrance to the north transept, the so-called Triangle Portal; a soaring Gothic chancel at the east end. A century later, the Romanesque nave was replaced by a nave in the Flamboyant Gothic style, with broad side aisles.

★★ Triangleportals – The entrance consists of two doors set obliquely and supporting elegant statuary groups – on the northwest side, the Wise and Foolish Virgins; on the northeast the Apostles at work, a group recalling the French master-masons.

Interior – There are several works of art worthy of attention: the Romanesque Altar of the Virgin (1160); the **statue candelabra★** known as "the Wolfram" (1160); the tombstone of the Count of Gleichen and his two wives; the intricately worked choir stalls (14C). The **stained-glass windows★** above the choir (c 1370-1420) depict the Old and New Testament.

★ Severi-Kirche (A) – Formerly the Benedictine monks' abbey church of St Paul and of the Augustines, this Early Gothic building is of the hall type, with five naves. The **sarcophagus★** of the saint (c 1365) is in the southern-most aisle.

Cross the Domplatz and take the Marktstraße.

Fischmarkt (A) – Inside the imposing neo-Gothic Rathaus (**R**) are **frescoes★** which illustrate the legends and the history of Thuringia. On the north side of the square (nos 13-16) there is a fine three-storey Renaissance building, "Zum Breiten Herd".

★ Krämerbrücke (B) – This bridge, built in 1325, is the only one north of the Alps on which the houses are inhabited. The narrow, half-timbered houses with their steeply pitched roofs date from the 16C to the 19C, but give the bridge something of a medieval air.

Augustinerkloster ⊘ (**AB**) – *Entrance at Augustinerstraße 10.*
The monastery church, founded by hermits in the mid 13C, has a window (c 1340) illustrating the life of St Augustine. The Gothic cloister leads to the abbey buildings where Luther lived and worked. The monastery serves as an ecumenical meeting place these days and also has an exhibition devoted to Martin Luther.

★ **Angermuseum** ⊘ (**B M'**) – *Anger 18.*
This museum in the middle of the city is located in a Baroque building dating from 1706 (the erstwhile weighing and packing house). The focal point of the museum is the exhibition of medieval art from Thuringia (14C and 15C **altarpieces**★★, including the Augustineraltar; a **Pietà**★★ by the Master of St Severinus' sarcophagus; paintings by Hans Baldung Grien depicting the Creation). In the paintings gallery is a collection of 18C-19C German landscape painting. Porcelain and faience produced in the workshops of Thuringia are a prominent feature of the craftwork on display. Note the gem of the museum – a mural by Erich Heckel (1923-24), entitled *Life of Man*.
The museum is being renovated, so some of the departments might be temporarily closed.

Barfüßerkirche (Franciscan Church) ⊘ (**B**) – The nave of this triple-aisle church has been left in a state of ruin since 1944. The reconstructed chancel (consecrated 1316) serves as an extension to the Angermuseum, housing the remaining furnishings (stained glass from 1235 to 1240; the earliest depiction of the Legend of St Francis north of the Alps; altars and impressive tombstones) and temporary exhibitions.

EXCURSIONS

Arnstadt – *16km/10mi to the south.*
A small Thuringian town dating from the 8C, but known above all for the fact that JS Bach stayed there from 1703 to 1707, when he was organist at the parish church, which today bears his name. There is a **Local History Museum** (Museum für Stadtgeschichte) ⊘ outlining the history of the town and displaying mementos of the composer and literary exhibits in the house named "Zum Palmbaum" on one side of the market place (Am Markt).
In the old cemetery (Alter Friedhof, Bahnhofstraße) are the graves of more than 20 members of the Bach family.
In the **New Palace** (Neues Palais, *August-Bebel-Straße*) ⊘, see the **collection of marionettes and dolls**★ (Mon plaisir Puppensammlung), the Brussels tapestries of the Renaissance period, and the **porcelain**★ from Meissen and the Far East.
Because of renovations, only the doll collection is open at present.

ERZGEBIRGE★

Sachsen

Michelin map 418/420 ○ 21-22

Known as the Ore Mountains, this medium-height massif owes its name to the many veins and deposits of silver, tin, cobalt, nickel and iron – a natural wealth which has brought prosperity to a number of small towns such as Zwickau, Annaberg and Schneeberg.
The ridge of peaks marking the frontier with the Czech Republic reaches a modest maximum height above sea level of 750m/2 461ft, and the relatively high altitude of the valley floors frequently gives the impression more of an upland plateau than a mountain range. The stretch of the mountain range which lies in Germany, however, features the impressive summit of the **Fichtelberg**, at 1 214m/3 950ft. Landscapes that are both open and wooded, reservoir lakes, forests crisscrossed by footpaths and picturesque holiday villages combine to make the region particularly attractive to visitors.
The itinerary described below, which explores the western part of the range, follows the Czech frontier to start with.

FROM ANNABERG-BUCHHOLZ TO KLINGENTHAL

81km/50mi (93km/58mi via Schwarzenberg) – 3hr
Annaberg-Buchholz – See ANNABERG-BUCHHOLZ. Leave Annaberg-Buchholz on road no 95 in the direction of Oberwiesenthal.

★ **Fichtelberg** – Towering above the health and winter sports resort of **Oberwiesenthal**, this peak is identifiable from far off by the meteorological equipment adorning its summit. The top is reached by ski lift or on foot *(30min there and back. Leave the car in the car park 455m/500yd after the lower ski-lift terminal).* A vast **panorama**★ opens out when the top is reached, showing all of the

surrounding country and, away in the south, the silhouette of Mount Klinovec in the Czech Republic. At 1 244m/4 800ft, this is the highest peak of the Erzgebirge.

From Oberwiesenthal to Ehrenzipfel there is a pretty forest road which follows the course of a river. At Rittersgrün, one can either take the detour via Schwarzenberg or continue along the direct route.

Schwarzenberg – Resting on a crag, this officially protected old town is nestled around its castle and church. The fortress, which was founded in 1150, was turned into the Elector's hunting lodge in 1555-58. Nowadays it harbours the "Schloß Schwarzenberg" museum. Next to it stands the **Pfarrkirche St.-Georg**★ (1690-99), a single-naved church with a grandiose wooden ceiling and a richly carved trinity pulpit. A beautiful wrought-iron grille separates the nave from the altar space.

Sosa Talsperre – *From the car park, walk to the kiosk and then the promontory. This small lake and its dam are in an idyllic forest setting.*

The road follows the northern bank of the reservoir formed by the Eibenstock barrage and then (Road 283) climbs the winding valley of the Zwickauer Mulde before it runs into Klingenthal.

Klingenthal – Built at the end of the 16C as a mining community, this town has been known as a centre of musical instrument building since the mid 17C. The Baroque church "Zum Friedenfürsten" is worth visiting.

Michelin Maps, The Red Guide and The Green Guide are complementary publications to be used together

ESSEN★

Nordrhein-Westfalen
Population 670 000
Michelin map 417 L 5 – Local map see RUHRGEBIET

Essen no longer lives up to its coal-bowl image. Three-quarters of the people in Europe's formerly largest mining town work in administration, service, and retail. The capital of the Ruhr has the air of a residential town, with attractive pedestrian precincts bordered by elegant shops, a lovely art gallery and pleasant suburbs in green surroundings (**Grugapark, RS**). Woods, extending southwards, border the Baldeneysee.

Neither steelworks nor blast furnace have been comissioned in the vicinity since the end of the Second World War. The main industry is now the manufacture of machine tools. Typical of the region is the reusing of industrial complexes for other purposes such as in Essen-Katernberg: the Zollverein Colliery *(Gelsenkirchener Staße 181)* is now home to the **Design-Zentrum Nordrhein-Westfalen** ⊘, located in the old boiler house, which was rebuilt by Norman Foster.

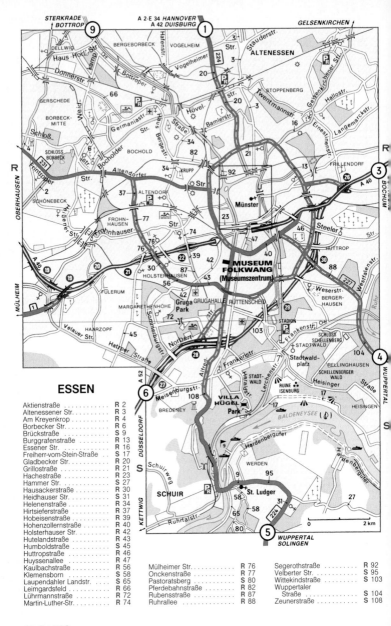

ESSEN

SIGHTS

★★ Museum Folkwang ⊘ (R) – *Museumszentrum.*

This museum houses a major collection of 19C and 20C painting, sculpture, graphic art and photography, particularly rich in works of art from Germany and France: German Romantics (Carus, CD Friedrich, Koch) and 19C Realists (Böcklin, Feuerbach, Leibl), French Realists (Corot, Courbet, Daumier) and Impressionists, and French Cubists (Braque, Delaunay, Léger, Picasso) and Surrealists (Dalí, Ernst, Magritte).

Works by the artists of the Brücke group (Heckel, Kirchner, Nolde, Pechstein), the Blauer Reiter (Kandinsky, Macke, Marc) and the Bauhaus (Feininger, Klee) demonstrate the tremendous variety of German Impressionism and art of the 20C. Note also sculptures by Rodin, Barlach, Lehmbruck and Archipenko, and the collection of post-1945 art, the Paris School and Art Informel, and works by Baselitz, Kiefer, Lüpertz, Penck and Richter, as well as Americans Pollock, Newman and Stella.

★ Ruhrlandmuseum (R) – *Museumszentrum.*

Besides its geological an archaeological collections, the focus of the museum is in the **social history of industrialisation★**. Authentic materials are used to depict the conditions of a working-class family and the lifestyle of the bourgeoisie in the Ruhr region around the turn of the century.

Münster (Cathedral) (DZ) – The 10C **west chancel**★, with three angled side walls, is the oldest part of the building. It was directly influenced by that in the cathedral at Aachen. The nave, a Gothic hall with ogive vaulting, dates from the end of the 13C; the Ottonian crypt now has stained-glass windows by Manessier. Off the northern aisle, there is a lateral chapel housing a priceless work: **The Golden Madonna**★★★, said to be the oldest (AD 980) statue of the Virgin in the West. In the western part of the church there is a gigantic seven-branch candelabra (c 1000) decorated with geometric motifs. The **cathedral treasury**★ (Domschatzkammer) ⊘ **(DZ M¹)** holds among other things four splendid **processional crosses**★★★ (10C and 11C), the Golden Madonna's crown, monstrances, gospels, and the "sword of the martyr-saints Cosmas and Damian" (parade sword from Otto III's treasure).

Johanniskirche (DZ A) – Originally a baptistery of the cathedral chapter – from which it is separated by an 11C atrium – this meditation chapel was transformed into a hall-church c 1470. In the south aisle, an **altarpiece**★ painted by Bartholomäus Bruyn the Elder (16C) represents scenes from the life of Jesus.

★ **Villa Hügel** ⊘ **(S)** – This imposing Gründerzeit mansion stands in an attractive **park** on the north shore of Lake Baldeney. The original house was built in 1870-73, after designs by Alfred Krupp. The complex included a residential wing and a guest wing, connected by a lobby, and could boast 269 bedrooms, 103 of which merit being classified as suites. Until 1945, the Villa Hügel was home to three successive generations of the Krupp family. Since 1953, it has been open to the public. The construction and fittings of the present great house date from 1915. The 15C-18C tapestries are one of the main features to have survived from the mansion's earlier magnificent decor. The villa now houses temporary exhibitions. The smaller house is used for permanent exhibitions. They offer an insight into the extraordinary success story of this family business, which started in 1811 with Friedrich Krupp's construction of the first steel-casting crucible and subsequently reflected the entire growth and development of heavy industry in Germany.

Abteikirche St.-Ludger (S) – The structure of this building is Romanesque (12C), but hints of Early Gothic design are already evident, particularly in the ogive vaulting of the nave. The transept crossing is surmounted by a **dome on pendentives**★. In the crypt is one of the rare **pierced galleries** in Germany, from which pilgrims praying could at the same time venerate the tomb of St Ludger, lying in a central vault.

The **treasury** ⊘ is situated in a museum on the south side of the church. Note the 11C bronze **crucifix**★ with a particularly pure line, as well as a **5C ivory pyx**★ (host holder, 5C-6C, with the oldest representation of the Christmas story in Germany).

ESSEN

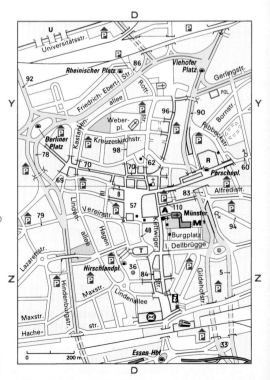

Johanniskirche . . . . **A**
Domschatzkammer . . . **M¹**

ESSLINGEN AM NECKAR

Baden-Württemberg

Population 95 000

Michelin map 419 T 11

Town plan in the current Michelin Red Guide Deutschland

The 1 220-year-old Swabian town of Esslingen nestles in the Neckar Valley sur-rounded by vineyards. The Golden Age of this Imperial city, which reluctantly lost its status in 1802 when it was given to Württemberg, was under the Staufen rulers, who often sojourned here. Indeed, the vital roadway between northern Italy and Flanders passed close by. The church belfries and the castle dominate the medieval townscape on the left bank of the Neckar.

Esslingen has a long tradition as a city of commerce. Early on and with a great deal of vim, it became an industrial city. Today its manufacturing focus is on engineering and car manufacturing. It is preparing for a future in the health industry, nutrition and environment, and multimedia.

SIGHTS

★ **Marktplatz** – The finest ornament to this picturesque, irregularly shaped square, which dates only from the 19C, is the Kielmeyer house. All the streets leading into the market are interesting, most of them bordered by old houses decorated with wood carvings.

★ **Altes Rathaus** – This 15C and 16C building combines the severe charm of old half-timbering with the gracefulness of decorated Renaissance façades. The curvilinear stepped gable overlooking the Rathausplatz is surmounted by a double lantern (carillon), vibrant with colour. But it is the south gable above all which must be seen – an outstanding feature typical of Swabian half-timbering, with heavy corbels and obliquely crossed beams.

Stadtkirche (City Church) – This Gothic building, with towers oddly linked by a footbridge, overlooks the Marktplatz. The name of its patron saint, St Dyonisius, recalls the fact that Esslingen, originally a hermitage, was given in the 8C to the great Frankish abbey of St Denis (north of Paris).

Inside the church, a rood screen divides the nave. To the left behind the screen is a 15C Pietà. Fine 13C and 14C **stained glass**★ illuminates the chancel. The Lutheran altar has painted panels.

Frauenkirche – A pleasing architectural unity distinguishes this Gothic church, which stands on a hillside and can be reached from the Marktplatz via the Untere Beutau rise. From the west there is a fine view of the ornate **church tower**★ flanked by twin staircase turrets. The interior is richly decorated. The doorways are especially noteworthy – in the southeast, the Life of the Virgin (1350); in the southwest a 15C Last Judgement. Note the stained-glass windows (1330) in the chancel.

FLENSBURG★

Schleswig-Holstein

Population 89 000

Michelin map 415 B 12

The port of Flensburg lies at the head of a sinuous arm of the sea, the **Flensburger Förde**★, appreciated by holidaymakers who can sail pleasure craft up numerous inlets shaded by beech trees. A glance at shop signs and newspaper kiosks along the quays or on the Holm, the town's principal artery, will confirm the immediate proximity of the **Danish border**. Germany's most northern town, Flensburg lives mainly from its naval shipyards and its rum and spirit trade.

SIGHTS

★ **Städtisches Museum (Municipal Museum)** ⊘ – *Museumsberg*. There is an attractive choice of antiques offering a perspective on the art and culture of Schleswig-Holstein (including that part of Schleswig that is now Danish). The **furniture and household items** on display include cupboards, trunks and marvellous wedding chests from the Gothic and Renaissance periods. Brass and copper gleam from the carefully reconstructed peasant and bourgeois interiors in the lower rooms. Note especially the small collection of works by the painter Emil Nolde.

Commercial and Warehouse Quarter – Maritime trade with Norway, the Baltic and the East Indies, inseparable from Flensburg's prosperous past, is recalled by these buildings **(Kaufmannshöfe und Speicherhäuser)**, mainly of the 18C, restored as part of an old town rehabilitation project. Note particularly the **Handelshof** *(at no 86 Norderstraße)*, the **Künstlerhof** *(no 22 in the same street)*, and the **Westindienspeicher** at Große Straße 24 *(in the courtyard)*.

Nikolaikirche – Overlooking the bustling Südermarkt, this massively proportioned brick church dates from the Gothic period (late 14C). There is a fine **Renaissance organ**★ (1609) inside.

Nordertor (North Gate) – This simply designed late-16C structure, with stepped gables over its brick façade, has become the symbol of the town.

EXCURSION

Glücksburg – *12km/7mi to the north.*
The road offers glimpses of the Flensburger Förde, and then suddenly the **Wasserschloß Glücksburg** ⊙ swims into view, apparently floating on the waters of its own lake. Four corner towers link the three wings of the 1585 building, said to have been inspired by the French Château de Chambord, on the Loire. The castle is distinguished by a simplicity of decoration typical of northern Renaissance architecture.
A visit recalls memories of the House of Oldenburg-Schleswig-Holstein, to which the Danish Royal Family is related. Do not miss the great **banqueting hall** (Roter Saal) on the first floor. The heavy vaulting is delicately embellished with coffering, between which stars, rosettes and miniature busts are inserted. Note also the unusual **leather hangings**, embossed with designs in silver and gold, which were crafted in Mechelen (Belgium) in 1703.

FRANKFURT AM MAIN★★

Hessen

Population 660 000
Michelin map 417 P 10

At the crossroads of the country's north-south and east-west communications, Frankfurt, a truly cosmopolitan city rich in traditions, is the commercial capital of Germany. Owing to its central position, numerous government organizations, including the Federal Bank, are based there. Research institutes, the university founded in 1914, the opera, theatres and an ever increasing number of museums have made the city the scientific and cultural metropolis of the Hessen Land.

HISTORICAL NOTES

The historic centre of the town is the **cathedral hill** (Domhügel), on which there were already fortifications and a palace in Roman and Carolingian times.

When the emperors ruled – In 1152, Frederick Barbarossa engineered his election as King of Germania at Frankfurt, thus inaugurating a tradition which was to be ratified by the Golden Bull of the Emperor Charles IV in 1356. Two centuries later, in 1562, the town replaced Aachen as the **coronation place** of the rulers of the Holy Roman Empire – a privilege it retained until the dissolution of the Reich in 1806. In Poetry and Truth *("Dichtung and Wahrheit")*, Goethe describes in great detail the sumptuous ceremonies and popular enthusiasm he witnessed as a boy when Josef II was crowned in 1764.

The young Goethe – Johann Wolfgang von Goethe was born in Frankfurt in 1749, the son of a worthy Imperial Counsellor and a lively, charming, much younger woman. The great writer frequently described his debt to his parents, especially in his memoirs *(Aus meinem Leben)*. To his father he owed his serious attitude to life, to his mother a happy temperament and a love of telling stories.
At the age of 14 he fell in love for the first time with a local girl called Gretchen (recorded in his autobiography *Dichtung and Wahrheit*, Book 5), about whom little is known other than that she kept somewhat questionable company which led to her having to leave Frankfurt, although her behaviour towards her lovelorn young swain seems to have been beyond reproach. She is thought by some to have later served as a model for elements of the character of Gretchen in **Faust**. After an emotionally turbulent period spent at Wetzlar while studying to be a lawyer, where he fell deeply in love with Charlotte Buff, who was betrothed to another, and where he was also profoundly affected by the suicide of Karl Wilhelm Jerusalem, a young diplomat whose career was foundering and who was disappointed in love, the young Goethe returned to Frankfurt via Strasbourg, where he completed his studies in law and embarked on an idyllic 10-month love affair with Friederike Brion which inspired some of his most enchanting love poetry. Back in Frankfurt, he enjoyed his most prolific period as a writer, between 1772 and 1775, producing among other great works **Werther**, based on his experiences in Wetzlar, in only four weeks (1774).

Finance and economy – In the 16C Frankfurt was granted the right to mint money. The money market rapidly flourished and the **stock exchange** was founded.

German banks dominated the economy in the 18C; in the 19C they acquired a worldwide reputation thanks to financiers such as **Bethmann** and above all **Rothschild** (1744-1812) whose sons, "the Five Frankfurters", established branches in Paris, London, Vienna and Naples. Profiting from such an economic climate, industries were not long in establishing themselves in the city. Chemicals and pharmaceuticals (Hoechst) remain the most active today.

The first Autumn Fair was held in 1240. The Spring Fair was added in 1330. Since the war the Fur Fair (Pelzmesse), the Motor Show (Automobilausstellung) and the famous **Book Fair** (Buchmesse) have confirmed Frankfurt as the country's commercial capital.

The fact that the EU decided in favour of Frankfurt as the headquarter for the European Central Bank is enhancing its undisputed reputation as Germany's financial and service sector metropolis.

FRANKFURT TODAY

City life – Despite its cosmopolitan character (one inhabitant in four is foreign), this "metropolis on the Main" has managed to preserve a typical Hessian atmosphere. It is around the **Hauptwache (GY)**, a square dating from 1729 at the junction of the Roßmarkt and the **Zeil (HY)**, that the life of Frankfurt is at its busiest. The Zeil is said to be the most shopped-in street in Germany.

To the north, the quarter known as the Westend, a tranquil, shady residential area from the Bismarck era, fights to stave off the encroaching office blocks of the commercial centre.

Cafés, cabarets, bars, and restaurants, often exotic, are grouped around the central station, while the taverns of the Alt Sachsenhausen quarter, on the south bank of the Main, specialize in the celebrated **Ebbelwei**, and Handkäs mit Musik (small yellow cheeses in an onion sauce).

A general view – The old town, almost entirely destroyed in 1943-44, lay within a green belt on the site of former fortifications razed in 1805. The **Eschenheimer Turm (GHY)** still stands however as a well-preserved example of the medieval defence system. The tower dates from 1428.

After 1945, a small kernel of the **old town** was reconstructed around the Römerberg. The contrast between its modest silhouettes and those of the business quarter skyscrapers is at its most striking when seen from the southern end of the **Untermainbrücke (GZ)** river bridge. Between the apse of the old Carmelite church and the cathedral, one can see (from left to right) the dome of the Paulskirche, the sharply pointed roofs of the Römer, the Leonhardskirche on the riverside, the soaring steeple of the Nikolaikirche and finally, at the end of the Eiserner Steg (a metal bridge), the Saalhof, a one-time Imperial Palace of which only the Gothic corner tower remains. The most imposing skyscrapers are the Fair Tower, the Deutsche Bank and the Dresdener Bank.

Frankfurt's economic wealth can be seen in the dense construction of skyscrapers in the bank and trade fair district. No other European metropolis has quite as many in the centre of town; and the building craze is by no means at an end.

Frankfurt's famous **skyline**, which has earned the city the nickname of the "German Manhattan", now features the 265m/870ft tall **Messeturm**, clad in red Swedish granite, designed by German-American architect Helmut Jahn, and the tallest – for the foreseeable future – office block in Europe, the headquarters of the Commerzbank (299m/980ft), built by Norman Foster. In the future, however, the new buildings in the bank district will not be allowed to pass the 200m/640ft mark. This is in contrast with the fairgrounds, where a 340m/1088ft Millennium Tower is in the planning.

From the 120m/394ft **Henninger Turm** ⊙ **(HZ)** *(leave by the Paradiesgasse)*, in the Sachsenhausen quarter, there is a **panorama**★ taking in the town, the river, the sprawling forest of the Stadtwald and the wooded massif of the Taunus.

OLD TOWN *half a day*

Römer and Römerberg (HZ R) – The **Römer** is a disparate collection of (reconstructed) medieval burghers' houses. From 1405 the block served as a town hall, and subsequently as the banquet hall for the election and coronation of the emperors. The most characteristic façade, with three stepped Gothic gables, overlooks the Römerberg. The name applied to the whole complex derives from the **Haus zum Römer**, the centre of three houses and also the oldest and most richly decorated. The four statues of emperors, above a balcony with a carved balustrade and beneath imperial eagles, are 19C additions. A graceful pierced Renaissance stairway adorns the small inner courtyard. In the 19C, to celebrate the 1 000-year history of the Holy Empire, 52 statues of emperors, from Charlemagne to Franz II (1806) were installed in niches hollowed from the walls of the **Imperial Hall** (Kaisersaal) ⊙.

G. Marth/Tourism Congress GmbH Frankfurt a. M.

A German Manhattan

The southern side of the **Römerberg** is closed off by the **Alte Nikolaikirche** (**A**), built in the 13C from the local red sandstone. The building is crowned by a gallery with four corner turrets, from which the city officials and their families would observe the lively popular fairs and fêtes. In the southwest corner is the **Haus Wertheim** (**B**), a fine half-timbered mansion in Late Renaissance (1600) style.

On the north side of the square, the 1464 **Steinernes Haus** (**C**) was clearly built in imitation of an Italian city mansion. A row of half-timbered houses dating from the 15C to the 18C (all reconstructed) flank the Römerberg to the east. In the centre of the square is the **Gerechtigkeitsbrunnen** (Fountain of Justice) (1543).

The restored sector of old Frankfurt is right next door to the post-modern **Kunsthalle Schirn** (**D**) – a long, low, domed cultural centre, stark and uncompromising, where exhibitions of contemporary art are organized.

★ **Dom (Bartholomäuskirche)** (**HZ**) – This church was designated a cathedral after it had been chosen first as the election and subsequently the coronation site of the emperors (1356 and 1562 – *see above*). A Gothic hall-church with three naves and a wide transept, it was built between the 13C and the 15C on a hill previously occupied by a Carolingian edifice. Its outstanding feature is the tall **west tower**★★ (Westturm), ornamented with a gabled polygonal crown topped by a dome and lantern, although this was not in fact completed until 1877, following the plans of the cathedral's original architect, Madern Gerthener.

In the columned peristyle erected in front of the tower in neo-Gothic style after the fire of 1867, note the outstanding grey-sandstone sculpture of **The Crucifixion** (1509) – the work of the Mainz artist Hans Backoffen.

Inside, the finely worked **choir stalls**★ are due to a master craftsman from the Upper Rhine (c 1350). The (restored) **mural paintings**, which date from 1427, are the work of a Master of the Cologne School. They illustrate the legend of St Bartholomew. In a niche on the south side of the chancel is the tombstone (1352) of Count Günther von Schwarzburg, unsuccessful rival to the Emperor Charles IV for the title of King of Germania. A door alongside leads to the chapel (Wahlkapelle: early 15C) where the seven Electors of the Holy Roman Empire in Germany made their final choice.

In the opposing chapel (north chancel) is the **Altar of Mary Sleeping** (Maria-Schlaf), which dates from 1434. Sole remaining altar from the church's original interior furnishings, this too is the work of the Cologne School. It represents the twelve Apostles grouped around the bed of the dying Mary. The large **Descent from the Cross** hanging on the west wall of the north chancel was painted by Anthony van Dyck in 1627.

Museum für Moderne Kunst

★ Dommuseum (Cathedral Museum) ⊘ – This has been installed in what remains of the Gothic cloister. Besides the cathedral treasure that is presented there, consisting of precious goldsmith works and splendid vestments from the high Middle Ages to the historicist period, it's the Late Merovingian **tomb of a young girl** that merits special attention.

West of the cathedral is an **Archeological Garden** (Historischer Garten), where the remains of Roman and Carolingian and Baroque fortifications can be seen.

Historisches Museum ⊘ (HZ **M¹**) – This museum retraces the history of the city of Frankfurt from the time of its earliest settlers to the present. Exhibits include sculpture, glassware, porcelain, items illustrating technological evolution, a numismatic collection and a display of graphics, paintings, photos, and toys.

Three models of the city (on the ground floor) represent Frankfurt in the Middle Ages, at the end of the Second World War and as it is at present. Behind this display, a passage leads off to a 12C chapel, the **Saalhofkapelle**, which is the oldest building in the city – in fact all that remains of the old king's Palace.

The historical museum also houses an **Äpfelwein-Museum** with 1 000 or so exhibits on the theme of apple wine.

★ Museum für Moderne Kunst (Modern Art Museum) ⊘ (HY **M¹⁰**) – The Viennese architect, Hans Hollein, has achieved a spacious custom-built gallery in spite of the rather cramped and awkwardly shaped site. The building in the form of a boat makes an interesting landmark in the cathedral quarter. The imaginatively designed interior is surprisingly large and makes an ideal setting for the mainly contemporary art collection. The New York School is represented by George Segal (Jazz Combo), Roy Lichtenstein (Brush-stroke), Claes Oldenburg and Andy Warhol. On the second exhibition level, there is a work by Katharina Frische (Tischgesellschaft) remarkable in its disproportion. Also represented are Joseph Beuys with a monumental bronze installation, Mario Merz and one of his famous Igloos and Gerhard Richter and his oppressive Stammhein Cycle (Stammhein Zyklus).

The modern art collection is complemented by a collection of photographs by Thomas Ruff (monumental portraits), the husband and wife team Becher and Blume and Jeff Wall.

Leonardskirche (HZ) – The outer aspect of this 15C Gothic church denies its Romanesque basilican origins. Two octagonal towers remain at the east end, along with the fine carvings of **Master Engelbert's Doorway** – although these can only be seen from inside (north aisle) now, as aisles were subsequently added on either side. The central nave, almost square, is surrounded on three sides by a gallery. Fine stained-glass windows illuminate the chancel. Left of the chancel are a superbly carved reredos representing scenes from the life of the Virgin, and a painting by Holbein the Elder depicting the **Last Supper**. The baptismal chapel of the north aisle displays a very large hanging keystone.

Paulskirche (HZ) – It was in this circular building dating from the beginning of the Classic era (again, reconstructed) that the German National Assembly, elected after the revolution of March, sat from 1848 to 1849. The church houses an exhibition devoted to the history of the German democratic movement.

Liebfrauenkirche (HY E) – The church, today a Capuchin monastery, was built as a Gothic hall-church in the 14C. The interior was remodelled in the Rococo style in the 18C.

The early-15C tympanum of the south doorway (the Adoration of the Magi, inside) is attributed to the architect and sculptor Gerthener (see above).

★ Goethe-Haus and Goethe-Museum ⊘ (GZ) – "The house is spacious, light and tranquil, with free-standing staircases, large vestibules and several windows with pleasant views of the garden" – it was thus that Goethe described the paternal home.

An atmosphere lingers in these rooms today of ease and serenity, of a taste for the good things of life, of a love of Italy transmitted from the father to the son. Paintings on the walls evoke memories of family friends, while details of the Goethes' day to day life are recalled by the pots and pans in the kitchen.

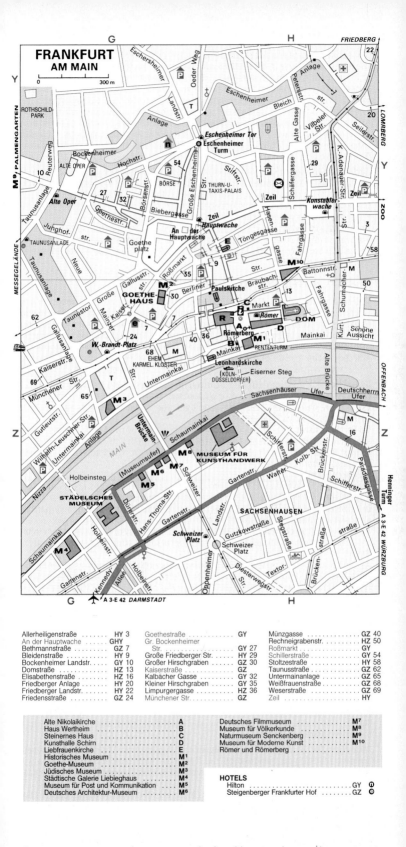

FRANKFURT
AM MAIN

0   300 m

Street names appear on the map or can be found by using the co-ordinates given in the caption below.

The room in which the poet wrote – reconstructed like the rest of the house after the war – is as it was in his lifetime, even a silhouette of Charlotte Buff, the object of his youthful passion, hangs there. Even his old marionette theatre is in its place in the next room. A separate exhibition shows the lifestyle of the Goethe family in 18C Frankfurt and has documents pertaining to Goethe's early work.

The **Museum** adjoining Goethe's birthplace has been arranged as a painting gallery of his era (Late Baroque to Romantic), and is otherwise devoted to his life-long close relationship with the visual arts. The works include paintings by, among others, Tischbein, Graff, Hackert, Fuseli and Friedrich (note especially Fuseli's *The Nightmare*, 1781).

Jüdisches Museum (Jewish Museum) ⊘ **(GZ M³)** – This museum in laid out in the Rothschild-Palais (a house dating to 1821). Organized according to the most modern of museographic procedures, the exhibits trace the history of the Jews in Germany and of the Frankfurt community – one of the largest in Germany – from the Middle Ages to the present day.

In the **Museum Judengasse** (Museum of Jew Street) – Kurt-Schumacher-Straße 10 – a branch of the Jewish Museum, you can see the foundations of five houses and two ritual baths from the Judengasse in Frankfurt. They were lived in by Jews from 1462 to 1796.

SOUTH BANK OF THE MAIN

The south bank of the river, between the Eiserner Steg and the Friedensbrücke, is known to Frankfurters as the **Museumsufer**. An impressive series of museums does in fact stretch the length of the Schaumainkai in a middle-class residential area attractively interspersed with green spaces. The creation and development of projects such as the Museum of Applied Arts and the Museum of Architecture, started in the 1980s and now enjoying worldwide renown, has been skilfully integrated within this area of well-kept gardens and quiet streets.

★★ **Städelsches Kunstinstitut and Städtische Galerie** ⊘ **(GZ)** – On the second floor there is an important collection of **old Masters**: the Holbein Room: altars from the Dominican church of Frankfurt: Holbein the Elder (*Christ's Family Tree*), Grünewald, Massys, and others.

Old German Cabinet: Schongauer, Altdorfer (*Adoration of the Magi*), Dürer, Holbein the Younger, Baldung named Grien (Birth and Baptism of Christ).

Lochner Room: Lochner (inside panel of an altar from the Laurentius church in Cologne), Altenberg altar.

Old Italian Room:

Room A: Van der Weyden, Hieronymus Bosch (*Ecce Homo*), Hans Memling (*Man in a Red Cap*), Jan van Eyck (the famous *Lucca Madonna*); **Room B:** Altdorfer (); **Room D:** H Baldung Grien (*Birth and Baptism of Christ*). There are also remarkable altarpieces, most of them from Frankfurt churches, including the main reredos of the Dominican church which embodies *The Genealogy of Christ* by Hans Holbein the Elder. In **Cabinets 19 and 20** there are several interesting works by Bruegel the Elder.

Added to this collection are early Renaissance paintings from Italy (Fra Angelico, Botticelli), including the Mannerists (Tintoretto, Veronese); **17C Flemish work** with the masters **Rubens** and **Rembrandt** (*The Blinding of Samson*, 1636); **French Baroque Painting** (Poussin, Lorrain, Watteau, Chardin); and the masterworks of **Adam Elsheimer**, an Early Baroque painter born in Frankfurt, who settled in Rome from 1600 (the Holy Cross altarpiece).

German works from the 18C and 19C dominate the first floor, among them the memorable meditation of *Goethe in the Roman Countryside*, painted by **JHW Tischbein** in 1787. French Impressionism is represented by **Renoir** and **Monet** (*The Breakfast Party*).

German Expressionists exhibited include Beckmann, Kirchner and Marc. Matisse, Picasso and Braque represent that part of the modern movement influenced by Fauvism and the Cubists. Max Ernst, Paul Klee and Feininger introduce Surrealism and the art of the Bauhaus. Contemporary art is represented by Dubuffet, Bacon, Tapiès and Yves Klein. Part of the museum display is also given over to an extensive **graphics collection**.

★ **Museum für Kunsthandwerk (Museum of Applied Arts)** ⊘ **(HZ)** – The museum building (1985) was designed by the New York architect Richard Meier, a pupil of Marcel Breuer at the Bauhaus. Integrated within the design is the classically styled Villa Metzler (1803).

Purity of line, richness of material and colour are all enhanced by the flood of light entering this airy, spacious building from every side. This is especially true of the furniture: medieval, 16C folding chairs, carved Renaissance and Baroque cupboards and chests, jewel-encrusted commodes and cabinets as well as Jugendstil items. The **glassware collection** (15C and 16C Venetian work) is particularly interesting; and plenty of space is given to German stoneware from the 15C to the 19C, and faience from Delft, Hanau and Berlin.

TIPS AND ADDRESSES

Prefix – 0 69

Information – *Tourismus + Congress GmbH*, ☎ 21 23 88 00, Monday-Friday 9.30am-5.30pm, Saturday-Sunday 9am-4pm. **Information offices**: Tourist Information at the main train station, entrance hall, Monday-Friday 8am-9pm, Saturday-Sunday 8am-6pm, ☎ 21 23 88 49; Tourist Information Römer, Römerberg 7, Monday-Friday 9.3am-5.30pm, Saturday-Sunday 9am-4pm; City Info Zeil, Monday-Friday 10am-6pm, Saturday 10am-4pm. The city magazines *Journal Frankfurt* (in newsagents), *Fritz* (free of charge) and *Welcome to Frankfurt* (in German) provide information on all events. Ticket sales (only on location) at the *Tourismus + Congress GmbH.*

Post offices with special: The post office on the Zeil is open Monday-Friday 9.30am-8pm, Saturday 9am-4pm; the branch office at the train station is open Monday-Friday 7am-9pm, Saturday 7am-6pm, Sunday 11am-6pm and at the airport daily 7am-9pm.

Newspapers – Frankfurter Allgemeine Zeitung, Frankfurter Rundschau, Frankfurter Neue Presse.

Internet – http://www.frankfurt.de; http://www.rhein-main.net; http://www.frankfurt-am-main.de; http://www.frankfurt-online.net

Public transport

The **RMV** (Rhein-Main-Verkehrsbund) is responsible for all public transport services, trams, buses, U-Bahns and S-Bahns, and regional trains in the greater Frankfurt region: ☎ 2 73 07 62 Monday-Friday 9am-8pm, Saturday 9am-4pm. The **VGF** (Verkehrsgesellschaft Frankfurt am Main) manages the local public transportation of the city of Frankfurt: ☎ 1 94 49 Monday-Friday 7am-3pm. Information: on the traffic island of the Hauptwache, Monday-Friday 9am-8pm, Saturday 9am-4pm, also at Konstablerwache, Passage B level and other underground (U-Bahn) and S-Bahn stations. The tariff rate 3 is for all rides inside Frankfurt. Normal fare is 3.60DM, day ticket 8.20DM (valid until the last ride of the day). Tickets are available at vending machines or from the bus drivers. Tickets are not available in the U-Bahn, S-Bahn or tram cars.

The **Frankfurt Card** costs 12DM (valid for 1 day) and 19DM (valid for 2 days) and can be used for the RMV network within city limits including the airport. It also gives a discount to 15 museums and other attractions, such as the zoo and the airport terraces, also 25-30 % for selected boat rides. The **Frankfurt Card** is available in many travel agencies, at tourist information offices and in both terminals at the airport.

Tip: For S-Bahn rides to the airport you need a ticket at tariff rate 4.

City sightseeing

City tours – 2hr 30min city tours (including the visit of the models of the old town in the Historical Museum and of the Goethe House) are offered by *Tourismus + Congress GmbH*: Departure daily at 2pm from Römerberg and 2.15pm from the main train station, April-October also at 10am and 10.15pm. The 6DM fare for the **Ebbelwei-Express** includes a 1hr tour (Saturday-Sunday afternoons only) with the tramway through the old town of Frankfurt and Sachsenhausen, a bottle of hard apple cider (Apfelwein) or apple juice, and a bag of pretzels; ☎ 21 32 24 25. For theme-related **city tours on foot** see *Kulturothek Frankfurt*; ☎ 28 10 10 and *Statt Reisen*; ☎ 46 33 59.

Lechthaler/TOURISMUS+CONGRESS GmbH, Frankfurt am Main

Ebbelwei-Express

Boat rides – Panorama rides lasting 50 and 100 minutes from April to October are provided by *Frankfurter Personenschiffahrt* ; ☎ 1 33 83 70

Shopping

Frankfurt's main shopping street (with department stores) is the Zeil – including among others the passage called *les facettes*. This is just a short way away from the **exclusive shops** in the streets around the Große Bockenheimer Straße (Freßgass) and Goethestraße. In Sachsenhausen interesting shopping opportunities are found at Schweizer Straße, in Bockenheim at Leipziger Straße.

Art galleries are ubiquitous in Frankfurt, though most of them are concentrated on the Braubachstraße. The **antique dealers** have settled in the Pfarrgasse in the vicinity of the cathedral (Dom).

The Flea market is always held on Saturday from 9am-2pm along the Main.

Markets – Every Saturday, the Konstablerwache is the site of a farmer's market. In Bornheim market day is Wednesday 7am-6pm on Berger Straße and in Sachsenhausen at the South Train Station (Südbahnhof) Friday 8am-6pm.

Hotels

BUDGET

A Casa – Varrentrappstraße 49; ☎ 97 98 88 21, Fax 97 98 88 22. 6 rooms, single rooms from 99DM. Small hotel in an old villa.

Kolpinghaus – Lange Straße 26; ☎ 29 90 60, Fax 29 90 61 00. 48 rooms, single rooms from 75DM. Functional house with simple furnishings.

Corona – Hamburger Allee 48, ☎ 77 90 77, Fax 70 86 39. 26 rooms, single rooms from 115DM. Hotel (without restaurant) with family feeling, near the fairgrounds.

OUR SELECTION

Courtyard by Marriott – Oeserstraße 180; ☎ 3 90 50, Fax 3 80 82 18. 236 rooms, single rooms from 165DM. Large conference hotel near the Frankfurt fairgrounds with inexpensive rooms.

Atlantic – Düsseldorfer Straße 20, ☎ 27 21 20, Fax 27 21 21 00. 60 rooms, single rooms from 210DM. Modern city hotel near the train station.

Liebig-Hotel – Liebigstraße 45, ☎ 72 75 51, Fax 72 75 55, 19 rooms. Single rooms from 205DM. Small, individual hotel in the bank district.

Imperial – Sophienstraße 40; ☎ 7 93 00 30, Fax 79 30 03 88. 60 rooms, single rooms from 210DM. Dignified hotel catering to the business crowd, timeless furnishings.

TREAT YOURSELF!

Steigenberger Frankfurter Hof – Bethmannstraße 33; ☎ 2 15 02, Fax 2 15 59 00. 332 rooms, single rooms from 431DM. Select grand hotel with long tradition right in the middle of town.

Hilton – Hochstraße 4; ☎ 1 33 80 00, Fax 13 38 13 38. 342 rooms, single rooms from 403DM. Modern business-style hotel right on the green inner city beltway, not far from the Alte Oper.

Restaurants

BUDGET

Bauer – Sandweg 113; ☎ 40 59 27 44. Main dishes from 24.50DM. Carefully furnished bistro with a casual atmosphere.

Tao – Friedberger Anlage 14; ☎ 44 98 44. Main dishes from 23DM. Excellent Vietnamese restaurant in the Nordend district, with garden terrace.

OUR SELECTION

Meyer's Restaurant – Große Bockenheimer Straße 54; ☎ 91 39 70 70. Main dishes from 28.50DM. Bistro-restaurant in the Freßgass'.

Stars and Starlets – Friedrich-Ebert-Anlage 49; ☎ 7 56 03 00. Main dishes from 26DM. Modern basement restaurant with designer look.

Eckstein – An der Staufenmauer 7; ☎ 1 31 07 27. Main dishes from 38DM. The restaurant is located in a small passageway near the Konstabler Wache right on the historical Staufen Wall.

Ernos Bistro – Liebigstraße 15; ☎ 72 19 97. Main dishes from 48DM. French cuisine, high level.

TREAT YOURSELF!

Humperdinck – Grüneburgweg 95; ☎ 72 21 22. Main dishes from 48DM. Gourmet locality (1 star) with garden.

Tigerpalast-Restaurant – Heiligkreuzgasse 20; ☎ 92 00 22 25. Main dishes from 50DM. Modern restaurant (1 star) with a bar in the famous variety theatre.

Cafés, Kneipen and Bars

Numerous restaurants and pavement cafés are located in the Freßgass'. The traditional quarter for "Ebbelwei" (apple cider, or "Apfelwein" in high German) is Sachsenhausen on the other bank of the Main. Bockenheim also offers numerous opportunities for going out.

CAFÉS

Altes Café Schneider – Kaiserstraße 12. "I want to stay as I am" – with nostalgic plush upholstery and scintillating chandeliers.

Café Hauptwache – At Hauptwache. With a terrace and loggias on the first floor.

Café im Liebighaus – Schaumainkai 71. Frankfurt's most beautiful museum café at a very idyllic location.

Stattcafé – Grempstraße 21. Pretty café in Bockenheim for breakfast or enjoying cakes.

Café Christine – Eschenheimer Landstraße 319. Lots of delicious titbits from Frankfurter Kranz cake to Swiss nut torte.

Krüger/TOURISMUS+CONGRESS GmbH, Frankfurt am Main

EBBELWEI IN SACHSENHAUSEN

Zum gemalten Haus – Schweizer Straße 67. Typical Ebbelwei place with the appropriate dishes.

Zum Eichkatzerl – Dreieichstraße 29. This squirrel establishment (the name of the place) has been around for over a century.

Klaana Sachsenhäuser – Neuer Wall 11. Old-fashioned establishment with a courtyard terrace, regional specialities.

Fichtekränzi – Wallstraße 5. Good beer in addition to Ebbelwei, and a good selection of wines.

Lorsbacher Tal – Große Ritterstraße 49-51. Everything needed for body and soul that Frankfurt offers can be found in this original establishment.

BARS

Oppenheimer Bar – Oppenheimer Straße 41. Happy hour from 8pm to 9pm.

Jimmy's – Friedrich-Ebert-Anlage 40. Piano bar located in the *Hessischer Hof*.

Havanna Bar – Schwanenstraße 2. A classic among cocktail bars in Frankfurt.

CAFÉ-KNEIPEN

Café Diesseits – Konrad-Broßwitz-Straße 1. Evergreen among bistros in Bockenheim.

Café Klatsch – Mainkurstraße 29. Multicultural patrons and corresponding menu.

Central Park – Kaiserhofstraße 12. Newest meeting spot in the city (with terrace).

Harveys – Bornheimer Landstraße 64. Some of the patrons look just as creative as the decorations.

Helium – Bleidenstraße 7. Some fun evenings can be spent in the Helium watching the other patrons.

GARDEN ESTABLISHMENTS

Römerbembel – Römerberg. Wonderful view of the Römer.

Zur Sonne – Berger Straße 312. Ideal place to catch the sun.

Zum Rad – Leonhardsgasse 2. Here (in Seckbach) people sit in the yard beneath old chestnuts or in the old house, leaning up against the original wooden panelling.

Entertainment

THEATER

Schauspiel Frankfurt – Neue Mainzer Straße 17; ☎ 21 23 79 99. The Schauspielhaus (Theatre), the Kammerspiele (Chamber Theatre), the Opera and ballet are located in the building of the Städtische Bühnen (Municipal Stages).

Die Komödie – Neue Mainzer Straße 18; ☎ 28 45 80. Comedies and variety theatre.

Volkstheater Frankfurt – Großer Hirschgraben; ☎ 28 36 76. Theatre in Hessian dialect.

Künstlerhaus Mousonturm – Waldschmidtstraße 4; ☎ 40 58 95 20. The Cultural Centre is located in a former soap factory offering professional free theatre and also a stage for various local and guest ensembles.

OPERA AND BALLET

Oper and Ballett Frankfurt – Willy-Brandt-Platz; ☎ 21 23 79 99. Daring staging and modern choreography under the direction of William Forsythe have earned the ensemble standing and fame.

VARIETY, REVUE AND CABARET

Schmiere – Seckbächer Gasse; ☎ 28 10 66. Satire in a cellar theatre.

Tigerpalast – Heiligkreuzgasse 16-10; ☎ 28 96 91. Cult establishment of Jonny Klinke offering variety and more.

CONCERTS

Alte Oper Frankfurt – Opernplatz; ☎ 1 34 04 00. The Alte Oper (Old Opera House) was reopened in 1981 as a concert and conference centre in 1981.

Jahrhunderthalle Hoechst – Pfaffenwiese, Hoechst; ☎ 3 60 12 40. The venue for classical concerts and other events in the entertainment sector.

JAZZ

Jazz-Keller – Kleine Bockenheimer Straße 18a; ☎ 28 85 37. Frankfurt's jazz scene was born here.

CLUBS, DISCOTHEQUES & LIVE MUSIC

Dreikönigskeller – Färberstraße 71; ☎ 62 92 73. Music of all sorts in a cellar near the Dreikönigskirche.

Sinkkasten – Brönnerstraße 5; ☎ 28 03 85. Music club with a long past.

Dorian Gray – FRA Terminal 1, Halle C; ☎ 69 02 21 21. This discotheque in the airport has been around for a long time, today it specialises in techno.

KINO

Most of the premiere cinema houses are located in the inner city in the vicinity of the Konstablerwache/Zeil/Hauptwache. The Weißfrauenstraße also boasts numerous film theatres. The Kommunale film theatre in the Deutsches Filmmuseum shows many interesting films.

Special dates

Dippemess (pottery) end of March-early April and in September, *Mainfest* end of July-early August, *Apfelwein festival on the Römerberg* early August, *Museumsuferfest* in August, *Christmas market on the airport gallery in terminal 1* in December.

The **Islamic department** *(second floor)* contains carpets from Persia and Anatolia, furniture and weapons, and above all glassware and faience from 9C to the 15C. The **Far East department** *(also on the second floor)* displays bronze statues (14C-17C) from China and Tibet; Chinese porcelain from the Ming and Ch'ing periods, including the white and the blue porcelain from the 17C and 18C; and a fine collection of lacquer.

Objects from the Rococo and Classical periods are exhibited in the former Villa Metzler.

It is here that there is another remarkable **porcelain collection** assembled from the major European manufacturers in Meißen, Berlin, Fürstenberg, Nymphenburg, Vienna, Höchst and Sèvres.

The **book and calligraphy section** *(in the new building)* has temporary exhibitions of selected highlights from its rich collection of material.

★ **Deutsches Filmmuseum (German Cinema Museum)** ⊘ (**GZ M**[7]) – Here, the film buff may examine *(first floor)* the different inventions relating to the discovery of animation: stroboscopic discs, Emile Reynaud's 1882 Praxinoscope, a Thaumatrope, Edison's Kineto-scope (1889), and a copy of the Lumière Brother's Cinematograph (1894). A reconstruction of the Meliès studio recalls the first film director. Daguerreotypes, a magic lantern and a dark room conjure up the beginnings of cinema.

On the second floor, visitors – introduced backstage, as it were, in both silent and talking studios faithfully reconstructed – can amuse themselves composing different shots. Designs, drawings and models illustrate the techniques of special effects (*King Kong*, for instance). A small working cinema shows newsreels, publicity shots and shorts several times a day.

On the premises are also a **film and video library** and the local cinema.

Städtische Galerie Liebieghaus (Liebieg Museum of Sculpture) ⊘ **(GZ M⁴)** – Here there are fine examples of sculpture and statuary from different civilizations, from **ancient Egypt** to the **Classical era**. Egypt: head of a dignitary (Middle Kingdom). Greece and Rome: statuettes; small bronze horse (8C BC); woman's head (2C BC); Tanagra figurines.

There are also Roman copies of the great Greek sculptures: Myron's Athena, the Torso of Polycletus, and the famous Praxiteles Satyr.

Equally interesting is the section devoted to the Middle Ages. A Virgin and Child (Trier, 11C), the Head of Bärbel von Ottenheim (NG van Leyden, 1463), the Rimini Reredos (c 1430), another Virgin and Child (French, 14C) and a Madonna by Riemenschneider – all these convey an idea of the wealth of talent working in that period. The genius of the Renaissance is exemplified by Andrea della Robbia's altarpiece of The Madonna of the Girdle (c 1500) and a small Black Venus with Mirror (16C).

Museum für Post and Kommunikation (German Postal Museum) ⊘ **(GZ M⁵)** – The history of communications systems from the earliest prototypes to state-of-the-art modern technological developments, displayed in appropriate historical contexts.

Deutsches Architektur-Museum (German Architectural Museum) ⊘ **(GZ M⁶)** – For this museum, inaugurated in 1984, the architect Oswald Mathias Ungers designed an original and extremely controversial complex incorporating a magnificent villa of the Bismarck period into an ultra-modern construction.

Examples of modern architecture from all over the world are on display, as well as the best of interior design. A collection of architects' **plans and models** (19C and 20C) is on display.

A series of tableaux illustrates the evolution of human settlement with different types of houses from various civilizations.

Museum für Völkerkunde (Museum of Ethnography) ⊘ **(GZ M⁸)** – This museum puts on special exhibitions only, on themes to do with either comparative ethnography or individual ethnic groups. The museum collections are particularly well-endowed with exhibits from South America (especially Bolivia), Sumatra, Flores and East Indonesia, Central Africa and Ethiopia, and the Sepik river basin in Papua-New Guinea.

ADDITIONAL SIGHTS

★★★ **Zoo** ⊘ – *Leave by Zeil* **(HY)**.

The Frankfurt zoo is famous for its rare species (over 5 000 examples of 600 species), which are encouraged, successfully, to reproduce. The animals live in their natural habitat. The bird section, with its huge free-flight aviary, is particularly colourful, the occupants at liberty to fly around the visitors.

Penguins, reptiles, fish and insects inhabit the Exotarium. There is an amazing beehive with thousands of bees busily at work. In the **Grzimek-Haus**, darkened by day, nocturnal animals such as the desert fox can be observed.

★ **Naturmuseum Senckenberg (Senckenberg Natural History Museum)** ⊘ – *Leave by the Bockenheimer Landstraße* **(GY M⁷)**. Opened in 1821, this museum is distinguished by its remarkable **Department of Paleontology**★★ *(ground floor).* Fossils from the

Naturmuseum Senckenberg

211

Lower Jurassic (Lias) are on display in the entrance hall, most discovered near Holzmaden, in Württemberg. They include ichthyosaurus, sea crocodiles and crinoids – which despite their vegetal appearance were in fact marine animals. In the **Hall of Dinosaurs** (Room 5), the skeletons of huge beasts from the Secondary Era are on view: diplodocus, iguanodon, triceratops, stegosaurus and plateosaurus (both original and in the form of mouldings). In Room 6 there are impressive fossils including sea crocodiles, ichthyosaurus and the placodus, a reptile with enormous teeth which fed on whole crustaceans. In Room 8 there are turtles, tortoises, whales and an anaconda in the act of swallowing a sea pig.

Room 9 (at the foot of the staircase) displays objects found in **Jurassic digs** – most of them near Solnhofen, on the banks of the Altmühl, where the archeopteryx was found.

See also an even older ancestor of the bird, the pterodactyl; a fish with circular teeth; and a dinosaur with a beak (tracodon), which lived in North America.

The great land and sea mammals (elephants, whales) are in Room 10. Nos 12 and 13 trace the evolution of the human race (numerous implements, weapons etc found in digs). In the rooms opposite, a geological display gives an insight into the dramatic forming of the Earth's crust and an overview of the evolution of life on Earth. A window into the geographical past is provided by the perfectly preserved fossils from the archeological dig at Messel near Darmstadt. An interesting collection of stuffed animals (armadillo, apes), reptiles (python with 377 vertebrae) and birds can be seen on the first floor. On the second are insects, and marine vertebrates and invertebrates. Dioramas show mammals in their natural habitat. Tanks house both freshwater and marine fish.

★ **Palmengarten (Tropical Gardens)** ⊘ – Leave by the Bockenheimer Landstraße (**GY**). These botanical gardens include a large area given over to various **greenhouses**, containing tropical plants, palms, Alpine plants etc and also exotic plants such as orchids, cacti and bromeliaceae (pineapples). The Palm House dating from 1869 is the oldest botanical building in Europe. The park itself is home to many beautiful old trees and features various types of specialized garden (herbaceous borders, rock gardens, rhododendrons, rose gardens).

EXCURSIONS

Offenbach – 7km/4.5mi to the east. Leave on the Deutschherrn-Ufer (**HZ**). Town plan in the current Michelin Red Guide Deutschland.

This town on the south bank of the Main is the centre of the German leather industry (International Leather Fair twice a year).

★★ **Deutsches Ledermuseum/ Deutsches Schuhmuseum** (Leather and Shoe Museum) ⊘ – At Frankfurter Straße 86.

The **Leather Museum** contains some interesting collections of articles made from leather, especially vellum and hides. There is an exhibition on tanning on the ground floor. On the first floor, the display covers the use of leather in various domains such as sport, travel and leisure, within Europe. The second floor looks at the use of leather in non-European countries (cowboys and Indians, Eskimos, shadow theatres). There is an interesting collection of handbags and suitcases, as well as some more unusual exhibits (such as one of Napoleon's portfolios). The **Shoe Museum** in the same building presents a history of foot fashion in all its variety, from Ancient Egyptian and Roman sandals to modern footwear. The section on shoes as works of art is particularly interesting.

★ **Friedberg** – 28km/17mi to the north on the Friedberger Landstraße (**HY**).

This is an attractive example of a medieval community with two distinct centres: the town enclosed within the imperial castle and the bourgeois town grouped at the foot of the church, at either end of the main street (Kaiserstraße).

The **castle** (Stauferburg) erected by Frederick Barbarossa in 1180 together with its outbuildings still has the air of a small, self-sufficient town. The ramparts, now a promenade, have been made even more attractive with bays of greenery and look-out points. **Adolf's Tower**★ (Adolphsturm, 1347) overlooks the assembled buildings. The **Jewish Baths**★ (Judenbad, 13C) – at Judengasse 20, in the bourgeois sector – is a deep, square well with a dome, which served originally for ritual ablutions required by Jewish law. Columns with Gothic capitals support the arches over the stairway (74 difficult steps) leading 25m/80ft to the water.

The **church** (Stadtkirche) is a 13C-14C building with a typically Hessian exterior – transverse attics with separate gables jutting from the roof above the aisles. The façade is unusual, its towers resting on Gothic arches. Inside, an unusually tall **ciborium**★ (1482) stands in the chancel. On the left of the rood screen is the **Friedberg Madonna** (c 1280).

★ **The Taunus** – Round tour of 62km/39mi – 4hr.

The Taunus is limited in extent, but reaches at the Großer Feldberg a greater height (880m/2 997ft) than any of the other Rhineland schist massifs. The area is covered by magnificent forests, and there are many mineral springs which have been developed into spas.

Verwalt. d. Straatl. Schlösser u. Gärten, Bad Homburg v. d. H.

Bad Homburg vor der Höhe

* **Königstein im Taunus** – The fortress here, on a height isolated from the main Taunus slopes, is a **feudal ruin** (Burgruine) ⊘ with impressive foundations: round 16C bastions and 17C projecting defences. Climb the keep *(166 steps)* for a **bird's-eye view** of the small town and the surrounding woods.

* **Großer Feldberg** – The tower and antennae of an important telecommunications centre top this height. From the tower's **observation platform** ⊘ visitors can enjoy an immense **panorama**★★ including the Westerwald tableland to the northwest, the Wetterau depression to the northeast and, in the southeast, the plain of the Lower Main invaded by the outskirts of Frankfurt.

Saalburg – This is a complete Roman fortress camp in the middle of the forest, reconstituted on the orders of Kaiser Wilhelm II on the Limes (fortified lines marking the northern limit of Roman occupation). Note the external trenches and, in the inner courtyard, buildings which now house a Roman museum.

* **Bad Homburg vor der Höhe** – *Town plan in the current Michelin Red Guide Deutschland.* In 1840, the opening of a casino by the **Blanc Brothers** transformed this little spa into one of Europe's gaming capitals. But the establishment was obliged to close its doors in 1872.
Today the life of most visitors centres on the **Spa Park**★ (Kurpark), where pavilions containing the health-giving springs are dispersed over shady lawns.
The **castle**, dominated by the tall White Tower – a survival of the original fortress – was successively the residence of the Landgraves of Hesse-Homburg, then the summer palace of the Prussian kings (who became, after Wilhelm I in 1871, the emperors of Germany).
A well-known exhibit in the castle is the artificial limb of Friedrich II (1633-1708), known locally as "the silver leg" because the joints of the wooden limb are fashioned from the precious metal.

FREIBERG★

Sachsen

Population 47 000
Michelin map 418 N 23/24

In an advantageous location at the foot of the eastern Erzgebirge mountain range, not far from Chemnitz and Dresden, Freiberg was the largest town in Saxony during the Middle Ages. It has the mineral resources to thank for its wealth, which is still evident in the proud bourgeois houses.

Saxon silver – Silver deposits were discovered in 1168 and were mined by men who were brought in from the Harz region. For 800 years mining contributed to the well-being of the town, for copper, lead, zinc, fluorspar and heavy spar and also agate were mined in addition to silver. A total of 1 000 mineral veins were mined, at a depth of up to 800m/2 624ft, until 1969. The first academy of mining in the world was founded in Freiberg in 1765, the Bergakademie, or Mining Academy, which is still a university today. Famous students there included the poets Novalis and Theodor Körner, together with Alexander von Humboldt.

Although today only a teaching and visitors' mine is still open, the town is nevertheless proud of its mining past and cultivates its traditions. This could not be expressed in a more beautiful way than during the annual mining parades (*see Calendar of events*).

Kidnapper of princes – Kunz von Kauffungen, castle governor at Altenburg in Thuringia, was beheaded in July 1455 at the Freiberg Obermarkt. His crime was that he had considered himself to have been unfairly treated by his sovereign, and had taken his revenge by abducting the king's two sons. A few days later however, the kidnapper had been captured and brought to Freiberg, where he had been given short shrift. A head on the town hall oriel serves as a reminder of "Der Prinzenräuber".

★★ DOM ⊙

The Late Gothic three-naved church was built between 1490 and 1501 and replaced an earlier Romanesque building which had fallen victim to fire. Its external appearance gives no indication of the immense treasure which it conceals. Two formidable towers flank the main entrance. The eastern gable with its blind niches, onto which the more richly composed burial chapel was built, is also characterized by its simplicity.

Interior – Three identical naves are supported by slim octangular pillars, from which the ribs of the net vault rise upwards. With its high pointed arched windows, the nave provides an impression of light-filled fluency. A tracery gallery encircles the interior at half height and leads around the pillars. The wall pillars are decorated by figures of the Apostles dating from 1505, whilst the central pillars bear a cycle of figures depicting the Wise and Foolish Virgins.

The rood screen is crowned by a Late Romanesque triumphal **Crucifixion group★**, produced around 1220 and one of the most important wooden sculptures of this period in Central Germany. Of the original 30 altars, only the Communion altar, dating from 1649 and a work from the Cranach area, remains.

★★ **Tulpenkanzel** – Hans Witten produced this splendid work (prior to 1505). The tulip pulpit (which was only given this name later, since Witten was not familiar with tulips, which were not introduced into Europe until 1647) with its quite unique shape, and its masterly artistic execution, represents a kind of tree of life, up whose trunk the steps climb and in whose boughs angels frolic. The male figures at the foot of the pulpit represent the prophet Daniel and a young miner, a reference to an old mining fable. The abat-voix pays homage to the Virgin Mary. Since the tulip pulpit is only used on public holidays, preaching has taken place since 1638 from the **Bergmann pulpit**, in itself a fine piece of work, but not worthy of comparison with Witten's work of genius.

M. Knopfe

"Tulip pulpit", Freiberg Cathedral

★★ **Silbermannorgel** – The harmonious shape and the delicate angel figures of the High Baroque organ front are beautiful indeed, but the actual sound of the instrument, which is considered to be Gottfried Silbermann's masterpiece, with its three keyboards, 45 stops (sets of pipes) and 2 674 pipes, is quite breathtaking. He combined Saxon and French musical traditions to create this organ, producing as a result a tone of exceptional quality.

★★ **Goldene Pforte** – The magnificent eight-stepped entrance portal was erected in around 1230 for the church's predecessor. In

> ## A family of organ builders
>
> **Gottfried Silbermann** (1683-1753) learnt his trade from his brother Andreas, who had set up in Strasbourg and whose masterpiece is the organ in Ebersmünster (Alsace). Gottfried Silbermann worked in Freiberg from 1710, and created instruments with an unusually fine tone. A total of 51 organs are ascribed to him, including that in the Hofkirche in Dresden. The Freiberg organ is the most important of those still in existence.
>
> His nephew Johann Andreas, Andreas Silbermann's son, built 54 organs in the Upper Rhine region.

1484 it was moved to the southeast side, having previously stood on the west side, between the towers. This is a Romanesque masterpiece, displaying major French architectural influence. The tympanum depicts the enthroned Madonna and the adoration of Christ by the Magi *(a leaflet is available which explains the complex figures)*. The iconography is said to have been designed by Abbot Ludeger von Altzella. The work was executed by master craftsmen from Goslar and Halberstadt. Although it was originally edged in colour, in particular in gold, only the name still bears witness to its early colour.

★ **Begräbniskapelle** – The chancel was converted in the 16C into the burial place of the Albertine line of the house of Wettin, and was reworked in the Mannerist style by Giovanni Maria Nesseni between 1586 and 1591. The tomb of Elector Moritz of Saxony (1563) is the first Renaissance tomb in Saxony and is the work of the sculptor Antonius van Zerroen from Antwerp. The railing with grotesque motifs originates from the year 1595. There are life-size kneeling figures of the monarchs in bronze and outstanding allegories of the Virtues by Balthasar Permoser.

ADDITIONAL SIGHTS

Obermarkt – The large square is dominated by the Late Gothic **town hall** (15C) with its square tower. The bourgeois houses around it, with their steeply pitched eaves, bear witness to the town's former prosperity. The splendid portal of the Schönlebe house (1 Obermarkt) and the Renaissance oriel at the corner of Obermarkt and Erbische Straße are worthy of note.

★ **Geowissenschaftliche Sammlungen der TU Bergakademie** ⊙ – *14 Brennhausgasse.* This geological collection at the Mining Academy, which includes 80 000 pieces of ore and whose variety and splendid colours are most impressive, is one of the largest in Europe. In addition to local minerals (silver ores), visitors can admire magnificent semi-precious and precious stones from around the world.

Stadt- und Bergbaumuseum ⊙ – *In the Untermarkt.* The former canon's house provides a worthy setting for a presentation of the history of the town and the development of mining in the area, of mining arts and crafts and of folk art. Two valuable portraits by Lucas Cranach the Younger, depicting Elector August and his wife Anna (1572) may be seen in the hall on the upper floor.

★ **Lehr- und Besucherbergwerk** ⊙ – This teaching and visitors' mine comprises two separate areas: the underground tour takes visitors around the silver and non-ferrous metal mine shaft, the **Reiche Zeche**, commencing with a man-haulage operation and covering four levels, in part with the pit railway *(tour 2hr)*. The above-ground mining installations around the **Alte Elisabeth mine shaft** originate from the 19C, and their original plant is impressive. Included are a beam engine (1849) with a historic piece of hoisting equipment, an ore separator and a mine forge. The only remaining prayer stall in the Saxon silver mining area is of particular interest *(tour 1hr)*.

To plan a special itinerary:
-consult the Map of Touring Programmes which indicates the recommended routes, the tourist regions, the principal towns and main sights;
-read the descriptions in the Sights section which include Excursions from the main tourist centres.
Michelin Maps nos 415, 416, 417, 418, 419 and 429 cover the different regions of Germany and indicate scenic routes, interesting sights, viewpoints, rivers, forests...

FREIBURG IM BREISGAU★★

Baden-Württemberg

Population 197 000

Michelin map 419 V 7 – Local map.see SCHWARZWALD

Freiburg, one of the most attractive cities in southern Germany, was founded in the 12C by the dukes of Zähringen, who conferred upon it a number of special privileges (Freiburg or "free town"). When the dynasty died out in 1388, the town passed under Habsburg rule. It was here, in May 1770, that the Archduchess Marie-Antoinette said farewell to Austrian territory and set out for Strasbourg, where she was greeted in the name of France by Cardinal Rohan as the bride of the future Louis XVI – and foredoomed victim of the guillotine in 1793.

Five centuries of Austrian rule, which was only ended by Napoleon, left the city with an agreeable, easygoing life style appreciated by young and old alike. The climate can be hot, but a refreshing breeze blows gently from the Upper Black Forest at nightfall and, streams ("Bächle") from the nearby mountains sweeten the air – many running in open gullies beside the streets of the old town.

SIGHTS

★★ **Münster (Cathedral)** (Y) – Of the original Romanesque building, started c 1200, only the transept crossing and the two "Cockerel Towers" flanking it remain. The octagonal towers are surmounted by Gothic superstructures. The technical progress characterising the Gothic period was reflected as building continued westwards culminating in the erection of the splendid tower which crowns the west façade. This feature, with its multiplicity of planes intersecting at sharp angles, is one of the few church towers in Germany to be wholly completed in the Middle Ages.

FREIBURG IM BREISGAU

Auf der Zinnen	Y 2
Augustinerplatz	Z 3
Bertholdstraße	Y
Eisenbahnstraße	Y 7
Eisenstraße	Y 9
Europaplatz	Z 12
Fahnenbergplatz	Y 13
Franziskanerstraße	Y 14
Friedrichring	Y 16
Gerberau	Z
Greiffeneggring	Z 19
Habsburgerstraße	Y 20
Herrenstraße	YZ 24
Holzmarkt	Z 26
Kaiser-Joseph-Straße	YZ
Münsterstraße	Y 30
Oberlinden	Z 31
Platz der Alten Synagoge	Y 32
Rathausgasse	Y 33
Salzstraße	YZ 38
Schiffstraße	Y 40
Schusterstraße	Z 43
Schwabentorplatz	Z 45
Schwabentorring	Z 47
Schwarzwaldstraße	Z 49
Turmstraße	Y 54
Universitätsstraße	Y 55
Unterlinden	Y 57
Werthmannplatz	Z 59

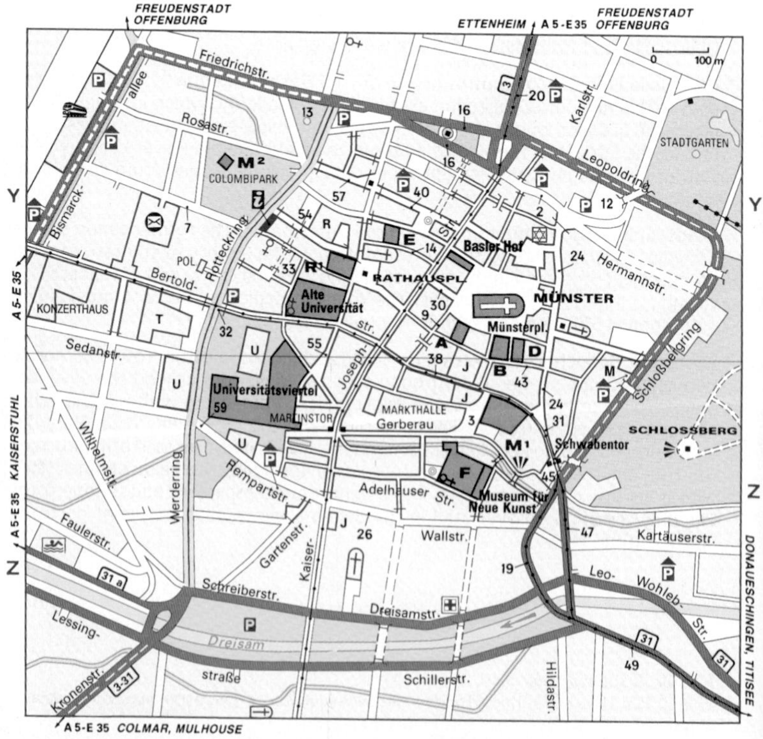

Erzbischöfliches Palais	A	Adelhauser Neukloster	F
Historisches Kaufhaus	B	Augustinermuseum	M¹
Wentzingerhaus	D	Colombischlößle	M²
Haus zum Walfisch	E	Neues Rathaus	R¹

In 1354, work started on the construction of a new chancel, but the grandeur of the design and the severity of the times were such that this huge addition was not finished and consecrated until 1513. The ambulatory, typically German in concept, has fan vaulting in keeping with its Late Gothic style.

North side – Above the door which leads to the chancel, the tympanum, carved c 1350, illustrates the theme of Original Sin, while the archivolt concerns itself with the Creation of the World according to Genesis. On the right of this, note the rare representation of the Creator resting on the seventh day.

★★★ **West Tower** – On the plain, square base of this stands a pierced octagonal belfry surmounted by a delicate openwork spire of stone. Four sharply jutting projections form a star at the foot of the tower house, the Sterngalerie. The gargoyles here are worth a closer look.

South side – Statues of the Apostles and the Old Testament kings stand on the buttresses of this richly ornate façade. A Renaissance porch shelters the south door.

West porch and doorway (Vorhalle) – Late-13C figures crowd this main entrance. On the left wall, facing the door, Satan, beguilingly disguised as "the Prince of this world", leads a procession. He is followed by his victim, sparsely clothed in a goat skin, the Wise Virgins, and a number of biblical characters. The Foolish Virgins, their expressions bitter, decorate the right wall. Behind them are statues of the liberal arts (painting and sculpture), St Margaret and St Catherine, the patronesses of Christian wisdom.

The doorway itself, flanked by statues representing the Church (left) and the Synagogue (with eyes covered; right) is entirely occupied by the mystery of the Redemption. The tympanum is unusual in that it portrays scenes from Christ's earthly life and an interesting Last Judgement.

Nave – Moderately tall, the nave is embellished with graceful galleries, their blind, trefoil arcades decorating the aisle walls from end to end. Furnishings and statuary of particular interest include:

1) The Virgin at the pillar (1270-80), worshipped by two angels (French-inspired art);

2) A Late Gothic pulpit with rustic themes (1560); the sculptor himself is represented in a window beneath the stairway;

3) A statue (originally recumbent, remodelled in the 17C) of Berthold V, last of the dukes of Zähringen, who founded the town;

4) The Holy Sepulchre, dating from 1340, behind a delicate Gothic grille;

5) In the three windows of the south transept, 13C stained-glass medallions, the oldest in the cathedral, which were probably originally in the old Romanesque chancel;

6) A 1505 group sculpture, the Adoration of the Magi.

Chancel ⓥ – Very well lit, the chancel invites appreciation of the skilful design of the ambulatory vaulting combined with that of the widely spaced side chapels. Among the many works of art note:

the **altarpiece★★** (Hochaltar) by Hans Baldung Grien (1512-16), which portrays the Coronation of the Virgin on the central panel;

a) a Rococo baptismal font by JC Wenzinger in the Stürzel Chapel;

b) the Oberried altarpiece (1521) in the Universität Chapel. The two side panels, the Nativity and the Adoration of the Magi, are by Hans Holbein the Younger;

c) in the Second Kaiser Chapel: an altarpiece from Schnewlin depicting Rest during the Flight to Egypt by Hans Wydyz. The paintings are from the Baldung Grien studio;

d) reverse of the large Baldung Grien altarpiece: a painting of the Crucifixion;

e) the Böcklin Chapel: the Romanesque Locherer Crucifix in beaten silver by Böcklin;

f) an altarpiece in the Locherer Chapel by Sixt von Staufen (1521-24). The carved part depicts the Virgin, with her cloak – held up by cherubim – shielding humanity.

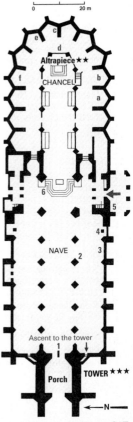

MÜNSTER

0   20 m

Altrapiece ★★

CHANCEL

6

5

4

3

NAVE   2

Ascent to the tower

1

Porch   **TOWER ★★★**

← N

Ascent of the West Tower (Turmbesteigung) ⊘ – *outside wall, southern side*. The first section of stairway leads to the star-shaped gallery, and then, after a further climb, visitors reach the upper platform beneath the beautiful perforated spire. From here there are **views**★ over the city, with distant perspectives of the Kaiserstuhl and the Vosges.

Münsterplatz (Y) – Facing the cathedral's south front across this square stand buildings whose ostentation declares them to have been designed for municipal or ecclesiastical prestige. They comprise the:

Archbishop's Palace (Erzbischöfliches Palais) **(Y A)** – A fine wrought-iron balcony decorates the façade of the archi-episcopal palace (1756).

★ **Historical department store** (Historisches Kaufhaus) **(YZ B)** – A picturesque medieval atmosphere is lent to the square by this roughcast red structure. The watchtowers on either side have pointed roofs; covered with glazed tiles and supported by an arcaded gallery, the Gothic façade shelters statues of the Habsburg emperors (1530) on the first floor. The building is still used for official receptions and other city functions.

Wentzingerhaus (Y D) – Built for himself in 1761 by the famous local painter and sculptor Christian Wentzinger, this mansion completes the layout of the square. A magnificent Baroque staircase adorns the interior which now houses the museum of local history (**Museum für Stadtgeschichte** ⊘).

ACCOMMODATION

BUDGET

Schwarzwälder Hof – Herrenstraße 43; ☎ 07 61/3 80 30, Fax 07 61/3 80 31 35. 47 rooms, single rooms from 70DM. Simple, well-attended rooms with comfortable, country furnishings rooms.

Hirschengarten Hotel – Breisgauer Straße 51; ☎ 07 61/8 03 03, Fax 07 61/8 83 33 39. 20 rooms, single rooms from 85DM. Inexpensive modern hotel in Freiburg-Lehen.

OUR SELECTION

Oberkirchs Weinstuben – Münsterplatz 22; ☎ 07 61/3 10 11, Fax 07 61/3 10 31. 26 rooms, single rooms from 125DM. Individually furnished rooms.

Zum Roten Bären – Oberlinden 12; ☎ 07 61/38 78 70, Fax 07 61/3 87 87 17. 25 rooms, single rooms from 195DM. The building originated in 1120, the tradition of hospitality goes back to 1311. The furnishings of the hotel, however, are contemporary modern.

TREAT YOURSELF!

Colombi-Hotel – Rotteckring 16; ☎ 07 61/2 10 60, Fax 07 61/3 14 10. 128 rooms, single rooms from 274DM. Elegant hotel with luxuriously furnished rooms.

RESTAURANTS

BUDGET

Charivari – Located in the Storchenpassage between Grünwälder- and Salzstraße; ☎ 07 61/2 24 01. Main dishes from 15DM. Not a common setting for a meal: a tortuous vaulted cellar with old, original furnishings.

Greifenegg-Schlößle – Schloßbergring 3, ☎ 07 61/3 27 28. Main dishes from 24DM. Restaurant with a terrace and a beer garden, with a wonderful view of the city in the summer, when one can sit outside.

OUR SELECTION

Schloßbergrestaurant Dattler – Am Schloßberg 1 (access via Wintererstraße or with the Schloßberg cable-car, DM 3); ☎ 07 61/3 17 29. Main dishes from 19.50DM. Restaurant in the mountains with a splendid view of Freiburg.

Weinstube zur Traube – Schusterstraße 17; ☎ 07 61/3 21 90. Main dishes from 28DM. Rustic furnishings, good, regional cuisine.

TREAT YOURSELF!

Eichhalde – Stadtstraße 91; ☎ 07 61/5 48 17. Main dishes from 30DM (lunch), 48DM (supper). Restaurant in Freiburg-Herdern with modern furnishings in a Jugendstil (Art-Nouveau) building, where light, modern food is served.

Colombi-Restaurant – Rotteckring 16; ☎ 07 61/2 10 60. Main dishes from 46DM. Country like, elegant restaurant with French cuisine.

★ Rathausplatz (Y) – The town hall square is a pleasant sight, with its flowered balconies and its scented chestnut trees surrounding the statue of Berthold Schwarz, a Franciscan said to have invented gunpowder in 1350.

★ Neues Rathaus (New town hall) (Y R¹) – Two 16C burghers' houses, once the heart of the old university, were linked in 1901 by a central arcaded portion to form the present town hall.
The oriel window at the corner of Rathausgasse is decorated with carvings illustrating the *Lady and the Unicorn*.

Haus zum Walfisch (Whale House) (Y E) – Of the original 1516 construction, there remains today an oriel which forms a canopy above a richly ornamented Late Gothic doorway.

★★ Augustinermuseum ⊘ (Z M¹) – The most interesting part of this museum is the **Medieval Religious Art Section★★** (Mittelalterliche Sakralkunst), housed in the church of an old Augustinian monastery and adjacent ground-floor galleries. The works, destined originally for churches and abbeys in the Upper Rhine districts, came from Alsace, the Baden region and the country around Lake Constance. The statuary, in particular, includes admirable 14C and 15C pieces. Among the museum's special treasures are the Malterer family rug dating to 1310 and the altarpiece panel (once at Aschaffenburg) depicting the miracle of the Snow, painted in 1519 by Matthias Grünewald. There are also works by Lucas Cranach the Elder, Hans Baldung Grien, Hans Wydyz and the Baroque masters Zürn and Wentzinger. Remarkable, too, is the collection of 19C masters from Baden.

Schwabentor (Swabian Gate) (Z) – From this remnant of the town's medieval fortifications, sightseers can walk down through the picturesque but poor Insel quarter to the quays bordering the Gewerbekanal, once the preserve of Freiburg's fishermen and tanners. A small bridge spanning the canal offers a view of the cathedral spire.

★ Schloßberg (Z) – A wooded walk climbs this last foothill of the Black Forest. The pathway, which starts from the Schwabentor, also offers fine views of the cathedral. A **cable-car** ⊘ operates from the Stadtgarten (Y).

EXCURSIONS

★ The Kaiserstuhl – *Round tour of 73km/45mi – allow 3hr. Leave Freiburg on Lessingstraße (Z) and go to Breisach via Gottenheim.*
A small volcanic massif rising in the Baden plain, the Kaiserstuhl (the Emperor's Throne: 538m/1 765ft) enjoys on its lower slopes a warm, dry climate particularly suitable for orchards and vineyards. The wines of Achkarren, Ihringen, Bickensohl and Oberrotweil are considered among the finest in the region.

★ Breisach – Breisach and its rock, crowned by a large church, tower above the Rhine, facing the twin town of Neuf-Brisach in France. The rock was the heart of one of the most redoubtable systems of fortification in Europe, the site serving at times as a French bridgehead, at times as an imperial advance post. French revolutionary troops sacked the town in 1793, and it was largely destroyed by the Allied armies in 1945.
As at Freiburg, the **Münster★** has a Romanesque nave, transept and two smaller twin towers, together with a Gothic chancel. The most important work of art is a carved **reredos★★** (1526) with an extraordinarily complex decoration of leaves, flowing hair and billowing draperies from which emerge a crowd of cherubim and the figures of the Eternal Father and Christ crowning the Virgin. Murals depicting the Last Judgement (in the first bay on the west side) were painted in the late 15C by Martin Schongauer of Colmar.

From the cathedral hill (Münsterberg) there is a good **view★** of the heights of the Black Forest to the south, the Sundgau and Lomont peaks, the Vosges from the Grand Ballon to Upper Königsburg Castle and, quite close, the Kaiserstuhl.

★ Burkheim – A village of wine-growers, Burkheim is picturesquely built on the southwest slope of the Kaiserstuhl. It rises in tiers above the roadway with three parallel streets giving access to the houses at different levels. The lowest of these, the Marktstraße, is delightful. Among the half-timbered buildings are a red, bow-windowed mansion and a town hall with a fine emblazoned doorway (1604).

★ Endingen – The elongated, historical Marktplatz is surrounded by fine buildings. Of particular note are the **Altes Rathaus** (old town hall) with impressive scrolled gables (16C) and the former Kornhalle (Granary) serving as the town hall today. This lengthy edifice dates from the same period and boasts gradated gables. On

Reredos, Breisach Münster

the northern side of the square is **Haus Krebs**, a former burgher's house dating to the 18C. The central part of its elegant façade is highlighted by a richly ornated portal and a balcony. A flying buttress connects the **Usenberger** Hof, a former noble's residence, with the main street (Hauptstraße).

Ettenheim – *33km/20mi to the north.*
Part of the Strasbourg bishopric until 1803, Ettenheim is worth seeing for the old residential quarter of Kirchberg, separated from the rest of the town by two 18C gates and clustered at the foot of the large parish church.
Facing the outer stairway of the Rathaus is the gable of the palace once owned by Cardinal Rohan, where the notorious "hero" of the celebrated affair of the diamond necklace lived out his eventful exile from 1790 to 1803. Higher up, where the Rohanstraße bends towards the church, is the house owned by the Duke of Enghien, complete with coat of arms above the door. The Duke, fiancé of the Cardinal's niece Charlotte, was arrested on the orders of Napoleon in violation of the sovereignty of the State of Baden on the night of the 14-15 March 1804 and executed by firing squad six nights later in the castle moat at Vincennes.
Cardinal Rohan's tomb lies beneath the chancel in the church.

★★★ **Upper Black Forest** – *See SCHWARZWALD* ③

FRITZLAR★

Hessen
Population 15 000
Michelin map 417 M 11

The placid waters of the Eder reflect the medieval towers and belfries of this small town.

A general view – From the end of the bridge that leads to the station on the south bank of the river's main stream, there is a fine view of the old town, its fortified walls overlooked by the towers of the collegiate church. The **ramparts** (Stadtmauer) retain almost all their ancient defence towers, in particular the impressive 13C spur structure, known locally as the **Grauer Turm★** (Grey Tower). Its the architectural ensemble of the Dom and its towers that dominates the cityscape.

SIGHTS

★ **Marktplatz** – The original half-timbered gables, some faced with wooden shingles, have been preserved in all their variety. Note especially the small, elongated, 15C shop with a square oriel that is crowned with a turret.
The stem of the fountain (1564) supports a statue of Roland – here, as in Bremen, the symbol of public liberty.

★ **Dom (Collegiate Church)** ⊘ – The present building was constructed in the 13C on the site of an earlier church of which only the west face, the lower parts of the towers and the crypt remained. A typical Rhineland feature is the dwarf gallery, adorned with blind arcades, which encircles the apse. The church's individuality lies in the interplay of the many gable roofs and the graceful half-timbered design of the chapter-house, built onto the north side of the apse.

Enter the church through the main door on the west side. The interior is noteworthy for an outstanding Gothic ciborium, and, on either side of the chancel opening, two Romanesque statues carved in wood. One of these represents the Virgin, the other St John (originals in the Treasury). Below ground, the crypts are vast. The most important, with three aisles, has fine, Romanesque cushion capitals with a simple, ribbed decoration. It houses the tomb of St Wigbert, the first abbot of Fritzlar.

Domschatz und Dommuseum (Museum and Treasury) ⊙ – *Enter through the cloister on the right of the chancel.*

Among the ritual objects, liturgical vestments and statues, the treasury displays the pearl-encrusted Cross of the Kaiser Heinrich II (1020), as well as cameos, precious stones and a 12C Romanesque reliquary plaque.

FÜSSEN★

Bayern

Population 16 500

Michelin map 419/420 X 16 – Local map see Deutsche ALPENSTRASSE

The importance of Füssen as a tourist centre lies in its position – at the foot of the gorge where the River Lech cascades down from the Alps, the town serves as a gateway to the Tyrol and departure point for trips to the Royal Castles built by Ludwig II of Bavaria (Neuschwanstein and Hohenschwangau). A number of small lakes downstream, as well as the **Forggensee** reservoir, offer opportunities for boating, bathing and sailing.

Below the **castle** (Hohes Schloß), which rises high above the roofs of the old town, are the remains of ancient fortifications and defensive towers.

SIGHTS

Ehemaliges Kloster St.-Mang – A Benedictine foundation, St.-Mang harks all the way back to the work of St Magnus (who died in 750) in Füssen. It was rebuilt in the Baroque style during the 18C and secularised in 1802.

Parish Church (Stadtpfarrkirche) – Rebuilt between 1701 and 1717, this church displays a remarkable unity, for Johann-Jacob Herkomer, born in the parish, was not only the architect but also the painter and stuccoworker. The Romanesque crypt in front of the high altar has frescoes from around AD 1000 that portray the two holy men Magnus and Gallus.

St Anne's Chapel (St. Anna-Kapelle) – *Access via the Museum der Stadt Füssen.* Within the chapel, there is a striking **Dance of Death★** (Totentanz, c 1602) by a local painter. There is also a group in the Gothic style portraying the Holy Family.

Abbey Buildings – The abbey buildings were also planned by Herkomer as a grandiose symmetrical Baroque complex in Venetian Baroque style. The **Museum der Stadt Füssen** ⊙, reached across the main quadrangle, is housed in the former state apartments of the abbey (banqueting hall, refectory, library etc) and contains displays on the history of the abbey itself including an excavated medieval cloister. There is also an interesting exhibition of string instruments, illustrating the evolution of the manufacture of violins and lutes locally.

OUR RECOMMENDATIONS

Landhaus Sommer – Weidachstraße 74, ☎ 083 62/14 70. Single rooms from 80DM. Nicely located holiday hotel right on the Forggensee with a terrific view of the mountains, with in-door pool and sauna.

Schloßgasthof "Zum Hechten" – Ritterstaße 6, ☎ 0 83 62/9 16 00. Fax 0 83 62/91 60 99. Single rooms from 85DM. In the middle of the old town

Geiger – Uferstraße 18 (in Hopfen am See), ☎ 0 83 62/70 74 , Fax 0 83 62/3 88 38. Single rooms from 75DM. Wonderful view of the mountains and of the Hopfensee.

Hirsch – Kaiser-Maximilian-Platz 7 18 (in Hopfen am See), ☎ 0 83 62/93 98 0, Fax 0 83 62/93 98 77. Single rooms from 90DM. A traditional family run hotel at the gates of the old town, decorated in old Bavarian painted furniture, with a good restaurant and a pub area where locals meet.

Hohes Schloß – The ramp leading up to the castle entrance starts behind the parish church.

In the late 15C, the castle was the summer residence of the Prince-Bishops of Augsburg. The surrounding property has been transformed into a **public park** (Baumgarten), picturesque and peaceful, affording unexpected views of the Säuling escarpment (alt 2 047m/6 716ft). The apartments housing the local museum, in particular the Knight's Hall (Rittersaal) with its sumptuous octagonally coffered ceiling, display a collection of Swabian painting from the 15C to the 18C.

Lechfall – *0.5km/550yd to the south.*

The river hurls itself tumultuously over a ledge in a small, rocky gorge. The falls are spanned by a footbridge which allows sightseers to return to Füssen by another route.

FULDA

Hessen

Population 60 000

Michelin map 417/418 ○ 13

The town's name is closely connected to the history of Christianity in Germany. But Fulda is not so much dominated by its medieval buildings, rather, its Baroque core, with the Dom, the Residence and the noble palaces harking back to the town's religious past, from the time of the prince-bishops who were guardians of the tomb of St Boniface. An overall view can be enjoyed from the top of the steps leading to the Frauenberg church. Fulda today is the economic and cultural centre of the region of eastern Hessen.

The upper platform of the stairs leading up to the Frauenbergkirche gives a good view of the city.

St Boniface, the Apostle of Germany – Wynfrith, an English missionary from a monastery in Exeter, was sent by Pope Gregory II in the 8C to preach the gospel to the heathen Germans. The Pope gave him the Latin name "Bonifatius", Boniface – he who does good deeds. Boniface charged Sturmius with building a monastery in Fulda. Work began on 12 March 744 and became Boniface's favourite monastery. In 754, Boniface was proselytising in Friesland when he was murdered at Dokkum in 754. His corpse was brought back to Fulda and lies buried in the monastery, founded on his orders, at Fulda.

The Benedictine abbey, especially under the rule of Abbot Raban Maur (822-42), subsequently became a centre of religious devotion, art and scholarship. The abbey in fact was responsible for the production of Germany's earliest literary works (*The Lay of Hildebrand* was copied by two monks c 820).

SIGHTS

Dom (Cathedral) – From the beginning of 1704, this church was rebuilt in a style inspired by Italian Baroque by the architect Johann Dientzenhofer. Pilgrims still worship the tomb of St Boniface, which lies in a crypt (Bonifatiusgruft) beneath the high altar. At the base of the **funerary monument**★, an 18C alabaster bas-relief represents Boniface, in his priestly vestments, raising the lid of his tomb on Judgement Day.

The reliquaries of the saint, the head reliquary and his sword, are conserved in the **museum** (Dommuseum – *access to the left of the cathedral*) ⊘, which also displays an important collection of liturgical vestments from the Baroque period. Baroque art is also represented by a splendid silver altar. There is a good collection of medieval artefacts.

★ **Michaelskirche** – This church, built around an early-9C rotunda, with a stout, square tower, overlooks the cathedral forecourt. The crypt, in which the vaulting rests on a single pillar, is Carolingian. The rotunda itself is supported on eight columns marking the outline of an impressive well-head.

Schloß – This formerly Renaissance construction was extended and rebuilt in 1706-21 to serve as a residence for the Prince-Bishops of Fulda according to blueprints by Johann Dientzenhofer. Their apartments and the Imperial and Princes' Halls – both heavily decorated with stucco and paintings – are part of the **Historical Rooms**. A collection of Fulda porcelain is also on display. The mirror room with its splendid Rococo furnishings is considered one of the high points. A stroll though the castle garden leads to the **Orangery** (1724), accessed by way of an oval free-standing stairway. Half way up there is a monumental "**Floravase**", a superb Baroque ornate masterpiece by Humbach dating from 1728.

EXCURSIONS

Probsteikirche St.-Petersberg – *4km/2.5mi, plus 30min walking and sightseeing. Leave Fulda by the Petersberger Straße and road no 458. Follow the Petersberg signposts to the foot of the rock on which the church is built, and leave the car there.*

A vast **panorama**★ is commanded from the summit: to the east is the Rhön massif (*see below*), the Milseburg spur and the rounded dome of the Wasserkuppe; southwest, behind Fulda, lies the Vogelsberg.

The Romanesque sanctuary built on this impressive **site**★ was largely remodelled in the 15C. It contains five 12C **low-relief sculptures**★★ – Christ in Glory and the Virgin on either side of a triumphal arch; St Boniface, Carloman and Pepin the Short on the walls. Mural paintings from the 9C decorate three niches in the Carolingian crypt.

Schloß Fasanerie ⊘ **or Adolphseck** – *6km/4mi to the south.*

Constructed between 1739 and 1754 by Prince-Bishop Amand von Buseck, this Baroque mansion with an expansive park owes to the Landgraves and Electoral Princes of Hesse its interior style, decoration and furnishing. The museum offers visitors an impressive overview of the evolution of noble lifestyles from the Baroque to the Historicist age and houses a fine collection of porcelain from Europe and the Far East and the largest private collection of antique art in Germany.

Schloß Fasanerie - Music room

Hessische Hausstiftung

★ **The Rhön** – *Round tour of 104km/65mi to the southwest of Fulda – allow 4hr.* The remnants of an enormous extinct volcano, the Rhön massif's craggy summits tower above the bleak moorlands clothing it, up to a height of 1 000m/3 280ft. These heights, swept by strong winds, have made the area a favourite among the organizers of gliding clubs.

Gersfeld – The most central resort in the Rhön district, Gersfeld has a Protestant **church** (1785) with interestingly placed furnishings: the grouping of organ, altar and pulpit in a single compact ensemble symbolizes liturgically the Lutheran reform.

★ **Kreuzberg** – From the Calvary – at 928m/3 044ft after a steep uphill climb – there is a splendid **view**★ of the massif. The Wasserkuppe can be seen to the north.

★★ **Wasserkuppe** – From the gliding centre, climb to the summit (950m/3 116ft), following the fencing on the left. The **panorama**★★ extends as far as Fulda and the Vogelsberg.

The length of time given in this guide
– for touring allows time to enjoy the views and the scenery;
– for sightseeing is the average time required for a visit.

GARMISCH-PARTENKIRCHEN★★★

Bayern

Population 26 500

Michelin map 419/420 X 17 – Local map see Deutsche ALPENSTRASSE

This is Germany's great winter sports resort, famed as the site of the fourth Winter Olympics in 1936 and the World Alpine Ski Championships in 1978. Worthy of its reputation internationally, the resort lies in an open mountain basin at the foot of the Wetterstein range, from which two massive silhouettes stand out. These are the Alpspitze and the axe-shaped Waxenstein, themselves masking the Zugspitze.

Despite its modest altitude (720m/2 362ft), favourable meteoric conditions assure the resort of a regular winter snowfall – from 30-50cm/12-20in in January and February, anything up to 1.8m/6ft in the areas served by the ski lifts. This is complemented by the Zugspitzplatt snowfield, accessible in autumn and springtime via a rack railway.

Summer visitors are offered numerous mountain walks (Höhenwege), crisscrossing the lower slopes of the Wank and the Kramer. Although more lively and sophisticated than the twin town of Partenkirchen, Garmisch nevertheless maintains certain customs and traditions. Thus, every evening around 6pm, there is the communal Return of the Herds – with cattle frisking through the streets and bringing traffic to a standstill.

The name of Richard Strauss is closely associated with Garmisch-Partenkirchen, as he lived here until his death in 1949. There is an annual Richard Strauss festival here in June.

WHERE TO STAY IN GARMISCH-PARTENKIRCHEN

Gasthof Fraundorfer – Ludwigstraße 24, ☎ 0 88 21/92 70, Fax 0 88 21/9 27 99. Single rooms from 70DM. Inn in good Bavarian style standing in the middle of Partenkirchen.

Berggasthof Panorama – St. Anton 3, ☎ 0 88 21/25 15, Fax 0 88 21/48 84. Single rooms from 95DM. Located above the town, 10min on foot. View of the Zugspitz range. The rooms are rustic and cozy.

Staudacherhof – Höllentalstraße 48, ☎ 0 88 21/92 90, Fax 0 88 21/92 93 33. Single rooms from 120DM. Quiet location and very well managed family run operation where the guest is well tended to. Indoor swimming pool, sauna, lawn for sunbathing.

Grand Hotel Sonnenbichl – Burgstraße 97, ☎ 0 88 21/70 20, Fax 0 88 21/70 21 31. Single rooms from 175DM. Hotel complex above town. A little bit of nostalgia here, excellent amenities.

SIGHTS

Olympia-Eissport-Zentrum (Ice Sports Centre) – *Garmisch.* Open all the year round, this comprises three separate skating rinks with a total surface of 6 500m²/7 800sq yd. The covered stands allow 12 000 spectators to watch skating competitions and ice hockey matches.

Skistadion (Ski stadium) – *Partenkirchen.* A ski-jump and a slalom course here are equipped for 80 000 spectators.

Alte Kirche – *Garmisch.* The parish church stands on the west bank of the River Loisach, in a picturesque neighbourhood where the old chalets have been carefully preserved. The interior embraces two equal naves, where a single central column supports 16C Gothic vaulting with liernes and tiercerons (ancillary ribs). A large number of 15C and 16C murals have been uncovered and restored as far as possible (note especially a huge representation of St Christopher and scenes from the Passion).

Wallfahrtskirche St.-Anton – *Partenkirchen.* To the octagonal nave of this 1708 pilgrim's sanctuary, a second nave, oval in shape, was added in 1734-36 by Joseph Schmuzer. The dome above this is decorated with frescoes by JE Holzer.

Philosophenweg (Philosophers' Way) – *Partenkirchen.* The park of **St.-Anton-Anlagen** is the departure point for this panoramic walk which offers fine, clear **views**★ of the surrounding massifs – with the Zugspitze visible this time behind the Waxensteine.

EXCURSIONS

★★★ **Zugspitze** – *For access and description, see ZUGSPITZE.*

★★ **Wank** ⊙ – *20min in a cable-car. Leave from the Schützenhaus inn, on the northern fringe of Partenkirchen.*
From the summit (1 780m/5 840ft) there is a comprehensive view of the Wetterstein chain – and a vertiginous appreciation of the Garmisch-Partenkirchen basin far below. A panorama of the surrounding mountains can be enjoyed from many of the footpaths crossing the Alpine meadows and skirting the forest.

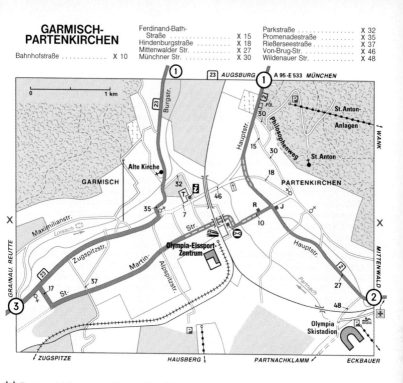

★★ Partnachklamm – *About 1hr 30min there and back, of which 5min are in a cable-car. (Remember to take rainwear.)*
From the Partenkirchen ski stadium, go to the lower terminus of the Graseck cable-car. The upper station is at the Forsthaus Graseck hotel, and from here a footpath leads up to the **gorges**. The route, carved from the solid rock, passes two spectacular bottlenecks amid the thunder of falling water and clouds of spray. At the Partnachklamm inn, the path rejoins the upward route. It is possible to make the same trip in wintertime, when the route will be decorated with a huge frieze of icicles.

★ Eibsee – *8km/5mi to the west.*
The calm waters of this lake occupy a superb forest site. It lies at the foot of the Zugspitze, at an altitude of 1 000m/3 280ft. A footpath *(2hr walk)* circles the lake.

★ Mittenwald – *20km/12mi to the east.*
Mittenwald, a community of violin makers on the old Augsburg-Verona trade route, still suffers from heavy traffic today. This is due to the large number of excursions possible in the nearby Kranzberg and Karwendel massifs, and to the beauty of the town itself. The **painted houses★★** lining the pavements of the main street are especially noteworthy.
If Mittenwald, as Goethe said, is "a living picture-book", a monument outside the church recalls that the town also has a place in the world of music. The memorial honours Matthias Klotz (1653-1743), who returned from Cremona in 1684 with a lute and, as an ex-pupil of Stradivarius, introduced the manufacture of stringed instruments to Bavaria despite the fact that it was then in the midst of an economic depression. A dozen artisans, a technical school, and a museum, the **Geigenbau-und- Heimatmuseum** ⊙, carry on that tradition today.

STAYING IN MITTENWALD

Arnspitze – Innsbrucker Straße 68, ☎ 0 88 23/24 25. Country inn at the southern end of town (no rooms). Good, upper scale regional cuisine.

Alpenrose – Obermarkt 1, ☎ 0 88 23/9 27 00, Fax 0 88 23/37 20. Single room from 85DM. Inn painted outside in "Lüftlmalerei". The cellar restaurant (the Josefikeller) has Bavarian specialities.

Alpengasthof Gröbl-Alm – Gröbl-Alm 1 (2km/1.25mi northwards), ☎ 0 88 23/91 10, Fax 0 88 23/29 21. Single rooms from 90DM. Lying above town on a deep green meadow. Grandiose view on Mittenwald and the mountains.

225

GELNHAUSEN

Hessen

Population 21 600
Michelin map 417 P 11

Emperor Frederick Barbarossa founded the Imperial city of Gelnhausen in 1170 by pooling three local settlements on a slope of the Kinzig Valley. A palace was built in which the Kaiser resided eight times, evidence shows. Thanks to its advantageous location and the imperial privileges, the city was one of the most prosperous at the time of the Staufer rule.

The townscape is dominated by towers, city gates and fountains as well as sections of the old wall, in part original, in part restored.

★ **Marienkirche** – Enter via the small south door that looks out over the valley. This solid, red-sandstone building, with its spires and gables, is typical of the Rhineland Romanesque style *(see Introduction)*. The **choir**★★ (Chorraum), adorned with trilobed blind arcades and heavily worked consoles, is considered to be one of the masterpieces of 13C religious architecture. The rood screen from the same century is a rarity.

Kaiserpfalz (Imperial Palace Ruins) ⊙ – This ruin, a fort on an island in the midst of greenery, is the best-preserved palace from the period of the Staufer rule. It is a superb document to their art of building. It was built between 1180 and 1195 during the reign of Kaiser Frederick I Barbarossa and comprises today – in various states of repair – a double-naved entrance hall, a colonnade with beautifully done capitals, the gate tower, the palace – the main residence – and the ring wall.

EXCURSIONS

Büdingen – *17km/10.5mi to the north.*
The 15C and 16C **fortified perimeter**★ (Stadtmauer) has fine decorative details. Note the 1503 Jerusalem gate, with its squat towers and Gothic embellishments.
The **castle** ⊙ of the Ysenburg princes is one of the few Staufen residences which is still inhabited. From the entrance arch to the interior courtyard, moving in a clockwise direction, the buildings around the inner courtyard decrease in age from the 12C to the 15C. The **choir stalls**★ of the 15C chapel are decorated with saints' effigies, rosettes and coats of arms.

Steinau – *25km/15.5mi to the northeast.*
The Brothers Grimm, sons of a magistrate, grew up in this small town *(see Kassel)*. They lived from 1791 to 1796 in the massive **Tribunal House** (Hanauisches Amtshaus), which stands back behind a courtyard at no 80, Brüder-Grimm-Straße, known as the Brüder-Grimm Haus Steinau, a documentary site for the life and work of the famous brothers.
There is a **Brothers Grimm museum** and a collection of marionettes in the **castle** ⊙, a fortified Renaissance ensemble with defensive towers and a square keep.

GÖRLITZ★

Sachsen

Population 70 000
Michelin map 418 M 28

Görlitz has spread out along the west bank of the Neiße, which has formed the frontier with Poland since 1945. Görlitz became extremely prosperous during the 15C and 16C in particular, through textile manufacture and trade in woad, and enjoyed privileges such as the right to mint coins and that of being the home of high judicial authority. The industrial revolution in the 19C contributed to the fame of the busy town, which is famous for its mechanical and optical industries.

Görlitz was largely spared during the Second World War, so that the huge legacy of historical buildings (the town boasts 3 500 listed houses) represents a major commitment, albeit also a challenge. Visitors will be gratified to see how the pearl of Lower Silesia is gaining shape and colour.

SIGHTS

Obermarkt (BXY 39) – On the north side of this square, fine Baroque houses have been preserved between the Reichenbacher Turm, a fortified gateway to the west, and the Dreifaltigkeitskirche to the east. Flamboyant Gothic **stalls**★ are worth looking at inside the church. At **no 29** (the Tourist Information Centre), the façade, including an entrance framed by sculpted columns, is adorned with impressive stuccowork.

GÖRLITZ

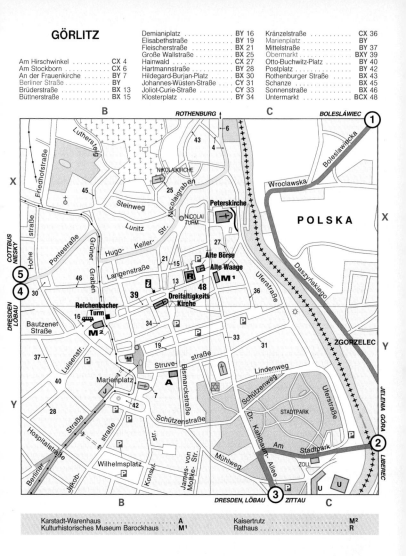

Dreifaltigkeitskirche ⊙ (**BX**) - A high, slim tower with a Baroque cupola is a major feature of this church in the Obermarkt. The interior with its two naves (15C) is extremely narrow and extends into the long chancel which dates from 1371 to 1381. Visitors will be impressed by the **choir stalls★** (1484), with the chronicle of the Franciscans above them, which will remind them that the church was formerly part of a Franciscan monastery. The Baroque high altar, which dates from 1713, was created by Caspar Gottlob von Rodewitz, a student of Permoser. The pulpit with the twelve Apostles is a work from the Late Renaissance era.

The **Barbarakapelle** houses some valuable works of art, for example the **Maria altarpiece★** (c 1510), a Late Gothic masterpiece. It depicts the Virgin Mary encircled by a glowing halo and also relates the Christmas story. When closed, the hinged panels of the altarpiece represent Christ's Passion. The burial group was created by Hans Olmützer in 1492, whilst the poignant **Christ at peace** (late 15C) is ascribed to a south German master.

★ **Untermarkt** (**BCX 48**) - Formerly the town's chief trading centre, the market place is overlooked by the tower (1378) of the **Rathaus** (town hall) (**BX R**). Note, on the corner of the Brüderstraße, the outside staircase (1537-38) encircling an elegant statue (a copy) representing Justice. To the right of the building's Renaissance doorway, a Late Gothic (1488) sculptured plaque displays the arms of Matthias Corvinus, King of Hungary. The central part of the town hall dates from Renaissance times, while the neo-Gothic additions are less than a century old.

In the middle of the market, the **Alte Börse** (former money exchange) (**BX**), with its entrance surrounded by allegorical figures, is the oldest Baroque monument in the town. Dating from 1706, the exchange is adjacent to the **Alte Waage** (Weigh-house) (**BX**), which combines three Renaissance upper storeys with a Baroque base at street level.

> ### "Silesian heaven"
>
> With a bit of luck, visitors to Görlitz will be able to sample *Schlesisches Himmelreich*, a typical Silesian sweet and sour dish, prepared from pickled pork and dried fruit and served with a light lemon sauce and white bread dumplings.

Arcaded houses bordering the southern side of the Untermarkt evoke the lives of the gentry and eminent burghers living there in the past.

Kulturhistorisches Museum Barockhaus (Museum of Cultural History in the Baroque House) ⊘ **(CX M¹)** – *At Neißstraße 30*.
This imposing Baroque mansion (1727-29) at the southeastern corner of the square houses an interesting collection of art, 16C to 19C decorative arts and beautiful Renaissance and Baroque furniture. There is a particularly fine collection of glassware on display. A collection of 18C **rustic cupboards and cabinets★** on the second floor is distinguished by the interesting painted decoration of the exhibits. The print room contains prints and graphic work from the 16C to the 20C.

★ **St. Peter und Paul** ⊘ **(CX)** – The mighty five-naved sandstone building of this place of worship, with its steep copper roof, towers high above the Neiße. It was built over a period of 75 years, being completed by the end of the 15C. Some Late Gothic additions were made to the Late Romanesque west portal (1235) of its predecessor.

Interior – The three central naves form a high, airy open space with a beautiful star vault. The windows are decorated with ornate tracery. The **pulpit**, which dates from 1693, with its gilded acanthus leaves, supported by a charming statue of an angel, is quite magnificent. The Baroque high altar (1695) was completed by Georg Heermann in sandstone and marble stuccowork. The altarpiece depicts the Ascension. The great organ was built by Eugenio Casparini, Andreas Silbermann's tutor, in 1703. The **Görlitz sun organ**, with its 56 organ stops and its radially arranged pipes, has an excellent reputation. The organ front, by the Görlitz artist Johann Conrad Buchau, is crowned by three groups of angels making music. A set of elaborate Baroque confessionals completes the ensemble. Beneath them, in the outer north nave, stands the Baroque confessional created by Caspar Gottlob von Rodewitz in 1717, with its statues of St Peter and Mary Magdalene.

The impressive feature of the lower church (Georgenkapelle) is its star-shaped vaulting.
The oldest secular building in the town, the former **woad house** (Waidhaus), in which the sought-after blue dye was stored, stands to the right of the church.

Kaisertrutz (Imperial Shelter) (BY M²) – *Demianiplatz*.
This solid-looking circular keep, 19m/62ft in diameter, was built as part of the town's fortifications between 1490 and 1541. It now houses the **Museum für Stadtgeschichte** ⊘ **und Kunst** (Local History and Art Museum).

Reichenbacher Turm ⊘ **(BY)** – Opposite the Kaisertrutz stands the symbol of the town, recorded for the first time in 1376. Some 165 steps lead up to the 52m/170ft high tower, and the little room at the top affords a wonderful **view★** over the town.

Karstadt-Warenhaus, Görlitz

Warenhaus Karstadt (BY A) – The steel-framed building faced with ashlar, built by the Potsdam architect Schmann, is the only remaining example of Jugendstil (Art Nouveau) department store architecture in Germany, and was built in 1912-13. Although from the outside it appears somewhat ponderous, its interior, with its central air well and the glazed barrel roof, its inspired staircase design and decorated columns, exudes an elaborate elegance.

EXCURSIONS

★ **St. Marienthal** – *15km/9mi south via B 66, in Ostritz.*
The Bohemian queen Kunigunde founded this Cistercian convent in 1234. It is still run by the Cistercian order today.
Picturesquely situated on a bend in the Lausitz Neiße, the convent institution built during the second half of the 17C and the first half of the 18C is surprisingly large, and the white and deep-red building is full of contrasts. Unmistakably Bohemian influences are evident in particular on the west façade with its central projection, in front of which lie an artesian well and a plague monument dating from 1704.

Klosterkirche ⊘ – Unusually for Cistercian architecture, which normally has only a roof turret, this church has a tower. The interior with its groined vaulting was painted in the narrative Romanesque style in 1850 by Nazarenes.
Germany's easternmost vineyard also lies within the boundaries of the convent estate.

GÖTTINGEN

Niedersachsen
Population 130 000
Michelin map 417/418 L 13

Along with Heidelberg, Tübingen and Marburg, Göttingen is one of the four German towns most deeply imbued with the university tradition. Student life, often noisy and highly coloured, lends a particular vivacity to the scene, especially at examination time and on Foundation Days (Stiftungsfeste). The streets of the old town, with their Gothic churches and neo-Classical university buildings, are frequently bustling with squads of students cycling to dispersed lecture halls and libraries.

A famous university – The university was founded in 1737 by George II of England in his capacity as Elector of Hanover. At first it tended to be an aristocratic institution, frequented by the sons of important English and Russian families and Hanoverian gentry. While lawyers and philologists studied, champion horsemen exercised their skills at the enormous riding school. In 1807, however, the nomination of **Carl Friedrich Gauß** (1777-1855) as Director of the Observatory and Professor of Astronomy ushered in a period of great learning and scientific achievement.
A mathematical genius even more precocious than Pascal, Gauß had, at the age of 16, envisaged the possibility of a non-Euclidian geometry. His name was later given to the international unit used in the measurement of magnetic field intensity, and to a society of learned researchers. Members of this body even today are still trying to distil the quintessence of Gauß's scientific testament, embodied in 145 enigmatic theses which are condensed into only 19 pages. Forty Nobel Prize winners studied or taught at the University of Göttingen; today it has 14 faculties with a total of about 33 000 students.
Since the end of the Second World War, Göttingen has become the headquarters of the Max Planck Society (successor to the Kaiser-Wilhelm-Gesellschaft), which groups together some 50 scientific research organisations in Germany and has been headquartered in Berlin since 1993. Author in 1900 of the revolutionary Quantum Theory, Max Planck (1858-1947) is buried in Göttingen.

SIGHTS

Rathaus (Town hall) – Students, tourists and citizens combine to make the market place and the wine cellars (Ratskeller) beneath the town hall the animated centre of social life in Göttingen. The 14C-15C building is constructed on the classic medieval pattern *(see Introduction)*. In front of it is the modern **Goosegirl Fountain** (Gänselieselbrunnen). Newly anointed Ph.D.s traditionally come to the fountain and give the girl a kiss.

Vierkirchenblick – A church is visible at each point of the compass from the southeast corner of the market: east, the countrified dome of St. Albanikirche; south, St. Michaelskirche; west, the octagonal towers of St. Johannis; and north, the lofty belfry of St. Jakobi – at 72m/236ft the tallest tower in town.

Half-timbered houses (Fachwerkhäuser) – Most of these are in the eastern part of the old town. Note particularly the ancient **Junkernschänke inn**★ (near the Rathaus, at the junction of the Barfüßerstraße and the Judenstraße). Medallions with portrait heads adorning this half-timbered Renaissance building are surmounted by biblical characters such as Adam and Eve, Samson and Delilah etc. The master and mistress of the house when it was built are depicted on the corner post.

Städtisches Museum (Municipal Museum) ⊘ – This museum, which is housed in a Renaissance building, is devoted to the historical and cultural development of Göttingen, both town and university, and the surrounding area. It also exhibits an interesting collection of religious art from the Midle Ages and Modern era, applied arts with Fürstenberg porcelain, faience from Hann. Münden, Göttingen silver and contemporary studio glass.

EXCURSION

★ **Duderstadt** – *31km/19mi to the east.*
Once known as "the Nuremberg of the Eichsfeld", Duderstadt retains from its colourful past more than 500 wonderfully unified half-timbered houses from various stylistic epochs. Most have sculpted exposed beams. Overlooking the Marktstraße are the pointed turrets of the **Rathaus**, built at the beginning of the 13C and enlarged between 1432 and 1533.
Not far away is **St. Cyriakus-Kirche**, an enormous eight-bay hall-church built in the 15C. Among the works of religious art inside are 15 Baroque statues – including the twelve Apostles – joined to the supporting columns.

GOSLAR★★

Niedersachsen
Population 47 000
Michelin map 418 K 15 – Local map see HARZ

This 1000-year-old imperial city lying on the northern rim of the Harz natural park exhibits its long and rich history in a large grouping of half-timbered houses and important monuments around its medieval centre.

A Mining Town – A former Free Imperial City, Goslar owed its prosperity to the mineral wealth of the Harz, and particularly to the Rammelsberg mines, worked during the Middle Ages for lead and silver. The city's commercial importance reached its height in the 15C and 16C, when profit accrued also from the vast surrounding forests which provided timber to fire the metal refineries. It was during this period that the fine houses of the city guilds were built.
Religious controversy between the Free City and the dukes of Brunswick, who owned the mines, brought an economic decline in the mid 16C. Today, although the Rammelsberg mines are still worked, tourism is Goslar's principal industry. The fact that the old town with the Imperial Palace and the Rammelsberg ore mines have been designated a World Heritage Site by UNESCO has also given the local economy a boost.
From the terrace of the **Georgenberg (Y)** there is a fine view of the town packed tightly against the mountain slope.

★★★ OLD TOWN (ALTSTADT) *3hr*

Beginning on Marktplatz

★ **Marktplatz (Z)** – The market square, dignified and austere in appearance, is surrounded by houses protected by slate cladding. Its architectural prestige derives from two Gothic buildings: the Kaiserworth and the Rathaus, behind which soar the spires of the 12C **Marktkirche**. In the centre of the square there is a **fountain** (Marktbrunnen) with two bronze basins (1230) surmounted by the crowned imperial eagle with outstretched wings. On the gable of a house opposite the Rathaus there is a **chiming clock** which animates four different scenes *(at 9am, noon, 3pm and 6pm)* representing the history of mining in the Harz mountains from the Middle Ages to the present day.

★ **Rathaus (Town hall) (YZ R)** – Following the medieval custom, this 15C building was designed with an open hall at street level, an arcaded gallery opening onto the Marktplatz.
On the south side, an exterior staircase leads to the first floor **State Room** (Diele). The lower part of the roof is masked by an ornate balustrade alternating with decorative gabling.

★★ **Huldigungssaal** (Chamber of Allegiance) ⊘ – This room, transformed into the **Municipal Council Chamber** in 1490, was magnificently decorated c 1520. Along the walls, beneath delicately carved upper panelling, Roman emperors alternate with

Rathaus, Goslar

sibyls in Renaissance costume; on the ceiling, scenes from the childhood of Christ are surrounded by figures of the Prophets and Evangelists. Concealed behind a door is a tiny chapel containing paintings of the Passion and an arm-reliquary (c 1300) of St Margaret.

Kaiserworth (Z **S**) - Built in 1494, this Gothic edifice, now a hotel, is embellished with a turreted oriel and Baroque statues of emperors beneath baldaquins. On a gable ridge, at the foot of an allegorical statue of Abundance, a grotesque figurine of **The Ducat Man** (Dukatenmännchen) vividly illustrates Goslar's ancient right to mint coins.

★★ **Carved half-timbered houses (Fachwerkhäuser)** - The Schuhhof (Y **76**), a small square to the northwest of the Rathaus, is entirely surrounded by half-timbered buildings, those on the right resting on arcades.

Further on, a passageway on the left leads to the narrow Münzstraße, which in turn passes an old staging inn, **Am Weißen Schwan** (Y **A**) and then the **Alte Münze** (Old Mint) (Y **Z**). Transformed today into a restaurant, this timbered building dates from 1500.

The fine house on the corner of the Münzstraße and the Marktstraße (Z **V**), with its splendid two-storey oriel, was constructed in 1526.

Facing the Marktkirche is the huge pointed roof of the **Brusttuch** (Z **B**), also dating from 1526, which was built for a rich mine owner and decorated, according to Renaissance taste, with a host of biblical, mythological and legendary characters and motifs. Not far away, the tall gable of the **Bäckergildehaus** (Bakers' Guild Hall) (Z **Y**), built between 1501 and 1557, rises into view.

The **Renaissance houses** at the Marktstraße-Bäckerstraße crossroads are adorned with friezes of the fan motif, so often found in Lower Saxony (no 2 Bäckerstraße), or a row of blind arcades (no 3 Bäckerstraße) (YZ **W**).

Siemenshaus ⊙ (Z **C**) - An impressive half-timbered house built in 1693 by Hans Siemens, ancestor of the founder of the celebrated industrial firm of the same name. There is a particularly fine tiled entrance hall (Däle), and a picturesque interior courtyard.

Stift zum Großen Heiligen Kreuz (Z **K**) - This former almshouse, founded in 1254, is on the banks of the River Gose, which has given its name to the delicious local beer (Gosebier).

The Gothic gable, beneath overhanging eaves, overlooks the Hoher Weg. Inside, the galleried **Great Hall** (Diele) communicates with an unadorned chapel.

ADDITIONAL SIGHTS

★ **Stiftskirche Neuwerk** (Y) - This former collegiate church (12C-13C) stands alone vis-à-vis the Rose gate (Rosentor) at the entrance of the town. The tall **polygonal towers** are among the most elegant ever built for a Romanesque church. The exterior decoration of the apse is exceptionally elaborate.

Heavily ribbed, pointed vaulting characterizes the interior. In the central bay, the columns carrying the transverse arches, two of which have a stone ring, are hollowed in their upper parts to form a curious handle. The former rood screen

GOSLAR

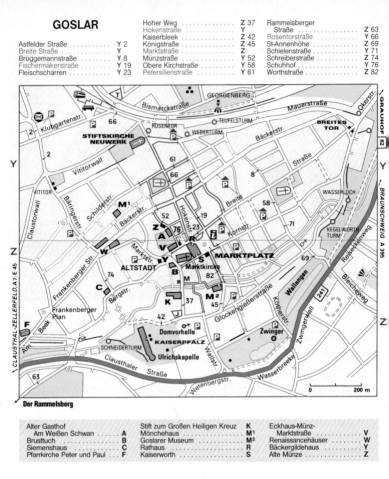

Der Rammelsberg

decorated with six low-relief sculptures dating to 1230-40, with figures (Christ, the Virgin, the four Apostles), whose clothing and artistic design appear manifestly Gothic, is used as an organ loft in the west. The Late Romanesque painting in the choir is particularly noteworthy.

★ **Pfarrkirche Peter und Paul** (Z F) – *Entrance on the Frankenberger Plan.*
This three-nave cruciform basilica built in the 12C stands at the highest point of the old town, the Frankenberg, in a quiet district of the town, which was once inhabited by miners and has hardly changed since the Middle Ages. The renovations done to the choir (c 1300) and the apse (c 1500) and the construction of a Baroque calotte instead of the double towered western nog, which was once part of the city's fortifications, have hardly altered the building's Romanesque character. The Romanesque arched frieze beneath the moulding is still intact.
The pillars and vaults of the interior are richly decorated with stone carvings. The work on the columns of the western choir, borrowed from those at Königslutter *(see Braunschweig: Excursions)* is particularly fine. Over the choir and upper loft are murals painted in the early 13C. The 12C altar bears a splendid Baroque retable dating to 1675, which, like the 1698 chancel, originated in the Goslar woodcarving workshop of Heinrich and Jobst Heinrich Lessen.

★ **Kaiserpfalz (Imperial Palace)** ⊙ (Z) – The castle, originally built for Kaiser Heinrich III in the 11C and reduced to ruins with the passage of years, was rebuilt and restored between 1868 and 1879. The impressive proportions of the whole give some idea of the power and prestige enjoyed by the imperial rulers. Ambitious historical paintings in the gigantic **Reichssaal** *(on the first floor)* chart the significant events affecting Saxony when Goslar was still an imperial residence. Beyond the Reichssaal is the early-12C **Palatine Chapel of St Ulrich**, where the plan passes, in elevation, from that of a Greek cross to that of an octagon. Inside the chapel is the tomb of Heinrich III, whose heart is preserved in the plinth. The recumbent effigy of the ruler dates from the 13C.

Domvorhalle (Z) – Of the cathedral built in the 11C by Heinrich III and demolished in 1822, all that remains is this deconsecrated chapel in the Romanesque style, which houses the late-11C imperial throne.

★ **Breites Tor (Wide Gate) (Y)** – This massive construction with its round towers, its barrack quarters and its two huge doors (only the inner one remains) is in fact a fortress in the form of a gateway. It was built c 1500.

★ **Mönchehaus (Monks' House) (Y M¹)** – A **museum of modern art**, housed in an ancient half-timbered house, displays works by Beuys, Hundertwasser, Serra and de Kooning. In the garden are sculptures by Ernst and Rennertz, and an interesting Calder mobile.

Goslarer Museum ⊙ **(Z M²)** – This museum outlines the history of the town. There is a fine collection of works of art from the Old Goslar Cathedral, such as the **Krodoaltar**, a large bronze reliquary altar dating from the 11C, from which the jewelled decorations and precious stones have unfortunately been stolen. Note also the Goslar Gospel, a 13C manuscript, and a 16C Crucifixion.
A numismatic chamber highlights Goslar's importance as a coin-minting centre. The exhibition on prehistory and early history is also well worth seeing.

The Zwinger (Z) – Built in 1517 as part of a defence ring, this fortified tower stands on the **ramparts** (Wallanlagen) south of the city centre. From the top of the tower, there is a fine view of the old town.

The Rammelsberg ⊙ – *To the south-west of town, via Clausthaler Straße and Rammelsberger Straße.*
Over the centuries the Rammelsberg mines with their rich deposits of non-ferrous metals – lead, zinc, copper, silver – have been largely responsible for Goslar's prosperity. The mines were worked continuously for at least 1 000 years, if not longer, giving up almost 30 million tons of ore during this period. During the museum visit, the Roeder gallery and other parts of the mine can be explored on foot or in a mining train. The mining museum and the public mine of Rammelsberg are connected, ie the mine can be visited above and below ground.

EXCURSIONS

★ **Grauhofer Kirche** – *3km/2mi. Leave Goslar by the Okerstraße (Y).*
Augustinian friars from Grauhof monastery (founded in 1527) employed an Italian architect to build this church in 1701. It was completed in 1717. The interior is remarkable both for its huge size and the restrained use of colour. Of particular interest are a pulpit in the form of a boat (1721), the splendid organ case, which dates from 1737, and the **choir stalls** in exotic woods, where 56 separate scenes represent the life and philosophy of St Augustine.

★★ **Harz Mountains** – *See HARZ.*

GOTHA

Thüringen
Population 51 000
Michelin map 418 N 16

This town, first mentioned in 775, flourished in the 15C and 16C thanks to its far-reaching commercial contacts. From 1640 to 1918, the town was the residence of the dukes of Saxe-Gotha. It won worldwide renown through the publication of the Gotha Almanac on the genealogy of the aristocracy. The market square, surrounded by beautiful town houses dating from a variety of periods, stretches as far as the ducal palace. In the lower part of the town, on the Hauptmarkt, stands the **Rathaus**, an elegant Renaissance building (1567-74), with an eye-catching, richly ornate north façade and beautiful doorway. The massive bulk of the Friedenstein palace, set back slightly from the main line of sight, dominates the town.

The Eckhof-Theater

In 1681, Duke Friedrich I von Sachsen-Gotha-Altenburg had the former ballroom turned into a theatre. The size and design we see today dates back to 1774. The 24m/77ft room is divided exactly down the middle by the stage portal. The entire Baroque machinery to change the scenes, while the curtain remains open, is still original as are the footlights. The Eckhof Theatre is also interesting from the standpoint of theatrical history as the site of the first permanent court theatre in Germany. Before that, the stage was used by members of the court or by wandering troops. It was here, then, that the way was paved towards social acceptance of the acting profession and towards the running of a modern theatre. The artistic director, Conrad Eckhof, after whom the theatre was named, was considered one of the most important actors of his day and is called the "father of German acting".

Schloßmuseum Gotha

Gotha Lovers by the Master of the Housebook

* **Schloß Friedenstein** ⊘ – This austere Early Baroque palace, which has three wings, was begun in 1643 under Ernst I the Pious, and finished in 1655. An arcaded gallery around the inner courtyard is the only decorative feature apart from the differently shaped roofs of the corner turrets. However, the visitor is amply compensated for this by the palace interior, which consists of more than 30 rooms decorated in the Baroque, Rococo and Classical styles, with fittings that verge in parts on the absolutely sumptuous. Note in particular the original stucco ceilings (late 17C), the beautiful marquetry flooring, and the fine quality furniture (from the workshop of Abraham Roentgen among others).

The palace houses numerous collections built up over the centuries by the Gotha dynasty with some later additions.

The **art collection** includes 17C Dutch and Flemish painting, while specializing in 15C and 16C German works. Note especially the **paintings by Lucas Cranach the Elder** and the charming **Gotha Lovers**★, painted by the Master of the Housebook in 1484, the first ever separate double portrait in German painting. The Gotha altarpiece is also a magnificent work, comprising 157 panels depicting the life of Christ, making it one of the most heavily illustrated of its kind in German art.

The collection of **Egyptian and Antique art** testifies to the enthusiasm of its founder. Finally, the visitor to the palace should not miss the **Ekhof-Theater** (1774).

Schloßpark – The extensive palace gardens, landscaped in the English style, with a number of beautiful old trees and an orangery built from 1747 to 1767, make a pleasant place for a stroll.

GREIFSWALD★

Mecklenburg-Vorpommern
Population 70 000
Michelin map 416 D 23

Greifswald dates from the foundation of Eldena Abbey. There is documentary evidence that the town had already been granted rights as early as 1250. Once it joined the Hanseatic League in 1281, Greifswald appears to have flourished. The construction at this time of three large parish churches, whose silhouettes still grace the town's skyline, provides evidence of its prosperity. In fact, Greifswald was to continue to expand and prosper for the next four centuries.

Swedish rule – Following the peace treaty of Osnabrück, which brought the Thirty Years War to an end, West Pomerania, and thus also Greifswald, passed into Swedish hands. The Swedes proved not to be oppressive rulers, exercising leniency for nigh on 200 years and granting the town an unusual degree of autonomy for the age, if not exactly furthering any particular economic growth. From 1815, when West Pomerania became part of Prussia, a busy period of construction began, to which the numerous well-preserved burghers' houses still testify.

The greatest German Romantic painter – Caspar David Friedrich, the epitome of the German Romantic painter and a revolutionary landscape painter, was born in Greifswald in 1774 (his place of birth at no 57 Lange Straße was destroyed by fire in 1901). Although he left Greifswald at the age of 20 (to settle in Dresden), he remained deeply attached to the town of his birth; Greifswald, and especially the ruins of Eldena Abbey, feature in many of his works. Friedrich's paintings are suffused with symbolism of the transitory nature of human existence and reflect intense and subjective emotions to a degree never before committed to canvas. Many of his very spiritual works evoke mankind's isolation in the face of nature and destiny. His austere compositions appeal strongly to modern viewers.

Present and future outlook – Greifswald's geographical location near a national frontier has its advantages and disadvantages; a significant upturn in the town's economic fortunes is hardly to be expected this close to the Polish border. The town does however still have a large number of its original buildings, since it escaped any destruction during the Second World War. Its charming appearance, in which a faint suggestion of Scandinavian influence can be detected, and its tranquil atmosphere will certainly stand it in good stead for future growth as a holiday destination.

OLD TOWN (ALTSTADT)

★ **Marktplatz** – To the west of this square stands the **Rathaus** (1738) with its distinctive curved, Renaissance style gables; the roof turret is nonetheless in the Baroque style. The arcades along the east gable, which were built according to medieval model, were uncovered in 1936. Around the square stand a number of architecturally interesting houses, the most noticeable of which is **no 11**★: this early 15C building with its ornately decorated crow-stepped gable is one of the most beautiful examples of north German Gothic architecture in brick.

★ **Marienkirche** ⊘ – This hall-church with three naves has no chancel. The elegantly structured east gable with its ornate tracery alleviates the somewhat heavy, stocky appearance of the rest of the brick church, which is known affectionately as "podgy Mary" by locals. Construction of the church was begun in 1280 and lasted into the 14C. Inside there is a beautiful carved **pulpit**★ dating from 1587, the work of Joachim Mekelenborg from Rostock. During the last phase of restoration work, Late Gothic frescoes from the 15C were uncovered, including one which depicts a whale caught in the fishing village of Wieck in 1545.

★ **Dom St. Nikolai** ⊘ – The cathedral is dwarfed by its tower, which is almost 100m/328ft in height and takes the form of a square base flanked by four small round towers, supporting a two-storey octagonal tower with blind double windows decorated with white plaster tracery. The crowning glory is a Dutch Baroque steeple dating from 1653. In the 14C the original hall-church was elevated to the rank of basilica, and the spaces between the flying buttresses were filled in to make a ring of 21 radiating chapels. In the 19C two students of Schinkel, Gottlieb Giese and Joachim Christian Friedrich (brother of Caspar David), undertook to remodel the church in the neo-Gothic style in the true spirit of Romanticism. The fruits of their labours are most apparent in the central nave, while the side chapels retain their medieval and Baroque features. Numerous oil paintings (16C-19C) and tombstones, including that of Heinrich Rubenow, founder of Greifswald University who was assassinated by his political opponents in 1462, are of interest. Note also the frescoes dating from c 1430.

St. Jakobikirche ⊘ – This is the smallest of the town's three medieval churches. Its core originates from the second half of the 13C, but it was rebuilt around 1400. The west door features a remarkable sandstone frieze and has an alternating pattern of dark glazing and natural stone around the door jambs. The painting in the vault of the eastern central nave dates to around 1400 as well and portrays the majestic being of God. Note the 13C granite font.

Ehemaliges Hospital St. Spiritus – *Lange Straße*.
The old hospital complex consisting of carefully restored 18C half-timbered single-storey buildings *(towards the courtyard)* and Classical town houses *(towards the street)* is now used as a community meeting centre. The charming inner courtyard is a pleasant place to linger.

Universität – *Rubenowplatz*.
The university of Greifswald is the second oldest in northern Europe after that at Rostock. It was founded in 1456 by local mayor Heinrich Rubenow, who was its first vice-chancellor. The university's most famous student is the poet **Ernst Moritz Arndt**, after whom the university is named, who went on to hold the university chair in history. He was also instrumental in the abolition of the feudal serf system in West Pomerania. The various university faculties are scattered all over town. The university's elongated main building, decorated in red and white plasterwork, stands on Rubenowplatz and was built in the mid 18C by Andreas Meyer from Augsburg. The triangular gable above the central façade bears the coats of arms of the Swedish royal family on the side facing the street, and of Pomerania on the side facing the courtyard.

Museum Greifswald ⊘ – *Theodor-Pyl-Straße 1*.
The local museum occupies the porter's lodge (Guardianshaus) of the old Franciscan abbey. Besides the exhibition on local history, there are displays on Caspar David Friedrich and Ernst Moritz Arndt.

ADDITIONAL SIGHTS

★ **Botanischer Garten** ⊙ – *Grimmer Straße 88/Münsterstraße 1, either side of the railway line.*
The pretty, well laid-out botanical gardens, which are affiliated with the university, offer 1ha/2.5 acres of plants, shrubs and trees, as well as a garden of herbs and medicinal plants. The **greenhouses** full of exotic flora are particularly well worth a visit. The university maintains an 8ha/20 acre **arboretum** divided by geography to the north of town *(Friedrich-Ludwig-Jahn-Straße)*.

★ **Klosterruine Eldena (Abbey Ruins)** – *Wolgaster Landstraße.*
The original Cistercian abbey was founded in 1199, and it appears to have reached the height of its wealth and power around the mid 14C. The Thirty Years War spelled large-scale destruction for it, and the remains were later used as a source of building materials by local people. Of the once splendid building, only fragments of the church, the cloisters and the east abbey building remain. They are nonetheless still as picturesque a scene as they were in the days of Caspar David Friedrich, who not only committed them to canvas, but campaigned for their preservation. The red brick of the buildings contrasts with the greenery of the surrounding park, landscaped by Peter Josef Lenné.

M. Buffard/MICHELIN

Swing bridge at Wieck

★ **Wieck** – *Can easily be reached on foot from the Eldena Abbey ruins.*
This little fishing village, now officially classified as a historical site, lies as the mouth of the River Ryck as it flows into Greifswald Bay. The shipmasters' and fishermen's cottages, the latter thatched with reeds, the idyllic little harbour and the wooden **swing bridge**★ make a delightful scene. The bridge, based on a Dutch design, is a technical monument in itself, dating from 1887. If you are lucky, you may get the chance to see it in action, being raised by a hand-wound winch.

GÜSTROW★

Mecklenburg-Vorpommern
Population 36 000
Michelin map 416 E 20

Güstrow was granted the civic charter in 1228 and went on from this promising start to become the residence of the dukes of Mecklenburg-Güstrow between 1556 and 1695. The wealth that accompanied this status continued to accumulate over the next few centuries, as can be seen from the elegant burghers' houses which line the cathedral and market squares and the streets surrounding them (Mühlenstraße nos 17 and 48, Grüner Winkel no 10). The **Rathaus** on the market square is an architectural oddity, comprising four gabled houses to which a decorative Classical façade was added in 1797.

Ernst Barlach – The name of this great Expressionist sculptor is linked with the town where he lived for nearly 30 years until his death in 1938. Barlach came to Güstrow in 1910, with the intention of settling, and produced some of his major work here.

SIGHTS

★ **Renaissanceschloß** – This Renaissance palace is one of the most important examples of its type in north Germany, combining Italian, French and German stylistic features. It was built from 1558 onwards for Duke Ulrich first by the north Italian architect Franziskus Parr, who completed the south and west wings, and then by his successor, Philipp Brandin from the Netherlands and his student Midow, who built the north and east wings (1587-88). The gatehouse in front of the palace was built in the Dutch Baroque style in 1671, following designs by Charles Philipp Dieussart. The building's exterior is clearly divided by horizontal ledges and has distinctively patterned plasterwork, whose element become smaller the closer they get to the ceiling. Although the west façade with its corner turrets and the striking entrance pavilion is undoubtedly the main decorative façade, the side of the south wing facing the courtyard is also charming with its staircase tower and three-storey colonnaded gallery. The Schloß contains a subsidiary of the **State Museum of Schwerin** (Staatliches Musum Schwerin) ⊘ with numerous rooms. Particularly remarkable is the **stuccowork** depicting exotic hunting and battle scenes decorating the banqueting hall; significant inventory of art and decorative arts, by Tintoretto, among others; weapons and glass collection.

★ **Dom (Cathedral)** ⊘ – The massive shape of this Gothic brick basilica, consecrated in 1335, is a distinctive feature on the town's skyline. Inside it is plain to see that the nave and chancel are set at an angle to each other, rather than being in alignment. Having been the court church of the dukes of Mecklenburg, the basilica is richly endowed with works of art. The **triumphal cross** (c 1370) in the south transept is portrayed as the tree of life. The altarpiece was produced by the workshop of Henrik Bornemann of Hamburg in about 1500 and depicts a Crucifixion scene on the central panel. The elaborately designed **Renaissance tombs**★ on the north side of the choir are the work of Philipp Brandin. A particular highlight among the cathedral's collection of art treasures are the **Güstrow Apostles**★, 12 almost life-size oak figures made by Claus Berg of Lübeck in c 1530. A stark contrast to these is Ernst Barlach's *Der Schwebende* (a recast, as the original was branded "degenerate art" and destroyed in 1937), an expressive figure with the features of Käthe Kollwitz in an attitude of meditation, above an ornate early-16C wrought-iron grille.

Pfarrkirche St. Marien ⊘ – The Gothic parish church has undergone many alterations over the centuries. The present building is a hall-church with three naves and a tower topped with a bulbous cupola in the Baroque style. The original **high altar**★, a fine example of wood carving from the Brabant, is the work of Jan Bormann of Brussels, who created it in 1522. He depicts Christ's Passion in 13 masterly crafted oak reliefs. The altarpiece has three different views and can be positioned in two different ways. The paintings on the wings are a masterpiece by Bernard van Orley. A Late Gothic **triumphal Crucifixion group** dating from 1516 unusually depicts Adam and Eve next to the Virgin Mary and St John.

★ **Ernst-Barlach-Stiftung** (Barlach Museum) ⊘ – This museum in honour of Barlach is located in three different parts of Güstrow: his religious works are exhibited in the Late Gothic **Gertrudenkapelle**, which the artist had always longed in vain to use as a studio. The "Barlachweg" leads to Barlach's **Heidberg studio**, on the shores of the Inselsee just outside of town: a collection of studio models is exhibited here. A few yards away is another building used for changing exhibitions, in fact it was the first brand new museum to be built in the former states of East Germany.

HAIGERLOCH★

Baden-Württemberg
Population 10 000
Michelin map 419 U 10

The attraction of Haigerloch lies in the two consecutive bends of the River Eyach that cuts deep into the shelly limestone slopes. The town, known as Lilac Town, Cliff Town or as the cradle of atomic research, is very picturesque.
After being ruled by the counts of Haigerloch and then Hohenberg, Haigerloch came under the Habsburgs and as then was passed on to the Hohenzollerns, who turned this little fortified bastion into an attractive castle.

SIGHTS

Start at the Marktplatz in the lower town. Climb the slope or stairway, both of which rise to the castle, built along the cliff-like promontory on the downstream bend of the Eyach.

Schloßkirche – Built on the end of the spur, this early-17C church is impressive with the splendour of its Baroque furnishings, which date from 1748.

Haigerloch

Stadt Haigerloch

Continue up the rise, cross the castle courtyard diagonally, and follow the signposted path to the Kapf.

Kapf – From the look-out point there is a view of the upstream river bend where it hugs the upper town, overlooked by the Roman Tower (Römerturm).

Return to the Marktplatz and take the Pfluggasse, on the left.

Atomkeller-Museum Haigerloch ⊘ – This small museum explains, with the help of display panels and three-dimensional material, how Professor Werner Karl Heisenberg and his colleagues constructed, deep inside the cliff beneath the Schloßkirche in the closing months of the Second World War, Germany's first experimental nuclear reactor.

Return once more to the Marktplatz and the car. Take the Oberstadtstraße and park opposite the church at the top of the hill.

★ **St. Anna-Kirche** – At the end of a shady avenue, this church looks across the Eyach gorge at the Schloßkirche, high up on the far side of the river. To get a clear **view★**, walk back a little down the approach road.

St. Anna-Kirche, a pilgrims' sanctuary built in 1755, together with its chaplain's house (Kaplaneihaus), forms a remarkably elegant Baroque ensemble. The interior, too, displays a remarkable sense of harmony and homogeneity. Inside, note the altars by Johann Michael Feuchtmayer bearing almost life-size statues of Johann Georg Weckenmann. The ceiling frescoes are the work of the Sigmaring painter Andreas Meinrad von Au, who displayed a great deal of skill here.

HALBERSTADT

Sachsen-Anhalt

Population 45 000

Michelin map 418 K 17

In 804, Charlemagne raised the mission of Halberstadt to the rank of bishopric. In the Middle Ages, this former Hanseatic city was a major economic centre whose main activity focused on the cloth and linen trade. An aerial bombardment on 8 April 1945, shortly before the end of the Second World War, destroyed most of the inner city; historical buildings were reconstructed, but during the following decades many of the smaller buildings gradually disappeared. Furthermore, the Socialist concept of urban planning played a weighty role in the architectural development of Halberstadt after 1945, and it is what marks the townscape today. Renovation work on the historical city centre was completed in 1998.

SIGHTS

★★ **Dom St. Stephanus** ⊘ – In its opulence and the spirit of its design, this church recalls the Gothic cathedrals of France. Building began in 1240 with the base of each tower and the western bays. A second stage of the work extended from 1354 to 1402. During this period, the chancel was erected, prolonged by the small chapel of St Mary (Marienkapelle) and the ambulatory, where the High Gothic influence resulted in lower walls and the installation of stained-glass windows in the space thus freed. The nave, completed towards the end of the 15C, has no triforium. Owing to the size of the chancel, the transept occupies an almost central position on the cathedral floor plan.

The **rood-screen hall**★ is finely worked in the High Gothic style (c 1510). Above it, a group representing the **Triumphal Cross**★ is a splendid example of Late Romanesque sculpture. Dating from c 1220, it is a relic from the Ottonian cathedral which once occupied the site of the present building. The figures of the Virgin Mary and St John, together with two seraphim, are represented on either side of the Saviour. The 15C choir columns are adorned with 14 statues of saints and the Apostles. A cloister decorated with 13C Stations of the Cross opens off the southern part of the nave.

★★ **Domschatz** (Treasury) ⊘ – Rare liturgical vestments and religious vessels from the 12C to the 16C are displayed here with a precious collection of altar paintings, manuscripts, and 12C tapestries, in particular the Abraham Tapestry, which is more than 10m/33ft long.

Liebfrauenkirche – *To the west of the cathedral.*
The choir screen of this 12C Romanesque basilica is embellished with **high-relief sculptures**★ representing Christ, the Virgin Mary and the Apostles. The workmanship, once again, rates them among the finest examples of late-12C Romanesque art.

Städtisches Museum (Municipal Museum) ⊘ – *At no 36 Domplatz.*
This regional museum devoted to the north of the Harz foothills displays exhibits on the city archeology, on the history of the town and the bishopric and romantic painting from the northern Harz region. The displays include the reconstruction of an old-fashioned pharmacy and of a shoemaker's workshop.

Marktkirche St. Martini – The saint is represented in a bas-relief on the south door of this 13C-14C church. A bronze baptismal font inside, dating from the beginning of the 14C, is decorated with scenes from the life of Christ.

HALLE★

Sachsen-Anhalt
Population 296 000
Michelin map 418 L 19

Halle, on the banks of the Saale between the great northern plain and the first heights of central Germany, is a town with a dual identity: on the one hand it is an important industrial centre specializing in mechanical engineering and chemical manufacture; on the other hand, an intellectual enclave whose university traditions go back to the 17C.

The Salt City – As early as 806 a fortress was built to safeguard the sources of salt extraction which formed the basis of Halle's wealth. The high point of the town's era of prosperity was between the 14C and the 16C, although Halle never attained the status of Imperial city. After this – especially during the Industrial Revolution – local lignite mines formed the commercial base on which the town's commercial development relied. Halle received a further boost to its economy from the mining of local seams of brown coal during the Industrial Revolution.

A Musical Tradition – The creation at the end of the 13C of the Brotherhood of Musicians and Fife Players (Spylleuten und Pfeiffern), and the foundation of an opera in 1654 by the Duke Augustus, illustrate the age-old support of music shown by the municipality. **Georg Friedrich Händel** was born in Halle in 1685. Organist at the cathedral in 1702, he composed many sonatas and cantatas before moving, after a period in Italy, to north Germany and then, in 1710, to London, where he set up residence. His compositions quickly won him an enthusiastic reception from the general public and, more importantly, royal favour and patronage. In 1726, he took British citizenship, after which he was appointed composer of the Chapel Royal. One of his major interests was the composition of large-scale choral works, of which perhaps the most famous example is the oratorio *Messiah*.

In 1713 Johann Sebastian Bach attempted – unsuccessfully – to obtain the post of organist at Halle's Marktkirche (a position, ironically enough, that went to his eldest son Wilhelm Friedemann 30 years later).

The city pays a tribute to the master of German Baroque music in the annual **Händel Festival.**

HALLE

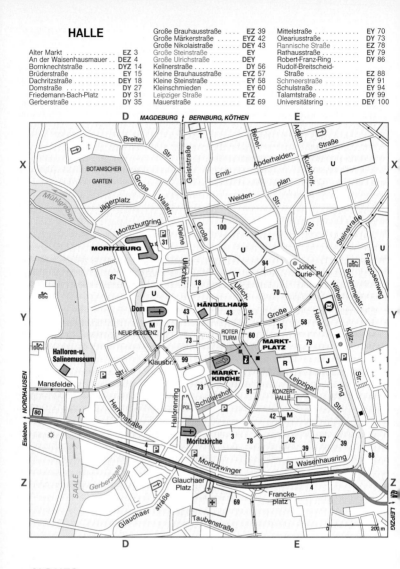

SIGHTS

★ **Marktplatz (EY)** – This huge square is dominated by the belfries of the Marktkirche and by the **Roter Turm** (red tower), built in the 15C and almost 80m/262ft high. An 1859 statue of Händel surveys the square from the centre. The market and the tramway junction there make this the most animated part of the town.

★ **Marktkirche (EY)** – A triple-aisle hall-church with no chancel, this building was constructed in 1529-1554 between the double towers of two Romanesque churhes, whose naves had been torn down. Inside, admire the delicate interlacing of ribs beneath the barrel vaulting, unusual in the absence of transverse arches corresponding to the bays – a feature which seems to confer on the vaulting its own existence independent of the columns supporting it. The side aisles are fitted with stone galleries. The pulpit, dating from 1547 with a sounding board (1596) by Heinrich Heidereiter, blends in harmoniously with its surroundings. The **reredos★** of the high altar carries a Virgin and Child painted by a pupil of the Cranach School (1529).

Moritzkirche (DZ) – *On the Hallorenring.* This, another triple-aisle hall-church, built between 1388 and 1511, displays a network of star-vaulting characteristic of the Flamboyant Gothic style. **Works★** by the sculptor Conrad of Einbeck are on view in the church, masterpieces distinguished at the same time by a naive realism and a great power of expression. Note in particular *The Man of Sorrows*, a statue (1411) of St Maurice, and a Pietà (1416).

★ **Händel-Haus** ⊙ **(DY)** – *Große Nikolaistraße 5.* The great composer's birthplace has been transformed into a museum outlining both his life and his work. One section of the museum exhibits period musical instruments, including several harpsichords dating from the 16C and 17C.

Dom (Cathedral) (DY) – *Am Domplatz; currently under restoration.* The original, monastery church, a three-naved Gothic hall-church was modified c 1520 by Cardinal Albert of Brandenburg, who transformed it into a collegiate church. The interior columns are decorated with statues of Christ, the Apostles and the saints, executed in the studios of Peter Schroh, one of the most talented sculptors of the time. Along with the pulpit (c 1525), they show signs already of a Renaissance influence.

Technisches Halloren -und Salinenmuseum (Saltworks Museum) ⊙ (DY) – *Mansfelder Straße 52*. This museum recounts the history of the exploitation of the local salt mines and the cultural development of the "Halloren" – the Halle salt miners guild. An evaporation vessel is demonstrated that still functions and produces regularly.

★★ **Staatliche Galerie Moritzburg Halle (Moritzburg National Gallery)** ⊙ (EY) – *Friedemann-Bach-Platz.*
In 1484, building began on the Moritzburg, a fortress complex with four wings. Until 1541, it was the preferred residence of the archbishops of Magdeburg and Mainz. Having been destroyed during the Thirty Years War, part of the fortress was restored and converted into a museum at the beginning of the 20C. It now houses the most significant art collection in Sachsen-Anhalt.
There is an excellent collection of **19C and 20C German painting**. The fine works on display embrace the periods of **Romanticism** (Hans von Marées, Caspar David Friedrich), **Impressionism** (Slevogt, Corinth, Liebermann) and **Expressionism**. Works by the artists of the **Brücke** group, as well as by Kandinsky and Feininger, are on display.
The department of **German sculpture of the 19C and 20C** includes works by, among others, Wilhelm Lehmbruck and Ernst Barlach. Numismatists will enjoy a fine collection of moneys and medals in the fortress tower. The museum also displays interesting collections of glassware and ceramics dating from the Middle Ages to the present, and also porcelain and gold ware.

EXCURSIONS

★ **Doppelkapelle Landsberg** ⊙ – *In* **Landsberg**, *19km/12mi west on B 100.*
The twin chapel of St. Crucis can be seen from way off, an elegant building with a tall hipped roof perched on a rocky spur. The plainness of the exterior is broken by three apsidal chapels adorning the east end. The building dates from 1195-1200, when the previous church was converted into a twin chapel under Margrave Konrad von Landsberg. This rare type of chapel – there are only about 30 such buildings recorded – separated the common people, who celebrated Mass in the lower chapel, from the nobility in the upper chapel. The two levels are linked by an open shaft, relatively large by Landsberg standards.
The **capitals**★ on the columns and pillars are adorned with extraordinarily beautiful motifs of plants, animals and figures. Other interesting features of the chapel include the so-called Blutsäule, or blood column, in the upper chapel, in reality booty brought back from Italy, and a magnificent carved altarpiece from 1525.
From the balcony, there is a superb **view**★ as far as Leipzig, Halle and Merseburg.

Eisleben – *34km/21mi to the west.*
Martin Luther was born – and died – in this small mining town within sight of the lower ranges of the Harz Mountains. Memories of the religious reformer are evoked in his **birthplace** (Luther-Geburtshaus, *Lutherstraße 16*) and the house where he died (Luther-Sterbehaus, *Andreaskirchplatz 7*). The historic old town is also worth the trouble. Here, too, much recalls Luther: the church of St Peter and St Paul in which he was baptised; St. Andreas, with the original Luther pulpit, from which he preached for the last time; the Marktplatz with its 1883 Luther statue.

HAMBURG★★★

Hamburg
Population 1 650 000
Michelin map 415/416 F 14

Hamburg, Germany's second largest city after Berlin, is one of the most important ports in Europe. Its old title of "Free and Hanseatic Town" and its status as a "City State" (Stadtstaat) testify to its eminence and influence through the centuries.

Each year, in May, there is an anniversary celebration in the port of Hamburg (Hafengeburtstag), commemorating Frederick Barbarossa's concession in 1189 of the right to free navigation on the lower Elbe. The exercise of this right, menaced by piracy and the feudal pretensions of neighbour states – especially Denmark – demanded a continual watch by the city authorities which could not be relaxed until the 17C.

The Hanseatic Town (13C-15C) – Originally a modest settlement on the banks of the Alster, a small tributary of the Elbe, Hamburg enjoyed its first taste of prosperity when it became a member of the Hanseatic League, headed at that time by Lübeck. It was then that merchants started to organize the banks of the Elbe itself for warehousing and the berthing of ships. The town profited from the particular conditions then of Baltic-North Sea trade: in those days only heavy cargoes of grain and timber took the long sea passage through the Kattegat and the Skagerrak; more valuable material was landed at Lübeck, transported overland to Hamburg, then re-embarked.

Hamburg skyline – the Port and the "Michel" tower

Liberty and Neutrality – The great geographic discoveries of the 16C, and the new sea routes they opened up, destroyed existing trade patterns and dislocated the Hanseatic monopoly. Hamburg traders were thus forced to become intermediaries in warehousing and distribution. The foundation of the first German Stock Exchange in 1558 reflected the intense business activity which resulted – a situation in no way worsened by the city's policy of strict neutrality, which kept it out of the Thirty Years War.

In 1618 Hamburg became a Free Imperial City. One year later the Bank of Hamburg was founded. From 1806 to 1814 French troops occupied the town. In 1842 it was ravaged by a disastrous fire.

But American independence and the emergence of Latin America lent an added impetus to the extraordinary expansion of the later 19C. By 1913, the Hamburg-Amerika steamship line was the largest in the world, and shipbuilding was the city's key industry. Today, port traffic in Hamburg has reached an annual turnover of 57 million tons.

LIFE IN HAMBURG

Business and Leisure – Like Sun many big ports, Hamburg has a reputation for night-life. This is mainly centred on the St. Pauli quarter, to the west of the city centre, where in the side streets flanking the **Reeperbahn (EZ 70)** and the Große Freiheit, in the gaudy illumination of multicoloured neon signs, bars, discotheques, exotic restaurants, clubs and the Eros Centre function day and night.

Many Hamburg residents are a little diffident about the fact that their city is known worldwide for the garish Reeperbahn district. They point to the elegance and attraction of the residential area around the northern end, and the business quarter around the southern part, and of Lake Alster which lies like a jewel in the heart of the city. Between the Staatsoper (Opera House) (FY) and the Rathaus (town hall), pedestrian precincts and covered malls form an almost uninterrupted labyrinth of art galleries, fashion shops, boutiques, jewellery stores and restaurants.

The Mönckebergstraße (GHY), which links the Rathaus with the railway station, is the city's other commercial artery. Antique shops around the Gänsemarkt (FY) specialize in oriental art. Between the Rathaus and the station, an impressive variety of old maps, prints, travel works and tourist guides can be found in a number of different booksellers', while philatelists and tobacco lovers will go to the small shops in the printing and counting house quarter.

The people of Hamburg are said to be very "British" Germans, as they tend to be more reserved and serious than their lively southern compatriots. For visitors, Hamburg is among the most welcoming of German cities, and English is spoken in many of the restaurants, stores and wine cellars.

Culinary Specialities – These often mix local produce with Eastern spices, sometimes combining in one dish meat, fruit and sweet-and-sour sauces. Typical are Aalsuppe – eel soup – and Labskaus, a seamen's dish of minced meat, herring, chopped gherkins and mashed potato, topped with fried eggs.

For visitors with a sweet-tooth, "Rote Grütze" is a local speciality dessert made of red fruit served with vanilla sauce or cream.

CITY CENTRE *allow one day*

*** **Außenalster (GHXY)** – This beautiful stretch of water offers sailing and canoeing in the centre of the city. A fleet of Alsterschiffahrt motorboats ferries passengers regularly between a series of landing-stages.

A boat trip (Alsterrundfahrt) on the lake allows the visitor to get far enough away to appreciate the city skyline punctuated by Hamburg's famous five towers, all of them over 100m/328ft high. They stand above the four main churches and the Rathaus.

It is equally pleasant to make a circuit of the Alster by car, driving clockwise around the long shaded avenues with blocks of luxury flats on one side and immaculate stretches of greensward between the water and the roadway on the other. Their use as **viewpoints** has conferred names on such quays as the **Fernsicht** (View. *Leave by the Alsterufer* – GX) and **Schöne Aussicht** (Beautiful Vista. *Leave by An der Alster* – HX).

* **Jungfernstieg (GY)** – Bordering the southern end of the Binnenalster (inner) basin, this famous street is perhaps the city's most cosmopolitan thoroughfare: the crowded terraces of the waterfront Alsterpavillon café-restaurant, the craft busily crossing and recrossing the basin, the presence nearby of one of the world's most famous hotels (Vier Jahreszeiten), and the imposing new office blocks lining the Ballindamm above the eastern quay all contribute to the general animation.

Rathausmarkt (GYZ) – This square, replanned after the fire of 1842, is dominated by the high campanile of the **Rathaus (R)**, built in the neo-Renaissance style in 1887 and supported by no less than 4 000 piles.

The bridge (Schleusenbrücke), which forms part of the lock controlling the level of the Alster, crosses the Alsterfleet, a final relic of the complex canal system once characteristic of the city. The monument at the end of the bridge with a plinth carving by Barlach is the First World War memorial. On the far bank the colonnade of the Alsterarkaden shelters elegant shops.

St. Jacobikirche (GZ) – Among the numerous treasures of this 14C-15C hall-church are the reredos of St Luke and the Fishers' Guild; a triptych of the Coopers' Guild on the high altar; Georg Bauman's alabaster and marble pulpit (1610); and finally the famous 1693 organ by Arp Schnitger.

Kontorhäuser (Counting House Buildings) (GHZ) – Massively constructed of sombre brick, these stand in the printing, press and business quarter around the Burchard-platz.

The **Chilehaus**, built in 1924, stands against the sky like the prow of a ship. The **Sprinkenhof** (1930) is a town within the town, an office complex complete with roadways that can be used by motor cars.

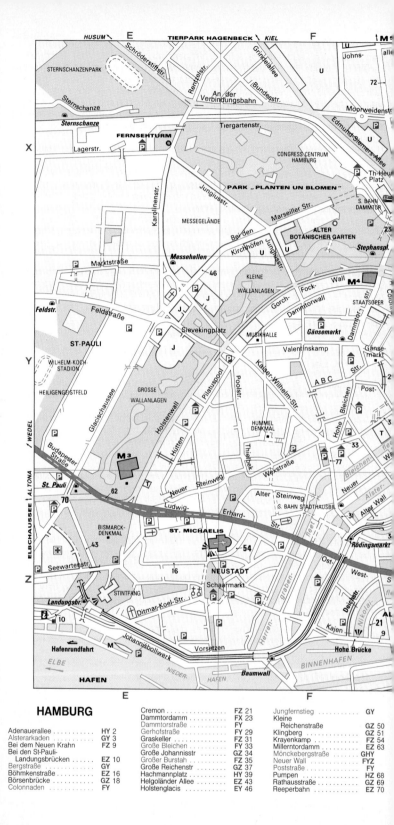

HAMBURG

The length of time given in this guide
  - for touring allows time to enjoy the views and the scenery;
  - for sightseeing is the average time required for a visit.

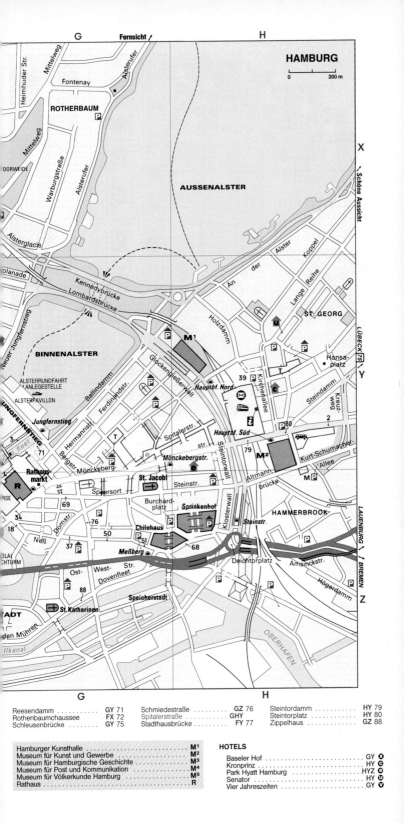

This guide, which is revised regularly, incorporates tourist information provided at the time of going to press. Changes are however inevitable owing to improved facilities and fluctuations in the cost of living.

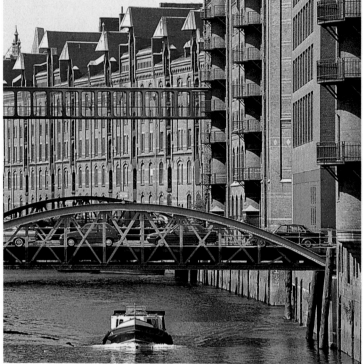

Speicherstadt warehouses

To the south, the squat **Speicherstadt (GZ)** warehouses rise above the Zoll (customs) Canal and its secondary channels. The severity of these dark brick masses is relieved only by an upper decoration of stepped gables and turrets. Built in the late 19C for the free trade zone, they store in their 373 000m²/447 000sq yd of floor space such valuable merchandise as coffee, tobacco, spices, raw silk and oriental carpets.

Altstadt (FGZ) – The old town is bounded by the Nikolaifleet, the Binnenhafen (docks reserved for river craft and tugboats) and the Zoll Canal.

Deichstraße (FZ) – 17C and 18C merchants' houses have today been converted mainly into bars and taverns. It was in the Deichstraße that the great fire of 1842 started.

The restored façades of warehouses opposite, lining the curve of the Nikolaifleet Canal, recall the Hamburg of yesteryear.

The best view is from the **Hohe Brücke**, which crosses the Nikolaifleet and lies parallel with the Binnenhafen. Pulleys once used for the transhipment of cargoes from ship to shore and vice versa can still be seen on the warehouse gables. Traces of the severe floods of 1962 and 1976 are visible on the walls.

Cremon (FZ 21) – From no 33 to no 36, this street is lined by warehouses and former lodging houses, each with dual entrances – one from the street, one from the canal.

St. Katharinen-Kirche (GZ) – This Gothic church, built of brick during the 14C and 15C, features a bulbous openwork tower that rises above the narrow streets of the old port.

★ **Hauptkirche St. Michaelis (EFZ)** – Another brick church, designed in 1762 by the architect Sonnin, this is one of the finest examples of the Baroque tradition in northern Germany. Intended for the Lutheran sect, the church is surprisingly spacious, well proportioned and well lit.

Its famous **tower** ⊘ (1786), rising high above the Elbe with a lantern turret in the form of a pillared temple, is known by local people simply as "**Michel**" and has become the emblem of the city.

The **view**★ from the platform takes in all of the town centre, but most particularly the river, zebra-striped with the wake of ships, and its docks, basins, warehouses and wharves. The ground floor of the second tower has a multivision slide show depicting the history of the city and the church.

Near the east end of the church, pass through the porch at no 10 Am Krayenkamp **(FZ 54)**. The blind alley beyond is lined with astonishing brick and timber houses built in 1670 as almshouses **(Krameramtswohnungen)** and today transformed into art galleries.

ENJOYING YOUR STAY IN HAMBURG

Telephone Prefix – 0 40

Information – *Tourismus-Zentrale Hamburg GmbH*, ☎ 30 05 13 00 Monday-Sunday 8am-8pm. **Information offices**: Main Train Station (Hauptbahnhof), main entrance Kirchenallee, Monday-Sunday 7am-11pm; Harbour, St. Pauli Landungsbrücken (piers) between piers 4 and 5, Monday-Sunday 10am-7pm (October-March only until 5.30pm). The fortnightly magazine *Prinz*, *Szene Hamburg* (every 4 weeks) and the *Hamburger Vorschau* (at the information offices) provide information on all sorts of events. Ticket sales for select events are at the *Tourismus-Zentrale Hamburg*.

Post offices with special opening times – Post office at the main train station (Hachmannplatz) Monday-Friday 8am-8pm, Saturday 9am-6pm, Sunday 10am-6pm.

Newspapers – Hamburger Morgenpost, Hamburger Abendblatt.

Internet – http://www.hamburg.de; http://www.hamburg-intern.de; http://www.hamburg-web.de; http://www.hamburg-information.de

Public Transport

Using the buses and underground trains of the **HVV** (Hamburger Verkehrsverbund, th Hamburg Transit Authority) is recommended. The lines stretch all the way into the surrounding region of Schleswig-Holstein, ☎ 1 94 49, Monday-Sunday 7am-8pm Uhr. Information at the HVV office at the Hauptbahnhof Monday-Friday 7am-8pm, Saturday 8.30am-5pm and Sunday 11am-8pm, and in U- and S-Bahn stations. Tickets are available from vending machines and from the bus drivers. Single tickets for rides into the centre of town from 2.70DM; a day ticket for one person costs 8DM, a group day ticket for up to five people costs 13.80DM (the two latter tickets are valid from 9am till the last ride).

The **Hamburg Card** costs 12.80DM and is valid for one person, the 24DM version is for up to five people (both are valid on the issue date and from 6pm onward on the day before). The three-day version costs 26.30DM or 42DM. Besides use of the HVV network, free entrance to 11 state-run museums and other discounts, the card also gives discounts for tours on water and on land. The Hamburg Card is available at the tourist information offices, in many hotels, at vending machines and in the HVV customer offices, as well as at many travel agents.

Sightseeing Tours

City tours – Tours by double-decker bus. Departure and arrivals at the Hauptbahnhof/Kirchenallee, Embarcation at several other stops. The *Top Tour Hamburg*, daily every 15min beginning at 9.30am (in winter only at 11am and 3pm) lasts about 1hr 30min; the *Gala Tour*, departs daily at 10am, 11am, 2pm and 3pm (in winter only at 10am and 2pm), includes the Elbe suburbs and lasts about 2hr 30min; ☎ 22 71 06 61. Tour with the *Hummel-Bahn* train from Hauptbahnhof/Kirchenallee, April to October from 10.30am-4.30pm daily every 2hr, November-March Saturday and Sunday 10.30am-2.30pm every 2hr (lasts just about 2hr); ☎ 7 92 89 79. **Foot tour of the city** under the heading of St. Pauli or the Speicherstadt for example: *Tourismus-Zentrale Hamburg* and *Stattreisen Hamburg e.V*; ☎ 4 30 34 81.

Boat rides – Tours in boats of various shapes and sizes through the Hamburg Harbour, last anywhere from 1hr, begin and end at the Landungsbrücken 1-9 in St. Pauli, April-October daily 9am-6pm every 30min, November-March 10.30am-4.30pm hourly. *HADAG* (Hafen-Dampfschiffahrts-Actien-Gesellschaft), is the biggest company ☎ 3 11 70 70 . In addition there is *Rainer Abicht*, ☎ 3 17 82 20, *Kapitän Prüsse*, ☎ 31 31 30 and other smaller shipping businesses offering tours of the harbour. Alster, Fleet an canal rides are also recommendable (departure from Jungfernstieg), by *Alster-Touristik GmbH*. ☎ 3 57 42 40.

Shopping

Jungfernstieg, Mönckebergstraße and Spitalerstraße are the big shopping miles with **department stores**. The many shopping passages in Hamburg's inner city are especially attractive for shopping, with over 300 speciality stores and boutiques. **Exclusive stores** have now settled at the Neuer Wall.

Art galleries are available in the inner city and in the various city districts; there is no area with an especially high concentration of galleries. For **antiques** try the *Quartier Satin* on ABC-Straße and the *Antik-Center* of the market hall at Klosterwall.

Flea markets – The *Menschen & Märkte* brochure has all the information on the more spontaneous flea markets in Hamburg (and all across northern Germany). Regular flea markets are held on Saturdays in Barmbek, (Hellbrockstraße) 7am-5pm, in Eppendorf (Nedderfeld/Parkhaus) 4.30pm-7.30pm.

Markets – The fish market is Hamburg's most famous market, held every Sunday, in summer from 5am-10am and in winter from 7am-10am. Weekly markets are held in all of the city's districts. The especially beautiful market held from Monday to Friday on the covered central strip of he elevated train at the U-Bahn station Eppendorfer Baum is highly recommendable.

Hotels

BUDGET

Kronprinz – Kirchenallee 46; ☎ 24 32 58, Fax 2 80 10 97. 73 rooms, single rooms from 130DM. Hotel near the train station, serves its purpose.

Elbbrücken-Hotel – Hamburg-Rothenburgsort, Billhorner Mühlenweg 28; ☎ 7 80 90 70, Fax 7 80 90 72 22. 40 rooms, single rooms from 90DM. Hotel near the Elbe bridges, practical for transport connections.

OUR SELECTION

Senator – Lange Reihe 18; ☎ 24 12 03, Fax 2 80 37 17. 56 rooms, single rooms from 185DM. Comfortable city hotel near the train station, well tended rooms.

Elbufer – Hamburg-Finkenwerder, Focksweg 40a; ☎ 7 42 19 10, Fax 74 21 91 40. 14 rooms, single rooms from 140DM. Hotel directly on the Elbe. The rooms are light.

Landhaus Flottbek (garni) – Hamburg-Flottbek, Baron-Voght-Straße 179; ☎ 8 22 74 10, Fax 82 27 41 51. 25 rooms, single rooms from 185DM. Hotel complex put together from several farm houses.

Baseler Hof – Esplanade 11; ☎ 35 90 60, Fax 35 90 69 18. 153 rooms, single rooms from 150DM. Central location, close to the Binnenalster, functional furnishings.

TREAT YOURSELF!

Vier Jahreszeiten – Neuer Jungfernstieg 9; ☎ 3 49 40, Fax 3 49 46 02. 158 rooms, single rooms from 433DM. Classic grand hotel, beautifully located on the Binnenalster, wide range of cuisine in four restaurants.

Park Hyatt Hamburg – Bugenhagenstraße 9; ☎ 33 32 12 34, Fax 33 32 12 35. 252 rooms, single rooms from 384DM. Modern elegant business hotel in a former office building.

Restaurants

BUDGET

Le Plat du Jour – Dornbusch 4; ☎ 32 14 14. Main dishes from 25DM. Typical French bistro.

Jena Paradies – Klosterwall 23; ☎ 32 70 08. Main dishes from 20DM. Modernly furnished restaurant in Bauhaus style, international, creative selection of dishes.

Rive Bistro – Hamburg-Altona, Van-der-Smissen-Straße 1; ☎ 3 80 59 19. Main dishes from 27DM. Restaurant in the harbour area in the building of a cruise ship centre. Nice view of the harbour, lively atmosphere, mainly fish dishes.

OUR SELECTION

Anna – Bleichenbrücke 2; ☎ 36 70 14. Main dishes from 39DM. Restaurant in the inner city at the Bleichenfleet, Mediterranean decor, international menu.

Il Ristorante – Große Bleichen 16; ☎ 34 33 35. Main dishes from 36DM. Italian restaurant in the inner city on the first floor of an office building. Lots of flowers and a classy atmosphere.

Zippelhaus – Zippelhaus 3; ☎ 30 38 02 80. Main dishes from 30DM. In a former warehouse. Modern atmosphere, international and regional cuisine.

Allegria – Hamburg-Winterhude, Hudtwalker Straße 13; ☎ 46 07 28 28. Main dishes from 24DM. Modern restaurant at the Winterhuder Fährhaus. Creative cuisine.

Lutz und König – Hamburg-Niendorf, König-Heinrich-Weg 200; ☎ 55 59 95 53. Main dishes from 28DM. In the north of Hamburg. Rustic furnishings, good cost/benefit ratio.

TREAT YOURSELF!

Jacobs Restaurant – Hamburg-Nienstedten, Elbchaussee 401; ☎ 82 25 50. Main dishes from 43DM. Restaurant of the luxury hotel Louis C Jacob in wonderful location. View of the harbour and the Elbe. Stylish, elegant restaurant rooms, very good cuisine.

Cölln's Austernstuben – Brodschrangen 1; ☎ 32 60 59. Main dishes from 37DM. Historical city mansion from 1760. Seven little separate rooms (reservations are a must), mostly fish dishes.

Tafelhaus – Hamburg-Bahrenfeld, Holstenkamp 71; ☎ 89 27 60. Main dishes from 38DM. Small restaurant in two rooms (reservations are a must), French cuisine.

Cafés, "Kneipen" and Bars

Hamburgs night-life has been associated with the name St. Pauli since time immemorial. In addition to its old and established temples of eroticism, the area around the Reeperbahn and Große Freiheit has become the site of the scene over the past few years. Around 400 food places are squeezed into these cramped quarters. The inner city, too, between the Gänsemarkt and Millerntor (especially around Großneumarkt) offers a great deal of opportunities to eat and drink; the passage quarter between Jungfernstieg and Stadthausbrücke is very pleasant. Eimsbüttel, in the Schanzenviertel, in Altona and in Eppendorf have a very lively "Kneipen" life.

CAFÉS

Alsterpavillon – Jungfernstieg 54. A true legend with a panoramic view of the Binnenalster.

Café Wien – Ballindamm/Binnenalster. Coffee variations like in Vienna, all on a remodelled Alster steamer.

Arkaden Café – Alsterarkaden 9-10. Wonderful view of the Alsterfleet and the town hall while enjoying coffee and cake.

Café Fees – Holstenwall 24. Cult café in the Museum für Hamburgische Geschichte; with a glass cupola over the winter garden.

Café Oertel – Esplanade 29. Quiet traditional café right on Stephansplatz.

COCKTAIL BARS

Angies's Nightclub – Spielbudenplatz 27. Classic mixes and live music in *Schmidts' Tivoli*.

Havanna Bar – Fischmarkt 4-6. Caribbean flair with the appropriate drinks.

Manhattan Bar – Große Bleichen. The Hamburg insiders meet here at the mahogany bar.

CAFÉ-KNEIPEN

Backatelle – Grindelallee 3. A recommendable import from Harburg.

Café Katelbach – Große Brunnenstraße 60. Alternative café in the multi-cultural district of Altona-Ottensen.

Café Loft – Große Bleichen 21. See and be seen in the inner city.

Factory – Hoheluftchaussee 95. This rather fun "Kneipe" opened in a former cigarette factory.

Café Unter den Linden – Juliusstraße 16. A place to discuss things and read the paper in the Schanzenviertel.

IN ST. PAULI

Café Absurd – Clemens-Schulz-Straße 84. Off the wall establishment in the vicinity of Hamburg's sinful sidewalk.

Christiansen's Fine Drinks and Cocktails – Pinnasberg 60. Cocktail bar in the quarter.

Haifisch-Bar – Große Elbstraße 128. Everything that St. Pauli has to offer seems to be located in this terrific Kneipe.

La Paloma – Gerhardstraße 2. St. Pauli's rebirth began in this establishment, decorated with the paintings of the owner Jörg Immendorf.

Hamborger Veermaster – Reeperbahn 62. Atmospheric place, with shanties and accordeon.

Grünspan – Große Freiheit 58. The city's oldest disco.

American

American Place – ABC Straße 52. A gastronomic trip through the USA.

Amtrak – Bahngärten 28. This restaurant, named after the American railway company, is settled in Hamburg's oldest train station.

City Rock Café – Welcker Straße 8. All American clichés are on tap here.

Entertainment

THEATER

Deutsches Schauspielhaus – Kirchenallee 39/41; ☎ 24 87 13. This theatre, built around 1900, was led at one time by Gustav Gründgens and later by Peter Zadek. The works played are marked by very sharp contrasts.

Hamburger Kammerspiele – Hartungstraße 9; ☎ 41 33 44 44. Contemporary pieces, cabaret and readings.

Thalia Theater – Alstertor; ☎ 32 81 44 44. The repertoire ranges from classical to modern, sometimes musicals appear on the programme.

Komödie Winterhuder Fährhaus – Hudtwalker Straße 13; ☎ 48 06 80 80. Popolar theatre with actors who have done tours of duty in television.

Ernst-Deutsch-Theater – Mundsburger Damm 60; ☎ 22 70 14 20. Small, highbrow private theatre.

Ohnesorg-Theater – Große Bleichen 25; ☎ 35 08 03 21. Light works, lust spiels and comedies in Low German (Platt).

OPERA, BALLET, OPERETTA AND MUSICALS

Hamburgische Staatsoper – Dammtorstraße 28; ☎ 35 17 21. Both the opera and the ballet ensemble (under John Neumeier) have a very good reputation.

Allee-Theater – Max-Brauer-Allee 76; 38 29 59. Hamburg chamber opera.

Buddy-Musicaltheater – Freihafen/Norderelbstraße 6; ☎ 30 05 11 50. Venue created for *Buddy-Das Musical* in the Hamburg Harbour, opposite the Landungsbrücken.

Neue Flora – Stresemannstraße/Alsenplatz; ☎ 30 05 13 50/0 18 05 44 44. The *Phantom der Oper* has been around here since 1990.

Operettenhaus – Spielbudenplatz 1; ☎ 30 05 13 50. The musical *Cats* has been on the program of the *Operettenhaus* since 1986.

VARIETY, REVUE AND CABARET

Pulverfaß Cabaret – Pulverteich 12; ☎ 24 97 91. Transvestite show, combining song, parodies and comedy with a shot of eroticism.

Schmidt-Theater – Spielbudenplatz 24; ☎ 31 77 88 99. Theatre, comedy, revue and variety are shown here and in the neighbouring *Schmidts Tivoli*.

Urs F. Kluyver/Wirtschaftsbehörde Domreferat

Roller-coaster on the Hamburg "Dom"

Imperial Theater – Reeperbahn 5; ☎ 31 31 14. Musical and comedy in St. Pauli.

Hansa-Theater – Steindamm 17; ☎ 24 14 14. Classic variety.

CONCERTS

Musikhalle – Johannes-Brahms-Platz; ☎ 34 69 20. This Baroque concert hall is the centre of Hamburg's musical life. All three Hamburg orchestras play here, the Philharmonische Staatsorchester, the North German Radio Symphony Orchestra and the Hamburger Symphoniker.

JAZZ

Cotton Club – Alter Steinweg; ☎ 34 38 78. Old-fashioned Jazz.

Dennis' Swing Club – Papenhuder Straße 25; ☎ 2 29 91 92. Important institution of Hamburg's jazz scene.

CLUBS, DISCOTHÈQUES & LIVE MUSIC

Traxx – Altländer Straße 10; ☎ 32 17 42. House and dance classics. The bouncer will not accept any leather.

Docks & Prinzenbar – Kastanienallee 20; ☎ 31 78 83 11. Venue for concerts and parties; one Sunday a month a flea market.

KINO

The two largest cinema houses are the *Cinemaxx* at Dammtor and the *UFA-Palast* on the Gänsemarkt. The leading programme cinemas are the *Abaton*, the *Zeise* and the *Grindel*.

Special events

Volksfest Dom, mid-March to mid-April, mid-July to mid-August, early November to December; *Flea market in Horn/at the galloping race track*, Easter Sunday, 2nd Sunday in July, 3 October; *Hafengeburtstag* (Harbour Birthday) early May; *Hamburger Ballettage* (Ballet Days) in July; *Alstervergnügen* (Alster Pleasure) end of August.

★★ **Hamburger Kunsthalle (Fine Arts Museum)** ⊘ (HY **M**¹) – This museum houses one of the largest art collections in Germany. The galleries have correspondingly been recently refitted and the paintings rehung to create a most attractive exhibition. The exhibition opens with medieval works. The **Grabow altarpiece** created in 1379 for St. Petri, Hamburg, by Master Bertram of Minden is one of the largest and most touching examples of primitive painting in north Germany. Its 24 separate panels are related to the concept of Salvation and comprise a variety of scenes from the naive to the animated. It is fascinating to compare this altarpiece with the polyptych of St Thomas of Canterbury by Master Francke.

The 17C Dutch School is represented by an early Rembrandt (*Simeon in the Temple*), and by land- and sea-scapes by Avercamp, Van Goyen, the Ruysdaels and Van de Velde. Genre paintings by Jan Steen and Pieter de Hooch are also exhibited. A particular strength of the exhibition is the section of 19C German painting. Prominently displayed are works by the Romantics Caspar David Friedrich (*Ice Field, Rambler above a Sea of Clouds*) and Philipp Otto Runge (*The Children of Hülsenbeck, Morning*), which are representative of the period when painting was breaking through into the realms of subjectivity. The museum also possesses major works by Feuerbach, Von Marées and Böcklin. An entire room is devoted to Menzel. Realists whose works are on display include Wilhelm Leibl, whose famous painting *Three Women in Church* can be found hanging here.

There is a dazzling display of work by Max Liebermann (*Women Repairing Nets*), Lovis Corinth and Edvard Munch (*Madonna*). The section on the Classical Modern artists is dominated by the works of Max Beckmann and Oscar Kokoschka, as well as the members of the **Brücke** and **Blauer Reiter** groups (Kirchner, Nolde, Marc). Paul Klee's enchanting painting *Goldfish* is also on display in this part of the museum. In 1997, an extension was added to the art gallery in the form of a building by **Oswald Mathias Ungers**. The new **Galerie der Gegenwart** has doubled the amount of exhibition space the gallery can devote to post-1960 art. In keeping with the architect's usual style, squares are a basic element of the design of this building, without in the least becoming monotonous. The effect is particularly charming seen from the central atrium.

Contemporary art is well served in this gallery, not least because many of the artists have taken a hand in setting up the display (Richard Serra, Claes Oldenburg, Hanne Darboven, Jenny Holzer). There are works by many of the famous names of the last few decades (Bruce Naumann, Andy Warhol, Donald Judd, Richard Long). German art is also well represented (Sigmar Polke, Georg Baselitz, Markus Lüpertz, Mario Merz, Gerhard Richter, Rosemarie Trockel). A central room is devoted to the work of Joseph Beuys.

★ **Museum für Kunst und Gewerbe (Museum of Decorative Arts)** ⊘ (HY **M**²) – Thousands of arts and crafts exhibits are displayed chronologically in this museum. Among the most fascinating are the medieval statuary, gold and silver plate (Reliquary of St George by Berndt Notke), sumptuous Renaissance furniture and fine examples of north German clockmaking as well as delicate 18C porcelain. There is a generous display of ornaments, furniture and artworks from the Jugendstil, and an interesting section of antiquities. Note also the departments of Chinese, Japanese and Islamic art, the hall of mirrors from the Budge-Palais, and collections on graphics, photography and design.

As of 2000, an annexe will be displaying a collection of historical keyboard instruments.

Model of Hamburg Port (1497)

★ **Museum für Hamburgische Geschichte** (Historical Museum) ⊘ (**EYZ M³**) – Here the visitor can browse over models of Hamburg in days gone by, a scale model of the city of yore, the harbour and shipping section (over 100 model ships and the impressive 1722 *Wappen von Hamburg*), and a model of the railway system. Other departments include one on clothing and fashion from several centuries and historic apartments with opulent furnishings.

★★ THE PORT (HAFEN) (EZ)

Apart from the tower of St. Michaeliskirche, the best **viewpoint**★ from which to see the port as a whole is the Stintfang (**EZ**) – a raised terrace below the youth hostel.

A few statistics – The Hamburg docks comprise 60 basins and more than 45km/27mi of quays, in addition to a great number of mooring buoys. Thanks to a relatively small tidefall (3.4m/11ft average), no locks are necessary in the basins accessible to ocean-going traffic able to navigate the Elbe (displacing up to 110 000t and drawing no more than 13.5m/44ft). The port's reputation relies on a speedy turnaround and on the wide variety of equipment, warehousing, transport and offloading machinery available for every kind of cargo. Some 340 shipping lines call regularly (about 650 departures a month) to transport merchandise to 1 000 ports all over the world.

Boat trip around the port (Hafenrundfahrt) ⊘ – *Boats leave from landing-stage no 2 in the St. Pauli district (St. Pauli-Landungsbrücken)* (**EZ**).
The visitor will be astonished by the sheer size of the dockyards – Five separate shipbuilders, 26 floating docks – and by the extraordinary activity on either side of the Elbe, where every type of vessel is constructed: tankers, lighters, tugs, cargo ships, containers, refrigerator craft and pleasure boats as well as police and customs launches. Motor ferries ply back and forth all day long, transporting south bank workers back to the city during the rush hour. One shouldn't leave the St. Pauli quays without visiting the lively St. Pauli Fischmarkt held every Sunday morning until 10am.

CITY OUTSKIRTS

★ **Museum für Post und Kommunikation** (Postal Museum) ⊘ (**FY M⁴**) – This museum, in Heinrich-von-Stephan-Platz, named after the Prussian director-general who inaugurated the World Confederation of Postal Services, outlines the evolution of mail transport and dispatches from the 16C to the present day. It has a particularly fine collection of **transmitting equipment**, concentrating especially on the pioneer period of long-distance communications. There are many examples of early telegraphic equipment, telephones invented by Bell and Siemens, instrument panels with warning lights, exchange keyboards, fax machines and radio installations.
Some of the modern instruments are displayed in working order and may be tried out by visitors to the museum.

★ Fernsehturm (Television Tower) ⊘ **(EX)** – A slender steel and concrete plinth whose highest aerials are almost 280m/919ft from the ground, the tower soars above the Planten un Blomen park to the west of the Alster. There is an observation platform at the top and, at a height of 132m/433ft above ground level, a revolving panoramic restaurant affording a fine **view**★★ of the entire city (one complete revolution takes 55min).

★ Erholungspark Planten un Blomen ⊘ **(EFX)** – Part of a green belt replacing the old fortifications which ran in an arc between the Elbe and the Alster to the west and north of the town, this park was laid out in 1936. Its geometrically arranged gardens are used as a proving ground for new species of flowers and trees. An artificial cascade tumbles into the main pool (Großer Parksee), where after dark the fountains act as background to a son et lumière performance (Wasserlicht-konzert). Nearby are the city conference centre (Congreß Centrum) and the Hamburg Plaza Hotel.

★ Museum für Völkerkunde Hamburg (Ethnographic Museum) ⊘ **(M⁵)** – *Rothen-baumchaussee 64* **(FX)**.

The collections in this museum – remarkable in their variety and rarity – are directly due to the commercial relations between this Hanseatic town and the rest of the world, Hamburg having been the departure point at the turn of the century for explorers' expeditions to Oceania and elsewhere. Well represented here are the civilizations of Europe, Asia (including the former Soviet Union and Turkey), Africa (Benin bronzes and cult objects from what is now Zaire), the Americas and the Pacific isles.

The **Golden Room** (Goldkammer), on the ground floor, has an exhibition of pre-Colombian jewellery. On the first floor, note the wand puppets used in shadow theatres from Bali and Java, a gallery of **Oceanian Masks**★, and the **Boat Hall** (Boot-shalle), which is devoted to Polynesian canoes and other craft. Symbolic figures decorate a fine **Maori Meeting Hall** from New Zealand, which is on the same floor.

★★ Tierpark Hagenbeck (Zoo) ⊘ – *Leave by the Grindelallee* **(FX)**.

This wonderful park of the zoo founded in 1907, with ancient trees, artificial lakes and crags, is a delightful place for a stroll and some communion with nature. Some 2 500 creatures of 360 species from five continents live in open corrals. Over the years, many rare fauna was successfully bred here. The zoo is especially proud of its Asian elephants and the excellent breeding results.

EXCURSIONS

Altona; Klein Flottbek; Wedel – *22km/14mi – allow half a day.*

★★ Altonaer Museum in Hamburg – Norddeutsches Landesmuseum (Altona and North German Museum) ⊘ – *Leave on the Reeperbahn* **(EZ 70)**.

Art, culture and day-to-day life in Schleswig-Holstein, the Lower Elbe Valley and along the North and Baltic Sea coasts are illustrated here. Note the exceptional collection of **ships' figureheads** from the 18C-19C. The recons-tructed interiors of farmers' cottages and a room containing traditional farmers' costumes are also interesting. The section for decorative arts displays skilfully done utility wars from the Late Renaissance until the Jugendstil period; the gallery with paintings of the north German landscapes contains works by Gurlit, Heckel, Schmidt-Rottluff and Radziwill.

A thatched cottage from the Vierlande, a fruit- and flower-producing region southeast of Hamburg, has been transformed into a small restaurant for the museum's visitors.

Altonaer Balkon (Altona Balcony) – From a terrace south of Altona's town hall, there is a **view**★ of the confluence of the two branches of the Elbe which marks the limit of Hamburg's industrial and port zone. The amount of shipping which passes each hour is astonishing.

Follow the **Elbchaussee**★, a spacious avenue bordered by great houses and superb properties developed since the beginning of the 19C by the grand Hamburg shipowning and trading dynasties.

At Klein Flottbek turn right and drive along the Baron-Voght-Straße as far as house no 50.

Jenisch-Haus ⊘ – A fine landscaped park planted with exotic trees surrounds this pleasant neo-Classical villa built between

"Terpsichore" ship's figurehead

Altonaer Museum in Hamburg – Norddeutsches Landesmuseum

1831 and 1834. The luxuriously furnished rooms illustrate the style of German bourgeois interiors from the Late Renaissance to the beginning of the Jugendstil period. Note the splendid marquetry flooring of the ground floor state rooms, and the Danish style furniture upstairs manufactured in Altona.

Ernst Barlach Haus ⊙ – *Baron-Voght-Straße 50A Jenischpark.*
This house, set up thanks to the donation of Hamburg tobacco tycoon Hermann Reemstma, contains an exceptional collection of sculptures, prints and drawings by local artist Ernst Barlach, born in Wedel near Hamburg. There is a particularly impressive display of sculptures in wood, including some powerfully expressive works such as *The Frieze of Listeners*, the figure of *Moses*, and the group of *Three Men Brandishing a Sword*.

Continue along the Elbchaussee, then head for Wedel after driving through the pleasant suburban resort of Blankenese.

Wedel – *Follow the Willkomm-Höft signposts to the café-restaurant beside the Elbe known as the "Schulauer Fährhaus".*
Above the terrace is a saluting base for passing ships (Schiffsbegrüßungsanlage). The ceremony – which many people come to watch – involves running up the flag and then playing the national anthem of the country of origin of every single vessel sailing upstream or downstream past the base.
There is an **Ernst-Barlach-Museum** ⊙ in the house where the artist was born (*Mühlenstraße 1*) which displays drawings and lithographs as well as fine bronzes, among them the impressive *Old Men Dancing*. The works on display here are a particularly good illustration of the artist's interest in exploring literary motifs and his creative working out of his personal dramas.

EXCURSION

Schloß Ahrensburg ⊙ – *23km/15mi to the northeast. Leave Hamburg by B25, the Lübeck road.*
The white bulk of this moated castle is framed by the green, leafy banks of the Hunnau. Built, like Schloß Glücksburg, by Peter Rantzau, it comprises three main blocks flanked by corner towers surmounted by lantern towers. Scrolled gables framed by obelisks decorate the castle, which was the last true Renaissance creation to be built in Schleswig-Holstein (1595).
The interior recalls the family of Count Heinrich Carl Schimmelmann, who bought the castle in 1759 and refurbished it. Note the stairwell, the oak-panelled dining room, and the Emkendorf Room with its elegant Louis XVI furnishings.

HAMELN★

HAMELIN – Niedersachsen
Population 60 000
Michelin map 417 J 12

Built on the banks of the Weser, Hamelin glories in fine old houses, of which the most typical belong to the **Weser Renaissance** (late 16-early 17C) period. The style is distinguished architecturally by ram's-horn scrollwork and pinnacled gables. Other characteristics include delicately worked stone bands encircling the building, forward projecting pavilions (Utlucht) treated as smaller extensions of the main façade, and large, well-developed lucarnes (Zwerchhäuser) with decorated gables at the base of the roof.
Hamelin is also a town with a special place in European folklore; it is the home of the celebrated rat-catcher immortalized by Goethe, and by Robert Browning as the **Pied Piper** (in English). In the summer, a dramatic version of the legend is performed each Sunday at noon on the terrace of the Hochzeitshaus. As souvenirs, toys or sweets, the rats are still to be seen in many of Hamelin's shop windows.

The Pied Piper of Hamelin – In 1284, a mysterious man in multicoloured clothes promised the townspeople that, for a substantial reward, he would free Hamelin from a plague of rats and mice. He played his pipe, and all the rodents emerged to follow him to the banks of the Weser, where they drowned.
But the reward was not forthcoming, so the piper returned on Sunday, when everyone was at church, and played again in revenge. This time it was the children who emerged from their houses. There were 130 of them, and they too followed him, never to be seen again. Only two escaped; one was dumb, the other blind.
The rather less romantic but historically more accurate version of the tale is that overpopulation in the 13C led to a troop of young people being sent by the authorities to colonize faraway lands to the east.

SIGHTS

★ **Rattenfängerhaus (The Rat-catcher's House)** – It is a large, well-proportioned building dating from 1603. The symmetrical decoration of the façade involves differently sculpted bands of stonework, further adorned with carved busts and masks. Typical Weser scrolls and pinnacles enrich the gable.

★ **Hochzeitshaus (Marriage House)** – The building, constructed between 1610 and 1617, acted as a reception centre for burghers' weddings. Three elegant gables break the horizontals of the façade, themselves emphasized by cornices and lateral bands of stonework.

Demptersches Haus – *In the market place.* An outstanding building, dating from 1607, is noteworthy especially for its fine Weser Renaissance projecting pavilion (Utlucht).

Stiftsherrenhaus (Canons' House) – *Osterstraße 8.* Another remarkable house, this one half-timbered and built in 1558. The sculpted consoles represent biblical figures.

Haus Lücking – *Wenden-straße 8.* This is a rich, half-timbered house of 1638 with a rounded doorway centred in a rectangular recess.

Rattenkrug – *Bäcker-straße 16.* A projecting pavilion (Utlucht) and a tall gable of no less than five floors distinguish this 1568 building.

Münster (Collegiate Church) – From the public gardens to the south, the church appears to cower beneath the protection of the massive polygonal tower over the transept – once part of a 12C Romanesque basilica

Stiftsherrenhaus (detail)

Rotzal/Tourist Information Hameln

which was transformed a century later into the existing Gothic hall-church. Inside, the layout of the columns and their capitals, checkered or carved with palm leaves, draws attention once more to the raised transept.

EXCURSIONS

★ **Hämelschenburg** – *11km/7mi to the south.*
The **Schloß**★ ⊘, which boasts both a moat and a lagoon, was built in the shape of a horse-shoe between 1588 and 1616. It is one of the masterpieces of the Weser Renaissance style.
The wing overlooking the road is the most ornate, with typical alternations of smooth and embossed stone bands, an oriel immediately above the moat, and four decorative gables. Weapons, trophies, paintings and furniture are on view in the interior.

Fischbeck – *7km/4mi to the northwest.*
The **abbey** ⊘ here was officially recognized by Otto I in the year 955 (photocopies of the original documents can be seen in the church). It is still used as a home for elderly Protestant women. The church itself dates from the 12C. It was equipped in the 19C with partitioned boxes, which allowed the noblewomen to take part in the services.
The **crypt** is in a pure Romanesque style, with each column topped by a capital embellished with a different motif. Left of the chancel is a moving Ecce Homo in sculpted wood; to the right of it hangs the famous 16C **Fischbeck tapestry** illustrating the foundation of the abbey. The figure of the Helmburgis, dating from the 13C, stands above the entrance to the sacristy. The cloister, in its present state, dates from the 13C and 14C (the original was burned down in the early 13C).

HANN. MÜNDEN**

Niedersachsen

Population 28 000

Michelin map 417/418 L 12

The town of Hann. Münden, or Hannoversch Münden, lies in a forest-covered valley where the Fulda and the Werra converge to flow on as the Weser. Excavations have revealed that a settlement already existed at the confluence of the three rivers in the time of Charlemagne. The actual foundation of the city, some say, dates back to Henry the Lion. The staple right for shipping which applied from 1247 to 1823 brought prosperity to the town that is mirrored in the grand half-timber ensemble of the old town.

Hann. Münden developed into quite a diversified little industrial city until the First World War. Its products – mostly in lead processing, abrasives and rubber products – were quite well-known throughout Europe. After the Second World War, industrial production dropped and the number of medium-sized enterprises and small crafts businesses grew.

★ **Altstadt** – The old town contains over 700 **half-timbered houses**★★ built over a period of six centuries, which have been restored and looked after in an exemplary fashion. Particularly beautiful examples lie along the streets between the town hall and the Werra. With its defensive towers and the remains of the town walls, the old town forms an extremely attractive self-contained, medieval townscape.

The name

The town was originally called Münden, but in the 18C the name Hannoversch Münden was coined to avoid confusions with Minden ("Preußisch Minden"). In 1870, the post office introduced the term Hann. Münden, the railway administration followed in 1909. In 1991, the City Council decided to make Hann. Münden the official name.

★ **Rathaus (Town hall)** – The main façade of this building is a typical Weser Renaissance design, its gables adorned with scrollwork, pyramids and statues.

St. Blasiikirche – Modified into a Gothic hall in the late 15C, this church with its steep slate roof is overlooked by a hexagonal tower. Inside, the south aisle contains the tomb of Wilhelm of Brunswick (d 1503), and there is an epitaph to his son in the northern part of the chancel. Note, in the north aisle, a 14C baptismal font.

EXCURSION

★ **Upper Weser Valley** – *67km/42mi – allow 2hr.*

From Hann. Münden to Bad Karlshafen, the Weser twists through a heavily wooded valley. In this otherwise deserted stretch of country, French Huguenot refugees, gathered together in the 18C by the Landgraves of Hessen, founded a number of villages baptised with such symbolically pious names as Gottstreu (Fidelity to the Creator) and Gewissensruh (Conscience in Repose). The valley is still without industry or railway.

Wahlsburg-Lippoldsberg – The old abbey church of Lippoldsberg (Ehemalige Klosterkirche St. Georg und Maria) was one of the first vaulted Romanesque churches erected in northern Germany.

Take the ferry across to the other side of the river.

Gewissensruh – Visit the tiny church (1779) here. Note the French inscriptions on the houses.

Bad Karlshafen – The town was founded in 1699 by the Landgrave Karl of Hessen with an eye to giving refuge to persecuted French Huguenots and to building a harbour with canal. It lies around a shipping basin at the confluence of the Weser and the Diemel.

A regular plan and uniform building design lend the place something of a monumental air. The **German Huguenot Museum** ⊘ (Deutsches Hugenottenmuseum, Hafenplatz 9) has been assigned to a former tobacco factory. The first floor presents the history of the Huguenots in France. The life of the famous ceramics artist Bernard Palissy is used as an illustration of an individual fate. The second floor is devoted to the reception given to the Huguenots in Germany and underscores their influence where crafts, science and decorative arts are concerned.

Fürstenberg – This has been the seat of the porcelain manufacturer of the same name, who produces the famous Fürstenberg porcelain, since 1747. Selected pieces may be admired in the **castle museum** ⊘. A video describes the manufacture of the porcelain and displays of manufactured work are held.

★ **Höxter** – Weser-type Renaissance and Baroque half-timber houses in bright colours are what make up the attraction of this town. The houses are decorated with wooden side walls and roofs of pink sandstone tiles. The most picturesque and pretty line the **Westerbachstraße**. In Kilianskirche, there is an outstanding **Renaissance pulpit★★** (1597) adorned with rare alabaster motifs.

Corvey – The only part of the original Carolingian **abbey church** that remains is the impressive **Westwerk★**. The lower parts can be traced back to the 9C. Above the pre-nave entrance is a square church, two storeys high, into which opened a gallery (the Johannischor) reserved for the emperor. The history of Corvey is outlined in a **museum** at the castle.

Following secularization, the landgrave of Hesse Rotenburg acquired the former convent building and made it into his residence. The castle is owned today by the dukes of Ratibor. The **Höxter-Corvey Museum** ⊘ is housed here.

HANNOVER

Niedersachsen
Population 518 000
Michelin map 415/416/418 I 13

Hanover, capital of Lower Saxony, is one of the main economic centres of northern Germany. Its two annual international fairs, held in special pavilions southeast of the town, stimulate an enormous amount of business. EXPO 2000 and the additional infrastructure has given the city even greater power of attraction. The Expo grounds alone are 160ha/395 acres in size.

The large waterways (Maschsee), the city forest and the Royal Gardens, which date back to the 17C, lie right in the heart of the city.

There is a good view over the whole district from the dome of the **Rathaus** ⊘ (**Z R**).

HISTORICAL NOTES

The House of Hanover – The principality of Hanover fell in the 17C to a branch of the House of Brunswick and Lüneburg. The Court moved to Hanover. The transformation of Herrenhausen began, and, under the aegis of the cultured Princess Sophia, a period commenced in which literature and the arts flourished. Handel, who composed his first operas in Hamburg, was frequently invited to give concerts. The philosopher **Gottfried Wilhelm Leibniz** arrived in 1676 to take up the position of Court Librarian, a post he held for 40 years. In 1692 the principality became the Electorate of Brunswick and Lüneburg, the ninth in Germany.

From the Hanoverian Court to the Court of St James – The marriage in 1658 of the Duke Ernst-Augustus with the Palatine Princess Sophia, granddaughter of the Stuart King James I, had given the Hanoverian succession a claim on the throne of England.

In 1714 the Elector Georg-Ludwig, son of Princess Sophia, did indeed find himself heir to the crown and became George I of England. He still remained Elector of the Electorate of Hanover. George III, who had been King of England since 1760, did not manage to become King of Hanover in his turn (Hanover became a kingdom after the Vienna Congress) until 1814. The union of Hanover and England

Hannover Trade Fair Centre

Schiller/Bildagentur SCHUSTER, Oberursel

257

HANNOVER

Kestner-Museum	M¹	Historisches Museum Hannover	M³
Niedersächsisches Landesmuseum	M²	Rathaus	R

ended in 1837, because the Salic Law (forbidding the accession of women to the throne) applied in Hanover. Victoria therefore became Queen of England, while in Hanover it was her uncle Ernst-Augustus who succeeded. Installing his Court in Hanover, the new monarch set about restoring the town to its former glory. But the year 1866 saw the fall of the House of Hanover and the annexation of the kingdom by Prussia.

★★ HERRENHÄUSER GÄRTEN (HERRENHAUSEN GARDENS)

Leave by the Leibnizufer (Y); *1hr 30min*

This beautiful 17C development, in the northwestern part of the city, comprises four separate and quite different gardens: the Großer Garten, the Berggarten, the Georgengarten and the Welfengarten. They are linked by an avenue of lime trees, the Herrenhäuser Allee, laid out in 1726 *(drivers take the Nienburger Straße)*.

★★ **Großer Garten** – Creation of the garden started in 1666. Between 1680 and 1710 Princess Sophia took it over, transformed it, and enlarged it, for – as she wrote more than once – "that garden is my very life". The oldest part is a formal French pleasure garden divided into flower borders punctuated by statues of allegorical figures and Roman gods. On one side is an open-air theatre, on the other a maze. At the southern end a mosaic of clipped hedges is cut by pathways between ornamental ponds. The powerful central fountain jets a plume of water no less than 82m/269ft into the air (as a comparison, Nelson's Column, in London, is 170ft high).

Georgengarten – This romantically landscaped park was laid out between 1835 and 1841 on a commission by the Hanoverian royal house. In its midst is the Leibniztempel and the Wallmodenschlößchen, a manor in which you find the **Wilhelm-Busch-Museum** ⊘. It is dedicated to the work of the famous poet, illustrator and humorist (1832-1908), who is immortalised in his illustrated stories such as "Max und Moritz", the forerunners of today's comic strips. He also produced caricatures and critical artwork, of contemporary artists among others. *(Renovation work in progress until 2000)*.

★ **Berggarten** – The greenhouses of this botanical garden display cactus plants and other succulents, as well as 2 500 varieties of orchid and flora native to the Canary Islands. At the far end of the garden's principal walk is the mausoleum of the Royal House of Hanover.

Welfengarten – The Welfenschloß, today the university, stands in the Welfengaten. In front of the building is the trademark of the state of Niedersachsen, the Saxon Steed, created in 1876 by Friedrich Wolff.

ADDITIONAL SIGHTS

Marktkirche (Y) – A four-gabled tower crowned by a sharp pinnacle presides over this church, rebuilt after 1945 in the style of the 14C original. An interesting contrast to the restored Gothic style are the modern (1957) bronze doors by Gerhard Marcks, depicting scenes from recent German history. Inside, note the 15C sculpted polychrome **reredos**★★ at the high altar, which represents the Passion. Also noteworthy are the stained-glass windows (14C) in the choir and the 15C baptismal font in bronze.

★ **Kestner-Museum** ⊘ **(Z M¹)** – This valuable collection was started by August Kestner, son of Charlotte Kestner, née Charlotte Buff and made famous thanks to Goethe. The museum is divided up into four topical areas:
The **Egyptian section** has objects dating from the 4th millennium BC to the Roman-Coptic era. The **Art of Antiquity section** covers classical cultures from the Mediterranean area – Greek, Etruscan, Roman. The collection of Greek vases and the portraits of Roman emperors are outstanding specimens.
The **Decorative Art section** exemplifies just about every kind of crafts techniques and European styles from the Middle Ages until our own day. The **Numismatic section** (Münzen und Medaillen) has everything from coins from the Roman Republic and Germany in the Middle Ages, to medals from the Renaissance, Baroque and Rococo eras from the area of modern-day Niedersachsen.

★ **Niedersächsisches Landesmuseum (Museum of Lower Saxony)** ⊘ **(Z M²)** – The museum is divided into four departments:
The **Lower Saxony picture gallery** exhibits paintings and sculptures from nine centuries, with the emphasis on German art from the Middle Ages to the Renaissance and from the 19C and 20C (Holbein, Cranach, Riemenschneider, CD Friedrich, Liebermann, Slevogt), Italian painting from the 14C to 18C (Botticelli, Tiepolo) and also Dutch and Flemish painting from the 17C (Rubens, Ruysdael).
The **nature department** concentrates on the Lower Saxony countryside, but also explains the process of earth's history and how oceans and continents were formed. The exhibition is brought to life by the presence of an aquarium.
The **prehistoric department**★ exhibits some significant original findings, reconstructions and models from the prehistoric and early history of Lower Saxony. The display includes some well maintained swamp findings dating from the Iron Age (including a prehistoric corpse found in the swamp).
The **folklore department** is thematic, using the example of New Guinea. There are also interesting exhibits from America, Africa and Indonesia (Gamelan orchestra).
(NB The museum building is being completely renovated, and as a result the museum is closed. Parts of it should reopen at the end of 1998).

★ **Sprengel-Museum Hannover** ⊘ **(Z)** – Not far from the Maschsee, a stabile by Calder indicates the entrance to the museum, which concentrates on art of the 20C. Among the Cubists who experimented with form and volume are Picasso (*Three Women*, 1908), Léger (*The Village*, 1912), and the sculptor Henri Laurens (*Head of a Young Girl*, 1920). Expressionism, starting with Edvard Munch (*Half-Nude*), developed in intensity with Karl Schmidt-Rottluff (*Four Bathers on the Beach*), Otto Mueller (*Lovers*) and Ernst Ludwig Kirchner of the Brücke movement, as well as members of the Blauer Reiter movement, whose research into different uses of colour is remarkable in the works shown here. They include Kandinsky's *Diagonal*, Jawlensky's *Turandot II*, Macke's *Nude With Coral Necklace*, a fascinating *Floral Myth* by Paul Klee, and *Horse with Eagle* by Marc. In a similar vein are Nolde (*Flowers and Clouds*), Rohlfs (*Birch Forest*), Kokoschka and Feininger. A key position is reserved for the portraits of Beckmann (*Woman with a Bouquet of Carnations*). Research in the Surrealist direction is represented by the pictures of Max Ernst (*Fascinating Cypress*), by Salvador Dalí and above all by Kurt Schwitters, Hanoverian by birth and the author of many different kinds of work (*Merz-Bau*). Contemporary tendencies have their spokesmen in Tapiès, Dubuffet, Lindner and W Baumeister.

★ **Historisches Museum Hannover** ⊘ **(Y M³)** – This museum illustrates the history and culture of the city and region of Hanover. Everything is put in the spotlight, from the rise of the medieval linen centre to the royal residence, from the path from the Principality of Calenberg to the Kingdom of Hanover, from the flourishing industrial centre to the top-notch fair and service sector hub. Among the items recalling the heydays when the Electoral principality of Hanover was connected by marital bonds to the British global empire are the valuable coaches from the possessions of the royal family, the splendid, gilt state carriage from the year 1783 that the Prince of Wales used to open the Parliament. The attractions for visitors include not only valuable items of decorative art, weapons, armours and textiles, but also objects that recall the rise of important enterprises in the city. Among the great favourites for young and old alike is the "world's most beautiful compact car", produced by the Hanomag company in 1924 already.

Merzkunst or the Art of 'Merce

To: Anna Blume
Oh you, Belovèd of my 27 sense, I you love!
You, yours, youse, you who, you mine, – – – we?

That is the beginning of perhaps the most famous poem of Kurt Schwitters. He pinned it onto all the advertising pillars of Hanover. Schwitters was born in the city in 1887, he completed his studies at the Dresden Academy. After passing through the influence of the futuristic "Sturm" circle in Berlin and the Club "Dada", Schwitters, now 32 years old, devised his own artistic orientation called Merz. He published his own magazine ("Merz") from 1923 to 1932. In 1937, he was forced to leave Germany, but he was also forced to flee from the Nazis from his Norwegian exile, and in 1940 he went to England, where he died in 1948.
What is particularly fascinating in Schwitters' work is that they follow no specific type; his goal was to create the *Merzgesamtkunstwerk*, a work of total art, as it were; he created image poems, object poetry, architectural sculptures and a "Primeval Sonata" with lutes. He also wrote numerous manifestos, critical articles and theoretical essays. The word "Merz" originated from a fragmenting of the word "Commerz" (commerce) in order to create a compositional element for a picture or poem. A Merzbild, or 'Merce Image, is a collage of everyday elements unrelated to art, a Merzgedicht, 'Merce Poem, consists of complete sentences taken from newspapers, posters and conversations.

A separate section illustrates the rural region around the city in olden and more recent times. It presents the different types of farmhouses and displays the festive costumes used by the people in the villages.

Zoologischer Garten (Zoological Garden) ⊙ - *Adenauerallee 3. Leave by the Schiffgraben* (Y).
The zoo has been steering an innovative course in recent times by conceiving new installations with an eye to the world of experience: the gorilla mountain with its waterfall and natural-looking landscaping; the "evolution path" that traces the Neanderthal; a 12 000m²/120 000sq ft jungle palace for elephants, tigers, leopards and tiger pythons; a Zambezi landscape with lions, giraffes and okapis; the African steppes for zebras, gazelles, antilopes and ostriches; and last but not least, the restored half-timbered barn for foul and hogs.

HARZ★★

HARZ MOUNTAINS – Niedersachsen and Sachsen-Anhalt
Michelin map 418 K 15-16

The wooded heights of the Harz form the northern foothills of those mountains of central Europe resulting from the Hercynian upthrust in the Primary Era. Standing at the southern extremity of the vast Germano-Polish plain and almost entirely covered in forests, they break the moisture-laden winds sweeping across from the west to create a hilly region plentifully supplied with watercourses. Numerous dams have transformed the Harz into an exceptional reservoir supplying the nearby areas.
The highest point of the range, the **Brocken** (alt 1 142m/3 747ft), site of the legendary Witches' Sabbath *(see Introduction)*, attracts a great number of walkers to its windswept slopes. The **Harzquerbahn**, a narrow-gauge railway with steam locomotives, penetrates the region from north to south, from Wernigerode to Nordhausen. This provides - especially between Wernigerode and the resort of Eisfelder Talmühle, but also from Schierke to the Brocken - an excellent way of exploring the heart of the eastern Harz.

① THE UPPER HARZ *81km/50mi - allow half a day*

This itinerary follows an admirable road network, passing through vast tracts of rolling country with rounded hills covered in conifers.

★★ **Goslar** - *See GOSLAR.*

Clausthal-Zellerfeld - This is the former mining capital of the Harz. At Zellerfeld, there is the **Upper Harz Mine Museum** (Oberharzer Bergwerksmuseum) ⊙ that illustrates mining techniques until 1930 and documents the technical and cultural history of the region.

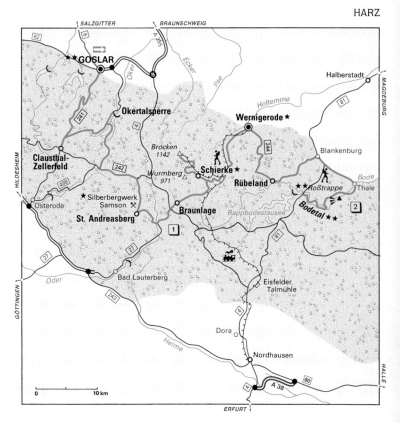

At Clausthal, in the Hindenburgplatz, the **Pfarrkirche zum Heiligen Geist**, built in 1642, is one of the largest wooden churches in the whole of Europe. Note the majestic positioning of the galleries and the light falling obliquely from windows placed just below the panelled vaulting.

Okertalsperre (Oker Dam) – From the top of the barrage there is a fine **view**★ over the widely dispersed waters of the reservoir.

St. Andreasberg – The road leads first to an **old silver mine**★ ⊙ (Silberbergwerk Samson) at the bottom of the valley. This was closed in 1910 but has been reopened for tourists.
The "Fahrkunst", a machine of ingenious simplicity which sent down and brought back the miners, can be seen at work. It consists of two bars side by side, each with steps cut into it, which move alternately up and down. All the miner had to do, effectively, was mark time on the steps with a foot on each bar.
A museum contains a collection of geological exhibits with Andreasberg calcite and numerous minerals.

Braunlage – Station on the Brocken railway. An important spa resort for its climate and for skiing lies high up on a plateau overlooked by the wooded slopes of the **Wurmberg** (971m/3 186ft).

★ **Schierke** – Station on the Brocken railway. A magnificent site here: a holiday centre from which many footpaths and ramblers' routes start – most of them leading towards the summit of the **Brocken**.

2 **THE EASTERN HARZ** 89km/55mi – allow half a day

In this part of the Harz, the forests have a greater proportion of deciduous trees. Even if it is on a smaller scale, the landscape is at times more spectacular.

★ **Wernigerode** – See WERNIGERODE.

Rübeland – In this area, where the chief activity is the exploitation of limestone, tourists enjoy exploring the many caves and grottoes formed by the erosion of the rock. In **Hermann's Grotto**★ (Hermannshöhle) ⊙, note particularly the Chamber of Crystals and the small pool stocked with "cave fish" (Grottenolmen) – blind creatures, living out their whole lives in darkness.

Continue via Blankenburg and Thale to reach the Bode Valley.

★★ Bodetal – The river here has gouged a passage as best it could through a maze of rock masses and now flows along the foot of impressive cliffs. The most spectacular site, without doubt, is the **Roßtrappe★★** (The Charger's Hoofmark). This is a 10min walk from the parking place. From the look-out point, which juts out dizzyingly above the river far below, there is an incredible **view★★★** of the sheer cliffs, the stream tumbling between crags at the foot of the chasm, and the distant woods. The place owes its name to a legend, according to which a horse ridden by a princess being chased by a giant pushed so hard while readying itself to spring across the gulf, that it left an imprint in the rock.

Following the course of the river, the scenic stretch of road twists and turns through the rugged forest landscape as far as the junction with Route 81. The beauty of the scenery and the frequent blind spots as the road winds through the undulating countryside all impose a reduced speed on drivers.

HEIDELBERG★★

Baden-Württemberg
Population 135 000
Michelin map 417 R 10

Heidelberg, the seat of Germany's most famous university since 1386, lies on the banks of the River Neckar. About 600 000 years ago, between Ice Ages, Heidelberg was home to Homo Heidelbergensis. It was in this city, in the early years of the 19C, that the poets Brentano, Eichendorff and Von Arnim united their talents to form the foundation of Germany's Romantic movement. Today, the city owes its liveliness to the presence of 30 000 students and innumerable foreign tourists, Anglo-Saxons in particular.

From the quays on the right bank of the Neckar, on either side of the picturesque bridge, the **Alte Brücke** or Karl-Theodor Brücke **(Y)**, there are splendid **views★★** of the castle ruins, their red sandstone ramparts distinct against the green of the forest, and of the old town clustered around the Heiliggeistkirche.

Further superb views of the castle and the city can be seen from the **Philosophenweg** (Philosophers' Walk) **(Y)** – reached by crossing the Alte Brücke and climbing the **Schlangenweg (Y)** *(steep steps)*.

HISTORICAL NOTES

The Rhineland Palatinate, of which Heidelberg was the political centre, owes its name to the title "palatines" given to the highest officers in the Holy Roman Empire who were in the sovereign's confidence. These functions and dignities disappeared in the 14C, except in the hereditary family ruling a group of territories whose appropriate centre was the confluence of the Neckar with the Rhine. Through the wise government of these palatine-electors (Kurfürsten), the **Electoral Palatinate** (Kurpfalz) became one of the most advanced states of Europe.

The "Orléans War" (1688-97) – In the 16C, the electors, who had become Protestant, were continually reinforcing and embellishing their castle at Heidelberg. The Elector Karl-Ludwig restored his states in an exemplary manner after the Thirty Years War. In the hope of ensuring peace in the Rhineland and extending the influence of his house he married his daughter Liselotte **(Elisabeth-Charlotte)** to Duke Philip of Orléans, brother of Louis XIV.

The **Palatine Princess** did not pass unnoticed at the Court of France. Saint-Simon in his *Memoirs* returns frequently to her loud voice, her endless chatter and her intractable dislike of Mme de Maintenon. When the son of Karl-Ludwig died without an heir in 1685, the marriage alliance, which was invoked by Louis XIV to assert his claim to the territories on the left bank of the Rhine, proved disastrous to the palatinate and to Heidelberg. The town was laid waste and the castle sacked in the brutal campaign of 1689. Total disaster followed in 1693, when the town was completely destroyed by fire. This catastrophe led to the rebuilding of the town in an uninspired Baroque style on the same foundations and with no thoroughfares. Before long the electors abandoned the ruined castle, turning their attention to their residences at Mannheim and Schwetzingen. Today it's precisely that ruin that makes Heidelberg so attractive.

★★★ SCHLOSS (CASTLE) *Cars approach via the Neue Schloßstraße (Z).*

The route marked on the plan leads to the **Rondell** promontory, once the site of a battery of cannons and now a **viewpoint★** looking out over the town, the Neckar Valley and the Rhineland plain. After this comes the **Dicker Turm** (Great Tower), and then the **Elisabethentor**, a gate which Friedrich V had built in a single night in 1615, as a surprise for his wife Elizabeth Stuart, daughter of James I of England.

Heidelberg Castle and the Neckar

The castle's southeast corner is formed by the **Gesprengter Turm** (Shattered Tower). A mine laid by French sappers in 1693 gutted one side of the edifice and destroyed the gun emplacements radiating from a solid central core.

The **gardens**★ were laid out in terraces under Friedrich V, after an enormous amount of earthworks lasting from 1616 to 1619. The east face of the castle, with its three towers (from right to left: the Glockenturm, the Apothekerturm, the Gesprengter Turm), is visible from the Scheffel terrace.

The courtyard and buildings

The courtyard is on the far side of a fortified bridge guarded by the **Torturm**. Immediately on the right is the fine Gothic hall of the **Brunnenhalle** (Well Wing), whose granite Roman columns came from Charlemagne's palace at Ingelheim, near Mainz.

Library (Bibliotheksbau) (6) – This Gothic building, set well back from the castle's west wing, is able thus to receive light from windows on all four sides. At one time it housed the personal library, art collections and treasure of the princely family. The loggia is charming.

★★ **Friedrich Wing (Friedrichsbau) (10)** – The façade design of this wing, with its two festooned gables, retains in its columns the classical orders of antiquity – Doric, Ionic and Corinthian – rediscovered during the Renaissance. But the composition of pilasters and corniches, creating contrasts of light and shade, presages already the subsequent taste for the Baroque. The **statues** (copies) represent the ancestors of Friedrich IV, who added the wing, among them princes of the house of Wittelsbach.

The rear of the building, the sole decorated wall directly facing the town, can best be seen from the **Great terrace** (Altan). Looking down on the roofs of old Heidelberg, this is approached via a vaulted passageway to the right of the palace.

Hall of Mirrors Wing (Gläserner Saalbau) (8) – Only a shell remains of this building, which retains, nevertheless, a series of tiered galleries in the Italian Renaissance manner.

Otto-Heinrich Wing (Otto-Heinrichsbau) (9) – This palace was built by the Elector Otto-Heinrich, one of the most enlightened rulers of the Renaissance. During the three years of his reign (1556-59), the sovereign opened the palatinate wide to innovative ideas, notably on religious and artistic matters. The wing inaugurated the fruitful Late Renaissance period in German architecture.

Horizontals predominate in the composition of the façade. In line with contemporary taste, the ornamentation combines biblical and mythological symbols. The famous sculptor Alexander Colin of Mechelen collaborated in the

263

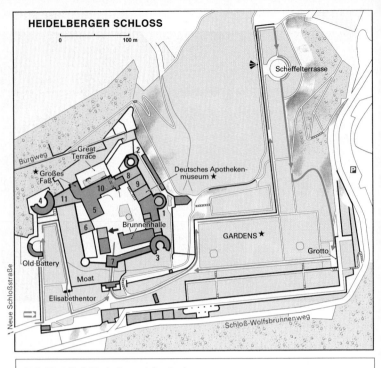

HEIDELBERGER SCHLOSS

0   100 m

Scheffelterrasse

Burgweg

Great Terrace

★ Großes Faß

Deutsches Apotheken-museum ★

Brunnenhalle

GARDENS ★

Grotto

Old Battery

Moat

Elisabethentor

Neue Schloßstraße

Schloß-Wolfsbrunnenweg

End of Feudal Period (and subsequent alterations)
1) Apothekerturm (14C) – **2)** Glockenturm (14C) – **3)** Gesprengter Turm (15C)
Gothic-Renaissance Transitional Period (Ludwig V – 1508-1544)
4) Dicker Turm (1533) – **5)** Ladies' Wing – **6)** Library – **7)** Torturm
Renaissance
8) Hall of Mirrors Wing (1549) – **9)** Otto-Heinrich Wing (1566)
Renaissance-Baroque Transitional Period
10) Friedrich Wing (Friedrich IV – 1592-1610), and below, Great terrace (Altan)
11) English Wing (Friedrich V – 1610-1632)

design of the entrance, which is in the form of a triumphal arch displaying the Elector's armorial bearings: the palatinate lion and the heraldic lozenges of the House of Wittelsbach framing the globe surmounted by a cross symbolizing the empire.

Interior ⊘

Two architectural models allow a comparison between the castle as it is today and as it was in the 17C. So far as the Renaissance decoration of the Friedrich Wing is concerned, this is largely due to a felicitous restoration (c 1900). Statues originally ornamenting the façades can be seen in the corridors. Baroque features were added to the chapel around 1720.

★ **Großes Faß (Great Vat)** – This colossal cask, with a capacity of 221 726l/48 780gal, was installed in the reign of Charles Theodore at the end of the 18C. Wine can be drawn from it, with the aid of a pump, in the royal banqueting hall (in the Ladies' Wing). The platform above the vat is large enough for dancing as well as wine tasting. The guardian of this Bacchic extravagance – today an idol of local folklore – was the dwarf court jester **Perkeo**, celebrated himself for the astonishing amount he could drink. The memory of Perkeo lives on in a wooden figurine and in the ingenious "surprise" clock he invented.

★ **Deutsches Apothekenmuseum (German Pharmaceutical Museum)** ⊘ (Z M') – *Entrance beneath the steps leading to the Otto-Heinrich Wing.*
Interesting 18C and 19C apothecaries' equipment. Collection of contemporary chemists' prescriptions. An alchemist's laboratory, complete with instruments, has been reconstructed in the Apothekerturm.
There is an excellent **view**★ of the castle from the **Molkenkur (Z)** restaurant, reached via the Molkenkurweg or by funicular railway. The restaurant is built on the site of an ancient fortification.

ADDITIONAL SIGHTS

★ **Kurpfälzisches Museum (Electoral Palatinate Museum)** ⊙ (**Z M²**) – *Hauptstraße 97.*
The archeological section exhibits a cast of the jaw of the prehistoric "Heidelberg Man" (500 000 BC). The department of German Primitives displays the **Altarpiece of the Twelve Apostles★★** (1509 – Windsheimer Zwölfbotenaltar) by Tilman Riemenschneider. The collection **Works from the Romantic Period★★** is devoted essentially to the iconography of the town and castle.

★ **Haus zum Ritter (The Knight's House) (Z N)** – This magnificent bourgeois mansion owes its name to a bust of St George in knightly armour which adorns the rich, scrolled pediment. Built in 1592 for the Huguenot merchant Charles Bélier, it was the only Late Renaissance masterpiece to be spared the devastations of 1689-93.

Studentenkarzer (Students' Prison) ⊙ (**Z B**) – From 1712 to 1914, students who were too rowdy or obtrusive ran the risk of incarceration here. Many of them left on the walls inscriptions, outlines darkened with soot, or coats of arms as a reminder to future generations of what they considered a particularly estimable episode in their career.

Heiliggeistkirche (YZ E) – The church is an example of the Late Gothic style. As in earlier times, covered stalls hug the walls between buttresses. From 1706 until 1936, the nave and chancel were separated by a wall, because the church was used by both Catholics and Protestants. The galleries in the hall apses were used for the Biblioteca Palatina, which ended up as war booty in the Vatican's possession after Tily took over Heidelberg in 1623 during the Thirty Years War. This famous library was considered the best in Europe, now most of it is found in Rome.
The well-lit **chancel** was formerly the sepulchre of the Palatine Electors, but since the pilaging wrought during the Orléans War in 1693 only the tomb of Ruprecht III and his wife remains.

Jesuitenkirche (Z F) – This Baroque church was built at the beginning of the 18C from plans drawn up by the Heidelberg architect JA Breunig. The main façade, based on the Gesù Church in Rome, was the work of the Palatinate court architect FW Rabaliatti (1716-82).
The luminous triple nave is supported by robust pillars whose capitals are decorated with Rococo stuccowork.

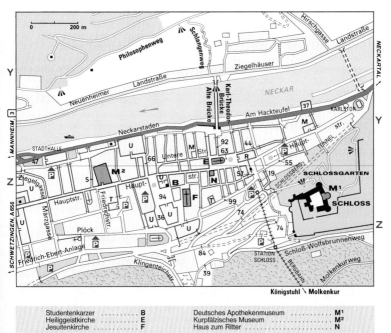

HOTELS

Backmulde – Schiffgasse 11, ☎ 0 62 21/5 36 60, Fax 0 62 21/53 66 60. Single rooms from 99DM. Old town house with a rustic look.

Schnookeloch – Haspelgasse 8, ☎ 0 62 21/13 80 80, Fax 0 62 21/13 80 813. Single rooms from 150DM. Old town hotel. Rough and rustic historical student establishment.

Weißer Bock – Große mantelgasse 24, ☎ 0 62 21/90 00 99, Fax 0 62 21/6 46 37. Single rooms from 155DM. Originally furnished small hotel, rooms in part with open beams; restaurant equally original with photos on the walls.

Romantik-Hotel Zum Ritter St. Georg – Hauptstrasse 178, ☎ 0 62 21/13 50, Fax 0 62 21/13 52 30. Single rooms from 175DM. Renaissance building rom 1592 with a beautiful sandstone façade. In the pedestrian zone.

The **Museum of Sacred and Liturgical Art** ⊙, which is reached through this church, houses religious artefacts (Madonnas, altar crosses, liturgical objects). In the museum treasury are examples (including chalices, monstrances) of the goldsmith's and silversmith's art.

EXCURSIONS

Schwetzingen – *10km/6mi to the west via the Friedrich-Ebert-Anlage* (**Z**) – *see Schwetzingen.*

Königstuhl – *5km/3mi to the southeast, via Neue Schloßstraße, Molkenkurweg, and then Gaisberger Weg; or take the* **funicular** ⊙ (*stops: Stadt – near the Kornmarkt* (**Z**), *Schloß, Molkenkur, Königstuhl*).
From the television tower on the summit (568m/1 864ft) there is a fine **panorama** of the Neckar Valley, from the Odenwald to the plain of the Rhine.

Insel HELGOLAND★★

Schleswig-Holstein
Population 1 700
Michelin map 415 D 7

Attracted by the idea of a short sea cruise, thousands of tourists each year head for the red-sandstone cliffs of the **island of Helgoland**, just 70km/43mi out from the estuary of the Elbe. English territory for many years, the island was exchanged for Zanzibar in 1890.

An unusual rock – Undermined for centuries by the sea, the island now covers an area of less than 1km²/0.5sq mi. In 1947, in accordance with the Potsdam Agreement, German military installations, including a submarine base, were totally destroyed by British sappers using 6 000t of high explosive.
Helgoland was returned to Germany in 1952, since when – thanks to a complete reconstruction of twin built-up areas divided by the form of the cliff (Unterland and Oberland) – it has once more become a tourist centre. An aquarium, an ornithological observatory and a marine biology station make the site of great scientific interest. The island has many attractions to offer the visitor: cliff walks, sea bathing from the lonely but sheltered sands of Düne Beach, even tax-free chocolates, cigarettes and spirits.

Access ⊙ – There is a daily car ferry service from Bremerhaven and Cuxhaven (passengers only), or a train-bus-boat linkup operated by the Sectouristik company from the main railway station (Hauptbahnhof) in Hamburg. A day excursion allows approximately 4hr on the island.

Michelin presents In Your Pocket
A new pocket-size collection of friendly, easy-to-use guides with the basics on what to see and do in some of the world's most attractive cities and regions. More than 30 destinations are now available :
Algarve – Amsterdam – Barcelona – Berlin – Brittany (France) – Bruges, Gand, Anvers – Budapest – Florida – Greek Islands – Istanbul – Italian Lakes – Jersey, Guernsey – Lisbon – London – Loire Valley – Madrid – Malta – Morocco – Munich – New Orleans – New York City – Paris – Prague – Rome – Saint Petersburg – San Francisco – Sicily – South of France : Riviera – Southern Spain – Thailand – Tuscany – Venice – Vienna

Bad HERSFELD★

Hessen
Population 33 000
Michelin map 417/418 N 13

The spa of Bad Hersfeld, set in a hilly section of the Hessian forest, is not only appreciated by those seeking health and wellness. Ever since 1951, crowds have flocked here from June to August to enjoy the festival of theatre, opera and musicals that is held before the extraordinary backdrop of the old abbey ruins.

The town arose in the 11C and 12C from a small trade settlement that had established itself at the gates of a monastery that later became an imperial abbey. The latter had originated in the 8C as a hermit's settlement but became a monastery that existed from 837 to 1606. In 1904, drilling in the earth tapped a source of healing waters, giving rise to a spa, which was officially placed on the Hessian roster of state spas in 1963.

★ **Stiftsruine (Abbey church ruins)** ⊘ – The remains of the abbey, destroyed by French troops in 1761, reveal the imposing proportions of its church, which was more than 100m/328ft long. The original building, which dated from the Ottonian period, was designed with an expanded transept forming a single uncluttered chamber. In the 11C and 12C, while retaining the general plan, the church was modified in the Romanesque style, with two chancels. The western apse, constructed on a rectangular base and flanked by a single Romanesque tower, is impressive, particularly when viewed from inside.

The Katharinenturm (1120), also in the Romanesque style, stands in an isolated position northeast of the church. Once part of the abbey complex, it houses the 900-year-old monastery bell.

Old Quarter – The blunt tower of the parish church emerges from a picturesque huddle of half-timbered burghers' houses near the market place (Marktplatz). Note especially the sacristan's house (Küsterhaus, 1452) and the Baroque residence of the pastor (Pfarrhaus, 1714), with its beautiful entrance.

Rathaus (Town hall) – This Gothic building, modified at the end of the 16C, is surmounted now by gables in the style of the Weser Renaissance. From the forecourt, there is a good **view★** of the church.

EXCURSION

Rotenburg an der Fulda – *21km/12mi to the north.*
Rotenburg lies in a particularly picturesque stretch of the Fulda Valley. The 750-year-old town has preserved its old-world charm, with fortifications, half-timbered houses and historical buildings (town hall with renaissance doorway and Rococo steps). The market square, attractive alleys and castle contribute to the delightful scene this small town makes.

HILDESHEIM★

Niedersachsen
Population 106 500
Michelin map 416/417/418 J 13

Louis the Pious founded a bishopric in 815, from which the town of Hildesheim evolved. As the capital of the Romanesque art which flowered in Germany during the Ottonian period, the town flourished under bishops Bernward (993-1022) and Godehard (1022-38). From the mid 13C to the 16C, feuds broke out repeatedly between the town's citizens and the bishops, who exerted their influence in a wide range of matters. Capricious turns of fate all too frequently prevented the town developing as it might, but over the centuries it managed to preserve its beautiful medieval buildings, until these were destroyed in an Allied Forces air attack in March 1945. After concerted efforts, the historical market square was rebuilt.

Hildesheim, which is linked by a secondary canal to the Mittellandkanal (which cuts across north Germany west to east from the Dortmund-Ems Kanal through Hannover to the River Elbe), has developed its economy largely in ecologically-friendly industries.

The thousand-year-old Rose Tree – As the legend goes, Louis I the Pious, exhausted after a day's hunting, hid his personal reliquary in a rose bush before he lay down to sleep. When he awoke the following morning, the precious casket was nowhere to be found. Interpreting this as a sign from Heaven, he founded a chapel – and subsequently a bishopric – on the spot, around which Hildesheim grew up.

SIGHTS

★ **Marktplatz** (Y) – The historical market square has been restored in an exemplary fashion. Visitors are greeted by the sight of buildings spanning eight centuries of architectural styles.

HILDESHEIM

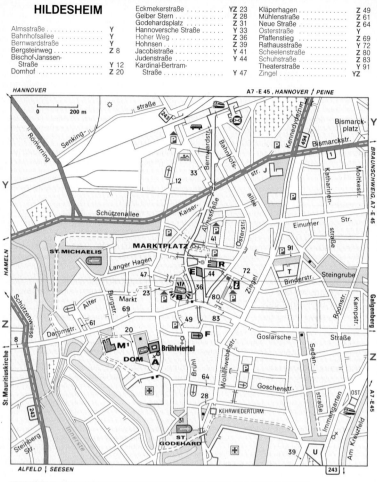

| Antoniuskapelle . . . . **A** | Tempelhaus . . . . **E** | Pelizaeus-Museum |
| St. Andreaskirche . . . . **B** | Heiligkreuzkirche . . . . **F** | und Roemer-Museum . . . **M¹** |

Rathaus – The east side of the square is lined with buildings in the Gothic style predominant between 1246 and 1290. Over the years, the Rathaus underwent numerous modifications and extensions, with the result that it clearly reflects three different periods of construction in three distinct sections. It was rebuilt in a simplified form of the original. *There is carillon daily at noon, 1pm and 5pm.*

Tempelhaus – This unusual, Oriental-looking building from 1320 to 1330 stands on the south side of the Marktplatz. The crow-stepped gable and two round turrets are probably 16C additions. The most distinctive feature is the ornate **Renaissance oriel★** dating from 1591, on which the parable of the Prodigal Son is depicted. The nearby **Wedekindhaus** has bay windows projecting from ground level up to the roof gable, a typical feature of the Renaissance architecture of Lower Saxony. The half-timbered building dates from 1598. Note the beautiful carved decoration. Not far off stands the **Lüntzelhaus** (1755), which now houses a local savings bank, and the 14C Gothic **Rolandstift** with a Baroque porch (c 1730).

The Bakers' and Butchers' Guild houses occupy the west side of the square. The original **Bäckeramtshaus** dated from 1451 but, like the impressive **Knochen-hauer-amtshaus★** (1529) next door, it is a faithful reproduction. The Knochen-haueramt-shaus is deservedly well-known as the "most beautiful half-timbered house in the world". This eight-storey building is the pride of the local citizens. The five upper floors house the **Municipal Museum** (Stadtmuseum).

The **Rokokohaus** on the north side of the square stands between the **Stadtschänke**, a local restaurant, and the Weavers' Guild House **(Wollenwebergildehaus)**.

★ Dom (Cathedral) ⊘ **(Z)** – The present building is a reconstruction, based on the original plans of an 11C Romanesque basilica, with later side chapels faithfully reproduced in the Gothic style and the dome above the transept modelled on the cupola added in the 18C. The interior retains the simplicity of the original. The alternate use of a single pillar and two columns in the nave is typical of the architectural school of Old Saxony.

Fine **works of art**★ can be seen in the cathedral. A huge chandelier dating from the 11C hangs above the transept crossing. On the north side, the last chapel contains a rare carved baptismal font (13C) supported by four figures representing the rivers of Paradise. In the south transept, an 11C bronze column depicting the life of Christ is displayed.

The two-storey Romanesque **cloister**★ abuts the eastern extremity of the cathedral. The legendary **rose** is trained along the outer wall of the apse.

Scenes from the Old and the New Testament are illustrated in the panels of **Bishop Bernward's bronze doors** beneath the west front porch – superb examples of early Romanesque sculpture.

Close to the cathedral, a magnificent Renaissance **rood screen**★ can be seen in the **Antoniuskapelle (Z A)**.

★ **Museums** ⊘ (Z **M'**) – The **Pelizaeus-Museum** houses a rich collection of Egyptian antiquities. *The museum is closed for restoration and scheduled to open in Summer 2000. During the restoration work, there are only temporary exhibitions.* The **Roemer-Museum** exhibits collections on natural and cultural history.

★ **St. Michaeliskirche (Y)** – Dating from the beginning of the 11C, this basilica is typical of Ottonian architecture in Old Saxony, with its double chancel and its alternation of pillars and columns. Note also the 13C **painted ceiling** depicting the Tree of Jesse in the nave, the two-tier galleries in the transepts, and the simplicity of the cushion capitals – again characteristic of Lower Saxony. Of the original decoration, an **Angel Screen** remains to the right of the west chancel *(on your left as you enter).* Above is a balustrade embellished with 13 angels.

★ **St. Godehardikirche (Z)** – This 12C church has an elegant silhouette marked by the slender spires crowning its three towers.

Andreaskirche (Z B) – Built by the town denizen in the 14C and 15C, this massive Gothic church was destroyed during the Second World War and then rebuilt. It contains the westworks of its Romanesque predecessor dating to 1140, whose façade is wonderfully structured in clear lines. The tower, rising with its spire to a height of 114m/355ft, is Niedersachsen's highest and it is the marking feature of the townscape.

The Brühl (Z) – Spared by the ravages of war, this quarter is typical of old Hildesheim. Note the Wernersches Haus dating from 1606 in the lower part of the district.

Heiligkreuzkirche (Z F) – Behind the Baroque façade of this building hides an Early Romanesque church (11C) originally refashioned from a fortified gateway. Gothic, Baroque and Ottonian elements jostle each other within.

St. Mauritius-Kirche – *Leave by the Bergsteinweg (Z).* This 11C church, with its 12C cloister, lies in the Moritzberg quarter, on the west side of Hildesheim. The interior was redone in the 18C, a great deal of stucco was added onto it.

HOHENLOHER LAND

Baden-Württemberg

Michelin map 419 S 13

The Hohenlohe plain separating the heights of the Swabian Forest from the Tauber Valley in northern Württemberg, remains a profoundly rural area. It is traversed by the tortuous valley of the wild Jagst and the lively Kocher Valley. Numerous castles along the way recall the glory of the Renaissance period.

THE JAGST VALLEY

① **From Bad Wimpfen to Schwäbisch-Hall**

114km/71mi - about 4hr

The route follows the sinuous course of the Jagst, along whose lush banks orchards, and sometimes vineyards, flourish.

★★ **Bad Wimpfen** – *See Bad WIMPFEN.*

Neudenau – Old houses with wooden-walled gables overlook the elegant and gracious **Marktplatz**.

Schöntal – The old **Cistercian abbey** ⊘, founded in 1157 and run by monks from Maulbronn, took on its present appearance under Abbot Knittel (1683-1732). The abbey complex was designed by **Dientzenhofer**. The 1727 **Baroque church**★ houses a high altar by Johann Michael Fischer and four rare alabaster **altarpieces**★★ (17C) against the pillars nearest the transept crossing. Among the old abbey buildings,

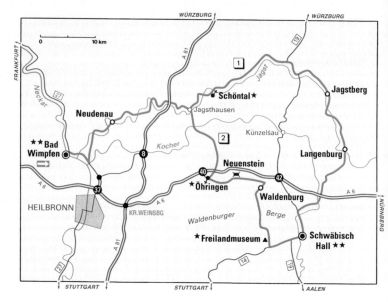

the abbot's antechamber, or **Orders Room**★ (Ordensaal) is especially noteworthy for its cladding of small panels painted to represent some 300 different costumes worn by the various religious orders.
The grave of Götz von Berlichingen, who died in 1562 and who was the subject of a play by Goethe, is in the cloisters.

Jagstberg – The village, sprawling over the crest of the valley's western slope, is dominated by a **church** (Pfarrkirche St. Burkhard) built at the beginning of the 17C to which Baroque features were added in 1765 by the stuccoworker Joseph Hell.
The route passes close by the famous wooden bridge of Unterregenbach.

Langenburg – This fortified town has been built along a crest encircled at its base by a bend in the river and crowned by the **castle** ⊘ of the Hohenlohe family. The **Renaisance inner courtyard**★, kernel of the original 12C fort which was enlarged in the 17C and 18C to become a castle, is framed by tiered galleries and overlooked by scrolled pediments. The castle rooms are furnished in grand style and contain numerous documents and souvenirs of the royal House of Hohenlohe.

★★ **Schwäbisch-Hall** – *See SCHWÄBISCH-HALL.*

② From Schwäbisch-Hall to Jagsthausen

73km/45mi – about 3hr

★ **Hohenlohe Open-Air Museum** – *See SCHWÄBISCH-HALL: Excursions.*

Waldenburg – From this town clustered on a narrow spur in the Waldenburg heights there is a good view as far as the Odenwald and Swabian Alps. The fortified town wall complete with defence towers and watch turrets has survived in good condition. The **castle** of the House of Hohenlohe-Waldenburg, destroyed in 1945, has been restored faithful to the original.
The road passes through the woods of the Waldenburger Berge before continuing downhill towards Neuenstein.

Neuenstein – Solidly constructed, the 16C-17C **castle** ⊘ here with its curved Renaissance gable dates from an 11C moated castle. A visit gives the impression of day-to-day life in a small German court, in this case that of the Hohenlohes. The Knights' Hall and Imperial Hall with its armoury, as well as masterpieces of the arts of furniture making and goldsmithing all evoke the magnificence of a bygone age. The kitchen, built in 1485, could still be used.

Öhringen – The late-15C **church**★ serves as a necropolis for the House of Hohenlohe. Enter through the Gothic hall-church's cloister and note in the chancel a monument to Philip of Hohenlohe (d 1609), son-in-law of William of Orange. Scenes from the Netherlands War of Independence are illustrated in relief at the base of the statue. The reliquary altar in the high chancel and the **Altarpiece of St Margaret**★ (Margarethen-Altar) in the large north chapel are beautifully executed works of art from the late 15C.
The crypt contains the funerary monument of the church's benefactor Adelheid, mother of Kaiser Konrad II.

Schloß HOHENSCHWANGAU★

Bayern
Michelin maps 419 and 420 x 16

Maximilian II of Bavaria, who was at the time still the Crown Prince, had this castle built between 1832 and 1836 on the remains of a fortress dating from the 12C. The neo-Gothic style, which was highly influenced by English castle and fortress architecture, was in accordance with current taste, which tended to be medieval, and the Prince's predilection for chivalric romance. It was in these surroundings that the unfortunate King Ludwig II of Bavaria dreamed away his youth.

The castle stands in a picturesque setting on a wooded hill. It is best to skirt this, following the road round to a beautiful **viewpoint**★ on a shaded rocky spur of the Pindarplatz on the north bank of the **Alpsee**★, from where it is possible to look out over the lake and its surroundings dotted with pines, which is overlooked by the steep slopes of the Säuling. Then cross the avenue to reach the castle.

TOUR ⊙ 1hr

In comparison to Neuschwanstein and despite many exaggerated features (there is an almost compulsive repetition of the etymological swan – *Schwan* – motif throughout the interior), an accumulation of rather cumbersome objets d'art, which had been left by Bavarian royal family corporations and institutions, Hohenschwangau has retained a very homely character. The length of time spent here by Queen Maria, Ludwig II's mother, explains the relatively personal atmosphere of the castle. Having endured the mania for over-decoration characteristic of the period, especially the High Gothic ceilings, visitors will welcome with relief the clean lines of the maple and cherrywood Biedermeier furniture. Oriental art, to which a great deal of space is given over, rubs shoulders with impressive murals, based on designs by Moritz von Schwind and which depict the life of the heroes celebrated in the medieval epics, and contributes to the sumptuous atmosphere which emanates from the castle. The old music room on the second floor contains moving evidence of the high esteem in which Ludwig II held Richard Wagner: the grand piano on which they both played, and also extracts from their correspondence. The fantastic and extravagantly romantic is again in evidence in the King's bedchamber, where the ceiling is painted to represent the stars in the night sky, which can be lit up like lamps. King Ludwig II was able to monitor the progress of the building work on Schloß Neuschwanstein with a telescope from his window.

EXCURSION

★★★ **Schloß Neuschwanstein** – *See Schloß NEUSCHWANSTEIN.*

The Green Guide includes fine art, historical monuments, scenic routes:
Europe: Austria – Belgium and Luxembourg – Berlin – Brussels – Europe – France – Germany – Great Britain – Greece – Hungary and Budapest – Ireland – Italy – London – Netherlands – Portugal – Rome – Scandinavia and Finland – Scotland – Sicily – Spain – Switzerland – Tuscany – Venice – Vienna – Wales – The West Country of England
North America : California – Canada – Chicago – Florida – New England – New York City – New York, New Jersey, Pennsylvania – Pacific Northwest – Quebec – San Francisco – Washington DC – USA East – USA West
And Mexico, Guatemala, Belize – Thailand and the complete collection of regional guides for France

Burg HOHENZOLLERN★

Baden-Württemberg
Michelin map 419 V 10 – Local map see SCHWÄBISCHE ALB

Built on a hill separated from the main massif of the Swabian Jura, Hohenzollern Castle, tall and bristling with turrets, looks from whichever side you see it like some fortress out of a fairytale. The **site**★★★, even more than the castle itself, is impressive enough to justify its fame.

The Cradle of the Hohenzollerns – The dynasty goes back to the counts of Zollern, originally overlords of the Hechingen region, and subsequently divided into several different branches. In 1415, the Hohenzollerns of Franconia became Margraves – and thus Elector-Princes – of Brandenburg. In 1618 they succeeded to the Duchy of Prussia.

Burg Hohenzollern

In the 18C, under the rule of the Hohenzollerns, the kingdom of Prussia became a leading power in Europe. It was a Hohenzollern, Wilhelm I, who was placed at the head of the German Empire, founded in 1871 at the instigation of Prussia. But less than half a century later, military defeat in the First World War and the revolution which followed it put an end to the domination of the Hohenzollern dynasty: on 9 November 1918, Kaiser Wilhelm II was forced to abdicate.

Castle ⊙ – A fortified ramp built in the form of a spiral leads to the courtyard. The castle as it is today was reconstructed from the original plans between 1850 and 1867 by the Prussian architects Von Prittwitz and Stüler. All that remains of the ancient fortress built by the counts of Zollern is the Roman Catholic chapel of **St.-Michael** (Michaeliskapelle), whose stained-glass windows are said to be the oldest in southern Germany. The neo-Gothic **Protestant chapel**, in the north wing of the castle, has contained since 1952 – when they were moved there from Potsdam – the tombs of the Soldier-King and of Frederick the Great. Mementoes of the latter (uniforms, decorations, snuffboxes, flutes) can be seen in the collections of the castle treasury (Schatzkammer).

Before leaving the castle, make a tour of the ramparts *(start on the left, after the drawbridge)* and enjoy the **panorama**★ of the Swabian Jura and the Upper Neckar Valley below.

HUSUM

Schleswig-Holstein
Population 21 000
Michelin map 415 C 11

"Yet my heart is always with you" – The birthplace of the writer **Theodor Storm** (1817-88), who wrote several of his principal works here and used many parts of Husum as settings, has seen its origins been subject to the coastal changes wrought by the North Sea. Today, this "grey city on the sea", as Storm described it in a poem, is the commercial hob of North Frisia thanks to the largest trade and fishing harbour on the west coast of Schleswig-Holstein. By the same token it is a modern holiday region with an abundance of cultural offerings.

Right in its midst is the tide-dependent interior harbour: depending on high or low tide, the boats are either afloat or lying in the sand. Some of the old merchants' houses, with their high and in part graduated gables, still stand in the **Großstraße**. The high attics were originally used as warehouses.

★ **Ludwig-Nisse-Haus-Nordfriesisches Museum (North Frisian Museum)** ⊙ – *Herzog-Adolf-Straße 25.*

The ground floor of this expressionistic brick construction displays the different types of German coastal landscape (Watt, Geest, Marsch, Polder etc), as well as the life and culture of its inhabitants. Natural catastrophes (the cataclysms – "Manndränken" – of 1362 and 1634, the high tide of 1962) are evoked in exhaustive detail, as are the construction of dykes and the reclamation of land by polders. A new section treats the emigration from Schleswig-Holstein across the seas from the 17C to the present. On the floor above, there is an exhibition of Frisian paintings (landscapes and scenes of everyday life).

Storm-Haus ⊙ – *Wasserreihe 31.* This typical Husum merchant's home was occupied by the writer Theodor Storm from 1866 to 1880; it has furniture from the Biedermeier age, paintings, documents and hand-written manuscripts from the writer's estate.

Marienkirche (St Mary's Church) – This church was built from 1829 to 1832 by the Danish state architect Christian Friedrich Hansen and is a perfect example of a Protestant sermon church in Classicist style. Dorian columns support the galleries, the view of the parishioners is guided towards the gabled pulpit altar.

Castle before Husum (Schloß vor Husum) – Built between 1577 and 1582 by Duke Adolf von Schleswig-Holstein-Gottdorf as a subsidiary residence in the Dutch Renaissance style and later as a widow's residence. The whole complex was renovated in the Baroque style after 1752. The castle park is beautiful, the blooming of the **crocuses**★ in spring is especially worth seeing.

EXCURSIONS

★ **Friedrichstadt** – *15km/9mi to the south.*
Dutch refugees, Remonstrants, hounded from their country for religious reasons and given sanctuary here by Duke Friedrich III of Schleswig-Holstein-Gottorf, founded this locality in 1621. The duke wanted the city planned according to Dutch models to become a major centre of trade and shipping. Friedrichstadt's unusual look has a special attractiveness to it. A rectilinear grid of canals with green banks crisscrosses the streets lined with houses topped with scrolled gables. The Marktplatz is the heart of the city and the point of departure for tours. It is well worth exploring the town from the water.

★ **Eidersperrwerk (Eider Dam)** – *35km/22mi to the south.*
Skirting a bird sanctuary, the road arrives at the mouth of the River Eider, closed off by a dam constructed between 1967 and 1972, after the catastrophic tidal wave of 1962. The five colossal steel sluice gates remain open when meteorological conditions are normal, permitting the customary rise and fall of tides. But they are closed when storms or abnormally high tides are threatened, preventing the sea from surging up the Eider to invade the low-lying country inland.

Friedrichstadt

Tourist Information Friedrichstadt

St. Peter Ording – *37km/23mi to the south.*
This well-known seaside town with 22km/7mi of sand beaches lies to the west of the Eiderstedt peninsula. This spa on the North Sea, with sulphurous waters has one of Germany's largest sulphur bases. The Seebrücke (Sea Bridge), 1 012m/3 239ft long, is especially lively.

★ **Nolde-Museum at Seebüll** ⊘ – *56km/35mi to the north.*
Known under the pseudonym of Nolde, the painter Emil Nansen (1867-1956), one of the most important representatives of the Expressionist School *(see Introduction: Art)* built himself a house of his own design in the solitude of the Seebüll marshes, between 1927 and 1937. Each year now, a different selection is displayed there of the works of Nolde – one of the most significant masters of German Expressionism. The *Life of Christ*, a series of nine canvases, is on permanent exhibition.

The chapter on Practical Information at the end of the guide lists:
local or national organisations providing additional information,
recreational sports,
thematic tours,
suggested reading,
events of interest to the tourist,
admission times and charges.

IDAR-OBERSTEIN

Rheinland-Pfalz

Population 36 000

Michelin map 417 Q 5

Twin towns here form a single built-up area – picturesque Oberstein lying along the foot of a gorge carved by the River Nahe and Idar spread out around a tributary beyond. The abundance in earlier times of nearby agate, jasper and amethyst deposits has left Idar-Oberstein a centre for the cutting and polishing of precious stones.

★★ **Deutsches Edelsteinmuseum (German Museum of Precious Stones)** ⓥ – *At Idar, in the Idar-Zentrum (Diamond Exchange), Hauptstraße 118.*
The museum presents precious stones from around the world, from agates to diamonds. Some 7 000 cut and polished stones as well as 1 000 intermediate precious stone and crystal phases are here to regale the eye. The Glyptothek is especially interesting, with its 6 000 year history of the gem-cutting industry and the engraving art of the Modern Age.

Idar-Oberstein – Deutsches Edelsteinmuseum

★ **Felsenkirche** – *Return trip 30min on foot. Access via a stairway (214 steps) rising from the Oberstein Marktplatz.*
Framed by a rock overhang in the cliff 50m/164ft above the river, this church, restored several times, is worth a visit for the **winged altarpiece** (beginning of the 15C) alone. The scenes of the Passion represented depict with a ferocious realism the hatred, the suffering and the annihilation involved.

Museum Idar-Oberstein ⓥ – *At Oberstein, in the Marktplatz (at the foot of the Felsenkirche stairway).*
Sizeable collections of minerals and precious stones, notably "Landschaftsachate" – paper-thin flakes of agate exhibiting in transparency the appearance of phantasmagoric landscapes. The museum also has displays of crystals, fluorescent stones and locally produced jewellery.

Burgruinen – *At Oberstein.*
Castle ruins with a view of the Nahe Valley.

Weiherschleife (Old Stonecutting Centre) ⓥ – *In the Tiefenstein district.*
The facetting and polishing of gems can be seen here, from the crude stone to the fine jewel. Skilled craftsmen still work in traditional fashion here, face down before sanded grindstones powered by a water-wheel.

EXCURSIONS

The Hunsrück – *Excursion 141km/88mi – allow about 5hr. Leave Idar-Oberstein to the northwest on road no 422.*
The Hunsrück forms the southern rim of the Rhenish schist massif (*see Introduction*). It is a region of low mountains and game-stocked forests, gashed by deep and steep-sided valleys.

Erbeskopf – Topping 818m/2 660ft, this is the highest summit of the massif. From the wooden tower, there is a panoramic view over the undulating, wooded countryside.
After Thalfang, the **Hunsrückhöhenstraße★** going northward offers fine views of the valleys, the forest-covered hills and numerous villages with ancient houses roofed by slabs of schist. The road passes the Stumpfer Turm, an old Roman watchtower.

Kirchberg – Perched on a hillside, this village retains many pretty half-timbered houses, especially around the Marktplatz. St. Michaelskirche dates back to the pre-Romanesque era, although the present building was constructed in the 15C.

Simmern – The farming centre of the Hunsrück. The parish church of St. Stephan (15C), with star-vaulting, houses the remarkable **tombs★** of the dukes of

Pfalz-Simmern. These are some of the finest works of Renaissance sculpture in the middle Rhineland. The Schinderhannesturm, once part of the city fortifications, was named after the bandit Schinderhannes, who was incarcerated here for a time.

It is also well worth exploring the old town centre around the church.

Ravengiersburg – Hidden away at the bottom of a valley, this village boasts a Romanesque church built on top of a spur. The imposing west front has a sculptured cornice and a miniature gallery. Above the porch: Christ in Majesty.

Dhaun – The castle here is built on a remarkable **site**★ on top of a sheer rock outcrop. On the esplanade, behind the statue, a staircase leads down to the gun positions.

The road on the final section of the excursion follows the valley of the Nahe before returning to Idar-Oberstein.

INGOLSTADT

Bayern
Population 112 000
Michelin map 419/420 T 18

Throughout its history, Ingolstadt has gone through many different phases. The layout of the streets and the buildings left over from this period mark the core of the old town. After a brilliant but short-lived period as the capital of a Bavarian partial Duchy (1392-1447) following Bavaria's third division, Duke Ludwig the Rich founded Bavaria's first university here in 1472. Later, 328 years to be exact, it was moved to Landshut and then to Munich.

At a Landtag (meeting of the Bavarian Parliament) held in 1516 in Ingolstadt, Duke Wilhelm IV announced the oldest still extant food law: the Purity Law for beer. From 1828 on, Ingolstadt served as an official fortress and became a military base. Today, this city in the middle of Bavaria is a major industrial hub with emphasis on motorcars (Audi). It is also a centre of oil refining.

★ **Maria-de-Victoria-Kirche** – This plain, single-nave praying room was transformed in 1732 by the Asam brothers. The huge ceiling fresco (490m²/5 200sq ft) illustrates the spreading of the Faith, through the intercession of the Virgin, to the four quarters of the earth. The perspective effect is astonishing.

The high altar, with a particularly rich canopy, is adorned by four statues representing Medicine, Theology, Law and Philosophy. The professors' seats along the side walls are also worthy of note.

Liebfrauenmünster – The interior of this church is in the form of an extended Gothic hall. It was built in the 15C, and the fine **reredos**★ of the high altar (1572) is a transitional work linking the Gothic with the Renaissance. The Virgin, patron saint of Bavaria, appears in the central panel in the form of a cloaked Madonna. Of particular note amid the rich furnishings are the choir stalls, the portrait of the saint and the Baroque crèche.

★ **Bayerisches Armeemuseum (Bavarian Army Museum)** ⊘ – Installed in the huge chambers of a 15C fortress (Herzogschloß), the rich collections of this museum trace the military history of Bavaria from the 14C to the present day. Numerous firearms illustrate the evolution of weaponry; an enormous diorama (17 000 model soldiers) stages the battle of Leuthen, which saw the victory of Friedrich II over the Austrians in 1757.

The Bavarian Army Museum also has a subsidiary in the fortification known as Reduit Tilly, not far from the Neues Schloß on the other bank of the Danube. The history of the First World War is displayed there.

Kreuztor – This octagonal, battlemented keep with six pointed turrets at the angles of the walls is the finest relic of the town's 14C and 15C fortifications.

Suit of armour, Bayerisches
Armeemuseum

Bayer. Armeemuseum Ingolstadt

275

EXCURSION

Neuburg an der Donau – *22km/14mi to the west.*
This small Renaissance Baroque town is built on a limestone ridge above the south bank of the river.

The **castle**, constructed between 1527 and 1546 by the Palatine count Otto-Heinrich, comprises a courtyard surrounded by a two-tier gallery, in the style of the early German Renaissance. The east wing, with its two towers, dates from 1665 to 1668.

The courtyard's western façade is decorated with murals representing scenes from the Old Testament. The arched gateway leads also to the **chapel**, which is embellished with frescoes (1543).

There is a **museum** (Schloßmuseum) ⊙ in the east wing, where neolithic remains, examples of sacred art, and exhibits charting the history of the princely House of Pfalz-Neuburg are on display.

The north wing boasts one of the finest Renaissance rooms in Germany, the **Knights' Hall**.

West of the castle is the **Hofkirche**, which was built at the end of the Renaissance (1607-27). The richly decorated **stucco ceiling**★ dates from the Counter-Reformation. The Baroque **reredos**★ (1752-54) is the work of JA Breitenauer, to whom the pulpit is also attributed.

JENA

Thüringen
Population 101 000
Michelin map 418 N 18

Northeast of the forest of Thuringia, midway along the course of the Saale, the town has developed steadily ever since the foundation of its university in 1558. From then on, numerous scientists and intellectuals such as the philologist Wilhelm von Humboldt, his brother Alexander, a geographer, Goethe and Schiller, contributed to Jena's importance.

Optics – In the mid 19C, Carl Zeiss and Ernst Abbe established an optical industry developed from their invention, the microscope. Jena today is a lively and future-oriented city.

SIGHTS

Johannistor (AY) – *Johannisplatz.*
Together with the Pulverturm (on the other side of the square), this gate is all that remains of the town's 14C fortifications.

Stadtmuseum Göhre ⊙ (AY **M²**) – *Markt.*
This local museum is housed in one of the town's most beautiful buildings, built around 1500. The four floors illustrate the history of Jena since its foundation. The collection includes some beautiful items of art and cultural history.

Jena – Optisches Museum

JENA

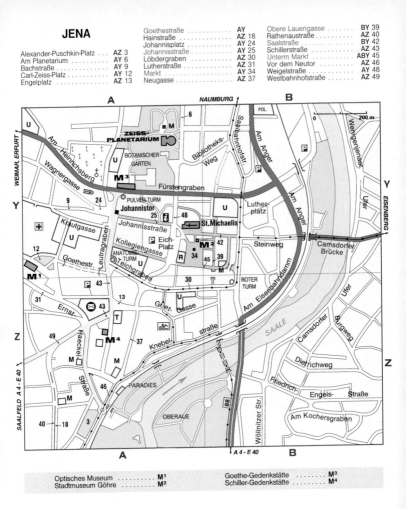

Optisches Museum .... M¹
Stadtmuseum Göhre .... M²

Goethe-Gedenkstätte .... M³
Schiller-Gedenkstätte .... M⁴

Stadtkirche St. Michaelis (AY) - *Kirchplatz.*
This ancient collegiate church of the Cistercians was completely transformed in the Gothic mode in the 15C. Note, on the south side, the canopied porch.

Goethe-Gedenkstätte (Goethe Museum) ⊘ (AY M³) - *Fürstengraben 26.*
The famous writer always said that it was in Jena that he found the tranquillity essential for literary creation. The inspector's house in the botanical gardens where he lived when he was in the town contains documents and items that recall his work in the field of natural science..

Schiller-Gedenkstätte (Schiller Museum) ⊘(AY M⁴) - *Schillergäßchen 2.*
Schiller lived in this summer house from 1797 to 1802. It now contains a display of memorabilia from Schiller's "Jena years".

★ Zeiss-Planetarium der Ernst-Abbe-Stiftung Jena ⊘ (AY) - *Am Planetarium 5.*
Built next to the botanical gardens by the Zeiss firm, this scientific spectacle permits visitors to voyage through the cosmos via the artful manipulation and movement of planets and the stellar systems. Varied laser and multi-visual show.

★ Optisches Museum ⊘ (AY M¹) - *Carl-Zeiss-Platz.*
Carl Zeiss started making microscopes in 1847. In collaboration with the physicist Ernst Abbe and the chemist Otto Schott, he laid the foundation stone for the construction of precision optical instruments. Part of the exhibition is dedicated to his work. This museum of science and technology contains a display on the history and technological developments in optical instruments over five centuries. The core of the exhibition is the development of the microscope, scpectacles, telescopes, photographic equipment and cameras as well as the life and work of Ernst Abbe, Carl Zeiss and Otto Schott.
There is also a reproduction of the "historical Zeiss workshop 1866" that gives insight into the production of a microscope.

KARLSRUHE★

Baden-Württemberg
Population 270 000
Michelin map 419 S 9

Karlsruhe is one of the "new towns" designed on a geometric plan in the 18C by the princely building enthusiasts of southern Germany. After the devastations of 1689 and the destruction of his family seat at Durlach, the Margrave of Baden decided to build a castle a little further west, among the trees of the Hartwald, his favourite hunting ground. The idea, put into operation in 1715 with the construction of an octagonal tower, was for the castle to be the hub of a network of radiating streets (hunting rides to the north, fan-shaped development for a future town to the south). This **"town fan"** was eventually fully realized in the 19C, when Karlsruhe became the capital of the Grand Duchy of Baden (1806).

The architect **Friedrich Weinbrenner** (1766-1826), a native of the town, was responsible for its neo-Classical aspect. From this period dates the **Marktplatz**, along with the town hall (Rathaus), the Protestant church (Evangelische Stadtkirche), and the modest pyramid of the founder's mausoleum. The Kaiserstraße (*pedestrian precinct*), today the city's commercial centre, was also designed by Weinbrenner. Cutting through the "fan" on an east-west axis, it follows the course of the old road from Durlach to the Rhine.

The former seat of the Grand Dukes today houses Germany's supreme courts (Court of Appeal and the Constitutional Court), together with the country's oldest School of Technology (1825). Among the eminent graduates of the latter are Hertz, who discovered electromagnetic waves, and Carl Benz, the motorcar pioneer. Karlsruhe is also the birthplace of the Baron Drais, inventor in 1817 of a vehicle – ancestor of the bicycle – known as the Draisienne.

SIGHTS

★ **Staatliche Kunsthalle (Fine Arts Museum)** ⊘ (**M¹**) – The building, erected between 1838 and 1846, houses a remarkable collection of **German Primitives**★★ (Gemälde Altdeutscher Meister). Among them the focal point in the Grünewald Room is a terrifying Crucifixion by the painter of the same name.

The golden age of Flemish and Dutch painting is represented by Rubens, Jordaens and Rembrandt (*Self-Portrait*). Still-life pictures by Chardin highlight a collection of 17C and 18C French paintings.

KARLSRUHE

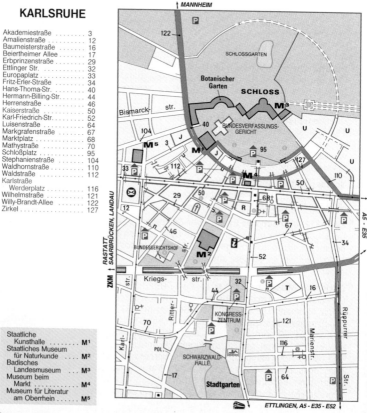

Staatliche Kunsthalle	**M¹**
Staatliches Museum für Naturkunde	**M²**
Badisches Landesmuseum	**M³**
Museum beim Markt	**M⁴**
Museum für Literatur am Oberrhein	**M⁵**

The **Hans Toma Collection**★ occupies a special place in German painting of the 19C. It is embedded in an almost complete presentation of famous German and French painters from Caspar David Friedrich to Paul Cézanne.

The adjacent **Orangery** houses an outstanding **collection**★ of Classical modern and contemporary art. Paintings by German Expressionists (*Deer in the Forest* by Franz Marc), artists of the Brücke group, artists who were influenced by Cubism (Léger, Delaunay), but also the *Hurricane* by Max Ernst and *The Seven Deadly Sins* by Otto Dix, stand alongside sculptures by Barlach, Lehmbruck and Henry Moore. The contemporary artists with work on display include Arnulf Rainer, Gerhard Richter, Yves Klein and Antoni Tapiès.

★ **Schloß** – Of the original castle building, only the tall octagonal tower that marks the centre of the city's radiating road system now remains. It was the grand-ducal residence up to 1918.

★ **Badisches Landesmuseum (Baden Regional Museum)** ⊘ (**M³**) – This museum has been arranged in the castle and consists of significant collections covering the region's prehistory and early history, the ancient cultures of the Mediterranean area and art, culture and regional history from the Middle Ages to the present. The famous **Turkish trophies** of the Margrave Ludwig Wilhelm, who was known as "Louis the Turk" (1677-1707) are particularly worthy of note. One section is reserved for the history of the castle and the court.

There is a wonderful view from the **tower** ⊘ over Karlsruhe as far as the Northern Black Forest, the Kraich region and the Palatinate hills.

From the castle park – which gives way, in the north, to a vast wooded area – there is access to the **Botanical Gardens** (Botanischer Garten) ⊘ , where the **greenhouses**★ (Gewächshäuser) offer a magnificent display of cactuses.

Museum beim Markt ⊘ (**M⁴**) *Between Marktplatz and the castle*. In another building of the Landesmuseum are collections of art from **Jugendstil**★ (Art Nouveau) and Art Deco to contemporary craft and design.

★ **ZKM** (Zentrum für Kunst und Medientechnologie) ⊘ – Access via Kriegsstraße. This former weapons and ammunition factory dating to the beginning of the 20C with a total of 10 roofed in patios now units research, teaching, workshops and museums revolving around media art.

Museum für Neue Kunst (Museum for New Art) – Access at the level of the blue cube (ZKM music studio).

At ground level of the eighth and ninth patios is an overview of the latest developments in the various types of new visual arts (painting, graphics, sculpture, holography, photo and media art, including installations by Plessi, Naumann and Nam June Paik).

The **Medienmuseum** is located on the first and second floors. The visitor must become active here in order to approach the exhibition items. Interactive presentation allows for a dialogue with form and impact of the new media technologies. In patio 10 at the southern end of the ZKM is the **Städtische Galerie** showing art from Baden after 1850 and German art after 1945.

Woven hanging by Sir Edward Burne-Jones and William Morris

Badisches Landesmuseum

KASSEL★

Hessen
Population 200 000
Michelin map 417/418 M 12

Once the seat of the Landgraves, today the economic, administrative and cultural capital of north Hessen, Kassel is situated on the banks of the River Fulda (*boat trips from Fuldabrücke*) (**Z**), in the heart of a hilly, lush and wooded countryside. To the west, at the foot of the Habichtswald heights, Wilhelmshöhe Palace and its park overlook the town. A natural spring at Wilhelmshöhe feeds the **Kurhessen thermal baths** (**X**).

Famous for its musical and dramatic activities, Kassel is nevertheless known best of all for the **Documenta**, an international exhibition of contemporary art which has been held every five years since 1955 (*next one is scheduled for the Summer of 2002*). The main centre for this event is the **Fredericianum** (**Z**), a pre-Classical building in the vast Friedrichsplatz designed by Simon Louis du Ry to be both museum and library for the Landgrave Frederick III. Germany's reunification has once again placed Kassel in the country's centre. The opening of a high-speed train ICE station in Wilhelmshöhe is yet another bonus.

The Brothers Grimm – **Jakob** (1785-1863) and **Wilhelm Grimm** (1786-1859) lived in Kassel from 1805 to 1830, both employed as Court Librarians. Through their shared work on literature and linguistics (a German basic grammar, the first volume of a German language dictionary) they can be considered the inaugurators of the science of German philology. Fascinated by legends and folklore, the brothers collected from all over the province a wealth of stories which they published between 1812 and 1822 under the general title of *Kinder und Hausmärchen* (Stories for Children and the Home, in English simply: *Grimms' Fairy Tales*).

★★ WILHELMSHÖHE (X) *allow half a day*

★★ Park – *West of the town.*

The landscaping of this huge 350ha/865 acre park was started in 1701 under the Landgrave Karl. It was based on a design by the Italian architect Guerniero. The Baroque-style park, in which almost 800 different species of trees grow, was transformed in the second half of the 18C into English-style gardens, complete with temples, pavilions, grottoes and artificial ruins. The ruins of **Löwenburg** (**A**), a fantasy castle built between 1793 and 1801, is an excellent example of the taste for sentimental romanticism current in that period (note inside the furnishings and the valuable collection of arms and armour).

At the highest point of the park stands **Hercules**★ (Herkules), emblem of the city of Kassel. This gigantic statue is a copy (1717) of the Farnese Hercules at the National Archeological Museum in Naples. It is 72m/236ft high (the Nelson monument in London's Trafalgar Square measures 52m/170ft). In the Wilhelmshöhe Park, the figure is placed on top of a pyramid, itself standing on a huge eight-sided pavilion, the Oktogon. From the base of the statue, there is a very fine **view**★★ over the park and the castle to Kassel.

Below the Oktogon is the great **Water Staircase** (Kaskadentreppe) – an enormous **cascade**★ with huge amounts of water falling in a sequence of steps to the Neptune Pool, before continuing past the rocks of the Steinhöfer waterfall, beneath the Devil's Bridge and along an aqueduct to the Fountain Pool (very high jets) in front of the castle. The Water Staircase falls 200m/656ft from top to bottom.

Schloß (Palace) ⊘ – This building in the Classical style was completed in 1803.

From 1807 to 1813, Jerome Bonaparte, the King of Westphalia, held a brilliant Court here.

The historic salons of the South Wing (**museum**), with their paintings and their Louis XV and Empire furniture, still recall the splendours of that period. Another famous guest was Napoleon III, held prisoner here after the Battle of Sedan in 1870. Heavily damaged during the Second World War, the building was reconstructed without its central cupola. At the end of the 1990s, work was begun on the castle to prepare it for housing the collections.

★ Antiquities – *Ground floor.*

In the entrance hall, 5C and 6C vases evoke echoes of Classical Greece. The Roman Empire is represented by an Apollo – referred to as the Kassel Apollo – a 2C work by Phydias and by a series of busts, a sarcophagus and some urns. Statuettes of gods and sacred animals in stone and bronze complete the section as examples of ancient Egyptian art.

During renovation work, the main pieces of the collection will be kept in the documents hall on Friedrichsplatz.

KASSEL

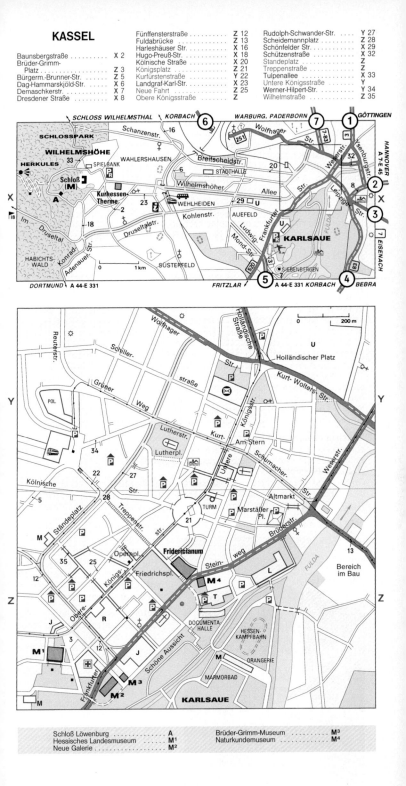

The chapter on Practical Information at the end of the guide lists:
local or national organisations providing additional information,
recreational sports,
thematic tours,
suggested reading,
events of interest to the tourist,
admission times and charges.

★★★ **Old Masters Gallery** – The rich, world-class exhibits here are derived from collections amassed by the Landgraves.
During restoration work some of the gallery's most interesting paintings are on display in other museums in Kassel:
German Primitive painting is in the **Hessisches Landesmuseum**: Altdorfer's Crucifixion, a triptych by Cranach the Elder, Dürer's *Portrait of Elizabeth Tucher*, *Hercules at Antioch* by Hans Baldung Grien. Also on display here are works by Italians (Tintoretto, Titian, Bassanoeni), Spanish (Ribera, Murillo) and French (Poussin's *Love's Victory Over the God Pan*) masters.
The **Neue Galerie** houses Dutch works: Rembrandt's *The Blessing of Jacob* (1656), *Portrait of Saskia van Uylenburgh* (the painter's first wife), *The Holy Family at the Screen*, *A Winter Landscape* and various self-portraits; lifelike portraits by Frans Hals, such as *Man with a Floppy Hat*; Rubens (*Crowning of a Hero; Mary and the Infant Jesus as a Refuge for Sinners*); Van Dyck (*Sebastian Leerse with his Wife and Son*); and Jordaens, who pictures himself as a lutenist in *The Painter's Betrothal*. Also on display here are landscapes and scenes of rustic and bourgeois life by Jan Brueghel, Jacob van Ruisdael, Gabriel Metsu and Jan Steen.

ADDITIONAL SIGHTS

★ **Karlsaue Park** (Z) – The most popular parts of this 18C riverside park are the steeply sloping gardens below the Schöne Aussicht terrace, and the Siebenbergen – an artificial island on the Fulda.
In the north corner of the park is the **orangery** (1710), home to the **Museum für Astronomie und Technikgeschichte mit Planetarium** ⊙. This museum's rich **collections**★★ of old astronomical instruments and clocks are the result of Landgrave Wilhelm IV's interest in astronomy, which led to his founding modern Europe's first permanently equipped observatory in Kassel in 1560. The great clockwork model of the planets was constructed in 1561 based on designs by "Milord-Astronomer". There are models demonstrating observable scientific phenomena and a display on the evolution of technology from Antiquity to the present (energy technology, data processing). The Planetarium has regular shows.
Not far from the orangery is the **Marmorbad** (1728), marble baths with an interior adorned with reliefs and statues on themes from Greek mythology.

★ **Hessisches Landesmuseum** ⊙ (Z M¹) – The street level is devoted to collections concerned with prehistory. There is a detailed display on the Stone Age. Subsequent periods are evoked by carefully selected exhibits (archeological finds from the Hallstatt and La Tène periods).
On the first floor is the **German Tapestry Museum**★★, where more than 600 pieces chart the evolution of wall coverings from the 18C to the 20C: wallpapers with Near-or Far-Eastern motifs, embossed leather, panoramic murals, printed papers with designs from famous workshops in Germany and France (Réveillon, Paris). The techniques of printing are also illustrated.
The second floor covers sculptures and porcelain from the manufacturers of Kassel and Fulda, and decorative art.

Panoramic mural tapestry, Deutsches Tapetenmuseum, Kassel

Verein Deutsches Tapetenmuseum

★ **Neue Galerie** ⊙ (Z M²) – Works ranging from the 18C to modern times are on display here, particularly those by German and European painters. Note the series of 18C portraits by the Tischbein family, among them *The Woman in Blue* (Amalie) and self-portraits. More classical in their approach are the mythological scenes by Nahl the Younger. The works of Lieber-mann, Trübner, and above all Corinth (*Walchensee Landscape, Woman with a Mask*), are close to those of the Impressionists, while Schlemmer and Kirchner (*Café at Davos*) are veering towards Expressionism.
One focus of the gallery is the department for art after 1960 and the "Space in the New Gallery" by Joseph Beuys. Its central object is *Das Rudel*, a composition consist-

ing of an old VW bus and sleds. The documental exhibitions are a must for those seeking to learn more about avant-garde art, with works of Mario Merz, Sigmar Polke and Gerhard Richter.
During the restoration of the Old Masters Gallery in the castle, Dutch masterpieces from the 16C and 17C are on display on the upper floor of the Neue Galerie.

Brüder-Grimm-Museum ⊘ (Z M³) – This is housed in Schloß Bellevue. Portraits, original manuscripts, letters, drawings and illustrations evoke the life and times as well as the works of the two scholars.

Naturkundemuseum (Natural History Museum) ⊘ (Z M⁴) – Divided into three sections – Geology, Botany and Zoology – this museum is in the former **Ottoneum**, Germany's oldest (1606) theatre. Note the remarkable **Ratzenberger Herbarium** (late 16C), also said to be the oldest in Germany, and the late-18C **Schildbach'sche Holzbibliothek**, a collection of 500 trees and shrubs in book shape, whose tomes have been made of various wood types illustrated inside with skillfully replicated blossoms, leaves and fruits of each species.
Until further notice, only the ground floor of this museum is open to the public.

EXCURSION

★ **Schloß Wilhelmsthal** ⊘ – *12km/8mi north on Rasenallee* (X).
This Rococo palace (1743-70), surrounded by a park in the English style, was built by François Cuvilliés. Interior decoration in the then current style, with fine panelling, elegant furniture (mother-of-pearl inlaid commode), Chinese porcelain and a gallery of beauties painted by JH Tischbein the Elder exemplify the taste of the Court.

KIEL★

Schleswig-Holstein
Population 240 000
Michelin map 415/416 D 14

Thanks to its location at the end of a 17km/10mi deep inlet in the Baltic Sea at the eastern end of the North Sea-Baltic Sea canal, Kiel, founded in the 13C, was always dominated by seafaring and mercantilism – even if this Hanseatic city never achieved more than regional importance, in contrast to Lübeck. For centuries, the city led a tranquil existence. This all changed in 1871, when Kiel was selected to become the main navy base for Germany. Within a few years, the little harbour city grew into a metropolis. It was heavily damaged during the Second World War. Ever since, today's capital of the state of Schleswig-Holstein was rebuilt from scratch, saving only little of the old buildings.
As a gateway to Scandinavia, Kiel plays an important role as a hub between north and south. After the Eastern Bloc was dissolved, Kiel was able to establish connections with eastern countries across the Baltic. The statistics of the harbour illustrate this clearly: 1.8 million ferry passengers, 5.5 million tonnes of goods transhipped. The Howaldtswerke on the Kieler Förde is still an important shipbuilding company.

★★ **Kieler Förde (Roadstead)** – The shores of this deep inlet are brightened by a series of sheltered resorts and bathing beaches, among them Schilksee, Strande, Laboe, Stein, Heikendorf and Schönberger Strand. In the northern part of the bay, regattas have been held for more than a century, including the events of the **Kiel Week**.

★★ **Hindenburgufer** – This promenade extends for almost 3km/2mi along the shore, with shady parks on one side and extended **views★** of the roadstead on the other.

Rathaus (Town hall) ⊘ – Built between 1907 and 1911, the building is noteworthy for its 106m/348ft tower. From the upper gallery of this, there is a splendid **view★** of the roadstead as far as the tall Laboe Memorial.

Wind in your sails

The Kiel Week held in June is the world's largest sailing event. 2.5 million visitors flock to the town and around 5 000 yachtsmen and women in 1 800 yachts and jolly boats can be observed at work. They embark in contests in 20 international classes and in the 11 Olympic sailing disciplines.
If you want to see the event at close range, you can go on one of the accompanying regatta's accompanying boats. Information at ☎ 04 31/6 79 10 16.

Regatta at Kiel

EXCURSIONS

★★ Schleswig-Holsteinisches Freilichtmuseum (Schleswig-Holstein Open-Air Museum) ⊙ – *6km/4mi to the south in Molfsee.*
Sixty rural buildings and farms typical of the country north of the Elbe are reconstructed here, arranged in groups according to their geographic origin. Those from the south, colour-washed or embellished with skilful designs in brick, resemble – inside as well as out – the rustic houses of Lower Saxony. The brick-built farms of the north Frisian area are more austere.
A forge, a potter's workshop, an old-fashioned bakehouse, flour mills and weavers' looms are all operated by local craftsmen in traditional manner.

★ Laboe – *20km/12mi to the north.*
This resort on the Baltic coast has a picturesque fishing and yachting harbour and is very popular with families because of its sandy dunes and calm waters. The memorial tower, 85m/279ft high, offers a wide **view★** of the outer part of the roadstead and, on a clear day, the Danish archipelago. Together with its underground galleries, the tower – which is built in the form of a ship's stern – constitutes the **German Naval War Memorial★** (Marine-Ehrenmal) ⊙. It includes a museum of navigation. Also on display is the U-995, a submarine launched in Hamburg in 1943, which operated in Norwegian waters and in the Barents Sea.

Kiel Canal (Nord-Ostsee-Kanal) – This link between the Baltic and the North Sea was inaugurated by Wilhelm II in 1895. From Kiel to Brunsbüttel, its 100km/62mi length is the world's busiest waterway: 38 000 vessels pass through it annually, not counting sports boats (although from the point of view of tonnage transported, it is relegated to third place).
From the second viaduct from Kiel to Holtenau (*Olympiabrücke, reached from Kiel via Holtenauer Straße and Prinz-Heinrich-Straße*) there is a good view of the **Holtenau locks**, linking the Kiel Canal and the Baltic Sea. On the island formed by the lock (Holtenauer Schleusen) there is an exhibition with a model of the canal and of the mechanics of the lock. Among the structures spanning the canal, the most impressive are the **Rendsburg Railway Viaduct★** *(see below)*, the **Grünental Bridge** on B 204, which has a viewing platform, and the **Hochdonn Railway Bridge**.

Rendsburg – *36km/22mi to the west.*
Rendsburg occupied one of the strategic points of northern Germany, where the main highway from Denmark crossed the Eider. The old town, tightly packed around its 16C town hall and the 13C Marienkirche, is built on a former island in the Eider. It is now hemmed in on either side by fortifications built in the 17C to defend the bridge. The **Neuwerk Quarter** in the south, between the Kiel Canal and the old town, is notable for its huge central esplanade (Paradeplatz), from which streets radiate out in different directions.
South of Rendsburg, the Kiel Canal can be crossed by a **railway viaduct★** (Eisenbahnbrücke), a **tunnel for road traffic** (Kanalbrücke) and a pedestrian footway. The viaduct is 42m/138ft above the water, with a transporter bridge below it. The tunnel beneath the canal is 640m/656yd long; the footway, in a second tunnel parallel with the first, is equipped with 1 278m/1 397yd of escalators and moving walkways.

* **Holstein's "Little Switzerland"** (Holsteinische Schweiz) – *51km/32mi – allow 2hr 30min.*
Between Kiel and the Bay of Lübeck (Lübecker Bucht), not far from the Baltic Sea, Holstein's "Little Switzerland" region is scattered with lakes separated by wooded hills formed from the glacial moraine (highest point: Bungsberg, 168m/550ft).
In the middle of the region, beside the biggest of the lakes (Großer Plöner See) is the town of **Plön**. From the terrace of its Renaissance castle, there is a pretty **view**★ of the surrounding lakes. Further east, **Eutin**, birthplace of the composer Carl Maria von Weber, has retained its 17C, brick-built town centre. The moated castle (1723) is surrounded by an English-style park bordering the lake.
Malente-Gremsmühlen, a small resort built on a wooded isthmus, is a departure point for boating trips.

KOBLENZ★

Rheinland-Pfalz
Population 108 000
Michelin map 417 O 6 – Local map see MOSELTAL

The prosperity of Koblenz (from the Latin confluentia) derives from its position at the confluence of the Rhine and the Moselle. Placed under the jurisdiction of the archbishops of Trier, the city came under French influence immediately after the Revolution, when refugees led by the counts of Artois and Provence, brothers of Louis XVI, fled there. But in 1794 troops of the Republic occupied the east bank of the Rhine, and four years later Koblenz became the Prefecture of the French Rhine-and-Moselle department. Subsequently the Prefect Lezay-Marnésia decided to beautify the city, and in 1809 he gave it the impressive **Rheinanlagen** (Z), a splendid riverside promenade.
The tomb of Hoche, at Weißenturm, and the Marceau cenotaph in the French cemetery at Lützel (*north of the town plan, via the Balduinbrücke* – Y), evoke memories of those young generals who fell during the first coalition.
Departure point for numerous excursions on both the Rhine and the Moselle, Koblenz also offers a summer festival, when the Rhine is set ablaze with flaming torches, many open-air concerts, and the celebrated taverns in its "wine village" (Weindorf). The old town (Altstadt) is centred on the Liebfrauenkirche.

SIGHTS

* **Deutsches Eck** (Y) – A gigantic equestrian statue of Wilhelm I presides over this tongue of land which marks the confluence of the Rhine and the Moselle. From the gallery crowning the base of the statue (*107 steps*), there is a fine view of the town, the port, the Moselle bridges and the east bank of the Rhine, overlooked by the fortress of Ehrenbreitstein.

Stiftskirche St. Kastor (Y) – This Romanesque church succeeded an earlier basilica in which the Treaty of Verdun, dividing Charlemagne's empire, was drawn up in 843. Heavy fan vaulting covers the nave and chancel. The furnishings are

---

Beer

Beer has been brewed in Germany since the beginning of the 9C. In 1516 a decree on quality (Reinheitsgebot) was passed which stated that only hops, malt, yeast and water should be used for brewing. This ruling still applies, and the following method is used:
Brewer's malt – obtained from barley after soaking, germination and roasting – is mixed with water and hops (which flavour the must) and boiled. Yeast is added and the must is left to ferment.
Nowadays about 1 400 breweries in Germany produce 4 000 kinds of beer, which vary greatly in taste, colour and alcohol content:
– Popular beers, such as Kölsch, Altbier, Export, Pils, Märzen and Weizenbier (beer made from wheat), are light and about 3-4% volume.
– Strong beers, or Starkbiere, such as Bockbier and Doppelbock, are rich in malt and about 5-6% volume. They tend to be lighter in the south (Munich, Stuttgart), stronger and more bitter in the Rhineland (Dortmund, Cologne), and sweeter in Berlin.
– Dark beers made with roasted malt can taste quite sugary (Rauchbier, Bockbier, Malzbier).
In restaurants and bars, beer is generally served on draught (*vom Faß*). If you prefer lighter beers such as Pils, be patient, for it takes a few minutes for the froth to settle!

KOBLENZ

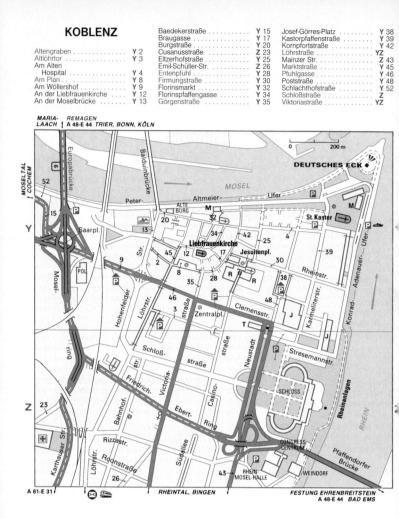

interesting: the tombs of two archbishops lie at the back of multicoloured Gothic bays and, in the south transept, there is a series of 16 painted wood panels, once part of a rood screen, with a picture of St Castor (bottom left).

Liebfrauenkirche (Y) – This originally Romanesque church was remodelled in the 13C and given a Late Gothic chancel in the 15C. Beautifully crafted, ornate keystones seem to grow from the ribs of the vault. The belfries were crowned with Baroque roofs towards the end of the 17C. The interesting windows in the chancel are the work of HG Stockhausen in 1992.

Jesuitenplatz (Y) – In the courtyard of a 17C Jesuit College, now serving as the town hall, is the "Schängelbrunnen" – a fountain evoking the mischief perpetrated by the street urchins of the city.

EXCURSIONS

★★★ Rhine Valley – See RHEINTAL.

★ Festung Ehrenbreitstein (Citadel) – 4.5km/3mi. Cross the Rhine on Pfaffendorfer Brücke (Z) then turn left.
This strategic stronghold, commanding the confluence of the two rivers, was the possession of the archbishops of Trier from the 10C until 1799, when it was destroyed by the French. Between 1816 and 1832 the Prussians, who had ruled the Rhineland since the Congress of Vienna (1815), constructed the powerful existing fortress.
From the terrace, there is a **view**★ of Koblenz, Schloß Stolzenfels to the south, the wooded plateau of Hunsrück and the volcanic massif of the Eifel.

★ Kloster Maria-Laach – 20km/12mi to the west.
The vast crater lake beside which this abbey stands emphasizes the monumental air of poise and solidity characterizing the abbey buildings. The 12C abbey church is a Romanesque basilica with three naves, whose exterior is reminiscent of the cathedrals of Worms, Speyer and Mainz.

The cloister-type entrance portico, added in the early 13C, has intricately worked capitals. An unusual hexagonal baldaquin - perhaps suggesting a Moorish influence - is stretched over the altar. The crypt is the oldest part of the church.

Andernach - *18km/11mi to the north.*
This small town on the west bank of the Rhine retains a strongly medieval atmosphere. Enter the old town through the **Rheintor**, a fortified double gateway whose oldest part dates back to the 12C, and continue to the **castle ruins** (14C-15C), which command the southern entry to the town.
The beautiful twin-towered façade of the **parish church** (Pfarrkirche) is a fine example of the early-13C Rhineland style - a transition between the Romanesque and the Gothic.

KÖLN ★★★

Cologne – Nordrhein-Westfalen
Population 1 008 480
Michelin map 417 N 4

Cologne is the capital of the Rhineland and one of the largest cities in Germany. On the Rhine's west bank, the old town forms a semicircle between the river and the Ring – a curving, 6km/4mi avenue, much of it dual carriageway, that follows the line of the city's 13C fortifications. Vestiges of these still remain at a few points, notably the **Severinstor** and **Ulrepforte** (FX). In the Middle Ages, 40 000 people lived within these walls, and Cologne was not only the biggest but also the most densely populated city in the whole country. At that time the two main thoroughfares were the **Hohe Straße** (GYZ) (north-south) and the **Schildergasse** (GZ) (east-west), both of them busy pedestrian precincts today. The more modern quarters, developed after the destruction of the ramparts in 1881, lie in concentric circles outside this ancient nucleus. A double **Green Belt** lends space and perspective to this outer urban area.

Many bridges link historic parts of the city with the industrial zones on the east bank of the river. It is here that the **exhibitions** and **fairs** which draw so many businessmen to Cologne are held – the photokina, Domotechnica, Möbelmesse (furniture), hardware and household goods exhibition and the international Süßwarenmesse (confectionery), for example.

Cologne's principal industries are mechanical (cars, machine tools), pharmaceutical, chemical and petrochemical – not forgetting the perfumery business, with its famous Eau de Cologne. The principal manufacturer of this toilet water, first elaborated in the early 18C by an Italian who settled in the city, is the cosmetic firm Muelhens KG, the old Glockengasse no 4711.

The Rhine Riverside – The most impressive view of the old city and its skyline can be found on the river's east bank, south of the Hohenzollernbrücke, at the level of Kennedy quay – or even from the Deutzer Brücke (FV). From these points the Rhine frontage, dominated by the bold cathedral spires and the square, steepled belfry of Groß St. Martin, is majestically attractive.

HISTORICAL AND ARTISTIC NOTES

Cologne in Roman Times – Once the Roman legions had extended the empire as far as the Rhine, General Agrippa, the colonizer of the region, allowed the Ubii, a Germanic people, to occupy (38 BC) the west bank of the river. The settlement was named the *Oppidum Ubiorum*. Then, in the year AD 50, Agrippina, the third wife of Emperor Claudius and the mother of Nero, obtained for her birthplace the official title of Roman Colony – *Colonia Claudia Ara Agrippinensium* (CCAA). "Colonia's" first defensive walls were then built, and the town became the residence of the Governor of Lower Germania. Roman ruins still exist in the (restored) Zeughausstraße, at the north gate of the town in front of the cathedral, and at the **Praetorium**, beneath the present town hall. From its official recognition onwards, the town flourished: it was the start of an era, rich in craftwork, trade and architecture, which did not end until the time of the Great Invasions, in the 5C.

The Holy City Beside the Rhine – Cologne's political power in the Middle Ages derived from the Church. The bishopric founded by Emperor Constantine in the 4C was upgraded to an archbishopric by Charlemagne. Until the Battle of Worringen in 1288, the archbishops of Cologne exercised powers that were not only spiritual but also temporal. Churches, of which the cathedral was one, monasteries and collegiates rose rapidly – more than 150 in all.

In the 13C and at the beginning of the 14C, the city became the enlightened religious, intellectual and artistic centre of the Rhine Valley. Eminent men came to preach: the Dominicans **Albertus Magnus** (the teacher of Thomas Aquinas) and **Master Eckhart**, as well as the Scottish Franciscan, **Duns Scotus**. It was the work of such religious scholars that led in 1388 to the creation of Cologne University by local lay burghers.

Trade and Commerce – Because of its favoured position on the banks of the Rhine and at the crossroads of important trade routes, Cologne soon became a power in the commercial world, imposing its own system of weights and measures over the whole of northern Germany. Such authority derived from a decree known as the **Stapelrecht** (Law of Stockage), under which all foreign merchants passing through the city were obliged to keep their goods there for at least three days, thus allowing Cologne residents a prior right to purchase. The town's first fair was held in 1360. Its elevation to the status of Free City in 1475 did no more than set an official seal on the preponderant role the burghers of Cologne had in fact been playing since the 13C.

ENJOYING YOUR STAY IN KÖLN

Local dialling code – 02 21

Tourist information – *KölnTourismus Office*, Tourist office opposite the cathedral (Unter Fettenhennen 19), open May-Oct, Mon-Sat 8am-10.30pm, Sun 9am-10.30pm, Nov-Apr, Mon-Sat 8-9pm, Sun 9.30am-7pm; ☎ 22 12 33 45. Every four weeks the following local publications list the cultural events and exhibitions that are on in town: *Kölner Illustrierte*, *Kölner Stadt-Revue* and *Monatsvorschau (KölnTourismus)*. Advance ticket bookings via *Köln-Ticket* on Roncalli-Platz; ☎ 28 01.

Post offices with extended opening hours – Main post office in Breite Straße Mon-Fri 8am-8pm, Sat 8am-4pm.

Daily newspapers – Kölner Stadt-Anzeiger, Express, Kölnische Rundschau.

Internet sites – http://www.koeln.org; http://www.koeln-online.de; http://www.cologne-in.de; http://koelnerkarneval.de

Public transport

The main operator of the local public transport network in Cologne is the Kölner Verkehrsbetriebe **(KVB)**, which runs most buses, underground trains (U-bahn) and trams (Straßenbahn). The KVB is linked with the Rhein-Sieg transport authority **(VRS)**, which covers the area as far as Bonn among other places.

Cologne city centre is divided into different price zones; the cost of single journeys *(Einzelfahrt)* comes to 2.20DM, 3.40DM or 5.30DM per trip. A *Minigruppenticket* costs 13DM, and is valid for up to 5 people after 9am allowing unlimited travel on all of Cologne's public transport. The 24hr ticket for one person costs 9.50DM, the 3-day ticket 23DM. For 24hr information ☎ 5 47 33 33. There are KVB information booths all over Cologne, the main ones are on the east side of the Hauptbahnhof, open Mon-Sat 7am-8pm, Sun noon-8pm; and at Neumarkt 25 and Ehrenfeldgürtel 14, both open Mon-Fri 7am-7pm, Sat 8.30am-2pm.

The **KölnTourismus Card**, available in hotels for 30DM (valid 72hr), allows the use of all of Cologne's public transport facilities, including a coach tour of the city, free entry to all the city's museums and discounts on tickets for the opera, boat trips, ascent of the cathedral tower, chocolate museum etc.

Sightseeing

City tours – Coach trip with guide, including a visit to a museum, available from *Köln Tourismus* office opposite the cathedral, Apr-Oct, daily at 10am, 11am, 2pm, 3pm, Fri and Sat also at 1pm, Nov-Mar at 11am and 2pm. Meeting point for tours of the cathedral is by the main door, Mon-Sat at 11am, 12.30pm, 2pm and 3.30pm, Sun at 2pm and 3.30pm only. **City tours on foot** organised by *StattReisen Köln*; ☎ 732 51 13 and *Inside Cologne – City Tours*; ☎ 52 19 77.

Boat trips – The *Köln-Düsseldorfer Deutsche Rheinschiffahrt (KD)* has the largest fleet of excursion boats on the Rhine, ☎ 208 83 18. Other boat companies include *Dampfschiffahrt Colonia* ☎ 257 42 25 and *Köln-Tourist Personenschiffahrt* ☎ 12 16 00.

Shopping

The cathedral is the best point of departure for any shopping trip in Cologne. It brings you straight to the main shopping street, the Hohe Straße. This is crossed by Schildergasse (department stores) at the far end. Not far from the shops along Neumarkt are numerous shopping arcades, such as Neumarktpassage and Neumarktgalerie. **Exclusive boutiques** are centred around Breite Straße, Mittelstraße and Pfeilstraße. There are further shopping opportunities besides these in other parts of town, such as the south around Chlodwigplatz; and in Bonner- and Severinstraße.

Köln – Hohe Straße

F. Damm/Köln Tourismus Office

Antique shops and **art galleries** are concentrated in St.-Apern-Straße; there are more galleries to the north of Neumarkt (Albertusstraße) and in the district around the cathedral. Tip: local artist Thomas Baumgärtner has sprayed his seal of approval – a banana – on the entrances to galleries, that he recommends.

Flea markets – In the old city centre around Groß St. Martin every third Saturday in the month from 9am to 6pm and between Breite Straße and Glockengasse in the city's main (pedestrianised) shopping zone every second Sunday from 11am-6pm.

Markets – City centre: Tuesday and Friday 7am-1pm on Sudermannplatz. The really original markets are to be found to the north of town, in the Köln-Nippes district on Wilhelmplatz, Mon-Sat 7am-1pm.

Where to stay

BUDGET

Ilbertz (B&B) – Mindener Straße 6; ☎ 88 20 49, Fax 88 34 84. 29 rooms, single rooms from 100DM. Family run hotel near the trade fair centre.

ETAP Köln-West – Toyotaallee 40 ☎ 0 22 34/ 957 78 20, Fax 0 22 34/597 78 30. 74 rooms, single rooms from 75DM. Modern and comfortably furnished accommodation in Marsdorf.

Brandenburger Hof – Brandenburger Straße 2; ☎ 12 28 89, Fax 13 53 04. 32 rooms, single rooms from 50DM. Practical overnight stop in the north of the old city centre.

OUR SELECTION

Savoy – Turiner Straße 9; ☎ 1 62 30, Fax 1 62 32 00. 103 rooms, single rooms from 175DM. Comfortable city hotel with fitness facilities.

Mercure Severinshof – Severinstraße 199 ☎ 2 01 30, Fax 2 01 36 66. 252 rooms, single rooms from 222DM. Modern, generously appointed hotel near the old city centre.

Brenner'scher Hof – Wilhelm-v.-Capitaine-Straße 15; ☎ 9 48 60 00, Fax 94 86 00 10. 40 rooms, single rooms from 255DM. Elegantly furnished hotel in the style of a country house in the quiet suburb of Köln-Junkersdorf.

TREAT YOURSELF!

Hyatt Regency – Kennedy-Ufer 2a; ☎ 8 28 12 34, Fax 8 28 13 70. 305 rooms, single rooms from 343DM. Modern luxury hotel in Deutz, a district on the east bank of the Rhine, with a view of the cathedral and the old city centre.

Excelsior Hotel Ernst – Domplatz; ☎ 27 01, Fax 13 51 50. 161 rooms, single rooms from 350DM. Top-class address right by the cathedral, classic elegant grand hotel.

Wasserturm – Kaygasse 2; ☎ 2 00 08, Fax 2 00 88 88. 90 rooms, single rooms from 449DM. This 19C water-tower has been converted into a modern hotel. Interior decor by Andrée Putman.

Eating out

BUDGET

Wackes – Benesisstraße 59; ☎ 2 57 34 56. Main courses from 16DM. This rustic inn serves predominantly Alsatian cuisine.

Höhn's Dombrauerei Ausschank – Goltsteinstraße 83, ☎ 3 48 12 93, Main courses from 14DM. This beer cellar In Bayenthal has a small beer garden and serves good wholesome cooking.

OUR SELECTION

Bruno Lucchesi – Dürener Straße 218, ☎ 40 80 22. Main courses from 39DM. Small corner restaurant with a typically Italian menu.

Paul's Restaurant – Bülowstraße 2; ☎ 76 68 39. Main courses from 36DM. Smartly furnished restaurant in a restored town house in Nippes.

TREAT YOURSELF!

Le Moissonnier – Krefelder Straße 25; ☎ 72 94 79. Main courses from 39DM. Typical French bistro in a Jugendstil setting.

Hanse Stube – Dompropst-Ketzer-Straße 2; ☎ 2 70 34 02. Main courses from 48DM. Elegant and comfortable hotel-restaurant in the Excelsior Hotel Ernst.

Cafés and bars

The old city centre offers a wealth of possibilities when it comes to eating out, having a drink or being otherwise entertained. Areas with the highest density of bars include the Belgian district between Aachener and Venloer Straße (beautiful part of town dating from the Gründerzeit), the university district (around Zülpicher Straße), south of town (around Chlodwigplatz) and the district around Friesenstraße.

CAFÉS

Café Reichard – Unter Fettenhennen 11. The best place for watching the comings and goings on the cathedral parvis is on the glazed veranda or the terrace.

Café Jansen – Obenmarspforten 7. Atmospheric 1950s decor in the protected interior.

Café Frommel – Breite Straße 122. This modern coffee house offers a selection of over 100 different pastries.

Café Schulte – Heumarkt 65. This bakery offers a marvellous overview of the art of baking in the Rhineland.

Café Zimmermann – Herzogstraße 11-13. This traditional café has always attracted locals and visitors alike.

TEA ROOMS

Café Storch – Aachener Straße 11. Tea here is prepared with specially filtered water.

Masal-Salon de Thé – Zülpicher Straße 85. 150 varieties of tea are listed on the menu in this Salon du Thé.

Schorschs Teestube – Schillingstraße 6. Impressive selection of aromatic green teas.

BEER CELLARS

Früh am Dom – Am Hof 12-14. The city's best-known beer cellar with three different levels of gastronomy. This is the place to meet.

Gaffel – Alter Markt 20-22. An archetypal beer cellar atmosphere reigns in this protected building.

Früh im Veddel – Chlodwigplatz 28. "Kölsch" in the south of town.

Em Golde Kappes – Neusser Straße 295. The beer cellar *Em Golde Kappes* acts as a local trademark for the district of Nippes.

Sion – Unter Taschenmacher 5-7. Besides the 500 seats inside the beer cellar, there are also seats outside in the covered beer garden.

WINE BARS

Beiss'l – Otto-Fischer-Straße 1. Wine-tasting in Art Deco surroundings.

Bacchus – Rathenauplatz 17. Friendly and welcoming wine bar.

Weinhaus Viertel – Darmstädter Straße 9. German wines are the focus of this wine bar in the south of town.

CAFÉ-BARS

Café Waschsalon – Ehrenstraße 77. The decor here consists of an arrangement of about 150 washing machines.

EWG – Aachener Straße 59. 1950s style bar; look out for the many original ceiling lights.

Scheinbar – Brüsseler Straße 10. Cocktail bar in the Belgian district

Café Central – Jülicher Straße 1. The ground floor of Hotel Chelsea houses one of Cologne's most popular bars with the "in" crowd.

Klein Köln – Friesenstraße 53. Open all hours for night-owls; take care with the saloon-style swing doors!

BEER GARDENS

Biergarten im Volksgarten – Volksgartenstraße 27. As soon as warm weather comes, half of Cologne gathers in this beer garden.

Em Birkenbäumchen – Neuenhöfer Allee 63a. This beer garden with about 340 seats is right next to the picturesque Beethovenpark.

Hyatt Regency Hotel – Kennedy-Ufer 2a. The hotel beer garden is right by the Deutz riverside walk. There is a great view of the cathedral and old city centre from here.

Entertainment

THEATRE

Bühnen der Stadt Köln – Offenbachplatz; ☎ 22 12 84 00. Cologne theatre has three very different stages on which to perform, namely *Halle Kalk*, *Schlosserei* and *West-end Theater*.

Volkstheater Millowitsch – Aachener Straße 5; ☎ 25 17 47. The Millowitsch family has been treading the boards of Cologne theatre since 1848.

Theater am Dom – Glockengasse 11; ☎ 2 58 01 53. Comedy and street-theatre; often with appearances by well-known German TV presenters.

Theater Der Keller – Kleingedankstraße 6; ☎ 31 80 59. The programme here is fresh, ambitious and exciting.

OPERA, BALLET, OPERETTAS AND MUSICALS

Opernhaus – Offenbachplatz; ☎ 22 18 48 00. Varied repertoire. The Tanz-Forum has won renown far beyond the local region.

Musical Dome – Hinter dem Hauptbahnhof; ☎ 28 01 (Köln-Ticket). This theatre was originally built for the Musiktheater Gaudi, but is now used for a rotating programme of musicals and other performances.

VARIETY, REVUE AND CABARET

Comedia Colonia – Löwengasse; ☎ 24 76 70. Cabaret and comedy.

Senftöpfchen-Theater – Große Neugasse; ☎ 2 58 10 58. This cabaret venue celebrated its 40th birthday in 1999.

Atelier-Theater – Roonstraße 78; ☎ 24 24 85. This underground theatre offers a variety of performances. The *Atelier-Café* opens at 4pm.

Die Machtwärter – Gertrudenstraße 24; ☎ 2 57 83 60. Cologne's oldest political cabaret.

CONCERTS

Kölner Philharmonie – Bischofsgartenstraße 1; ☎ 20 40 80. The heart of the city's musical life beats inside an inspired architectural setting.

Funkhaus Wallrafplatz – Wallrafplatz; ☎ 2 20 21 44. Broadcasting studio of the radio station Westdeutscher Rundfunk (WDR).

JAZZ

Stadtgarten – Venloer Straße 40; ☎ 9 52 99 40. The beer garden is inviting in summer months; otherwise the odd festival and some often progressive jazz concerts on frequently on offer here.

Subway – Aachener Straße 82-84; ☎ 51 79 69. Cologne's most famous jazz club; occasionally there are evenings dedicated to other styles of music.

Papa Joe's Biersalon "Klimperkasten" – Alter Markt 50-52; ☎ 2 58 21 32. A 1920s style beer hall, with jazz from 8pm onwards.

NIGHT-CLUBS, DISCOTHEQUES AND LIVE MUSIC

Alter Wartesaal – Im Hauptbahnhof; ☎ 9 12 88 50. Cologne's best-known disco is located in the station's converted first class waiting room, which originally dates from 1915.

E-Werk – Schanzenstraße 28; ☎ 96 27 90. Major concerts and mass-attendance discos in the old Mülheim electrical power station.

CINEMAS

The most modern cinema complex is the *Cinedom* (Media Park) with 13 screens. Most cinemas are located on the ring road between Rudolfplatz and Christophstraße. There are alternative cinemas in various locations in the city centre.

Dates for your diary

Carnival in February with the great Rosenmontag (Monday before Lent) parade (season traditionally begins at 11.11am), *Köln Comedy Festival* in October, *Ringfest der PopKomm* in August, *Art Cologne* in November.

The School of Cologne – Manuscript illumination and the decoration of altars were already blossoming local arts in Cologne at the beginning of the 14C. Painting attained its summit in the first half of the 15C, with the works of **The Master of St Veronica** and **Stephan Lochner**, a native of Meersburg. From 1450 onwards, under the influence of the Dutch schools, the artists of Cologne abandoned the idealistic mysticism of the Gothic period in favour of the more gracious realism of the Renaissance (Master of the Life of The Virgin, Master of the Reredos of St Bartholomew). This later work is characterized by a delicacy of colour and a certain suavity in the treatment of subjects.

Sculpture – Religious sculpture in Cologne reached its high point between the 14C and the 15C. The many **Madonnas** on display underline a particular sentimentality of approach: more than one can be classed in the so-called "style of tenderness" sweeping Europe around 1400 – the hinted smile, a softness of drapery, a lissom stance, these all mark the distinguishing traits of such Virgins of the Late Gothic School.

MODERN CITY

Industrialization in the second half of the 19C conferred on Cologne an expansion that was both rapid and remarkable. After the Second World War, **Konrad Adenauer** continued the process of modernization he had inaugurated while he was Mayor of the city between 1917 and 1933 – the year in which he was deposed by the Nazis. It was through the man destined to become the Federal Republic's first Chancellor that the university, shut down under the French occupation in 1798, was re-opened (1919); that the Deutz exhibition halls (Messehallen) were built; and that the green belts girdling the city were established. Much of the aspect of Cologne today is due to Adenauer.

War and Reconstruction – Between 1942 and 1945, continual air raids that were more than usually devastating destroyed 90% of the old town and 70% of the surrounding areas. Rebuilding of the city, under the direction of the architect **Rudolf Schwarz**, involved considerable modification of the original town plan, retaining at the same time the historic kernel at the heart of Cologne. A good example is the **Fest- und-Tanzhaus Gürzenich (GZ A)** – a municipal hall for fairs and balls which has been incorporated in the ruins of the church of St. Alban. The restored Gothic façade hides an ultra-modern interior. A copy (E Mataré) of **The Afflicted Parents**, by Käthe Kollwitz, is displayed in St Alban's church ruins as a memorial to the victims of war.

Roman Catholicism – Reverential, yet sumptuous and enormously popular, the **Corpus Christi Procession** ("Gottestracht") is an indication each year of the importance and vitality of the Church in Cologne. First winding around the cathedral, the procession subsequently embarks in boats plying between Mülheim and St. Kunibert **(FU)** on the Rhine. The city's many modern churches testify equally to the strength of faith today. The most influential figures in this renewal of sacred art are **Dominikus Böhm** and his son Gottfried.

Art and Culture – Diversity is the keyword in any consideration of cultural life in Cologne today. Apart from music and drama, the plastic arts hold pride of place: no less than 120 galleries are devoted to the exhibition of contemporary work. Two highly regarded international fairs take place here every year: the Westdeutsche Kunstmesse and **"Art Cologne"**, devoted to modern art. Beside the Schnütgen Museum, the **Josef-Haubrich-Halle (EV N)** mounts important permanent exhibitions.

Heinrich Böll (1917-85), one of the most eminent representatives of German post-war writing and winner of the Nobel Prize for Literature in 1972, was born in Cologne – and his work, sparing neither the Church nor society, is inseparable from his Rhineland birthplace.

Media City – There have been publishing houses and printers in Cologne for centuries. Building on this reputation, a great deal has been done over the past few years in the sphere of electronic media. Cologne, the media city, is currently Germany's TV capital, with eight television stations, including WDR (Westdeutscher

Carnival time in Cologne

Barten, KölnTourismus Office

293

Rundfunk), three RTL programmes, Viva, Vox and five radio stations (including Deutsche Welle, DeutschlandRadio, Westdeutscher Rundfunk, RadioKöln), with sound studios, a media park and an Academy of Media Arts. The media and communications business in Cologne brings in an annual turnover in the region of 20 billion DM.

The Carnival – The Rhinelanders' gaiety and sense of fun is evident on a daily basis throughout the year in Cologne, but it is during the carnival season that this proverbial good humour reaches its apogee.

Celebrations in Cologne start at 11min past 11 on the 11th day of the 11th month, and gradually build up to a climax during the three days preceding Ash Wednesday. Things get under way beforehand with **Weiberfastnacht**, or the Women's Carnival (on the Thursday before Shrove Tuesday – no man in a tie is safe; women go round indiscriminately cutting them off!). Then there is the people's carnival on the Sunday before Shrove Tuesday with the **Veedelszöch** and the Schullzöch (dialect words), **Rosenmontag**, the day before Shrove Tuesday with its legendary procession which includes elaborately decorated floats, bands and a cavalcade of giants, each in its own way caricaturing or parodying some aspects of current affairs *(a brochure and a leaflet detailing the routes of the processions and plenty of other important details, such as stand tickets, traffic direction and room reservation, are obtainable from the Cologne tourist office)*, and finally Shrove Tuesday (Fastnachtsdienstag), which ends at midnight with the burning of straw dolls ("Nubbel"). The carnival associations meet up on the evening of Ash Wednesday for a meal of fish.

During the carnival season, the inhabitants of Cologne and the many visitors who come for the event go wild, no one gets much sleep and peace and quiet are out of the question.

Town Life – If a sense of humour is characteristic of the city, conviviality is not far behind in the life of Cologne. This party spirit is inseparable from the "**Kölsch**" – a word standing at the same time for the local dialect and a famous beer, brewed in the region and served in huge stemmed glasses.

There is a strong sense of neighbourhood – almost rural – unity in the relationship linking the Cologne locals with their "**Veedeln**": the traditional quarters of the old town, each centred on a parish church, each preserving its own traditions. St. Severin is the oldest and most typical *(see below)*.

Cologne Carnival cast list

Funkenmariechen – This is a general description for the dancers in a troupe. In earlier times only the daughters of the regiment (from the guards) and the female sutler of the Jan van Werth cavalry bore this name.

Kölner Dreigestirn – This group, basically a Carnival committee, comprising a "Carnival Prince", a "Farmer" and a "Virgin", is enthroned in January and is in charge until midnight on Shrove Tuesday. During this period the characters represent the Cologne Carnival at official events.

The Carnival **Prince** has been in existence since 1871. His dress however is based on Burgundian fashion from the end of the 15C. His get-up is completed by a wand (a sort of "tickling stick"), a fertility symbol borrowed from Germanic rite.

The **Virgin** stands for the independent city of Cologne. The crown which she wears is intended to represent the medieval city wall. In fact, "she" is traditionally played by a man in drag, since in times gone by only men were allowed to take part in the carnival.

Finally the **Farmer** signifies that Cologne is part of a greater German farming community. His hat is decorated with 125 peacock feathers as a symbol of immortality, and thus of the continued existence of the free city of Cologne. His flail symbolizes his fitness to fight and his city keys the force of law.

The Dreigestirn resides in the so-called "Hofburg", a suite in a top Cologne hotel, during the period between the proclamation and Ash Wednesday.

But in addition to their particular corner, all Cologne citizens appreciate that part of the old town bordering the Rhine. Remodelled in the 1980s, this is now, night and day, one of the liveliest parts of the city.

Since the riverside highway has been diverted through tunnels between the Hohenzollern and Deutzer bridges, land has been freed for the establishment of attractive **gardens** (Rheingarten) (**GYZ**) where the inhabitants can walk or relax in calm surroundings immediately above the water. **Boat excursions** leave from this point.

Rudolph, KölnTourismus Office

KÖLN

The **Dance Fountain** (Tanzbrunnen), which holds open-air events, situated in the 40ha/100-acre **Rheinpark** on the far (eastern) side of the river, continues nevertheless to be very popular. The best way to get there is by ferry or by **cable-car** (Rheinseilbahn), which runs from Easter until the end of October from a terminal near the zoo. Leave by the Konrad-Adenauer-Ufer (**FU**). Events held at the **Kölnarena** in Deutz are very popular. With 18 000 seats, this is the largest multi-purpose venue in Germany.

CATHEDRAL ⊘ (GY)

The cultural heart of Cologne beats in the immediate vicinity of the central station and the **Hohenzollernbrücke** – the busiest railway bridge in the world, with a train crossing it every two minutes, day and night. Not far from Germany's best-known church, Cologne Cathedral, are several outstanding museums. The Römisch-Germanisches Museum and Diözesanmuseum rub shoulders with the Wallraf-Richartz-Museum/Museum Ludwig, built in 1986 by P Busmann and G Haberer – a piece of modernistic architecture whose saw-tooth roofing contrasts with the Gothic spires of the cathedral and the silhouette of the Gründerzeit railway station. The complex also includes, at basement level, the **Philharmonia** auditorium. From the Heinrich-Böll-Platz, where the museums are located, a series of terraces leads down to the northern part of Rheingarten.

★★★ **Dom (Cathedral)** – It took more than 600 years to complete this gigantic edifice. In 1164, when Frederick Barbarossa donated **relics of the Magi** to the town of Cologne, an accelerating influx of pilgrims began, and by 1248 the need for a new and larger place of worship had become pressing. Thus began the construction of a new cathedral, the first Gothic church in the Rhineland, its original design based on those in Paris, Amiens and Reims, although the size of its exterior far exceeds theirs.

The chancel was completed c 1300. The south tower was built in two levels by 1410. Almost the whole of the ground plan of the present building had taken shape up to the level of the ground floor by 1560, when the medieval construction project was called off.

More than three centuries elapsed before the gap in the building was to be filled: it was not until 1842, when neo-Gothic fever shook Romantic Germany, that work on the original plans was resumed. In 1880 the cathedral was at last ceremoniously consecrated in the presence of Emperor Wilhelm I. UNESCO has declared the cathedral one of the world's cultural heritage sites.

At first, the modern visitor is overwhelmed by the sheer size of the building and the profusion of its ornate decoration. The **twin-towered western façade** marks the peak of achievement in the style known as Flamboyant Gothic. Stepped windows, embellished gables, slender buttresses, burst upwards, ever upwards, slimly in line with the tapering spires that reach a height of 157m/515ft. The apse facing the Rhine, spined with a multitude of turrets and pinnacles is a bravura expression of architectural prowess and enthusiasm. The **bronze doors** (1) in the south transept entrance (1948-53) are by Mataré (Celestial Jerusalem above; Cologne in flames on the right). Entering the cathedral by the west door, one appreciates the sweep of the nave

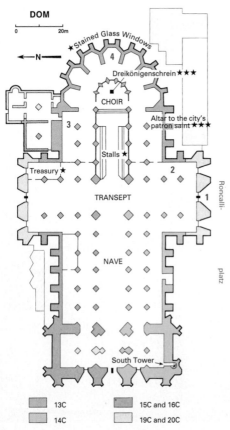

DOM

0   20m

★ Stained Glass Windows

← N

Dreikönigenschrein ★★★

CHOIR

Altar to the city's patron saint ★★★

Stalls ★

Treasury ★

TRANSEPT

Roncalli-platz

NAVE

South Tower

13C
14C
15C and 16C
19C and 20C

in a single glance, but until the transept is reached, the building's colossal proportions cannot truly be taken in. The nave, as far as the choir, is 144m/472ft long, 45m/148ft wide, and 43.5m/143ft high. Seen from the nave, the choir appears to float at some infinite distance, while the vaulting arched far above seems to reach a height that is completely unreal.

The five Late Gothic **stained-glass windows**★ in the north aisle (1507-08) depict the lives of The Virgin and St Peter. The Kreuzkapelle, a chapel off the north ambulatory, houses the **Cross of Gero**★ (Gerokreuz) (3), a unique example of 10C Ottonian art. In the axial chapel (Dreikönigskapelle) is a very old stained-glass window, the **Ältere Bibelfenster** (4), which was put in place in 1265. Behind the High Altar is the shrine of the Three Magi, the **Dreikönigenschrein**★★★. This masterpiece of medieval goldsmithing, intricately decorated with different figures, contains the relics said to be of the Three Magi. The reliquary, in the form of a basilica with unusually large dimensions (2.20m/7ft long), was begun in 1190 and completed in 1225 by Cologne master craftsmen. The last chapel in the south ambulatory (Marienkapelle) contains the celebrated altarpiece of the city's patrons, the **Altar der Stadtpatrone**★★★, painted c 1440 by **Stephan Lochner** and illustrating The Adoration of the Magi (centre section). Side panels portray the patron saints of the city of Cologne: St Ursula and her Virgins on the left; St Gereon on the right. Against a pillar on the south wall nearby stands a figure of **The Madonna of Milan**, a Virgin and Child which resembles in style the figures on the pillars in the choir which date from 1270 to 1280.

The south transept houses a large Flemish polyptych of 1521 with double side panels known as the Altarpiece of the Five Moors (2) **(Agilolphusaltar)**.

Choir ⊘ – The finely carved **choir stalls**★ (Chorgestühl), the most extensive medieval example in Germany, contain 104 places. High up above the stalls, on each of the chancel walls, frescoes dating from c 1332 to 1340 represent the legends of various saints.

The 14 **statues** incorporated in the pillars of the chancel (Chorpfeilerstatuen) are of Jesus, Mary and the 12 Apostles.

★ **Treasury** (Domschatzkammer) ⊘ – *Enter via the north transept.* The cathedral treasury contains gold and silver liturgical plate, crosiers, pectoral crosses, the baroque shrine to St Engelbert, St Peter's crosier and a reliquary monstrance with St Peter's chain, and Late Antique fabric with the Three Magi. *A new treasury was opened in the Gothic vaults beneath the sacristy at the end of 1999.*

South Tower (Südturm) – A very steep stairway *(509 steps)* leads to a **platform** from which, at a height of 97m/318ft, a splendid panorama of Cologne and the surrounding country can be enjoyed. Do not neglect the **belfry** (Glockenstube). The largest of the nine bells, **St Peter's Bell** (Petersglocke) was cast in 1923. At an overall weight of 24t (the clapper alone accounts for 800kg/1 763lb) this is the biggest swinging church bell in the world.

OLD TOWN

★ **Historisches Rathaus** (Historic town hall) (GZ) – The building with its reconstructed Gothic **tower** dating from 1407 to 1414 (61m/200ft high, *carillon at noon and 5pm*) and the Flemish style **Renaissance pavilion** (1569-73) lies at the heart of the old Jewish quarter, which is evoked by street names such as Judengasse and Salomonsgasse. In 1349, the ghetto was stormed, despite its defensive gates and

---

Eau de Cologne

The people of Cologne were familiar with this "aqua mirabile" in as early as the 16C, although it did not become a commercial success until the 18C. The fact that it finally did is thanks to the enterprising spirit of a family of Italian immigrants, the Farinas, of whom the most famous is **Johann Maria Farina**. "Cologne water" (Kölnisch Wasser) was considered to have medicinal properties and was believed to cure a number of diverse ills. In the wake of the Farina family's success, a number of other producers of the wonder-water sprang up, with the result that "Eau de Cologne" became famous and a best-seller for the export market. The new wave of producers included a certain Wilhelm Mühlens, who founded a company in Glockengasse in 1792. Under Napoleon, the use of Eau de Cologne as a medicine was banned, whereupon the manufacturers hastily began marketing their cure-all as toilet water. Also during the French occupation of Cologne, the city's street numbering was radically altered and as a result the house where Mühlens' business was located became no 4711 Glockengasse. In 1875, this number was registered as a trade mark for authentic Eau de Cologne. *(Carillon in the gable of no 4711 Glockengasse plays the Marseillaise every hour from 9am to 9pm).*

KÖLN

curfew system; its inhabitants were murdered and their homes set alight. Right by the town hall, part of the Jewish baths, or **Mikwe** (c 1170), have been preserved and are now covered by a glass pyramid *(it is possible to visit the baths Monday to Friday – the key is held by the porter of the town hall)*.

Prätorium ⊙ **(GZ C)** – *The entrance is a little hard to find as it is tucked away near the underground car park in Kleine Budengasse* **(GZ 68)**. The foundations of the Roman governor's palace (1C-4C) were excavated after the war and are largely preserved. Cracks in the mighty walls suggest that the previous, and also largest, building on this site must have collapsed. In the antechamber are small sculptures, bricks and receptacles dating from Roman times. Vistors can also view the Roman **sewer**, which was used as an air-raid shelter by Cologne townspeople during the Second World War.

Gürzenich (GZ A) – This was one of the first secular Gothic buildings (1441-44) and served as a model for many of the townhouses. The "council's dance hall" was used for receptions and banquets in the Middle Ages and then, after a break, from the 19C on, when the carnival in its present form was born.
Down towards the banks of the Rhine lies the Heumarkt, currently the site of archeological excavations, although there are plans to turn it into an underground car park eventually. To the north is the **Alter Markt** with Jan van Werth's fountain (1895), a major role-player in the carnival, as it is from here that Weiberfastnacht gets underway the Thursday before the three "crazy days" at the climax of the carnival (before Ash Wednesday).
Between Alter Markt and the Rhine lies the **Martinsviertel**, a district famous for its tourist cafés and bars. In front of the Romanesque church of St. Martin stand bronze sculptures of two local characters: Tünnes, a well-meaning if somewhat naive peasant, and Schäl, an altogether more worldly wise businessman. This pair are supposed to encapsulate the characteristics of local people.

MUSEUMS

★★★ **Wallraf-Richartz-Museum/Museum Ludwig** ⊙ **(FV M²)** – This double museum on the banks of the Rhine boasts 60 rooms – a complex including not only the Philharmonia but also a whole series of cultural institutions: a museum of photography (Agfa Foto-Historama, *see below*), a graphics collection, the Cologne cinematheque, and a library.

In summer 2000, the Wallraf-Richartz-Museum is scheduled to move home. It will occupy a generously proportioned new building designed by Oswald M. Ungers in Martinstraße (GZ M¹², next to the Gürzenich). As a result, the Museum Ludwig in the present building on the south side of the cathedral will gain more space for its rapidly expanding collection.

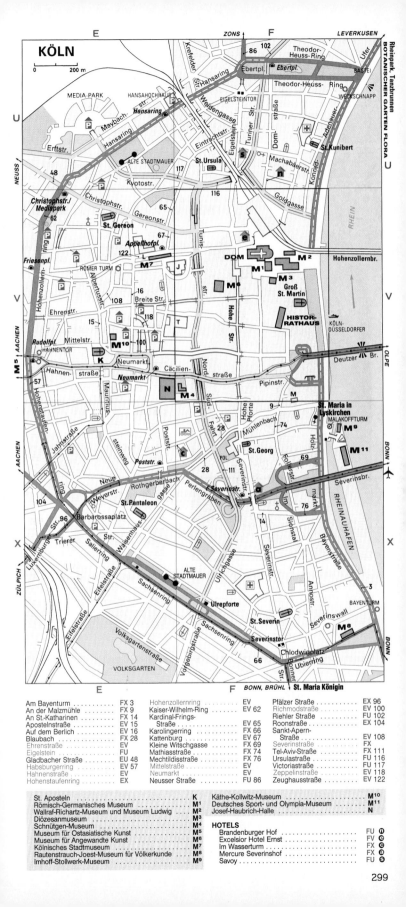

KÖLN

This change means that the locations given below for the following works of art, both for the Wallraf-Richartz-Museum (which will then be in its new site) and the Museum Ludwig, will no longer be correct. The new arrangements were not known at the time of going to press.

Wallraf-Richartz-Museum – *First floor*. Works by German, Italian, Flemish, Dutch and French painters from the 14C to the 19C are on display here. The priceless **Medieval Painters of Cologne** collection, culminating with the Late Gothic work of Stefan Lochner and his contemporaries, is unique. Note in particular the **Master of St Veronica** with the early 15C triptych *The Holy Family*; the **Master of Life of the Virgin** with an Annunciation triptych and *The Vision of St Bernard* (late 15C); and **Stefan Lochner's** own **Virgin and the Rose Bush** (c 1450) – a masterpiece which impresses not only by its use of colour, the delicacy of yellows and golds, but also by the serenity of expression on the faces.

Piper and drummer by Albrecht Dürer

Rheinisches Bildarchiv, Köln

Works by the **Italian Old Masters** Martini and Lorenzetti show the pan-European dimension of religious painting in the Middle Ages. Display panels with text and illustrations explain the techniques of medieval painting, the use of illustrative themes in those times, and the history of Cologne.

Bartholomäus Bruyn the Elder (1493-1555) was one of the rare painters who took orders for portraits from private individuals. Influenced by the Mannerists of Antwerp, he was much esteemed and sought after by the patrician burghers of Cologne. Note, in this gallery, the portraits of *Gerhard Pilgrim* and *Heinrich Salsburg.*

Among the **German Old Masters** on view are **Dürer** *(The Fife Player* and *The Tambourine Player)* and Lucas Cranach the Elder *(Virgin and Child)*. The 16C Italians are represented by Titian and Tintoretto.

The collection of **Dutch and Flemish painting of the 17C** offers such great names as Rubens *(The Holy Family* and *The Stigmata of St Francis)*, Ruisdael *(View of a River)*, Frans Hals *(The Fisherman's Daughter)* and **Rembrandt**, with the famous self-portrait in which the artist, already old, wearing a turban, regards the spectator obliquely, a smile on his lips. After this comes the section featuring 17C and 18C painters: Spanish (Murillo), Italian (Tiepolo, Bordone), and French (Boucher: *Young Girl Resting*; landscapes by Claude Lorrain).

French and German artists dominate the section devoted to the 19C. The German Romantics are represented by, among others, CD Friedrich; the Realists by the Cologne-born Wilhelm Leibl (Portrait of *H Pallenberg*). The German Impressionist School offers work by Liebermann, Corinth and Klinger. With the Romantic movement (Delacroix) as a point of departure, French painting advances via Realism (Courbet) to the Impressionists: Renoir, Monet, Sisley, Cézanne, Van Gogh *(The Railway Bridge)* and Gauguin. Sculptures by Degas and Rodin are also on display.

Museum Ludwig – First and second floor (modern classics); basement. There is an important collection of 20C art in this museum, with the **Expressionist** movement particularly well represented. Among the painters of the **Brücke** group, Kirchner is noteworthy with his *Five Women in the Street*, as are his associates Heckel and Nolde.

The **Blauer Reiter** movement is represented by Macke, Marc, Kandinsky and Jawlensky; Expressionism by **Kokoschka** and Beckmann. A separate section is reserved for art between the two World Wars: Constructivism, the Bauhaus (for example Klee's *Highway and Byways*), New Objectivity, the Cologne Progressionists.

One of the museum's strong points is embodied in a collection of **Russian Avant-Garde Art** (1910-30). Paintings and "spatial constructions" by Gontscharova, Larinov, Malevitz and Popova vividly convey the strength of the country's artistic renewal before the cultural freeze under Stalin.

The department devoted to the Surrealists reveals that the **Dada** movement was in fact born in Cologne, just before the First World War. Apart from oil paintings, gouaches and collages by Max Ernst (Friend's Meeting), who was born in Brühl, near Cologne, exhibits include work by Hans Arp, Schwitters, Miró, Dalí and Magritte.

French modern art is represented by Modigliani, Maillol, and above all the **Cubists** Braque, Léger, Delaunay and Juan Gris. A highlight of this section is the display of Pablo Picasso's work, which covers all phases of its development in one of the world's most comprehensive collections.

Paintings by Baumeister and Nay introduce the visitor to post-war German art and the "renewal" of the 1960s, in which **Joseph Beuys** and the Group Zero played an important part. American abstract painting is well represented, (Rothko, Newman, de Kooning). A further strength of the museum's collection is the display of **Pop Art** – oriented once more towards the object – which had its heyday in the United States in the 1960s. The paintings, silk-screen prints and environments by Rauschenberg, Warhol and Segal are reflections of modern consumerism with a note of social criticism. European art of this period is represented by works by the artists of **Nouveau Réalisme**: Arman, Klein, Saint-Phalle, Tinguely, Tàpies, Burri and Dubuffet.

German contemporary art on display includes works by Baselitz, Richter, Polke, Penck and Kiefer, among others, giving an overview of the evolution in German art over the last few decades.

Numerous works by contemporary artists from Europe, America, Japan and China, complete with a whole series of giant installations, illustrate the most recent artistic trends.

Visitors should not forget the **sculpture terrace** on the second floor, from where there is also a good view of the east end of the cathedral.

Prints, drawings and photographic collections – First floor. Guided tour possible. Temporary exhibitions.

Agfa Foto-Historama (Museum of Photography) ⊘ – Ground floor and first floor. Compiled from various private collections (the Stengler Collection, the archives of the Agfa company etc), these three galleries present an overall view of 150 years of photography. The impact of the displays derives from the juxtaposition of ancient exhibits and photographs of great historical or cultural value. Thus the history of photography can be followed through its

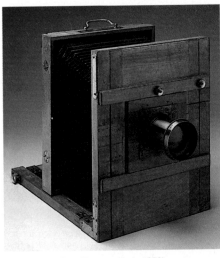

Travelling camera (c 1880)

Rheinisches Bildarchiv, Köln

various stages – magic lantern, daguerreotype (1839), calotype (Talbot's negative process, 1841), amateur interest, spooled film (Eastman, 1888) – to the invention of microfilm and the small, high-tech cameras of today.

★★ **Römisch-Germanisches Museum** ⊘ (FV **M'**) – Capital of the Roman province known as Lower Germania, Cologne enjoyed immense prosperity between the 1C and the mid 4C, due largely to fruitful exchanges between the civilization of the colonizers and the Germanic culture of the Ubii. In this museum, such evidence of the period as has been discovered over the centuries is on display in this building south of the cathedral. The exhibits are presented thematically. (For those preferring to avoid school parties, for which this museum is a popular attraction, we recommend a visit in the afternoon or at weekends).

In the basement is the **Dionysius Mosaic★**, an exceptionally well-preserved Roman mosaic made of one and a 1.5 million fragments of stone (measuring 14.5x7m/48x23ft). The larger pictures depict a drunken god of wine surrounded by people dancing and playing musical instruments. The banqueting hall (part of a Roman villa) was uncovered during the construction of an air-raid bunker in

1941 and preserved on its original site. The adjacent rooms evoke not only funerary rites (tombstones and votive items) but also the everyday life of the ancient Romans: games, pots, leather sandals, writing equipment and a cut-throat razor.

Another highlight of the museum is the **Mausoleum of Lucius Poblicius**, an officer of the Roman 5th Legion who settled in Cologne for his retirement in 1C AD. The tomb, which was reconstructed in the 1960s, stands 14.6m/48ft high and is best viewed from the upper floors. It is easy enough to distinguish the original stones, which were discovered and dug up by residents of the south of Cologne, from those added during reconstruction.

The different levels of the museum introduce the visitor to Roman statuary as well as architecture (fortified gateway inscribed with the abbreviated Roman name for the town: CCAA). There are also examples of transport, port activity, coinage, Roman religion and games. An interesting exhibit, although it is not the original, is the **Philosophers' Mosaic** with Pompeiian-style frescoes.

A valuable collection of **glassware**★★ testifies to the incredible wealth of imagina-tion in Roman glassmaking workshops up to the 4C. The 2C **Schlangenfadergläser** (an early form of filigree glass) made in Cologne were a big hit for the ancient Roman export market. Note also the unique 4C **vasa diatreta** blown several times to produce a thick glass which is then cut and undercut to give an outer tracery in coloured relief and a Greek inscription on the rim. There are only six of this kind of vessel in the world. Some of the ancient Roman, Frankish and "Barbaric" **jewellery** and ornaments which are on display would not look out of place in a modern jeweller's window.

★ **Diözesan-Museum (Diocesan Museum)** ⊘ **(M³)** – The relatively small Diocesan Museum regards itself as an art museum, and has recently moved resolutely in a new direction, by increasingly acquiring examples of contemporary art on Christian themes. The result is a vigorous interplay between old and new art.

The most famous piece is Stefan Lochner's **Virgin with Violets**, where each flower represents one of the virtues of Mary. An item by **Joseph Beuys** with a munitions chest and crucifix is particularly impressive.

A particular highlight of the collection is the 11C-16C sculpture and gold work, including the "Herimannkruzifix", a crucifix with little Roman lapis lazuli heads.

There are plans for a new museum building, scheduled to open in 2003, on the site of the ruins of the Late Gothic Kolumbakirche. The designs are the work of Swiss architect Peter Zumthor.

Additional Museums

★★ **Schnütgen-Museum** ⊘ **(GZ M⁴)** – The 12C former **Cäcilienkirche**, one of the dozen Romanesque religious edifices still standing in the city, makes a suitable site for this museum devoted to sacred art from the 6C to the 19C, but essentially concentrated on the Middle Ages.

Numerous **Madonnas in wood** illustrate the local "tender" style in statuary. **St Hieronymus and the Lion** (Erkelenz, 1460-70) is a masterpiece of Late Gothic woodcarving. The Wassenberg choir stalls and a series of marble portrait statues from the cathedral (c 1300-10) are additional, important examples of work from the Gothic period. The gold altar panel (c 1170) is from St Ursula's Church.

A collection of medieval items in **ivory**, most of them from Byzantium, France or other parts of Germany, is of particularly fine workmanship. It includes figurines, boxes, portable altars and copies of the Gospels. **Goldsmiths' and silversmiths' work** on display (reliquaries, busts, liturgical items) is equally impressive. Note, too, the items in bronze made by Christians from the East. The museum furthermore boasts a comprehensive collection of textiles dating from the Middle Ages to the 18C.

★★ **Museum für Ostasiatische Kunst (Museum of Far Eastern Art)** ⊘ **(EV M³)** – Univer-sitätsstraße 100.

Germany's oldest museum of Far Eastern art (founded in 1909), was relocated in 1977 to a modern building designed by Kunio Maekawa (1905-86), a student of Le Corbusier. The Japanese garden was laid out by contemporary artist Masayuki Nagare (b 1923).

The permanent exhibition displays works of Chinese, Japanese and Korean art, from the Neolithic Age to the present. Among the oldest exhibits are some **bronze vessels** from China (16C-12C BC). The museum also has a vast collection of **Buddhist art** from China and Japan. The collection of Chinese ceramics covers all phases of the evolution of this craft until the end of Imperial rule. The reconstruction of the study of a man of letters, complete with 17C Chinese furniture and writing equipment, gives an insight into the culture of the scholarly elite. There is a beautiful collection of Chinese landscape paintings and Japanese painted screens.

Ceremonial urn, Museum
für Ostasiastische Kunst

For those less well acquainted with the culture of the Far East, the museum provides a series of detailed and informative commentaries on the exhibits.

* **Museum für Angewandte Kunst (Museum of Applied Arts)** ⊘ **(GYZ M⁶)** - This museum contains a comprehensive collection of applied arts from the Middle Ages to the present. It boasts an extensive collection of furniture, and a **ceramics** section which gives an overview ranging from stoneware from the Rhineland, to Islamic and Italian majolica, to European porcelain over the last three centuries.

As far as metalwork is concerned, there are excellent displays of 16C and 17C pewter and of **jewellery**. German Waldglas ("forest glass", thick greenish, yellowish or brownish glassware produced in the Middle Ages), Venetian filigree glasses, Baroque goblets and Jugendstil glasses (Emile Gallé) represent some of the **glassware** on display.

Among **textiles**, there are Late Gothic woven hangings from the upper Rhine, 13C to 18C silk fabrics and a collection of fashion ware.

Visitors should not miss the **sculpture** department which contains works by Tilman Riemenschneider, small bronze sculptures from the Renaissance and large animal figures from the Meissen porcelain manufacture (Kirchner, Kändler).

The **design** department gives a comprehensive overview of 20C design right through to the present.

Kölnisches Stadtmuseum (Metropolitan Historical Museum) ⊘ **(EV M⁷)** - Cologne's eventful past is evoked in the old arsenal by arms and armour, pictures of battles, weights and measures, episcopal tombstones and portraits of eminent townspeople. There is an interesting **historical model** of the city.

Käthe-Kollwitz-Museum ⊘ **(EV M¹⁰)** - This museum in Neumarktpassage displays, in between special exhibitions, the largest collection in the world of the work of Käthe Kollwitz, first woman art professor at the Prussian Academy in Berlin. This graphic artist and sculptress (1867-1945) devoted her life's work to fighting against war and for social justice, paying particular attention to the plight of women and children (she lost her own son in the First World War).

Rautenstrauch-Joest-Museum für Völkerkunde (Ethnographic Museum) ⊘ **(FX M⁸)** - This museum offers fine displays of **Thai and Khmer ceramics and sculpture** from the 8C to the 16C and a good collection of ancient Egyptian art. The recently renovated section on the art of north American Indians and Eskimos is very interesting.

A new building is planned in which it will be possible to exhibit the large collection in more detail.

* **Imhoff-Stollwerck-Museum** ⊘ - *Rheinauhafen*.
This highly original museum takes as its subject that most fascinating of foodstuffs, **chocolate**. The museum's architecture and **site★** are fascinating in themselves: a customs warehouse from the Gründerzeit period has been integrated into a modern glass building, which visitors get to across a historical swing bridge over the Rhine. The building looks for all the world like a ship floating on the river.

Visitors are greeted by a chocolate fountain, which they may sample, thus setting an appropriately self-indulgent mood for the rest of the tour. Besides various delicious end-products, the display includes interesting information on the 3000-year history and production of chocolate, a miniature chocolate factory, old-fashioned chocolate-vending machines, a greenhouse that visitors may enter full of cocoa plants and other tropical plants, and a collection of beautiful silver and porcelain drinking vessels reflecting the fact that chocolate was once an expensive luxury drink enjoyed only by the aristocracy. The museum also recounts the history of the traditional chocolate-

Chocolate-vending machine

making firm of Stollwerck, founded in Cologne in 1839. This is presented in a very accessible way in a cinema dedicated to chocolate, in which adverts from 1926 to the present are screened – to the delight of nostalgia buffs.

Since autumn 1999, the **German Sports and Olympics Museum** (FX **M¹¹**, Deutsches Sport- und Olympia-Museum) has been open, occupying a listed customs warehouse directly next to the Stollwerck Chocolate Museum. It is dedicated to presenting the various aspects of national, international and Olympic sports.

ROMANESQUE CHURCHES

The Romanesque period in Cologne, from the mid 10C to the mid 13C, saw the construction of numerous churches. In the old town alone, 12 churches from that era are still standing, one of which now houses the Schnütgen-Museum (see above). The damage from the Second World War has now nearly all been repaired. Strolling through its old streets, therefore, the visitor gets a good idea of the different periods and varying styles of Rhineland Romanesque architecture. Certain concepts of religious design – the **trefoil chancel**, for instance – originated indeed in the city (see Introduction).

Groß St. Martin (GZ) – This church, once a monastery, is built on what was once an island in the river, opposite the Roman port. The imposing square tower, rising 84m/276ft above the transept crossing, lends, with its four octagonal turrets, a fortress-like aspect to the whole. In the forecourt, on the corner in front of the hostel, note the life-size bronze statues of well-known local figures (**Tünnes** and **Schäl**).

★ **St. Maria im Kapitol** (GZ B) – This late Ottonian church (11C), built on the site of a Roman capitol temple, features the oldest **trefoil chancel**★ (clover-leaf) in Cologne. The crypt extends beneath almost the entire body of the chancel;

it is the largest in Germany after the crypt in Speyer Cathedral.

On the left side of the east clover-leaf is the Madonna of St Hermann-Joseph altarpiece (c 1180). The **Renaissance choir screen** is richly decorated with sculpture (c 1525). In front of it, to the left, is the Limburg Madonna (late 13C). At the west end of the nave there are two memorial slabs dedicated to Plectrudis, wife of Pepin the Middle; that on the left dates from 1160, that on the right from 1280.

At the west end of the south side aisle are some Romanesque **wooden doors**★ dating from 1065.

St. Maria in Lyskirchen (FX) – This triple-aisle basilica was built opposite the entrance to the Rhine port (c 1220). The exterior is uninteresting (the south tower is unfinished), but

St. Maria-im-Kapitol

there are splendid 13C **frescoes**★★ inside. A series of 24 biblical scenes appears among the ribbed vaulting of the central nave.

St. Georg (FX) – This church, a flat-roofed basilica with colonnades, dates from the 11C. The vaulting above the choir and nave is 12C, the same period as the west end, with 5m/16ft-thick walls and something of the air of a fortified tower. It encloses the west chancel, in which there is a 14C forked Cross and a Late Romanesque font.

St. Severin (FX) – This is the oldest Christian foundation in Cologne, dating back to the 4C. It is built on the site of a **Roman-Frankish burial ground**. The present building dates from the 13C (chancel) and 15C (west tower and nave). There is a fine Gothic nave in the **interior**★. Note, in the main chancel, paintings by the **Master of St Severinus**; a 13C forked Cross above the parish altar; and behind the high altar, a shrine to the saint (restored in the 19C). The actual **tomb of St Severinus**, Bishop of Cologne c 400 and now one of the patron saints of the city, is kept in the crypt (11C-13C).

★ **St. Pantaleon (EX)** – The nave and impressive Westwerk, which originally served as a law court and musicians' gallery, are examples of Ottonian architecture (10C). The **rood screen★** closing off the chancel is Late Gothic. The 10C tombs of Archbishop Bruno of Cologne, brother of Otto the Great, and Empress Theophanu, wife of Otto II, are in the crypt and south side aisle. Lapidarium with Ottonian stonework fragments in the west gallery; treasury.

St. Aposteln (EV K) – Pure Rhineland Romanesque, this 11C church has a **trefoil chancel★** which was possibly built after a fire in c 1200. The painted decor is the work of church painter Hermann Gottfried (1988-93). Outside, the 13C apse, flanked by two octagonal lantern turrets, is adorned with a beautiful Romanesque gallery and blind arcading. An octagonal tower tops the transept crossing.

★ **St. Gereon (EV)** – *Entrance via Christopherstraße.*
A Christian memorial church to St Gereon (one of Cologne's patron saints) and other unknown martyrs of the Theban Legion, said to have been butchered during Diocletian's persecution of Christians, was built on the site of a Roman graveyard in the 4C. This ancient elliptical building with its eight niches was extended in the 11C and 12C by the addition of nave, towers and crypt (11C mosaic floor, stone altar from 1540). At the beginning of the 13C, a monumental **decagon★** was built above the church. The baptismal chapel also dates from this period; it is adorned with 13C murals (of St Gereon and the Theban martyrs) and contains an early-16C altarpiece.
In the nave (north side) is an interesting tabernacle (1608), depicting the Last Supper (carved in relief); on the south side of the decagon is a colourfully painted Madonna and Crescent Moon (1430). The modern windows in the decagon were created by Wilhelm Buschulte and Georg Meistermann.

St. Andreas (GY) – This Late Romanesque church was built in the first quarter of the 13C, as a vaulted basilica on pillars with a two-storey west transept, short nave, octagonal transept tower and transept with a trefoil apse. It features some remarkable architectural sculpture. At the beginning of the 15C, the chancel was demolished and a Gothic chancel added, modelled on the glass architectural shrine at Aachen (1414-20). The Gothic side chapels contain murals from the first half of the 13C.
The sarcophagus of **Albert the Great** (c 1200-80) lies in the crypt, which also contains the remnants of 14C murals.

St. Ursula (FU) – In the north aisle are 30 plates (1456) by **Stephan Lochner** depicting the martyrdom of St Ursula. The daughter of a British king was murdered by Huns along with 10 of her companions in the 5C. As the story was passed down through the ages, the number of martyred maidens increased to 11 000. In the south transept is the treasury, **Goldene Kammer★** ⊙, built by Johannes Crane in 1643, which contains over 120 reliquary busts and 700 skulls. The shrine of St Ursula (1256) and the **Aetherius Shrine** (1170-80) are to be found in the high chancel.

St. Kunibert (FU) – The last wholly Romanesque church in Cologne was completed in 1247, a year before building began on Cologne Cathedral. The twin towers flanking the chancel are intact. Highlights of the Romanesque decor include the **stained-glass windows★** in the chancel (1230) and the murals in the baptistery, painted at almost the same time (scenes from the life of the Virgin Mary). In 1998, St Kunibert's Church was made into a basilica.
The Annunciation group (Virgin Mary and Angel at the Lectern) in the transept crossing is the work of Gothic sculptors (1439). The folds of clothing and the gestures of the larger than life-size subjects already herald the development towards Realism. The treasury contains precious reliquary busts and a length of silk Sassanid fabric (Byzantine or Syrian, c 800).

ADDITIONAL SIGHTS

Botanischer Garten und Flora(Botanical Park) ⊙ – *Leave by the Konrad-Adenauer-Ufer* (**FU**).
In the **botanical gardens** there are plants from all over the world, either growing in the open air or in hothouses (tropical and subtropical). The **Florapark** is a historical garden laid out following designs by Peter Josef Lenné and including formal French-Baroque style, Italian Renaissance and a vast English style landscape garden. There is also some contemporary landscape gardening.

St. Kolumba (GZ) – This 1950 church by **Gottfried Böhm** is built on the site of a Gothic church destroyed during the war. Note the luminosity of the chancel with its blue stained-glass windows, and a 1450 statue of the **Mater Dolorosa**, saved from the ruins.

St. Peter (GZ) – This Late Gothic gallery-basilica was built in 1525, and the **stained-glass windows** date from this period. Displayed in the choir is the **Crucifixion of St Peter** (1639), one of the last works by Rubens, who grew up in St Peter's parish and whose father is interred in this church. Annexed to the church is an international exhibition centre for contemporary art.

St. Mariä Himmelfahrt (GY F) – The spirit of the Counter-Reformation which inspired the building of this Jesuit church (1618-78) led to a conscious blending of Romanesque, Gothic and Baroque styles, inside as well as outside. Among Gothic elements borrowed by the Alsatian architect Christoph Wamser are the vaulting in the nave and the windows in the entrance façade. Rich Baroque decorations (restored) adorn the pillars which support galleries above the side aisles.

St. Maria-Königin – *Access via Bonner Straße southeast of the plan* **(FX)**.
This modern church of vertically laid red brick was designed by **Dominikus Böhm** in 1954. Shades of grey predominate in the **glass wall**★ *(south)* illuminating the interior.

EXCURSIONS

★★ **Schloß Augustusburg** – *13km/8mi to the south. See BRÜHL.*

★ **Altenberger Dom** – *20km/12mi to the northeast.*
This former Cistercian abbey church (still known locally as the Bergischer Dom – cathedral of the Berg Duchy) lies in a green valley much appreciated by the city dwellers of Cologne. The pure Gothic building (1259-1379) has been a "parallel church" since 1857, celebrating Roman Catholic and Protestant rites alternately. Note especially the huge (18x8m/59x26ft) **coloured glass canopy** (c 1400) above the west entrance, considered to be the largest stained-glass window in Germany, and the **grisaille stained-glass windows** in the chancel.

★ **Zons** – *24km/15mi to the north.*
This picturesque Rhineland fortified village had a **toll-house** added to it in the 14C, which has survived virtually intact and therefore represents a good example of a medieval fortification. Its walls and numerous towers lend particular charm to the site.

KONSTANZ★

CONSTANCE – Baden-Württemberg
Population 75 000
Michelin map 419 X 11 – Local map see BODENSEE

A German enclave on the Swiss shore of Lake Constance and the southern bank of the Rhine, Constance occupies an agreeable **site**★ opposite the narrows which separate the main body of the lake (known as the Bodensee in German) from its picturesque prolongation (Untersee). The foundation of the town, long attributed to the Roman emperor Constantius Chlorus (292-306), played a prominent part in the Great Schism of the West (1378-1429).

Constance, Capital of Christianity – From 1414 to 1418, a council convened in the town to attempt to re-establish the unity of the Church, which had been compromised by the pretentions of three ecclesiastical dignitaries, each claiming the right to be elected to the papal throne.
After long negotiations, two of the three rival Popes, Gregory XII and John XXIII, agreed to stand down; only Benedict XIII, who had taken refuge in Spain, remained adamant about the validity of his claim.
In 1417, the election of Martin V, who was universally recognized as the true Pope, put an end temporarily to the schism.
Three years previously, the council had summoned before it the religious reformer **Jan Hus**, Rector of the University of Prague. Hostile to German influence, Hus expounded his theses – which contested papal primacy and certain rites – was declared a heretic, and burned alive. This precursor of Protestantism was hailed as a national hero in his native Bohemia.

★THE LAKE SHORE (SEEUFER) (Y)

The lakeside part of the town is the most attractive, with the port, shady public gardens, a casino (Spielbank), ancient defensive towers such as the Rheintorturm and the Pulverturm, and the quays – especially the Seestraße – competing for the attention of the discerning tourist. The lake itself, busy with all kinds of water traffic, offers numerous opportunities for excursions. The Untersee, with its steep, indented shores, is particularly appealing.

WHERE TO STAY AND WHERE TO EAT OUT

OUR RECOMMENDATIONS

Barbarossa - Obermarkt 8-12, ☏ 0 75 31/2 20 21, Fax 0 75 31/2 76 30. Single rooms from 71DM. Historical hotel in the centre of the old town of Constance; welcoming wine bar on the first floor.

Bayerischer Hof - Rosgartenstraße 30, ☏ 0 75 31/1 30 40, Fax 0 75 31/13 04 13. Single rooms from 115DM. Classical town house in the centre of town.

Schiff am See - William-Graf-Platz 2, ☏ 0 75 31/3 10 41, Fax 0 75 31/3 29 81. Single rooms from 130DM. House on the shores of the lake with a fine view. 2min by ferry to Meersburg.

TREAT YOURSELF!

Steigenberger Inselhotel - Auf der Insel 1, ☏ 0 75 31/12 50, Fax 0 75 31/2 64 02. Single rooms from 220DM. This old Dominican monastery on a small island is not far from the old town. Splendid view.

Seehotel Siber - Seestraße 25, ☏ 0 75 31/6 30 44, Fax 0 75 31/6 48 13. Single rooms from 305DM. Modernised Jugendstil villa with terrace. Star-rated restaurant. Main courses from 60DM.

ADDITIONAL SIGHTS

★ **Münster** (Y) – Since its construction was spread over a period from the 11C to the 17C, this former cathedral lacks any artistic unity.
The **panels**★ (Türflügel) of the porch doors in the main façade are decorated with bas-relief sculptures representing scenes from the life of Christ (1470).
The 17C vaulting in the central nave rests on the arcades of the original 11C sanctuary, achieving a visual harmony that is completely Romanesque. The decoration of the organ case and the loft itself preview the Renaissance. In the north transept, a spiral staircase turret (Schnegg), finely decorated in the French Late Gothic style, leads to the vault of the east end of the building *(access to the treasury is beneath the Schnegg.)*
The 13C Mauritiuskapelle houses the Münster's most priceless piece of sculpture, the **Holy Tomb**★, a vaulted dodecagon containing three statuary groups. It is one of the few examples of its kind from the High Middle Ages, bearing a stylistic resemblance to the sculpture of Bamberg and Naumburg.
In the crypt are four plaques of gilded copper, each from a different period (11C-13C). They represent Christ in Majesty, the symbolic Eagle of St John, and St Conrad and St Pelagius, patrons of the diocese. They are known as the **Konstanzer Goldscheiben** (gilded plaques of Constance). A staircase to the right of the main door leads to a tower platform from which there is a fine view over the town and the lake.

Rathaus (Z R) – The façade of this Renaissance building is embellished with paintings that illustrate the history of Constance. In the inner courtyard – a quiet spot in the tourist season – is an elegant 16C house between two round towers.

Rosgartenmuseum ⊘ (Z M¹) – This regional museum devoted to the lakeshore areas is housed in a former corporation building. It contains a famous Paleolithic wall carving of a reindeer as well as a copy of the 1440 Ulrich Richental Chronicle. The latter is vividly illustrated, evoking the atmosphere of council meetings of the period. The museum houses comprehensive collections of artistic and cultural artefacts from the Middle Ages to the 19C.

Konzilgebäude (Z) – This former warehouse, built at the end of the 14C, was used by the Conclave of 1417 which proclaimed the election of Pope Martin V. Across the road, in a garden bordering the pleasure boat harbour, is a monument to Count Zeppelin (1838-1917), the celebrated airship inventor, who was born in Constance.

Archäologisches Landesmuseum ⊘ (Y M²) – This local archeological museum is housed in an old conventual building of the Peterhausen Abbey, which makes a very attractive setting. History comes to life in 3 000m²/32 280sq ft of exhibition space,

Roman door knocker,
Archäologisches Landesmuseum

KONSTANZ

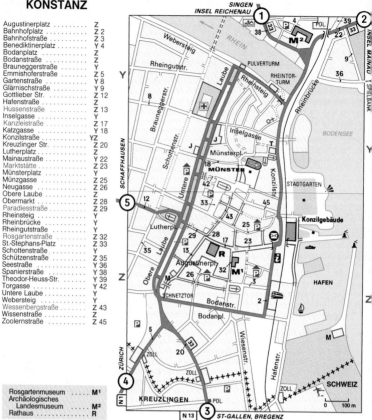

beginning with the buildings on stilts dating from 4000 BC and continuing to the industrial archeology of Ludwigsburg. Methods of archeological research are also described in an interesting way. Archeological finds from the Roman and Celtic periods form a particularly strong feature of the exhibition, while another highlight is the illustration of medieval archeology from the towns of Baden-Württemberg. Exhibits are presented by theme with clear explanatory notes. Besides the displays and reconstructions of archeological digs, there are interesting slide shows and video presentations.

EXCURSIONS

★★ **Mainau Island (Insel Mainau)** ⊙ – *7km/4.5mi. 2hr sightseeing. Leave by ② on the plan.*
The Grand Dukes of Baden laid out a large park on this 45ha/110-acre island on Lake Constance. The property of Count Lennart Bernadotte since 1932, it is a paradise for all plant enthusiasts. The juxtaposition of the palace, charming Baroque church and colourful flower beds set in green parkland contributes to the magic of the island. The mild climate means that exotic plants also thrive here. Further attractions include Germany's largest butterfly house and floral displays that change with the seasons.

★ **Reichenau Island (Insel Reichenau)** – *7km/4.5mi to the west. Leave by ① on the plan.* St Pirmin founded the first German Benedictine monastery to the east of the Rhine on Reichenau Island in 724, and the seeds which he sowed germinated into a centre for arts and science which flourished for centuries. Some quite outstanding book illuminations were produced here during the Ottonian period. Unfortunately for visitors, there are no longer any monks here, but gardeners have transformed the 430ha/1 063 acres of the island into a fertile market garden. However the three churches are its main attraction.
The late-9C Carolingian St. Georgskirche of **Oberzell** – remarkable for the harmonious design of its stepped elements – contains a series of **wall paintings**★★ (c 1000 AD), depicting the miracles of Jesus.
At **Mittelzell**, the chief town on the island, there is an **old abbey**★ (Münster St. Maria und Markus) which was built between the 8C and 12C. The robust Romanesque tower of the Westwerk is lightened in appearance by a decorative band of Lombard pilasters and friezes. The open oak **roof frame** of the nave of the church is

particularly noteworthy, being an outstanding example of medieval workmanship. The oaks are believed to have been felled in around 1236, making this possibly the oldest roof frame in Germany. There is a very beautiful sandstone Madonna in the chancel (c 1300). In the abbey **treasury★** there is a reliquary of St Mark (c 1305) fashioned in beaten silver enriched with gilt and enamels.

The former collegiate church (Stiftskirche) of St Peter and St Paul (11C-12C) stands in **Niederzell** on the western tip of the island. The wall paintings in the choir are thought to date from the beginning of the 12C. They show Christ surrounded by an almond-shaped glory, with the Apostles and Prophets beneath him.

Bad KREUZNACH ★

Rheinland-Pfalz

Population 43 000
Michelin map 417 Q 7

This mineral spa, whose origins go back to Roman times, lies in the Lower Nahe Valley, surrounded by vineyards and mixed woodland. Bad Kreuznach is celebrated both for the health-giving qualities of its **mineral springs** and for the **wines** of the Nahe region – whose qualities lie between the fresh, strong taste of the Moselle and the lighter appeal of Rhine wines. The centre of the thermal resort is on **Badewörth Island** – its downstream tip spanned by the **Alte Nahebrücke.** Both **Gothic houses** on the bridge, a trademark of the town, were first recorded in 1495. The salt-mining valley with its tiers of mineworkings is an open-air inhalation clinic. From the **Kauzenburg** *(café-restaurant on the Kauzenberg),* there is a fine view of the town and its surroundings.

★ **Römerhalle** ⊙ – *Hüffelsheimer Straße 11.* The museum is on a former smallholding at the western end of the castle park. Items discovered during archeological excavations in Bad Kreuznach and the surrounding district are on display. There are two exceptional exhibits, both of them 13C **mosaic floors★★**: one depicts the Sea god in his element; the other illustrates wild animals and gladiators in combat. Below, a **Roman central heating system** has been unearthed (hypocaust). Nearby, a **Roman villa** has been uncovered. Also close at hand is the historical Schloßpark with a small lake, tropical trees and a **museum**.

EXCURSIONS

★ **Bad Münster am Stein-Ebernburg** – *By car, 4.5km/3mi. Leave the car near the cure centre (Kurhaus); then 1hr there and back on foot.*
Go into the thermal **park★** and walk through the gardens to the Nahe. On the far side of the river is the **Rheingrafenstein★★**, a 136m/446ft rock face surmounted by the ruins of an ancient castle.
Take the ferry across and, from the Hüttental café-restaurant, climb to the panoramic platform on top.
From here, there is a fine **view★** of the Bad Münster basin and, downstream, the Rotenfels, whose sheer porphyry cliffs tower 214m/700ft above the river.

LAHNTAL

LAHN VALLEY – Hessen and Rheinland-Pfalz
Michelin map 417 O 7-9

The winding course of the lower Lahn, which is navigable although no longer used by commercial shipping, its sombre waters overlooked by wild scenery and steeply wooded banks, makes a charming setting for excursions to a number of castle ruins, castles and delightful old towns steeped in history. The 7km/4mi long meander by Balduinstein is particularly impressive. At the narrowest point, the valley sides are only 700m/2 300ft apart.

FROM BAD EMS TO WETZLAR *89km/55mi – about 4hr 30min*

Bad Ems – The Lahn valley, separating the Westerwald and the Taunus-Rhine schist massif, is rich in mineral springs, like all areas on the fringe of a volcanic region. Bad Ems, treating mainly rhino-pharyngeal affections, is one of the oldest spas in the area. In the 19C Emperor Wilhelm I of Germany was a familiar figure in the town. The modern spa centre blends harmoniously with the preserved historical spa architecture (eg in Römerstraße).
Opposite the assembly rooms, set into the quay-promenade near the Roman springs, is a flagstone (Benedettistein) bearing the date 13 July 1870 commemorating the meeting between Wilhelm and the French Ambassador, Benedetti. The Emperor categorically refused the French request that the

Hohenzollerns renounce "forever" their claims to the throne of Spain. A report of the meeting, distorted and then leaked by Bismarck, hastened the Franco-Prussian War of 1870.

Nassau – This climatic health resort in the Lahn Valley was the cradle of the counts of Laurenburg, from whom the Nassau-Orange royal line of the Netherlands (House of William of Orange, King William III of England) is descended. Points of interest include the Adelsheimer Hof (town hall), the Stammburg (ancestral castle) Nassau-Oranien and the Steinisches Schloß (birthplace of Prussian Baron von Stein).

Kloster Arnstein – *1km/0.6mi by a steep uphill road from the Obernhof bridge.* The church of this former Premonstratensian monastery stands alone on a wooded spur. The Romanesque west chancel contrasts with that in the east, which is Gothic.

Balduinstein – Ruins of a castle built in 1320 by Baudouin of Luxembourg, Archbishop of Trier, to rival that of Schaumburg.

Schloß Schaumburg ⊘ – A neo-Gothic reconstitution after the English manner. There is a fine **view** from the tallest of the crenellated towers overlooking the valley.

Diez – Dominating the small town clustered around its ramparts is the tall mass of the 17C **Schloß Oranienstein** ⊘. The castle was built 1672-1684 as one of the first ancestral castles of the Nassau-Orange royal house. In 1811, Napoleon dissolved the principality of Orange, as Prince William IV, later King William I of the Netherlands, had not joined the Confederation of the Rhine. In 1867, Schloß Oranienstein was transformed into a cadet school. The modern castle serves as a barracks for an armoured brigade and houses the **Oranien-Nassau-Museum**, devoted to the history of the House of Orange *(apply to the guard)*.

★ **Limburg** – *See LIMBURG.*

★ **Burg Runkel** – The picturesque **setting**★★ of the castle, built into the rock face, and the ancient village below it, can best be appreciated from the 15C bridge over the river.

Weilburg – Once the residence of the Counts of Nassau, this Baroque town is built on a promontory enclosed by the Lahn. Of the many different structures which comprised the Renaissance **castle** ⊘, note especially the turreted clock tower and the elegant 1573 gallery, where the twinned Ionic columns of the arcades are topped by a glazed gallery with Corinthian columns. About 30 **rooms** are open to visitors.

The **Mining and town museum** (Bergbau-und Stadtmuseum) ⊘ is devoted to the history of the local Iron Mountain mining industry and to the culture of the Weilburg region.

Schloß Braunfels – This massive castle, built over 800 years, seen unexpectedly after a fork in the road, has a superb and exciting feudal outline with its many towers etched against the sky. The perimeter wall encloses the whole village. Inside the castle are fine pieces of 15C-19C furniture, paintings, Gobelins tapestries and a collection of weaponry. There is an audio-visual presentation on the history of mining in the castle chapel.

Follow the road as far as **Wetzlar**.

LANDSBERG AM LECH★

Bayern

Population 25 000
Michelin map 419/420 V 16

A fortified frontier town between Swabia and Bavaria in the Middle Ages, Landsberg – on the old road from Salzburg to Memmingen – prospered through trade and the levying of tolls. Fortress gates, towers and perimeter walls still preserve a most attractive medieval atmosphere as one approaches the place.

There is a fine view of the tiered **site**★ and the original Lech weir from the shady riverside promenade on the west bank of the Lech, where it meets the Karolinen-brücke *(the best place to park if the Marktplatz below is full)*.

SIGHTS

★ **Marktplatz** – Triangular in shape, this market place is surrounded by a remarkable group of gaily coloured roughcast town houses. The **fountain** (Marienbrunnen), in the centre, falls into a marble basin surmounted by a statue of the Virgin Mary.

Rathaus – The façade of this building was executed c 1720 by Dominikus Zimmermann, one of the greatest artists of the Wessobrunn School, who went on to be burgomaster of Landsberg (1749-54). The gable of the elegant structure is ornamented with finely worked stucco. The rest of the town hall was built between 1699 and 1702.

In the far corner of the square stands the **Schmalztor**, through which the upper town can be reached. Hemmed in on all sides by old houses, the 14C tower-gate is topped by a lantern turret roofed with glazed tiles.
The Alte Bergstraße climbs steeply to the "Bavarian Gate".

Bayertor (Bavarian Gate) – With its projecting porch flanked by turrets and sculptures, this 1425 town gateway is one of the best preserved of its period in the whole of Germany. Outside the ramparts, which continue on either side, the gateway is embellished with carved and painted coats of arms and with a Crucifixion.

LANDSHUT*

Bayern
Population 58 660
Michelin map 420 U 20

Landshut on the Isar, once capital of the Lower Bavaria dukedom, has kept its medieval centre practically intact.
Memories of the Ingoldstadt and Landshut branches of the House of Wittelsbach, whose members until the 16C outshone even their extravagant Munich cousins, remain very much alive in the valleyed countryside surrounding the town. Every four years, Landshut commemorates with great pomp the marriage in 1475 of the son of Duke Ludwig the Rich with Hedwige, daughter of the king of Poland (*see Calendar of events*).

SIGHTS

* **Martinskirche** – Designed by Master Hans von Burghausen and built of rose-coloured brick, this 14C-15C church impresses above all by its outstanding elevation. The **tower★★**, square at the base, slims and becomes octagonal as it soars to a height of more than 130m/426ft. Circle the outside of the building, which is adorned with tombstones. The five Flamboyant doorways show an Early Renaissance influence.
The well-lit interior shows a splendid unity of design. Octagonal pillars, deceptively fragile in appearance, support in a single thrust, vaulting which rises to 29m/95ft. There is a delicate Virgin and Child by Leinberger (1518) on the altar in the south aisle.

* **Altstadt** – The town's most important monuments are to be found in this wide, slightly curving main street with its arcaded 15C and 16C houses, between the Rathaus and the Martinskirche. Note especially the variety and inventiveness of

Altstadt, Landshut

M. Thonig

the gables, which can be seen again – though perhaps to a lesser extent – in the Neustadt, which runs parallel to the Altstadt. The façades in this second street have had many Baroque features added.

Stadtresidenz (Palace) ⊘ – Two main blocks linked by narrow wings comprise this charming palace (1536) arranged around an arcaded courtyard, which faces the town hall. The German building is on the Altstadt (18C furniture, decorations etc); the 16C Italian Renaissance one looks onto the courtyard (large rooms with painted, coffered ceilings).

Burg Trausnitz ⊘ – The fortress founded in 1204 was decorated during the Renaissance with fine arcaded galleries. Interesting features include the chapel, the Gothic hall known as the Alte Dürnitz, and several rooms embellished in 16C style are open to the public. The chapel is remarkable for its Early Gothic statuary. Note also the Jesters' Staircase (Narrentreppe), painted in the 16C with scenes from the Commedia dell'Arte.

From an upper loggia (Söller), there is an exceptional **view** across the town to the spire of the Martinskirche.

LEIPZIG★

Sachsen
Population 450 000
Michelin map 418 L 21

Leipzig stands at the confluence of the River Weiße Elster and River Pleiße. The city is famous as a centre for trade fairs, conferences and culture.

HISTORICAL NOTES

The Leipzig Fairs – The first mention of the locality historically was in the Chronicle of Bishop Thietmar of Merseburg (975-1018), who noted the death of the Bishop of Meißen in "Urbs Lipzi". The township of "Lipzk" was granted a city charter c 1165. Subsequently, a situation at the crossing of several important trade routes, plus the bestowal by the Margrave Otto the Rich of the right to levy tolls – one of the oldest feudal privileges enjoyed by burghers – established Leipzig as a commercial centre of more than local influence. From the 12C onwards, markets were held over the Easter period and on the Feast of St Michael. A third event – during the New Year celebrations – was added in 1485. The Spring and Autumn international trade fairs, symbolized by the famous "Double M", have been held since 1896.

Neue Messe Leipzig

The Leipzig Trade Fair Centre inaugurated in 1996 after three years construction not only continues an 800-year-old tradition but is one of the most state-of-the-art trade fair venues in the world. The focal point is the central entrance hall by architect Volkwin Marg, a steel and glass construction which is the only one of its kind in Europe. This glass edifice spanning 80m/260ft, 243m/800ft in length and almost 30m/100ft high at its apex incorporates light and vibrancy.

Railway stations can look good...

Leipzig railway station, which had become seriously rundown, despite being Europe's largest railway terminus, was given a major facelift in 1995. Within two years, the station lobbies had been renovated and a three-storey shopping centre covering 30 000m²/322 800sq ft installed. Travellers arriving in Leipzig by train nowadays are overwhelmed by the original 1915 building with its huge oblong hall, measuring 267m/876ft long by 32m/105ft wide, and two entrance lobbies, which has become a cathedral to consumerism, home to 130 business concerns. Art is also given a good deal, with Jean Tinguely's *Luminator* making a striking impression.

Leipzig, City of Books – One of the world's earliest books, the Glossa Super Apocalipsim, was printed in Leipzig in 1481 by an itinerant craftsman. The German Book Exchange was founded in 1825, and this was followed in 1912 by the German Library (Deutsche Bücherei) and the Museum of Books and Literature (Deutsches Buch- und Schriftmuseum). More than 35 established publishers are based in Leipzig today, among them Kiepenheuer, Brockhaus and Reclam.

The city also enjoys a fine reputation in the musical world, thanks to the Choir of St Thomas **(Thomanerchor)**, the Gewandhaus Orchestra, and the Mendelssohn-Bartholdy National College of Music.

Science and Industry – The "Alma Mater Lipsiensis", founded in 1409, the present university, and numerous colleges of higher education testify to the importance of intellectual and scientific activity in Leipzig. The most striking development in Leipzig is its transformation from an industrial centre to a metropolis specializing in service industries.

MARKT (AY)

★ **Altes Rathaus (Former Town Hall) (AY)** – This long, low building with its fine Renaissance façade is crowned with dwarf gables which are pierced by windows – one of the earliest examples of an architectural style typifying town hall design during the German Renaissance. It was completed in 1556 after plans drawn up by Hieronymous Lotter, architect and burgo-master of Leipzig, and restored for the first time in 1672. The tower above the main doorway features a special balcony for the town pipers or heralds. Today the building houses the local history museum, the **Stadtgeschichtliches Museum** ⊘.

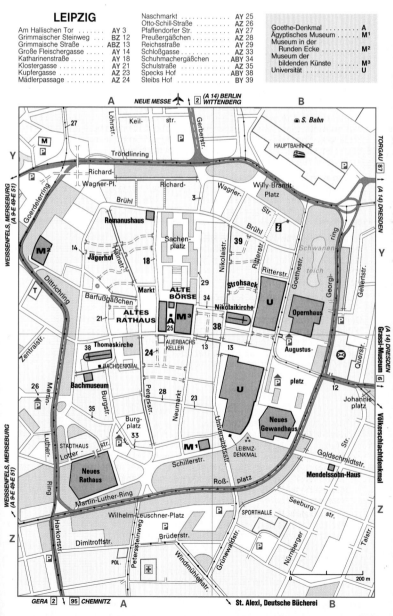

Musicians in Leipzig

Johann Sebastian Bach worked in Leipzig from 1723 until his death in 1750. As choirmaster and director of music at St. Thomas he was responsible for the religious and secular musical life of the entire city. His enormous output includes 200 religious cantatas, 3 oratorios, 2 Passions, 5 masses, 1 Magnificat, 6 motets and 190 four-part chorales. However, during his lifetime, his inspired work was considered "difficult".

Bach had faded into relative obscurity by the time **Felix Mendelssohn-Bartholdy** took up the post of director of music of the Gewandhaus orchestra in 1835. In the decade he occupied this position he transformed the city into a musical centre of international renown. He decisively turned to reviving forgotten works during this period, including the works of Bach, whose Matthew Passion he had already performed in 1829. Mendelssohn founded Germany's first musical Conservatory in Leipzig in 1843.

Clara Wieck and **Robert Schumann** spent the early years of their marriage in Leipzig. They lived in a fine neo-Classical house at 16 Inselstraße, which is now fitted out as a memorial to them. Among other works, the *'Spring' Symphony* was composed here.

★ **Thomaskirche (AZ)** – Recorded for the first time in 1212 in the report of the foundation of the abbey for canons of the Augustinian order, this Late Gothic triple-aisle hall-church took on its present appearance towards the end of the 15C. On Whit Sunday in 1539, Martin Luther gave a sermon here to inaugurate the Reformation.
The church became famous through **Johann Sebastian Bach**, who was cantor for 27 years and who is buried here, and through the celebrated **Thomanerchor**. Originating at the School of St Thomas, founded after 1212, this choir at first had no more than 12 singers. It now has about 80 members and performs on Fridays at 6pm (choral evensong), Saturdays at 3pm (sacred choral music and Bach cantatas) and Sundays at 9.30am (main service).
In front of the church stands a **Bach memorial statue** by Carl Seffner (1908).

Bachmuseum ⊘ – *Thomaskirchhof 16*. The museum and Bach archive were founded in 1586 and installed in the converted home of the Bose family, who had been friends of Bach's, in the 18C. The life, work and legacy of the great composer are documented in detail, with the main emphasis on his Leipzig period.

★ **Alte Börse (Former Produce Exchange) (AY)** – *On the Naschmarkt*.
Built between 1678 and 1687 after plans by Johann Georg Starcke, this one-time commodity market was Leipzig's first Baroque edifice. It is used today for fairs and festivals.
The statue outside (by Carl Seffner in 1903) represents **Goethe** as a student.

★★ **Museum der Bildenden Künste (Fine Arts Museum)** ⊘ **(AZ M³)** – *Grimmaische Straße 1-7*.
One of Europe's most important art collections, with works from the Late Middle Ages to the present, is temporarily housed in this trade fair hall until the new building planned on Sachsenplatz, a 34m/112ft high glass cube, can be inaugurated in 2002. Due to the temporary nature of the accommodation, the following works of art on display may be subject to change:

FANCY A COFFEE?

The **Café zum Arabischen Coffebaum** *(at the junction of Barfußgäßchen and Kleiner Fleischergasse)* offers more than just coffee. This is possibly the oldest coffee house in Europe, a favourite haunt of Goethe, Klopstock, Robert Schumann, and Richard Wagner, which continues to attract followers of art and the humanitites nowadays. It houses the tiny, but nonetheless interesting, **Museum on the History of European Coffee Culture**. It rubs shoulders with an oriental coffee house, a Viennese-style café and a Parisian-style café.

The **Kaffeehaus Riquet** at no 1 Schuhmachergäßchen is certainly eye-catching. The roof of this narrow corner house is crowned by a pagoda-style lantern and the entrance doorway is flanked by a pair of elephant heads. The interior is not quite so exotic. The atmosphere here is more like that of a Viennese coffee house.

It's Jugenstil that you're after? The **Café Maître** in Karl-Liebknecht-Straße has not only retained something of the spirit of old Leipzig coffee houses, but also its fine Jugendstil decor.

German Primitives: *The Man of Agonies* (c 1425) by **Master Francke**; *Portraits of Luther and Junker Jörg* (1521) by **Lucas Cranach the Elder**; *The Seven Ages of Woman* (1544) by **Hans Baldung Grien**.

Flemish Painting: *Portrait of an Old Man* (1430-40) by a **disciple of Jan van Eyck**; *Visitation* (c 1435) by **Rogier van der Weyden**; a portrait (c 1653) by one of Rembrandt's circle; *The Mulatto* (c 1630) by **Frans Hals**; and works by Gerard Honthorst, Van Goyen, Van Ostade, Van Ruisdael.

Italian Painting: Cima da Conegliano, Francesco Francia, **Tintoretto** (*The Resurrection of Lazarus*, c 1565).

German Painting: Anton Graff, **JFA Tischbein**, JA Koch, **CD Friedrich** (*The Ages of Life*, c 1835), Carl Spitzweg, Moritz von Schwind, Arnold Böcklin (*The Island of the Dead*, c 1886), Max Liebermann (*The Bottlers*, 1879), Max Klinger (*Blue Hour*, 1890) and Wilhelm Leibl.

In the **Sculpture Department** there are works by, among others, Balthazar Permoser, Berthel Thorvaldsen, Auguste Rodin and Max Klinger. The museum's **collection of prints and drawings** offers a virtually unbroken panoramic survey of graphic art from medieval times (Martin Schongauer) to the present.

ARCADES

It is fun to stroll along some of Leipzig's characteristic glass-roofed arcades. Many have been remarkably well restored and offer a colourful variety of shops and bars, which are appreciated by local residents and tourists alike.

Mädlerpassage (**AZ 24**) – *Opposite Naschmarkt*. This is the grandest and perhaps the best-known of Leipzig's arcades, not least because it is home to Auerbachs Keller, where Goethe set some of the scenes in his great work Faust. There is good food and a great atmosphere in the vaulted underground rooms. Before going downstairs, pause to admire the bronze groups by Matthieu Molitor, depicting Faust, Mephistopheles and revellers.

Specks Hof (**ABY 38**) – *Schuhmachergäßchen*. The restoration of this 1911 trade fair hall provoked some controversy, but the result is a success. Old features have been preserved and new ones added with a sensitive touch. Specks Hof leads into the Hansahaus with its latched light well.

Strohsack (**BY**) – This modern arcade links Nikolaistraße with Ritterstra ße. Check the time on the glass-covered clock in the floor.

Steibs Hof (**BY 39**) – *Between Brühl and Nikolaistraße*. This trade fair house with its blue and white tiled inner courtyards was built in 1907 for a furrier. Leipzig was the European centre for tanned goods until the 1930s.

Jägerhofpassage (**AY**) – *Between Hainstraße and Großer Fleischergasse*. This arcade with its ivory coloured tiled walls is a late Jugendstil work dating from 1913-14 and houses a cinema.

Katharinenstraße (**AY 18**) – Some Baroque houses survive on the west side of this street. The finest is definitely the **Romanushaus** *(on the corner with Brühl)*, built in 1701-04 after designs by Johann Gregor Fuchs for burgomaster Franz Conrad Romanus. This man financed the construction of his house with uncovered borrower's notes and was punished with a 41 year sentence in the Königstein Fortress, where he ended his days. The neighbouring houses *(nos 21 and 19)* were built in the mid 18C and feature charming façades. The Fregehaus *(no 11)*, also built by Fuchs, belonged to the wealthy banker Christian Gottlob Frege, the Fugger *(see AUGSBURG)* of Leipzig, whose trade emporium stretched across Europe and as far as America.

Nikolaikirche (**BY**) – *Nikolaistraße*.
Originally built in the Romanesque style, this church has since undergone various modifications: the Gothic chancel and west towers date from the 14C, the Late Gothic triple nave surrounded by a double gallery from 1523 to 1526, and the central tower from 1555.

The church's classical **interior**★ (1784-97) by Carl Dauthe is particularly impressive. The effect is simultaneously spacious and dramatic. The pale, fluted pillars end in light green palm leaves. The vaulting is coffered in old rose with stucco flowers. There are 30 paintings hanging in the narthex and chancel by Adam Friedrich Oeser, a contemporary of Dauthe. The Late Romanesque wooden crucifix in the chancel is believed to be the oldest surviving work of art in Leipzig. The organ (1858-62) is the work of renowned Weißenfels organ-builder Friedrich Ladegast.

AUGUSTUSPLATZ AND SURROUNDING AREA (BYZ)

On the north side of the Augustusplatz stands the **opera house**, built in 1956-60, with its widely praised acoustic. Its high quality, innovative musical productions have attracted much approbation over the years.

On the west side of the square is the eye-catching **Krochhaus**, the city's first "skyscraper". It was built in 1928-29 and is crowned by a replica of the Mori, the chime from the belfry in Venice. The building that dominates the west side is however the **Leipzig University building** (BYZ), 142m/466ft high, dating from 1973. The Schinkeltor, a gate designed by Karl Friedrich Schinkel and E Rietschel in 1836, has been incorporated in the amphitheatre wing.

A monument to the memory of **Leibniz** stands on the south side of the university. It is not far from here to the Egyptian Museum.

Ägyptisches Museum (Egyptian Museum) ⊘ (AZ **M¹**) – *Schillerstraße 6.*
Five thousand years of the Pharaohs' civilization, represented by more than 8 000 separate exhibits, are covered by the splendid collections in this museum, which is attached to the university. A particular highlight is the cedarwood sarcophagus of Hed-Bast-Iru (c 400 BC).

Neues Gewandhaus (New Concert Hall) (BZ) – This superb auditorium to the south of the square was inaugurated in 1981. More than 1 900 enthusiasts can be seated to hear the famous Gewandhaus Orchestra. The bust of Beethoven (1902) is the work of Leipzig-born Max Klinger. In front of the concert hall is a **fountain** (Mendebrunnen, 1886) which is an allegory on the world of water.

Cross the Georgiring and go into Goldschmidtstraße.

Mendelssohn-Haus ⊘ (BZ) – *Goldschmidtstraße 12.* Felix Mendelssohn Bartholdy spent the last two years of his life in this magnificent house, which has now been turned into a memorial to him. The composer died here on 4 November 1847 at the age of only 38 years. Original furniture and items from among his possessions recreate the environment in which he lived. Concerts are held in the fine music room.

From Goldschmidtstraße turn left into Talstraße and go to Johannisplatz.

Grassi Museum – *Johannisplatz.*
This impressive complex with its four inner courtyards was built in 1925 to 1929 in the Expressionist style, with echoes of Art Deco, by architects Carl William Zweck and Hans Voigt. Funding has now been found for the urgent renovation of this fine building, so that British architect David Chipperfield's project may be implemented. The results are eagerly anticipated. The Grassi-Museum houses three important collections.

★ **Museum für Kunsthandwerk** (Museum of Arts and Crafts) ⊘ – The renovated galleries house displays of European arts and crafts from the Middle Ages right up to the first half of the 20C. Exhibits include furniture (Nuremberg hall cabinet, 16C), porcelain (Meissen), glassware (Venetian, Bohemian), and valuable Jugendstil pieces (Gallé, Lalique). There are also exhibits of work from the Vienna Workshops. An extremely rare objet d'art is the delicate Buchsbaum jointed doll dating from 1521.

★ **Museum für Völkerkunde** (Museum of Ethnography) ⊘ – This is one of the oldest and most important museums of its kind in Europe. It illustrates the history, culture and way of life of the peoples of Asia, Africa, America, Australia and Oceania by

---

It started with prayer group on Mondays...

From 1982, a prayer group used to meet at the Nikolaikirche every Monday at 5pm to pray for peace. This was attended by Christians and non-Christians, young and old alike. Some weeks there were many present, and others only a few. In summer 1989, as the wave of emigration hit the DDR, this prayer group assumed increasing significance. From May of that year, the streets leading to the Nikolaikirche were guarded by the People's Police. Notwithstanding, on some weeks the 2 000 seats in the church were no longer enough to accommodate those who came. Many people were arrested following the prayer meetings. Tension rose to breaking point. After uniformed troops had attacked unarmed civilians in Leipzig on 7 October, people feared the worst for the prayer meeting scheduled for Monday 9 October, to which 1 000 members of the socialist unity party (SED) had been summoned. When these people left the church, there was a crowd of 10 000 or more waiting for them in the square, all holding candles. The miracle of the peaceful revolution had happened. A member of the SED said afterwards, "We had planned everything. We were ready for anything. But not for candles and prayers."

Leipziger Gewandhaus Orchestra

Many orchestras were founded as court orchestras, as in the case of the Dresden "Staatskapelle". Not so the Leipziger Gewandhaus Orchestra, which was founded thanks to a donation by wealthy local burghers and merchants in 1743. In 1781, the 500-seat hall in the Clothworkers' Guildhall was made into a concert hall, and thus the orchestra got its name. Famous composers and performers have appeared in this temple to music over the centuries. Among the very first star performances were Beethoven's Triple Concerto, Franz Schubert's Symphony in C major, Mendelssohn's "Scottish" Symphony, and Brahms' Violin Concerto in D major. In 1884, the city built the orchestra its own concert hall, but the name "Gewandhaus" was retained. This building was destroyed by fire-bombs in 1944. Until the third "Gewandhaus" was opened in 1981, the orchestra had to make do with temporary accommodation in the congress centre.

Since 1998, Swedish conductor Helmut Blomstedt has wielded the baton in the long line of music directors, preceded by such illustrious forebears as Felix Mendelssohn, Arthur Nikisch and Kurt Masur.

means of a wealth of cultural artefacts and informative documentary photographs and drawings. It is rare to find such detailed documentation on the people of Siberia, for example, as there is here. In the African department, there is a fascinating collection of Benin bronze ware, including a remarkable 18C aquamanile in the shape of a leopard.

* **Musikinstrumenten-Museum** (Museum of Musical Instruments) ⊘ – This is the second most important collection in Europe after Brussels. It displays instruments spanning five centuries, including a clavichord, made in Venice in 1543, a spinet (1693) and a hammer piano from Florence (1726). Note the guitar by Antonio Mariani (Venice, 1680) with its finely worked mother-of-pearl inlay. Some of the more original and innovative exhibits include a rare ivory racket (Tyrol, second half of the 16C), a glass harmonica and a piano that plays itself, driven by hole-punched tape.

ADDITIONAL SIGHTS IN THE CITY CENTRE

Neues Rathaus (New town hall) (AZ) – Built on the foundations of the old Pleißenburg Castle, the town hall marries both Renaissance and Baroque elements with features that are more modern.

Museum in der Runden Ecke ⊘ (AY M²) – This contemporary exhibition on the sinister methods of the infamous old East German Ministry for State Security, known as the *"Stasi"* (short for *"Staatssicherheit"*), shows the terrible aspects of this instrument of oppression. It employed 85 000 staff and hardly missed a thing that went on. This detailed exhibition has been put together by a committee of local townspeople in the original setting of the offices that were the Leipzig administrative headquarters of the Stasi. While visitors might be tempted to laugh at the "smell samples" of potential opponents of the regime, kept in glass jars, one look at the prison cell and the literature on the systematic surveillance of the townspeople is enough to wipe any smile off their faces.

AROUND THE OLD EXHIBITION CENTRE (ALTES MESSEGELÄNDE)

Via Windmühlenstraße (BZ)
The old sites for Leipzig's annual trade and book fairs extend from the Deutscher Platz to the Wilhelm Külz Park, in the eastern part of the city.

Völkerschlachtdenkmal (Battle of the Nations Monument) ⊘ – *Via Johannisplatz* (BZ).
Inaugurated in 1913, on the 100th anniversary of the Allied victory over the armies of Napoleon (Battle of Leipzig), this memorial took 15 years to build. Some 500 steps lead to a terrace from which the entire city and its surroundings can be seen.

St. Alexi-Gedächtniskirche – *Philipp-Rosenthal-Straße.*
Dedicated to the 22 000 Russian soldiers who fell in the above battle, this church in the old Tzarist style was built by WA Pokrowski between 1912 and 1913.

Deutsche Bücherei (German National Library) – *Deutscher Platz.*
Founded, again, in 1912, the huge library attempts to group together all known books in the German language – a collection that already comprises 7.5 million titles. On the same premises the **German Museum of Books and Literature** is open to the public.

LEMGO ★

Nordrhein-Westfalen
Population 42 000
Michelin map 417 J 10

This town, founded shortly before 1200 by the noble Bernhard zur Lippe, owes its growth into the largest town in the earldom of Lippe to a favourable site at a ford and the junction of old trade routes. A second town was founded in 1265, directly to the south and adjacent to Lemgo – the new town. In 1365, the old and new towns combined and were surrounded by a town wall which survives to this day. The relationships forged by the merchants of Lemgo were far-reaching – to Lübeck as far as Finland, and to Bremen and Elberfeld as far as Flanders. Cloth, linen and cotton were the main commodities. Lemgo later became a centre for book-printing (from 17C) and publishing.

The grand town houses from the Late Gothic and Renaissance periods testify to the grandeur of the once-wealthy Hanseatic city. The fine old buildings, every single one spared during the Second World War, are inhabited and put to use. Lemgo town centre is therefore saved from the risk of becoming a museum. Besides timber production, the main branches of local industry include dentistry, lighting, mechanical engineering and automobile supply industry.

★ OLD TOWN

From the Ostertor to the east, approach the Mittelstraße, which is the main street. Note especially the fine façades of no 17 (with wood carving on all four floors) and no 36, known as the House of Planets (Planetenhaus).

★★ **Rathaus (Town hall)** – Comprising eight buildings side by side, the civic centre of Lemgo is exceptional for its oriel windows, its arcades and its unique gables. The elegantly worked façade of the old apothecary's shop on the corner of the Marktplatz displays, on the first floor, the sculpted portraits of 10 famous philosopher-physicians, from Aristotle to Paracelsus. Beneath the central arcades, brutal witchcraft trials were held in about 1670.

Bear left into Breite Straße.

Hexenbürgermeisterhaus (House of the Witches' Burgomaster) ⊘ – *19 Breite Straße.* The house, with its splendid façade, was built between 1568 and 1571 and is an outstanding memorial to Weser Renaissance urban architecture. It houses the **city museum**, which focuses on housing and everyday culture, craft and trade.
A special exhibition is dedicated to the history of witch-hunting in Lemgo.

Witch-hunting in Lemgo

During the Inquisition, the death penalty existed for heresy and sorcery. Great waves of persecution ran through the country, also affecting the town of Lemgo. They were the result of the "witch-hunt" by the inquisitor J Sprenger. Between 1564 and 1681, more than 200 were persecuted as witches. The accused were tortured and false confessions were wrung out of them. The Lemgo mayor Herrmann Cothman ingloriously distinguished himself as a particularly cruel "director of the criminal court".

The persecutions finally came to an end when a young woman withstood the torture, was banished from the region but sued her torturers before the imperial supreme court.

Marienkirche – A Renaissance organ with a finely carved case, among the oldest in Germany (1587-1613), adorns this triple-aisle Gothic church constructed at the end of the 13C and the beginning of the 14C (about 1260-1320). Admire too the baptismal font (1592), the pulpit (1644) and the Cross Triumphant (c 1500).

Return to Papenstraße, following it to the right.

St. Nikolaikirche – Appropriately dedicated to the patron saint of merchants, the church combines features that are both Romanesque (a three-figure tympanum in the south aisle; a stone triptych in the north) and Gothic (frescoes and vault keystones). The pulpit and the font are Late Renaissance (c 1600).

Papenstraße leads back to the starting point.

ADDITIONAL SIGHTS

★ **Junkerhaus (Karl Junker's House)** ⊘ – *Hamelner Straße 36.*
Karl Junker (1850-1912), painter, sculptor and architect, a contemporary of the blossoming Jugendstil, left in his own house a memorial to his highly personal style. His design is organized around a spiral which relies for its effect on an arcane play of movements alternately balanced and opposed. Surprise is

everything in this design: the visitor's perception of Junker's sculpted and painted decor (note the Pointillist medallions adorning the ceilings) is of an infinite diversity, constantly changing with each different point of view.

Schloß Brake – *Schloßstraße 18*. This mighty castle was built between the 12C and 19C, although the predominant style is Weser Renaissance. Nothing couldbe more apt, therefore, than to have a **Weserrenaissance-Museum** installed here, in which the various aspects of art and culture between the Reformation and the Thirty Year War are clearly explained.

EXCURSION

Herford – *20km/12.5mi to the west.*
This town between Teutoburger Wald and the Weser was a member of the Hanseatic League until the 17C. The historic town centre contains numerous half-timbered houses from the 16C to the 18C. Herford is home to one of the oldest hall-churches in Westphalia, the late Romanesque **Münsterkirche** (1220-80). Modifications during the Gothic period bequeathed it some beautiful window tracery. The Protestant **Johanniskirche** is garnished with fine 17C **wood carving**★, both sculpted and painted. Galleries, stalls and pulpit were all donated by different city corporations, whose shields and emblems can be recognized in the design. The chancel has interesting 15C stained-glass windows.

LIMBURG AN DER LAHN★

Hessen
Population 35 000
Michelin map 417 O 8

This site on the banks of the Lahn, between the Taunus heights to the south and the Westerwald to the north, was originally based around a ford, then from the mid 12C a wooden bridge, and finally, according to the Limburg annuls, a stone bridge, construction of which was begun in 1315. Tolls from the bridge were a source of wealth for centuries. The powerful yet elegant silhouette of the cathedral overhanging the Lahn dominates the Limburg skyline. The town centre, a protected site, consists largely of half-timbered houses with lavish woodcarving dating from the 13C to the 18C.

★ CATHEDRAL (DOM) *30min*

Built on a rocky spur, St. Georgsdom is in a picturesque **setting**★★. Apart from that, it is remarkable for the style of its architecture: a classic example of Romanesque-Gothic Transitional, which was prevalent in Germany between 1210 and 1250.
The outside remains Romanesque and closely resembles the Rhineland cathedrals *(see Introduction)*, but the interior is already Gothic, with a structure directly inspired by the cathedral of Laon, in Picardy, France. Here we find superposed galleries, arcades, a triforium and clerestory windows as typical of the early Gothic period as the distinctive crochet capitals. Diagonal ribs characterize the vaulting. The transept crossing lies beneath a domed lantern tower. The original multicoloured decoration has been uncovered and restored.
From the **cemetery terrace** (Friedhofsterrasse) on the north side of the church, there is a good **view**★ of the river, the old bridge, and a new motorway viaduct.

★ **Diözesanmuseum** (Diocesan Museum) ⊘ – *Domstraße 12*.
The 10C Byzantine reliquarycross known as the Limburger Staurothek is

Limburg an der Lahn

Werner OTTO Reisefotografie, Oberhausen

the jewel of the religious art collection displayed in this museum, which occupies a historical building along with the cathedral treasury. Another highlight is the sheath encasing the reliquary Staff of St Peter, completed in 980 in Trier under Archbishop Egbert. On display in the medieval sculpture department, is an admirable terracotta Lamentation of Christ, a moving work that dates from the "soft" style period c 1415.

ADDITIONAL SIGHT

* **Old Town (Alstadt)** – In the old town, whole streets are preserved with their original buildings, some of which have fine half-timbering *(Domplatz, Fischmarkt, Brückengasse, Römer, Rütsche, Bischofsplatz)*. Walderdorffer Hof (Fahrgasse) is a Renaissance construction with four wings. Taking time to discover the beautiful old houses in the winding alleys is one of the joys of a visit to Limburg.

LINDAU IM BODENSEE★★

Bayern
Population 24 000
Michelin map 419 X 13

Lindau is popular with visitors. The former Free Imperial City (1275-1802) adds to the charm of its old streets, island setting, harbour lights, and a magnificent panorama visible from the windows of all its hotels.

Lindau – im Bodensee (in the lake) and not am Bodensee (by the lake) like its neighbours Überlingen and Meersburg – boasts a number of churches with belfries crowned by an onion dome. The gabled burghers' houses in the old town testify still to the prosperity of bygone days when it was an important trading centre, particularly for commerce with Italy.

There is an almost Mediterranean quality to life in this lakeside island resort at the gates of Austria – a retro charm which can be savoured to the full during an evening stroll between the port and the Maximilianstraße.

SIGHTS

Stadtmuseum Lindau (Municipal Museum) ⊙ (Y M¹) – Installed in the **Haus Zum Cavazzen**★, a typical example of bourgeois Baroque architecture (1729), the museum houses a gallery of painting and sculpture. It also has an exhibition on home decor, including arts and crafts and an interesting collection of mechanical musical instruments.

Maximilianstraße (Z) – This, the main artery leading through the old town, is a picturesque street lined by old houses and inns. Narrow, half-timbered façades with the oriel windows characteristic of the Alpine Rhine Valley and the Vorarlberg huddle together with the stepped gables of Old Swabia (the former town hall (**A**) – **Altes Rathaus** – is a fine example of the latter style).

Turn right into the Zeppelinstraße and walk to the **Brigands' Tower** (Diebesturm), a well-known Lindau silhouette with its crown of bartizans.

Lindau

B. Duke/SUPERBILD, München

Altes Rathaus . . . . . **A**   Stadtmuseum . . . . . **M¹**

Hafen (Port) (Z) – Tourists crowd the quays, many of them waiting to embark on one of the large white Bodensee pleasure boats. In the centre of the activity stands the Mangturm, a fortified 12C tower once used as a lighthouse. The present lighthouse commands, along with a monument to the Lion of Bavaria (1856), the entrance to the roadstead. A few steps lead up to the **Römerschanze**★ viewpoint – a pleasant, shady place from which to admire the Rhine Gap and the Alpine landmarks surrounding the "Bodan" (the ancient form of Bodensee). These are: Kanisfluh, the Hoher Freschen, the Drei Schwestern and (in Switzerland) Säntis and Altmann.

WHERE TO STAY AND WHERE TO EAT OUT

OUR SELECTION

Hoyerberg-Schlössle – Hoyerbergstraße 64, ☎ 0 83 82/2 52 95, Fax 0 83 82/18 37. Small historical castle (no rooms) on the Hoyerberg with magnificent view of Lake Constance and the Alps; enjoy all this over a delicious meal. Main courses from approximately 50DM.

Brugger – Bei der Heidenmauer 11, ☎ 0 83 82/9 34 10, Fax 0 83 82/41 33. Single rooms from 80DM. Small family run business by the town wall (B&B).

Lindauer Hof – Seepromenade, ☎ 0 83 82/40 64, Fax 0 83 82/2 42 03. Single rooms from 130DM. Historical hotel by the port. Stylish rooms; garden for guests by the lakeside promenade.

TREAT YOURSELF!

Bayerischer Hof – Seepromenade, ☎ 0 83 82/91 50, Fax 0 83 82/91 55 91. Single rooms from 200DM. Classic grand hotel, by the lakeside promenade.

Schloß LINDERHOF★★

Deep in the forest, in one of the most secluded valleys of the Ammergau Alps – a region where the royal hunters of the House of Bavaria reserved for their own use – **Ludwig II** had this small villa-like palace built. Designed in the style of the 18C, it served as a background, along with its Moorish pavilion, Moroccan House, Hundinghütte, Gurnmanzklause and grotto, for the romantic fancies of the young king, obsessed by oriental fables and the heroic legends of Germany. The extraordinary contrasts provided by a Rococo building surrounded by gardens and terraces inspired by the Italian Renaissance, set in the middle of a park landscaped in the English manner – the whole planted in an Alpine valley – lend the project its own peculiar charm.

TOUR ⊘ *allow 2hr*

NB During high season queues can be over 3hr long.

Palace – Built between 1869 and 1879, in a style intermingling the second Italian Renaissance and the Baroque, Linderhof was intended by the king to achieve a certain intimacy. Inside, nevertheless, one finds a state bedchamber surpassing in luxury even those of Versailles, a hall of mirrors, cloth panels painted to resemble tapestries, pastels and statues of Louis XIV, Louis XV, Madame de Pompadour, Madame du Barry and others. The magnificent decor never fails to impress visitors.

★★ **Park** – The natural slopes of the valley have been used to lay out a vista in line with the castle in which pools, cascades and terraced gardens in the style of an Italian villa have been devised. Fountains of water and the blaze of formal flower beds strike yet another bizarre note in this wooded Alpine landscape. The east-west lateral borders, on the other hand, with their beech hedges and boxwood trained in pyramids, suggest a more placid approach in the French manner.

Climb to the Temple of Venus rotunda, which closes off the perspective above an ornamental lake (a fine view, especially when the fountains play). Then descend, keeping to the right of the castle, and climb the opposite slope to reach the Moorish pavilion and the grotto. It is here that the skill of the landscape gardener, Karl von Effner, is most in evidence, with plantations of oak, maple and decorative beech placed with consummate art against a backdrop of clumps of conifers into which they gradually blend to form a sombre natural density.

Moorish Pavilion (Maurischer Kiosk) – Acquired by Ludwig II after the 1867 Exposition Universelle in Paris (which was really the world's first International fair), this metallic structure was used by him when he wished to play the oriental potentate.

Moroccan House (Marokkanisches Haus) – This timber building was acquired by Ludwig II at the World Exhibition in Paris in 1875.

Grotto of Venus – A cavern, fashioned with the aid of artificial rocks and intended to recreate the atmosphere of the Venusberg sequence in the Wagnerian opera *Tannhäuser*, the conceit here displays once more the king's taste for theatrical

FOTOGRAM/STONE, Paris

Schloß Linderhof

effect: by the royal throne is a rock evoking the Loreley, which is set beside a lake, illuminated by the play of coloured lights, on which floats a golden skiff in the form of a huge conch shell.

Hundinghütte – This pavilion was built with the backdrop of Wagner's opera *The Valkyrie* in mind. It was originally located in the Ammerwald. The present building is a reconstruction (1990) in the castle grounds faithful to the original, which was burned down in 1945.

Gurnemanzklause – This too is a reconstruction of a stage set from a Wagner opera, this time *Parzifal*. It was originally in the Ammerwald in view of the Hundinghütte.

LUDWIGSBURG★

Baden-Württemberg
Population 86 000
Michelin map 419 T 11

This former royal seat and garrison town on the River Neckar owes its development to the Baroque palace set in beautiful palace grounds, that Duke Eberhard Ludwig von Württemberg had built along the lines of Versailles at the beginning of the 18C. The straight streets following a grid pattern testify to the deliberate planning behind the town. Leading Swabian politician and first President of the Federal Republic of Germany Theodor Heuss (1884-1963) said of Ludwigsburg's arcaded market square that it was the grandest square in all Württemberg.
The Ludwigsburg film academy, founded in 1991 on premises that were once used by the military and manufacturing industry, is the youngest up-and-coming production unit of the German film industry. It already enjoys a global reputation: for the blockbuster "Independence Day", three students from the Ludwigsburg film academy were flown specially to Hollywood, where they were in charge of a substantial proportion of the digital special effects and computer animation.

★ SCHLOSS (PALACE)

This monumental quadrilateral, known as the "Versailles of Swabia", has no less than 452 rooms, 75 of them open to the public.

Tour of the Apartments ⊘ – *Entrance: first courtyard on the right on the road from Stuttgart (access also through the park).* Inside, the "best rooms" (on the first floor of the new building, facing the park) are the apartments of the first king of Württemberg, furnished in the Empire style. Through the Ancestors' Gallery (Ahnengalerie) and the castle's Catholic Church (Schloßkirche), decorated with lavish Italian stucco, visitors arrive at the Fürstenbau state apartments. These are in the oldest and highest part of the palace, which closes off the north side of the court.

★ **Blühendes Barock (Park)** ⊘ – Green Baroque arbours and terraces clothed with an embroidery of flowers have been reconstituted in the southern part of the park, in front of the newest part of the palace. The terrain to the north and east, more broken up, has been landscaped in the English manner.

★★ **Märchengarten** (Fairy-tale Garden) – Fairy stories, legends and folk tales from Germany (the Brothers Grimm) and elsewhere (Hans Christian Andersen) are illustrated here with performances by mechanical figures, some activated by the sound of children's voices.

EXCURSIONS

Marbach am Neckar – *9km/5mi to the northeast.*
This small town cultivates the memory of the poet Schiller (1759-1805), its most illustrious son. The huge **Schiller-Nationalmuseum** ⊘, is the largest literary museum in the former West Germany, running six permanent exhibitions on German literature from the mid 18C to the present drawing on the resources of the German national literature archive. A visit to **Schiller's birthplace** (Schiller-Geburtshaus) completes the pilgrimage.

Schloß Monrepos – *2km/1mi to the northwest.*
Built in 1767 on a site bordering a small lake, this gracious Rococo palace encircles a rotunda.

Markgröningen – *5km/3mi to the west.*
The 15C **Rathaus**★ in this picturesque small town is, by virtue of its impressive size and its skilful construction, a monument to German half-timbering craftsmanship. Many wood-framed houses still exist in Markgröningen.

LUDWIGSLUST★

Mecklenburg-Vorpommern
Population 13 500
Michelin map 416 G 18

The town was founded by Duke Friedrich von Mecklenburg, who moved his residence from Schwerin to Ludwigslust in 1764. He chose the name in honour of his father, Christian II Ludwig, who owned a hunting lodge here. The castle and town were built at the same time, under the supervision of the court master builder Johann Joachim Busch. Only the single and two-storey buildings in Schloßstraße bear witness today to the town's unity of design; the subsequent classical style of Johann Georg Barca is apparent along Kanalstraße and Schweriner Straße.

Ludwigslust cardboard decor – Although Duke Friedrich's intensive building activity had exhausted his funds, he was determined to decorate his castle in an appropriate, not to say sumptuous manner, and he managed to make a virtue out of necessity. The precious and expensive materials, such as marble and fine wood, used elsewhere, were substituted at Ludwigslust by papier mâché. A malleable substance was produced from used paper, glue and water in a time-consuming process (labour was after all cheap), and after it had set, it could be ground, polished and painted. Works of art made of it were even able to withstand the weather. The Ludwigslust workshop achieved such mastery that its products (decorative strips, busts, magnificent vases, centrepieces etc) were exported as far afield as Russia. Production stopped in 1835 through lack of demand, and the original recipe was kept a closely guarded secret which has never been divulged. Plans are now afoot to study and if possible revive this papier mâché tradition, of which some remarkable examples can be seen in the castle.

SIGHTS

★ **Schloß** ⊘ – The E-shaped Late Baroque building (1772-76) already features some Classical elements. Made of brick, the façade was faced with Pirnau sandstone. Three projections divide the frontage, with the portico in the centre extending over the side sections. The attic parapet which crowns the roof is still adorned with the original 18 vases and 40 statues, produced by the Bohemian sculptor Rudolph Kaplunger. The figures represent the arts, sciences and virtues, and symbolize the special interests of the Duke, so that at his request, allegories were even invented to convey hydraulics and hydrostatics!

The interior – *(Only some of the rooms are open to the public).* White and gold dominate the rooms which are decorated in the German version of the Louis XVI style, with tendrils and shells being replaced by medallions and festoons. Oil paintings

Papier mâché decor at Schloß Ludwigslust

above the doors show countryside and animal motifs. The furniture is original, being for the most part gifts or else having been manufactured in Ludwigslust itself.

The **Golden Room★**, a banqueting hall, which is two storeys high and contains exclusively papier mâché ornamentation, is particularly sumptuous. The Venus Medici in the salon just before the gallery, made to look deceptively like marble, is in fact also made of papier mâché. The former Sala terrana facing the garden was converted into a trophy room in 1878 and is now a café.

An oval lake with a **waterfall** lies in front of the castle, with a sandstone sculpture by Rudolph Kaplunger displaying two river gods on either side of the Mecklenburg coat of arms.

★ **Stadtkirche** ⊘ – In accordance with the preference of the time, the castle and church lie along a single line of vision (great importance was attached to such relative position during the Baroque period). The church was built between 1765 and 1770, before the castle, and is an impressive building. The exterior resembles a temple, the interior an ancient church, and surprisingly enough, the idea works extremely well. Standing in front of the castle, you can see at a distance the huge monogram of Christ, 7m/23ft in height, which towers over the building. The porch with its six Doric Tuscan pillars supports a tympanum and a portico on which four sandstone figures depict the Evangelists. Unusually, the chancel is on the southern side and is dominated by an enormous **concave painting** depicting the Annunciation to the Shepherds. The picture is the work of the court painter

Dietrich Findorff, and was completed by Johann Heinrich Suhrland. What cannot be seen, although it could of course be guessed, is the fact that it is made up of painted papier mâché panels. Another original feature, which the visitor will search for in vain, is the organ, which is hidden behind the giant painting. The richly adorned **Prince's seat**, with the court loge and the choir's rostrum above it, stands on the northern side. The ceiling, which is barrel-vaulted and coffered, is supported by two rows of columns.

* **Schloßpark** – The park covers an area of 135ha/334 acres and is one of the largest of its kind in Mecklenburg-Vorpommern. It was originally created by Johann Joachim Busch, and was transformed in the mid 19C by Peter Josef Lenné. Take a stroll around the park and you will constantly discover new points of interest, including streams, monuments, mausoleums and a limonite grotto (earth containing iron, which produces a porous stone when dried out).

LÜBECK★★★

Schleswig-Holstein – Population 216 000 – Michelin map 415 E 16

Girdled with canals, crowned by belfries and towers, Lübeck has retained much of its medieval character as business centre of the Hanseatic League; many of its buildings and monuments are still decorated with alternating bands of red and glazed black-brick courses. Today the city remains the busiest German port on the Baltic and a focal point for shipbuilding and heavy industry.

At the head of the League – The 14C marked the summit of Lübeck's power as Hanseatic capital – the most influential town of that association of Dutch and north German cities which from the 12C to the 16C monopolized trade with Scandinavia and Russia. In the 16C, the business acumen of merchants and shipowners combined to extricate the port from a long period of decline, thanks largely to the establishment of new relations with Holland, and also with France and the Iberian countries, who sent cargoes of wine. For a long time, Dutch architecture was the preferred style for the rich burghers on the banks of the Trave.

In the 19C, Lübeck's seaport status was menaced by the Prussian port of Stettin (now Szczecin) and the opening of the Kiel canal. But the construction of a canal linking the Trave with the Elbe, plus an influx of almost 100 000 refugees in 1945, have together permitted the city to maintain its importance in present-day Germany. Among other assets it has the reputation of being the country's chief importer of the French red wines, which are matured in the celebrated **Lübeck Cellars** beneath the River Trave.

★★★ OLD TOWN (ALTSTADT) *3hr*

Leave from the Holstentor (follow the itinerary marked on the town plan)

★★ **Holstentor** (Y) – This fortified gate with its enormous twin towers was built between 1469 and 1478, before the construction of the city's perimeter wall, more as a matter of prestige than protection. The most impressively designed façade, that towards the town, has three tiers of blind arcades with ornamented ceramic friezes. The building houses the **Local History Museum** (Museum im Holstentor).

The Holstentor at Lübeck

W. Kaehler/FOVEA, Paris

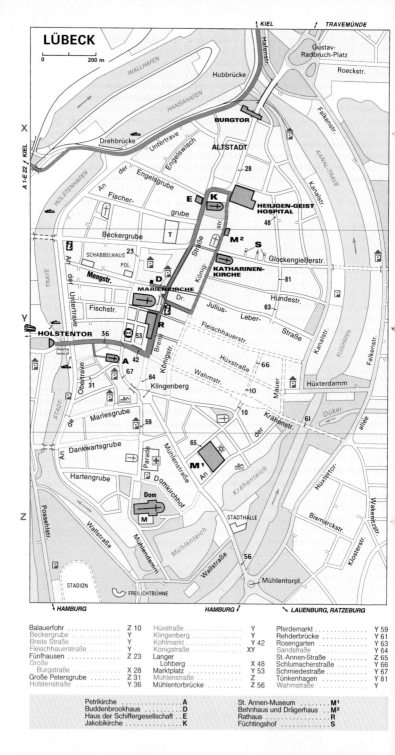

LÜBECK

200 m

Petrikirche (Y A) – The triple nave of the original Romanesque church (completed c 1240) was modified in the Gothic style in the first half of the 14C. A fourth aisle on the south side was added in the mid 15C, and then a fifth, on the north, at the beginning of the 16C. From the tower platform (lift), there is an aerial **view**★ of the port and the town – unique in its central nucleus surrounded by a double ring of canals separated by a circle of narrow islands.

★ **Rathaus** (Y R) – Built from 1250 onwards, on two sides of the Marktplatz, the town hall is an elegant edifice in dark glazed brick, raised, in accordance with municipal tradition, on a gallery of arcades. Note the high protective walls, sometimes pierced with blind arcades or by gaping round openings decorated and strengthened by slender turrets with "candle-snuffer" roofs.

In front of the north wing, a Renaissance superstructure in ornately carved sandstone has been added. The building at the extremity of the east wing, the Neues Gemach (1440), is interesting for the heightened effect lent to it by an imaginative openwork wall.

Pass beneath the arcades to see, on the Breite Straße, a stone staircase (1594) in Dutch Renaissance style.

Continuing the circuit of the Rathaus, arrive at the foot of the north façade.

The wall here displays an impressive layout, with immense bays lined up across almost its entire height.

Buddenbrookhaus

★★ Marienkirche (Y) – One of the finest brick-built Gothic churches in Germany. The original designers in 1250 planned a hall-type church without a transept, but the concept was changed while work was in progress. Subsequently, under the influence of French cathedral architecture, the main buttress-supported vaulting was raised to a height of 38.5m/126ft. The 125m/410ft spires were completed in 1350. The composer Buxtehude (1637-1707) was the church's official organist. The interior, audacious in design, has grandiose proportions. A fire, started by an air raid in 1942, exposed the original polychromatic 13C and 14C decoration. At the end of the south aisle is an elegant 14C chapel, the **Briefkapelle**, with tall lancet windows recalling the High Gothic style. The star vaulting rests on two monolithic columns of granite. Inside the south tower, two huge church bells, which were brought down during the raid, remain embedded in the ground. The ambulatory vaulting covers in a single sweep both the radial apsidal chapels and the axial Lady Chapel, which contains an altarpiece to the Virgin made in Antwerp in 1518.

Outside the church, walk around the east end and go through the arcade of the former town hall Chancellery (15C-16C) to the Mengstraße.

Buddenbrookhaus ⊙ **(YD)** – *4 Mengstraße.*
However attractive the concept may be, **Heinrich** and **Thomas Mann** were unfortunately not born in Buddenbrookhaus. It is however a fact that in 1841 their grandfather Johann Siegmund Mann bought the Baroque house with its beautiful façade, which was built in 1758 and the brothers were frequently guests there during their childhood and adolescence. Thomas Mann used the house in his world-renowned book *The Buddenbrooks*, in which he described the greatness and fall of a patrician family in Lübeck.
The house is now the home of the Heinrich and Thomas Mann Centre, which is dedicated to the life and works of Lübeck's most famous sons.

★ Haus der Schiffergesellschaft (House of the Seamen's Guild) (X E) – Behind the stepped Renaissance gable, the **interior★★** (now a restaurant) still preserves the picturesque furnishings of a seamen's tavern, with rough wooden tables, copper lamps and model ships hanging from the beams.

★ Heiligen-Geist-Hospital (Hospice of the Holy Spirit) (X) – Since the end of the 13C, the three turret-bordered gables of this almshouse have stood above the Koberg. The chapel, a large Gothic hall embellished with 13C and 14C paintings, is just outside the even bigger Great Hall of the hospice (Langes Haus).

★ Jacobikirche (X K) – The magnificent woodwork of the two **organ lofts★★** (16C-17C) in this small Gothic hall-church is noteworthy. Larger than life-size representations of Apostles and saints adorn the pillars of the central nave. A chapel on the south aisle contains an altar known as the "Brömbse" (c 1500), with bas-relief sculptures of very fine workmanship. The chapel to the north

ENJOYING YOUR STAY IN LUBECK

WHERE TO STAY

Wakenitzblick – Augustenstraße 30, ☎ 04 51/79 12 96, Fax 04 51/79 17 92. Single rooms from 95DM. Central, but relatively quietly situated, hotel with fine views of Wakenitz and the river traffic.

Jensen – Obertrave 4, ☎ 04 51/7 16 46, Fax 04 51/7 33 86. Single rooms from 125DM. Comfortably appointed, gabled house between Trave and Holstentor.

Lindenhof – Lindenstraße 1a, ☎ 04 51/8 40 15, Fax 04 51/86 40 23. Single rooms from 125DM. Good value for money town hotel.

Kaiserhof – Kronsforder Allee 11, ☎ 04 51/70 33 01, Fax 04 51/79 50 83. Single rooms from 145DM. Fine patrician houses which have been joined together. Original and comfortably furnished rooms.

WHERE TO EAT OUT

Schiffergesellschaft – Breite Straße 2, ☎ 04 51/7 67 76, Fax 04 51/7 32 79. Menus from 28DM. Historical house with stepped gable. This has been an inn since 1535. Numerous mementoes of Lübeck seamen.

Wullenwever – Beckergrube 71, ☎ 04 51/70 43 33, Fax 04 51/7 06 36 07. Main courses from 44DM. Historical 16C patrician house with a good atmosphere and star-rated cooking.

of the tower is arranged as a memorial to the shipwrecked, and displays a lifeboat from the *Pamir*, the full-rigged Lübeck training ship lost with all hands in 1957.

★ **Katharinenkirche** (Y) – The lower niches of the 14C façade contain modern statues★, the first three on the left being by Ernst Barlach. Inside the church, which is a museum, note, on the right side as you enter, *The Resurrection of Lazarus* by Tintoretto.

The "Höfe und Gänge" – At the corner of the church, turn left into the Glockengießerstraße, on which open the courts (Höfe), set back from the street, which are typical of Lübeck – social amenities donated in the 17C by local benefactors. Note, successively, the delightful **Füchtingshof**★ (no 25 – Y S), with its Baroque doorway dating from 1639; the Glandorps-Gang, a simple alignment of small houses along an alley (no 41); and, from nos 49 to 51, the Glandorps-Hof.

ADDITIONAL SIGHTS

★ **Burgtor** (X) – This fortified gateway defended the narrow isthmus – now cut by a canal – which was once the only land approach to Lübeck. The structure is a fine example of military architecture (13C-15C) with a design of superimposed tierce point bays.

Mengstraße (Y) – Much of the original character remains in this street, with its varied brick gables at the lower end recalling the rivalries of rich neighbours in years gone by. The two houses now occupied by the Schabbelhaus restaurant have been restored with great care.

Dom (Cathedral) (Z) – The 14C enlargement of the chancel in the Gothic style transformed this Romanesque church. A covered entrance and a very fine porch were added to the north transept in the mid 13C. Inside, there is an imposing monumental Late Gothic **Crucifix**★ made between 1470-77 by Bernt Notke. A stone screen (second half of the 14C) with a wooden tracery balustrade closes off the choir. There are some fine altarpieces against the pillars in the transept: the altarpiece of the Merchants of Stecknitz (1422); the altarpiece of the canonical daily offices, from the early 15C; altarpiece of the millhands (c 1460); and the altarpiece of Our Lady (1506).

★ **St. Annen-Museum** ⊙ (Z M¹) – Installed in a former monastery, this museum devoted to the art and cultural history of the town has a rich department of religious sculpture, including works by the master sculptors of Lübeck. Note also an altarpiece depicting the Passion, painted by Hans Memling in 1491.

Behnhaus and Drägerhaus ⊙ (XY M²) – The **Behnhaus** (1780-1810) with its classic façade and beautiful interior provides an attractive setting for paintings, sculptures and commercial art from the Romantic period up to the present time. The **Drägerhaus**, formerly a merchant's meeting place, displays works by artists up to Edvard Munch, in addition to paintings by the Lübeck artist Johann Friedrich Overbeck (1789-1869). The beautiful banqueting halls and living areas are furnished in historical style.

EXCURSION

★ Travemünde – *20km/12.5mi to the northeast.*
This smart Baltic health resort boasts a fine sandy beach, a 2.5km/1.5mi-long promenade and a casino. **Travemünde week** is an annual event for German and foreign yachtsmen. Travemünde is also a well-known port, with links to Scandinavia and Estonia.
The old town, with its half-timbered houses and the fishermen's church of St. Lorenz, is charming. Along the seafront there are some typical local gabled houses dating from the 18C and 19C. The four-masted bark *Passat*, a former trading ship, lies at anchor on the **Priwall** peninsula, on the opposite bank (*accessible by ferry*).
The steep coastline of the **Brodten shore** stretches for several miles behind the promenade. A walk as far as **Niendorf** affords wonderful views over Lübeck Bay and the coastline. The popular Baltic Sea resort of **Timmendorfer Strand** lies further to the north.

LÜNEBURG★★

Niedersachsen

Population 65 000

Michelin map 415/416 G 15

The Salt Town – The town of Lüneburg is built on a salt deposit from which brine was extracted until as recently as 1980. Salt has thus been at the source of Lüneburg's prosperity since the 10C. In the Middle Ages the town was the principal supplier of the mineral to many places, notably Scandinavia, where, because of the Baltic's low saline content, it was always in short supply. Traffic followed the **Old Salt Route**, via Lauenburg, Ratzeburg and Lübeck.

Brick houses – The traditional architecture of Lüneburg is distinguished by stepped and scrolled gables, cornices with rounded or tierce point blind arcades, and the "Tausteine" – a local twisted brick feature producing an effect like a cable stitch.

SIGHTS

★★ Rathaus ⊘ (Y R) – The municipal headquarters is an assembly of different buildings dating from the 13C to the 18C. The **Great Council Chamber★★** (Große Ratsstube), on the right of the entrance hall, is a Renaissance masterpiece (1566-84). Panelled throughout, it is adorned with intricate wood sculptures by Albert von Soest: note the wealth of expression in the small heads rhythmically animating the frieze beneath allegorical paintings. The fine door frames also are worth attention.
The **Princes' Apartment** (Fürstensaal), on the first floor, is equally rewarding. It is Gothic, with lamps fashioned from stags' antlers and a superbly beamed and painted ceiling.
The **Hall of Justice** (Gerichtslaube, c 1330), with its cradle vaulting, is decorated on walls and ceilings with paintings inspired by the etchings of Hans Burgkmair and Heinrich Aldegrever.

★ Old Town – The houses here are characterized by the traditional brick architecture. Typical are those lining the long, narrow square known as **Am Sande★** (Z), especially no 1, the 16C **Black House** (Schwarzes Haus or Schütting), which was once a brewery and now houses the International Chamber of Commerce.
In the Große Bäckerstraße (no 10) stands the **Rathsapotheke** (pharmacy) (Y A), which dates, with its fine twisted brick gables, from 1598. The Reitende-Diener-Straße (Y 40) comprises a double row of identical low houses, each embellished with medallions and, again, twisted brick cornices.
Rotehahnstraße (Y 43) is a particularly picturesque street. Note especially no 14, the **Haus Roter Hahn** (Y D), a former 16C hospice with three half-timbered gables and a pretty inner courtyard.

St. Johanniskirche (Z E) – The robust **west tower** (108m/354ft high) is displaced from the vertical at the top by 2m/6ft 6in and has been refurbished several times. The church itself dates from the 13C. The huge interior, with five naves and two rows of side chapels, forms a perfect square, closed at the east end by plain polygonal apses.
The most valuable item of the furnishings is the sculpted reredos of the high altar, which has painted panels depicting scenes from the lives of John the Baptist, St Cecilia, St Ursula and St George (1482). The 16C **organ**, enlarged in the early 18C, is one of the oldest in Germany. Note also the 15C candelabra in honour of the Virgin Mary (north side aisle) and sandstone epitaphs by Albert von Soest.

LÜNEBURG

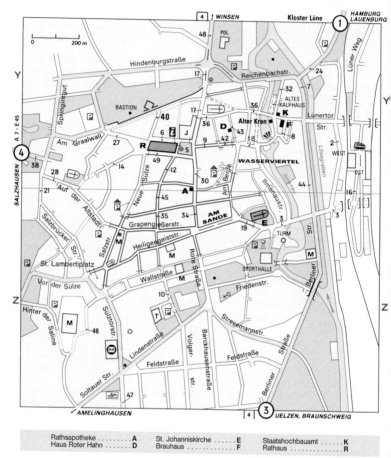

Rathsapotheke ....**A**	St. Johanniskirche .....**E**	Staatshochbauamt ......**K**
Haus Roter Hahn ......**D**	Brauhaus ....**F**	Rathaus ....**R**

★ **Old Port Quarter (Wasserviertel)** – There is a particularly fine view of this district from the bridge across the Ilmenau. To the left is the Alter Kran (Y), a crane dating from the 14C, converted in the 18C. Looking upstream ,there is a good view of the Lüner Mühle, a grand half-timbered mill building dating from the 16C, of the Abtswasserturm (water-tower) in the centre and, to the right, of the rear of the old houses along Am Stintmarkt. A **brewery**★ (Brauhaus) (Y **F**) stands at the corner of the Am Werder square and Lünertorstraße. This is a Renaissance building, its gables once more decorated with medallions and twisted brick motifs. The oriel construction on the front of this 1550 building was not added until the 17C. Further on, at the corner of Lünertorstraße and Kaufhausstraße, is a striking house (Staatshochbauamt) (Y **K**) built in 1574 with remarkable rusticated half-pilasters in sandstone and a solid cornice. Beside it, note the Baroque façade (1741-45) of an old warehouse (Altes Kaufhaus).

EXCURSIONS

Kloster Lüne – 2km/1.2mi via ① on the plan.
This abbey dates from the 15C and makes a harmonious complex set among its conventual buildings. It has housed a community of Protestant nuns since the Reformation. Particularly fine features include the Gothic **cloister** and fountain, the nuns' choir, the refectory and the summer refectory. Inside the abbey church are a fine altarpiece from 1524 and a Baroque organ from 1645. There is an interesting little **tapestry museum**★ with Gothic tapestries and finely worked embroidery.

Lauenburg an der Elbe – *25km/15.5mi via ① on the plan.*
A sleepy township today, Lauenburg commands a point where the ancient salt route from Lüneburg to Lübeck crossed the Elbe. At the foot of a steep, wooded slope, lie old **half-timbered houses** clustered along Elbstraße. These were built from the 16C to the 19C. They are dwarfed by the tower of the Maria-Magdalena-Kirche dating from 1227. All that remains of the mighty fortress begun in 1182 is the castle tower of 1477. The other extant parts of the castle date from the late 17C and early 18C.

The **Elbe Navigation Museum** (Elbschiffahrtsmuseum) ⊙ – in the lower town, at no 59 Elbstraße – relates the history of river traffic between Bohemia and Hamburg with the help of models, documents, illustrated panels and even ships' engines (*demonstrations*).

LÜNEBURGER HEIDE

LÜNEBURG HEATH – Niedersachsen

Michelin map 415/416 G 13-15

The great expanse of Lüneburg Heath stretches between the glacial valleys of the Aller to the south and the Elbe to the north.

It is Pastor of the heath Wilhelm Bode (1860-1927), who initiated the transformation of the Lüneburg Heath into a nature reserve, whom visitors have to thank for the fact that they are able to enjoy the delights of this once undervalued region. To preserve the heath from the increasing advances of agriculture and forestry, a 200km²/77sq mi **nature reserve** has been created in the neighbourhood of the **Wilseder Berg**, where the flora and fauna are protected and motor cars only permitted on the main roads which cross the heath. Considerable effort is being made to preserve the rural character of Lower Saxony housing, and even outside the reserve villages on the heath have retained much of their old-world charm – notably in the case of their wooden belfries, separated from the church and half hidden in plantations of trees.

TOWNS, LANDSCAPES AND SIGHTS

Bergen-Belsen – *7km/4mi southwest of Bergen.*
The **memorial** (Gedenkstätte) raised to the victims of the Bergen-Belsen concentration camp – erected in 1946 on the orders of the British Military Government – stands in solitude in a clearing on Lüneburg Heath surrounded by pines and birch trees. There is a **documentation centre** (Dokumentenhaus) at the entrance, with a permanent exhibition retracing the history of the camp.

The Monument – *From the car park, 45min there and back on foot.* The monument is beyond the tumulus which marks the site of the mass graves. It is a simple obelisk in pale volcanic tufa, with inscriptions in 13 languages honouring the memory of those who fell victim to the Nazis' "extermination" policy.

★★ **Celle** – *See CELLE.*

Ebstorf – *26km/16mi south of Lüneburg.* Do not miss the former **Benedictine abbey** (Ehemaliges Benediktinerkloster) ⊙ in this small town, where the 14C and 15C cloister and nuns' gallery are the most impressive features among the ruins. A life-size wooden statue of St Maurice (1300) and several Romanesque and Gothic Virgins can be seen in the gallery. Visitors interested in cartography can see a reproduction **Mappa Mundi**★ (Ebstorfer Weltkarte). The famous 13C original, once preserved

in the abbey, was destroyed during the Second World War.

Lönsgrab – *Between Fallingbostel and Walsrode, in the bird reserve (Vogelpark-Region).*

Sheep keeping the Lüneburg Heath in trim

The tomb of the poet **Hermann Löns** (1866-1914), who celebrated the beauties of the heath with extravagant lyricism, can be seen here in a setting of junipers.

Handwerksmuseum am Mühlenberg in Suhlendorf ⊙ – The location of this craft museum is indicated by a tall windmill visible from some way off. The museum, which has a sizeable collection of mills, documents the work of a miller. Various workshops contain displays on other professions (saddler, smith, cobbler).

The Heath

In the Middle Ages, the name "heath" signified the boundary of a village. Only later did it come to mean the common heather (Calluna vulgaris) which carpets the whole area with its rose-pink hue in August and September. The bell-heather (Erica tetralix) which blooms in July is also found on the heath, but it is very rare, preferring moorland and damp areas.

Although we may be tempted to think of the term heath as the epitome of a natural landscape, in reality it is man-made dwarf shrubland. 5 000 years ago the area was covered in forest, which was uprooted by farmers. Cattle were then driven into the forest to finish off the farmers' work. Only then was the light-hungry heath able to spread. To prevent the forest taking hold again, the practices of burning, allowing cropping by moorland sheep, or lifting turf (the heath was grubbed up using a hoe) were employed.

Flora and fauna – The **Juniper** (Juniperus communis) gives the region a quite special character. The bushes appear either individually or in groups. The heath is also home to birch, mountain ash, pine and oak, together with common gorse and broom, silver grass and matgrass, crowberries, bilberries and cranberries.

The **moorland sheep** are "living mowers". Where they are still used as such, they maintain the heath heather at an optimum height of 20cm/8in. Both the males and the females have horns, those of the male being spectacularly coiled. They have dark heads and legs. There were one million moorland sheep on the heath around 1800, when it was much larger, but there are only a few thousand head left today.

The bees are also an intrinsic feature of the heath. They frequently belong to travelling beekeepers, who bring their swarms to the heath flowers, sometimes in the baskets known as "Lüneburger Bogenstülpern".

The largest bird seen on the heath is the blackcock with its lyre-shaped tail, although it is now virtually extinct. There are plenty of buzzards, red kites, hobbies and kestrels, not forgetting the herons and snipes in the lowlands and high moors. Autumn visitors include flocks of fieldfares.

Boulders – Large and small boulders made of granite, and in some cases porphyry, are scattered all over the heath. They came from Scandinavia as boulder clay and were left behind when the glaciers of the last Ice Age retreated over 18 000 years ago. The angular or sharp polished stones known in German as Windkanter were formed by corrosion.

Heide-Park Soltau

Mountain rafting at Heide-Park Soltau

★ **Heide-Park Soltau** ⊙ – This well-maintained leisure park offers 40 different kinds of ride. It is organized into areas on various themes, such as the heath itself, a Dutch village, or Little America, and some of the attractions on offer involve roller-coasters, cable railways and water flumes. The park is home to animals such as dolphins, sea-lions and crocodiles. A particular favourite with visitors is the mountain rafting in circular rafts, or a breathtaking ride on the "Limit" roller-coaster.

★ **Undeloh** – The charming village of Undeloh, with its old houses sheltered beneath huge oak trees, is the departure point for the 4km/2.5mi trip to Wilsede, a nature reserve village which has been kept untouched by the onward march of a mechanised civilization *(cars are not allowed: there is a service of horse-drawn vehicles from Undeloh).*

★ **Vogelpark Walsrode** ⊙ – *Follow the itinerary sign: Rundgang.*
Almost 5 000 birds (850 species, from all parts of the world) live in this fine 22ha/54-acre **ornithological park**, most of them in their natural habitat and at semi-liberty. Waders and web-footed birds, as well as parrots and budgerigars, are particularly well represented in the ornithological park, the largest of its kind in the world. A tropical plant house is occupied by a range of exotic bird-life unlike any to be found in a zoo.
A historic half-timbered house (1717) contains the **German Birdcage Museum** (Deutsches Vogelbauermuseum), where an incredible number of birdcages are on display.

★ **Kloster Wienhausen** – *See CELLE: Excursions.*

★ **Wilseder Berg** – From the summit (there is a marker post: 169m/554ft), a vast **panorama**★ of heath and woodlands is visible. On a clear day, the spires of the churches of Hamburg can be seen, 40km/25mi away to the north.

MAGDEBURG★★

Sachsen-Anhalt
Population 240 000
Michelin map 416/418 J 18

Mid-way along the 1 100km/683mi course of the Elbe, on its journey from northern Bohemia to the North Sea, lies Magdeburg, regional capital of Sachsen-Anhalt. This town in the German heartlands was an important trade centre before the Middle Ages and has had an eventful history. From the original Carolingian fortress evolved the favourite imperial palace of Otto the Great. The town subsequently became an important centre for the Premonstratensian Order in Germany, a place of refuge during the Reformation, Prussia's most secure stronghold and an industrial capital. Despite the ravages of the Thirty Years War and the bombardments of the Second World War, Magdeburg is now a thriving centre for culture and the service industries, situated between Hanover and Berlin. Many of its major sights and architectural witnesses to its turbulent 1 200-year history have happily survived. Magdeburg's mid-way location on the "Straße der Romanik" tourist route (retracing evidence of the Romanesque period) offers possibilities further afield to its visitors.

Famous local figures include Archbishop Norbert of Xanten, the medieval mystic Mechthild of Magdeburg, Bürgermeister **Otto von Guericke** (1602-86), German physicist who carried out experiments in creating vacuums using water pumps, and the composer **Georg Philipp Telemann** (1681-1767), one of the luminaries of Baroque music, who composed about 600 overtures, not to mention many operas, oratorios and concertos.

National garden display – Magdeburg made good use of the opportunity presented by the 1999 national garden display (Bundesgartenschau). The 140ha/345 acre green to the east of the Elbe, the Cracauer Anger, which was the home of a Russian tank unit during the days of the German Democratic Republic, was transformed into a variety of styles of garden. A 60m/200ft "millennium tower", the world's tallest wooden construction, was used as an exhibition centre. Further possibilities for leisure entertainment are offered by a 3km/2mi long elevated railway on stilts, open-air stages and a summer toboggan run.

★★★ DOM ST. MAURITUS UND ST. KATHARINA (z)

In the Domplatz. Entrance through the north doorway.

At a time when the Romanesque style in Germany was losing its impetus, the construction of Magdeburg Cathedral at the beginning of the 13C marked the first attempt to impose a Gothic style derived from the architectural precepts of the great French cathedrals. The decision was taken by Archbishop Albrecht II, who had studied in France and witnessed the new cathedrals being built there, and following a fire in the original Ottonian building the foundation stone of the new cathedral was laid in 1209. Several of the architects commissioned to work on the project were French.

If certain alterations which supervened at different stages of the construction denied the building as a whole a stylistic unity, Magdeburg Cathedral can nevertheless be considered the first great German Gothic religious edifice, well ahead of its time.

Outside, the three levels of the east end (absidioles, ambulatory, apse) at once give an impression of power.

On the north side, the **Paradise Doorway** *(reached from inside the cathedral)* displays **statues★★** of the Wise and Foolish Virgins. Dating from c 1245, these, in common with statuary at Strasbourg, Bamberg and Naumburg, mark a stage in the evolution of Gothic sculpture, which became more and more inclined towards the expression of emotional feeling.

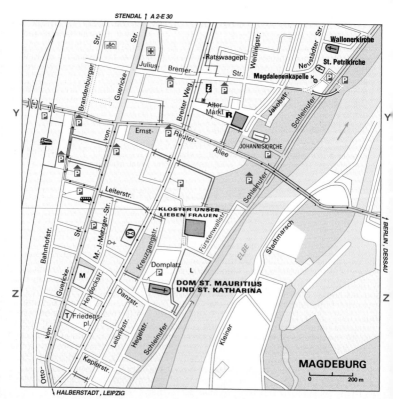

A statue of Emperor Otto I stands at the late-15C west door. In the cloister's north gallery, the **chapel of the fountains** (Brunnenkapelle) is remarkable for the elegance of its rib vaulting.

Interior – Slender divided pillars framed by columns of Italian porphyry distinguish the polygonal chancel. The upper gallery, built between 1232 and 1240 by Cistercian workers from Maulbronn, combines forms of great simplicity not unlike those characterizing the monastic style of Burgundy.

A 1240 modification of the original plan having suppressed the intermediate pillars, the tall nave with its wide bays admits an abundance of light to illuminate the works of art displayed.

Sculpture – A southeast transept pillar incorporates a sandstone **statue**★ (c 1240) of St Maurice, with black African features. In the high chancel, there are **bronze funerary plaques**★★ in memory of the archbishops Friedrich of Wettin (d 1152) and Wichmann of Seeburg (d 1192).

Seated **statues**★ said to represent Christ and the Church are more likely in fact to be Otto I and his wife, the Anglo-Saxon princess Edith. Dating from c 1245, they are housed in a small 16-sided chapel off the north aisle. The emperor's tomb is located in the high chancel. Further interesting sculpture includes the

Statue of Otto I and Empress Edith in the cathedral of St. Mauritius und St. Katharina

statue of St Catherine and the Annunciation group (smiling angel) of 1240, the choir stalls of 1360 with outstanding carved decoration, and the remarkable Renaissance pulpit. In between the cathedral towers there is a **bronze tomb**★ of the Archbishop Ernst, which was cast in 1495 in the foundry of Peter Vischer of Nuremberg. Note also the memorial to those who fell in the First World War by Ernst Barlach (1929).

ADDITIONAL SIGHTS

★★ **Kloster Unser Lieben Frauen** ⊙ (Z) – *Regierungsstraße*. This abbey was founded in 1017 and 1018 by Archbishop Gero on the fringe of the Germanic lands – separated from the Slav countries at the time by the Elbe. In 1064 Archbishop Werner authorised the reconstruction of the site, which was completed in 1170. The Premonstratensian Order took over the abbey in 1129 and ran it until 1632. After they moved out the abbey was used as a seminary and school until 1945. Since 1974 it has been a concert venue and art museum.

Gothic vaulting was added to the church in 1220-40. North of the church lie the **cloisters**★, some of the best preserved in Germany; the west gallery was almost entirely rebuilt in 1945.

Rathaus (Y R) – In front of the two-storey Baroque town hall (1691-98) stands the famous statue of **The Magdeburg Knight** (c 1240 - copy), one of the oldest equestrian sculptures in Germany. Next to the town hall is a monument to Otto von Guericke (*see above*).

Petriberg (Y) – North of the town hall, on the banks of the Elbe. Three churches stand on the riverside rise: the **Magdalenenkapelle**, with a single Gothic nave; **St. Petrikirche**, a Gothic hall-church with three aisles (1380-1490); and the **Wallonenkirche**, a former abbey church (1285-1366) built by a community which came from the Netherlands (thus its Walloon name).

The Michelin on-line route planning service is available on a pay-per-route basis, or you may opt for a subscription package. This option affords you multiple route plans at considerable savings. Plan your next trip in minutes with Michelin on Internet: www.michelin-travel.com.

MAINZ★

Rheinland-Pfalz
Population 186 000
Michelin map 417 Q 8

Formerly the episcopal seat of the influential Prince-Electors, Mainz – elevated in 1949 to be the capital of the Land of Rheinland-Pfalz – is ideally placed for trade. Situated at the confluence of the Rhine and the Main, the city is Germany's largest and most important wine market. It is also the site of a famous annual carnival, the gaiety and colourful buffoonery of which are televised all over the country (*see Calendar of events*). **Johannes Gutenberg** (c 1394-1468), the father of modern printing, is the city's most prominent son.

Bird's-eye view – The restaurant An der Favorite, at the highest point of the **Stadtpark (BY)**, affords a general view of the city on either side of the Rhine.

CATHEDRAL QUARTER (Z) *allow 2hr*

Leaving the Liebfrauenplatz, walk down the Domstraße and then left around the cathedral.

From the Leichhof square, there is a **view★★** of the cathedral in its entirety, the west chancel and transept rising loftily, their complex ridge roofs overlooked by the lantern tower which crowns the transept crossing. Baroque as well as Gothic elements adorn the upper part of this tower, which rests on a Romanesque base showing a Lombard influence.

The adjoining square, known as the Höfchen, is extended towards the south by the Gutenbergplatz (containing Thorwaldsen's statue of the craftsman printer, a theatre and the House of German Wines) and to the northeast by the market square, embellished with a **Renaissance fountain** (Renaissancebrunnen) (**Z A**).

Enter via the doorway opening onto the market square (Marktportal).

★ **Dom (Cathedral)** – The cathedral is an enormous reconstructed Romanesque building – a basilica with two chancels, one in the west, leading off a wide transept whose crossing is illuminated by a fine Rhenish dome and one in the east of simpler architectural style.

Fixed to the massive Romanesque columns is a collection of archiepiscopal **funerary monuments★** (Grabdenkmäler der Erzbischöfe).

Turn left into the north aisle on entering the church.

In the second chapel (**1**), there is a moving late-15C Entombment. A multicoloured Gothic funerary monument is attached to one of the main pillars (**2**).

In the east crypt, beneath the chancel, a modern **gold reliquary** (**3**) of the Saints of Mainz stands upon the altar.

A pillar (**4**) on the south side of the east chancel steps bears another Gothic funerary monument in many colours, surrounded by statuettes of St Benedict, St Catherine, St Maurice and St Clare.

A door in the south aisle leads to the **cloisters★** (Kreuzgang). In addition to the tombstones, there is a low relief (**5**), remodelled in 1783, of the master-singer Heinrich von Meißen, known as "Frauenlob" – a man who, having sung the praises of women all his life, was finally laid to rest by the burgesses of Mainz in 1323.

Fine statues adorn the doorway (**6**) of the former chapter-house (Kapitelsaal), built in the 15C in an elegant Rhineland style. Cross the transept below the west chancel steps and go into the opposite arm, where there is a fine 1328 baptismal font in pewter (**7**), ornamented with deli-

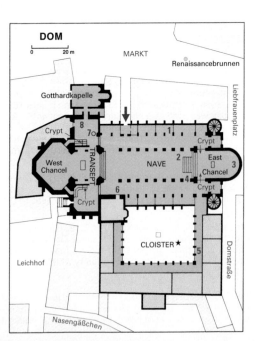

DOM
0   20 m
MARKT
Renaissancebrunnen
Gotthardkapelle
Liebfrauenplatz
Crypt   8   7o   1
Crypt
West Chancel   TRANSEPT   NAVE   2   East Chancel   3
Crypt
6   4
Crypt
CLOISTER ★   5
Leichhof   Domstraße
Nasengäßchen

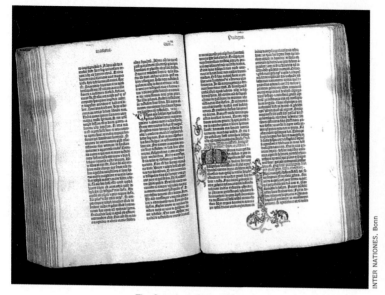

The Gutenberg Bible, Mainz

cately worked figures. Beyond, a Romanesque doorway (8) leads to the Gotthardkapelle, built in the same style with a square plan and a two-storey elevation.

★★ Gutenberg-Museum ⊘ (Z M¹) – The visitor to this museum is reminded how, over the centuries, men of taste and discrimination have nurtured the art of the printed word, regarding it as one of the most precious treasures of civilization, to be guarded and passed on as a sacred trust as its usage developed and spread.

In the basement of the building, the reconstruction of an early print shop (15C), the so-called "Gutenberg-Werkstatt", gives an idea of the developments in working conditions and technology in the world of printing. On the first floor, along with incunabula and ancient presses, there is a collection of editions published between the 16C and the 19C. The museum's prize exhibit, two original editions of the world-famous **Gutenberg Bible★★★** (1452-55), with 42 lines to the page, are on display in a second floor strong room. This three volume work in Latin is the earliest complete book printed using movable type to have survived in the West. It is sometimes known as the Mazarin Bible, as the first documented copy was kept in the Paris Library of Cardinal Mazarin.

Polychromatic wood engravings and printed works from China, Japan and Korea can be seen in the Far East Department on the third floor. Displays on modern book production and "paper" are on the fourth floor.

ADDITIONAL SIGHTS

★ **Römisch-Germanisches Museum** (Romano-German Museum) ⊘ (BV M²) – Installed in the one-time Electors' Palace (15C-17C) and the Steinhalle opposite, the three departments of this museum house collections on the pre- and proto-history of ancient Europe and the advanced Mediterranean civilizations, and ancient Roman and early medieval archeology.

★ **Landesmuseum Mainz** ⊘ (Z M³) – The Department of Antiquities traces Rhineland civilization from prehistory to the present. Of particular interest is the Steinhalle which houses some 300 stone memorials dating from the Roman colonization of Germany, including Jupiter's Column (Jupitersäule). A copy of this column stands in the Deutschhaus-Platz (BV D). The museum's medieval and Baroque sections and its extensive collections of Höchst porcelain and Jugendstil glassware are also well worth seeing. The 20C Department houses the largest collection of works by Tàpies in Germany.

Schillerplatz and Schillerstraße (Z) – The Baroque mansions in this square and street now house (after restoration) the ministries of the Rheinland-Pfalz. In the centre of Schillerplatz, a fountain is decorated with scenes illustrating the carnival.

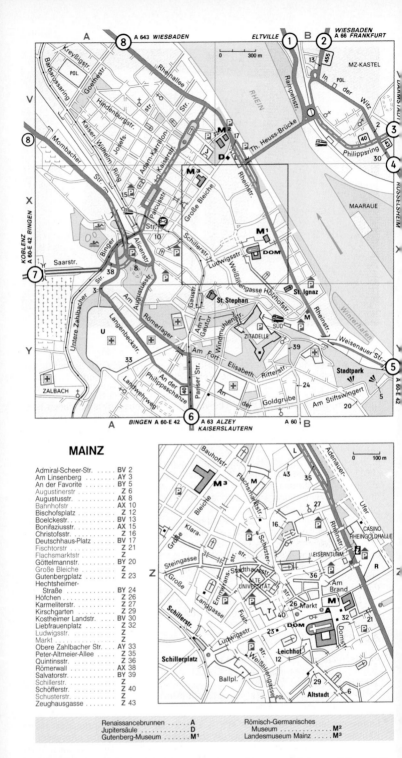

MAINZ

Renaissancebrunnen	A		
Jupitersäule	D		
Gutenberg-Museum	M¹		
Römisch-Germanisches Museum		M²	
Landesmuseum Mainz		M³	

Old Town (Altstadt) (BYZ) – Off Augustinerstraße, the chief thoroughfare of the old quarter, which is virtually intact, opens the picturesque Kirschgarten square, lined with pretty half-timbered houses. Kapuzinerstraße (note several houses with sandstone door frames and Rococo panels) leads to the church of St. Ignaz, past several inviting little streets.

Stephanskirche (ABY) – Virtually all that remained of this late 13C church, severely damaged in the Second World War, were the outside walls and Gothic pillars. It was rebuilt between 1946-63. The east chancel is renowned for its remarkable series of modern **stained-glass windows★★**, by Marc Chagall between

1978-85, illustrating themes from the Bible. There are a further 19 windows by Charles Marq (1989-2000). Built against the south wall is a restored **cloister**★ (1465-99) of which the intricate and varied vaulting expresses all the virtuosity of Late Gothic design.

Ignazkirche (BY) – This church is the work of JP Jäger, built in 1763-75 and illustrating the transition from Rococo to neo-Classicism. Outside the church, on the left, stands an imposing 16C group of the **Crucifixion**★ (Kreuzigungsgruppe), by Mainz artist Hans Backoffen (1519), who designed it as his own funerary monument.

MANNHEIM

Baden-Württemberg

Population 324 000

Michelin map 417/419 R 9

Mannheim, at the confluence of the Rhine and the Neckar, is the second largest river port in Europe *(motorboat trips around the port area start from the Kurpfalzbrücke, the bridge spanning the Neckar)*. The town, founded in 1607 by the Palatine elector Friedrich IV, was conceived as a fortified residential enclave. Conforming to a rigid plan, the centre comprises a checkerboard of 142 identical blocks **(Quadratstadt)**, each identified only by a letter and number according to its coordinates on the city plan. Local enthusiasm for the arts – especially the theatre, where the works of Schiller were first performed – soon made Mannheim a cultural as well as a trade centre.

SIGHTS

★★ **Städtische Kunsthalle (Fine Arts Museum)** ⊘ (DZ **M¹**) – Installed in a Jugendstil building designed by H Billing in 1907, the museum concentrates on works of the 19C and 20C. Sculpture, including works by Rodin, Lehmbruck, Barlach, Brancusi, Giacometti, Moore, Nam June Paik, Richard Long and Mario Merz, form the focal point of the art collection. Important works from the collection of paintings include the *Execution of Emperor Maximilian* by Manet and *The Pipe Smoker* by Cézanne, together with paintings by Corot, Monet and Pissarro.

The German Secession artists are represented by Slevogt and Corinth, and the Expressionists by Beckmann, Heckel *(Sunflowers)*, Kokoschka *(View of Amsterdam)* and the Belgian James Ensor *(Still-life)*. Other departments exhibit works from the New Objectivity period and post-1945 art.

The museum is famous for holding special exhibitions on classical modern and contemporary art which are particularly rich in content.

★ **Museum für Kunst-, Stadt- und Theatergeschichte im Reiß-Museum** ⊘ (CY **M²**) – *In the Arsenal (Zeughaus, built 1777-79).*

The **Art History** Department houses mainly sculpture and painting of the Palatinate electorate dating from the 18C, together with Baroque and Rococo furniture. There is an outstanding, even on an international scale, collection of **European porcelain and faience**★, with the highlight of this comprehensive display being Frankenthal porcelain from the Palatinate.

The **local history** collections chronicle the development of the town.

The **theatre collection** is housed in the basement, and retraces the history of the Mannheim national theatre through costumes, props and audio-visual media.

★ **Museum für Archäologie, Völker- und Naturkunde (Museum of Archeology, Ethnology and Natural History)** ⊘ (CY **M³**) – *In the Mutschler-Bau opposite the arsenal.* The archeology collections include important artefacts from the Paleolithic and Mesolithic eras to the Carolingian period, as well as finds from Ancient Greece, Antique Italy and the Roman Empire. High and Late Middle Ages are represented, as is the archeology of the modern period with town centre excavations.

The exhibition of **folklore**★ is conceived as a tour around the Old World, from the Tuareg in North Africa via the Islamic cultures of the Near East, to India. The **Benin collection**★ is of international significance.

Schloß ⊘ (CZ) – The building of this Baroque palace, the biggest in all of Germany (400 rooms, 2 000 windows), lasted from 1720 to 1760. Restored after the Second World War, the palace is now occupied by departments of the university. Two wings at right angles to the central block enclose an enormous main courtyard. The palace church terminates the right wing, the former palace library the left.

From the state staircase inside, there is a view down the entire perspective of Kurpfalzstraße, the street that bisects the chessboard centre from one end to the other, as far as the River Neckar.

The painted ceilings have been restored after the original work of Cosmas Damian Asam. The same artist was responsible for the ceiling of the church (Schloßkirche) and the frescoes in the **Knights' Hall** (Rittersaal). The most interesting apartment is the green and rose **Rococo library** in the university wing, which is embellished with stucco-work, panelling and camaïeu (monochrome) paintings.

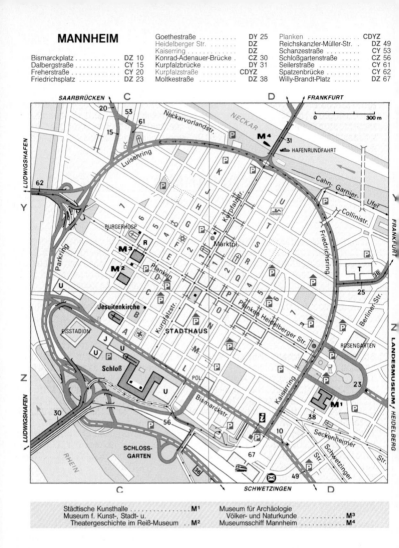

Städtische Kunsthalle .... M¹
Museum f. Kunst-, Stadt- u.
    Theatergeschichte im Reiß-Museum .. M²

Museum für Archäologie
    Völker- und Naturkunde .... M³
Museumsschiff Mannheim .... M⁴

★ **Jesuitenkirche** (CZ) – Founded at the same time as the palace (building in fact lasted from 1733 to 1769), this massive edifice is said to be the biggest Baroque church of the Upper Rhine. The façade is Classical with the three orders superposed. The green and red marble stuccowork lends colour to the well-lit interior. The high altar by Peter Anton von Verschaffelt, which was destroyed in the Second World War, is currently being rebuilt, as are the former electoral court galleries. The contemporary design of the chancel is the work of the sculptor Klaus Ringwald from Schonach. **The Silver Virgin with her Crown of Light** (Silbermadonna im Strahlenkranz), in the northern aisle, is the work of the Augsburg silversmith JI Saler (1747).

★ **Landesmuseum für Technik und Arbeit in Mannheim** (Regional Museum of Industrial Techniques) ⊘ – At Museumsstraße 1 (DZ).
Two hundred and fifty years of industrial development in southwest Germany are retraced in this modernistic building, which impresses with the elegance, lightness and transparence of its architecture. Over 7 500m²/80 700sq ft of floor space, the museum, which was opened in 1990, examines the relationship between industrialisation and the evolution of society, together with innumerable demonstrations of various technologies (weaving, papermaking, printing, plastics manufacture, steam locomotives etc).

Museumsschiff Mannheim (Boat Museum) ⊘ (DY M⁴) – This museum, an annexe of the Landesmuseum für Technik und Arbeit, is installed in the paddle-steamer *Mainz*, which was built in 1929 and is now moored beneath the Kurpfalzbrücke, on the Neckar.
The engine room and galley are well worth a visit. Many models are on display, along with river charts, photographs and equipment illustrating the history of navigation on the Rhine and Neckar.

MARBURG★★

Hessen

Population 85 000
Michelin map 41.7 N 10

Marburg was once a great pilgrimage centre, with crowds being drawn to the town to venerate the relics of St Elizabeth of Hungary. Since the Reformation, and still maintaining the magnificent Gothic cathedral dedicated to the saint and the equally impressive Landgraves' castle, Marburg has, thanks to its university founded in 1527, become a centre of Protestant scholarship and theology. Highlights of the town are the Landgraves' palace and the Early Gothic Elisabethkirche.

St Elizabeth (1207-31) – Princess Elizabeth, daughter of the King of Hungary and the intended bride of the Landgrave Ludwig of Thuringia, was brought to the Thuringian court at Wartburg Castle near Eisenach at the age of four. Early in her life she became known for her kindness to the sick and unfortunate, and there are many stories concerning the ruses she employed to help them. In 1227 her husband Ludwig died of the plague, and Elizabeth resolved to withdraw from the world. She was given Marburg, in the far west of Thuringian territory, as her widow's seat. The hard work of her daughter Sophie of Brabant later made this into the seed from which Hessen would grow. Elisabeth died of exhaustion at the age of 24. Canonized only four years later (1235), she was to have her remains exhumed the following year in the presence of Emperor Friedrich II, to be immortalized in the superb Gothic church built by the members of the Teutonic Order to receive them. This was also to become the burial place for the Landgraves of Hessen.

In 1529 one of her descendants, the **Landgrave Philip the Magnanimous**, one of the most important Protestant princes of the Reformation period, decided to abolish the cult of relics. He had the shrine forced open and personally removed his ancestor's bones to bury them in a nearby cemetery. This is the same Philip who invited the Reformers Luther and Zwingli to a meeting that was to become known as the "Marburg Religious Discussion" (1-3 October 1529).

★★ OLD MARBURG AND THE ELISABETHKIRCHE *allow 2hr*

★★ **Elisabethkirche** ⊙ (BY) – The first truly Gothic church in Germany, this was built between 1235 and 1283. Its regional character derives from the stylistic unity of the chancel and transepts, each terminating in an apse, and from its three aisles of equal height – making it in fact the first hall-church. Transverse roof timbers covering the side aisles are typically Hessian. The towers, surmounted by stone spires, rest on massive buttresses.

Enter through the main doorway.

Nave – Note the following works:

1) A statue of St Elizabeth (c 1470) wearing an elegant court gown.

2) An openwork Gothic rood with finely decorated consoles; on the altar *(nave side)*, a modern Crucifix by Ernst Barlach.

Chancel and transepts – A collection of exceptional works of art★★★:

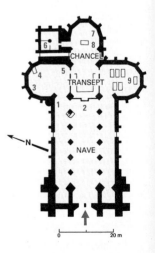

3) Altarpiece of the Virgin; 1360 Pietà in the predella.

4) Tomb of St Elizabeth (after 1250). The 14C bas-relief on the sarcophagus represents the saint's burial.

5) The remains of frescoes visible in the niches date from the 14C and 15C. On the right, a scene evoking St Elizabeth's charitable activities (the Landgrave sees in his imagination the Saviour, in a bed in which Elizabeth placed a sick man); the formal exhumation of 1236.

6) **St Elizabeth's Shrine**★★ (Elisabethschrein) in the old sacristy. This masterpiece of the goldsmith's art was completed by craftsmen from the Rhineland c 1250. Scenes from the saint's life enrich the casket's sloping panels.

7) St Elizabeth's Window. Assembled from a collection of 13C medallions, this illustrates the charitable works of the saint.

8) Above the former priest's seat, a statue of St Elizabeth as the personification of Charity (the work, dating from 1510, is attributed to Ludwig Juppe, one of the most illustrious Marburg artists).

9) "The Landgraves' Chancel" *(in fact the south transept)*. Necropolis of the Landgraves of Hessen descended from St Elizabeth.

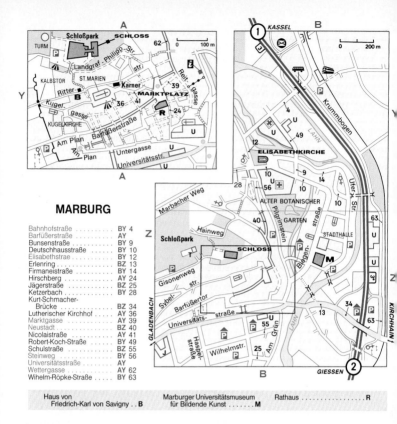

MARBURG

Haus von Friedrich-Karl von Savigny **B**	Marburger Universitätsmuseum für Bildende Kunst **M**	Rathaus **R**

The chapel beneath the tower immediately on the left contains the tomb of Field-Marshal von Hindenburg (1847-1934).

Leaving the church, climb up into the old town by way of the Steinweg – an unusual ramp with three different levels, which continues as the Neustadt and then the Wettergasse.

Turn right into the Marktgasse.

★ **Marktplatz (AY)** – Only the upper part, the Obermarkt, has retained its original old houses. Particularly outstanding examples among them include nos 14 and 21, dating from 1560, no 23, and no 18, a stone house of 1323 and the oldest preserved house still inhabited.

The market fountain, dedicated to St George who is depicted vanquishing the dragon, is a popular student's meeting place.

Rathaus (AY R) – A Gothic building built in 1512-27. Above a door in the staircase tower is a fine carving by Ludwig Juppe, representing Elizabeth bearing her coat of arms of the House of Hessen-Thuringia. A mechanical cock crows the hours from the gable.

Past the Gothic ossuary (Karner), the Nikolaistraße now leads to the forecourt of the Marienkirche (late 13C), from which there is a fine view over the roofs of the old town to the valley beyond. Past the church façade, at the top of a steep slope, there is a glimpse of the castle above.

At the end of the esplanade, a passage leads down to the Kugelkirche, a fine small church in the Late Gothic (end of the 15C) style. Climbing again, the route leads past the Kalbstor fortified gate at the top of the Kugelgasse, turns right into Ritterstraße, and finally passes above the Marienkirche to rejoin Marktplatz. In Ritterstraße, at no 15 (**B**), is the house which belonged to the famous legal historian Friedrich Karl von Savigny (1779-1861), one of the founders of the "historical school" of the study of law and a man who was the nucleus of the Marburg Romantics (Clemens von Brentano, Achim and Bettina von Arnim, Jakob and Wilhelm Grimm).

ADDITIONAL SIGHTS

★ **Schloß** ⊙ **(AY)** – From the 13C to the 17C, the castle was the home of the Landgraves of Hessen, descendants of St Elizabeth and Ludwig. From the terrace beside the first entrance esplanade on the south side, there is a view along the Lahn Valley. The historic buildings (13C-15C) on top of the spur include the Gothic Princes' Hall with its double nave, the west hall which gives a view of the excavations of the remains of the previous fortress (9C and 11C), the south hall with its memorials of the founding of the university (1527) and of the religious debate that took place in Marburg in 1529, and finally the castle chapel with its medieval ceramic floor.

The **Regional and Art History Museum**★ (Museum für Kulturgeschichte), housed in the 15C Wilhelmsbau wing, displays among other things precious artefacts from the Elisabethkirche (fragments of stained glass, a 15C tapestry depicting the story of the Prodigal Son). There is also an exhibition of medieval shields.

There is a pleasant walk through the park at the foot of the buttress.

Marburger Universitätsmuseum für Bildende Kunst (Fine Arts Museum) ⊘ **(BZ M)** – Mainly German paintings from the 16C to the present are on view here, including Carl Spitzweg's *Der Briefbote*.

Kloster MAULBRONN★★

Baden-Württemberg

Michelin map 419 S 10

This was one of the earliest Cistercian foundations in Germany, an enormous abbey complex, very well preserved, with all its outbuildings and dependencies enclosed within a perimeter wall. The school established here since the Reformation (1556) has seen the flowering of such diverse literary and philosophical talents as those of Johannes Kepler, Friedrich Hölderlin, Justinus Kerner and Hermann Hesse.

★★ ABBEY ⊘ *1hr 30min*

The abbey was founded in 1147 and passed into the hands of the dukes of Württemberg after the Reformation, managing to escape any Baroque transformations. It is now the property of the Baden-Württemberg region and has been inscribed on UNESCO's World Heritage List since 1993.

★ **Abbey Church** – This was consecrated in 1178.

The early 13C Paradise Porch (1) is the first German example of the Romanesque-Gothic transition.

Inside, the fan vaulting of the nave and south aisle, which was not added until the 15C, changes the impact of the original flat ceiling of Romanesque design. The 10-bay nave is separated into two sections – one for the monks, the other for the lay brothers – by a Romanesque rood screen (2), which is topped by a dog-tooth frieze. A large Crucifix (1473) stands before the screen. The chapels off the transept are all that remain of an earlier church. Note a beautiful 14C Virgin to the left of the high altar (3). In the north side aisle is a set of choir stalls with 23 seats dating from the early 15C. More impressive still are the richly carved monks' choir stalls (behind the choir screen), to seat 92, made in c 1450 and clearly influenced by the Ulm School.

★★ **Cloister and Monastery Buildings** (Kreuzgang und Klosterbauten) – The old stone walls of the cloister galleries and adjoining buildings, together with the idyllic cloister garth make a pleasant and harmonious setting for a stroll.

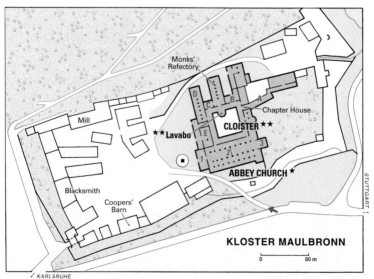

KLOSTER MAULBRONN

0   50 m

The Cistercians

This Benedictine Reformist order derives its name from the monastery of Cîteaux in Burgundy, France, which was founded by Robert of Molesmes in 1098. The order expanded rapidly, until by the 12C and 13C it was represented throughout Europe, with 742 monasteries between Ireland and Syria. In Germany, it was the monks of Morimond who were largely responsible for spreading the influence of the movement in their country. Early foundations include the abbeys of Camp in the Rhineland, Ebrach in Bavaria, Altenberg south of Cologne and Maulbronn in Württemberg, all of which gave rise to daughter abbeys in their turn. Among the monasteries which are still extant, those in the Roman Catholic regions of Germany have been transformed by the Baroque style, whereas those in regions affected by the Reformation, as is the case with Maulbronn, have survived in their original state.

St Bernard of Clairvaux (1090-1153) formally laid down the Benedictine Rule of his predecessors in uncompromising terms and ensured that his monks followed it to the letter. Cistercian rule tolerates only what is essential to the development and expansion of the monastic way of life, hence the strict discipline imposed on the monks and the extreme austerity of their abbeys. These tend to be located in an isolated spot, tucked at the bottom of a secluded valley or in a forest clearing, and they share practically identical architectural features: blind nave, barrel-vaulted side aisles, a square and not very deep chancel ending in a flat east end, no bell-tower (a discreet lantern turret above the transept crossing would be all that signalled the abbey's presence). In the absence of any decorative elements, such as sculpted or painted motifs, or stained-glass windows, the characteristic beauty of Cistercian architecture is embodied in its well-proportioned dimensions and clarity of line.

The south gallery, running between the church and the close, is designed with slender columns grouped in clusters, a feature noticeable also in the church porch. Opening off the east gallery are the chapter-house, whose 14C groined vaulting springs from central pillars, and the connecting building (**A**), thought but not proven to have been used as a parlatory, which has fan vaulting.

The **monks' refectory**★, completed c 1220-30 by the master who did the Paradise Porch, is flanked by the calefactory (**B**) and the kitchens (**C**) to the north. With its tall columns, featuring an annulet halfway up, and its early Gothic vaulting, the refectory is one of the most impressive rooms in the abbey complex. Opposite the entrance door, a charming **lavabo**★★ (Brunnenkapelle, c 1350) with quadri-lobed blind arcades juts out into the cloister garden.

The west gallery leads to the lay brothers' refectory (rebuilt in 1869-70), where groined vaulting arches low over the two aisles (**D**), and to the Romanesque storeroom (**E**), now a lapidarium. The storeroom vaulting is square-ribbed.

An **abbey museum** has been installed in the quarters for those attending early mass and the top floor of the old Coopers' Barn (now an information centre).

MECKLENBURGISCHE SEENPLATTE★★★

Mecklenburg-Vorpommern

Michelin map 416 F 20-22

The Mecklenburg lake district lies in the area between the Elbe-Lübeck canal and the Ucker march. It was formed during the last Ice Age, when glaciers pushed up the terminal moraine into mounds and the glacial tongues produced depressions, troughs and basins. This unique region contains over 1 000 lakes, most of which are linked by natural or artificially created canals, making it a paradise for water sports enthusiasts. The area has not yet been particularly developed as a tourist attraction or marketed in the same way as the lakes of Upper Bavaria. Nor has it yet been taken over by motor boats. Only a very few lakes have roads along their shores, and motorists only get the odd magical glimpse across a shining expanse of water. It is almost as if the lakes were hiding, despite the fact that most are quite large.

The principal lakes, from west to east, are:

Schweriner See, with the provincial capital **Schwerin**★ *(see SCHWERIN)* on its banks;
Krakower See, where the Mecklenburg regional poet Fritz Reuter dreamt of paradise;
Plauer See, the third largest lake in Mecklenburg-Vorpommern, with the town of Plau on its eastern banks, and which, together with the Müritz, forms the heart of the Mecklenburg lake district;

Lakeside houses on piles, Müritzsee

North of these lie the **Malchiner See** and the **Kummerower See** in **Mecklenburg's** **"Switzerland"** with the town of **Malchin** (the interior of the brick basilica of St. Maria and St. Johannes is sumptuously decorated);

The **Müritz**, the second largest lake in Germany, 115km²/44sq mi in size. The name comes from the Slavonic word *"morcze"* meaning small sea. The town of **Waren**, the main tourist centre of the region, lies on its northern shores. In addition to the two parish churches of St. Georg and St. Maria, the old and new town halls and the Löwenapotheke (pharmacy) draw the eye. **Röbel** is developing into a pretty port, with its attractive boathouses on the shores of the lake.

* **Müritz-Nationalpark** – This national park *(east of Müritz)* is 318km²/123sq mi in size, and covers a charming and representative section of the tremendous variety encompassed by the Mecklenburg lake district. Woodland, numerous lakes, heathland and marshes constitute the countryside, underlaid by terminal moraine and sand.

The area is particularly popular with bird-watchers *(we recommend taking a good set of binoculars with you)*. The **sea eagle**, Germany's heraldic bird, can often be spotted at the fish pools at Boek from hides by the road from Rechlin to Boek. There are observation shelters by the **osprey nests** on the road from Federow to Speck *(park the car at Federow)*.

The last fortnight in October is the climax of the migration season for **cranes**. Thousands of them flock here and nest by the lakes at night.

During the winter, birds of prey can be seen on the open foreshores of the lakes. To find out more about these and other birds, as well as on flora and other fauna, it is well worth going on one of the **guided nature walks** which are organized in the area *(details from the tourist offices in Waren and Neustrelitz and from the information centres of the national park)*.

MEISSEN★

Meissen's skyline is characterised by the Albrechtsburg, cathedral and former bishops' palace. To understand the development of Meissen, only 15km/9mi northwest of Dresden, the foundation of the town has to be placed in the military and historical context of the campaigns waged against the Slav tribes east of the Saale and the Elbe by King Heinrich I. In 929, he fortified a height commanding a strategic ford crossing the Elbe. The fortress was built on a rocky plateau where a tributary, the Triebisch, precipitated itself into the main river. And the town grew up around the foot of the castle hill from the 12C. Since the 18C, of course, Meissen has been famous worldwide for its porcelain. From the vineyards in the river valley it also produces wine which is appreciated by connoisseurs.

THE PORCELAIN OF SAXONY

It was in the reign of Augustus the Strong that the alchemist **Johann Friedrich Böttger** (1682-1719) revealed that he had discovered the formula for creating the white hard-paste porcelain until then made only in China. The formula is based on kaolin (china clay), large quantities of which could be – and still are – mined only a short

Staatl. Porzellanmanufaktur Meißen

Pepper Eater by Paul Walther

distance northwest of Meissen. Böttger made the discovery in 1708, although he did not reveal the secret until 29 March 1709. A year later, Augustus, Elector of Saxony and King of Poland, founded the Royal Saxon Porcelain Manufactory, which he installed in the castle – an isolated, well-guarded site, ideal for the protection of secrets. Böttger, who had until then produced only hard red stoneware, was its first director.

The Motifs – Initially, the lavish decoration imitated Chinese and Japanese models. The period of plant designs, red and green dragons, a yellow lion, flowers, birds and mythical creatures dates from the directorship of Böttger's successor, Johann Gregorius Höroldt (1720-55), who was responsible for the factory's first flush of prosperity (Old Saxony).

It was Höroldt who produced the famous "**Blue Onion**" (Zwiebelmuster) tableware design, based on the use of cobalt, which was to become one of the most celebrated glazed designs in the world. Innumerable elegant services, along with individual vases, pots, giant animals and "conversation pieces", were also created by Johann Joachim Kändler (1706-75). The factory mark distinguishing Meissen Porcelain is a pair of crossed swords in blue.

★ **Staatliche Porzellanmanufaktur (National Porcelain Factory)** ⊘ (**AZ**) – In 1865, the studios and workshops of the Meissen factory were transferred from the castle (Albrechtsburg), where they had been for more than 150 years, to a site in the Triebisch Valley.

Today the history of the industry is retraced here via a large number of superb exhibits. In a demonstration workshop, the preparation of paste and the processes of painting, fabrication and firing can be observed.

OLD MEISSEN (AY)

Old town – The old town has plenty of witnesses to the Gothic and Renaissance periods. On **Marktplatz**, stand the Late Gothic Rathaus (town hall, 1472-85), the Bennohaus from the second half of the 15C, the Marktapotheke, a Renaissance building from 1555-60, and the Hirschhaus with a fine 1642 doorway. Not far from this is the Tuchmachertor, a Late Renaissance gateway (c 1600), and the Brauhaus (brewery) from 1569-74.

Frauenkirche (**AY**) – Also standing on the Marktplatz is this three-aisle Late Gothic hall-church with its fine star-vaulting dating from the late 15C. The bells of the carillon are made of Meissen porcelain.

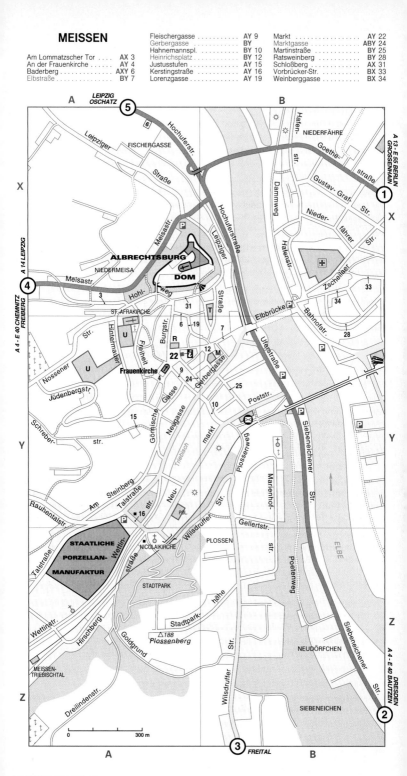

MEISSEN

★★ BURGBERG (ABX)

The castle, the cathedral and its subsidiary buildings are all grouped on this hill which was the original site of the town.

★ **Albrechtsburg** ⓥ **(ABX)** – Arnold von Westfalen, one of the most esteemed architects of late medieval times, was commissioned to build this castle in 1471 by the Margrave Albert. The finished work is considered to be one of the finest civic examples of the Late Gothic style. The **spiral staircase** (Großer Wendelstein)

347

adorning the façade is a model of its kind. Although the castle housed the first European porcelain factory from 1710 to 1865, most of the exhibits on view in the elegant, frescoed apartments are purely historical or concerned with other types of art – principally German painting of the 16C. Note the murals on Saxon history from the period of Historicism, an eclectic movement inspired by a great variety of past styles.

From the Burgberg there is a good **view** of the historic town centre, the vineyards and the Elbe Valley.

★ **Dom (Cathedral)** (ABX) – Another Gothic hall with a transept and three naves, this church was built from 1250 onwards on the remains of a Romanesque sanctuary and not completed until the end of the 15C. The west towers were begun in 1315 and, following damage suffered between 1904 and 1908, completed after designs by Carl Schäfer (81m/265ft high). Early 16C sketches for bronze **funerary plaques★** in the Dukes' Chapel (Fürstenkapelle) are said to be due in part to Albrecht Dürer and Lucas Cranach the Elder, and came from the famous Peter Vischer studio in Nuremberg. In front of the rood screen, parts of which were sculpted between 1260 and 1270 in Naumburg, is the **Lay Brothers' Altar★** (Laienaltar), which is again due to Cranach the Elder. The **Benefactors' Statues★★** (Stifterfiguren) in the chancel, from the same studio, represent Emperor Otto I and his second wife, Empress Adelaide. In style, they are reminiscent of the statues in the chancel of Naumburg Cathedral.

The cathedral square (Domplatz) is surrounded by **monastic buildings**. The Dean's residence, at no 5, dates from 1526; next door at no 6 is the Canons' House (1728); the Priory (c 1500) is at no 7.

MEMMINGEN

Bayern
Population 40 000
Michelin map 419 W 14

Memmingen grew from a small Late Roman settlement into a free city in the Swabian-Bavarian Pre-Alps.

In the old town, surrounded by a largely preserved fortified wall, the characteristic appearance of a medieval trading centre remains. Gothic buildings, medieval guildhalls, and also lavishly decorated Rococo buildings give a vivid picture of over 850 years of local history.

Old Town – This lies on either side of the stream canalized through the city centre. Its character is exemplified by such ancient buildings as the **Siebendächerhaus** (House with Seven Roofs), once the tanners' headquarters. Interesting buildings also surround Marktplatz: the **Steuerhaus** (1495), with its ground floor opened by arcades; the 1589 **Rathaus**, which was remodelled in the Rococo style in 1765. The design of this is unusual, with three oriel windows on different floors, each with an onion dome. A further highlight is the Late Gothic Antonierhaus with an arcaded courtyard, which houses a museum with works by Memmingen painter Bernhard Strigel (1460-1528) and another on the Antonine Order.

Martinskirche – The Gothic basilica dates from the 14C and 15C. It has a fine chancel (1496-1500), a masterpiece by architect of the Münster at Ulm, Matthias Böblinger. The **choir stalls★** (Chorgestühl), dating from 1501 to 1507, are one of the best examples of their kind from this period, intricately carved with 68 figures of the Prophets, sibyls and church benefactors.

Kreuzherrenkirche – *On the Hallhof square.* The final octagon on the 1617 belfry surpasses the town's other towers in the refinement of its decoration.

Bad MERGENTHEIM★

Baden-Württemberg
Population 23 000
Michelin map 419 R 13

Lying in the charming valley of the Tauber, the old town of Bad Mergentheim, chosen as a base for the Knights of the Teutonic Order in the 16C, owes its popularity as a health and leisure resort to its position on the "Romantic Road" (*see ROMANTISCHE STRASSE*), its historic old town, its castle and grounds, and its spa.

Deutschordensschloß (Castle of the Teutonic Order) ⊘ – The castle, which was built in the 12C as a moated castle, was extended in the mid 16C to become the residence of the Teutonic Order and its Grand Master, following which other structural changes were gradually made. The coat of arms of the Grand Master Maximilian, Archduke of Austria (1590-1618), is displayed above the richly decorated main entrance to the inner courtyard, whilst the corner towers in the inner courtyard house intricate Renaissance spiral stairways.

The Teutonic Order

The order was founded as a Germanic hospitaller community in the Holy Land and became a religious order in 1190 after the fall of the Kingdom of Jerusalem, when the knights were forced to return home. They became princes in their own right of sizeable territories and estates, either by conquering them (Prussia and Livonia) or by accepting them as gifts.

In 1525 the Grand Master of the order, Albrecht von Brandenburg-Ansbach, who resided in Königsberg, adopted the teaching of Luther and suppressed the religious side of the organization. The community's patrimony of Prussia became a secular principality.

Dispossessed of its seat, the Teutonic Order elected Schloß Mergentheim in Franconia as its new headquarters during the same year. The castle had been in its possession since 1219 and remained the residence of the Teutonic and Grand Master for almost three centuries. In 1809 the order was abolished by Napoleon throughout all the states of the Rhine Confederation.

Nowadays the order has resumed existence as a religious and charitable body, and has its headquarters in Vienna.

The **museum on the Teutonic Order** occupies three floors of the castle. On the second floor, the royal apartments with their Baroque stucco ceilings and the classical chapter-house form the setting for a presentation on the history of the order. The department on the history of the town focuses on local history from its beginnings until the present. The Adelsheim antiques collection includes porcelain, faience, carved ivory pieces and religious works of art. An extensive and attractive **dolls' house collection** includes 40 exhibits from the 19C and 20C. Styles may easily be compared, as the exhibition is in chronological order, and it is even possible to imagine the technical developments which were taking place in the home over this period. In addition to dolls' houses and kitchens, the collection also includes shops and apothecaries.

Castle of the Teutonic Order, Bad Mergentheim

Deutschordensmuseum Bad Mergentheim GmbH

EXCURSION

Stuppach - *6km/4mi on the Schwäbisch Hall road.*
The **parish church** ⊘ of this village now boasts the central panel of the celebrated altarpiece from the Chapel of Our Lady of the Snow in Aschaffenburg, kept in a side chapel. The panel, known as the **Stuppacher Madonna**★★ (1519), depicts a Virgin and Child and is the work of Matthias Grünewald.

MERSEBURG

Sachsen-Anhalt
Population 40 000
Michelin map 418 L 19

An episcopal town since the end of the 10C and seat of the dukes of Saxe-Merseburg from 1685 to 1738, Merseburg has enjoyed a substantial industrial development during the present century. Symbolizing the commercial success of this small town is the gigantic Buna petrochemical complex (synthetic rubbers, hydro-carbon derivatives), which was built in 1936 a little way to the south. The town has considerable potential as a tourist destination, since it stands at the gateway to the Saale-Unstrut Valley region with its wealth of castles and is itself home to some fine historic monuments, the cathedral and the castle, which overlook the River Saale from their site on Domberg hill.

SIGHTS

★★ **Dom (Cathedral)** – Three separate styles can be distinguished in this church. The crypt testifies to the Romanesque origins of the earliest structure; the porch, transept, apse and chancel owe their Early Gothic character to remodelling carried out in the first half of the 13C; and the three-aisle nave, originally Romanesque, was transformed between 1500 and 1517 into the purest of High Gothic, with reticulated vaulting and slender octagonal pillars.
The **pulpit**★ (1514-26) is richly carved in a fashion distinctively Late Gothic. The bronze **funerary plaque**★ of King Rudolph of Swabia (d 1080), which is in the choir, is remarkable for the mastery of its workmanship. It is believed to be the oldest funerary image in Germany.

Schloß (Castle) – The impressive Late German Renaissance palace complex was converted in 1605-08 by Melchior Brenner, who included the main parts of Bishop Tilo von Trotha's Late Gothic castle. The typical Late Renaissance dwarf gables lend the building its special character. The east wing is connected to the cathedral via a raised passage. Heraldic plaques, doorways and oriels from different periods contribute to the building's overall splendour. In the palace grounds, there is a delightful two-storey Baroque **Schloßgartensalon** (1727-38).

MINDEN

Nordrhein-Westfalen
Population 87 000
Michelin map 417 J 10

An important junction at the Porta Westfalica gap, the last point on the Weser before the river, the road and the railway branch out across the north German plain, Minden has long been a key crossroads on Europe's trade routes. The former stronghold bears the stamp of its 1 200-year history and is now the cultural and economic centre of the region.

SIGHTS

★ **Dom (Cathedral)** – The Romanesque **Westwerk**★★ is beautiful. It has a porch (the "Paradies") in front of it, fretted with delicate blind arcades, above which rises the great wall of the belfry.
The interior is notable for the rounded Westphalian-style vaulting which covers the transept, and for the chancel's tiered Romanesque blind arcades in the Rhineland tradition. A copy of the celebrated Minden Cross hangs above the altar in the transept crossing (the original is in the cathedral treasury). On the front right pillar of the transept crossing is a fresco with the oldest depiction of St Francis north of the Alps. The Frieze of the Apostles (c 1270), now in the south transept, once crowned the cathedral rood screen.

★ **Domschatzkammer (Cathedral Treasury)** ⊙ – *On the right-hand side of the Westwerk, beneath the arcades.*
Aside from the **Minden Cross**★★ masterpiece (a Crucifix dating from the second half of the 11C), a very fine Virgin in Majesty (the Silberne Madonna, c 1230-40) is on display along with a beautifully worked gold reliquary dating from 1070. Episcopal awards and liturgical items (13C-20C) are on view in glass cases.

Mindener Museum für Geschichte, Landes- und Volkskunde (Local History Museum) ⊙ – *Ritterstraße 23-31.*
Apart from displays on shipping on the Weser and agricultural life, this museum formed from six Weser Renaissance houses offers a fine selection of traditional regional costumes, interiors in the Biedermeier style, and reconstructed craft workshops and studios (shoemakers, photographers, leatherworkers, cobblers etc). It also contains north Germany's only coffee museum, covering the history of this beverage.

By way of Marienstraße, drive out of town in the direction of Bremen. Soon after the bridge over the canal, turn right and continue around the dock basin after crossing the Great Lock. There is a visitors' car park after the bridge.

★★ **Schachtschleuse (Great Lock)** – This engineering marvel, 85m/280ft long and 10m/33ft wide, lowers or raises shipping between the canal and the Weser, 14m/46ft below. *Information centre.*

Return to the car and continue around the port. After the exit from a tunnel beneath the canal, it is possible to climb, on foot, up the embankment and reach the aqueduct towpath.

★ **Wasserstraßenkreuz** – It is always a spectacular sight when waterways cross, but here it is especially interesting. The Mittelland canal crosses a navigable river, the Weser, so that there are occasions when ships cross their paths on both stretches of water. The 375m/410yd aqueduct has enabled canal traffic to treat the 211km/131mi separating Münster from Hanover as a single reach, obviating the necessity of any more locks.

Directly north of this aqueduct is a new aqueduct built in 1997 which provides a second route over the Weser.

Return to Minden via Werftstraße.

EXCURSION

Porta Westfalica – *Tour of 28km/17mi. Leave Minden via Portastraße (Bundesstraße 61). At Barkhausen, take a right turn towards the Kaiser-Wilhelm-Denkmal.*

Kaiser-Wilhelm-Denkmal – There is a fine view of the Weser Gap from the foot of this enormous statue, raised to the memory of Emperor Wilhelm I in 1896.

Return to Barkhausen, take Bundesstraße 61 on the right and cross the Weser in the direction of the Porta Westfalica. Follow the signs for Fernsehturm.

Fernsehturm (Television Tower) ⊘ – Built on the site of the former Bismarckturm, the tower has 129 steps which lead to a viewing platform. The panorama visible from this terrace embraces the Porta Westfalica gap with its intense road and rail traffic, the Wilhelm I monument, the town of Minden and the north German plain. The horizon is blocked on the east by the Wesergebirge, and towards the south by the Lippisches Bergland.

Return to Minden on B 482.

MÖNCHENGLADBACH

Nordrhein-Westfalen
Population 270 000
Michelin map 417 M 3

A Benedictine abbey founded in 974 was at the origin of this thriving industrial town. The oldest part, bordered on the south by the Late Gothic Roman Catholic parish church, **Hauptpfarrkirche St. Mariä Himmelfahrt**, lies around the **Alter Markt**, behind which are the cathedral and the ancient abbey buildings. The former Prelate's residence, dating from the 17C, is well preserved and serves today as the town hall. To the southwest of the old market, stepped alleys and cobbled streets lead down to the park through a quarter where there are still traces of the old medieval fortifications, notably the **Dicker Turm** (Great Tower).

SIGHTS

★ **Städtisches Museum Abteiberg (Municipal Museum)** ⊘ – *Abteistraße 27.*
The use of space and light in this modern building, with its complex, overlapping and interlinked storeys, makes it an ideal site for the exhibition of 20C art. Expressionism is represented by Pechstein, Kirchner, Heckel and Rohlfs; there are also Constructivist works. But above all it is the post-1950 avant-garde artists who predominate: Pien, Mack and Uecker of the Group Zero, Pop Art, Op Art, Nouveau Réalisme, Conceptual Art and Process Art (many exhibits by Beuys, sculptures by Richard Serra, and works by S Polke, Palermo and G Richter).

Münster St. Vitus – The former abbey church, a marriage of the Gothic and Romanesque styles, overlooks the southern flank of the hill (Abteiberg). The powerful three-tower ensemble of the Westwerk dates from 1180 to 1183, while the three aisles of the long nave, with their quadripartite vaulting supported on massive pillars, were constructed between 1228 and 1239. The **Gothic chancel** (1256-77) was designed by Master Gerhard, the chief architect of Cologne Cathedral. The interior is relatively plain, following damage sustained during the Second World War. A Romanesque **baptismal stone** remains in the Apostles' chapel.

Mönchengladbach – Städtisches Museum Abteiberg

Above the altar in the chancel hangs a modern triumphal crucifix by Elmar Hillebrand. The oldest part of the church is the great Romanesque **crypt-hall** (c 1100) beneath the choir. The **treasury** (Schatzkammer) is reached through the northern part of the cloister.

Schloß Rheydt ⓥ – *Leave the town centre southwards via Theodor-Heuss-Straße and then take a left turn into Breite Straße-Ritterstraße.*
This castle and its grounds are set in a picturesque conservation region on the green banks of the Niers. It is one of the best-preserved Renaissance castles in the lower Rhineland. The castle comprises a gatehouse, a front wing and a manor and is surrounded by a star-shaped fortified wall with a moat and casemates, some of which are open to the public.
The castle houses a **museum** of local art and cultural history from the Renaissance, Mannerist and Baroque periods. There is a section on local history in the front wing.

EXCURSION

★ **Schloß Dyck** – *9km/5mi to the east.*
This picturesque moated castle, consisting of four wings flanked by towers, dates from the 17C. The inner and outer front wings were built in the 17C and 18C. *The castle is not open to the public.*
A 40ha/100-acre **park**, laid out as landscape gardens since the early 19C, is open all year. It features a stone bridge with a charming pavilion (1767).

MONSCHAU★★

Nordrhein-Westfalen
Population 13 000
Michelin map 417 O 2

From a **viewpoint** lay-by on Bundesstraße 258, coming from Aachen, there is a superb **view**★★ of this ancient Eifel village, with its tall, narrow, slate-roofed houses huddled together at one end of a winding gorge carved from the rock by the River Rur.
Monschau owes its wealth, apparent from the considerable number of grand houses, to the clothmaking industry brought to the small farming town by Protestants from Aachen in c 1600. The town flourished in the 18C and its buildings are therefore predominantly Baroque in style. Visitors should keep an eye open for the wonderful Baroque doors which can adorn even the most modest of houses, contributing to the overall charm of the locality.

SIGHTS

Village centre – The **half-timbered façades**★★ (Fachwerkhäuser) of the old buildings overlook the stream and crowd the twisting streets.
Leaving the market place via the Unterer Mühlenberg slope, on the right of the Kaular café, turn right again along the Knieberg and climb to the chapel (Friedhofkapelle) which lies beyond the cemetery. From here, again, there is a good **view**★ of the town, the castle, and the ruins of the Haller watchtower.

The oldest part of Monschau is in the Kirchstraße quarter (note especially the period house at no 33).

★ **Rotes Haus (Red House)** ⊘ – The draper and merchant Johann Heinrich Scheibler had this house built in 1762-65 as his place of residence and business. He paid 90 000 Thaler, a considerable sum in those days. However, Scheibler was well able to afford this, with about 6 000 people working for him. The remarkable **interior decor**★ has a harmoniousness rare for the time and is an exceptional example of middle-class home decor in the 18C and 19C: fine collection of oak furniture from Aachen and Lüttich; hand-painted wall-hangings; and 6 000 textile designs from the heyday of Monschau's draper's industry. All this is overshadowed by the magnificent **Rococo staircase**★, however, probably the work of craftsmen from Lüttich. The free-standing staircase serves three storeys and features rocaille cartouches illustrating the various stages of the clothworker's trade.

Haus Troistorff – *Laufenstraße 18.*
This magnificent house was built by a cloth manufacturer in 1783. In comparison with the Rotes Haus, it takes architectural evolution a step further. It is much more like a town house, and its central façade with heraldic gables and balconies supported by atlantes stands apart from the otherwise more rustic architecture of the rest of the town.

EXCURSION

The North Eifel Lakes – *85km/53mi – allow half a day.*
Still on B 258, leave Monschau. The road rises rapidly, and after a mile there is yet another **look-out point**★ giving a good view over the village. From Imgenbroich onwards, particularly between Strauch and Schmidt, there are attractive glimpses, on the right, of the Rur lake region. Leaving Schmidt, the Nideggen ruin lies straight ahead.

Nideggen – Until the 15C the rose-coloured sandstone **castle** ⊘ – a true "eagle's eyrie" site – was the residence of the counts and dukes of Jülich, after which it fell into disuse. From the 12C keep (partially restored and turned into a **museum** – Burgenmuseum – devoted to the castles and fortresses of the Eifel), there are fine **views**★ to the south of the Rur Valley cutting into the Eifel plateau, and of the Aachen basin to the north. The restored 12C church has a Romanesque chancel with frescoes.

★ **Rur Dam** (Rurtalsperre) – In a wild stretch of country, the reservoir here, known also as the "Stausee Schwammenauel", forms with the Urft reservoir to the south the largest stretch of water in the Eifel. **Motor boat services** operate on each of them. The road crosses the dam to enter the Kermeter forest. From Einruhr, the route skirts the southern end of the Rursee, which is overlooked from a viewpoint laid out at the top of the hill beyond.

MOSELTAL★★★

MOSELLE VALLEY – Rheinland-Pfalz
Michelin map 417 Q 3 – O 6

The wide, peaceful curves of the River Moselle flow between two massifs of Rhineland schist, the Eifel to the west and the Hunsrück to the east. Most of the steep slopes are planted with wonderful vines, producing dry white wines largely from Riesling stock. Here the schistous subsoil plays a vital part in the maturing of the grapes, the decomposed rock absorbing heat during the day and breathing it out at night among the vines. The harvest is late and sometimes continues until the Feast of St Nicholas (6 December).
The wines are light, sometimes pungent, but with an extremely delicate bouquet. The further north the vines are planted, the more acid the wine becomes.
The river, canalized from Thionville onwards, comprises 12 separate sectors, the locks beside each dam taking barges of up to 1 500t, or towed convoys of 3 200t. On this navigable part of the Moselle **river cruises** ⊘ between Trier and Koblenz are available.

FROM TRIER TO KOBLENZ *195km/121mi – one day*

★★ **Trier** – *See TRIER.*

Neumagen-Dhron – This town is known for its Roman discoveries, which have been transported to the Rhine Museum at Trier. A copy of the famous *Wine Ship* can be seen beside the chapel opposite the Am Römerweinschiff café.

★ **Bernkastel-Kues** – *See BERNKASTEL-KUES.*
One magnificent vineyard follows another on this route. Note the oversize sundials (Sonnenuhren) fixed here and there to bare rock outcrops, which have given their names to some of the better-known vintages (Wehlen and Zeltingen, for instance).

The road passes through many villages typical of this wine-growing region: **Ürzig**, **Kröv**, **Enkirch** and **Pünderich** among them. From Enkirch, make a 5km/3mi detour to **Starkenburg**. From the terrace, there is a splendid **view**★ over the river's lazy Mont-Royal meanders. Some 3km/2mi after the bridge at **Zell**, which offers a fine perspective of the riverside houses lining the bank on the far side of the water, take the left turn

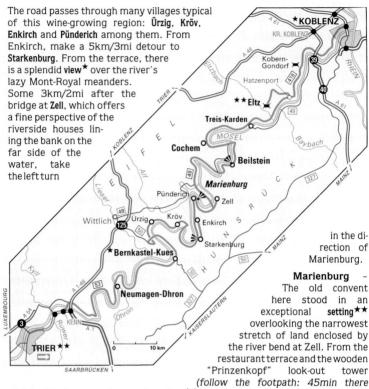

in the direction of Marienburg.

Marienburg – The old convent here stood in an exceptional **setting**★★ overlooking the narrowest stretch of land enclosed by the river bend at Zell. From the restaurant terrace and the wooden "Prinzenkopf" look-out tower *(follow the footpath: 45min there and back)*, there are impressive **views**★★ of the various curves in the course of the river and the vineyards on either bank, the Kondel forest and the Hunsrück slopes.

Beilstein – This tiny fortified town, whose last squire was the Chancellor Metternich, is huddled at the foot of a huge church and an enormous castle. From the ruins of the **castle** ⊙ *(30min back on foot there and, from the banks of the Moselle via Bachstraße)* there is, again, a splendid **view**★ of the ever-curving valley.

Cochem – Leave the car on the outskirts and follow the river bank to discover one of the most celebrated **sites**★★ of the region: towering above the river, the castle crowns a conical hill entirely covered with vines.
Of the original castle, the **Reichsburg** ⊙, *(30min on foot there and back, from Marktplatz)*, only the keep and the foundations of the walls remained after the destructions of 1689 – but the ruins were rebuilt in 14C style during the 19C, bristling with turrets and pinnacles. The **interior** has been refurnished in an opulent "feudal" manner.

Moselle wines are made from the Riesling grape stock, and are typically fruity with a hint of acidity.

Treis-Karden – The **church of St. Castor**, in the Karden quarter, exemplifies a transitional style halfway between Rhineland Romanesque (the "dwarf gallery" in the apse) and Gothic (ribbed vaulting).
Inside, there is a 1420 high altarpiece in carved wood representing the Three Magi and, in the chapel on the left-hand side of the chancel, a small wooden shrine to St Castor in the Gothic style (1490).

★★ **Burg Eltz** ⊙ – *10km/6mi from Hatzenport, plus 40min on foot or 5min by bus.*
From the promontory at the first hairpin bend after the car park, there is an awe-inspiring view looking down on this romantic **site**★★: the fortress, bristling with eight towers and numerous turrets, pinnacles and spires, rises majestically above the trees at the far end of the wild Eltz Valley. The castle courtyard also makes an impressive scene. There are period furnishings inside, as well as weapons and armour. Not to be missed are the Rübenach lower hall with a 15C timber ceiling and the upper hall with Gothic ornamentation, the knights' hall and the late medieval Rodendorf kitchen, still intact. Among the paintings, note Lucas Cranach's *Madonna with Grapes*.

Burg Eltz

Returning to the main road, the visitor soon sees the twin-tower silhouette of Thurant Castle on the east bank of the river. At **Kobern-Gondorf**, not long before the final twist in the river, the road passes right through an enormous restored 15C-17C castle – one of two overlooking this stylish small town and blending remarkably well with the landscape. Opposite the upper castle and the plain square keep stands the hexagonal Romanesque chapel of St. Matthias.

★ **Koblenz** – *See KOBLENZ.*

MÜHLHAUSEN★

Thüringen

Population 41 000
Michelin map 418 M 15

This Rhineland town is mentioned for the first time in 967 in one of Otto II's manuscripts. It had developed into a town by the 12C and was enclosed by a town wall which is largely still extant. Its prosperity was based on manufacture of drapery, leatherwork and dyer's woad (blue dyestuff). In 1525 Mühlhausen was transformed into a centre of the Thüringian peasant revolt against the feudal overlords fomented by **Thomas Müntzer**, a local Reformist.
The old town has been restored since 1991, with obvious success. It won distinction in the German Federal competition for best preserved historic town.

SIGHTS

★ **Town Walls (Stadtmauer)** – Built in the 12C and 14C, this peripheral fortification is still largely intact, with its defence towers, and reveals the oval town outline dating from medieval times. Only the Frauentor has survived of the original seven gateways, however. *We recommend starting the tour of the town from inside the Frauentor.*

Old town – There is a particularly charming view of the town from the rampart walkway, which visitors can walk along between the Raben and Hospital towers. Numerous well-preserved historic townhouses dating from the 13C to the 18C are to be found in Mühlhausen, mainly along Herrenstraße, Holzstraße, Erfurter Straße and Untermarkt. Note the richly decorated doorways and house signs.

★ St. Marien – Müntzergedenkstätte – Apart from Erfurt Cathedral, this is the largest church in Thuringia. Its tower reaches a height of 86m/282ft. The 14C exterior is notable for the exuberance of its decoration: gargoyles, statues, cornices, pinnacles and gables rival each other in the elegance and inventiveness of their design. Oddly placed on the south porch balustrade are the statues of Emperor Karl IV and his wife. Fashioned between 1360 and 1380, these came from the Parler studios in Prague.

Inside the church, with its five aisles, the **folding altarpieces★** are finely crafted, especially the one depicting the life of St Nicholas and that relating to the Crowning of the Virgin. The latter, dating from 1530, betrays in its treatment of faces the strong influence of Lucas Cranach the Elder. On the western pillars of the transept crossing, note the Adoration of the Magi (early 16C): the treatment of draperies and the bearing of the figures already hints at the Renaissance.

Thomas Müntzer, who preached in this church in 1525, lived nearby, at no 9 Bei der Marienkirche.

Rathaus (Town hall) – *Ratsstraße.*
This comprises blocks built at different times between the 13C and the 17C. The main block (14C) houses the former prison, a wine cellar (Ratsstube), and the local council chamber.

Blasiuskirche – *Johann-Sebastian-Bach-Platz.*
In 1707 and 1708, Bach was organist at this church, which was built between 1235 and 1260 and transformed into a three-aisle Gothic hall in the first half of the 14C. Worth seeing are the mid-14C stained-glass windows in the choir as well as the Late Gothic central reredos, executed by craftsmen from Erfurt.

MÜNCHEN★★★

MUNICH – Bayern
Population 1 298 537
Michelin map 419/420 V 18

The Bavarian capital, third largest and one of the most important cities in Germany, lies not far from the Alps. Munich is not only a first-class cultural centre (with over 40 theatres, three orchestras of global renown, an academy of fine arts, one of Europe's largest film studios, dozens of museums, the headquarters of the Goethe-Institut and 10 university colleges), but also the most flourishing economic zone in the southern part of the country. Especially in recent years, the development of high-tech industries allied to the production of motor vehicles, locomotives, rubber, chemicals and machine tools has enormously increased the commercial influence of the town. Nor have such trades as printing, publishing and craftwork been ignored: exhibitions such as the International Crafts Fair (Handwerksmesse) attract almost 2 400 exhibitors each year, and the products of Munich's Breweries are known worldwide.

The choice of Munich as seat of the European Patents Office (opened in 1980) recognizes the city's illustrious scientific past, resounding with such famous names as Fraunhofer, Liebig, Ohm and Sauerbruch.

Among writers working in Munich were Lion Feuchtwanger, Thomas Mann, Frank Wedekind and Ludwig Thoma – the last two also being collaborators in the production of the satirical weekly *Simplicissimus*. It is however in the absurd, surrealistic logic of the stand-up comedian Karl Valentin that the spirit of Munich most popularly expresses itself.

With the foundation of the review *Jugend* in 1896, the city became the centre of the Jugendstil movement; and then, after the **Blauer Reiter** exhibition in 1911, one of the meccas of modern art.

Munich's cultural wealth, its special atmosphere – a blend of gaiety, tolerance and respect for tradition – and the beauty of the surrounding countryside have combined to make it one of the most appreciated German cities.

HISTORICAL NOTES

The foundation of the town – A small village founded in the 9C near a Benedictine abbey identified itself by taking the name of the monks – in German Mönch, in Old High German Munich. Ever since, the town's emblem has been a little monk (Münchner Kindl).

In 1156 Emperor Frederick Barbarossa ceded a part of Bavaria to Henry the Lion, Duke of Saxony. Two years later, the Duke decided to take for himself the salt trade taxes formerly levied by the Bishop of Freising, and to this end destroyed the bridge,

Munich

TIPS AND ADDRESSES

Telephone prefix – 0 89

Tourist information – *Fremdenverkehrsamt München*, ☎ 2 33 03 00, Mon-Thur 9am-3pm, Fri 9am-12.30pm. **Information points**: Tourist information at the Hauptbahnhof, Mon-Sat 9am-8pm, Sun 10am-6pm, ☎ 23 33 02 57/58; Tourist information in the Neues Rathaus (Marienplatz), Mon-Fri 10am-8pm, Sat 10am-4pm, ☎ 23 33 02 72/73. A detailed overview of events is given in the following local newspapers available from news kiosks: *Prinz* and *Münchner*. Every 4 weeks the tourist office publishes a calendar of events. Advance ticket bookings via the tourist information point in the Neues Rathaus or at the numerous advance tickets booths. It is well worth making sure to buy tickets in plenty of time.

Post offices with extended opening hours – Postfiliale 32, Bahnhofsplatz, Mon-Fri 7am-8pm, Sat 8am-4pm, Sun 9am-3pm. Postfiliale 24 at the airport (central area level 3) in McPaper, Mon-Fri 8am-7pm, Sat 8am-noon, Sun 10am-noon.

Daily newspapers – Süddeutsche Zeitung. Münchner Merkur, AZ

Internet sites: http://www.intermunich.de; http://www.munich-online.de; http://www.munich-info.de; http://www.muenchen-tourist.de

Public transport

Munich and its surroundings are divided into four ring-shaped price zones. The local transport and fare association **MVV** (Münchner Verkehrs- und Tarifverbund) covers underground trains (U-Bahn), **SWM** (Stadtwerke München) buses and trams (Straßenbahn), rail (S-Bahn) and the transport authorities for the surrounding area; ☎ 41 42 43 44. Information at the Hauptbahnhof on the mezzanine level, Mon-Sun 7am-8pm, and Marienplatz basement level, Mon-Fri 9am-8pm, Sat 9am-4pm. Tickets are available from any underground or rail station and in trams, from ticket machines or from bus drivers. Tickets from the central zone, which includes Munich city centre: single ticket 3.60DM, 10-trip ticket (10er Streifenkarte) 15DM (in Munich city centre, two strips on this ticket must be validated), single day ticket 9DM, "Partner" day ticket for up to five people 13DM (both valid from when they are stamped to 6am the following day). There is a 3-day ticket costing 22DM for one person, and 33DM for two to five people.

There are three varieties of **München Welcome Card:** 1 day single 12DM, 3 day single 29DM, 3-day "Partner" (two adults and up to three people under 18 years) 42DM. The ticket is valid for use of public transport in Munich city centre and gives discounts of up to 50% for more than 30 sights, museums, castles and palaces, tourist attractions, city tours and bicycle hire.

Tip: Bus line 53 running between Nordbad and Ostbad links many of the city's most important museums; the best stops for getting on and off are Schellingstraße, Odeonsplatz and Haus der Kunst/Nationalmuseum.

Sightseeing

City tours – *Münchner Stadt-Rundfahrten – Panorama Tours*; ☎ 55 02 89 95: *Höhepunkte Münchens* (1hr) daily at 10am, 11am, 11.30am, noon, 1pm, 2.30pm, 3pm, 4pm, *Olympiatour* round tour including the Olympic complex (2hr 30min) daily at 10am and 2.30pm and *Schloß Nymphenburg* (2hr 30 min) daily except Mon; departure in each case from the Bahnhofplatz (in front of Hertie department store), all tours accompanied by a guide. Tickets also available from hotels. *Stattreisen* offers a programme of city tours on 60 different themes, eg beer, tours on foot, by tram or by bicycle, ☎ 54 40 42 30.

Shopping

Many consider Munich to be Germany's best city by far for shopping. The old town has numerous shopping arcades with shops to cater for all budgets. *Beck am Rathauseck* and other department stores are located between Marienplatz and Stachus. Another good shopping district is Schwabing (on and to the west of Leopoldstraße). **Exclusive boutiques** are to be found in Residenzstraße, Brienner Straße and of course Maximilianstraße.

Art galleries – Most of Munich's galleries are in Maximilianstraße and the nearby streets, also in Residenzstraße and on Odeonsplatz. In the old artists' district of Schwabing, the most interesting streets in this respect are Türken-, Schelling and Franz-Joseph-Straße.

Antiques – Munich covers the whole range from elegant, exclusive antique dealers' establishments to inexpensive bric-à-brac shops. Schwabing boasts a wealth of antiques shops in the area around Amalien-, Türken-, Barer-, Kurfürsten- and Hohenzollernstraße, as does the city centre around Lenbach-and Promenadenplatz.

Flea markets – Arnulfstraße by the old container depot and Kunstpark Ost behind the Ostbahnhof Fri-Sat 7am-6pm.

Markets – The best market in town is, as it has always been, the Viktualienmarkt; smaller permanent markets are held on Wiener Platz in Haidhausen and on Elisabethplatz in Schwabing.

R. Chéret/MICHELIN

Maypole at the Viktualienmarkt

Where to stay

BUDGET

Jedermann (B&B) – Bayerstraße 95; ☎ 53 36 39, Fax 53 65 06. 55 rooms, single rooms from 95DM. Family run B&B between the Hauptbahnhof and Theresienwiese.

Uhland (B&B) – Uhlandstraße 1; ☎ 54 33 50, Fax 54 33 52 50. 25 rooms. single rooms from 120DM. Small city hotel in a neo-Renaissance style villa.

Lutter (B&B) – Eversbuschstraße 109; ☎ 8 92 67 80, Fax 89 26 78 10. 22 rooms, single rooms from 110DM. Well-run small hotel in the Munich suburb of Allach which offers good value for money.

OUR SELECTION

Platzl – Platzl 1; ☎ 23 70 30, Fax 23 70 38 00. 167 rooms, single rooms from 235DM. First class hotel in the centre of the old historic town (opposite the Hofbräuhaus).

Brack (B&B) – Lindwurmstraße 153; ☎ 7 47 25 50, Fax 74 72 55 99. 50 rooms, single rooms from 150DM. Modern central city hotel near the Theresienwiese.

Drei Löwen (B&B) – Schillerstraße 8; ☎ 55 10 40, Fax 55 10 49 05. 97 rooms, single rooms from 175DM. Renovated city hotel near the Hauptbahnhof.

Schlicker (B&B) – Tal 8; ☎ 22 79 41, Fax 29 60 59. 69 rooms, single rooms from 130DM. Original hotel with view of Marienplatz and the town hall.

TREAT YOURSELF!

Bayerischer Hof – Promenadeplatz 2; ☎ 2 12 00, Fax 2 12 09 06. 396 rooms, single rooms from 377DM. Grand traditional hotel in the city centre with a variety of gastronomy on offer (from a gourmet restaurant to Polynesian cuisine to Bavarian specialities).

Rafael – Neuturmstraße 1; ☎ 29 09 80, Fax 22 25 39. 73 rooms, single rooms from 508DM. Elegant luxury city hotel in a palace. There is a fine view of Munich from the roof garden with its swimming pool.

Eating out

BUDGET

Straubinger Hof – Blumenstraße 5; ☎ 2 60 84 44. Main courses from 14DM. Typical Bavarian inn by the Viktualienmarkt.

Weichandhof – Betzenweg 81; ☎ 8 91 16 00. Main courses from 10DM. Attractive rural inn at Obermenzing.

OUR SELECTION

Weinhaus Neuner – Herzogspitalstraße 8; ☎ 2 60 39 54 Main courses from 24DM. Cosy restaurant in a 19C wine tavern.

Lenbach – Ottostraße 6; ☎ 5 49 13 00. Main courses from 24DM. Modern, spacious restaurant with designer decor.

Bogenhauser Hof – Ismaninger Straße 85; ☎ 98 55 86. Main courses from 36DM. Stylish restaurant in Bogenhausen in a hunting lodge dating from 1825. Garden terrace.

Käfer Schänke – Prinzregentenstraße 73; ☎ 4 16 82 47. Main courses from 38DM. Restaurant of the well-known local delicatessen store.

TREAT YOURSELF!

Tantris – Johann-Fichte-Straße 7; ☎ 3 61 95 90. Main courses from 56DM. Unconventional concrete building housing an outstanding gourmet restaurant.

Am Marstall – Maximilianstraße 16; ☎ 29 16 55 11. Main courses from 48DM. Elegant restaurant opposite the opera house.

Cafés and bars

Munich's café and bar scene is not concentrated only in the old town. The best-known area for spending leisure time is Schwabing: around the university there is a plethora of student bars, and along Leopoldstraße south of Münchner Freiheit a range of smarter establishments where people go to "see and be seen". Other parts of town which offer a good evening out are Haidhausen (around Pariser and Weißenburger Platz) and the area around Gärtnerplatz.

CAFÉS

Café Arzmiller – Salvatorstraße 2. "Kaffee und Kuchen" in the peace and quiet of the Theatinerhof.

Café Luitpold – Brienner Straße 11. The palm garden and glass dome come as a surprise in this coffee house redolent of a bygone age.

Café Reber – Herzogspitalstraße 9. Offshoot of the legendary café in Bad Reichenhall.

Café in der Glypthothek – Königsplatz 8. A refreshing oasis in the museum building of court architect Leo von Klenze.

BEER GARDENS

Aumeister – Sondermeier Straße 1. Beer garden located in the far north of the Englischer Garten, a Munich institution.

Chinesischer Turm – Englischer Garten 3. The place to meet in the Englischer Garten – near the Monopteros – recognised by the sign over the beer garden.

Seehaus – Kleinhesselohe 3. Idyllic setting by Lake Kleinhesseloher in the Englischer Garten. Adjoining the beer garden are a café and a restaurant.

Hirschgarten – Hirschgarten 1. The largest beer garden in town is located near the Nymphenburg in Laim.

BAVARIAN BARS

Augustiner – Neuhauser Straße 27. Parent house of the oldest surviving brewery in Munich, with a historic beer hall and a snug inner courtyard.

Hofbräuhaus – Am Platzl. Local and foreign visitors vie with one another propping up the bar in the *Schwemme*. In the more spacious first floor bar, there are comfy seats, but the best of all is the beer garden in the inner courtyard.

Löwenbräukeller – Nymphenburger Straße 2. In summer visitors can choose whether to drink their Löwenbräu in the beer cellar or in the neighbouring beer garden under the shade of the chestnut trees.

Weisses Bräuhaus – Talstraße 10. Traditional inn with a mixed clientele.

Hofbräukeller – Innere Wiener Straße 19. Not to be confused with the more famous Hofbräuhaus; this smaller beer cellar offers a pleasant local atmosphere and incorporates a jazz bar.

CAFÉ-BARS

Baader Café – Baaderstraße 47. About half the guests here are involved in the music industry in some form or other.

Café Extrablatt – Leopoldstraße 7. Atmosphere ripe with witty journalists' anecdotes; this bar was founded by gossip columnist Graeter.

Café Wiener Platz – Innere Wiener Straße 48. This bar in Haidhausen is frequented by a youthful clientele.

Atzinger – Schellingstraße 9. The Atzinger is the epitome of a student bar.

...AND FOR NIGHT-OWLS

Schumann's – Maximilianstraße 36. This is where Munich's glitterati meet to enjoy top quality cocktails.

Nachtcafé – Maximiliansplatz 5. Well-known focus for night-life, often with live music.

Brasserie Tresznjewski – Theresienstraße 72. Stylish bar, soigné atmosphere, excellent cocktails.

Hotel Bayrischer Hof – Promenadenplatz 2-6. Elegant atmosphere in the old school piano bar of Munich's Grand Hotel.

Entertainment

THEATRE

Münchner Kammerspiele-Schauspielhaus; Maximilianstraße 26; ☎ 23 33 70 00 This famous company offers superb spoken theatre.

Bayrisches Staatsschauspiel – Max-Joseph-Platz; ☎ 21 85 19 40. Performance venues are the *Residenztheater* and the *Altes Residenztheater* (Cuvilliés-Theater).

Münchner Volkstheater – Stiglmaierplatz/Eingang Brienner Straße; ☎ 5 23 46 55. High-quality popular theatre, a cut above farce.

Blutenburg-Theater – Blutenburgstraße 35; ☎ 1 23 43 00. Munich's whodunnit theatre.

Georg Maiers's Iberl Bühne – Wilhelm-Leibl-Straße 2; ☎ 79 42 14. Popular theatre in Bavarian dialect.

Teamtheater Tankstelle – Am Einlaß; ☎ 2 60 43 33. Small but active theatre often with amusing productions.

OPERA, BALLET, OPERETTAS AND MUSICALS

Nationaltheater – Max-Joseph-Platz; ☎ 21 85 19 20. The Nationaltheater is the main stage venue for the Bavarian State Opera, which also offers ballet performances as part of its programme. From time to time the Rococo treasure that is the *Cuvilliés-Theater* and the *Prinzregententheater* are used.

R. Chéret/MICHELIN

Nationaltheater

Staatstheater am Gärtnerplatz – Gärtnerplatz 3; ☎ 2 01 67 67. Reopened in November 1999 following renovation, the programme mainly offers opera evenings.

Deutsches Theater – Schwanthaler Straße 13; ☎ 55 23 44 44. Theatre for musicals and operettas, in which the Paris Lido also makes an appearance during its tour.

VARIETY, REVUE AND CABARET

Münchner Lach- und Schießgesellschaft – Haimhauser/Ursulastraße; ☎ 39 19 97. This cabaret theatre was jointly founded by Dieter Hildebrandt, Werner Schneyder and Ursula Noack.

Theater im Fraunhofer – Fraunhofer Straße 9; ☎ 26 78 50. Literary, musical and cabaret entertainment in the Hinterhoftheater.

Drehleier – Balanstraße 23; ☎ 48 27 42. Long-standing venue for local artists.

CONCERTS

Philharmonie im Gasteig – Rosenheimer Straße 5; ☎ 48 09 80. The Munich Philharmonic Orchestra has been based at this modern cultural centre since 1985. The Bavarian Radio Symphony Orchestra also performs concerts here.

Herkulessaal der Residenz – Residenzstraße 1/entrance Hofgartenstraße; ☎ 29 06 71. Classical music in a classical setting.

Prinzregententheater – Prinzregentenplatz 12; ☎ 21 85 29 59. This magnificent concert hall was built c 1900 as a theatre and has been recently renovated.

JAZZ

Unterfahrt – Kirchenstraße 96; ☎ 4 48 27 94. This jazz bar in Haidhausen hosts celebrated names and promising newcomers alike.

NIGHTCLUBS, DISCOTHEQUES AND LIVE MUSIC

Nachtwerk – Landsberger Straße 185; ☎ 5 78 38 00. This discotheque for young people is located in what used to be a warehouse.

Muffathalle – Zellstraße 4; ☎ 45 87 50 10. A place for the multicultural scene to meet, offering concerts theatre and dance.

CINEMAS

The latest, mainly American, films are shown in the cinemas and multi-screen complexes near the Stachus and Münchner Freiheit. Some of Munich's many preview cinemas are located in Schwabing. There is a panoramic screen IMAX-Kino in the Forum der Technik (Deutsches Museum).

Dates for your diary

Starkbierzeit beer festival in March, *Auer Dult* late April to early May, late July and mid October, *TollWood Sommerfestival* mid June to mid July, *Opernfestspiele* in July, *Oktoberfest* late September to early October, *Christkindlmarkt* in December.

---

warehouse and customs building set up 9.5km/6mi from the town. He then built a new bridge over which traders had to pass, forcing all commercial transactions into the town. The stratagem, subsequently legalized by Barbarossa, proved to be the beginning of a long and flourishing history for Munich, which until then had been no more than a cluster of unimportant houses.

The Rise of the Wittelsbachs – In 1180 Henry the Lion was stripped of his titles and banished from his lands in southern Germany. Barbarossa replaced him with the Palatine count Otto von Wittelsbach, and from then on that house became closely linked with Bavaria. In 1225 Munich became the ducal seat. In 1314 one of the dukes, Ludwig the Bavarian, became King of Germany, and then Emperor (1328). After the demise of the Wittelsbachs of Landshut in 1503, Munich was created the sole capital of the Bavarian Duchy, rivalling as a trade centre both Augsburg and Nuremberg.

In 1623, Duke Maximilian I exercised the function of Prince-Elector and made the town, during the turbulence of the Thirty Years War, the bastion of German Catholicism. During the 17C and 18C, religious and civil architecture sprang up everywhere: Theatinerkirche, Nymphenburg Castle, Heiliggeistkirche, the Asam brothers' church and the ducal theatre (Residenztheater) among them. The ramparts were demolished and replaced by spacious, well-laid-out gardens, the finest of them in the English style.

The Kings of Bavaria – It was under the enlightened rulers of the 19C that Munich reached its artistic zenith. **Max Joseph** (1799-1825), who had at first remained neutral in the conflict opposing Napoleon and the European coalition, finally took sides with the latter – a ploy which rewarded him in 1806 with the crown of Bavaria under the name of **Maximilian I**. Despite the Napoleonic Wars, in which large numbers of Bavarian troops were involved, Munich continued to flourish, embellished now with monuments in the Classical style, such as the Palace of Prince Karl and the buildings of Karolinenplatz and Brienner Straße.

Maximilian's son, **Ludwig I** (1825-48), a great admirer of classical antiquity, welcomed to his court the best of Europe's architects, painters and sculptors. In his desire to make his capital the most beautiful in Europe, he enriched the city with the Alte and the Neue Pinakothek, the university, the Glyptothek and the Propylaea. He cut a swathe through the old town with the construction of Ludwigstraße and had the ducal residence greatly enlarged. But in 1848, faced with a rebel movement provoked by the scandal of his liaison with the Spanish dancer Lola Montez, he was obliged to abdicate in favour of his son, Maximilian. A younger son, Otto, had already become King of Greece (1832).

Maximilian II (1848-64) continued the artistic traditions of his father, founding in 1855 the Bavarian National Museum.

In the history of the Wittelsbach dynasty, a special place must be reserved for **Ludwig II** (1864-86). This tormented romantic, a passionate admirer of Wagner, succeeded to the throne at the age of 18. Beloved by his subjects, he was nevertheless restless and unpredictable, a young man prey to extreme depression – especially in the face of political setbacks. After his disastrous choice of an alliance with Austria (their combined armies were beaten by the Prussians at Sadowa in 1866), he switched sides a year later and supported the proclamation of Prussia's Wilhelm I as Emperor of all Germany. But the young ruler, craving solitude and living in a fantasy world, largely withdrew from his court and built himself the three extravagant and isolated castles of Neuschwanstein, Linderhof and Herrenchiemsee. Mentally unstable, Ludwig II (whose tragic life has been the subject of books and films) was deposed in 1886 and confined to Schloß Berg, on the shores of Lake Starnberg. He was found drowned there shortly afterwards.

In the absence of a direct heir – and in face of the fact that the younger brother Otto, the King of Greece, was also mentally ill – the son of Ludwig I, **Prince Luitpold**, assumed the Regency. An able and inventive man, always open to new ideas, the Regent improved the Bavarian capital with a zoological garden, an ethnographic museum, a new town hall, the German Museum and the impressive avenue named after him, Prinzregentenstraße. His son, crowned as **Ludwig III** (1912-18), was the last King of Bavaria: under pressure from a workers' revolutionary movement after the defeat of Germany in the First World War, he was forced to abdicate.

In between two wars – The months following the cessation of hostilities were turbulent with strife, nowhere more so than Munich. In February 1919 Kurt Eisner, the social democrat Bavarian President, was assassinated. A month earlier, Adolf Hitler's **German Workers' party** had been formed and its aims announced by the leader at the Munich Hofbräuhaus. Meanwhile, a republican **Council of State** had been proclaimed, only to be annihilated by Imperial troops in May of the same year.

King Ludwig II of Bavaria

Bayer. Verwalt. der Staatl. Schlösser, Gärten und Seen

In 1923, Hitler and Ludendorff fomented a popular uprising (the **Munich Putsch**), but it was unsuccessful, the party was dissolved and Hitler imprisoned. Released before the sentence had run its term, he reorganized the group as the National Socialist (Nazi) Party. After he had become Chancellor, it was Munich that Hitler chose in 1938 for the notorious meeting with Chamberlain, Daladier and Mussolini at which the annexation by Germany of the Sudetenland was agreed.

LIFE IN MUNICH

The most animated part of the town is concentrated in the pedestrian precincts of Neuhauser Straße and Kaufingerstraße, between Karlsplatz (or "Stachus") and Marienplatz. The most elegant shops, however, are to be found along Maffeistraße, Pacellistraße, Maximilianstraße and Brienner Straße. Beneath the colonnades of Hofgartenstraße are the art galleries, and most of the antique dealers congregate near Maximilianplatz, in Ottostraße. The **Schwabing** quarter (via Ludwigstraße **KLY**), deployed around Leopoldstraße, enjoyed its hour of glory as the city's artistic and intellectual hub at the turn of the century – but with its boutiques, its pavement cafés and its nightspots remains one of the most brilliant and lively after-dark centres in Germany.

Munich Food – Local specialities include the white sausages known as Weißwurst, roast knuckle of pork (Schweinshaxe) and Leberkäs, a meat and offal pâté which can be bought in slices, hot, from most of the butchers any time after 11am. At the beer festivals, a favourite offering is Steckerlfisch (small fish grilled on a skewer). White radishes (Radi), pretzels and Munich Salzstangen (small salt rolls) are often served with beer.

Cherville/FOTOGRAM-STONE, Paris

Munich beer tankard

Beer – Five million hectolitres – 110 000 000 gallons – of beer are brewed in Munich every year, most of it being drunk in the beer cellars, taverns and beer gardens of the town itself. There is a season of strong beers, starting in March. The names of these more alcoholic drinks ("Which at least" – as the local people say – "help us to get through Lent!") are distinguished by the suffix "-ator". The arrival of the month of May is celebrated by the drinking of Maibock.

Holidays and Feast Days – The term Fasching is the Munich name for a carnival traditional throughout western Germany and the southwest (where it is known as Fastnacht). This festival in honour of Shrovetide, just before Lent, is a period of unbridled and uninhibited public merriment, frequently involving masked costume balls, both indoors and outdoors.

The origins of the famous early autumn **Oktoberfest**, which is held on the **Theresienwiese** (via the Mozartstraße **JZ**) goes back to the official marriage of the heir to the throne, Prince Ludwig, and Princess Theresa in 1810. Almost six and a half million visitors flock to Munich each year for this gigantic public fair, for which the local breweries produce a special drink, the Wiesenbier, delivered in the old style by horse-drawn drays. Under canvas marquees and in stands ranged around the base of a huge statue representing Bavaria, nearly five million tankards of this beer are handed out during the festivities. The party is complemented by roasts of poultry and beef (two entire oxen are cooked on a spit each day). The Oktoberfest goes on for 16 days. **Corpus Christi** (Fronleichnam) is the most important religious holiday of the year. An immense procession winds its way through beflagged streets garlanded with branches of young birch trees, the vast crowd preceded by the clergy and members of the religious orders, Roman Catholic personalities, Catholic student organizations and representatives of the various city guilds.

★★ OLD TOWN (ALTSTADT) *allow one day*

The tour indicated starts at the Karlstor.

Richard-Strauss-Brunnen (KZ A) – Bas-relief sculptures on the central column of this fountain illustrate scenes from the opera *Salome*, which the famous Munich composer wrote in 1905.

★ **Michaelskirche (KYZ B)** – This Jesuit sanctuary was built between 1583 and 1597 on the model of the society's Roman church (Gesù). It was the first Renaissance church north of the Alps. The façade is decorated with pilasters and bands of script. The 15 statues are of sovereigns descended from the church's patron, the Archangel Michael, who is depicted between the two entrances. This superb Mannerist statue in bronze is the work of Hubert Gerhard (1588).

The single nave – which inspired many builders of the Baroque School in south Germany – is covered by a 20m/65ft wide cradle vault resting on massive pillars abutting the walls. At the far end of the well-lit chancel the high altar rises to the level of the vaulting like a triumphal arch. The pulpit and seven side altars date from 1697. The tomb of Eugène de Beauharnais, stepson to Napoleon and son-in-law to King Maximilian I, is in the north transept. Thirty of the Wittelsbach princes, including **Ludwig II** of Bavaria, are buried in the **crypt** (Fürstengruft).

★★ **Deutsches Jagd- und Fischereimuseum (German Hunting and Fishing Museum)** ⊙ (**KZ M**[1]) – The museum, housed in a disused Augustinian church, displays on three different levels a splendid collection of ancient and modern arms, trophies (including the skeleton of a giant Irish stag from the Stone Age), paintings and drawings of hunting scenes, and stuffed animals. Different species of freshwater fish, stuffed and mounted, are shown in their separate groups against a diorama.

★ **Frauenkirche** (**KZ**) – The architect of this vast Late Gothic hall-church (1468-88) was **Jörg von Halspach**, who also designed the old town hall. The exterior of the church, in dark-red brick, is extremely sober; only the side entrances and tombstones built into the walls break the tall façades. The onion domes, which since 1525 have crowned the two towers at the west end (just over 98m/320ft high), have become the symbol of the city.

Interior – In striking contrast to the exterior, the nave makes an immediate impression with its simplicity and its height. Eleven pairs of powerful octagonal pillars support the reticulated vaulting. Seen from the entrance, the perspective of these columns forms a continuous line, effectively hiding the aisles. The pillars and walls are in an off-white and the ribs of the vaulting are picked out in ochre. The south side aisle contains the lavishly built monumental **cenotaph**★ to Emperor Ludwig of Bavaria, worked in black marble by Hans Krumper (1619-22). The four knights in armour come from another funerary monument (c 1595).

Furnishing and works of art blend the old and the new. Thus the 32 carved wood busts representing the Apostles, the saints and the Prophets, attributed to the sculptor **Erasmus Grasser** (c 1500), are placed immediately above the modern **choir stalls**. All the chapels contain high quality paintings and altarpieces. The main chapel off the chancel contains a fine Robed Madonna by Jan Polack, c 1510; the image of Our Lady of Mercy in the shrine was donated by the citizens of Munich in 1659. Above the retable in the chapel of Our Lady's Sacrifice (to the right of the main chapel) is an altar panel dating from 1445 with a Crucifixion and scenes from the life of Christ.

The chapels off the ambulatory contain 15C **stained-glass windows**; that in the main chapel is the work of Strasbourg stained-glass artist Peter Hemmel of Andlau. The chapels in the nave have resolutely modern stained-glass windows.

A staircase at the far end of the choir leads to the **Bishops' and Princes' Crypt** (Bischofs- und Fürstengruft), with the burial vaults of certain cardinals of Munich and Wittelsbach princelings.

In the **south tower**, there is now a lift taking visitors to the platform (April to October), from which there is a fine **view**★ of the town.

★ **Marienplatz** (**KZ**) – This square is the heart of Munich. In the centre rises the **Mariensäule**, a column erected by the Prince-Elector Maximilian in 1638. The north side is occupied by the neo-Gothic **Neues Rathaus** (1867-1908) (**R**), whose **carillon** (Glockenspiel) installed in the tower's oriel window, is a favourite tourist attraction. When the mechanism is activated (at 11am, noon and 5pm), brightly coloured figures in enamelled copper emerge and enact the Dance of the Coopers (Schäfflertanz, below) and the Tournament which accompanied royal weddings in the 16C (above).

From the town hall tower (85m/279ft: lift) there is another lovely **view** of the city. The façade of the **Altes Rathaus** (**D**), with its stepped gables and bell turrets, occupies the eastern side of the square. There is a **toy museum** (Spielzeugmuseum) in the tower.

Peterskirche (**KZ E**) – Baroque vaulting remodelled this 13C, three-aisle Gothic church in the 17C and 18C. The centre section of the enormous high altar is occupied by an Erasmus Grasser statue of St Peter (1492). Slightly lower down, the flanking figures representing the four Fathers of the Church were sculpted by Egid Quirin Asam in 1732. The church's 1386 bell-tower is affectionately nicknamed "Old Pete" by the people of Munich. Visitors braving the climb to the top (306 steps) are rewarded with a splendid **view**.

Viktualienmarkt (Food Market) (**KZ Q**) – This market can certainly claim to have tradition; it has been held here since 1807. Fresh fruit and vegetables, meat and fish are on sale here every day. The market stalls and kiosks, not to mention the beer garden during warm weather, ensure that the atmosphere on this centrally located square is always lively. Two of the six fountains recall the famous local comedian Karl Valentin and his partner Liesl Karlstadt.

Heiliggeistkirche (**KZ F**) – Another Gothic original which paid later tribute to the local taste for the Baroque, this hall-church was completely transformed between 1723 and 1730. The façade however is neo-Baroque, and dates only from 1888.

MÜNCHEN

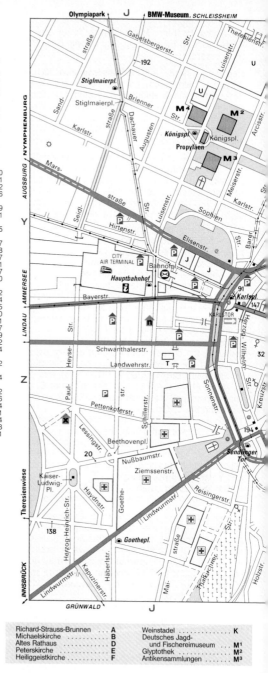

Richard-Strauss-Brunnen	A	Weinstadel	K
Michaelskirche	B	Deutsches Jagd- und Fischereimuseum	M¹
Altes Rathaus	D	Glyptothek	M²
Peterskirche	E	Antikensammlungen	M³
Heiliggeistkirche	F		

The painting above the **high altar** is by U Loth (1644), and the two angels with large wings in front of the altar pillars are the work of JG Greiff (1730). The mid-15C Virgin in the north aisle, said to be by Hammerthal, was once in the Benedictine abbey at Tegernsee.

Cross the Talstraße, take the passage beneath the old town hall, and turn right into Burgstraße.

Weinstadel (KZ K) – *Burgstraße 5.*
The oldest house (1552) in Munich, in days gone by the municipal office of the Clerk of the Court. The façade is decorated in trompe-l'œil. The fine doorway has a basket-handle arch.

At no 10 Burgstraße, take the vaulted passageway to reach Ledererstraße, then cross diagonally (left) into Orlandostraße.

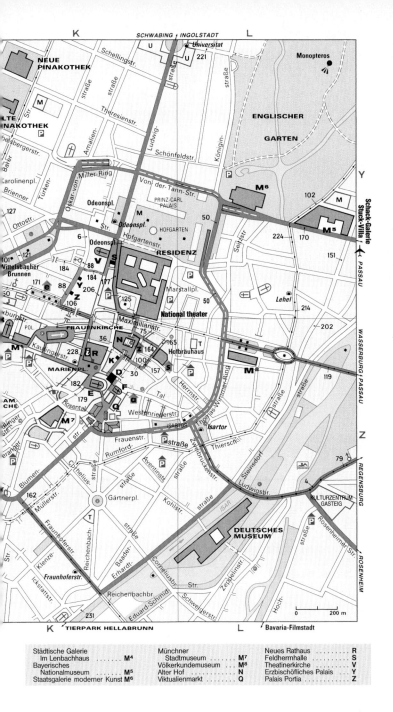

Städtische Galerie Im Lenbachhaus	M⁴	Münchner Stadtmuseum	M⁷	Neues Rathaus	R
Bayerisches Nationalmuseum	M⁵	Völkerkundemuseum	M⁸	Feldherrnhalle	S
		Alter Hof	N	Theatinerkirche	V
		Viktualienmarkt	Q	Erzbischöfliches Palais	Y
Staatsgalerie moderner Kunst	M⁶			Palais Portia	Z

Hofbräuhaus (KZ) – The best-known of the famous Munich beer halls stands on Platzl and dates from 1589. The present building was constructed at the end of the 19C, the original brewery having already been transferred to the east bank of the Isar through lack of space. Every day, in this great temple of beer, perspiring waiters serve 100 hectolitres (17 500 pints) of beer in one-litre (1.75 pints) tankards (Maßkrug). In many of the rooms and in the shaded courtyard, orchestras add to the festive atmosphere with renditions of popular songs – frequently with additional help from the drinking public. The huge vaulted **Bierschwemme**, on the ground floor, where the odours of strong tobacco mingle with those of sausages and beer, is the rowdiest part of the building. Customarily there is a police presence to ensure that high spirits do not degenerate into brawls.

At the far end of the square, turn left into Pfisterstraße.

Marienplatz and the Neues Rathaus

Alter Hof (Old Castle) (KZ N) – This building, a quadrilateral opening onto an inner courtyard, was the official Wittelsbach residence from 1253 to 1474. The south wing has an elegant tower with half-timbered corbelling (late 15C). The courtyard with its fountain is charming.

The Hofgraben leads to Max-Joseph-Platz, enclosed on the north and east by the imposing mass of the palace.

★★ RESIDENZ (KY)

In 1385, the Wittelsbachs started the building of this new royal **palace** (Neuveste) which, with the passing of time, expanded into an ever more vast complex around seven courtyards. Work was well advanced in the Renaissance period (Antiquarium, Kaiserhof, the Residenzstraße façade) and the subsequent Classical era (Festsaalbau, Königsbau).

This tremendous building now houses the municipal collection of Egyptian art and the municipal numismatic collection. Visitors who are pressed for time, however, should direct their attentions first of all to the treasury and the palace museum. The 130 rooms of this museum contain trappings of royal domestic life spanning four centuries.

★★ **Schatzkammer (Treasury)** ⊘ – This is one of the most important collections of its kind in Europe, a testimony to three centuries of Bavarian rulers' passion for collecting things. The magnificent displays of gold work, enamels, crystal ware and carved ivories will fascinate every visitor.

Among the highlights of the collection are the superb cross executed for Queen Gisela of Hungary (after 1006), Heinrich's crown from 1280, a domestic altar depicting the Flagellation of Christ and a dazzling example of the goldsmith's art inlaid with precious stones, a statue of **St George** (1586-97). The **royal insignia** of the House of Bavaria – crown, orb, sceptre, royal sword, and chest of seals – were made in Paris in 1806-07 for the first king of Bavaria, Maximilian I.

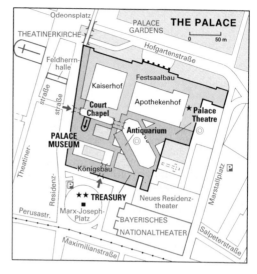

THE PALACE

✦✦ Residenzmuseum ⓥ

– Visitors should do both the morning and afternoon guided tours (which are different) if nothing is to be missed. It is possible that the morning and afternoon tours may be reversed. Since the rooms contain such a wealth of material, we recommend that visitors hire an official guide for detailed information on the fittings and furnishing.

It is impossible to give due praise to every room, not to mention the outstanding decor and contents, in these pages. The description which follows is therefore necessarily a selection from the many highlights on offer.

Morning Tour – A room embellished with gilded stuccowork and carvings houses the Wittelsbach **Ancestors' Gallery**. The enormous **Antiquarium** (1570) inlaid with marble, the oldest part of the palace, impresses with its painted ceilings and innumerable Antique busts. The **State Rooms** (Die Reichen Zimmer - 1730-37), decorated by Effner and Cuvilliés, illustrate in great style the early version of the Rococo style. A particular highlight of the tour is the **Royal Apartments** in the Königsbau (King's Wing), which Ludwig I had built by court architect Leo von Klenze between 1826 and 1835. The building suffered extensive damage in the Second World War. However the contents that were not permanent fixtures were removed in time, so that the rooms can once more be viewed in their former glory, since restoration work begun in 1980, as a complete work of art including paintings, sculpture and furniture.

Afternoon Tour – Masterpieces from the workshops of Meissen, Nymphenburg and Sèvres ("Bird Service" of 1759) are on display in the **Porcelain Rooms**. The 17C **Hofkapelle** (Court Chapel) is dedicated to the Virgin Mary, patron saint of Bavaria. The Reiche Kapelle, severely damaged in 1944 but whose furnishings it was possible to save, now lives up to its name. Close at hand is the **Reliquary Room** (Reliquienkammer), with valuable exhibits of 16C-18C gold and silver plate. The **Silver Rooms**, magnificent **Stone Room** with its marble, stucco and scagliola decor, and reconstructed **Imperial Room** are also worth seeing.

P. Tetrel/EXPLORER, Paris

Water ewer from the Palace Treasury

✶ Altes Residenztheater ⓥ – This enchanting Rococo theatre was built by François Cuvilliés between 1751 and 1753 (and is therefore also known as **Cuvilliéstheater**), with four tiers of Court boxes, each different from the others in design and decoration. The Prince-Elector's box, in the centre, is set apart by the elegance and richness of its carved decoration with hangings, rocaille, putti etc. The harmonization of colours in red, gold and ivory is particularly beautiful.

369

RESIDENZ QUARTER

Nationaltheater – Built between 1811 and 1818, the national theatre, home to the **Bavarian State Opera**, was endowed with one of the largest stages in the world, on a par with the Scala in Milan or the Viennese Opera. The five-tier auditorium can seat 2 100 spectators.

★ **Theatinerkirche** (KY V) – A fine example of Baroque ecclesiastical architecture, this church was built between 1663 and 1688, first under the direction of the Italian Barelli and later by Zuccalli, who came from Graubünden. The well-proportioned Late Rococo façade was added a century afterwards, by Cuvilliés. Inside, the dome of this very tall building, which rises to a height of 71m/233ft, emphasizes a grandiose impression of space. The stuccowork is particularly rich, the Italian stuccodore having paid special attention to the smaller load-bearing arches and the pendentives. The wreathed double colonnade of the monumental high altar is also very generously embellished. The dark wood of the pulpit, designed in 1681 by Faistenberger, makes a striking contrast with the whites and greys in the nave and elsewhere. More princes from the Wittelsbach dynasty are buried in the crypt beneath the chancel.

Odeonsplatz (KY) – On the westside of this square stands the Leuchtenberg-Palais, built for Eugène de Beauharnais, Count of Leuchtenberg, in 1816-21 by Leo von Klenze. It now houses the Bavarian Finance Ministry. To the south, the **Feldherrnhalle** (S) portico, erected in 1840-44 by F von Gärtner in imitation of the Loggia dei Lanzi in Florence, Italy, closes the long perspective of Ludwigstraße. The far (northern) end of this splendid avenue leads in a straight line to a triumphal arch.

From Salvatorstraße turn into Kardinal-Faulhaber-Straße.

Erzbischöfliches Palais (Episcopal Palace) (KY Y) – *Kardinal-Faulhaber-Straße 7.* François Cuvilliés built his finest palace between 1733-35, once called the Palais Holnstein and destined for the natural son of Electoral Prince Karl Albrecht. The magnificent façade of this rectangular complex features a central projection and nine colossal pilasters.

Palais Portia (KY Z) – *Kardinal-Faulhaber-Straße 12.* This mansion, designed by Enrico Zuccalli in 1694, was transformed in the Rococo style by Cuvilliés in 1735, for one of Karl Albrecht's favourites, later to become Countess Portia. The façade, in tones of pink and grey, is charming.

Return to Marienplatz via Maffaistraße and Weinstraße.

ALTE PINAKOTHEK QUARTER (KY)

★★★ Alte Pinakothek ⊘

This colossal building (the word Pinakothek means art gallery) was destined to house the collections of paintings amassed by the House of Wittelsbach from the beginning of the 16C onwards. It was built between 1826 and 1836 by the architect Leo von Klenze, in the Venetian Renaissance style. The collection was started by Duke Wilhelm IV, who commissioned historical scenes from the most eminent painters of his time, Altdorfer and Burgkmair. The Duke's great grandson, the Elector Maximilian I, continued the tradition by founding a home for the collection, the Kammergalerie, in the 17C. And this, under King Ludwig I, developed into the finest exhibition of art in the whole of Europe. The Alte Pinakothek houses outstanding works by European painters from the 14C to the 18C.

FIRST FLOOR

Early Flemish painting

Gallery I – The extraordinarily beautiful Altarpiece of the Three Magi (c 1455) from St Columba's Church in Cologne, a masterpiece by **Rogier van der Weyden**, catches the eye with the luminescence of its colour and purity of its draughtsmanship. By the same master, *St Luke drawing the Madonna.* Dirk Bouts is the artist responsible for the *Imprisonment and Resurrection of Christ* (c 1450). There is a circular work by the Master of the Joseph Series *Joseph and Potiphar's Wife.* The many layered *Seven Joys of Mary* is by **Hans Memling** (c 1480).

Gallery IIa – Further works by Hans Memling.

Old German masters

Gallery II – **Albrecht Dürer** painted the fascinating *Self-portrait in Fur Coat* (1500), depicting himself at 28 years of age; *Lamentation of Christ,* 1500; the Paumgartner altarpiece, 1502-04; *Four Apostles,* 1526. **Hans Holbein the Elder** painted the St Sebastian altarpiece, in 1516; Hans Burgkmair the St John altarpiece in 1518 and **Lucas Cranach the Elder** *Lamentation at the Foot of the Cross* in 1503.

Gallery IIb – This houses the Oswolt Krel triptych by Albrecht Dürer (1499); *Susanna Bathing* (1526), with complex architectural detail, and *Virgin Mary and Child in Glory* (c 1525) by Albrecht Altdorfer.

Gallery III – We encounter Altdorfer again here, in the *Battle of Alexander* (1529) with its interesting light effect. Bernhard Strigel painted both the panel portraits of *Konrad Rehlinger and his eight children* (1517). **Lucas Cranach the Elder** painted *Suicide of Lucretia* (1524) and *The Golden Age* (c 1530). Works by **Mathias Grünewald** include *St Erasmus and St Mauritius* (1520-24) and *Mocking of Christ* (1503).

15C and 16C Italian painting

Gallery IV – *Lamentation of Christ* (after 1490) is a late work by Florentine artist Sandro **Botticelli**. Lorenzo di Credo is represented by a circular painting, the *Birth of Christ*, Domenico Ghirlandaio by parts of the high altar from Santa Maria Novella in Florence (1490), **Raphael** by one of his masterpieces *Madonna Tempi* from 1507, and also the *Holy Family from the Canigiani House* (c 1505-06) and *Madonna della Tenda* (1513-14). Note also **Leonardo da Vinci**'s *Madonna and Child*.

Gallery V – Here are two late works by Venetian artist **Veronese**: *Cupid with two Hounds* (after 1570) and *Portrait of a Lady* (after 1570). The *Crowning of Thorns* is one of **Titian**'s masterpieces, along with *Madonna and Child in an Evening Landscape* (c 1560). *Vulcan surprising Venus and Mars* is an early work by **Tintoretto** (c 1555) and the eight Gonzaga cycle paintings are also by him; they were commissioned by the Court at Mantua. *Bust of a Young Man* by Giorgione is an outstanding example of Venetian portraiture.

17C Flemish painting

Gallery VI – This gallery houses several fine works by **Sir Anthony van Dyck**: *St Sebastian*, *Susanna Bathing*, and *Rest on the Flight to Egypt*. Peter Paul Rubens painted *Seneca Dying* (c 1611), **Jacob Jordaens** the extravagant *Allegory of Fertility* (c 1616-17) and *Satyr and Peasant* (after 1620).

Gallery VII – This whole gallery documents the remarkably rich collection of paintings by **Peter Paul Rubens**: *Self-portrait with Isabella Brant under a Honeysuckle Bower* (1609), *The Great Last Judgement* (c 1614-16); *Hunt Scene with Hippopotamuses and Crocodiles* (1615-16), *Drunken Silenus* (1617-18), *Hélène Fourment in her Wedding Dress* (1630-31).

Gallery VIII – The apocalyptic *Descent into Hell* and *Massacre of the Innocents at Bethlehem* (c 1635-39) are by Rubens. The painting of the *Madonna with Floral Wreath* is a joint work by Rubens and Jan Brueghel the Elder (c 1620) – it was not uncommon for two artists to work together like this in 17C Flemish painting. There are some large-format landscapes by Jacques d'Arthois: *Woodland Path*, *Canal through Woods*, *Ford in Woods* (c 1660).

17C Dutch painting

Gallery IX – *Portrait of a Man in Oriental Costume* (c 1633), *The Holy Family* (c 1633), *Sacrifice of Isaac* (c 1636) by **Rembrandt**. An example of the group portrait so popular in Dutch painting is Ferdinand Bol's *Leaders of the Amsterdam Wine Merchants' Guild* (1659). Full-length portrait of the artist *Willem van Heythuyzen* (1625-30) by **Frans Hals**.

17C and 18C Italian painting

Gallery X – **Giovanni Battista Tiepolo** is represented by two outstanding examples of his craft: *Veneration of the Holy Trinity by Pope Clemens* (1739) and *Adoration of the Magi* (1753). The *Ascension of the Blessed Virgin Mary* was painted by Guido Reni in 1631 for a church in Modena.

17C French painting

Gallery XI – The great landscape painter **Claude Lorrain** is represented here by *Sea Port at Sunrise* (1674). Simon Vouet's *Judith* (1620-25) reveals the influence of Caravaggio. In the paintings *Midas and Bacchus* (before 1627) and *Apollo and Daphne* (c 1627) **Nicolas Poussin** takes his subjects from Ovid's *Metamorphoses*.

18C French painting

Gallery XII – **François Boucher**'s talent is reflected in his full portrait of *Madame Pompadour* (1756) and the sensitive portrayal of a *Girl at Rest* (1752). Typical of Boucher's landscape painting is the pair of paintings *Rest by the Spring* and *Rural Idyll* (after 1730). **Hubert Robert**, famed for his paintings of architecture, painted *Landscape with Roman Temple Ruin* and *Park Landscape* in 1773. A favourite subject of his is *Demolition of Houses on the Pont du Change in Paris* (1788).

Gallery XIIa – Pastels by Maurice Quentin de la Tour: *Abbé Nollet*, *Mademoiselle Ferrand*, both from 1753. Jean Liotard in his *Breakfast* shows a highly realistic method of representation for his age. Nicolas Lancret's *Concert* reveals the influence of Watteau.

ALTE PINAKOTHEK

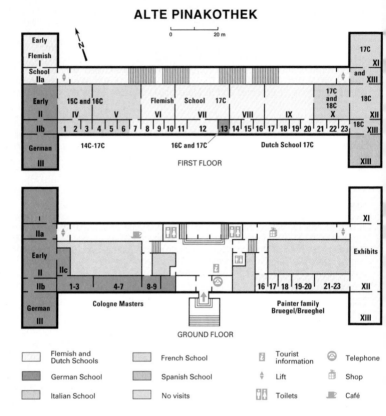

18C Italian painting

Gallery XIIb – Works by **Antonio Canaletto** and **Francesco Guardi** celebrate the art of the Venetian *vedutisti*. Guardi painted the magical *Venetian Gala Concert* in 1782.

Spanish painting

Gallery XIII – The harshness of works by El Greco (*Stripping of Christ*) and the seriousness of those by Velázquez (*Young Spaniard*, after 1623) are in stark contrast to the lively genre scenes by **Bartolomé Esteban Murillo**, of which the Alte Pinakothek only possesses five, including the famous *Grape and Watermelon Eater* (1645-46).

14C to 17C Italian painting

Rooms 1-6 – Four small-format predella paintings by **Fra Angelico** (Room 1); *Still-life with Partridge* by Jacopo de' Barbari (Room 2); *Virgin Mary and Child*, c 1465 (Room 4), by Fra Filippo Lippi; *Portrait of a Sculptor* by Domenico Tintoretto (Room 5); *Death of Cleopatra* by Johann Liss (Room 6).

17C Flemish painting

Rooms 7-12 – Works by **Sir Anthony van Dyck** (*Lamentation of Christ*, Room 7; *Self-portrait as a Young Man*, 1621, Room 9), **Peter Paul Rubens** (*Hélène Fourment putting on a Glove*, 1630-31, Room 9) and a whole series of small-format peasant scenes by **Adriaen Brouwer** and genre paintings by **David Teniers the Younger** (Room 11). Room 12 contains Rubens' Medici cycle and *The Small Last Judgement*.

16C to 17C German painting

Room 13 – *Flight into Egypt* (1609) by **Adam Elsheimer**; *Victory of Truth* and *Birth of Christ* by Johann Rottenhammer.

17C Dutch painting

Rooms 14-23 – Room 14 contains Cornelius von Poelenburgh's *Portrait of a Young Girl*; Room 15 Jacob Pynas' *Nebuchadnezzar has Royal Dignity returned to him*, 1616; Room 16 is devoted to **Rembrandt**: *Self-portrait*, 1629, and his Passion cycle. Fine landscape paintings by **Salomon van Ruysdael** in Room 17, and a strikingly harmonious composition by Dutch seascape painter Willem van de Velde (*Calm Sea*) in Room 18. **Gerard ter Borch** is celebrated in Room 19: *Portrait of a Gentleman and a Lady*, 1642, *Boy whipping his Dog*, c 1655. The virtuoso and at the same time naive art of Frans Post in his Brazilian landscapes of 1649 comes as a surprise in Room 20. Jacob van Ruisdael shows his precocious talent in *Sand Dunes*, painted when he was about 18 or 19 years old (Room 21). **Gabriel Metsu** is represented by genre scenes in Room 22: *The Cook*, c 1665, *Bean Feast*. One of Jan Davidsz de Heem's Vanitas still-life paintings full of hidden symbolism, from c 1665 together with Nicolaes van Veerendael, is a pleasure to examine in Room 23.

GROUND FLOOR

Old German painting

Gallery 1 – Seven panels depicting events from the life of the Mother of Christ are the work of the master of the Life of Mary, who was active in Cologne c 1460-90. The Hofer altarpiece (1465) by **Hans Pleidenwurff** is composed with a landscape that stretches consistently over four panels.

Gallery IIa – *Palatine Count Philip the Warlike* (1517) by **Hans Baldung Grien**; *Portrait of Hieronymus Seiler and his Wife* (1537-38) by Christoph Amberger; *St Anne* (c 1516) and *Adam and Eve* by Lucas Cranach the Elder.

Gallery II – Masterly Altarpiece of St Lawrence and the Fathers of the Church by **Michael Pacher** (c 1480).

Gallery IIb – Hans Funk Diptych by **Bernhard Strigel**, also the artist behind *Sleeping Grave Attendants* (after 1520).

Gallery III – **Hans Holbein the Elder** painted the Kaisheimer Altarpiece in 1502. The outer panels depict Christ's Passion, the inner scenes from the life of Mary. The Wettenhausen High Altar (1523-24) is by Martin Schaffner. When open, it is adorned with scenes from the life of Mary, when closed with *Christ taking leave of the Women*.

Cologne School

Rooms 1-9 – Some works by **Bartholomäus Bruyn the Elder**, including the Crucifixion Altarpiece (1515-20). *Portrait of Johann von Melem* (c 1495-1500) by the Master of the Aachen Altarpiece (Room 4). Several very fine works by **Stefan Lochner**, who lived in Cologne from 1442 until his death in 1451, including the outer panels of the Last Judgement Altarpiece, c 1440-45 (Room 6), *Virgin Mary and Child in front of a Grassy Bank*, c 1440, *Adoration of the Child by Mary*, 1445 (Room 7). Also in Room 7, *The Holy Family* (1475-80) by **Martin Schongauer**. Room 8 contains *Story of Lucretia* (1528) by Jörg Breu the Elder and *Story of Susanna* (1537) by Hans Schöpfer the Elder.

Brueghel family

Rooms 16-23 – The collection of works by this famous family of painters includes *The Land of Milk and Honey* by **Pieter Bruegel the Elder**, painter of famous country scenes. There is a particularly strong collection – the third largest after Madrid and Vienna – of works by **Jan Brueghel the Elder**. This master of landscape and still-life painting earned himself the nickname "Velvet" Brueghel because of his skill in depicting delicate textures in his exquisite flower paintings. *Bouquet of Flowers*, painted after 1607, is a luxuriant example of his work, containing no fewer than 130 different types of flower. The master's talent for narrative scenes is reflected in *Large Fish Market* and *Fish Market on the Bank of a River*, both painted between 1603 and 1605. *Sea Port with the Sermon of Christ* and *Calvary* (1598) represent a particular peak in the artist's creativity.

Galleries XI-XIII – Home to temporary exhibitions.

★★ Neue Pinakothek ⊙ (KY)

The post-modernist style building, completed in 1981 and faced with light sandstone, was designed by Alexander von Brancas. This well-proportioned construction with charming light effects replaces the building erected under Ludwig I, which had to be demolished due to serious war damage. The Neue Pinakothek is dedicated to 19C art.

Galleries 1, 2, 2a – International art from c 1800. **Thomas Gainsborough**'s portraits and landscapes are characterised by delicate colour tones. The display includes works by **Jean Louis David** *(Marquise de Sorcy)*, **Joshua Reynolds** *(Captain Pownall)*, **William Turner** *(Ostend)* and **Francesco Goya** *(Marquesa de Caballero*, 1807). Antonio Canova is represented by the statue of *Paris* (1807).

Galleries 3, 3a – Early German Romantic works from Dresden, Berlin and Munich; highly spiritual symbolic landscapes by **Caspar David Friedrich**; landscapes by Johann Christian Dahl *(Frederiksholm Canal in Copenhagen*, 1817), and works by Karl Blechen *(View of Assisi*, 1830), Johann Georg Dillis and Carl Rottmann.

Galleries 4, 4a – Art from the court of Ludwig I. Famous portrait of the great German poet *Johann Wolfgang von Goethe* painted by **Joseph Karl Stieler** in 1828, who is known principally for the captivating portraits in the "Gallery of Beauties" in Schloß Nymphenburg. Two large-format paintings of the *Arrival of King Otto in Greece* by Peter von Hess.

Galleries 5, 5a – German Classicists in Rome. Heroic landscapes by Josef Anton Koch; views of Rome by Johann Christian Reinhart; famous painting by **Ludwig Richter** *The Night-Watchman*, 1824.

Gallery 6 – The paintings destined for this gallery were not known at the time of going to press.

Gallery 7 – Nazarenes, who drew their inspiration from mythological symbols and the work of Raphael and Dürer: Johann Friedrich Overbeck (*Italia and Germania*, 1828, *Vittoria Caldoni*, 1821). Charming statue of *Woman fastening her Sandal* (1813) by Rudolf Schadow.

Galleries 8, 9 – Biedermeier. **Moritz von Schwind** (*Cinderella*, 1852, *The Visit*, 1855). Small-format paintings and landscapes by Ferdinand Georg Waldmüller. *Portrait of Fanny Eber* (1826) by Friedrich Wilhelm von Schadow.

Galleries 10, 10a – French late Romantics and Realists. Works by **Gustave Courbet** (*Horse in Motion*, *River Landscape*, 1872), Eugène Delacroix (*Ophelia's Death*, *Liberation of Olindo and Sophronia*), Théodore Géricault (*Artillery Moving to the Front*, 1814), Camille Corot (*Woman in Meditation*, 1850-55, *Bridge and Mill at Mantes*, 1860-65).

Galleries 11, 11a – German late Romantics and Realists. Andreas Achenbach (*Landscape with Rune-Stone*, 1841, *Beach Scene*, 1880) and **Carl Spitzweg** (*The Hussar*, *The Poor Poet*, 1839, *The Writer*, 1850) represent late Romantics, and **Adolf Menzel** Realism with *Menzel's Sister* (1847) and *Procession in Hofgastein* (1880).

Gallery 12 – Works by Munich court painter **Wilhelm von Kaulbach**.

Galleries 13, 13a – Historical and genre painting. Large-format works by Wilhelm von Kaulbach (*Destruction of Jerusalem*, 1846) and Karl Theodor von Piloty (*Seni by the body of Wallenstein*, 1855).

Galleries 14, 14a – Gründerzeit painting. Eye-catching painting of *The Limestone Gatherers* (1883) by Joseph Wenglein, one of the late but significant landscape painters of the Munich School. *Peasant Boy on a Wooden Bridge* (c 1859), *Russian Princess* (1863), *Ignaz von Döllinger* (1874) by Franz von Lenbach. *The Woman Falconer* (c 1880) by Hans Makart.

Gallery 15 – Devoted to **Hans von Marées**: *Three Boys beneath Orange Trees*, the triptych *The Hesperides* and *The Recruitment*.

Gallery 16 – Böcklin, Feuerbach, Thoma. **Arnold Böcklin**'s *Pan in the Reeds* (1859), and *In the Play of the Waves* (1883). **Anselm Feuerbach**'s famous painting *Medea's Farewell* (1870), and portrait of *Nanna* (1861). **Hans Thoma**'s two *Taunus Landscapes*. Bronze by Reinhold Begas (*Venus and Amor*, 1864).

Gallery 17 – Leibl and his circle. Works by **Wilhelm Leibl**: *Portrait of Mina Gedon* (1868), *Girl with White Headscarf* (1875), *In the Farmer's Parlour* (1890).

Gallery 18 – French Impressionists: paintings by **Edouard Manet** (*Breakfast in the Studio*, 1868, *Barque*, 1874), Camille Pissarro (*Street in Upper Norwood*, 1871), **Edgar Degas** (*Woman Ironing*, c 1869), Claude Monet (*Bridge over the Seine at Argenteuil*, 1874).

Gallery 19 – **Vincent van Gogh** (*Vase with Sunflowers*, 1888, *The Plain at Auvers*, 1890). **Paul Gauguin**'s complex *Birth of Christ*, symbolically transferred to the setting of the South Seas (1896). Paul Cézanne (*Still-life with Chest of Drawers*, c 1885, *Railway Cutting*, 1870).

Gallery 20 – Social Realism, represented by **Max Liebermann** (*Munich Beer Garden*, 1884, *Woman with Goats in the Dunes*, 1890) and Max Slevogt (*Closing Time*, 1900).

Gallery 21 – German Impressionists: Friedrich von Uhde (*Summer Holiday*, 1883), Lovis Corinth (*Portrait of the Writer Eduard Graf von Keyserling*, 1901).

Gallery 21a – Munich Secession. Albert Weisgerber (*Somali Woman*, 1912), Leo Putz (*Mrs Putz in the Garden*, 1907).

Gallery 22, 22a – Symbolism and Jugendstil (Art Nouveau). Marble bust of *Helene of Nostiz* by **Auguste Rodin**. Works by Ferdinand Hodler (*Disappointed*), **Gustav Klimt** (*Margarethe Stonborough-Wittgenstein*, 1905), Egon Schiele (*Agony*, 1912), Giovanni Segantini (*Ploughing*, 1890), Franz von Stuck (*War*, 1894, bronze statue of *Helena*, c 1906), Fernand Khnopff (*Closing Myself In*, 1891), *Neptune's Horses* by Walter Crane and *Elsa Asenijeff*, a marble bust by Max Klinger (c 1900).

Not far from the Alte and Neue Pinakothek (on the corner of Barer Straße and Gabelsberger Straße) is the site of the new building Pinakothek der Moderne, scheduled to open in late summer 2000. The building was designed by Munich architect Stephan Braunfels, and will be an impressive and original sight with its glass rotunda and glazed sawtooth roofs. It will house three museums: the Municipal Gallery of Modern Art, the Neue Sammlung (Craft and Design), and the Institute of Technology's Museum of Architecture. A later section is planned to accommodate an extension of the Prints and Drawings Collection.

Propyläen (Propylaea) (JY) – This imposing gateway by Leo von Klenze (1784-1864) was completed two years before the Munich architect died. Inspired by the Propylaea of the Acropolis, it stands on the west side of the Königsplatz (which is thus flanked on three sides by monuments in the Classical style). The frieze represents the war of liberation against the Turks; Otto I of Wittelsbach, King of Greece from 1832 to 1862, is commemorated in a statue on the pediment above the Doric colonnade.

★ **Glyptothek** ⊘ **(JY M²)** – One thousand years of Greek and Roman sculpture are gathered together under the roof of this museum, built with its Classical porch and Ionic colonnade, by the architect **Leo von Klenze** (1816-30). The **Tenea Apollo**, with his handsome, smiling face, is typical of the Kouros – those large naked figures, half human, half divine, who spread through Greece in the 6C BC *(Gallery I)*. The **Barberini Faun** *(Gallery II)*, which appears sated with drink and half asleep, dates from the Hellenistic epoque (c 220 BC). The Classical period is represented by Roman copies of ancient Greek statues and funerary stones (5C-4C BC): here the **bas-relief by Mnesarete** displays a magisterial harmony of proportion, and the sculptor's handling of the draperies swathing Irene, the Goddess of Peace, is equally fine *(Gallery V)*.

Note too, in the original works from the east and west pediments of the Temple of Aphaia on the island of Aegina, which were sculpted from Paros marble, how finely detailed is the shaping of the warriors' musculature. These statues *(Galleries VII-IX)* date from the end of the Archaic era (500-480 BC).

Finally *(Galleries X to XIII)*, the visitor can judge to what state of virtuosity the Romans had brought the arts of portraiture and the decoration of sarcophagi.

★ **Antikensammlungen (Collection of Antiquities)** ⊘ **(JY M³)** – *Opposite the Glyptothek.* A building by GF Ziebland (1838-48) which, with its Corinthian colonnade, forms an architectural counterpart to the sculpture museum across the road.

An important display of **ceramics** on the ground floor traces the evolution of pottery and the painting of vases in Greece, which reached its zenith during the 6C and 5C BC. Geometric decoration was succeeded by the representation of black figures on a red background – illustrated by an amphora and a goblet by the painter Exekias. The amphora depicts Ajax carrying the body of Achilles; Dionysius decorates the goblet, in a boat escorted by dolphins *(Gallery II, showcases 10 and 12)*. The transition towards the use of red figures against a background of varnished black can be seen on another amphora, where a single subject – Hercules' banquet in the presence of Athena – is treated in the two styles *(Gallery III, showcase 6)*.

Certain vases (loutrophora and lecythus on a white ground) were destined for funerary worship; others – such as the elegant canthare (drinking vessel in the shape of a female head) – for domestic use *(Gallery II, showcase 7 – 540 BC)*. **Bronzes** on the first floor (ceremonial vessels, engraved plaques, statuettes), and particularly the **Etruscan jewellery** in the basement *(Galleries VII and X)* testify to the enormous craftsmanship enjoyed by these workers in metal: necklaces, fibula, rings, in filigree or with granulations, rival each other in the delicacy and elegance of their execution.

★ **Städtische Galerie im Lenbachhaus (Lenbach Collections)** ⊘ **(JY M⁴)** – Built between 1883 and 1889 in the style of a Florentine villa, the house containing the Lenbach collections is devoted mainly to the works of **Munich painters of the 19C**. Among these are the landscapes of EB Morgenstern *(Starnberg Lake)* and portraits by FA von Kaulbach and F von Defregger. There is also a set of powerful **portraits** by Franz von Lenbach himself *(King Ludwig I, Bismarck, Wagner)*.

But the gallery's international reputation is built above all on the avant-garde **Blauer Reiter collection**. Born in the tumultuous period just before the First World War, the movement is represented by its founder members, Kandinsky, Marc *(Blue Horse)* and Kubin, as well as by paintings from the hands of Jawlensky, Klee and Macke. Contemporary art is also displayed in the Lenbach villa.

★★★ **DEUTSCHES MUSEUM** ⊘ **(LZ)**

Allow at least half a day

Founded in 1903, this museum – one of the most important in the world for scientific and technical matters – is built on an isle in the Isar (Museumsinsel). It traces the history of science and technology from the beginning of time to the present day. Over 1.25 million people visit it each year.

Apart from a large number of original items and reconstructions, most of them of great value, the exhibits comprise dioramas, synoptic tables, scale models and examples of working apparatus. In line with the expressed wish of the museum's founder, the Bavarian pioneer of electricity **Oskar von Miller**, the display system is pedagogic: the visitor is there to inquire, to touch, and to discover. Thus there are innumerable **working models** and workshop and laboratory **demonstrations** to explain the relevant techniques in a way that even a beginner can understand.

Such physics experiments as Faraday's Cage and Foucault's Pendulum, for example, are reproduced. And there are regular performances illustrating such manufacturing processes as papermaking, glass-blowing, smelting and the fabrication of tiles. Some of the demonstrations are accompanied by a commentary on film.

A library endowed with 900 000 different volumes is associated with the museum, as well as privately donated collections and archives including documents, plans, maps, blueprints and drawings.

In view of the huge scope of subjects covered, visitors are advised to choose a particular theme to follow. There are some 18 000 exhibits displayed over an area of 45 000m²/484 200sq ft. A brochure in English and a plan of the museum's layout are available at the entrance.

In view of necessary and ongoing modernisation, two or three of the museum's departments may as a rule be temporarily closed.

Ground Floor – Environment; metallurgy; machine tools; machines powered by different types of energy (wind, water, steam); applications of electrical current; bicycles and barouches; civil engineering (roads, bridges, tunnels, railways, canals etc). In the **Railway Hall**, there are famous steam engines, including the 1912 S-3/6 which powered the Bavarian Express, and the first electric locomotive *(Werner von Siemens, 1879)*. The **Aeronautical Section** (Modern Division) exhibits early jet planes, including the Messerschmitt Me-262, the first jet fighter made on a production line, helicopters, gliders and vertical take-off machines.

An Elbe sailing ship (1880) and an Italian steam tug (1932) stand at the entrance to the Navigation Department *(continued in the basement)*.

First electric locomotive (1879)

Basement – Among many other displays, the **Navigation Section** highlights naval construction, warships (including U-1, the first German submarine, built in 1906), methods of navigation, fishing techniques, and Jacques Piccard's 1958 bathysphere.

A section on **mining** details the working of a coal mine, the extraction of salt, and the treatment of ores. There is a model salt mine.

The **Automobile Department** shows an 1885 carriage with a Benz motor, an 1891 steam driven Serpollet, luxury cars of the 1920s and 1930s (Daimler, Opel, Horsch, Bugatti), utility vehicles, racing cars (1936 Auto-Union Grand Prix Type-C), an assembly line, and motorcycles. Note the 1885 Daimler-Maybach (a replica, built in 1906).

First Floor – The most interesting section here is perhaps **Aeronautics**. Gliders built by the engineer Lilienthal (c 1885), the pioneer of this form of flight, can be seen. Also a **1917 Fokker Dr I Triplane**, of the type made famous by Baron von Richthofen's "circus" in the First World War (a replica including parts from the original). Note also the Wright Brothers' Type-A Standard (USA, 1909), a Blériot

Type XI (1909), a Junkers F-13 (the first true air liner, 1919), and the legendary Junkers Ju-52 (built under licence in France, 1947). Military aircraft of the 1930s and 1940s are on show, including the Messerschmitt Bf-109.

From this most recent gallery devoted to aeronautics, there is direct access *(by escalator)* to the second floor section on space flights. Technologies from the earliest attempts at rocketry (Hitler's V2, code-named A4) to the current Spacelab are illustrated.

Department of Physics – Physical laws and their application: optics, mechanics, electronics, thermology, nuclear physics; **chemistry:** alchemy, Liebig's laboratory, pharmacy, biochemistry; media technology; musical instruments.

Second Floor – Manufacture of glass and ceramics (beautiful 17C earthenware stove from the Thurgau area in Switzerland); paper printing; photography (Daguerre's apparatus, 1839); textile processes (Jacquard's 1860 loom).

Third Floor – Weights and measures; climatic forecasts; agriculture (dairy farming, flour milling, breweries); data processing and computer science; robotics and microelectronics. Access to the **fourth floor** observatory *(visits must be booked in advance)*.

Fifth Floor – Astronomy (celestial globes, sundials, astrolabes, quadrants, etc).

Sixth Floor – Planetarium.

★ ENGLISCHER GARTEN QUARTER

★ **Englischer Garten (English Garden)** (LY) – Not far from the city centre, this park, with its broad sweeps of tree-bordered lawn, its streams and its lake, was designed in the late 18C by **Friedrich Ludwig von Sckell** and the British-American scientist **Sir Benjamin Thompson**, Count von Rumford. It is particularly popular in summer, when an open-air beer garden seating 7 000 people is open near the **Chinese Tower** (Chinesischer Turm). From the **Monopteros**, a circular temple built on a knoll by Leo von Klenze, there is a fine **view★** of the belfries in Munich's old town.

★★ **Bayerisches Nationalmuseum (Bavarian National Museum)** ⊘ (LY M⁵) – Maximilian II created this museum in 1885 with the aim of preserving Bavaria's artistic heritage. The rooms on the ground floor offer a survey of Bavarian **arts and crafts** from Romanesque to Renaissance, including silver and gold plate and religious statuary, tapestry, furniture, altarpieces and a model of the city.

The German and Italian Renaissance is evoked in other sections by jewellery, clocks, clothing, bronzes and glazed earthenware.

On the first floor, there are displays of musical instruments, silverware and porcelain from different periods. The basement contains a very large collection of **Christmas cribs**.

Staatsgalerie moderner Kunst(Modern Art Collection) ⊘ (LY M⁶) – In the west wing of the Haus der Kunst, built between 1933 and 1937 in the heavy, pompous "National Socialist" style.

The ground floor concentrates on "classic" modern art: Matisse, Picasso, Braque, Léger and Juan Gris represent Cubism and Fauvism; Kirchner *(Interior)*, Schmidt-Rottluff, Marc, Kandinsky and Beckmann (remarkable self-portrait of 1943) the different tendencies of German Expressionism. Examples of the Blauer Reiter and Die Brücke movements are shown with paintings from the Bauhaus (Feininger's *Halle Church*). Surrealism is present with Ernst, Miró, De Chirico and Dali; sculpture with Lehmbuch, Barlach, Giacometti and Mario Marini. The upper floor is reserved for late-20C art (Abstract Expressionism, Pop Art, Photorealism, Group Zero, CoBrA and Vasarely).

In summer 2000, it is planned to move the modern art collection to the new Pinakothek der Moderne building, located close to the Alte and Neue Pinakothek.

ADDITIONAL SIGHTS

★ **Schack-Galerie** ⊘ – *Prinzregentenstraße 9.*
Those interested in 19C German painting must not fail to visit this collection, which is exceptionally comprehensive. It is on display in a house that was built especially for the purpose and therefore provides the perfect setting for it. The collection is a real treasure, with works by the most renowned artists of the period. It was assembled by Count Adolf Friedrich von Schack (1815-94), who showed both idealism and, as it turns out, good taste in his patronage of the artists of his day. He was forced to live in modest style, however, in order to afford his works of art.

The collection spans Early to Late Romanticism and includes numerous works by landscape painter **Carl Rottmann** *(Kochelsee)*, **Moritz von Schwind** *(Rübezahl, Morning Hour)*, **Carl Spitzweg** *(Hermit, A Hypochondriac)*, Fritz Bamberger *(View of*

Gibraltar), **Arnold Böcklin** *(Spring Landscape Ideal, Villa by the Sea I and II)*, **Franz von Lenbach** *(Shepherd Boy, Self-portrait)*, **Anselm Feuerbach** *(Paolo and Francesca, Hafis by the Well, Portrait of Nanna)*, Georg Köbel *(Nymph Egeria's Spring near Rome)*. Hans von Marées is represented by copies of Old Masters that Schack had commissioned from him.

Museum Villa Stuck ⓥ – *Prinzregentenstraße* 60(**LY**).

Professor at the Munich Academy of Fine Arts from 1895 and one of the founding members of the Munich Secession, **Franz Stuck** (1863-1928) built this Jugendstil villa with an Italian influence after his own plans. The interior of the house is magnificent: it was Stuck himself who made the furniture, the panelling, the bas-reliefs and coffered ceilings. Note in particular the famous canvases by the artist, including *The Guardian of Paradise* and *The Sin*, and his sculptures *(Dancer, Amazon)*. The museum also hosts temporary exhibitions.

★ Münchner Stadtmuseum (City Historical Museum) ⓥ (KZ M⁷) – *In the stables of the old Arsenal.*

This museum houses comprehensive collections on local history, including a display of home decor in Munich, crafts, paintings, musical instruments, marionette theatres, photography and film. Do not fail to see the **Moorish Dancers**★★ (Moriskentänzer), 10 carved wooden figures painted and gilded in 1480 by **Erasmus Grasser** *(ground floor)*.

★ Asamkirche (St Johannes Nepomuk) (KZ) – The church, built in 1733, is always

referred to locally under the name of the men who constructed it, the Asam Brothers: **Cosmas Damian Asam**, who specialized in the painting of frescoes, and **Egid Quirin Asam**, sculptor and stucco-worker. The church's remarkable unity of style is due to the fact that the two brothers drew up the plans themselves, and both executed and supervised every stage of the work.

The design of the interior is strikingly harmonious. A curved gallery links the choir, the nave and the organ loft; above, supported on pillars, a second gallery is adorned with stuccowork and statues of angels or cherubim. The frescoed ceiling, lit by windows concealed behind mouldings, depicts episodes in the life of St John of Nepomuk.

To the left of the church stands **Egid Quirin Asam's House** *(Sendlinger Straße 61)* with a richly stuccoed Baroque façade.

Völkerkundemuseum (Ethnology Museum) ⓥ (LZ M⁸) – *Maximilianstraße 42.*

This imposing building was built by Eduard Riedel between 1858 and 1867. It is the setting for one of the richest collections of this kind in Germany. It has its origins in the collections built up so enthusiastically by the Wittelsbachs, who had begun to bring artefacts back from the Far East already in the 16C. Later rulers were likewise fascinated by the culture of far-off lands, and so Ludwig I systematically acquired Indian art, while Ludwig II bought the collection of a well-known researcher into Japanese culture in 1874. Ludwig II was also responsible for setting up a gallery devoted to ethnology.

Schloß Nymphenburg

The **Indian and Far Eastern collection** on the first floor, housed in part in rooms decorated with beautiful frescoes from 1860, gives a splendid overview of the art and culture of these regions with its wealth of exhibits. The Buddha Hall is very impressive, with a monumental statue of Amitabha Buddha, as are the 2C BC stone sculptures from Mathura (India), remarkably naturalist in style, and the wooden façade of a Jaina shrine from Gujarat (19C). In the stairwell on the way to the second floor is a striking gable end from a ceremonial storehouse in north New Guinea.

The **South American department** on the second floor is devoted to the Pre-Columbian cultures of the Central Andes (vessels, woven fabric from Ancient Peru, feather ponchoes) and the Amazon region (face and full-length masks). Note the fascinating stone stele with a representation of a jaguar from Costa Rica.

Wittelsbacher Brunnen (Wittelsbach Fountain) (KY) – *Between the Lenbachplatz and the Maximiliansplatz.*
Adolf von Hildebrand built this neo-Baroque fountain in 1895 to mark the completion of a water canalization programme which provided the city with clean drinking water.

★★ NYMPHENBURG *allow half a day*

6km/4mi from the city centre, leaving Munich on Marsstraße (JY).

The oldest part of the palace, once the summer residence of the Bavarian sovereigns, is the five-storey central pavilion, built by Barelli between 1664 and 1674 in the style of an Italian palazzo. The Prince-Elector Max Emmanuel, who reigned from 1679 to 1726, added two lateral pavilions on either side which were linked to the main building by arcaded galleries. At the same time he remodelled the central block, accentuating the verticals by the addition of pilasters. His successors, Karl-Albrecht (1726-45) and Max III Josef (1745-77), then constructed a semicircle of outbuildings and dependencies, which underlined the castle's resemblance to Versailles.

From 1701 onwards, the surrounding park too was enlarged under the direction of Carbonet and Girard, the pupils of Le Nôtre. The formal French gardens date from this period, as do the various park pavilions: Pagodenburg (1719), Badenburg (1721), Magdalenenklause (1728) and Amalienburg (1739).

★ **Palace** ⊘ – The splendid **banqueting hall**, a symphony of white, gold and pale green, was richly adorned with coloured stuccowork and frescoes by Johann Baptist Zimmermann and his son Franz. A musicians' gallery is placed beneath the high windows looking out over the park.

The rooms in the north wing of the central block – antechamber, bedroom, study – are panelled, with tapestry hangings and paintings. Beyond this the north pavilion contains views of the castle and park in the early 18C.

The most fascinating room in the main block's south wing is the one devoted to a collection of **Chinese lacquer**. The south gallery contains further images of Wittelsbach castles. In the south pavilion, the apartments of Queen Carolina contain the famous **Gallery of Beauties**★ conceived by King Ludwig I. Commissioned by the King to immortalize the most beautiful women of the epoch (Lola Montez, among others), these paintings were executed by the portraitist Joseph Karl Stieler (1781-1858).

★ Park - *See itinerary on Nymphenburg map.*

Most of the park can be seen from the top of the steps in front of the palace's main entrance. Below the steps, beyond the formal rectilinear flower gardens lined with white marble urns and the statues of gods, the Grand Canal, which ends in a waterfall, flows straight as an arrow away into the distance.

★★ Amalienburg ○ - This charming little hunting lodge by **Cuvilliés** is one of his most accomplished designs - a model for the many Rococo country pavilions which so delighted the courts of 18C Germany. The simplicity and sobriety of the exterior is in vivid contrast with the extraordinary richness of the interior. Beyond the curious Kennel - a panelled central room surrounded by the quarters of hunting dogs - are the Blue Room and a beautiful bedchamber, with silver woodwork on a background of lemon yellow.

In the centre of the building is the **Hall of Mirrors** rotunda. Here the combination of blue walls and ceiling, silver-plated stucco and wood-framed glass forms a marvellous ensemble. A Hunting Room, the Pheasant Room, and kitchens whose walls are tiled with blue Delft complete this masterpiece of Bavarian Rococo.

Badenburg - A luxurious heated swimming pool, with a ceiling decorated by mythological motifs, is the centrepiece of this 18C bathhouse. A dressing-room, and an antechamber serving as games and rest room are also included in the pavilion.

Pagodenburg - The 18C taste for exoticism and the Far East is exemplified in the design of this octagonal tea house. A drawing room, a Chinese room and a boudoir occupy the first floor. *Currently under restoration.*

Magdalenenklause - A "hermitage" or folly built in the then popular style of "artificial ruins", this pavilion is dedicated to St Mary Magdalene.

Marstallmuseum und Porzellansammlung (Carriage Museum and Porcelain Collection) ○ **(M)** - The museum is housed in the castle's former stables. Besides superb 18C and 19C harnesses, broughams, coaches, carts, sledges and sedan chairs used by the Wittelsbachs are on display. Note especially the coronation coach of Emperor Karl VII, and the state coach and personal sleigh of Ludwig II, all of them equipped with quite incredible luxury.

Above the old stables, a series of rooms exhibits the **Bäuml Collection of Nymphenburg Porcelain**. Painted figurines by Franz Anton Bustelli, master modellist of the factory between 1754 and 1763, are particularly fine. The **reproductions in porcelain ★** - miniature copies in extraordinary detail of paintings in the Alte Pinakothek - were commissioned by King Ludwig I.

Museum Mensch und Natur ("Man and Nature" Natural History Museum) ○ - *In the north wing of Nymphenburg Palace.*

Rarely is a natural history museum so interesting and accessible, especially to younger visitors. The first room on the **ground floor** is devoted to the evolution and physical composition of the planet Earth. A large slide display shows how the

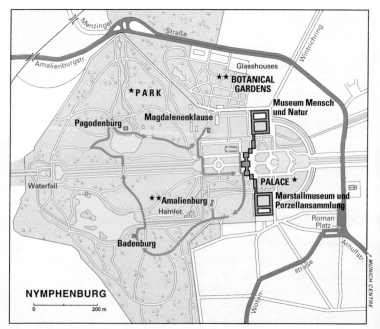

NYMPHENBURG

Earth looked four billion years ago. Room 2 contains a colourful display on minerals. This is followed by a section entitled "History of Life", in which the evolution of life on Earth is retraced. The "Window on the Past" displays life-size copies of life forms and plant species long since extinct.

On the **first floor**, the exhibition takes as its theme the Earth's environment and how it supports the billions of people who now live on it, from the earliest days of the plough to modern farming methods. Interactive games and quizzes test visitors' knowledge of the plant and animal kingdoms. The final room explores the topic of man and nature in America, again with interesting interactive programmes.

Museum Mensch und Natur

Museum Mensch und Natur

★★ **Botanischer Garten (Botanical Gardens)** ⊙ – Reputed to be among the finest and most richly stocked in Europe. A stroll through the Schmuckhof (*opposite the main building*), the Spring Garden and the Rosery, past masses of rhododendrons shaded by pines and around the Alpine Garden by the Great Lake is not only a feast for the eyes but a horticultural lesson in itself. There are marvellous orchids among the tropical and sub-tropical species flowering in the **greenhouses**.

EXCURSIONS

★ **Tierpark Hellabrunn (Hellabrunn Zoological Gardens)** ⊙ – *6km/4mi from the city centre, leaving via Wittelsbacherstraße (**KZ**).*
Munich's zoo was founded as the world's first nature reserve and zoo combined in 1911, occupying an idyllic site on the banks of the Isar. The generous enclosures are home to about 5 000 animals. Main attractions include the giant aviary, elephant house, jungle pavilion with primeval forest biotope, tortoise house, polar zone and children's zoo. The Villa Dracula may well send a shiver down your spine with its resident bats, although they are only the fruit-eating variety. The zoo is world-famous for its breeding programmes for Przewalski's horses and Mhorr gazelles.

Bavaria-Filmstadt Geiselgasteig (Bavaria Film Studios) ⊙ – *10km/6mi from the centre via Hochstraße (**LZ**), Grünwalderstraße and Geiselgasteigstraße.*
The first film shot in these studios was made in 1919. Since then, the Bavaria Film Studios can pride themselves on a long line of successes in the great tradition of the cinema. Visitors here will learn all about film and television and be able to admire the original sets for famous features such as *The Boat* and *Neverending Story*. They can even visit the set of the Asterix film shot here.
During the tour of the studios, visitors are shown what goes on behind the cameras. In the Showscan-Kino, the seats move in coordination to the action on the screen. Stuntspeople demonstrate their dangerous work in the **Action Show**.

Olympiapark ⊙ – *5km/3mi from the centre, via Dachauer Straße (**JY**).*
Munich was host to the XX Olympic Games in 1972. The many sports and leisure facilities (Olympic stadium, Olympic swimming pool and skating rink, open-air theatre with stage in the Olympiasee) are now used by the people of Munich. There is a museum on the Olympic Games in the old cycling stadium.
The 1968 **Olympiaturm** (television tower) is no less than 290m/951ft high. At the 190m/623ft level (*lift*), there is a terrace with **panorama**★★★, which offers an exceptional view over the city to the Bavarian Alps.

BMW 502

BMW-Museum ⊘ – *Petuelring 130. 5km/3mi to the north, via Schleißheimer Straße* (**JY**) *and Lerchenauer Straße.*
This strange silver building shaped like a cup lies at the foot of the administration tower – which enhances the futuristic effect by being built in the form of four linked cylinders. The guided tour, which progresses in a spiral, retraces technical developments, social history of the 20C and examines prognoses for the future. Examples from BMW used to illustrate each of these themes include aircraft engines (from 1916), motorcycles (from 1923) and motor cars (from 1928), and besides the exhibits there are explanatory films, videos and slide shows.

★ **Schloß Schleißheim** ⊘ – *15km/9mi to the north. Leave via Schleißheimer Straße* (**JY**).
Neues Schloß, the so-called "new" castle, a majestic 330m/1 083ft in length, was built between 1701 and 1727 under Elector Max II Emanuel. The grand staircase leads to the State Apartments on the upper floor, the highlight of which is the huge banqueting hall in dazzling white. The adjacent Hall of Victory is adorned with gleaming gold stuccowork by JB Zimmermann depicting battle scenes. Next come the princely apartments and **galleries** *(temporarily still empty)*, hung with European Baroque painting and works by 16C and 17C Dutch and Flemish masters, including the great gallery taking up the whole of the garden side of the central block *(the paintings are scheduled to be rehung from 2000 or 2001)*.
On the ground floor, a second series of galleries follows on from the music room. The castle **grounds** are laid out in formal geometric French style by Carbonet and Girard, with a central canal as their main axis. At the far end of the park, enclosed by a circular canal, stands a small Baroque folly, the **Lustheim**, built by Zuccali in 1684-89; it houses a collection of Meissen porcelain.

★ **Flugwerft Schleißheim** ⊘ – *Right next to Schloß Schleißheim.*
The **hangar** was built between 1912 and 1919 for the Bavarian air corps. The Deutsches Museum has set up a new branch in the historic hangar and the newly built glass exhibition hall, the **Museum of Air and Space Travel**, which has proved popular with the public. There is a variety of interesting exhibits, including The 1959 Olympia-Meise DFS glider, the Heinkel He III bomber, or the 1943 Douglas DC-3 commercial aircraft, which between them embody the most important areas of air travel, namely sport, military and commercial flight. Some variants of the legendary Russian MiGs are represented, as is the notorious Starfighter, with which the German Air Force was equipped from 1960 and of which no fewer than 269 aircraft crashed before the model was withdrawn from service.
The collection of historic aircraft or the airmen's radio training college with its original fittings are also informative. From the visitors' gallery in the restoration workshop, it is possible to view the restorers at work on weekdays.

★ **Ammersee** – *Round tour of 116km/72mi – allow 4hr.*
Lying at an altitude of 533m/1 749ft, this lake of glacial origin is cradled in a pretty landscape of wooded hills. Swimming, sailing and **boat trips** can be enjoyed at small resorts such as Dießen and Herrsching. Enthusiasts of the Rococo style must be sure to visit the abbey church at Andechs.
Follow the western lake shore to reach Dießen.
Dießen – The **church**★ (Marienmünster) was built between 1732 and 1739 to replace a former monastery collegiate. The architect was Johann Michael Fischer, one of the most celebrated of the late, south German Baroque. The Asam brothers and François Cuvilliés also contributed to the design.

The church is an impressively harmonious blend of rich decoration, in the stuccowork by Augsburg and Wessobrunn masters, frescoes by Johann Georg Bergmüller and valuable altarpieces crafted by south German and Italian masters (including Straub and Tiepolo). The imposing chancel altar, over 20m/65ft high, with a fold-away image, unusually features a Mysteries stage.

The climb from Fischen to Andechs offers fine views of the lake.

★ **Andechs** – Crowning the Heiliger Berg ("holy hill"), this **Benedictine abbey** overlooks the Ammersee by more than 200m/656ft. Its **church**★★ ⊙, erected on a Gothic base, was remodelled as a Rococo building. The architect JB Zimmermann (1680-1758), then at the height of his powers as a mature artist, was responsible both for the frescoes and the stuccowork. An elegant gallery, its balustrade decorated with painted panels evoking the history of the abbey, surrounds the main body of the church. The treatment of the vault frescoes, in various shades of pastel, shows an exceptional talent in the handling of colour. Bavarian composer Carl Orff, famous for the Carmina Burana, is buried in the Chapel of Suffering.

About 1.5 million visitors come to Andech every year to visit the church (and sample the famous local beer). At the foot of the hill a new brewery has been built, which has an annual production of about 90 000hl/1 980 000gal. The beer is highly regarded both locally and much further afield.

Return to Munich via Herrsching and Seefeld.

Dachau Concentration Camp (KZ-Gedenkstätte) ⊙ – *19km/12mi to the northwest.* Nazi Germany's first concentration camp was organized near the pleasant, terraced town of Dachau on the orders of Heinrich Himmler in 1933. Originally designed for the detention of German political opponents of the Nazi regime, the camp was soon flooded by tens of thousands of deportees, the majority of them Jews of diverse nationalities. More than 32 000 died there – without counting the several thousand Russian prisoners-of-war shot dead on the nearby SS firing range. The system was described by Joseph Rovan, one of the few who escaped from the camp, as "implacable, perverted, an organization that was totally murderous, a marvellous machine for the debasement and de-humanizing of man".

Ruins, Commemorative Monuments, Museum – *Follow the signposting "KZ-Gedenkstätte"*. A Jewish memorial, a Protestant commemorative sanctuary and a Catholic expiatory chapel in the form of an open tower have been built within the precincts of the old camp. The huts were razed, but two, complete with their interior layout, have been reconstructed. On the Appelplatz (roll-call square), where prisoners were forced to muster morning and evening whatever the weather, a monument has been erected by the International Community. Behind, outside the camp perimeter, is a Carmelite convent with a chapel which may be visited. The Museum, which outlines the punitive penal system established there by the Nazis, is housed in the former camp administration buildings. Land surrounding the cremation ovens, outside the camp, has been turned into a park-necropolis. The bodies of other victims have been buried in the cemeteries of Dachau (Waldfriedhof) and Leitenberg, 2km/1.2mi to the northeast.

MÜNSTER★★

Nordrhein-Westfalen

Population 279 000
Michelin map 417 K 6
Local map see MÜNSTERLÄNDER WASSERBURGEN

Münster, the historical capital of Westphalia, where the local lords used to stay in winter, lies in the middle of a wooded plain studded with castles and manor houses. The city, one of Germany's most important university centres, has been restored to give full value to its many fine Gothic, Baroque and Renaissance façades.

The Peace of Westphalia – This treaty, signed on 24 October 1648, ended the Thirty Years War. During the five years of negotiations, the Emperor shuttled between the plenipotentiaries of the Protestant states in Osnabrück and those from the Catholic states in Münster, where the documents were finally agreed. As a result, much of Germany was carved up, to the detriment of Imperial prestige. The treaty recognized or confirmed the cession to France of Alsace and the bishoprics of Metz, Toul and Verdun, guaranteed the independence of Switzerland and the Netherlands, and favoured the development of Prussia. Three religious faiths were recognized, the Calvinists receiving the same rights as the Lutherans.

SIGHTS

★★ **Dom (Cathedral)** (Y) – A squat building with two towers, two chancels and two transepts, this church is in the transitional style typical of Westphalia in the 13C. Entering via the 16C south porch, the visitor sees that the inner door is surrounded by 13C statues and overlooked by a Christ in Judgement. A 16C statue of St Paul, patron saint of the cathedral, looks down from the pier.

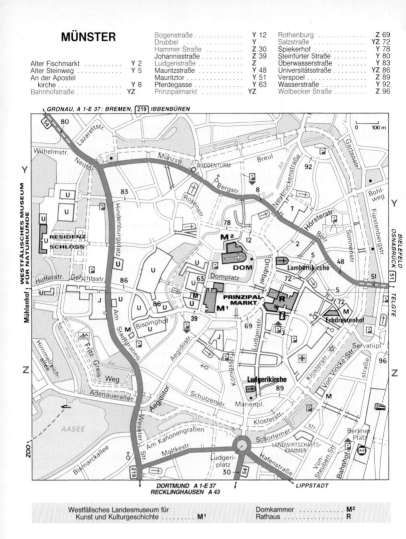

		Bogenstraße	Y 12	Rothenburg	Z 69
		Drubbel	Y	Salzstraße	YZ 72
		Hammer Straße	Z 30	Spiekerhof	Y 78
		Johannisstraße	Z 39	Steinfurter Straße	Y 80
Alter Fischmarkt	Y 2	Ludgeristraße	Z	Überwasserstraße	Y 83
Alter Steinweg	Y 5	Mauritzstraße	Y 48	Universitätsstraße	YZ 86
An der Apostel		Mauritztor	Y 51	Verspoel	Y 89
kirche	Y 8	Pferdegasse	Y 63	Wasserstraße	Y 92
Bahnhofstraße	YZ	Prinzipalmarkt	YZ	Wolbecker Straße	Z 96

Westfälisches Landesmuseum für Kunst und Kulturgeschichte	M¹	
Domkammer	M²	
Rathaus	R	

Visit the interior anti-clockwise.

The wide central nave and its bays lie beneath rounded vaulting. The side aisles are very low. In the ambulatory there is a 1540 **astronomic clock**★ in which the hours are struck by metal figurines wielding hammers. The spectators' gallery, high up in the church, was painted by Tom Ring the Elder.

The Chapel of the Holy Sacrament, left of the entrance to the cloister, is **richly furnished**★ (note especially an 18C silver tabernacle, made by a craftsman in Augsburg). The cloister entrance is reached through the north transept crossing.

★★ **Treasury** (Domkammer) ⊙ (**M²**) – *Off the cloister.* This is a modern building, blending perfectly with the structure of the cathedral, to which it is indirectly attached by the cloister.

On the ground floor, fourteen 15C reliquary-busts of the Prophets in copper and silver, the 11C head-reliquary of St Paul, together with a 13C Virgin – both of them in chased gold – surround the **Processional Cross** of the Chapter. And this, due to superimposed openings adjusted on the three levels, becomes the focal point of the whole treasure house. In the basement there is a fine collection of liturgical vestments (copes, stoles, chasubles), particularly from the 17C and 18C, and ritual items. In the centre stands a portable altar (12C) hung with a cloth embroidered in pearls.

Noteworthy on the first floor, amid a collection of Gothic and Baroque statuary, is the 1520 **Altarpiece of St John.**

★ **Westfälisches Landesmuseum für Kunst und Kulturgeschichte (Fine Arts Museum)** ⊙ (**YZ M¹**) – The medieval art of Westphalia lives on, thanks to the Gothic statuary of the cathedral and churches of Münster, a series of stained-glass windows in this museum, and the sculptures of Johann and Heinrich Brabender. There is a remarkable collection of **altarpieces**★★ by Konrad von Soest, Koerbecke and the Masters of Liesborn and Schöppingen. Flemish influence is noticeable in the works of the Tom Ring family (Ludger Tom Ring's painting was a precursor

H. Lohse

Landscape near Hammamet by August Macke

of the still-life). Interesting portraits of Luther and his wife are by Lucas Cranach. 20C masterpieces by August Macke, Ernst Ludwig Kirchner and Josef Albers, among others, round off this overview of artistic creativity from the Middle Ages to the present.

★ **Prinzipalmarkt** (YZ) – Running in a semicircle to the east of the cathedral, this is the busiest – and at the same time the most historic – street in town. The elegant houses, with Late Gothic or Renaissance gables, which have been restored since the Second World War, were once the homes of rich burghers. Under the arcades, attractive shops compete for space with restaurants and beer halls. The northern end of the street opens into the Bogenstraße, a wide space equally inviting for window-shoppers and strollers (the statue halfway up, a pedlar with his basket, is known as the Kiepernkerl).

Rathaus (YZ **R**) – The late-14C gabled façade of the town hall, with pinnacles and fine stone window tracery, is one of the most impressive examples of Gothic civic architecture.

★ **Friedenssaal** (Peace Hall) ⊘ – The wood-panelled council chamber, now named after the peace treaty, dates from the second half of the 12C. In 1648 it was the backdrop to the peace between Spain and the Netherlands, which heralded the whole Treaty of Westphalia. The original fittings, which were put out to store during the Second World War, are preserved just as they are recorded in the painting of the peace treaty by Gerhard Terborch.

The woodwork on the doors of the filing cabinet behind the burgomaster's table are some of the most original produced by German sculptors at the beginning of the 16C. The colourful mixture of religious and amusing motifs nonetheless raises the suspicion that the present arrangement is not that of the original. Note also the portraits of the rulers and their delegates who participated in the treaty and the beautiful wrought-iron chandelier.

The Anabaptists

This Reformist movement, which refused to acknowledge infant baptism, advocating baptism for believing adults only, originated in Zürich. What began as a peaceful movement aiming to change the Church from within, evolved over time into a more radical revolutionary sect under the pressure of savage persecution (since they dared to voice criticism of the state). One of the places they achieved supremacy was Münster, where one of their more radical branches effectively set up a reign of terror in 1534, which was brought to an end only after a 16-month state of siege; whereupon its ringleaders were hung.

The Anabaptists, or Rebaptists, were in some ways the spiritual forerunners of the Baptists.

★ **Residenzschloß** (Y) – Once the Prince-Bishops' residence, this Baroque palace is now part of the university. The red brick of the elegant three-part façade designed by Johann Conrad Schlaun is variegated with sandstone facings which enliven any monotony of style. At the back, surrounded by water, lies a park (Schloßgarten) with an adjoining botanical garden. This green space is continued south of the castle by the Rampart Walk (Wallpromenade), from which there is a view of Lake Aasee.

Lambertikirche (Y) – Groined vaulting over the centre nave and star vaults above the side aisles are the striking features of this Gothic hall-church. The neo-Gothic tower with its openwork spire was added in the 19C. It stands 90m/295ft tall. Still visible hanging from the tower are the iron cages in which the bodies of the Anabaptist rebel leaders were displayed to the public following the defeat of their uprising in 1535. Behind the east end of the church is the Krameramtshaus, a fine guild house with a gable end (1588).

Ludgerikirche (Z) – Romanesque multi-level hall-church dating from 1180. Modern stained-glass windows (1961) illustrating the life of Jesus have been added to the chancel. Note in particular the Renaissance choir stalls from 1540, the winged altarpiece (1480) above the tabernacle wall and the *Madonna of Joy*, a Burgundian work (1450).

Erbdrostenhof (Z) – This palace, dating from 1757, was built with a majestic concave façade and a triangular forecourt testifying to the skill of architect Johann Conrad Schlaun.

★ **Westfälisches Museum für Naturkunde (Westphalian Museum of Natural History)** ⊙
– *Sentruper Straße 285. Entrance signposted from the Hüfferstraße* (Y).
Departments of geology, paleontology, mineralogy, botany and zoology, all beautifully laid out, offer a huge, panoramic survey of our environment and its evolution. There are further displays on specific topics, such as dinosaurs, Indians of the prairies and plains, and on human evolution.
The displays in the **planetarium**★ provide an excellent introduction to astronomy.

Mühlenhof-Freilichtmuseum (Open-Air Windmill Museum) ⊙ – *Signposted from the Hüfferstraße* (Y), *south of the Residenzschloß gardens.*
In a peaceful setting on the shores of the Aasee, a mill house, a 1748 windmill and a large farm dating from 1619 are surrounded by such traditional rural features as a forge, a Westphalian chapel, different kinds of barn, a bread oven, a local well etc.

EXCURSIONS

Telgte – *12km/8mi to the east on B 51.*
In the historic town centre of Telgte, next to the Baroque pilgrimage chapel in which there is a Pietà dating from 1370 visited by numerous pilgrims, is the local museum, **Heimathaus Münsterland** ⊙. One of its prize exhibits is a folk art masterpiece on cloth, the **Lenten Veil**★ (Hungertuch, 1623), which measures no less than 32m²/344sq ft. Both the Heimathaus and the nearby **Christmas crib museum** explore the way religious faith is expressed in local art and customs.

Freckenhorst – *26km/16mi to the east on B 51.*
The **Collegiate Church**★ (Stiftskirche) with its fortified façade, is a fine example of pre-Romanesque German architecture *(see Introduction)*. Note the magnificent **baptismal font**★ in the north aisle, inscribed with the date of the church's consecration (1129). On a tomb in the crypt is the recumbent statue of Geva, the church's founder.
Fine twinned columns support the remaining (west) gallery of the cloister.

Ostenfelde – *36km/22mi to the east on B 51.*
The graceful **Vornholz Castle**★ (1666) stands in a rolling landscape forested with ancient oaks. Built on two islets, its tall, roofed main block flanked by two wings, this is a typical Münsterland "water castle" (Münsterländer Wasserburg – *see below*).

To plan a special itinerary:
-consult the Map of Touring Programmes which indicates the recommended routes, the tourist regions, the principal towns and main sights;
-read the descriptions in the Sights section which include Excursions from the main tourist centres.
Michelin Maps nos 415, 416, 417, 418, 419 and 429 cover the different regions of Germany and indicate scenic routes, interesting sights, viewpoints, rivers, forests...

MÜNSTERLÄNDER WASSERBURGEN★

MOATED CASTLES OF THE MÜNSTER REGION
Nordrhein-Westfalen
Michelin map 417 K 3-8

The charming **Wasserburgen** ⊙ – literally "water castles" – are to be found all over the Münster region. Witness to the incessant fighting between rival nobles in order to protect their territories, they are built on the sites of temporary encampments set up by the Teutons. They first appeared in the 12C in the form of wooden strongholds erected on artificial hills ("Motten") which were protected at the base by a surrounding stockade or defensive wall and a moat full of water. The invention of firearms at the beginning of the 16C made this system of defence precarious, and it was replaced, little by little, with proper fortifications isolated still more by moats or lagoons.

Many of these fortresses spread over two islands, joined by a bridge. The first isle, or "Vorburg", would be used for the outbuildings; the second, or "Hauptburg" for the dwelling. Subsequently, two separate influences could be detected in their design: that of the Weser Renaissance from the east, and that of the Dutch architectural school coming from the west. Their defensive character became less distinct over the centuries, and especially after the Thirty Years War (1618-48). After that, virtual palaces set in formal gardens began to appear. In the 18C, a taste for the Baroque manifested itself in the treatment of façades and gateways. Such water-surrounded castles, situated in pleasant landscapes, fascinate still with their old-world charm. Descriptions of several of them are given below.

★ **Anholt** ⊙ – Surrounded by a 34ha/84-acre landscaped park and restored Baroque garden, this moated castle (main and fore castle 12C-17C, converted into a Baroque place in c 1700) is built around a square inner courtyard. The museum contains evidence of three centuries of royal home decor: collection of paintings (Rembrandt, Brueghel, Murillo), tapestries, furniture, porcelain and weapons.

Gemen ⊙ – The towers, battlements and buildings of this **castle** (15C, remodelled in the 17C) are grouped on a fortified islet which arises from beautiful, shaded stretches of water. The original keep was later crowned with a Baroque roof. Today, the moated castle is a youth centre.

★ **Hülshoff** ⊙ – The massive square towers of the outbuildings (first island) complement a **manor-house** (second island) constructed in 1545. The brick and stonework manor is distinguished by gable ends and a turret with cupola and lantern. A neo-Gothic chapel was added in 1870. The poetess **Annette von Droste-Hülshoff** was born here in 1797 (small museum).

★ **Lembeck** ⊙ – The approach to this castle is impressive – a long perspective of driveway punctuated by a series of Baroque gateways and flanked by the arched entrances to various parts of the central complex. The monumental edifice spread over two islands today was built at the end of the 17C on the site of a 14C fortress. Huge towers with Baroque roofs stand at every corner. A few salons inside can be visited. The biggest (Großer Saal) is embellished with fine panelling and stuccowork. Valuable furniture, Gobelins tapestries, porcelain and paintings from the 17C to the 19C are on display.

In the spring the rhododendron park is an absolute riot of colour.

Raesfeld ⊙ – Raesfeld castle, built between 1643 and 1658 by Alexander von Velen, now consists only of a building with two wings, the Vorburg and the castle chapel. The tower (49.5m/162ft) and onion dome are visible from afar.

★ **Vischering** ⊙ – Built on two islands and protected by a double fortified wall, Vischering is still one of the most formidable fortresses in the Münster region. A Renaissance building has been constructed on the medieval foundations of the

Rundburg. The fortress now houses a museum, with special emphasis on furniture from various eras, for example a state bed from the 16C. The wall and ceiling paintings and splendid sandstone fireplaces are particularly impressive. The Vorburg, which stands on a separate island, used to house the fortress' farm outbuildings. Today visitors can see an exhibition of life and work in the rural environment. There is also a richly decorated carriage house.

Not far from Vischering, 8km/5mi southeast of Lündinghausen, is the impressive 18C moated castle of **Nordkirchen**, known as "Westphalia's miniature Versailles". This beautiful palace also houses a school of finance.

★ **Vornholz** – *See MÜNSTER: Excursions.*

On all town plans north is at the top of the page.

NAUMBURG★

Sachsen-Anhalt
Population 31 000
Michelin map 418 M 19

Naumburg, seat of a bishopric (since 1028), lies on the edge of the Thuringian basin, surrounded by vineyards and wooded hillsides in the middle of the "Saale-Unstrut-Triasland" national park. In the 12C, the town was already developing as a civic entity independent of the cathedral city. The city, which was largely spared damage during the Second World War, was an important trading centre in the Late Middle Ages and Renaissance period. The "Peter-Pauls-Messe" held here was a serious rival to the trade fair in Leipzig. Naumburg became part of Prussia under the Vienna Congress and was transformed into a local government and administration centre for the province of Saxony.

In 1991, Naumburg was one of five cities in the nine new Federal German states selected as a model for restoring old city centres. Its economic structure is essentially composed of administration and service facilities, and small- and medium-sized craft industries.

★★ DOM ST. PETER UND ST. PAUL (CATHEDRAL)

Access via Domplatz

This double-chancel church is a perfect example of the architectural evolution from Late Romanesque to Early Gothic. The Romanesque nave was built in the beginning to mid 13C. Between 1250 and 1270, the western section was completed by a chancel already displaying certain Early Gothic features. The east chancel, under which there is still a Romanesque crypt, was itself transformed into a Gothic structure in the 14C. The eastern chancel is separated from the central nave by the eastern **rood screen**, the only remaining hall-church rood screen in Germany.

West Chancel – The western **rood screen★★** is a magnificent work by the Master of Naumburg, who created it as a partition wall, in which the incredibly poignant, life-like scenes represent the Passion as a human tragedy. The splendid central portal depicts a Crucifixion group, surmounted by the Majesty of God as a fresco in a quatrefoil. The same Master also created the famous statues of the cathedral's **benefactors★★★**, which decorate the chancel and which undoubtedly took medieval sculpture in Germany to the summit of its glory. The individual personification of these figures, their penetrating expressions, the overall impression of seriousness all add up to an exceptional effect of humanity and grandeur. The best-known are those of the founders of the town, Margrave Ekkehardt and his wife Uta *(centre, right)*.

H. Champollion/MICHELIN, Paris

Benefactors' statues,
Naumburg Cathedral

ADDITIONAL SIGHTS

★ **St.-Wenzel** – Th original church on this site was first recorded in 1228. The present building was constructed as a Late Gothic hall-church with an unusual floor plan in the 15C. The width of the west octagon matches the distance west to east as far as the junction with the east chancel, to which extra elevation has been added (33m/108ft). Between 1610 and 1618, five Renaissance tribunes were added, and up to the mid 18C the interior was transformed into the Baroque style with a mirror-vaulted ceiling, magnificent carved altar, pulpit and organ. This 18C instrument is one of the largest surviving works by Zacharias Hildebrand. It was put through its paces by Johann Sebastian Bach, no less.

There are two fine paintings by Lucas Cranach the Elder: *The Adoration of the Magi*, facing the choir (1522); and, on the south side of the choir, *The Blessing of the Children* (1529).The artist is supposed to have portrayed himself in both these scenes. The second shows Katharina von Bora, Luther's wifer, surrounded by her sons and daughters.

Marktplatz – The large market square is edged with 16C-17C houses. The **town hall**, a Late Gothic building with a beautiful portal dating from 1612, boasts six transverse gables with tracery decoration. The same façade design is repeated on the **Schlößchen** (1543), behind which towers the church of St. Wenzel. The "Hohe Lilie" (municipal museum), with its Late Gothic corbie gable and traced transom, stands at the entrance to Herrenstraße.

Townhouses – In Jakobstraße note the Alte Post (1574) with its three-storey oriel. In **Marienstraße** there are plenty of interesting old houses to look at. The extravagantly ornate portals, testifying to the town's prosperity, for example the Samson portal on Peter-Pauls-Haus illustrating the fight between Samson and the lion. **Herrenstraße** features some fine oriels, for example the oldest in Naumburg at house no 1.

Doorway on Marktplatz, Naumburg

The "Lorbeerapotheke", chemist's shop adjacent to it also boasts a splendid oriel, as does the house at no 8 (1525).

Marientor – This is the only one of the five original town gates to have survived. It is a rare example of a double gate with gatehouses, a courtyard with a bend in it to trap intruders, and a watchpath. Its nucleus dates from the 14C, but it was extended in the 15C.

Nietzsche-Haus – *On Weingarten*. The philosopher Nietzsche spent a brief part of his childhood in this well-proportioned, neo-Classical building. Later, when his mental health was failing, his mother took him in here once again. The museum contains a permanent exhibition on "Nietzsche in Naumburg".

EXCURSIONS

Freyburg – *7km/4.5mi to the north*. This wine-growing centre stands in a picturesque location on the banks of the Unstrut, dominated by the Neuenburg which stands high above the town. Visitors can travel by steamer along the river through attractive countryside as far as the Naumburg flower fields.

★ **Neuenburg** ⊙ – The Neuenburg was founded in 1090 by Ludwig der Springer, the Landgrave of Thuringia. It represented the eastern counterpart to the Wartburg fortress in the west. The **double chapel**★, an extremely unusual type of building, of which the lower floor was reserved for the people and the upper floor for the higher nobility, is of considerable interest. Its origins date back to c 1230. The two floors are linked by a small grille in the ceiling. The rich architectural design and ornamentation is copied from the Lower Rhine area. The serrated transverse arches of the upper floor are in the same style, as is the splendid gilded **capital**★ with its decorative figures. The superb Renaissance spiral staircase, which leads from the lower to the upper floor, was moved here from another part of the castle in the 19C.

There are around a dozen beautifully furnished rooms to visit in the **royal apartments**, including the banqueting hall and the royal hall with a whole series of portraits of various princes and a portal which dates from 1552.

The **Dicker Wilhelm**, a Romanesque keep with a domed slate roof, is said to have been built at the end of the 12C. An exhibition retraces the history of the tower and the town.

Schulpforte ⊘ – *On B 87, just before Bad Kösen, around 6km/3.5mi southwest.* The Cistercian monastery, which was founded in 1137, was closed in 1540. Since then it has been the home of the renowned provincial school, whose famous scholars include Schlegel, Fichte and Klopstock, together with Friedrich Nietzsche, who joined the school in 1858 ("I longed for Pforta, only for Pforta") and which is still in existence today. The monastery church, with its imposing west façade dating from c 1300 has been under restoration for some considerable time. The well maintained monastery contains the interesting **Panster mill**★, a technically most impressive monument to the technology of its era *(the mill is put into operation during guided tours)*.

★ **Bad Kösen** – *On B 87, around 7km/4.25mi.* This attractive little health resort on the Saale boasts a technical monument which is quite unique in Europe, the **brine extraction unit**★, which comprises an undershot water wheel, a 180m/590ft long double set of artificial rods which originates from 1780, and a 320m/1 050ft refinery.

The **Romanesque house** ⊘ *(by the double set of rods)*, now used as a museum, was first recorded in 1138 as the Schulpforte monastery guesthouse. The exhibits illustrate this past, for example there is a Romanesque store cabinet from the 13C. Since there was a doll workshop run in Bad Kösen by Käthe Kruse between 1912 and 1950, there is also an area of the museum given over to a display of dolls of yesteryear.

The ruined fortresses of **Rudelsburg** ⊘ and **Burg Saaleck**, which were destroyed during the Thirty Years War, lie in an attractive **site**★ high above the Saale 3km/2mi to the south of Bad Kösen. They are a popular tourist destination. Built in the 12C, they have fallen into disrepair over the years, but the walls were repaired and the towers made safe during the castle blessing which took place in the 19C.

Römische Villa in NENNIG★

Saarland

Michelin map 417 R 3 – 3km/2mi southeast of Remich

The foundations of this immense **Roman villa** were excavated in 1852. Built on a splendid site overlooking the Moselle Valley in the 2C or 3C AD, the façade was no less than 120m/394ft long.

Tour ⊘ – The superb reception hall **mosaic floor**★★, in a fine state of preservation, measures 16x10m (52x33ft). It comprises eight cartouches, framed by intricate geometric designs, illustrating gladiatorial combats between men and beasts in the arena of the Trier amphitheatre. One of the medallions, no longer extant, has been replaced by a text explaining the restoration of the site. The seven mosaic pictures depict the following motifs: tiger and wild ass; lion and slave; bear with three swordsmen (in the centre, beneath the marble basin); panther and spear-thrower; swordsman with rod and whip; organ player and horn blowers. The main picture, a rectangle, depicts a pair of gladiators and an arbitrator.

NEUBRANDENBURG

Mecklenburg-Vorpommern

Population 75 000

Michelin map 416 F 23

The town is not as new as its name suggests, since it was founded in 1248 at the behest of Margrave Johann von Brandenburg, its name serving to distinguish it from the previously existing town of Brandenburg. Built on an almost circular ground plan, crisscrossed by a grid-like network of streets, the town has retained its original layout. Its later development took place outside the town walls. When 80% of the old town was destroyed in 1945, the fortifications with their four unique gates were quite remarkably spared from damage, making them a principal point of attraction to the tourist, in conjunction with the Tollensesee close by.

NEUBRANDENBURG

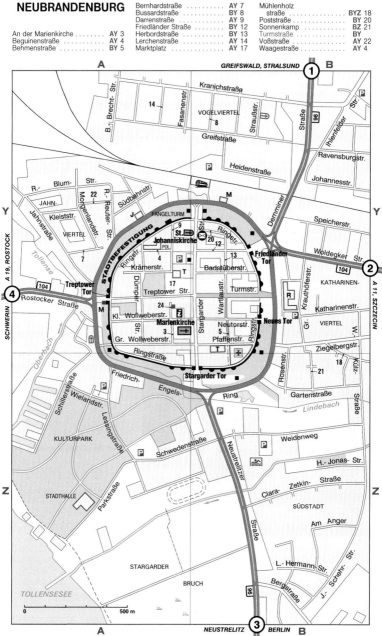

SIGHTS

★★ **Fortifications** – Some 50 years after the town was founded, it became obvious that considerable defences were needed to protect it. Consequently, work was begun on a 2 300m/1.4mi long town wall, over 7m/23 ft in height, 1.40m/4ft 7in wide at the base and 0.60m/1ft 10in at the top. Boulders from the vicinity were used to build the wall, capped by several rows of bricks. Four gates were incorporated into the wall, and these were closed every evening and only opened in return for payment. These remained the only access to the town right up to the mid 19C when a fifth opening was made to provide access to the station.

The gates are all of the same design. The main gate is inside the wall, and is connected with an outer gate via keep walls. Each gate constitutes an individual fortification. The outer gates were secured with portcullises. As if this was insufficient to secure the town, a semicircular battle tower with 4m/13ft thick walls, the Zingel or circular wall, was erected 19m/62ft away from the outer gate.

391

So that the town could be safely defended, 3- to 4-floor bastions, known as **Wiekhäuser**, were built into the town wall every 30m/98ft. There were 56 of them in the 16C, 26 of which have been reconstructed. All the able-bodied citizens were called upon to maintain the Wiekhäuser, whilst defence of the gates was the duty of the four principal guilds: Bakers, Wool Weavers, Shoemakers and Blacksmiths.

"Die Jungfrauen" ("The Maids") **(BZ)** – Nine terracotta sculpted female figures, all with long, stiffly pleated skirts, from beneath which their feet peep out, stand on the top of the Stargarder Tor, with their backs against the town wall. On the Neues Tor there are eight of them. No-one knows their connection with the gates. One historian may see them as the Wise and Foolish Virgins of the Bible story, whilst another may interpret them as "Worshipping Figures", since their arms are help up in an attitude of prayer. They cannot be there to welcome visitors, since they are on the inside of the gates. They have managed to keep their secret intact, and so continue to arouse fascination.

Friedländer Tor (BY) – This is the oldest gate, built just after 1300. It is 19m/62ft high. On the outside it is possible to see the transition from the Romantic to the Gothic period, whilst the town side, built later, is entirely Gothic. The houses of the former keeper of the circular defence wall, the gate recorder and the tax collector are incorporated into the 48m/157ft long wall between the main gate and the outer gate.

Stargarder Tor (BZ) – Built during the first half of the 14C. The body of the tower and the gable ends form a unit in which the Perpendicular style is emphasised by the nine terracotta figures. The outer gate is especially sumptuously decorated.

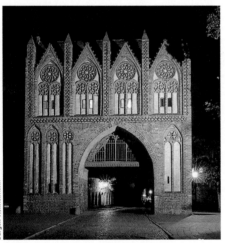

Neubrandenburg – Stargarder Tor

Jürgen Henkelmann

Treptower Tor (AY) – Built before 1400. At 32m/105ft, this is the highest of the gate towers. Both the main gate and the outer gate are sumptuously decorated with brick tracery. On this High Gothic masterpiece, the outside is for the first time more highly decorated than the inside, an expression of the town's desire to appear imposing.

Neues Tor (BY) – Built after 1550. The Late Gothic structure features no fresh influences, but instead combines the decorative elements of the other three gates. The outer gate no longer exists.

Fangelturm (AY) – Of the two towers which provided reinforcement to the fortifications, only the 19m/62ft high Fangelturm remains. It is 6.5m/21ft 4in in diameter with 2.3m/7ft 6in thick walls. The spire was added in 1845.

Marienkirche (AY) – The brick church, whose naves are of equal height and which was built at the end of the 13C, was seriously damaged in 1945. Nevertheless the eastern gable with its tracery is still impressive. The church has been renovated into a concert hall.

St. Johanniskirche ⊘ **(AY)** – The 13C-14C church of the former Franciscan monastery features a surprising lack of symmetry, having only a single side aisle. The paintings with their plant motifs were produced in the 19C. The **Baroque altar** with its extravagant woodcarving depicts the crucifixion. The **Renaissance pulpit★** supported by a figure of Moses, which dates from 1598, is particularly worthy of note. It is made of limestone and displays alabaster reliefs (Christ, the Evangelists).

EXCURSIONS

Tollensee (AZ) – This lake, which is 10.4km/6.5mi in length and almost 3km/2mi wide, lies to the south of the town, in the middle of an extremely attractive glacial (terminal moraine) landscape. The western bank slopes steeply up to Brodaer woods.

★ **Feldberger Seenlandschaft** – *75km/47mi round trip.*
The road leads, via the site of **Burg Stargard**, whose castle ruins dominate their surroundings, to the town of **Woldegk** with its five windmills, to the south west of which lies a lovely hilly lake region. It is home to the rare old-world otter, and also

to the sea eagle, osprey and lesser spotted eagle. Woods, meadows, moors and lakes alternate attractively between **Fürstenwerder** and **Feldberg**. The former house of the writer **Hans Fallada** ("If you ever eat from a tin bowl") in **Carwitz**, which stands in an idyllic lakeside location, is now a memorial.

Neustrelitz – *27km/17mi to the south.*
The former residence of the dukes of Mecklenburg-Strelitz still bears witness today to their proud past. Visitors can admire the **Schloßgarten**★ with its graceful buildings and monuments, part of which was laid out in the 19C as an English country park, the orangerie with is remarkable Pompeii style **paintings**★, the Baroque **town church** (1768-78), the classical **Rathaus** dating from 1841, and the neo-Gothic Schloßkirche (1855-59).

The length of time given in this guide
  – for touring allows time to enjoy the views and the scenery ;
  – for sightseeing is the average time required for a visit.

Schloß NEUSCHWANSTEIN★★★

Bayern
Michelin map 419/420 X 16

Neuschwanstein castle, with its countless towers and light limestone merlons, is a fairy tale castle come true, and is a product of the imagination of **King Ludwig II of Bavaria** (1845-86). The young ruler was an ardent admirer of the composer Richard Wagner, whose theatrical world he wished to recreate in this castle "in the true style of the old German knights' castles". At his request the building was to contain "features reminiscent of Tannhäuser and Lohengrin". He was unquestionably inspired, when planning Neuschwanstein, by the Wartburg, which he had seen in 1867.
King Ludwig found the ideal location for "Neu-Hohenschwangau" (which did not become commonly known as Neuschwanstein until after 1890) not far from Hohenschwangau castle *(see under this name)*, where he had spent part of his childhood and youth, on a rocky ridge high above the Pöllat gorge.
In 1868 he commissioned Eduard Riedel to design the castle and the latter's plans were recorded by the stage painter Christian Rank in painted backdrops, thus producing further theatrical effect. The foundation stone was laid a year later. In view of the fact that three architects were involved in the building (Georg Dolmann from 1874 and Julius Hoffmann from 1886), each of whom had to adapt to the king's ideas, the consistency of the building work is quite impressive. The castle was not quite complete when Ludwig died, but the great hall was finished and the interior of the 3rd and 4th floors were almost ready.
Ludwig II only lived at Neuschwanstein for 170 days. It was here, on 10 June 1886, that a government commission from Munich brought him news of his dethronement. The king was found dead three days later in Lake Starnberg.

TOUR ⏱ 1hr 15min

The most distinctive rooms are on the 3rd floor, and include the artificial stalactite cave with the adjacent small conservatory reminiscent of the Tannhäuser legend, the sitting room decorated to represent scenes from the Lohengrin legend (once again many pictures of swans) and the throne room, (uncompleted) which is in reality an imitation of a Romanesque-Byzantine chapel, in whose apse the throne was to stand. The 4th floor of the castle is taken up almost entirely by the **minstrels' room**, with its coffered ceiling and its many candelabra and chandeliers. The architect based its design on the Wartburg, in which the legendary competition among the singers featured in

WHERE TO STAY

SCHWANGAU-HOHENSCHWANGAU

Weinbauer – Füssener Straße 3, ☎ 0 83 62/98 60, Fax 0 83 62/98 61 13. Single rooms from 58DM. Welcoming country inn. From the terrace there is a view of the mountains and Schloß Neuschschwanstein.

Schloßhotel Lisl und Jägerhaus – Neuschwansteinstraße 3, ☎ 0 83 62/88 70, Fax 0 83 62/8 11 07. Single rooms from 128DM. Hunting lodge fitted out in the turn-of-the-century style. Both houses give a partial view of the royal castles.

Rübezahl – Am Ehberg 31 (Horn), ☎ 0 83 62/83 27, Fax 0 83 62/81 17 01. Single rooms from 90DM. Hotel complex in Alpine style.

Wagner's opera *Tannhäuser* was said to have been held. Richard Wagner, who was a guest at Hohenschwangau, in the event never went to Neuschwanstein or to Linderhof or Herrenchiemsee.

Visitors who still have some time after they have toured the castle might like to go up to the Marien bridge over the Pöllat gorge. The bridge spans the gorge at a height of 90m/295ft *(this walk takes another hour)*. Ludwig II used to gaze at the empty castle from this bridge in the dark, having had the lights in the minstrels' room lit earlier.

NB Visitors should be prepared to queue for as long as 3hr in high season.

EXCURSION

★ **Schloß Hohenschwangau** – *See Schloß HOHENSCHWANGAU.*

NÖRDLINGEN★

Bayern
Population 21 000
Michelin map 419/420 T 15

The former Free Imperial Town of Nördlingen lies in the middle of the Ries basin, along the Romantic Road. It is first mentioned in records in 898. Its development throughout the centuries has been by concentric extension, witnessed by the street pattern and the ring of fortifications. Occupying an important position at the gates of the Bavarian Plateau, Nördlingen saw the armies of the French subdue the Austrians in 1796 and 1800.

SIGHTS

★ **St.-Georgskirche** – *Am Obstmarkt.*
This late-15C hall-church is surmounted by a majestic, 90m/295ft high bell-tower, known as Daniel, on which a look-out still keeps watch round the clock. Fan vaulting covers the interior in splendid style. The pulpit (1499) is reached via a corbelled staircase with only three steps. The 15C high altar has been replaced by a Baroque altarpiece. The wings of the first altarpiece painted by Friedrich Herlin are now on display in the Stadtmuseum. The Late Gothic altarpiece casing is located in the nave, opposite the side organ. The Crucifixion group and the statues of St George and **Mary Magdalene**★, created by Nikolaus Gerhaert von Leyden, still remain. Note the expression of the Saviour, moving in its sweetness and humility.

★ **Stadtmauer (Town Walls)** – The Nördlingen town walls are the only remaining fully accessible walls of their kind in Germany. Access to the historic, picturesque old town is possible through just one of the five gates, and a walk right around the town walls, which are for the most part covered, reveals 11 watchtowers. One of the most attractive parts of the walk is along the battlements from the Berger Gate via the Alte Bastei, or old bastion, to the Reimlinger Gate. The history of the town wall is documented in the Löpsinger gate tower.

★ **Stadtmuseum (Local Museum)** ⓥ – The museum displays cover the pre- and early history of the Ries basin, along with the history of the Imperial Town of Nördlingen. There is a collection of 19C painting, and altar panels by Old German masters, such as the wings (1462-77) of the altarpiece from St. Georgskirche by Friedrich Herlin. The display includes other panel paintings by Hans Schäufelin and Sebastian Taig. The "Battle of Nördlingen" (1634) is reproduced in the form of a pewter figure diorama.

ENJOYING NÖRDLINGEN

WHERE TO STAY

Goldene Rose – Baldinger Straße 42, ☎ 0 90 81/8 60 19, Fax 0 90 81/2 45 91. Single rooms from 65DM. Small, well-run family business with good value rooms.

Sonne – Marktplatz 3, ☎ 0 90 81/8 80 54, Fax 0 90 81/2 27 40. Single rooms from 95DM. City centre, located near the town hall.

EATING OUT

Meyers Keller – Marienhöhe 8, ☎ 0 90 81/44 93, Fax 0 90 81/2 49 31. Main courses from 30DM. Former brewery located in front of the town wall with restaurant and bistro. Large beer garden beneath old chestnut trees. Good cooking.

* Rieskrater-Museum ⊙ – *Next to the Stadtmuseum.*
The Nördlingen Giant Crater was formed approximately 15 million years ago when a **meteorite** hit the earth. Just imagine it – a giant stone sphere, 1km/0.6mi in diameter, leaves its orbit between Mars and Jupiter and hits the earth at a speed of 70 000kph/44 000mph, penetrating up to 1km/0.6mi into the rock! The energy of 250 000 Hiroshima atom bombs is released, and a wave of pressure and heat extinguishes all life within a range of 100km/62mi. The heat generated by the impact is so great that the meteorite evaporates. A crater 14km/9mi in diameter is formed, which eventually spreads to 25km/16mi due to all the rock that subsequently falls in. The crater, which was originally 4km/2.5mi deep, is gradually filled in over the course of millions of years, but later partially excavated and opened out again.
The Rieskrater-Museum, which is housed in a carefully restored barn (1503), attempts to give the general public an understanding of this scarcely imaginable phenomenon. An ambitious venture, which succeeds admirably using modern didactic methods (a slide show and videos to watch, stone to touch). There is even a lump of moon rock, which is on permanent loan to the museum from NASA.

EXCURSION

* Neresheim Abbey – *19km/12mi to the southwest.*
The huge white buildings of the Benedictine abbey stand out in the largely undeveloped landscape east of the Swabian Jura. The abbey church (Klosterkirche), started in 1747 under the direction of Balthasar Neumann, was the last work of the great Baroque architect. It was not finished until 1792. Inside, the seemingly weightless ceiling decoration painted between 1770 and 1774 by Martin Knoller is entirely in keeping with the tremendous sense of light in the building's interior.

NORDFRIESISCHE INSELN*

Northern Frisians – Schleswig-Holstein
Michelin map 415 A-C 8-10

Since the melting of the great Quaternary Era glaciers, the wind and sea have been the agents crafting the landscape of the Northern Frisians, restoring islands to the mainland and breaking chunks off the mainland to become islands. These islands in the mudflats off the Danish-German coast fall into two groups: the islands of Sylt, Föhr and Amrum, consisting mainly of sandy moorland *(Geest)* formed by moraine deposits from the Ice Age, and Pellworm and Nordstrand, island strips of marshland *(Marschen)* which were formed during the great storm floods of 1634. Beach life and the fresh North Sea air make the Northern Frisians a popular holiday destination.

** Sylt – *See SYLT.*

Föhr ⊙ – This is a peaceful, charming island which boasts an exceptionally mild climate thanks to its sheltered site in the mudflats behind a protective outer circle of smaller islands and the Halligens. The second largest island off the west Schleswig-Holstein coast consists of broad expanses of green marshland and gently undulating moorland, dotted with pretty villages, their houses thatched with reeds (eg Nieblum, Süderende or Oldsum). The beaches stretch round the south of the island. The small, windswept woods frequented by bird colonies are in the more remote north of the island.
The delightful port and main town of the island, **Wyk**, is located in the southeast. It features well-tended narrow streets which are a pleasure to explore, such as Carl-Hälberlin-Straße and the tree-lined grand promenade (Sandwall) above the beach, laid in honour of summer visits by the Danish royal family. Visitors interested in the nature, history and culture of the Northern Frisians should not miss the **Friesenmuseum** ⊙, with its wealth of exhibits on Föhr and the surrounding islands. In Boldixum, St.-Nikolaikirche dates from the second half of the 13C (Late Romanesque-Early Gothic) with the original painted vaulted ceiling which has been uncovered and restored. **Dunsum** is the departure point for a walk across the mudflats to Amrum.

Amrum ⊙ – Amrum is possibly the oldest and certainly the most unspoiled of the Northern Frisians. The west coast is protected from the full force of the North Sea by a 1.5km/1mi wide strip of sand – a sandbank that has been formed over centuries. Behind this lie sand dunes, heaths (which reach full bloom in August/September), woods, farmland and finally the mudflats of the east coast, a rich habitat for sea birds.

There have been various pre- and early historical artefacts found near the hamlet of Steenodde, which make the island culturally and historically interesting. The **Esenhugh**, measuring 4.7m/15ft high and with a diameter of 26.5m/87ft, is the largest stone grave site on the island. The prettiest hamlet on the island is **Nebel**, which grew up around the medieval church of **St. Clemens** in the 16C. The graveyard contains some interesting tombstones with inscriptions dating back to the 18C. Also of interest is the **Öömrang Hüs**, a sea captain's house built in 1736. The far north of the island, in the bird sanctuary area of **Amrum Odde**, is the departure point for walks across the mudflats to Föhr.

* **Halligen** – This collection of tiny islands is all that remains of mainland marshes that were once part of the much more extensive coastal region in prehistoric times. In c 1600, there were more than 25 documented islands here, but the number has since fallen to 10, of widely differing sizes. The other Halligens fell victim to storm floods or simply merged into one another over the centuries. In contrast to the other North Sea islands, most of the Halligens are not protected by sea dykes, with the result that it can be a case of "total submersion" up to 50 times a year. At these times only the houses on the man-made mounds (terps) can be seen above water level. A total of about 400 people inhabit the Halligens; the largest with 18 mounds is **Langeneß**, linked with **Oland** (mainland connection), and **Hooge** (Queen of the Halligens). Various shipping companies offer boat trips to the Halligens.

Hallig Langeneß

Fremdenverkehrsbüro, Hallig Langeneß

Pellworm ⓥ – Those who are looking first and foremost for peace and quiet, rather than sandy beaches, should go to Pellworm. The island is enclosed by a 25km/15mi long and 8m/20ft high dyke, without which Pellworm would be inundated twice a day, since the island lies below sea level. Sheep graze on the dykes, as much as part of the island landscape as the distinctive black and white cows.

The island's main feature is the mighty ruined tower of the **Alte Kirche St. Salvator**, whose origins date back to the 11C-12C. Nearby lies the **Friedhof der Heimatlosen**, where the bodies of strangers washed up on the island's shores by the sea are buried. Traces and artefacts from the settlement inundated in 1634 are on display, along with other exhibits, in the **Wattenmuseum Liermann**. The museum collections are based around those of postman Heinrich Liermann, who spent almost 50 years assuring postal deliveries on foot across the mudflats to Hallig Süderogg.

Nordstrand – This marshland island is now linked to the mainland by a 4km/2mi causeway. Nordstrand consists of a tapestry of reclaimed farmland (polders) and villages on man-made mounds (terps). Arable fields rub shoulders with fertile pastureland in what was once a landscape crisscrossed with sea dykes. The island's centre is at **Süden**, in one of the most picturesque stretches of countryside, where many craftspeople have made their home. Part of the bird-nesting area set up in 1905 and then allowed to become overgrown with woods again since 1930 has now been restored as a cultural and historical monument, while an area has been sectioned off as a completely untouched microclimate of indigenous island vegetation.

NÜRBURGRING★

Michelin map 417 O 4 – Local map see EIFEL

This motor racing track, laid out over a stretch of wooded, undulating country, has taken the name of the Nürburg ruin *(see EIFEL)*, which stands inside its northern loop. The new circuit, opened in 1984, is used for such prestigious events as Formula 1, motorcycle Grand Prix, International Touring Cars and Super Touring Wagen races and truck Grand Prix. Open-air concerts are also held here. The 4.542km/2.82mi circuit includes 14 corners, with a height differential of 56m/184ft. Aside from competitions and practice sessions, the circuits are open for normal use *(apply at the Information Bureau on B 258)*. The old northern loop is 20km/12mi long.

Erlebnispark Nürburgring ⊙ – Motor racing enthusiasts will find plenty to interest them in these four exhibition halls. Hall 1 contains the **Collection of Nürburgring Legends★**, with numerous veteran and racing cars, which will set many a heart beating faster. Hall 2 involves visitors actively in motor racing, with racing and shock absorber simulators and an indoor roller coaster. Hall 3 is devoted to technological and natural mobility, with crash simulation, transport systems, literature on recycling and some test seats. The indoor go-carting track in Hall 4 will give would-be racing drivers a chance to test their skills.

NÜRNBERG★★

NUREMBERG – Bayern
Population 500 000
Michelin map 419/420 R 17

Before the Second World War, Nuremberg was one of the most beautiful medieval cities in Germany. Whole blocks of half-timbered burgher's houses with embellished gables made a setting so typically "Germanic" that the city was chosen by the Nazi party for its huge annual rallies each September. Some of the buildings used for the rallies still stand in Luitpoldhain park in the southeast suburbs. It was in this "ideological capital" of the Reich that the notorious anti-Semitic laws were promulgated in 1935; and it was here that the Allies held the war crimes trials when the fighting was over.

Today, with many of those medieval quarters completely destroyed, the old bronze caster's and gold-beaters' town, together with its neighbour Fürth, is one of the main industrial centres of southern Germany. Machine tools, tractors, electrical and electronic apparatus, motorcycles, typewriters and toys are among its principal manufacturing products. Gastronomically, the Franconian capital offers a number of specialities: carp, either fried or poached in wine; Bratwurst (small grilled sausages); and **Lebkuchen** – fragrant gingerbread sold in attractive coloured boxes.

From the Friday before the first Sunday in Advent until the end of December the market place is occupied by the famous Christmas market, known locally as the **Christkindlesmarkt** (Christ-child Market). A wide choice of Christmas tree decorations and gifts are on offer.

The Golden Age – Nuremberg was at the peak of its fame and fortune during the 15C and 16C. Located at the crossroads of major trade routes and a shop window for Franconian craftsmanship, the city at that time rivalled Augsburg in importance. Nor was its renown purely commercial; literature, the arts and sciences flourished. The first German science university was founded in Nuremberg in 1526. At the same time the local humanist Willibald Pirkheimer (1470-1530) was translating texts from Latin and Greek. From 1510 onwards the locksmith Peter Henlein manufactured fob watches. In the world of art, the audacious sculptors **Veit Stoß** (c 1445-1533) and **Adam Krafft** (c 1460-1508); the talented bronze caster **Peter Vischer the Elder** (1460-1529); **Michael Wolgemut** (1434-1519), the painter of altarpieces – and above all his pupil **Albrecht Dürer** – all profoundly influenced the German scene with their works. Finally, the Nuremberg **Mastersingers** brought new life to German poetic form.

Erhard Etzlaub's Street Plans

The first street plans – not to be confused with country maps which had been around for some time – on which the European street network north and south of the Alps was modelled, were published from the workshop of Nuremberg sundial and compass maker Erhard Etzlaub. The increase in pilgrims travelling to Rome in 1500 and in European foreign trade made the design of such a plan necessary. Progress in printing technology made it possible to produce one. For the first time, Europe was represented as a geographical area, united by a network of roads and cities.

★★★ GERMANISCHES NATIONALMUSEUM ⊙ (JZ)

Allow half a day

We recommend that you study the plan in the entrance hall to enable you to find your way around the various sections of this extensive museum.

Germanisches Nationalmuseum, Nürnberg

Harpsichord (c 1750)

The museum, which was founded in 1852, houses the largest collection of art and culture in the German-speaking world, with 1.2 million exhibits. Its 20 000 principal items are on permanent display. The heart of the truly massive and richly stocked museum is a former Carthusian monastery dating from the 14C. In 1993 it was extended across the Kartäusergasse by the addition of a large new building. The Israeli artist Dani Karavan has redesigned the street itself, which is fully integrated into the museum complex, as a **street of human rights**.

The central section is the **picture gallery**, with works by **Albrecht Dürer** (*Portrait of Michael Wolgemut, Emperor Charles the Great in his Coronation Robes*), Hans Baldung Grien, Hans Holbein the Elder, Albrecht Altdorfer, Lukas Cranach the Elder (*Portrait of Martin Luther, Venus with Cupid the Honey Thief*). Works by Veit Stoß (*The Archangel Raphael and The Young Tobias*), Tilman Riemenschneider (*The Lamentation of Christ*) and Ignaz Günther are especially outstanding within the **sculpture collection**.

Many types of **decorative arts** are represented, including glass, ceramics, furniture and textiles. The gold and silversmith's work should not be missed. The collection includes numerous medieval religious art treasures.

The **folk art collection** is impressive, with its many traditional costumes, rural household effects and exhibition areas featuring rooms decorated in rustic style. Not only children find the **toys and doll's houses** section (including one dating from 1639) fascinating. The collection of **ancient musical instruments**, with the largest collection in the world of historical pianos, is extremely varied and comprehensive. The most noteworthy of the very many scientific instruments is the so-called **Behaim terrestrial globe**, dating from 1492 to 1493, which is the oldest surviving depiction of the earth in globe form. In addition to the **pre- and proto-historic** collection, the museum also boasts a collection of historical **arms and hunting pieces** and a **medical history** collection, which includes complete sets of apothecary's equipment and medical and pharmaceutical instruments. Further exhibits includes examples of work produced by the trades and guilds.

There is an extensive **prints and drawings section** with 300 000 exhibits, including miniatures, freehand drawings and printed graphics. The **numismatic collection** contains 60 000 coins and around 20 000 medals, together with seal and coinage stamps.

The Germanisches Nationalmuseum complex also houses the **Industrial Museum**, which is linked with the Bavarian Industrial Institute. Its exhibits include examples of craftsmanship, commercial art and design dating from Antiquity right up to the 20C.

OLD TOWN *allow half a day*

* **Albrecht-Dürer-Haus (Dürer's House)** ⊙ (JY) – This restored 15C burgher's house with jutting eaves lies at the base of the fortifications. Dürer bought it in 1509 and lived here until his death in 1528. The interior, soberly furnished, gives some idea of the life of the artist. A 15min video presentation gives a brief introduction on Dürer's life and work. *Closed until further notice.*

Burg (Castle) ⊙ (JY) – Symbol of the city, the castle stands proudly on a sandstone outcrop a little way to the north. The original **castle of the Burgraves** (Burggrafenburg), almost entirely destroyed in 1420, had been completed in the 12C by the part known as the **Kaiserburg**; its present appearance dates from the 15C and 16C. From the outside terrace or the **Sinwellturm**, a 25m/82ft high keep, there is an exceptional **view★** of the steeply sloped roofs and belfries of the old town. In an adjoining courtyard, the **well** *(under cover inside the building)* is an impressive 50m/165ft deep.

Among the dependencies near the apartments, the **Imperial Chapel**, a Romanesque double-chapel, is particularly interesting with its special Imperial Gallery from which the Emperor could survey his court assembled below. The castle contains an exhibition on the significance of the Imperial Palace in the history of the Empire and a display of historical weapons.

★ **Stadtbefestigung (Fortifications)** – Completed in the mid 15C, these have remained practically intact, which is unique for a large town in Germany. They comprised an inner and an outer ring (Zwingermauer), the ramparts of the former with a covered parapet walk. A wide dry moat (in which modern avenues now run) lay outside the latter. No less than 67 defensive towers still exist. Among them are the four **Great Towers**, dating from the 16C and protected by colossal shells of cannon-proof masonry, sometimes 6m/20ft thick (Frauentor – **KZ**, Spittlertor – **HZ**, Neutor – **JY**, Laufertor – **KY**).

The most interesting sector lies between the Kaiserburg and the Spittlertor *(west side)*. An instructive 30min **walk** starts from the castle gardens (Burggarten) *(outside, below the Kaiserburg)*. From the ramparts it is possible to reach the watch-path, which can be followed as far as the Neutorzwinger. Continue inside the ramparts. The River Pegnitz is crossed via a suspension footbridge beside the fortifications, before the promenade is concluded, once more on the outside (there is an attractive view of the castle from this point).

Stadtmuseum Fembohaus (Fembo Municipal Museum) Ⓥ **(JY M²)** – The museum is housed in a sandstone Renaissance mansion with a scrolled gable embellished by cornucopiae and obelisks. It is concerned with the history of Nuremberg, and in particular the homelife of the town's gentry between the 16C and the 19C.

Sebalduskirche (JY) – This Late Romanesque basilica with a triple nave and two chancels was begun in 1230-40. The church was modified and enlarged subsequently until the Late Gothic period. The towers, which burned down during the Second World War, and the major part of the east chancel, which was also destroyed, have been rebuilt. The sobriety of the west front, which is plain, with two Romanesque doorways framing the projecting chancel, is in vivid contrast with the huge Gothic east chancel, intricately worked and adorned with statues and pinnacles. Inside, the Romanesque and transitional Gothic western section (central and side aisles) is easily distinguished from the radiating High Gothic style of the east chancel and its ambulatory.

Works of Art★★:

1) St Peter Altarpiece (1485), painted on a gold background in the Wolgemut studio.
2) Richly decorated bronze baptismal font (Gothic, c 1430), including a hearth – the oldest religious work cast in bronze in Nuremberg.
3) St Catherine (1310).
4) St Sebald (1390).
5) Emperor Heinrich II (1350) and Empress Kunigunde.
6) The Virgin Mary in Glory (1420).
7) St Sebald's tomb. The Gothic shrine is part of a bronze display shelf by Peter Vischer (1519), supported by dolphins and snails and adorned with a host of statuettes. On the side panels, St Sebald is represented, and the artist himself in working clothes.
8) A Crucifixion group (1520) by Veit Stoß.
9) From the studio of the same artist: (above) Christ Transfigured and Mater Dolorosa (wood); (below) The Last Supper, The Mount of Olives and Christ Taken Prisoner (bas-relief in stone). Both groups date from 1499.
10) The Bearing of the Cross, by Adam Krafft (1506).
11) (Outside the church) Funerary monument of the Schreyer family: the Passion and The Resurrection, by Adam Krafft.

A fine series of **stained-glass windows** (14C-15C) illuminate the east chancel.

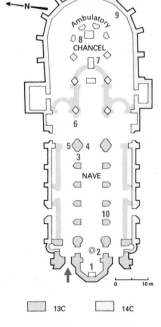

13C	14C

▨ Non-extant parts

★ **Schöner Brunnen (Beautiful Fountain) (JY C)** – This 14C Gothic fountain in the old market place is one of the best-known sights of Nuremberg. Comprising 40 separate figures arranged in the form of a pyramid, the structure is 19m/62ft high. At the top, Moses is surrounded by the Prophets; around the base are the seven Electors and a series of nine Old Testament and medieval heroes: three forefathers, three Jews and three Christians. The figures decorating the fountain today are copies.

★ **Frauenkirche (JY E)** – A Late Gothic church on the east side of the market, built on the site of a destroyed synagogue, this sanctuary was erected during the reign of Emperor Karl IV and served as Imperial chapel (1352-61). The Imperial jewels were kept here. The gable, with its pinnacles, niches and small oriel window, was designed by Adam Krafft (early 16C).

Dating from the same period, the clock above the balcony attracts visitors each day at noon, when a series of jacks appear to strike the hour. These colourful metal figures (Männleinlaufen) represent the seven Electors coming to swear allegiance to the Emperor after the enactment of the Golden Bull in Nuremberg in 1356.

The roof above the main body of the church, which is almost square in plan, is supported by four columns. On the north wall of the building is Adam Krafft's **Peringsdorffer Epitaph** (a robed Madonna), which dates from 1498. The **Tucher Altar** in the chancel, garnished with human figures, is a masterpiece of the pre-Albrecht Dürer Nuremberg school of painting: the triptych (c 1445-50) depicts the Crucifixion, the Annunciation and the Resurrection.

Spielzeugmuseum (Toy Museum) ⊙ **(JY M³)** – *Karlstraße 13-15*. The museum, housed in a modernised 17C burgher's house, illustrates the important role played by Bavaria, and Nuremberg in particular, in the intricate skills of miniaturism. Doll's houses, tin soldiers, clockwork toys, and model cars, railways and aeroplanes here will delight children and adults alike.

Heilig-Geist-Spital (Hospital) (JKY F) – This 14C-15C building, spread over two wide arches, spans a branch of the Pegnitz. Its graceful corbelled tower, and the oriel window embellishing the façade, can be seen from the Museumsbrücke. The central courtyard *(reached from an islet upstream)*, with its wooden galleries above wide sandstone arches, recalls a rich patrician's mansion of times gone by.

Banks of the Pegnitz – Parts of the old city still standing can be seen from here. Those crossing the Maxbrücke **(JY 90)** enjoy a fine view of the ancient, half-timbered wine hall (Weinstadel) and its flanking tower, together with the Henkersteg covered footbridge.

★ **Lorenzkirche (JZ)** – A magnificent rose window enlivens the west face of this 13C-14C Gothic church. The impressive hall-type chancel was added in the 15C. Inside *(enter via the south door)*, from the nave, two outstanding works of art can be seen: the 1400 rood-beam Crucifix, with delicate medallions fashioned from its outer ends; and Veit Stoß's **Annunciation**★★ (Engelsgruß, 1517-18), which is suspended from the chancel vaulting. The larger-than-life-size figures of the Virgin Mary and the Angel Gabriel dominate the proceedings, in an oval frame decorated with seven medallions. The reliefs in the medallions depict the Seven Joys of Mary after the Annunciation. The richly ornamented **tabernacle**★★ (1493-96) by Adam Krafft, the rounded pinnacle of which extends right up to the vault, stands to the left of the main altar (with a crucifix by Veit Stoß). The stonemason has depicted himself life-sized beneath the gallery.

The ambulatory is lit by superb stained-glass windows from the workshop of the Alsatian Peter Hemmel of Andlau, notably that representing the Tree of Jesse (1487, *second on the right, starting from the central window*).

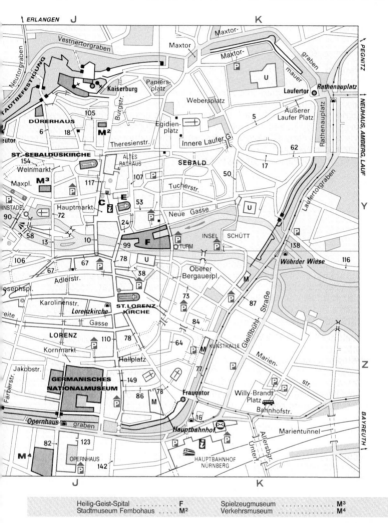

Heilig-Geist-Spital	F	Spielzeugmuseum	M³
Stadtmuseum Fembohaus	M²	Verkehrsmuseum	M⁴

Verkehrsmuseum (Transport Museum) ⊘ **(JZ M⁴)** – The chief attraction in the **German Rail Museum**★ is the replica of the very first German train, drawn by an Adler locomotive, which linked Nuremberg and Fürth in 1835. There are a great many scale models. Note also the interesting **Post and Communications Museum**, where there is a fine collection of postage stamps, together with sections describing the development of the telephone, of transmission technology, of radio and television.

On the far side of the Sandstraße, all kinds of railroad vehicles, ancient and modern, are on display in a special hall.

EXCURSIONS

Hersbrucker Alb – *Round tour of 109km/68mi – allow half a day. Leave on Sulzbacherstraße* **(KY)**, *then take the A 9 motorway in the direction of Bayreuth, leaving at the Plech exit.*

★ **Neuhaus an der Pegnitz** – This charming locality comes suddenly into view after a bend in the road, with the tall tower of Burg Veldenstein dominating the town.

Continue following the course of the Pegnitz in the direction of Hersbruck. The valley is steeply enclosed, overlooked here and there by tall, pointed crags.

Hersbruck – An attractive little town situated at a point where the valley of the Pegnitz opens out, with stately burghers' houses and the remains of its medieval fortifications. The town church contains an important Late Gothic altar-shrine, the altarpiece of the Fathers of the Church. The **Deutsche Hirtenmuseum** (German Shepherds' Museum, *Eishüttlein 7*) in a fine half-timbered building contains collections of popular arts and traditions.

Continue towards Happurg over the Pegnitz bridge, from which, looking back, there is a fine view of the Wassertor (fortified gate) with its stone customs house, and over the roofs of the adjacent old town centre at the foot of the Michelsberg hill.

Return to Nuremberg, taking B 14.

Erlangen – *17km/10.5mi to the north.*
This residential town of the Baroque period, with its rows of uniform houses, was one of the places where the French Huguenots settled. The Protestant church marks the centre of the quarter built for them. Sharing with Nuremberg the functions of a university city, Erlangen was the birthplace of the physicist **Georg Ohm** (1789-1854), who formulated the law relating to the resistance of electrical circuits. In an early-18C **English garden** behind the castle stands the strange **Fountain of the Huguenots**, built by the French in 1706 as a gesture of thanks to their protector, the Margrave of Bayreuth.

OBERSTDORF★★

Bayern
Population 11 000
Michelin map 419/420 X 14

The well-known mountain and skiing village (843m/2 765ft above sea level) lies in the southernmost corner of Germany. This charming mountain-air health resort is also the departure point for numerous walking tours. It lies at the junction of the valley of the Iller, deeply incised into the Allgäu Alps, and seven other valleys. Following a fire in 1865, Oberstdorf town centre had to be rebuilt. Motor traffic is banned from the centre of town.

★★ **Nebelhorn** ⊘ – *1hr 30min there and back, of which 20min are by* **cable-car** *(3 stages to the trip).*
The highest cable railway in the Allgäu leads to the 2 224m/7 296ft high summit of the Nebelhorn, from where, in clear weather, there is a **panoramic view**★★ over more than 400 Alpine summits: extending from the Zugspitze in the east to the Säntis (the Swiss Appenzell Alps) in the west and, beyond the bold outlines of the Allgäu itself, even the snows of the Bernese Oberland can be seen.
The destination of numerous hikes, the Nebelhorn is also the point of departure for the demanding "Hindelang climb". A **geological footpath** explains the origins and structure of the Alps.

★★ **Fellhorn** ⊘ – *Take the Fellhorn* **cable-car** *in two stages up to the station at the summit (1 967m/6 452ft).*
There is a wonderful **panoramic view**★★ over the Allgäu mountains, the Austrian and Swiss Alps, from the 2 037m/6 683ft high summit of the Fellhorn.
The Fellhorn has an easily accessible network of paths for hikes 1 500-2 000m/4 922-6 562ft long, including a very interesting flower footpath (Blumen- und Wanderlehrpfad), with rare Alpine flowers, including orchids, to be seen along it. In summer these bloom all the way to the summit. The **Alpine Rose**, which blooms between about mid June to mid July, is particularly captivating.

EXCURSIONS

★★ **Breitachklamm** ⊘ – *6.5km/4mi to the southwest, plus a 1hr 30min walk there and back. (Recommended also in winter, when fantastic "curtains" of ice are formed.)*
In the lower gorge, galleries lead down to a cutting with sheer, polished walls, where the turbulent mountain stream has carved a course 100m/300ft deep into the bedrock. At the foot of this path it is possible to turn back and re-mount by the long series of stairways that lead to the upper gorge (which is, however, less impressive). To return to Oberstdorf without a car, leave the gorge path at the top of these stairways. Walkers will then arrive at the Walserschanze, on the Kleinwalsertal road, from which there is a frequent bus service to the resort.

★ **The Kleinwalsertal** – *17km/11mi – allow 30min.*
The name identifies a high valley of the River Breitach, a mountain area some 100km²/38sq mi in size, which was settled in the 13C by the **Walsers** – emigrants of Germanic origin from the Upper Valais. Cut off from the rest of the Vorarlberg

View of Oberstdorf

by the peaks of the Allgäu, the Walsers found themselves Austrian subjects when national frontiers were established in 1453, although such culture and traditions as they had were oriented exclusively towards Germany.

In 1891 the area was granted a special status whereby, still under Austrian sovereignty, it was nevertheless economically regarded as part of Germany. Today the Kleinwalsertal has Austrian police, German customs, a German postal service but Austrian stamps, and the only legal tender is the German mark. Until a modern road was built in 1930, the valley remained isolated and the Walsers, like other hardy pioneers, retained a reputation of grim individualism and dourness of character – traits still reflected in the sombre buildings of their scattered homesteads.

Riezlern, Hirschegg and **Mittelberg** are the main resorts of the Kleinwalsertal, popular with tourists everywhere.

ODENWALD★

Bayern and Hessen
Michelin map 417 R 10-11

A popular excursion for the inhabitants of big cities nearby, this huge natural park lies between the Rhine, the Main and the Neckar, undulating and rural to the west, forested and with steeper hills east of the River Mömling.

EXCURSION FROM MILTENBERG 92km/57mi – allow 4hr

★ **Miltenberg** – A remarkable row of half-timbered houses lines the main street leading to the **Marktplatz★**. This small town is overlooked by the wooded heights bordering the final curve of the Main.

★ **Amorbach** – On the eastern slopes of the Odenwald, Amorbach is dominated by two pairs of belfries, those with red-stone courses belonging to the former **abbey church★** ⊘ (Abteikirche).

This was built between 1742 and 1747, respecting the plan of the Romanesque building which preceded it. Even the old towers were left, the architect simply adding a Rococo sandstone façade. Note the **chancel grilles**, the Rococo pulpit and the 1782 organ.

The abbey **library★** has rich Baroque decorations (1789-99). The neo-Classic ornamentation in the **Green Room★** is a rare feature for a German abbey.

403

★ **Park von Eulbach** ⊘ – This romantic landscaped park, with a lake and excavations of the ancient Roman limes, also incorporates a nature reserve with various species of wild deer and wild boars and an enclosure of European wild oxen (bison).

Michelstadt – Ancient houses, a flowered 16C fountain, and the town hall **façade**★, topped by a very steep roof flanked by two oriel windows, combine to form a striking ensemble in the market place. Follow the road beside the town hall and turn right into the Einhardtspforte alley: the **Odenwald-Museum** ⊘ (rural activity, craftwork) and the **toy museum** (toys, dolls' kitchens, interiors, shops etc) are housed in a fine group of half-timbered buildings, the former **cellars** (Kellerei) around an ancient courtyard.

Leave Michelstadt to the south in the direction of Erback. Shortly after Hetzbach, turn left to Kailbach and Amorbach. The road winds through the hills and wooded valleys.

OLDENBURG

Niedersachsen
Population 155 000
Michelin map 415 G 8

Steeped in tradition, this capital and lively university city is the cultural and economic focus of northwest Germany. Its river port is linked to the Weser and the North Sea by the Hunte, and to the Benelux countries by a coastal canal (Küstenkanal). Seat of government for the Weser-Ems region of Lower Saxony, Oldenburg is becoming an increasingly popular and successful commercial centre. An orbital motorway keeps traffic away from the city centre, improving air quality and therefore quality of life. Oldenburg is the birthplace of philosopher Karl Jaspers.

The old city, which includes Germany's oldest pedestrian precinct, also houses monumental buildings spanning five centuries, generous parkland and its former ramparts.

★ **Schloßgarten (Castle Park)** – A mild, moist coastal climate has favoured the growth of magnificent trees and shrubs in this landscaped garden, such as rhododendrons and tulip trees. From the weeping willows on the lake shore there is an attractive view of the towers of the Lambertikirche.

Landesmuseum für Kunst und Kulturgeschichte (Regional Art and History Museum) ⊘ – The museum, housed since 1923 in the former seat of the counts and grand dukes of Oldenburg, was built in the 17C and remodelled in the 18C and again the 19C.

The first floor houses among other things the Old Masters' gallery, which includes mainly 16C-18C Italian and Dutch masters and 18C-19C European paintings. The series of small pictures depicting idyllic scenes by **Johann Heinrich Wilhelm Tischbein** (1751-1829) is particularly interesting.

Items relating to Oldenburg's provincial history and culture are exhibited with commentaries on several floors.

★ **Stadtmuseum Oldenburg** ⊘ – Of interest here are rooms from the villas Francksen (1877), Jürgens and Ballin, with paintings, furnishings and decor dating from the 17C to the early 20C. There are also departments on local history and an antiques collection.

Augusteum ⊘ – *Elisabethstraße 1.*
Works by painters from the Worpswede colony are on show here along with such German Expressionists as Erich Heckel. Among the Surrealists, note Franz Radziwill – who classes himself as a "symbolic realist".

Staatliches Museum für Naturkunde und Vorgeschichte (Natural History Museum) ⊘ – *Damm 38-44.*
These exhibitions are focused on the northwest region of Germany with its varied landscapes and traces of pre- and early historic settlements. Natural, archeological and cultural aspects are presented in a display entitled "Neither sea nor land – the peat bogs, a lost landscape". A huge block of peat, in which ancient bodies were found buried, always attracts attention.

EXCURSIONS

★ **Museumsdorf Cloppenburg** ⊘ – *31km/19mi to the south.*
In an area of about 20ha/50 acres, 53 historic buildings from the 15C to the 19C have been constructed around a lake and a church. Most of the reconstructed buildings come from the region between the River Weser and River Ems. Large farmsteads, two types of mill, peasants' and tenants' houses, a blacksmith's and a bleachery illustrate aspects of the history of everyday life in Lower Saxony. The houses are fitted out with furnishings, household goods, clothing and work tools.

Landesmuseum, Oldenburg

★ **Steindenkmäler von Visbek (Megalithic Monuments)** – *38km/24mi to the south.*
In this group collectively known as "The Intended", the **Bride** (Visbeker Braut) is
a collection of granite blocks arranged in a rectangular pattern in a clearing that
measures 80x7m/262x23ft.
The **Groom** (Visbeker Bräutigam) comprises a dolmen, considered as a sacrificial
altar (Opfertisch), and, again, an alignment of 80 blocks in a rectangle
108x10m/354x33ft. At the western extremity of the site a funerary chamber
recalls – it is thought – the dwellings of this period. The site is a 30min walk, there
and back, from the Engelmannsbäke inn.

OSNABRÜCK

Niedersachsen
Population 162 000
Michelin map 415 J 8

Lying between the Teutoburger Wald and the Wiehengebirge heights, Osnabrück
developed around two separate centres: in the 9C the old town spread from the
ancient market and the episcopal quarter; and from the 11C onwards, a new town
proliferated around the Johanniskirche. When they united within a single city wall
(c 1300), Osnabrück became an important commercial centre.
The all-important linen trade has now been supplanted by metallurgy and paper mills.

Before the Peace in 1648 – Preliminaries to the **Peace of Westphalia** started in
Osnabrück between the emperor and the Protestant belligerents (Sweden and the
Lutheran princes of Germany) five years before the end of the Thirty Years War. On
the other side, the Roman Catholic powers negotiated with the emperor in Münster.
News of the treaties' final signature was announced in Osnabrück on 25 October
1648 to a crowd, at first incredulous and then bursting into a spontaneous hymn of
thanksgiving.

SIGHTS

Rathaus ⊙ – This early-16C building had to be restored after the Second World
War, but still retains its Gothic look beneath a wide pavilion roof. The peace of
1648 was announced from its steps. The statue of Charlemagne, above the
entrance, is surrounded by the effigies of eight other emperors and kings.

★ **Friedenssaal** (The Peace Chamber) – The hall in which the long-drawn-out peace
negotiations were held is adorned with portraits of the heads of state and their
delegates. The floor and ceiling have been rebuilt; the carved wooden seats and
the chandelier are authentic and date from 1554. Among the gold plate in the
Treasury is the priceless 14C Kaiserpokal (imperial goblet).

Marienkirche – A 14C Gothic hall-church which, with its elegant transverse
gables, closes off the northern end of the Marktplatz. Its most interesting work
of art is the early-16C **Altarpiece of the Passion**★, originally from Antwerp.

Dom St.-Peter – The squat outline of this 13C Transitional Gothic church is distinguished by large towers differing both in shape and size. The north face boasts a fine Romanesque embellishment of blind arcades and cornices. The interior is equally unusual, with a flat chevet and squared-off ambulatory. The chapels leading off this contain a few works of art, notably a 15C Pietà and a 16C stone Crucifixion.

The ogive vaulting in the nave is rounded; from the triumphal arch hangs an early-13C Crucifix. There is a good view of the two towers from the asymmetrical cloister, entered via the south aisle.

Osnabrück – Felix-Nussbaum-Museum

Johanniskirche – This Early Gothic hall-church dates from the 13C. The carved Passion altarpiece (16C) is the work of Edvard van Rodens. The church also features some interesting figures sculpted in stone: Christ, the Virgin Mary and the Apostles (c 1400-40). The cloisters enclose a graveyard.

Felix-Nussbaum-Haus ⊘ – *Lotter Straße 2.* This Deconstructivist museum building (1998) was designed by **Daniel Libeskind**. Its broken architectural lines, sloping floors, non-parallel walls and other resolutely non-standard details all combine to disorientate the visitor. This language turned to stone is supposed to symbolise the turmoil and disorientation in the life of Jewish painter Felix Nussbaum.

The artist was born in Osnabrück in 1904, and his work ranks him under Neue Sachlichkeit (New Objectivity), although it also contains echoes of Surrealism. After years of productive creativity in Berlin, Nussbaum emigrated to Belgium in 1935. His short life ended in 1944 in Auschwitz. Anticipating his tragic early death, Nussbaum had expressed the wish that his paintings not be allowed to die with him, but that they be shown to posterity. Some 160 paintings from his huge output are on display in this building.

EXCURSION

★ **Tecklenburg** – *23km/14mi to the southwest. About 30min. Leave the car in the parking area at the entrance to the town.*

Famous for its half-timbered houses and its position on the crest of the Teutoburger Wald, this is a very popular small town. We recommend heading for the main square and then west, through the Legge gateway, to the oldest part, at the foot of the **castle**. Of this, nothing remains but a monumental Renaissance gateway and a look-out tower.

OSTFRIESISCHE INSELN★

Eastern Frisians – Niedersachsen

Michelin map 415 E-F 3-7

The seven inhabited Eastern Frisian islands lie between the Ems and the Weser deltas off the North Sea coast of Germany. To the north and east of land formations dating from the modern era and ranging in area from 6.5km²/2.5sq mi to 38km²/15sq mi, stretch sandy beaches, which are covered with wicker-hooded deck chairs and windbreaks during the summer. Dune formations grouped by age are characteristic of the island interiors, while to the south of the sea is reclaimed fertile pastureland. Between the islands and the mainland are the mudflats which were declared a national park (Niedersächsisches Wattenmeer) in 1986. The islands' evolution is by no means finished; due to the prevailing northwesterly tides and winds, they are drifting ever further southeast. Their climate reflects the influence of the North Sea: relatively small variations in annual and daily temperatures, but highly changeable weather and almost constant winds.

Motor vehicles are banned on all the islands (except Borkum and Norderney). The only transport is by horse-drawn carts or handcarts. Some of the islands have a railway.

Borkum ⊘ - The largest of the Eastern Frisians (38km²/15sq mi) boasts an impressive beach promenade with grand hotel façades from the turn of the century. In fine weather, there is a good view of the mainland and the "Hohes Riff" (high reef) seal bank from the 60m/200ft tall **Neuer Leuchtturm**, a lighthouse built in 1879 *(315 steps)*.

Juist ⊘ - This island (17km/11mi long) is home to an interesting **Küstenmuseum** (Coastal Museum) in the attractive village of Loog. The museum documents the local daily life on the coast, the history of the lifeboat service, the importance of dyke building and includes literature on drilling for oil and gas in the North Sea. At the exit to the village of Loog is the start of the nature conservation zone of **Bill**, a windswept but fascinating landscape of sand dunes.

Norderney ⊘ - The most urbanised of the Eastern Frisians was once the summer residence of the royal House of Hanover. Its main town still has much of its old charm with the spa rooms on the Kurplatz, well-tended spa gardens and 19C houses in some of the side streets.

Baltrum ⊘ - On the smallest of the Eastern Frisians, it is relatively calm even in high season. The main sight here is the **old church** in Westdorf, built one year after the great floods of 1826. The church bell next to the simple place of worship was originally a ship's bell, which was washed up as jetsam on the coast of Baltrum. Nature has been left to its own devices on the east side of the island and the impressive valley of **sand dunes** (Großes Dünental) here is well worth a visit.

Langeoog ⊘ - The house on this island houses the **Schiffahrtsmuseum** (Museum of seafaring). In front of the building is Langeoog's lifeboat, in service between 1945 and 1980. From the raised promenade along the chain of sand dunes, near Ebbe, there is a fine view of 14km/9mi of beach and sand banks many hundred yards long.

Spiekeroog ⊘ - The striking thing about this island is the fact that, despite the numerous contemporary spa and holiday facilities, the traditional village and island infrastructure has remained virtually intact. The **Alte Inselkirche** of 1696 is the oldest surviving place of worship in the Eastern Frisians. A Pietà made of wood and fragments of a pulpit are said to have come from a ship in the Spanish Armada that sank in 1588. One of the island's more unusual sights is the **Muschelmuseum** (Mussel Museum) in the basement of the seaside hall.

Wangerooge ⊘ - Over the course of history, the furthest east of the Eastern Frisians has belonged to Holland, France, Russia (twice) and since 1818 to the Grand Duchy of Oldenburg. This much sought after island is now a peaceful family holiday destination. The colourful island train runs from the isolated port on the southwest point past lagoons rich in bird life straight to the centre of the village.

The local brew

Statistics show that the inhabitants of the Eastern Frisians drink 14 times more tea per head than the inhabitants of the whole of the rest of Germany. Tea-drinking is a way of life here (so British visitors will feel quite at home). The beverage was introduced to the region by the Dutch in c 1670 and soon caught on. Frederick the Great attempted to implement a tea ban in 1777, but was forced to repeal it two years later as so many people were leaving the region. Even during rationing in the Second World War, the Eastern Frisians were allocated a much more generous tea allowance than elsewhere.

An essential aspect of the Eastern Frisian "tea ceremony" is the sequence of events: first warm the teapot, then pour boiling (not just hot) water onto the tea leaves in the pot and leave to draw for 5min. Place a piece of white sugar crystal into a porcelain cup and pour on the strong, hot tea, which will make an enticing crackling sound as it hits the sugar. Finally, with infinite care, add the merest splash of cream over the back of a special curved spoon made for this purpose. On no account should the cup of tea be stirred; in Eastern Frisian circles this would be a grave breach of etiquette.

Bayern
Population 8 000
Michelin map 419/420 W 14

Ottobeuren abbey, the jewel of German Baroque, stands in a small town surrounded by pleasant, hilly country, with the dramatic outline of the Allgäu in the background.

The Climax of the Baroque Style – Founded in 764, the Benedictine abbey prospered from the start, when its patron, Charlemagne, granted it extensive rights. The early 16C saw one of the first printing presses working here. Soon afterwards, a college was established whose fame spread far beyond Bavaria but which unfortunately did not stay open for very long.

In the 18C the abbey was totally transformed into a Baroque style mingling the influences of Salzburg (rounded transept arms), the Vorarlberg School (dividing columns) and Rome (domes). In 1748, **Johann Michael Fischer**, the great architect of southern Germany, put the finishing touches on what was to be his masterpiece. But in the realms of Rococo decoration, the names of Johann Jakob Zeiller and his cousin Franz Anton Zeiller must be associated with his (for the frescoes), and also that of Johann Michael Feuchtmayer (stuccowork and statues). Under their direction, a number of artists helped with the church's interior ornamentation.

Secularized in 1802, the abbey was re-established as a priory in 1834 and regained its former status in the Benedictine Order in 1918.

TOUR *allow 30min*

★★★ **Klosterkirche (Abbey church)** ⊘ – The squat outside appearance of the church gives no clue to its actual size. The towers are 82m/272ft high; the length of the nave is 90m/295ft; and the transept is no less than 60m/200ft wide. It is in fact an enormous building, one of the largest Baroque churches in the whole of Germany, with an overall length outside of 480m/1 575ft. The secret of course lies in its perfect proportions (and it is here that the theory of certain German art critics can be tested: that the exterior of a Baroque church has no intrinsic value, but serves only to reflect in its arrangement of masses the powerful influences of the interior).

Once inside, the visitor is struck by the luminosity of the nave: as a result of this astonishing church, in defiance of tradition, being oriented north-south, the light effects are often unexpected – particularly when the sun's rays slant low, in early morning and evening.

CESA, Marburg

Interior view of Ottobeuren abbey church

The colours are harmonious. Half-tones of rose, amber, violet and ochre predominate, while the vault frescoes adopt warmer tints. In the chancel, relatively shadowed, more sombre shades complement gold ornamentation and the patina of natural wood.

Transept crossing (Vierung) – The transept – being angled of course east-west – could in fact be a church in itself. Every architectural element derives from the central dome. Johann Michael Fischer has even furnished the crossing piers with cut-off corners. Noteworthy here are the altars of St Michael, patron of the Ottobeuren region and of the empire; of the Saintly Guardian Angel; of St Joseph and of St John the Baptist. But the most interesting works are the pulpit and, opposite, a group above the font representing the baptism of Christ himself, the work of the sculptor Joseph Christian. The paving is based on the motifs of the cross, the circle and the star. Franz Anton and Johann Jakob Zeiller painted the grandiose composition embellishing the interior of the cupola, The Miracle of Pentecost.

Chancel (Chor) – At the entrance, the small altar of the Holy Sacrament is surmounted by a much venerated Crucifix, dating from c 1220, surrounded by stars symbolizing the sovereignty of the universe.

The high altar glorifies the Holy Trinity. At the foot of the reredos columns are statues of St Peter and St Paul; of St Ulrich, Bishop of Augsburg and patron saint of Swabia; and of St Konrad, bishop and patron saint of the nearby diocese of Constance.

The walnut **choir stalls★★** (1764) form, with the organ loft, a fine ensemble. The backs of the stalls are decorated with gilded limewood low-relief sculptures by Joseph Christian depicting events from the life of St Benedict *(right)* and his models from the Old Testament *(left)*.

Karl Joseph Riepp (1710-75), a pupil of famous organ builder Silbermann who worked for a long time in Burgundy (churches at Dijon, Beaune and Besançon), built both the chancel **organs★★** (1766). The instruments' musical and decorative properties, already impressive, were supplemented in 1958 by a third organ, the "Marienorgel", installed in the same loft.

Klostergebäude (Abbey buildings) ⊘ – These were constructed between 1711 and 1731. Inside the abbey museum the state apartments can be viewed, including the abbatial palace (Prälatur), magnificent **library**, theatre and Emperor's Hall, with a frescoed ceiling depicting the coronation of Emperor Charlemagne. There is an exhibition on the abbey's 1 200 year history.

PADERBORN

Nordrhein-Westfalen

Population 132 000
Michelin map 417 K 10

Paderborn, the city of 200 springs, was founded by Charlemagne in 777 and ranked for many years among the central royal and episcopal seats of the Middle Ages. Evidence of this is the reconstructed Imperial palace and the cathedral. In 1614, the first university in Westphalia was founded in Paderborn. After the Thirty Years War, numerous grand buildings were built under the prince-bishops of the Baroque period, many of which still adorn the city.

Economically, Paderborn remained a rural city until the 20C. After the Second World War a transformation took place, and Paderborn became a centre for research and teaching, as well as for information and communications technology, while retaining its charm as a "city with green spaces".

SIGHTS

★ **Dom (Cathedral)** – A massive tower, pierced with many Romanesque bays, overlooks the church, most of which dates from the 13C.

The entrance porch (Paradiesportal) is on the north side, where the doors are flanked by statues of bishops and saints (among them St Julian, the first Bishop of Le Mans), with the Virgin (c 1250) above on the pier.

The 13C interior, modelled on Poitiers Cathedral, France, demonstrates the evolution from Romanesque (in the western part of the huge hall) to Gothic (in the east). Off the north chancel is a small atrium with three equal aisles and some arches dating back to the year 1000. The crypt, reached from the transept, houses the relics of St Liborius.

Cloister *(entrance via the atrium)* – Note the funerary chapel of the Westphalian Counts, with a graceful Gothic altarpiece (1517), and the amusing "Three Hares Window". The animals, visible from the outside only, each have a pair of ears and yet there are only three ears in all.

Bartholomäuskapelle – A small Romanesque hall chapel, built apart, a little way north of the main structure, by Byzantine masons in 1017. The slender columns with ornate capitals in Late Corinthian style support a domed vaulting.

Diözesanmuseum ⊘ – The attractive interior is the setting for this important collection of religious art from the 10C to 20C. The fine **Madonna of Bishop Imad★** (1050) is outstanding. Also on display are two small portable altars of Roger von Helmarshausen (c 1100), and the 1627 St Liborius' shrine.

★ **Rathaus** – This magnificent building with a main gable and two gabled oriels was built in 1613-20 in the style of the Late Weser Renaissance. Its rich decoration reflects the rise of the bourgeoisie.

Paderquellen (The Pader Springs) – Below the cathedral, more than 200 springs bubble from the ground, merging to form streams strong enough to turn a water-wheel, before flowing into the River Pader.

The first all-electronic digital computer (ENIAC)

Heinz Nixdorf MuseumsForum ⊘ – This museum takes as its theme "From Cuneiform Script to Computers", retracing over 5 000 years of information technology and posing pertinent questions about society and the individual. As much space is devoted to cultural history as to speculation on future developments. This breathtaking journey through the ages begins with the invention of writing and counting in Mesopotamia and finishes in the age of modern information technology. Attractions include flight simulators, recognition of faces by computers, computer-game arcades and software theatres, video, audio and multimedia presentations – so visitors have no excuse to get bored!

Traktoren-Museum ⊘ – *Karl-Schoppe-Weg 8. Entrance on Steubenstraße.* This museum contains a display of more than 100 tractors of German manufacture, including the legendary Lanz-Bulldog, which began its long and successful career after 1921. There are also examples of rural technology and crafts. A collection of model aircraft numbering about 10 000 items in total is also on display.

PASSAU★★

Bayern
Population 50 000
Michelin map 420 U 24

Passau, a frontier town between Bavaria and Austria and known as the "Town of the Three Rivers", lies in a marvellous **setting**★★ at the junction of the Inn, the Danube (Donau) and the small River Ilz. The old town, with its Baroque churches and patrician houses, lies crowded onto the narrow tongue of land separating the Inn and the Danube. Northwards, on the far bank of the Danube, rises the wooded bluff on which the Oberhaus fortress is built.

Passau's cultural and economic influence on eastern Bavaria was reinforced in 1978, when a new university was opened. In summertime, the European Weeks attract a large number of music – and theatre – lovers.

A Powerful Bishopric – The see was founded in the 8C by St Boniface, the English-born "Apostle of Germany". By the end of the 10C it had become so powerful that it rivalled that of Salzburg. In 1217 the bishops were created by Princes of the Empire. Until the 15C the diocese was so huge that it encompassed the entire Danube Valley in Austria, even including Vienna.

A commercial base – The arrival of the Inn waters at Passau almost doubles the flow volume of the Danube; from there on it becomes a really big river. From the Middle Ages, river trade played an important role in the town's prosperity, including such essentials as cereals, wine and salt, for which the Passau merchants enjoyed the "right of storage". Business with Bohemia, which was conducted via the valley of the Ilz, was also important. Today, when barges can go upriver as far as Kelheim, the "Town of Three Rivers" also offers excursions, cruises and passenger traffic to Vienna and Budapest.

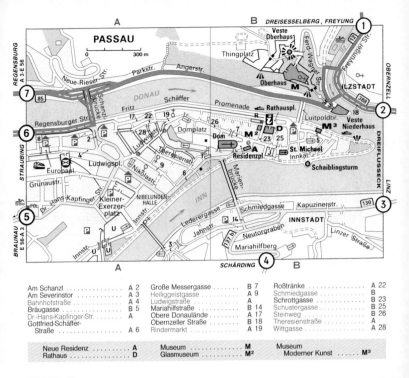

Am Schanzl	A 2	Große Messergasse	B 7	Roßtränke	A 22
Am Severinstor	A 3	Heiliggeistgasse	A 9	Schmiedgasse	B
Bahnhofstraße	A 4	Ludwigstraße	A	Schrottgasse	B 23
Bräugasse	B 5	Mariahilfstraße	B 14	Schustergasse	B 25
Dr.-Hans-Kapfinger-Str.	A	Obere Donaulände	A 17	Steinweg	B 26
Gottfried-Schäffer-		Obernzeller Straße	B 18	Theresienstraße	A
Straße	A 6	Rindermarkt	A 19	Wittgasse	A 28

Neue Residenz .... **A**	Museum .... **M**	Museum	
Rathaus .... **D**	Glasmuseum .... **M²**	Moderner Kunst ..... **M³**	

SIGHTS

Veste Oberhaus (Fortress) (B) – Work on this imposing citadel, which served the bishops as a refuge against continuous rebellions by the burghers, started in 1219. It is linked with the **Veste Niederhaus** by a fortified road along the spit of land separating the Danube and the Ilz. From the belvedere marked Zur Aussicht, near the car park – or from the top of a tower inside the compound (*142 steps*) – there are magnificent **views**★★ over the rocky promontory dividing the Inn from the Danube, with the town's churches and houses jumbled close together upon it. Some of the houses, following a former Inn Valley tradition, have ridge roofs behind façades – masking the many sloping angles from street level.

The history of the town and its craftwork, folk art, and religious past are traced in a small **museum (B M¹)** which also displays paintings of the Danube School.

Dom St.-Stephan (B) – Apart from the east chancel and the transept, the original Late Gothic cathedral was destroyed by fire in the 17C. Once rebuilt, the greater part of it was in the Baroque style. The majestic west front is so severe in concept that the late 19C addition to the two towers of a final, octagonal stage seems almost frivolous.

The huge interior is overloaded with frescoes and stuccowork. There are four **lateral chapels** with fine paintings by the Austrian artist JM Rottmayr (1654-1730). The first on the south side shows *The Beheading of John the Baptist*. Opposite is *The Conversion of St Paul*. In the two remaining chapels are *St Sebastian Succoured by St Irene (north)* and *The Martyrdom of St Agnes (south)*.

The pulpit, lavishly decorated with figures, is a Viennese work (1722-26). Henselmann's modern (1953) high altar represents the stoning of St Stephen (figures in silvered poplar wood). The organ, rebuilt in 1928 with 17 388 pipes and 231 stops, is the largest in the world.

From the Residenzplatz, visitors can admire the cathedral's **east end**★★, a remarkable Late Gothic work (1407-1530) whose slender outline is emphasized by the domed belfry which tops the transept cupola.

Residenzplatz (B) – The square is bordered on the south by the bishops' **New Residence (A)**, which dates from the beginning of the neo-Classical period. The surrounding streets are still lined with many old houses above arcades, with corbelling and concealed Inn valley ridge roofs.

Danube School

The German painters working in the Danube Valley in the 16C were among the first to depict landscape for its own sake. The best masters of this so-called school were Albrecht Altdorfer, Lucas Cranach the Elder, Wolf Huber and Jörg Breu the Elder.

411

Jugendstil glassware (c 1900)

Rathausplatz (B) – One of the town's most picturesque squares. The painted façade of the **Rathaus** (D) dates from the 14C; the building's tower was built in the late 18C.

★★ **Glasmuseum** ⊘ (B M²) – *In the "Wilder Mann" on Rathausplatz.* Glassware from Bohemia, Bavaria and Austria, from the late 18C to the 1930s, makes up most of this fine collection. The most important display comes from **Bohemia** (Biedermeier, Historicism, Jugendstil); coloured glass, vases, pots and figurines attest to the great skill of the Bohemian glassblowers.

St.-Michaels-Kirche (B) – This 17C church built by the Jesuits overlooks the north bank of the Inn. The over-rich gilding and stuccowork date from c 1720. A reredos painted by Carlone hides the squared-off chevet.

★ **Dreiflußeckspaziergang** (Three Rivers Walk) (B) – *From St.-Michaels-Kirche, go down to the Inn quayside.*
The fast, at times almost torrential, river runs at the foot of the **Schaiblingsturm** (1481), which was once part of Passau's defence system. At the **confluence**, the green current of the Inn can be seen running alongside the brown Danube waters for a long time before they mingle. From the Danube bank, on the far side of the promontory, there is a fine **viewpoint**, looking across the river at the wooded, rocky height of the Oberhaus fortress.

Museum Moderner Kunst ⊘ (B M³) – The Modern Art Museum is housed in a beautiful, part-Gothic and part-Baroque house in the old city, right on the banks of the Danube, whose elegant architecture with its atrium, vaults and arcades provide an attractive and contrasting framework for modern art. Originally the priest's house of the former Benedictine monastery opposite, it has retained much of its atmosphere through exemplary restoration work. The collection of contemporary painting belonging to the Wörlen foundation is extremely interesting. The works exhibited are not by major, internationally famous artists, but are substantial works by less well-known masters, for example the Donau-Wald (Danube Forest) Group and the community of artists known as "Der Fels" (the Rock), all of which are well worth discovering.

EXCURSIONS

★ **Dreisesselberg** – *48km/30mi to the northeast.*
The drive to this curious group of granitic rocks, eroded into flat, saucer-like shapes, runs through some of the wildest forest regions of the Bavarian forest. The inn at the foot of the formation is soon reached from the road. Green triangles bordered with white waymark the path leading to the lowest rock outcrop. From there, steps rise to the **Hochstein** (1 332m/4 370ft). The viewpoint at the summit affords a splendid **panorama**★ which reveals the immensity of this Bohemian forest.

Osterhofen Church – *36km/22mi to the northeast. Leave Passau by ⑥ on the town plan.*
Three great names of the Bavarian Baroque style have vent here the fullness of their talent: Johann Michael Fischer for the architecture and the Asam brothers for the decoration. The alternation of the convex lines of the balustrades and concave lines of the pilasters as well as the almost total absence of right angles gives many contours to the buildings. Note in particular the monumental high altar with its wreathed columns and its angels with enraptured smiles surrounding a radiant almond-shaped glory.

Die PFALZ★

RHINELAND PALATINATE – Rheinland-Pfalz

Michelin map 417/419 S 7 – R 9

The palatinate mountains are a continuation of the northern Vosges, with a similar forested aspect broken up by escarpments of red sandstone.

The **Pfälzer Wald**, densely wooded and sparsely inhabited, is a huge natural park in the northern part of the massif much favoured by walkers; further south lies the broken country of the **Wasgau**, where tree-clad heights crowned by ruins or rock outcrops overlook the valley clearings which shelter the villages.

The Wines of the Palatinate – The most extensive wine-growing region of the country, the Palatinate produces almost one-third of Germany's total output: a long reach of suitable country, calcareous, protected and facing the sun it stretches along the foot of the **Haardt** – the steep eastern flank of the massif overlooking the Rhine. The highest point of the Haardt is the Kalmit, at 673m/2 208ft. The strip below being almost flat, vines can be cultivated in the traditional way on low cordons. This permits late-harvested grapes to ripen more and produce fruity wines of fairly high alcoholic content, the most appreciated being the whites. The most famous vintages come from the villages of Bad Dürkheim, Forst, Deidesheim and Wachenheim. The itinerary suggested below follows part of the celebrated Deutsche Weinstraße (German Wine Road), which begins at Schweigen, on the French frontier, and ends at Bockenheim, west of Worms.

FROM WORMS TO BAD BERGZABERN

158km/98mi - allow one day

South of **Worms★**, cultivation of the Rhine plain becomes progressively devoted to the vine. Soon, the steep barrier of the Haardt appears in the distance.

Freinsheim – A large wine town, encircled by ramparts. The town hall, beside a 15C church, occupies an elegant Baroque house with an overhanging roof that protects an outside staircase.

The road continues through vineyards, past pretty villages.

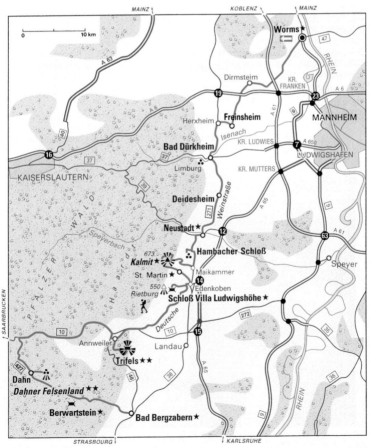

Bad Dürkheim – Sheltered by the Pfälzer Wald, this thermal cure town enjoys a mild climate in which fig, almond and chestnut trees in the **Spa Park** flower early. A couple of miles west *(via Schillerstraße and Luitpoldweg)* are the ruins of Limburg abbey. From here there are picturesque views – to the east across the vineyards of the Rhine plain; westwards along the Isenach Valley to the Hardenburg ruins.

Deidesheim – One of the most typical and prosperous towns on the German Wine Road with its smart market place, bordered by half-timbered and patrician houses.

The traditional goat auction, which takes place in historical costumes on the steps of the town hall (16C), is held every year on Whit Tuesday.

* **Neustadt an der Weinstraße** – Narrow, picturesque lanes in this small town surround a pretty market place with a 16C town hall. The **old town*** is attractive and boasts the largest number of old houses in the region.

Hambacher Schloß ⊘ – *On the outskirts of Hambach.*
Founded by the Salian Franks in the 11C, this castle was for some considerable time the summer residence of the Speyer bishops before being destroyed in 1688. The ruins of this old fortress are famous in Germany because it was here, in 1832, that militant patriots demanding a more liberal approach raised for the first time the black, red and gold flag adopted as the German national emblem in 1919, and again in 1949. A permanent exhibition in the fully restored ruins commemorates this event, the first major rally in German history.

* **The Kalmit** – *8km/5mi, leaving from Maikammer, then 15min on foot there and back.*
At 673m/2 208ft above sea level, the Kalmit is the highest outcrop in the Rhineland Palatinate. It is a good departure point for numerous walks through beautiful woodland. There is a viewpoint at the summit. From the Kalmithaus terrace, there is a splendid **view*** of the Rhine plain and, in the east, Speyer cathedral. Return to the Wine Road via the charming village of **St. Martin***.

* **Schloß Villa Ludwigshöhe** ⊘ – *2km/1mi from Edenkoben.*
Built by Ludwig I of Bavaria in the "Italian villa" style, this castle now houses a **gallery*** devoted to the works of the German Impressionist painter **Max Slevogt** (1868-1932). The castle apartments with Pompeian-style murals and fine **parquet flooring*** are also open to the public. There is a superb **view*** of the River Rhine plain from the castle terrace.

A chair-lift carries sightseers to the **Rietburg** (550m/1 804ft), departure point for forest walks. The return journey in the chair-lift affords superb views over the vine-covered slopes.

** **Trifels** ⊘ – *7km/4.5mi from Annweiler, plus 1hr 30min walking and sightseeing.*
This castle is of considerable historic importance and dates back to a foundation by the Salian Franks. It was the Hohenstaufen imperial stronghold and in the 12C and 13C, the temporary residence of the crown jewels and royal treasury.

Trifels and surrounding landscape

Südl. Weinstraße e. V., Zentrale für Tourismus, Landau

Legend even has it that the Holy Grail was found here. It is proven fact, however, that Emperor Henry IV held **Richard the Lionheart** prisoner in the fort, while the latter was returning from the Third Crusade in 1193. The enormous ransom that Henry IV received for Richard's release enabled him to fund a military campaign against the Norman kingdom in south Italy. He set off from Trifels on 9 May 1194.

On a superb **site**★★ crowning the summit of a bluff, Trifels makes an imposing sight even from a distance. It is clear to see how strategic a role the fortress played in protecting the route from Metz via Pirmasens to the Rhine plain. The sandstone outcrop on which it rests, seemingly fused at the base, is 145m/4765ft long and only 40m/130ft wide.

★★ **Dahner Felsenland** – The climatic health resort of **Dahn** is surrounded by one of the best areas for walking in Germany, featuring breath-taking mountains and numerous interesting rock formations from red sandstone, of which 47 have been singled out as protected natural monuments. The **castle ruins**★ of Altdahn dominate the town. Flights of steps and guard rooms hewn into the rocks add to the charm of the castle, the heart of which probably dates from c 1100. From the towers, there are fine **views**★ of the Wasgau.

★ **Burg Berwartstein** ⊘ – *Turn off towards Erlenbach (B 427).* This former robber baron's lair, situated at the intersection of several valleys, is perched 100m/330ft above the village of Erlenbach. The upper castle dates back to the 12C, and the lower to the 15C. The castle was destroyed by a fire in 1591, and then rebuilt at the end of the 19C. The knights' hall, hunting room, a 104m/340ft deep well, the old kitchen, casemates and subterranean passages cut into the rock are open to the public. From the terrace there is a **view**★ "beyond frontiers" of the undulating Wasgau landscape as far as France.

Winding through a landscape scattered with rock outcrops, the road arrives at Bad Bergzabern.

★ **Bad Bergzabern** – This charming health resort features numerous half-timbered houses (Königstraße, Marktstraße). Among the ornate residences dating from the 17C and 18C, note in particular the **Gasthaus zum Engel**★ (1579), which is said to be the finest Renaissance building in the region. The **palace** with its sturdy round towers was built in 1720-25. All that remains of the previous building is a polygonal staircase tower on the courtyard side, dating from 1530.

Rhine-Main-Danube Canal

Ever since Roman times emperors, kings, engineers and visionaries have dreamt of linking the Rhine and Danube waterways. Charlemagne began the great enterprise, hence the name Charlemagne's Ditch (Fossa Carolina). Bavaria's Ludwig I made another attempt when he built the Ludwig Canal. However it was barge loads of 20C dignitaries who were the first to cross the watershed between the Rhine and the Danube on 25 September 1992.

The 177km/110mi canal with its hundreds of locks takes the barges up and down the 245m/800ft climb. Some 12 centuries after it was originally conceived, the idea of a waterway linking Europe from the North Sea to the Black Sea has become a reality.

Brandenburg
Population 140 000
Michelin map 416/418 I 23

Located in delightful countryside only a few miles west of Berlin, Potsdam was chosen at the beginning of the 17C as the official residence of the electors of Brandenburg because of its ideal setting – a natural wooded site dotted with lakes and crisscrossed by canals and arms of the River Havel. Sacked by Swedish troops during the Thirty Years War, the town was revived by Friedrich Wilhelm I. After the Revocation of the Edict of Nantes, many French Huguenots emigrated to Potsdam, among them merchants and craftsmen who contributed to the subsequent economic development of the area.

A Prussian Versailles – Under the rule of Friedrich Wilhelm, "the King-Sergeant" (1713-40), Potsdam became an administrative centre and above all a garrison town (to the extent that at one time three-quarters of the population were military).

The King's son, **Frederick the Great** (Friedrich II: 1740-86), was on the contrary a patron of the arts and man of letters. Most of the prestigious monuments for which the city is famous today were due to him, notably Sanssouci and the Neues Palais. Frederick, as eloquent in French as in his own language, welcomed many eminent Frenchmen to his court, among them **Voltaire**, who lived in Potsdam for three years.

In 1991, 205 years after his death, the remains of Frederick the Great were reinterred in the crypt of his beloved palace of Sanssouci in Potsdam.

The Potsdam Conference – The treaty defining the role of the victors in the occupation and future of Germany after the Second World War was signed here at Cecilienhof Palace on 2 August 1945 by the leaders of the Allied powers (Churchill – subsequently Attlee – Truman and Stalin).

Schloß Sanssouci

★★★ SANSSOUCI PALACE AND PARK

Follow the itinerary suggested on the map.

Designed by Peter Joseph Lenné (1789-1866), the most talented landscape gardener in Prussia, the 300ha/740-acre park contains several hundred different species of tree. The various palaces and pavilions were all built between 1744 and 1860. This huge complex marrying architecture with the landscape is undoubtedly the best example of its kind in Germany. Wandering here and there it is easy to understand why Frederick the Great, turning his back momentarily on affairs of state, took such delight coming here to steep himself in the arts, especially music. In fact, Sanssouci has become his final resting place. His body was brought from Burg Hohenzollern in 1991 and interred in a vault above the terraces of the palace. His father, Friedrich Wilhelm I, is buried in a mausoleum in the Friedenskirche near the Marly Gardens.

Friedenskirche – This church was built under Friedrich Wilhelm IV, who is buried here, in 1844-54. It was modelled on the basilica of San Clemente in Rome. The apse contains a fine **mosaic★** made during the first half of the 18C and from the island of Murano. The mausoleum houses the recumbent statues of Emperor Friedrich III and his wife, and the sarcophagus of Friedrich Wilhelm I, the King-Sergeant.

Neptungrotte (Neptune's Grotto) – This is the last building (1751-57) designed by Georg Wenzelaus von Knobelsdorff. The fountain decorated with shell motifs was not installed until the 19C.

★ Bildergalerie (Paintings Gallery) ⊘ – This is one of the oldest museums in Germany. It was built between 1755 and 1763. Amid the rich Rococo decor of the great rooms visitors can admire works mainly from the Italian (Bassano, Tintoretto and Caravaggio), Flemish (Van Dyck, Rubens and Terbrugghen) and French (Simon Vouet and Van Loo) schools, all bought by Friedrich II.

★★★ Schloß Sanssouci ⊘ – *There may be a wait, because only a limited number of visitors are allowed in at once.*
It is impossible to remain unmoved by the progressive appearance of this majestic façade as one climbs the great staircase rising through the tiers of terraces before it. The original idea of the architect (Knobelsdorff again) was for the façade, adorned with 36 atlantes, to encompass the entire terrace area. But the king preferred a generous proportion of space which indeed became one of his favourite places to relax in. On the far side of the palace the state entrance is flanked by an elegant semicircular colonnade.
A walk through the rooms inside reveals the enormous skill and artistry in the Rococo style of the craftsmen who decorated them.

Ante-chamber – Grey and gold, the decoration here is elegant and sober. The ceiling was painted by Swedish artist Johann Harper in 1746.

Small Gallery – Paintings by Nicolas Lancret (1690-1743) and Jean-Baptiste Pater (1695-1736), both of them followers of Watteau. On the chimney-piece are busts of Frederick and his brother Henry.

Library – This small rotunda is the cosiest room in the palace. Beautiful panelling in cedarwood with gilded bronze decoration.

Bedchamber and Study of Frederick the Great – Portraits of the royal family as well as the King's table and the chair in which he died.

Concert Hall – This was Frederick the Great's favourite room. It is a masterpiece of Prussian Rococo. The walls are hung with paintings by Antoine Pesne with motifs from Ovid's *Metamorphoses*. There is a painting by Menzel representing the King playing the flute.

Reception Hall – The ceiling was painted by Antoine Pesne. Paintings by Coypel and Van Loo.

Hall of Marble – This hall, which opens onto the terrace through large French windows, hosted the "philosophical discussions". The marble used for the floor of this hall comes from Silesia and Carrara. Beneath the cupola there is a Bernini bust of Richelieu, also statues of Apollo and Venus by François Gaspard Adam (1710-61).

Four Guest Rooms – The fourth is supposed to have been Voltaire's, from 1750 to 1753. There is a replica of the great writer's bust by Jean Antoine Houdon (1741-1828). In all probability, however, Voltaire stayed in Stadt-schloß.

★ Neue Kammern (New Rooms) ⊘ – Designed in 1747 by Knobelsdorff in the form of an orangery, this block was transformed into the palace guesthouse by Georg Christian Unger from 1771 to 1774. The Rococo interior decor is bright and captivating. Note in particular the **Ovid-Galerie★**, in which the panelling is decorated with scenes from Ovid's *Metamorphoses*.

Historische Mühle – This mill is the subject of a well-known anecdote, which is an excellent observation on the role of the State and of Frederick the Great's enlightened despotism. The King was disturbed by the noise of the mill, so made efforts to persuade the miller to discontinue his business or go somewhere else. He began by offering compensation, and when this did not work proceeded to

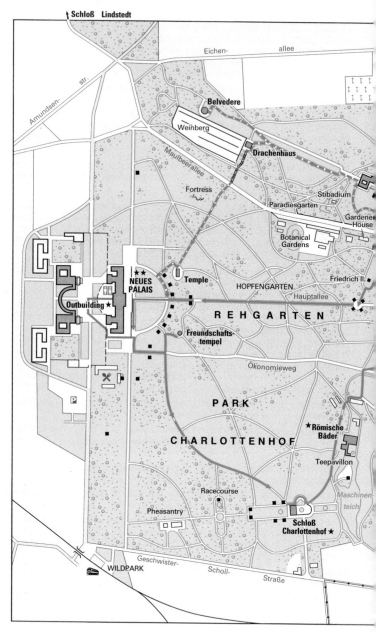

threats, but to no avail. The King then took the miller to court, but lost the civil case, on the principle that in a court of law it is the law that speaks while the King must remain silent.

Sizilianischer Garten – These charming gardens were designed in the Renaissance style by Lenné.

Neue Orangerie ⊘ – The orangery was built in the style of an Italian Renaissance palace between 1851 and 1860, after plans by Friedrich Wilhelm IV. Among the magnificent apartments occupied by Czar Nicolas I and his wife, the malachite hall is particularly impressive. Even more of a find, however, is the **Raphael Hall**★, which houses 47 copies of paintings by Raphael.

Drachenhaus – This small pagoda (with 16 copper dragons on the roof ridge) is now a café. It was built by Karl von Gontard in 1770, near a vineyard planted in 1769, and was used by the wine-grower as his home.

Belvedere – This charming building dates back to 1770-72 and was the last Potsdam construction commissioned by Frederick the Great.

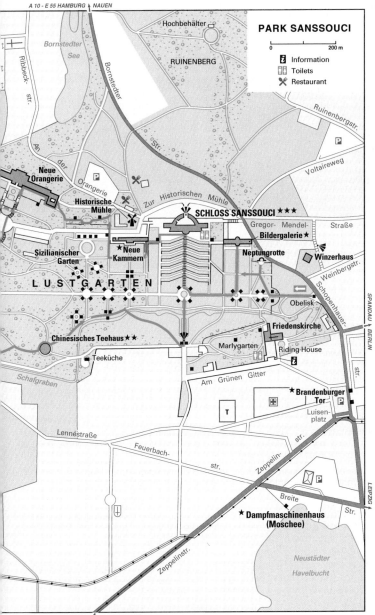

PARK SANSSOUCI

0   200 m

🅸 Information
🚻 Toilets
✗ Restaurant

Before reaching the Neues Palais, note the **Antique temple**, which was to house part of the King's collections.

★★ **Neues Palais** ⊘ – This imposing – and in fact rather pompous – building was commissioned by Frederick the Great to demonstrate that the economic power of Prussia remained intact after the arduous Seven Years War. Some 400 rooms behind a frontage of almost 213m/700ft, together with over-lavish decorations and a superabundance of sculpture, themselves alone testify to the over-ambitious nature of the project – which was nevertheless completed in a relatively short time, from 1763 to 1769. The style of architecture, an unrestrained Baroque, today seems both heavy and over mannered, very far from the elegant simplicity of Sanssouci.

Behind the palace, the so-called Communs, or outbuildings and servants' quarters, take the form of small pavilions linked by a curved colonnade (1766-69).

Neues Palais

Since the number and nature of rooms open to visitors can vary, only the most important rooms are described below.

Ground floor

Shell Room – Sea-shells and minerals contribute to the exuberant decor of this fantasy room. The ceiling fresco, *Venus and the Graces*, is by JG Niedlich.

Marble Gallery – Red jasper and white Carrara marble decorate the floor and walls of this hall. The allegorical frescoes on the ceiling, based on the hours of the day, are by CB Rode, a pupil of Pesne.

Red Damask Room – The eight canvases depicting members of the royal family were executed by Pesne when he was the official Court Painter. Note especially *Frederick II as Crown Prince*.

Oval Office – A barrel-vaulted room with a magnificent parquet floor. The marquetry, in floral motifs, was laid by the Spindler Brothers.

First floor

Marble Room – The stone floor is an elegant grey-blue, enhanced by discreet gilding. Statues in the same stone represent the electors of Brandenburg. The ceiling fresco, by Van Loo (1769), depicts *Ganymede and Hebe on Olympus*.

Upper Gallery – This is neo-Classical in style, with stuccowork antique heads on plinths. The 17C Italian paintings include Giordano's *Judgement of Paris* and *The Suicide of Lucretia* and *Diogenes in his Tub* by Reni.

Theatre – Designed as part of the palace's south wing, this is a fine example of Germany's Late Rococo style (1766-68). The auditorium is encompassed by two galleries supported by gilded Hermes.

★ Schloß Charlottenhof ⊘ – Karl-Friedrich Schinkel and his pupil Ludwig Perseus drew up the plans for this palace, which was built in the Classical Italian style between 1826 and 1829. Visitors can see, among other things, the bedchamber and office of **Alexander von Humboldt**.

Römische Bäder (Roman Baths) – Schinkel designed this group of buildings, Perseus executed it between 1829 and 1835, and Lenné planted the garden. The guiding principle was to blend a group of different buildings harmoniously with their natural setting. The **interior decor★** of the baths is tastefully done.
A pergola leads to the **Tea Pavilion**, not unlike a temple, with a single room decorated all in blue, which has a good view of the lake and gardens.

★★ Chinesisches Teehaus (Chinese Tea House) – A circular pavilion decorated with gilded statues, this structure arose from the "Sino-mania" so popular in 18C Germany. There is an exhibition of Chinese porcelain inside.

SIGHTS ABOUT TOWN

★ **Brandenburger Tor** - *Luisenplatz.* A monumental gateway in the form of a triumphal arch, Roman style, built in the Baroque fashion in 1770 based on designs by Karl von Gontard and Georg Friedrich Unger.

★ **Dampfmaschinenhaus (Moschee) (Hydraulic Waterworks)** ⊘ - *Take Schopenhauerstraße, and then, on the right, Breite Straße.*

Installed in a most unusual building imitating a mosque, complete with minarets, this pumping station (1841-42) supplies water to the fountains, pools and cascades in Sanssouci Park. The ingenious machinery can be seen at work.

Marstall (Old Stables) – *Breite Straße.* Dating from 1675 and modified by Knobelsdorff in 1746. Groups of horse trainers decorate the attics. There is an interesting **film museum**★ here with reconstructions of Marlene Dietrich's and Lilian Harvey's dressingrooms. The museum also contains a lot of literature on German Expressionist films and émigré film directors.

★ **Nikolaikirche** - Built on the site of an old Baroque church destroyed by fire in 1795, this is a perfect example of German Classicism as conceived by Karl Friedrich Schinkel. Construction of the squared nave and preceding porch was completed in 1837. The cupola was added two years later.

Ph. Gajic/MICHELIN

Potsdam's Dutch quarter

★ **Holländisches Viertel (Dutch Quarter)** - It is on each side of the **Mittelstraße** that one can still see these gabled houses in varying colours, built by the Dutch architect Boumann around 1740 for Netherlands artisans working in Potsdam. There is a good view of the row of houses from the corner of Benkerstraße and Mittelstraße.

★★ NEUER GARTEN

This park was laid out at the end of the 18C by Peter Lenné on the shore of Heiliger See for Frederick the Great, who was a great fan of English-style landscaped gardens. Interesting follies and features in the park include the Holländisches Etablissement, where servants were quartered; the **orangery**; the pyramid; the kitchens, which Langhans incorporated into a building in the style of an ancient ruin; and finally the marble palace.

★ **Marmorpalais** ⊘ - This marble palace was built by Karl von Gontard and converted into a summer residence for Friedrich Wilhelm II by Langhans (1744-97). The ceremonial rooms and apartments are sumptuously furnished, particular highlights being a Fiedler chest of drawers in mahogany with a marble panel and Wedgwood vases.

★ **Schloß Cecilienhof** ⊘ - This English-style country residence built during the First World War for the Crown Prince (1882-1951) and his wife Cecilia of Mecklenburg-Schwerin has been converted into a luxury hotel.

Historische Stätte der Potsdamer Konferenz - Besides the Crown Princess's private office, furnished like a ship's cabin, visitors can see the conference and meeting rooms used by the members of the Allied delegations and where the Potsdam Agreements were signed (2 August 1945).

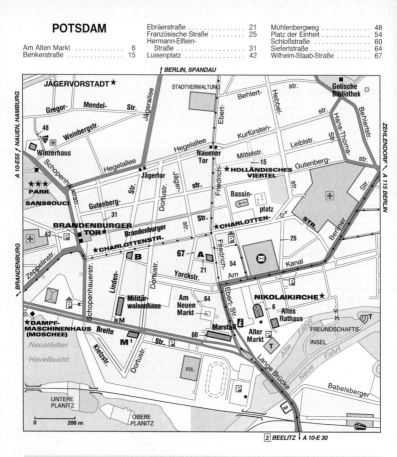

Acht-Ecken-Haus . . . . **A**   Ehemalige Hauptwache . . . . . **B**   Hiller-Brandtsche Häuser . . . **M¹**

EXCURSIONS

Brandenburg – *38km/24mi to the west.*
It was in the 14C that this small town in the heart of the Havelland (an area of scattered lakes fed by the River Havel) began to prosper, mainly through the cloth trade. The **Dom St.-Peter und St.-Paul**★, founded in 1165 and remodelled in the 14C, is furnished with several Gothic altarpieces. In the two-aisle crypt there is a mausoleum in memory of the clergy murdered during the Nazi regime.
Rich exterior decoration distinguishes the 15C **St.-Katharinenkirche**★, which boasts a polygonal chancel. The ambulatory *(currently under restoration)* is a typical example of brick-built Gothic.

★ **Kloster Lehnin** (Abbey) ⊘ – *28km/17mi to the southwest.*
Brick-built again, this three-aisle basilica, founded in 1180 by the Cistercian Order, has all the hallmarks of Early Gothic. Worth seeing: a Triumphal Cross dating from 1225 and the funerary stone of the Margrave Otto IV.

QUEDLINBURG★

Sachsen-Anhalt
Population 27 000
Michelin 418 K 17

Nestling at the foot of a rock pinnacle crowned by a castle and an abbey church, the picturesque half-timbered houses and narrow, winding streets of Quedlinburg form a picture that corresponds to everyone's idea of a 17C German town. The old town, in which no less than 770 houses are classified as historical monuments, has been inscribed on UNESCO's World Heritage List.

The Abbesses of Quedlinburg – A convent for the daughters of the nobility was founded on this height by Otto I around AD 930. Thanks to certain privileges, and to the lands with which it was endowed, the religious community prospered to the extent that Quedlinburg was chosen as a residence by the Saxon kings, and six Diets, or Councils of State were convened there.

WHERE TO STAY

Acron – Oeringer Straße 7, ☎ 0 39 46/7 70 20, Fax 0 39 46/77 02 30. Single rooms from 79DM. Good value place to stay.

Zur goldenen Sonne – Steinweg 11, ☎ 0 39 46/9 62 50, Fax 0 39 46/96 25 30. Single rooms from 90DM. Renovated half-timbered house in the centre of town. Some rooms in the style of a country house.

Am Brühl – Billungstraße 11, ☎ 0 39 46/9 61 80, Fax 0 39 46/9 61 82 46. Single rooms from 120DM. Former manor. Well-run establishment.

Theophano – Markt 14, ☎ 0 39 46/0 63 00, Fax 0 39 46/96 30 36. Single rooms from 130DM. Half-timbered house on the historic market square. Each room has its own individual decor. Restaurant in vaulted cellars.

★ OLD TOWN

★ **Markt** – The early-17C Renaissance **Rathaus**, a two-storey building flanked by a gateway showing the town's armorial bearings, borders the northern side of the market place. On the left of the façade is a statue of Roland (c 1420). Houses built in the 17C and 18C line the other three sides of the square.

★ **Old streets** – Circle St.-Benediktkirche via Marktstraße and Kornmarkt to explore the cobbled lanes behind the Rathaus, then return to the Markt along Breitstraße, which has several picturesque alleyways opening off it. On the far side of the square, stroll to the hill that leads up to the castle by way of Wordgasse, Hohe Straße and Blasiistraße.

Klopstock-Haus ⊘ – The poet **Friedrich Gottlieb Klopstock** was born in 1724 in this late-16C house (no 12) on one side of the charming **Schloßbergplatz**★. Drawing on sources close to the German psyche, inspired by ancient Teutonic myths, he composed a saga glorifying the hero Arminius, but he is best-known for the huge religious epic, *Messias (The Messiah)*, said to be inspired by Milton's *Paradise Lost*. Various rooms in the house recall his life and his work.

Feininger-Galerie ⊘ – *Behind the Klopstock Museum, entry at no 5A, Finkenherd.* This small gallery houses an interesting collection of drawings and water-colours by the Expressionist painter Lyonel Feininger (1871-1956). Born in New York City, Feininger trained in France and Germany, where he exhibited with the Blauer Reiter group in 1913. After the First World War he joined the staff of the Bauhaus.

★ SCHLOSSBERG

The ramp leading up to the castle ends in a wide terrace with a fine general **view**★ of the town.

★★ **Stiftskirche St.-Servatius** – On the site of the original 9C church, the present basilica, in the form of a Latin cross, was started in 1070 and consecrated in 1129. The **capitals**★ and **friezes** above the central nave were sculpted by craftsmen brought

Interior of St. Servatius, Quedlinburg

H. Champollion/MICHELIN, Paris

especially from northern Italy. Beneath the chancel, the **crypt**★★ is divided by three aisles with diagonal rib vaulting decorated by **frescoes**★ depicting scenes from the Bible. Note the sarcophagi of King Heinrich I and his wife Matilda, interred here in the 10C, and the funerary stones of abbesses. The **treasury**★★ (Domschatz) – manuscripts, 10C **Gospel**, and, above all, the **Quedlinburg Knotted Carpet**★ – is kept in the sacristy.

Schloß – Construction of the castle building, which formed part of the abbey, extended from the late 16C to the mid 17C. The irregularity of the floor plan was imposed on the architects by the nature of the rocky base onto which the castle was built.

In the **Schloßmuseum**★ ⊘, 16C and 17C paintings from the Flemish and Italian schools are on display. The Abbess' Reception Room, the Throne Room and the Princes' Hall (mid 18C) can be visited.

EXCURSION

Gernrode – *7km/4.5mi to the south.*
Here, the **collegiate church of St.-Cyriacus**★, built at the end of the 10C, was designed with the three-aisle nave and flat ceiling characteristic of the Ottonian basilica. The crypt was excavated and the west chancel added at the beginning of the 12C. A late-12C baptismal font in the Romanesque style, together with the funerary plaque of the Margrave Gero, one of the convent founders, can be seen in the crypt. Upstairs, in the south aisle, is the **Holy Sepulchre group**★, a handsome and rare example of Ottonian sculpture.

RASTATT★

Baden-Württemberg
Population 50 000
Michelin map 419 T 8

Rastatt has never regained the prestige it enjoyed at the beginning of the 18C, when it was ruled by the **Margrave Ludwig of Baden** (1665-1707), known as **Ludwig the Turk** *(see KARLSRUHE)*. Faced by the threat of an invasion arising from the political ambitions of Louis XIV, the gallant captain abandoned the ruins of Baden-Baden and turned Rastatt into a stronghold, at the same time building a castle that was in line with his own ambitions.

The town is connected with two treaties between France and the Holy Roman Empire. The first, in 1714, ended the War of the Spanish Succession. The second in fact came to nothing: the congress discussing the enforcement of the Peace of Campo Formio, inaugurated in 1797, came to a tragic end two years later when two of the French plenipotentiaries were assassinated.

★SCHLOSS ⊘

Ludwig the Turk's enormous red-sandstone palace was designed by **Domenico Egidio Rossi**, the architect to the Viennese court. It was built between 1698 and 1707, and was only just completed when Ludwig died. The three wings of the castle, based on Italian models, enclose a vast state courtyard on the town side.

Royal Apartments – The nucleus of the central block is the tall, sumptuous **Hall of Ancestors** (Ahnensaal), with the column capitals decorated will stucco figures representing Turkish prisoners. The Margrave's apartments are in the south wing, those of his wife in the north. Both are richly embellished with frescoes and stuccowork. The **Collection of Porcelain** (Porzellankabinett) is worth seeing.

★ **Schloßkirche** – *Enter from Lyzeumstraße.* This Baroque church constructed between 1720 and 1723 by the architect **Michael Ludwig Rohrer** is attached to the north wing of the castle. The centrepiece of the magnificently decorated interior is the high altar, the columns of which have been hollowed and can be illuminated from inside. The legend of the Holy Cross is represented in the ceiling paintings. *Currently closed. Reopening date not known at time of going to press.*

Wehrgeschichtliches Museum (Military Museum) ⊘ – *On the ground floor of the main block (south side).* German military history from the end of the Middle Ages up to 1815 is displayed here. The exhibits include weapons, uniforms and pictures.

Schloß Favorite, Rastatt

Freiheitsmuseum (Liberty Museum) – *Also on the ground floor of the main block, but on the north side.* The displays here evoke the history of the 19C German Liberation Movement. The exhibition is oriented around the struggles arising from the 1849 Constitution of the Empire (the Baden War).

EXCURSION

★★ Schloß Favorite ⊘ – *5km/3mi to the southeast.*
This charming Baroque palace was built between 1710 and 1712 for the Margravine Sybilla Augusta, widow of Ludwig the Turk. The architect was again Michael Ludwig Rohrer, who had designed the church attached to her old apartments in Rastatt Palace. He coated the outside of this much smaller building with an unusual matrix of roughcast gravel and granite chips. The **interior★★** is particularly fine: floors of brilliant **scagliola** (stucco imitating encrusted marble), shiny as glass; mirror decorations; mosaics; chinoiserie. Note especially the **Florentine Room**, embellished with miniatures; the **Mirror Study**; Sybilla Augusta's apartments; sumptuous kitchen quarters with pottery from Frankfurt, Delft and Strasbourg; and a collection of Meissen, Nymphenburg and Chelsea porcelain.

RATZEBURG★

Schleswig-Holstein
Population 12 500
Michelin map 415/416 E 16

The island town of Ratzeburg is built attractively in the middle of a **lake★**, the biggest of many in the morainal hills between the Elbe and Lübeck. The tower *(129 steps)* rising from the woods on the eastern shore of the lake *(access via the Hindenburghöhe avenue)* provides the best **view★** of the town dominated by the squat outline of its cathedral.

★ Dom (Cathedral) – Brick-built and Romanesque in style, this 12C construction lies in a stretch of parkland on the northern point of the island. Outside, note the lavish gable decorations of the south porch, remodelled as a chapel. The entrance now is through doors beneath the tower. Above the high altar is an altarpiece in the form of a triptych, illustrating the **Crucifixion★** (1430), on the superb central shrine. Beautiful ecclesiastic vestments embroidered with gold thread may be seen in a chapel off the north aisle.

Ernst-Barlach-Museum ⊘ – *At no 3 Barlachplatz, in the town centre, beside the Peterskirche.*

The sculptor, artist, graphic designer and author Ernst Barlach (1870-1938), one of the leading exponents of German Expressionism, spent part of his youth in Ratzeburg and was buried here at his own request (suburban cemetery, Schweriner/Seedorfer Straße).

The 25 original bronze sculptures on display include *The Singer*, *The Flautist* and *The Reader*. There are also lithographs, drawings and woodcuts to be seen. The exhibition includes examples both of the artist's early work and from his years in Güstrow.

EXCURSION

Mölln - *11km/7mi to the southwest.*
A stage on the old Salt Road, this small town is famous for the memory of **Till Eulenspiegel**, whose tombstone is at the foot of **St Nicholas' church tower** (13C-15C). A statue of the celebrated jester, who died at Mölln in 1350, adorns the fountain in the market below. There are many lakes in the wooded countryside around Mölln (Seenlandschaft), the most popular of which is the romantic **Schmalsee★**, easily reached on foot from the Kurhaus Waldhalle.

RAVENSBRÜCK

Brandenburg

Michelin map 416 G 23 – 1km/0.6mi northeast of Fürstenberg

Built in 1938 on the shores of Lake Schwedtsee, and continuously extended over the next few years, Ravensbrück soon became Nazi Germany's largest camp for the detention of women: more than 132 000 women and 20 000 men of over 40 different nationalities were deported here until 1945. Conditions of work and the harshness of the imprisonment were so terrible that the camp had the highest mortality rate of any in Europe, with women, children and men dying in their tens of thousands.

Mahn- und Gedenkstätte Ravensbrück (Memorial) ⊘ – Evidence of the camp, the crematorium, the cell block and parts of the camp perimeter wall are still to be seen. Laid out in the SS camp commander's headquarters, a permanent exhibition evokes with horrifying realism the life (and death) of the victims through biographies and other exhibits, and also their solidarity and will for survival. By the lakeside, there is a monument in memory of the victims.

RAVENSBURG

Baden-Württemberg

Population 46 000
Michelin map 419 W 12

Ravensburg remains to this day an ancient Swabian town, bristling with many towers, still sheltering behind a well-preserved rectangular city wall. The road from Wangen passes beneath the Obertor, a gateway with stepped gables near the Mehlsack *(see below)*. At the end of Marktstraße is a block of old buildings comprising the Rathaus and the Blaserturm, a square clock tower with a polygonal coping and lantern.

The Mehlsack ("Sack of Flour") – In order to overlook and spy on the activities of the constables of Veitsburg, on a nearby hill, the burghers of Ravensburg erected this grey stone **tower**, which rises to a height of 50m/164ft. Looking out over the city wall from the top *(240 steps)*, the view extends as far as the church at Weingarten.

Liebfrauenkirche – A 14C building which has been completely modernized. It is worth visiting for its best-known work of art, which is exposed on an altar in the south aisle. This is a copy of **The Ravensburg Madonna★★**, a poignant 15C sculpture of the Virgin Mary in a mantle (the original is in the Gemäldegalerie in Berlin).

EXCURSION

★ **Wangen im Allgäu** - *23km/14mi to the east.*
Lying within sight of the first crests of the Allgäu Alps, this small Swabian town has been built with its colourful houses arranged in a simple cruciform plan, the two main streets crossing at right angles in **Marktplatz★**. Herrenstraße, running as it were from side to side, is lined with attractive houses, many with decorative shop signs. At the far end is the Ravensburger Tor (or Frauentor), a square gateway of which the 17C coping, confined by engaged turrets, is topped by an elegant ribbed roof. Perpendicular to this street, the other main thoroughfare ends at St. Martin-stor. Painted outside like the Ravensburger Tor, this entrance is crowned with a pyramidal roof, beneath which very finely worked gargoyles jut out.

REGENSBURG★★

Bayern
Population 138 000
Michelin map 420 S 20

Regensburg, originally a Celtic colony (Radasbona), later became a Roman garrison town *(Castra Regina)* guarding the natural frontier of the Danube at its most northerly point. Some evidence of Roman occupation remains (Porta Praetoria). The town was converted to Christianity by St Emmerammus in the 7C, and St Boniface founded a bishopric there in 739, making it a centre for religious life in the Middle Ages, a role reflected by the extraordinary density of religious buildings in the city centre. As the seat of the Bavarian dukes (6-13C), the town developed into an important trading post, and in 1245 it was made a Free Imperial City. The wealth and ambition of local merchants was manifested in the Italian style **towers** (Goldener Turm, Baumburger Turm) they had built all over town between the 12C and 14C. A 14C fortified gateway, the **Ostentor**, is all that remains of the medieval fortifications. Nowadays Regensburg is the economic and, not least thanks to its university, the cultural hub of eastern Bavaria.

The City of Diets – Once a Free Imperial City, Regensburg was privileged on occasion to be the seat of plenary sessions of the Royal Diet (Reichstag), which was charged with responsibility for the internal peace and external security of the immense and confused federation of states forming the Holy Roman Empire. From 1663 to 1806, date of the Empire's dissolution by Napoleon, the city was the seat of a **Permanent Diet** – the first indication of a continuing, overall German government. The Diet drew representatives from up to 70 other states to Regensburg.

OLD QUARTER *allow half a day*

Follow the itinerary suggested on the town plan below.

★ **Dom St.-Peter (E)** – Based on the design of certain French cathedrals, this pillared Gothic church has three naves and a non-projecting transept. Building began after 1260 and the major part of the work was completed by 1525, but the spires were not added until the 19C. The **Donkey Tower** (Eselsturm), above the northern part of the transept, is all that remains of the original Romanesque sanctuary built on this site.

The **west front**, richly decorated, is the work of a local family of sculptors named Roritzer. The main entrance, flanked by two neo-Gothic towers, is unusual, with a triangular, jutting porch. St Peter can be seen on the pier, and there are beautiful statues in the niches – particularly the meeting of the Virgin and St Elizabeth.

Go inside via the south porch.

The huge Late Gothic interior measures: 85m/279ft long and 32m/105ft high. On each side of the nave, the aisles are encircled by a gallery, that on the south side being supported by fine carved consoles. Two masterpieces of local Gothic

Regensburg (by a schoolchild)

Nübler/Fremdenverkehrsamt Regensburg

statuary – the Archangel Gabriel, and Mary at the Annunciation, by the Master of Erminold (c 1280) – stand in front of the west transept pillars. The three chancel windows are adorned with beautiful 14C **stained glass★★**.

Treasury (Domschatz) ⊘ – *In the south wing of the former bishops' residence (Bischofshof), entrance via the courtyard.* Liturgical items from the 11C to the 18C – vestments, chalices, monstrances, reliquaries – are on display here. Among the rarest and finest, note the Ottocar Cross (c 1430), a Venetian reliquary chest in the form of a tiny house (c 1430), and the Schaumberg Altar (1534-40), in the Zwölf-Boten-Kapelle.

Cloister (Kreuzgang) ⊘ – *Access through the cathedral garden.* This is divided by a central gallery paved with tombstones. On the right is the Romanesque **Allerheiligenkapelle**, on the walls of which are traces of ancient frescoes. Another gallery leads to the Alter Dom – the old 11C **Stefanskirche**, with an altar reliquary. This is a box-shaped, limestone monolith, hollow underneath, with blind windows, dating from the 10C or 11C.

★ **Diözesanmuseum St.-Ulrich** ⊘ **(E)** – The museum is installed in the **Ulrichskirche**, an Early Gothic galleried church (c 1225-40) decorated with 1 571 murals. Among other exhibits, visitors can see antique bishops' crosses (including the 12C Cross of St Emmerammus), fine medieval reliquaries, gold and silver plate, and religious paintings such as *The Legend of St Severinus* (a gift from the Regensburg Wool Merchants' Guild in 1456).

Taking the covered passageway that links the Herzogshof (Ducal Palace) with the massive quadrilateral of the Römerturm (Roman tower), visitors arrive at a wide, paved square, **Alter Kornmarkt★**, where a grain market used to be held.

★ **Alte Kapelle (E)** – The basilica of Our Lady associated with this chapel stands on the south side of Alter Kornmarkt. Originally Carolingian, Alte Kapelle was completely transformed in the Rococo style in the 18C. The two double oratories in the chancel, the splendid reredos, the painted ceiling and the gilded stuccowork executed by a Master of Wessobrunn, Anton Landes, combine to form a harmonious ensemble admirably set off by the light penetrating the tall windows.

Kassianskirche (E) – *Enter by the west door.*
A Romanesque basilica with pillars and later (18C) Rococo decoration. On the left of the main doorway, a Gothic low relief represents the Visitation. On an altar in the south aisle is a Schöne Maria (Lovely Mary) sculpture by Hans Leinberger, the Master of Landshut (1520).

Hinter der Grieb (D) – In this ancient alleyway with its old burghers' houses, the visitor is transported back to the Middle Ages. Looking back from the far end, there is a fine view of one of the cathedral spires.

★ **Haidplatz (D)** – A square surrounded by historic buildings, among which (at no 7) is an inn, **Zum Goldenen Kreuz**, with a grey-stone tower and façade, and a crenellated pediment. In the centre of the square is the 1656 **Justitiabrunnen** (Fountain of Justice).

★ **Altes Rathaus (D)** – The eight-storey tower of the old town hall dates from c 1250. The Gothic western section (Reichssaalbau) was built c 1360. The façade includes a gabled doorway and a pedestal supporting a charming oriel window which lights the Imperial Hall (Reichssaal).

Reichstagsmuseum ⊘ – The centrepiece of this museum is the splendid **Gothic hall**, where the "Permanent Diet" used to meet. In the same building the Reichsstädtisches Kollegium houses an exhibition tracing the history of all the Regensburg Diets.
On the ground floor, the interrogation room (Fragestatt) and the dungeons are also open to the public.

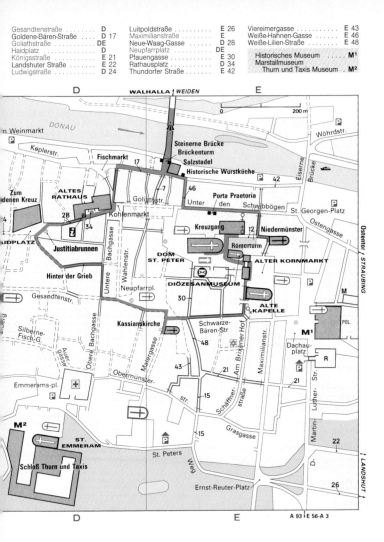

Fischmarkt (Fish Market) (D) – This is one of Regensburg's oldest market squares. It was built in 1529 in Italian style, as the original stone benches indicate. The fountain, Fischbrunnen or Georgsbrunnen, is one of three in Regensburg depicting local virtues; this one represents Fortitude.

Steinerne Brücke (Stone Bridge) (E) – Built between 1135 and 1146, this 310m/1 017ft bridge rests on no less than 16 arches. From the middle, there is a fine **view**★ of the old town, its medieval roofs dominated by the cathedral's spires. In the foreground is the 14C **Brückenturm** gateway, flanked, on the left, by the huge roof of the **Salzstadel** (early-17C salt loft). Beside this building, on the quayside, is the **Historische Wurstküche**, the oldest cooked sausage kitchen in Germany.

Porta Praetoria (E) – This is the remains of the north gateway of the ancient Roman stronghold Castra Regina, a garrison which covered an area of almost 25ha/62 acres. The west arch of the gateway and the east corner tower are all that are still standing.

Niedermünster (E) – A Romanesque basilica with two towers that was originally the church of a convent of nuns. The interior was remodelled in the Baroque style in the 17C and 18C. The stuccowork is good. The tomb of St Erhard, surmounted by an altar and baldaquin (c 1330), is in the north aisle.

ADDITIONAL SIGHTS

★ **St.-Emmeram** (D) – This was once the abbey church of an 8C Benedictine monastery. A Gothic gateway on Emmeramsplatz leads to a close from which visitors pass through the huge Romanesque **porch** (12C) to the double doors at the church entrance. The 11C **sculptures** by these doors (Jesus Christ, St Emmerammus and Dionysius) are among the oldest in Germany.

429

The original Romanesque aspect of the church was lost when the Asam brothers introduced a Baroque decorative scheme. Light from the clerestory windows highlights the ceiling's frescoes and stuccowork. Among the numerous tombs is the **tombstone of Queen Hemma**★ (c 1280), by the north wall, depicting the queen with an expression of profound sadness.

Schloß Thurn und Taxis ⊙ (D) – The Thurn and Taxis princes held the monopoly of German postal services until the 19C. As partial compensation for losing the monopoly, they were given the St. Emmeram abbey buildings. They occupied these as their home from 1816 and converted them into a good example of historicist style. Visitors can visit the state apartments (including the ballroom and throne room), with their fine fittings and furnishings, as part of a guided tour. The Romanesque-Gothic **cloister** ⊙, built between the 11C and 14C, can be visited separately. The Benedictus portal dating from the first half of the 13C is especially impressive.

The **Marstallmuseum (D M²)** houses a fine collection of coaches, sleighs and sedan chairs, with space allocated to ceremonial harnesses and riding accessories.

Thurn und Taxis Museum ⊙ – This branch of the Bavarian Nationalmuseum was installed in the north wing of the coach house in 1998, and regroups numerous handcraft items from the royal family's possessions. The collection is well presented in the available space. The most interesting exhibits are the gold work, clocks, furniture, porcelain and valuables dating from the 17C to the 19C.

★ **Historisches Museum** ⊙ **(E M¹)** – A former Minorite monastery, now deconsecrated, houses this museum, which traces the cultural and artistic history of Regensburg and eastern Bavaria from the Stone Age to the present day. In the 13C building's **Roman section** is the town's "Act of Foundation" – a stone slab 8m/26ft long on which an inscription recalls the implantation of the Roman garrison in AD 179. On the second floor there is an exhibition of paintings by **Albrecht Altdorfer** and other masters of the Danube School.

Schottenkirche St.-Jakob (C) – This sanctuary church was built at the beginning of the 12C for Irish monks. The Romanesque **main entrance**★ (north side) is famous for its statuary: on the tympanum, Christ is between St John and St James; above, on the frieze, the Saviour and the Apostles are flanked by Adam and Eve.

Dominikanerkirche (C) – A building that is bare to the point of severity – but nevertheless one of the oldest of all Gothic churches in Germany.

EXCURSIONS

★ **Walhalla** ⊙ – *11km/7mi to the east. Leave Regensburg on the Steinerne Brücke.*
Built between 1830 and 1842 by Ludwig I of Bavaria, this Doric temple – which seems strangely out of place in the Danube Valley – was intended to honour all the great men in German history (in Nordic mythology, Valhalla is the final resting place built by Odin for the souls of heroes who have died in battle, where they train to fight with the gods in the Last Battle by drinking until they drop every night, fighting to the death by day, and then rising to do it all over again). Inside the memorial are 121 busts of famous soldiers, artists, scientists etc and, beneath a gallery, 64 plaques of older or lesser-known heroes.
From the peristyle there is a good view of the river bend above which the temple is built, the ruins of Schloß Donaustauf, and the distant spires of Regensburg Cathedral.

★ **Befreiungshalle (Liberation Monument)** ⊙ – *32km/20mi to the southwest just outside Kelheim.*
The liberation is that of Germany from Napoleonic rule. It was, again, Ludwig I who conceived the idea of a memorial while returning from a visit to Greece in 1836. It takes the form of a huge rotunda, which was built between 1842 and 1863 by Bavarian court architect **Leo von Klenze**. The central hall is supported by 18 buttresses, each bearing an allegorical statue representing a Germanic people. The coping, which partly hides the cupola roof, is adorned with trophies. Inside, 34 victory tableaux form a homogenous ring. From the outside gallery *(staircase)*, there is a fine view of the Altmühl Valley.

★ **Kloster Weltenburg (Abbey)** ⊙ – *30km/19mi to the southwest.*
Set in a delightful landscape, right on the banks of the Danube, Weltenburg Abbey has a truly majestic appearance. The **abbey church** was built by Cosmas Damian Asam in 1718, with an ante-nave – or narthex – and a nave proper, both of them oval. The attention is drawn immediately to a statue of St George, theatrically illuminated in the central arch of the reredos by light from a hidden source. Visible through an aperture in the lower dome is a trompe-l'œil Asam composition in the upper dome on the theme of the Church Triumphant. Most of the sculptural decoration is the work of Cosmas' brother Egid Quirin Asam.

Bad REICHENHALL*

Built where the last of the Saalach gorges finally opens out, Bad Reichenhall is the city of salt. The cures at the spa are mainly for people with respiratory trouble. This thermal establishment extends for just over 1.5km/1mi along the busiest section of **Ludwigstraße**, the main street linking the St.-Zeno-Kirche with the bridge over the River Saalach.

The town has produced domestic salt since Celtic times. The success of the industry is based on the fact that the concentration of the mineral (a maximum of 24%) is the highest in Europe – and the fact that the salt derives from abundant springs, not from rock brine as at Berchtesgaden or the mines of the Salzkammergut.

Until 1958 the waters were piped through a 79km/49mi conduit (Soleleitung) to extraction and refining plants at Traunstein and Rosenheim; today, together with brine from Berchtesgaden, they are treated in new saline works at Bad Reichenhall itself.

St. Zeno-Kirche – *On the street that cuts across the northern part of the town*. This late-12C church (remodelled in the 16C and later decorated in the Baroque style) corresponds on the north side of the Alps to the well-known Romanesque church dedicated to the same saint in Verona. Lombard influence can be seen in the design and decoration of the main doorway, with its arch stones of alternating shades and slender outside columns resting on couched lions. On the tympanum, a Virgin and Child are depicted between St Rupert, first Bishop of Salzburg, and the patron saint himself, invoked in the Alps against flooding.

Bad Reichenhaller Salzmuseum ⊘ – Ludwig I of Bavaria had this salt-working plant built in 1834 in the so-called "Troubadour" style in vogue at that time. Entering the huge machine room, where two immense paddle wheels operate the pumps, visitors could imagine themselves part of a mid-19C steel engraving in *The Illustrated London News*. Beyond this, caverns and galleries with marble cladding lead to different catchment areas where some of the archaic equipment still works – for example the 103m/113yd transmission shaft which, thanks to five separate joints, actuates the pump at the Karl-Theodor spring.

Schloß RHEINSBERG*

The castle, in its idyllic location on Lake Grienerick, is inseparably linked with Kurt Tucholsky and his charming novella *Rheinsberg – A picturebook for lovers*, and above all with Friedrich II, or **Frederick the Great**, although he only lived here for four years.

These were however the four best years of his life. In retrospect he reflected "I have always been dogged with bad luck, the only place where I was happy was Rheinsberg". He had serious differences of opinion with his father, which led to an attempted flight to England (1730) and the execution of his friend Katte. His imprisonment, which was ordered by his father, ended when Frederick agreed to become engaged to Elisabeth-Christine of Brunswick. As a result, Friedrich Wilhelm I purchased the estate of Rheinsberg for his son in 1734 and furnished him with sufficient funds for converting the old 16C moated castle.

The building director of the Mark of Brandenburg, Johann Gottfried Kemmeter designed the Baroque structure with three wings. The Crown Prince and **Georg Wenzeslaus von Knobels-**

Frederick the Great as Crown-Prince by Antoine Pesne

J. P. Anders/Gemäldegalerie Preußischer Kulturbesitz

Schloß Rheinsberg

dorff, who took over direction of the site in 1737, were also involved in the planning. It was here that the young Frederick, in the company of his friends and in conflict with the philosophical ideas of his time, came to the conclusion that the Prince should be the "chief servant of his country". It was here too that his correspondence with Voltaire began, which lasted until the latter's death in 1778. In Rheinsberg, the master builder Knobelsdorff, the painter Antoine Pesne and the sculptor Friedrich Christian Glume created a style which was subsequently to reach its zenith in the Rococo of Frederick the Great in Charlottenburg and Sanssouci.

From 1752 to 1802, the castle was used as a residence by Prince Heinrich, Frederick's brother, who was not much liked by him. However Frederick was indulgent towards Heinrich, and apparently only once admonished him with the words "I cannot believe that you are serious in what you say. There is no doubt that neither you nor I are responsible for current events, and only when we have done everything in our power will our own conscience and the people grant us justice". During Prince Heinrich's time, under the management of Georg Friedrich Boumann the Younger, the corner buildings on the town side were built, an obelisk was erected in honour of the Prussian Generals in the Seven Years War and the Baroque garden was redesigned as a "natural landscape".

After the Second World War the castle was used as a sanatorium. Its complete restoration will take some considerable time, but already around 20 rooms can be visited.

TOUR ⓥ

The Corps de Logis or main structure, the central projection of which was the work of Knobelsdorff, is reached via a bridge. The building is enclosed by a roof parapet, which bears four statues, allegories of Rhetoric, Music, Painting and Sculpture. The colonnaded side wings end in round towers.

Interior – The hall of mirrors, the Bacchus Room and the anterooms with their remarkable ceiling paintings by Antoine Pesne are open to visitors. There are a large number of paintings, including a portrait of the Marquise de Sabran by Elisabeth Vigée-Lebrun, in the red room in Princess Amalie's quarters. The so-called Ferdinand apartment was designed in 1767 based on plans by Carl Gotthard Langhans. The same artist was responsible for the shell room in Prince Heinrich's quarters. The castle also houses the **Kurt-Tucholsky Memorial**.

Park – The garden dates back essentially to plans by Knobelsdorff and Johann Samuel Sello, and took account of Frederick the Great's particular interest in garden culture. The aim was to combine kitchen and pleasure gardens. The geometrical grid layout of paths was retained under Prince Heinrich, who had the park extended over onto the other side of Lake Grienerick (this side gives an attractive view of the castle). Most of the varied garden architecture from the Crown Prince's time remains, for example the sphinx steps, and the park gate with the figures of Flora and Pomona.

> **Kurt Tucholsky** (1890-1935), poet, short story writer and critic, he also wrote witty satirical essays, directed in particular at German nationalism and militarism. Much of his poetry was immortalised as German cabaret songs. Tucholsky left Germany in 1924, and eventually settled in Sweden. He was stripped of his German nationality and his work was banned by the Nazis in 1933; Tucholsky committed suicide in 1935.

Jürgen Henkelmann

RHINE VALLEY – Rheinland-Pfalz and Hessen
Michelin map 417 O 6 – Q 7

The river, 1 320km/820mi long, flows through four different countries and has often been a source of controversy between neighbours: below Basle, for instance, no town has ever completely settled both sides of the stream. At the same time it has always been a unique highway for the exchange of commercial, intellectual, artistic and religious ideas, a vital artery of the West.

Shipping companies today organize many **excursions and Rhine cruises**, especially from Cologne, Koblenz and Rüdesheim or Bingen.

The Rhine Legends – There is not, along the whole length of the river, a castle, an island, even a rock without its tale of chivalry or legend. **Lohengrin**, the Knight of the Swan, appeared at the foot of the castle of Kleve (Cleves); Roland escaped from Roncesvalles to arrive too late before the island of Nonnenworth, where his fiancée, inconsolable at the rumour of his death, had taken the veil (Roland in despair withdrew to the neighbouring castle of Rolandsbogen); at the **Loreley**, the Rock of Lore, a beautiful enchantress bewitched boatmen with her song, leading their vessels to disaster.

The outstanding legend associated with the Rhine however is the story of the Nibelungen, an inexhaustible source of inspiration from which Wagner borrowed both names and ideas for his opera tetralogy *The Ring* (*Walküre*, *Siegfried*, *Götterdämmerung* and *Rheingold* as Introduction). Inspired by Germanic and Scandinavian myths, the **Song of the Nibelungen** was probably composed towards the end of the 12C. It tells of the splendours of the 5C Burgundian court at Worms, and of the passions inflaming the hearts of its heroes, known also under the name of Nibelungen.

Brunhilde, the wife of the Burgundian king Gunther, learns from her arch-rival, the latter's sister Kriemhild, that it was not Gunther, but Kriemhild's husband Siegfried who had won her in the trial of strength which her suitors had had to fight to win her hand. Siegfried had however secretly been in love with Kriemhild all along.

Proud Brunhilde swears revenge. She persuades a fellow conspirator, Gunther's henchman Hagen (so the story goes), to murder Siegfried during a hunting party and then throw into the Rhine the Burgundian treasure which had been Siegfried's wedding present to Kriemhild. This is to stop Kriemhild using the treasure to pay someone to avenge Siegfried in turn.

Kriemhild has to wait 13 years for her revenge. Then, having in the mean time married Attila, the King of the Huns, she invites her three brothers and Hagen to a royal banquet at Etzelburg, in Hungary. But the feast turns out to be an ambush, which turns into a general massacre. Hagen, beheaded by Kriemhild with Siegfried's sword, takes the secret of the treasure's whereabouts with him to the grave.

W. Wilke/FOTOGRAM-STONE. Paris

Burg Gutenfels and the fortified island of Pfalz on the Rhine

The Loreley

From the Alps to the North Sea – At the beginning of its journey to the north, the Rhine is a typical Alpine river, with little water in the winter and a full flood after spring when the snows melt. Lake Constance (Bodensee), through which the Rhine flows, and the lakes of the Swiss plateau which drain into its tributary, the Aar, help to moderate this irregularity.

Reception of the Neckar at Mannheim and the Main at Frankfurt, each with a more regular flow, tend to even out that of the main stream, and the process is completed with the arrival of the Moselle at Koblenz.

After the exit from Lake Constance, rock outcrops from the Black Forest and the foothills of the Jura impede the force of the current and produce the famous Rhine Falls *(see the Michelin Green Guide Switzerland)*.

Further downstream, limestone strata result in rapids (Laufen). These obstacles, although they inhibit the use of shipping, do allow the installation of powerful hydroelectric projects. At Basle, the Rhine abruptly changes direction, veering north to follow and fertilize the subsidence fault separating the Vosges and the Black Forest. In Alsace, a canal draws off some of the excess water, but after Breisach this is fed only from power station dams.

From Bingen to Neuwied, north of Koblenz, the Rhine cuts its way through the Rhineland schist massif, where the hard rock – especially the quartzites exposed in the neighbourhood of the Loreley – can foment dangerous whirlpools. This so-called **"romantic" stretch** of river valley, with its alternation of vineyards, woods and impressive escarpments, punctuated by ruins perched on rock spurs, is the most picturesque part of what is known as the Rhine Gorge. Later, having passed through the industrial region around Duisburg, the river turns west and curls slowly across the plain towards the sea.

An Exceptional Shipping Lane – The traditional strings of Rhine barges, displacing anything from 1 000 to 2 000t each as they are towed, have been supplanted latterly by self-powered "auto-barges" and convoys towed or pushed by tugs which can comprise anything up to six 2 000 or 3 000t freight carriers.

Recent work carried out on the more difficult reaches upstream from St Goar have guaranteed shipping a uniform navigation channel 120m/394ft wide.

Today, the Rhine, navigable over the 850km/528mi between Rotterdam and Rheinfelden (upstream from Basle), handles an annual traffic of 265 million tons. Linked both to Rotterdam and to Antwerp, it boasts also in Duisburg-Ruhrort the world's largest river port (18 million tons annually).

Next in order of importance, on the river's German sector, are Cologne-Godorf, Karlsruhe, Ludwigshafen and Mannheim.

★★ THE LORELEY

① From Rüdesheim to Koblenz *75km/47mi – about 4hr*

This route, following the Rhine's east bank, passes through the wildest and steepest part of the valley, with splendid views of the castles and fortresses on the far side of the river.

After **Rüdesheim★** *(see entry)*, the road runs at the foot of terraced vineyards overlooked by the ruins of Burg Ehrenfels, built by the archbishops of Mainz at the same time as the Mäuseturm, a tower on the opposite bank to supervise the collection of tolls from shipping on the river. After Assmannshausen, silhouetted high up on the west bank, the castles of Rheinstein, Reichenstein and Sooneck appear one after the other. The crenellated tower of Fürstenberg, on the wooded slopes facing Lorch, marks the start of a more open stretch. And then the vineyards and towers of Bacharach slide into view. After that the fortified isle of Pfalz comes into view in the middle of the river.

Kaub – One of the outstanding landmarks in the valley, this village dominated by the restored ruins of Gutenfels is worth exploring on foot by way of Metzger-straße, the picturesque main street.

★ **Pfalz bei Kaub (Pfalzgrafenstein)** ⊘ – The massive five-sided keep of this **toll fortress** rises from the centre of the river, encircled by a turreted fortified wall.

Before a sharp, almost right-angled bend in the river, admire the **setting★★** of the towers of Oberwesel as they succeed one another at the foot of the Schönburg, on the far side of the water. The sharp bend, veering northeast and then northwest, leads to the most untamed stretch on this part of the Rhine.

★★★ **The Loreley** – This legendary spur, towering 132m/433ft above the rock-strewn river, has become the symbol of the Romantic Rhine and has a very special place in German literature. Heine's poem, *I Know Not Whence Cometh My Sadness*, set to music by Friedrich Silcher, is traditionally played aboard ship when the promontory appears around a curve in the valley.

St. Goarshausen – The town, strung out along the river bank (which makes a very pleasant walk), is dominated by the **Katz** (Cat) stronghold *(not open to the public)*, said to have been built to neutralize the **Maus** (Mouse), a little further downstream. From St.-Goarshausen, just beyond the famous rock, take the road signposted Loreley-Burgenstraße and drive up to the Hotel Auf der Loreley. From the car park, walk *(15min there and back)* to the **Loreley viewpoint★★**. There are impressive **views★★** plunging down into the "romantic gorge" from several accessible spurs here.

Wellmich – In the church of this small riverside town, there are traces (restored) of 15C wall paintings. Note: in the nave, the Crucifixion and the Last Judgement; in the Gothic chancel, the Legend of St Mary the Egyptian.

The Rival Brothers – *At Kamp-Bornhofen, turn right towards Dahlheim, and then right again at the sign "Zu den Burgen".*

The hill slopes become wild again. Beyond Kestert there is a fine **panorama★★**; from the ruins of **Liebenstein Fortress**, **Sterrenberg** and the valley below can be admired (the two castles are traditionally linked to an ancient legend concerning two rival brothers).

From Boppard onwards, where the Rhine swings lazily into a huge double loop, dense cultivation of vines appears and the landscape becomes less wild. Soon the fortress of Marksburg emerges on its promontory.

At Braubach, take the road to Nastätten.

★ **Marksburg** – The **castle** ⊘, the only one in the whole Rhine Valley never to have been destroyed, is built on a **site★★** above the river that is almost aerial. Particularly notable are the fortress' great battery, a medieval herb garden with more than 170 different species of plant, and a collection of armour ranging from 600 BC to the 15C.

Lahneck – *3km/2mi from Lahnstein, near the confluence of the Rhine and the Lahn.*

The ruins of this **fortress** ⊘, originally built in the 13C to protect neighbouring silver mines, were reconstructed in neo-Gothic style in the 19C. From the keep there is a view of the junction of the two rivers and the troubadour castle of Stolzenfels, on the far side of the Rhine.

Soon afterwards, the road arrives on the outskirts of Koblenz.

★★★ THE RHINE CASTLES

② From Koblenz to Bingen 63km/39mi – allow one day

This itinerary in effect retraces the previous one, in the opposite direction, on the other side of the river. Soon after leaving Koblenz, Lahneck comes into view again, with its tower overlooking the river confluence. Above, on the right, is Stolzenfels.

Stolzenfels – This enormous **castle** ⊘ was reconstructed, with its many crenellations, by Friedrich-Wilhelm IV in 1842. The style is now neo-Gothic, inspired by certain English manor houses. The sumptuous **interior**★ is arranged as a museum. From the slope against which Stolzenfels is built, the terrace offers a view of Koblenz and the citadel of Ehrenbreitstein.

Rhens – A town of pretty colour-washed houses with half-timbered facades. The old town hall juts out into the main street.

Gedeonseck – 1hr there and back, including 20min on a **chair-lift** ⊘.
Southwards, there is a superb **view**★ of the great convex loop of the Rhine as it flows around the Boppard curve.

Boppard – A residential town where several small valleys meet. The **Rheinallee** makes a particularly pleasant riverside walk. Near the quay, the Gothic Carmelite church with its single tower still has its 15C choir stalls, and a very fine Renaissance funerary monument depicting the Eternal Father receiving the dead Christ.

The beginning of the "romantic" Rhine Gorge is marked by the two Rival Brothers fortresses (*see above*) on the opposite slopes. After Hirzenach, the Cat and Mouse towers are visible, standing above St.-Goarshausen.

St. Goar – The village, clinging to the hillside at the foot of the impressive **Burg Rheinfels★★** ⊙, commands with St.-Goarshausen the Loreley passage. The river here, obstructed and narrowed by the legendary rock, swirls and eddies dangerously as it races through the defile. Rheinfels, which threw back the assaults of Louis XIV, was until it fell to the French in 1797 the most powerful fortress in the whole valley. It is worth climbing to the top of the clock tower to get an overall view of the turbulent Rhine, the Cat and Mouse castles, and the maze of towers, gates, courts and casemates comprising the Rheinfels complex.

The banks of the river remain steep and heavily wooded until Oberwesel.

Oberwesel – South of the town, the Gothic **Liebfrauenkirche★** has a fine high altarpiece, one of the oldest in Germany (early 14C), a Gothic rood screen and, in the north aisle, a most unusual 1510 triptych illustrating the 15 cataclysms presaging the end of the world.

From the terrace of **Schönberg Castle★**, a little further on, there is a view of Kaub, on the far side of the river, and the fortified

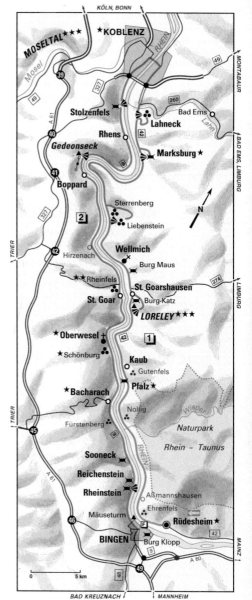

isle of Pfalz. Schönberg is in fact a block of three forts sheltered by a common – and impressive – defence wall.

Pfalz, with the Gutenfels ruins perched on the heights far above it, is an astonishing sight: a massive stone ship, anchored in the middle of the fast-running river.

★ **Bacharach** – Once the property of the counts of the Palatinate, Bacharach – a town of vineyards and ancient towers, relics of medieval fortifications – is one of the most popular resorts in the Rhine Valley. The houses in **Marktplatz** and **Oberstraße**, wooden-walled and decked with flowers, are a delight. One of the last Romanesque naves built in Germany can be seen in **Peterskirche**, although its four-stage elevation (arcades, galleries, triforium and clerestory windows) already heralds French Gothic. The ruins of the Gothic **Wernerkapelle** are nearby. The ruined towers of Nollig and Fürstenberg mark the end of the valley's most grandiose stretch; from here onwards it is less winding, the river running between the steep eastern bank, topped by a few vines, and the cliffs on the opposite shore. The road on this side passes below castles whose sites are ever more audacious, from Sooneck to Reichenstein and finally Rheinstein.

Burg Sooneck ⊙ – This fortress is much restored and tiered to suit the terrain with a maze of staircases, platforms and terraced gardens beneath the turrets.

Burg Reichenstein ⊘ - Well-situated at the mouth of a rural valley, this neo-feudal castle has a fine collection of arms and hunting trophies.

Burg Rheinstein ⊘ – The castle is perched on a perpendicular rock spur, in a commanding position above the Rhine. From the foremost watchtower there is a **bird's-eye view**★★ of the valley.

Once past the **Mäuseturm**, balanced on its tiny islet in the middle of the river, the valley widens out and the east bank becomes covered with terraced vines.

Bingen – Founded by the Romans at the confluence of the Rhine and the Nahe (Castel Bingium), this small river port today serves chiefly the wine-growing hinterland.

Burg Klopp, an ancient stronghold built by the bishops of Mainz, has been razed to the ground more than once – in particular by the troops of Louis XIV in 1689, during the "Orléans War". From the terrace there is a fine **view**★ of the Binger Loch, between Hunsrück and the hills of the Rheingau, upstream from the Niederwald monument on the outskirts of Rüdesheim.

ROMANTISCHE STRASSE★★

Baden-Württemberg and Bayern

Michelin maps 419 folds 6-38/420 folds 17-42

From the Main Valley to the foot of the Bavarian Alps, by way of peaceful valleys and an idyllic, rolling countryside, the "Romantic Road" tourist itinerary recalls at every stage of its course some aspect of the past that could only belong to the history of Germany. As the route unfolds, It evokes life in the great medieval cities (Rothenburg, Nördlingen and Dinkelsbühl), the religious sensibility of artists like Tilman Riemenschneider, the prestige of German chivalry (Bad Mergentheim), the sumptuously Baroque character of the old episcopal courts and such imperial towns as Würzburg and Augsburg.

FROM WÜRZBURG TO ROTHENBURG o. d. T.

100km/62mi – about 4hr

Leaving **Würzburg**★★, B 27 winds down towards the valley of the Tauber, which it reaches at Tauberbischofsheim.

★ **Bad Mergentheim** – *See Bad MERGENTHEIM.*

Weikersheim – Once the seat of the Hohenlohe princes, this small town has retained its 18C architectural unity, especially noticeable in the layout of the market, built in a semicircle on the palace side to provide a splendid vista.

The **castle** ⊘ was built between 1580 and 1680 on the banks of the Tauber, in a sober style divorced from Baroque influences. Two hundred years of decorative art (c 1550-1750) are illustrated by the remarkable collection of **furniture**★★. The magnificent **Knights' Hall**★★ (Rittersaal), completed in 1603, is typical of the transition between the Renaissance style and the Baroque. Note the sculptured figures above the monumental doorway of emperors and empresses. The perspective of formal gardens (1710), peopled with statues in caricature in the style favoured by the Franconian courts of the period, ends in a charming perforated orangery.

The picturesque section of the run, in the narrow part of the Tauber Valley, begins above the attractive town of Bieberehren. The road rises and falls over slopes covered at times by natural woodland, at times by orchards, above the willow-fringed river banks. Occasionally the stream forms a loop to feed a sawmill or watermill. This countryside is at its loveliest in springtime.

Creglingen – The isolated **Herrgottskirche** – about 1.5km/1mi along the road to Blaufelden – contains the precious **Altarpiece of the Virgin Mary**★★ sculpted by Tilman Riemenschneider. The theme of the Assumption in the central motif has permitted the artist to translate all his own sensitivity into the attitude and expression of the Madonna.

Detwang – In the church at Detwang another Riemenschneider **altarpiece**★ portrays the Crucifixion.

★★★ **Rothenburg ob der Tauber** – *See ROTHENBURG OB DER TAUBER.*

FROM ROTHENBURG o. d. T. TO DONAUWÖRTH

105km/65mi – about 5hr

Feuchtwangen – A small town with an attractive market place surrounded by pretty houses and overlooked by a parish church housing another **Altarpiece of the Virgin** - this time the work of Albrecht Dürer's teacher, Michael Wolgemut. Near the café Am Kreuzgang there is a Romanesque **cloister**. Installed in a 17C peasant house is a **Museum of Franconian Folklore** (Heimatmuseum) displaying fine rustic furniture with regional pottery and costumes.

A. Forkel/Touristik Service Dinkelsbühl

Dinkelsbühl

★ Dinkelsbühl – Ramparts and watchtowers still surround this medieval town which wakes up every year in mid July with a colourful children's festival (Kinderzeche) commemorating the relief of Dinkelsbühl in the Thirty Years War (*see Calendar of events*).

The **Georgskirche★** has retained its Romanesque tower. The interior, a Gothic hall-church, is a remarkable sight, with all three naves decorated with skilfully designed fan vaulting. Among the town's many ancient buildings, note the **Deutsches Haus★** (*Am Weinmarkt*), and its richly decorated Renaissance façade, as well as the **Hezelhof** (*Segringer Straße 7*), remarkable for the long, two-tiered balconies hung with flowers that overlook its inner courtyard.

The undulating landscape of the Feuchtwangen-Dinkelsbühl region is supplanted, after Nördlingen, by the bleak wastes of the **Ries Basin**. This practically treeless depression amid the heights of the Swabian Jura forms a symmetrical bowl 20km/12mi across and a regular 200m/656ft deep, which is thought by some geologists to have been caused millions of years ago by the fall of a gigantic meteorite.

Wallerstein – From the summit of the rock, reached by a pathway and then steps cut in the strata, there is a vast panorama over the Ries Basin (*access via the Fürstlicher Keller*).

WHERE TO STAY IN DINKELSBÜHL

OUR SELECTION

Kunststuben – Segringer Straße 52, ☎ 0 98 51/67 50, Fax 0 98 51/55 35 27. Single rooms from 70DM. Very friendly small hotel incorporating an artist's workshop.

Zum Goldenen Anker - Untere Schmiedgasse 22, ☎ 0 98 51/5 78 00, Fax 0 98 51/57 80 90. Single rooms from 80DM. This inn has good, spacious rooms decorated in a rustic style. Traditional Franconian cooking.

Goldene Rose – Marktplatz 4, ☎ 0 98 51/5 77 50, Fax 0 98 51/57 75 75. Single rooms from 85DM. A 500-year-old house in the historic town centre. Fine half-timbering.

Blauer Hecht – Schweinemarkt 1, ☎ 0 98 51/58 10, Fax 0 98 51/58 11 70. Single rooms from 99DM. Smart hotel in a former brewery inn dating from 1684. Some of the furnishings in the rooms are antiques. Rustic old German restaurant.

Travellers' addr

★ **Nördlingen** – See NÖRDLINGEN.

Schloß Harburg ⊙ – A large fortified castle whose buildings, considerably enlarged and remodelled in the 18C, look down on the picturesque houses of a village tightly packed along the banks of the Wörnitz. On display are extensive **collections**★ of sculpture, ivory, enamel, tapestry and gold and silver plate.

Kaisheim – The former Cistercian **abbey church** (Zisterzienserkloster) was built at the end of the 14C in the full flower of the Gothic era. Around the chancel, very pure in style, is a 12-sided **ambulatory**★ with ogive vaulting, divided into two galleries. *(To visit, apply at the presbytery.)* The abbey itself is now used as a prison.
The valley of the Wörnitz, commanded by Schloß Harburg, peters out after a final, narrow, twisting section, allowing the Ries to connect with the Danube Valley.

Donauwörth – On a hillside running steeply down to the Danube, the town is dominated by the **Heiligkreuzkirche**. The large 1720 Baroque building, with its concave interior galleries, is decorated with Wessobrunn stuccowork.

FROM DONAUWÖRTH TO FÜSSEN

148km/92mi – about one day

This drive along the ancient Via Claudia, one of the main arteries of the old Holy Roman Empire, owes its interest less to the route (which follows the Lech Valley, by now largely widened) than to the historical souvenirs evoked by the sites on the way. These include **Augsburg**★★, **Landsberg**★, **Königsschlösser**★★★ and (well worth the price of a small detour) **Wieskirche**★★.

ROSTOCK★

Mecklenburg-Vorpommern
Population 240 000
Michelin 416 D 20

Rostock, with its widespread port installations, shipyards and huge fishing fleet, was until reunification East Germany's only major sea outlet to the Baltic and the rest of the world. In order to get some idea of the scope of maritime activity in this city of 500 000 people, a **boat trip** ⊙ around the International Port is strongly recommended.

A busy (and coveted) port – A particularly choice situation on the wide Warnow estuary favoured the development of Rostock from its earliest days: by the beginning of the 13C, the town was already a member of the Hanseatic League, was minting its own money and was in the process of asserting its independence from the princes of Mecklenburg. In 1419, Rostock founded the first Baltic university, which earned it the nickname of "Light of the North". Such a position and such a reputation soon excited the envy of powerful and covetous neighbours. The Danes and then the Swedes occupied the city during the Thirty Years War (1618-48), returning for a second time while the Nordic countries were struggling for supremacy in the war raging from 1700 to 1721. Nor was the port spared during the Napoleonic Wars; it was occupied by French troops until 1813.

SIGHTS

★★ **Marienkirche** (CX) – *Am Ziegenmarkt.*
The building as it is today – an imposing basilica in the form of a cross – results from a transformation in the second half of the 15C of a hall-church built in the previous century. It is one of the biggest churches in northern Germany.
The massive tower, lightened by pierced sections, was not completed until the end of the 18C. From the top there is a **panorama**★ of the city and the dock area.
Inside the church, the overriding impression is one of height and verticality. Note especially the 1472 **astronomic clock**★★ (its face was remodelled in 1643), which comprises a calendar valid until the year 2017. The delicately worked bronze **baptismal font**★, decorated with scenes from the life of Christ, is supported by the figures of four men. The Baroque organ dates from 1770.

Rathaus (Town hall) (CX R) – *Neuer Markt.*
This is composed of three 13C-14C gabled houses topped by a brick-built arcaded gallery supporting seven towers. In front of the block is a Baroque façade added in 1727. Across the square stand some fine gabled houses.

★ **Schiffahrtsmuseum** (Navigational Museum) ⊙ (CX M') – *At the corner of August-Bebel-Straße and Richard-Wagner-Straße.*

ROSTOCK

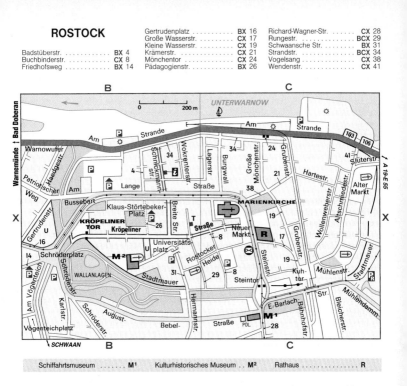

Schiffahrtsmuseum . . . . **M¹**   Kulturhistorisches Museum . . **M²**   Rathaus . . . . **R**

Models, paintings and navigational instruments chart the history of maritime activity from the time of the Vikings to the present day. Note in particular the full-size reconstruction of a tramp steamer bridge, and a model of the present international port.

Kröpeliner Straße (BCX) – This pedestrian precinct, crossing the old city from the Rathaus to the Kröpeliner Tor, has become the town's shop-window and commercial centre. It is bordered by the familiar gabled houses dating from Baroque and Renaissance times. At no 82, the brick façade of the old (late 15C) Heilig-Geist-Spital presbytery is distinguished from the other buildings by a stepped gable.

★ **Kröpeliner Tor (BX)** – The 14C brick gate, six floors high, closes off the western end of Kröpeliner-Straße. The interior has been turned into a **museum** evoking the history of the town (Stadtgeschichtliches Museum).

★ **Kulturhistorisches Museum (Historical Museum)** ⊘ **(BX M²)** – Collections of paintings and sacred art are displayed in this former Cistercian convent joined to Heilig-Kreuz-Kirche – a brick-built, triple-aisle hall-church dating from the late 13C. On the late-15C **Altarpiece of the Three Kings★**, the background gives a good idea of Rostock in the Middle Ages.

EXCURSIONS

★ **Warnemünde** – *11km/6mi to the northwest.*
This one-time fishing village, "bought" by the town from the Prince of Mecklenburg in 1323, has become Rostock's most popular holiday beach. From the ferry terminal, services run to Denmark. Warnemünde has also become the most important German destination port for cruisers from all over the world. In summer, some 50 such floating hotels are moored here.

Bad Doberan – *15km/9mi to the west. See Bad DOBERAN.*

★ **Fischland, Darß and Zingst** – *To the northeast of Rostock.*
The peninsular chain of Fischland-Darß-Zingst is an attractive natural area in which woods, salt-marshes, moorland and broad stretches of water alternate. The narrow tongue of land extends northwards and eastwards parallel to the mainland, separated from it by a lagoon (flat bays) in which brackish water from the Baltic and freshwater from the rivers leading down to it mingle. The artists' village of **Ahrenshoop** in the slightly hilly **Fischland** is a very popular Baltic resort. The holly tree is especially characteristic of the Ahrenshoop woods. **Darß and Zingst** form part of the National Park of the West Pomeranian lagoon area. The **sea eagle** nests here, and during the spring and autumn, whole colonies of cranes can be seen. The quiet charm of the salt-marshes with their typical flora, such as samphire and sea asters, bewitches many a visitor. The contemplative nature of the little villages and seaside resorts with their reed-covered houses and cottages makes them especially attractive.

ROTHENBURG OB DER TAUBER★★★

Bayern
Population 12 000
Michelin map 419/420 R 14

One of the oldest towns on the "Romantic" tourist road, Rothenburg overlooks four ox-bow bends in the River Tauber from its rocky crag. As well as being old, the town is both picturesque and unspoiled. Once behind the ramparts in the car-less central enclave, the visitor faced with Rothenburg's ancient houses, street signs, fountains and narrow, cobbled lanes seems all at once in some kind of time-warp plunged back into the mid 16C.

HISTORICAL NOTES

The Burggarten spur, whose steep-sided promontory is enclosed within the tightest of the ox-bow curves, was a strongpoint, according to tradition, as far back as the time of King Pharamund. What is certain is that, from the 12C onwards, two castles – the first imperial, the second belonging to a count – stood successively on this rock platform so ideally placed to command the winding valley below. At first the town itself was small; the outline of its earliest circle of fortifications can be seen, with two towers (Markusturm and Weißer Turm), in the arc formed by the Judengasse and the Alter Stadtgraben.

In the 13C the town spread out... then lost both its castles, destroyed in an earthquake in 1356. From then on the ambition of the local Rothenburg worthies inclined more and more towards the building, and then the embellishment, of such public works as might enhance their own importance: the Rathaus, Jakobskirche, the long line of merchants' houses, with their impressive gables, on the Herrngasse.

But Rothenburg, now won over to the Protestant side, failed to recover from the recession and economic stagnation engendered by the rigours of the Thirty Years War. Reduced to the status of an obscure regional market, too poor even to rebuild its houses in line with the prevailing taste, the town vegetated ingloriously throughout the 17C and 18C, unable to expand beyond its own walls. In the 19C however this very antique aura became an asset: strict preservation orders were placed on the steep-roofed houses with their tall gables, inherited from the Gothic period; no staircase turrets or corner oriels could be dismantled. Tourists of today, therefore, are granted a genuine glimpse into the past.

They will notice that half-timbering above a stone base or foundation is the general building rule, although roughcast or pebble-dash usually hides the beams. In the Spital quarter, nevertheless, the woodwork of many lovely old houses remains exposed.

A Long Drink (Meistertrunk) – During the Thirty Years War, the Protestant Rothenburg fell to the Imperial army commanded by General Tilly. Tilly decided to raze the town. All pleas for mercy having been rejected, the burgomaster as a last resort offered the victorious general a goblet of the very best local wine... and the miracle occurred. His heart warmed by generosity, Tilly offered a way out. He would spare the town if some eminent local could empty in a single draught a hanap (a 6-pint tankard) of the same wine. A man named Nusch, a former burgomaster, succeeded in this exploit and Rothenburg was saved (the after-effects on the courageous drinker are not recorded).

Every year now, on the three days of the Pentecost (Whitsun) weekend and certain other occasions, the population of Rothenburg takes part in a huge fête which is in effect a reconstitution of this event *(see Calendar of events)*.

★★★ OLD TOWN (ALTSTADT) *allow 3hr 30min*

Starting at Marktplatz, follow the itinerary marked on the town plan.

★ **Rathaus (Town Hall)** – The Gothic part, its gable topped by a 60m/197ft belfry,
is 14C, while that facing Marktplatz, with its octagonal staircase tower, is a Renaissance work, completed by an 18C portico. Visitors can inspect various state or council chambers, or climb the tower for a **view**★ of the fortified town.

North of Marktplatz is the gable of an ancient inn, the Ratstrinkstube, on which the figures of a clock re-enact mechanically *(at 11am, noon, 1pm, 2pm, 3pm, 9pm and 10pm)* the famous legend of the Long Drink.

Baumeisterhaus – The steps on the gables of this Renaissance house serve as pedestals for dragon motifs. Statues on the first floor represent the seven cardinal virtues, those on the second the seven deadly sins.

Mittelalterliches Kriminalmuseum (Museum of Medieval Justice) ⊙ – Medieval attitudes towards crime and dissidence are reflected in this museum installed in the former headquarters of the Knights of the Order of St John of Jerusalem. Law

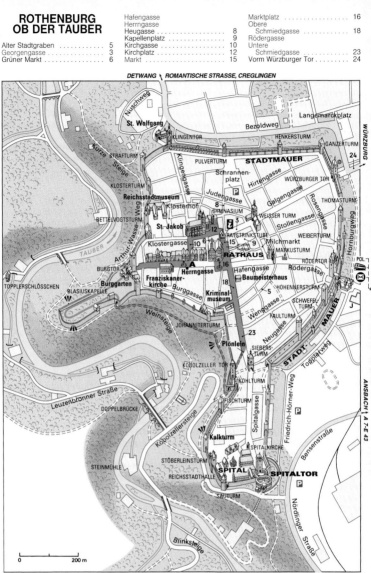

books, seals, engravings, along with instruments of torture, punishment and execution are exhibited on four different floors. Among the most typical are a spiked chair used in witchcraft trials, iron-collared yokes, and "masks of shame".

Plönlein – A picturesque corner formed by the bifurcation of two streets, one level, one descending – but both ending at the same fortified gateway.

Leave the town by the Koboldzell gate, on the right, turn sharp right again, and follow the path circling the spur some way below the ramparts.

In the valley below, there is a remarkable arched, two-storey, **fortified bridge** (Doppelbrücke) which crosses the Tauber. Return to the old town via the Burggarten.

Burggarten – All that remains of the double fortress erected on this promontory is a chapel, the Blasiuskapelle, which has been turned into a war memorial, and a fortified gateway, the Burgtor. The area is now a public garden with views of the river, the two tier bridge, the Topplerschlößchen (a riverside tower oddly topped by apartments) and, some way to the north, the village of Detwang.

Herrngasse – The mansions of formerly well-known personages line this busy commercial street. Those interested should look into some of the courtyards, for instance no 15 (**A**), where the half-timbered gallery rests on embossed wooden pillars.

ENJOYING ROTHENBURG

WHERE TO STAY

Zum Greifen – Obere Schmiedgasse 5, ☎ 0 98 61/22 81, Fax 0 98 61/8 63 74. Single rooms from 64DM. Inn near the town hall. Simple, good value accommodation.

Spitzweg – Paradeisgasse 2, ☎ 0 98 61/9 42 90, Fax 0 98 61/14 12. Single rooms from 95DM. Peaceful hotel in the centre of town, in a building dating from 1536.

Romantik-Hotel Markusturm – Rödergasse 1, ☎ 0 98 61/9 42 80, Fax 0 98 61/26 92. Single rooms from 150DM. Former 13C toll house, later a brewery and an inn. Comfortable rooms with some antique furnishings.

Burg-Hotel – Klostergasse 1, ☎ 0 98 61/9 48 90, Fax 0 98 61/94 89 40. Single rooms from 160DM. Fine hotel located by the town wall with a good view of the Tauber Valley. Tasteful and original decor in guestrooms.

WHERE TO EAT OUT

Mittermeier – Vor dem Würzburger Tor 9, ☎ 0 98 61/9 45 40, Fax 0 98 61/94 54 94. Single rooms from 98DM, main courses from 28DM. Country house style hotel by the town wall. Good, inventive cooking.

Louvre – Klingengasse 15, ☎ 0 98 61/8 78 09, Fax 0 98 61/48 81. Main courses from 38DM. Small restaurant and exhibition gallery with an artistic atmosphere.

St.-Jakobskirche – Building of the Gothic church's east chancel started in the mid 14C. The foundation of the west chancel is penetrated by a vaulted passageway that leads to the Klingengasse. This chancel also houses the most precious work of art: Tilman Riemenschneider's **"Holy Blood" altarpiece**★★ (1504).

The composition of the main scene, the Last Supper, is original. Judas is shown from behind, facing Christ. The expressions are tense and perplexed, except for that of Jesus, which is full of compassion.

The east chancel overlooks a square on which stands the 1593 Renaissance building of the former college (Gymnasium).

ADDITIONAL SIGHTS

★ **Spital (Hospital)** – A picturesque group of buildings, mostly 16C and 17C, built on the southern extremity of the plateau known locally as the Kappenzipfel (peak of the cap).

There are works of art in the Gothic chapel and, in the middle of the courtyard, the Hegereiterhäuschen – a graceful pavilion with a pointed roof and turrets.

From the hospital courtyards, the **Kalkturm** viewpoint can be reached (also accessible from outside), with its **view**★ over the town centre and the watch-path linking the Stöberleinsturm and the Sauturm.

★ **Stadtmauer (The Ramparts)** – Constructed in the 13C and 14C, these ramparts, complete with gates and towers, are still in a state of perfect preservation. Long stretches are open to the public. Near the hospital, the southern entry to the town is defended by the **Spitaltor**★, a massive 16C bastion enclosing two inner courtyards, both oval.

Wolfgangskirche – North of the Klingentor. A curious late-15C Gothic church, fortified and incorporated into the barbican doubling the defences of the gateway. The casemates and the parapet walk can still be viewed.

Franziskanerkirche – The rood screen, as well as walls and columns in this church, are decorated with fine 15C and 16C sculptures. Note also, on the left above a funerary niche, the Creglingen Madonna (1400).

Reichsstadtmuseum ⊘ – A Dominican monastery from 1258 to 1544, this building is now a local museum showing, among other collections in its spacious, oak-beamed rooms, the Rothenburg Stations of the Cross (1494). Perhaps the most fascinating exhibit is the original hanap drained by ex-Burgomaster Nusch in front of General Tilly *(see above)*. The tankard's design depicts the emperor and the seven electors. It was made in 1616.

ROTTWEIL ★

Baden-Württemberg
Population 24 000
Michelin map 419 V 9

Rottweil, a charming, fortified town on a spur circled by a meander in the Upper Neckar, occupies a pleasant site, between the Swabian Jura and the Black Forest.

The town was founded in 1140 by the Zähring duke Konrad and became a Free Imperial Town in 1268. In the 15C it joined in an "everlasting league" with the Swiss Confederation. Traces of the Baroque era are still evident, in the church buildings in particular. Part of Württemburg since 1802, Rottweil has become a tourist centre.

Old Alemannic customs still dictate events on Shrove Tuesday, with the celebrations culminating in the famous **Rottweiler Narrensprung** (fools' parade) when traditional carved wooden masks are worn.

Rottweiler Narrensprung

SIGHTS

It is best to park in car park P 1 (am Kriegsdamm) or P 2 (Nägelesgraben). Both are only around 2min walk from the town centre.

★ **Old town** – The almost fully preserved late medieval town centre with its burghers' houses adorned with oriels (Hauptstraße) and its fountains is just as remarkable as the churches and museums.

From Hauptstraße there is a delightful **view**★ of the distant Swabian Alps.

Heiligkreuzmünster – *On the left, past the Rathaus.*
The Late Gothic minster was built between 1430 and 1534. On the top of the church there is a crucifix which is attributed to the leading Nürnberg master Veit Stoß (c 1445-1533). **Altarpieces**★ from various periods decorate the side chapels. These include the Late Gothic St Peter's altarpiece in the north side aisle, the St Nicholas altarpiece in the south side aisle and the Virign Mary and Apostles altarpieces, both dating from the 15C. The 17C chancel is richly carved.

Outside, on the square in front of the minster, stands the Georgsbrunnen, a Gothic fountain ornamented with three charming sculpted figures: the Virgin Mary, St George and St Catherine.

Go through the Pfarrgasse, left along Schulgasse and then onto Kriegsdamm.

Dominikanermuseum ⓥ – The museum owes its name to a Dominican monastery which was founded on this site in 1266. Of the monastery buildings, only the Baroque church remains. The architecturally attractive museum, which was built in 1992, exhibits the most important local finds dating from Roman times. The beautiful **Orpheus Mosaic**★ from the 2C AD, which is composed of 570 000 small stones, is well worth seeing. In addition the museum houses a high quality collection of **Swabian sculptures**★ from the 14C to the 16C with works by famous artists (Multscher, Michel Erhart).

Take Lorenzgasse to Lorenzkapelle.

Lorenzkapelle – This former cemetery chapel was built in 1580, and now houses a collection of **Rottweil stonemasonry**. It displays the best work produced by the Rottweil stonemason's lodge in late medieval Swabia.

Turn left, and take Hauptstraße back to the town's central crossroads.

Kapellenkirche – The **tower**★ of this Gothic church, Baroque on the inside, is a splendid example of the Flamboyant style. The square base, quartered with graceful staircase turrets, supports on the façade an unusual pierced loggia. The upper part of the tower, in two octagonal tiers, is lit by windows with a fine tracery of stonework.

The three entrances retain their original Gothic carvings: the Last Judgement (west face) and the Knight's Betrothal (right corner turret) are outstanding.

EXCURSION

★ **Dreifaltigkeitsberg (Trinity Hill)** – *20km/12mi to the southeast.*
A minor road leads up to the pilgrimage church here from Spaichingen, on the edge of the Swabian Jura. From the top of the hill a wide **panorama**★ includes the Baar Depression and, in the distance, the dark outline of the Black Forest.

RÜDESHEIM AM RHEIN★

Hessen
Population 10 000
Michelin map 417 Q 7 – Local map see RHEINTAL

The wine town of Rüdesheim lies at the southern end of the Rhine Gorge – where the river, deflected westwards through the Rheingau vineyards by the Taunus massif, decides to turn north again. Here at the Bingen Gap, gateway to the "Romantic Rhine", Rüdesheim has become the most popular tourist centre in the whole valley: the narrow streets, including the famous **Drosselgasse**, are crammed with visitors, attracted by the wine bars offering a taste of the celebrated local Riesling. There are also distilleries to be visited and cellars where sparkling wine can be drunk.

Brömserburg – Residence-cum-refuge for the bishops of Mainz until the 13C, this stronghold passed into the hands of the knights of Rüdesheim, and then became a meeting-place for brigands. It was retaken in 1281 by Archbishop Wernherr. Today, it is arranged as a **wine museum**. The outstanding exhibits are 21 old winepresses and a collection of amphorae (vases, jars, bins for storage or transport of wine).

EXCURSIONS

Niederwald Monument – *Access by road (2km/1mi) or by cable-car (terminal on the Oberstraße: 20min there and back).*
Built (1877-83) to commemorate the re-establishment of the German Empire in 1871, the monument comprises a statue of Germania (which alone weighs 32t) on a plinth with bronze bas-relief sculptures showing Bismarck, Emperor Wilhelm I, the German princes and their armies. From the terrace there is a **view** of the vineyards, Bingen, and the confluence of the Rhine and Nahe. The heights of the Palatinate are visible in the distance.

★ **The Rheingau** – *23km/14mi – allow 2hr.*
A southern exposure allows successful cultivation of vines high up on the foothills of the Taunus. Before passing through these vineyards to reach Eberbach Abbey, the road passes the picturesque villages of Geisenheim, Winkel and Hattenheim.

SELECTED HOTELS

Rüdesheim

Trapp – Kirchstraße 7, ☎ 0 67 22/9 11 40, Fax 0 67 22/4 77 45. Single rooms from 115DM. Peaceful but central location. Welcoming atmosphere.
Rüdesheimer Schloß – Steingasse 1, ☎ 0 67 22/29 62, Fax 0 67 22/34 85. Single rooms from 160DM. Historic building dating from 1729. Designer furnishings in rooms.

Rüdesheim-Assmannshausen

Altes Haus – Lorcher Straße 8, ☎ 0 67 22/4 03 50, Fax 0 67 22/4 03 51 50. Single rooms from 80DM. Half-timbered house dating from 1578, located in the town centre. Very comfortable rooms.
Jagdschloß Niederwald – On the road to the Niederwald Monument, ☎ 0 67 22/10 04, Fax 0 67 22/4 79 70. Single rooms from 185DM. Former hunting lodge in the middle of a landscaped park.

★★ Kloster Eberbach – *See Kloster EBERBACH.*

Kiedrich – The 15C **church** in this wine-growers' market town is still furnished in its original, rare Flamboyant form: the early-16C carved **pews★★** and choir stalls are still adorned with polychromatic embellishment; they still have their Gothic inscriptions. The 14C **Kiedrich Madonna★**, beneath the rood screen, shows French influence.

Eltville – The oldest town in the Rheingau makes a picturesque scene with its narrow streets and fine old town houses dating from the 16C and 17C. Built beside the Rhine, the castle here was the residence of the prince-electors of Mainz in the 14C and 15C. Living quarters in the tower can still be viewed. In the church of St Peter and St Paul *(Rosengasse 5)*, there is a very fine baptistry from the Mainz studio of Hans Backhoffen, with the symbols of the Four Apostles worked into the base.

Insel RÜGEN★

Mecklenburg-Vorpommern
Michelin 416 C 23-24

Joined to the mainland by a long bridge (2.5km/1.5mi) straddling the straits opposite the town of **Stralsund★**, Rügen is Germany's largest island. In a total area of 926km²/358sq mi, the Baltic island offers a surprising variety of scenery. In the west, as the straits widen towards the open sea, the coastline is indented, following the irregular contours of many inlets. Chalk cliffs and sandy beaches in the east attract summer crowds; the wooded southern shores face the wide, shallow waters of the Greifswalder Bodden (Gulf); and to the north Rügen is cut almost in two by the deep, extraordinarily jagged penetration of the Jasmunder Bodden – which is practically an inland sea.

The poet, travel writer, historian and polemicist **Ernst Moritz Arndt** (1769-1860) was born on Rügen.

MAIN SIGHTS

★ Putbus – The "white town" in the southeast of the island was founded in 1810 by Prince William Malte of Putbus, in imitation of Bad Doberan, as a royal seat and bathing resort. Although the princely castle was demolished in 1960, the neo-Classical town has miraculously remained. A surprising harmonious picture of a homogenous whole, such as is rarely found in Germany, greets the visitor. It is not without justification that Putbus is known as "the pearl of Rügen".

★ Circus – The round circus, from which the roads radiate in a star shape, is surrounded by eave-fronted houses, many with neo-Classical ornamentation. Finished in dazzling white, they stand out from the green of the oaks. The 21m/69ft high obelisk, which bears the Prince's crown on the top, stands in the centre of the circus.

★ Theatre – *Alleestraße.* The building was erected between 1819 and 1821 by the Berlin architect Steinmeyer (a student of Schinkel). The portico is made up of four Tuscan columns. Above the entrance, a blue stucco frieze, depicting Apollo and the Muses, stands out from the bright white of the building. The theatre is famous for its acoustics.

★ Schloßpark – The 75ha/185 acre Schloßpark with its **orangery** (converted in 1853 by Friedrich August Stüler), **royal stables** and **parish church**, is laid out in the style of an English landscape garden.

Jagdschloß Granitz ⊙ – *South of Binz.* In 1837 Prince William Malte I of Putbus had a hunting castle, the most important secular building on the island, built in the neo-Gothic Tudor style on the 107m/351ft high Tempelberg, the highest point in Eastern Rügen. The four crenellated corner towers of

SELECTED HOTELS ON RÜGEN ISLAND

Binz

Villa Schwanebeck – Margarethenstraße 18, ☎ 03 83 93/20 13, Fax 03 83 93/3 17 34. Single rooms from 120DM. Fully restored villa in the style of spa architecture.

Strandhotel Lissek – Strandpromenade 33, ☎ 03 83 93/38 10, Fax 03 83 93/38 14 30. Single rooms from 130DM. Carefully restored spa architecture with great attention to detail. Modern comforts. Some rooms give a fine view of the Baltic Sea.

Villa Salve – Strandpromenade 41, ☎ 03 83 93/22 23, Fax 03 83 93/3 26 53. Single rooms from 150DM. Jugendstil building from the turn of the century, catering for every comfort.

Am Meer – Strandpromenade 34, ☎ 03 83 93/4 40, Fax 03 83 93/4 44 44. Single rooms from 150DM. Modern architecture with some features from the turn of the century.

Putbus

Am Bodden – In Lauterbach. Chausseestraße 10, ☎ 03 83 01/80 00, Fax 03 83 01/8 00 20. Single rooms from 75DM. Modernised inn.

Wreecher Hof – Kastanienallee, ☎ 03 83 01/8 50, Fax 03 83 01/8 51 100. Single rooms from 155DM. Peaceful hotel village located off the beaten track, with reed-thatched buildings. Modern comfortable rooms, many with living room area.

the square castle rise up in the middle of Granitz woods. A 38m/125ft high viewing tower was built in the inner courtyard in 1844, based on plans by Karl Friedrich Schinkel. The viewing platform is reached up the 154 steps of the fine cast-iron **spiral staircase** (recommended as a subject for amateur photographers). From the top, the **view**★★ of Rügen Island is breathtaking. The rooms inside the castle are open to the public.

★ **Bathing resorts** – These are all in the southwest of the island. Binz, Sellin, Baabe and Göhren await the visitor with their inviting sandy beaches, beautiful seaside resort architecture and a woodland backdrop.

They can be reached in the "Rasender Roland", a little train that connects Putbus to Göhren (via Granitz).

Saßnitz – Ferries to Scandinavia leave from this port. There are very beautiful beech forests in the north.

★★ **Stubbenkammer** – The **Königsstuhl**, a 117m/384ft high cliff, towers over the impressive chalk bluff which projects out into the sea. If you are lucky enough to visit on a sunny day you will see the breathtaking sight of the white cliff,

---

Störtebeker

Klaus Störtebeker is one of the more colourful characters from this stretch of the Baltic coast. This notorious pirate is said to have been born in the village of Ruschwitz on Rügen in 1370. As a young man, feeling thirsty one day while at work, he seized his master's tankard of beer and took a generous gulp of the contents. Unfortunately, he was seen by his employer, who had him chained up and beaten. Störtebeker was so strong, however, that he managed to break free of his chains and set about thrashing his tormentors. He then fled in a fishing boat which took him as far as the cape of Arkona, where he made the acquaintance of a certain Michael Gödecke, leader of a band of brigands whose reputation struck terror into all those who sailed the seas anywhere near this stretch of coast. He passed a number of trials of strength with flying colours, thus qualifying to join the band. Having embarked on his new career, he became one of the most feared buccaneers of his age as he proceeded to scour the seas, until he was betrayed by one of his followers, eventually being run to ground in Hamburg in 1401 and condemned to death beneath the guillotine. As a mark of the respect he commanded, his last request, that the lives of some of his companions arrested with him should be saved, was granted.

Legend has it that Störtebeker hid his booty beneath the cliffs of the Stubbenkammer, and once a year a ship in full sail, steered by a phantom crew of buccaneers, is said to haunt this part of the coast. Every summer, at Ralswiek, several of the islanders put on a play commemorating the adventurous life of this local anti-hero, scourge of the rich and benefactor of the poor.

JÜRGENS OSTEUROPA, Köln

The Königsstuhl at Stubbenkammer, Rügen

surrounded by green foliage, shining brightly above the deep blue sea. This postcard idyll (marred nowadays only by the many visitors) also inspired the painter Caspar David Friedrich.

*★ Kap Arkona** – Kap Arkona, with its 50m/164ft high chalk cliffs, is the northernmost point of the island. The **old lighthouse** ⊘, a square three-storeyed brick building on a granite base, was built in 1826-29 based on plans by Karl Friedrich Schinkel. There is a wonderful **view★★** from here right across to the neighbouring island of **Hiddensee**. Not far from the lighthouse, an embankment recalls the Jaromarsburg fortification, which was built there by the Slavs, but was destroyed by the Danes in 1168.

EXCURSION

*★ Hiddensee** – *For details of* **ferry connections** ⊘, *consult the Admission times and charges chapter at the end of the guide. Motor traffic (except service vehicles) is forbidden on the island. We recommend catching the ferry from Kloster and hiring a bicycle once on Hiddensee. Allow 5hr to visit the island.*

Hiddensee Island, the little "pearl of the Baltic", is to be found 17km/10mi off the west coast of its larger neighbour, Rügen. Like the neighbouring peninsula of Fischland, Darß and Zingst *(see ROSTOCK)*, it falls almost entirely within the boundaries of the Nationalpark Vorpommersche Boddenlandschaft. The island belongs to the few Central European natural coastal landscapes, with towering cliffs, land spits, lagoons and deeply incised coastal inlets, which are all undergoing continual change. The island's relief was sculpted by retreating Scandinavian glaciers some 10 000 years ago and rises to its highest point in the north, at the **Dornbusch** peak (72m/236ft), site of the island's trademark **lighthouse**, put into operation in 1888 and measuring 28m/90ft in height. There is a good view from the top terrace of the lighthouse of the Bessin sand spits stretching away along the coastline. This landscape is ideal habitat for migrating birds in the spring and autumn. The Neue Bessin is growing at a rate of 30-60m/100-200ft a year, due to accretion.

Hiddensee Island is crisscrossed by footpaths and cycle paths, giving visitors ample opportunity to explore the individual villages and other sights. The small village of **Grieben** is famous on the island for its fine thatched houses. The village of **Kloster** has developed into a pleasant bathing resort. The graveyard next to the church here is the final resting place of writer **Gerhart Hauptmann** (1862-1946), best-known for his Naturalist dramas. Hauptmann's summer residence, **Haus Seedorn** on Kirchweg street, is open to the public. The island's administrative centre is at **Vitte**, which has evolved from a fishing village to a tourist resort. Heading south from Vitte, the countryside is a charming one of vast dunes interspersed with marshland (Dünenheide). **Neuendorf**, the island's most southerly village, has its fishermen's houses arranged along an east-west axis, so that the living area is facing the sun.

The island's most southerly point is Gellen, formed of shifting sands and growing at an annual rate of 5m/16ft.

RUHRGEBIET

RUHR BASIN – Nordrhein-Westfalen

Michelin 417 L 4 – M 9

The Ruhr Basin (5 000km²/1 930sq mi) lies between three rivers: the Ruhr, the Rhine and the Lippe, and is home to a total population of 5.4 million. The infrastructure provided by the rivers encouraged settlement here in pre-Roman times. However, it is the last two centuries with the rise of mining and heavy industry that left their mark most noticeably on the landscape and employment structures of the Ruhr Basin. This has tended to overshadow the fact that, for example, Duisburg already had a town charter by the 12C and Dortmund was a member of the Hanseatic League.

The Ruhr is still one of the world's most important industrial centres. A large proportion of German steel production is manufactured here; Duisburg inland port is the largest in Europe and the largest river port in the world. The landscape in the north of the region is shaped by the chemical industry and ultra-modern mining operations, reaching depths of 1 000m/3 300ft or more. To the south, the perimeter strip is home to staff-intensive businesses, heralding the light industry of the hillsides delimiting the Ruhr Valley, the Bergisches Land.

Since the period following the Second World War, the **Ruhrfestspiele** have held a special place in the Ruhr-Rhine region's annual calendar of events. Theatres, opera houses, and even local churches host national and international figures in performances of theatre or classical music.

INDUSTRIAL RE-ORGANISATION

Numerous towns and cities that had spread and virtually merged with one another during the course of industrialisation make up the dense concentration of urban settlement, seemingly with a life of its own, between Duisburg and Dortmund. Characteristically, people from the Ruhr Basin identify themselves more with their home region than their home town. The prevalent attitude in the Ruhr Basin is deeply influenced by lively activity and constant change. This is not least down to the centuries-long influx of workers from every country in the world.

Since the 1960s, there has been a shift away from the heavy industry with which the Ruhr Basin was once overwhelmingly identified, to service industries. Only a small proportion of the workforce is now employed in traditional industries such as coal mining and iron and steel production. Mergers by steel companies and pit closures led to a steady rise in unemployment, which it was and still is necessary to counteract with imagination and pragmatism. In the mean time, 60% of the workforce are now employed in the service indus-

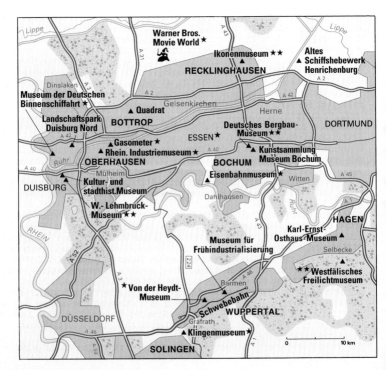

tries sector. The main objective of Ruhr Basin economic policy is to continue to attract new branches of industry to the region and establish new firms there. Research and education are also being encouraged, with six universities and nine colleges of further education training executives in the most state-of-the-art technologies in some cases.

THE RUHR BASIN GETS A NEW IMAGE

The reorganisation of the Ruhr Basin has been and is being implemented in a variety of ways. The legacy of heavy industry has been seized upon as an opportunity of reworking the Ruhr's old "Black Country" image and using it to create a region characterised by a new culture and activities. The Emscherpark international construction exhibition, the Westphalian and Rhineland countryside associations, and the Ruhr Basin municipal association have agreed upon and implemented year-long projects for reconstructing countless industrial plants that had been closed down.

In this way, for example, one of Europe's most modern shopping centres has sprung up on a disused factory site in **Oberhausen**. CentrO occupies 70 000m²/753 200sq ft and offers shoppers some 200 shops and boutiques. For those vital breaks, there are 20 restaurants and bars, as well as variety performances, jazz, cinema and concerts. Old pits and factories are not only doing business, but have been converted in many cases into **industrial museums**. In this way they give educational insight into the production methods and social history of heavy industry.

MUSEUMS AND SIGHTS OF THE RUHR BASIN
AND BERGISCHES LAND (IN ALPHABETICAL ORDER)

Bochum

Kunstsammlung Museum Bochum ⊘ – *Kortumstraße 147, opposite the park.*
The collections in this spacious, airy modern building concentrate mainly on **contemporary East European art** and modern art from Germany (including Gruppe Zero).

★★ **Deutsches Bergbau-Museum (German Mining Museum)** ⊘ – *Am Bergbau-Museum 28.*
Founded in 1930, this museum is on the site of the old Germania mine (recognizable by its 68m/223ft pithead frame). On more than 9 300m²/ 100 000sq ft of floor space it gives a complete picture of mining from antiquity to the present. Models, reconstructions, graphics and original equipment cover every aspect of extraction, along with such techniques as drilling, ventilation and the use of explosives. Fifty feet underground, in the **Schaubergwerk**, more than 1.5km/1mi of abandoned workings have been restored to illustrate various methods of coalface extraction and transport. There are demonstrations of modern mining machinery. The tour of the mine workings ends with a trip to the top of the 68m/220ft high mining tower. There is a good view of Bochum and the surrounding area from the platform.

★ **Eisenbahnmuseum (Railway Museum)** ⊘ – *At* **Bochum-Dahlhausen**, *C.-Otto-Straße 191, halfway between Essen and Bochum. Car park.*
Founded by a society of railway enthusiasts, this museum is installed in a disused station and rolling-stock repair shop on the north bank of the Ruhr. Equipment dating from 1914 (an engine house, a turntable, a hydraulic crane) is for the most part still in mint condition. More than 100 machines

Bochum – Deutsches Bergbau-Museum

Deutsches Bergbau-Museum

451

that ran on rails retrace the evolution of this form of transport from the beginnings to the end of the steam era. The highlights of the collection are 15 **steam locomotives**, the oldest of which is a Prussian T-3 of 1882. A postal locomotive built by AEG in 1913 marks the start of electrification. Railcars, hand-operated gangers' trucks, many types of wagon and a rail-or-road motor bus can also be seen. Map printing. **Train trips**.

Bottrop

Quadrat ⊘ – *Im Stadtgarten 20 (near town centre)*.
The Constructivist work of Bottrop painter and educational art theorist Josef Alber gave rise to the name of this museum centre. The former Bauhaus lecturer called the pictorial results of his research on changing effects of colour *Hommage an das Quadrat* (Homage to the Square). True to its origins, the museum is dedicated to Constructivism. The adjoining **sculpture park** contains works by Max Bill, Donald Judd, Norbert Kricke etc.
Next to the Quadrat is the **Museum of Pre- and Local History**. The **Ice Age Hall**★ houses Germany's largest Quaternary Era collection.

★ **Warner Bros. Movie World** ⊘ – *In Bottrop-Kirchhellen, via A 31, exit Kirchhellen*. This 40ha/100-acre film and amusement park, under the motto "Hollywood in Germany", will take your breath away, with a total of 27 different attractions and shows. They include the Bermuda Triangle with its rapids and raging waterfalls, the **Batman adventure** in the breathtaking flight simulator, the **Police Academy Stunt Show**, which presents a robbery with plenty of thrills and surprises, a 3D animated film theatre, the **Neverending Story**, which includes a trip on rapids through caverns and gorges, the breakneck Lethal Weapon roller-coaster and the studio tour with its special effects.

Batman at Warner Brothers Movie World

Visitors finding themselves in need of a little peace and quiet can visit the **Museum of German Film History**★, a look back over 100 years of film in Germany, which also traces the development of photographic and film cameras, beginning with the camera obscura.

Dortmund – *see DORTMUND*.

Duisburg

★★ **Wilhelm-Lehmbruck-Museum** ⊘ – *In Duisburg town centre, Kantpark*.
The "European Centre for Mmodern Sculpture" is home to over 700 20C sculptures and objets (Arp, Barlach, Beuys, Calder, Dalí, Giacometti, Kollwitz, Kricke, LeWitt, Magritte, Moore, Tinguely, Uecker etc). Part of the museum is given over to an exhibition of works by Duisburg sculptor Wilhelm Lehmbruck (1881-1919) which were considered quite radical in their day. The surrounding park (7ha/17 acre) contains outdoor sculptures by international artists against a backdrop of the area's original trees.

Kultur- und stadthistorisches Museum ⊘ – *At Duisburg river port*.

In addition to a large numismatic collection, part of which dates from Celtic days, this museum contains some impressive amber work from its partner museum at Königsberg. A highlight of the collection is the section with globes and atlases dedicated to Dutch cartographer Gerhardus Mercator, who died in Duisburg in 1594.

★ **Museum der Deutschen Binnenschiffahrt** ⊙ – *Duisburg-Ruhrort, Apostel-straße 84.*
The swimming pool at Ruhrort was given to the townspeople at the turn of the century, in order to improve standards of hygiene in this part of town. It was intended to take the place of a bathroom, which was a rarity in most industrial workers' houses at that time. The building has been preserved and is now in use as a museum, illustrating the history of shipping from dugouts to modern transport craft. The **museum ships** are 10min walk away along a path through Ruhrort port.

Landschaftspark Duisburg Nord – *In Duisburg-Meiderich, Emscherstraße 71. Car park.*
The centrepiece of the park is the disused Thyssen iron and steel works with its three blast furnaces towering skywards. The various foundry and compression halls now host cinema, concerts and other events. The old sintering area has been converted into an amphitheatre. This is the best place from which to appreciate the Jonathan Park's **lighting effects** ⊙. A total of 126 relays bathe the iron and steel works in a new flood of colour every four seconds with the aid of 400 lamps.

Essen – *see ESSEN.*

Hagen

Karl-Ernst-Osthaus-Museum ⊙ – *Hochstraße 73.*
This museum steeped in tradition dates back to industrialist and patron Karl Ernst Osthaus, who founded the Museum Folkwang for art and crafts here in 1902 (the collections were donated to the city of Essen in 1922), with the aim of bringing the fine arts to this culture-starved region and to its socially deprived inhabitants. The museum is housed in a Wilhelminian building with Jugendstil interior decor designed by Henry van de Velde. There is a collection of furniture and craft work from this period on display.
Part of the collection of 20C German art begun in 1945 (including works by Kirchner, Nolde and Dix, among others) consists of paintings and drawings by the artist Christian Rohlfs, who worked in Hagen until his death in 1938.
The collection has been augmented with contemporary art from Germany and abroad.

★★ **Westfälisches Freilichtmuseum (Open-Air Technical Museum)** ⊙ – *At Hagen-Selbecke, in the valley of Mäckingerbachtal. Leave Hagen heading south on the Frankfurt, then the Eilpe road. At Eilpe, turn right towards Breckerfeld-Halver and continue for just over 1.5km/1mi to Selbecke. From the museum car park (Museumsparkplatz), on the left of the road, 15min on foot.*
Along 2.5km/1.5mi of this valley, more than 70 installations or buildings have been reconstructed to illustrate the evolution of crafts and techniques in Westphalian industry. Traditional metalwork displays (at the foot of the valley) include giant iron and copper hammers activated by water from artificial lakes. A half-timbered 18C house has been turned into a **Blacksmith Museum** with a working forge. There are also examples of James Nasmyth's steam hammer (c 1840) and the zinc rolling mill of Hoesch (1841), both of which marked the start of true industrialization.
Higher up the valley an 18C paper mill houses a **Printing Museum**. Finally there is a whole village of traditional craftsmen, where not only saddlers and smiths and rope makers and dyers, but also bakers and brewers ply their trade. *We recommend visiting on weekday mornings to see the craftsmen in action.*

Oberhausen

★ **Gasometer** ⊙ – *Oberhausen new town centre (near CentrO shopping centre).*
The present exhibition hall used to be Europe's largest blast furnace gas storage tank in its heyday (117.5m/385ft high, 68m/220ft in diameter, built in 1928-29). The outside staircase has 592 steps leading up to the viewing platform, from where there is a view over the site of the 1999 regional garden show towards the lower Rhine. Inside, a panoramic lift takes visitors up to a height of 106m/350ft. The impressive spatial effect of the rotunda opens out from the second level.

★ Rheinisches Industriemuseum ⊘ – *In Oberhausen town centre (behind the main station), Hansastraße 18.*

The Altenberg zinc works was closed down in 1981, after 130 years of processing raw zinc from Mülheim and Essen. The heavy industry museum was housed in the old rolling hall. It is dedicated not only to the history of technological progress since the mid 19C, but also underlines the political and economical importance of iron and steel production to the Rhine and Ruhr regions. Original components from the factory building have been retained and incorporated into the exhibition, eg the 9m/30ft high steam power hammer dating from 1900.

Recklinghausen

★★ Ikonenmuseum (Icon Museum) ⊘ – *Kirchplatz.*

The marvellous specimens exhibited here are arranged by theme: the Holy Trinity and the Celestial Hierarchy (a theme rich in symbolism); the Virgin Mary; the Saints and their Days (a splendid calendar of all the religious feasts). To these are added a collection of iconostases (screens separating the sanctuary from the rest of the church).

Altes Schiffshebewerk Henrichenburg ⊘ – *In Recklinghausen-Waltrop, Am Hebewerk 2.*

In 1899 Emperor Wilhelm II inaugurated this construction, which was one of a kind at the time. It provided a means of bridging a stretch of land with a 14m/46ft difference in height via the Dortmund-Ems canal (1892-99), the waterway to the North Sea. The Westphalian industrial museum now illustrates how the ship's hoist, which has been restored, works. It also contains displays on the technical, political and economical requirements of canal building, and life and work on and along the canal. The museum ship **MS Franz Christian** gives an insight into life aboard a canal boat.

Solingen

★ Klingenmuseum (Blade Museum) ⊘ – *At Solingen-Gräfrath. Car park at the museum.*

Known the world over for its knives and its scissors, Solingen is the centre of fine metalwork in Germany. The museum is located in the former Gräfrath Abbey, an elegant Baroque building charmingly converted with considerable imagination by Joseph Paul Kleihues, making the architectural backdrop to the exhibits well worth taking note of. The museum traces the history of side arms (magnificent dress swords). A further highlight of the collections is the cutlery, and by extension tableware, from the 18C, which give those visitors less interested in matters military plenty to admire. The museum basement houses the treasury of the neighbouring church of St. Maria Himmelfahrt.

From the abbey gardens, go down some steps to the historic **Marktplatz**. The houses around the square have been restored in the traditional half-timbered style of the Bergisches Land, with slate shingles cladding roofs and walls and green wooden shutters at the windows.

Wuppertal

★ Von der Heydt-Museum ⊘ – *At Wuppertal-Elberfeld.*

This museum, housed in the old Elberfeld town hall (1827-42), has an interesting collection of paintings and sculpture. The museum is named after the Wuppertal family of bankers, the Von der Heydts, who were its generous patrons. The collections include 16C and 17C Flemish and Dutch painting; French and German painting from the 19C to Impressionism, Expressionism (Kirchner, Beckmann), Fauvism, Cubism (Braque) and the present. Sculptures from the 19C and 20C are also on display (Rodin, Maillol). The cafeteria was designed by French artist Daniel Buren.

Museum für Frühindustrialisierung (Early Industrialization Museum) ⊘ – *At Wuppertal-Barmen.*

Housed in a disused factory, this museum traces the economic and social history of the Wupper Valley since the mid 18C.

Schwebebahn (Cable railway) – An interesting mode of transport for getting around Wuppertal is the cable railway (1898-1903). This is the world's oldest suspended railway for transporting passengers and is also one of the safest means of public transport, carrying 22.6 million passengers a year. Most of the station buildings date from the turn of the century.

For a quiet place to stay, consult The Red Guide Deutschland, published annually, which offers a selection of pleasant and quiet hotels in a convenient location.

Rising on high ground at the eastern extremity of the Thüringer Wald, the River Saale flows 427km/265mi to the north before joining the Elbe upstream from Magdeburg. Its winding course forms a natural link between such towns as Jena and Halle, masterpieces of sacred architecture like Merseburg and Naumburg, and the innumerable castles – Heidecksburg, Weißenfels, Dornburg – built on its banks.

The itinerary suggested below heads south through a countryside of woods and fields and small market towns to an attractive upland region dotted with lakes, in a corner formed by the old East- and West-German demarcation line and the Czech frontier.

FROM RUDOLSTADT TO SAALBURG

61km/38mi – allow 4hr

Rudolstadt – Once the seat of the princes of Schwarzburg-Rudolstadt, this town is dominated by the fine silhouette of **Schloß Heidecksburg**★ ⊙, which dates from 1737. Several **rooms**★★ magnificently decorated in the Rococo style are open to the public.

Saalfeld – In medieval times, Saalfeld was among the most important towns in Thuringia, thanks to local silver and copper mines and a position on the main trade route to Bohemia which assured its commercial prosperity.

The Renaissance **Rathaus** in Marktplatz is designed around a façade that centres on a staircase tower with two oriel windows. On the other side of the square, the **Stadtmarktapotheke** (pharmacy) is one of the rare Romanesque (restored) buildings in the area. The **Johanniskirche** displays a late-14C Last Judgement above its main entrance. Several altarpieces from a Saalfeld studio (late 15C) can be seen in the **Thüringer Heimatmuseum** ⊙, which has been installed in a former Franciscan abbey.

★ **Feengrotten (Fairy Grottoes)** ⊙ – *1km/0.6mi southeast of Saalfeld on B 281.* Stalactites, stalagmites, concretions and petrifications... such near-magical subterranean decor can be found in the abandoned galleries of this disused mine.

Leave Saalfeld on B 85. Cross the Saale at the Hohenwarte dam.

Saalfelder Feengrotten

Saalfeld Fairy Grottoes

The artificial lake at **Hohenwarte** (Hohenwarte-Talsperre) curves for 10km/6mi, in a series of wide arcs magnificently incorporated into the existing landscape. Woodland scenery alternates with crops as the road crosses the plateau.

Via Drognitz and Remptendorf, the suggested route arrives at the Bleiloch reservoir. Driving across the dam, sightseers regain the river's east bank.

This reservoir, 29km/18mi long, with an enormous volume of water retained, is the largest of the five artificial lakes between Blankenstein and Saalfeld.

Saalburg – Now a lakeside town, Saalburg lost part of its outskirts when first the valley was flooded. Remains of the 16C fortifications, however, can still be seen.

SAARBRÜCKEN★

Saarland

Population 200 000

Michelin map 417 S 5

The capital of the Saarland was first mentioned in the record books in AD 999, although it dates back to Celtic and Roman times. During the 1C, the Romans built a vicus (small market town) at a river crossing of the Saar, crossroads of the Metz to Worms road and the link between Trier and Strasbourg. They also built a stone bridge over the river, which was used right up to the Middle Ages. The medieval settlement was the seat of the counts of Saarbrücken. In 1321 it was given the status of a town, together with St Johann on the north bank of the Saar. It came to the house of Nassau by marriage in 1381.

Baroque Saarbrücken – In 1738 Count Wilhelm Heinrich von Nassau (1741-88) summoned the master builder **Friedrich Joachim Stengel**, who originally came from Zerbst, to the court in Saarbrücken. A time of intensive and fruitful building activity began, and the city's architecture today owes its character to the large number of buildings that have been preserved. The castle, the Ludwigskirche, the collegiate church in St.-Johann, all originate from this period. Under the influence of Palladio, Stengel created impressive works in a Classical Late Baroque style. Alt-Saarbrücken was therefore to gradually take on a new aspect, from 1752, as the seat of the court. During the 19C, industrialisation along the Saar brought Saarbrücken economic growth, change and prosperity, but also monostructure. In 1909 (Alt) Saarbrücken, St Johann and Malstatt-Burbach joined together to become the city of Saarbrücken, following the incorporation of St.-Arnual in 1896. Although it was seriously damaged during the Second World War, the city has developed into a regional metropolis, especially since 1950, when it became the capital of the 11th German province and completed the secession of the Saarland from France. It has since taken full advantage of its border situation.

Saarbrücken, full of the joys of living – People from the Saarland in general, and those from Saarbrücken in particular, are extremely convivial and enjoy celebrations. They will find any excuse to celebrate. You only have to visit the St.-Johann market in the old city to see what we mean. Ludwig Harig, a well-known Saarland writer, once said: "People from Saarbrücken iron out differences, they can lead the wolves to the lambs", which sums up the Saarlanders' flexible and tolerant mentality extremely well.

ALT-SAARBRÜCKEN *(on the south bank of the Saar)*

Schloß – The medieval fortress was succeeded at the beginning of the 17C by a Renaissance castle, which was demolished in 1738 to make way for a Baroque castle designed by the court architect Friedrich Joachim Stengel. Wars and conversion work left deep marks, so that reconstruction was necessary in 1982 and the new design was entrusted to **Gottfried Böhm**. The Classical three-winged structure was renovated and the central façade was determinedly given a modern look, becoming a glass building through which the light floods. The banqueting hall is a successful symbiosis of glass and colour (the attentive visitor will not fail to miss three painted doves and a snake with a rose in its mouth, although Böhm has hidden them well).

The **Saar Historical Museum** ⊘, a glass and steel construction and a further creation of Gottfried Böhm, adjoins the right wing of the castle. Its permanent exhibition "Ten years, not a thousand" deals with National Socialism in the Saar region. Another important exhibition shows development since the post-war era and during the 1950s, up to the point at which the Saarland became part of Germany.

Schloßplatz – A darkly paved central strip, in reality an invisible memorial, leads to the castle. The artist **Jochen Gerz** and students of the Saarland Academy of Art carved out all the names of the Jewish cemeteries known in Germany in 1933, on the underside of 2 146 stones. These were relaid with the inscription facing downwards.

The **pump room** on the left should be seen, according to Gottfried Böhm, as a derivation from the Baroque guard-houses. It enlivens the extremely simple Schloßplatz.

Museum für Vor- und Frühgeschichte ⊘ – *First building on the left in Schloßplatz.*

Housed in the former district Parliament house, a neo-Baroque building. Inside there is a remarkable cast iron bannister from a Saarbrücken wealthy middle-class house, the Bodesch Palais (25 Altneugasse), created by court blacksmith Höer. On the ground floor, finds mainly from Roman times can be admired. The central feature of the museum is however the **Celtic princess's grave**★★ from Reinheim on the first floor, which dates back to 400 BC. The find is considered one of the most important in Central Europe from the Early Celtic period. The princess' jewellery and the tomb furnishings, which include a gilded bronze pitcher, are wonderfully well preserved.

A further building by Stengel, the old town hall, or **Altes Rathaus**, with its clock tower and its imperial roof (1748-50) stands at the western end of the Schloßplatz. The Saarbrücken city coat of arms is visible on the gable end. The **Abenteuermuseum** (Museum of Adventure) ⊘ housed on the upper storey contributes to an understanding of foreign peoples and foreign countries.

The **Erbprinzenpalais** stands on the southern side of Schloßplatz, a building converted by Stengel for the hereditary prince Ludwig von Nassau between 1760 and 1766 from three older houses and adapted to the style of the castle, with a triaxial central projection and a mansard roof. It has been used for many purposes since the French Revolution, for example as the seat of the Prussian mountain authority, the mining administration or police headquarters, and today the offices of municipal institutions.

Schloßkirche – *Am Schloßberg.*

The church was built at the end of the 15C and reconstructed in the Late Gothic style in 1683 after a serious fire, badly damaged during the Second World War and rebuilt again in 1956-58.

Twenty six glass paintings by **Georg Meistermann** must be admired, together with Baroque **tombstones** of the graves of Nassau-Saarbrücken, including that of Wilhelm Heinrich and his wife from the year 1772 (in the tower), created by the court sculptor Johann Philipp Mihm.

★★ **Ludwigsplatz and Ludwigskirche** – This is Stengel's masterpiece, one of the most beautiful and uniform Late Baroque complexes in Germany, erected between 1762 and 1775.

Ludwigsplatz – The square is bordered in the north, south and west by eight palaces of various sizes. All with three storeys and mansard roofs, they illustrate the transition from the Late Baroque to the neo-Classical style. Their white and silver-grey colouring enhances the effect of the Ludwigskirche, which is built in yellow and red sandstone in the centre of the square. The long building (front elevation) on the western side is the former orphanage. The Minister-President also has his offices in Ludwigsplatz.

Ludwigskirche and Ludwigsplatz, Saarbrücken

Marion Worm/Amt für Öffentlichkeitsarbeit

Ludwigskirche ⊘ – A successful restoration project has allowed this unique Baroque Protestant church to radiate its former glory once again. The east and west ends of this building in the shape of a cross are slightly shorter and polygonal. The east end exhibits a degree of splendour which is quite unusual in a Protestant church, with elaborate window frames and statues of the Evangelists by Franziskus Bingh in the splays either side of the projecting building. A stone-roof balustrade with further statues by Bingh (now copies), representing figures from the Old and New Testaments, runs around the church.

The **interior**, with its restrained elegance, forms a contrast to the sumptuous iconological exterior. The extremely light and airy impression is enhanced by the light delicate colouring of the stucco ornamentation. Of the original four galleries, only those in the east and west ends (choirs) have so far been reconstructed. They are supported by canephori, which symbolise worldly and spiritual power (east end) and the sacraments, the sermon, the vocal and instrumental church music (they support the organ). The golden shining eye of God, a frequent image of the Baroque and Enlightenment age, watches in the central dome, which is supported by four pillars.

The **Friedenskirche** built by Stengel, completes the harmonious impression of this beautiful ensemble beyond the eastern side of Ludwigsplatz.

ST.-JOHANN *(on the north bank of the Saar)*

★ **St.-Johanner Markt** – The old city around the market is the true heart of Saarbrücken. The focal point is the beautiful market fountain, with its obelisk and cast-iron railing, which was built in 1759-1760. Life pulses in the crooked streets and the numerous bistros (France is very close by). No 22, the seat of the former freemasons' lodge with its beautiful wooden door is worthy of note. No 19 is said to feature the oldest window in the old city, dating from 1668.

★ **Basilika St.-Johann** ⊘ – Built by the princely master builder Stengel between 1754 and 1758, and consecrated to St John the Baptist and St.-Ludwig, this church with its onion tower and lantern is another jewel of the Late Baroque period. The tympanum over the main doorway shows the Synagogue and the Church. The balconies were built in 1789 by Heinrich Heidehoff, and are supported by six oak beams surrounded by artificial marble. The four confessionals, which date back to original plans by Stengel and already hint at the Louis XVI style, are noteworthy. The paintings in the medaillons show King David, St Mary Magdalene, Peter and Dismas (the penitent thief). The pulpit is original and its shell-shaped niches show the four Evangelists and Christ as a teacher. The side altars are copies (from the church of St.-Nicolas in French Sarreguemines). However the figures of the saints, which were produced by Wunnibald Wagner, are originals.

The mirrored ceiling above the high altar (original) shows the rose motif which also appears elsewhere in the church, as a symbol of discretion, but also as the coat of arms of the town of St.-Johann.

A **Pietà** of beautiful quality stands in the right-hand chapel of the chancel. It dates from the first half of the 15C, and has been restored in colour.

ADDITIONAL SIGHTS

Saarland-Museum – Alte Sammlung ⊘ – *Karlstraße 1 (opposite the Moderne Galerie).*
Paintings and decorative arts (including a remarkable Renaissance cabinet from Limburg Monastery) from southwest Germany and Lorraine from the Middle Ages up to early modern times. There is an extensive collection of ceramics and porcelain.

Moderne Galerie ⊘ – *Bismarckstraße, on the banks of the Saar.*
20C art (paintings, sculptures, graphic art). The main emphasis is on German Impressionism and above all **Expressionism**★. There are major works by artists of international stature, such as Picasso, Léger, Tàpies, Beuys, Polke.

★ **Stiftskirche St.-Arnual** – *In the district of St.-Arnual, via Talstraße and Saargemünder Straße.*
The Gothic church was erected between the end of the 13C and the early 14C, and was given a Baroque domed roof in 1746, based on plans by Stengel. It was named after Bishop Arnuald von Metz, who lived in the 7C. The cross-shaped three naved vaulted basilica which incorporates the west tower and the projecting porch is one of the most important religious buildings in southwest Germany, a transitional building of French Gothic design in the east, but restrained by influence from Trier.

Having been the burial place of the dukes of Nassau-Saarbrücken since the 15C, the church houses 50 **tombs**★★ dating from the 13C to the 18C, some of which are masterly and are decorated in colour. The tomb of **Elisabeth von Lothringen** (who died in 1446 and won a name for herself as a translator and writer of medieval prose) is to be found in the chancel. The northern wall of the chancel features the larger than life-size Renaissance grave of **Count Philipp von Nassau-Saarbrücken** (who died in 1621) with his mother Anna Maria von Hesse and his sisters Dorothea and Luise Juliane. In the northern transept, note the altar tomb of **Count Johann III** (who died in 1472), in full armour, with his two wives Johanna von Heinsberg and Elisabeth von Württemberg, a work of considerable artistic merit. Above it stands the wall tomb of **Count Johann Ludwig** (who died in 1545) with his two sons. The octagonal **font**★ (15C) made of red sandstone shows the Ecce Homo motif and an angel with the instruments of the Passion.

Deutsch-Französischer Garten – *Deutschmühlental, towards Forbach.*
A park (50ha/124 acres) with a Lilliputian world straight out of Gulliver's Travels, chair-lift and Europe's largest water organ beckons visitors to promenade outside the gates of Saarbrücken.

EXCURSIONS

★ **Alte Völklinger Hütte** ⊙ – *In Völklingen, 10km/6mi west of Saarbrücken.*
This **iron and steel works** was established in 1873, initially manufacturing only iron girders. After being taken over by the Röchling family in 1881, it developed into a major industrial centre, ultimately covering all stages of iron and steel manufacture. For a century the town of Völklingen was dominated by the iron and steel works, which brought work and prosperity to the whole region. When the blast furnaces were closed down in 1986, it signalled the end of an era. During its heyday, the monumental works employed more than 16 000 people.
This plant, with its six blast furnaces and blast preheaters, is quite unique within Europe, and in 1994 it became the first industrial monument to be included in the UNESCO world cultural inheritance.
Under the expert guidance of former factory employees *(meeting point at the information centre in the old station)*, visitors are familiarised with the various stages of pig iron manufacture, namely the sintering plant, coking plant, blast furnaces, charging floor and discharge level. They also learn a little about the social environment and the everyday life of the iron and steel worker. The high spot of the tour, apart from climbing up to the blast furnace feed hopper, is the visit to the vast **gas blower hall**★, a cathedral of industrial culture with its heavy machinery dating from the early 20C.
In conjunction with this chapter of technical history, the neo-Baroque Church of Reconciliation, **Versöhnungskirche** ⊙ *(Poststraße)*, is well worth a visit. Its ceiling fresco, which dates from 1936, glorifies the industrial plant and the Röchling dynasty.

Fotodesign/Siegfried Layda

Alte Völklinger Hütte

Schloßberghöhlen ⊙ – *In* Homburg, *20km/12mi to the east on the A 6 motorway.*
The largest coloured sandstone caves in Europe are man-made. Mile long corridors, 2km/1mi of which can be visited, extend over 12 levels. The caves were built between the 11C and 17C and were mainly used for defence purposes. They served as munitions and food stores, and during the Second World War they were used as air raid shelters. At a constant temperature of 10ºC/50ºF, the humidity is between 80 and 90%. Ventilation is natural.
The stone out of which the caves are hollowed is a sedimentary rock formed by wind and sea deposits during the Triassic period (230-160 million years ago). The beautiful yellowish red sandstone gives the underground world unexpected colour.

Römermuseum Schwarzenacker ⊙ – *2km/1mi to the east of Homburg, on* B 423.
The Roman settlement of Schwarzenacker was apparently as large as the medieval town of Worms. It was founded at around the time of the birth of Christ and was destroyed by the Alemanni in AD 275. The excavations uncovered roads, buildings and also many examples of different skills. The house of an optician and a columned house with a cellar have been reconstructed and are graphic examples of Roman architecture. The finds are exhibited in a Baroque house, the Edelhof, from where a Baroque garden leads to the open-air museum.

Between Mettlach and Konz, where it flows into the Moselle, the River Saar cuts its way through the crystalline Hunsrück massif, the resistance of which reduces this stretch of the river valley to a winding defile at times visible only from the top of its steeply sloping sides. Ten percent of the total vineyard coverage of the area between the Moselle, Saar and Ruwer rivers lies between Konz and Serring. Grapes, predominantly Riesling, have been cultivated here since the 18C.

Streichan/ZEFA, Paris

Saar meander at Cloef

FROM METTLACH TO TRIER 57km/35mi - about 2hr

Mettlach – The Baroque, red sandstone façade of the old abbey – now the offices of a ceramics factory – rises above the trees bordering the road leading uphill towards Merzig. Downstream, in a public park nearby, stands the Alter Turm, a ruined octagonal funerary chapel dating from the 10C.

★★ Cloef – *7km/4mi west of Mettlach then 15min on foot there and back.*
From a viewpoint high above the river, there is a view of the Montclair loop, a hairpin curve enclosing a long, densely wooded promontory.

German wines

Since legislation passed in 1971 and 1982, German wines can be divided into four categories:

(Deutscher) Tafelwein – table wine with no clearly defined region of origin, which may in fact be a blending of other Common Market wines or of purely German ones.

Landwein – medium quality wine which carries a general indication of origin (eg Pfälzer Landwein) and can only be made from officially approved grapes; it must have at least 55° "Öchslegrade" and be dry or medium dry,

Qualitätswein bestimmter Anbaugebiete – wine of superior quality which carries an allocated control number and originates from one of the officially recognised regions (Gebiet), eg Moselle, Baden, Rhine,

Qualitätswein mit Prädikat – strictly regulated wine of prime quality, grown and made in a clearly defined and limited area or vineyard and generally carrying one of the following descriptions: Kabinett (a perfect reserve wine), Spätlese (wine from late-harvest grapes), Auslese (wine from specially selected grapes), Beerenauslese and Trockenbeerenauslese (sweet wine), Eiswein (wine produced from grapes harvested after a minimum -7°C frost).

Return to Mettlach.

From Mettlach to Saarburg, the road runs at the foot of the valley, forested on the lower slopes, with tall escarpments above. Vines appear as the valley widens.

Saarburg – The setting of this small town is typical of the valley's final section, with terraced vineyards now on every side. There is an attractive view of the town from a knoll crowned with the ruins of a 10C castle. In the old quarter, near the Markt, a 20m/66ft cascade plunges between houses built on the rock.

After Konz, where the Saar joins the Moselle, follow the river to Trier.

★★ **Trier** – *See TRIER.*

SÄCHSISCHE SCHWEIZ★★★

SWISS SAXONY – Sachsen
Michelin map 418 N 26

Lying between Dresden and the Czech frontier, the region known as Swiss Saxony is one of Germany's most popular – and most spectacular – natural wonders. It is an area of sheer sandstone cliffs, of table-shaped outcrops and isolated pillars, of deep gorges gouged from the rock and fantastically shaped formations through which the upper reaches of the Elbe flow in wide curves.

This huge depression can be explored by road, following the itinerary suggested below, or from the river, taking one of the "Weiße Flotte" boats plying between Dresden and Bad Schandau.

Geological Formation – The Elbe sandstone massif (Elbsandsteingebirge) resulted from the raising up – and subsequent decomposition – in the Tertiary Era of sedimentary limestones originally laid down over the Primary bedrock.

Vertical faulting of the horizontal sandstone beds, followed by the action of erosion, then produced over the millennia the flat-topped maze of fantasy formations through which the river today winds its way.

ROUND TOUR FROM DRESDEN 78km/49mi – one day

★★★ **Dresden** – *See DRESDEN.*

Leave the city to the east by Pillnitzer Landstraße (Y) on the town plan.

★ **Schloß Pillnitz** – *See DRESDEN: Excursions.*

★★★ **Bastei** – The **view**★★ from this rocky spine across the Elbe Valley to the table mountains of Swiss Saxony is famous. The top of the ridge is split by numerous fissures. The narrow rocky outcrop projecting furthest towards the Elbe is the Bastei itself, the top of which towers 190m/620ft above river level. The

Jogschies/EXPLORER, Paris

The Bastei viewpoint, Swiss Saxony

spectacular, almost lunar, landscape of these unusual rock formations is all the more impressive for being seen close at hand, with visitors actually able to touch the rocks that make up this dramatic scenery.

*A short stretch downhill leads to the 76m/250ft long **Basteibrücke**. There are numerous waymarked footpaths through the surrounding rocks.*

★ **Bad Schandau** – Apart from being the main tourist centre of the region, Bad Schandau is also a spa renowned for the properties of its iron-rich waters, which have been exploited since 1730. At the exit from the town, in the direction of Schmilka, a lift and a footpath lead to the Ostrauer Scheibe, from which there is a superb **view**★ of the Schrammsteine – a chaotic rock massif much favoured by amateur mountaineers.

The **Kirnitzsch Valley**★ (Kirnitzschtal), which can be followed by mountain railway, is hemmed in by steep cliffs.

Cross the Elbe at Bad Schandau and turn right along the south bank (B 172) towards Königstein fortress.

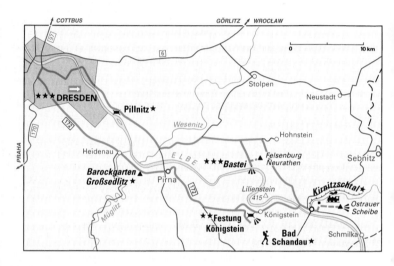

★★ **Festung Königstein** – The great sweep of the Elbe here is overlooked by the 415km/1 362ft Lilienstein on the east bank, and the Königstein (360m/1 181ft) on the west. The formidable fortress crowning the latter was built between the 13C and the 16C, strengthened and enlarged in the 17C and 18C, and served several times as a refuge for the Court of Saxony. Prisoners held there had very little chance of escaping. Among the most famous internees were Böttger, the inventor of hard-paste porcelain *(see MEISSEN)*; August Bebel, founder with Karl Liebknecht of the Social Democrat party in 1869; and the Second World War French General Giraud. (Giraud was one of the few who did get away, a celebrated escape accomplished with the help of a rope tied to the bars of a loophole in the castle's outer wall.) From the old rampart walk, which follows the edge of the Erzgebirge, there are splendid **views**★★ of the Lausitz foothills and the distant mountains of Bohemia.

Continue along B 172 as far as Pirna, then turn left towards the Barockgarten.

★ **Barockgarten Großsedlitz** ⊙ – This **Baroque pleasure ground** was partly laid out by Pöppelmann in the French style in 1719. It is still possible to see the orangery, the Stille Musik – a double-flight stairway surrounding an ornamental pool – and statues of mythological Greek heroes sculpted by Kirchner and Thoma.

Return to Dresden on B 172.

Bad SÄCKINGEN★

Baden-Württemberg
Population 16 800
Michelin map 419 X 7

Bad Säckingen can probably trace its origins back to a missionary cell founded by St Fridolin in 522. The convent of Benedictine nuns recorded for the first time in 878 determined the town's fortunes for many centuries. Town and convent passed into the hands of the Habsburgs in 1173 where it remained until 1805. The abbesses of the convent, who had been elevated to imperial royal rank in 1307, were also rulers of the town until secularisation in 1806.

The warm springs at Bad Säckingen were no doubt already in use in the Middle Ages, although the town was only officially dubbed "Bad" (the German prefix for a spa town) in 1978. It is used in cures for patients who cannot move, or have difficulty moving. There is clear evidence of the architectural influence of nearby Switzerland in the buildings of this town on the banks of the Rhine south of the Black Forest.

★ **Fridolinsmünster** – This church is named after the missionary who converted the Alemanni in the 6C. The barrel-vaulted processional crypt has survived from the Carolingian era. The present basilica was built in the Gothic style in the 14C and later had Baroque features added to it: the once pointed arcades were filled in to become round arches; the vaulting lowered in order to decorate it with Wessobrunn School rocaille ornamentation (*see WESSOBRUNN*); and the clerestory windows rounded off. The church treasury contains the **Shrine of St Fridolin**, a magnificent 18C piece of gold work from Augsburg, in the form of a carriage chest.

★ **Gedeckte Brücke (Roofed Bridge)** – The stone pillars of this wooden bridge, which has been re-roofed on numerous occasions, were put up in 1575. The bridge is 200m/650ft long, the longest of its kind in Europe, and spans the Rhine, leading to Stein in the Swiss canton of Aargau. The basic design of the bridge itself is attributed to the bridge constructor Blasius Baldischweiler from Laufenburg, who built it between 1785 and 1803.

Schloßpark (Palace gardens) – These pleasant grounds are the setting for the Trompeterschloß (Trumpeter's Palace), which was built c 1600 essentially by the lords of Schönau, the stewards of the religious foundation since 1360. The palace now houses a museum, which contains the largest **collection of trumpets** in Europe. From the corner of the park, which boasts a mini-golf course, there is a good view of the old wooden roofed bridge.

EXCURSION

Waldshut – *26km/16mi to the west.*
Halfway up a wooded, semicircular slope rising from a curve in the Rhine, this small town retains its two fortified gateways. The heart of the historic **old town**★ is **Kaiserstraße** – a street whose orderly line of houses is broken only by overhanging eaves. It is delimited to the west by the Lower or Basle Gate and to the east by the Upper or Schaffhaus Gate.

The Late Baroque **town hall**, built in 1770, is thought to have been designed by Johann Caspar Bagnato. This fine building boasts a magnificent doorway with cartouches and a turret with a sundial. Among the grand houses along Kaiserstraße, note in particular the "Wilder Mann", a 16C town house with a typical overhanging gable. The "Alte Metzig" (Butcher's Gateway) built in 1588 now houses the **Local Museum** (Heimatmuseum).

SALEM★

Baden-Württemberg
Michelin map 419 W 11

This Cistercian abbey, founded in 1137, was at its most influential under the Abbot Anselm II (1746-1778), the builder of Birnau (*see BODENSEE*). Secularised in 1803, the abbey buildings have since been used as the palace of the Grand Dukes of Baden (Margraves since 1918).

★ **Münster** – The former abbey church was constructed between 1299 and 1414. Outside, the austere Gothic façade is relieved by the delicate tracery of the bays lightening the east and west gables.
Inside, the design is typical Cistercian Gothic, with a large chancel and flattened chevet, soaring vaults and side aisles supporting the nave through walls abutting on wide arcades.

★ **Schloß** ⊘ – The abbey buildings were almost completely destroyed by fire in 1697 and were rebuilt in the Baroque style at the beginning of the 18C. Visitors can follow the evolution of the stuccowork entrusted to artists of the Wessobrunn School over a whole century.
The ceiling of the old summer refectory still boasts its fine Wessobrunn stucco ornamentation, the work of the Schmuzer brothers. These artists were also responsible for decorating the library ceiling with its fine basket-handle vaulting.

Further highlights of a tour round the palace must include the Bernardus passage, the **Imperial Hall** completed in 1707 – the first great State Hall in the Baroque style in any German abbey – and the Rococo study of Abbot Anselm II.

Untertor-Haus (Lower Gatehouse) – Between the pilasters of this strikingly elegant Baroque entrance, the decorative window lintels have a different design on each storey.

ADDITIONAL SIGHTS

The 17ha/42 acre site at Salem offers further points of interest:

Feuerwehr-Museum ⊘ – 500 years of the history of the fire brigade is brought to life here, with equipment from around the world.

A **distillery museum** in a show distillery explains the production of spirits (Branntwein), while the **Cooperage Museum**, housed in an old winepressing room with a huge winepress dating from 1706, sheds light on this old profession. Craftsmen and women demonstrate their art in a special **handcrafts village**.

ST. BLASIEN★

Baden-Württemberg
Population 4 200
Michelin map 419 W 8

The majestic domed church dedicated to St Blaise comes suddenly into view at the far end of a wooded valley in the Hotzenwald, in the southern part of the Black Forest. It stands in the grounds of a medieval monastery founded in 835 by a brotherhood of hermit monks whose influence extended all over the southern part of Germany. The area is popular with holidaymakers, who come here to enjoy some fresh air and peace and quiet.

★★ **Dom** – This Baroque church, following a ground plan much favoured during that period, is built in the middle of what would have been the north wing of the old abbey complex, which had four wings. The French architect, Pierre-Michel d'Ixnard (1726-95), graced it with a central dome, which rises 64m/210ft from

Domed church of St. Blasien

the ground, behind a peristyle. After those of St Peter's in Rome and Les Invalides in Paris this is the third largest dome in Europe. Inside the dome, which is lit through windows set in deep niches, is a false cupola, suspended from the true dome although it appears to be supported by the columns of the central rotunda. Behind the high altar lies the chancel, which is quite long and roofed with cradle vaulting.

EXCURSIONS

The Hochkopf Massif – *45km/28mi to the west; allow 3hr. Drive via Todtmoos to the Weißenbachsattel pass.*

Hochkopf – *1hr on foot there and back.* From the car park, to the right of the road, a footpath leads up to the look-out tower, from which there are superb **views**★★ of the barren peaks of the Belchen and the Feldberg, to the west, and – on clear days – the Alps to the southeast.

★ **Bernau** – In a fertile mountain valley are several picturesque hamlets composed of the attractive farmhouses of this region.
At Bernau-Innerlehen, the town hall (Rathaus) houses the **Hans-Thoma-Museum**, an exhibition of paintings by this local artist, notably some of his Black Forest landscapes executed with great sensitivity.

The Alb Valley (Albtal) – *30km/18.5mi to the south; allow 1hr.*
The road runs high above the Alb gorges, alternating stretches along the edge of the cliffs with tunnels through the rock, before it reaches the Rhine at Albbruck.

SAUERLAND★

Nordrhein-Westfalen
Michelin map 417 M 6-8

The Sauerland, which forms the hinterland to the Ruhr Basin, is the most mountainous, if not actually the highest part, of the Rhineland Schist Massif.
It is crowned by the **Langenberg** (843m/2 766ft), near Niedersfeld, which is already in effect a transitional area linking the Sauerland with the Waldeck heights.
Numerous artificial lakes in the region supply water and hydroelectric energy to the industrial towns of the Ruhr, serving also as centres for water sports. The Upper Sauerland, especially the Roth-aargebirge, a range covered by forests of beech and fir, is very popular with tourists.

FROM SOEST TO BAD BERLEBURG

181km/112mi – allow one day

★ **Soest** – See SOEST.

★ **Möhnesee** – See SOEST: Excursions.

Arnsberg – The old town is built on a spur enclosed by a bend in the River Ruhr, rising in tiers above the waterside. To the north, a clock tower commands the approach to the

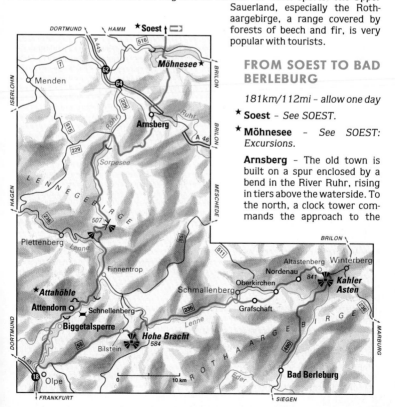

Schloßberg ruins *(good view)*; to the south, near the old abbey, stands a superb Rococo gate, the Hirschberger Tor, decorated with hunting scenes.

Beyond Arnsberg, the road skirts the right bank of the Sorpesee reservoir *(water sports)* and then crosses the Lennegebirge massif. There are many attractive viewpoints, particularly near the pass. On the far side of Finnentrop, the Bigge Valley is punctuated by a number of rock-strewn passages.

★ **Attahöhle (Grotto)** ⊙ – *On the right-hand side of the road (signposted), just before Attendorn.*
This strange cavern eroded from the limestone cuts into the bedrock for no less than 3km/2mi. Apart from a multitude of stalactites and stalagmites, curious stone "draperies" are visible, some of them translucent.

Attendorn – The reputation of Attendorn was at its height in the Middle Ages, as witness the splendid 14C **town hall** (Historisches Rathaus) with its stepped gable, the open, arcaded hall of the old covered market (Alter Markt), and the "**Sauerland cathedral**" (Sauerländer Dom). This Gothic hall-church has magnificent 14C interior decorations.
Southeast of Attendorn, on the other side of the Bigge, is **Burg Schnellenberg**, which dates, in its present form, largely from the 17C.

Biggetalsperre – This dam, in service since 1964, forms with the Lister barrage – which has flooded an adjacent valley – the largest reservoir in Westphalia.
About 2km/1mi before Olpe, fork left on B 55. Soon after Bilstein, on a small mountain road, take a right turn in the direction of the Hohe Bracht.

Hohe Bracht – Alt 584m/ 1 916ft. From the viewing tower (620m/2 034ft), there is a fine panorama, including the hummocked Rothaargebirge massif as far as Kahler Asten.

After crossing the rural landscape of the Lenne Valley, the route passes **Grafschaft** and **Oberkirchen**, two villages with charming half-timbered houses, and then the country becomes wilder and more hilly. Beyond **Nordenau**, a typical Upper Sauerland village where the houses are roofed with slate, is the ski station of Altastenberg. Finally, on the far side of an open upland plateau with splendid views all around, the road arrives at Kahler Asten.

Kahler Asten – At 841m/2 759ft above sea level, this is the highest point of the Rothaargebirge. From the look-out tower, as might be expected, there is a superb **view** all around. To the northeast is the spa and winter sports centre of Winterberg. Slate quarries flank the road back down, which twists and turns but is well-made. There are many attractive views towards the south.

Bad Berleburg – The townscape of the Kneipp spa resort Bad Berleburg is definitively characterised by the **castle** of the princes of Sayn-Wittgenstein at the heart of the historic town centre. The origins of the castle date from the 13C, although the present building's appearance bears the stamp of later Baroque additions. The castle now serves as a venue for concerts.

SCHLESWIG★

Schleswig-Holstein
Population 27 000
Michelin map 415 C 12

Schleswig, an old maritime town of white houses, was built on low-lying banks at the inner end of an arm of the sea, the **Schlei**, which penetrates the coast for 43km/27mi. From the car park on B 76, there is an attractive **view**★ of the old town below the cathedral, on the far side of the water.

The Vikings – Merchants were settled on the south bank of the Schlei at the beginning of the 9C. Their favoured position at the crossroads of the old north-south road to Jutland and the east-west route used to transport light loads from the Baltic to the North Sea, soon made the settlement an important North European trade centre.
A century later, Vikings from Sweden invaded the region. They renamed the area **Haithabu** ("the town in the heather") and encircled it with a vast defence system of which the **semicircular retrenchment** beside the Haddebyer Noor remains today.
Near this lagoon, stones with runic carvings such as the **Busdorfer Runenstein** *(access via Busdorfer Straße)* are visible at another archeological site. There are further Viking remains at Gottorf Castle.
In the 11C, the townspeople of Haithabu, seeking better defences against Scandinavian marauders, crossed to the north bank of the Schlei to found the town of Schleswig.

Schloss GOTTORF ⊙

Two large museums devoted to the Schleswig-Holstein Land are housed in this 16C-18C castle, once the seat of the Holstein-Gottorf ducal family, which in 1762 became the Imperial House of the Czars of Russia. *The collections merit at least half a day to be fully appreciated.*

★★ **Schleswig-Holsteinisches Landesmuseum** – This museum contains extensive cultural and historical collections (local arts, crafts and traditions). Note in particular the Gothic hall (medieval religious art), the **collections of porcelain and faience**★ and the antique furniture. Another highlight is the **Renaissance chapel**★★ with its ducal loggia and oratory. Finally, visitors should be sure not to miss the **Jugendstil collection**★, without peer in north Germany.

An adjacent building houses Rolf Horn's fine collection of works spanning Expressionism to the present. The luminosity of the paintings by Emil Nolde and Alexei von Jawlensky are especially striking. One room is given over to sculptures by Ernst Barlach.

Works by artists of the Brücke are on display on two floors in the old stable – this is the largest collection after the Brücke-Museum in Berlin.

★ **Archäologisches Landesmuseum** – This museum offers a systematic presentation of Schleswig-Holstein's pre- and early history from the Paleolithic Age to the time of the Vikings. There are spectacular finds dating from the 4C (bodies found perfectly preserved in peatbogs, fragments of clothing, shoes, weapons) rescued from the peatbogs before their decay.

★★★ **Nydam-Boot** – *In the Nydam Hall.*
This oak-hulled longship with its fine lines dates from about AD 320 and was excavated in 1863 from the Nydam marshes, on Danish territory. It is 23m/75ft long by 3m/10ft wide and was powered by 36 oarsmen. It is the oldest surviving Germanic longship, and was probably sunk in the peatbogs as a sacrifice in c 350 AD.

ADDITIONAL SIGHTS

★ **Dom St. Peter** – Thanks to its graceful spire, this brick-built Gothic hall-church can be seen from far off. Enter by the south doorway (St Peter's), which is of stone, with a carved tympanum dating from 1170. The most remarkable work of art is the 1521 **Bordesholm Altarpiece**★★, which can be seen in the chancel. Northwest of the nave lies the 14C **cloister**, with stylized vine-leaf motifs painted on the vaulting.

Wikinger Museum Haithabu

★ **The Holm** – This picturesque old sailors' and fishermen's quarter with its low houses (18C) is centred around a small cemetery and chapel.

Wikinger Museum Haithabu (Viking Museum) ⊙ – *Access via B 76, direction Kiel.*
This annexe to the Archäologisches Landesmuseum is near the Haddebyer Noor lagoon, next to the old Viking site *(see above)*, whose history it traces. A large number of objects unearthed in various digs (jewels, weapons, tools and domestic implements) are on display, along with graphics and models of the Viking settlement. The galleries are

Ferslev fibula in the Viking museum

very well laid out, with a wealth of information on the life and times of the Haithabu inhabitants. In the **Boat Hall** (Schiffshalle) there is a Viking longship, partly reconstituted from contemporary fragments dredged up in the ancient port site.

EXCURSION

Eckernförde – *23km/14mi to the east, again via B 76.*
The town lies at the inner end of the Eckernförder Bucht, a deep, wide inlet penetrated by the waters of the Baltic. It is a picturesque fishing port which existed already in the 12C (a document dating from that period mentions a "fishermen's community"). Eckernförde is the home of a Holsteiner delicacy known as Kieler Sprotten (smoked fish).

Nikolaikirche, a sober triple-aisle brick church, stands in the market place. The **interior**★, supported by four massive columns, is lavishly decorated. The Early Baroque **altarpiece** (1640) is said to be the most accomplished work of the wood carver Hans Gudewerdt the Younger, whose father sculpted the Renaissance pulpit with its biblical scenes. The bronze **baptismal font** in the middle of the church, also richly decorated, dates from 1588. On either side of the west tower are the tombs of the nobility (17C), and the **Sintflutbild** – a large oil painting dating from 1632 which recalls floods, plagues and the horror of the Thirty Years War.

SCHWÄBISCHE ALB★

SWABIAN JURA – Baden-Württemberg

Michelin map 419 V 10 – T 15/420 U 13 – T 15

The high limestone plateaux of the Swabian Jura, watershed between the Rhine (Neckar Basin) and the Danube, lie between the Black Forest and the Nördlinger Ries and form in effect the "roof" of southern Germany. The highest point is at Lemberg (1 015m/3 330ft). From this summit, the Jura plateaux drop no less than 400m/1 312ft to the Neckar Basin in the northwest.

Mountain outcrops detached from the main block form natural fortresses, and some have been chosen as castle sites by familes subsequently to enjoy great glory and dynastic fame (the Hohenstaufens, the Hohenzollerns).

An ingenious population – As in many mountainous regions, the length and harshness of the winters have resulted in the formation of numerous small family businesses or cottage industries. In the 19C, through the philanthropic activities of pastors, schoolteachers and imaginative inventors, the whole northern fringe of the massif became covered with workshops, studios and small factories turning out toys, precision instruments, musical accessories, clothing etc.

① FROM KIRCHHEIM UNTER TECK TO BURG HOHENZOLLERN *125km/78mi – allow one day*

Kirchheim unter Teck – The pinnacled tower of the half-timbered **Rathaus** overlooks the main crossroads. The building dates from 1724.

Holzmaden – Follow the arrows leading to the **Urwelt-Museum Hauff**★ ⊙: an astonishing assembly of saurian fossil skeletons immured in the local schists and dating back almost 160 million years.

Burgruine Reußenstein (Castle ruins) – *20min on foot there and back.*
Make for the edge of the escarpment to appreciate to the full the **setting**★★ of Reußenstein as it dominates the coomb of Neidlingen. From the look-out point built into the castle ruins, there is a **view**★ of the whole narrow valley and, beyond it, the plain of Teck.

After Wiesensteig (half-timbered houses), the route follows one section of the **Schwäbische Albstraße,** *which is marked by blue-green indication arrows.*

Bad Urach – A pretty town, enclosed deep in the Erms Valley, with half-timbered houses clustered round a central Marktplatz.

Uracher Wasserfall (Urach Falls) – *15min on foot there and back. Leave the car in the parking area marked "Aussicht 350m".*
Impressive **view**★ of the valley and the waterfall (flow reduced in summer).

Schloß Lichtenstein ⊙ – Built on a rock spur protected by a natural cleft, Lichtenstein was completely redesigned and decorated in the "troubadour" style in 1842. Before crossing the entrance bridge, turn right and make for two viewpoints: one overlooks the Echaz Valley, the other the castle itself.

Bärenhöhle ⊙ – *In Erpfingen.* The biggest cavern in this "Bear Grotto" contains well-preserved stalactites and stalagmites.

At Onstmettingen, follow the signs "Nädelehaus" and "Raichberg".

★ **Raichberg** – *30min on foot there and back.*
Leave the car at the hotel and walk past a brown-stone tower, across the fields to the lip of the plateau. From here there is a fine **view**★ of the downward sweep of the Jura and, 3km/2mi away, Burg Hohenzollern.

Return to Burg Hohenzollern via Tannheim and Hechingen.

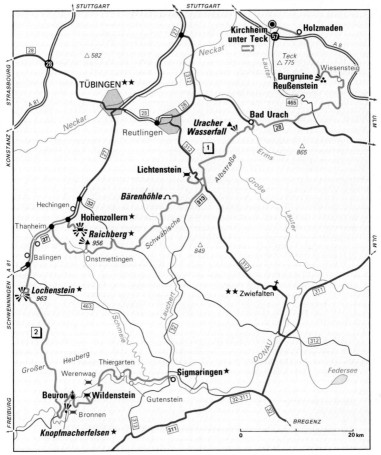

★ 2 FROM HOHENZOLLERN TO THE DANUBE GAP

89km/55mi - allow half a day

★ **Burg Hohenzollern** - *See Burg HOHENZOLLERN.*

★ **Lochenstein** - *30min on foot there and back.*
Leave the car at the saddle (Lochenpaß) and climb to the summit (alt 963m/3 160ft) of the Lochenstein, which is surmounted by a Cross. From here there is a **view**★ of the Balingen-Hechingen depression, and still - away in the distance - Hohenzollern Castle.
Beyond the pass, the road sweeps downhill in tight curves and then crosses the bare, rolling uplands of the Großer Heuberg plateau.

★ **Knopfmacherfelsen** - Below the car park, make your way to a viewpoint from which there is a **view**★ of the Danube Valley as far as Beuron Abbey and, on the right, Schloß Bronnen.

Kloster Beuron - A flourishing Benedictine congregation at Beuron contributed greatly to the revival of monastic life, the liturgy and the use of the Gregorian chant in Germany. The Gnadenkapelle, abutting the Baroque **abbey church** ⊙, is treated in the "Beuron style" - derived from a late-19C school of sacred art much influenced by Byzantium.

Burg Wildenstein - *7km/4.5mi from Beuron via Leibertingen.*
This small citadel commanding the Danube was designed with two moats and a forward defence system on the plateau side comprising two towers linked by a long wall.

Below Beuron, the road follows the **Danube Valley**★ past the rocky fortresses of Wildenstein and Werenwag on the way to Sigmaringen. Approaching the town, the cliffs give way to curious rock needles which form a fantastic ensemble between Thiergarten and Gutenstein.

★ **Sigmaringen** - *See SIGMARINGEN.*

SCHWÄBISCH GMÜND

Baden-Württemberg
Population 63 000
Michelin map 419 T 13

This former free city lies in the Rems Valley north of the three distinctive conical peaks of the Kaiserberge, which are a popular destination for day trippers.
The settlement of Gamundia, through which the Roman Limes demarcation
once ran, was first documented in 782 and was granted its town charter by
Konrad III (1138-52) of the Hohenstaufen dynasty. Medieval half-timbered
houses and Baroque town houses line the market square at the heart of the
city.

Traditionally, Schwäbisch Gmünd is a centre for the working of precious metals, and
its silverware is seen on many German tables. There are still about 70 gold- and
silverworking firms in business here.

* **Heiligkreuzmünster** – The cathedral was built in the 14C by Heinrich Parler, a
  Swabian master whose descendants designed cathedrals as far apart as Prague,
  Vienna and Milan. Surprisingly, it has no towers. The pinnacles, balustrades and
  exterior tracery are Flamboyant Gothic. The architect skilfully worked the
  decoration into a grid over the west gable, and both chancel doors are sculpted
  beneath porches which were once also fully decorated. The two-tier chevet is
  gracefully conceived.

  The interior is a perfect hall, the chancel – which has a similar layout to the nave
  – profiting from more intricately worked ribbed vaulting. The early Renaissance
  choir stalls and radiating chapels are rich in statuary: note especially, in the axial
  chapel, an early-15C Holy Sepulchre watched over by the three Marys. The
  Baptismal Chapel contains the Tree of Jesse (1520), composed of 40 sculpted
  figurines.

  Marktplatz – A huge square whose Baroque character is emphasized by
  the prosperous-looking houses surrounding it and a twin-statue fountain
  dedicated to the Virgin Mary. Several half-timbered buildings, the hospital
  and the Gräth (old town hall) nevertheless recall the medieval existence of the
  town.

  Johanniskirche – This church is a good example of Swabian Romanesque
  architecture and is lavishly decorated with sculpture, mainly of people, animals
  and mythological figures executed in a traditional popular style.

EXCURSIONS

* **Hohenstaufen** – *14km/8.5mi to the southwest, plus 30min on foot there and
  back.*
  From the two churches at the top of the town, a shady footpath leads to the
  summit at 684m/2 244ft. Nothing remains of the castle, the one-time seat of the
  Staufer, but the climb is worthwhile for the **panorama★** of the two remaining
  Kaiserberge, Stuifen and Rechberg, and, on the horizon, the Swabian Jura. *The
  car should be left on the central esplanade in the village.*

  Hohenrechberg – *12km/7.5mi, plus 1hr on foot there and back.*
  The castle ruins, again, command a vast horizon. Visitors can stroll around the
  ancient rampart walk or, higher up, walk around the ruined walls whose crests
  have been converted into a walkway. In the foreground is the massive cone of
  Hofenstaufen.

SCHWÄBISCH HALL★★

Baden-Württemberg
Population 34 000
Michelin map 419 S 13 – Local map see HOHENLOHER LAND

This old town, built in tiers up the steep flank of the Kocher Valley, grew up around
salt springs known as far back as Celtic times. In the Middle Ages, it was famous for
the Imperial silver coins, the Häller or Heller, minted there.

From Mauerstraße (the quay on the west bank), at the level of the Löwenbrauerei
(brewery), there is a fine **general view★** of the old town, with its roofs stepped one
above the other at the foot of Michaelskirche, and the imposing 1527 **Büchsenhaus** or
Neubau (the former arsenal). Below, the arms of the river are spanned by attractive
roofed wooden bridges. Still in the old town opposite, the two parallel streets of the
Obere and the **Untere Herrengasse**, linked by stone stairways, are bordered by several 15C
and 16C half-timbered houses.

★★ MARKTPLATZ *allow 45min*

Laid out on a slope, this square is dominated by the monumental stone steps of Michaelskirche (where actors, during a festival from June to August each year, perform a repertory of the world's theatre classics). In the square itself, only a characteristic alignment of half-timbered gables on the south side – spared by the great fire of 1728 – remains to remind us of what the town must have looked like in the early 18C.

★ **Rathaus** – An elegant building in the Late Baroque style.

Marktbrunnen – Dating from 1509, the fountain stands against a decorative wall adorned with statues of Samson, St Michael and St George. The rectangular design, unusual in a Gothic work, includes the old pillory post.

Pfarrkirche St. Michael – The church's position at the top of 53 steps is impressive. The octagonal porch, opening beneath a Romanesque tower with a Renaissance top, has a statue of its patron saint in front of its central pillar. The interior★, originally Romanesque also, was transformed into a Gothic hall-church in the 15C. The Flamboyant chancel was added in the 16C.

ADDITIONAL SIGHTS

Hällisch-Fränkisches Museum (Regional Museum) ⊘ – This museum is housed in six historical buildings, the centrepiece of which is a 10-storey high Romanesque tower, once inhabited. The collections include mementoes of the region's past in general, and that of the town in particular (as an industrial salt centre, as a mint etc). Several rooms are devoted to Württemberg-Franconian regional art.

Gräterhaus – This beautiful half-timbered house, so exquisitely decorated, stands in the town's northern suburb. It dates from 1605.

Henkersbrücke – There is an attractive view from this bridge of the mass of half-timbered buildings of the Ilge quarter, and their reflection in the waters of the Kocher. The **view** is perhaps even better from the junction of the street named Am Spitalbach and the Salinenstraße quay, from which the east end of the old church of St. Johann can also be seen.

EXCURSIONS

★ **Großcomburg** – *3km/2mi to the south.*
The church of this old fortified **Benedictine abbey** ⊘ still has its three Romanesque towers. The rest of the building was reconstructed in 1715, the interior taking the form of a Baroque hall. Along with those of Aachen and Hildesheim, the church's chandelier is one of the most precious in the West. Dating from 1130 and designed in the shape of a crown, the **chandelier**★★★ (Radleuchter) is made of iron, subsequently copper-plated and then gilded. In front of the high altar is an **antependium**★ of the same period, made of gilded beaten copper representing Christ among the Apostles. The framework supporting this is treated with cloisonné enamel and filigree work.

★ **Hohenloher Freilandmuseum (Hohenlohe Open-Air Museum)** ⊘ – *At Wackershofen, 5km/3mi to the northwest – local map see HOHENLOHER LAND.*
Over 30 buildings from the 16C to the 19C, which originally stood in different locations, have been reconstructed here and faithfully recapture the rural life of this area from the mid 16C to the end of the 19C. There is an exhibition of furniture and agricultural implements.

The Hohenlohe – *See HOHENLOHER LAND.*

THE GREEN GUIDE:
Landscapes
Monuments
Scenic routes, touring programmes
Geography
History, Art
Places to stay
Town and site plans
Practical information
Desinations around the world and
a collection of regional guides to France

SCHWARZWALD★★★

The Black Forest, stretching for 170km/106mi from Karlsruhe to Basle, is separated from the Vosges by the subsided plain of the Rhine. The two ranges, facing one another across this consequence of the Alpine Fold, have much in common. Both are densely wooded, rising from a crystalline base in the south, sloping gently towards the north, where the massif is covered by limestone beds; both drop steeply in the direction of the Rhine, less abruptly on the far side of the crests – to the Swabian plateaux of the Upper Neckar in one case, to the plateau of Lorraine on the other. Even the highest points of each range correspond: the Feldberg at 1 493m/4 899ft and the Grand Ballon at 1 424m/4 674ft.

Unlike the Vosges, however, the Black Forest – the larger and denser of the two massifs – displays no marked north-south line of crests, and no coherent east-west arrangement of passes.

The economy of the region has always been linked to the **forest**, wood being practically the sole construction material and the base of all crafts. The trunks of trees, often 50m/165ft long, were floated away as far as the Netherlands, where they were much in demand by boatbuilders. **Clockmaking**, symbolized by the famous cuckoo clock, remains a fruitful activity.

Fruit farms and **vineyards** are cultivated on the foothills along the western limits of the forest.

Northern Black Forest – Drained by the Murg, the Nagold and the two Enz rivers, this sandstone area is almost entirely covered by conifers. The contrast, within a few miles, between the upper parts of the Grinde moors and the orchards and vineyards flourishing south of Baden-Baden, is remarkable.

Central Black Forest – The main axis of this region follows the valleys of the Kinzig and the Gutach – a gap through which the main road and rail arteries cut diagonally towards the Upper Danube and Lake Constance. The patchiness of the infertile sandstone topsoil is reflected in the forest's separation into groves, distanced by fields and meadows. South of the Elz and Berg valleys, the Upper Black Forest, notably in the Feldberg region, forms a landscape that is almost Alpine in character.

Southern Black Forest – Gashed by the racing watercourses of the Wehra, the Alb and the Schlücht, the land drops progressively towards the Rhine. The climate, favourable to mountain cures, has led to the establishment of health resorts in the region.

★★★ SCHWARZWALD-HOCHSTRASSE (CREST ROAD)

① From Baden-Baden to Freudenstadt

80km/50mi – about 4hr

Amply provided with viewpoints and car parks, the Black Forest crest road, or Hochstraße, runs past many winter ski slopes with ski lifts. Much of the route is at heights approaching 1 000m/3 280ft.

Black Forest landscape

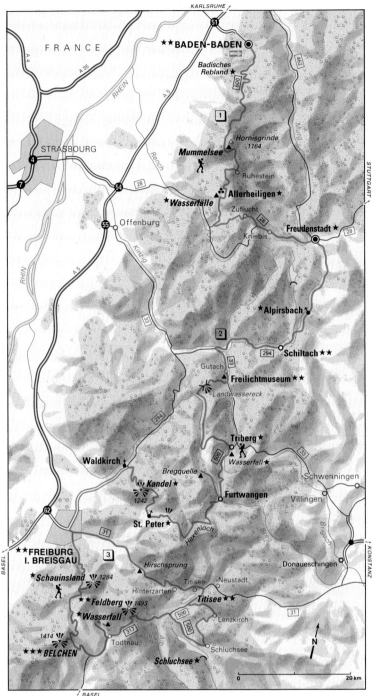

★★ **Baden-Baden** – *See BADEN-BADEN.*

Mummelsee – This small, dark glacial lake is at the foot of the **Hornisgrinde** (1 164m/3 819ft), the highest point of the Northern Black Forest. It is named after the "Mümmeln" (water sprites) that inhabit its icy depths, according to local legend. In days gone by, the Black Forest breweries would obtain blocks of ice chopped out of the frozen lake until well into spring.

At Ruhestein, the itinerary leaves the Hochstraße temporarily to plunge towards the **Allerheiligen Valley**★ and then climb back from Oppenau towards Zuflucht by way of an extremely steep mountain road.

* **Allerheiligen** – The ruins of a late-13C church, built for a Premonstratensian monastery, add a romantic touch to this lonely dell. The vaulted porch and the walls of the transept are still standing, together with a polygonal Gothic chapel leading off them. A footpath leads from the ruins to the celebrated waterfall.

* **Allerheiligen-Wasserfälle** – *45min on foot there and back from the car park at the foot of the falls (2km/1.2mi beyond the abbey ruins).*
A steep, stepped path climbs beside the torrent between rock walls overhung by huge trees.
From Zuflucht to Kniebis, the route crosses an upland plateau, most of it marshy moorland typical of the Grinde.

* **Freudenstadt** – At the crossing of several routes, the town, built in the 17C by order of the Duke of Württemberg, was destroyed by fire in 1945. Rebuilt since, it now follows a checkerboard plan centred on the **Marktplatz★**, a huge square surrounded by houses with arcades.
The 17C **church** (Stadtkirche) is oddly placed: its two naves, arranged at right-angles, form one corner of Marktplatz. The pulpit, supported by the four evangelists, and the carved 12C **lectern★★**, come from Alpirsbach Abbey, the most important Romanesque church in the Black Forest. A further treasure is the Romanesque **font★** dating from c 1100.

★★ CENTRAL BLACK FOREST

[2] **From Freudenstadt to Freiburg** *152km/94mi – one day*

The itinerary follows the foot of the Kinzig and Elt valleys, passing through a number of busy villages before reaching the Upper Black Forest at Kandel.

* **Alpirsbach** – The church, joined to the old **Benedictine abbey★** buildings, has a 12C apse with unusual lines: the Romanesque lower floor supports a Gothic chancel in which the buttresses do not reach the floor but stand on free columns. Inside, at the apse's lower level, a hollowed-out niche – the central one out of three – bears traces of 12C **wall paintings**: Christ in Glory between the Chosen and the Damned on the vaulting; The Crucifixion on the hemispherical surface. In the **cloisters** *(ring for the caretaker)*, the vault tracery and the bays, much restored, are in the Gothic Flamboyant style.

★★ **Schiltach** – At the confluence of the Schiltach and the Kinzig lies this picturesque half-timbered village. The double valley and the unusually complete collection of well-preserved historic buildings around the steeply sloping **Marktplatz★** lend this village an idyllic aspect.

★★ **Schwarzwälder Freilichtmuseum Vogtsbauernhof** (Black Forest Open-Air Museum) ⊘ – In Gutach. *Allow 2hr for visit.*
The skills of the people of the Black Forest in matters of rural building, craftwork and agriculture are celebrated in this admirable open-air museum in the Gutach Valley. The Vogtsbauern farm, still in its original (1570) state, is set amid five more reconstituted farmhouses with their outbuildings. At the **Hotzenwaldhaus**, replicas of a cowshed and interior furnishings are confined to an inner gallery to protect them from the weather. The **Falkenhof** from the Dreisam Valley is the museum's only example of a building with a two-storey residential section and a threshing floor separating the living quarters and the animals' stalls. The **Schauinslandhaus** is well adapted to the harsh conditions of the Black Forest mountain plateaus. Living quarters, stalls and workshops are all under one roof.
The **Hippenseppenhof** farm represents the commonest type, especially of those found in the wilder upland valleys; its position on the slope allows farm carts direct access to the hayloft. There is no trouble identifying the **Vogtsbauernhof** itself: the central portion is stone-built. Inside, note the timber roof framework, with the load-bearing beams set horizontally. Crafts connected with forest life are on display on the ground floor of the **Lorenzerhof** farm.
The road leading through the Landwassereck pass offers a number of fine **views★** over the undulating landscapes of the central Black Forest. Upstream from Oberprechtal, the beautiful cascades of the Elz border the route.

* **Triberg** – This centre of the clockmaking industry is also a favourite health resort. The **Waterfall Walk★** *(1hr on foot there and back)* follows the Gutach rapids in a natural setting of boulders and tall trees. The **Schwarzwald Museum** ⊘ specializes in the exhibition of traditional costumes and local craftwork: watch and clock-making, ceramics, wood veneers etc. The church of **Maria in den Tannen** (Our Lady of the Firs), one of the most popular pilgrims' sanctuaries in the Black Forest,

displays carved and painted Baroque **furnishings**★ in an exuberant style that is wholly rustic.

Furtwangen – This health resort lies in a mountain valley 850m/ 2 790ft above sea level. It has a population of 10 000 and is the cultural

and economic centre of this agricultural region. Cases and movements from all over the world, selected for their value, their artistic character or the ingeniousness of their conception are on display at the **Deutsches Uhrenmuseum**★ ⊘ in this small clock-making town. Also on view are fantasy clocks, cuckoos, singing birds, wooden clocks and a reconstruction of a period watchmaker's workshop. The museum does not leave the social and cultural aspects of clockmaking unexplored.

From the town it is only 6km/4mi to the **source of the Breg** (signposts *"Katzensteig-Martinskapelle" and then "Donauquelle"*). The Breg, one of the rivers flowing into the Danube which lies furthest from its mouth, rises here

Deutsches Uhrenmuseum Furtwangen

Double Basket Clock (18C), Deutsches Uhrenmuseum, Furtwangen

at a height of 1 078m/3 537ft. The source of the Danube itself is located at Donaueschingen.

Soon after leaving Furtwangen, turn right for **Hexenloch**. Pass through a deep, steeply wooded gorge enlivened by many waterfalls. Between St. Märgen and St. Peter, the twists and turns of the road allow plenty of clear **views**★★ of the central Black Forest.

★ **St. Peter** – This Baroque church, attached to the huge **abbey** (1727), is the burial place of the Dukes of Zähringen, the founders of Freiburg-im-Breisgau (statues by the great sculptor JA Feuchtmayer).
The extravagance of the Late Rococo style is exemplified in the high altar and the ceiling paintings. The elegant (restored) Baroque **library**★ ⊘ is decorated with delicate stuccowork.

★ **Kandel** – From the viewing table here *(30min on foot there and back)* there is a splendid **panorama**★ taking in the Vosges, the Feldberg, the Belchen, and the isolated Kaiserstuhl massif.

★ **Waldkirch** – Lovely 18C houses, once part of the chapter of canons, surround the former collegiate church of St. Margaretha in a tranquil, shady quarter of this small industrial town.

★★★ UPPER BLACK FOREST

③ Round tour leaving from Freiburg-im-Breisgau

142km/88mi - one day

This circuit, mountainous in the first part, passes the three principal summits of the Black Forest (Schauinsland, Belchen and Feldberg), and then the two best-known lakes (Schluchsee and Titisee) in the massif.

★ **Schauinsland** – The mountain road, extremely twisty, leads to the upper teleferic station. From the car park, climb to the top of the viewing tower *(91 steps)* after following the signs "Rundweg" and "Schauinsland Gipfel" *(30min on foot there and back)*. The look-out point offers a **view★** across upland meadows to the Feldberg.

Follow the road for 1km/0.5mi, and take the right-hand fork towards Stohen, and the Münstertal. Winding down through the meadows, the route finally plunges once more into the forest. At Wiedener Eck, turn right towards the Belchen.

★★★ **Belchen** – *From the end of the road, walk (30min there and back) to the viewing table on the summit.*

This rounded mountain with its steep, bare flanks, dominates the Wiesenthal and the valleys which, like the Münstertal, interlace the western fringe of the Black Forest. The Belchen summit is at a height of 1 414m/4 637ft. When visibility is good, it makes a magnificent **observation point★★★** over the Rhine plain, the rounded heights of the High Vosges, and the Alps from Säntis to Mont Blanc.

★ **The Falls of Todtnau** – *1.5km/1mi from Todtnau.*
Climbing through a wooded combe, a footpath leads *(1hr there and back)* to an impressive series of cascades.

★★ **Feldberg** – A chair-lift conveys sightseers to the Seebuck (1 448m/4 750ft), which is crowned by the Bismarck monument. From here there is a **view★** of the symmetrically perfect, circular bowl of the Feldsee, a small lake at the bottom of a glaciated circus or amphitheatre. It is possible to reach the Feldberg summit at 1 493m/4 897ft *(1hr 30min there and back)*, to enjoy, again, a vast **panorama★★** stretching as far as the Alps.

★ **Schluchsee** – This lake, originally glacial, has become – thanks to a dam built in 1932 – the most immense stretch of water in the Black Forest. On its shore is a small climatic health resort which shares its name.

The Titisee is reached via Lenzkirch. During the final part of the descent, the road overlooks the lake.

★★ **Titisee** – This pretty lake, formed by a moraine barrier, is at the junction of several tourist routes. Because of its position, it has developed both into a health centre (Titisee-Neustadt and **Hinterzarten★**) and a departure point for many Black Forest excursions. The return to Freiburg is through the **Höllental★** ("The Vale of Hell"), which – except perhaps in the Hirschsprung Gorge – does nothing to justify its nickname.

SCHWERIN★

Mecklenburg-Vorpommern
Population 130 000
Michelin map 416 F 18

Magnificently situated in a landscape of lakes and forests, Schwerin renewed its links with an administrative past by becoming a Land capital in 1990. The origins of the town go back to the 11C, when the Slavs built a fortress on what is now an island – Schloßinsel. It was not long, however, before they were expelled by Henry the Lion, the Duke of Saxony, who used the emplacement as a base for the construction of the first German town east of the Elbe. For almost five centuries after that (1358-1918), Schwerin was capital of the Duchy of Mecklenburg.

★★ SCHLOSSINSEL (CZ) 2hr

The island, and the two bridges linking it with the town, separate the smaller Burgsee from the 21km/13mi stretch of Lake Schwerin.

★ Schloß ⊘ (CZ) – Built between 1845 and 1857 in the neo-Renaissance style – with elements borrowed from the Gothic and the Baroque styles – this is one of the most important civic constructions of 19C Germany. From the outside, it recalls the Château of Chambord on the Loire, by which in fact the architects Demmler and Stüler were inspired.
The rooms inside are lavishly decorated, with particularly **fine floors**. Note especially the **Throne Room**★ (Thronsaal), the Ancestors' Gallery (Ahnengalerie) and the Smoking Room (Rauchzimmer).

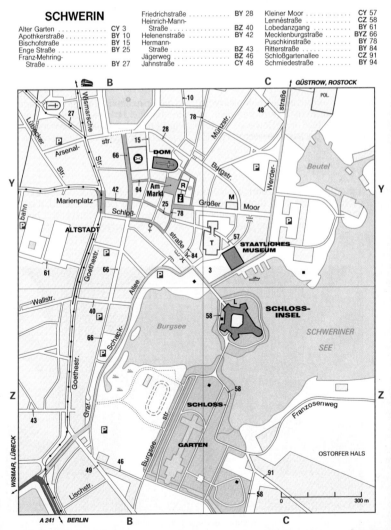

★ **Kapelle** – The castle chapel is much older; it was built between 1560 and 1563. The Renaissance galleries and vaulting are supported by Tuscan columns.

★ **Schloßgarten** – Created in the mid 18C, this formal Baroque garden is organized around canals in the form of a cross and rectilinear walks. It is peopled with statues (copies) by Balthazar Permoser.

ADDITIONAL SIGHTS

★ **Staatliches Museum** (National Museum) ⊙ **(CY)** – *Werderstraße.*
Important Flemish and Dutch paintings of the 17C (Brueghel, Brouwer, Jordaens and Van Ruisdael) are on display in this museum, a neo-Classical block built between 1877 and 1882 beside an old public garden (Alter Garten) near the theatre. The outside is adorned with Italian Renaissance decorations.
A department of 18C and 19C European painting houses works by Houdon, Pesne, Friedrich, Liebermann, Corinth etc.
Relics of Slav settlements established in the region during the Stone Age are on view in a prehistoric section.

Markt (BY) – Four late-17C half-timbered houses with gables have been preserved next to the town hall. On the north side of the square, the so-called **New Building** (Neues Gebäude) was erected between 1783 and 1785 in the Classic style, with Doric columns and attics, to be used as a chamber of commerce.

★ **Dom (Cathedral) (BY)** – Brick built in the Gothic style during the 14C and 15C, the church contains several works of art worth a visit. They include a Gothic altarpiece (from a Lübeck workshop, c 1480); a number of 14C funerary plaques; and, in the Chapel of the Assumption, frescoes dating from c 1335.

SCHWETZINGEN

Baden-Württemberg
Population 22 000
Michelin map 417/419 R 9

Schwetzingen lies in the Rhine plain with its favourable climate. During the asparagus season, gourmets flock to the town, while in May and June music lovers come for the festivals held here. However, the town is best known for having been the summer residence of the Palatine electoral princes, as testified by the magnificent palace and gardens.

★ SCHLOß ⊙

The castle, destroyed during the Orléans War, was rebuilt in 1700-17 as a Baroque palace complex with three wings. The most splendid period of its history was under Prince Elector Carl Theodor, who spent every summer here with his wife Elisabeth Augusta from 1742 to 1778. In 1803, the palace passed to the House of Baden.

Rococo theatre, Schloß Schwetzingen

Staatl. Schlösser u. Gärten B.-W. Schloßverwaltung Schwetzingen

About 40 of the palace rooms are open to the public. One set of the apartments has been restored in the style of the 19C, including the Swiss Room with its remarkable original panoramic tapestries from 1804, while the rooms on the first floor are resplendently fitted out as they would have been c 1775.
The charming **Rococo theatre** ⊘, built in the mid 18C by Lorraine architect Nicolas de Pigage (1723-96), is open throughout the summer. During the Schwetzingen festival it makes an ideal tranquil setting for concerts.

★★ **Schloßgarten** ⊘ – This 72ha/178 acre park was laid out stage by stage and is undoubtedly one of the finest examples of 18C parks in Europe. The French garden, with its rigorously geometric design (circular parterre with fountains along the central axis), is also the work of Nicolas de Pigage. A little later, the English style gardens were landscaped by Friedrich Ludwig von Sckell, with streams, lakes and trees. The Late Rococo taste for mock ancient buildings gave rise to a number of little temples and artificial ruins dotted around the grounds, such as the Apollo temple, the **Mosque**, a Roman moated castle and the charming bathing house with "perspective" (artificial view onto a painted landscape).

SIGMARINGEN★

Baden-Württemberg
Population 16 000
Michelin map 419 V 11 – Local map see SCHWÄBISCHE ALB

The strong defensive position of Sigmaringen – a rocky spur rising from the valley at the mouth of the Upper Danube Gap – made the town an ideal choice as minor capital of the principality ruled by the Swabian (Catholic) branch of the Hohenzollerns. The castle rises in traditional style from the edge of the cliff, but the only feudal parts remaining are the site and its general appearance: all the buildings and their interior decoration are pastiches of different styles.

The Castle and its Annexes – *1hr.*
The approach ramp starts at the highest point reached by the road cutting across the land enclosed by the loop of the Danube *(leave the car in front of the Stadthalle, the Rathaus, or the fortified gateway to the castle)*.

Schloß (Castle) ⊘ – The State Apartments adorned in the 16C style with coffered ceilings and tapestries (Royal Bedchamber, Ancestral Hall etc) will be of most interest to those versed in the history of European royalty. Fine **collection of arms and armour**.

Church – Luminous with Rococo stuccowork, the church clings to the castle rock. A shrine in a transept chapel on the left contains the cradle of St Fidelio of Sigmaringen (1577-1622), first Capuchin martyr, Patron of the Order and local patron saint.

Museums – On view here are paintings (Swabian Primitives) and an exhibition of means of transport (Marstallmuseum).

SOEST★

Nordrhein-Westfalen
Population 43 000
Michelin map 417 L 8 – Local map see SAUERLAND

This town has existed probably since the 7C, located on the Hellweg, an important route for trade, armies, pilgrims and monarchs, in the middle of fertile countryside. The rapid growth and increase in wealth of this former Hanseatic League member can be traced to salt extraction in the Early Middle Ages. This generated considerable trade far afield, with the result that by the High Middle Ages, by dint of its economic and cultural success, Soest was considered the unofficial capital of Westphalia. In 1444, Soest parted company with its feudal lord, the Archbishop of Cologne, and allied itself with the Duke of Cleves, unleashing a five year military conflict known as the **Soest Feud** (Soester Fehde). The town eventually emerged victorious, but at a price, having lost its strategic trade advantage. In the 17C, it passed to Brandenburg.
Soest is distinguished by the use of markedly greenish sandstone, and a very individual style of garden wall. The town features numerous half-timbered houses lining a star-shaped network of streets. The towers of various churches can be seen above the rampart enclosing the town centre.

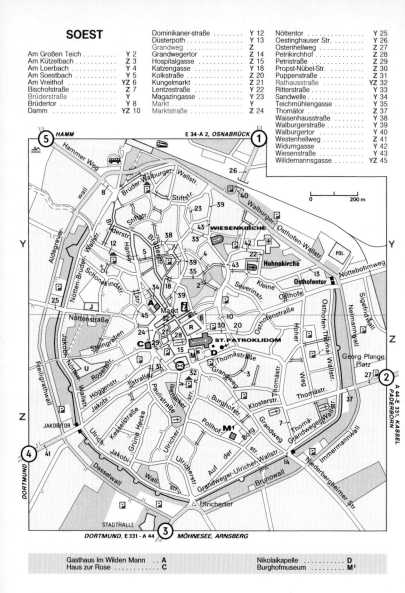

SOEST

Gasthaus Im Wilden Mann .. **A**
Haus zur Rose .... **C**

Nikolaikapelle .... **D**
Burghofmuseum .... **M¹**

SIGHTS

One of the most remarkable half-timbered buildings is the twin-gabled hotel, **Im Wilden Mann** (**Y A**), in the Markt. Another, decorated with motifs in colour, is the **Haus zur Rose** (**Z C**), at the corner of Marktstraße and Rosenstraße. The well-preserved **Osthofentor** (East Gate) (**Y**), with its fine Gothic embellishments, formed part of later 16C fortifications. The past history of the town can be traced in the **Burghofmuseum** (**Z M¹**).

Pumpernickel, the black rye bread baked for 24hr which is found in so many German breakfast tables, is made in Soest.

★ **Patroklidom** (**Z**) – The interest in this massive 11C-12C Romanesque building lies entirely in the **Westwerk**★★ and its perfectly balanced square **tower**★★ austerely decorated with blind arcades and blind rose windows. The two tiers of arcades lightening the upper part of the tower are matched by two more at the base, the lower of which is furnished with very delicate small columns. The Romanesque frescoes in the apse of the north transept are original, having survived the Second World War. The others were restored to Romanesque designs in 1950. A fine 15C Crucifix stands on the altar. Parts of the original furnishings salvaged from the war damage can be seen in the Treasury.

Nikolaikapelle (**Z D**) – In the chancel of this two-aisle chapel is the **St Nicholas Altarpiece**★, painted on a gold background in about 1400 by Conrad von Soest, a great name in Westphalian art. St Nicholas is shown as the patron of merchants and mariners.

★ **Wiesenkirche** (Y) – Length, width and height are virtually identical in the nave of this beautifully lit 14C Gothic hall-church. A late-14C Virgin and Child can be seen at the pier of the south doorway.

The 1520 **stained-glass window of the Last Supper**, above the north doorway, gave the artist the chance to advertise some local specialities: boar's head, ham, pitchers of beer and small loaves of rye bread can be recognized on the table. The most important work of art in the church is the 1525 **Aldegrever Altarpiece★** – the Virgin Mary between St Anthony and St Agatha, bathed in a halo of light – in the south apsidal chapel.

Hohnekirche (Y) – This bizarre, squat church of Romanesque origin was built with a flat chancel and apsidal chapels out of line with the main block. It was converted into a hall-church in the 13C. The whole interior – walls, vaults and roofing included – is covered with frescoes. In the chancel, the **Dance of the Angels** (c 1280) depicts the Virgin in Majesty surrounded by a ring of 16 angels with stylized wings in the form of flames.

A **funerary niche** (Grabnische) with 13C frescoes faces the south entrance; on the left, half hidden by three short, thick columns, is the baptistry with its Romanesque font.

EXCURSIONS

★ **Möhnesee** – *11km/7mi to the south. Leave by ③ on the town plan.*
This artificial lake on the northern edge of the Sauerland is 10km/6mi long. The dam retaining the reservoir is 650m/over 700yd across and almost 40m/131ft high. To the north, the lakeshore is open to tourists and those practising water sports. On the other hand, the south bank, which is well forested, is a nature reserve harbouring many species of birds, some of them very rare.

The Sauerland – *See SAUERLAND.*

SPEYER★

Rheinland-Pfalz
Population 46 000
Michelin map 417/419 S 9 – Local map see PFALZ AM RHEIN

The old Imperial City of Speyer lies in the Rhine plain and is easily distinguished from some way off by its belfries. It effectively has its back to the Rhine, which cuts a meander at this point, and is linked to the river only by the Rheinallee and the port. Once favoured as a place to stay by the Salian emperors, and having been an episcopal seat since the 7C, Speyer enjoyed considerable importance from the 11C on. It was made Imperial City in 1294. More than 50 Imperial Diets were held here, the last one taking place in 1570. Speyer was the seat of the Imperial Council from 1526 to 1688. However, Speyer was burned to the ground in 1689 by Louis XIV's troops during the Orléans War. For this reason, the only evidence of its medieval splendour that survives is the Kaiserdom, fragments of the town wall in the cathedral grounds and the Altpörtel, a tall tower at the west end of Maximilianstraße that was once the town's main gateway.

After a brief period under French rule – the town was handed over to France in 1797 – Speyer passed into the hands of the Bavarian monarchs, along with the rest of the Palatinate east of the Rhine. During this period, numerous authorities were based here, including archives and libraries, with the result that Speyer now has a reputation as an administrative centre.

The "Protestants" – The Edict of Worms, in fact never enacted, was confirmed by the Diet of Speyer in 1529. The Lutheran states then made a solemn protest against the Diet's decisions, from which derives the label "Protestant" to identify partisans of the Reformation. The fact is commemorated in the existence of a neo-Gothic church, Gedächtniskirche, built early this century on Bartholomäus-Weltz-Platz.

★★ KAISERDOM ⊘

This fine cathedral building, founded by Konrad II in 1030 and remodelled at the end of the 11C, is a Romanesque basilica with four towers and two domes.

Exterior – There is an interesting **view★★** of the east end from the garden approach to the 13C **Heidentürmchen** (Pagan Tower). An elegant dwarf gallery circles the nave and transept just below the roof. The finely carved capitals display a wide variety of motifs on the garden side of the apse. On the lower part of one of the blind arcades, in the centre, a worn 11C relief depicting the Kingdom of Peace can be distinguished. The window arches of the east transept show Lombard influence and – especially on the south side – a lavish decoration of palm leaves and scrollwork. Similar motifs are repeated on the cornice below the roof.

The east end, Speyer Cathedral

Interior – The most impressive way to enter is via the door in the west face (rebuilt in the mid 19C). On the right of the porch is a statue of Rudolph of Habsburg. The huge, well-lit nave has groined vaulting with prominent transverse arches. The half columns engaged in the main pillars are cut by rings and capitals with acanthus leaves.

The sobriety of the side aisles, also with groined vaulting, is remarkable. There is a good view of the building's harmonious proportions from the top of the south aisle stairway.

The raised **transept**★★ is a masterpiece of unity and balance. Note particularly, above the transept crossing, the octagonal cupola on squinches with its small lantern tower. The lack of texture and ornamentation on the walls emphasizes the natural decorative character of the architecture itself. The **Chapel of the Holy Sacrament** (Afrakapelle) *(on the left, before the north transept)* houses two 15C low-relief sculptures: the Bearing of the Cross and the Annunciation. Opposite, before the south transept, eight groined vaults surround a two-tier central rotunda in which are the **baptistry** (Chapel of St Emmerammus) and, above, a chapel dedicated to St Catherine.

★★★ **Crypt** ⊘ – This is probably the finest and largest Romanesque crypt in Germany. Beneath the chancel and the transept, whose crossing above is marked by four columns with splendid cushion capitals, Romanesque groined vaulting spreads out like a net supported by transverse arches of alternately pink and white sandstone. Four Holy Roman Emperors and four German Kings are buried in the impressive **Royal Vault**. The 13C tombstone of Rudolph of Habsburg stands guard at the entrance.

In the gardens south of the cathedral is the **Ölberg** (1502-12), once the centre of the cloisters. A large stone trough – the **Domnapf** – stands in the forecourt. In days gone by, each time a bishop was enthroned, it was filled with wine and anyone who wished to could drink until he dropped.

ADDITIONAL SIGHTS

Old town – This stretches from the cathedral west towards the **Altpörtel**★, a fine 12C-13C gateway tower. Maximilianstraße is a lively street, whose crowning glory is the Late Baroque town hall. At the fork with Korngasse stands the "Alte Münze" (Old Mint) built in 1748; its name is derived from the coin minters' guildhall which stood on this spot in the Middle Ages. There are old houses to be admired in Kleine and Große Greifengasse, Hagedorngasse and Gutenberggasse. The district around the timber and fish market is also picturesque.

★ **Judenbad (Jewish Baths)** – *Access via Judengasse, southwest of the cathedral (signposted).*
Ritual ablutions were performed here. The building (Judenhof), in the centre of the medieval Jewish quarter, was erected in the 12C, probably by workmen engaged in the construction of the cathedral.
A stairway with double doors leads down to the first chamber, which has groined vaulting and, on the left, an anteroom for changing. A second, semicircular staircase then descends to the level of the water-table, where the actual bath is situated.

Dreifaltigkeitskirche – *In Große Himmelsgasse.*
The **interior**★ of this enormous Baroque church (1701-17) is surrounded by a two-storey gallery with a balustrade adorned by paintings. The wooden capped vaulting is painted too.

★ **Historisches Museum der Pfalz (Palatinate Museum)** ⊙ – In Gallery 4 on the ground floor of this museum is the celebrated **Golden Hat**★ of Schifferstadt, the rarest, most valuable item in the Prehistoric Department. In the shape of a cone, this solid gold religious cult object dates from the 12C BC.

Further focal points of the museum are the Roman, Medieval and Modern departments. The sumptuous collection of art and decorative arts from the 16C to the 19C, which includes some beautiful Frankenthal porcelain, should not be missed.

Cathedral treasury (Domschatzkammer) – *In both the basement storeys of the new building*. There is no doubt that the tomb furnishings of the emperors and kings from the vault of the cathedral are the main points of attraction, for example the funerary crown of Konrad II, the first Salian emperor, the Imperial orb of Heinrich III, the crown of the Canossa penance of Heinrich IV. A little piece of German history is brought to light. There are some magnificent liturgical robes and articles.

Weinmuseum – The museum presents 2 000 years of wine history. The showpiece is the **Roman wine**★, which is the oldest still liquid wine in the world, in its aphora-like bottle. It was found in Palatinate in a Roman stone sarcophagus dating from the 3C AD. There is a sumptuous collection of decorated barrels, and imposing winepresses dating from the 16C and 18C.

★ **Technik-Museum** ⊙ – The **Technology Museum** situated south of the cathedral will interest young and old alike. Displayed in exhibition halls and the open air are an impressive number of aircraft (Fokkers, Junkers, Dornier, Antonov, Douglas), railway engines, but mainly classic veteran cars by every famous manufacturer, not forgetting a whole range of fire engines. There is a submarine with which visitors can quite literally enjoy a hands-on visit. Being able to go inside the U 9, built in 1966, gives visitors a vivid insight into how terribly cramped conditions are inside a submarine. Further attractions on offer at this museum include a marine museum with model ships and an extensive collection of historical musical instruments.

Those who enjoy big thrills and being able to see things in close-up must be sure not to miss the **IMAX-Filmtheater**★, either for conventional cinema or the dome version with an 800m²/8 600sq ft screen.

Purrmann-Haus ⊙ – A selection of fine works from every period of his creative output testifies to the artistic skill of painter **Hans Purrmann**, born in this house in 1880. His contact with Henri Matisse, who was his student, greatly inspired Purrmann in his own art, resulting in paintings with some exuberant palettes. Matisse's influence is evident right up to Purrmann's last works. His powerful, yet sensitive, brush strokes are as well suited to portraits and still-life as to landscape painting.

Feuerbachhaus ⊙ – **Anselm Feuerbach**, nephew of the famous philosopher Ludwig Feuerbach, was born in this simple house in 1829. The artist, best known for his monumental canvases (*Medea, Iphigenia*) and portraits of women (*Nanna Risi*), was, together with Arnold Böcklin and Hans von Marées, one of the most important representatives of the avant-garde school of artists who took many of their themes from Classical Antiquity. He lived in Rome for 17 years which is where he honed his style to one which idealised Classicism.

SPREEWALD★★

Brandenburg

Michelin map 418 K 25-26

A network of more than 300 waterways crisscrosses this lush countryside, declared a biosphere reserve by UNESCO – site of an ancient forest swamp painstakingly cleared and drained – lending it the appearance of a "Venice in the Woods". The region's special interest lies also in its **Sorbian minority**, descendants of western Slav people who settled in the Lausitz area of Germany after the migrations of the 6C and who remain fiercely proud of their language, traditions and culture today (*see the Sorbian museums at Bautzen and Cottbus*).

Basically agricultural, the Spreewald specialises in the cultivation of cucumbers and horseradish.

Barge Trip (Kahnfahrt) ⊙ – *Boat trips are available in most places in the Spreewald, although* **Lübbenau** *has established itself as the centre for such trips. In Lübbenau, leave the main road opposite the railway station and take Maxim-Gorki-Straße to one of the car parks near the landing-stage.*

From here, boatmen/guides organize excursions aboard flat-bottomed craft which ferry passengers to the heart of a leafy paradise shaped by man into a limitless garden. Only the ripple of water, the singing of birds and the quacking of ducks break the silence.

R. Chérey/MICHELIN

In the Spreewald

A stop at **Lehde**★, a tiny lagoon village with a population of 150 and which boasts almost as many islands as houses, allows sightseers to visit the **Open-Air Museum** (Freilandmuseum Lehde). Here, three early-19C farms, complete with living quarters and outbuildings, display rustic furniture, folk art, costumes and agricultural implements. Visitors to the museum can learn about barge-building in the Spreewald and about matters related to nature conservation.

Visitors preferring to make these discoveries on foot can choose between three different footpaths starting from Lübbenau: one leading towards Lehde (1hr there and back), another to Wotschofska and a third to Leipe (3hr there and back).

Lübbenau – In addition to a visit to the old town, the town church of **St. Nikolai**★ ⊘, built in 1738-41 by the Dresden master and fortifications builder Findeisen, is well worth a visit. The interior is in an impressively harmonious Dresden Baroque style. Two-storey galleries extend along the sides, opening out into glazed loges in the chancel. There are some impressive tombs, including the high **tomb** (c 1765) of the mediatized (i.e. no longer an immediate vassal of the Holy Roman Empire and thus deprived of some of his rights of government) prince Moritz Carl, Count of Lynaer. Lübbenau castle and grounds are well worth a trip, for the chancellery building (1745, now a museum), the neo-Classical castle (1817, now a hotel) and the Orangery.

STADE

Niedersachsen

Population 47 000
Michelin map 415 F 12

This town with over 1 000 years of history lies on the bank of the navigable stretch of the Schwinge, which flows into the Elbe to the northeast. In the Middle Ages, Stade was a port in the same league as Hamburg. The Swedes occupied the town during the Thirty Years War and transformed it is the 70 years their troops were stationed here into a garrison stronghold and administrative centre, the capital of their north German territory. Most buildings in the fine **old town**★ are from after 1659, date of the great fire in which two thirds of the town's dwellings were destroyed. Between 1960 and 1970, Stade more or less became a port once again as a result of the new industrial region on the Lower Elbe.

Alter Hafen (Old Port) – Traditionally handling wood on the ancient Hanseatic route, the winding basin is now almost deserted, leaving only a nostalgic stretch of still water bordered by rusting iron. An idea of how it must have looked in the 17C is nevertheless provided by the fine houses, meticulously restored, which stand on either side.

★ **Schwedenspeicher-Museum** ⊘ – *Wasser West*.
Built between 1692 and 1705 on one of the quays, this brick granary now houses a museum illustrating the town's commercial history and its old system of defences. There is also a prehistoric department exhibiting four magnificent **bronze wheels**★ (c 700 BC) from a funerary carriage, as well as antique jewellery, weapons and pots.

Not far from the museum (*Wasser West* 7), the Kaufmann Collection, housed in a handsome building (the **Kunsthaus**), displays paintings of the Worpswede School. The artists include Fritz Mackensen, Otto Modersohn (*Marsh, Barns and Silver Birches*, 1896), Paula Modersohn-Becker (*Peasant Woman with Red Scarf*, 1900) and Fritz Overbeck (*Flooding in the Marsh*, 1903).

St.-Cosmae und Damianikirche – The Baroque spire of this 13C-15C church, complete with onion bulb, rises above a picturesque old quarter where the wooden houses are bricked in between the beams. Inside, the fine 17C furnishings (organ, pulpit, copper chandeliers) are intact. The wrought iron grille work (1670) is imaginative.

EXCURSION

★ **Altes Land** – *Round tour of 51km/32mi to the southeast; about 2hr. Narrow, twisting and cobbled roads. Take the main Hamburg road for Buxtehude.*
Between Stade and Buxtehude, the flat land beside the Elbe is a countryside of apple and cherry orchards, enchanting in the spring when the blossoms are out. Leave Buxtehude via the Jork road, which runs northwards beside the winding Este embankment. After the pretty village of Estebrügge, turn left in Königreich towards **Jork**★. Towards the far end of this village, just where there is a left turn towards the Museum Altes Land, there is a series of fine thatched **farmhouses**★ (Bauernhäuser). At Mittelnkirchen, stay on the east bank of the canal, crossing further downstream at the Steinkirchen weighbridge. Return to Stade via Grünendeich (splendid view of the Elbe from the top of the embankment).

Abbot Albert's Travel Guide

A discussion between two holy brothers, Tirri and Firri, on the journey to Rome and back, recorded in Abbot Albert's "Stade Annuls" (written c 1250), is the oldest known example of a travel guide in the German-speaking world. Besides descriptions of individual routes, giving very precise indications of distances (instead of saying how many days' travel), the author provides a considerable amount of practical information, including advice on what action to take if the Rhine has flooded at Duisburg, the best time to travel in view of being able to cross the Alpine passes, evaluations of tourist infrastructures (for example, the facilities in Pustertal were judged to be bad quality and expensive), cultural background and suggestions on what to visit.

STENDAL

Sachsen-Anhalt
Population 48 500
Michelin map 416/418 I 19

Founded c 1160 by the Margrave Albrecht the Bear, Stendal soon developed into an important trade centre. The town was a member of the Hanseatic League from 1359 to 1518, and until the mid 16C remained the most influential in the Brandenburg March. The ravages of the Thirty Years War, however finally dealt it a death blow. Several monuments typical of Gothic brick architecture can still be seen from its period of prosperity.
Stendal was the birthplace of **Johann Joachim Winckelmann** (1717-68), considered to be the founder of a scientific approach to archeology. One of his admirers, the French novelist **Henri Beyle** (1783-1842), liked the name of the town so much that he adopted it as a pseudonym, adding an extra "h" to become world famous as **Stendhal**.

SIGHTS

Rathaus – *On the Markt.*
The oldest part of the town hall, in exposed brick, dates from the beginning of the 15C. The gables are stepped. Added at the end of that century, the main wing was later remodelled in the Renaissance style. On the square stands a copy of the statue of Roland destroyed by a hurricane in 1972.

Marienkirche – *Behind the Markt.*
The triple-aisle hall-church was built between 1435 and 1477. The chancel, surrounded by an ambulatory, is separated from the nave by a delicately worked partition. The high altar (Coronation and Death of the Virgin) is in the Flamboyant Gothic style.

★ **Dom St. Nikolaus** – The former Augustinian monks' church was supplanted in the 15C by a cathedral of much larger size, the square ground-plan recalling the hall-churches of Lower Saxony, in particular St.-Johanniskirche in Lüneburg. The

stained-glass windows★ (1420-60) are remarkable. Note especially those in the chancel, which, because of the amount of wall they replace, suggest a huge conservatory.

★ **Uenglinger Tor (Uenglingen Gate)** – Northwest of the old town.
Dating from c 1380, this is one of the most interesting fortified medieval gateways in the region. From the outside, the two lower storeys present an aspect that is purely defensive, while the upper part, added in the 15C, is much more decorative.

EXCURSIONS

★ **Tangermünde** – *10km/6mi to the southeast.*
Situated, as its name suggests, where the waters of the River Tanger join those of the Elbe, Tangermünde's history closely follows the history of Stendal. The small town, still enclosed within its late-14C ramparts, is crossed by two parallel streets, bordered by half-timbered houses with finely worked doorways. The brick-built 1430 **Rathaus★** has a three-gable façade garnished with a superb lacework of carved decorations.
The town's ancient gateways retain their monumental aspect, particularly the **Neustädter Tor★**, an imposing circular tower on the south side.

Havelberg – *46km/29mi to the north; cross the Elbe at Tangermünde.*
Overlooking this small, pretty town on the banks of the River Havel the **cathedral of St.-Marien★** ⊙ was founded at the end of the 12C but almost entirely rebuilt in the Gothic style between 1279 and 1330. The sculpturing of the chancel partition and the rood-screen **panels★★** (c 1400) is greatly to be admired. Illustrating scenes from the life of Jesus, these were probably the work of craftsmen from the Parler studio in Prague. Note also three **sandstone candelabra** and a **Triumphal Cross** (c 1300). The Early Gothic cloister dates from the 13C.

STRALSUND★

Mecklenburg-Vorpommern
Population 70 000
Michelin map 416 D 23 – Local map see RÜGEN

Separated from the island of Rügen by a narrow sea channel and surrounded by lakes, the Baltic town of Stralsund has developed since the earliest times as a centre of maritime navigation and long-distance trade. Its Gothic brick buildings, inspired by those of Lübeck, its more powerful neighbour, are among the best-known in northern Germany.

A Coveted City – From the moment of its foundation by Prince Jaromir of Rügen in 1209, Stralsund was subjected to assaults from envious neighbours: from Lübeck, from Denmark, from Sweden and even Holland they came with their troops to seize this port, so admirably situated. Protected by its massive rampart belt, the town was able during the Thirty Years War to beat off the forces of the all-conquering Imperial General Albrecht von Wallenstein. Subsequently taken – several times – by Sweden, it returned to Prussian rule after the Napoleonic Wars. Today, Stralsund's prosperity depends mainly on its shipyards and its fishing fleet.

SIGHTS

★ **Rathaus (Town hall) (BY R)** – Built in the 13C and 14C, this splendid edifice comprises two separate, parallel blocks. The magnificent **north façade★**, crowned by a pediment with openwork gables – again, inspired by the Rathaus in Lübeck – was added c 1450. The ground floor arcades open onto a covered market hall. From this a passageway leads to the west porch of Nikolaikirche. Among the old houses bordering the market place, the **Wulflammhaus** (no 5, **BY A**), brick built in the mid 15C, is noteworthy for its odd three-storey gable pierced by small windows.

★ **Nikolaikirche (BY)** – Modelled on Marienkirche of Lübeck, this 13C-14C hall-church has seen its central nave raised and its single tower replaced by a powerful façade with two towers. The relatively low ambulatory at the east end is dominated by solid buttresses.
Inside, there is a striking contrast between the modest height of the side aisles, flanked by low chapels, and the spectacular, soaring nave. Certain columns and several chapels still have Late Gothic frescoes.
Among the altarpieces, note the stone group figuring St Anne (c 1290) and the central reredos, made at the beginning of the 18C based on designs by Andreas Schlüter.

★ **Deutsches Meeresmuseum (Oceanographic Museum)** ⊙ **(BY M)** – Buildings which once belonged to a former abbey (the Katharinenkloster) have been transformed into galleries devoted to the Baltic Sea – its flora and fauna, the exploitation and refinement of salt etc – and to the fishing industry. Among the aquaria installed in the old church crypt is a huge 50 000l/11 000gal tank stocked with tropical species. In the old chancel hangs the eye-catching 15m/50ft long skeleton of a fin-back whale that was stranded on the west coast of Rügen in 1825.

Kulturhistorisches Museum (Historical Museum) ⊘ (**BY M**) – Sacred art from the Middle Ages, gold and silver plate from the isle of Hiddensee (Rügen), and the history of Stralsund itself, are among the diverse exhibits displayed here.

Deutsches Meeresmuseum

★ **Marienkirche** (**BZ**) – Apart from the impressive 104m/340ft west tower, which was added between 1416 and 1478, this church was built towards the end of the 14C. Its originality lies in the fact that the flying buttresses of the chancel are concealed below the roof. The interior of the west tower comprises a central portion flanked by side aisles, in the manner of a transept. The organ, which dates from the 17C, is the last work of organ builder F Stellwagen from Lübeck.

Stadtbefestigung (Ramparts) (**BY**) – The sections on the west side of the town are in the best condition, between the Kniepertor and the Kütertor, beside the lake.

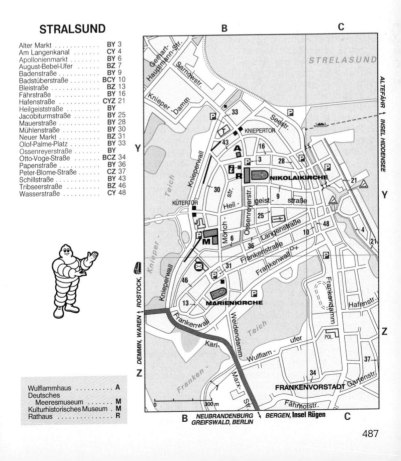

STRALSUND

487

STRAUBING

Bayern

Population 44 000

Michelin map 420 T 21

This town embraced by a loop of the Danube evolved from a Roman military camp. The present town centre, the Neustadt, is however a Wittelsbach addition dating from the early 13C. The town's site in the fertile Gäuboden region, the granary of Bavaria, contributed in no small terms to its prosperity. Another decisive factor was the fact that Straubing was governmental seat of the Dukes of Straubing-Holland between 1353 and 1425 and an important administrative centre for the old kingdom of Bavaria until the early 19C. Modern Straubing is still the economic focus of the region as far as deep into the Bavarian Forest.

★ **Stadtplatz** – In the centre of the huge main square stands an original 13C **tower** crowned by five pointed turrets, the remains of an old town hall. The tower lends a final flourish to a vista which begins with the gabled houses of the Theresienplatz, continuing with a beautiful Renaissance fountain and the Dreifaltigkeitssäule (Column of the Trinity), adorned with swirling statuary. The whole is an elegant reminder that Austria is not far off.

Jakobskirche – Just off Stadtplatz, this large brick hall-church was built in the 15C. The ribless vaulting of interpenetrating ovals above the nave is supported by round, slender pillars. This almost total lack of Baroque decoration is unusual for this part of Bavaria.

The panels of the high altar reredos, bought in 1590 from a church in Nuremberg, frame some 16C statuary. Note particularly the figure of the Virgin, in the middle, and Mary Magdalene, at the far left. In the first chapel north of the axial chapel is the admirable tomb of Ulrich Kastenmayer (1430), his effigy costumed as a magistrate of the town. The features and expression are of a poignant realism. The church pulpit dates from 1753.

Ursulinenkirche – This is the last joint piece of work by the Asam brothers. It was built between 1736 and 1741 during the transition from Baroque to Rococo and features a rare blend of architecture and decor. Egid Quirin Asam was architect, sculptor and stuccoworker, while his brother Cosmas Damian was responsible for the paintwork.

St. Peter – *1.5km/1mi. Leave the town in the direction of the Danube by B 20 (signposted Cham). Turn right before the bridge. St Peter's is the second church.* The old burial ground surrounding the Romanesque church contains many crosses made of wrought iron, of which the town was once a manufacturing centre. Ask the caretaker to open the chapel of the Dance of Death (Totentanzkapelle) and the chapel of **Agnes Bernauer**, a touching and popular folk heroine in Germany.

EXCURSIONS

The Abbeys of the Danube – *Round trip of 46km/29mi, downstream, on the north bank of the river. Allow 2hr 30min.*

Agnes Bernauer

Agnes, a beautiful young commoner from Augsburg, was married in secret to Albrecht III, son of Duke Ernst of Bavaria. The Duke took exception to the match, for reasons of State, and had Agnes condemned as a witch and a sorceress. In 1435 she was drowned in the Danube not far from Straubing. The tragic fate of this beautiful country girl captured many a heart, inspiring Friedrich Hebbel to write a political tragedy (1855) and Carl Orff to compose an opera (1946).

Oberalteich – *1km/0.6mi south of Furth.* Founded by Count Friedrich von Bogen, Bailiff of Regensburg Cathedral around 1100, this Benedictine monastery church was transformed between 1622 and 1630 into a hall-church with five aisles. Note especially the hanging staircase that leads to the gallery, a technical feat at that time, and the Rococo tabernacle with its furiously busy embellishments, realized by Matthias Obermayer in 1759.

Metten – *4km/2.5mi northwest of Deggendorf.*

The onion-domed towers of the **Benedictine abbey** ⊘ of Metten rise at the lower fringe of the Bavarian Forest. The church, whose foundations are pre-Romanesque, was remodelled in the Gothic era but was given its final facelift between 1720 and 1729.

Tall windows illuminate the frescoes on the cradle vaulting. The high altarpiece, a work due to Cosmas Damian Asam, represents St Michael slaughtering the dragon. It is possible to visit the old abbey **library**★, decorated in the Baroque style by FJ Holzinger from 1706 to 1720. There are no less than 160 000 volumes on the shelves, among them one of the first Bibles to be translated into German (1477) and the original Nuremberg Chronicle (1493).

Niederalteich – *14km/9mi southeast of Deggendorf.*
The present **abbey church**★ is the result of a Baroque remodelling of the original Gothic hall-church, of which nothing but the nave columns were re-used. The chancel was again rebuilt in 1726 with flattened vaulting. The upper parts of the aisles are interrupted by galleries oddly pierced by lantern-windows which afford an astonishing view of the vaulting.

From here it is possible to reach the church at **Osterhofen***, on the south bank of the Danube (10km/6mi – see PASSAU: Excursions).*

Michelin on Internet:
www.michelin.com.fr
for general information on the manufactory.
www.michelin-travel.com
For travel products:
  – route planning service
  – travel resources (hotels and restaurants)
  – catalogue of Michelin products
  – message service

STUTTGART★

Baden-Württemberg
Population 559 000
Michelin map 419 T 11

The capital of the Baden-Württemberg Land lies in a valley surrounded by wooded hills opening to the northeast onto the Neckar. The site itself is undulating, with an encircling belt of trees separating the city centre from extensive suburbs. The finest overall **view**★ of Stuttgart is from the upper platform of the **Fernsehturm** (television tower) (*access via the Hohenheimer Straße* – **LZ**), which soars 400m/1 312ft above the woods on the southern side of town.
The name of the city, originally **Stutengarten**, derives from a 10C seigniorial stud farm which flourished in the region, the German word "Stute" meaning "mare". By the 14C, the town which had grown up there was significant enough to be protected by fortified walls and had become the seat of the counts of Württemberg. Soon, supplanting such older burgs as Cannstatt, Waiblingen and Esslingen, which were equally part of the Hohenstaufen heritage, it became also the home of the dukes and kings of the realm.

Two Motor Car Pioneers – An engineer who lived in Bad Cannstatt, **Gottfried Daimler** (1834-1900) pioneered the adaptation of the internal combustion engine to the powering of vehicles. Collaborating with the brilliant designer Wilhelm Maybach, he developed a vertical motor which was patented in 1883.
Unlike Daimler, **Carl Benz** (1844-1929) was less concerned with the actual invention of a new motor than with its universal application. Born and educated at Karlsruhe, he envisaged an entire motor vehicle, which he elaborated himself in every detail at Mannheim. Soon he was able to start manufacturing in series and put his cars on the market. In 1899 he sold his 2 000th vehicle and thus became the world's leading automobile manufacturer. Then, in 1901, Daimler's company marketed a model baptized **Mercedes**, after the daughter of its most important foreign agent. The name was to make a fortune. And since the two firms amalgamated in 1926 Mercedes-Benz has been synonymous with luxury cars built to a high standard of excellence and technical prowess. Today, above the roofs of the city, the night sky over Stuttgart blazes with the illuminated three-point-star within a circle – the firm's world-famous trademark.

Urban Landscape – The former appearance of the city is only apparent nowadays on **Schillerplatz** (**KLY**), which is flanked by the Stiftskirche (collegiate church) and the Altes Schloß (Old Castle). The **statue of Schiller** in the centre of the square is the work of the Danish sculptor Thorwaldsen (1839).
In front of the **Neues Schloß** (New Palace) (**LY**) is the wide **Schloßplatz** (**LY 72**), off which a tree-lined avenue leads through the castle gardens to **Rosenstein-Park** (*access via the Heilbronner Straße* – **LY**) in the north. The Neues Schloß was built between 1746 and 1807 after a design by L Retti. It is now the home of regional ministerial departments. Modern Stuttgart's business centre is based on Königstraße (**KLY**), in the pedestrian zone.

CENTRAL SIGHTS

★★ **Linden-Museum** ⊘ (**KY M¹**) – Exhibits in this museum consecrated to fine arts and folk arts worldwide are beautifully presented, falling under six main headings: America; the Pacific (ground floor); Africa; the Middle-East (first floor); Southern and Eastern Asia (second floor).

America – Highlights include a display of **ancient Peruvian ceramics** (1500 BC to 1500 AD), and the section on **North-American Indians** (19C artefacts).

The Pacific – Here the interest is concentrated on the inhabitants of **New Guinea** and neighbouring isles in the **Papuan archipelago** (New Britain, New Ireland) where the indigenous culture is centred on belief in spirits and the cult of ancestors. There is also a section on Central Australian indigenous culture.

Africa – Displays on Africa's rural and urban culture (Reconstitution of a typical North Nigerian market, royal palace). The traditions of African tribal life and its superstitions are evoked in fantasy **masks**.

The Middle-East – Visitors to this department pass through an oriental **bazaar** which gives a good overview of Islamic culture and history (religion, science, social hierarchy).

The Far East – Highlights include sections on Japan (reconstruction of a Japanese tea house and a traditional Japanese room, silk painting) and China (funerary ceramic ware, porcelain, lacquer work).

Southern Asia – Main focuses of the collections are art from India, Nepal and Tibet and the development of Hinduism and Buddhism. Shadow theatre puppets and marionettes from Indonesia.

★★ **Staatsgalerie** (**Art Gallery**) ⊘ (**LYM**) – The building commissioned under King Wilhelm I of Württemberg in 1838-1843 houses European painting from medieval times to Impressionism. Note especially the **Old German Masters Section★★**, in which Swabian painting from the 14C to the 16C is pre-eminent. One of the masterpieces exhibited is the **Herrenberg Altar** by Jerg Ratgeb (1519), which portrays – from left to right – the Last Supper, the Martyrization of Jesus, the Crucifixion and the Resurrection. Venetians and Florentines from the 14C dominate an excellent collection of Italian painters. Among the Dutch Old Masters are Hans Memling (Bethsheba Bathing), Rembrandt (St Paul In Prison), Jacob van Ruisdael and Rubens.

The 19C art department contains a special display on "Swabian Classicism" and works from the most important artistic movements of the age, from the Pre-Raphaelites to the Impressionists.

An annexe (opened in 1984) designed by the British architect James Stirling houses the department of **20C Art**. Among the "modern classics" on display are

works by the Fauvists and French Cubists (Matisse, Braque, Juan Gris), the German Expressionists (a fine selection of Kokoschka paintings), the artists of Neue Sachlichkeit (Dix, Grosz) and artists of the Bauhaus School. A special place is reserved for the work of **Willi Baumeister** (1889-1955) and **Oskar Schlemmer** (1888-1943) of the Bauhaus, both natives of Stuttgart. Schlemmer's famous six-figure Triadic Ballet is on view, as well as certain enormous sketches for murals (the finished works, painted in 1929, were victims of the Nazi crusade against the so-called "degenerate art"). Another highlight of this museum is a collection of 12 works by **Picasso** covering every period of his creative life. Among them is the world-famous sculpture group in wood, The Bathers.

W.H. Müller/ZEFA, Paris

Neue Staatsgalerie, Stuttgart

STUTTGART

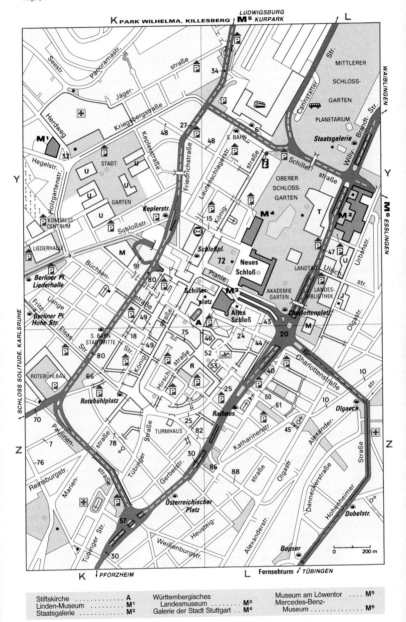

The section on contemporary art covers the half century since the Second World War, starting with Dubuffet and Giacometti and ending with the latest works of Baselitz and Kiefer, by way of American Pop Art (Warhol, Segal), Italy's Arte Povere and the "installations" of Beuys.

Altes Schloß (Old Castle) (LY) – Four wings flanked by round towers comprise this building, most of which dates from the 16C. The **Renaissance Courtyard★** is surrounded by three floors of arcaded galleries. The interior now houses the **Württembergisches Landesmuseum★** ⊘ (**M³**).

On the ground floor and the mezzanine, the exhibits include rare tapestries, craftwork in ceramics, glass and silver tableware (14C-19C), and clothes worn by the nobility (especially in the 18C). Ancient history and prehistory are also represented on the first floor (important finds from the excavation of the **Hochdorf royal tomb**, a 5C BC Celtic burial site near Ludwigsburg), while the second contains an extremely interesting collection of **religious statuary★★**. Note above all the eight Scenes of the Passion (in the central octagon) executed by the sculptor Jörg Syrlin in 1515 for the church at Zwiefalten.

Funerary objects (weapons, jewels and household items) can be seen in the section devoted to the **Franks and the Alemanni★**, which is also on the second floor, and gives some idea of the civilization of these peoples between the 5C and the 8C.

There is a fine collection of **musical instruments and clocks** on the third floor, which also houses a numismatic gallery.

The Treasury Tower (Kunstkammerturm – entrance on the ground floor or second floor) contains items from the "Ducal Chamber of Arts and Marvels" (Herzogliche Kunst-und-Wunderkammer) which range from the 15C to the 18C. They include the **crown jewels** of the kings of Württemberg (19C).

Stiftskirche (KY A) – The most impressive part of this church, built in the mid 15C, is the west tower belfry porch with superposed polygonal copings (1490-1531). When the church was restored after the war damage of 1945, the nave and former aisles were combined into a single hall covered with panelled vaulting. A large funerary **monument★**, a memorial to the dukes of Württemberg, stands in the chancel. Commissioned by Duke Ludwig III, this was executed by the sculptor S Schlör c 1580. Eleven armoured figurines representing ancestors of the Duke are standing in front of a decor of Renaissance arcades.

Restoration work is in progress on the Stiftskirche; the date of completion was not known at the time of going to press.

Galerie der Stadt Stuttgart (City Gallery) ⊘ **(LY M')** – Between-the-wars painting (1918-39) figures prominently in this museum. Note particularly the **work★** of Neue Sachlichkeit artist **Otto Dix**, famous for the ferocity of his criticism of modern society and its depravities, and his disgust at the horrors of war. Typical of his approach are the Big City (Großstadt) triptych and the anti-war picture Grabenkrieg. Young Stuttgart artists of the 1980s are represented, and so too are the local painters Hölzel, Schlemmer and Baumeister (see above).

ADDITIONAL SIGHTS

★ **Wilhelma Park and Zoo** – Leave by Heilbronner Straße **(LY)**.
This **botanical and zoological garden** (one of Europe's finest) laid out at the request of King Wilhelm I in the mid 19C is furnished with hothouses displaying many fascinating tropical plants and a celebrated exhibition of orchids. The zoo is home to more than 8 000 animals (1 000 species). Worth seeing also: the **aquarium and terrarium**.

Staatliches Museum für Naturkunde (National Museum of Natural Sciences) ⊘ – In Rosenstein-Park.
There is a Zoology Department in the museum in **Schloß Rosenstein** which features a collection of stuffed creatures (especially mammals and birds) from all over the world, displayed in their natural habitat. The most imposing exhibit is a 13m/43ft northern whale, reconstituted around a genuine skeleton.
The department consecrated to the origins of planet Earth is now installed in the new **Museum am Löwentor★** ⊘ **(LY M⁵)** – a collection of spacious modern galleries in the same park. Here, through a fine assembly of Baden-Württemberg **fossils**, beautifully displayed, 600 million years of world history can be skimmed over. Fossil birds, fish, reptiles, tortoises and even dinosaurs can be seen. There are also actual skeletons of large prehistoric mammals (c 200 000 year old elephant discovered near Steinheim am Murr), excavated bones, and a section dealing with man in the glacial period in different parts of the museum.

★ **Höhenpark Killesberg** – Leave by Heilbronner Straße **(LY)**.
A little way to the west of the Rosenstein, this park is a continuation of the green belt encircling the inner city. Laid out on a height to the north of the centre, it integrates perfectly with the undulating terrain. Terraced cascades, fountains and brilliantly coloured flower beds invite the visitor to relax and admire, and there is a **miniature train** on which a tour of the whole park can be made.
A panoramic view of Stuttgart can be enjoyed from a **look-out tower** at the highest point (Aussichtsturm).

★ **Kurpark Bad Cannstatt (Spa Park)** – Leave by Cannstatter Straße **(LY)**.
The old town of Bad Cannstatt, now the city's largest residential suburb, has retained its function as a spa. The 18 thermal springs – feeding a fountain and three swimming-pools – have made the place, after Budapest, Europe's second

largest producer of mineral water. The park (Kurpark) is attractive. Once a year, in late September-early October it hosts a **funfair** as part of the Cannstatter Volksfest.

★ **Mercedes-Benz Museum** ⊘ – *Leave by Schillerstraße* (**LY M⁴**). *At 136 Mercedesstraße, in a block of the company's main factory, located at Stuttgart-Untertürkheim.*
Nearly 100 vintage and veteran motor cars are on show here, the models ranging from the earliest to the most recent, as well as video films tracing the history of engines and cars, especially at Daimler-Benz. The racing car collection testifies to the success of Mercedes worldwide until 1955. Engines powering aircraft, airships (Zeppelin) and rail buses complete the exhibition.

INTER NATIONES, Bonn

A 1927 Mercedes Sportwagen "S" (Mercedes-Benz Museum, Stuttgart)

EXCURSIONS

★ **Schloß Solitude** ⊘ – *Leave by Rotebühlstraße* (**KZ**).
The former summer residence of the Württemberg Court stands on the edge of a plateau about 8km/5mi from the city centre, west of the Botnang suburb. Flanked by lateral wings, the castle is centred on an oval pavilion with a cupola, the whole being majestically raised on a base of open arcades. Around this, the lower outbuildings lie in an immense arc. The design was by the French Court architect, La Guépière, who supervised construction between 1764 and 1769. A certain restraint, tempering the sumptuousness of the concept, can be traced to the architect's admiration for the buildings of ancient Greece.
Inside, the decorations of the central rotunda (Weißer Saal) and the small marble room are in the neo-Classical tradition. The other apartments, which are panelled, are French Rococo. One of the more bizarre items on view is the desk used by Friedrich I of Württemberg – generously hollowed out to accommodate the corpulent figure of its owner.

★ **Schwäbisches Brauereimuseum (Swabian Brewery Museum)** ⊘ – *Robert-Koch-Straße 12, Stuttgart-Vaihingen.*
Five thousand years of beer making are traced in this museum. Objects discovered in Mesopotamian and Ancient Egyptian digs (some of them reproductions) prove that, even in the mists of antiquity, appreciation of this liquid with a base of hops and barley was not confined to Europe. The principles and techniques of brewing are explained in the lower basement. Well-chosen instruments and plants illustrate the different stages in the making of beer (malting, crushing, wort preparation, fermentation, filtering, bottling etc).

★ **Porsche-Museum** ⊘ – *Leave on Heilbronner Straße* (**LY**), *in the direction of the motorway. Before the motorway, take the exit signposted Zuffenhausen-Industriegebiet, and then turn right into Porschestraße. The museum is at no 42.*
In 1934, the engineer **Ferdinand Porsche** (1875-1951), already distinguished by his work at Daimler-Benz, produced a design for the famous "people's car" – the Volkswagen. His prototype evolved into the celebrated "Beetle". Porsche himself, from 1948 onwards, devoted himself to a sports model bearing his own name, which was developed from the original VW chassis and engine and subsequently manufactured at Zuffenhausen. In one of the factory buildings 30 different Porsches are now on show, along with a display of high-performance engines.

★ **Tiefenbronn** – *38km/24mi to the west.*
This village is home to the **Pfarrkirche St. Maria Magdalena**, which boasts unusually rich and well-made interior decor. Besides murals (late-14C *Last Judgement* above the interior of the triumphal arch; altar murals on the east wall of the nave from

c 1400), stained-glass windows (late 14C) and numerous tombs, there are some particularly fine Late Gothic altarpieces. The high altar by Ulm master Hans Schüchlin (1469) depicts scenes from the life of the Virgin Mary and the Passion of Christ. On the end wall of the south side aisle there is a magnificent **altarpiece of St Mary Magdalene**★★ (1432) by **Lucas Moser**, illustrating various episodes from the life of the saint.

In the chancel, to the left of the high altar, is a **monstrance**★ dating from c 1500, which must be a masterpiece of Late Gothic gold- and silversmiths judging by its shape and wealth of figures.

SWABIAN JURA★

See SCHWÄBISCHE ALB

SWISS SAXONY★★★

See SÄCHSISCHE SCHWEIZ

SYLT★★

Schleswig-Holstein

Michelin map 415 B 8

The popular holiday island of Sylt, the most northerly point of German territory, stretches in a north-south direction for 40km/25mi, although in parts it is less than 457m/500yd across. Since 1927, it has been connected to the mainland via a rail link across the Hindenburgdamm causeway. Despite the reduced area (100km²/39sq mi) of this long, narrow isle, the landscape of this island with origins in the Geest is varied. The west coast features a long stretch of fine sandy beach running for miles. The rest of the island landscape is characterised by dunes and marshes, salt pastures and mudflats, fields and meadows, open heathland and primeval burial mounds. Sylt offers spas, North Sea bathing and climatic health resorts. There are official nudist beaches, although the demarcation between clothed and unclothed bathing areas is frequently not clearly indicated.

Access by rail ⊘ – Train-car ferries depart from Niebüll and cross the arm of sea separating Sylt from the mainland via the Hindenburgdamm causeway.

Access by car-ferry ⊘ – There is a seaborne car ferry service between Havneby (*on the Danish island of Römö – accessible by road*) and List, on the northern tip of Sylt.

★ **Westerland** – This is the largest resort on the island and the most popular North Sea spa and cure establishment in Germany. The cure establishment boasts a leisure pool – the Sylter Welle – in the form of a ship and a 7km/4mi long sandy

Sylt – Red cliffs at Kampen

Nick Bock/Kurverwaltung Kampen

beach with foaming breakers. The aim is to see and be seen on the Promenade, which is centred around the large music hall. There is also plenty of action in the bars, bistros and nightclubs. As the island's metropolis, Westerland has everything visitors could desire, from window-shopping (Strandstraße and Friedrichstraße), galleries, boutiques and a casino (in the old Jugendstil spa building). There are also various sports facilities and cultural events to be enjoyed.

★ Keitum – This idyllic village with numerous craft workshops is the other face of the island. Keitum's ancient traditional thatched Frisian houses, almost hidden among trees and lilac bushes, drystone embankments overgrown with dog roses, and the view from the **Grünes Kliff** over endless miles of water and the mudflats of the Schleswig-Holstein National Park have earned it the nickname of being the island's "green heart". At the edge of the village, on the side towards Munkmarschen, lies the early-13C seafarers' church of **St. Severin** with a Late Romanesque font.

To the north of Sylt, near the port of List, lie the **Wanderdüne**, 1 000m/3 280ft long and 30m/10ft high dunes made of quartz sand and moving several miles further east every year. South of **Kampen**, a resort favoured by VIPs and artists, the **Rotes Kliff★** towers above the sea. In Wenningstedt-Braderup, the **Denghoog** is a megalithic grave over 4 000 years old which is open to the public. Three massive roof stones weighing 2t each are supported by 12 load-bearing stones. **Morsum-Kliff**, on which 10 million years of geological history can be seen, is an interesting geological feature.

THÜRINGER WALD★★

THURINGIA FOREST – Thüringen

Michelin map 418 N 14 – O 16

Much in the same way as the Harz, the Thuringia Forest is a wooded massif, orientated northwest-southeast, with an average height of 1 000m/3 300ft. Granite, gneiss and porphyry formations underlie the central nucleus of the forest, while the foothills are composed mainly of sandstone and limestone sedimentary deposits. This is one of the most beautiful natural regions in Germany, and the massif is scattered with charming villages whose inhabitants still retain their traditional skills and craftsmanship. Many of Germany's most famous historical figures have close links with the Thuringia Forest: Goethe, Schiller, Bach, Cranach and Müntzer. A wealth of tourist amenities, particularly at Oberhof, and the development of several resorts have made the region popular with a large number of ramblers and summer holidaymakers.

Flora and fauna – The forest covering practically the whole area is largely beech, pine and fir. Marshy plateaux have developed in some of the higher reaches, and there is moorland on the approaches to some crests. Among the larger varieties of game, stags, roe deer and wild boar are abundant.

THÜRINGER HOCHSTRASSE (FOREST HIGH ROAD)

From Eisenach to Ilmenau *110km/68mi – one day*

This fascinating forest road mainly follows the **Rennsteig**, a ramblers' path 160km/100mi long which keeps to the highest parts of the forest and includes such major summits as the Großer Inselsberg (916m/3 005ft) and the Großer Beerberg (982m/3 222ft).

Leave **Eisenach★** *(see under this name) in the direction of Gotha.*

Großer Inselsberg – *1hr on foot there and back.*
The **panorama★★** extending from the summit takes in the greater part of the forest.

★ Marienglashöhle ⊙ – Crystalline gypsum is extracted from this natural cavity. The use of this mineral in the decoration of church altars has led to the grotto's unusual name (Marienglas means Glass of Mary).

The road cuts across the Rennsteig and twists between the Regenberg (727m/2 385ft) and the Spießberg (749m/2 457ft), offering numerous possibilities for sightseeing and walks, especially in the direction of **Ebertswiese**, a zone of marsh and meadows. Steinbach is overlooked by the Hallenburg ruins. The road continues towards Oberhof via the Kanzlergrund, a valley with wide stretches of grass and meadowland.

★ Oberhof – At 800m/2 625ft altitude, this town is the most important leisure centre and winter sports station in the Thuringia Forest.
In the **Rennsteiggarten**, a botanical park specializing in Alpines and the flora of Central European heights, more than 4 000 varieties of plant can be seen.

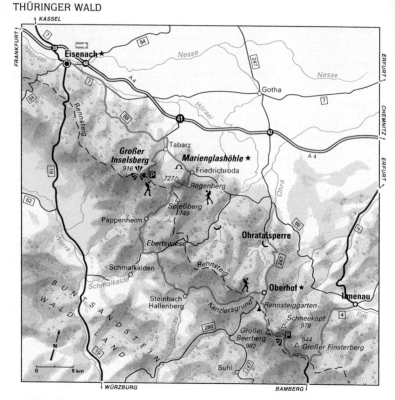

Ohratalsperre (Dam) - *Follow road B 247 to the large car park.*
The reservoir dammed by this barrage, the surface of which extends over 88ha/218 acres, supplies water to Weimar, Jena, Gotha and the Thuringian capital, Erfurt.
Leaving Oberhof in the direction of Schmücke, the country road winds once again sinuously between the Großer Beerberg (982m/3 222ft) and the Schneekopf (978m/3 209ft). From the hotel car park at Schmücke, there is a fine viewpoint looking out over the valley. The 944m/3 097ft Finsterberg is visible on the left.

Ilmenau - This locality on the northern fringe of the Thuringia Forest has always been associated with **Goethe**, who is said to have been particularly fond of its natural beauties. There is a plaque in his memory on the wall of the town's municipal headquarters (Amtshaus, in Marktplatz), which has been transformed into a Goethe museum, and another in the Gabelbach hunting lodge. A pathway called **"In Goethe's Footsteps"** (Auf Goethes Spuren) links the places associated with the great writer.

Bad TÖLZ

Bayern
Population 16 000
Michelin map 419/420 W 18

There was already a river crossing on this site in Roman times. A settlement, "Tollenz", is first recorded in 1180. Tölz was finally granted official market rights by Emperor Ludwig the Bavarian in 1331. In the years that followed, the town prospered thanks to rafting. The discovery of exceptionally pure iodine springs (at 41.5mg/l, the richest in Germany) in 1845 transformed Tölz (670m/2 200ft above sea level) into a spa town famous throughout Europe. The spa resort was raised to the status of town in 1906.
The Isar flowing down from the Alps cuts Bad Tölz into two: the modern spa district and the picturesque old town with colourfully painted houses. The Blomberg peak (1 248m/4 095ft) is a favourite day-trip destination (*chair-lift*).

★ **Marktstraße** - Much of the character of this street derives from its wide curve and steep slope, bordered by multicoloured façades beneath overhanging eaves.

Kalvarienberg (Calvary Hill) - At the top of the Kalvarienberg pathway, which is flanked by the Stations of the Cross, stands a small chapel (1743) dedicated to St Leonard, whose powers are still widely revered among the peasants of Bavaria and Austria. In this part of the country his intercession is sought not only for the deliverance of prisoners (note the chain surrounding the chapel), but also for the protection of horses. The saint's anniversary, 6 November, is celebrated each year by a parade of rustic wagons and carts, colourfully decorated and drawn by teams of brilliantly harnessed horses *(see Calendar of events)*.

EXCURSIONS

Benediktbeuern – *15km/9mi to the southwest.*
Built on the lower slopes of the Bavarian Alps foothills, this imposing complex dating from AD 739 is the oldest Benedictine abbey in Upper Bavaria. The **abbey church** ⊙ as it is now was remodelled between 1681 and 1686. On those parts of the cradle vaulting left free of stuccowork, Georg Asam – father of the famous Asam Brothers – painted the first complete cycle of frescoes dating from the beginning of the Bavarian Baroque period: the Birth, Baptism, Transfiguration and Resurrection of the Saviour, the Descent of the Holy Spirit and the Last Judgement.
Elegant frescoes and finely worked stucco make the **Anastasiakapelle**★ (1751-53), a chapel a little to the north of the church, one of the most charming examples of Rococo art. The designer, Johann Michael Fischer, and the craftsmen who carried out the work for him, were commissioned a few years later to repeat their artistry at Ottobeuren.

★ **Walchensee** – *40km/25mi to the southwest.*
Framed by dense woods, this deep blue reservoir lake is one of the beauties of the Bavarian Alps. Its waters serve the power station on the Kochelsee, some 200m/600ft lower down. A chair-lift rises to the Fahrenberg, from which a path leads in 30min to the summit of the **Herzogstand** (1 731m/5 679ft). From the observation deck, there is a superb **all-round view**★★ taking in the Walchensee, the Kochelsee, the Karwendel massif and the rock wall of the Wetterstein, which culminates in the Zugspitze.

TRIER★★

Rheinland-Pfalz
Population 99 000
Michelin map 417 Q 3
Local map see MOSELTAL

This venerable episcopal city on the banks of the Moselle is the oldest city in Germany. After the status of Prince Electors was conferred upon the archbishops of Trier in the 14C, the city flourished. In the wake of the French Revolution, it was made capital of the French administrative region of Saar before falling into the hands of Prussia in 1815. Trier is now a focal point of the region, not only as a major centre of wine production and trade but also of culture. The city's well-preserved monuments from Ancient Roman and later periods attract a large number of tourists here every year.
The philosopher and economist **Karl Marx** (1818-83) was born in Trier.

A SECOND ROME

Trier became the meeting point very early on for the Celtic, Germanic and Latin cultures which evolved to form Western civilization.
After the conquest of the Treveri, a Celtic tribe from the eastern part of Gaul, the Roman Emperor Augustus founded on their territory the town of **Augusta Treverorum** (c 16 BC), which soon became a centre of intense economic, cultural and intellectual activity, continuing to develop until the invasion of Germanic tribes in AD 274. Essentially a civic and residential settlement, the town fell before the onslaught.
Later, however, when Diocletian reorganized the Roman Empire, Trier was retaken and became capital of the western territories (Gaul, Spain, Germania and Britain). As the town regained its former eminence, the Emperor Constantine (306-337) surrounded it with a defensive wall within which magnificent buildings were erected. In this second period of prosperity, Trier was given the status of Imperial Residence.
In the year 313, the Edict of Milan put an end to the persecution of Christians, and a year later the See of Trier, the oldest in Germany, was created. But towards the end of the 4C, renewed pressure from the Germanic tribes became so strong that the imperial residence was transferred to Milan and the prefecture to Arles. In 470, Trier finally fell into the hands of the Franks. During the Middle Ages, the archbishops of Trier wielded a great deal of power as prince-electors.

OLD TOWN *allow one day*

★★ **Porta Nigra** ⊘ **(DX)** – This magnificent four-storey structure – originally the northern entrance to the walled town – dates from the 2C and is the most important Roman relic on German soil. Its name derives from the dark patina forming over the centuries on the sandstone blocks used in its construction. The stones are fitted together without mortar, held only here and there with iron crampons. The gateway was designed for military use: the double arcade of the central block, flanked by two massive towers, leads to an inner court where only the upper arcades are pierced – and assailants forcing the outer gates would find themselves exposed here to attack from all sides.

In the 11C, the fortified gateway was transformed into a church on two levels, dedicated to St Simeon. The Romanesque apse can still be seen on the east side, and there are traces of additional alterations – Rococo decoration, for example – in the upper galleries (on the inner courtyard side). It was Napoleon who ordered the monument to be restored to its original form in 1804. There is a fine view from the tower terrace.

Nach Foto Gerd Schneider

The Porta Nigra at Trier

Städtisches Museum ⊘ **(DX M²)** – This municipal museum is installed in a Romanesque convent, the **Simeonstift**, built beside the Porta Nigra at the same time as the church (11C). The history of Trier is illustrated with models, paintings, engravings, maps and sculptures, among them the original figures surrounding the fountain in the market place (the Four Virtues and St Peter, late 16C). Above the arcades, the old **cloister** is being transformed into a lapidary museum.

★ **Dreikönigenhaus (House of the Three Kings) (DX K)** – This Early Gothic town house (c 1230), with its arched windows, recalls the Italianate towers of the patricians of Regensburg.

★ **Hauptmarkt (DX)** – One of the finest old squares in Germany. In the middle is the **Market Cross**★ (Marktkreuz), erected in the year 958 when the town was granted the right to hold a market. The **fountain**, with its painted figures, dates from the late 16C. Standing by the Cross (which was restored in the 18C), the visitor can see 15 centuries of history encapsulated in the monuments around the square. To the north is the Porta Nigra, to the east the Romanesque cathedral, to the south the Gothic **Gangolfkirche**, whose early 16C tower was once used as a look-out post.

Picturesque half-timbered houses, both Renaissance and Baroque, stand on the west side. The **Steipe (D)**, a medieval (15C) municipal building with a steep, tall roof, is elegantly built over an open gallery. Beside it, the 17C **Rotes Haus** (Red House) **(E)**, bears the proud inscription: "There was life in Trier for 1 300 years before Rome even existed".

NB Both these houses were rebuilt after the Second World War.

Frankenturm (CX) – A heavily built Romanesque tower (c 1100) with small windows.

★ **Dom (Cathedral) (DX)** – Seen from its forecourt (Domfreihof), Trier Cathedral looks more like a fortress than a church. A rounded apse projects from a massive, austere façade which, with its squat, square towers, is a fine example of Early Romanesque architecture.

From the north side, different stages in the construction are evident. A flattened gable and rectangular plan distinguish the 4C Roman heart of the building. West of this central block is the 11C Romanesque section; east of it the polygonal chancel, which is furnished with a dwarf gallery and dates from the 12C *(see Introduction)*. Unfortunately, a Baroque axial chapel crowned by a dome was added to this in the 18C.

Entering the cathedral from the forecourt, note near the main door the fallen section (Domstein) of a Roman column which supported part of the former church. Inside, the decoration is principally Baroque and includes some interesting

TRIER

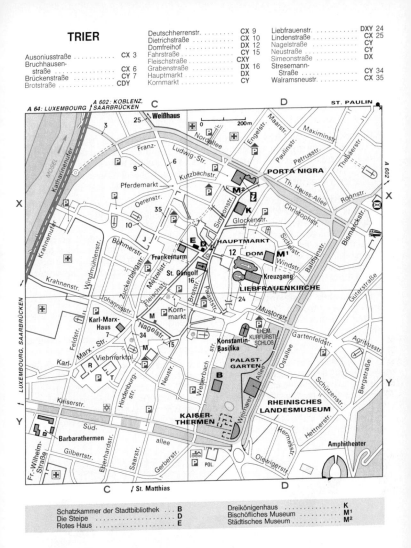

altarpieces. In the west chancel *(on the left of the entrance)* there is a Gothic funerary monument of the Archbishop and Prince-Elector Baldwin of Luxembourg. A splendid **tympanum**★ in the south aisle depicts Christ between the Virgin Mary and St Peter. Another Madonna, a graceful 16C example, stands in the stuccoed chapel on the right of the chancel.

★ **Treasury** (Domschatz) ⊙ – Silver and gold plate (portable altar of St Andrew, richly enamelled), valuable ivories, and magnificently illuminated Gospels are on view here, in the domed axial chapel.

Cloister (Kreuzgang) – From the Gothic cloister, there is a good **view**★ of the cathedral and the Liebfrauenkirche. In the northeast corner is the 15C Malberg Madonna.

★ **Liebfrauenkirche (Church of Our Lady) (DX)** – One of the earliest Gothic sanctuaries in Germany (1235-60), this church was directly inspired by one in the Champagne region of France, with the ground plan in the form of a Greek cross. There are thus four apsidal chapels, between each pair of which two smaller, three-sided chapels have been interposed, giving the whole church the highly original form of a rose with 12 petals.

The **tympanum** over the west porch shows the Virgin Mary Enthroned, the Annunciation, the Adoration of the Magi, the Massacre of the Innocents and the Presentation in the Temple. The Coronation of the Virgin is represented at the north entrance.

The interior has an incomparable elegance, enhanced by rings of foliage carved around each column, by the finesse of the public gallery, and the richness of the high central vaulting. There is a fine 17C **funerary monument**★ (north chapel) to Metternich's personal canon.

* **Bischöfliches Dom- und Diözesanmuseum (Episcopal Museum)** ⊘ **(DY M¹)** – The most interesting exhibits here are the frescoes (Deckenmalerei, 4C) of the Palace of Constantine, discovered beneath the cathedral. It is supposed that they represent St Helen, the Emperor's mother, and his wife Fausta. The colours are extraordinarily fresh and the technique highly skilled.

The first floor of the museum is reserved for sacred art (note the original statues which once adorned the west face of Liebfrauenkirche).

Basilika (DY) – Once the main hall of the building, this "Aula Palatina" is all that remains of the imperial palace built by Constantine c 310. Modified many times over the centuries, it was finally restored to its original form in the 19C and early 20C. The basilica is used today as a Protestant church. The sheer size of the interior is breathtaking, although the decor is restrained.

Ehem. Kurfürstliches Schloß (DY) – Only the north and east wings remain of the former Renaissance electoral castle, on which building was begun in 1615. The Rococo wings were built between 1756 and 1762, based on plans by the court master builder Johannes Seitz. His virtuosity (he was a student of Balthasar Neumann) is expressed in a magnificent **staircase**, one of the most beautiful creations of its kind in Germany. The south façade with its gentle colouring looks out over the **palace gardens★**, laid out in the French style with ponds, flower borders and Baroque statues.

★★ **Rheinisches Landesmuseum (Rhineland Museum)** ⊘ **(DY)** – The department of prehistory *(ground floor)* and a section on **Roman antiquities** *(basement, ground floor and first floor)* are particularly interesting.

Paleolithic Age: Stone Age implements, ceramics and weapons; objects found in Bronze Age tombs; jewels set in gold from Iron Age sepulchres.

Roman Period: marvellous mosaics; bronze statuettes; sculptures and bas-reliefs (including a school scene and one depicting the payment of farm rent). Among the sculpture discovered at Neumagen *(see MOSELTAL)* is the representation of a ship sailing down the Moselle loaded with wine. Included in this Neumagen ship carving is the figure of "the jolly sailor" – a mariner with a broad grin who has passed into the folklore of the Moselle. Regional ceramics and jewels and glassware found in Frankish tombs are also on display.

Neumagen ship carving

★★ **Kaiserthermen (Imperial Roman Baths)** ⊘ **(DY)** – Among the largest in the Roman Empire, these baths date from the time of Constantine, but appear never to have been used. The construction of the rounded walls – alternate layers of brick and rubble – is typically Roman. The window openings are wide and arched. Inside, the hot water caldarium is preceded by a tepidarium (warm water baths), a frigidarium (cold) and a gymnasium for physical exercises. The two floors below ground where the heating and circulating plant were installed are particularly interesting to see.

★★ **Schatzkammer der Stadtbibliothek (Minicipal Library Treasury)** ⊘ **(DY B)** – Fascinating exhibits are on view here. The collection includes rare ancient manuscripts, beautifully illuminated (medieval Bibles, homilies, fables etc);

WHERE TO STAY

Berghotel Kockelsberg – Auf dem Kockelsberg, ☎ 06 51/8 24 80 00, Fax 06 51/8 24 82 90. Single rooms from 65DM. Idyllic isolated setting with panoramic view of Trier.

Alte Villa – Saarstraße 133, ☎ 06 51/93 81 20, Fax 06 51/9 38 12 12. Single rooms from 98DM. Villa converted into a hotel, located on the edge of the town centre.

Römischer Kaiser – Porta-Nigra-Platz 6, ☎ 06 51/9 77 00. Fax 06 51/97 70 99. Single rooms from 130DM. Modernised town house, right next to the Porta Nigra.

examples of the earliest books to be illustrated (Gospels, teaching manuals, legal volumes); and many old documents, treaties, letters of credit and safe conduct passes.

Karl-Marx-Haus ⊘ (**CY**) – *Brückenstraße 10*.
The birthplace of the socialist theoretician has been turned into a museum. Letters, manuscripts, first edition of Communist Manifesto etc.

ADDITIONAL SIGHTS

★ **Pfarrkirche St.-Paulin** – *Access via Thebäerstraße* (**DX**).
Tall windows illuminate the single nave of this church, the interior of which was designed by Balthazar Neumann and completed in 1754. The martyrdom of the saint and members of the Theban Legion in AD 268 is illustrated in paintings on the ceiling. Rococo stucco decorates the vaulting.

Barbarathermen ⊘ (**CY**) – Roman baths from the 2C, used for several centuries, are now in ruins.

Amphitheater (Roman Amphitheatre) ⊘ (**DY**) – Once seating 20 000 spectators, this arena was used as a quarry in the Middle Ages, and became so damaged by the 18C that vines were grown on the terraces. The cellars below ground house theatrical equipment.

St.-Matthias – *Access via Saarstraße* (**CY**).
A 12C pillared Romanesque basilica, now a Benedictine convent church housing the St Matthias reliquary shrine. Apart from Romanesque, the façade shows traces of Baroque and neo-Classical influence.

Weißhaus – Restaurant with a terrace giving a good **view** of the west bank of the Moselle and Trier on the opposite bank.

Take the cable railway from the Zurlauben stop, or drive there, crossing the river over the Kaiser-Wilhelm-Brücke and then taking Bitburger Straße and the Stückradweg.

TÜBINGEN★★

Baden-Württemberg
Population 83 500
Michelin map 419 U 11 – Local map see SCHWÄBISCHE ALB

This town on the banks of the Neckar and Ammer, between the slopes of Schloßberg and Österberg, was lucky enough to escape unharmed during the Second World War. It therefore gives an unbroken picture of its evolution from the Middle Ages to the 19C. The labyrinth of narrow sloping streets lined with ancient houses and its animated student life combine to create a delightful atmosphere, making Tübingen one of the most attractive towns in south Germany.

The University – The saying goes that, rather than having a university, Tübingen is a university, so closely linked are the town's history and cultural life with its Alma Mater. It all began in 1477, when Count Eberhard took the risk of founding a university in a small town with only 3 000 inhabitants. A success story that is still going strong started with 300 matriculations. Tübingen University now has 16 faculties, and 25 000 students registered in 74 different subjects.
The university and the Protestant "seminary" founded in 1536 have schooled important figures such as the poets Hölderlin, Mörike and Uhland, the philosophers Hegel and Schilling. The astronomer Kepler worked here, as did Greek scholar and theologian Melanchthon. In 1623, Wilhelm Schickard invented the first calculating machine in Tübingen, which was attributed to Blaise Pascal for many years. In 1869, 25-year-old Friedrich Miescher discovered deoxyribonucleic acid, or DNA, here.

Neckar riverfront, Tübingen

SIGHTS

Visitors with enough time to ramble as whim dictates will be delighted to discover Tübingen's twisting alleys, magnificent half-timbered architecture and sleepy squares. For those whose time is limited, we recommend the following tour of the old town, which includes the main points of interest. Leave from the **Eberhards-brücke** (Z), which gives a scenic **view**★ over the Neckar. The roofs of the houses and the Hölderlin Tower rise above the light foliage of the weeping willows. The **Platanenallee** (Z) leads off to the left, a beautiful walkway along the bank of the Neckar. From here visitors may be fortunate enough to see some punts, the gondolas of Tübingen, which make trips from the Hölderlin Tower along past the river front and round the island in the Neckar. To the right, a small path leads along the river front.

Hölderlinturm ⊘ (Z A) – Once part of the fortifications, this tower was turned into a residence and inhabited by **Friedrich Hölderlin** from 1807 until his death. Now a museum, it displays many souvenirs of the poet.

Schloß Hohentübingen (YZ) – The present castle was built during the Renaissance on the foundations of an earlier 11C fortress built by the archdukes of Tübingen. It houses several university institutes. A magnificent Renaissance portal, the work of sculptor Christoph Jelin, gives access to the four-wing complex.

★ **Museum** ⊘ – The castle contains the university's collections, part of which are the result of private donations, in a delightful setting. The pre- and early history department displays numerous captivating exhibits, such as the tiny ivory

---

Friedrich Hölderlin in Tübingen

Friedrich Hölderlin was born at Lauffen am Neckar in 1770. He studied theology at the Protestant seminary in Tübingen in preparation for entering the church as a minister, a vocation chosen for him by his mother. Here he befriended the philosophers Hegel and Schelling. He had begun writing poetry while still at school (in Maulbronn), and continued to write at Tübingen, finally rebelling against a career in the Church. He spent some time in Frankfurt, Switzerland and Bordeaux as a private tutor. The first signs of his mental illness (he is thought to have been suffering from schizophrenia) manifested themselves in 1802. In 1806, he returned to Tübingen where he was promised a recovery from his condition if he put himself into the hands of the professor of medicine Autenrieth at the residential home (in the former hostel, the oldest surviving original university building). When the treatment failed to produce any results, he went to stay with the family of carpenters called Zimmer at no 6 Bursagasse. He spent the remaining 36 years of his life in the tower room at this address.

"Vogelherdpferdchen"★, the figure of a horse named after the cave near Ulm in which it was discovered in 1931, which is one of the oldest works of art on display from the New Paleolithic Age. There are outstanding exhibits from Classical Antiquity, Ancient Egypt and the Ancient Orient. Note in particular the **religious chamber**★ from a tomb dating from the Old Kingdom (3rd millennium BC), which is completely covered in bas-relief sculptures. There is an interesting collection of castings of ancient sculpture in the knights' hall, which features a state oriel with stellar rib vaulting dating from 1537. The museum also has an ethnology department.

There is a good view of the Neckar and the roofs of the old town from the castle terrace.

★ **Am Markt** (Y) – An old square, very animated on market days (Mondays, Wednesdays and Fridays). In the centre, Renaissance fountain and statue of Neptune.

★ **Rathaus** (Y R) – The sgraffito decoration of this 15C building dates from 1876 and depicts the allegories of Justice, Agriculture and Science, as well as famous local figures. The astronomic clock (1511) on the façade is the work of Johann Stöfler.

Fruchtschranne (Y) – The roof of this imposing 15C half-timbered house is broken by four rows of shed dormers. The house, now a grammar school, was once a ducal grain store.

Bebenhausener Pfleghof (Bebenhausen Hospital) (Y B) – This 15C building was once the administrative seat and tithe barn of Bebenhausen Abbey *(see below)*. Jutting from the tall, steep roof is a three-storey dormer through the windows of which the grain was passed into the lofts. This grand complex has served many purposes over the years, but now houses student lodgings and a small police station.

Stiftskirche ⊙ (Y) – A Gothic hall-church built in the 15C. The rood screen (1490) and the **pulpit**★ (1509) are Flamboyant in origin. Beneath the rood screen with its reticulated rib vaulting stands a fine three-panelled Passion altarpiece (1520),

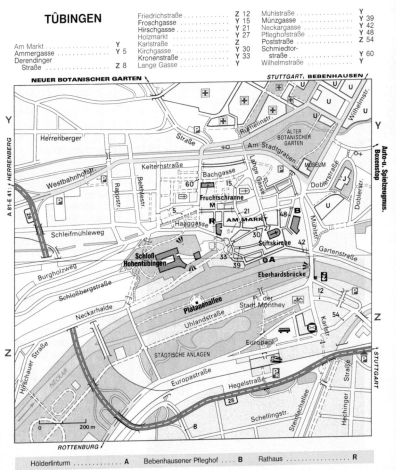

Hölderlinturm .... **A**   Bebenhausener Pfleghof .... **B**   Rathaus .... **R**

Castle residents

Schloß Hohentübingen is home to south Germany's largest colony of **bats**. Disturbed by the renovation of the roof framework in 1995, the bats decided to move home, choosing the castle cellars as their new abode. For this reason, it is no longer possible for visitors to see the giant vat dating from 1548 which has a capacity of 850hl/18 700gal.

---

attributed to Dürer's pupil Hans Leonhard Schäufelein. The chancel is in fact the burial place of the princes of Württemberg. Note the funerary monument of Eberhard the Bearded, original founder of the university, and the Renaissance **tombs**★★ of Duke Ludwig and his wife, adorned with fine alabaster relief work.

From the top of the church tower, there is an interesting **view**★ of the river, the castle promontory and, in the distance, the Swabian Jura.

At the foot of the perron leading to Stiftskirche stretches the **Holzmarkt** (woodwork market) with the Georgsbrunnen fountain lending added charm to the scene. The old Heckenhauer bookshop (now a travel agent) is where the writer and poet **Hermann Hesse** spent his apprenticeship from 1895 to 1899.

ADDITIONAL SIGHTS

★ **Neuer Botanischer Garten** ⊙ – *Hartmeyer Straße 123, best reached via the north ring road (Nordring).*
These botanical gardens north of town are part of the university and are home to more than 12 000 plant species from all over the world. The well established outdoor beds with an arboretum are laid out in over 5ha/12 acres. The **greenhouses**★ (tropical and sub-tropical plants, succulents) are particularly interesting.

Kunsthalle Tübingen – *Philosophenweg 76, via the north ring road (Nordring).*
Tübingen's art gallery has won itself a good reputation far beyond the local region with its excellent temporary exhibitions of 19C and 20C art.

Auto- und Spielzeugmuseum Boxenstop (Car and Toy Museum) ⊙ – *Brunnenstraße 18.*
Motor enthusiasts will be delighted with the fine vehicles on display here. Sports cars, such as the Mercedes-Benz 300 SL (1955), rub shoulders with luxury vehicles, such as the Jaguar 100 from 1935, or racing cars, such as the Lola Type T 212 from 1971. The museum also houses an impressive collection of old toys, which will tweak many a memory.

EXCURSION

★ **Kloster Bebenhausen** ⊙ – *6km/4mi to the north via Wilhelmstraße* (**Y**).
This ancient monastery, founded in 1180 in the solitude of Schönbuch Forest, is an interesting example of Romanesque-Gothic architecture in Germany. Together with Maulbronn and Eberbach, it is the best preserved Cistercian monastery in Germany. Built to the classic Cistercian plan, but much restored, the abbey church still shows traces of Romanesque design.

In the 15C, Bebenhausen was the wealthiest monastery in Württemberg, owning a vast estate (over 30 000ha/74 000 acres). The famous **roof turret**★, which has become the monastery's trademark, dates from this period of prosperity. It was built by a lay-brother from Salem Abbey between 1407 and 1409 and its filigree stonemasonry is a masterpiece of Gothic architecture. In 1535, the monastery was dissolved, but a Roman Catholic convent remained here until 1560. In the same year, a Protestant monastic school was founded

R. Chéret/MICHELIN

Kloster Bebenhausen

here, which remained in place until 1807. Finally, between 1947 and 1952, these historic walls housed the State Parliament (*Landtag*) of the then mini-state of Württemberg-Hohenzollern.

The **cloister** (1475-1500), in the Flamboyant style, has splendid fan vaulting. Facing the lavabo is the **summer refectory**★ with delicate painted ornamentation; it was built in c 1335 and its vaulting is supported by three detached pillars. The chapter-house, parlatory and common eating room (frater) are also worth a closer look. The west wing houses the winter refectory, which is like a small slice of history from 1490. The tiled stove dates from the mid 16C. On the first floor is the **monks' dormitory**, which was divided into separate cells in the early 16C.

Schloß Bebenhausen ⊘ – King Karl of Württemberg had a hunting lodge built in the old monastery manor house after 1870. This is where the last king of Württemberg, Wilhelm II, retired after his abdication. His widow, Charlotte, lived here until her death in 1946. The rooms have a homely atmosphere, as Charlotte lived modestly, in style far removed from royal pomp and s plendour.

Michelin maps (scale 1/200 000), which are revised regularly, indicate:
golf courses, sports stadiums, racecourses, swimming-pools, beaches, airfields, scenic
routes, public and long-distance footpaths, viewpoints, forest parks, interesting sights...
The perfect complement to the The Green Guide for planning holidays and leisure time.
Keep current Michelin Maps in the car at all times

ÜBERLINGEN★

Baden-Württemberg
Population 21 000
Michelin map 419 W 11 – Local map see BODENSEE

This former Imperial City on the northwest arm of Lake Constance was founded c 1180 by Frederick I Barbarossa. Its growth and prosperity in the Middle Ages were largely due to harvests from the vineyards and trade in salt and grain. In 1379 Überlingen was granted Imperial freedom, a status that it retained until 1802. From the mid 19C, the tourist industry, fostered by the mild climate, played an increasingly important role in local economy. Überlingen has been an officially recognised Kneipp spa resort since 1956.

West of the town there is a pleasant **moat walk** (Stadtbefestigungsanlagen) (**A**) which leads to the lakeside **Seepromenade** (**AB**).

SIGHTS

Münsterplatz (**B**) – The square lies between the Gothic cathedral, the north façade of the town hall, and the Renaissance municipal chancellery (Alte Kanzlei).

★ **Münster** (**B**) – The cathedral, or minster, has an enormous central portion with five aisles covered by Gothic fan vaulting. A graceful Swabian work of 1510, the Virgin of the Crescent Moon, stands in St Elizabeth Chapel off the south aisle.

ÜBERLINGEN

Bahnhofstraße	A 2
Christophstraße	A 3
Franziskanerstraße	B 5
Gradebergstraße	B 6
Hafenstraße	B 8
Hizlerstraße	B 9
Hochbildstraße	B 10
Hofstatt	A
Jakob-Kessenring-Str.	A 12
Klosterstraße	A 14
Krummebergstraße	B 15
Landungsplatz	B 17
Lindenstraße	B 19
Luziengasse	B 20
Marktstraße	AB 22
Münsterstraße	B
Obertorstraße	B 23
Owinger Straße	B 25
Pfarrhofstraße	B 26
St.-Ulrich-Straße	B 28
Seestraße	B 29

Städtisches Museum	**M**
Rathaus	**R**

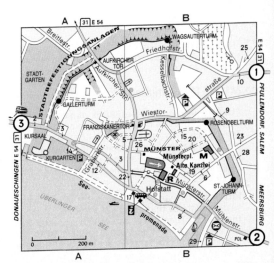

505

WHERE TO STAY

OUR SELECTION

Bürgerbräu – Aufkircher Straße 20, ☎ 0 75 51/9 27 40, Fax 0 75 51/6 60 17. Single rooms from 85DM. Beautiful half-timbered house.

Seegarten – Seepromenade 7, ☎ 0 75 51/6 34 98, Fax 0 75 51/39 81. Single rooms from 110DM. Hotel right by the lake, with a terrace shaded by chestnut trees. Comfortable rooms.

Rosengarten – Bahnhofstraße 12, ☎ 0 75 51/9 28 20, Fax 0 75 51/80 85 31. Single rooms from 140DM. Modernised Jugendstil villa peacefully located in the park (Stadtgarten). Rooms fitted with every comfort.

Rathaus (Town hall) (B R) – *Enter through the turret on the right and walk up to the first floor.* The **Council Chamber★** ⊘ (Ratssaal) is decorated with great finesse in the Gothic manner: panelled walls embellished with projecting arches; ribbed, and slightly rounded, wooden ceiling; a series of 15C statuettes.

Städtisches Museum ⊘ **(B M)** – Among the exhibits, housed in a late-15C mansion, is a collection of cribs (Krippen): 18C wood carvings in the folk tradition, representing scenes from the life of Jesus in miniature.

EXCURSION

★ **Salem** – *11km/7mi to the east. See SALEM.*

Pfahlbaumuseum Unteruhldingen ⊘ – *In* **Uhldingen-Mühlhofen**, *taking Seepromenade 6-7km/4mi southeast.*
Reconstructions of prehistoric dwellings on stilts (Stone and Bronze Ages).

ULM★★

Baden-Württemberg
Population 110 000
Michelin map 419/420 U 13

The royal palace of "Hulma" recorded for the first time in 854 was one of Europe's most important cities in the Middle Ages and acknowledged leader of the Swabian League of Cities. After the Thirty Years War and the Spanish War of Succession, Ulm's political and economic strength declined, and in 1802 it was stripped of its Imperial City status. Between 1842 and 1859 Ulm and Neu-Ulm, on the opposite bank of the Danube and now part of Bavaria, were made into a stronghold as part of the German Federation and enclosed in a 9km/6mi long fortified wall. Ulm's most famous local figure is Nobel Prize winner **Albert Einstein**, born here in 1879.
Trade and industry, especially in the manufacturing sector, have long been established in these sister cities situated at the crossroads of several major communications routes. Vehicle construction is a particularly important branch of local industry. A university was founded here in 1967, which is now the model for building cooperation between science, research and production in the technologies of the future.

★★ **General view** – A walk along the **Jahnufer** (the south bank of the Danube) (Z) opens a fine view of gabled houses crowning the ramparts on the far side of the river, of the Metzgerturm (Butchers' Tower) and the cathedral.

★★★ **MÜNSTER (CATHEDRAL) (Y)** *45min (not counting ascent of the spire)*

At a total height of 161m/528ft, Ulm cathedral spire is the tallest in the world. It appears to arrow the entire Gothic building skywards in its slender trajectory. The church's sweeping vertical lines, added to the lightness of the pierced masonry, are wholly admirable. Although the foundation stone was laid in 1377, the two towers and the spire were not erected until 1890. A beautiful porch with three arcades and a very fine profile precedes the double Renaissance entrance doors.

Interior – The upswept nave, with sharply pointed arches, is emphasized in its soaring flight by the absence of a transept, which also concentrates attention on the chancel. The chancel arch bears the largest **fresco** north of the Alps. It depicts the Last Judgement and was created in 1471. To the right on the chancel arch stands the *Man of Sorrows*, an early work by Hans Multscher, a native of Ulm (1429).

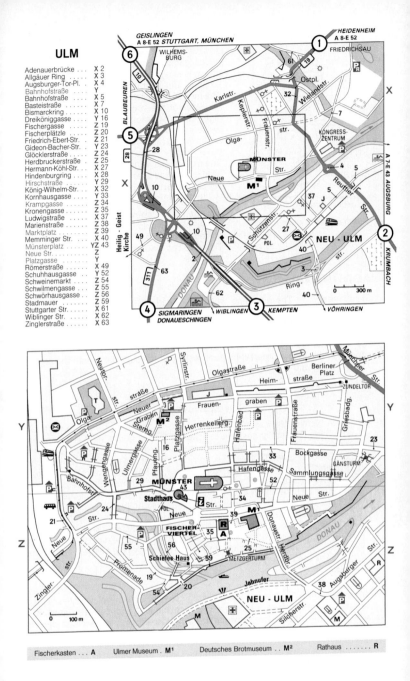

ULM

Fischerkasten ... **A** Ulmer Museum . **M¹** Deutsches Brotmuseum .. **M²** Rathaus .... **R**

The pillars of the central nave support a series of graceful early-15C consoles. The pulpit is surmounted by a splendid wooden sounding board dating from 1510, the work of Jörg Syrlin the Younger, and above this is what appears to be a second pulpit in the Flamboyant style. This is intended for the Holy Spirit, the invisible preacher. The ciborium, left of the chancel entrance, is in the same style, and so are the four side aisles with fine fan vaulting.

★ **Tabernacle** – *Left of the entrance to the chancel*. At 26m/85ft it is the tallest in Germany. The masterpiece, chiselled out of limestone and sandstone, was produced c 1460-80. Three rows of wooden figures depict the prophets and lawbringers. Visitors should note the small figures of people and animals, which have been carved into the handrail of the banister and on which the artist has allowed his imagination to run riot.

★★★ **Choir stalls** (Chorgestühl) – A marvellous example of wood carving, executed by Jörg Syrlin the Elder between 1469 and 1474, faces two series of characters, from the Bible and from pagan antiquity, one opposite the other. Men are

507

Sibilla amend petsanao oen oe Vagit

Ulm cathedral choir stalls:
a sibyl

grouped on the left, women on the right, the upper gables being devoted to the Church's apostles and martyrs, and the high backs of the stalls to Old Testament figures.

The most expressive sculptures are carved from the sides of the stalls and include sibyls on the right, busts of Greek and Latin philosophers and writers (Pythagoras, Cicero etc) on the left. The sculptor and his wife head the ranks nearest the nave.

The **triple throne**, which Jörg Syrlin the Elder created in 1468 as a test of his skill, stands beneath the chancel arch. Only after completing this work was he commissioned to produce the choir stalls.

Ascent of the spire – *(768 steps)*. From the tower platform or the bulb of the spire, the all-round **panorama**★★ includes the town, the Danube, the plateaux of the Swabian Jura and the Alps.

ADDITIONAL SIGHTS

Stadthaus (Z) – The gleaming white town hall (1991-93) with its avant-garde architecture, has been the subject of considerable controversy. It was unquestionably somewhat daring to erect this work, by the American architect **Richard Meier**, right next to the venerable cathedral. However it provides an exciting link between the past and the present, takes away a little of the severity of the cathedral square, and brings a cheerful note, especially in the summer, when the terrace is full of young and old.

The Sparrow of Ulm

The emblem of the city of Ulm is a sparrow in flight, carrying a long straw in its beak. The story goes that in the days when goods were transported by horse and cart, some timber merchants arrived at the gates of Ulm with a cartload of logs. To their dismay, the load of logs was too wide to fit through the gate. While they were pondering how to solve this dilemma, one of them caught sight of a sparrow building her nest. She was carrying a long straw in her beak and flying towards a tiny gap in the hedge. "Aha," thought the man, "She's going to have the same problem as us, as that straw is too long to fit through the gap." However, at the last minute the sparrow twisted her head so that the straw fitted through the gap lengthways. The cart-driver and his fellows followed the bird's example and adjusted the angle of their load of logs so that they could drive through the gate into the city.

★ **Ulmer Museum** ⊙ **(Z M¹)** – The museum consists of a complex of four adjacent houses, with its main entrance in a 15C mansion with a well-preserved vault. The works by the Ulm masters are particularly noteworthy, and include the Virgin Mary of Bihlafingen by Hans Multscher.

One of the most arresting exhibits is the charming *Mary of Sorrows*, edged in blue and gold, the work of a master from the Lake Constance area of Upper Swabia (early 13C). The easternmost of the houses, the Kiechelhaus, is the only one among the very many Ulm mansions from the 16C and 17C which has survived fully intact. It features, among other things, a beautiful Renaissance **coffered ceiling** on the second floor. Several rooms are dedicated to the guilds, which were of course especially important in a rich town like Ulm. The **master craftsman's plaques**, which date from the 16C to the 18C, bear witness to the strict guild regulations. The museum also boasts a prehistoric section and, even more interesting, a **collection of 20C art**, which includes paintings by Picasso, Klee, Stella and Rothko.

Rathaus (Town hall) (Z R) – An elegant Gothic and Renaissance building with pierced gables and painted facades, richly decorated in trompe-l'œil. An astronomic clock adorns the fine west façade.

On the market square in front of the town hall is the **Fischerkasten (Z A)**, a fountain thus named because fishermen would cool their wares in it. The spiral stem was fashioned by Jörg Syrlin the Elder in 1482.

★ **Mühlen-, Fischer- und Gerberviertel (Z)** – The little alleys which extend along the Blau in the quarter formerly inhabited by millers, fishermen and tanners, are very appealing. A good place to start an exploration is Fischerplätzle, a small square shaded by a lime tree. Turn left into a narrow street and pass over the little bridge, which leads to the so-called crooked house (**Schiefes Haus**, mid 15C) on the banks of the Blau. The tiny alley opposite is known as the "kissing alley" (Kußgasse), because the roofs of the houses touch one another. The house of oaths (**Schwörhaus**) nearby (the main part of which originates from 1613) is the scene every year on Oath Monday of the ceremonial statement of account by the chief burgomaster and of the renewal of his oath.

The **town walls** afford a wonderful close-up view of the gables of the old houses. Visitors cannot fail to notice the crooked **Metzger tower**, erected in 1349, since it stands 2.05m/nearly 7ft out of true. Go through the rose garden to reach the eagle bastion (**Adlerbastei**), where the unfortunate **tailor of Ulm** attempted to fly in 1811.

★ **Deutsches Brotmuseum** ⊘ (**Y M²**) – This collection, unique in Germany, has found a worthy setting in the Salzstadel or salt barn, a Renaissance building dating from 1592. It was established when an Ulm entrepreneur realised that no museum existed for **bread**, which is so important to humanity. Starting around 1950 he and his son meticulously put together a collection, with enormous professional and artistic understanding, which represents 8 000 years of the cultural and social history of bread. The links between this basic nutrient and religion, tradition and politics are emphasised, with videos and dioramas being used whenever they contribute towards a better understanding of the subject.

Baker's sign dating from 1820

Deutsches Brotmuseum Ulm

Exhibits range from ovens, models, guild symbols, coins and stamps, to specially selected works of art (by Brueghel, Corinth, Kollwitz, Picasso). Everything in the museum is related to grain (its cultivation and trade) or bread. A critical examination is made of the world food situation.

Heilig-Geist-Kirche – *To the southwest, accessible via Römerstraße* (**X**). This modern church, distinguished by its bell-tower pointing upwards like a finger, stands on a fine panoramic site above the town.

EXCURSIONS

Kloster Wiblingen (Abbey) ⊘ – *5km/3mi to the south, via Wiblinger Straße* (**X**). Although its foundation dates back to the 11C, the final touches were not put to the **abbey church** until the 18C. As at Vierzehnheiligen, more than a third of the abbey church's floor plan is occupied by the transept, where pilgrims worshipped relics of the Holy Rood. The flattened domes of this Baroque building could give visitors the impression of being crushed, but this is compensated for by the illusion of height provided by the painter Januarius Zick in the frescoes which cover them. This artist is also responsible for the High Altar. The abbey **library**★, completed in 1760, is one of the finest examples of the Rococo in Swabia.

The main interest lies in a gallery, supported by 32 columns, which projects into the centre of the room and at each end. The rhythmically placed columns, painted alternately pink and blue, combine with the large false-relief fresco on the ceiling to create an ensemble rich in colour and movement.

★ **Blaubeuren** – *18km/11mi to the west.*
Follow the signposts Blautopf-Hochaltar, in this village of the Swabian Jura renowned for its fine setting among the rocks, then leave the car near the monumental abbey entrance.

Blautopf – *15min on foot there and back.* This deep blue pool was formed by a natural embankment of glacial origin. The shady approaches have been laid out as walks.

Old Benedictine Abbey – *Allow 30min. Follow the "Hochaltar" signs.* The premises include a picturesque group of ancient half-timbered buildings. In the chancel of the old **abbey church** (Klosterkirche) ⊘ is a magnificent **altarpiece**★★ (Hochaltar), a masterpiece of Gothic sculpture and a collective work created by the principal studios of Ulm in the 15C. The themes treated are Christ's Passion, the life of John the Baptist, and the Virgin Mary among the Saints. The beautiful **choir stalls**★ of 1493 and the **triple throne** are the work of Ulm master Syrlin the Younger.

Insel USEDOM★

Mecklenburg-Vorpommern
Michelin map 416 D 25 – E 26

Usedom is Germany's easternmost island and at 445km²/172sq mi it is the largest after Rügen. The eastern part of the island, with the town of Swinoujscie, covering around one fifth of the total area, belongs to Poland. Usedom displays a wonderfully unspoilt natural landscape, alternating between moors, inland seas, forest, dunes, sandy beaches, with steep cliffs here and there. The flat northwest contrasts with the hilly southeast part, which likes to be known as Usedom's Switzerland. The island is part of the Usedom-Oderhaff Nature Reserve. Its extremely irregular outline can best be compared with a wide-open crocodile's jaw. At the narrowest point, at Koserow, the island is barely 200m/220yd wide. Its main industry is tourism, since the elegant bathing resorts on the Baltic coast developed after 1820. At the turn of the century it became known as "Berlin's bathtub", since it was mainly the residents of the capital who came here to relax and recuperate. Notable bathing resort architecture from this period remains, and has been carefully restored everywhere.

Wolgast - *On the mainland.*
One point of access to Usedom is in the south at Zecherin, and the other lies in the northwest, from Wolgast over the River Peene. The parish church, **Pfarrkirche St.-Petri** ⊙ in the birthplace of the Romantic painter Philipp Otto Runge, with its formidable octangular tower, dating back to the year 1370, is a must for visitors. Its unadorned exterior contrasts with its sumptuous interior. There are wall paintings from the 15C and 16C, a danse macabre cycle, which was painted around 1700 by Caspar Sigmund Köppe based on a woodcut by Hans Holbein the Younger, and a Renaissance gravestone.

Krummin - *To the east of Wolgast.*
The most beautiful **avenue of lime trees★** (Lindenallee) in Usedom leads to the right off the main 111 road, down to the little fishing village which lies on the Krummin cove.
The surfaced road is only just two kilometres long, but it is quite marvellous. The rounded canopy formed by the leaves overhead gives one the impression of being in a high Gothic cathedral. It gives the visitor pause for thought and soothes many a troubled breast.

Hist.-techn. Informationszentrum Peenemünde ⊙ - The army test establishment of Peenemünde, the development site of the V2 rockets, which cost thousands their lives during the Second World War, but which signalled the beginning of modern space travel, was built right in the north of the island in 1936. This double-edged sword is described and explained in a video presentation.

The "Taille" Usedoms - At the narrowest point or waist of the island, the white sandy beaches of the resorts of **Zinnowitz, Koserow, Kölpinsee** and **Ückeritz** stretch out, interrupted from time by the steep cliff.

★ **Bansin, Heringsdorf, Ahlbeck** - These "three sisters" in the southeast of the island, are linked by a 10km/6mi-long beach promenade. During the 19C these were fashionable resorts, the rendezvous of the aristocracy and the wealthy. The many imposing villas and hotels, which have happily stood the test of time and make these resorts so attractive, bear witness to the past. Despite its rather ordinary name, **Heringsdorf** was an extraordinarily fashionable resort, and Emperor Wilhelm II was a regular visitor. He resided in the Villa Staudt (*Delbrückstraße 6*), which still stands today. **Ahlbeck** is justifiably proud of its attractive historical **pier★**, which was

Pier, Ahlbeck

built in 1898. A restaurant was added in 1902, and with its white walls, red roof and the four green-roofed corner towers, it is one of the most favoured photographic subjects on the island.

Mellenthin – *Northeast of the town of Usedom, 2km/1mi to the north of B 110.* This little-visited village radiates peace, and with its Renaissance castle, it forms a rural idyll. The three winged building surrounded by a moat is unadorned, whilst a colourfully mounted Renaissance fireplace from the year 1613 in the entrance hall is quite magnificent. The 14C **village church** in the centre of a cemetery full of 600-year-old oak trees is urgently in need of restoration, but it is still a little pearl with its **interior decoration**★ dating from the 17C. The painted Baroque gallery from 1755 in particular radiates fresh and simple belief. The offertory dates from 1125.

Wallfahrtskirche VIERZEHNHEILIGEN★★

Bayern

Michelin map 418/420 P 17

This pilgrimage church dedicated to the 14 Auxiliary Saints (Holy Helpers) stands on an open hillside overlooking the beautiful Upper Main Valley, opposite Kloster Banz. The bold concepts of Balthasar Neumann, master of the Baroque, are evident in the interior.

The Pilgrimage – In 1445 and 1446, a herdsman on this hillside was blessed with a number of visions, the last of them identified as the Christ Child among the "Fourteen Holy Helpers". The worship of this group of saints, actively encouraged by German Dominicans and Cistercians, must be seen in the context of the mysticism which prevailed at the beginning of the 15C, when "visions" were frequent (the "voices" heard by Joan of Arc – born in 1412 – were those of St Catherine and St Margaret, themselves members of this group of Auxiliary Saints). This devotion to the Holy Helpers remained alive for many years among local people, attracting crowds of pilgrims to a chapel which was to be superseded, in the 18C, by a sumptuous Rococo church.

TOUR ⏱ *about 30min*

The church was built in handsome yellow ochre sandstone following designs by Balthasar Neumann between 1743 and 1772. The west façade is framed by domed towers unusually tall for a Baroque building. The design of the façade itself is bold indeed, with jutting cornices to emphasize the tiered arrangement of pilasters and columns and the sinous lines of the convex front. In accordance with the taste of the time – Rococo rather than purely Baroque – these elements do not simply constitute a covering, as at Ottobeuren, but form an embellishment in its own right. The four rows of windows, small at mezzanine or attic level, wide and spacious elsewhere, together with a broken pediment crowned with statues, are reminiscent of the castles of the period. The statues, once gilded, represent Jesus Christ between Faith and Charity.

511

Interior – The interior layout is organized as a succession of three oval bays framed by colonnades and covered by low inner domes. The true centre of the church is the bay containing the altar to the Auxiliary Saints – to the detriment of the transept crossing, which is invaded by the bay's colonnade. Circular domes, again, cover the transepts. Such geometric subtleties create an overall perspective concentrating the worshippers' view relentlessly on a central focal point – an ideal striven for by 18C architects who were wearied of an endless succession of rectangular bays.

Many visitors will be surprised by the restraint and elegance of the church's Rococo interior decoration. Outstanding are the colour combinations of the painting inside the domes, the lightness of the stuccowork, the richesse of the gold outlines defining the woodwork of the galleries, and the grace of putti surmounting confessionals and cornice.

★★ **Altar to the Fourteen Auxiliary Saints** (Nothelfer-Altar) – A Rococo pyramid with a pierced baldaquin, where every line is nevertheless convex or concave, this remarkable work was executed by Johann Michael Feichtmayr and stucco-workers of the Wessobrunn School in 1764. It stands on the spot where the herdsman's visions are said to have occurred.

The Altar Statues

Balustrade: 1) St Denys – **2)** St Blaise – **3)** St Erasmus – **4)** St Cyriacus (delivery from the Devil at the final hour).

Altar niches: 5) St Catherine, patron saint of the learned, of students and girls wishing to get married (the model of Christian wisdom). – **6)** St Barbara, patron saint of miners, artillerymen and prisoners (the grace of a noble death).

Buttresses: 7) St Acacius (the agonies of death). – **8)** St Giles, the only intercessor not to suffer martyrdom (to obtain the grace of a true confession). – **9)** St Eustace (converted by the vision of a stag with a Cross between its antlers). – **10)** St Christopher, patron saint of travellers.

On top of the baldaquin: 11) St Vitus (epilepsy). – **12)** St Margaret (intercession for the forgiveness of sins). – **13)** St George, patron saint of peasants and their possessions – **14)** St Pantaleon.

Those who enjoy seeing – or photographing – unusual views should climb the slopes above the church. Before long, Banz Abbey comes into view on the far side of the valley, framed by the Vierzehnheiligen towers, in line with – and apparently resting on – the ridge pole of the church roof.

WALDECKER BERGLAND ★

Hessen

Michelin map 417 M 10-11

This small stretch of countryside in the Hessen mountains, under the rule of the Waldeck Princes until 1918, has developed into one of the most popular tourist areas of central Germany thanks to its forests, the magnificent lake retained by the Eder dam offering a wide variety of sports, and the well-known spa resort of Bad Wildungen.

ROUND TOUR STARTING FROM BAD WILDUNGEN

145km/90mi – allow 1 day

Bad Wildungen – The most impressive bathing installations of this spa follow one another on either side of the Brunnenallee, through the Kurpark and as far as the horse-shoe buildings of the George-Viktor spring – the busiest centre of this picturesque region. Visitors should explore the historic town centre with its fine half-timbered houses.

In the middle of the old town, the **Evangelical church** (Evangelische Stadtkirche) contains an altarpiece said to be one of the earliest milestones in German painting: the **Wildunger Altar★★**, which dates from 1403. Embellishing the high altar, these scenes from the life and Passion of Christ are notable for their profundity and for the stylized elongation of the idealized figures.

Heading north, the road comes to the steep, tortuous banks of the Edersee, a reservoir created in 1914 which contains 200 million m³/7 billion cu ft of water.

★ **Waldeck** – Rising above the steep, wooded shores of the artificial lake, the castle seat of the Waldeck Princes, abandoned in the 17C, is now part hotel, part museum. From the terrace there is a fine **view**★ of the lake, curving away out of sight between the wooded heights. The **Burgmuseum** ⊙ galleries evoke the history of the House of Waldeck. The castle boasts a Witches' Tower (Hexenturm) with three prison cells, one below the other. The Eder dam, completed in 1914, retains 200 million m³/44 000 million gallons of water. In 1943, during the Second World War, a specialized raid by the RAF breached the dam with a single 4-ton bomb, blowing a gap in the stonework 70m/230ft wide and 22m/72ft high, resulting in catastrophic floods.

Drive to Arolsen via Nieder-Werbe, Sachsenhausen, Freienhagen and Landau.

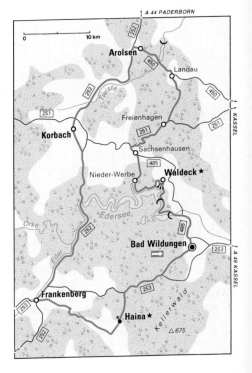

Arolsen – Formerly the residence of the Waldeck princes, this is a small town whose symmetrical plan testifies to its aristocratic origins.
The **Schloß** ⊙, its design inspired by the Château de Versailles, was built between 1714 and 1728, although the interior decoration was to continue until the beginning of the 19C. The apartments, adorned with stuccowork and painted ceilings (1715-19), are gained via a vestibule and double staircase. Together with the Baroque Garden Chamber (Gartensaal) and the Great Hall (Großer Saal), these complete the state rooms.

Korbach – The present town was formed by joining together two fortified settlements: Alstadt (built around the church of St Kilian – without a tower) and Neustadt (built around the church of St Nicolai – a tower with a spire). Many old half-timbered houses have been preserved. **St Kilian's** is a Gothic hall-church wider than it is long, a particularity showing Westphalian influence. There is a fine group of statues at the south door: the Virgin Mary stands against the pier, while the Last Judgement is depicted on the tympanum.

Frankenberg an der Eder – The upper town contains impressive wooden houses dating from the 16C, especially around the two central squares, the Obermarkt and Untermarkt. A particularly interesting feature of the latter is the **Rathaus**★ (1509), bristling with turrets. On the crest behind stands the 13C-14C Liebfrauenkirche, with the **Lady Chapel** (Marienkapelle) abutting on the south transept. The chapel is Gothic, built with an asymmetric polygonal floor plan. It contains a stone altarpiece, now lacking its statues but with a rare decorative perfection.

★ **Haina** – The **church** of the former Cistercian abbey, built here in the heart of the woods, is a huge, rather plain Gothic hall. The flat east end, the small columns in the nave broken halfway up by historiated consoles, and the six transept chapels are Romanesque.
The cloister, however, shows both Romanesque and Gothic features (note the Romanesque "Lamb of God" entrance).

The road passes through the beechwoods and plantations of oak forming the Kellerwald forest massif before regaining the outskirts of Bad Wildungen.

Use the Index to find more information about a subject mentioned in the guide people, towns, places of interest, isolated sites, historical events or natural features...

WALDSASSEN★

Bayern

Population 8 000
Michelin map 420 P 20

Waldsassen lies between mountains and forest – the Fichtelgebirge and the Oberpfälzer Wald – in a thickly wooded region. The first residents were Cistercian monks in a monastery founded under Margrave Diephold III. The monastery was dissolved when the Protestant Palatinate gained possession of the abbey. The Cistercians returned, however, after the Oberpfalz region was seized by Bavaria in the 17C. After secularisation the abbey was once more closed in 1803. Modern Waldsassen owes its economic prosperity to the glass and ceramics industry.

★ **Stiftsbasilika** – Completed in 1704, mainly on plans drawn up by Georg Dientzenhofer, this building is distinguished by its unusual length (83m/272ft) and a chancel occupying more than one third of the floor space – a feature recalling the design of Cistercian churches.

The aisles and galleries form two storeys of chapels which communicate vertically by apertures in the vaulting. The decoration is particularly lavish: the stuccowork is by GB Carlone; the **choir stalls**★ are by local craftsmen, and so is the red- and black-marble high altar, with its sculpted reredos (the Annunciation) incorporating a tabernacle in the form of a gilded globe.

On the pillars of the transept crossing are imposing statues of the four Fathers of the Church. The overall effect of the church is that it is an example of an early attempt to adapt Italian Baroque to German taste.

★★ **Bibliothek** ⊙ – This library is a real treasure. The visitor will be spellbound with admiration before the carved woodwork framing the shelves, decorating the balustrade and, above all, forming the 10 life-size statues supporting the gallery. Karl Stilp and Andreas Witt, the local artists who created these masterpieces, brought a profound realism, touched with wry humour, to their task.

The 10 figures symbolize, with wit and accuracy, the different guilds involved in the production of a book. They include, among others, the rag sorter who provides the raw materials, the shepherd who delivers the animal skins to the bookbinder, the bookseller who distributes the finished work. The stance and characterization of each one is remarkable – and each face, according to the viewpoint of the observer, can show opposing expressions. Thus the oriental bookseller (second statue on the left of the entrance) presents a noble profile on one side, and features twisted by illness and cunning on the other. The butcher, brandishing a knife, leers maliciously in the direction of his neighbour, the shepherd. The strangest figure is that of the critic (second on the left side of the end door): his hands are tied, and a bird of prey, emerging from his head, has seized him by the nose – the inference being that the character has a sharp wit but is nevertheless a prisoner of his pride.

Completed in 1726, this library is one of the finest manifestations of lay Baroque art.

EXCURSION

★ **Kappel Church** – _6.5km/4mi to the north._
Isolated in a pastoral **setting**★★, this church dedicated to the Holy Trinity stands within sight of the Cheb Basin in the Czech Republic. It was built in 1689 by Georg Dientzenhofer in the shape of a trefoil rotunda punctuated by three towers. Inside, three apses, each dedicated to one of the three characters forming the Trinity, radiate from a central triangular bay with three columns. Three altar niches have been hollowed out from each apse.

WASSERBURG AM INN

Bayern

Population 10 500
Michelin map 420 V 20

Wasserburg owes its existence to its site, on a rise encircled by a loop of the River Inn, and its name to a castle built there by the Wittelsbachs. River navigation and the trade in salt contributed to the town's rapid development in the Middle Ages. Coming from the south, the bridge over the river affords an attractive **view**★ of the old town, with the tall façades of the quayside houses reflected in the water. The mixture of flat roofs, stepped gables and ridged roofs behind copings give Wasserburg the half-German, half-Italian look typical of the Inn and Salzach valleys.

SIGHTS

Marienplatz – Bordered by arcaded houses, this main square is closed off by the tall, stepped gable of a **Rathaus** decorated with paintings in which religious subjects alternate with armorial bearings. The façade has Renaissance windows. On the first floor, next to the banqueting hall, there is a **room** with painted panels and walls covered by 16C woodwork beneath carved beams of the same period. On the opposite side of the square, the lovely **Patrizierhaus Kern** features an outstanding façade with two-storey oriel windows, paintings, and richly ornamented stucco-work by Johann Baptist Zimmermann.

Pfarrkirche St Jakob – The church is crowned by a tall, square tower. The interior, in the Gothic style, contains a carved wood pulpit dating from 1638.

★ **Heimatmuseum** ⊙ – The four floors of this huge Gothic building house many different displays. Note Bavaria's oldest postal sleigh *(ground floor)*, exhibitions of furniture *(first and second floors)*, and the craft workshops on the third floor. Examples of religious art from the 15C to the 18C can be seen behind the building in a gallery housed in the former stable block.

EXCURSION

Rott am Inn – *15km/9.5mi to the south.*
Of the former Benedictine abbey founded in the 11C, only an interesting **church**, to which a number of Baroque features were added in the 18C, remain in Rott today. The remodelling was carried out by Johann Michael Fischer (architect), Franz Xavier Feuchtmayer and Jakob Rauch (stuccowork), Matthäus Günther (frescoes) and Ignaz Günther (sculpture). Together, they achieved a quite remarkable visual harmony.

WEIMAR★★

Thüringen
Population 58 000
Michelin map 418 N 18

To most non-Germans, the name of Weimar recalls the ill-fated republic which existed uneasily between the end of the First World War and the Hitler years. But the city's claim to a place in European history rests unshakeably on the extraordinary flowering of intellectual and artistic talent here over the centuries, as it attracted great names as diverse as Luther, Cranach, Bach, Wieland, Schiller and Liszt. The one genius whose traces it is impossible to escape in Weimar, however, is that greatest of all German classicists, Johann Wolfgang von Goethe.

THE "GERMAN ATHENS"

The first historical mention of Weimar occurs in a document dated 975. By 1348 the town had been granted an urban charter, and in 1547 it became the capital of the Duchy of Saxe-Weimar. From this time onwards dates the formidable cultural expansion which made the town the true spiritual capital of Germany.

An Intellectual and Cultural Centre – Weimar's hour of glory coincided with the succession, in 1758, of the Duchess Anna Amalia. It was during her reign that the town's intellectual reputation grew, largely because of **Goethe** (1749-1832). He had first been summoned to the court at the age of 26 by Amalia's son, Duke Carl August. In the small provincial capital – at that time numbering no more than 5 000 inhabitants – he was appointed Minister and raised to a peerage, and it was in Weimar that he produced the majority of his life's work, including his dramatic masterpiece *Faust*. Goethe's reputation and influence spread far beyond the city's boundaries. For more than 25 years he directed the Weimar Theatre, which soon became accepted as the German National Theatre, renowned for its staging of international classics.

This was the result of a fruitful collaboration with **Friedrich von Schiller**, who moved permanently to Weimar in 1799. The

Goethe and Schiller, Weimar

H. Champollion/MICHELIN, Paris

515

work produced by these two friends, along with the writings of the theologian **Johann Gottfried Herder** (1744-1803, moved to Weimar in 1776), a disciple of Kant, raised Weimar's literary reputation to the point where the town was considered "the home of German classicism". In the **Goethe-Schiller Archives** (*Jener Straße*), which are among the most important literary collections in the country, several posthumous works are conserved, together with letters from almost 1 000 personalities worldwide.

Art and Music in Weimar – It was in Weimar that **Lucas Cranach the Elder** worked – from 1552 until his death a year later – on his final masterpiece: the altarpiece triptych for the local church of St Peter and St Paul (*see Stadtkirche below*). **Johann Sebastian Bach** was organist and choirmaster there from 1708 to 1717. In 1848 **Franz Liszt** in his turn became choirmaster and surrounded himself with the artistic elite of the period. It was Liszt who was the driving force behind the creation of Weimar's famous School of Music, which still bears his name today.

In 1860, an establishment was founded which left an indelible mark on 20C German painting. This was the School of Fine Arts – later to be transformed into the College of Architecture. It was under the influence of such celebrated graduates as **Arnold Böcklin** (1827-1901) that painters spearheading the contemporary avant-garde movement developed what is known as "the Weimar School".

Jugendstil and Bauhaus – The famous Belgian exponent of Jugendstil, or Art Nouveau, **Henri van de Velde**, was called to Weimar in 1902. In the company of other artists he stood for the "new Weimar", founded an applied arts school (the present day Van-de-Velde building in the Academy of Architecture and Building) and built a number of Jugendstil houses, examples of which are at nos 15 and 47 Cranachstraße. His own house, the "Hohe Pappeln" house (*Belvederer Allee 58*), completed in 1907 and recently restored, is a fine example of his work.

Further Jugendstil buildings by other architects can be seen in Gutenbergstraße and Humboldtstraße.

In 1919 the State Bauhaus was established in Weimar under the management of Walter Gropius. The interdisciplinary interaction between artists and craftsmen was to lead to a new style of building and living. This "Bauhaus style" took shape in Weimar, where beauty of form and practicality were expressed in cubic architectural and commercial art designs. Traditional Weimar was not capable of taking advantage of this opportunity for radical renewal, with the result that the Bauhaus was obliged to cease its work in 1925 and moved to Dessau (*see DESSAU*).

The Weimar Republic (1919-33) – The constitution of the Weimar Republic was set up in 1919 by the German National Assembly, which sat at that time in the Weimar National Theatre (*see Introduction: History*).

HISTORIC CENTRE

Lucas-Cranach-Haus (BZ) – The famous painter spent the last year of his life in this Renaissance house (1549) with scrolled gables. His studio was on the third floor. The **Rathaus** (R), opposite, was built c 1500 but heavily remodelled in the mid 19C.

Platz der Demokratie (BZ) – The equestrian statue of the Grand Duke Carl August of Saxe-Weimar-Eisenach (1757-1828), executed by Adolf von Donndorf, stands in this square. On the south side, the former palace (1757-74) is occupied by the **Franz Liszt Hochschule für Musik.**

The 16C-18C **Grünes Schloß** today houses the **Central Library of German Classics.** It contains medieval manuscripts, very early printed works, rare documents dating from the 16C and 17C, and above all original, priceless 18C volumes. For many years now, the museum has been collecting manuscripts, publications and translations relating to the "Age of Enlightenment" (Aufklärung) – Kant, Locke, Leibniz etc.

To the west of the square stand the 16C **Rotes Schloß**, with a Renaissance doorway, and the Baroque **Gelbes Schloß** (18C).

Haus der Frau von Stein (BZ A) – *Ackerwand 25.*

Goethe met Charlotte von Stein, lady-in-waiting to the Duchess Anna Amalia, in November 1775. The first 10 years of his stay in Weimar were profoundly influenced by his feelings for her. The house was remodelled in 1776 to his own design.

★★ **Goethes Wohnhaus** ⊘ (BZ) – *Frauenplan.*
The dramatist-politician lived in this Baroque mansion (1709) for half a century, from 1782 until his death in 1832. The interior is for the most part the way he left it. The living rooms, workroom and library (5 400 volumes) can all be visited. An annexe has been turned into a museum which gives an idea of his personality, his poetical works and his scientific research.

★ **Schillers Wohnhaus** ⊘ (BZ) – *Schillerstraße 12.*
The writer moved here in 1802 to be nearer to his great friend Goethe. It was here that *William Tell* and *The Bride of Messina* were written. The **Schiller Museum** offers a rundown on his life and his work.

Follow Schillerstraße as far as Theaterplatz.

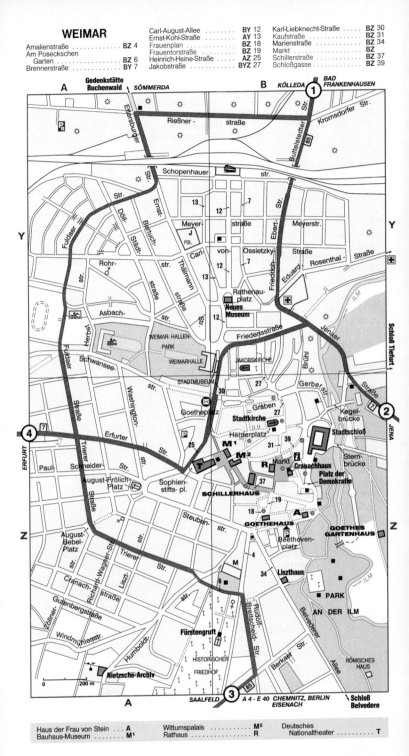

WEIMAR

Deutsches Nationaltheater (ABZ **T**) – The present structure, which dates from 1907, was built on the site of a 1779 Baroque building. It was in this old theatre that Schiller's great plays were staged and directed by Goethe; it was here, in 1850, that the first performance of Richard Wagner's Lohengrin was given. And it is in front of the present-day building that the **statues★★** of Goethe and Schiller, sculpted in 1857 by Ernst Rietschel, are to be found.

Bauhaus-Museum ⊘ (BZ **M¹**) – The selection of exhibits illustrates artistic development in Weimar from 1900 to 1930, with the emphasis on the activities of the Bauhaus during this period. Thus designs and finished work from

Van de Velde's School of Applied Arts rub shoulders with items relating to the Bauhaus. On the ground floor is the collection accumulated by Walter Gropius.

Wittumspalais ⊙ (BZ M²) – After the death of her husband the Duchess Anna Amalia moved to this 1767 Baroque palace with two wings; it was here that she organized the famous salons of which Goethe, Schiller, Herder and Wieland were so important a part. The **Wielandmuseum** illustrates the lifework of this fervent supporter of German classicism, translator and spokesman for the Aufklärung.

Stadtkirche (BY) – This triple-nave Gothic hall-church (see Art and Music in Weimar above) was built between 1498 and 1500 and much remodelled in the Baroque style between 1735 and 1745. It is also known as the **Herderkirche**, in memory of the sermons preached there by the philosopher, who is buried in the church. The famous **Cranach Triptych★★**, started by Lucas Cranach the Elder and finished by his son in 1555, represents the Crucifixion on its central panel. This is surrounded by scenes from the Old and New Testmanents. On the right, Luther and Cranach the Elder himself are depicted.
Sumptuous **Renaissance gravestones★** adorn the chancel of this otherwise relatively plainly decorated church.

Schloßmuseum ⊙ (BZ) – The original palace burned down in 1774 and was rebuilt in the neo-Classical style under Duke Carl August from 1789 to 1803. The addition of a south wing in 1914 completed the four-wing layout. Some of the apartments are open to the public: the banqueting hall, the great gallery and rooms dedicated to the writers Goethe, Schiller, Wieland and Herder. The galleries house the Weimar art collections: numismatics, prints and – perhaps of wider interest – galleries of paintings. Here, visitors can see: Thuringian altarpieces of the Flamboyant Gothic period; an important **Cranach collection★★** (Sybil of Cleves, Portrait of Luther); Flemish and Italian paintings; and work by Hans Baldung Grien, Albrecht Dürer and Bartholomäus Bruyn the Elder. The Weimar School (Von Schwind and Rohlfs) and German Impressionists and Expressionists (Max Beckmann, Max Liebermann) are also represented.
In the southwest wing of the complex is the castle tower (1729-32) with its Baroque cupola, and the 1545 (renovated) keep.

ILM PARK

"Weimar is in fact a park in which they happened to build a town." This approving comment was written by Adolf Stahr in 1851 – and indeed modern Weimar is still a city of green spaces, indissolubly linked with its riverside park. From the palace of Tiefurt to the Belvedere, there is a single stretch of greenery centred on the gardens laid out on each side of the Ilm. There was no intention of restraining nature – said Goethe, planning the English-style landscaping – but simply of guiding and at the same time respecting her. The gardens are only a few yards from the city centre.

★★ Goethes Gartenhaus (BZ) – Duke Carl August made a present of this summer residence to Goethe, and the great man liked it so much that he lived there permanently from 1776 to 1782. It remained his favourite retreat until the end of his life.
Among his works there is even a short poem recording his delight in the place.

> "It is an unpretentious
> Small house beneath a tall roof.
> Everyone who came there
> Felt light-hearted;
> Trees I had planted grew strong and green,
> And the spirit as well
> Thrived on this blessed ground."

It was in this house that Goethe wrote Wilhelm Meister's Theatrical Mission, major parts of Iphigenia, and early drafts of Egmont and Torquato Tasso.
Facing it is the **Borkenhäuschen**, Augustus' own favourite retreat. Only 10min walk away is the **Römisches Haus**, a classical building (1791-97) designed by Goethe for the Grand Duke.

Cross the park now in the direction of the Belvederer Allee.

Liszt-Haus ⊙ (BZ) – Belvederer Allee.
In this one-time gardeners' lodge at the entrance to the park it is possible to visit the apartments lived in by the composer during his second stay in Weimar, from 1869 to 1886.

Geschwister-Scholl-Straße leads to the old cemetery (Alter Friedhof).

ADDITIONAL SIGHTS

Neues Museum ⊘ **(BY)** - *Rathenauplatz.*
The grand and well-proportioned neo-Renaissance building was put up as archducal museum between 1863 and 1869 following designs by Czech architect Josef Zítek. During the Third Reich it was the headquarters of the Nazi administration for Thuringia. It has now been restored to its original vocation as museum, thanks to the collection of gallery owner Paul Maenz from Cologne. The museum is dedicated to the international Avant-Garde since 1960 with special emphasis on German art and Italian Arte Povera, and American Minimal and Conceptual Art.

Visitors are greeted on the perron by a polished bronze sculpture by Robert Schüte, *The Great Spirit.* Sol LeWitt painted the black-grey mural in the entrance lobby, with Pipilotti Rist's colourful *Weimar Installation* providing quite a contrast. The imaginative wall reflections and stripes of bare masonry on the central staircase are the work of **Daniel Buren.** The historical mural cycle (1869) by Friedrich Peller on the first floor has been restored and is now displayed in exciting juxtaposition with works by **Anselm Kiefer.**

Fürstengruft (BZ) – This is the central focus of the ancient cemetery and was built in 1825-27 by CW Coudray as the burial place of the princely family. In addition to Duke Wilhelm IV and Grand Duke Carl August (his duchy having been elevated to the status of Grand Duchy during the Congress of Vienna in 1815), the two princes of poetry **Goethe** and **Schiller** found their last resting place here. The **Russian Orthodox Church** nearby was built between 1859 and 1862 specially for Maria Pavlova, Grand Duchess and daughter-in-law of Carl August.

S. Geske/A. Kittel/Stiftung Weimarer Klassik

Music room, Nietzsche-Archiv, Weimar

Nietzsche-Archiv ⊘ **(AZ)** – The philosopher **Friedrich Nietzsche** spent the last three years of his life, until his death in 1900, in this house. During this final stage of his 12-year decline into paralysis and madness he was cared for by his sister Elisabeth. After Nietzsche's death, Elisabeth set up an archive on her brother's work and commissioned Van de Velde to adapt the ground floor of the house to accommodate it in 1903. From the vestibule with its brass fittings to the furniture, the covers, lamps and vases in the dining room and study, almost every item is based on the designs of Van de Velde.

A highlight of the visit has to be the **library★**, in which the furniture and fittings combine to make the room a work of art in itself. Note the bust of Nietzsche by Max Klinger. The archive houses literature and photographic material on the life and work of this brilliant, although tragically misinterpreted, philosopher.

EXCURSIONS

Schloß Tiefurt ⊘ – *2km/1mi to the east.*
The former summer residence (18C) of Duchess Amalia is surrounded by English-style gardens. Both palace and gardens were frequently the scene of the literary gatherings she loved. Goethe, the Humboldt brothers and the other members of her cultural coterie were welcome guests. The apartments, in the neo-Classical style, evoke the classical era of Weimar.

Schloß Belvedere ⊙ - *4km/2.5mi to the southeast.*
This is one of the most delightful – and the most artistically successful – stately homes of Thuringia. Comprising a large central block flanked by two low wings, the mansion is completed by four outbuildings and an orangery harbouring a **collection of carriages and barouches.**
The grounds, originally formal in the Baroque style, were redesigned and laid out as an English garden between 1814 and 1840.

Buchenwald - *8km/5mi to the northwest.*
Only a few miles from Weimar, cradle of Humanism and first capital (1918) of a democratic Germany, the Ettersberg beech forests concealed one of the largest concentration camps of the Hitler regime for eight years.

Between Beeches and Wolves – Established in July 1937 for the internment of Germans who opposed the Nazi ethos, the camp was quick to take the Jews and gypsies persecuted by the National Socialists – and then, as the invasion of Europe expanded, victims from the occupied countries. A total of almost 300 000 human beings, including innumerable children, took the road that led to Buchenwald; for 65 000 of them, it was a one-way trip.
The camp was liberated by the Americans on 11 April 1945.

Gedenkstätte Buchenwald (Memorial Centre) ⊙ – *Map and descriptive brochure at entrance.*
The Information Centre shows a film tracing the history of the camp.
A tour of the camp starts at the gatehouse, which still retains above the entrance the chilling slogan: **"Jedem das Seine"** ("You get what you deserve").
The position of each hut is marked out on the ground; at the far end, on the right, is the building which was used for storing the inmates' possessions and effects, now transformed into a museum. Outside the camp, a road leads to the quarry where excessively rigorous working conditions resulted in a particularly high death rate among those sent there. Nearly 20 000 Buchenwald prisoners were transferred to a camp named **Dora** *(local map see HARZ)*, for forced labour in an underground factory developing secret weapons. The nature of their work meant that none of them ever saw daylight again.

Special camp 2 – From 1945 to 1950, the Soviet occupation force set up a special camp here, in which Nazi criminals and officials, and also arbitrarily arrested individuals, were interned. According to Soviet sources, over 7 000 people died in this camp.

Memorial (Mahnmal der Gedenkstätte Buchenwald) – *1km/0.6mi in the direction of Weimar.* From the entrance, the Steles' Way leads to the Avenue of Nations, which links three mass graves. From the last of these, Liberty Avenue brings you to the memorial bell-tower, in front of which is the statuary group of *Eleven Buchenwald Prisoners,* by Fritz Cremer.

WERNIGERODE★

Sachsen-Anhalt
Population 37 000
Michelin map 418 K 16 – Local map see HARZ

On a marvellous site at the foot of the Harz Mountains, with many of its narrow streets bordered by old, half-timbered houses still intact, Wernigerode is one of the most delightful small towns in this region and an ideal starting point for exploration of the massif.

SIGHTS

★★ **Rathaus (Town hall)** - *Marktplatz.*
Considered to be one of the finest half-timbered buildings in Germany, this municipal treasure dates from the first half of the 16C. Its splendid façade includes superposed oriel windows surmounted by slender spires. Note the double staircase and the carved wood features representing town aldermen.

★★ **Half-timbered houses (Fachwerkhäuser)** - The most picturesque group is on the **Breite Straße**, as it leaves Marktplatz – several rows of town houses built by the rich burghers of Wernigerode in the 16C, 17C and 18C. The wooden sections and joists are often decorated with masks or carved patterns – as for instance on the 1674 house at no 72 known as the "Krummelsches Haus".
An exploration of the lanes between Breite Straße and the castle hill to the south is also worthwhile. The houses here are smaller but full of charm. At the highest part of Kochstraße (no 43) is the tiniest house of all, which is only 3m/10ft wide.

STAYING IN WERNIGERODE

Am Anger – Breite Straße 92, ☎ 0 39 43/9 23 20, Fax 0 39 43/92 32 50. Single rooms from 70DM. Historic house which has been fully modernised in a calm town centre location.

Parkhotel Fischer – Mauergasse 1, ☎ 0 39 43/69 13 50, Fax 0 39 43/69 13 60. Single rooms from 85DM. Peaceful location on the edge of the old town. Tastefully decorated rooms.

Weißer Hirsch – Marktplatz 5, ☎ 0 39 43/60 20 20, Fax 0 39 43/63 31 39. Single rooms from 125DM. Hotel dating from 1760 opposite the historic town hall. Renovated and well fitted out.

Gothisches Haus – Marktplatz, ☎ 0 39 43/67 50, Fax 0 39 43/67 55 37. Single rooms from 158DM. A 15C house steeped in tradition.

Pfarrkirche St.-Johannis – *Take Breite Straße and then, on the left, Grüne Straße.*
This late-15C, triple-aisle Gothic hall-church has a four-panel altarpiece in carved wood dating from 1425. It depicts the Virgin Mary with angels.

Schloß – Extensively remodelled in the late 19C, the castle is in a magnificent position overlooking the town. The main apartments house a museum, the **Zentrum für Kunst- und Kulturgeschichte des 19. Jh.s.** ⊘, outlining the origins and development of feudalism, with a selection of craftwork and sacred art of the time.

WERTHEIM *

Baden-Württemberg
Population 21 700
Michelin maps 417 Q 12

Wertheim lies at the foot of a mighty fortress. This beautiful location, together with the well-preserved architecture of the town, contribute to the attraction of this small town to painters. Pretty, half-timbered houses, mainly from the 16C, border its twisting, narrow streets.

Marktplatz – Among the half-timbered houses around the market place, the 16C **Zobelhaus** is especially worth seeing. The "**angels' well**" (Engelsbrunnen) which dates from the Renaissance period, stands at the end of the square next to the collegiate church. The sandstone draw well, which was built in 1574, is decorated with figures which depict the citizens of Wertheim and the planets of Mercury, Mars, Jupiter, Saturn and Venus. It is crowned by two angels.

The **Grafschaftsmuseum** is not far away in the Rathausgasse. It is housed in the old town hall, a building dating from the 16C. Note in particular the stair tower with its **double spiral staircase** (1540). Opposite the museum stands the **Haus der Vier Gekrönten** (house of the four crowned heads), a fine half-timbered structure from the second half of the 16C.

Stiftskirche – The Gothic building erected between 1384 and 1445 has been left unadorned, with the exception of the oriel-type "little chancel" (next to the north porch). This makes the sumptuous sculpture on the 40 or so **tombs★★** inside all the more impressive. They were erected from 1407, when the church was selected as the burial place of the counts of Wertheim. The tombs in the chancel, including the **Isenburg gravestone** *(on the left)*, the **Eberstein tomb** *(in the centre)* and the **Stohberg gravestone**, are of particular importance. The free-standing tomb known as the "Bedstead" stands alone in the centre of the chancel, and was created in 1618 by Michael Kern for Count Ludwig III zu Löwenstein (who died in 1611) and Countess Anna zu Stolberg.

Burg – A well-fortified castle was created over the centuries, from a fortress built in the 13C. It was destroyed during the Thirty Years War by the emperor's troops. The outer fortress gate was extended into an archive library between 1742 and 1745. From the castle ruins, the visitor looks down on the town, the confluence of the rivers and the wooded heights of Spessart (to the north) and the Odenwald (west).

EXCURSION

Ehemaliges Kloster Bronnbach ⊘ – *10km/6mi to the south.*
The late-12C **church★** here has retained its original Romanesque design and, in particular, the groined vaulting above the nave. This was specially designed to make it possible to fit tall, deeply pierced windows, thus providing much brighter lighting than was customary in the period. From the Gothic cloister, with its triple-arched windows, there is a good view of the church's south wall, and the tiered roofs above it.

WESSOBRUNN★

Bayern
Population 1 740
Michelin map 419/420 W 17

This locality in Upper Bavaria is known for the famous **Wessobrunn Prayer** (Wesso-brunner Gebet), one of the oldest known documents in the German language. The 9C manuscript, in a Bavarian dialect of Old High German, is kept in the Munich Civic Library (Staatsbibliothek).

School of Wessobrunn – In the 17C and 18C, Wessobrunn produced a series of architects and artists of multiple talents who, according to the needs of construction projects or the dictates of their own inspiration, were able to exchange the compass at will for the paintbrush or the tools of the stuccoworker. Working in a corporate and family framework known as the Wessobrunn School, these artists of Baroque genius, who were in no way specialists, beautified churches and civic buildings all over Bavaria, Swabia and the Tyrol. The names of the **Feuchtmayer** and **Schmuzer** families are eminent within the group, though the most celebrated is perhaps **Dominikus Zimmer-mann**, who was responsible for the church at Wies *(see entry)*.

Ehemalige Benediktinerabtei (Former Benedictine abbey) ⊘ – The history of the abbey goes back to the 8C. After its secularization in 1803, the mother church was destroyed and only the 13C clock tower with its saddleback roof is still extant. On the first floor of the old monastic block is the magnificent **Princes' Gallery**★ (Fürstengang), a 17C masterpiece due to the Wessobrunn School, whose versatility is exemplified in the long hall where painted medallions adorn a vaulted roof covered in stuccowork mingling acanthus leaves, the heads of cherubim and other motifs.

WETZLAR

Hessen
Population 54 000
Michelin map 417 O 9

Until the beginning of the 19C, Wetzlar was a town of lawyers, the seat of one of the law courts of the Holy Roman Empire. Today it is famous for the manufacture of optical and photographic equipment (Leitz). The small format (35 mm) film was invented here by the engineer Oscar Barnack in 1924.
The cathedral quarter and three ancient squares, **Eisenmarkt**, **Kornmarkt** and **Schillerplatz**, still bear witness to the town's illustrious past.

SIGHTS

Dom (Collegiate Church) – Of the original 12C Romanesque building, only the north tower of the façade – a sombre construction of dark sandstone and basalt – is still standing. Of the subsequent Gothic façade, again, only one Flamboyant 14C tower was completed (in the south). Since this particular stage of the work seems to have been interrupted, the central doorway (embellished with a completed work, the Coronation of the Virgin) opens upon nothing.
The sandstone of the south tower is red, in contrast both with the north tower and the light stone in which nave and chancel were eventually finished in the 13C Gothic style. Despite its rather bizarre outside appearance, however, the church has two interesting works inside: an ensemble of Gothic frescoes in the south transept and a fine 14C Pietà in the first chapel off the south aisle.

The Sorrows of Young Werther

In May 1772, Goethe moved to Wetzlar with the aim of completing his legal training as an articled clerk with the Imperial Supreme Court. This was at the behest of his father, who was less than satisfied with his son's legal endeavours to date. Wetzlar proved to be the setting for an unhappy love affair for the young poet, who fell in love with Charlotte Buff. The young woman liked him well enough as a friend, but remained faithful to her fiancé, the diplomat Johann Christian Kestner. At the same time, and also in Wetzlar, a young man called Carl Wilhelm Jerusalem shot himself over his own unrequited love affair. Luckily, rather than following his example, Goethe wrote *The Sorrows of Young Werther* as his way of coming to terms with a broken heart. This work, the first novel to be written in the form of letters, aroused an unheard-of response from the reading public, due to the intensity of the emotions it expressed and its closeness to real events. It was even banned in a few regions, as there were one or two cases of suicide which were exactly modelled on that described by Goethe.

Stadt- und Industrie-Museum ⊘ – The buildings of the former Teutonic Order foundation serve as the backdrop for this museum. Both the history of the town and the significance of industry in the Wetzlar area are emphasised. The museum contains some beautiful furniture from the 17C and 18C.

Lottehaus ⊘ – "Lotte" was Charlotte Buff, the diplomat's fiancée to whom the young Goethe was passionately, but unrequitedly, attracted and whom he immortalised as the heroine in his novel *The Sorrows of Young Werther*. In this house, which was the young woman's birthplace, glass cases of souvenirs, furniture and other mementoes recall the personality of Goethe's heroine.
First editions of *The Sorrows of Young Werther*, and copies of translations in 30 different languages underline the enormous success of the novel (which Napoleon claimed to have read seven times, one after the other).

Sammlung Dr. Irmgard von Lemmers-Danforth ⊘ – *Kornblumengasse 1.*
The rooms of a fine 18C house have been transformed into examples of the Renaissance and Baroque styles in Italy, France, Holland and Germany. Paintings, furniture, clocks, jewellery and work by goldsmiths and silversmiths can be admired.

Reichskammergerichtsmuseum (Tribunal Museum) ⊘ – *Hofstatt 19.*
The history of the Holy Roman Empire court in Wetzlar (1693-1806) is evoked by ancient law books, court documents and verdicts, and the portraits of personalities concerned with these trials.

EXCURSIONS

Burg Greifenstein – *17km/11mi to the northwest.*
This castle was built in the 12C, on a rise overlooking the road from Frankfurt to Cologne – an important trade route in need of protection in the Middle Ages. One of the fortress bastions houses a collection of bells, the oldest of which dates from the 11C.

★ **Münzenberg** – *28km/17.5mi to the southeast.*
Together with those of Gelnhausen and Büdingen, this **feudal stronghold** formed a defensive line destined to protect the Wetterau – an open depression between the Taunus and Vogelsberg massifs. The whole of the depression is visible from the top of the east tower. The ruins are very well preserved, with the outer wall and its bastions emerging from the surrounding greenery. Between the two keeps, fine examples of Romanesque interior decoration can be seen in the living quarters.

★ **Arnsburg** – *30km/18.5mi to the southeast.*
The Early Gothic chapter-house of this one-time **Cistercian abbey** is still standing; the abbey **church**★, entirely in ruins, was built to the Cistercian plan, with a flat chevet. The remains of massive columns with Romanesque capitals can be seen in the old transept crossing.

WIESBADEN★

Hessen
Population 271 000
Michelin map 417 P 8

Lying at the foot of the Taunus mountains and favoured by the mild climate of the Rhine Valley, the capital city of Hessen has great variety to offer visitors. The refined atmosphere of a spa town, the flair of an elegant city, its proximity to the Rhine region, its attractive surroundings, all serve to contribute to its special attraction. First mentioned during the 9C as "Wisibada" (spa in the meadows), the city was owned from the 13C on by the House of Nassau, and from 1806 it became the seat of government of the newly founded Duchy of Nassau. For a time the city blossomed and enjoyed an upturn in its economy, which is evident from the generous layout of the roads and in the spa quarter built by Christian Zais in the Classical style. During the time of Emperor William II, when the Emperor brought his court to Wiesbaden every summer, new quarters with elegant villas and new roads were built, for example Wilhelmstraße and Ringstraße, which still afford visitors an insight into the city's original style.

The "world spa town" – The ancient Romans were aware of the benefits of the 26 hot sodium chloride springs (46-66°C/115-150°F), and Pliny noted with surprise that the water from the springs stayed warm for three days. The middle of the 19C saw the start of Wiesbaden's heyday as a spa town, when it became a rendezvous for the crowned heads and higher nobility of the world. Nowadays the spa business has a different clientele, although it is still booming. Equipped to the standards of a modern health resort, Wiesbaden has achieved an excellent reputation as a spa for sufferers of rheumatism.

OLD TOWN

Schloß – The former residence of the dukes of Nassau was built between 1837 and 1841 in the unadorned Classical style. The main entrance lies on the diagonal and is emphasised by a rotunda. Today the palace is the seat of the Hessen Provincial Parliament.

Altes Rathaus (Old town hall) – The oldest building in the city, whose ground floor has been kept in the Late Renaissance style, it was built in 1609-10, whilst the upper storey in the Romantic Historicist style originates from the year 1828.

Neues Rathaus (New town hall) – Georg Hauberisser, the architect of the Munich town hall, erected this building in the German Renaissance style, divided by oriels and projecting bays, in 1886-87. It is somewhat free of adornment, but is impressive due to the considerable use of sandstone and the beautiful proportions on the ground floor and in the central part.

Marktkirche – This first brick-built church in the Nassau region was erected in the mid 19C. Its architect, Carl Boos, copied the Friedrichwerder church in Berlin which was created by Schinkel. *Carillon rung daily at 9am, noon and 5pm.*

SPA QUARTER

Kaiser-Friedrich-Bad – *38-42 Langgasse.*
The Jugendstil building at the beginning of the 20C cost 3 million Gold Marks. The Late Jugendstil frescoes in the entrance hall are worth seeing, as is the Roman-Irish steam bath with its majolica glazed tiles manufactured in Darmstadt and Karlsruhe.

Kochbrunnen – This fountain is made up of 15 springs. Its hot salty water contains iron, as is easy to tell from the reddish scale deposit on the granite fountain basin. Among Roman women the reddish powder was highly regarded, as they used it to colour their hair red. The octangular **Kochbrunnen Temple** dates from 1854.

★ **Kurhaus (Spa house)** – A lawn as flat as a bowling green, flanked on either side by the hydro and the theatre colonnades and by lofty plane trees, planted at the beginning of the 19C, leads up to what is, according to Emperor Wilhelm II, "the most beautiful spa house in the world".
The spa house itself was built in 1907. The inscription "Aquis Mattiacis" refers to the springs and the Germanic Mattiaker tribe who settled here in Roman times. The sumptuous interior decoration was restored to its original state in 1987. Although visitors don't get to see the magnificent rooms, unless they are attending an event or trying their luck in the casino which is located in the left wing, they should at least have a look in the **foyer**, in order to get a glimpse of the splendid decor.

Staatstheater – The impressive Renaissance style building, built in 1892-94, lies to the south of the theatre colonnade. The taste for lavish decoration which existed at the turn of the century is evident in its **foyer**, redolent of the Rococo, with a double flight of outdoor stairs.

★ **Kurpark und Kuranlagen (Spa park and grounds)** – A vast park, laid out in 1852, stretches away to the east behind the spa house. Sonnenberger Straße *(to the north)* and Parkstraße *(to the south)* feature magnificent villas dating from the Gründerzeit.

FROM WILHELMSTRASSE TO THE NEROBERG

Museum Wiesbaden ⊙ – This museum is in fact made up of three separate museums: the **natural sciences collection**, the **collection of Nassau antiquities** and most importantly the **art collections**, which proudly boast the largest **Jawlensky collection**★ in the world. The artist lived in Wiesbaden from 1921 up his death in 1941. The exhibition includes significant works from the 16C and 17C as well as Classical modern paintings and contemporary art. Substantial renovation has made this museum into a real treasure, in which works of art are displayed to their optimum advantage.

Wiesbaden's main street, the **Wilhelmstraße**, is flanked on one side by elegant shops and on the other by the "Warmer Damm" park, which leads to the Staatstheater.

Taunusstraße, which leads to the Nerotal park, will make the heart of every lover of antiques beat faster, since a large number of antique dealers have set up shop here.

Whilst walking through the **Nerotal**, a beautiful park with lakes, it is impossible not to admire the magnificent Gründerzeit villas along Wilhelminenstraße.

★ **Nerobergbahn** ⓥ – The cable, rack railway, which still runs as well and safely today as it did when it was built in 1888, is a very special monument to technical achievement. It leads up the Neroberg, Wiesbaden's local mountain, 245m/804ft in height. Driven with water ballast (a 7 000l/1 540gal tank), the car descending into the valley hauls the car going up the mountain. When it arrives at the bottom, the water is pumped back up to the top to be reused. It couldn't be more environmentally friendly!

Russische Orthodoxe Kirche ⓥ – Also known as the Griechische Kapelle, or Greek Chapel. It was built by Duke Adolf of Nassau in 1847-55 for his wife Elisabeth, a Russian grand duchess, who died at the tender age of 19. It includes a central building with five gilded cupolas, which overlook the whole of the city. The elegant marble tomb was created by Emil Alexander Hopfgarten, a copy of Rauch's tomb of Queen Luise in Berlin-Charlottenburg.

EXCURSION

★ **Schloß Biebrich** – *South of the city on the banks of the Rhine.* The uniformity of this horseshoe-shaped building, the residence of the princes and dukes of Nassau, is deceptive, since several master builders worked on its construction over time. Most notable among these were Maximilian von Welsch and Friedrich Joachim Stengel, the creator of the castle at Saarbrücken (Saarbrücken belonged to Nassau at the time), who built the Baroque palace, with a long pink and white façade facing the Rhine, between 1700 and 1744. The round central build-

Russian Orthodox Church, Wiesbaden

Kurbetrieb Wiesbaden

ing with the roof balustrade and the roof parapet figures is an architectural success. The palace chapel, whose vault has plaster of Paris decoration by CM Pozzi, is located on the ground floor. The cupola of the round banqueting hall above it rests on eight marble pillars. The so-called winter building (the northwest wing) contains Baroque and neo-Classical plaster of Paris decoration. Schloß Briebrich is used by the Hessen government to hold official receptions.

The **castle park**, originally laid out as formal Baroque-style gardens, was converted into an English landscaped garden in 1817-23 by Friedrich Ludwig von Sckell. The 35ha/86-acre park, home to the Moosburg (Moss Castle), a folly or artificial castle ruin (1805-16), is a popular destination for an excursion.

WIESKIRCHE★★

WIES CHURCH – Bayern
Michelin map 419/420 W 16 – Local map see Deutsche ALPENSTRASSE

A masterpiece of Bavarian Rococo, Wieskirche stands amid the forests, meadows and peatbogs whose gentle undulations characterize the final slopes of the Ammergau Alps between the Lech and the Ammer.

The Architect – It was **Dominikus Zimmermann** (1685-1766), one of the most gifted members of the **Wessobrunn School**, who was entrusted with the task of building this pilgrimage church "in der Wies" (in the meadow), and dedicated to Jesus Scourged. Aided by his brother Johann Baptist, a painter at the Bavarian court, Zimmermann started the work in 1746, soon after he finished Steinhausen, and completed it in 1754. Indeed, much of the church was based on the Steinhausen design: the focal point, as in the earlier edifice, was an oval cupola, which lent itself to painted decorations and emphasized the Rococo approach.

Zimmermann was so pleased with the result, which he considered the most successful of all his works, that he spent the last 10 years of his life in a small house near the church.

The Church ⊙ – A certain sobriety in the exterior leaves the visitor unprepared for the splendour and magnificence of the oval bay and the long, narrow chancel which prolongs it. Gilded stucco, wood carvings and vividly coloured frescoes stand out from the whitewashed walls, while the richly glowing effect is enhanced by an abundance of light entering through windows whose elaborate design is typical of the architect – an essential feature of the whole, both inside and out. It is in fact this same finesse in the adaptation of detail to the global effect that strengthens the balance between architecture and ornamentation and achieves that visual harmony for which Wieskirche is renowned. The lower parts of the interior, for example – the walls and paired pillars defining the ambulatory in the usual manner of pilgrimage churches – are deliberately sparsely decorated because they symbolize, in the mind of the designer, the Earth. The upper reaches, on the other hand, symbolizing the heavens, vibrate with a profusion of paintings, stucco and gilded work. The immense **cupola fresco** represents the Second Coming, the Gates of Paradise (still closed) and the Court of the Last Judgement with the throne of the Judge himself yet to be occupied.
The decoration of the choir is unparalleled: columns, balustrades, statues, gilded stuccoes and frescoes combine to form a symphony of colour. The wide reredos painting is of Christ Made Man. The richness and delicacy of the lavish ornamentation adorning the organ loft and pulpit mark the high point of the Rococo style in southern Germany.

Bad WIMPFEN★★

Baden-Württemberg
Population 6 000
Michelin map 417/419 S 11 – Local map see HOHENLOHER LAND

Imperial residence of the Hohenstaufens in the 13C, this small fortified town, with its network of narrow streets lined with numerous old half-timbered houses, is built on a rise overlooking the River Neckar.
Along the foot of the hill stretch the Ludwigshalle salt works, the product of which once brought prosperity to the whole surrounding region, and the built-up area of Bad Wimpfen im Tal, which grew up around an old collegiate church.

★★BAD WIMPFEN AM BERG (UPPER TOWN) *allow 1hr 30min*

Follow the itinerary on the town plan, starting at Marktplatz.

Kaiserpfalz (Remains of the Imperial Palace) – Standing behind the Rathaus is the **Blauer Turm** (Blue Tower) (**A**), whose "neo-feudal" top dates only from the 19C. From the top of the tower – occupied today as in medieval times by a watchman – there is a panoramic view of the town and the Neckar Valley. A little further on is the Romanesque **Steinhaus** (**B**), with its 16C stepped gable, where there is a museum tracing the history of Bad Wimpfen since the Roman occupation.
Eight steps down from the Steinhaus terrace, on the right at the foot of the wall, note the twin-columned Romanesque arcading through which light entered the gallery of the old palace. The decorative intricacy of the arcades demonstrates the building talents of the Hohenstaufens, under whose rule Romanesque civic architecture reached its peak.

Continue to follow the wall as far as a flight of steps, on the right, which leads to the tip of the spur on which the town is built, at the foot of the **Roter Turm** (Red Tower) (**C**), the fortress' final defensive point.
Return to the town centre, descending to pass beneath the **Hohenstaufentor** (**D**), which was the castle's main entrance in medieval times, and join Klostergasse.

Nach Foto R. Schuler

Bad Wimpfen am Berg

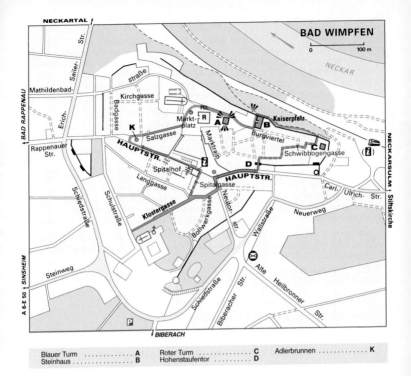

Blauer Turm	.... A	Roter Turm	 C	Adlerbrunnen	.... K
Steinhaus	.... B	Hohenstaufentor	.... D		

Old Streets – In **Klostergasse**, which has considerable rustic charm, there are a number of half-timbered houses standing in their own gardens. On the left are the former spa bathhouses, recognizable by their outside galleries. To explore more of the town's old streets, return to the Langgasse crossroads and take a narrow alley on the right which leads to **Hauptstraße**★. At no 45 is the courtyard of a former hospital (Spitalhof), with beautiful half-timbered houses which are among the oldest buildings in Bad Wimpfen. Return along Hauptstraße, with its many picturesque, finely worked signs, and pass the beautiful 1576 **Eagle Fountain** (Adlerbrunnen) (**K**) before regaining Marktplatz via Salzgasse.

BAD WIMPFEN IM TAL (LOWER TOWN)

Stiftskirche St.-Peter und St.-Paul – This Gothic parish church has retained a strikingly crude Westwerk from an earlier Romanesque building. The **cloister**★★ ⊘ (Kreuzgang) clearly shows the evolution of the Gothic style, though the late-13C east gallery is an example of the period at its best: a true purity of line informs the sculpted decor and the tri- and quadri-lobed windows. The north gallery (c 1350), already more angular in design, marks the transition to the style of the west gallery, which is more austere, heralding the sober forms of the Renaissance.

EXCURSIONS

★ **Auto- und Technikmuseum** (Automobile and Technical Museum) ⊘ – At **Sinsheim**, *25km/15.5mi to the west.*
Mechanical vehicles of many types are brought together in this collection. In the first building are impressive early-20C tractors, steam locomotives, luxury motor cars (Bugatti, Mercedes), and a replica of the first hang-glider to be commercially marketed, the Lilienthal, which dates from the late 19C.
A second building exhibits a collection of mainly military vehicles (tanks, motorized artillery, aeroplanes).

★ **The Neckar Valley** (Neckartal) – *Round tour of 74km/46mi – about 4hr.*
Downstream from Bad Wimpfen, the Neckar, cutting once more through the sandstone massif of the Odenwald, runs through an area of wooded hills, many of them crowned by castles. Linked now with the great flow of navigation on the Rhine, river traffic is heavy.

Burg Guttenberg ⊘ – A massive defence wall protects this castle on the side facing the mountain. Inside, there are unusual **collections of objets d'art**★ and a series of archives. Note especially the odd 18C "Library-Herbarium", in which the plants are encased in 92 pseudo-"books" made of wood. A 15C altarpiece, The Virgin Mary in her Cloak, is on display. There is a fine **view** of the river from the keep.

Burg Hornberg ⊙ – *1.5km/about 1mi outside Neckarzimmern.*
Crowning a hill planted with vines, this castle – now partly in ruins – can be recognized from far away by its tall keep. In the part now turned into a **museum**, note the body armour of Götz von Berlichingen, who died here in 1562. This knight, popularised in German folklore as a Robin Hood figure, was immortalised in a play by Goethe. From the keep, the **view**★ stretches a long way down the valley.

In the village of Hirschhorn am Neckar, turn right towards Beerfelden, then right again to reach the entrance to Hirschhorn Castle.

★ **Hirschhorn am Neckar** – The castle stands on a fortified spur. From the tower *(121 steps, a difficult climb)* the **view**★ extends over the meander and wooded slopes of the Neckar Valley.

Neckarsteinach – Four castles stand guard on a narrow ridge overlooking the village: the Vorderburg and Mittelburg castles are privately owned. Hinterburg Castle, built shortly after 1000, is the oldest of the four and was the seat of the lords of Steinach; it is now in ruins. Burg Schadeck, also in ruins, is a small 14C castle which has earned itself the local nickname of "swallow's nest" because of its site.

Dilsberg – *4.5km/3mi from Neckarsteinach.* Follow the signposts "Burgruine" to reach the ruined castle. From the tower *(97 steps)* there is another **panorama**★ over the winding River Neckar.

The best way to get to **Heidelberg**★★ *(see under this name)* is along the east bank road, which leads straight to the castle.

Jagst Valley (Jagsttal) – *See HOHENLOHER LAND.*

Neckarsulm – *10km/6mi to the southeast.*
The castle once belonged to the Teutonic Order. It now houses the **German Cycle and Motorcycle Museum** ⊙ (Deutsches Zweiradmuseum, NSU-Museum). Nearby is the NSU motor factory which produced the first bicycles in Germany.

WISMAR★

Mecklenburg-Vorpommern
Population 52 000
Michelin map 415/416 E 18

Wismar dates back to the year 1226. It enjoyed its heyday for a time as a Hanseatic city, relying principally on trade with the main countries in Europe. The brewery trade (Wismar was known for its excellent beer) and wool weaving were further sources of wealth. Its downfall came with the Thirty Years War. The peace of Osnabrück meant that the town came under Swedish rule in 1648, under which it remained until 1803. Industrial operations only started up at the end of the 19C, and the town revived again as merchant shipping grew in importance.

During the last few decades, shipbuilding, merchant shipping and fishing have determined the fate of the town. As the 21C dawns, Wismar will have to move in a new direction. Tourism will play a decisive role, since the town has a large number of old gabled houses and other admirable buildings.

SIGHTS

Remarkable houses can be discovered everywhere in the old town. They are either noticeable because they have been renovated, or are still eking out their humble existence. With a little imagination, the visitor will be able to picture what a treasure Wismar once was and promises to become again.

★ **Marktplatz** – Of considerable size (10 000m²/107 600sq ft), this square is dominated to the north by the white silhouette of the neo-Classical **Rathaus**, which dates from 1817 to 1819. The gabled houses date from a number of different periods, each of them recording a chapter of architectural and art history. On the eastern side stands the oldest well-to-do middle-class house in the town, an eye-catching red-brick building, known as the "Old Swede" and built around 1380. On its right stands the Reuterhaus, where the works of the Mecklenburg writer Fritz Reuter were published and on its left, a house with charming Jugendstil ornamentation. On the southeastern side of the market place an artistic pavilion, the **waterworks**★, draws the eye. It was built in 1580-1602 in the Dutch Renaissance style and served to supply the town with water for centuries.

Marienkirchturm – Only the 80m/262ft high tower remains of the mighty Marienkirche which was built during the first half of the 13C and destroyed during the Second World War. *(Carillon at noon, 3pm and 7pm)* The brick built **archdeaconry** at the corner of Marienkirchhof and Sargmacherstraße dates from 1450.

Fürstenhof – *To the west of the Marienkirchturm.*
The building, which was erected in two phases, is thought to be the northernmost Renaissance castle in Europe. The more recent, long section in particular, built in 1553-54 by Gabriel von Aken and Valentin von Lyra, is impressive with the ornaments on the pilaster and friezes. Those facing the road represent the Trojan Wars, and those facing the courtyard represent the parable of the Prodigal Son. The gateway and window frames are sumptuously decorated.

St.-Georgen-Kirche – The Late Gothic brick church (begun in 1290 and completed during the 15C) was seriously damaged during the Second World War. Extensive restoration work should help to restore it to its former splendour and dignity.

Grube – The "Grube" is a watercourse laid in 1255, where washing was done right up into the 20C. It is the only artificial stream of its kind still existing in Germany. After careful renovation, the streets which flank it could become one of the most picturesque corners of Wismar.

★ **Schabbellhaus** – The sumptuously decorated red-brick building in the Dutch Renaissance style, which stands on the corner of Schweinsbrücke and Frische Grube, was erected between 1569 and 1571 by the Dutch master builder Philipp Brandin for Hinrich Schabell. It bears witness to the wealth of the owner, a respected merchant and mayor of the town (his gravestone is in the Nikolaikirche). The house is on two floors, but the four-storey gable end pointing towards the Grube adds a certain cachet. The house is home to a **Museum of Local History** ⊙.

★ **Nikolaikirche** ⊙ – Beyond the Grube looms the dark mass of this, the highest brick church in the world, after the Marienkirche in Lübeck. The basilica was built between 1381 and 1487. Arched buttresses over the side aisles support the considerable pressure and at the same time alleviate the austere appearance of the building. The southern gable with its glazed figures is attractive. The interior is impressive with its sumptuous decor, with some valuable pieces from both the other destroyed churches contributing to the decorations. The **Altar der Krämergilde**★ (Grocers' Guild Altarpiece), a hinged, panelled altarpiece in a later softer style, erected in 1430, is worth a closer look. The figures on the central panel, the Virgin Mary, the Archangel Michael and St.-Mauritius, exude a strong, expressive sensitivity. A bronze font cast in 1335 depicts the Life of Christ, the Last Judgement and the Wise and Foolish Virgins. The "Devil's railing" around the font originates from the 16C. The Triumphal Cross group (15C) is captivating, thanks to the quality of the crucifix. The frescoes in the side halls of the tower, including an immense St Christopher, date from the period around 1450.

Alter Hafen (Old Harbour) – From the Grube and the idyllic street "Am Lohberg", just a few steps lead to the harbour, at the end of which stands an unadorned Baroque building, the Baumhaus (tree house). Here the harbour used to be locked

Wismar harbour

by the lock keeper at fixed times with a tree trunk. The function of the two "Swedish heads" executed in colour is not clear. Were they intended to frighten people off? In any event, they are known to date from 1672.

EXCURSION

Neukloster – *17km/11mi to the east of Wismar.*
The **monastery church** ⓥ of the former Cistercian convent was built around 1219-40 under the influence of Ratzeburg Cathedral, and served in turn as a model for very many Mecklenburg churches. It is a cross-shaped, well-proportioned brick building, characterised by its excellent workmanship. The remains of Late Romanesque **stained glass★**, dating from before 1245, are of particular interest.

Lutherstadt WITTENBERG

Sachsen-Anhalt
Population 55 000
Michelin map 418 K 21

In a pleasant situation between the wooded hills of Fläming and the Elbe, this small town is known mainly because of its connection with Martin Luther.

A Key Town in the Reformation – Summoned by the Elector Friedrich the Wise (1502) to teach philosophy in the university he had just founded, **Martin Luther** was at the same time appointed the town preacher. After the celebrated public burning of a Papal Bull, Luther was forced to appear before the Imperial Diet at Worms. Then, installed again in Wittenberg in 1522, he was obliged to temper the excesses of his own followers, especially Thomas Müntzer. A year after Luther's death, in 1546 at Eisleben, and eight years before he signed the Peace of Augsburg, allowing freedom of worship to the Lutherans, Emperor Charles V seized Wittenberg and is said to have meditated over the tomb of the great Reformer.

SIGHTS

★ **Schloßkirche (Castle Church)** – *Am Schloßplatz, in the western part of the town.*
The church attached to the royal residence was burned down in 1760 and rebuilt in the Baroque style. It was on the original doors that Luther had pinned up his famous 95 Articles condemning the abuses practised by the Church (1517). The new church contains the text, which was cast in bronze in 1855. Luther's tomb is also in this church, as is that of Melanchthon *(see below)*, as well as the bronze epitaph to Friedrich the Wise executed in 1527 by Peter Vischer.

★ **Markt** – In front of the Late Gothic (1440) town hall stand statues of Luther (by Schadow, 1821) and of his friend and disciple Melanchthon (Drake, 1860). The square is bordered by houses with gables, that in the southwest corner having been the home of the painter Lucas Cranach the Elder from 1505 to 1547, when he was the town's mayor.

Stadtkirche – *On Kirchplatz, east of the Markt.*
This triple-aisle Gothic (14C-15C) church was redecorated in neo-Gothic style in the 18C. The fact that Luther preached here is celebrated in one panel of the 1547 Cranach **Reformation Altarpiece★**. Melanchthon is depicted on the left-hand panel.

Melanchthon-Haus ⓥ – *Collegienstraße 60.*
The building in which Luther's companion lived and died is a Renaissance edifice topped by a gable of particularly elegant form. A man of moderate temperament, more tolerant than Luther, the author of the Confession of Augsburg worked for most of his life trying to reconcile the different factions of the Reformation. His study, and many documents relating to his work, can be seen in this house.

★ **Lutherhalle** ⓥ – *At the far end of Collegienstraße.*
Occupied by Luther from 1524 onwards, this house faces the courtyard of the Collegium Augusteum, the town's old university. The **Reformation Museum**, housed here since 1883, exhibits collections of antique Bibles, manuscripts, and original editions of Luther's works. One department displays a selection of fine arts from Luther's time: portraits of the Reformer, prints and paintings by Cranach the Elder, canvases by Hans Baldung Grien etc.

EXCURSIONS

★★ **Wörlitzer Park** – *18km/11mi to the west. Take the car ferry across the Elbe in Coswig. See WÖRLITZER PARK.*

WÖRLITZER PARK★★

Sachsen-Anhalt

Michelin map 418 K 21

Prince Leopold III Friedrich Franz von Anhalt-Dessau (1740-1817), known as "Father Franz" to his subjects, was an enlightened ruler, to whom the welfare of his small state was paramount (*see DESSAU*). His interest extended from the modernisation of agriculture and the processing of products within his own country, to road building, health and social policy. However his endeavours extended far beyond merely material matters, and he sought to link the beautiful with the useful and promoted literature, music, architecture and garden design.

A number of trips to England provided him with food for progressive thought, strengthened his philanthropic tendencies and paved the way for his planned reforms. It was also in England that he saw his first landscaped parks, which with their attempt to create unity between nature and reason were so in keeping with his own beliefs and with the fundamental tenets of the Enlightenment. He wanted to create such a park environment in his own kingdom. His friend, the master builder **Friedrich Wilhelm von Erdmannsdorff**, who had accompanied him on his trips, was to act as his assistant and like-minded adviser.

The work began in 1764 and incorporated the countryside into the park. The result was a garden which appears natural at first sight, but which is in reality artificially shaped nature. In the park, axes of vision were created (sometimes up to 14 "eye lines"). A castle and a Gothic house were the most striking buildings here, and a whole series of smaller buildings, such as the Flora and Venus temples, synagogues, a pantheon, the Villa Hamilton, the Egeria grotto, a reproduction of Vesuvius and numerous bridges in a whole range of designs, created a kind of Arcadian paradise. This work of art took shape during three stages of building, which extended to around 1800, with Erdmannsdorff being responsible for the architectural design and **Johann Leopold Schoch** for the garden design, at all times however under the overall management of the Prince. As a witness to a garden design which was revolutionary at the time, this park has retained all its original magic. It was the first landscaped park on the European mainland, open to the public even then, and served a model for the gardens which were later created in Prussia. It remains one of the most significant landscaped gardens in Europe.

TOUR *allow at least half a day to view the entire park and also the castle and Gothic house*

★ **Schloß** ⊙ – Erdmannsdorf built the castle between 1769 and 1773, making it the earliest neo-Classical building on the European mainland. He modelled it on Claremont Castle in Surrey, which was inspired by Andrea Palladio (1508-80). The splendid two-storey yellow and white plastered building stands out boldly against a backdrop of trees. The entrance hall, supported by four immense Corinthian

The pantheon in Wörlitzer Park

R. Chéne/MICHELIN

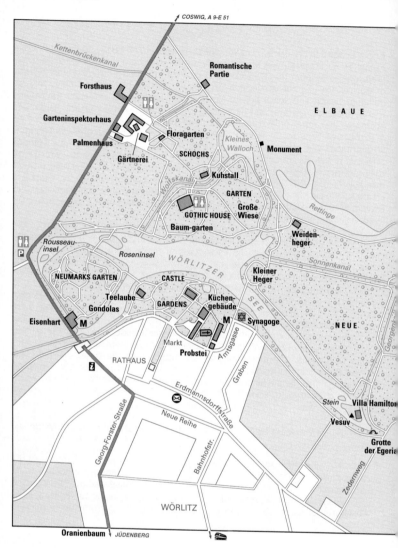

COSWIG, A 9-E 51

Kettenbrückenkanal

Forsthaus

Romantische Partie

Garteninspektorhaus

ELBAUE

Palmenhaus

Floragarten

Kleines Walloch

Monument

Gärtnerei

SCHOCHS

Kuhstall

GARTEN

Rettinge

Große Wiese

GOTHIC HOUSE

Baum-garten

Weiden-heger

Rousseau-insel

P

Roseninsel

WÖRLITZER

Kleiner Heger

Sonnenkanal

NEUMARKS GARTEN

CASTLE

Teelaube

Gondolas

GARDENS

Küchen-gebäude

Eisenhart

M

SEE

M

Synagoge

NEUE

Markt

Probstei

Amtsgasse

RATHAUS

Graben

Erdmannsdorffstraße

Stein

Villa Hamilton

Neue Reihe

Vesuv

Georg-Forster-Straße

Bahnhofstr.

Grotte der Egeria

WÖRLITZ

Zederweg

Oranienbaum   JÜDENBERG

pillars, is crowned by a simple tympanum. An inscription explains that Prince Franz had the castle built for his wife Luise. He attached great importance to practical accoutrements, as indicated by the water pipes, lifts, folding beds and cupboards fitted into the walls. All the sculpture and carpentry work was undertaken by local people, whom Erdmannsdorff insisted, as far as he was able, on having properly trained.

Luckily the original interior and artistic decoration have survived virtually intact. The rooms are no more than moderate in size, with the result that visitors find it easier to take them in. The elegant **dining room** with its elaborate stucco decoration and slim Corinthian pillars, and the great **banqueting hall**, which is two storeys high, are particularly striking. In the latter, the eye is drawn to the beautiful coffered ceiling with its fresco paintings in the style of Carracci. The **library** with its waxed limewood bookcases is as successful a composition as the rest of the rooms (the Prince's and the Princess' apartments), richly hung with paintings (Cranach the Elder, Snyders, Van Ruysdael, Antoine Pesne) and fitted with furniture, the highlight of which is unquestionably the suite of furniture from the Roentgen workshop, which can be found in the Princess' cabinet.

★ **Gotisches Haus** ⊙ – The canal side façade of this building, built in several stages between 1773 and 1813, is modelled on the Gothic church of Santa Maria dell'Oro in Venice, whilst the side facing the garden, with its brick

WÖRLITZER PARK

ℹ Information

🚻 Toilets

0 ——————— 300 m

Pantheon

Großes Walloch

Amalieninsel

Rotes Wachhaus

ANLAGEN

Italienisches Bauernhaus

Holzhof

façade and the white pointed arch windows, is based on the English Tudor style. This "Gothic house" is the first neo-Gothic building outside England, with the exception of the Nauener Gate in Potsdam.

While the castle served for official purposes, the Gothic house was a refuge for the Prince, to which he could withdraw and in which he would frequently come and live for a spell. Through the mediation of the Swiss scholar Johann Caspar Lavater he was able to acquire an outstanding collection of **Swiss stained glass**★ dating from the 15C to the 17C. This has survived intact and adorns the windows of the Gothic house.

The many corners and narrow corridors of the building give visitors the impression of being in an English castle. This impression is reinforced by the neo-Gothic interior design, which is particularly marked in the so-called church-hall and above all in the **knights' hall**, evocative of the Middle Ages. The latter boasts a beautiful window with 18 stained-glass panels, depicting Swiss standard-bearers. In the **bedchamber** the Prince's practical streak is clearly evident: wall cupboards and fold-out writing desks and shelves are incorporated into the wooden panelling. All the rooms house numerous paintings (portrait of a macho-looking Tintoretto in the war cabinet and several works by Lucas Cranach the Elder in the library and the dining room).

EXCURSION

Oranienbaum - *6km/4mi south*. This Baroque town was named after the Dutch Princess Henri-ette Catharina of Nassau-Orange, who was married to Johann Georg II of Anhalt-Dessau. The estate, with its castle, orangery and extensive park, to which a Chinese pagoda lends an exotic air, is preserved more or less in its original form. The town is divided into squares. An iron orange tree in a beautiful sandstone tub in the market place embodies the name of this small town which was once a royal seat.

Use the Map of Principal Sights to plan an itinerary.

WOLFENBÜTTEL★★

Nierdersachen
Population 54 000
Michelin map 416/418 J 15

For three centuries, until the court transferred to Brunswick in 1753, Wolfenbüttel was the seat of the cukes of Brunswick and Lüneburg. The precise, spacious plan of the small town, with die-straight streets linking large symmetrical squares, makes it one of the most successful examples of Renaissance town planning in Germany.

SIGHTS

★★ **Half-timbered houses (Fachwerkhäuser) (ABYZ)** - Picturesque groups of these houses in different styles reflect the town's social structure under the Dukes. Lining Kanzleistraße, Reichstraße and the west end of Harzstraße, for instance, majestic façades with overhangs on either side of the main entrance distinguish the homes of High Court officials, most of them built c 1600. The corbelled upper floors of these houses are supported on brackets. The decoration of smaller houses owned by lesser dignitaries and merchants, oddly enough, is more elaborate. A single gable normally tops their wide, flat façades (Lange Herzogstraße, Brauergildenstraße, Holzmarkt, Krambuden). At no 12 Harzstraße, note the curious grimacing heads above cornices carved with biblical inscriptions. The simpler, two-storey houses of the less well-to-do (Krumme Straße, Stobenstraße) are prettily ornamented with coloured fan designs. The corner houses with only slightly projecting oriels are characteristic of Wolfenbüttel. The most harmonious single group of these half-timbered houses is to be found surrounding the main town square (Stadtmarkt).

★ Stadtmarkt (AZ) – On the north and west side of the square, the Rathaus comprises a number of buildings with splayed beams filled in by brickwork. The Weights and Measures Office has a distinctive arched doorway surmounted by King Solomon's Edict and the Wolfenbüttel coat of arms. Picturesque weather vanes creak in the wind. The philologist **Schottelius**, or Justus Georg Schottel, known as "the father of German grammar", lived in the square in about 1650. A statue of Duke Augustus the Young (1635-66) honours one of the most cultivated princes of the House of Brunswick and Lüneburg.

Schloß ⊘ (AZ) – This is reached via an attractive narrow street bordered by arcades known as the Krambuden. Originally a 12C stronghold conquered by Henry the Lion of Brunswick, the building was the subject of many transformations before it evolved into the present Baroque residence, complete with several pediments and overlooked by a fine Renaissance **tower★**. In the 16C and 17C, under the rule of several ducal patrons, the castle became a centre of literature and sacred music.

The Ducal Apartments – *Access via a stairway, on the right beneath the porch.* Rare furniture, tapestries, porcelain and valuable paintings recreate the atmosphere of court life, especially during the reigns of Duke Anton-Ulrich and Augustus-Wilhelm (early 18C). Mythological scenes, executed in marquetry with an ivory inlay, adorn the walls of the small study.

Herzog-August Bibliothek (Library) ⊘ (AYZ) – Founded in 1572 by Augustus the Young, and rebuilt at the end of the 19C, this was the largest, most important library in Europe in the 17C. Still an invaluable treasure house for researchers and scholars, it houses today some 600 000 volumes. Among the priceless manu-

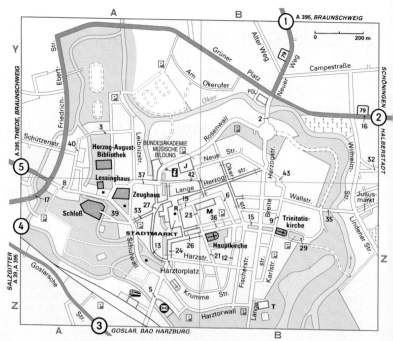

scripts and illuminated documents from the Middle Ages are *The Story of the Lovely Melusina*, by Jean d'Arras (1478), a rare example of the 14C *Saxon Mirror*, and the first *Helmarshausen Gospel* (12C) said to have belonged to Henry the Lion. These are exhibited in the Augusteer-Halle and in the room below it. On the left of the latter are two globes, terrestrial and celestial, as well as ancient maps and a portolan (marine chart) which provide interesting information on the state of geographic knowledge and the advances in cartography during the 15C, 16C and 17C. On the right *(shown in rotation)* are books illustrated by great artists of the 20C.

Lessinghaus ⊘ (AZ) – **Gotthold Ephraim Lessing**, the great innovator of German drama, lived in Wolfenbüttel from 1770 to 1781, working as official ducal librarian and writing, among other works, *Emilia Galotti* and *Nathan the Wise*. His last home was this mansarded pavilion just before the library on the north side of the esplanade. An evocation of his life and works (writings on philosophy, theology, literary criticism and aesthetics, besides drama) is on view inside.
On the right of the Lessing house is the **Zeughaus** (Arsenal, 1613), a distinctive Renaissance building with projecting gables flanked by obelisks and scrolls. Note the fine rusticated west doorway.

Hauptkirche (BZ) – Built on Kornmarkt in 1608, this Protestant church is laid out in the Gothic manner, with very tall windows and pointed vaulting, but it also has features characteristic of the Late Renaissance.
Note the lateral gables, on which the pediments embellished with niches and columns boast a curiously thick decoration of twisted scrollwork. The massive tower with its Baroque roof resembles the castle tower in shape.

Trinitatiskirche (BZ) – The church, which closes off the east end of the Holzmarkt, was built in 1719. In its construction, the architects made use of an existing, twin-towered structure which was once a city gate. This explains the strangely flat silhouette of the church. Behind it, a deconsecrated burial ground has been transformed into an inviting **public garden**.

WORMS★

Rheinland-Pfalz
Population 80 000
Michelin map 417/419 R 9 – Local map see PFALZ AM RHEIN

The city of Worms was, like Speyer and Mainz, an Imperial Residence on the banks of the Rhine, a town with a legendary past, a town of history and prestige. Today it extends along the river irrigating the rich soil of the Palatinate Plain vineyards. The **Liebfrauenkirche** (*leave on Remeyerhofstraße – B*), which stands amid the vines in the northern suburb, has given its name to the most famous of all Hocks: Liebfraumilch. Remains (now restored) of the medieval walled town destroyed during the Thirty Years War are visible near the **Torturmplatz** (B) and the **Karolingerstraße** (B 22).

Luther before the Diet – Everyone knows the old chestnut about Luther and the "diet of worms", bandied about to much hilarity during school history lessons. In fact this particular Diet had perhaps the most far-reaching consequences of any conference before the two world wars (*see Introduction: History – "The Reformation and the Thirty Years War: Luther"*). Summoned before it by the young Charles V in 1521, after a Papal Bull condemning everything he believed in, Luther arrived in Worms "as though going to the torture chamber". He went nevertheless without hesitation, held back by the anxiety of his friends but acclaimed by enthusiastic crowds. Refusing to retract his beliefs, he was banned to the outer parts of the empire (*see also WITTENBERG*).

★★ DOM ST.-PETER (A) allow 30min

Worms Cathedral is a Romanesque building with two apses quartered in each case by two round towers. From the outside, the **west chancel**★★ of this four-towered structure, completed c 1230, is one of the finest Romanesque creations in Germany, with its double tier of Rhenish dwarf galleries.

Interior – The best way to go in is through the south (Gothic) doorway. On the tympanum: the Coronation of the Virgin. A splendid Christ In Judgement is on the far side of the door, dating from the 12C. A very old sculpture in the first chapel on the south side represents Daniel in the Lions' Den.
The east chancel, with its pointed vaulting, is the older of the chancels: the high altar is the work of Balthasar Neumann. Nine Imperial tombs of relatives of Emperor Konrad II are beneath the choir. Note the transept crossing, surmounted by a Rhenish cupola on squinches.
The Romanesque nave, which has five bays with diagonally ribbed vaulting, is embellished with blind arcades featuring intricate carving typical of the later development of the style. The west chancel, the last to be built, is extremely elegant, with rose windows, a chequered frieze and arches added to its blind arcades.
Five **Gothic relief sculptures**★ in the north aisle (Scenes from the Life of Christ) represent the Annunciation, the Nativity, the Entombment, the Resurrection and the Tree of Jesse.

WORMS

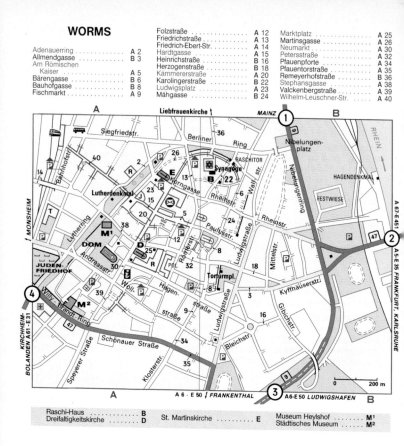

ADDITIONAL SIGHTS

Lutherdenkmal (Luther Monument) (A) – Unveiled in 1868, the monument commemorates the Reformer's appearance before the Diet. Luther himself, in the centre, is surrounded by the precursors of the Reformation: Pietro Valdo, John Wycliffe, Jan Hus and Savonarola. At the four corners are *(back)* the Reformist theologians Melanchthon and Reuchlin, *(front)* the Landgrave of Hessen Philip the Magnanimous *(see MARBURG)* and the Elector of Saxony who protected Luther. Seated women symbolize the towns of Speyer, Augsburg and Magdeburg.

★ **Museum Heylshof** ⊘ (A M¹) – This museum installed in the salons of a former town house displays **paintings**★ from the 15C to the 19C, including works by Rubens, Van Loo, Mignard and Knaus. Also on view are ceramics (from Winterthur, Delft and China), glassware and crystal, 300 pieces of Frankenthal porcelain, and examples of 15C and 16C stained-glass windows.

★ **Judenfriedhof (Jewish Cemetery)** (A) – Worms was one of the most highly esteemed centres of Jewish culture in Germany. This ancient burial ground, in use since the 11C, is studded with more than 2 000 steles carved in Hebrew.

Synagogue (B) – Dating also from the 11C (and rebuilt in 1961), this is the oldest synagogue in Germany. Nearby is the Mikwe (Women's Bathhouse) and the **Raschi-Haus** (B B), an old Jewish school restored to exhibit archives, ceremonial items and other examples of life in the Rhineland Jewish community.

Städtisches Museum ⊘ (A M²) – The historic and prehistoric exhibits are displayed in the Romanesque buildings of a former monastery. Note the collection of helmets in the Roman section. The church contains sacred art, with a lapidary museum in the cloister.

Dreifaltigkeitskirche (A D) – Only the tower and façade of the original Baroque (18C) church buildings remain. The interior commemorates the Reformation.

St.-Martinskirche (A E) – The Romanesque west door is flanked by eight columns with crocketed capitals. Note the decorative interlacing of vine stems and leaves on the tympanum.

EXCURSION

★ **Rhineland Palatinate** – *See PFALZ AM RHEIN.*

WÜRZBURG★★

Bayern
Population 129 000
Michelin map 417/419/420 Q 13

Würzburg lies in the middle of the Franconian vineyards on the banks of the Main, at the foot of the episcopal citadel of Marienberg. The town which grew up around a Franconian ducal court (7C) had become important enough by the Middle Ages to host the marriage of Hohenstaufen emperor Frederick I Barbarossa and Beatrice of Burgundy in 1156. Würzburg took on its present appearance from the mid 17C to mid 18C under three prince-bishops of the **Schönborn** family, who were also responsible for the Baroque churches of the old town and the Residenz Palace.
At Würzburg **University**, founded in 1582 under Prince-Bishop Julius Echter von Mespelbrunn, **William Conrad Röntgen** discovered X-rays in 1895.

The Master of Würzburg – This was the title bestowed on the great Flamboyant Gothic sculptor **Tilman Riemenschneider** (1460-1531), who came to live in Würzburg in 1483 and who was also the town's mayor in 1520 and 1521. Riemenschneider's work was never purely decorative: his whole interest centred on human beings, whose faces and hands – even their clothes – served as vehicles to express emotion and sensitivity. A gravity that is almost melancholy distinguishes his finest work, which includes the magnificent altarpieces at Creglingen and Rothenburg, the statues in Würzburg's local museum, and the tomb of Heinrich II in Bamberg cathedral – all priceless treasures of Franconian art.

★★RESIDENZ ⊙ (Z) *guided tour: 1hr*

This superb Baroque palace, one of the biggest in Germany, was built between 1720 and 1744 under the direction of that architect of genius, **Balthasar Neumann**, supplanting the old Marienberg stronghold as the bishops' residence.
The monumental **Grand Staircase★★** (Treppenhaus), which ends in a double flight and occupies the whole northern part of the vestibule, is one of Neumann's masterpieces. The huge **fresco★★** (600m²/6 400sq ft) decorating the vaulted ceiling is by the Venetian, **Tiepolo** (1753). This gigantic work depicts the homage of the four then known continents to the Prince-Bishop Carl Philipp von Greiffenclau. In the White Room (Weißer Saal), between the Grand Staircase and the Imperial Hall, the stuccoes, also Italian, are the work of Antonio Bossi.

The oval **Imperial Hall★★** (Kaisersaal) is splendid. Situated on the first floor, it, too, is adorned with **frescoes by Tiepolo**. Following a fashion current in the Baroque period, the artist makes an impeccable transition, moving imperceptibly from sculpture to false-relief painting.
It is also possible to visit the **Imperial Apartments** (Paradezimmer), a luxurious suite of rooms restored in all their splendour with Rococo stuccowork, tapestries and German furniture.

★★ Hofkirche – The architectural fantasy and audacity displayed by Neumann in the royal chapel are astonishing. The complex positioning of oval arching, the pink-veined marble columns, the white and gold of false marble highlighting the

Fresco by Tiepolo in the Imperial Hall of Würzburg Residenz

H. Veiller/EXPLORER, Paris

537

A masterpiece in 210 days

Having initially commissioned an artist from Milan to paint the residence, who "painted it so atrociously badly", Prince-Bishop Carl Philipp von Greiffenclau hesitated no longer: only **Giovanni Battista Tiepolo**, the best fresco painter of his age, could meet his demands. The painter arrived, in the company of his two sons aged 23 and 14, on 12 December 1750. He was entertained in a princely style, ".. and was given eight courses at lunch and seven in the evening. In other respects, he wanted for nothing and was generally treated quite admirably". He was to receive 10 000 Gulden for his work, three times more than he earned in Venice.

During the barely three years he stayed in Würzburg, Tiepolo created the frescoes adorning the imperial hall and the staircase, two altars for the Würzburg court church, one for Schwarzach Abbey (now located in the Alte Pinakothek in Munich) and also worked for some other families in Würzburg. Since he was not able to paint his frescoes during the winter months, he must have worked day and night for the rest of the year. It took him only 210 days to complete the staircase fresco, which is 32x19m/105x62ft in size and features an overwhelming range of people, allegories and details, virtually a theatre of the world. In the frescoes in the Würzburg residence the artist, who was well known in his youth for the amazing speed at which he painted and for his creativity, produced his greatest and most important work.

warm tints of frescoes by the court painter Rudolf Byss – all of these combine to form a colourful composition rich in contrasts. Two more Tiepolo paintings hang above the side altars: the Assumption and the Fall of the Angels.

★ **Hofgarten** – Astute use of old, stepped bastions has produced a layout of terraced gardens with majestic ramp approaches. From the eastern side, the whole 167m/545ft of the palace façade, with its elegant central block, is visible. The stucco is the work of Johann Peter Wagner.

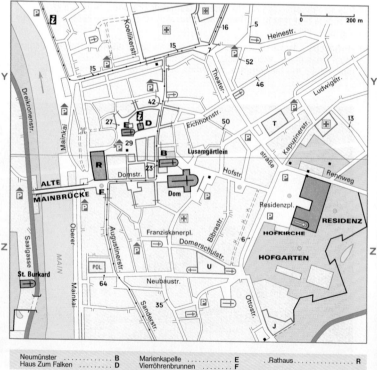

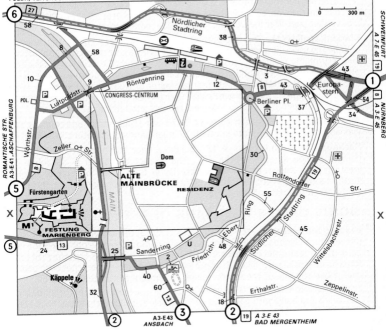

★ **Martin-von-Wagner-Museum** ⊘ – *In the south wing.*
On the second floor there is a **painting gallery**★ exhibiting German and other European work from the 14C to the 19C. Particularly noteworthy: altar paintings by the masters of Würzburg (14C-16C) and Franconian sculpture, especially that of Riemenschneider. Dutch and Italian painters from the 16C to the 18C are well represented (Tiepolo again).
On the third floor, there is a collection of **antiquities**★ displaying an interesting series of **painted Greek vases**★★ (predominantly from the 6C to the 4C BC). The department also exhibits Roman pottery, earthenware items, and jewellery from Ancient Egypt. Note the Greek and Roman sculpture and implements made from bronze.

ADDITIONAL SIGHTS ON THE EAST BANK OF THE MAIN

Dom (Cathedral of St Kilian) (Z) – This basilica with columns and four towers, rebuilt in 1945, has retained its original (11C-13C) silhouette, although the interior is marked by many other centuries. The Baroque stuccowork of the chancel contrasts with the high ceiling and simplicity of the Romanesque nave; the **Altar of the Apostles** in the south transept was conceived in 1967 by H Weber as a resting place for three **sandstone sculptures**★ by Riemenschneider which were created between 1502 and 1506.
Against the pillars on either side of the great nave, **funerary monuments**★ to the prince-bishops, ranging from the 12C to the 17C, stand in proud array. Those by the seventh and eighth pillar on the north side (Rudolf von Scherenberg and Lorenz von Bibra) are also by Riemenschneider.
The **crypt**, accessible via the north transept, houses a monument (13C) to the founder of the cathedral, Archbishop Bruno. Off the north transept is the **Schönborn Chapel**, built between 1721 and 1736 by Balthasar Neumann and the architect Maximilian von Welsch to take the tombs of the prince-bishops of that house. The 15C Gothic **cloister** abuts on the south face of the cathedral.

Neumünster (YZ B) – The imposing Baroque **west façade** of this church (1710-16) is attributed to Johann Dientzenhofer. The twin superposed gables of the central section, sharply curved and richly decorated, lend power to the whole façade.

The three-aisle nave inherited from the original Romanesque building was extended at the beginning of the 18C by a huge domed bay at the western end. In niches below this cupola are a Riemenschneider Virgin and Child and a Christ in an unusual pose with arms folded below the chest (14C).

In the west crypt is the **tomb of St Kilian**, apostle, patron of Franconia and missionary, executed in Würzburg in 689.

North of the chancel, on the left, is the entrance to the **Lusamgärtlein**, a small garden laid out on the site of a medieval cloister. It was here, so they say, that the troubadour-poet Walther von der Vogelweide, who died in 1231, is buried.

Marienkapelle (Y E) – This fine Gothic hall-church with its lovely upswept lines was built by the town burghers in the 14C and 15C. There is an attractive Annunciation on the tympanum of the north doorway (c 1420). Inside the west front is the 1502 tombstone of Konrad von Schaumberg, carved by Riemenschneider and, on the north side, a **silver Madonna** made by the Master of Augsburg, J Kilian, in 1680. East of the chapel is the **Haus zum Falken**★ (Falcon House) (**D**), with its graceful 1752 façade decorated in the Rococo style (reconstructed after the war).

★ **Alte Mainbrücke** (Z) – Built between 1473 and 1543, the bridge over the Main was adorned in the Baroque era with 12 huge sandstone statues of saints.

Rathaus (Town Hall) (YZ **R**) – A 13C building, once an episcopal residence. The painted façade dates from the 16C. The interior courtyard is charming. The western part, known as the **red building** (Roter Bau), is an example of the Late Renaissance (1659) architectural art. The **fountain** (Vierröhrenbrunnen) (**F**) in front of the town hall dates from 1765.

SIGHTS ON THE WEST BANK OF THE MAIN

★ **Festung Marienberg** ⊘ (X) – From 1253 to 1719, this stronghold was the home of the prince-bishops of Würzburg. Built on a commanding height above the west bank of the Main, the original early-13C medieval castle was transformed into a Renaissance palace by Julius Echter c 1600. It was under the Schönborn bishops that it became one of the fortresses of the empire from 1650 onwards.

Fürstenbaumuseum ⊘ – This comprises the prince-bishops' apartments, richly furnished and hung with paintings and tapestries. These include the huge Echter family tapestry dating from 1564. The treasury contains valuable items (church plate etc) from the cathedral, royal chapel and Marienberg Chapel.

Marienberg forms a complex around a rectangular central courtyard in which stand a fine 13C **circular keep**, a circular chapel dedicated to the Virgin Mary (Marienkirche) and a Renaissance covered well that is 104m/341ft deep. The chapel, crowned by an impressive cupola decorated with Baroque stuccowork, dates back to the early 8C (it was consecrated in 706). It houses many episcopal tombstones.

From the terrace of the **Fürstengarten** (Princes' Garden) there is a fine **view**★ of the town.

★★ **Mainfränkisches Museum (Franconian Museum of the Main)** ⊘ (X **M¹**) – *The entrance is on the right in the fortress' first courtyard.*

Among the displays of local art and crafts in this former arsenal (Zeughaus, 1702-12) is the world's most significant collection of **Riemenschneider sculptures** (first floor), with 80 of his works including Adam and Eve, Virgin Mary and Child and The Apostles.

The Irony of Fate

It is certainly a tragic irony that **Tilman Riemenschneider** is now fêted in a town where he spent some of the darkest days of his life. During the Peasants' Uprising of 1525, the artist took the side of the peasants, and when they were defeated he was imprisoned and tortured in Marienberg Fortress on the orders of the bishop. He was released after only nine weeks, but fell out of favour with his clients and lost all his property. This experience understandably had an adverse effect on his creativity, and there are no pieces of work attributed to his final years.

In the splendid vaulted galleries of the **Echterbastei**, gold and silver religious plate, Gothic easel paintings and examples of Franconian folk art can be seen. In the **cellars** are old winepresses.

St.-Burkard (Z **K**) – The chancel of the Romanesque-Gothic (11C-15C) riverside church straddles the Uferstraße *(covered passageway)*. The bust of a Riemenschneider **Madonna** enlivens the south transept. Nearby there is a late-16C altarpiece and in the middle of the church is an offertory box in a Late Romanesque cubic capital.

THE BEST OF WURZBURG

WHERE TO STAY

Zur Stadt Mainz – Semmelstraße 39, ☎ 09 31/5 31 55, Fax 09 31/5 85 10. Single rooms from 110DM. Well-run family business in the centre of town. Very welcoming rooms decorated in typical local style.

Schloß Steinburg – Auf dem Steinberg, ☎ 09 31/9 70 20, Fax 09 31/9 71 21. Single rooms from 130DM. Palace-hotel built in 1897 in a beautiful site with a view of the town and the Main Valley. Comfortable rooms.

Walfisch – Am Pleideturm 5, ☎ 09 31/3 52 00, Fax 09 31/3 52 05 00. Single rooms from 165DM. Centrally located hotel near the bank of the Main with view of the vineyards and fortress. Good, freshly cooked food in the Walfisch-Stube.

Rebstock – Neubaustraße 7, ☎ 09 31/3 09 30, Fax 09 31/3 09 31 00. Single rooms from 172DM. Fine Rococo façade. Luxurious rooms with individual decor and good level of comfort.

EATING OUT

Weinhaus Stachel – Gressengasse 1, ☎ 09 31/5 27 70, Fax 09 31/5 27 77. Main courses from 20DM. Fine old town house, furnished in a cosy rustic style with wood panelling. The popular Stachelhof is especially recommended for warm summer days.

Bürgerspital – Theaterstraße 19, ☎ 09 31/35 28 80, Fax 09 31/3 52 88 88. Main courses from 20DM. Wine cellar belonging to the Bürgerspital wine estate. Rustic vaulting and bar tables, which are always laid with good things. Franconian specialities to go with the local wine.

Schiffbäuerin – Katzengasse 7, ☎ 09 31/4 24 87, Fax 09 31/4 24 85. Main courses from 28DM. Rustic restaurant with good cooking, well known for its fish dishes.

Käppele (X) – At the top of a monumental Way of the Cross, this well-situated pilgrim sanctuary, the work of Balthasar Neumann, comprises a central Baroque chapel with curious bulbous domes and decorations that include Matthäus Günther frescoes and Rococo stuccowork by Johann Michael Feuchtmayer. The adjoining chapel of mercy is connected via a "miracle passage".

The finest **view**★★ of Würzburg and the river is from the chapel terrace, with the fortress of Marienberg rising from the vineyards in the foreground.

EXCURSIONS

★ **Schloß Veitshöchheim** Ⓥ – *7km/4mi to the northwest by ⑥ on the town plan.*
The castle, built at the end of the 17C and enlarged around 1750 after plans drawn up by Balthasar Neumann, contains splendid Rococo and Empire furniture, including gaming and billiard tables. But it was above all the **park**★ that received particular attention from the prince-bishops, who improved it so consistently that by the end of the 18C it was an entirely Rococo creation. In the southern part, formalized in the French manner, about 200 statues people the shaded walks and leafy arbours, brightening avenues bordered by artistically clipped lime trees. In the middle of the great lake stands the superb **Parnassus Group** (Pegasus, the Muses and Apollo), which was carved in 1766.

★ **The Main Valley Vineyards** (**Bocksbeutelstraße**) – *Round tour of 87km/55mi – allow 1 day. Leave Würzburg via ③ on the town plan.*
It was monks at the beginning of the Middle Ages who introduced viticulture to the Franconian region of the Main – an area with a mild climate and hot, dry summers. The 4 500ha/11 115 acres under the vine produce mainly white wines from the **Müller-Thurgau** and traditionally fruity **Silvaner** grape stock. Such wines adapt perfectly to the essentially rich Franconian cooking.

Sommerhausen – A small Franconian walled town. The picturesque gables of the 16C town hall and the castle overlook the main street.

Ochsenfurt – Another town still encircled by ancient **ramparts**★ punctuated by gates. In the centre, many old half-timbered houses and hotels are adorned with wrought-iron statuettes or signs. A clock with mechanical figurines striking the hours is an attraction at the **Neues Rathaus** (late 15C). At the southwest corner of the building is a graceful 1498 statue of the Virgin Mary. The **Andreaskirche**, built between the 13C and the 15C, is noteworthy for its interior decoration.

Frickenhausen – A fortified town dating from late medieval times. There is a beautiful **Renaissance gateway** with ramshorn scrollwork decorating the pediment. The town hall is Late Gothic.

Marktbreit – Here there is a fine **Renaissance ensemble**★ formed by the town hall, dating from 1579, a bridge (Breitbachbrücke) and the gateway beyond it (Maintor, c 1600). Two Baroque houses with corner oriels complete the picture.

Sulzfeld – Another fortified town. The gables of the 17C town hall are decorated with projecting scrollwork.

Pass through Kitzingen and Mainstockheim (on the east bank of the Main), and take the road for Dettelbach.

★ **Dettelbach** – This charming fortified market town stands on the northern slopes of the Main Valley. See the Late Gothic (c 1500) town hall and the mid-15C parish church, whose principal tower is linked by a wooden bridge to the smaller staircase tower. Northeast of the upper town is the **pilgrimage church "Maria im Sand"** (1608-13), an interesting example of the transition between Flamboyant Gothic and a Renaissance already tainted by the Baroque. The 1623 **Renaissance doorway**★ was made by Michael Kern, who was also responsible for the sandstone and alabaster **pulpit**★ (1626).

From Dettelbach to Neuses am Berg, the road crosses an open plateau planted with vines, with good views of the neighbouring slopes. It then drops down again to the valley of the Main and the peaceful village of **Escherndorf**. From Escherndorf, a small ferry crosses the river to Nordheim.

★ **Volkach** – This delightful little wine-growing town lies on the east (outer) side of a wide oxbow curve in the Main. Of the original medieval enclave only two gates remain: the **Gaibacher Tor** and the **Sommeracher Tor**, one at each end of the main street. On one side of Marktplatz is the **Renaissance town hall** (Tourist Information Centre), built – with its double-flight outside stairway and corner turret – in the mid 16C. In front of it is a 15C fountain with a statue of the Virgin Mary and slightly further south is the **Bartholomäuskirche**, a Late Gothic building with Baroque and Rococo interior decor.

The building known as the **Schelfenhaus**, a civic mansion in the Baroque style dating from c 1720, is worth seeing for its interior decorations (*in the Schelfengasse, north of the market place*).

At the northwestern limit of the town (*about 1km/0.5mi, in the direction of Fahr*) stands the 15C **pilgrimage church "Maria im Weingarten"**, in the middle of vineyards covering the Kirchberg. Inside is the famous **Virgin with Rosary**★ (Rosenkranzmadonna), a late work (1512-24) of Tilman Riemenschneider, in carved limewood. From the Kirchberg there is a superb **panorama** including Volkach, the vineyards and the valley of the Main.

In town, unless otherwise indicated, our itineraries are walking tours.

XANTEN

Nordrhein-Westfalen
Population 19 000
Michelin map 417 L 3

Xanten, birthplace of Siegfried, hero of the Nibelungen saga, was originally a Roman town and honours St Victor, martyr of the Theban Legion. Traces of the medieval fortifications, such as the 1393 **Cleves Gate** (Klever Tor), can still be found.

★ **Dom (Cathedral)** – *The south doorway is being restored.*
This cathedral is one of the finest Gothic buildings in the Lower Rhineland. A Romanesque church was erected here in the 12C on the site of an earlier sanctuary founded by St Helen to house the relics of St Victor. The towers and Westwerk of this, damaged in the Second World War, are nevertheless still standing. The present Gothic structure was begun in 1263, although the five-aisle nave was not completed until the 16C.

The high altar, harbouring the shrine of St Victor, has a handsome reredos by Bartholomäus Bruyn the Elder (1530) which illustrates the lives of St Victor and St Helen. Heinrich Douvermann, the Master Sculptor of Kalkar, created the 1536 Altarpiece of the Virgin, with its intricately worked predella, in the south aisle. The north aisle houses the altarpiece of St Anthony, which dates from 1500. The outer panels were painted by Derick Baegert. The Gothic **cloister** is 16C.

Cathedral Museum – *Closed for renovation.*

Regionalmuseum ⊙ – Roman and Celtic discoveries from archeological excavations nearby are exhibited on the ground floor. There is a department of prehistory. The first floor is reserved for temporary exhibitions.

Archäologischer Park ⊙ – North of the town, near the site of the digs, a Roman town has been reconstituted, complete with perimeter wall, amphitheatre, bathhouse etc.

ZITTAUER GEBIRGE*

Michelin map 418 N 27-28

This mountain range extends for 20km/12mi in a southeast-northwest direction, forming an abrupt barrier towering over the Zittau Basin. A favourite region for rock climbers, mountaineers and winter sports enthusiasts, it is also noted for such spas as Lückendorf, Oybin and Jonsdorf, and the trips that can be made from them. The highest peaks in the range – Lausche (793m/2 602ft), Hochwald (749m/2 457ft) and Jonsberg (681m/2 234ft) – are steep phonolithic (clinkstone) cones protruding from sandstone bedrock. This juxtaposition of sandstone and limestone heights with the remains of volcanic and igneous eruptions is characteristic of the Zittau mountains.

ROUND TOUR STARTING FROM ZITTAU

50km/31mi – allow a day

Zittau – The depression in which the town lies is hemmed in by the Zittau mountains, the Lausitz range and its eastern foothills, and the region drained by the River Neiße. This was the richest of the towns in the Oberlausitz town league (founded in 1346), whose other members included Bautzen, Görlitz, Kamenz, Lauban and Löbau.

The famous **Zittau Lenten veils** (1472 and 1573) originated here. Only a very few examples of these testimonies to medieval piety, which hid the chancel during Lent, and of which there were at one time many, remain in Europe. The great Zittau Lenten veil is the most important example, measuring 56m2/600sq ft and representing 90 scenes from the Creation to the Last Judgement, a Late Gothic illustrated Bible. It is on display in the **Kreuzkirche**.

The town's **Marktplatz** is dominated by the **Rathaus** (1840-45), which was built after plans originally drawn up by Karl-Friedrich Schinkel in the Italian Renaissance style. The **Johanniskirche** (15C-19C) has also been restored on the basis of plans by Schinkel. The **church of St.-Peter und Paul**, once part of a Franciscan monastery, is a Flamboyant Gothic structure (15C) built on Romanesque foundations. The upper part of the tower is Baroque.

Stadtmuseum ⊙ – This museum, with its interesting collections relating to the history of the town and to folk art, is housed in the former Franciscan museum. The **Grüner Born**★, a well with an elaborate cast-iron cupola (1679), stands in front of the building.

Leave Zittau and take the road signposted to Lückendorf.

The road runs through delightful, hilly countryside dotted with woods and forests of conifers. The many sandstone outcrops make this landscape not unlike that of the "Swiss Saxony" area *(see SÄCHSISCHE SCHWEIZ)*.

At Lückendorf, leave the car in the parking place on the right of the road, opposite the Kurhaus "Karl Lucas".

The post-and-beam frame house

This rural method of building, which is quite unique within Europe, combines the half-timbering of the German conquerors (the Thuringians and Franks) with the log cabin method of building of the Slavs who lived here originally. Although log cabins are excellent for the climatic conditions, their structural design does not permit an upper storey to be added. Therefore a supporting framework is erected around the core of the house, the log cabin itself. This post-and-beam structure, which is frequently arch-shaped, carries the upper floor together with the roof framework.

R. Chéret/MICHELIN

543

R. Chérer/MICHELIN

Oybin monastery ruins

Oybinblick – After a 10min walk, there is a fine view of Lückendorf and, on the far side of the frontier, the nearer reaches of the Czech Republic. Continue 23m/25yd past the viewpoint then bear left in the direction of Oybinblick, from where there is another splendid view of the Oybin spa and the rock masses of the Großer Wetterstein and the Kelchstein.

★ **Oybin** – This attractive holiday resort nestles at the foot of Oybin mountain. The Baroque **Bergkirche**★, also known as the "wedding church", is a little jewel, with its double painted wooden galleries and its coffered ceiling. It stands on the road leading to Oybin **fortress and monastery estate**★ ⊙. Work began on the fortress in around 1316, and on the monastery in around 1365. The Gothic monastery church was built by stonemasons from the cathedral building site in Prague. The entire construction has fallen into disrepair since the 16C, but provides a splendid example of Romantic ruins, which also inspired the painter Caspar David Friedrich. There is a magnificent **view**★ to the Lausche, at 793m/2 602ft the highest point in the Zittau range, and in good weather, as far as the Riesen range.

There are some beautiful post-and-beam construction houses in **Jonsdorf** and **Waltersdorf**, which have been lovingly restored and smartened up by their owners. In Waltersdorf the entrances have been designed with particular care and feature elaborately worked lintels dating from the second half of the 18C.

At the exit from Jonsdorf, there is a large car park from which there are opportunities for interesting walks and rambles towards the Steinbruchschmiede, the Waldbühne and the Carolafelsen.

Großschönau – This town was formerly Germany's damask weaving centre. Several of the historic weaving looms are on display and, more importantly, can be seen in action in a museum, the **Deutsches Damast-und Frottiermuseum**★ ⊙, including the only still operational damask weaving loom in Europe. The range of patterns on the valuable fabrics woven here for over three centuries is quite extraordinary. In contrast to damask, one of the oldest woven fabrics in Europe, the museum is also concerned with the production of towelling and there is a demonstration of how this is woven. We recommend that visitors take their time over this museum, as they will be richly rewarded by the demonstrations and detailed explanations.

A number of post-and-beam frame houses can be seen in the immediate vicinity of the museum.

Return through Jonsdorf to Zittau.

A trip on the **Zittau narrow-gauge railway**, which runs to Jonsdorf and Oybin, among other places, is a peaceful, pleasant way of getting to know the Zittau mountain range.

Michelin publications:

more than 220 maps, atlases and town plans;

12 editions of The Red Guide to hotels and restaurants in European countries;

more than 200 editions of The Green Guide in 8 languages to destinations around the world.

ZUGSPITZE★★★

Bayern

Michelin map 419/420 X 16

With a summit at 2 964m/9 724ft above sea level, the Zugspitze is the highest peak on German territory. It is the northwest pillar of the Wetterstein limestone massif, a rocky barrier enclosing the valley of the Loisach. The matchless panorama it offers, added to extensive ski slopes which can be used up to the beginning of summer in the Schneeferner corrie, have meant that the mountain is particularly well served so far as tourist facilities are concerned. It can be reached by cable-car (Gletscherbahn) from Zugspitzplatt station, the terminus of the rack railway rising from Garmisch, or directly from the Eibsee, or again from Ehrwald with the Tyrolean Zugspitz train.

THE ASCENT ⊘ (Be sure to wear warm clothing)

From Garmisch-Partenkirchen – Departure from the Zugspitzbahn station or the terminus at the Eibsee, accessible by road from Garmisch. The whole trip lasts 1hr 15min, a 4.6km/2.9mi tunnel bored through the mountain ending the rack-railway climb to Zugspitzplatt station. As long as the snow is good (from October to May), the lower part of the corrie known as the Zugspitzplatt offers a skiing area of some 7.5km²/almost 3sq mi, equipped with many ski-tow installations.

From the Eibsee – By rack railway (see above). Cable-car direct to the summit in 10min.

From the Zugspitzkamm (Austrian Tyrolese side) – See the Michelin Green Guide Austria. From Ehrwald, the Tyrolean cable-car (which carries 100 people) takes you from the valley station to the summit in 10min.

★★★ THE SUMMIT (ZUGSPITZGIPFEL)

The upper terminals of the Gletscherbahn and the Eibsee cable-car are on the German side, next to the eastern peak of the mountain where a cross has been planted. After that come the "Münchner Haus" refuge and an observatory. The look-out terrace by the Gipfelbahn is at an altitude of 2 964m/9 724ft. On the Austrian side is the upper station of the Tyrolean Zugspitzbahn. The crossing from Austria to Germany at the summit has been redesigned and revised.

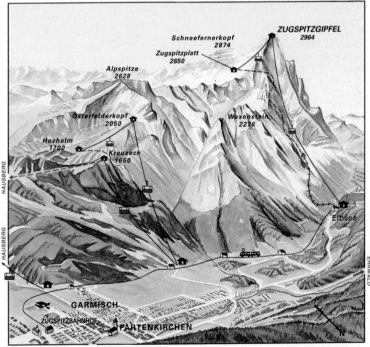

The **panorama**★★★ to the east reveals the forward bastions of the Kaisergebirge, the Dachstein and the Karwendel, the glacial peaks of the Hohe Tauern (Großglockner, Groß Venediger), the High Alps of the Tirol (Zillertal, then Stubai and Ötztal to the south) as well as the Ortler and the Bernina.

Nearer, towards the southwest, the mountains of the Arlberg (Silvretta, Rätikon) stand in front of the Säntis in the Appenzell Alps and, further away to the west and northwest, the Allgäu and Ammergau ranges. To the north, the Bavarian lowlands are visible, together with lake Ammersee and Lake Starnbergersee.

The Green Guide includes fine art, historical monuments, scenic routes:
Europe: Austria – Belgium and Luxembourg – Berlin – Brussels – Europe – France – Germany – Great Britain – Greece – Hungary and Budapest – Ireland – Italy – London – Netherlands – Portugal – Rome – Scandinavia and Finland – Scotland – Sicily – Spain – Switzerland – Tuscany – Venice – Vienna – Wales – The West Country of England
North America: California – Canada – Chicago – Florida – New England – New York City – New York, New Jersey, Pennsylvania – Pacific Northwest – Quebec – San Francisco – Washington DC – USA East – USA West
And Mexico, Guatemala, Belize – Thailand and the complete collection of regional guides for France

ZWICKAU

Sachsen

Population 107 000

Michelin map 418 N 21

The geographic site of Zwickau (recorded for the first time in 1118), on the northern edge of the Erzgebirge ("the ore mountains"), has played an all-important role in the town's economic development. Since 1316, mines south of the town have been exploited for copper, iron and silver, but it was above all the discovery in 1470 of richer silver-bearing lodes at Schneeberg, a few miles away, which brought prosperity to the city.

On the cultural level, Zwickau is famous as the birthplace of the composer **Robert Schumann** (1810-56).

SIGHTS

★ **Dom St.-Marien** (DZ) – This three-aisle hall-church in the Flamboyant Gothic style was built between 1453 and 1565 on an earlier (13C) construction. Successive stages in the work were directed by the architects N Eichhorn, P Harlaß and C Teicher. The Baroque octagonal superstructure crowning the west tower was designed by J Marquardt (1671-77). The austerity of the cathedral's exterior contrasts vividly with an interior bathed in light, where star vaulting which appears to leap upwards and outwards from well-spaced slender pillars forms an audacious visual statement.

The jewel of the cathedral's interior decorations is the 1479 **high altar**★★ *(sometimes on display in the Städt. Museum, see below)*. The six painted panels of the altarpiece, depicting the life of Mary and the Passion of Christ, were executed by Michael Wolgemut of Nuremberg. Also from the School of Nuremberg is the major work of Michael Heuffner, the 1507 **Holy Sepulchre**★ *(between the two south pillars of the chancel)*. **The Lamentation of Christ**★ (1502), carved in lime wood, is by Peter Breuer, a Master of Zwickau. Paul Speck, a sculptor from Freiberg, executed the **pulpit**★ and the **baptismal font** (1538). The decorations embellishing the various parts of the entrance and the rail leading to the pulpit foreshadow already in their richness the style of the Renaissance (note for instance the terracotta medallions with portraits created by J Elsesser in 1560).

Robert-Schumann-Haus ⊘ (DZ M¹) – The birthplace of the composer (1810-56) was demolished in 1955 due to its dilapidated state, and subsequently rebuilt true to the original. Schumann passed his childhood in Zwickau but left it at the age of 18 when his education was complete. At the age of 46 he died in the health resort of Endenicht (near Bonn). Many documents and articles belonging to Robert Schumann and his wife, the pianist Clara Wieck, can be seen.

ZWICKAU

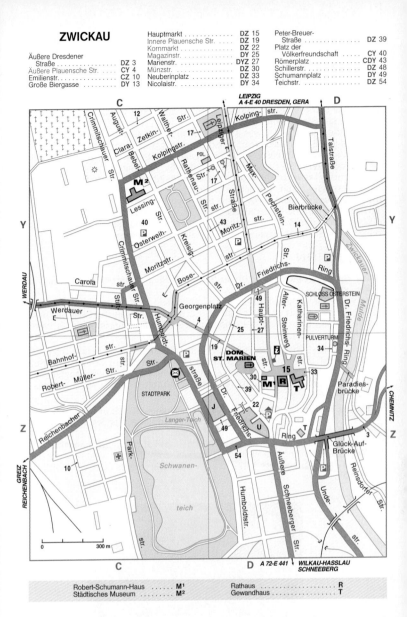

The historical room is decorated with original furniture. For example, visitors can admire the grand piano on which Clara performed for the first time when she was nine years old.

Hauptmarkt (DZ 15) – The main square is surrounded by burghers' houses built at various times between the 15C and the 19C. The **town hall (R)** was restored in neo-Gothic style in 1862, although the Council Chamber (formerly the Jakobskapelle) has preserved its original Late Gothic style.
The **Gewandhaus (T)**, which has served as a municipal theatre since 1823, combines elements from the Late Gothic and Early Renaissance. It dates from 1525.

Städtisches Museum ⊘ **(CY M²)** – Documentation on the history and development of Zwickau, the museum houses an important collection of minerals and fossils, and sculptures and painting ranging from the 16C to the mid 20C (including works by local artist Max Pechstein).

Admission times and charges for the sights described are listed at the end of the guide. Every sight for which there are times and charges is identified by the symbol ⊘ in the Sights section of the guide.

ZWIEFALTEN★★

Baden-Württemberg
Population 2 300
Michelin map 419 V 12

This village, on the Danubian edge of the Swabian Jura, has a remarkable **Baroque church**. Like most Baroque edifices in this region, the building's sober exterior conceals a lavishly decorated interior.

Entering the church, which was built by Johann Michael Fischer between 1739 and 1753, the initial impression is of an extraordinary profusion of luminous colours, a richness and exuberance in the decoration and an extreme virtuosity on the part of the stuccoworkers. The eye, intoxicated at first by this deluge of painting, stucco and statues, finally settles on the details: the ceiling paintings devoted to the Virgin Mary, the Feuchtmayer pulpit, the angels and cherubs, in every attitude and from every corner, addressing themselves to the pilgrims.

The choir is separated from the nave by an altar to the Virgin surrounded by superb grilles dating from 1757. The stalls are richly carved and gilded. Before leaving the church, note the most unusual confessionals built to resemble grottoes.

EXCURSION

★★ **The Baroque Churches of Upper Swabia** – *Round tour of 84km/52mi – allow 4hr.*

Between Ulm and Lake Constance (Bodensee), the Upper Swabian Plateau, with its gentle hills and soft light, is scattered with beautiful Baroque churches whose fluid, low-key decorations in pastel tints harmonize perfectly with the landscape.

Obermarchtal – The old **abbey church** ⊙ in this small town, dating from 1686, was one of the first to be completed by the Vorarlberg School. The rigidity of the architecture – a Baroque still undeveloped – is accentuated by the heaviness of the furnishings: only the Wessobrunn stuccowork lightens the overall effect.

★ **Steinhausen** – Designed by Dominikus Zimmermann, master of the Baroque in this part of the country, the abbey church in this hamlet comprises a single nave and a small chancel, both of them oval in shape.

A crown of pillars, which supports the inner shell of the vaulting, marks the limit of a gallery circling the nave. The capitals, cornices and window embrasures, carved and coloured, are adorned with birds and insects or flowers with heavy corollas.

Interior of Zwiefalten Church

Bad Schussenried – A pleasant small town. The old abbey buildings (now a psychiatric hospital) and the **abbey church** owe their sumptuous Baroque appearance to former Premonstratensian abbots. In the church, the upper panels of the intricately decorated choir stalls (1717) are separated by 28 statuettes representing men and women who founded religious orders. The **library**★ ⊘ has a huge painted ceiling by Franz Georg Herrmann, court painter to the Prince-Abbot of Kempten, and a sinuous gallery and Rococo balustrade supported by twin columns, the work of Fidelis Sporer. The column pedestals are embellished alternately with vivacious cherubim in burlesque costumes and effigies of Fathers of the Church.

★★ **Weingarten** – A dominant position in this town of 23 000 inhabitants is held by the abbey church, with its fine bare-sandstone façade. Consecrated in 1724, the church rivals Ottobeuren as the largest Baroque sanctuary in Germany. It is 102m/335ft long and 44m/144ft wide at the

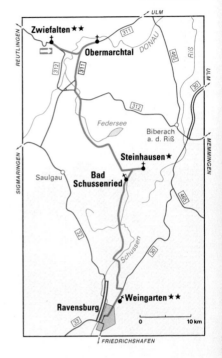

transepts. The west front, framed by two short but elegant towers, is rounded. This, with the construction of a dome on a drum with wide window openings above the transept crossing, betrays an Italian influence transmitted by way of Salzburg.

The interior vistas are amplified by openings pierced through the dividing piers in a manner typical of the Vorarlberg School. The painting and stuccowork, relatively restrained, were entrusted to the masters of the day. Scenes on the vaulting by Comas Damien Asam are full of virtuosity. The choir stalls by Joseph Anton Feuchtmayer are also interesting.

Take Bundesstraße 30 to **Ravensburg** *(see under this name).*

Cruisng the River Elbe in Swiss Saxony

Practical information

Travelling to Germany

Entry Formalities – Proof of identity in the form of a valid passport, identity card or equivalent is required by foreigners entering Germany. No visa is required for visitors with a valid passport visiting Germany for up to three months from the following countries: Australia, Canada, Ireland, New Zealand, UK, USA.

Customs Regulations – Since the implementation of the single European market in 1993, there are effectively no longer any restrictions on the quantities of goods which can be purchased within the EU by private travellers from its member states. A leaflet entitled *A Guide for Travellers* is available from HM Customs, UK.

Non-residents of EU member states should enquire about customs regulations at their local customs service. US residents can obtain a free publication *Know Before You Go* from the US Customs Service, PO Box 7407, Washington, DC 20044, ☎ 202-927-5580.

Duty-free allowances for goods purchased in non-EU countries are: gifts to the value of 115DM (this includes items for your personal consumption); 200 cigarettes; 100 cigarillos; 50 cigars; 250g tobacco; 1l of spirits (over 22%) or 2 litres of wine/sparkling wine; 50g perfume.

Medical treatment – British citizens should apply to their local post office for an **E111 Form** (application form included in the brochure *Health Advice for Travellers* available from the post office), which entitles the holder to emergency treatment for accidents or unexpected illness in EU countries. Non-EU residents should check that their private health insurance policy covers them for travel abroad, and if necessary take out supplementary medical insurance with specific overseas coverage. All prescription drugs should be clearly labelled, and we recommend that you carry a copy of the prescription with you.

Disabled travellers – A book entitled *Handicapped-Reisen in Deutschland* by Yvo Escales (38 DM, including postage) is published by FMG Fremdenverkehrsmarketing GmbH, Postfach 15 47, 53005 Bonn, ☎ 02 28/61 61 33, Fax 02 28/62 35 00. Besides listing 1 250 hotels, leisure complexes, apartments and youth hostels with wheelchair facilities, it gives detailed information on local facilities and infrastructures for the disabled.

Disabled motorists should take note that a disabled car badge/sticker does not entitle them to unrestricted parking, as it does in the UK (local disabled residents are granted special parking permits only in exceptional circumstances). Apart from this, Germany is on the whole a well-equipped country for disabled visitors.

By air – Various international airline companies operate regular services to one or all of Germany's international airports (Berlin, Bremen, Dresden, Düsseldorf, Frankfurt/Main, Hamburg, Hannover, Köln/Bonn, Leipzig, München, Münster/Osnabrück, Nürnberg, Saarbrücken, Stuttgart). The international German airline **Lufthansa** can be contacted in the UK at Starline Ticket Office, 7/8 Conduit Street, London, W1R 9TG, ☎ 0845 773 7747, or in the Republic of Ireland at Lufthansa German Airlines, Link Building, Room 118, Dublin Airport, ☎ (353) (0)1 844 5000, or on their Web site: www.lufthansa.uk for information about flights to and in Germany.

By rail and sea – The principal travel routes by rail and sea are from:
London, Victoria Station, via Dover and Ostend (sailing: 4hr; jetfoil: 1hr 40min) or Sheerness and Vlissingen (sailing: 9hr);
London, Liverpool Street Station, via Harwich and the Hook of Holland (sailing: 7-9hr) or Hamburg (sailing: 20hr);
London to Brussels via Folkestone and Calais (the Channel Tunnel);
Hull to Rotterdam (sailing: 13hr).
For details of rail tickets, see *Travelling In Germany, By Train* below.

By road – When driving to the continent the ideal ports of entry for Germany are Hamburg (from Harwich), Rotterdam (from Hull), the Hook of Holland (from Harwich), Zeebrugge (from Hull, Felixstowe and Dover) as well as Ostend (from Dover) and Calais (from Dover, or Folkestone via the Channel Tunnel). From these ports there is a wide choice of routes using motorway or national roads into Germany.

Hamburg to Berlin 289km/180mi.
Rotterdam to Berlin via Hanover 721km/448mi.
Vlissingen to Munich via Cologne, Bonn, Mainz, Stuttgart and Augsburg 895km/556mi.
Ostend to Munich via Regensburg 787km/489mi.

Travelling in Germany

BY CAR

Documents – A valid national or international driving licence is required (enquire at your local German tourist office to check whether it is necessary to obtain an accompanying translation in German) and third-party insurance cover is compulsory; it is advisable to obtain an International Motor Certificate or Green Card issued by insurance companies.

Driving Regulations – Traffic in Germany drives on the **right**. Drivers in cities in which **trams** operate should be extra careful when looking to check that the road is clear before crossing tramlines. The **maximum speed** permitted in built-up areas is 50kph/31mph. On the open road the maximum increases to 100kph/62mph. There is no official limit on motorways (Autobahnen), but drivers are recommended not to exceed 130kph/81mph. There is a compulsory speed limit of 80kph/50mph on roads and motorways for vehicles with trailers. In Germany careless or reckless driving is considered a serious offence and fines can be stiff. The maximum limit for **level of alcohol** in the blood is 0.8ml/g.

German **motorways** are toll-free and are well equipped with service areas. These are usually open round the clock and provide the following facilities: petrol, spare parts and accessories, washrooms, toilets, public telephones, refreshments, accommodation and first-aid equipment.

The wearing of **seat belts** is obligatory, in the back as well as in the front of the car. Children under the age of 12, or less than 1.5m/4ft 11in tall, are required by law to be seated and fastened in a suitable **child car seat**; fines for non-compliance. It is a legal requirement to carry the regulation **red emergency triangle**, for warning other motorists of a breakdown or enforced roadside halt, and a first-aid box.

In Germany emergency services are always given priority and drivers should pull over to the side of the road.

Breakdown Service – For 24-hour breakdown service, call ☏ 01 30/ 81 92 11. This is taken care of on main roads and motorways by the ADAC (the Auto Club Europa in the eastern part of the country). Roadside break-down services can be called from one of the emergency phones – small

Emergency telephone numbers:
Police: 110
Fire brigade: 112

arrows on the posts along the road indicate the direction of the nearest emergency phone. On-the-spot repairs are free, as only the cost of replacement parts or towing is charged. Motorists ringing this service should ask specifically for the "Straßenwachthilfe".

The Michelin Red Guide Deutschland lists the numbers to use to contact the ADAC service in all big towns.

Petrol – The following grades of petrol (gas) are available in Germany:
Super Plus Bleifrei: Super unleaded (98 octane)
Super verbleit: 4-star leaded (likely to be phased out)
Normal Bleifrei: Standard unleaded (95 octane)
Normal verbleit: 2-star leaded (not very common)
Diesel

Car Hire – Cars may be hired only if the driver is over 23 and has held a driving licence for more than one year.

The major car hire firms have offices at airports and main stations and in large towns. Some useful numbers include:
Avis: ☏ 018 05/55 77, Fax 061 71/68 10 01
Europcar: ☏ 018 05/80 00, Fax 040/52 01 86 13
Hertz: ☏ 018 05/33 35 35, Fax 061 96/93 71 16
Sixt: ☏ 018 05/25 25 25, Fax 018 05/22 11 20

Important warning signs:

Anfang	start, beginning
Ausfahrt	exit
Baustelle	roadworks, building site
Einbahnstraße	one-way street
Ende	end
Einfahrt	entrance
Gefahr/gefährlich	danger

LKW	heavy lorries (HGVs), trucks
PKW	private cars
Rechts einbiegen	turn right
Links einbiegen	turn left
Rollsplitt	gravel chippings
Stau	hold-up, traffic jam
Unfall	accident
Umleitung	deviation
Verengte Fahrbahn	road narrows
Vorrang	priority
Vorsicht	attention! Look out!

BY TRAIN

Tickets and fares – Germany's leading transport organisation, **Deutsche Bahn AG** (DB) has a network of some 43 000km/26 700mi and provides a quick and reliable means of transport. Over 50 cities are served by the InterCity (supplement fare payable) and Inter-Regional (IR) services. The DB InterCity express (ICE) operates on certain high-speed routes (special fares payable). Special offer tickets (**Eurodomino** – for unlimited travel all over Germany, **German Regional Rail Pass** – 5 or 10 days of travel in a particular region within a 31 day period, Bahncards – for frequent travellers to Germany and discount fares for children, students and senior citizens) are available from your local German Rail office or travel agents (such passes should be obtained before you leave home, as they are not available in Germany). Generally speaking, children under four travel free and children aged 4-11 years inclusive pay half fare. Motorail bookings are also available.

For further information and reservations apply to:

DER Travel Service, 18 Conduit Street, London W1R 9TD, ☏ 020-7290-1111, Fax 020-7629-7442, e-mail sales@dertravel.co.uk, Web site www.dertravel.co.uk; German Rail Telesales, ☏ 0870 243 5363.

Rail Europe, 179 Piccadilly, London W1, ☏ 08705 848 848, Web site www.raileurope.co.uk

Deutsche Bahn's Web site: www.bahn.de (to get English text, select the "International guests" option from the menu down the left of the screen).

General information

Electricity – The power supply in Germany is currently being changed from 220V to 230V, to comply with standards in the rest of Europe. This change will have no effect on most 220-240V appliances.

Money – The unit of currency in Germany is the Deutsche Mark (DM), subdivided into 100 Pfennige (Pf). German coins come in values of 1, 2, 5, 10 and 50Pf and 1, 2 and 5DM. Notes are issued to the values of 5, 10, 20, 50, 100, 200, 500 and 1 000DM. Credit cards (European and Japanese) are increasingly accepted throughout Germany, but it unwise to rely on them entirely, especially in smaller towns or villages, or out-of-the-way petrol stations. It is advisable to make sure your credit card is accepted before making your purchase, even when there is a sign saying that credit cards are accepted. At times it may be more convenient to make a purchase in cash obtained with a Eurocard (Mastercard), Visa or American Express card. **Cash dispensers** at banks such as Citibank, Deutsche Bank and Commerzbank in large towns or cities, or at main railway stations, generally accept Visa and Eurocard.

Banks are generally open Mon to Fri 8.30am to 12.30pm and 2pm to 4pm, sometimes to 6pm. They are closed at weekends and on public holidays.

Post Offices – Post offices are open Mon to Fri 8am to 6pm and Sat 8am to noon. Postal rates at the time of going to press were: 1.10DM for letters up to 20g and 1DM for postcards (within the EU).

Post offices with poste restante facilities (postlagernde Sendungen) are shown on the town plans in this guide. Poste restante mail is only issued on presentation of a passport or identity card.

Public holidays – **1 Jan**, **6 Jan** (in Baden-Württemberg, Bayern and Sachsen-Anhalt only), **Good Fri**, **Easter Day**, **Easter Mon**, **1 May**, **Ascension**, **Whit Sun and Mon**, **Corpus Christi** (in Baden-Württemberg, Bayern, Hessen, Nordrhein-Westfalen, Rheinland-Pfalz, Saarland, Sachsen, Thüringen and those communities with a predominantly Roman Catholic population only), **15 Aug** (in Roman Catholic communities in Saarland and Bayern only), **3 Oct** (Day of German Unity), **31 Oct** (Reformation Day, celebrated in the new Federal States ie Brandenburg, Mecklenburg-Vorpommern, Sachsen, Sachsen-Anhalt and Thüringen only), **1 Nov** (in Baden-Württemberg, Bayern, Nordrhein-Westfalen, Rheinland-Pflaz and Saarland only), **Buß- und Bettag** (Day of Repentance and Prayer, usually third Wed in Nov, observed in Sachsen only), **24 and 25 Dec.**

Shops – On the whole, shops open between 9am and 10am, and close between 6.30pm and 8pm (earlier in smaller localities or rural villages). On Sat they are generally open until 4pm. Some bakeries are also open on Sun mornings.

Telephone – Off-peak rates apply at weekends. Phonecards (Telefonkarten) for use in the increasingly card-operated public call-boxes can be bought from any post office (in 12DM and 50DM denominations).
The **international dialling code** for Germany is 49, so from the UK you would dial 00 49, followed by the local dialling code (omitting the initial 0) and the subscriber's number. Telephoning overseas from Germany, dial 00, followed by the country code (UK: 44, Ireland: 353, USA and Canada: 1, Australia: 61, New Zealand: 64) then the local code (omitting the initial 0) and the subscriber's number.

Time – Germany follows **Central European Time** (GMT+1). Clocks are put forward 1hr from the end of Mar to the end of Sept for daylight saving time.

Accommodation

Germany offers a wide range of traditional (Hotel, Gasthof, Gasthaus) accommodation. Lists of local hotels, pensions and boarding houses can be obtained at any Tourist Information Centre.

Hotels – The **Michelin Red Guide Deutschland** is revised annually and gives a selection of hotels and restaurants based on impartial inspectors' reports, ranging from a modest inn to the most luxurious grand hotel, or from the centrally situated modern establishment catering for the needs of today's business person to the secluded retreat.
Places listed in the Red Guide are underlined in red on the Michelin map series at a scale of 1:300 000 (maps 415, 416, 417, 418, 419 and 420).

German Hotel Reservation Service (HRS) – Reservations in all hotels, inns and pensions can easily be made through this German reservation service:
HRS, Drususgasse 7-11, 50667 Köln, ☎ 02 21/2 07 70, Fax 02 21/2 07 76 66, Web site www.hrs.de. Immediate reservation. English spoken.

Bed and Breakfast (Garni) – The sign **Zimmer frei** outside private houses indicates that guest rooms are available. Final prices quoted usually include tax, service charges etc. The DZT (Deutsche Zentrale für Tourismus) produces a Bed and Breakfast brochure with further information (address lists) and lists of cities and towns in which bookings may be made through local tourist offices during office hours, Mondays to Fridays. Guest rooms can also be booked through the agency "bed & breakfast", Methfesselstraße 49, 20257 Hamburg, ☎ 0 40/4 91 56 66, Fax 0 40/4 91 42 12.

Camping and Caravanning – Numerous camp sites are available to tourists. To obtain a full list and discover the amenities offered by each site, write to:
– Deutscher Camping-Club (DCC), Mandlstraße 28, 80802 München, ☎ 0 89/3 80 14 20, Fax 0 89/33 47 37.
– ADAC, Am Westpark 8, 81373 München, ☎ 0 89/7 67 60, Fax 0 89/76 76 25 00.

Youth Hostels (Jugendherbergen – JH) – German youth hostels are open to all young people who are members of the German Youth Hostel Association or of another youth hostel association affiliated to the International Youth Hostel Federation. Priority is given to young people under 26. The stay may not exceed three consecutive nights at any one youth hostel. For lists of all youth hostels apply to the German Youth Hostel Association:
Deutsches Jugendherbergswerk, Hauptverband, Bismarckstraße 8, 32756 Detmold, ☎ 0 52 31/7 40 10, Fax 0 52 31/74 01 66.

Country holidays – Details from the German National Tourist Office (DZT). Details of holidays "on the farm" (Urlaub auf dem Bauernhof) are also available from the Deutsche Landwirtschaftgesellschaft e.V. (DLG), Eschborner Straße 122, 60489 Frankfurt/Main, ☎ 0 69/24 78 84 53, Fax 0 69/24 78 84 80 (catalogue costs 14.50DM plus postage). Alternatively, there is another catalogue called *Raus aufs Land* published by the association for country holidays, Zentrale für den Landurlaub, available from Landschriften Verlag, Heerstraße 73, 53111 Bonn, ☎ 02 28/96 30 20, Fax 02 28/9 63 02 33 (costs 14.80DM plus postage).

Where to eat – The current **Michelin Red Guide Deutschland** lists a large selection of restaurants in which tourists can taste for themselves the best and most original specialities of each German region (see Introduction: Food and Drink).
Generally speaking, hotel breakfasts are substantial. Notwithstanding, that familiar sinking feeling at midday can easily be assuaged at an "Imbiß", a small fast-food concern to be found everywhere, in town, on motorways or at the roadside. These offer the traditional snack of **Bratwurst** (grilled sausage), sometimes accompanied by a potato salad or chips, and usually washed down with beer (often on draught – Bier vom Faß).

One of the most delightful of German eating habits – Kaffee und Kuchen – is observed mid-afternoon in one of the many coffee houses to be found nationwide. These veritable havens for the weary traveller always smell delicious and customarily have a large selection of revitalising cakes, such as Schwarzwälder Kirschtorte (Black Forest cherry cake), unctuous Käsekuchen (cheesecake) or delicious fruit tarts. The coffee served with these pastries is always accompanied by cream (Kaffeesahne), and the pastries themselves are frequently adorned with a generous dollop of whipped cream (Schlagsahne).

The Weinstube (wine cellar or wine bar) is an agreeable place to spend an afternoon or evening, with a pleasant atmosphere, where the best wines can be bought and tasted by the glass.

Tourist information

GERMAN NATIONAL TOURIST OFFICES (DZT)

Information on travel arrangements and accommodation and a variety of brochures are available from the German National Tourist Office. For on-line information (also in English), refer to www.germany-tourism.de, the German National Tourist Office Web site.

Local tourist office details are listed in the Admission times and charges section of this guide, indicated by the symbol **B**. Most German cities have Web sites, the addresses of which are generally composed of the city name, eg www.karlsruhe.de is the Web site for Karlsruhe.

Chicago: German National Tourist Office, 401 N Michigan Avenue, Chicago, IL 60611, ☎ 312-644-0723, Fax 312-644-0724.

Johannesburg: German National Tourist Office, c/o Lufthansa German Airlines, 22 Girton Road, Parktown, PO Box 10883, Johannesburg 2000, ☎ 011-646-1615, Fax 011-484-2750.

London: German National Tourist Office, P.O. Box 2695, London W1A 3TN, ☎ 09001 600 100 (information line, calls cost 60p/min), Fax 020 7495 6129.

New York: German National Tourist Office, Chanin Building, 52nd floor, 122 East 42nd Street, New York, NY 10168-0072, ☎ 212-661-7200, Fax 212-661-7174.

Sydney: German National Tourist Office, P.O. Box A980, Sydney South, NSW 1235, ☎ 012-9267 8148, Fax 012-9267 9035.

Toronto: German National Tourist Office, 175 Bloor Street East, North Tower, 6th floor, Toronto, ONT M4W 3R8, ☎ 416-968-1570, Fax 416-968-1986.

REGIONAL TOURIST OFFICES IN GERMANY

Allgäu – Bavarian Swabia: Tourismusverband Allgäu/Bayrisch-Schwaben, Fuggerstraße 9, 86150 Augsburg, ☎ 08 21/3 33 35, Fax 08 21/3 83 31.

Altmark: Fremdenverkehrsverband Altmark, Marktstraße 13, 39590 Tangermünde, ☎ 03 93 22/34 60, Fax 03 93 22/35 60.

Baden: Touristikgemeinschaft Baden-Elsass-Pfalz, Baumeisterstraße 2, 76137 Karlsruhe, ☎ 07 21/35 50 20, Fax 07 21/3 55 02 22.

Baden-Württemberg: LFV-Marketing Baden-Württemberg, Esslinger Straße 8, 70182 Stuttgart, ☎ 07 11/23 85 80, Fax 07 11/2 38 58 99.

Baltic Sea (Mecklenburg-West Pomerania)**:** Verband Mecklenburgische Ostseebäder, Kühlungsborner Straße 14, 18209 Bad Doberan, ☎ 03 82 03/6 21 20, Fax 03 82 03/6 21 20.

Baltic Sea (Schleswig-Holstein)**:** Verband Ostseebäder Schleswig-Holstein, Vorderreihe 57, 23570 Lübeck-Travemünde, ☎ 0 45 02/68 63, Fax 0 45 02/42 34.

Bavaria: Bayerischer Tourismusverband, Prinzregentenstraße 18, 80538 München, ☎ 0 89/21 23 97 30, Fax 0 89/29 35 82.

Berlin: Berlin Tourismus Marketing, Am Karlsbad 11, 10785 Berlin, ☎ 0 30/25 00 25, Fax 0 30/25 00 24 24.

Black Forest: Tourismus Marketing Schwarzwald, Bertoldstraße 45, 79098 Freiburg i. Breisgau, ☎ 07 61/2 96 22 71, Fax 07 61/2 92 15 81.

Brandenburg: Tourismusverband des Landes Brandenburg, Schlaatzweg 1, 14473 Potsdam, ☎ 03 31/27 52 80, Fax 03 31/2 75 28 10.

East Bavaria: Tourismusverband Ostbayern, Luitpoldstraße 20, 93047 Regensburg, ☎ 09 41/58 53 90, Fax 09 41/5 85 39 39.

Eifel: Eifel Touristik, Marktstraße 15, 53902 Bad Münstereifel, ☎ 0 22 53/60 75, Fax 0 22 53/53 06.

Erzgebirge: Fremdenverkehrsverband Erzgebirge, Adam-Ries-Haus, Johannisgasse 23, 09456 Annaberg, ☎ 0 37 33/2 35 53, Fax 0 37 33/2 35 53.

Franconia: Tourismusverband Franken, Fürther Straße 21, 90428 Nürnberg, ☎ 09 11/26 42 02, Fax 09 11/27 05 47.

Hamburg: Tourismus-Zentrale Hamburg, Steinstraße 7, Postfach 10 22 49, 20095 Hamburg, ☎ 0 40/30 05 10, Fax 0 40/30 05 12 20.

Harz: Harzer Verkehrsverband, Marktstraße 45, 38640 Goslar, ☎ 0 53 21/340 40, Fax 0 53 21/34 04 66.

Hessen: Hessischer Fremdenverkehrsverband, Abraham-Lincoln-Straße 38-42, 65189 Wiesbaden, ☎ 06 11/77 88 00, Fax 06 11/78 80 40.

Holstein's "Little Switzerland": Fremdenverkehrsgemeinschaft Holsteinische Schweiz, Bleekergang 7, 23701 Eutin, ☎ 045 21/7 09 70, Fax 0 45 21/7 09 20.

Lake Constance – Upper Swabia: Tourismusverband Bodensee-Oberschwaben, Schützenstraße 8, 78462 Konstanz, ☎ 0 75 31/9 09 40, Fax 0 75 31/90 94 94.

Lower Saxony – Bremen: Fremdenverkehrsverband Nordsee-Niedersachsen-Bremen, Bahnhofstraße 19-20, 26104 Oldenburg, ☎ 04 41/92 17 10, Fax 04 41/9 21 71 90.

Lüneburg Heath: Fremdenverkehrsverband Lüneburger Heide, Barckhausenstraße 32, 21335 Lüneburg, ☎ 0 41 31/7 37 30, Fax 0 41 31/4 26 06.

Mecklenburg – West Pomerania: Tourismusverband Mecklenburg-Vorpommern, Platz der Freundschaft 1, 18059 Rostock, ☎ 03 81/4 03 06 00, Fax 03 81/4 03 05 55.

Mecklenburg Lake District: Fremdenverkehrsverband Mecklenburgische Seenplatte, Turnplatz 2, 17207 Röbel/Müritz, ☎ 03 99 31/5 13 81, Fax 03 99 31/5 13 86.

Moselle: Mosellandtouristik, Gestade 12-14, 54470 Bernkastel-Kues, ☎ 0 65 31/20 91, Fax 0 65 31/20 93.

Munich – Upper Bavaria: Tourismusverband München-Oberbayern, Bodenseestraße 113, 81243 München, ☎ 0 89/8 29 21 80, Fax 0 89/82 92 18 28.

North Sea (Schleswig-Holstein): Nordseebäderverband Schleswig-Holstein, Parkstraße 7, 25813 Husum, ☎ 0 48 41/8 97 50, Fax 0 48 41/48 43.

Odenwald: Touristikgemeinschaft Odenwald-Bergstraße-Neckartal, Marktplatz 1, 64711 Erbach, ☎ 06 62/94 33 30, Fax 0 60 62/94 33 17.

Palatinate: Pfalz Touristik, Landauer Straße 66, 67434 Neustadt/Weinstraße, ☎ 0 63 21/3 91 60, Fax 0 63 21/39 16 19.

Rhineland: Landesverkehrsverband Rheinland, Rheinallee 69, 53173 Bonn, ☎ 02 28/36 29 21-22, Fax 02 28/36 39 29.

Rhineland Palatinate: Fremdenverkehrs- und Heilbäderverband Rheinland-Pfalz, Löhrstraße 103-105, 56068 Koblenz, ☎ 02 61/91 52 00, Fax 02 61/9 15 20 40.

Rhön: Fremdenverkehrsverband Rhön, Wörthstraße 15, 36037 Fulda, ☎ 06 61/6 00 61 11, Fax 06 61/6 00 61 20.

Ruhr Basin: Kommunalverband Ruhrgebiet, Kronprinzenstraße 35, 45128 Essen, ☎ 02 01/2 06 90, Fax 02 01/2 06 95 01.

Saale: Fremdenverkehrsverband Saaleland, Im Oberhof 108, 07407 Uhlstädt, ☎ 0 36 47/6 35 34, Fax 0 36 47/6 35 36.

Saar: Saarland Touristik, Dudweiler Straße 53, 66111 Saarbrücken, ☎ 06 81/92 72 00, Fax 06 81/9 27 20 04.

Sauerland: Fremdenverkehrsverband Sauerland, Heinrich-Jansen-Weg 14, 59929 Brilon, ☎ 0 29 61/94 32 29, Fax 0 29 61/94 32 47.

Saxony: Landesfremdenverkehrsverband Sachsen, Friedrichstraße 24, 01067 Dresden, ☎ 03 51/49 17 00, Fax 03 51/4 96 93 06.

Saxony – Anhalt: Tourismusverband Sachsen-Anhalt, Große Diesdorfer Straße 12, 39108 Magdeburg, ☎ 03 91/7 38 43 00, Fax 03 91/7 38 43 02.

Schleswig-Holstein: Fremdenverkehrsverband Schleswig-Holstein, Niemannsweg 31, 24105 Kiel, ☎ 04 31/5 60 00, Fax 04 31/5 60 01 40.

Spreewald: Tourismusverband Spreewald, Lindenstraße 1, 03226 Raddusch, ☎ 03 54 33/7 74 33, Fax 03 54 33/7 74 34.

Swabia: Touristikgemeinschaft Neckarland-Schwaben, Lohtorstraße 21, 74072 Heilbronn, ☎ 0 71 31/7 85 20, Fax 0 71 31/78 52 30.

Swiss Saxony: Tourismusverband Sächsische Schweiz, Am Bahnhof 6, 01814 Bad Schandau, ☎ 03 50 22/49 50, Fax 03 50 22/4 95 33.

Teutoburg Wald: Fremdenverkehrsverband Teutoburger Wald, Bad Meinberger Straße 1, 32760 Detmold, ☎ 0 52 31/9 58 50, Fax 0 52 31/62 34 78.

Thuringia: Thüringer Landesfremdenverkehrsverband, Tschaikowskistraße 11, 99096 Erfurt, ☎ 03 61/3 73 54 68, Fax 03 61/3 73 54 64.

Thuringian Forest: Fremdenverkehrsverband Thüringer Wald, August-Bebel-Straße 16, 98527 Suhl, ☎ 0 36 81/3 94 50, Fax 0 36 81/72 22 79.

Weser Valley: Fremdenverkehrsverband Weserbergland-Mittelweser, Inselstraße 3, 31787 Hameln, ☎ 0 51 51/9 30 00, Fax 0 51 51/93 00 33.

Westerwald: Fremdenverkehrsamt Westerwald-Lahn-Taunus, Schiede 43, 65549 Limburg, ☎ 0 64 31/29 62 21, Fax 0 64 31/29 64 44.

Westerwald: Westerwald Gäste-Service, Kirchstraße 48a, 56410 Montabaur, ☎ 0 26 02/3 00 10, Fax 0 26 02/30 01 15.

Westphalia: Landesverkehrsverband Westfalen, Friedensplatz 3, 44135 Dortmund, ☎ 02 31/52 75 06-07, Fax 02 31/52 45 08.

Discovering Germany

If the traditional summer holiday tour allows visitors to discover the richness and beauty of Germany under the best possible conditions (pleasant climate, plenty to see and do), there are many other ways to appreciate the warmth of German hospitality and explore the charms of this great country.

CRUISES

For information on river cruises along the Rhine, Moselle, Main, and Elbe, contact KD Deutsche Flußkreuzfahrten GmbH, Frankenwerft 15, 50667 Köln, ☎ 02 21/2 08 82 88, Fax 02 21/2 08 82 31.
Another possibility is Transocean Tours (catalogues are available from travel agents).

PARKS

Amusement parks – The following list includes some of the best-known and popular of Germany's amusement parks:

Park/Place	☎	Nearest motorway exit (no)
Bavaria-Filmtour/ Geiselgasteig (Bayern)	0 89/64 99 23 04	A 99 Oberhaching (4)
Churpfalzpark Loifling/ Cham (Bayern)	09 91/3 03 40	A 3 Straubing (106)
Erlebnispark Schloß Thurn/ Heroldsbach (Bayern)	0 95 56/2 24	A 73 Baiersdorf Nord (10)
Erlebnispark Tripsdrill/ Cleebronn-Tripsdrill (Baden-Württemberg)	0 71 35/99 99	A 81 Mundesheim (13)
Erlebnispark Ziegenhagen/ Witzenhausen (Niedersachsen)	0 55 45/2 46	A 75 Hann.-Münden (75)
Europa-Park/ Rust (Baden-Württemberg)	0 78 22/7 70	A 5 Ettenheim (57)
Fränkisches Wunderland/ Plech (Bayern)	0 92 44/98 90	A 9 Plech (46)
Freizeit-Land/ Geiselwind (Bayern)	0 95 56/2 24	A 3 Geiselwind (76)
Filmpark Babelsberg/ Potsdam (Brandenburg)	03 31/7 21 27 50	A 115 Potsdam-Babelsberg (5)
Fort Fun Abenteuerland/ Bestwig-Wasserfall (Nordrhein-Westfalen)	0 29 05/8 11 23	A 46 Bestwig (71)
Hansa-Park/ Sierksdorf (Schleswig-Holstein)	0 45 63/47 42 22	A 1 Eutin (15)
Heide-Park/ Soltau (Niedersachsen)	0 51 91/91 91	A 7 Soltau-Ost (44)
Holiday Park/ Haßloch (Rheinland-Pfalz)	0 63 24/5 99 33 18	A 65 Neustadt-Süd (13)
Phantasialand/ Brühl (Nordrhein-Westfalen)	0 22 32/3 62 00	A 553 Brühl-Süd (2)
potts park/ Minden-Dützen (Nordrhein-Westfalen)	05 71/5 10 88	A 2 Porta Westfalica (33)

Ravensburger Spieleland/ Weitnau (Bayern)	0 75 42/40 00	A 96 Wangen-West (5)
Safari- und Hollywood-Park/ Schloß Holte-Stukenbrock (Nordrhein-Westfalen)	0 52 07/8 86 96	A 2 Stukenbrock-Senne (23)
Serengeti-Safaripark/ Hodenhagen (Niedersachsen)	0 51 64/5 31	A 7 Westenholz (7)
Taunus-Wunderland/ Schlangenbad (Hessen)	0 6 24/40 81	A 66 Wiesbaden-Frauenstein (2)
Vogelpark Walsrode/ Walsrode (Niedersachsen)	0 51 61/6 04 40	A 27 Walsrode-Süd (28)
Warner Bros. Movie World/ Bottrop-Kirchhellen (Nordrhein-Westfalen)	0 20 45/89 98 99	A 31 Kirchhellen-Feldhausen (40)

National parks – There are over a dozen national parks in Germany, including:

Bavaria: Bavarian Forest (Bayerischer Wald); Berchtesgaden.

Brandenburg: Lower Oder valley (Unteres Odertal).

Hamburg: Hamburg mudflats (Wattenmeer).

Lower Saxony: Lower Saxon mudflats (Niedersächsisches Wattenmeer); Harz.

Mecklenburg-West Pomerania: West Pomeranian coastline and gulfs (Vorpommersche Boddenlandschaft); Jasmund (on Rügen); Müritz.

Saxony: Swiss Saxony (Sächsische Schweiz).

Saxony-Anhalt: Hochharz.

Schleswig-Holstein: Schleswig-Holstein mudflats (Wattenmeer).

Thuringia: Hainich.

Further information is available from Europarc Deutschland, Postfach 1154, 94475 Gräfenau, ☎ 0 85 53/28 39, Fax 0 85 52/32 42.

SPAS AND HYDROTHERAPY

Germany has a wide selection of spas and health resorts, equipped with well-run establishments with modern facilities. These resorts prove popular because of their beautiful settings, well-suited climate and excellent accommodation. Brochures and further information can be obtained from the **Deutscher Heilbäderverband**, Schumannstraße 111, 53113 Bonn, ☎ 02 28/26 20 10, Fax 02 28/21 55 24. Apart from the towns traditionally known for their cures (water or mud), a series of medium-altitude health resorts, and seaside thermal establishments, Germany offers a wide choice of spas specializing in what is known as the **Kneipp System**. Details of resorts specialising in this system can be obtained from the Kneippbund, Adolf-Scholz-Allee 6, 86825 Bad Wörishofen, ☎ 0 82 47/ 3 00 20, Fax 0 82 47/3 00 21 99, or from the Verband Deutscher Kneippheilbäder und Kneippkurorte, 57334 Bad Laasphe, ☎ 0 27 52/8 98, Fax 0 27 52/77 89.

Waldkirch/Bildagentur SCHUSTER, Oberursel

The Spa Establishment, Baden-Baden

Sebastian Kneipp (1821-97), curate and then priest at Wörishofen, developed the set of treatments named after him following an illness. His cure system combines baths, an alternation of warm and cold showers and a "healthy" life-style, involving a strictly controlled diet, plenty of walking and herbal medication.

The German regions with the highest density of health resorts are Baden-Württemberg (information from Heilbäderverband Baden-Württemberg, Luisenstraße 4, 78073 Bad Dürrheim, ☎ 0 77 26/66 62 83, Fax 0 77 26/66 63 03), Bavaria (Bayerischer Heilbäderverband, Rathausstraße 8, 94072 Bad Füssing, ☎ 0 85 31/97 55 90, Fax 0 85 31/2 13 67) and Lower Saxony (Heilbäderverband Niedersachsen, Unter den Eichen 15a, 26160 Bad Zwischenahn, ☎ 0 44 03/5 86 89, Fax 0 44 03/6 14 90).

The principal German **spa towns** include: Baden-Baden, Badenweiler, Bad Berka, Bad Brückenau, Bad Doberan, Bad Düben, Bad Ems, Bad Homburg, Bad Kissingen, Bad Kreuznach, Bad Langensalza, Bad Muskau, Bad Orb, Bad Pyrmont, St. Peter-Ording, Bad Reichenall, Bad Saarow, Bad Salzungen, Bad Sulza, Bad Tölz, Bad Vilbel, Bad Wiessee, Bad Wildbad and Bad Wildungen.

The best-known **climatic health resorts** are: Bayrischzell, Bad Bergzabern, Braunlage, Freudenstadt, Garmisch-Partenkirchen, Hahnenklee, Bad Herrenalb, Königstein im Taunus, Isny, Oberstdorf, Rheinsberg, Rottach-Egern, St. Blasien, Schönwald, Bad Suderode and Titisee-Neustadt.

Coastal health resorts include Ahlbeck, Baltrum, Binz, Borkum, Damp, Grömitz, Heiligendamm, Heiligenhafen, Helgoland, Heringsdorf, Hiddensee, Juist, Kampen, Langeoog, Norddeich, Norderney, Nordstrand, Pellworm, Scharbeutz-Haffkrug, Spiekeroog, Timmendorfer-Strand, Travemünde, Wangerooge, Westerland and Wyk.

SPORT

Cycling

Information, maps and leaflets available are from the Deutsche Fahrrad-Club (ADFC), Hollerallee 23, 28209 Bremen, ☎ 04 21/34 62 90, Fax 04 21/3 46 29 50. This organisation also arranges trips of one day or longer and produces cycling maps and information brochures on various themes. *Deutschland per Rad entdecken* describes 30 cycle routes in Germany, giving detailed information on distances, requirements, useful addresses and route-finding. A useful brochure entitled *Radfernwanderwege in Deutschland*, describing 170 long-distance cycle routes nationwide, is also available.

Those wishing to combine rail and cycle travel will need special tickets; call the Deutsche Bahn hotline on ☎ 0 18 03/19 41 94. It is necessary to reserve a space for the bicycle (no extra fee) in many trains.

Rambling and climbing

Those who long for peaceful holidays will delight in the countrywide network of footpaths and ramblers' routes, all of them clearly waymarked. Whether it is a matter of a three-day hike or a simple walk around a chosen area, many maps are available to help you prepare an itinerary. KOMPASS maps and guides cover the most popular tourist regions.

The German mountaineering club (**Deutscher Alpenverein**, DAV), Von-Kahr-Straße 2-4, 80997 München, ☎ 0 89/14 00 30, Fax 0 89/1 40 03 11, gives useful information on routes and accommodation in the mountains. Their Alpine information centre at Praterinsel 5, 80538 München, ☎ 0 89/29 49 40 can be contacted by telephone Monday to Thursday 9am to noon and 1pm to 4pm for details on mountain refuge opening times, weather reports, guides and maps.

Most of the local ramblers' associations, which oversee 200 000km/124 280mi of paths, belong to the **Verband Deutscher Gebirgs- und Wandervereine**, Wilhelmshöher Straße 157-159, 34121 Kassel, ☎ 05 61/93 87 30, Fax 05 61/9 38 73 10. This organisation will provide details on specific routes and even organises hikes.

Winter Sports

In Germany there is a wide variety of ski resorts (12 ski regions in all), all well equipped and easy to reach, with facilities to cater for every level of skill on the piste. The **Allgäu** can be divided into three regions: west, upper and east. Well-known resorts here include Oberstaufen, Oberstdorf and Pfronten. The other German Alpine ski regions are in **Upper Bavaria** around Berchtesgaden, Reit im Winkel, Tegernsee/Schliersee and Garmisch-Partenkirchen/Mittenwald, **East Bavaria** caters for cross-country skiers as well as downhill (Bayerischer Wald, Oberpfälzerwald, Fichtelgebirge), as does the **Black Forest** (Feldberg and Belchen). Other ski regions, mainly for cross-country, include the **Rhön**, **Sauerland**, **Taunus**, **Eifel** and **Swabian Alp** ranges. The **Harz** has plenty to offer skiers, both downhill and cross-country, to the west and east of the massif. The main ski resort of the **Thuringian Forest** is Oberhof, while Oberwiesenthal (downhill) and Zinnwald-Georgenfeld (cross-country) are the ski centres in the **Erzgebirge**.

TOURIST ROUTES

Very clearly signposted, there are some 150 "thematic" itineraries providing an original means of crisscrossing the country and getting to know it better. They include:

Baden Wine Route (Badische Weinstraße), from Baden-Baden to Lörrach;

Beer and Castle Route (Bier- und Burgenstraße), from Passau to Bad Frankenhausen;

Black Forest Crest Road (Schwarzwald Hochstraße), from Baden-Baden to Freudenstadt;

Black Forest Panoramic Road (Schwarzwald Panoramastraße), from Waldkirch to Hinterzarten;

Castle Roa (Burgenstraße), from Mannheim to Bayreuth and then on to Prague (975km/605mi in total);

Clock Route (Deutsche Uhrenstraße), circuit from Villingen-Schwenningen;

Franconian Wine Route (Bocksbeutelstraße), five different routes through the Main valley vineyards leaving from Würzburg;

German Alpine Road (Deutsche Alpenstraße – described in this guide), from Lindau to Berchtesgaden;

German Avenues (Deutsche Alleenstraße), from Sellin on Rügen Island to Goslar;

German Holiday Route (Deutsche Ferienroute Ostsee-Alpen), which links the Baltic Sea (Puttgarden) with the Alps (Berchtesgaden);

German Wine Road (Deutsche Weinstraße), from Bockenheim/Pfalz to Schweigen;

Green Coast Road (Grüne Küstenstraße), from Westerland (Sylt) to Wischhafen;

Half-timbered Buildings (Deutsche Fachwerkstraße), six local routes through Lower Saxony and Hessen;

Old Salt Road (Alte Salzstraße), from Lüneburg to Lübeck;

Romanesque Road (Straße der Romanik), circuit through Saxony-Anhalt leaving from Magdeburg;

Romantic Road (Romantische Straße), from Würzburg to Füssen;

Royal Road (Straße der Kaiser und Könige), from Frankfurt to Vienna (Austria);

Silver Route (Ferienstraße Silberstraße), from Zwickau to Dresden;

Thuringian Classical Route (Klassikerstraße Thüringen), circuit from Meiningen;

Upper Swabian Baroque Route (Oberschwäbische Barockstraße), various routes from Ulm to Lake Constance;

Weser Renaissance Route (Straße der Weser-Renaissance), from Hann. Münden to Bremen.

On the Michelin maps at a scale of 1: 300 000, some of these tourist itineraries are indicated by a black dotted line running beside the road.

Further reading

HISTORY AND BIOGRAPHY

A Concise History of Germany. M Fulbrook (CUP)
A History of Germany 1815-1985. W Carr (Edward Arnold)
Exploring the Roman World: Roman Gaul and Germany. A King (British Museum Press)
Frederick the Great: Absolutism and Administration. W Hubatsch (Thames & Hudson)
Hitler, A Study in Tyranny. A Bullock (Pelican)
The Concise German History: A Survey of the Development of German History Since 1815. AJP Taylor (Routledge)
The Last Days of Hitler. H Trevor-Roper
The Past is Myself. C Bielenberg
The Saddled Cow. East Germany's Life and Legacy. A McElvoy (Faber and Faber)

THE ARTS

An Outline of European Architecture. N Pevsner (Penguin)
Art in Germany: 1990-1939 From Expressionism to Resistance. R Heller (Prestel Art Books)
Baroque Art and Architecture in Central Europe. E Hempel (Pelican)
Bauhaus. F Whitford (Thames & Hudson)
Caspar David Friedrich. H Börsch-Supan (Prestel Art Books)
Early Medieval Art – Carolingian, Ottonian and Romanesque. J Beckwith (Thames & Hudson)

German Architecture and the Classical Ideal 1740-1840. D Watkin and T Mellinghoff (Thames & Hudson)
German Cathedrals. J Baum (Thames & Hudson)
The Expressionists. W-D Dube (Thames & Hudson)
The Weimar Years: A Culture Cut Short. J Willett (Thames & Hudson)

LITERATURE

Heinrich **Böll** – *The Lost Honour of Katharina Blum*
Bertolt **Brecht** – *The Caucasian Chalk Circle; Threepenny Novel; Mother Courage*
Elias **Canetti** – *Auto da Fé*
Erskine **Childers** – *The Riddle of the Sands*
Günter **Grass** – *The Tin Drum; The Flounder; From the Diary of a Snail*
Hermann **Hesse** – *The Glass Bead Game; Narcissus and Goldmund; Steppenwolf*
Ernst Theodor Amadeus **Hoffmann** – *Tales of Hoffmann*
Thomas **Mann** – *Buddenbrooks; The Magic Mountain*
Rudolph Erich **Raspe** – *The Adventures of Baron Münchhausen*
Erich Maria **Remarque** – *All Quiet on the Western Front*
Christa **Wolf** – *Kindheitsmuster*

TRAVEL AND MODERN GERMAN SOCIETY

A Guide to Eastern Germany. J Bentley (Penguin)
A Time of Gifts. P Leigh Fermor (Penguin)
Atlas of German Wines. H Johnson (M Beazley)
A Tramp Abroad. M Twain
Berlin: Coming in from the Cold. K Smith
Berlin: The Dispossessed City. M Simmons (Hamish Hamilton)
Deutschland: A Winter's Tale. H Heine
Germany and the Germans. J Ardagh (Penguin)
Goodbye to Berlin. C Isherwood (Penguin)
Guide to the Wines of Germany. I Jamieson (Reed International)
The Germans. GA Craig
The New Germany. D Marsch (Random Century Group)
The Origins of Modern Germany. G Barraclough (Blackwell Publishers)
The Rhine. J Bentley (George Philip)
Three Men on the Bummel. JK Jerome (JM Dent & Sons)
To the End of the Rhine. B Levin
Vanishing Borders. M Farr
Winter – A Berlin Family 1899-1945. L Deighton (Random Century Group)

Calendar of events

See also the "Travellers' Addresses" sections under Berlin, Dresden, Frankfurt, Hamburg, Köln and München.

1 January
Garmisch-Partenkirchen . . . . . New Year's Day International Ski Jump, part of the Four Jump Tournament

Sunday before Shrove Tuesday
Munich . . . . "München narrisch" Carnival

Shrove Monday
Cologne, Düsseldorf, Mainz . Rosenmontagszug: procession and street carnival

Shrove Monday and Tuesday
Rottweil . . . . Narrensprung Carnival: elaborate traditional costumes and expressive wooden masks; Dance of the Fools

Maundy Thursday to Easter Monday
Bautzen . . . . Traditional Sorbian Easter Egg Market

Easter
Oberlausitz . . . . Sorbian Easter celebrations, Easter parade

Sorbian Mass

30 April/1 May
Towns in the Harz region . . . Walpurgisnacht: Witches' Sabbath Festival

Marburg . . . . Marburg townspeople and students sing in the month of May

End of April to end of May
Wiesbaden . . . . International May Festival: theatre, music

Mid-May to mid-September every Sunday at noon
Hamelin . . . . Rattenfängerspiel: pageant retracing the legend of the Pied Piper

Friday after Ascension
Weingarten . . . . Blutritt: mounted cavalcade in honour of the Holy Blood

Schwetzingen .... Music Festival

Baden-Baden .... International horse racing at Iffezheim

Merfelder Bruch .... Rodeo: catching and harnessing one-year-old stallions

Schwäbisch Hall .... Kuchen und Brunnenfest: dance of the salt-workers in traditional costume
Rothenburg ob der Tauber .. Meistertrunk: performance of the legend of the "Long Drink" (period costumes, local festival)

Kötzting .... Pfingstritt: mounted cavalcade

Deidesheim .... Historische Geißbockversteigerung: auctioning of a goat; period costumes; folk dancing; local fair

Merfelder Bruch .... Roundup of wild horses, rodeo

Munich .... Solemn procession through the decorated town
Cologne .... Mühlheimer Gottestracht: procession of boats along the Rhine
Hüfingen .... Procession through flower-decked street

Schwalmstadt .... Salatkirmes: Salad Fair commemorating the introduction of the potato to the Hessen region; traditional local costumes

Traditional local
Schwalm costume

Heidelberg .... Castle illuminations; firework displays

Chorin .... Summer Music Festival: concerts of classical music in the Cistercian abbey
Bad Hersfeld .... Festival of Drama and Opera in the abbey ruins; theatre, opera

Kassel .... Documenta: world's largest international exhibition of contemporary art

Kiel .... Kiel Week: international sailing regatta; local festival

Freiberg .... Bergparade in historical costumes

Landshut .... Fürstenhochzeit (Landshut Royal Marriage): historical pageant in period costume

Various places in Mecklenburg-Vorpommern .... Mecklenburg-Vorpommern Summer Music Festival, held in historic houses, castles and churches

Bergparade in Freiberg

Saturday after 24 August
Markgröningen .... Schäferlauf: shepherds' race (barefoot over a field of stubble)

Last week in August
Baden-Baden .... International horse racing at Iffezheim

September
Rothenburg o. d Tauber ..... Festival with fireworks display

End of September to beginning of October
Bad Cannstatt .... Cannstatter Volksfest: popular local fair (with fairground)

1st and 2nd weekend in October
Neustadt an der Weinstraße Weinlesefest: Wine Fair and election of the Queen of Wine

Last 10 days in October
Bremen .... Bremer Freimarkt: largest popular fair in northern Germany

6 November (St Leonard)
Bad Tölz .... Leonhardifahrt: prior to a Mass in honour of St Leonard, gaily decorated horse-drawn carts process through town to the church

Sunday after 6 November
Benediktbeuern .... Leonhardifahrt: similar celebration to that at Bad Tölz

Friday before Advent to 24 December
Nuremberg .... Christkindlesmarkt: Christmas market (Christmas tree decorations and gifts); seasonal performances by children

24 December and New Year's Eve
Berchtesgaden .... Weihnachtsschießen und Neujahrsschießen: Christmas and New Year shooting matches

Glossary

Abtei	abbey	*Fremden verkehrsamt*	tourist office
Ausfahrt	(motorway/highway) exit	*Garten*	garden(s)
Aussicht	view	*Gebirge*	mountain range
Autobahn	motorway (highway)	*Gedenkstätte*	memorial
Bad	spa	*Gletscher*	glacier
Bahnhof	railway station	*Grotte*	cave
Berg	mountain	*Hauptbahnhof*	mainline railway station
Botschaft	embassy		
Brücke	bridge	*Hafen*	port, harbour
Brunnen	fountain	*Höhle*	cave
Burg	castle, fortress	*Insel*	island
Denkmal	memorial	*Jugendherberge, JH*	youth hostel
Dom	cathedral	*Kap*	cape, headland
Dorf	village	*Kapelle*	chapel
Einbahnstraße	one-way street	*Kirche*	church
Fels	rock, cliff	*Kloster*	abbey, monastery
Fernsehturm	television tower	*Krankenhaus*	hospital
Flughafen	airport	*Münster*	cathedral, collegiate church
Fluß	river		

Platz	(town) square	*Straße*	road
Polizei	police	*Tal*	valley
Quelle	fountain, spring	*Talsperre*	dam
		Thermalbad	spa
Rathaus	town hall	*Tierpark*	zoo
Residenz	palace	*Turm*	tower
Sankt-, St.-	Saint-, St-	*Wache*	guardhouse, police station
Schloß	castle, palace		
Schlucht	gorge	*Wald*	forest
See	lake, reservoir	*Wasserfall*	waterfall
Stadt	town, city	*Zeughaus*	arsenal
Staudamm	dam	*Zoll*	customs

Admission times and charges

As admission times and charges are subject to modification due to increases in the cost of living, the information printed below is for guidance only.

The following list details the opening times and charges (if any) and other relevant information concerning all sights in the descriptive part of this Guide accompanied by the symbol ⊙. The entries below are given in the same order as in the alphabetical section of the Guide.

Normally, especially in the case of large towns, the telephone number and/or address of the local tourist office (Fremdenverkehrsamt), indicated by the symbol ⊟, is given. Generally most efficient, these organizations are able to help passing tourists find accommodation (hotel, pension, camp site, youth hostel) as well as providing information on exhibitions, performances, guided tours and other items of interest locally.

The prices quoted apply to individual adults, but many places offer reduced rates for children, OAPs, and some a discount family ticket.

The times are those of opening and closure, but remember that some places do not admit visitors during the last hour or half hour.

The symbol ♿ denotes sights that are accessible to wheelchair users.

NB In German alphabetical order, adopted below, ä = ae, ö = oe and ü = ue.

A

AACHEN   ⊟ Friedrich-Wilhelm-Platz - 52062 ☎ 02 41/1 80 29 60 - Fax 02 41/1 80 29 31

Dom und Domschatzkammer – ♿ Open Mon 10am to 1pm, Tues, Wed, Fri, Sat and Sun 10am to 6pm, Thur 10am to 9pm. 5 DM. ☎ 02 41/47 70 91 27.

Rathaus – Open daily 10am to 1pm and 2pm to 5pm. Closed 1 Jan, 1 May, Ascension, 1 Nov, 24 to 26 and 31 Dec and during special exhibitions. 3 DM. ☎ 02 41/4 32 73 10.

Couven-Museum – Open Tues, Wed and Fri to Sun 10am to 5pm, Thur 10am to 1pm. Closed 1 Jan, Thur and Sun before Shrove Tues, Good Fri, Ascension, Corpus Christi, 24 to 26 and 31 Dec. 2 DM. ☎ 02 41/4 32 44 21.

Suermondt-Ludwig-Museum – ♿ Open Tues to Fri 11am to 7pm, Wed 11am to 9pm, weekends 11am to 5pm. 6 DM. ☎ 02 41/47 98 00.

Ludwig Forum für Internationale Kunst – Open Tues and Thur 10am to 5pm, Wed and Fri 10am to 8pm, weekends 11am to 5pm. Closed 1 Jan, Thur and Sun before Shrove Tues, 24 to 26 and 31 Dec. 6 DM. ☎ 02 41/1 80 71 04.

Deutsche ALPENSTRASSE

Wendelstein rack-railway – From the valley station at Brannenburg, between May and Oct hourly departures 9am to 3pm; 2 Nov to 30 Apr Mon to Fri at 9am, 10am, noon and 2pm, weekends at 9am, 10am, 11am, 1pm and 2pm. Journey time: 30min. Enquire about closure periods. Return fare 42 DM. ☎ 0 80 34/30 81 02.

ALSFELD   ⊟ Rittergasse 5 - 36304 ☎ 0 66 31/18 21 65 - Fax 0 66 31/7 38 96

ALTENBURG   ⊟ Moritzstraße 21 - 04600 ☎ 0 34 47/59 41 74 - Fax 0 34 47/59 41 79

Schloß- und Spielkartenmuseum – Open Tues to Sun 9.30am to 5.30pm. Closed 1 Jan, 25 and 31 Dec. 4 DM (free on 1st Fri of month). ☎ 0 34 47/31 51 93.

Lindenau-Museum – Open Tues to Sun 10am to 6pm. 7 DM (free on 1st Fri of month). ☎ 0 34 47/25 10.

ANNABERG-BUCHHOLZ   ⊟ Markt 1 - 09456 ☎ 0 37 33/42 51 39 –
Fax 0 37 33/42 51 38

Erzgebirgsmuseum mit Besucherbergwerk – Open Tues to Sun 10am to 5pm. 10.50 DM (museum and mine). ☎ 0 37 33/2 34 97.

Technisches Museum Frohnauer Hammer – Guided tours (50min) daily 9am to 11.45am and 1pm to 4pm. Closed 1 Jan, 24, 25 and 31 Dec. 5 DM. ☎ 0 37 33/2 20 00.

ANSBACH   ⊟ Johann-Sebastian-Bach-Platz 1 ☎ 09 81/5 12 43 - Fax 09 81/5 13 65

Residenz – Guided tours (50min) Apr to Sept Tues to Sun at 10am, 11am, 1pm, 2pm, 3pm and 4pm; Oct to Mar Tues to Sun at 10am, 11am, 2pm and 3pm. Closed 1 Jan, Shrove Tues, 1 Nov, 24 to 26 and 31 Dec. 6 DM. ☎ 09 81/31 86.

ASCHAFFENBURG
🚌 Schloßplatz 1 - 63739 ☎ 0 60 21/39 58 00 - Fax 0 60 21/39 58 02

Schloß Johannisburg

Staatsgalerie – Open Apr to Oct Tues to Sun 9am to 11.30am and 1pm to 4.30pm; Nov to Mar Tues to Sun 11am to 3.30pm. Closed 1 Jan, Shrove Tues, 1 Nov, 24, 25 and 31 Dec. 5 DM. ☎ 0 60 21/2 24 17.

Städtisches Schloßmuseum – ♿ Open Apr to Oct Tues to Sun 9am to noon and 1pm to 5pm; Nov to Mar Tues to Sun 11am to 4pm. Closed 1 Jan, Shrove Tues, 1 Nov, 24, 25 and 31 Dec. 5 DM. ☎ 0 60 21/38 67 40.

AUGSBURG
🚌 Bahnhofstraße 7 - 86150 ☎ 08 21/50 20 70 - Fax 08 21/5 02 07 45

Städtische Kunstsammlungen – Open Wed to Sun 10am to 4pm. Closed Good Fri, Easter Mon, Whit Mon, 24, 25 and 31 Dec. 4 DM (free on 1st Sun of month). ☎ 08 21/3 24 41 02.

Maximilianmuseum – Open Wed to Sun 10am to 4pm. Closed Good Fri, Easter Mon, Whit Mon, 24, 25 and 31 Dec. 4 DM (free on 1st Sun of month). ☎ 08 21/3 24 41 02.

Mozarthaus – Open Wed to Sun 10am to 4pm. Closed 24, 25 and 31 Dec. 2.50 DM. ☎ 08 21/3 24 38 94.

Staatsgalerie in der Kunsthalle – ♿ Open Wed to Sun 10am to 4pm. Closed Good Fri, Easter Mon, Whit Mon, 24, 25 and 31 Dec. 4 DM (free on 1st Sun of month). ☎ 08 21/3 24 41 02.

B

BADEN-BADEN
🚌 Augustaplatz 8 - 76530 ☎ 0 72 21/27 52 00 - Fax 0 72 21/27 52 02

Römische Badruinen – Closed until further notice due to renovation (details not available at time of going to press).

BADENWEILER
🚌 Ernst-Eisenlohr-Straße 4 - 79410 ☎ 0 76 32/7 21 10 - Fax 0 76 32/7 21 70

Excursion

Schloß Bürgeln – Guided tours (40min) Mar to Nov daily (except Tues) at 11am, 2pm, 3pm, 4pm and 5pm. 5 DM. ☎ 0 76 26/2 37.

BAMBERG
🚌 Geyerswörthstraße 3 - 96047 ☎ 09 51/87 11 61 - Fax 09 51/87 19 60

Diözesanmuseum – Open Tues to Sun 10am to 5pm. Closed Good Fri, 25 and 31 Dec. 4 DM. ☎ 09 51/50 23 25.

Neue Residenz – ♿ Guided tours (45min) Apr to Sept daily 9am to noon and 1.30pm to 5pm; Oct to Mar 9am to noon and 1.30pm to 4pm. Closed 1 Jan, Shrove Tues, 1 Nov, 24, 25 and 31 Dec. 5 DM. ☎ 09 51/5 63 51.

E.-T.-A.-Hoffmann-Haus – Open May to Oct Tues to Fri 4pm to 6pm, weekends and public holidays 10am to noon. 2 DM.

Excursion

Schloß Pommersfelden – Guided tours (30min or 1hr) Apr to Oct Tues to Sun at 9am, 10am, 11am, 2pm, 3pm and 4pm, shorter tours also at 11.30am and 4.30pm. Closed Tues after Easter and Whitsun. 5-7 DM. ☎ 0 95 48/2 03.

Staircase in Schloß Pommersfelden

SCALA

🛈 Hauptmarkt 1 - 02625 ☎ 0 35 91/4 20 16 - Fax 0 35 91/53 43 09

Reichenturm – Open Apr to Oct daily 10am to 5pm. 1 DM. ☎ 0 35 91/4 41 98.

Serbski Muzej (Sorbian Museum) – ♿ Open Apr to Oct daily 10am to 5pm; Nov to Mar daily 10am to 4pm. Closed 24 and 31 Dec. 3 DM. ☎ 0 35 91/4 24 03.

Alte Wasserkunst – Open Apr to Oct daily 10am to 5pm. 2 DM. ☎ 0 35 91/ 4 15 88.

Excursion

Löbau: König-Friedrich-August-Turm – Open May to Sept Mon to Fri 9am to 8pm, weekends 9am to 10pm; Oct to Apr Mon to Fri 10am to 6pm, weekends 10am to 8pm. May be closed during bad weather. Use the car park outside the nature reserve or obtain a special permit for the trip from Löbau-Information, Altmarkt 1. 3 DM. ☎ 0 35 85/45 04 50.

BAYERISCHER WALD

Großer Arber: Chairlift – Operates 8am to 4.45pm. Closed Nov to the beginning of the ski season. Journey time: 10min. 12 DM. ☎ 0 99 25/2 45.

BAYREUTH 🛈 Luitpoldplatz 9 - 95444 ☎ 09 21/8 85 88 - Fax 09 21/8 85 38

Markgräfliches Opernhaus – Guided tours (20min) Apr to Sept Tues to Sun 10am to 5pm; Oct to Mar 10am to 3pm (last admissions 30min before closing). Closed 1 Jan, 1 Nov, 24, 25 and 31 Dec. 6 DM. ☎ 09 21/7 59 69 22.

Neues Schloß – Guided tours Apr to Sept Tues to Sun 10am to 5pm; Oct to Mar Tues to Sun 10am to 3pm (last admissions 30min before closing). Closed 1 Jan, 1 Nov, 24, 25 and 31 Dec. 4 DM. ☎ 09 21/75 96 90.

Richard-Wagner-Museum – Open Apr to Oct daily 9am to 5pm (until 8pm on Tues and Thur); Nov to Mar daily 10am to 5pm. Closed 1 Jan, Easter Day, Whit Sun, 24 and 25 Dec. 4 DM (5 DM in July and Aug). ☎ 09 21/7 57 28 16.

Festspielhaus – Guided tours (45min) Tues to Sun at 10.45am and 2.15pm. During the Wagner festival (June to Aug) guided tours should be requested by telephone. 2.50 DM. ☎ 09 21/7 87 80.

Schloß Eremitage – Guided tours (30min) Apr to Sept Tues to Sun 10am to 5pm; Oct and Nov Tues to Sun 10am to 3pm. Closed 1 Jan, Shrove Tues, 1 Nov, 24, 25 and 31 Dec. 5 DM. ☎ 09 21/7 59 69 15.

Excursions

Teufelshöhle – Guided tours (45min) Apr to Oct daily 9am to 5pm; Nov to Mar Tues and weekends 10am to 3pm. 5 DM. ☎ 0 92 43/7 08 41.

Sanspareil: Burg Zwernitz – Open mid-Apr to mid-Oct Tues to Sun 10am to 5pm. 4 DM. ☎ 0 92 74/3 30.

Kulmbach: Plassenburg – Open Tues to Sun 10am to 5pm. Closed 1 Jan, 24, 25 and 31 Dec. 4 DM. ☎ 0 92 21/9 58 80.

Kulmbach: Deutsches Zinnfigurenmuseum – Open daily 10am to 5pm. Closed 24 and 31 Dec. 4 DM. ☎ 0 92 21/9 58 80.

BERCHTESGADEN 🛈 Königsseer Straße 2 - 83471 ☎ 0 86 52/96 70 – Fax 0 86 52/6 33 00

Schloß – Guided tours (50min) Easter to Sept daily (except Sat) 10am to 1pm and 2pm to 5pm; Oct to Easter, open Mon to Fri 10am to 1pm and 2pm to 5pm. 7 DM. ☎ 0 86 52/20 85.

Salzbergwerk – Guided tours (1hr) May to mid-Oct daily 9am to 5pm; mid-Oct to Apr Mon to Sat 12.30pm to 3.30pm. Closed Shrove Tues, Good Fri, Whit Mon, 24 and 31 Dec. 21 DM. ☎ 0 86 52/60 02 60.

Excursions

Obersalzberg and the Kehlstein – Bus connection between Obersalzberg and Kehlstein from May to mid-Oct daily 7.40am to 4pm (last departure for Kehlstein). Journey time: about 1hr. 20 DM for bus and lift. ☎ 0 86 52/96 70.

Königssee – Boat trips (round trip of about 1hr 45min) July and Aug daily 7.45am to 5.30pm; May, June and Sept daily 8.30am to 4.15pm; Jan to Apr and Oct to Dec daily 9.45am to 3.30pm. Closed 24 Dec. 18.00-22.50 DM. ☎ 0 86 52/96 36 18.

Roßfeld-Höhenringstraße – Toll: 10 DM per car. ☎ 0 86 52/96 70.

Lorsch: Torhalle – Guided tours (1hr) Tues to Sun 10am to 5pm. Reserve in advance. 6 DM. ☎ 0 62 51/59 67 73.

Bensheim-Auerbach: Auerbacher Schloß – Open 10am to 6pm. Admission free. ☎ 0 62 51/7 29 23.

BERLIN 🚇 Europa-Center, Budapester Straße - 10787 ☎ 0 30/25 00 25 - Fax 0 30/25 00 24 24

Friedenswerdersche Kirche – Open Tues to Sun 10am to 6pm. 4 DM. ☎ 0 30/2 08 13 23.

Berliner Dom – ♿ Open Apr to Sept Mon to Sat 9am to 8pm, Sun noon to 8pm; Oct to Mar Mon to Sat 9am to 7pm, Sun noon to 7pm. 5 DM (admission free on religious festivals). ☎ 0 30/20 26 91 36.

Knoblauchhaus – Open Tues to Sun 10am to 6pm. Closed 24 and 31 Dec. 4 DM (admission free on Wed). ☎ 0 30/24 00 20.

Ephraim-Palais – Open Tues to Sun 10am to 6pm. Closed 24 and 31 Dec. 5 DM (admission free on Wed). ☎ 0 30/24 00 20.

Nikolaikirche: Permanent Exhibition from the Märkisches Museum – Open Tues to Sun 10am to 6pm (last admission 30min before closing). Closed 24 and 31 Dec. 5 DM (admission free on Wed). ☎ 0 30/24 00 20.

Pergamonmuseum – Open Tues to Sun 10am to 6pm. 8 DM. ☎ 0 30/24 00 20.

Antikensammlung – Same admission times and charges as Pergamonmuseum.

Vorderasiatisches Museum – Same admission times and charges as Pergamonmuseum.

Museum für Islamische Kunst – Open Tues to Fri 9am to 5pm, weekends and public holidays 10am to 5pm. Closed 1 Jan, Easter Tues, Whit Tues, 1 May, 24, 25 and 31 Dec. 8 DM.

Alte Nationalgalerie – Closed for refurbishment until 2001. ☎ 0 30/20 90 55 55.

Bode-Museum – Currently closed for renovation. ☎ 0 30/20 90 55 55.

Altes Museum – Open Tues to Sun 10am to 6pm. 8 DM. ☎ 0 30/20 90 50.

Siegessäule – Open Apr to Sept 9.30am to 7pm; Oct to Mar 9.30am to 5pm. Closed 24 and 31 Dec. 2 DM. ☎ 0 30/3 91 29 61.

Zoologischer Garten – Open 28 Mar to 26 Sept daily 9am to 6.30pm; 27 Sept to 31 Dec daily 9am to 5pm; 1 Jan to 27 Mar 9am to 5.30pm. 13 DM (21 DM for the zoo and aquarium). ☎ 0 30/25 40 10.

Aquarium – Open daily 9am to 6pm. 13 DM. ☎ 0 30/25 40 10.

Gemäldegalerie (Kulturforum) – Open Tues to Sun 10am to 6pm. 4 DM. ☎ 0 30/2 66 20 01.

Kunstgewerbemuseum (Kulturforum) – ♿ Open Tues to Fri 10am to 6pm, weekends 11am to 6pm. Closed 24 and 25 Dec. 4 DM (admission free on 1st Sun of month). ☎ 0 30/2 66 29 02.

Kupferstichkabinett – Open Tues to Fri 10am to 6pm, weekends 11am to 6pm. 4 DM. ☎ 0 30/2 66 20 01.

Neue Nationalgalerie – Open Tues to Fri 10am to 6pm, weekends 11am to 6pm. 8 DM. ☎ 0 30/2 66 26 51.

Philharmonie – ♿ Guided tours (1hr) daily at 1.30pm. ☎ 0 30/25 48 80.

Musikinstrumenten-Museum – Open Tues to Fri 9am to 5pm, weekends 10am to 5pm. 4 DM (admission free on 1st Sun of month). ☎ 0 30/25 48 11 78.

Gedenkstätte Deutscher Widerstand – Open Mon to Fri 9am to 6pm, weekends 9am to 1pm. Admission free. ☎ 0 30/26 99 50 00.

Kaiser-Wilhelm-Gedächtniskirche – Open daily 9am to 7pm. ☎ 0 30/2 18 50 23.

Schloß Charlottenburg – Open Tues to Fri 9am to 5pm, weekends 10am to 5pm. 8 DM. ☎ 0 30/32 09 12 75.

Royal Apartments – Guided tours (50min) Tues to Fri 9am to 5pm, weekends 10am to 5pm (last tour at 4pm). 8 DM. ☎ 0 30/32 09 12 75.

Gallery of Romanticism – Open Tues to Fri 10am to 6pm, weekends 11am to 6pm. 4 DM. ☎ 0 30/32 09 12 02.

Museum of Pre- and Proto-History – Open Tues to Fri 10am to 6pm, weekends 11am to 6pm. 4 DM. ☎ 0 30/32 09 11.

Sammlung Berggruen: Picasso and his age – Open Tues to Fri 10am to 6pm, weekends 11am to 6pm. 8 DM. ☎ 0 30/20 90 55 66.

Ägyptisches Museum – Open Tues to Fri 10am to 6pm, weekends 11am to 6pm. 4 DM (admission free on 1st Sun of month). ☎ 0 30/32 09 12 61.

Bröhan-Museum – ♿ Open Tues to Sun 10am to 6pm. Closed 24 and 31 Dec. 6 DM. ☎ 0 30/3 21 40 29.

Dahlem Museums

Museum für Völkerkunde – Open Tues to Fri 10am to 6pm, weekends 11am to 6pm. Closed 1 Jan, 24, 25 and 31 Dec. 4 DM (admission free on 1st Sun of month). ☎ 0 30/8 30 14 38.

Museum für Indische Kunst – Open Tues to Fri 9am to 5pm, weekends 10am to 5pm. Closed 1 Jan, Easter Tues, Whit Tues, 1 May, 24, 25 and 31 Dec. 4 DM. ☎ 0 30/8 30 13 61.

Museum für Ostasiatische Kunst – Open Tues to Fri 9am to 5pm, weekends 10am to 5pm. Opening hours on public holidays are the same as they would be for the equivalent normal day. Closed 1 Jan, Easter Tues, Whit Tues, 1 May, 24, 25 and 31 Dec. 8 DM (ticket allows admission to all municipal museums on day of purchase). ☎ 0 30/8 30 13 81.

Museum europäischer Kulturen – Exact details of opening hours not available at the time of going to press. Telephone to enquire. ☎ 0 30/83 90 12 95.

Museum für Post und Kommunikation – Guided tours (1hr) every Wed at 2pm. Admission free. ☎ 0 30/75 01 68 77.

Deutsches Technikmuseum Berlin – ♿ Open Tues to Fri 9am to 5.30pm, weekends 10am to 6pm. Closed 1 May, 24, 25 and 31 Dec. 5 DM. ☎ 0 30/25 48 40.

Hamburger Bahnhof: Museum für Gegenwart Berlin – Open Tues to Fri 10am to 6pm, weekends 11am to 6pm. 8 DM. ☎ 0 30/3 97 83 40.

Käthe-Kollwitz-Museum – Open daily (except Tues) 11am to 6pm. Closed 24 and 31 Dec. 8 DM. ☎ 0 30/8 82 52 10.

Martin-Gropius-Bau – ☎ 0 30/25 48 60.

Topographie des Terrors – ♿ Open May to Sept daily 10am to 8pm; rest of the year 10am to 6pm. Admission free. ☎ 0 30/25 48 67 03.

Museum Haus am Checkpoint Charlie – Open daily 9am to 10pm. 8 DM. ☎ 0 30/2 53 72 50.

Märkisches Museum – Open Tues to Sun 10am to 6pm (last admission 30min before closing). Closed 24 and 31 Dec. 8 DM (admission free on Wed). ☎ 0 30/30 86 60.

Botanischer Garten Berlin-Dahlem

Botanischer Garten – ♿ Open May to July daily 9am to 9pm; Apr and Aug and September 9am to 8pm; Sept 9am to 7pm; Mar and Oct 9am to 6pm; Feb 9am to 5pm, Nov to Jan 9am to 4pm. Closed 24 and 31 Dec. 6 DM. ☎ 0 30/83 00 61 27.

R. März/Brücke-Museum

Berlin Street Scene by Ernst Ludwig Kirchner. in the Brücke-Museum

Botanisches Museum – ♿ Open Tues to Sun 10am to 5pm. Closed 24 and 31 Dec. Admission free. ☎ 0 30/83 00 61 27.

Brücke-Museum – ♿ Open daily (except Tues) 11am to 5pm. Closed 24 and 31 Dec. 7 DM. ☎ 0 30/8 31 20 29.

Jagdschloß Grunewald – Open May to Oct Tues to Sun 10am to 5pm; Nov to Apr weekends 10am to 4pm. 4 DM. ☎ 03 31/9 69 42 02.

Pfaueninsel: Schloß – Guided tours (30min) Apr to Oct daily (except Mon) 10am to 5pm. 4 DM. ☎ 03 31/9 69 42 02.

Funkturm – Open daily 10am to 11pm (Mon 11am to 9pm). If temperatures drop below freezing, the viewing platform is closed. 6 DM. ☎ 0 30/30 38 19 05.

Olympiastadion – Open Apr to Sept daily 8am to 8pm; Oct to Mar daily 8am to 4pm. Since the stadium is frequently closed for setting up or dismantling exhibitions, visitors are advised to telephone in advance. 2 DM. ☎ 0 30/30 06 33.

Bauhaus-Archiv, Museum für Gestaltung – ₺ Open daily (except Tues) 10am to 5pm. Closed 1 Jan and 25 Dec (1pm to 5pm). 5 DM. ☎ 0 30/2 54 00 20.

Maria Regina Martyrum – Open Mon to Fri 9am to 4pm, Sat 9am to 6pm, Sun and public holidays 9am to noon. If the church is locked, ask for the key at the abbey door. ☎ 0 30/3 82 60 11.

Gedenkstätte Plötzensee – ₺ Open Mar to Oct 9am to 5pm; Nov to Feb 9am to 4pm. Closed 1 Jan, 24, 25, 26 and 31 Dec. Admission free. ☎ 0 30/26 99 50 00.

Schloß Tegel (Humboldtschloß) – Guided tours (45min) May to Sept Mon 10am to noon and 3pm to 5pm. Closed on public holidays. 12 DM. ☎ 0 30/4 34 31 56.

Stadtgeschichtliches Museum Spandau – Open Tues to Fri 9am to 5pm, weekends 10am to 5pm. Closed 1 Jan, 1 May, 3 Oct, 24, 25 and 31 Dec. 4 DM. ☎ 0 30/3 54 94 42 97.

St.-Nikolai-Kirche – Open Tues, Fri, Sun and public holidays 3pm to 6pm, Sat 1pm to 6pm. Closed at Easter, Whitsun and Christmas. ☎ 0 30/3 33 80 54.

Excursion

Oranienburg: Gedenkstätte und Museum Sachsenhausen – ₺ Open Apr to Sept Tues to Sun 8.30am to 6pm; Oct to Mar Tues to Sun 8.30am to 4.30pm (last admission 30min before closing). Admission free. ☎ 0 33 01/80 37 19.

BERNKASTEL-KUES
🛈 Gestade 5 - 54470 ☎ 0 65 31/40 23 - Fax 0 65 31/79 53

St. Nikolaus-Hospital – Open Mon to Fri 9am to 6pm, weekends 9am to noon. Admission free. Guided tours of library on Tues at 10.30am and Fri at 3pm. 5 DM. ☎ 0 65 31/22 60.

BODENSEE

Zeppelin-Museum – Open May to Oct Tues to Sun 10am to 6pm; Nov to Apr Tues to Sun 10am to 5pm. Closed 1 Jan, 24 and 25 Dec. 12 DM. ☎ 0 75 41/38 01 33.

BONN
🛈 Münsterstraße 20 - 53111 ☎ 02 28/77 34 66 - Fax 02 28/69 03 68

Beethovenhaus – Open Apr to Sept Mon to Sat 10am to 6pm, Sun 11am to 4pm; Oct to Mar Mon to Sat 10am to 5pm, Sun 11am to 4pm (last admission 30min before closing). Closed 1 Jan, Mon before Shrove Tues, Good Fri, Easter Day, 24, 25 and 26 Dec. 8 DM. ☎ 02 28/9 81 75 25.

Haus der Geschichte der Bundesrepublik Deutschland – Open Tues to Sun 9am to 7pm. Admission free. ☎ 02 28/9 16 54 00.

Kunstmuseum Bonn – ₺ Open Tues to Sun 10am to 6pm, Wed 10am to 9pm. Closed during Carnival period (Thur, Sun and Mon before Shrove Tues), 24, 25 and 31 Dec. 5 DM. ☎ 02 28/77 62 60.

Kunst- und Ausstellungshalle der Bundesrepublik Deutschland – Open Tues and Wed 10am to 9pm, Thur to Sun 10am to 7pm. Closed 24, 25 and 31 Dec. 8 DM. ☎ 02 28/9 17 12 00.

Deutsches Museum Bonn – ₺ Open Tues to Sun 10am to 6pm. Closed during Carnival period (Thur before Shrove Tues and Shrove Tues), Good Fri, 1 May, 24, 25 and 31 Dec. 7 DM. ☎ 02 28/30 22 55.

Godesburg castle – Open Apr to mid-Oct Wed to Sun 10am to 6pm. 1 DM. ☎ 02 28/31 60 71.

Excursions

Funicular to Drachenfels ruins – Operates May to Sept 9am to 8pm every half hour; Jan, Feb and Nov departures depending on demand Mon to Fri noon to 5pm, weekends 11am to 6pm (hourly); Mar and Oct 10am to 6pm (every half hour); Apr 10am to 7pm (every half hour). Return fare: 13 DM. ☎ 0 22 23/9 20 90.

Remagen: Friedensmuseum – Open May to Oct daily 10am to 6pm; early Mar to Apr and first fortnight of Nov daily 10am to 5pm. 2.50 DM. ☎ 0 26 42/2 18 63.

BRAUNSCHWEIG
🛈 Lander Hof 6 - 38100 ☎ 05 31/27 35 50 - Fax 05 31/2 73 55 19

Herzog-Anton-Ulrich-Museum – ₺ Open Tues to Sun 10am to 5pm, Wed 1pm to 8pm. Closed Easter Day, 1 May, Whit Sun, 24, 25 and 31 Dec. 5 DM. ☎ 05 31/4 84 24 00.

Medieval Art Collection in the Burg Dankwarderode – Open Tues to Sun 10am to 5pm, Wed 1pm to 8pm. Closed Easter Day, 1 May, Whit Sun, 24 and 25 Dec. 5 DM. ☎ 05 31/4 84 24 00.

🚇 Am Bahnhofsplatz - 28195 ☎ 04 21/30 80 00 - Fax 04 21/3 08 00 30

Bremen museums pass – This pass covers entrance to six of Bremen's main cultural sights (Bremer Landesmuseum, Kunsthalle, Gerhard-Marcks-Haus, Kunstsammlungen Böttcherstraße, Neues Museum Weserburg, Übersee-Museum). The pass costs 18 DM and is valid for three successive days, allowing access to the museums as often and for as long as ticket holders choose.

Boat trip round the port – Embarcation from the quay by the St. Martinikirche. Duration of trip: 1hr 15min. Departures Apr to late Oct daily at 11.45am, 1.30pm and 3.15pm. 13 DM. ☎ 0 18 05/10 30 30.

Rathaus – Guided tours (45min) Mon to Sat at 11am, noon, 3pm and 4pm, Sun at 11am and noon. 5 DM. ☎ 0 18 05/10 10 30.

Paula Modersohn-Becker Museum – Open Tues to Sun 11am to 6pm. Closed Good Fri, 24 and 31 Dec. 8 DM. ☎ 04 21/3 36 50 77.

St. Martinikirche – ♿ Open Apr to Sept Mon to Sat 10.30am to 12.30pm; Oct to Mar Tues 3pm to 5pm, Thur 10am to noon. Admission free. ☎ 04 21/32 48 35.

Kunsthalle – ♿ Open Tues 10am to 9pm, Wed to Sun 10am to 5pm. 8 DM. ☎ 04 21/32 90 80.

Übersee-Museum – ♿ Open Tues to Sun 10am to 6pm. Closed Good Fri, Easter Mon, 1 May, Whit Mon, 3 Oct, 24, 25 and 31 Dec. 6 DM. ☎ 04 21/3 61 97 51.

Focke-Museum – ♿ Open Tues 2pm to 10pm, Wed to Sun 10am to 6pm. Closed 1 Jan, Good Fri, Easter Day, 1 May, Ascension, Whit Sun, 3 Oct. 6 DM. ☎ 04 21/3 61 34 55.

🚇 Columbus-Center, Obere Bürger 17 - 27568 ☎ 04 71/4 30 00 - Fax 04 71/4 30 80

Deutsches Schiffahrtsmuseum – Open Apr to Oct daily 10am to 6pm; Nov to Mar Tues to Sun 10am to 6pm. Closed 24, 25 and 31 Dec. 6 DM including Freilichtmuseum. ☎ 04 71/48 20 70.

Freilichtmuseum – Open Apr to Oct daily 10am to 6pm. 6 DM including Deutsches Schiffahrtsmuseum. ☎ 04 71/48 20 70.

Technikmuseum U-Boot Wilhelm Bauer – Open Apr to Oct daily 10am to 5.30pm. 4 DM. ☎ 04 71/4 82 07 52.

Zoo am Meer – ♿ Open May to Sept daily 8am to 7pm; Nov to Mar 8am to 5pm; Apr and Oct 8am to 4.30pm (last admissions 30min before closing). 4 DM. ☎ 04 71/4 20 71.

Excursion

Cuxhaven: Wrackmuseum – Open mid-Mar to late Oct Tues to Fri 9am to 1pm and 3pm to 6pm, weekends 10am to 1pm and 3pm to 6pm. 4.50 DM. ☎ 0 47 21/2 33 41.

🚇 Am alten Schloß 2 - 76646 ☎ 0 72 51/7 27 71 - Fax 0 72 51/7 27 71

Schloß – ♿ Open Tues to Sun 9am to 5pm. Closed 1 Jan (am), Shrove Tues, 24, 25 and 31 Dec. 5 DM. ☎ 0 72 51/74 26 61.

Museum Mechanischer Musikinstrumente – ♿ Guided tours (1hr) Tues 10am to 5pm, Wed to Sun 9.30am to 5pm. Closed 1 Jan (am), Shrove Tues, 24, 25 and 31 Dec. 7 DM. ☎ 0 72 51/74 26 61.

Städtisches Museum – Open Tues to Fri 1pm to 5pm, weekends 9am to 1pm and 2pm to 5pm. Closed Shrove Tues, 24, 25 and 31 Dec. Admission free. ☎ 0 72 51/7 92 53.

🚇 Uhlstraße 3 - 50321 ☎ 0 22 32/7 93 45 - Fax 0 22 32/7 93 46

Schloß Augustusburg – Guided tours (1hr) Feb to Nov Tues to Sun 9am to noon and 1.30pm to 4pm. 6 DM. ☎ 0 22 32/4 40 00.

Schloß Falkenlust – Open Feb to Nov Tues to Sun 9am to 12.30pm and 1.30pm to 4.30pm. 4.50 DM. ☎ 0 22 32/1 21 11.

Phantasialand – Open Apr to late Oct daily 9am to 6pm (9am to 8pm in July). Day ticket: 36 DM. ☎ 0 22 32/3 62 00

🚇 Marktplatz 4 - 31675 ☎ 0 57 22/20 61 81 - Fax 0 57 22/20 62 10

Schloß Bückeburg – Guided tours (45min) Apr to Sept daily 9.30am to 6pm; Oct to Mar daily 9.30am to 5pm. Closed 1 Jan, 24, 25, 26 and 31 Dec. 8 DM. ☎ 0 57 22/50 39.

Hubschraubermuseum – ♿ Open daily 9am to 5pm. 6 DM. ☎ 0 57 22/55 33.

Excursion

Kleinenbremen: Besucherbergwerk – Guided tours (1hr 30min) Apr to late Oct on Tues and Fri to Sun 10am to 4pm (by prior appointment only on Tues and Fri). 12 DM. ☎ 05 71/9 34 44 38.

BURGHAUSEN 🛈 Rathaus, Stadtplatz 112 - 84489 ☎ 0 86 77/24 35 - Fax 08677/887155

Burg – Open Apr to Oct daily 9am to 5.30pm; Nov to Mar daily 10am to 4.30pm (last admission 30min before closing). Closed 1 Jan, Shrove Tues, 1 Nov, 24, 25 and 31 Dec. 4 DM. ☎ 0 86 77/46 59.

C

CELLE 🛈 Markt 6 - 29221 ☎ 0 51 41/12 12 - Fax 0 51 41/1 24 59

Schloß – Guided tours (1hr) Apr to Oct Tues to Sun at 10am, 11am, noon, 1pm, 2pm, 3pm and 4pm; Nov to Mar Tues to Sun at 11am and 3pm. 5 DM. Telephone bookings in advance. ☎ 0 51 41/1 23 73.

Bomann-Museum – ♿ Open Tues to Sun 10am to 5pm. Closed 1 Jan, 24, 25 and 31 Dec. 4 DM. ☎ 0 51 41/1 23 72.

Excursion

Kloster Wienhausen – ♿ Guided tours (1hr 15min) Apr to Oct Mon to Sat and on public holidays not linked with a religious festival at 10am, 11am, 2pm, 3pm, 4pm and 5pm; on Sun and religious holidays tours every hour from noon to 5pm. During the 1st fortnight in Oct the last tour leaves at 4pm. Closed Tues to Thur before Whitsun and before Michaelmas (29 Sept), also the Thur after Whitsun. 7 DM. ☎ 0 51 49/3 59.

CHEMNITZ 🛈 Stadthalle, Rathausstraße 1 - 09111 ☎ 03 71/1 94 33 - Fax 03 71/4 50 87 25

Museum für Naturkunde – ♿ Open Tues to Fri 9am to noon and 2pm to 5pm (Wed until 7.30pm), weekends 11am to 5pm. 4 DM. ☎ 03 71/4 88 45 51.

Kunstsammlung Chemnitz – Open Tues to Sun 11am to 5pm (Wed until 7.30pm). Closed 24 and 31 Dec. 4 DM. ☎ 03 71/4 88 44 24.

Excursion

Schloß Augustusburg

Museum für Jagdtier und Vogelkunde – Open Apr to Oct daily 10am to 6pm; Nov to Mar daily 10am to 5pm. Closed 24 and 25 Dec. 5 DM. ☎ 03 72 91/38 00.

Motorradmuseum – Open Apr to Oct daily 10am to 6pm; Nov to Mar daily 10am to 5pm (last admission 30min before closing). Closed 24 and 25 Dec. 5 DM. ☎ 03 72 91/38 00.

CHIEMSEE

Prien-Stock landing stage – Boat trips all year round. 15min trip to Herreninsel, Return fare 10 DM; 30min trip to Fraueninsel, Return fare 12.50 DM; longer round trip 17.50 DM. ☎ 0 80 51/60 90.

Schloß Herrenchiemsee – Guided tours (35min) Apr to Sept daily 9am to 5pm; Oct to Mar 9.30am to 4pm. Closed 1 Jan, Shrove Tues, 1 Nov, 24, 25 and 31 Dec. 8 DM. ☎ 0 80 51/30 69.

Kloster CHORIN

Ehemaliges Kloster – ♿ Open Apr to Oct daily 9am to 6pm; Nov to Mar 9am to 4pm. 3.50 DM. ☎ 03 33 66/7 03 77.

Excursion

Schiffshebewerk Niederfinow – Operates daily 9am to 4pm (until 7pm in summer). 2 DM. ☎ 03 33 36/22 15.

COBURG 🛈 Herrngasse 4 - 96450 ☎ 0 95 61/7 41 80 - 0 95 61/74 18 29

Kunstsammlungen – Open Apr to Oct Tues to Sun 10am to 5pm; Nov to Mar Tues to Sun 1pm to 4pm. Closed 24, 25 and 31 Dec. 6 DM. ☎ 0 95 61/8 79 79.

Schloß Ehrenburg – Guided tours (1hr) Tues to Sun at 10am, 11am, 1.30pm, 2.30pm, 3.30pm and (in summer only) 4.30pm. Closed 1 Jan, Shrove Tues, 1 Nov 24, 25 and 31 Dec. 5 DM. ☎ 0 95 61/8 08 80.

Excursion

Schloß Callenberg – Guided tours (1hr) Apr to Oct daily 10am to noon and 2pm to 4pm; Nov to Mar Tues to Sun 2pm to 4pm. Closed 7 to 31 Jan, 24 and 31 Dec. 5 DM. ☎ 0 95 61/5 51 50.

Schloß Rosenau – Guided tours (40min) Tues to Sun at 10am, 10.45am, 11.30am, 1.30pm, 2.15pm, 3pm, 3.45pm and (in summer only) 4.30pm. Closed 1 Jan, Shrove Tues, 1 Nov, 24, 25 and 31 Dec. 4 DM. ☎ 0 95 63/47 47.

COTTBUS 🛈 Karl-Marx-Straße 68 - 03044 ☎ 03 55/2 42 55 - Fax 03 55/79 19 31

Schloß Branitz – Open Apr to Oct daily 10am to 6pm; Nov to Mar Tues to Sun 10am to 5pm. 5 DM. ☎ 03 55/7 51 50.

Niederlausitzer Apothekenmuseum – Guided tours (1hr) Tues to Fri at 11am and 2pm, weekends at 2pm and 3pm. 4 DM. ☎ 03 55/2 39 97.

Wendisches Museum – Open Tues to Fri 8.30am to 5pm, weekends 2pm to 6pm. Closed 24 and 31 Dec. 4 DM. ☎ 03 55/79 49 30.

Oberkirche St. Nikolai – Open Mon to Sat 10am to 5pm, Sun 1pm to 5pm. Admission free, but donations welcome. To climb the church tower: 2 DM. ☎ 03 55/2 47 63.

Excursion

Altes Schloß Bad Muskau – Open May to Sept Tues to Fri 10am to noon and 1pm to 4pm; Oct to Apr Tues to Fri 10am to noon and 1pm to 4pm, Sun 1pm to 4pm. 3 DM. ☎ 03 57 71/6 03 52.

D

DARMSTADT 🛈 Luisen-Center, Luisenplatz 5 - 64283 ☎ 06151/132781 - Fax 06151/20228

Hessisches Landesmuseum – Open Tues to Sat 10am to 5pm (Wed until 9pm), Sun 11am to 5pm. Closed Shrove Tues, Good Fri, Easter Day, 24, 25 and 31 Dec. 5 DM. ☎ 0 61 51/16 57 03.

Schloß – Guided tours (1hr) Mon to Thur 10am to 1pm and 2pm to 5pm, weekends 10am to 1pm. Closed 1 Jan, Shrove Tues, Easter Day, Whit Sun, 1 May, 3 Oct, 25 and 31 Dec. 3.50 DM. ☎ 0 61 51/2 40 35.

Prinz-Georg-Palais – ☎ 0 61 51/78 14 14.

Jagdschloß Kranichstein – Open Wed to Fri from 10am to noon and 2.30pm to 6pm, weekends 2.30pm to 6pm. Closed over New Year period. 5 DM. ☎ 0 61 51/71 86 13.

DESSAU 🛈 Zerbster Straße 2c - 06844 ☎ 03 40/2 04 14 42 - Fax 03 40/2 04 11 42

Bauhausgebäude – Open Tues to Sun 10am to 5pm (May to Oct Sat until 8pm). 5 DM. ☎ 03 40/6 50 82 51.

Feiningerhaus – Open Tues to Fri 10am to 5pm, weekends noon to 5pm. 5 DM. ☎ 03 40/61 95 95.

Anhaltische Gemäldegalerie (Georgium) – Open Tues to Sun 10am to 5pm. Closed 24 and 31 Dec. 5 DM (admission free on 1st Fri in month). ☎ 03 40/61 38 74.

Excursions

Luisium – Open Apr to Oct Tues to Sun 10am to 6pm; Nov to Mar Tues to Sun 11am to 4.30pm. Closed 24, 25 and 31 Dec. 8 DM. ☎ 03 40/2 18 37 11.

Schloß Mosigkau – Guided tours (1hr) May to Sept Tues to Sun 10am to 6pm; Apr and Oct Tues to Sun 10am to 4.30pm; Nov to Mar Tues to Sun 10am to 4pm. 6 DM. ☎ 03 40/6 46 15 41.

R. Chéret/MICHELIN

Schloß Mosigkau, Dessau

DETMOLD
🇩 Rathaus, Lange Straße - 32754 ☎ 0 52 31/97 73 27 - Fax 0 52 31/97 74 47

Residenzschloß – Guided tours (40min) Apr to Oct daily at 10am, 11am, noon, 2pm, 3pm, 4pm and 5pm; Nov to Mar at 10am, 11am, noon, 2pm, 3pm and 4pm. 6 DM. ☎ 0 52 31/7 00 20.

Westfälisches Freilichtmuseum – Open Apr to Oct Tues to Sun 9am to 6pm. 7 DM. ☎ 0 52 31/70 61 04.

Hermannsdenkmal – Open Mar to Oct daily 9am to 6.30pm; Nov to Feb daily 9.30am to 4pm. 2.50 DM. ☎ 0 52 61/2 50 20.

Excursion

Externsteine – Site accessible all year round. Low relief of the Descent from the Cross can be viewed Apr to Oct daily 9am to 7pm. 2 DM. ☎ 0 52 34/20 12 62.

Bad DOBERAN
🇩 Goethestraße 1 - 18209 ☎ 03 82 03/6 21 54 - Fax 03 82 03/6 21 54

Cathedral – ♿ Open May to Sept Mon to Sat 9am to 6pm, Sun noon to 6pm; Oct, Mar and Apr Mon to Sat 9am to 4.30pm, Sun noon to 4.30pm; Nov to Feb Tues to Fri 9am to noon and 2pm to 4pm, Sat 9am to 4pm, Sun noon to 4pm. 2 DM. ☎ 03 82 03/6 27 16.

DONAUESCHINGEN
🇩 Karlstraße 58 - 78166 ☎ 07 71/85 72 21 - Fax 0771/85 72 28

Fürstenberg-Sammlungen – Open Tues to Sun 9am to noon and 1.30pm to 5pm. 5 DM. ☎ 07 71/8 65 63.

Schloß – Guided tours (40min) Easter to Sept daily (except Tues) 9am to noon and 2pm to 5pm. 5 DM. ☎ 07 71/8 65 09.

DORTMUND
🇩 Am Hauptbahnhof - 44137 ☎ 02 31/5 02 56 66 - Fax 02 31/16 35 93

Westfalenpark – Open daily 9am to 9pm (automatic ticket entry). 2.50 DM. ☎ 02 31/5 02 61 00.

Marienkirche – Open Tues to Fri 10am to noon and 2pm to 4pm, Sat 10am to 1pm. ☎ 02 31/52 65 48.

Brauerei-Museum – Open Tues to Sun 10am to 6pm. Closed 1 Jan, 1 May, 24, 25 and 31 Dec. Admission free. ☎ 02 31/5 02 48 50.

Museum für Kunst und Kulturgeschichte – ♿ Open Tues to Sun 10am to 5pm. Closed 1 Jan, Easter Mon, 1 May, Whit Mon, 24, 25 and 31 Dec. 4 DM. ☎ 02 31/5 02 55 22.

Museum am Ostwall – ♿ Open Tues to Sun 10am to 5pm (Wed until 8pm). Closed 1 Jan, Easter and Whit Mon, 1 May, 24, 25 and 31 Dec. 4 DM. ☎ 02 31/5 02 32 47.

DRESDEN
🇩 Prager Str. 10 - 01069 ☎ 03 51/49 19 20 - Fax 03 51/49 19 20

Day-ticket for all Dresden museums (Staatliche Kunstsammlungen): 10 DM.

Zwinger

Gemäldegalerie Alter Meister – ♿ Open Tues to Sun 10am to 6pm. 7 DM. ☎ 03 51/4 91 46 19.

Rüstkammer – Open Tues to Sun 10am to 6pm. 3 DM. ☎ 03 51/4 91 46 19.

Porzellansammlung – Open daily (except Thur) 10am to 6pm. 5 DM. ☎ 03 51/4 91 46 19.

Mathematisch-Physikalischer Salon – Open daily (except Thur) 10am to 6pm. 3 DM. ☎ 03 51/4 91 46 19.

Diana's Bath (1704), Grünes Gewölbe

DRESDEN

Albertinum

Gemäldegalerie Neuer Meister – Open daily (except Thur) 10am to 6pm. 7 DM. ☎ 03 51/4 91 46 19.

Grünes Gewölbe – Open daily (except Thur) 10am to 6pm. 7 DM. ☎ 03 51/4 91 46 19.

Stadtmuseum – Open daily (except Fri) 10am to 6pm. 4 DM. ☎ 03 51/49 86 60.

Museum für Sächsische Volkskunst – Open Tues to Sun 10am to 6pm. 3 DM. ☎ 03 51/4 91 46 19.

Deutsches Hygiene-Museum – ♿ Open Tues, Thur and Fri 9am to 5pm, Wed 9am to 8.30pm, weekends 10am to 5pm. 5 DM. ☎ 03 51/4 84 66 70.

Excursions

Schloß Moritzburg – Open Apr to Oct daily 9am to 5.30pm (last admission 30min before closing). The rest of the year tours only: Nov to Mar Tues to Sun at 10am, 11am, 1pm, 2pm, 3pm and 4pm; in Jan at weekends only. Closed 24 and 31 Dec. 7 DM. ☎ 03 52 07/87 30.

Schloß Pillnitz – The Bergpalais (Decorative Arts Museum) is open May to Oct Tues to Sun 9.30am to 5.30pm, and the Wasserpalais May to Oct daily (except Tues) 9.30am to 5.30pm. 3 DM. ☎ 03 51/4 91 46 19.

DÜSSELDORF   🛈 Immermannstraße 65b - 40210 ☎ 02 11/17 20 20 - Fax 02 11/16 10 71

Kunstmuseum – ♿ Open Tues to Sun 11am to 6pm. Closed 24 and 31 Dec. 5 DM. ☎ 02 11/8 99 24 60.

Kunstsammlung Nordrhein-Westfalen – ♿ Open Tues to Thur and weekends 10am to 6pm, Fri 10am to 8pm. 12 DM. ☎ 02 11/8 38 10.

Hetjens-Museum/Deutsches Keramikmuseum – ♿ Open Tues to Sun 11am to 5pm (Wed 11am to 9pm). 6 DM. ☎ 02 11/8 99 42 10.

Löbbecke-Museum und Aquazoo – ♿ Open daily 10am to 6pm. Closed 1 Jan, Mon before Shrove Tues, 1 May, 24, 25 and 31 Dec. 10 DM. ☎ 02 11/8 99 61 50.

Excursions

Benrath: Schloß – Guided tours (1hr) Apr to Oct Tues to Sun 10am to 5pm; Nov to Mar Tues to Sun 11am to 5pm. 7 DM. ☎ 02 11/8 99 72 71.

Neanderthal Museum – ♿ Open Tues to Sun 10am to 6pm, also open Easter and Whit Mon. Closed 24 Dec. 10 DM. ☎ 0 21 04/97 97 97.

E

Kloster EBERBACH

Tours – Apr to Oct daily 10am to 6pm; Nov to Mar Mon to Fri 10am to 4pm, weekends 11am to 4pm. 5 DM. ☎ 0 67 23/9 17 80.

EICHSTÄTT   🛈 Kardinal-Preysing-Platz 14 - 85072 ☎ 0 84 21/9 88 00 - Fax 0 84 21/98 80 30

Diözesanmuseum – Open Apr to Oct Wed to Sun 10am to 5pm. Closed Good Fri. ☎ 0 84 21/5 02 66.

Fürstbischöfliche Residenz – Guided tours (20min) Thur at 11am and 3pm, Fri at 11am, weekends at 10am, 10.30am, 11am, 11.30am, 2pm, 2.30pm, 3pm and 3.30pm. Admission free. ☎ 0 84 21/7 00.

Jura-Museum – ♿ Open Apr to Sept Tues to Sun 9am to noon and 1pm to 5pm; Oct to Mar Tues to Sun 10am to noon and 1pm to 4pm. Closed 1 Jan, Shrove Tues, 1 Nov, 24, 25 and 31 Dec. 6 DM. ☎ 0 84 21/29 56.

Museum für Ur- und Frühgeschichte – Open Apr to Sept Tues to Sun 9am to noon and 1pm to 5pm; Oct to Mar Tues to Sun 10am to noon and 1pm to 4pm. Closed 1 Jan, Shrove Tues, 1 Nov, 24, 25 and 31 Dec. 6 DM. ☎ 0 84 21/8 94 50.

Excursions

Weißenburg: Römische Thermen – ♿ Open late Mar to 1 Nov Tues to Sun 10am to 12.30pm and 2pm to 5pm. 2 DM. ☎ 0 91 41/90 71 24.

Weißenburg: Römermuseum – Open Mar to Dec Tues to Sun 10am to 12.30pm and 2pm to 5pm. Closed 24, 25 and 31 Dec. 3 DM. ☎ 0 91 41/90 71 24.

Weißenburg: Reichsstadtmuseum – Open Mar to Dec Tues to Sun 10am to 12.30pm and 2pm to 5pm. Closed 24, 25 and 31 Dec. 2 DM. ☎ 0 91 41/90 71 24.

Ellingen: Schloß – Guided tours (50min) Apr to Sept at 10am, 11am, 1pm, 2pm, 3pm and 4pm; Oct to Mar at 10am, 11am, 2pm and 3pm. Closed 1 Jan, Shrove Tues, 1 Nov, 24, 25 and 31 Dec. 5 DM. ☎ 0 91 41/33 27.

EINBECK   🚹 Rathaus, Marktplatz 6 - 37574 ☎ 0 55 61/91 61 21 - Fax 0 55 61/91 63 00

Excursions

Alfeld: Stadtmuseum – Open Tues to Fri 10am to noon and 3pm to 5pm, weekends 10am to noon; May to Sept also open Sun 3pm to 5pm. Closed between Christmas and New Year. Admission free. ☎ 0 51 81/70 31 81.

EISENACH   🚹 Markt 2 - 99817 ☎ 0 36 91/7 92 30 - Fax 0 36 91/79 23 20

Schloß: Thuringian Museum – Open Tues to Sun 9am to 5pm. 5 DM. ☎ 0 36 91/78 46 78.

Lutherhaus – Open May to Oct daily 9am to 5pm; Nov to Apr daily 10am to 5pm. Closed Good Fri. 5 DM. ☎ 0 36 91/2 98 30.

Bachhaus – Open Apr to Sept Mon noon to 5.45pm, Tues to Sun 9am to 5.45pm; Oct to Mar Mon 1pm to 4.45pm, Tues to Sun 9am to 4.45pm. 5 DM. ☎ 0 36 91/7 93 40.

Automobilbaumuseum – Open Tues to Sun 10am to 5pm. 4 DM. ☎ 0 36 91/7 72 12.

Fritz-Reuter- und Richard-Wagner-Museum – Open Tues to Sun 10am to 5pm. 4 DM. ☎ 0 36 91/74 32 93.

Wartburg – Guided tours (1hr) Mar to Oct daily 8.30am to 5pm; Nov to Feb daily 9am to 3.30pm. 11 DM. ☎ 0 36 91/25 00.

EMDEN   🚹 Alter Markt - 26721 ☎ 0 49 21/9 74 00 - Fax 0 49 21/9 74 09

Ostfriesisches Landesmuseum – Open Apr to Sept daily 11am to 5pm; Oct to Mar Tues to Sun 11am to 4pm. 6 DM. ☎ 0 49 21/87 20 57.

Kunsthalle (Stiftung Henri und Eske Nannen) – Open Tues 10am to 8pm, Wed to Fri 10am to 5pm, weekends 11am to 5pm. Closed 1 May, 24, 25 and 31 Dec. 9 DM. ☎ 0 49 21/97 50 50.

ERFURT   🚹 Fischmarkt 27 - 99084 ☎ 03 61/6 64 00 - Fax 03 61/6 64 02 90

Augustinerkloster – Guided tours (45min) Apr to Oct Tues to Sat at 10am, 11am, noon, 2pm, 3pm and 4pm, Sun at 10.45am; Nov to Mar Tues to Sat at 10am, 11am, noon and 2pm, Sun at 10.45am. 5.50 DM. ☎ 03 61/57 66 00.

Angermuseum – Open Tues to Sun 10am to 6pm. 3 DM. ☎ 03 61/5 62 33 11.

Barfüßerkirche – Open Easter to late Oct Tues to Sun 10am to 1pm and 2pm to 6pm. 2 DM. ☎ 03 61/5 62 33 11.

Excursions

Arnstadt: Museum für Stadtgeschichte und Bachgedenkstätte – Open Mon to Fri 8.30am to noon and 1pm to 4.30pm, weekends 9.30am to 4.30pm. Closed 1 Jan, 24 and 31 Dec. 4 DM. ☎ 0 36 28/60 29 78.

Arnstadt: Neues Palais, Mon Plaisir Puppensammlung – Open Apr to Oct Tues to Sun 8.30am to noon and 1pm to 4.30pm; Nov to Mar Tues to Sun 9.30am to 4pm. 3.50 DM. ☎ 0 36 28/60 29 32.

ESSEN   🚹 Am Hauptbahnhof 2 - 45127 ☎ 02 01/1 94 33 - Fax 02 01/8 87 20 44

Design-Zentrum Nordrhein-Westfalen – Open Tues to Sun 11am to 8pm. Closed 24 and 31 Dec. 10 DM. ☎ 02 01/3 01 04 17.

Museum Folkwang – 🕭 Open Tues to Sun 10am to 6pm (Thur until 9pm). Closed 1 Jan, Easter Mon, 1 May, 24 and 31 Dec. 5 DM. ☎ 02 01/8 84 53 14.

Ruhrlandmuseum – Open Tues to Sun 10am to 6pm (Fri until midnight). Closed 1 Jan, 1 May, 24 and 31 Dec. 8 DM. ☎ 02 01/8 84 52 00.

Domschatzkammer – Open Tues to Sat 10am to 5pm, Sun 12.30pm to 5pm. Closed 1 Jan, Good Fri, Easter Day, 1 May, Whit Sun, 1 Nov, 24 to 26 and 31 Dec. 2 DM. ☎ 02 01/2 20 42 06.

Villa Hügel – 🕭 Open mid-Jan to mid-Dec Tues to Sun 10am to 6pm. 1.50 DM. ☎ 02 01/1 88 48 37.

Abtei St. Ludger: Treasury – Open Tues to Sun 10am to noon and 3pm to 5pm. Closed 24 Dec to 1 Jan. 2 DM. ☎ 02 01/49 18 01.

F

🚉 Speicherlinie 40 - 24937 ☎ 04 61/2 30 90 - Fax 04 61/1 73 52

Städtisches Museum – Open Apr to Oct Tues to Sun 10am to 5pm; Nov to Mar Tues to Sun 10am to 4pm. 5 DM. ☎ 04 61/85 29 56.

Excursions

Glücksburg: Wasserschloß – Open Apr to Oct daily 10am to 5pm; Jan to Mar and Nov to Dec, weekends only 10.30am to 4pm. Closed 24 and 31 Dec. 7.50 DM. ☎ 0 46 31/22 43.

FRANKFURT AM MAIN   🚉 Hauptbahnhof - 60329 ☎ 0 69/21 23 88 49 - Fax 0 69/21 24 85 12

Henninger Turm – Open noon to 10pm. 5 DM. ☎ 0 69/6 06 36 01.

Kaisersaal – Open daily 10am to 1pm and 2pm to 5pm. 3 DM. ☎ 0 69/21 23 49 19.

Dommuseum – ♿ Open Tues to Fri 10am to 5pm, weekends 11am to 5pm; also open on Easter and Whit Mon. Closed 1 Jan, Easter Tues, Whit Tues, 24, 25 and 31 Dec. 3 DM. ☎ 0 69/13 37 61 86.

Historisches Museum – ♿ Open Tues to Sun 10am to 5pm (Wed until 8pm). Closed Easter Mon, 1 May, Whit Mon. 8 DM. ☎ 0 69/21 23 55 99.

Museum für Moderne Kunst – ♿ Open Tues to Sun 10am to 5pm (Wed until 8pm). Closed on certain public holidays. 7 DM (admission free on Wed). ☎ 0 69/21 23 04 47.

Goethe-Haus und Frankfurter Goethe-Museum – Open Apr to Sept Mon to Fri 9am to 6pm, weekends 10am to 4pm; Oct to Mar Mon to Fri 9am to 4pm, weekends 10am to 4pm. Closed 1 Jan, Good Fri, 24, 25 and 31 Dec. 7 DM. ☎ 0 69/13 88 00.

Jüdisches Museum – ♿ Open Tues to Sun 10am to 5pm (Wed until 8pm). 5 DM (admission free on Sat). ☎ 0 69/21 23 50 00.

Städelsches Kunstinstitut und Städtische Galerie – Open Tues to Sun 10am to 5pm (Wed until 8pm). 5 DM. ☎ 0 69/6 05 09 80.

Museum für Kunsthandwerk – ♿ Open Tues to Sun 10am to 5pm (Wed until 8pm). 8 DM (admission free on Wed). ☎ 0 69/21 23 40 37.

Deutsches Filmmuseum – ♿ Open Tues, Thur, Fri and Sun 10am to 5pm, Wed 10am to 8pm, Sat 2pm to 8pm. 5 DM (admission free on Wed). ☎ 0 69/21 23 88 30.

Städtische Galerie Liebieghaus – Open Tues to Sun 10am to 5pm (Wed until 8pm). Closed Easter Mon, 1 May, Whit Sun, Corpus Christi, 24, 25 and 31 Dec. 5 DM. ☎ 0 69/21 23 86 17.

Museum für Post und Kommunikation – ♿ Open Tues to Sun 9am to 5pm. Closed 1 Jan, 24 and 31 Dec. Admission free. ☎ 0 69/6 06 00.

Deutsches Architektur-Museum – Open Tues to Sun 10am to 5pm (Wed until 8pm). 8 DM. ☎ 0 69/21 23 88 44.

Museum für Völkerkunde – Open Tues to Sun 10am to 5pm (Wed until 8pm). 6 DM (admission free on Wed). ☎ 0 69/21 23 59 13.

Zoo – ♿ Open summer season Mon to Fri 9am to 7pm, weekends 8am to 7pm; winter season daily 9am to 5pm. 11 DM. ☎ 0 69/ 21 23 37 35.

Naturmuseum Senckenberg – Open Mon to Fri 9am to 5pm (Wed until 8pm), weekends 9am to 6pm; on Shrove Tues and the Tues after Whitsun (Wäldchestag) open 9am to 1pm. Closed Good Fri. 7 DM. ☎ 0 69/7 54 20.

Palmengarten – ♿ Open Mar to Oct daily 9am to 6pm; Nov to Jan daily 9am to 4pm; Feb 9am to 5pm. 7 DM. ☎ 0 69/21 23 39 39.

Excursions

Offenbach: Deutsches Ledermuseum/Deutsches Schuhmuseum – ♿ Open Mon 10am to 1pm, Tues and Thur to Sun 10am to 5pm, Wed 10am to 8pm. Closed 1 Jan, 24, 25 and 31 Dec. 5 DM. ☎ 0 69/8 29 79 80.

Königstein im Taunus: Burgruine – Open Apr to Sept daily 9am to 7pm; Mar and Oct 9.30am to 4.30pm; Nov to Feb Mon to Fri 9.30am to 3pm, weekends 9.30am to 4pm. 3 DM. ☎ 0 61 74/20 22 51.

Großer Feldberg: Observation platform – Ascent of tower (163 steps) daily from 9am until nightfall. Closed the 1st 3 weeks in Nov. 3 DM. ☎ 0 61 74/2 22 19.

FREIBERG
🏛 Burgstraße 1 - 09599 ☎ 0 37 31/2 36 02 - Fax 0 37 31/27 32 60

Dom – Guided tours (45min) May to Oct Mon to Sat 10am to noon and 2pm to 5pm, Sun 11am to noon and 2pm to 5pm; Nov to Apr daily from 11am to noon and 2pm to 4pm. 3 DM. ☎ 0 37 31/2 25 98.

Geowissenschaftliche Sammlungen der TU Bergakademie – Open Wed to Fri 9am to noon and 1pm to 4pm, Sat 9am to 4pm. Closed on public holidays. 4 DM. ☎ 0 37 31/39 22 64.

Stadt- und Bergbaumuseum – Open Tues to Sun 10am to 5pm (last admissions 30min before closing). 4 DM. ☎ 0 37 31/2 31 97.

Lehr- und Besucherbergwerk - Guided tours (2hr 30min) Mon to Fri at 9.30am; May to Aug additional tours on Sat at 8am, 11am and 2pm; Sept to Apr additional tours on 1st Sat of the month at 8am, 11am and 2pm. 15 DM. ☎ 0 37 31/39 45 71.

FREIBURG IM BREISGAU
🏛 Rotteckring 14 - 79098 ☎ 07 61/3 88 18 81 - Fax 07 61/3 88 18 87

Münster: Chancel – Open Mon to Fri 10am to noon and 2.30pm to 5pm, Sat 10am to noon. Guided tours (50min) mid-June to late Sept Mon to Sat at 2pm, Sun at 2.30pm; Octo to mid-June Mon to Fri at 11am ands 2pm, Sun at 2.30pm. 1 DM, 2 DM including guided tour. ☎ 07 61/20 27 90.

Münster: Tower – Open Apr to Oct Mon to Sat 9.30am to 5pm, Sun 1pm to 5pm; Nov to Mar Tues to Sat 9.30am to 5pm, Sun 1pm to 5pm. 2 DM. ☎ 07 61/20 27 90.

Wentzingerhaus - Museum für Stadtgeschichte – Open Tues to Sun 10am to 5pm. Closed 24 and 31 Dec. 4 DM. ☎ 07 61/2 01 25 15.

Augustinermuseum – Open Tues to Sun 10am to 5pm. Closed 24 and 31 Dec. 4 DM. ☎ 07 61/2 01 25 31.

Schloßberg: Cable-car – Operates June to Sept 10am to 7pm or 8pm; Oct to Feb 11.30am to 6pm. Closed in Feb. Return fare: 6 DM. ☎ 07 61/3 98 55.

FRITZLAR
🏛 Rathaus - 34560 ☎ 0 56 22/98 86 43 - Fax 0 56 22/98 86 27

Dom – Open Mon to Sat 10am to noon and 2pm to 5pm (4pm in winter), Sun 2pm to 5pm (4pm in winter). 4 DM. ☎ 0 56 22/9 99 90.

Domschatz und Dommuseum – Open May to Oct Mon to Sat 10am to noon and 2pm to 5pm, Sun 2pm to 5pm; Nov to Apr open until 4pm. 4 DM. ☎ 0 56 22/99 99 21.

FÜSSEN
🏛 Kaiser-Maximilian-Platz 1 - 87629 ☎ 0 83 62/9 38 50 - Fax 0 83 62/93 85 20

Museum der Stadt Füssen (Kloster St. Mang) – Open Apr to Oct Tues to Sun 11am to 4pm; Nov to Mar 2pm to 4pm. Closed Shrove Tues, Easter Mon, Whit Mon, 24 and 31 Dec. 5 DM. ☎ 0 83 62/90 31 46.

FULDA
🏛 Schloßstraße 1 - 36037 ☎ 06 61/10 23 46 - Fax 06 61/10 27 75

Dommuseum – ♿ Open Apr to Oct Tues to Sat 10am to 5.30pm, Sun 12.30pm to 5.30pm; Nov to Mar Tues to Sat 10am to 12.30pm and 1.30pm to 4pm, Sun 12.30pm to 4pm. Closed in Jan and on Easter day and Whit Sun. 4 DM. ☎ 06 61/8 73 30.

Excursion

Schloß Fasanerie – Guided tours (45min) Apr to Oct Tues to Sun 10am to 5pm. 8 DM. ☎ 06 61/9 48 60.

G

GARMISCH-PARTENKIRCHEN
🏛 Dr.-Richard-Strauss-Platz - 82467 ☎ 0 88 21/18 06 - Fax 0 88 21/18 07 55

Wank: Cable-car – Operates daily 9am to 5pm. Closed for the 6 weeks following Easter and from mid-Nov until Christmas. Return fare: 28 DM. ☎ 0 88 21/79 79 79.

Excursion

Mittenwald: Geigenbau- und Heimatmuseum – Open late Dec to Oct Mon to Fri 10am to noon and 2pm to 5pm, weekends 10am to noon. 3 DM. ☎ 0 88 23/25 11.

GELNHAUSEN
🏛 Am Obermarkt - 63571 ☎ 0 60 51/83 03 00 - Fax 0 60 51/83 03 03

Kaiserpfalz – Open Tues to Sun 9am to 4pm (5pm Mar to Oct). Closed in Jan, and on 24, 26 and 31 Dec. 3 DM. ☎ 0 60 51/38 05.

Excursions

Büdingen: Castle – Guided tours (1hr) mid-Mar to end of Oct Tues to Fri and on Sun 11.30am to 5pm, Sat 2pm to 5pm. 6.50 DM. ☎ 0 60 42/88 92 03.

Steinau: Castle – &. Open Tues to Sun 9am to 5pm. 3 DM. ☎ 0 66 63/68 43.

GÖRLITZ

🛈 Obermarkt 29 - 02826 ☎ 0 35 81/4 75 70 - Fax 0 35 81/47 57 27

Dreifaltigkeitskirche – &. Open May to Oct Mon to Fri 2pm to 5pm. ☎ 0 35 81/31 13 11.

Kulturhistorisches Museum Barockhaus – Open Tues to Sun 10am to 5pm. Closed Easter Mon, Whit Mon, 24 and 31 Dec. 3 DM. ☎ 0 35 81/67 13 55.

St. Peter und Paul – Open Apr to Oct Mon to Sat 10.30am to 4.30pm, Sun 11.30am to 4.30pm; Nov to Mar Mon to Sat 10.30am to 4pm, Sun 11.30am to 4pm. ☎ 0 35 81/40 21 00.

Kaisertrutz: Museum für Stadtgeschichte und Kunst – Open May to late Oct Tues to Sun 10am to 5pm. Closed Whit Mon. 3 DM. ☎ 0 35 81/67 13 55.

Reichenbacher Turm – Open May to late Oct Tues to Sun 10am to 5pm. Closed Whit Mon. 3 DM. ☎ 0 35 81/67 13 55.

Excursion

Klosterkirche St. Marienthal – Open daily 9am to 5pm (9.30am to 4pm in winter). ☎ 03 58 23/88 60.

GÖTTINGEN

🛈 Altes Rathaus, Markt 9 - 37073 ☎ 05 51/5 40 00 - Fax 05 51/4 00 29 98

Städtisches Museum – Open Tues to Fri 10am to 5pm, weekends 11am to 5pm. Closed 1 Jan, Good Fri, Easter Day, 1 May, Ascension Day, Whit Sun, 3 Oct, 24, 25 and 31 Dec. 3 DM (admission free on 18 May). ☎ 05 51/4 00 28 43.

GOSLAR

🛈 Markt 7 - 38640 ☎ 0 53 21/7 80 60 - Fax 0 53 21/78 06 44

Huldigungssaal – Closed for restoration work. ☎ 0 53 21/7 57 80.

Siemenshaus – &. Open Tues and Thur 9am to noon. Closed on public holidays. Admission free. ☎ 0 53 21/2 38 37.

Kaiserpfalz – Open Apr to Oct daily 9.15am to 4.30pm; Nov to Mar daily 10am to 3.30pm; 26 and 31 Dec open 10am to 1pm (last admissions 30min before closing). Closed 1 Jan, 24 and 25 Dec. 3.50DM. ☎ 0 53 21/70 43 92.

Goslarer Museum – Open Apr to Oct Tues to Sun 10am to 5pm; Nov to Mar 10am to 4pm; 26 and 31 Dec open 10am to 1pm (last admissions 30min before closing). Closed 1 Jan, 24 and 25 Dec. 3.50 DM. ☎ 0 53 21/70 43 58.

Rammelsberger Bergbaumuseum – Guided tours (1hr) daily 9am to 6pm. Closed 24 and 31 Dec. 9 DM, 13.50 DM or 17 DM depending on tour. ☎ 0 53 21/3 43 60.

GOTHA

🛈 Blumenbachstraße 1 - 99867 ☎ 0 36 21/85 40 36 - Fax 0 36 21/22 21 34

Schloß Friedenstein – Open May to Oct Mon to Sat 10am-5pm; Nov to April 10am-4pm. Closed 24 and 31 Dec. 8 DM. ☎ 0 36 21/8 23 40.

GREIFSWALD

🛈 Schuhhagen 22 - 17489 ☎ 0 38 34/34 60 - Fax 0 38 34/37 88

Marienkirche – &. Open June to Sept Mon to Fri 10am to noon and 2pm to 4pm, Sat 10am to noon and Sun 10.30am to noon; Apr, May and Oct Mon to Fri 10am to noon. Closed 1Jan, Easter Mon, 1 May, Whit Mon, 3 Oct. Admission free. ☎ 0 38 34/22 63.

Dom St. Nikolai – &. Open May to Oct Mon to Sat 10am to 4pm, Sun 11am to 1pm; Nov to Apr daily 11am to noon. To climb the tower: 3 DM. ☎ 0 38 34/26 27.

St. Jakobikirche – Open May to Oct Mon to Fri 10am to noon and 2pm to 4pm, Sat 10am to noon, Sun 11.30am to noon; otherwise by appointment. ☎ 0 38 34/50 22 09.

Museum Greifswald – Open Wed to Sun 10am to 6pm (Fri 10am to 4pm). 3 DM. ☎ 0 38 34/27 20.

Botanischer Garten – Greenhouses and gardens open May to Sept Mon to Fri 9am to 3.45pm, weekends 1pm to 6pm; Mar, Apr, Oct and Nov Mon to Fri 9am to 3.45pm, weekends 1pm to 4pm; Jan, Feb and Dec Mon to Fri 9am to 3.45pm, weekends 1pm to 3pm. Arboretum is open May to Sept daily 9am to 6pm; Apr and Oct daily 9am to 3.45pm. Admission free. ☎ 0 38 34/86 11 30.

GÜSTROW

🛈 Domstraße 9 - 18273 ☎ 0 38 43/68 10 23 - Fax 0 38 43/68 20 79

Schloßmuseum – Open Tues to Sun 9am to 5pm; 1 Jan open 11am to 5pm; 25 Dec open 10am to 5pm; 31 Dec open 9am to 4pm. Closed 24 Dec. 5 DM. ☎ 0 38 43/75 20.

Dom – ♿ Open June to Sept Mon to Sat 10am to 5pm, Sun 11am to noon and 2pm to 4pm; Apr, May and Oct Tues to Sat 10am to noon and 2pm to 4pm, Sun 11am to noon and 2pm to 4pm; Nov to Mar Tues to Sun 11am to noon and 2pm to 3pm. Admission free. ☎ 0 38 43/68 24 33.

Pfarrkirche St. Marien – ♿ Open July to Sept Mon to Sat 10am to 4pm, Sun 2pm to 4pm; Apr to June Tues to Sat 10am to noon and 2pm to 4pm, Sun 2pm to 4pm; Oct Tues to Sat 11am to noon and 2pm to 4pm, Sun 2pm to 4pm; Nov to mar Tues to Sat 11am to noon and 2pm to 3pm, Sun 2pm to 3pm. Admission free. ☎ 0 38 43/68 20 77.

Ernst-Barlach-Gedenkstätte

Gertrudenkapelle – Open Mar to Oct Tues to Sun 10am to 5pm; Nov to Feb Tues to Sun 11am to 4pm. Closed 1 Jan, 24 and 31 Dec. 6 DM. ☎ 0 38 43/8 22 99.

Atelierhaus am Heidberg – Same admission times as the Gertrudenkapelle.

H

HAIGERLOCH   🄸 Rathaus, Oberstadtstraße - 72401 ☎ 0 74 74/6 97 27 - Fax 0 74 74/60 68

Atommuseum – ♿ Open Mar to Nov Mon to Sat 10am to noon and 2pm to 5pm, Sun 10am to 5pm. 2 DM. ☎ 0 74 74/6 97 27.

HALBERSTADT   🄸 Düsterngraben 3 - 38820 ☎ 0 39 41/55 18 15 - Fax 0 39 41/55 10 89

Dom St. Stephanus – ♿ Open Mon to Fri 10am to 5pm, Sat 10am to 4.30pm, Sun 11am to 4.30pm. Closed 24 and 31 Dec. ☎ 0 39 41/2 42 37.

Domschatz – Guided tours (1hr) Apr to Oct Tues to Fri at 10am, 11.30am, 2pm and 3.30pm, Sat at 10am and 2pm, Sun at 11.30am and 2.30pm; Nov to Mar Tues to Sun at 11.30am and 2.30pm. ☎ 0 39 41/2 42 37.

Städtisches Museum – Open Tues to Fri 9am to 5pm, weekends 10am to 5pm. Closed 1 Jan, 25 Dec. 5 DM. ☎ 0 39 41/55 14 71.

HALLE   🄸 Roter Turm, Marktplatz - 06108 ☎ 03 45/2 02 33 40 - Fax 03 45/50 27 98

Händel-Haus – Open daily 9.30am to 5.30pm (Thur until 7pm). Closed 24 and 25 Dec. 4 DM (admission free on Thur). ☎ 03 45/50 09 00.

Technisches Halloren- und Salinenmuseum – ♿ Open Tues to Sun 10am to 5pm. Closed 1 Jan, 24, 25 and 31 Dec. 3 DM. ☎ 03 45/2 02 50 34.

Staatliche Galerie Moritzburg Halle – Open Tues 11am to 8.30pm, Wed to Sun 10am to 6pm. Closed 24 and 31 Dec. 5 DM (admission free on Tues). ☎ 03 45/2 81 20 10.

Excursion

Doppelkapelle Landsberg – Guided tours (1hr) May to Oct weekends at 11am and 3pm. 3 DM. ☎ 03 46 02/2 06 90.

Halle Cathedral by Lyonel Feininger, Galerie Moritzburg

© VG Bild-Kunst, Bonn 1994

☐ Hauptbahnhof - 20099 ☎ 0 40/30 05 13 00 - Fax 0 40/30 05 13 33

Hauptkirche St. Michaelis – Open Apr to Sept Mon to Sat 9am to 6pm, Sun 11am to 6pm; Octo to Mar Mon to Sat 10am to 5pm, Sun 11am to 5pm. Crypt 2.50 DM, tower 4 DM. ☎ 0 40/37 67 80.

Hamburger Kunsthalle – ♿ Open Tues to Sun 10am to 6pm (Thur until 9pm). Closed 24 and 31 Dec. 15 DM. ☎ 0 40/24 86 26 12.

Museum für Kunst und Gewerbe – ♿ Open Tues to Sun 10am to 6pm (Thurs until 9pm). Closed 1 Jan, 1 May, 24 and 31 Dec. 8 DM. ☎ 0 40/24 86 27 32.

Museum für Hamburgische Geschichte – ♿ Open Tues to Sat 10am to 5pm, Sun 10am to 6pm. Closed 1 Jan, 1 May, 24 and 31 Dec. 8DM. ☎ 0 40/35 04 23 61.

Boat trip around the port – Departures Apr to Oct daily every half hour 9am to 6pm; Nov to Mar daily every hour 10.30am to 4.30pm. Embarcation: St. Pauli-Landungs-brücken, landing stages 1-9. Trip takes 1hr. 15 DM. ☎ 0 40/3 11 70 70.

Museum für Post und Kommunikation – ♿ Open Tues to Sun 9am to 5pm. Closed 1 Jan, 24, 25 and 31 Dec. Admission free. ☎ 0 40/3 57 63 60.

Fernsehturm – Panorama viewpoint open daily 10am to 11pm. Lift: 6.50 DM. ☎ 0 40/43 80 24.

Erholungspark "Planten un Blomen" – Illuminated fountain displays with musical accompaniment Apr to Aug at 10pm and Sept at 9pm. ☎ 0 40/30 05 13 00.

Museum für Völkerkunde Hamburg – Open Tues to Sun 10am to 6pm (Thurs until 9pm). 7 DM. ☎ 0 40/4 28 48 25 24.

Tierpark Hagenbeck – ♿ Open daily 9am to 6pm (until 4.30pm in winter). 21 DM. ☎ 0 40/54 00 01 47.

Excursions

Altonaer Museum – Norddeutsches Landesmuseum – Open Tues to Sun 10am to 6pm. Closed 1 May, 24 and 31 Dec. 8 DM. ☎ 0 40/42 81 15 14.

Jenisch-Haus – Open Apr to Sept Tues to Sun 10am to 5pm; Oct to Mar Tues to Sun 10am to 4pm. Closed 1 Jan, Easter Day, 1 May, 24, 25 and 31 Dec. 5 DM. ☎ 0 40/82 87 90.

Ernst-Barlach-Haus – Open Tues to Sun 11am to 5pm. Closed 24 and 31 Dec. 6 DM. ☎ 0 40/82 60 85.

Wedel: Ernst-Barlach-Museum – Open Tues to Sun 10am to noon and 3pm to 6pm. 5 DM. ☎ 0 41 03/91 82 91.

Schloß Ahrensburg – Open Apr to Sept Tues to Sun 10am to 12.30pm and 1.30pm to 5pm; Feb, Mar and Oct Tues to Sun 10am to 12.30pm and 1.30pm to 4pm; Nov to Jan Tues to Sun 12.30pm to 3pm. Closed 24 Dec to 1 Jan and on Good Fri. 6 DM. ☎ 0 41 02/4 25 10.

☐ Deisterallee - 31785 ☎ 0 51 51/20 26 17 - Fax 0 51 51/20 25 00

Excursions

Hämelschenburg: Schloß – Guided tours (45min) Apr to Oct Tues to Sun at 10am, 11am, noon, 2pm, 3pm, 4pm and 5pm. 8 DM. ☎ 0 51 55/97 08 41.

Fischbeck: Abbey – Guided tours (1hr 30min) during summer months Tues to Sun 2pm to 4pm, also Tues and Fri 9am to 11am. 4 DM. ☎ 0 51 52/86 03.

☐ Rathaus, Lotzestraße 2 - 34346 ☎ 0 55 41/7 53 13 - Fax 0 55 41/7 54 04

Bad Karlshafen: Deutsches Hugenottenmuseum – ♿ Open Mar to Oct Tues to Sat 9am to 1pm and 2pm to 6pm, Sun 11am to 6pm; Nov to Feb open Wed and Sat 9am to 1pm and 2pm to 5pm, Sun 11am to 5pm. Closed 24 and 25 Dec. 4 DM. ☎ 0 56 72/14 10.

Fürstenberg: Schloßmuseum – Open Apr to Oct Tues to Sun 10am to 6pm; Jan to Mar and in Nov and Dec weekends 10am to 5pm (until 6pm on Sun in Advent). Closed from 24 Dec to 1 Jan. 6 DM. ☎ 0 52 71/40 11 61.

Museum Höxter-Corvey – ♿ Open Apr to Oct daily 9am to 6pm. 6.50 DM (castle), 1 DM (church). ☎ 0 52 71/68 10.

☐ Ernst-August-Platz 2 - 30159 ☎ 05 11/3 01 40 - Fax 05 11/30 14 14

Rathaus – Open Mon to Fri 8am to 6pm, weekends 10am to 5pm. Access to dome (ascent of tower) Apr to Oct daily 10am to 4.30pm. Closed 1 Jan, 24, 25, 26 and 31 Dec. 3 DM. ☎ 05 11/1 68 45 33.

Wilhelm-Busch-Museum – Closed for renovation until 17 June 2000. ☎ 05 11/71 40 76.

Kestner-Museum – Open Tues to Sun 10am to 6pm (Wed until 8pm). Closed 1 Jan, Good Fri, 1 May, Ascension, 24, 25 and 31 Dec. 3 DM (admission free on Fri). ☎ 05 11/16 84 21 20.

Niedersächsisches Landesmuseum – ♿ Open Tues to Sun 10am to 5pm (until 7pm Thur). Closed Easter Day, 1 May, Whit Sun, 24, 25 and 31 Dec. 6 DM. ☎ 05 11/9 80 76 26.

Sprengel-Museum Hannover – ♿ Open Tues 10am to 8pm, Wed to Sun 10am to 6pm. Closed Good Fri, 1 May, 25 Dec. 7 DM. ☎ 05 11/16 84 38 75.

Historisches Museum Hannover – ♿ Open Tues 10am to 8pm, Wed to Fri 10am to 4pm, weekends 10am to 6pm. Closed 1 Jan, Good Fri, 1 May, 24, 25 and 31 Dec. 5 DM (admission free on Fri). ☎ 05 11/16 84 39 49.

Zoologischer Garten – ♿ Open Mar to Oct daily 9am to 7pm (last tickets at 5.30pm); Nov to Feb daily 9am to 4pm (last tickets at 3pm). 21 DM. ☎ 05 11/28 07 40.

HARZ

Clausthal-Zellerfeld: Oberharzer Bergwerksmuseum – Open daily 9am to 5pm. Closed 24 Dec. 7 DM. ☎ 0 53 23/9 89 50.

St. Andreasberg: Silberbergwerk Samson – Guided tours (1hr) daily 8.30am to 4.30pm. Closed 1 Jan, 24 Dec. 6.50 DM. ☎ 0 55 82/12 49.

Rübeland: Hermannshöhle – Guided tours (45min) June to Oct daily 9am to 5.30pm; Jan to May and in Nov and Dec daily 9.30am to 3.30pm. Closed 24 Dec. 7 DM. ☎ 03 94 54/4 91 32.

HEIDELBERG   🚉 Hauptbahnhof – 69115 ☎ 0 62 21/1 94 33 – Fax 0 62 21/16 73 18

Schloß – Guided tours of the interior (1hr) daily 8am to 5.30pm; on 24 and 31 Dec 1pm to 5.30pm only. 4 DM. The courtyard and the Großes Faß can be visited separately. Closed 25 Dec. 4 DM. ☎ 0 62 21/53 84 14.

Deutsches Apothekenmuseum – Open 10am to 5.30pm. Closed 1 Jan and 25 Dec. 3 DM. ☎ 0 62 21/2 58 80.

Kurpfälzisches Museum – Open Tues to Sun 10am to 5pm (Wed until 9pm). 5 DM. ☎ 0 62 21/58 34 02.

Studentenkarzer – Exact details not known at time of going to press. ☎ 0 62 21/2 95 45.

Museum of Sacred and Liturgical Art – Open June to Oct Tues to Sat 10am to 5pm, Sun 1pm to 5pm; Nov to May Sat 10am to 5pm, Sun 1pm to 5pm. Closed 1 Jan, Good Fri, Easter Day, 24 to 26 Dec. 4 DM. ☎ 0 62 21/47 56 22.

Excursions

Königstuhl: Funicular – Operates Mon to Fri 9am to 7.20pm every 10min, weekends 10.10am to 5.10pm every 20min. Return fare: 8.50 DM (from Heidelberg-Kornmarkt stop). ☎ 0 62 21/51 30.

HELGOLAND   🚉 Rathaus – 27498 ☎ 0 47 25/8 13 70 – Fax 0 47 25/81 37 25

Access – Mar to Oct daily boat connections from Cuxhaven (foot passengers only). A day trip to Helgoland allows about 3hr 30min on the island itself (departure from Cuxhaven at 10.30am). There are also connections from Büsum, Bremerhaven, Wilhelmshaven or Hamburg. For details of boat connections from Cuxhaven Nov to Feb, enquire at the shipping company Cassen Eils: ☎ 0 47 21/3 50 82.

Bad HERSFELD   🚉 Am Markt 12 – 36251 ☎ 0 66 21/20 12 74 – Fax 0 66 21/20 12 44

Stiftsruine – Open Mar to end of Oct Tues to Sun 10am to noon and 2pm to 4pm. No admission during festival period. 1 DM. ☎ 0 66 21/20 12 74.

HILDESHEIM   🚉 Am Ratsbauhof 1c – 31134 ☎ 0 51 21/1 79 80 – Fax 0 51 21/17 98 88

Dom – ♿ Open Apr to Oct Mon to Sat 9.30am to 5pm, Sun noon to 5pm; Nov to Mar Mon to Fri 10am to 4.30pm, Sat 9.30am to 2pm, Sun noon to 5pm. Closed Good Fri. 0.50 DM. ☎ 0 51 21/1 79 17 60.

Roemer- und Pelizaeus-Museum – The Roemer-Museum is open Tues to Sun 9am to 4.30pm. 3 DM. ☎ 0 51 21/9 36 90. Due to renovation and extension work only part of the collections in the Pelizaeus-Museum are on display. There are still special exhibitions, however, details of which can be obtained by calling the above number.

Schöntal: Abbey – ♿ Guided tours (45min) Apr to Oct daily at 11am, 2pm and 4pm; Nov to Mar daily at 11am and 2pm. 4 DM. Closed 1 Jan, Easter, 24 to 26 Dec. ☎ 0 79 43/89 40.

Langenburg: Castle – Guided tours (45min) daily Good Fri to 1 Nov daily 10am to 5pm every hour. 4.50 DM. ☎ 0 79 05/2 64.

Neuenstein: Castle – Guided tours (50min) mid-Mar to mid-Nov Tues to Sun 9am to noon and 1.30pm to 6pm. 8 DM. ☎ 0 79 42/22 09.

HOHENSCHWANGAU

Guided tours (30min) mid-Mar to mid-Oct daily 8.30am to 5.30pm; mid-Oct to mid-Mar daily 10am to 4.30pm. Closed 24 Dec. 12 DM. ☎ 0 83 62/8 11 27.

Burg HOHENZOLLERN

Castle – Guided tours (35min) mid-Mar to mid-Oct daily 9am to 5.30pm; mid-Oct to mid-Mar daily 9am to 4.30pm. Closed 24 Dec. 9 DM. ☎ 0 74 71/24 28.

HUSUM
🖫 Großstraße 27 - 25813 ☎ 0 48 41/8 98 70 - Fax 0 48 41/47 28

Nissenhaus-Nordfriesisches Museum – ♿ Open Apr to Oct daily 10am to 5pm; Nov to Mar Tues to Fri and on Sun 10am to 4pm. 5 DM. ☎ 0 48 41/25 45.

Storm-Haus – Open Apr to Oct Tues to Fri 10am to noon and 2pm to 5pm, Mon and weekends 2pm to 5pm; Nov to Mar Tues, Thur and Sun 2pm to 5pm. Closed 24 and 31 Dec. 4 DM. ☎ 0 48 41/66 62 70.

Excursion

Seebüll: Nolde-Museum – Open Mar to Oct daily 10am to 6pm; Nov daily 10am to 5pm. 7 DM. ☎ 0 46 64/3 64.

I – J

IDAR-OBERSTEIN
🖫 Georg-Maus-Straße 2 - 55743 ☎ 0 67 81/6 44 21 - Fax 0 67 81/6 44 25

Deutsches Edelsteinmuseum – ♿ Open May to Oct daily 9am to 6pm; Nov to Apr daily 9am to 5pm. Closed the 1st 3 weeks in Dec. 8 DM. ☎ 0 67 81/94 42 80.

Museum Idar-Oberstein – Open daily 9am to 5.30pm. Closed 25 Dec. 6 DM. ☎ 0 67 81/2 46 19.

Weiherschleife – ♿ Guided tours (30min) mid-Mar to mid-Dec daily 9am to 5pm; mid-Feb to mid-Mar Mon to Fri 9am to 5pm. 5 DM. ☎ 0 67 81/3 15 13.

INGOLSTADT
🖫 Rathaus, Rathausplatz - 85049 ☎ 08 41/30 54 17 - Fax 08 41/3 05 10 99

Bayerisches Armeemuseum – Open Tues to Sun 8.45am to 4.30pm. Closed Shrove Tues, Good Fri, 1 Nov, 24, 25 and 31 Dec. 7.50 DM. ☎ 08 41/9 37 70.

Excursions

Neuburg an der Donau: Schloßmuseum – ♿ Open Tues to Sun 10am to 5pm. Closed 1 Jan, Shrove Tues, 1 Nov, 24, 25 and 31 Dec. 4 DM. ☎ 0 84 31/88 97.

JENA
🖫 Johannisstra ße 23 - 07743 ☎ 0 36 41/5 86 30 - Fax 0 36 41/58 63 22

Stadtmuseum Göhre – Open Tues to Sun 10am to 5pm (Wed until 6pm). Closed 24 and 31 Dec. 5 DM. ☎ 0 36 41/44 32 45.

Goethe-Gedenkstätte – Open Tues to Sun 11am to 3pm. 2 DM. ☎ 0 36 41/93 11 88.

Schiller-Gedenkstätte – Open Apr to Oct Tues to Sun 11am to 3pm; Nov to Mar Tues to Sat 11am to 3pm. 2 DM. ☎ 0 36 41/93 11 88.

Zeiss Planetarium – ♿ Presentations (50min) Tues and Thur at 11am and 3pm, Wed and Fri at 11am, weekends at 2pm and 4pm. There are additional laser shows and children's presentations at varying times. 8 DM. ☎ 0 36 41/88 54 88.

Optisches Museum – ♿ Open Tues to Fri 10am to 5pm, Sat 1pm to 4.30pm, Sun 9.30am to 1pm. 8 DM. ☎ 0 36 41/44 31 65.

K

KARLSRUHE   🚻 Bahnhofplatz 6 - 76137
   ☎ 07 21/3 55 30 - Fax 07 21/35 53 43 99

Staatliche Kunsthalle – ♿ Open Tues to
Fri 10am to 6pm, weekends 11am to 7pm.
Closed Shrove Tues, 31 Dec. 8 DM.
☎ 07 21/9 26 31 88.

Badisches Landesmuseum – ♿ Open
Tues to Fri 10am to 5pm (Wed until 8pm),
Sat noon to 6pm, Sun 10am to 6pm.
Closed 24 and 31 Dec. 8 DM (museum and
tower). ☎ 07 21/9 26 65 42.

Schloß: tower – Open Tues to Fri 10am to
5pm (Wed until 8pm), Sat noon to 6pm,
Sun 10am to 6pm. Closed 24 and 31 Dec.
8 DM (tower and Badisches Landesmuseum). ☎ 07 21/9 26 65 42.

Botanischer Garten – Open daily 8am to
nightfall.   Admission   free.   The
greenhouses are open Tues to Fri 9am to
4pm, weekends 9am to noon and 1pm to
5pm (4pm Oct to Mar). 2.50 DM. ☎ 07
21/9 26 30 08.

Museum beim Markt – ♿ Open Tues to
Thur 11am to 5pm, Fri to Sun 10am to
6pm. Closed 24 and 31 Dec. ☎ 07 21/9 26
65 78.

ZKM (Zentrum für Kunst und Medientechnologie)
– ♿ Open Wed to Sat noon to 8pm, Sun
10am to 6pm. 10 DM. Joint ticket for ZKM
and Städtische Galerie 12 DM. ☎ 07 21/8
10 00.

Badisches Landesmuseum

Nature by Alfons Mucha, Museum beim
Markt, Karlsruhe

KASSEL   🚻 Königplatz 53 - 34117 ☎ 05 61/7 07 71 63 - Fax 05 61/7 07 71 69

Schloß Wilhelmshöhe – Closed until June 2000. ☎ 05 61/9 37 77.

Museum für Astronomie und Technikgeschichte mit Planetarium – ♿ Open Tues
to Sun 10am to 5pm. Closed 1 May, 24, 25 and 31 Dec. 5 DM (admission free on
Fri). ☎ 05 61/7 15 43.

Hessisches Landesmuseum – Open Tues to Sun 10am to 5pm. Closed 1 May, 24,
25 and 31 Dec. 5 DM (admission free on Fri). ☎ 05 61/7 84 60.

Neue Galerie – ♿ Open Tues to Sun 10am to 5pm. Closed 1 May, 24, 25 and 31 Dec.
5 DM (admission free on Fri). ☎ 05 61/70 96 30.

Brüder-Grimm-Museum – Open daily 10am to 5pm. Closed 1 Jan, Good Fri, 24, 25
and 31 Dec. 3 DM. ☎ 05 61/7 87 40 64.

Naturkundemuseum – ♿ Open Tues to Sun 10am to 5pm. Closed 24 and 31 Dec.
3 DM. ☎ 05 61/7 87 40 14.

Excursion

Schloß Wilhelmsthal – Guided tours (1hr) Mar to Oct Tues to Sun 10am to 4pm;
Nov to Feb Tues to Sun 10am to 3pm. Closed 1 Jan, 24, 25 and 31 Dec. 6 DM. ☎ 0
56 74/68 98.

KIEL   🚻 Andreas-Gayk-Straße 31 - 24103 ☎ 04 31/67 91 00 - Fax 04 31/6 79 10 99

Rathaus – ♿ Open Mon to Wed 8am to 5pm, Thur 8am to 6pm, Fri 8am to 3pm.
Closed on public holidays. ☎ 04 31/67 91 00.

Excursions

Schleswig-Holsteinisches Freilichtmuseum – ♿ Open Apr to Oct daily 9am to 6pm;
Nov to Mar Sun 11am to 4pm. 7 DM. ☎ 04 31/65 96 60.

Laboe: Marine-Ehrenmal – ♿ Open mid-Apr to mid-Oct daily 9.30am to 6pm; mid-Oct to
mid-Apr daily 9.30am to 4pm (24 and 31 Dec until 1pm). 5 DM. ☎ 0 43 43/4 27 00.

KOBLENZ   🚻 Pavillon gegenüber Hauptbahnhof - 56068 ☎ 02 61/3 13 04 -
Fax 02 61/1 29 38 00

KÖLN   🚻 Am Dom - 50667 ☎ 02 21/2 21 33 45 - Fax 02 21/2 21 33 20

Cathedral – Open daily 6am to 7.15pm. Guided tours of the excavations Tues and
Thur at 4.30pm. 10 DM. ☎ 02 21/92 58 47 30.

Choir – Same admission times as the Cathedral. There may be occasions when the choir is closed for liturgical reasons. ☎ 02 21/92 58 47 30.

Treasury – Open Apr to Dec Mon to Sat 9am to 5pm, Sun 1pm to 4pm; Jan to Mar Mon to Sat 9am to 4pm, Sun 1pm to 4pm. 3 DM. ☎ 02 21/2 57 76 74.

Prätorium – Open Tues to Fri 10am to 4pm, weekends 11am to 4pm. Closed during the Carnival, 24 Dec to 1 Jan. 3 DM. ☎ 02 21/2 21 23 94.

Wallraf-Richartz-Museum/Museum Ludwig – ♿ Open Tues 10am to 8pm, Wed to Fri 10am to 6pm, weekends 11am to 6pm. Closed 1 Jan, during the Carnival, 24, 25 and 31 Dec. 10 DM. ☎ 02 21/22 12 23 79.

Museum of Photography – Open Tues 10am to 8pm, Wed to Fri 10am to 6pm, weekends 11am to 6pm. ☎ 02 21/2 21 22 41.

Römisch-Germanisches Museum – ♿ Open Tues to Sun 10am to 5pm. Closed 1 Jan, during the Carnival, 24, 25 and 31 Dec. 5 DM. ☎ 02 21/22 12 23 04.

Diözesanmuseum – Open daily (except Thur) 10am to 6pm. Closed Mon before Shrove Tues, 24 and 31 Dec. Admission free. ☎ 02 21/2 57 76 72.

Schnütgen-Museum – ♿ Open Tues to Fri 10am to 5pm (every 1st Wed in month until 8pm), weekends 11am to 5pm. Closed 1 Jan, during the Carnival, 24, 25 and 31 Dec. 5 DM. ☎ 02 21/22 12 36 20.

Museum für Ostasiatische Kunst – ♿ Open Tues to Sun 11am to 5pm (Thur until 8pm). Closed 1 Jan, during the Carnival, 24, 25 and 31 Dec. 5 DM. ☎ 02 21/9 40 51 80.

Museum für Angewandte Kunst – ♿ Open Tues to Sun 11am to 5pm (Wed until 8pm). Closed 1 Jan, during the Carnival, 24, 25 and 31 Dec. 5 DM. ☎ 02 21/22 12 67 14.

Kölnisches Stadtmuseum – ♿ Open Tues 10am to 8pm, Wed to Sun 10am to 5pm. Closed 1 Jan, during the Carnival, 24, 25 and 31 Dec. 5 DM. ☎ 02 21/22 12 57 89.

Käthe-Kollwitz-Museum – Open Tues to Fri 10am to 6pm, weekends 11am to 6pm. Closed 1 Jan, 24, 25 and 31 Dec. 5 DM. ☎ 02 21/2 27 23 63.

Rautenstrauch-Joest-Museum für Völkerkunde – Open Tues to Fri 10am to 4pm, weekends 11am to 4pm. Closed 1 Jan, during the Carnival, 24, 25 and 31 Dec. 5 DM. ☎ 02 21/3 36 94 13.

Imhoff-Stollwerck-Museum – ♿ Open Tues to Fri 10am to 6pm, weekends 11am to 7pm (last admissions 1hr before closing). Closed 1 Jan, during the Carnival, 24, 25 and 31 Dec. 10 DM. ☎ 02 21/9 31 88 80.

St. Ursula (Goldene Kammer) – Open Mon and Wed to Sat 9am to noon and 1pm to 5pm, Sun 3pm to 5pm. Closed Maundy Thur to Easter Day and all public holidays. ☎ 02 21/13 34 00.

Botanischer Garten und Flora – Gardens open daily 8am to nightfall. Greenhouses open daily 10am to noon and 1pm to 6pm (until 4pm during winter). Admission free. ☎ 02 21/76 43 35.

KONSTANZ 🚉 Bahnhofplatz 13 - 78462 ☎ 0 75 31/13 30 30 - Fax 0 75 31/13 30 80

Rosgartenmuseum – Closed for renovation work. ☎ 0 75 31/90 02 46.

Archäologisches Landesmuseum – ♿ Open Tues to Sun 10am to 6pm. 4 DM. ☎ 0 75 31/9 80 40.

Excursion

Mainau Island – ♿ Open mid-Mar to 24 Oct 7am to 8pm; the rest of the year open 9am to 6pm. 18 DM (admission free 25 Oct to mid-Mar). ☎ 0 75 31/30 30.

Italian water steps, Mainau Island

S. Rosenhall/Blumeninsel Mainau GmbH

Bad KREUZNACH 🚉 Kurhausstraße 23 - 55543 06 71/8 36 00 50 - Fax 06 71/8 36 00 80

Römerhalle - ♿ Open Tues to Sun 10am to 5pm. Closed 24 and 31 Dec. 3 DM. ☎ 06 71/80 02 48.

L

LAHNTAL

Schloß Schaumburg - Open Mar to Oct Tues to Sun 10am to 5pm. 5DM. ☎ 0 64 32/37 84.

Diez: Schloß Oranienstein - Guided tours (1hr) Apr to Oct Tues to Fri at 9am, 10.30am, 2pm and 3.30pm, Sat, Sun and public holidays at 10.30am, 2pm and 3.30pm; Nov to Mar Wed to Fri at 9am, 10.30am, 2pm and 3.30pm, Sat and Sun at 10.30am, 2pm and 3.30pm. Apply to guard about tours. 3DM. ☎ 0 64 32/3 05 12 96.

Weilburg: Castle - Guided tours (45min) May to Sept daily 10am to 4pm; Mar, Apr and Oct Tues to Sun 10am to 4pm; Nov to Feb Tues to Sun 10am to 3pm (last tour 1hr before closing). 6DM. ☎ 0 64 71/22 36.

Weilburg: Mining and Town Museum - Open Apr to Oct Tues to Sun 10am to noon and 2pm to 5pm; Nov to 19 Dec and 21 Jan to end of Mar Mon to Fri 10am to noon and 2pm to 5pm. 4DM. ☎ 0 64 71/3 14 59.

LANDSBERG AM LECH
🚉 Hauptplatz - 86899 - ☎ 0 81 91/12 82 46 - Fax 0 81 91/12 81 60

LANDSHUT
🚉 Altstadt 315 - 84028 - ☎ 08 71/92 20 50 - Fax 08 71/8 92 75

Stadtresidenz - Guided tours (45min) Apr to Oct daily 9am to noon and 1pm to 4pm; Nov to Mar daily to noon and 1pm to 5pm (last tour 30min before closing). Closed 1 Jan, Shrove Tues, 24, 25 and 31 Dec. 4DM. ☎ 08 71/92 41 10.

Burg Trausnitz - Same admission times as the Stadtresidenz. 5DM. ☎ 08 71/92 41 10.

LEIPZIG
🚉 Sachsenplatz 1 03 41/10 40

Stadtgeschichtliches Museum - Open Tues 2pm to 8pm, Wed to Sun 10am to 6pm. Closed 24, 25 and 31 Dec. 5DM (admission free on 1st Sun of month). ☎ 03 41/9 65 13 60.

Bach-Museum - Open daily 10am to 5pm. Closed 1 Jan (after 1pm), 24, 25 and 31 Dec. 4DM. ☎ 03 41/9 64 41 35.

Museum der bildenden Künste - ♿ Open Tues, Thur to Sun 10am to 6pm, Wed 1pm to 9.30pm. Closed 24 and 31 Dec. 5DM (admission free on 2nd Sun of month). ☎ 03 41/2 16 99 14.

Ägyptisches Museum - Open Tues to Sat 1pm to 5pm, Sun 10am to 1pm. Closed 1 Jan, Easter Mon, Whit Mon, 1 May. 3DM. ☎ 03 41/9 73 70 10.

Mendelssohn-Haus - Open daily 10am to 6pm. Closed 24 and 31 Dec. 5DM. ☎ 03 41/1 27 02 94.

Grassi-Museum:

Museum für Kunsthandwerk - Open Tues to Sun 10am to 6pm (Wed until 8pm). Closed 24 and 31 Dec. 5DM (admission free on 1st Sun of the month). ☎ 03 41/2 14 21 75.

Museum für Völkerkunde - Open Tues to Fri 10am to 5.30pm, Sat and Sun 10am to 5pm. Closed Good Fri, 24 and 31 Dec. 5DM (admission free on 1st Sun of month). ☎ 03 41/2 14 22 18.

Musikinstrumenten-Museum - Open Tues to Sat 10am to 5pm, Sun 10am to 1pm. Closed 1 Jan, Good Fri, 24 and 31 Dec. 5DM. ☎ 03 41/2 14 21 20.

Museum in der runden Ecke - Open Wed to Sun 2pm to 6pm. Closed 1 Jan, 24 to 26 and 31 Dec. Admission free although donations requested. ☎ 03 41/9 61 24 43.

Völkerschlachtdenkmal - Open Apr to Oct daily 10am to 5pm; Nov to Mar 9am to 4pm. Closed 1 Jan, 24, 25 and 31 Dec. 5DM. ☎ 03 41/8 78 04 71.

LEMGO
🚉 Papenstr. 7 - 32657 - ☎ 0 52 61/21 33 47 - Fax 0 52 61/21 34 92

Hexenbürgermeisterhaus - Open Tues to Sun 10am to 12.30pm and 1.30pm to 5pm. ☎ 0 52 61/21 32 76.

Junkerhaus - Open Tues to Sun 10am to 12.30pm and 1.30pm to 5pm. ☎ 0 52 61/21 32 76.

🚉 Hospitalstraße 2 - 65549 - ☎ 0 64 31/61 66 - Fax 0 64 31/32 93

Diözesanmuseum – ⚘ Open mid-Mar to mid-Nov Tues to Sat 10am to 1pm and 2pm to 5pm, Sun 10am to 5pm. 3DM (admission free on 1st Sun of month). ☎ 0 64 31/29 52 33.

🚉 Am Hauptbahnhof - 88131 - ☎ 0 83 82/26 00 30 - Fax 0 83 82/26 00 26

Stadtmuseum Lindau – Open Apr to Dec Tues to Sun 10am to noon and 2pm to 5pm. Closed 1 Jan, Easter Day, 1 May, Whit Sun, 25 and 31 Dec. 4DM. ☎ 0 83 82/94 40 73.

Tour – Guided tours (45min) Apr to Sept daily 9am to 5.30pm; Oct to Mar daily 9.30am to noon and 1pm to 4pm. Closed 1 Jan, Shrove Tues, 1 Nov, 24, 25 and 31 Dec. 10DM in summer, 7DM in winter. ☎ 0 88 22/9 20 30.

🚉 Wilhelmstraße 10 - 71638 - ☎ 0 71 41/9 10 22 52 - Fax 0 71 41/9 10 27 74

Schloß: Tour of the Apartments – Guided tours (1hr 15min) Mar to Oct daily 9am to noon and 1pm to 5pm; Nov to Feb 10am to noon and 1pm to 4pm. 7DM. ☎ 0 71 41/18 64 40.

Schloß: Blühendes Barock – ⚘ Open end of Mar to beginning of Nov daily 7.30am to 8.30pm (Märchengarten open 9am to 6pm). 12DM. ☎ 0 71 41/97 56 50.

Excursions

Marbach am Neckar: Schiller-Nationalmuseum – Open daily 9am to 5pm. Closed 25 and 26 Dec, and 24 and 31 Dec in the afternoon. 4DM. ☎ 0 71 44/84 86 01.

🚉 Schloßfreiheit 8 - 19288 - ☎ 0 38 74/2 90 76 - Fax 0 38 74/2 90 76

Schloß – Open Apr to Oct Tues to Sun 10am to 6pm; Nov to Mar Tues to Sun 10am to 5pm. 5DM. ☎ 0 38 74/2 81 14.

Stadtkirche – ⚘ Open May to Sept Tues to Sat 11am to 4pm, Sun 3pm to 4pm; Oct and Apr 3pm to 4pm. ☎ 0 38 74/2 84 57.

🚉 Beckergrube 95 - 23552 - ☎ 04 51/1 22 81 09 - Fax 04 51/1 22 81 90

Buddenbrookhaus – ⚘ Open daily 10am to 5pm. Closed 1 Jan, 25 and 26 Dec. 5DM. ☎ 04 51/1 22 41 92.

St. Annen-Museum – Open Apr to Sept Tues to Sun 10am to 5pm; Oct to Mar Tues to Sun 10am to 4pm. Closed 24, 25 and 31 Dec. 5DM (admission free on 1st Fri of month). ☎ 04 51/1 22 41 37.

Behnhaus und Drägerhaus – Same admission times and charges as St. Annen-Museum. ☎ 04 51/1 22 41 48.

🚉 Am Markt - 21335 - ☎ 0 41 31/3 22 00 - Fax 0 41 31/30 95 98

Rathaus – Open daily 10am to 5pm. Closed 1 Jan, 24 to 26 and 31 Dec. 6DM. ☎ 0 41 31/30 92 30.

Excursion

Lauenburg an der Elbe: Elbe Navigation Museum – Open Mar to Oct Mon to Fri 10am to 1pm and 2pm to 5pm, Sat and Sun 10am to 5pm; Nov to Feb Wed and Fri to Sun 10am to 1pm and 2pm to 4.30pm. Closed 1 Jan, 24 to 26 Dec. 2DM. ☎ 0 41 53/5 12 51.

Ebstorf: Benedictine abbey – Guided tours (1hr 30min) Apr to mid-Oct Mon to Sat 10am to 11am and 2pm to 5pm, Sun at 11.15am and 2pm to 5pm; 2nd fortnight of Oct 1 tour only at 2pm. Closed Good Fri. 5DM. ☎ 0 58 22/23 04.

Handwerksmuseum am Mühlenberg in Suhlendorf – ⚘ Open Apr to Sept Tues to Sun 10am to 6pm; Oct to Mar Tues to Sun 10am to 4.30pm. 4DM. ☎ 0 58 20/3 70.

Heide-Park Soltau – ⚘ Open mid-Mar to Oct daily 9am to 6pm. 36DM. ☎ 0 51 91/91 91.

Vogelpark Walsrode – ⚘ Open Mar to Oct daily 9am to 7pm; Nov to Feb daily 10am to 4pm. 18DM. ☎ 0 51 61/20 15.

M

🏛 Alter Markt 12 - 39104 - ☎ 03 91/5 40 49 03 - Fax 03 91/5 40 49 10

Kloster Unser Lieben Frauen – Open Tues to Sun 10am to 6pm. 4DM (admission free on 1st Fri of month). ☎ 03 91/56 50 20.

MAINZ 🏛 Brückenturm 28 - 55116 - ☎ 0 61 31/28 62 10 - Fax 0 61 31/2 86 21 55

Gutenberg-Museum – Closed for renovation until 2000. ☎ 0 61 31/12 26 40.

Römisch-Germanisches Museum – Open Tues to Sun 10am to 6pm. Closed Mon before Shrove Tues, Shrove Tues, 1 Nov, 24, 25 and 31 Dec. Admission free. ☎ 0 61 31/9 12 40.

Landesmuseum Mainz – ♿ Open Tues 10am to 8pm, Wed to Sun 10am to 5pm. Closed 1 Jan, Good Fri, Sat before Easter, 1 May, Whit Sun, 24, 25 and 31 Dec. 5DM. ☎ 0 61 31/28 57 28.

MANNHEIM 🏛 Willi-Brandt-Platz 3 - 68161 - ☎ 06 21/21 44 99 - Fax 06 21/2 41 41

Städtische Kunsthalle – ♿ Open Tues, Wed and Fri to Sun 10am to 5pm, Thur noon to 5pm. Closed during Carnival, Good Fri, 1 May, 24 and 31 Dec. 4DM. ☎ 06 21/2 93 64 11.

Museum für Kunst-, Stadt- und Theatergeschichte im Reiß-Museum – ♿ Open Tues, Wed, Fri to Sun 10am to 5pm, Thur noon to 5pm. Closed 1 May, 24 and 31 Dec. 4DM. ☎ 06 21/2 93 31 50.

Museum für Archäologie, Völker- und Naturkunde – ♿ Same admission times as Museum für Kunst-, Stadt- und Theatergeschichte. 4DM. ☎ 06 21/2 93 31 51.

Schloß – ♿ Open Tues to Sun 10am to 1pm and 2pm to 5pm. Closed 25 Dec. 4DM. ☎ 06 21/2 92 28 90.

Landesmuseum für Technik und Arbeit in Mannheim – ♿ Open Tues and Thur 9am to 5pm, Wed 9am to 8pm, Fri 9am to 1pm, Sat 10am to 5pm, Sun 10am to 6pm. Closed 24, 25 and 31 Dec. 5DM (admission free on Wed from noon). ☎ 06 21/4 29 87 50.

Museumsschiff Mannheim – Same admission times as Landesmuseum. 2DM (admission free on Wed from noon). ☎ 06 21/4 29 87 50.

MARBURG 🏛 Pilgrimstein 26 - 35037 - ☎ 0 64 21/9 91 20 - Fax 0 64 21/99 12 12

Elisabethkirche – ♿ Open Apr to Oct daily 9am to 5pm; Nov to Mar daily 10am to 4pm. Shrine: 3DM. ☎ 0 64 21/6 55 73.

Schloß – Open Apr to Oct Tues to Sun 10am to 6pm; Nov to Mar Tues to Sun 11am to 5pm. Closed 24, 25 and 31 Dec. 3DM. ☎ 0 64 21/28 23 55.

Marburger Universitätsmuseum für Bildende Kunst – Open Tues to Sun 11am to 1pm and 2pm to 5pm. Closed 24, 25 and 31 Dec. Admission free. ☎ 0 64 21/28 23 55.

Kloster MAULBRONN

Abbey – Open Mar to Oct daily 9am to 5.30pm; Nov to Feb Tues to Sun 9.30am to 5pm. Closed 24, 25 and 31 Dec. 8DM. ☎ 0 70 43/92 66 10.

MEISSEN 🏛 Markt 3 - 01662 ☎ 0 35 21/45 44 70 - Fax 0 35 21/45 82 40

Staatliche Porzellanmanufaktur – Museum open daily 9am to 5pm (last admissions at 4.30pm). Showcase workshop: guided tours (30min) 9am to noon and 1pm to 4pm. Closed 1 Jan, 24 to 26 and 31 Dec. 9DM museum, 5DM workshop. ☎ 0 35 21/46 82 08.

Albrechtsburg – Open Mar to Oct daily 10am to 6pm; Nov to Feb daily 10am to 5pm (last admissions 30min before closing). Closed first 3 weeks in Jan, 24, 25 and 31 Dec. 6DM. ☎ 0 35 21/4 70 70.

MEMMINGEN 🏛 Marktplatz 3 - 87700 - ☎ 0 83 31/85 01 72 - Fax 0 83 31/85 01 78

Bad MERGENTHEIM 🏛 Marktplatz 3 - 97980 - ☎ 0 79 31/5 71 31 - Fax 0 79 31/5 73 00

Deutschordensschloß – ♿ Open Tues to Sun 10am to 5pm. Closed 24, 25 and 31 Dec. 6DM. ☎ 0 79 31/5 22 12.

Doll's room, Deutschordensschloß, Bad Mergentheim

Excursion

Stuppach: Parish church – ♿ Open May to Oct daily 9am to 5.30pm; Mar to Apr 10am to 5pm. 2DM. ☎ 0 79 31/26 05.

MERSEBURG   🛈 Burgstraße 5 - 06217 - ☎ 0 34 61/21 41 70 - Fax 0 34 61/21 41 77

MINDEN   🛈 Großer Domhof 3 - 32423 - ☎ 05 71/8 29 06 59 - Fax 05 71/8 29 06 63

Domschatzkammer – ♿ Open Tues, Thur, Sat and Sun 10am to noon, Wed and Fri 3pm to 5pm.

Mindener Museum für Geschichte, Landes- und Volkskunde – Open Tues to Fri 10am to 1pm and 2.30pm to 5pm (Thur until 6.30pm), Sat 2.30pm to 5pm, Sun 11am to 6pm. 3DM. ☎ 05 71/8 93 16.

Excursion

Porta Westfalica: Fernsehturm – Open Easter to Oct daily 10am to 6pm. 1DM. ☎ 05 71/7 11 76.

MÖNCHENGLADBACH   🛈 Bismarckstraße 23-27 - 41061 - ☎ 0 21 61/2 20 01 - Fax 0 21 61/27 42 22

Städtisches Museum Abteiberg – Open Tues to Sun 10am to 6pm. Closed 1 Jan, 24, 25 and 31 Dec. 5DM. ☎ 0 21 61/25 26 37.

Schloß Rheydt: Museum – Open Apr to Sept Tues to Sun 11am to 7pm; Oct to Mar Tues to Sat 11am to 4pm, Sun 11am to 6pm. Closed 1 Jan, 24, 25 and 31 Dec. 5DM. ☎ 0 21 66/92 89 00.

MONSCHAU   🛈 Stadtstraße 1 - 52156 - ☎ 0 24 72/33 00 - Fax 0 24 72/45 34

Rotes Haus – Guided tours by appointment Good Fri to end of Nov Tues to Sun at 10am, 11am, 2pm, 3pm and 4pm. 5DM. ☎ 0 24 72/50 71.

Excursion

Nideggen: Castle – Open Apr to Oct Tues to Sun 10am to 5pm; Nov to Mar Sat and Sun only 10am to 5pm (last admissions at 4.30pm). 3.50DM. ☎ 0 24 27/63 40.

MOSELTAL

River cruises along the Moselle – May to Oct 10am to 2.30pm and 3.50pm to 8.10pm. There are connections from Koblenz to Cochem. Enquire at the offices along the pier or at Köln-Düsseldorfer, Frankenwerft 1, 50667 Köln, ☎ 02 21/2 08 83 18.

Beilstein: Castle – Open Apr to Sept daily 9am to 6pm; Oct daily 9am to 5pm. 3DM. ☎ 0 26 73/9 36 39.

Cochem: Reichsburg – Guided tours (40min) mid-Mar to end of Oct daily 9am to 5pm; Nov to beginning of Jan 11am to 3pm. 7DM. ☎ 0 26 71/2 55.

Burg Eltz – Guided tours (40min) Apr to 1 Nov daily 9.30am to 5.30pm. 9DM. ☎ 0 26 72/95 05 00.

MÜHLHAUSEN 🖪 Ratsstraße 20 - 99974 - ☎ 0 36 01/45 23 35 - Fax 0 36 01/45 23 16

MÜNCHEN 🖪 Hauptbahnhof - 80335 - ☎ 0 89/2 33 03 00 - Fax 0 89/23 33 02 33

Deutsches Jagd- und Fischereimuseum – Open 9.30am to 5pm (Mon and Thur until 9pm). Closed Shrove Tues, 24 and 31 Dec. 6DM. ☎ 0 89/25 02 22.

Residenz: Schatzkammer – Open daily 10am to 4.30pm. 7DM. ☎ 0 89/29 06 71.

Residenzmuseum – Same admission times as Schatzkammer. 7DM. ☎ 0 89/29 06 71.

Altes Residenztheater (Cuvilliés-Theater) – Open Mon to Sat 2pm to 5pm, Sun 10am to 5pm. 3DM. ☎ 0 89/29 06 71.

Alte Pinakothek – ♿ Open Tues to Sun 10am to 5pm (Tues and Thur until 8pm). Closed Shrove Tues, 1 May, Corpus Christi, 24 and 31 Dec. 7DM (admission free on Sun). ☎ 0 89/23 80 52 16.

Neue Pinakothek – ♿ Open Tues to Sun 10am to 5pm (Wed until 8pm). Closed Shrove Tues, Good Fri, Easter Mon, 1 May, Whit Mon, 1 Nov, 24, 25 and 31 Dec. 7DM (admission free on Sun). ☎ 0 89/23 80 51 95.

Glyptothek – Open Tues to Sun 10am to 5pm (Thur until 8pm). 6DM. ☎ 0 89/28 61 00.

Antikensammlungen – Open Tues to Sun 10am to 5pm (Wed until 8pm). 6DM (admission free on Sun). ☎ 0 89/59 83 59.

Städtische Galerie im Lenbachhaus – ♿ Open Tues to Sun 10am to 6pm. Closed Shrove Tues, 24 and 31 Dec. 8DM. ☎ 0 89/23 33 20 20.

Deutsches Museum – Open daily 9am to 5pm. Closed 1 Jan, Shrove Tues, Good Fri, 1 May, Corpus Christi, 1 Nov, 24, 25 and 31 Dec. 10DM. ☎ 0 89/2 17 91.

Bayerisches Nationalmuseum – ♿ Open Tues to Sun 9.30am to 5pm. Closed Sun before Shrove Tues, Good Fri, 1 May, Whit Sun, 1 Nov, 25 Dec. 3DM (admission free on Sun). ☎ 0 89/21 12 42 16.

Staatsgalerie moderner Kunst – ♿ Open Tues to Sun 10am to 5pm (Fri until 8pm). Closed Good Fri, 1 May, Corpus Christi, 1 Nov, 24 and 31 Dec. 6DM. ☎ 0 89/21 12 71 37.

Schack-Galerie – Open daily (except Tues) 10am to 5pm. Closed 1 Jan, Good Fri, Easter Day, Easter Mon, 1 May, Whit Sun and Mon, Corpus Christi, 1 Nov, 24 and 25 Dec, 31 Dec (pm). 4DM (admission free on Sun). ☎ 0 89/23 80 52 24.

Museum Villa Stuck – Open Tues to Sun 10am to 6pm. ☎ 0 89/4 55 51 10.

Münchner Stadtmuseum – ♿ Open Tues to Sun 10am to 6pm. Closed Shrove Tues, 24 and 31 Dec. 5DM (admission free on Sun). ☎ 0 89/23 32 23 70.

Völkerkundemuseum – Open Tues to Sun 9.30am to 4.30pm. Closed Good Fri, 1 May, 1 Nov, 24 and 25 Dec, 31 Dec (pm). 6DM. ☎ 0 89/10 13 60.

Nymphenburg Palace – Open Apr to Sept Tues to Sun 9am to 12.30pm and 1.30pm to 5pm; 1st fortnight in Oct Tues to Sun 9am to 12.30pm and 1.30pm to 4pm; mid-Oct to Mar Tues to Sun 10am to 12.30pm and 1.30pm to 4pm. Closed 1 Jan, Shrove Tues, 1 Nov, 24, 25 and 31 Dec. 5DM. ☎ 0 89/17 90 80.

Lola Montez by Josef Stieler, Nymphenburg Palace

Amalienburg – Same admission times as Nymphenburg. 3DM. ☎ 0 89/17 90 80.

Marstallmuseum und Porzellansammlung – Open Apr to Sept Tues to Sun 9am to noon and 1pm to 5pm; 1st fortnight in Oct Tues to Sun 9am to noon and 1pm to 4pm; mid-Oct to Mar Tues to Sun 10am to noon and 1pm to 4pm. Closed 1 Jan, Shrove Tues, 1 Nov, 24, 25 and 31 Dec. 4DM. ☎ 0 89/17 90 80.

Museum Mensch und Natur – ♿ Open Tues to Sun 9am to 5pm. Closed Shrove Tues, 24, 25 and 31 Dec. 3DM (admission free on Sun). ☎ 0 89/17 64 94.

Botanischer Garten – Open May to Aug daily 9am to 7pm; Apr and Sept 9am to 6pm; Feb, Mar and Oct 9am to 5pm; Jan, Nov and Dec 9am to 4.30pm. Closed 24 and 31 Dec. 4DM. ☎ 0 89/17 86 13 10.

Excursions

Tierpark Hellabrunn – ♿ Open Apr to Sept daily 8am to 6pm; Oct to Mar 9am to 5pm. 10DM. ☎ 0 89/62 50 80.

Bavaria-Filmstadt Geiselgasteig – ♿ Guided tours (1hr 30min) May to Oct daily 9am to 5pm; Mar and Apr 9am to 4pm; Nov to Feb 10am to 3pm. Closed 1 Jan, 24 to 26 and 31 Dec. 17DM. ☎ 0 89/64 99 23 04.

Olympiapark – The park itself is open all the time and can be visited free of charge. In summer there are guided tours of the sports facilities. The Olympia tower is open daily 9am to midnight, although the last lift up leaves at 11pm. 5DM. ☎ 0 89/30 67 24 14.

BMW-Museum – ♿ Open daily 9am to 5pm (last admissions 4pm). Closed 1 Jan (until noon), 24 and 31 Dec. 5.50DM. ☎ 0 89/38 22 33 07.

Schloß Schleißheim – Open Apr to Sept Tues to Sun 10am to 12.30pm and 1.30pm to 5pm; Oct to Mar Tues to Sun 10am to 12.30pm and 1.30pm to 4pm. Closed 1 Jan, Shrove Tues, 24, 25 and 31 Dec. 2DM. ☎ 0 89/3 15 87 20.

Flugwerft Schleißheim – Open daily 9am to 5pm. Closed 1 Jan, Shrove Tues, Good Fri, 1 May, 24, 25 and 31 Dec. 5DM. ☎ 0 89/3 15 71 40.

Andechs: Benedictine Abbey Church – ♿ Only the abbey church and brewery are open to the public: May to Sept daily 8am to 7pm; Oct to Apr daily 8am to 6pm. ☎ 0 81 52/37 60.

Dachau Concentration Camp Memorial – ♿ Open Tues to Sun 9am to 5pm. Admission free, but donations are appreciated. ☎ 0 81 31/17 41.

MÜNSTER   🛈 Klemensstraße 9 – 48127 – ☎ 02 51/4 92 27 10 – Fax 02 51/4 92 77 43

Dom: Treasury – ♿ Open Tues to Sun 11am to 4pm. 2DM. ☎ 02 51/4 24 71.

Westfälisches Landesmuseum für Kunst und Kulturgeschichte – ♿ Open Tues to Sun 10am to 6pm. Closed 1 Jan, 24, 25 and 31 Dec. 5DM (admission free on Fri). ☎ 02 51/59 07 01.

Rathaus: Friedenssaal – Open Mon to Fri 9am to 5pm, Sat 9am to 4pm, Sun 10am to 1pm. ☎ 02 51/4 92 27 24.

Westfälisches Museum für Naturkunde – Open Tues to Sun 9am to 6pm. Closed 24 and 25 Dec. 6DM. ☎ 02 51/5 91 05.

Mühlenhof-Freilichtmuseum – ♿ Open mid-Mar to end of Oct daily 10am to 6pm (last admissions 5pm); Nov to mid-Mar Tues to Sat 1pm to 4.30pm, Sun 11am to 4.30pm (last admissions 4pm). 5DM. ☎ 02 51/98 12 00.

Excursion

Telgte: Heimathaus Münsterland – ♿ Open Tues to Sun 10am to 6pm. Closed 24, 25 and 31 Dec. 5DM. ☎ 0 25 04/9 31 20.

MÜNSTERLÄNDER WASSERBURGEN

Wasserburgen – From Münster there are **bus trips** to the various castles in the surrounding area Apr to Sept Sat at 2pm; Oct Sat at 1pm. 32-49.50DM, depending on route. ☎ 02 51/4 92 27 10.

Anholt – Guided tours (1hr) Apr to Sept Tues to Sun at 11am, 1pm, 2pm, 3pm and 4pm; Oct to Mar Sat and Sun at 11am, 1pm, 2pm, 3pm and 4pm. Closed 1 Jan, 24 to 26 and 31 Dec. 10DM. ☎ 0 28 74/4 53 53.

Gemen – Since the castle is an educational centre, it is not always open to the public. Enquire in advance. ☎ 0 28 61/9 22 00.

Hülshoff – Open mid-Mar to mid-Dec daily 9.30am to 6pm. 5DM. ☎ 0 25 34/10 52.

Lembeck – Guided tours (45min) Mar to mid-Nov daily 10am to 6pm. 7DM. ☎ 0 23 69/71 67.

Raesfeld – Guided tours (1hr) only by reservation at the tourist office. ☎ 0 28 65/95 51 27.

Vischering – Open Apr to Oct 10am to 12.30pm and 1.30pm to 5.30pm; Nov to Mar Tues to Sun 10am to 12.30pm and 1.30pm to 4.30pm. Closed 1 Jan, 16, 24, 25 and 31 Dec. 4DM. ☎ 0 25 91/79 90 10.

N

NAUMBURG   🛈 Markt 6 – 06618 – ☎ 0 34 45/20 16 14 – Fax 0 34 45/26 60 47

Excursions

Freyburg: Neuenburg – Open Apr to Oct Tues to Sun 10am to 6pm; Nov to Mar Tues to Sun 10am to 5pm. 8DM. ☎ 03 44 64/2 80 28.

Schulpforte – The grounds of the monastery are open to the public at all times (admission free). The buildings can be visited only as part of a guided tour (1hr to 1hr 30min): Apr to Oct Sat at 10.30am and 2pm. 3DM. ☎ 03 44 63/3 50.

Bad Kösen: Romanesque house – Open Apr to Oct Tues to Sun 10am to 5pm (Wed 10am to noon and 1pm to 5pm); Nov to Mar Tues to Sun 10am to 4pm (Wed 10am to noon and 1pm to 4pm). Closed mid-Dec to mid-Jan. 4DM. ☎ 03 44 63/2 76 68.

Bad Kösen: Rudelsburg – Open Apr to Dec daily 10am to 6pm; Jan to Mar Tues to Fri 10am to 5pm, Sat and Sun 10am to 6pm. 1DM (to climb the tower). ☎ 03 44 63/2 73 25. **Burg Saaleck** – Open Apr to Oct Tues to Fri 10am to 5pm, Sat and Sun 10am to 6pm. 2DM. ☎ 03 44 63/2 77 45.

NENNIG

Roman Villa and tour – Open Apr to Sept Tues to Sun 8.30am to noon and 1pm to 6pm; Jan to Mar and Oct to Nov Tues to Sun 9am to 11.30am and 1pm to 4.30pm. Closed Dec to mid-Jan. 3DM. ☎ 0 68 67/6 60.

NEUBRANDENBURG

🛈 Waagestraße – 17033 – ☎ 03 95/1 94 33 – Fax 03 95/5 44 23 18

St. Johanniskirche – ♿ Open May to Sept Mon to Fri 10am to 4pm. ☎ 03 95/5 82 34 75.

NEUSCHWANSTEIN

Roman mosaic at Nennig

Waldow Fotografie/Gemeinde Perl

Tour – Guided tours (35min) Apr to Sept daily 9am to 5.30pm; Oct to Mar daily 10am to 4pm. Closed 1 Jan, Shrove Tues, 1 Nov, 24, 25 and 31 Dec. 12DM. ☎ 0 83 62/8 10 35.

NÖRDLINGEN   🛈 Marktplatz 2 – 86720 ☎ 0 90 81/43 80 – Fax 0 90 81/8 41 02

Stadtmuseum – Open Mar to Oct Tues to Sun 1.30pm to 4.30pm. Closed Good Fri, 1 May, 1 Nov. 5DM. ☎ 0 90 81/2 73 82 30.

Rieskrater-Museum – Open Tues to Sun 10am to noon and 1.30pm to 4.30pm. Closed 1 Jan, Shrove Tues, Good Fri, 24 to 26 and 31 Dec. 5DM. ☎ 0 90 81/2 73 82 20.

NORDFRIESISCHE INSELN

Boat connections to Föhr – Dagebüll to Föhr (45min): 10-15 trips per day. Return fare 15DM. Dagebüll to Amrum (1hr 30min to 2hr): 8-10 trips per day. Return fare 23.50DM. Timetables vary. For information and reservations for cars, contact Wyker Dampfschiffs-Reederei GmbH in Wyk on Föhr ☎ 0 46 81/8 01 47.

Wyk: Friesenmuseum – Open Mar to Oct Tues to Sun 10am to 5pm; Nov to Feb Tues to Sun 2pm to 5pm. Closed 24 and 31 Dec. 7.50DM. ☎ 0 46 81/25 71.

Boat connections to Amrum – Schlüttsiel to Amrum (2hr 30min): 1-2 trips per day. Return fare 23.50DM. Timetables vary. For information and reservations for cars, contact Wyker Dampfschiffs-Reederei GmbH in Wyk on Föhr ☎ 0 46 81/8 01 47.

Boat connections to Pellworm – Landing-stages: Strucklahnungstörn, Nordstrand, Pellworm. Trips (35min) between 4 and 7 times per day depending on tides. Return fare 17DM/person, 73-83DM/vehicle (passengers not included). ☎ 0 48 44/7 53.

NÜRBURGRING

Erlebnispark Nürbürgring – Open 10am to 6pm. 9.50DM. ☎ 0 26 91/30 26 02.

NÜRNBERG   🛈 Hauptmarkt 18 – 90403 – ☎ 09 11/2 33 61 35 – Fax 09 11/20 43 59

Germanisches Nationalmuseum – ♿ Open Tues to Sun 10am to 5pm (Wed until 9pm). Free guided tours of museum Tues to Sat at 10.30am and 3pm, Sun at 3pm. Closed Shrove Tues, Good Fri, 24, 25 and 31 Dec. 6DM. ☎ 09 11/1 33 11 61.

Albrecht-Dürer-Haus – Open Mar to Oct Tues to Sun 10am to 5pm (Thur until 8pm); Nov to Feb Tues to Fri 1pm to 5pm, Sat and Sun 10am to 5pm. Closed 1 Jan, Shrove Tues and Mon before it, Good Fri. 5DM. ☎ 09 11/2 31 25 68.

Burg – Guided tours (45min) Apr to Sept daily 9am to 5pm; Oct to Mar daily 9.30am to 4pm. Closed 1 Jan, Shrove Tues, 1 Nov, 24, 25 and 31 Dec. 9DM. ☎ 09 11/22 57 26.

Stadtmuseum Fembohaus – Currently closed for restoration. ☎ 09 11/2 31 25 95.

Spielzeugmuseum – Open Tues to Sun 10am to 5pm (Wed until 9pm). Closed 1 Jan, Shrove Tues and Mon before it, Good Fri, 24 to 26 and 31 Dec. 5DM. ☎ 09 11/2 31 31 64.

Verkehrsmuseum – ♿ Open Tues to Sun 9am to 5pm. Closed 1 Jan, Good Fri, 24 and 31 Dec. 6DM. ☎ 09 11/2 19 24 28.

○

OBERSTDORF   🛈 Marktplatz 7 – 87561 – ☎ 0 83 22/70 00 – Fax 0 83 22/70 02 36

Nebelhorn: Cable-car – Operates every 20min. First departure is at 8.30am, last trip down from Höfatsblick is at 4.30pm or 5pm. Closed mid-Apr to mid-May, and early Nov to mid-Dec. 42DM to summit and back. ☎ 0 83 22/96 00 96.

Fellhorn: Cable-car – Operates mid-May to early Nov 8.20am to 4.50pm every 20min; mid-Dec to mid-Apr (depending on snow) 8.30am to 4.30pm (until 5pm from Feb) every 15min. Closed early Nov to mid-Dec and mid-Apr to mid/late May. 38DM to summit and back. ☎ 0 83 22/9 60 00.

Excursion

Breitachklamm – Accessible May to Oct daily 8am to 5pm; Dec to Apr daily 9am to 4pm. Not accessible in Nov. 4.50DM. ☎ 0 83 22/48 87.

ODENWALD

Amorbach: Abbey church – ♿ Guided tours (45min) Apr to Oct Mon to Sat 9am to 4.30pm, Sun 11.15am to 4.30pm; Mar Mon to Sat 9.45am to 11.45am and 1.30pm to 3.45pm, Sun 11.15am to 3.45pm; Jan and Feb Sat 9.45am to 11.45am and 1.30pm to 3.45pm, Sun 1.30pm to 3.45pm. 4.50DM. ☎ 0 93 73/97 15 451.

Park von Eulbach – ♿ Open Apr to Oct daily 9am to 6pm; Nov to mid-Jan daily 9am to 4pm; mid-Jan to Mar daily 9am to 5pm. 6DM. ☎ 0 60 62/9 59 20.

Michelstadt: Odenwald-Museum – Open 2nd Sat before Easter to end of Oct Tues to Fri 10am to 12.30pm and 2pm to 5pm, Sat and Sun 10am to 12.30pm and 2pm to 5.30pm. 2DM. ☎ 0 60 61/7 41 39.

OLDENBURG   🛈 Wallstraße 14 – 26122 – ☎ 04 41/1 57 44 – Fax 04 41/2 48 92 02

Landesmuseum für Kunst und Kulturgeschichte – ♿ Open Tues to Fri 9am to 5pm, Sat and Sun 10am to 5pm. Closed 1 Jan, Good Fri, Easter Day, 1 May, Whit Sun, 24, 25 and 31 Dec. 4DM. ☎ 04 41/2 20 73 00.

Stadtmuseum Oldenburg – Open Tues to Fri 9am to 5pm, Sat 9am to noon, Sun 10am to 5pm. Closed 1 Jan, 1 May, 24 and 31 Dec. Admission free. ☎ 04 41/2 35 28 81.

Augusteum – ♿ Open Tues to Fri 9am to 5pm, Sat and Sun 10am to 5pm. Closed 1 Jan, Good Fri, Easter Day, 1 May, Whit Sun, 24, 25 and 31 Dec. 4DM. ☎ 04 41/2 20 73 00.

Staatliches Museum für Naturkunde und Vorgeschichte – ♿ Open Tues to Thur 9am to 5pm, Fri 9am to 3pm, Sat and Sun 10am to 5pm. Closed 1 Jan, Good Fri, Easter Day, Whit Sun, 24, 25 and 31 Dec. ☎ 04 41/9 24 43 00.

Excursion

Museumsdorf Cloppenburg – ♿ Open Mar to Oct daily 9am to 6pm; Nov to Feb daily 10am to 4pm. Closed 24 and 31 Dec. 7DM. ☎ 0 44 71/9 48 40.

OSNABRÜCK   🛈 Krahnstraße 58 – 49074 – ☎ 05 41/3 23 22 02 – Fax 05 41/3 23 27 09

Rathaus – Open Mon to Fri 8.30am to 6pm, Sat 9am to 4pm, Sun 10am to 4pm. Closed on public holidays. Admission free. ☎ 05 41/3 23 21 52.

Felix-Nussbaum-Haus – Open Tues to Sun 11am to 6pm (Thur until 8pm). Closed 1 Jan, Good Fri, 1 May, 24 and 31 Dec. 8DM. ☎ 05 41/3 23 24 15.

OSTFRIESISCHE INSELN

Boat connections to Borkum – Car ferry from Emden (approx 2hr) 2-4 trips per day. Return fare 46DM, cars 14DM. ☎ 0 49 21/89 07 22.

Boat connections to Juist – From Norddeich (approx 1hr 15min). Return fare 42DM. Timetable information: ☎ 0 49 31/98 70.

Boat connections to Norderney – From Norddeich (journey time approx 1hr). Return fare 23.50DM, cars from 99DM. Timetable information: ☎ 0 49 32/9 13 13.

Boat connections to Baltrum – Landing-stages: Neßmersiel and Baltrum. Trips (30min) twice a day depending on tides. Return fare 24DM. ☎ 0 49 69/9 13 00.

Boat connections to Langeoog – From Bensersiel (approx 1hr) daily between 9.30am and 5.35pm. From Langeoog daily between 8.15am and 4.15pm. Return fare 31DM. No cars. ☎ 0 49 72/69 32 60.

Boat connections to Spiekeroog – Landing-stages: Neuharlingersiel and Spiekeroog. Trips (50min) 2-4 times per day depending on tides. Return fare 28-35DM. ☎ 0 49 76/91 93 33.

Boat connections to Wangerooge – From Harlesiel (approx 50min). No cars. Return fare 46DM. ☎ 0 44 64/94 94 11.

OTTOBEUREN   🛈 Marktplatz 14 – 87724 – ☎ 0 83 32/92 19 50 – Fax 0 83 32/92 19 92

Klosterkirche – Open Apr to Sept daily 7am to 7pm; Oct daily 7am to 6pm; Nov to Mar daily 7am to 5pm. Admission free. ☎ 0 83 32/79 80.

Klostergebäude – Open 20 Mar to 1 Nov daily 10am to noon and 2pm to 5pm; 2 Nov to 19 Mar Mon to Fri 2pm to 4pm, Sat and Sun 10am to noon and 2pm to 4pm (last admissions 20min before closing). Closed 1 Jan, Good Fri, 24 and 31 Dec. 4DM. ☎ 0 83 32/79 80.

P – Q

PADERBORN   🛈 Marienplatz 2a – 33098 – ☎ 0 52 51/88 29 80 – Fax 0 52 51/88 29 90

Diözesanmuseum – Open Tues to Sun 10am to 6pm (10am to 8pm on 1st Wed in month). Closed 24, 25 and 31 Dec. 4DM. ☎ 0 52 51/12 54 00.

Heinz Nixdorf MuseumsForum – ♿ Open Tues to Fri 9am to 6pm, Sat and Sun 10am to 6pm. 6DM. ☎ 0 52 51/30 66 00.

Traktoren-Museum – Open Tues to Sun 10am to 6pm. Closed 24, 25 and 31 Dec. 10DM. ☎ 0 52 51/49 07 11.

PASSAU   🛈 Rathausplatz 3 – 94032 – ☎ 08 51/95 59 80 – Fax 08 51/5 72 98

Glasmuseum – Open Apr to Sept daily 10am to 4pm; Oct to Mar 1pm to 4pm. 5DM. ☎ 08 51/3 50 71.

Museum Moderner Kunst – Open Tues to Sun 10am to 6pm (Thur until 8pm). Closed 24 and 25 Dec. 8DM. ☎ 08 51/3 83 87 90.

Die PFALZ

Hambacher Schloß – Open Mar to Nov daily 10am to 6pm (last admissions 30min before closing). 9DM. ☎ 0 63 21/3 08 81.

Schloß Villa Ludwigshöhe – Guided tours (45min) week before Easter to end of Sept 10am to 1pm and 2pm to 6pm; Oct to Sun before Easter 10am to 1pm and 2pm to 5pm (last admissions 45min before closing). Closed in Dec. 5DM (including Max-Slevogt-Galerie). The Max-Slevogt-Galerie can be visited independently of the guided tour. ☎ 01 80/5 22 13 60.

Trifels – Open Apr to Sept 9am to 6pm; Oct to Mar 9am to 5pm. Closed Dec. 5DM. ☎ 0 63 46/84 70.

Burg Berwartstein – Open Mar to Oct 9am to 6pm; Nov to Feb Sat and Sun only 1pm to 6pm. 5DM. ☎ 0 63 98/2 10.

🚹 Friedrich-Ebert-Straße 5 - 14467 - ☎ 03 3127 55 80 - Fax 03 31/2 75 58 99

Sanssouci: Bildergalerie – Open 15 May to 15 Oct 10am to 5pm. 4DM. ☎ 03 31/9 69 42 02.

Schloß Sanssouci – Guided tours (40min) Apr to Oct Tues to Sun 9am to 5pm; Jan to Mar, Nov to Dec 9am to 4pm. 10DM. ☎ 03 31/9 69 42 02.

Neue Kammern – ♿ Open 15 May to 15 Oct daily 10am to 5pm; 1 Apr to 14 may and last fortnight in Oct Sat and Sun 10am to 5pm. 4DM. ☎ 03 31/9 69 42 02.

Neue Orangerie – Open 15 May to 15 Oct Tues to Sun 10am to 5pm. 5DM. ☎ 03 31/9 69 42 02.

Neues Palais – Guided tours (1hr) Apr to Oct Mon to Thur, Sat and Sun 9am to 5pm; Jan to Mar and Nov to Dec 9am to 4pm. 8DM. ☎ 03 31/9 69 42 02.

Schloß Charlottenhof – ♿ Guided tours (30min) mid-May to mid-Oct Tues to Sun 10am to 5pm. 6DM ☎ 03 31/9 69 40.

Dampfmaschinenhaus (Moschee) – ♿ Guided tours (30min) 15 May to 15 Oct Sat and Sun 10am to 5pm. 4DM. ☎ 03 31/9 69 42 02.

Marmorpalais – Guided tours (1hr) Apr to Oct Tues to Sun 10am to 5pm; Nov to Mar Sat and Sun 10am to 4pm. Closed 24 and 31 Dec. 10DM. ☎ 03 31/9 62 42 00.

Schloß Cecilienhof – ♿ Open Apr to Oct Tues to Sun 9am to 5pm; Nov to Mar 9am to 4pm. Closed 24, 25 and 31 Dec. 6DM. ☎ 03 31/9 69 42 44.

Excursion

Kloster Lehnin – Open Apr to Oct Mon to Fri 9.30am to 5.30pm, Sat and Sun 10.30am to 5pm; Nov to Mar Mon to Fri 9.30am to 4.30pm, Sat and Sun 10.30am to 4pm. Closed 1 Jan, 24 Dec. ☎ 0 33 82/76 88 42.

QUEDLINBURG 🚹 Markt 2 - 06484 - ☎ 0 39 46/77 30 00 - Fax 0 39 46/77 30 16

Klopstock-Haus – Open Tues to Sun 10am to 5pm. Closed 24 and 31 Dec. 5DM. ☎ 0 39 46/27 30.

Feininger-Galerie – ♿ Open Apr to Oct Tues to Sun 10am to 6pm; Nov to Mar Tues to Sun 10am to 5pm. Closed 1 Jan, 24 and 31 Dec. ☎ 0 39 46/22 38.

Schloßmuseum – Open May to Sept Tues to Sun 10am to 6pm; Oct to Apr Tues to Fri 9am to 5pm, Sat and Sun 10am to 5pm (last admissions 30min before closing). Closed 24 and 31 Dec. 5DM. ☎ 0 39 46/27 30.

R

RASTATT 🚹 Kaiserstraße - 76437 - ☎ 0 72 22/97 24 62 - Fax 0 72 22/97 21 08

Schloß – Guided tours (1hr) Apr to Oct Tues to Sun 10am to 5pm; Nov to Mar Tues to Sun 10am to 4pm (last tour 1hr before closing). 6DM. ☎ 0 72 22/97 83 85.

Wehrgeschichtliches Museum – ♿ Open Tues to Sun 9.30am to 5pm. Closed 24 and 31 Dec. 3DM. ☎ 0 72 22/3 42 44.

Excursion

Schloß Favorite – Guided tours (1hr) mid-Mar to Sept Tues to Sun 9am to 5pm; Oct to mid-Nov Tues to Sun 9am to 4pm. 8DM. ☎ 0 72 22/4 12 07.

RATZEBURG 🚹 Schloßwiese 7 - 23909 - ☎ 0 45 41/80 00 80 - Fax 0 45 41/53 27

Ernst-Barlach-Museum – Open Mar to Nov Tues to Sun 10am to 1pm and 2pm to 5pm. 5DM. ☎ 0 45 41/37 89.

RAVENSBRÜCK

Mahn- und Gedenkstätte Ravensbrück – Open Tues to Sun 9am to 5pm (last admissions at 4.30pm). Admission free. ☎ 03 30 93/3 92 41.

Detail from the Florentine Room, Schloß Favorite, Rastatt

Staatl. Liegenschaftsamt, Karlsruhe

🏛 Kirchstraße 16 - 88212 - ☎ 07 51/8 23 24 - Fax 07 51/8 24 66

🏛 Altes Rathaus - 93047 - ☎ 09 41/5 07 34 16 - Fax 09 41/5 07 44 19

Dom St.-Peter: Treasury - Open Apr to 1 Nov Tues to Sat 10am to 5pm, Sun noon to 5pm; Dec to Mar Fri and Sat 10am to 4pm, Sun noon to 4pm; 25 Dec to 6 Jan Tues to Sat 10am to 4pm, Sun noon to 4pm. Closed 1 Jan and 24 Dec. 3DM. ☎ 09 41/5 10 68.

Dom St.-Peter: Cloister - Guided tours (1hr 15min with cathedral) May to Oct Mon to Sat at 10am, 11am and 2pm, Sun at noon and 2pm; Nov to Apr Mon to Sat at 11am, Sun at noon. 4DM. ☎ 09 41/5 97 10 02.

Diözesanmuseum St. Ulrich - Open Apr to 1 Nov Tues to Sun 10am to 5pm. 3DM. ☎ 09 41/5 10 68.

Reichstagsmuseum - Guided tours Apr to Oct Mon to Sat every 30min 9.30am to noon and 2pm to 4pm, Sun 10am to noon and 2pm to 4pm; Nov to Mar every hour Mon to Sat 9.30am to 11.30am and 2pm to 4pm, Sun 10am to noon. Closed 24 and 25 Dec. 4DM. ☎ 09 41/5 07 14 40.

Schloß Thurn und Taxis - Guided tours (1hr 30min) Apr to Oct Mon to Fri at 11am, 2pm, 3pm and 4pm, Sat and Sun at 10am, 11am, 2pm, 3pm and 4pm; Nov to Mar Sat and Sun at 10am, 11am, 2pm and 3pm. Closed 24 Dec. 12DM (castle and cloister). ☎ 09 41/5 04 81 33.

Cloister - Same admission times and charges as Schloß Thurn und Taxis.

Marstallmuseum - Open Apr to Oct Mon to Fri 11am to 5pm, Sat and Sun 10am to 5pm; Nov to Mar guided tours only Sat and Sun at 11.30am and 2pm. Closed 24 Dec. 7DM. ☎ 09 41/5 04 81 33.

Thurn und Taxis Museum - Open Mon to Fri 11am to 5pm, Sat and Sun and public holidays 10am to 5pm. 8DM (joint opening with Marstallmuseum Apr to Oct), 6DM (Nov to Mar). ☎ 09 41/5 07 44 10.

Historisches Museum - ♿ Open Tues to Sun 10am to 4pm. Closed 1 Jan, Good Fri, Easter Mon, 1 May, Whit Mon, 1 Nov, 24, 25 and 31 Dec. 4DM (admission free on 1st Sun of month). ☎ 09 41/5 07 14 40.

Excursions

Walhalla - Open Apr to Sept daily 9am to 5.45pm; Oct daily 9am to 4.45pm; Nov to Mar daily 10am to 11.45am and 1pm to 3.45pm. Closed Shrove Tues, 24, 25 and 31 Dec. 3DM. ☎ 0 94 03/96 16 80.

Befreiungshalle - Open May to Aug daily 9am to 6pm; Mar, Apr, Sept and Oct daily 9am to 5.30pm; Nov to Feb 9am to noon and 1pm to 4pm (last admissions 30min before closing). Closed Shrove Tues, 1 Nov, 24 and 25 Dec. 4DM. ☎ 0 94 41/15 84.

Kloster Weltenburg - Only the abbey church is open to visitors: in summer 7am to 8.30pm; in winter 8am to 5pm. ☎ 0 94 41/20 40.

🏛 Wittelsbacherstraße 15 - 83435 - ☎ 0 86 51/60 63 03 - Fax 0 86 51/60 63 11

Bad Reichenhaller Salzmuseum - Guided tours (1hr) May to Oct daily 10am to 11.30am and 2pm to 4pm; Nov to Apr Tues and Thur 2pm to 4pm (and also Jan to Apr every 1st Sun in month). 8.50DM. ☎ 0 86 51/7 00 20.

Tour - Open Apr to Oct Tues to Sun 9.30am to 5pm; Nov to Mar Tues to Sun 10am to 4pm. Closed 25 Dec. 8DM. ☎ 03 39 31/21 05.

Pfalz bei Kaub - Open Tues before Easter to late Sept Tues to Sun 10am to 1pm and 2pm to 6pm; Jan to Palm Sun, Oct and Nov Tues to Sun 10am to 1pm and 2pm to 5pm (last admissions 30min before closing). The fortress is on an island: take the ferry there from Kaub. 4DM plus fare for crossing. ☎ 01 80/5 22 13 60.

Marksburg: Castle - Guided tours (50min) Easter to Oct daily 10am to 5pm; Nov to Easter daily 11am to 4pm. Closed 24 to 31 Dec. 8DM. ☎ 0 26 27/2 06.

Lahneck: Fortress - Guided tours (40min) Apr to Oct daily 10am to 5.30pm, on the hour. 6DM. ☎ 0 26 21/27 89.

Schloß Stolzenfels - Guided tours (45min) week before Easter to Sept Tues to Sun 10am to 1pm and 2pm to 6pm; Jan to Sun before Easter, Oct and Nov Tues to Sun 10am to 1pm and 2pm to 5pm (last admissions 45min before closing). 5DM. ☎ 02 61/5 16 55.

Gedeonseck: Chair-lift - Operates mid-June to Aug daily 9.30am to 6.30pm; May to mid-June Mon to Sat 10am to 6pm, Sun until 6.30pm; Sept and Oct Mon to Sat 10am to 6pm; last fortnight in Apr Mon to Sat 10am to 5.30pm. Return fare 10DM. ☎ 0 67 42/25 10.

RHEINTAL

St. Goar: Burg Rheinfels – Open Apr to Sept daily 9am to 6pm; Oct daily until 5pm. 5DM. ☏ 0 67 41/3 83.

Burg Sooneck – Guided tours (45min) Apr to Sept Tues to Sun 9am to 6pm; Oct to Mar Tues to Sun 9am to 5pm (last admissions 45min before closing). 5DM. ☏ 0 67 43/60 64.

Burg Reichenstein – Open Mar to mid-Nov daily 9am to 6pm. 6DM. ☏ 0 67 21/61 17.

Burg Rheinstein – Open May to Sept 9.30am to 5.30pm; mid-Mar to end of Apr and Oct to mid-Nov daily 10am to 5pm. 6.50DM. ☏ 0 67 21/63 48.

ROMANTISCHE STRASSE

Weikersheim: Castle – & Guided tours (1hr) Apr to Oct daily 9am to 6pm; Nov to Mar 10am to noon and 1.30pm to 4.30pm. Closed 24 and 31 Dec. 7DM. ☏ 0 79 34/83 64.

Schloß Harburg – Guided tours (50min) mid-Mar to Sept Tues to Sun 10am to 5pm; Oct 10am to 4pm. 7DM. ☏ 0 90 80/9 68 60.

ROSTOCK   🛈 Schnickmannstraße 13 - 18055 - ☏ 03 81/49 79 90 - Fax 03 81/4 97 99 23

Boat trip – Departures from landing-stages in the harbour (Stadthafen, by Schnickmannstraße), at Stadthafen/Portcenter and at Warnemünde/Alter Strom. Details of timetables and fares from the tourist office: ☏ 03 81/1 94 33.

Schiffahrtsmuseum – Open Tues to Sun 9am to 5pm. Closed Good Fri, Whit Sun, 24 and 31 Dec. 4DM. ☏ 03 81/4 92 26 97.

Kulturhistorisches Museum – Open Tues to Sun 9am to 5pm. Closed Good Fri, Whit Sun, 24 and 31 Dec. 4DM. ☏ 03 81/45 59 14.

ROTHENBURG OB DER TAUBER   🛈 Marktplatz 2 - 91541 - ☏ 0 98 61/4 04 92 - Fax 0 98 61/8 68 07

Mittelalterliches Kriminalmuseum – Open Apr to Oct daily 9.30am to 6pm; Jan, Feb and Nov daily 2pm to 4pm; Mar and Dec daily 10am to 4pm (last admissions 30min before closing). 6DM. ☏ 0 98 61/53 59.

Reichsstadtmuseum – Open Apr to Oct daily 9.30am to 5.30pm; Nov to Mar 1pm to 4pm. Closed 24 and 31 Dec. 5DM. ☏ 0 98 61/93 90 43.

ROTTWEIL   🛈 Rathaus, Rathausgasse - 78628 - ☏ 07 41/49 42 80 - Fax 07 41/49 43 73

Dominikanermuseum – & Open Tues to Sun 10am to 1pm and 2pm to 5pm. Closed on public holidays. 3DM. ☏ 07 41/49 43 30.

Insel RÜGEN

Jagdschloß Granitz – Open May to Oct daily 9am to 6pm; Nov to Apr Tues to Sun 10am to 4pm (last admissions 30min before closing). Closed 25 Dec. 5DM. ☏ 03 83 93/22 63.

Kap Arkona: Old Lighthouse – Open June to Aug daily 9.30am to 8pm; Sept daily 10am to 7pm; Apr, May and Oct daily 10am to 6pm; Jan to Mar, Nov to Dec daily noon to 4pm. Closed 24 Dec. 5DM. ☏ 03 83 91/1 21 15.

Excursion

Hiddensee: Ferry connections – Boat trips to the island from Wiek, Breege and Schaprode on Rügen and from Stralsund, journey time 30-45min. Details from Reederei Hiddensee GmbH, Stralsund Office, Fährstraße 16, 18439 Stralsund. ☏ 0 38 31/26 81 16. On arrival, health resort tickets cost 3DM.

RUHRGEBIET

Bochum

Kunstsammlung Museum Bochum – Open Tues, Thur-Sat 11am to 5pm, Wed 11am to 8pm, Sun 11am to 6pm. Closed 1 Jan, Good Fri, 1 May, 24, 25 and 31 Dec. 5DM. ☏ 02 34/5 16 00 30.

Deutsches Bergbau-Museum – & Open Tues to Fri 8.30am to 5.30pm, Sat and Sun 10am to 4pm. Closed 1 Jan, 1 May, 24, 25 and 26 and 31 Dec. 6DM. ☏ 02 34/5 87 70.

Eisenbahnmuseum – & Open Apr to Oct Wed and Fri 10am to 5pm, Sun 10m to 3pm; Nov to mid-Dec, mid-Jan to Mar Wed and Fri 10am to 5pm, Sun 10am to 1pm (last admissions 45min before closing). 7.50DM. ☏ 02 34/49 25 16 (Wed and Fri only).

Bottrop

Quadrat – Open Tues to Sun 10am to 6pm. Closed 1 Jan, 24, 25 and 31 Dec. Admission free. ☎ 0 20 41/2 97 16.

Warner Bros. Movie World – ♿ Open July and Aug daily 9am to 9pm; end of Mar to June and Sept to 24 Oct Mon to Fri 9.30am to 6pm, Sat and Sun 9.30am to 7pm. Day ticket: 38DM. ☎ 0 20 45/89 98 99.

Duisburg

Wilhelm-Lehmbruck-Museum – Open Tues to Sat 11am to 5pm, Sun 10am to 6pm. Closed 1 Jan, 1 May, 24, 25 and 31 Dec. 6DM. ☎ 02 03/2 83 26 30.

Kultur- und stadthistorisches Museum – Open Tues to Thur, Sat 10am to 5pm, Fri 10am to 2pm, Sun 10am to 6pm. Closed 1 Jan, 1 May, 24, 25 and 31 Dec. 5DM. ☎ 02 03/2 83 26 40.

Museum der Deutschen Binnenschiffahrt – Open Tues to Sun 10am to 5pm (museum ships Apr to Oct only). 5DM. ☎ 02 03/80 88 90.

Landschaftpark Duisburg Nord Lighting Effects – Operate Fri to Sun from dusk to 2am. ☎ 02 03/4 29 19 42.

Hagen

Karl-Ernst-Osthaus-Museum – Open Tues to Sun 11am to 6pm (Thur until 8pm). Closed 1 Jan, 1 May, 24, 25 and 31 Dec. Admission free, except during special exhibitions. ☎ 0 23 31/2 07 31 31.

Westfälisches Freilichtmuseum – Open Mar to Oct Tues to Sun 9am to 6pm (last admissions 1hr before closing). 7DM. ☎ 0 23 31/78 07 39.

Oberhausen

Gasometer – Open May to Oct daily 10am to 8pm; Nov to Apr Tues to Sun 10am to 5pm (Wed until 3pm). Closed 24 to 26 Dec. 4DM. ☎ 02 08/80 37 45.

Rheinisches Industriemuseum – Open Tues to Sun 10am to 5pm (Thur until 8pm). Closed Good Fri, 24 and 31 Dec. 5DM. ☎ 02 08/8 57 90.

Recklinghausen

Ikonenmuseum – Open Tues to Fri 10am to 6pm, Sat and Sun 11am to 5pm. 5DM. ☎ 0 23 61/50 19 41.

Altes Schiffshebewerk Henrichenburg – Open Tues to Sun 10am to 6pm. 4DM (joint ticket with new lift 6DM). ☎ 0 23 63/9 70 70.

Solingen

Klingenmuseum – ♿ Open Tues to Thur, Sat and Sun 10am to 5pm, Fri 2pm to 5pm. Closed 1 Jan, 24, 25 and 31 Dec. 6DM. ☎ 02 12/25 83 60.

Wuppertal

Von der Heydt-Museum – ♿ Open Tues to Sun 11am to 6pm (Thur until 8pm). Closed 1 Jan, 1 May, 24 and 25 Dec. 6DM. ☎ 02 02/5 63 62 31.

Museum für Frühindustrialisierung – ♿ Open Tues to Sun 10am to 1pm and 3pm to 5pm. Closed 1 Jan, Easter Day, Whit Sun, 24 and 25 Dec. 3DM. ☎ 02 02/ 5 63 64 98.

S

Oberes SAALETAL

Rudolstadt: Schloß Heidecksburg – Open Tues to Sun 10am to 6pm. 6DM. ☎ 0 36 72/4 29 00.

Saalfeld: Thüringer Heimatmuseum – Open Tues to Sun 10am to 5pm. Closed 24 and 31 Dec. 3.50DM. ☎ 0 36 71/59 84 71.

Saalfeld: Feengrotten – Guided tours (45min) Mar to Oct daily 9am to 5pm; Nov Sat and Sun 10am to 3.30pm; Dec to Feb daily 10am to 3.3.0pm. 8DM. ☎ 0 36 71/5 50 40.

SAARBRÜCKEN 🏢 Hauptbahnhof 4 - 66111 - ☎ 06 81/3 65 15 - Fax 06 81/9 05 33 00

Saar Historical Museum – ♿ Open Tues to Sun 10am to 6pm (Thur 10am to 8pm, Sat noon to 6pm). Closed 1 Jan, Good Fri, Corpus Christi, 24, 25 and 31 Dec. 5DM. ☎ 06 81/50 65 49.

Banqueting hall, Schloß, Saarbrücken

Museum für Vor- und Frühgeschichte – Open Tues to Sat 9am to 5pm, Sun and public holidays 10am to 6pm. Admission free. ☎ 06 81/9 54 05 11.

Abenteuermuseum – Open Tues and Wed 9am to 1pm, Thur and Fri 3pm to 7pm, 1st Sat in month 10am to 2pm. 3DM. ☎ 06 81/5 17 47.

Ludwigskirche – &. Open Tues 3pm to 5pm, Wed 10am to noon (Apr to Sept also 4pm to 5.30pm), Sat 4pm to 6pm, Sun 11am to noon. ☎ 06 81/5 25 24.

Basilika St. Johann – Open Mon, Wed and Fri 8.30am to 7.15pm, Tues and Thur 9.30am to 7.15pm, Sat 9am to 7.30pm, Sun 9.30am to 7.30pm. Admission free. ☎ 06 81/3 29 64.

Saarland Museum: Alte Sammlung – &. Open Tues, Thur to Sun 10am to 6pm, Wed noon to 8pm. 3DM. ☎ 06 81/9 96 40.

Moderne Galerie – &. Open Tues, Thur to Sun 10am to 6pm, Wed noon to 8pm. 3DM. ☎ 06 81/9 96 40.

Excursions

Alte Völklinger Hütte – Guided tours (2hr) Mar to Nov Tues to Sun at 10am and 2pm. 6DM. ☎ 0 68 98/2 77 34.

Versöhnungskirche – Can be viewed by appointment only. ☎ 0 68 98/13 21 16.

Homburg: Schloßberghöhlen – Open Mar to Nov Tues to Sun 9am to 6pm; Dec to Feb daily 9am to 4pm. Closed 2 weeks in Dec and 1 week in Jan. 5DM. ☎ 0 68 41/20 64.

Römermuseum Schwarzenacker – Open Mar to Nov Tues to Sun 9am to 6pm; Dec to Feb Sat and Sun 10am to 4.30pm. 5DM. ☎ 0 68 48/8 75.

SÄCHSISCHE SCHWEIZ

Barockgarten Großsedlitz – &. Open Apr to Sept 7am to 8pm; Oct to Mar 8am to 4.30pm. 3DM. ☎ 0 35 29/5 63 90.

Bad SÄCKINGEN

🛈 Waldshuter Straße 20 – 79713 – ☎ 0 77 61/5 68 30 – Fax 0 77 61/56 83 17

SALEM

Schloß and museums – &. Open Apr to 1 Nov Mon to Sat 9.30am to 6pm, Sun 10.30am to 6pm. 21DM. Price includes guided tour of abbey, abbey buildings (palace) and fire brigade museum, visit to craftworkers' village, gardens, cooperage and distillery museums, and a welcoming drink. ☎ 0 75 53/8 14 37.

ST. BLASIEN

🛈 Am Kurgarten – 79837 – ☎ 0 76 72/4 14 30 – Fax 0 76 72/4 14 38

SAUERLAND

Attahöhle – Guided tours (40min) May to Oct daily 9.30am to 4.30pm; Nov to Feb Tues to Sun 10.30am to 3.30pm; Mar and Apr daily 10.30am to 4pm. Closed 24 and 25 Dec. 9.50DM. ☎ 0 27 22/9 37 50.

🛈 Plessenstraße 7 - 24837 - ☎ 0 46 21/2 48 78 - Fax 0 46 21/2 07 03

Schloß Gottorf – Open Mar to Oct daily 9am to 5pm; Nov to Feb Tues to Sun 9.30am to 4pm. Closed 1 Jan, 24, 25 and 31 Dec. ☎ 0 46 21/81 33 00.

Wikinger Museum Haithabu – Open Apr to Oct daily 9am to 5pm; Nov to Mar Tues to Sun 9.30am to 4pm. 4DM. ☎ 0 46 21/81 33 00.

SCHWÄBISCHE ALB

Holzmaden: Urwelt-Museum Hauff – Open Tues to Sun 9am to 5pm. Closed 1 Jan, 24, 25 and 31 Dec. 7DM. ☎ 0 70 23/28 73.

Schloß Lichtenstein – Guided tours (30min) Apr to Oct Mon to Sat 9am to noon and 1pm to 5.30pm, Sun 9am to 5.30pm; Feb, Mar and Nov Sat and Sun 9am to noon and 1pm to 5pm. 6DM. ☎ 0 71 29/41 02.

Bärenhöhle – Open Apr to Oct daily 9am to 5.30pm; Mar and Nov Sat and Sun 9am to 5pm. 5DM. ☎ 0 71 28/6 35.

Kloster Beuron: Abbey church – & The abbey church is open daily 5am to 8pm. Admission free. ☎ 0 74 66/1 70.

SCHWÄBISCH GMÜND
🛈 Im Kornhaus - 73525 - ☎ 0 71 71/60 34 55 - Fax 0 71 71/60 34 59

SCHWÄBISCH HALL
🛈 Am Markt 9 - 74523 ☎ 07 91/75 12 46 - 07 91/75 13 75

Hällisch-Fränkisches Museum – Open Tues to Sun 10am to 5pm (Wed until 8pm). Closed Good Fri, 24, 25 and 31 Dec. Admission free. ☎ 07 91/7 5 13 60.

Excursions

Groß-Comburg: Benedictine abbey – Guided tours Apr to Oct Tues to Fri at 10am, 11am, 2pm, 3pm and 4pm, Sat and Sun at 2pm, 3pm and 4pm. 4DM. ☎ 07 91/93 81 85.

Hohenloher Freilandmuseum – Open May to mid-Nov Tues to Sun 9am to 6pm (June to Aug also open on Mon); mid-Mar to Apr Tues to Sun 10am to 5pm. 9DM. ☎ 07 91/97 10 10.

SCHWARZWALD

Schwarzwälder Freilichtmuseum Vogts-bauernhof – Open Apr to early Nov daily 8.30am to 6pm. 8DM. ☎ 0 78 31/9 35 60.

Triberg: Schwarzwald Museum – & Open May to Oct daily 9am to 6pm; Nov to Apr daily 10am to 5pm; mid-Nov to mid-Dec Sat and Sun only 10am to 5pm. Closed 24 and 25 Dec. 5DM. ☎ 0 77 22/44 34.

Furtwangen: Deutsches Uhrenmuseum – & Open Apr to Oct daily 9am to 6pm; Nov to Mar 10am to 5pm. Closed 24 to 26 Dec. 5DM. ☎ 0 77 23/92 01 17.

St. Peter: Abbey Library – & Guided tours (1hr) Tues at 11am, Thur at 2.30pm, Sun at 11.30am. Closed the week before Easter and 1 week in Sept. 5DM. ☎ 0 76 60/9 10 10.

SCHWERIN
🛈 Am Markt 10 - 19055 - ☎ 03 85/5 92 52 12 - Fax 03 85/55 50 94

Schloß – Open 15 Apr to 14 Oct Tues to Sun 10am to 6pm; 15 Oct to 14 Apr Tues to Sun 10am to 5pm (last admissions 30min before closing). Closed 24 and 31 Dec. 6DM. ☎ 03 85/56 57 38.

Staatliches Museum – Open 15 Apr to 14 Oct Tues 10am to 8pm, Wed to Sun 10am to 6pm; 15 Oct to 14 Apr Tues 10am to 8pm, Wed to Sun 10am to 5pm. Closed 24 Dec. 7DM. ☎ 03 85/5 95 80.

Table clock (Augsburg, c 1650), Deutsches Uhrenmuseum, Furtwangen

Deutsches Uhrenmuseum, Furtwangen

SCHWETZINGEN

Schloß – Guided tours (1hr) Apr to Sept Tues to Fri 10am to 4pm, Sat and Sun 10am to 5pm; Mar and Oct Tues to Sun 10am to 4pm; Nov to Feb Fri at 4pm, Sat and Sun at 11am, 2pm and 3pm. Closed 25 Dec. 9DM. ☎ 0 62 02/8 14 81.

Rococo theatre – Guided tours (20min) July to Sept daily at 11.30am, 2pm, 3pm and 3.30pm. 2DM. ☎ 0 62 02/8 14 81.

Schloßgarten – ও Open Apr to Sept daily 8am to 8pm; Mar and Oct daily 9am to 6pm; Nov to Feb 9am to 5pm. 4.50DM. ☎ 0 62 02/8 14 81.

SIGMARINGEN
🖪 Schwabstraße 1 – 72488 – ☎ 0 75 71/10 62 23 – Fax 0 75 71/10 61 66

Schloß – Guided tours (45min) May to Oct daily 9am to 4.45pm; Feb to Apr and Nov daily 9.30am to 4.30pm. 7DM. ☎ 0 75 71/72 92 30.

SOEST
🖪 Am Seel 5 – 59494 – ☎ 0 29 21/10 33 23 – Fax 0 29 21/3 30 39

SPEYER
🖪 Maximilianstraße 11 – 67346 – ☎ 0 62 32/14 23 92 – Fax 0 62 32/14 23 81

Kaiserdom – Open Apr to Oct daily 9am to 7pm; Nov to Mar daily 9am to 5pm. Admission free. ☎ 0 62 32/10 22 98.

Crypt – Open Apr to Oct daily 9am to 7pm; Nov to Mar daily 9am to 5pm. ☎ 0 62 32/10 22 98.

Historisches Museum der Pfalz – ও Open Tues to Sun 10am to 6pm (Wed until 8pm). Closed 31 Dec. 8DM. ☎ 0 62 32/13 25 33.

Technik-Museum – Open daily 9am to 6pm. 12DM museum, 12DM IMAX-Filmtheater, 22DM joint ticket. ☎ 0 62 32/6 70 80.

Purrmann-Haus – Open June to Sept Tues to Fri 10am to noon and 4pm to 6pm, Sat and Sun 11am to 1pm; Oct to May Tues to Fri 4pm to 6pm, Sat and Sun 11am to 1pm. Closed Easter, Whitsun, Christmas. 4DM. ☎ 0 62 32/7 79 11.

Feuerbachhaus – Open Mon to Fri 4pm to 6pm, Sun 11am to 1pm. 1DM (donation). ☎ 0 62 32/7 04 48.

SPREEWALD

Lübbenau: Barge trip – Embarcation in Lübbenau harbour. Apr to Oct (weather permitting) from 9am. Duration: 2-8hr, with a stopover. ☎ 0 35 42/22 25.

Stadtkirche St. Nikolai – ও Open May to Sept Mon to Sat 2pm to 4pm, Sun 10am to noon. ☎ 0 35 42/26 62.

STADE
🖪 Pferdemarkt 11 – 21682 – ☎ 0 41 41/40 91 70 – Fax 0 41 41/40 91 10

Schwedenspeicher-Museum – Open Tues to Fri 10am to 5pm, Sat and Sun 10am to 6pm. 2DM. ☎ 0 41 41/32 22.

STENDAL
🖪 Kornmarkt 8 – 39576 – ☎ 0 39 31/65 11 90 – Fax 0 39 31/56 11 95

Excursion

Havelberg: Cathedral of St.-Marien – Open Apr to Oct daily 10am to 6pm; Nov to Mar daily 10am to 4pm. ☎ 03 93 87/8 93 80.

STRALSUND
🖪 Alter Markt 9 – 18409 – ☎ 0 38 31/2 46 90 – Fax 0 38 31/24 69 49

Deutsches Meeresmuseum – ও Open July and Aug daily 9am to 6pm; Sept to June daily 10am to 5pm. Closed 24 and 31 Dec. 7DM. ☎ 0 38 31/2 65 00.

Kulturhistorisches Museum – Open Tues to Sun 10am to 5pm. Closed 24 and 31 Dec. 6DM. ☎ 0 38 31/29 21 80.

STRAUBING
🖪 Theresienplatz 20 – 94315 – ☎ 0 94 21/94 43 07 – Fax 0 94 21/94 41 03

Excursion

Metten: Benedictine abbey – ও Guided tours (45min) daily (apart from the week before Easter) at 10am and 3pm. 3DM. ☎ 09 91/9 10 81 12.

STUTTGART
🖪 Königstraße 1a 70173 ☎ 07 11/2 22 82 40 – Fax 07 11/2 22 82 53

Linden-Museum – ও Open Tues, Thur, Sat and Sun 10am to 5pm, Wed 10am to 8pm, Fri 10am to 1pm. Admission free. ☎ 07 11/2 02 24 56.

Staatsgalerie – ও Open Tues to Sun 11am to 7pm, every 1st Sat in month 11am to midnight. Closed Good Fri, 24 and 25 Dec. 9DM (admission free on Wed). ☎ 07 11/2 12 40 50.

Württembergisches Landesmuseum – Open Tues 10am to 1pm, Wed to Sun 10am to 5pm. Closed 1 Jan, Good Fri, 24, 25 and 31 Dec. 5DM. ☎ 07 11/2 79 34 00.

Galerie der Stadt Stuttgart – Open Tues to Sun 11am to 6pm (Wed until 8pm). Closed 1 Jan, 1 May, 24 and 25 Dec. Admission free. ☎ 07 11/2 16 21 88.

Staatliches Museum für Naturkunde

Museum Schloß Rosenstein – ♿ Open Tues to Fri 9am to 5pm, Sat and Sun 10am to 6pm. Closed 24 and 31 Dec. 4DM. ☎ 07 11/8 93 60.

Museum am Löwentor – ♿ Open Tues to Fri 9am to 5pm, Sat and Sun 10am to 6pm. Closed 24 and 31 Dec. 4DM. ☎ 07 11/8 93 60.

Mercedes-Benz-Museum – ♿ Open Tues to Sun 9am to 5pm. Closed on public holidays. Admission free. ☎ 07 11/1 72 25 78.

Excursions

Schloß Solitude – Guided tours (30min) Apr to Oct Tues to Sun 9am to noon and 1.30pm to 5pm; Nov to Mar Tues to Sun 10am to noon and 1.30pm to 4pm. 4DM. ☎ 07 11/69 66 99.

Schwäbisches Brauereimuseum – Open Thur to Sat 11am to 5.30pm. Closed on public holidays. Admission free. ☎ 07 11/7 35 78 99.

Porsche-Museum – ♿ Open Mon to Fri 9am to 4pm, Sat and Sun 9am to 5pm. Closed 23 Dec to 6 Jan. Admission free. ☎ 07 11/9 11 56 85.

Insel SYLT

Rail connection – From Niebüll to Westerland, fare for car plus passengers: 135DM there and back. ☎ 0 46 61/7 18.

Ferry connection – From Havneby (Denmark): 4 to 9 crossings per day depending on the season. Journey time about 1hr. Return fare 80-88DM per vehicle including passengers, 8DM for foot passengers. Information and reservations: ☎ 0 46 51/87 04 75 or from travel agents.

T

THÜRINGER WALD

Marienglashöhle – Guided tours Apr to Oct daily 9am to 5pm; Nov to Mar daily 9am to 4pm. 7DM. ☎ 0 36 23/30 49 53.

Bad TÖLZ   🛈 Ludwigstraße 11 – 83646 – ☎ 0 80 41/7 86 70 – Fax 0 80 41/78 67 56

Excursion

Benediktbeuern: Abbey church – ♿ Guided tours (1hr 30min) mid-May to June Wed and Sat at 2.30pm, Sun at 10.30am and 2.30pm; July to Sept Mon-Fri at 2.30pm, Sat and Sun at 10.30am and 2.30pm; Oct to mid-May Sat and Sun at 2.30pm. 5DM. ☎ 0 88 57/8 80.

TRIER   🛈 An der Porta Nigra – 54290 – ☎ 06 51/97 80 80 – Fax 06 51/4 47 59

Porta Nigra – ♿ Open the week before Easter to Sept daily 9am to 6pm; Jan to the Sun before Easter, Oct and Nov daily 9am to 5pm; Dec daily 10am to 4pm (last admissions 30min before closing). 4DM. ☎ 06 51/97 80 80.

Städtisches Museum – Open Easter to Oct daily 9am to 5pm; Nov to Easter Tues to Fri 9am to 5pm, Sat and Sun 9am to 3pm. Closed 1 Jan, 24 to 26 Dec. 3DM. ☎ 06 51/7 18 14 50.

Dom: Treasury – Open Apr to Oct Mon to Sat 11am to 5pm, Sun 1.30pm to 5pm; Nov to Mar Mon to Sat 11am to 4pm, Sun 1.30pm to 4pm. 2DM. ☎ 06 51/7 58 01.

Bischöfliches Dom- und Diözesanmuseum – ♿ Open Apr to Oct Mon to Sat 9am to 5pm, Sun 1pm to 5pm; Nov to Mar Tues to Sat 9am to 1pm and 2pm to 5pm, Sun 1pm to 5pm (last admissions 30min before closing). Closed 1 Jan, Mon before Shrove Tues, 24 to 26 and 31 Dec. 4DM. ☎ 06 51/7 10 52 55.

Rheinisches Landesmuseum – Open Tues to Fri 9.30am to 5pm, Sat and Sun 10.30am to 5pm. Closed 1 Jan, during the Carnival, 24 to 26 Dec. 7DM. ☎ 06 51/9 77 40.

Kaiserthermen – Same opening times as the Porta Nigra. 4DM. ☎ 06 51/97 80 80.

Schatzkammer der Stadtbibliothek – Closed at the time of going to press (further details not available). ☎ 06 51/7 18 14 29.

Karl-Marx-Haus – Open Mon 1pm to 6pm, Tues to Sun 10am to 6pm. Closed 23 Dec to 2 Jan. 3DM. ☎ 06 51/4 30 11.

Barbarathermen – Open the week before Easter to Sept Tues to Sun 9am to 1pm and 2pm to 6pm; Jan to the week before Easter, Oct and Nov Tues to Sun 9am to 1pm and 2pm to 5pm (last admissions 30min before closing). 4DM. ☎ 06 51/97 80 80.

Amphitheater – Same opening times as the Porta Nigra. 4DM. ☎ 06 51/97 80 80.

TÜBINGEN

☑ An der Eberhardsbrücke – 72072 – ☎ 0 70 71/9 13 60 – Fax 0 70 71/3 50 70

Hölderlinturm – Open Tues to Fri 10am to noon and 3pm to 5pm, Sat and Sun 2pm to 5pm. 3DM. ☎ 0 70 71/2 20 40.

Schloß Hohentübingen: Museum – Open May to Sept Wed to Sun 10am to 6pm; Oct to Apr Wed to Sun 10am to 5pm. Closed 24, 25 and 31 Dec. 4DM. ☎ 0 70 71/2 97 73 84.

Stiftskirche – Open Easter to Sept Fri and Sat 11am to 5pm, Sun noon to 5pm (open daily Aug to mid-Sept). 2DM. ☎ 0 70 71/4 20 46.

Neuer Botanischer Garten – Open daily 8am to 4.45pm (greenhouses are closed beween noon and 1.30pm). Admission free. ☎ 0 70 71/2 97 26 09.

Auto- und Spielzeugmuseum Boxenstop – Open Apr to Oct Wed to Sun 10am to noon and 2pm to 5pm; Nov to Mar Sun and public holidays 10am to noon and 2pm to 5pm. Closed 24 Dec. 5DM. ☎ 0 70 71/55 11 22.

Excursions

Kloster Bebenhausen – Open Tues to Sun 9am to noon and 1pm to 6pm. Closed 1 Jan, 24, 25 and 31 Dec. 5DM (join ticket with Schloß 8DM). ☎ 0 70 71/60 21 80.

Schloß Bebenhausen – Guided tours (1hr) Tues to Sun 9am to noon 1pm to 6pm. Closed 1 Jan, 24, 25 and 31 Dec. 6DM. ☎ 0 70 71/60 21 80.

U – V

ÜBERLINGEN

☑ Landungsplatz 14 – 88662 – ☎ 0 75 51/99 11 22 – Fax 0 75 51/99 11 35

Rathaus: Council chamber – Open Apr to Oct Mon to Fri 9am to noon and 2.30pm to 5pm, Sat 9am to noon; Nov to Mar Mon to Fri 9am to noon and 2.30pm to 5pm. Admission free. ☎ 0 75 51/99 10 11.

Städtisches Museum – Open Tues to Sat 9am to 12.30pm and 2pm to 5pm; Apr to Oct also open Sun 10am to 3pm. Closed on the Tues after Easter and Whitsun. 4DM. ☎ 0 75 51/99 10 71.

Excursions

Uhldingen-Mühlhofen: Pfahlbaumuseum Unteruhldingen – Guided tours (45min) Apr to Sept daily 8am to 6pm; Oct daily 9am to 5pm; Mar and Nov Sat and Sun only 9am to 5pm. ☎ 0 75 56/85 43.

ULM

☑ Münsterplatz – 89073 – ☎ 07 31/1 61 28 30 – Fax 07 31/1 61 16 41

Ulmer Museum – Open Tues to Sun 11am to 5pm (Thur until 8pm). Opening times vary during the Easter, Whitsun and Christmas periods. 5DM (admission free on Fri). ☎ 07 31/1 61 43 00.

Deutsches Brotmuseum – ♿ Open Tues to Sun 10am to 5pm (Wed to 8.30pm) (last admissions 1hr before closing). Closed Good Fri, 24 and 31 Dec. 5DM. ☎ 07 31/6 99 55.

Excursions

Kloster Wiblingen: Abbey Library – Open Apr to Oct Tues to Sun 10am to noon and 2pm to 5pm; Nov to Mar Sat and Sun 2pm to 4pm. Closed 24, 25 and 31 Dec. 3DM. ☎ 07 31/1 89 30 04.

Blaubeuren: Abbey Church – Open Palm Sun to 1 Nov daily 9am to 6pm; 2 Nov until Sat before Palm Sun Mon to Fri 2pm to 4pm, Sat and Sun 10am to noon and 1pm to 4pm. 3DM. ☎ 0 73 44/9 62 60.

Insel USEDOM

Wolgast: Pfarrkirche St. Petri – Open May to Oct Mon to Fri 10am to 12.30pm and 1.30pm to 5pm, Sat 10am to 5pm, Sun 11.30am to noon and 2pm to 4pm; Nov to Apr Mon to Fri 10am to 12.30pm and 1.30pm to 4.30pm. Admission to the church is free, St. Petri tower: 3DM. ☎ 0 38 36/20 22 69.

Hist.-techn. Informationszentrum Peenemünde – ♿ Open Apr to Oct 9am to 6pm; Nov to Mar 10am to 4pm. Closed Oct to May on Mon, 25 and 26 Dec. 6DM. ☎ 03 83 71/2 05 73.

Wallfahrtskirche VIERZEHNHEILIGEN

Tour – ♿ Open Sun before Easter to Oct daily 7am to 5pm; Nov to Sun before Easter 8am to 4pm. ☎ 0 95 71/9 50 80.

W

WALDECKER BERGLAND

Waldeck: Burgmuseum – Open Mar to Oct daily 9am to 5pm; Nov to Dec Sat and Sun 10am to 4pm. Closed 24 to 26 Dec. 3DM. ☎ 0 56 23/58 90.

Arolsen: Schloß – Guided tours (45min) May to Sept daily 10am to 4.15pm. 6DM. ☎ 0 56 91/8 95 50.

WALDSASSEN   🛈 Johannisplatz 11 - 95652 - ☎ 0 96 32/8 81 60 - Fax 0 96 32/54 80

Bibliothek – Guided tours (25min) Sat before Easter to Oct Mon to Sat 10am to 11.30am and 2pm to 4.45pm, Sun 10am to 11am and 2pm to 4.45pm; Nov to Easter daily 1pm to 4pm (last tour 30min before closing). Closed Maundy Thur, Good Fri and for the fortnight leading up to Christmas. 4DM. ☎ 0 96 32/9 20 00.

WASSERBURG AM INN   🛈 Rathaus, Marienplatz 2 - 83512 ☎ 0 80 71/1 05 22 - Fax 0 80 71/4 06 01

Heimatmuseum – Open May to Sept Tues to Fri 10am to noon and 1pm to 4pm, Sat and Sun 11am to 4pm; Oct to Apr Tues to Fri 1pm to 4pm, Sat and Sun 1pm to 3pm. Closed 16 Dec to 31 Jan. 3DM. ☎ 0 80 71/92 52 90.

WEIMAR   🛈 Markt 10 - 99423 - ☎ 0 36 43/2 40 00 - Fax 0 36 43/24 00 40

Goethes Wohnhaus – Open 10 May to 29 Aug Tues to Sun 9am to 7pm; 30 Aug to 24 Oct and 15 Mar to 9 May Tues to Sun 9am to 6pm; 25 Oct to 14 Mar Tues to Sun 9am to 4pm. ☎ 0 36 43/54 51 02.

Schillers Wohnhaus – Same opening times as Goethes Wohnhaus. Closed Tues. 5DM. ☎ 0 36 43/54 51 02.

Bauhaus-Museum – Open Apr to Oct Tues to Sun 10am to 6pm; Nov to Mar 10am to 4.30pm. 5DM. ☎ 0 36 43/56 41 61.

Wittumspalais – Same opening times as Goethes Wohnhaus. Closed Mon, 24 and 31 Dec. 6DM. ☎ 0 36 43/54 51 02.

Schloßmuseum – Open Apr to Oct Tues to Sun 10am to 6pm; Nov to Mar Tues to Sun 10am to 4.30pm. 6DM. ☎ 0 36 43/54 61 60.

Liszt-Haus – Open 10 May to 29 Aug Tues to Sun 9am to 1pm and 2pm to 7pm; 30 Aug to 24 Oct and 15 Mar to 9 May Tues to Sun 9am to 1pm and 2pm to 6pm; 25 Oct to 14 Mar Tues to Sun 9am to 1pm and 2pm to 4pm. Closed 24 and 31 Dec. 4DM. ☎ 0 36 43/54 51 02.

Neues Museum – Open Apr to Oct Tues to Sun 10am to 6pm; Nov to Mar Tues to Sun 10am to 4.30pm. Closed 24 Dec after 1pm and 25 Dec. 5DM. ☎ 0 36 43/54 61 63.

Nietzsche-Archiv – Open 10 May to 29 Aug Tues to Sun 1pm to 7pm; 30 Aug to 24 Oct and 15 Mar to 9 May 1pm to 6pm; 25 Oct to 14 Mar Tues to Sun 1pm to 4pm. Closed 24 and 31 Dec. 4DM. ☎ 0 36 43/54 51 02.

Excursions

Schloß Tiefurt – Same opening times as Goethes Wohnhaus. Closed 24 and 31 Dec. 6DM. ☎ 0 36 43/54 51 02.

Schloß Belvedere – Open Apr to Oct Tues to Sun 10am to 6pm. 5DM. ☎ 0 36 43/54 61 62.

Gedenkstätte Buchenwald – ♿ Open May to Sept Tues to Sun 9.45am to 6pm; Oct to Apr Tues to Sun 8.45am to 5pm (last admissions 45min before closing). Closed 22 Dec to 3 Jan. Admission free. ☎ 0 36 43/43 00.

WERNIGERODE   🛈 Nikolaiplatz - 38855 - ☎ 0 39 43/63 30 35 - Fax 0 39 43/63 20 40

Zentrum für Kunst- und Kulturgeschichte des 19. Jh.s – Open May to Oct daily 10am to 6pm (last admissions at 5.30pm); Nov to Apr Tues to Sun 10am to 4pm. Closed 24 Dec. 8DM. ☎ 0 39 43/55 30 30.

WERTHEIM   🛈 Am Spitzen Turm - 97877 ☎ 0 93 42/10 66 - Fax 0 93 42/3 82 77

Excursion

Ehemaliges Kloster Bronnbach – Guided tours (1hr) Apr to Oct Mon to Sat 9.30am to 11.30am and 2pm to 4pm, Sun 1pm to 4pm. 7DM. ☎ 0 93 42/3 95 96.

WESSOBRUNN

Ehemalige Benediktinerabtei – Guided tours (45min) Mar to Oct Mon to Sat at 10am, 3pm and 4pm, Sun at 3pm and 4pm; Nov to Feb daily at 3pm. 2DM. ☎ 0 88 09/9 21 10.

🏛 Domplatz 8 - 35573 - ☎ 0 64 41/9 93 38 - Fax 0 64 41/9 93 39

Stadt- und Industrie-Museum – Open Tues to Sun 10am to 1pm and 2pm to 5pm. Closed 1 Jan, Good Fri, 24, 25 and 31 Dec. 3DM. ☎ 0 64 41/9 92 69.

Lottehaus – Open Tues to Sun 10am to 1pm and 2pm to 5pm. Closed 1 Jan, 24, 25 and 31 Dec. 3DM. ☎ 0 64 41/9 92 69.

Sammlung Dr. Irmgard von Lemmers-Danforth – Open Tues to Sun 10am to 1pm and 2pm to 5pm. Closed 1 Jan, Good Fri, 24 and 31 Dec. 3DM. ☎ 0 64 41/9 93 66.

Reichskammergerichtsmuseum – Open Tues to Sun 10am to 1pm and 2pm to 5pm. Admission free. ☎ 0 64 41/9 96 12.

🏛 Marktstraße 6 - 65183 - ☎ 06 11/1 72 97 80 - Fax 06 11/1 72 97 98

Museum Wiesbaden – Open Tues 10am to 8pm, Wed to Fri 10am to 4pm, Sat and Sun 10am to 5pm. Closed 1 Jan, Sun before Shrove Tues, Tues after Easter and Whitsun, 24, 25 and 31 Dec. 5DM. ☎ 06 11/3 35 22 50.

Nerobergbahn – Operates May to Aug daily 9.30am to 7pm; Apr and Sept Wed and Sat noon to 7pm, Sun 10am to 7pm; Oct Wed, Sat and Sun noon to 6pm. Departures every 15min. 3DM there and back. ☎ 06 11/7 80 22 22.

Russische Orthodoxe Kirche – Open May to Sept daily 11am to 4pm; Oct to Apr Sat and Sun only 11am to 4pm. 1DM. ☎ 06 11/52 84 94.

Church – ♿ Open Apr to Sept daily 8am to 7pm; Oct to Mar daily 8am to 5pm. Admission free. ☎ 0 88 62/5 01.

🏛 Carl-Ulrich-Straße 1 - 74206 - ☎ 0 70 63/9 72 00 - Fax 0 70 63/97 20 20

Stiftskirche St.-Peter und St.-Paul: Cloister – Guided tours (1hr) by prior appointment. ☎ 0 70 63/97 04 24.

Excursions

Sinsheim: Auto- und Technikmuseum – ♿ Open daily 9am to 6pm. 14DM. ☎ 0 72 61/9 29 90.

Burg Guttenberg – Open Mar to Oct daily 10am to 6pm. 5DM. ☎ 0 62 66/13 73.

Burg Hornberg – Open daily 8am to 8pm. 4.50DM. ☎ 0 62 61/50 01.

Neckarsulm: German Cycle and Motorcycle Museum – ♿ Open Mon to Fri 9am to noon and 1.30pm to 5pm, Sat and Sun 9am to 5pm (last admissions 30min before closing). Closed 24 and 31 Dec. 7DM. ☎ 0 71 32/3 52 71.

🏛 Am Markt 11 - 23966 ☎ 0 38 41/1 94 33 - Fax 0 38 41/25 18 19

Schabbellhaus: Museum of Local History – Open May to Oct Tues to Sun 10am to 8pm; Nov to Apr Tues to Sun 10am to 5pm. Closed 24 and 31 Dec. 3DM. ☎ 0 38 41/28 23 50.

Nikolaikirche – Open Apr and May Mon to Sat 10am to noon and 1pm to 3pm, Sun 1pm to 3pm; June to Oct Mon to Sat 10am to noon and 1pm to 5pm, Sun 1pm to 5pm; Nov to Mar Mon to Sat 11am to noon and 1pm to 3pm, Sun 1pm to 3pm. Admission free, but donations welcome.

Excursion

Neukloster: Monastery Church – ♿ Open May to Sept Mon to Fri 10am to noon and 2pm to 5pm, Sun 11am to noon; Oct to Apr Mon to Fri 10am to noon, Sun 11am to noon. Admission free. ☎ 03 84 22/2 54 51.

🏛 Schloßplatz 2 - 06886 - ☎ 0 34 91/49 86 10 - Fax 0 34 91/49 86 11

Melanchthon-Haus – Open Apr to Oct daily 9am to 6pm; Nov to Mar Tues to Sun 10am to 5pm. Closed 31 Dec. 5DM. ☎ 0 34 91/40 32 79.

Lutherhalle – Open Apr to Oct daily 9am to 6pm; Nov to Mar Tues to Sun 10am to 5pm. Closed 31 Dec. 7DM. ☎ 0 34 91/4 20 30.

Schloß – Guided tours (1hr) May to Sept Mon 1pm to 6pm, Tues to Sun 10am to 6pm; Apr and Oct Mon 1pm to 4.30pm, Tues to Sun 10am to 4.30pm; Nov to Mar Tues to Sat 11am to 4pm, Sun 11am to 4.30pm (last admissions 45min before closing). 6DM. ☎ 03 40/6 46 15 41.

Peacock in Wörlitzer Park

Gotisches Haus – Guided tours (1hr) May to Sept Mon 1pm to 6pm, Tues to Sun 11am to 6pm; Apr and Oct Mon 1pm to 4.30pm, Tues to Sun 10am to 4.30pm; Nov to Mar Tues to Sat 11am to 4pm, Sun 11am to 4.30pm (last admissions 45min before closing). 5DM. ☎ 03 40/6 46 15 41.

WOLFENBÜTTEL 🄱 Rosenwall 1 – 38100 – ☎ 0 53 31/29 83 46 – Fax 0 53 31/29 83 47

Schloß – ♿ Open Tues to Sun 10am to 5pm. Closed 1 Jan, Good Fri, Easter Day, 1 May, Corpus Christi, Whit Sun, 3 Oct, 24, 25 and 31 Dec. 3DM. ☎ 0 53 31/9 24 60.

Herzog-August-Bibliothek – Open Tues to Sun 10am to 5pm. Closed Good Fri, 24, 25 and 31 Dec. 6DM. ☎ 0 53 31/80 82 14.

Lessinghaus – Same admission times as Herzog-August-Bibliothek. 6DM. ☎ 0 53 31/80 82 14.

WORMS 🄱 Neumarkt 14 – 67547 – ☎ 0 62 41/2 50 45 – Fax 0 62 41/2 63 28

Museum Heylshof – Open May to Sept Tues to Sun 10am to 5pm; Oct to Dec and 16 Feb to Apr Tues to Sat 2pm to 4pm, Sun 10am to noon and 2pm to 4pm. Closed Good Fri, 25 and 31 Dec. 3DM. ☎ 0 62 41/5 75 42.

Städtisches Museum – Open Tues to Sun 10am to 5pm. Closed 1 Jan, 24 to 26 Dec. 4DM. ☎ 0 62 41/94 63 90.

WÜRZBURG 🄱 Congress Centrum – 97070 – ☎ 09 31/37 25 35 – Fax 09 31/37 36 52

Residenz – ♿ Open Apr to Oct Tues to Sun 9am to 5pm; Nov to Mar Tues to Sun 10am to 4pm (last admissions 30min before closing). Closed 1 Jan, Shrove Tues, 1 Nov, 24, 25 and 31 Dec. 8DM. ☎ 09 31/35 51 70.

Martin-von-Wagner-Museum – Picture gallery open Tues to Sat 9.30am to 12.30pm. Antiques collection open Tues to Sat 2pm to 5pm. Prints and drawings open Tues and Thur 4pm to 6pm. Picture gallery and antiques collection open alternately Sun 9.30am to 12.30pm. Closed 1 Jan, Good Fri, 1 May, 1 Nov, 24, 25 and 31 Dec. Admission free. ☎ 09 31/31 28 66.

Festung Marienberg – Tours Apr to Oct Sat and Sun at 10am, 11am 1pm, 2pm, 3pm and 4pm. Closed 1 Jan, Shrove Tues, 1 Nov, 24, 25 and 31 Dec. 2DM. ☎ 09 31/35 51 70.

Fürstenbaumuseum – Open Apr to Oct Tues to Sun 10am to 5pm; Nov to Mar Tues to Sun 10am to 4pm (last admissions 30min before closing). Closed 1 Jan, Shrove Tues, 24, 25 and 31 Dec. 4DM. ☎ 09 31/4 38 38.

Mainfränkisches Museum – Open Apr to Oct Tues to Sun 10am to 5pm; Nov to Mar Tues to Sun 10am to 4pm (last admissions 30min before closing). Closed 24, 25 and 31 Dec. 5DM. ☎ 09 31/4 30 16.

Excursion

Schloß Veitshöchheim – Guided tours (40min) June to Aug Tues to Sun 10am to noon and 1pm to 5pm (last admissions 30min before closing); Easter to May, Sept and Oct by appointment only. 3DM. ☎ 09 31/35 51 70.

X – Z

XANTEN   🏛 Rathaus, Karthaus 2 – 46509 – ☎ 0 28 01/77 22 98 – Fax 0 28 01/77 22 09

Regionalmuseum – Open May to Sept Tues to Fri 9am to 5pm, Sat and Sun 11am to 6pm; Oct to Apr Tues to Fri 10am to 5pm, Sat and Sun 11am to 6pm. 4DM. ☎ 0 28 01/71 94 15.

Archäologischer Park – ♿ Open Mar to Nov daily 9am to 6pm; Dec to Feb 10am to 4pm. 8DM. ☎ 0 22 34/29 99.

Das ZITTAUER GEBIRGE

Zittau: Stadtmuseum – Open Tues to Sun 10am to noon and 1pm to 5pm. Closed 1 Jan, 25 and 31 Dec. 3DM. ☎ 0 35 83/51 02 70.

Oybin: Fortress and monastery estate – Open May to Oct 9am to 6pm; Nov to Apr 10am to 4pm. 5DM. ☎ 03 58 44/73 40.

Großschönau: Deutsches Damast- und Frottiermuseum – Guided tours (1hr 15min) May to Oct Tues to Sun 10am to noon and 2pm to 5pm; Nov to Apr Tues to Fri 10am to noon and 1pm to 4pm, 1st and 3rd Sat and Sun of month 1pm to 4pm. 3DM. ☎ 03 58 41/3 54 69.

ZUGSPITZE

Ascent – From Eibsee, cable-car daily 30min 8.30am to 4pm. Journey time: 10min. Return fare: 77DM. ☎ 0 88 21/79 79 79.

ZWICKAU   🏛 Hauptstraße 6 – 08056 – ☎ 03 75/1 94 33 – Fax 03 75/29 37 15

Robert-Schumann-Haus – Open Tues to Sat 10am to 5pm. Closed Good Fri, Easter Mon, 2 May, Whit Mon, Buß- und Bettag (a Wed in Nov), 24, 25 and 31 Dec. 5DM. ☎ 03 75/21 52 69.

Städtisches Museum – Open Tues to Fri 9am to 5pm, Sat and Sun 10am to 5pm; during Christmas exhibition 10am to 5pm. Closed 1 May. 5DM. ☎ 03 75/83 45 10.

ZWIEFALTENExcursions

Obermarchtal: Abbey Church – Viewing by appointment only. ☎ 0 73 75/9 50 51 12.

Bad Schussenried: Abbey Library – Open Apr to Oct daily 10am to noon and 2pm to 5pm; Nov to Mar Mon to Fri 2pm to 5pm, Sat and Sun 10.30am to noon and 2pm to 5pm. Closed 20 Dec to mid-Jan. 4.50DM. ☎ 0 75 83/33 10 01.

Index

Ludwigsburg .... Towns, sights and tourist regions followed *Baden-Württemberg* by the name of the *Land*.

Barlach, Ernst .... People, events and artistic styles mentioned in the guide.

Botanical Gardens .... Sights in major cities.

This index, like the other alphabetical lists in this guide, follows the normal German alphabetical order, where the vowels ä, ö and ü are classified under ae, oe and ue respectively, ß is classified under ss, and St. under Sankt (Saint).

H

S